GREAT BOOKS
OF THE WESTERN WORLD

ROBERT MAYNARD HUTCHINS, *EDITOR IN CHIEF*

6.

HERODOTUS

THUCYDIDES

THE HISTORY OF HERODOTUS

THE HISTORY OF
THE PELOPONNESIAN WAR
THUCYDIDES

WILLIAM BENTON, *Publisher*

ENCYCLOPÆDIA BRITANNICA, INC.

CHICAGO · LONDON · TORONTO · GENEVA · SYDNEY · TOKYO · MANILA

THE TEXTS OF THE HISTORY OF HERODOTUS
AND THUCYDIDES' THE HISTORY OF THE PELOPONNESIAN WAR
IN THIS EDITION
ARE DERIVED FROM THE EDITIONS IN EVERYMAN'S LIBRARY
BY PERMISSION OF J. M. DENT & SONS LTD., LONDON,
AND E. P. DUTTON & CO. INC., NEW YORK.

THE UNIVERSITY OF CHICAGO

The Great Books
is published with the editorial advice of the faculties
of The University of Chicago

GENERAL CONTENTS

《《-《《-《《

THE HISTORY OF HERODOTUS, Page 1
Translated by GEORGE RAWLINSON

THUCYDIDES: THE HISTORY
OF THE PELOPONNESIAN WAR, Page 349
Translated by RICHARD CRAWLEY
Revised by R. FEETHAM

》》-》》-》》

THE HISTORY OF HERODOTUS

BIOGRAPHICAL NOTE
HERODOTUS, *c*.484–*c*.425 B.C

HERODOTUS was born about four years after the battle of Salamis in Halicarnassus in Asia Minor. Although a Greek colony, the city had been subject to Persia for some time, and it remained so for half of Herodotus' life. He came from a Greek family which enjoyed a position of respect in Halicarnassus, and his uncle, or cousin, Panyasis, was famous in antiquity as an epic poet.

The Persian tyranny made any free political life impossible, and Herodotus, after his elementary education, appears to have devoted himself to reading and travelling. In addition to his unusually thorough knowledge of Homer, he had an intimate acquaintance with the whole range of Greek literature. In his *History* he quotes or shows familiarity with, among others, Hesiod, Hecataeus, Sappho, Solon, Aesop, Simonides of Ceos, Aeschylus, and Pindar. Whether or not the plan of his *History* governed or grew out of his travels is not known. All the dates of his travels are uncertain; it is thought that most of them were made between his twentieth and thirty-seventh year. The *History* reveals the elaborateness of his observation and inquiry. He traversed Asia Minor and European Greece probably more than once, visited all the most important islands of the Archipelago—Rhodes, Cyprus, Delos, Paros, Thasos, Samothrace, Crete, Samos, Cythera, and Aegina—, made the long journey from Sardis to the Persian capital of Susa, saw Babylon, Colchis, and the western shores of the Euxine as far as the Dnieper, travelled in Scythia, Thrace, and Greater Greece, explored the antiquities of Tyre, coasted along the shores of Palestine, saw Gaza, and made a long stay in Egypt.

Apart from the travels undertaken in his professional capacity, political developments involved Herodotus in many shifts of residence. About 454 B.C. his relative, Panyasis, was executed by Lygdamis, the tyrant of Halicarnassus. Herodotus left his native city for Samos, which was then an important member of the Athenian Confederacy. He was there for

seven or eight years and perhaps took part in the preparations for the overthrow of Lygdamis. After the expulsion of the tyrant, in which the Athenian fleet may have been a decisive factor, he returned to Halicarnassus, which then became a member of the Confederacy. He remained there less than a year. It is surmised that an unfavorable reception to parts of his *History* and the ascendency of the anti-Athenian party caused Herodotus to leave Halicarnassus for Athens.

At Athens, Herodotus seems to have been admitted into the brilliant Periclean society. He was particularly intimate with Sophocles, who is said to have written a poem in his honour. Plutarch records that the public readings he gave from his *History* won such approval that in 445 B.C., on the proposal of Anytus, the Athenian people voted to award him a large sum of money. At one of his recitations, the story is told that the young Thucydides was present with his father and was so moved that he burst into tears, whereupon Herodotus remarked: "Olorus, your son has a natural enthusiasm for letters."

Despite his fame in Athens, Herodotus may not have been reconciled to his status as a foreigner without citizenship. He was either unwilling or unable to return to his native land. When in 443 B.C. Pericles sent out a colony to settle Thurii in southern Italy, Herodotus was one of its members. He was then forty years old.

From this point in his career Herodotus disappears completely. He may have undertaken some of his travels after this time, and there is evidence of his returning to Athens, but it is inconclusive. He was undoubtedly occupied with completing and perfecting his *History*. He may also have composed at Thurii the special work on the history of Assyria to which he refers and which Aristotle quotes.

From the indications afforded by his work it is inferred that he did not live later than 425 B.C. Presumably he died at Thurii; it was there that his tomb was shown in later ages.

CONTENTS

The First Book, Entitled
CLIO

⋙⋙⋙⋙⋙⋙⋙⋙⋙⋙⋙⋙⋙⋙⋙⋘⋘⋘⋘⋘⋘⋘⋘⋘⋘⋘⋘⋘⋘⋘⋘

THESE are the researches of Herodotus of Halicarnassus, which he publishes, in the hope of thereby preserving from decay the remembrance of what men have done, and of preventing the great and wonderful actions of the Greeks and the Barbarians from losing their due meed of glory; and withal to put on record what were their grounds of feud.

1. According to the Persians best informed in history, the Phœnicians began to quarrel. This people, who had formerly dwelt on the shores of the Erythræan Sea,[1] having migrated to the Mediterranean and settled in the parts which they now inhabit, began at once, they say, to adventure on long voyages, freighting their vessels with the wares of Egypt and Assyria. They landed at many places on the coast, and among the rest at Argos, which was then preeminent above all the states included now under the common name of Hellas.[2] Here they exposed their merchandise, and traded with the natives for five or six days; at the end of which time, when almost everything was sold, there came down to the beach a number of women, and among them the daughter of the king, who was, they say, agreeing in this with the Greeks, Io, the child of Inachus. The women were standing by the stern of the ship intent upon their purchases, when the Phœnicians, with a general shout, rushed upon them. The greater part made their escape, but some were seized and carried off. Io herself was among the captives. The Phœnicians put the women on board their vessel, and set sail for

Egypt. Thus did Io pass into Egypt, according to the Persian story, which differs widely from the Phœnician: and thus commenced, according to their authors, the series of outrages.

2. At a later period, certain Greeks, with whose name they are unacquainted, but who would probably be Cretans, made a landing at Tyre, on the Phœnician coast, and bore off the king's daughter, Europé. In this they only retaliated; but afterwards the Greeks, they say, were guilty of a second violence. They manned a ship of war, and sailed to Æa, a city of Colchis, on the river Phasis; from whence, after despatching the rest of the business on which they had come, they carried off Medea, the daughter of the king of the land. The monarch sent a herald into Greece to demand reparation of the wrong, and the restitution of his child; but the Greeks made answer that, having received no reparation of the wrong done them in the seizure of Io the Argive, they should give none in this instance.

3. In the next generation afterwards, according to the same authorities, Alexander the son of Priam, bearing these events in mind, resolved to procure himself a wife out of Greece by violence, fully persuaded, that as the Greeks had not given satisfaction for their outrages, so neither would he be forced to make any for his. Accordingly he made prize of Helen; upon which the Greeks decided that, before resorting to other measures, they would send envoys to reclaim the princess and require reparation of the wrong. Their demands were met by a reference to the violence which had been of-

[1] The Indian Ocean, or rather both the Indian Ocean and the Persian Gulf, which latter Herodotus does not consider distinct from the Ocean, being ignorant of its shape.
[2] The ancient superiority of Argos is indicated by the position of Agamemnon at the time of the Trojan war and by the use of the word Argive in Homer for Greek generally. No other name of a single people is used in the same generic way.

1

fered to Medea, and they were asked with what face they could now require satisfaction, when they had formerly rejected all demands for either reparation or restitution addressed to them.

4. Hitherto the injuries on either side had been mere acts of common violence; but in what followed the Persians consider that the Greeks were greatly to blame, since before any attack had been made on Europe, they led an army into Asia. Now as for the carrying off of women, it is the deed, they say, of a rogue: but to make a stir about such as are carried off, argues a man a fool. Men of sense care nothing for such women, since it is plain that without their own consent they would never be forced away. The Asiatics, when the Greeks ran off with their women, never troubled themselves about the matter; but the Greeks, for the sake of a single Lacedæmonian girl, collected a vast armament, invaded Asia, and destroyed the kingdom of Priam. Henceforth they ever looked upon the Greeks as their open enemies. For Asia, with all the various tribes of barbarians that inhabit it, is regarded by the Persians as their own; but Europe and the Greek race they look on as distinct and separate.

5. Such is the account which the Persians give of these matters. They trace to the attack upon Troy their ancient enmity towards the Greeks. The Phœnicians, however, as regards Io, vary from the Persian statements. They deny that they used any violence to remove her into Egypt; she herself, they say, having formed an intimacy with the captain, while his vessel lay at Argos, and perceiving herself to be with child, of her own free will accompanied the Phœnicians on their leaving the shore, to escape the shame of detection and the reproaches of her parents. Whether this latter account be true, or whether the matter happened otherwise, I shall not discuss further. I shall proceed at once to point out the person who first within my own knowledge inflicted injury on the Greeks, after which I shall go forward with my history, describing equally the greater and the lesser cities. For the cities which were formerly great have most of them become insignificant; and such as are at present powerful, were weak in the olden time. I shall therefore discourse equally of both, convinced that human happiness never continues long in one stay.

6. Crœsus, son of Alyattes, by birth a Lydian, was lord of all the nations to the west of the river Halys. This stream, which separates Syria[1] from Paphlagonia, runs with a course from south to north, and finally falls into the Euxine. So far as our knowledge goes, he was the first of the barbarians who had dealings with the Greeks, forcing some of them to become his tributaries, and entering into alliance with others. He conquered the Æolians, Ionians, and Dorians of Asia, and made a treaty with the Lacedæmonians. Up to that time all Greeks had been free. For the Cimmerian attack upon Ionia, which was earlier than Crœsus, was not a conquest of the cities, but only an inroad for plundering.

7. The sovereignty of Lydia, which had belonged to the Heraclides, passed into the family of Crœsus, who were called the Mermnadæ, in the manner which I will now relate. There was a certain king of Sardis, Candaules by name, whom the Greeks called Myrsilus. He was a descendant of Alcæus, son of Hercules. The first king of this dynasty was Agron, son of Ninus, grandson of Belus, and great-grandson of Alcæus; Candaules, son of Myrsus, was the last. The kings who reigned before Agron sprang from Lydus, son of Atys, from whom the people of the land, called previously Meonians, received the name of Lydians. The Heraclides, descended from Hercules and the slave-girl of Jardanus, having been entrusted by these princes with the management of affairs, obtained the kingdom by an oracle. Their rule endured for two and twenty generations of men, a space of five hundred and five years; during the whole of which period, from Agron to Candaules, the crown descended in the direct line from father to son.

8. Now it happened that this Candaules was in love with his own wife; and not only so, but thought her the fairest woman in the whole world. This fancy had strange consequences. There was in his bodyguard a man whom he specially favoured, Gyges, the son of Dascylus. All affairs of greatest moment were entrusted by Candaules to this person, and to him he was wont to extol the surpassing beauty of his wife. So matters went on for a while. At length, one day, Candaules, who was fated to end ill, thus addressed his follower: "I see thou dost not credit what I tell thee of my lady's loveliness; but come now, since men's ears are less credulous than their eyes, contrive some means whereby thou mayst behold her naked." At

[1] By Syria Herodotus here means Cappadocia, the inhabitants of which he calls Syrians (i. 72, and vii. 72), or Cappadocian Syrians (Συρίους Καππαδόκας i. 72).

this the other loudly exclaimed, saying, "What most unwise speech is this, master, which thou hast uttered? Wouldst thou have me behold my mistress when she is naked? Bethink thee that a woman, with her clothes, puts off her bashfulness. Our fathers, in time past, distinguished right and wrong plainly enough, and it is our wisdom to submit to be taught by them. There is an old saying, 'Let each look on his own.' I hold thy wife for the fairest of all womankind. Only, I beseech thee, ask me not to do wickedly."

9. Gyges thus endeavoured to decline the king's proposal, trembling lest some dreadful evil should befall him through it. But the king replied to him, "Courage, friend; suspect me not of the design to prove thee by this discourse; nor dread thy mistress, lest mischief befall thee at her hands. Be sure I will so manage that she shall not even know that thou hast looked upon her. I will place thee behind the open door of the chamber in which we sleep. When I enter to go to rest she will follow me. There stands a chair close to the entrance, on which she will lay her clothes one by one as she takes them off. Thou wilt be able thus at thy leisure to peruse her person. Then, when she is moving from the chair toward the bed, and her back is turned on thee, be it thy care that she see thee not as thou passest through the doorway."

10. Gyges, unable to escape, could but declare his readiness. Then Candaules, when bedtime came, led Gyges into his sleeping-chamber, and a moment after the queen followed. She entered, and laid her garments on the chair, and Gyges gazed on her. After a while she moved toward the bed, and her back being then turned, he glided stealthily from the apartment. As he was passing out, however, she saw him, and instantly divining what had happened, she neither screamed as her shame impelled her, nor even appeared to have noticed aught, purposing to take vengeance upon the husband who had so affronted her. For among the Lydians, and indeed among the barbarians generally, it is reckoned a deep disgrace, even to a man, to be seen naked.

11. No sound or sign of intelligence escaped her at the time. But in the morning, as soon as day broke, she hastened to choose from among her retinue such as she knew to be most faithful to her, and preparing them for what was to ensue, summoned Gyges into her presence. Now it had often happened before that the queen had desired to confer with him, and he was accustomed to come to her at her call. He therefore obeyed the summons, not suspecting that she knew aught of what had occurred. Then she addressed these words to him: "Take thy choice, Gyges, of two courses which are open to thee. Slay Candaules, and thereby become my lord, and obtain the Lydian throne, or die this moment in his room. So wilt thou not again, obeying all behests of thy master, behold what is not lawful for thee. It must needs be that either he perish by whose counsel this thing was done, or thou, who sawest me naked, and so didst break our usages." At these words Gyges stood awhile in mute astonishment; recovering after a time, he earnestly besought the queen that she would not compel him to so hard a choice. But finding he implored in vain, and that necessity was indeed laid on him to kill or to be killed, he made choice of life for himself, and replied by this inquiry: "If it must be so, and thou compellest me against my will to put my lord to death, come, let me hear how thou wilt have me set on him." "Let him be attacked," she answered, "on the spot where I was by him shown naked to you, and let the assault be made when he is asleep."

12. All was then prepared for the attack, and when night fell, Gyges, seeing that he had no retreat or escape, but must absolutely either slay Candaules, or himself be slain, followed his mistress into the sleeping-room. She placed a dagger in his hand, and hid him carefully behind the self-same door. Then Gyges, when the king was fallen asleep, entered privily into the chamber and struck him dead. Thus did the wife and kingdom of Candaules pass into the possession of Gyges, of whom Archilochus the Parian, who lived about the same time, made mention in a poem written in iambic trimeter verse.

13. Gyges was afterwards confirmed in the possession of the throne by an answer of the Delphic oracle. Enraged at the murder of their king, the people flew to arms, but after a while the partisans of Gyges came to terms with them, and it was agreed that if the Delphic oracle declared him king of the Lydians, he should reign; if otherwise, he should yield the throne to the Heraclides. As the oracle was given in his favour he became king. The Pythoness, however, added that, in the fifth generation from Gyges, vengeance should come for the Heraclides; a prophecy of which neither the Lydians nor their princes took any account till it was fulfilled. Such was the way in which the Mermnadæ deposed the Heraclides, and themselves obtained the sovereignty.

14. When Gyges was established on the throne, he sent no small presents to Delphi, as his many silver offerings at the Delphic shrine testify. Besides this silver he gave a vast number of vessels of gold, among which the most worthy of mention are the goblets, six in number, and weighing altogether thirty talents, which stand in the Corinthian treasury, dedicated by him. I call it the Corinthian treasury, though in strictness of speech it is the treasury not of the whole Corinthian people, but of Cypselus, son of Eetion. Excepting Midas, son of Gordias, king of Phrygia, Gyges was the first of the barbarians whom we know to have sent offerings to Delphi. Midas dedicated the royal throne whereon he was accustomed to sit and administer justice, an object well worth looking at. It lies in the same place as the goblets presented by Gyges. The Delphians call the whole of the silver and the gold which Gyges dedicated, after the name of the donor, Gygian.

As soon as Gyges was king he made an inroad on Miletus and Smyrna, and took the city of Colophon. Afterwards, however, though he reigned eight and thirty years, he did not perform a single noble exploit. I shall therefore make no further mention of him, but pass on to his son and successor in the kingdom, Ardys.

15. Ardys took Priêné and made war upon Miletus. In his reign the Cimmerians, driven from their homes by the nomads of Scythia, entered Asia and captured Sardis, all but the citadel. He reigned forty-nine years, and was succeeded by his son, Sadyattes, who reigned twelve years. At his death his son Alyattes mounted the throne.

16. This prince waged war with the Medes under Cyaxares, the grandson of Deïoces, drove the Cimmerians out of Asia, conquered Smyrna, the Colophonian colony, and invaded Clazomenæ. From this last contest he did not come off as he could have wished, but met with a sore defeat; still, however, in the course of his reign, he performed other actions very worthy of note, of which I will now proceed to give an account.

17. Inheriting from his father a war with the Milesians, he pressed the siege against the city by attacking it in the following manner. When the harvest was ripe on the ground he marched his army into Milesia to the sound of pipes and harps, and flutes masculine and feminine. The buildings that were scattered over the country he neither pulled down nor burnt, nor did he even tear away the doors, but left them standing as they were. He cut down, however, and utterly destroyed all the trees and all the corn throughout the land, and then returned to his own dominions. It was idle for his army to sit down before the place, as the Milesians were masters of the sea. The reason that he did not demolish their buildings was that the inhabitants might be tempted to use them as homesteads from which to go forth to sow and till their lands; and so each time that he invaded the country he might find something to plunder.

18. In this way he carried on the war with the Milesians for eleven years, in the course of which he inflicted on them two terrible blows; one in their own country in the district of Limeneium, the other in the plain of the Mæander. During six of these eleven years, Sadyattes, the son of Ardys, who first lighted the flames of this war, was king of Lydia, and made the incursions. Only the five following years belong to the reign of Alyattes, son of Sadyattes, who (as I said before) inheriting the war from his father, applied himself to it unremittingly. The Milesians throughout the contest received no help at all from any of the Ionians, excepting those of Chios, who lent them troops in requital of a like service rendered them in former times, the Milesians having fought on the side of the Chians during the whole of the war between them and the people of Erythræ.

19. It was in the twelfth year of the war that the following mischance occurred from the firing of the harvest-fields. Scarcely had the corn been set alight by the soldiers when a violent wind carried the flames against the temple of Minerva Assesia, which caught fire and was burnt to the ground. At the time no one made any account of the circumstance; but afterwards, on the return of the army to Sardis, Alyattes fell sick. His illness continued, whereupon, either advised thereto by some friend, or perchance himself conceiving the idea, he sent messengers to Delphi to inquire of the god concerning his malady. On their arrival the Pythoness declared that no answer should be given them until they had rebuilt the temple of Minerva, burnt by the Lydians at Assêsus in Milesia.

20. Thus much I know from information given me by the Delphians; the remainder of the story the Milesians add.

The answer made by the oracle came to the ears of Periander, son of Cypselus, who was a very close friend to Thrasybulus, tyrant of Miletus at that period. He instantly despatched a messenger to report the oracle to him, in order that Thrasybulus, forewarned of its tenor, might the better adapt his measures to the posture of affairs.

21. Alyattes, the moment that the words of the oracle were reported to him, sent a herald to Miletus in hopes of concluding a truce with Thrasybulus and the Milesians for such a time as was needed to rebuild the temple. The herald went upon his way; but meantime Thrasybulus had been apprised of everything; and conjecturing what Alyattes would do, he contrived this artifice. He had all the corn that was in the city, whether belonging to himself or to private persons, brought into the market-place, and issued an order that the Milesians should hold themselves in readiness, and, when he gave the signal, should, one and all, fall to drinking and revelry.

22. The purpose for which he gave these orders was the following. He hoped that the Sardian herald, seeing so great store of corn upon the ground, and all the city given up to festivity, would inform Alyattes of it, which fell out as he anticipated. The herald observed the whole, and when he had delivered his message, went back to Sardis. This circumstance alone, as I gather, brought about the peace which ensued. Alyattes, who had hoped that there was now a great scarcity of corn in Miletus, and that the people were worn down to the last pitch of suffering, when he heard from the herald on his return from Miletus tidings so contrary to those he had expected, made a treaty with the enemy by which the two nations became close friends and allies. He then built at Assêsus two temples to Minerva instead of one, and shortly after recovered from his malady. Such were the chief circumstances of the war which Alyattes waged with Thrasybulus and the Milesians.

23. This Periander, who apprised Thrasybulus of the oracle, was son of Cypselus, and tyrant of Corinth. In his time a very wonderful thing is said to have happened. The Corinthians and the Lesbians agree in their account of the matter. They relate that Arion of Methymna, who as a player on the harp, was second to no man living at that time, and who was, so far as we know, the first to invent the dithyrambic measure, to give it its name, and to recite in it at Corinth, was carried to Tænarum on the back of a dolphin.

24. He had lived for many years at the court of Periander, when a longing came upon him to sail across to Italy and Sicily. Having made rich profits in those parts, he wanted to recross the seas to Corinth. He therefore hired a vessel, the crew of which were Corinthians, thinking that there was no people in whom he could more safely confide; and, going on board, he set sail from Tarentum. The sailors, however, when they reached the open sea, formed a plot to throw him overboard and seize upon his riches. Discovering their design, he fell on his knees, beseeching them to spare his life, and making them welcome to his money. But they refused; and required him either to kill himself outright, if he wished for a grave on the dry land, or without loss of time to leap overboard into the sea. In this strait Arion begged them, since such was their pleasure, to allow him to mount upon the quarter-deck, dressed in his full costume, and there to play and sing, and promising that, as soon as his song was ended, he would destroy himself. Delighted at the prospect of hearing the very best harper in the world, they consented, and withdrew from the stern to the middle of the vessel: while Arion dressed himself in the full costume of his calling, took his harp, and standing on the quarter-deck, chanted the Orthian. His strain ended, he flung himself, fully attired as he was, headlong into the sea. The Corinthians then sailed on to Corinth. As for Arion, a dolphin, they say, took him upon his back and carried him to Tænarum, where he went ashore, and thence proceeded to Corinth in his musician's dress, and told all that had happened to him. Periander, however, disbelieved the story, and put Arion in ward, to prevent his leaving Corinth, while he watched anxiously for the return of the mariners. On their arrival he summoned them before him and asked them if they could give him any tiding of Arion. They returned for answer that he was alive and in good health in Italy, and that they had left him at Tarentum, where he was doing well. Thereupon Arion appeared before them, just as he was when he jumped from the vessel: the men, astonished and detected in falsehood, could no longer deny their guilt. Such is the account which the Corinthians and Lesbians give; and there is to this day at Tænarum, an offering of Arion's at the shrine, which is a small figure in bronze, representing a man seated upon a dolphin.

25. Having brought the war with the Milesians to a close, and reigned over the land of Lydia for fifty-seven years, Alyattes died. He was the second prince of his house who made offerings at Delphi. His gifts, which he sent on recovering from his sickness, were a great

bowl of pure silver, with a salver in steel curiously inlaid, a work among all the offerings at Delphi the best worth looking at. Glaucus, the Chian, made it, the man who first invented the art of inlaying steel.

26. On the death of Alyattes, Crœsus, his son, who was thirty-five years old, succeeded to the throne. Of the Greek cities, Ephesus was the first that he attacked. The Ephesians, when he laid siege to the place, made an offering of their city to Diana, by stretching a rope from the town wall to the temple of the goddess, which was distant from the ancient city, then besieged by Crœsus, a space of seven furlongs. They were, as I said, the first Greeks whom he attacked. Afterwards, on some pretext or other, he made war in turn upon every Ionian and Æolian state, bringing forward, where he could, a substantial ground of complaint; where such failed him, advancing some poor excuse.

27. In this way he made himself master of all the Greek cities in Asia, and forced them to become his tributaries; after which he began to think of building ships, and attacking the islanders. Everything had been got ready for this purpose, when Bias of Priêné (or, as some say, Pittacus the Mytilenean) put a stop to the project. The king had made inquiry of this person, who was lately arrived at Sardis, if there were any news from Greece; to which he answered, "Yes, sire, the islanders are gathering ten thousand horse, designing an expedition against thee and against thy capital." Crœsus, thinking he spake seriously, broke out, "Ah, might the gods put such a thought into their minds as to attack the sons of the Lydians with cavalry!" "It seems, oh! king," rejoined the other, "that thou desirest earnestly to catch the islanders on horseback upon the mainland, —thou knowest well what would come of it. But what thinkest thou the islanders desire better, now that they hear thou art about to build ships and sail against them, than to catch the Lydians at sea, and there revenge on them the wrongs of their brothers upon the mainland, whom thou holdest in slavery?" Crœsus was charmed with the turn of the speech; and thinking there was reason in what was said, gave up his ship-building and concluded a league of amity with the Ionians of the isles.

28. Crœsus afterwards, in the course of many years, brought under his sway almost all the nations to the west of the Halys. The Lycians and Cilicians alone continued free; all the other tribes he reduced and held in subjection. They were the following: the Lydians, Phryg-ians, Mysians, Mariandynians, Chalybians, Paphlagonians, Thynian and Bithynian Thracians, Carians, Ionians, Dorians, Æolians and Pamphylians.[1]

29. When all these conquests had been added to the Lydian empire, and the prosperity of Sardis was now at its height, there came thither, one after another, all the sages of Greece living at the time, and among them Solon, the Athenian. He was on his travels, having left Athens to be absent ten years, under the pretence of wishing to see the world, but really to avoid being forced to repeal any of the laws which, at the request of the Athenians, he had made for them. Without his sanction the Athenians could not repeal them, as they had bound themselves under a heavy curse to be governed for ten years by the laws which should be imposed on them by Solon.

30. On this account, as well as to see the world, Solon set out upon his travels, in the course of which he went to Egypt to the court of Amasis, and also came on a visit to Crœsus at Sardis. Crœsus received him as his guest, and lodged him in the royal palace. On the third or fourth day after, he bade his servants conduct Solon over his treasuries, and show him all their greatness and magnificence. When he had seen them all, and, so far as time allowed, inspected them, Crœsus addressed this question to him. "Stranger of Athens, we have heard much of thy wisdom and of thy travels through many lands, from love of knowledge and a wish to see the world. I am curious therefore to inquire of thee, whom, of all the men that thou hast seen, thou deemest the most happy?" This he asked because he thought himself the happiest of mortals: but Solon answered him without flattery, according to his true sentiments, "Tellus of Athens, sire." Full of astonishment at what he heard, Crœsus demanded sharply, "And wherefore dost thou deem Tellus happiest?" To which the other replied, "First, because his country was flourishing in his days, and he himself had sons both beautiful and good, and he lived to see children born to each of them, and these children all grew up; and further because, after a life spent in what our people look upon as comfort, his end was surpassingly glorious. In a battle between the Athenians and their

[1] It is not quite correct to speak of the Cilicians as dwelling *within* (i.e., west of) the Halys, for the Halys in its upper course ran *through* Cilicia (διὰ Κιλίκων, I. 72), and that country lay chiefly *south* of the river.

neighbours near Eleusis, he came to the assistance of his countrymen, routed the foe, and died upon the field most gallantly. The Athenians gave him a public funeral on the spot where he fell, and paid him the highest honours."

31. Thus did Solon admonish Crœsus by the example of Tellus, enumerating the manifold particulars of his happiness. When he had ended, Crœsus inquired a second time, who after Tellus seemed to him the happiest, expecting that at any rate, he would be given the second place. "Cleobis and Bito," Solon answered; "they were of Argive race; their fortune was enough for their wants, and they were besides endowed with so much bodily strength that they had both gained prizes at the Games. Also this tale is told of them:— There was a great festival in honour of the goddess Juno at Argos, to which their mother must needs be taken in a car. Now the oxen did not come home from the field in time: so the youths, fearful of being too late, put the yoke on their own necks, and themselves drew the car in which their mother rode. Five and forty furlongs did they draw her, and stopped before the temple. This deed of theirs was witnessed by the whole assembly of worshippers, and then their life closed in the best possible way. Herein, too, God showed forth most evidently, how much better a thing for man death is than life. For the Argive men, who stood around the car, extolled the vast strength of the youths; and the Argive women extolled the mother who was blessed with such a pair of sons; and the mother herself, overjoyed at the deed and at the praises it had won, standing straight before the image, besought the goddess to bestow on Cleobis and Bito, the sons who had so mightily honoured her, the highest blessing to which mortals can attain. Her prayer ended, they offered sacrifice and partook of the holy banquet, after which the two youths fell asleep in the temple. They never woke more, but so passed from the earth. The Argives, looking on them as among the best of men, caused statues of them to be made, which they gave to the shrine at Delphi."

32. When Solon had thus assigned these youths the second place, Crœsus broke in angrily, "What, stranger of Athens, is my happiness, then, so utterly set at nought by thee, that thou dost not even put me on a level with private men?"

"Oh! Crœsus," replied the other, "thou askedst a question concerning the condition of man, of one who knows that the power above us is full of jealousy, and fond of troubling our lot. A long life gives one to witness much, and experience much oneself, that one would not choose. Seventy years I regard as the limit of the life of man. In these seventy years are contained, without reckoning intercalary months, twenty-five thousand and two hundred days. Add an intercalary month to every other year, that the seasons may come round at the right time, and there will be, besides the seventy years, thirty-five such months, making an addition of one thousand and fifty days. The whole number of the days contained in the seventy years will thus be twenty-six thousand two hundred and fifty, whereof not one but will produce events unlike the rest. Hence man is wholly accident. For thyself, oh! Crœsus, I see that thou art wonderfully rich, and art the lord of many nations; but with respect to that whereon thou questionest me, I have no answer to give, until I hear that thou hast closed thy life happily. For assuredly he who possesses great store of riches is no nearer happiness than he who has what suffices for his daily needs, unless it so hap that luck attend upon him, and so he continue in the enjoyment of all his good things to the end of life. For many of the wealthiest men have been unfavoured of fortune, and many whose means were moderate have had excellent luck. Men of the former class excel those of the latter but in two respects; these last excel the former in many. The wealthy man is better able to content his desires, and to bear up against a sudden buffet of calamity. The other has less ability to withstand these evils (from which, however, his good luck keeps him clear), but he enjoys all these following blessings: he is whole of limb, a stranger to disease, free from misfortune, happy in his children, and comely to look upon. If, in addition to all this, he end his life well, he is of a truth the man of whom thou art in search, the man who may rightly be termed happy. Call him, however, until he die, not happy but fortunate. Scarcely, indeed, can any man unite all these advantages: as there is no country which contains within it all that it needs, but each, while it possesses some things, lacks others, and the best country is that which contains the most; so no single human being is complete in every respect—something is always lacking. He who unites the greatest number of advantages, and retaining them to the day of his death, then dies peaceably, that man alone, sire, is, in my judgment, entitled to bear

the name of 'happy.' But in every matter it be-
hoves us to mark well the end: for oftentimes
God gives men a gleam of happiness, and then
plunges them into ruin."

33. Such was the speech which Solon addressed to Crœsus, a speech which brought
him neither largess nor honour. The king saw
him depart with much indifference, since he
thought that a man must be an arrant fool who
made no account of present good, but bade
men always wait and mark the end.

34. After Solon had gone away a dreadful
vengeance, sent of God, came upon Crœsus, to
punish him, it is likely, for deeming himself
the happiest of men. First he had a dream in
the night, which foreshowed him truly the
evils that were about to befall him in the person of his son. For Crœsus had two sons, one
blasted by a natural defect, being deaf and
dumb; the other, distinguished far above all
his co-mates in every pursuit. The name of the
last was Atys. It was this son concerning whom
he dreamt a dream that he would die by the
blow of an iron weapon. When he woke, he
considered earnestly with himself, and, greatly
alarmed at the dream, instantly made his son
take a wife, and whereas in former years the
youth had been wont to command the Lydian
forces in the field, he now would not suffer
him to accompany them. All the spears and
javelins, and weapons used in the wars, he removed out of the male apartments, and laid
them in heaps in the chambers of the women,
fearing lest perhaps one of the weapons that
hung against the wall might fall and strike
him.

35. Now it chanced that while he was making arrangements for the wedding, there came
to Sardis a man under a misfortune, who had
upon him the stain of blood. He was by race a
Phrygian, and belonged to the family of the
king. Presenting himself at the palace of Crœsus, he prayed to be admitted to purification
according to the customs of the country. Now
the Lydian method of purifying is very nearly
the same as the Greek. Crœsus granted the request, and went through all the customary
rites, after which he asked the suppliant of his
birth and country, addressing him as follows:—
"Who art thou, stranger, and from what part
of Phrygia fleddest thou to take refuge at my
hearth? And whom, moreover, what man or
what woman, hast thou slain?" "Oh! king,"
replied the Phrygian, "I am the son of Gordias,
son of Midas. I am named Adrastus. The man
I unintentionally slew was my own brother.

For this my father drove me from the land,
and I lost all. Then fled I here to thee." "Thou
art the offspring," Crœsus rejoined, "of a house
friendly to mine, and thou art come to friends.
Thou shalt want for nothing so long as thou
abidest in my dominions. Bear thy misfortune
as easily as thou mayest, so will it go best with
thee." Thenceforth Adrastus lived in the palace of the king.

36. It chanced that at this very same time
there was in the Mysian Olympus a huge monster of a boar, which went forth often from this
mountain country, and wasted the corn-fields
of the Mysians. Many a time had the Mysians
collected to hunt the beast, but instead of doing
him any hurt, they came off always with some
loss to themselves. At length they sent ambassadors to Crœsus, who delivered their message
to him in these words: "Oh! king, a mighty
monster of a boar has appeared in our parts,
and destroys the labour of our hands. We do
our best to take him, but in vain. Now therefore we beseech thee to let thy son accompany
us back, with some chosen youths and hounds,
that we may rid our country of the animal."
Such was the tenor of their prayer.

But Crœsus bethought him of his dream, and
answered, "Say no more of my son going with
you; that may not be in any wise. He is but just
joined in wedlock, and is busy enough with
that. I will grant you a picked band of Lydians, and all my huntsmen and hounds; and I
will charge those whom I send to use all zeal
in aiding you to rid your country of the brute."

37. With this reply the Mysians were content; but the king's son, hearing what the
prayer of the Mysians was, came suddenly in,
and on the refusal of Crœsus to let him go with
them, thus addressed his father: "Formerly,
my father, it was deemed the noblest and most
suitable thing for me to frequent the wars and
hunting-parties, and win myself glory in them;
but now thou keepest me away from both, although thou hast never beheld in me either
cowardice or lack of spirit. What face meanwhile must I wear as I walk to the forum or
return from it? What must the citizens, what
must my young bride think of me? What sort
of man will she suppose her husband to be?
Either, therefore, let me go to the chase of this
boar, or give me a reason why it is best for me
to do according to thy wishes."

38. Then Crœsus answered, "My son, it is
not because I have seen in thee either cowardice or aught else which has displeased me
that I keep thee back; but because a vision

which came before me in a dream as I slept, warned me that thou wert doomed to die young, pierced by an iron weapon. It was this which first led me to hasten on thy wedding, and now it hinders me from sending thee upon this enterprise. Fain would I keep watch over thee, if by any means I may cheat fate of thee during my own lifetime. For thou art the one and only son that I possess; the other, whose hearing is destroyed, I regard as if he were not."

39. "Ah! father," returned the youth, "I blame thee not for keeping watch over me after a dream so terrible; but if thou mistakest, if thou dost not apprehend the dream aright, 'tis no blame for me to show thee wherein thou errest. Now the dream, thou saidst thyself, foretold that I should die stricken by an iron weapon. But what hands has a boar to strike with? What iron weapon does he wield? Yet this is what thou fearest for me. Had the dream said that I should die pierced by a tusk, then thou hadst done well to keep me away; but it said a weapon. Now here we do not combat men, but a wild animal. I pray thee, therefore, let me go with them."

40. "There thou hast me, my son," said Crœsus, "thy interpretation is better than mine. I yield to it, and change my mind, and consent to let thee go."

41. Then the king sent for Adrastus, the Phrygian, and said to him, "Adrastus, when thou wert smitten with the rod of affliction— no reproach, my friend—I purified thee, and have taken thee to live with me in my palace, and have been at every charge. Now, therefore, it behoves thee to requite the good offices which thou hast received at my hands by consenting to go with my son on this hunting party, and to watch over him, if perchance you should be attacked upon the road by some band of daring robbers. Even apart from this, it were right for thee to go where thou mayest make thyself famous by noble deeds. They are the heritage of thy family, and thou too art so stalwart and strong."

42. Adrastus answered, "Except for thy request, Oh! king, I would rather have kept away from this hunt; for methinks it ill beseems a man under a misfortune such as mine to consort with his happier compeers; and besides, I have no heart to it. On many grounds I had stayed behind; but, as thou urgest it, and I am bound to pleasure thee (for truly it does behove me to requite thy good offices), I am content to do as thou wishest. For thy son,

whom thou givest into my charge, be sure thou shalt receive him back safe and sound, so far as depends upon a guardian's carefulness."

43. Thus assured, Crœsus let them depart, accompanied by a band of picked youths, and well provided with dogs of chase. When they reached Olympus, they scattered in quest of the animal; he was soon found, and the hunters, drawing round him in a circle, hurled their weapons at him. Then the stranger, the man who had been purified of blood, whose name was Adrastus, he also hurled his spear at the boar, but missed his aim, and struck Atys. Thus was the son of Crœsus slain by the point of an iron weapon, and the warning of the vision was fulfilled. Then one ran to Sardis to bear the tidings to the king, and he came and informed him of the combat and of the fate that had befallen his son.

44. If it was a heavy blow to the father to learn that his child was dead, it yet more strongly affected him to think that the very man whom he himself once purified had done the deed. In the violence of his grief he called aloud on Jupiter Catharsius to be a witness of what he had suffered at the stranger's hands. Afterwards he invoked the same god as Jupiter Ephistius and Hetæreus—using the one term because he had unwittingly harboured in his house the man who had now slain his son; and the other, because the stranger, who had been sent as his child's guardian, had turned out his most cruel enemy.

45. Presently the Lydians arrived, bearing the body of the youth, and behind them followed the homicide. He took his stand in front of the corse, and, stretching forth his hands to Crœsus, delivered himself into his power with earnest entreaties that he would sacrifice him upon the body of his son—"his former misfortune was burthen enough; now that he had added to it a second, and had brought ruin on the man who purified him, he could not bear to live." Then Crœsus, when he heard these words, was moved with pity towards Adrastus, notwithstanding the bitterness of his own calamity; and so he answered, "Enough, my friend; I have all the revenge that I require, since thou givest sentence of death against thyself. But in sooth it is not thou who hast injured me, except so far as thou hast unwittingly dealt the blow. Some god is the author of my misfortune, and I was forewarned of it a long time ago." Crœsus after this buried the body of his son, with such honours as befitted

the occasion. Adrastus, son of Gordias, son of Midas, the destroyer of his brother in time past, the destroyer now of his purifier, regarding himself as the most unfortunate wretch whom he had ever known, so soon as all was quiet about the place, slew himself upon the tomb. Crœsus, bereft of his son, gave himself up to mourning for two full years.

46. At the end of this time the grief of Crœsus was interrupted by intelligence from abroad. He learnt that Cyrus, the son of Cambyses, had destroyed the empire of Astyages, the son of Cyaxares; and that the Persians were becoming daily more powerful. This led him to consider with himself whether it were possible to check the growing power of that people before it came to a head. With this design he resolved to make instant trial of the several oracles in Greece, and of the one in Libya. So he sent his messengers in different directions, some to Delphi, some to Abæ in Phocis, and some to Dodôna; others to the oracle of Amphiaraüs; others to that of Trophonius; others, again, to Branchidæ in Milesia. These were the Greek oracles which he consulted. To Libya he sent another embassy, to consult the oracle of Ammon. These messengers were sent to test the knowledge of the oracles, that, if they were found really to return true answers, he might send a second time, and inquire if he ought to attack the Persians.

47. The messengers who were despatched to make trial of the oracles were given the following instructions: they were to keep count of the days from the time of their leaving Sardis, and, reckoning from that date, on the hundredth day they were to consult the oracles, and to inquire of them what Crœsus the son of Alyattes, king of Lydia, was doing at that moment. The answers given them were to be taken down in writing, and brought back to him. None of the replies remain on record except that of the oracle at Delphi. There, the moment that the Lydians entered the sanctuary, and before they put their questions, the Pythoness thus answered them in hexameter verse:—

I can count the sands, and I can measure the ocean;
I have ears for the silent, and know what the dumb man meaneth;
Lo! on my sense there striketh the smell of a shell-covered tortoise,
Boiling now on a fire, with the flesh of a lamb, in a cauldron—
Brass is the vessel below, and brass the cover above it.

48. These words the Lydians wrote down at the mouth of the Pythoness as she prophesied, and then set off on their return to Sardis. When all the messengers had come back with the answers which they had received, Crœsus undid the rolls, and read what was written in each. Only one approved itself to him, that of the Delphic oracle. This he had no sooner heard than he instantly made an act of adoration, and accepted it as true, declaring that the Delphic was the only really oracular shrine, the only one that had discovered in what way he was in fact employed. For on the departure of his messengers he had set himself to think what was most impossible for any one to conceive of his doing, and then, waiting till the day agreed on came, he acted as he had determined. He took a tortoise and a lamb, and cutting them in pieces with his own hands, boiled them both together in a brazen cauldron, covered over with a lid which was also of brass.

49. Such then was the answer returned to Crœsus from Delphi. What the answer was which the Lydians who went to the shrine of Amphiaraüs and performed the customary rites obtained of the oracle there, I have it not in my power to mention, for there is no record of it. All that is known is that Crœsus believed himself to have found there also an oracle which spoke the truth.

50. After this Crœsus, having resolved to propitiate the Delphic god with a magnificent sacrifice, offered up three thousand of every kind of sacrificial beast, and besides made a huge pile, and placed upon it couches coated with silver and with gold, and golden goblets, and robes and vests of purple; all which he burnt in the hope of thereby making himself more secure of the favour of the god. Further he issued his orders to all the people of the land to offer a sacrifice according to their means. When the sacrifice was ended, the king melted down a vast quantity of gold, and ran it into ingots, making them six palms long, three palms broad, and one palm in thickness. The number of ingots was a hundred and seventeen, four being of refined gold, in weight two talents and a half; the others of pale gold, and in weight two talents. He also caused a statue of a lion to be made in refined gold, the weight of which was ten talents. At the time when the temple of Delphi was burnt to the ground, this lion fell from the ingots on which it was placed; it now stands in the Corinthian treasury, and weighs only six talents and a half, having lost three talents and a half by the fire.

51. On the completion of these works Crœsus sent them away to Delphi, and with them two bowls of an enormous size, one of gold, the other of silver, which used to stand, the latter upon the right, the former upon the left, as one entered the temple. They too were moved at the time of the fire; and now the golden one is in the Clazomenian treasury, and weighs eight talents and forty-two minæ; the silver one stands in the corner of the ante-chapel, and holds six hundred amphoræ. This is known because the Delphians fill it at the time of the Theophania. It is said by the Delphians to be a work of Theodore the Samian, and I think that they say true, for assuredly it is the work of no common artist. Crœsus sent also four silver casks, which are in the Corinthian treasury, and two lustral vases, a golden and a silver one. On the former is inscribed the name of the Lacedæmonians, and they claim it as a gift of theirs, but wrongly, since it was really given by Crœsus. The inscription upon it was cut by a Delphian, who wished to pleasure the Lacedæmonians. His name is known to me, but I forbear to mention it. The boy, through whose hand the water runs, is (I confess) a Lacedæmonian gift, but they did not give either of the lustral vases. Besides these various offerings, Crœsus sent to Delphi many others of less account, among the rest a number of round silver basins. Also he dedicated a female figure in gold, three cubits high, which is said by the Delphians to be the statue of his baking-woman; and further, he presented the necklace and the girdles of his wife.

52. These were the offerings sent by Crœsus to Delphi. To the shrine of Amphiaraus, with whose valour and misfortune he was acquainted, he sent a shield entirely of gold, and a spear, also of solid gold, both head and shaft. They were still existing in my day at Thebes, laid up in the temple of Ismenian Apollo.

53. The messengers who had the charge of conveying these treasures to the shrines, received instructions to ask the oracles whether Crœsus should go to war with the Persians, and if so, whether he should strengthen himself by the forces of an ally. Accordingly, when they had reached their destinations and presented the gifts, they proceeded to consult the oracles in the following terms:—"Crœsus, king of Lydia and other countries, believing that these are the only real oracles in all the world, has sent you such presents as your discoveries deserved, and now inquires of you whether he shall go to war with the Persians,

and if so, whether he shall strengthen himself by the forces of a confederate." Both the oracles agreed in the tenor of their reply, which was in each case a prophecy that if Crœsus attacked the Persians, he would destroy a mighty empire, and a recommendation to him to look and see who were the most powerful of the Greeks, and to make alliance with them.

54. At the receipt of these oracular replies Crœsus was overjoyed, and feeling sure now that he would destroy the empire of the Persians, he sent once more to Pytho, and presented to the Delphians, the number of whom he had ascertained, two gold staters apiece. In return for this the Delphians granted to Crœsus and the Lydians the privilege of precedency in consulting the oracle, exemption from all charges, the most honourable seat at the festivals, and the perpetual right of becoming at pleasure citizens of their town.

55. After sending these presents to the Delphians, Crœsus a third time consulted the oracle, for having once proved its truthfulness, he wished to make constant use of it. The question whereto he now desired an answer was—"Whether his kingdom would be of long duration?" The following was the reply of the Pytheness:—

Wait till the time shall come when a mule is
*   monarch of Media;*
Then, thou delicate Lydian, away to the pebbles
*   of Hermus;*
Haste, oh! haste thee away, nor blush to behave
*   like a coward.*

56. Of all the answers that had reached him, this pleased him far the best, for it seemed incredible that a mule should ever come to be king of the Medes, and so he concluded that the sovereignty would never depart from himself or his seed after him. Afterwards he turned his thoughts to the alliance which he had been recommended to contract, and sought to ascertain by inquiry which was the most powerful of the Grecian states. His inquiries pointed out to him two states as pre-eminent above the rest. These were the Lacedæmonians and the Athenians, the former of Doric, the latter of Ionic blood. And indeed these two nations had held from very early times the most distinguished place in Greece, the one being a Pelasgic, the other a Hellenic people, and the one having never quitted its original seats, while the other had been excessively migratory; for during the reign of Deucalion, Phthiôtis was the country in which the Hellenes dwelt, but under Dorus,

the son of Hellen, they moved to the tract at the base of Ossa and Olympus, which is called Histiæôtis; forced to retire from that region by the Cadmeians,[1] they settled, under the name of Macedni, in the chain of Pindus. Hence they once more removed and came to Dryopis; and from Dryopis having entered the Peloponnese in this way, they became known as Dorians.

57. What the language of the Pelasgi was I cannot say with any certainty. If, however, we may form a conjecture from the tongue spoken by the Pelasgi of the present day—those, for instance, who live at Creston above the Tyrrhenians, who formerly dwelt in the district named Thessaliôtis, and were neighbours of the people now called the Dorians—or those again who founded Placia and Scylacé upon the Hellespont, who had previously dwelt for some time with the Athenians—or those, in short, of any other of the cities which have dropped the name but are in fact Pelasgian; if, I say, we are to form a conjecture from any of these, we must pronounce that the Pelasgi spoke a barbarous language. If this were really so, and the entire Pelasgic race spoke the same tongue, the Athenians, who were certainly Pelasgi, must have changed their language at the same time that they passed into the Hellenic body; for it is a certain fact that the people of Creston speak a language unlike any of their neighbours, and the same is true of the Placianians, while the language spoken by these two people is the same; which shows that they both retain the idiom which they brought with them into the countries where they are now settled.

58. The Hellenic race has never, since its first origin, changed its speech. This at least seems evident to me. It was a branch of the Pelasgic, which separated from the main body, and at first was scanty in numbers and of little power; but it gradually spread and increased to a multitude of nations, chiefly by the voluntary entrance into its ranks of numerous tribes of barbarians. The Pelasgi, on the other hand, were, as I think, a barbarian race which never greatly multiplied.

59. On inquiring into the condition of these two nations, Crœsus found that one, the Athenian, was in a state of grievous oppression and distraction under Pisistratus, the son of Hippocrates, who was at that time tyrant of Athens.

[1] The race (their name merely signifying "the Easterns") who, in the ante-Trojan times, occupied the country which was afterwards called Bœotia.

Hippocrates, when he was a private citizen, is said to have gone once upon a time to Olympia to see the Games, when a wonderful prodigy happened to him. As he was employed in sacrificing, the cauldrons which stood near, full of water and of the flesh of the victims, began to boil without the help of fire, so that the water overflowed the pots. Chilon the Lacedæmonian, who happened to be there and to witness the prodigy, advised Hippocrates, if he were unmarried, never to take into his house a wife who could bear him a child; if he already had one, to send her back to her friends; if he had a son, to disown him. Chilon's advice did not at all please Hippocrates, who disregarded it, and some time after became the father of Pisistratus. This Pisistratus, at a time when there was civil contention in Attica between the party of the Sea-coast headed by Megacles the son of Alcmæon, and that of the Plain headed by Lycurgus, one of the Aristolaïds, formed the project of making himself tyrant, and with this view created a third party. Gathering together a band of partisans, and giving himself out for the protector of the Highlanders, he contrived the following stratagem. He wounded himself and his mules, and then drove his chariot into the market-place, professing to have just escaped an attack of his enemies, who had attempted his life as he was on his way into the country. He besought the people to assign him a guard to protect his person, reminding them of the glory which he had gained when he led the attack upon the Megarians, and took the town of Nisæa, at the same time performing many other exploits. The Athenians, deceived by his story, appointed him a band of citizens to serve as a guard, who were to carry clubs instead of spears, and to accompany him wherever he went. Thus strengthened, Pisistratus broke into revolt and seized the citadel. In this way he acquired the sovereignty of Athens, which he continued to hold without disturbing the previously existing offices or altering any of the laws. He administered the state according to the established usages, and his arrangements were wise and salutary.

60. However, after a little time, the partisans of Megacles and those of Lycurgus agreed to forget their differences, and united to drive him out. So Pisistratus, having by the means described first made himself master of Athens, lost his power again before it had time to take root. No sooner, however, was he departed than the factions which had driven him out quarrelled anew, and at last Megacles, wearied

with the struggle, sent a herald to Pisistratus, with an offer to re-establish him on the throne if he would marry his daughter. Pisistratus consented, and on these terms an agreement was concluded between the two, after which they proceeded to devise the mode of his restoration. And here the device on which they hit was the silliest that I find on record, more especially considering that the Greeks have been from very ancient times distinguished from the barbarians by superior sagacity and freedom from foolish simpleness, and remembering that the persons on whom this trick was played were not only Greeks but Athenians, who have the credit of surpassing all other Greeks in cleverness. There was in the Pæanian district a woman named Phya, whose height only fell short of four cubits by three fingers' breadth, and who was altogether comely to look upon. This woman they clothed in complete armour, and, instructing her as to the carriage which she was to maintain in order to beseem her part, they placed her in a chariot and drove to the city. Heralds had been sent forward to precede her, and to make proclamation to this effect: "Citizens of Athens, receive again Pisistratus with friendly minds. Minerva, who of all men honours him the most, herself conducts him back to her own citadel." This they proclaimed in all directions, and immediately the rumour spread throughout the country districts that Minerva was bringing back her favourite. They of the city also, fully persuaded that the woman was the veritable goddess, prostrated themselves before her, and received Pisistratus back.

61. Pisistratus, having thus recovered the sovereignty, married, according to agreement, the daughter of Megacles. As, however, he had already a family of grown up sons, and the Alcmæonidæ were supposed to be under a curse, he determined that there should be no issue of the marriage. His wife at first kept this matter to herself, but after a time, either her mother questioned her, or it may be that she told it of her own accord. At any rate, she informed her mother, and so it reached her father's ears. Megacles, indignant at receiving an affront from such a quarter, in his anger instantly made up his differences with the opposite faction, on which Pisistratus, aware of what was planning against him, took himself out of the country. Arrived at Eretria, he held a council with his children to decide what was to be done. The opinion of Hippias prevailed, and it was agreed to aim at regaining the sovereignty The first step was to obtain advances of money from such states as were under obligations to them. By these means they collected large sums from several countries, especially from the Thebans, who gave them far more than any of the rest. To be brief, time passed, and all was at length got ready for their return. A band of Argive mercenaries arrived from the Peloponnese, and a certain Naxian named Lygdamis, who volunteered his services, was particularly zealous in the cause, supplying both men and money.

62. In the eleventh year of their exile the family of Pisistratus set sail from Eretria on their return home. They made the coast of Attica, near Marathon, where they encamped, and were joined by their partisans from the capital and by numbers from the country districts, who loved tyranny better than freedom. At Athens, while Pisistratus was obtaining funds, and even after he landed at Marathon, no one paid any attention to his proceedings. When, however, it became known that he had left Marathon, and was marching upon the city, preparations were made for resistance, the whole force of the state was levied, and led against the returning exiles. Meantime the army of Pisistratus, which had broken up from Marathon, meeting their adversaries near the temple of the Pallenian Minerva, pitched their camp opposite them. Here a certain soothsayer, Amphilytus by name, an Acarnanian, moved by a divine impulse, came into the presence of Pisistratus, and approaching him uttered this prophecy in the hexameter measure:—

Now has the cast been made, the net is out-spread
    in the water,
Through the moonshiny night the tunnies will
    enter the meshes.

63. Such was the prophecy uttered under a divine inspiration. Pisistratus, apprehending its meaning, declared that he accepted the oracle, and instantly led on his army. The Athenians from the city had just finished their midday meal, after which they had betaken themselves, some to dice, others to sleep, when Pisistratus with his troops fell upon them and put them to the rout. As soon as the flight began, Pisistratus bethought himself of a most wise contrivance, whereby the Athenians might be induced to disperse and not unite in a body any more. He mounted his sons on horseback and sent them on in front to overtake the fugitives, and exhort them to be of good cheer, and return each man to his home. The Athenians

took the advice, and Pisistratus became for the third time master of Athens.

64. Upon this he set himself to root his power more firmly, by the aid of a numerous body of mercenaries, and by keeping up a full exchequer, partly supplied from native sources, partly from the countries about the river Strymon. He also demanded hostages from many of the Athenians who had remained at home, and not left Athens at his approach; and these he sent to Naxos, which he had conquered by force of arms, and given over into the charge of Lygdamis. Farther, he purified the island of Delos, according to the injunctions of an oracle, after the following fashion. All the dead bodies which had been interred within sight of the temple he dug up, and removed to another part of the isle. Thus was the tyranny of Pisistratus established at Athens, many of the Athenians having fallen in the battle, and many others having fled the country together with the son of Alcmæon.

65. Such was the condition of the Athenians when Crœsus made inquiry concerning them. Proceeding to seek information concerning the Lacedæmonians, he learnt that, after passing through a period of great depression, they had lately been victorious in a war with the people of Tegea; for, during the joint reign of Leo and Agasicles, kings of Sparta, the Lacedæmonians, successful in all their other wars, suffered continual defeat at the hands of the Tegeans. At a still earlier period they had been the very worst governed people in Greece, as well in matters of internal management as in their relations towards foreigners, from whom they kept entirely aloof. The circumstances which led to their being well governed were the following:—Lycurgus, a man of distinction among the Spartans, had gone to Delphi, to visit the oracle. Scarcely had he entered into the inner fane, when the Pythoness exclaimed aloud,

Oh! thou great Lycurgus, that com'st to my
    beautiful dwelling,
Dear to Jove, and to all who sit in the halls
    of Olympus,
Whether to hail thee a god I know not, or only
    a mortal,
But my hope is strong that a god thou wilt
    prove, Lycurgus.

Some report besides, that the Pythoness delivered to him the entire system of laws which are still observed by the Spartans. The Lacedæmonians, however, themselves assert that Ly-

curgus, when he was guardian of his nephew, Labotas, king of Sparta, and regent in his room, introduced them from Crete; for as soon as he became regent, he altered the whole of the existing customs, substituting new ones, which he took care should be observed by all. After this he arranged whatever appertained to war, establishing the Enomotiæ, Triacades, and Syssitia, besides which he instituted the senate,[1] and the ephoralty. Such was the way in which the Lacedæmonians became a well-governed people.

66. On the death of Lycurgus they built him a temple, and ever since they have worshipped him with the utmost reverence. Their soil being good and the population numerous, they sprang up rapidly to power, and became a flourishing people. In consequence they soon ceased to be satisfied to stay quiet; and, regarding the Arcadians as very much their inferiors, they sent to consult the oracle about conquering the whole of Arcadia. The Pythoness thus answered them:

Cravest thou Arcady? Bold is thy craving. I shall
    not content it.
Many the men that in Arcady dwell, whose food
    is the acorn—
They will never allow thee. It is not I that am
    niggard.
I will give thee to dance in Tegea, with noisy
    foot-fall,
And with the measuring line mete out the glorious champaign.

When the Lacedæmonians received this reply, leaving the rest of Arcadia untouched, they marched against the Tegeans, carrying with them fetters, so confident had this oracle (which was, in truth, but of base metal) made them that they would enslave the Tegeans. The battle, however, went against them, and many fell into the enemy's hands. Then these persons, wearing the fetters which they had themselves brought, and fastened together in a string, measured the Tegean plain as they executed their labours. The fetters in which they worked were still, in my day, preserved at Tegea where they hung round the walls of the temple of Minerva Alea.

67. Throughout the whole of this early contest with the Tegeans, the Lacedæmonians met with nothing but defeats; but in the time of

[1] It is quite inconceivable that Lycurgus should in any sense have instituted the senate. Lycurgus appears to have made scarcely any changes in the constitution. What he did was to alter the customs and habits of the people.

Crœsus, under the kings Anaxandrides and Aristo, fortune had turned in their favour, in the manner which I will now relate. Having been worsted in every engagement by their enemy, they sent to Delphi, and inquired of the oracle what god they must propitiate to prevail in the war against the Tegeans. The answer of the Pythoness was that before they could prevail, they must remove to Sparta the bones of Orestes, the son of Agamemnon. Unable to discover his burial-place, they sent a second time, and asked the god where the body of the hero had been laid. The following was the answer they received:—

*Level and smooth is the plain where Arcadian
    Tegea standeth;
There two winds are ever, by strong necessity,
    blowing,
Counter-stroke answers stroke, and evil lies upon
    evil.
There all-teeming Earth doth harbour the son of
    Atrides;
Bring thou him to thy city, and then be Tegea's
    master.*

After this reply, the Lacedæmonians were no nearer discovering the burial-place than before, though they continued to search for it diligently; until at last a man named Lichas, one of the Spartans called Agathoërgi, found it. The Agathoërgi are citizens who have just served their time among the knights. The five eldest of the knights go out every year, and are bound during the year after their discharge to go wherever the State sends them, and actively employ themselves in its service.

68. Lichas was one of this body when, partly by good luck, partly by his own wisdom, he discovered the burial-place. Intercourse between the two States existing just at this time, he went to Tegea, and, happening to enter into the workshop of a smith, he saw him forging some iron. As he stood marvelling at what he beheld,[1] he was observed by the smith who, leaving off his work, went up to him and said,

"Certainly, then, you Spartan stranger, you would have been wonderfully surprised if you had seen what I have, since you make a marvel even of the working in iron. I wanted to make myself a well in this room, and began to dig it, when what think you? I came upon a coffin seven cubits long. I had never believed that men were taller in the olden times than they are now, so I opened the coffin. The body inside

[1] Herodotus means to represent that the forging of *iron* was a novelty at the time.

was of the same length: I measured it, and filled up the hole again."

Such was the man's account of what he had seen. The other, on turning the matter over in his mind, conjectured that this was the body of Orestes, of which the oracle had spoken. He guessed so, because he observed that the smithy had two bellows, which he understood to be the two winds, and the hammer and anvil would do for the stroke and the counterstroke, and the iron that was being wrought for the evil lying upon evil. This he imagined might be so because iron had been discovered to the hurt of man. Full of these conjectures, he sped back to Sparta and laid the whole matter before his countrymen. Soon after, by a concerted plan, they brought a charge against him, and began a prosecution. Lichas betook himself to Tegea, and on his arrival acquainted the smith with his misfortune, and proposed to rent his room of him. The smith refused for some time; but at last Lichas persuaded him, and took up his abode in it. Then he opened the grave, and collecting the bones, returned with them to Sparta. From henceforth, whenever the Spartans and the Tegeans made trial of each other's skill in arms, the Spartans always had greatly the advantage; and by the time to which we are now come they were masters of most of the Peloponnese.

69. Crœsus, informed of all these circumstances, sent messengers to Sparta, with gifts in their hands, who were to ask the Spartans to enter into alliance with him. They received strict injunctions as to what they should say, and on their arrival at Sparta spake as follows:—

"Crœsus, king of the Lydians and of other nations, has sent us to speak thus to you: 'Oh! Lacedæmonians, the god has bidden me to make the Greek my friend; I therefore apply to you, in conformity with the oracle, knowing that you hold the first rank in Greece, and desire to become your friend and ally in all true faith and honesty.'"

Such was the message which Crœsus sent by his heralds. The Lacedæmonians, who were aware beforehand of the reply given him by the oracle, were full of joy at the coming of the messengers, and at once took the oaths of friendship and alliance: this they did the more readily as they had previously contracted certain obligations towards him. They had sent to Sardis on one occasion to purchase some gold, intending to use it on a statue of Apollo—the statue, namely, which remains to this day at Thornax in Laconia, when Crœsus, hearing of the matter, gave them as a gift the gold which they wanted.

70. This was one reason why the Lacedæmonians were so willing to make the alliance: another was, because Crœsus had chosen them for his friends in preference to all the other Greeks. They therefore held themselves in readiness to come at his summons, and not content with so doing, they further had a huge vase made in bronze, covered with figures of animals all round the outside of the rim, and large enough to contain three hundred amphoræ, which they sent to Crœsus as a return for his presents to them. The vase, however, never reached Sardis. Its miscarriage is accounted for in two quite different ways. The Lacedæmonian story is that when it reached Samos, on its way towards Sardis, the Samians having knowledge of it, put to sea in their ships of war and made it their prize. But the Samians declare that the Lacedæmonians who had the vase in charge, happening to arrive too late, and learning that Sardis had fallen and that Crœsus was a prisoner, sold it in their island, and the purchasers (who were, they say, private persons) made an offering of it at the shrine of Juno: the sellers were very likely on their return to Sparta to have said that they had been robbed of it by the Samians. Such, then, was the fate of the vase.

71. Meanwhile Crœsus, taking the oracle in a wrong sense, led his forces into Cappadocia, fully expecting to defeat Cyrus and destroy the empire of the Persians. While he was still engaged in making preparations for his attack, a Lydian named Sandanis, who had always been looked upon as a wise man, but who after this obtained a very great name indeed among his countrymen, came forward and counselled the king in these words:

"Thou art about, oh! king, to make war against men who wear leathern trousers, and have all their other garments of leather; who feed not on what they like, but on what they can get from a soil that is sterile and unkindly; who do not indulge in wine, but drink water; who possess no figs nor anything else that is good to eat. If, then, thou conquerest them, what canst thou get from them, seeing that they have nothing at all? But if they conquer thee, consider how much that is precious thou wilt lose: if they once get a taste of our pleasant things, they will keep such hold of them that we shall never be able to make them loose their grasp. For my part, I am thankful to the gods

that they have not put it into the hearts of the Persians to invade Lydia."

Crœsus was not persuaded by this speech, though it was true enough; for before the conquest of Lydia, the Persians possessed none of the luxuries or delights of life.

72. The Cappadocians are known to the Greeks by the name of Syrians. Before the rise of the Persian power, they had been subject to the Medes; but at the present time they were within the empire of Cyrus, for the boundary between the Median and the Lydian empires was the river Halys. This stream, which rises in the mountain country of Armenia, runs first through Cilicia; afterwards it flows for a while with the Matiêni on the right, and the Phrygians on the left: then, when they are passed, it proceeds with a northern course, separating the Cappadocian Syrians from the Paphlagonians, who occupy the left bank, thus forming the boundary of almost the whole of Lower Asia, from the sea opposite Cyprus to the Euxine. Just there is the neck of the peninsula, a journey of five days across for an active walker.

73. There were two motives which led Crœsus to attack Cappadocia: firstly, he coveted the land, which he wished to add to his own dominions; but the chief reason was that he wanted to revenge on Cyrus the wrongs of Astyages, and was made confident by the oracle of being able so to do: for Astyages, son of Cyaxares and king of the Medes, who had been dethroned by Cyrus, son of Cambyses, was Crœsus' brother by marriage. This marriage had taken place under circumstances which I will now relate. A band of Scythian nomads, who had left their own land on occasion of some disturbance, had taken refuge in Media. Cyaxares, son of Phraortes, and grandson of Deïoces, was at that time king of the country. Recognising them as suppliants, he began by treating them with kindness, and coming presently to esteem them highly, he intrusted to their care a number of boys, whom they were to teach their language and to instruct in the use of the bow. Time passed, and the Scythians employed themselves, day after day, in hunting, and always brought home some game; but at last it chanced that one day they took nothing. On their return to Cyaxares with empty hands, that monarch, who was hot-tempered, as he showed upon the occasion, received them very rudely and insultingly. In consequence of this treatment, which they did not conceive themselves to have deserved, the

Scythians determined to take one of the boys whom they had in charge, cut him in pieces, and then dressing the flesh as they were wont to dress that of the wild animals, serve it up to Cyaxares as game: after which they resolved to convey themselves with all speed to Sardis, to the court of Alyattes, the son of Sadyattes. The plan was carried out: Cyaxares and his guests ate of the flesh prepared by the Scythians, and they themselves, having accomplished their purpose, fled to Alyattes in the guise of suppliants.

74. Afterwards, on the refusal of Alyattes to give up his suppliants when Cyaxares sent to demand them of him, war broke out between the Lydians and the Medes, and continued for five years, with various success. In the course of it the Medes gained many victories over the Lydians, and the Lydians also gained many victories over the Medes. Among their other battles there was one night engagement. As, however, the balance had not inclined in favour of either nation, another combat took place in the sixth year, in the course of which, just as the battle was growing warm, day was on a sudden changed into night. This event had been foretold by Thales, the Milesian, who forewarned the Ionians of it, fixing for it the very year in which it actually took place. The Medes and Lydians, when they observed the change, ceased fighting, and were alike anxious to have terms of peace agreed on. Syennesis of Cilicia, and Labynetus of Babylon, were the persons who mediated between the parties, who hastened the taking of the oaths, and brought about the exchange of espousals. It was they who advised that Alyattes should give his daughter Aryênis in marriage to Astyages, the son of Cyaxares, knowing, as they did, that without some sure bond of strong necessity, there is wont to be but little security in men's covenants. Oaths are taken by these people in the same way as by the Greeks, except that they make a slight flesh wound in their arms, from which each sucks a portion of the other's blood.

75. Cyrus had captured this Astyages, who was his mother's father, and kept him prisoner, for a reason which I shall bring forward in another part of my history. This capture formed the ground of quarrel between Cyrus and Crœsus, in consequence of which Crœsus sent his servants to ask the oracle if he should attack the Persians; and when an evasive answer came, fancying it to be in his favour, carried his arms into the Persian territory. When he reached the river Halys, he transported his army across it, as I maintain, by the bridges which exist there at the present day; but, according to the general belief of the Greeks, by the aid of Thales the Milesian. The tale is that Crœsus was in doubt how he should get his army across, as the bridges were not made at that time, and that Thales, who happened to be in the camp, divided the stream and caused it to flow on both sides of the army instead of on the left only. This he effected thus:—Beginning some distance above the camp, he dug a deep channel, which he brought round in a semicircle, so that it might pass to rearward of the camp; and that thus the river, diverted from its natural course into the new channel at the point where this left the stream, might flow by the station of the army, and afterwards fall again into the ancient bed. In this way the river was split into two streams, which were both easily fordable. It is said by some that the water was entirely drained off from the natural bed of the river. But I am of a different opinion; for I do not see how, in that case, they could have crossed it on their return.

76. Having passed the Halys with the forces under his command, Crœsus entered the district of Cappadocia which is called Pteria. It lies in the neighbourhood of the city of Sinôpé upon the Euxine, and is the strongest position in the whole country thereabouts. Here Crœsus pitched his camp, and began to ravage the fields of the Syrians. He besieged and took the chief city of the Pterians, and reduced the inhabitants to slavery: he likewise made himself master of the surrounding villages. Thus he brought ruin on the Syrians, who were guilty of no offence towards him. Meanwhile, Cyrus had levied an army and marched against Crœsus, increasing his numbers at every step by the forces of the nations that lay in his way. Before beginning his march he had sent heralds to the Ionians, with an invitation to them to revolt from the Lydian king: they, however, had refused compliance. Cyrus, notwithstanding, marched against the enemy, and encamped opposite them in the district of Pteria, where the trial of strength took place between the contending powers. The combat was hot and bloody, and upon both sides the number of the slain was great; nor had victory declared in favour of either party, when night came down upon the battle-field. Thus both armies fought valiantly.

77. Crœsus laid the blame of his ill success on the number of his troops, which fell very

short of the enemy; and as on the next day Cyrus did not repeat the attack, he set off on his return to Sardis, intending to collect his allies and renew the contest in the spring. He meant to call on the Egyptians to send him aid, according to the terms of the alliance which he had concluded with Amasis, previously to his league with the Lacedæmonians. He intended also to summon to his assistance the Babylonians, under their king Labynetus, for they too were bound to him by treaty: and further, he meant to send word to Sparta, and appoint a day for the coming of their succours. Having got together these forces in addition to his own, he would, as soon as the winter was past and springtime come, march once more against the Persians. With these intentions Crœsus, immediately on his return, despatched heralds to his various allies, with a request that they would join him at Sardis in the course of the fifth month from the time of the departure of his messengers. He then disbanded the army —consisting of mercenary troops—which had been engaged with the Persians and had since accompanied him to his capital, and let them depart to their homes, never imagining that Cyrus, after a battle in which victory had been so evenly balanced, would venture to march upon Sardis.

78. While Crœsus was still in this mind, all the suburbs of Sardis were found to swarm with snakes, on the appearance of which the horses left feeding in the pasture-grounds, and flocked to the suburbs to eat them. The king, who witnessed the unusual sight, regarded it very rightly as a prodigy. He therefore instantly sent messengers to the soothsayers of Telmessus, to consult them upon the matter. His messengers reached the city, and obtained from the Telmessians an explanation of what the prodigy portended, but fate did not allow them to inform their lord; for ere they entered Sardis on their return, Crœsus was a prisoner. What the Telmessians had declared was that Crœsus must look for the entry of an army of foreign invaders into his country, and that when they came they would subdue the native inhabitants; since the snake, said they, is a child of earth, and the horse a warrior and a foreigner. Crœsus was already a prisoner when the Telmessians thus answered his inquiry, but they had no knowledge of what was taking place at Sardis, or of the fate of the monarch.

79. Cyrus, however, when Crœsus broke up so suddenly from his quarters after the battle at Pteria, conceiving that he had marched away with the intention of disbanding his army, considered a little, and soon saw that it was advisable for him to advance upon Sardis with all haste, before the Lydians could get their forces together a second time. Having thus determined, he lost no time in carrying out his plan. He marched forward with such speed that he was himself the first to announce his coming to the Lydian king. That monarch, placed in the utmost difficulty by the turn of events which had gone so entirely against all his calculations, nevertheless led out the Lydians to battle. In all Asia there was not at that time a braver or more warlike people. Their manner of fighting was on horseback; they carried long lances, and were clever in the management of their steeds.

80. The two armies met in the plain before Sardis. It is a vast flat, bare of trees, watered by the Hyllus and a number of other streams, which all flow into one larger than the rest, called the Hermus. This river rises in the sacred mountain of the Dindymenian Mother, and falls into the sea near the town of Phocæa.

When Cyrus beheld the Lydians arranging themselves in order of battle on this plain, fearful of the strength of their cavalry, he adopted a device which Harpagus, one of the Medes, suggested to him. He collected together all the camels that had come in the train of his army to carry the provisions and the baggage, and taking off their loads, he mounted riders upon them accoutred as horsemen. These he commanded to advance in front of his other troops against the Lydian horse; behind them were to follow the foot soldiers, and last of all the cavalry. When his arrangements were complete, he gave his troops orders to slay all the other Lydians who came in their way without mercy, but to spare Crœsus and not kill him, even if he should be seized and offer resistance. The reason why Cyrus opposed his camels to the enemy's horse was because the horse has a natural dread of the camel, and cannot abide either the sight or the smell of that animal. By this stratagem he hoped to make Crœsus's horse useless to him, the horse being what he chiefly depended on for victory. The two armies then joined battle, and immediately the Lydian war-horses, seeing and smelling the camels, turned round and galloped off; and so it came to pass that all Crœsus's hopes withered away. The Lydians, however, behaved manfully. As soon as they understood what was happening, they leaped off their horses, and engaged with the Persians on foot. The combat was long; but at last, after a great slaughter on both sides, the Lydians turned and fled. They were driven within their walls, and the Persians laid siege to Sardis.

81. Thus the siege began. Meanwhile Crœsus, thinking that the place would hold out no inconsiderable time, sent off fresh heralds to his allies from the beleaguered town. His former messengers had been charged to bid them assemble at Sardis in the course of the fifth month; they whom he now sent were to say that he was already besieged, and to beseech them to come to his aid with all possible speed. Among his other allies Crœsus did not omit to send to Lacedæmon.

82. It chanced, however, that the Spartans were themselves just at this time engaged in a quarrel with the Argives about a place called Thyrea, which was within the limits of Argolis, but had been seized on by the Lacedæmonians. Indeed, the whole country westward, as far as Cape Malea, belonged once to the Argives, and not only that entire tract upon the mainland, but also Cythêra, and the other islands. The Argives collected troops to resist the seizure of Thyrea, but before any battle was fought, the two parties came to terms, and it was agreed that three hundred Spartans and three hundred Argives should meet and fight for the place, which should belong to the nation with whom the victory rested. It was stipulated also that the other troops on each side should return home to their respective countries, and not remain to witness the combat, as there was danger, if the armies stayed, that either the one or the other, on seeing their countrymen undergoing defeat, might hasten to their assistance. These terms being agreed on, the two armies marched off, leaving three hundred picked men on each side to fight for the territory. The battle began, and so equal were the combatants, that at the close of the day, when night put a stop to the fight, of the whole six hundred only three men remained alive, two Argives, Alcanor and Chromius, and a single Spartan, Othryadas. The two Argives, regarding themselves as the victors, hurried to Argos. Othryadas, the Spartan, remained upon the field, and, stripping the bodies of the Argives who had fallen, carried their armour to the Spartan camp. Next day the two armies returned to learn the result. At first they disputed, both parties claiming the victory, the one, because they had the greater number of survivors; the other, because their man remained on the field, and stripped the bodies of the slain, whereas the two men of the other side ran away; but at last they fell from words to blows, and a battle was fought, in which both parties suffered great loss, but at the end the Lacedæmonians gained the victory. Upon this the Argives, who up to that time had worn their hair long, cut it off close, and made a law, to which they attached a curse, binding themselves never more to let their hair grow, and never to allow their women to wear gold, until they should recover Thyrea. At the same time the Lacedæmonians made a law the very reverse of this, namely, to wear their hair long, though they had always before cut it close. Othryadas himself, it is said, the sole survivor of the three hundred, prevented by a sense of shame from returning to Sparta after all his comrades had fallen, laid violent hands upon himself in Thyrea.

83. Although the Spartans were engaged with these matters when the herald arrived from Sardis to entreat them to come to the assistance of the besieged king, yet, notwithstanding, they instantly set to work to afford him help. They had completed their preparations, and the ships were just ready to start, when a second message informed them that the place had already fallen, and that Crœsus was a prisoner. Deeply grieved at his misfortune, the Spartans ceased their efforts.

84. The following is the way in which Sardis was taken. On the fourteenth day of the siege Cyrus bade some horsemen ride about his lines, and make proclamation to the whole army that he would give a reward to the man who should first mount the wall. After this he made an assault, but without success. His troops retired, but a certain Mardian, Hyrœades by name, resolved to approach the citadel and attempt it at a place where no guards were ever set. On this side the rock was so precipitous, and the citadel (as it seemed) so impregnable, that no fear was entertained of its being carried in this place. Here was the only portion of the circuit round which their old king Meles did not carry the lion which his leman bore to him. For when the Telmessians had declared that if the lion were taken round the defences, Sardis would be impregnable, and Meles, in consequence, carried it round the rest of the fortress where the citadel seemed open to attack, he scorned to take it round this side, which he looked on as a sheer precipice, and therefore absolutely secure. It is on that side of the city which faces Mount Tmolus. Hyrœades, however, having the day before observed

a Lydian soldier descend the rock after a helmet that had rolled down from the top, and having seen him pick it up and carry it back, thought over what he had witnessed, and formed his plan. He climbed the rock himself, and other Persians followed in his track, until a large number had mounted to the top. Thus was Sardis taken, and given up entirely to pillage.

85. With respect to Crœsus himself, this is what befell him at the taking of the town. He had a son, of whom I made mention above, a worthy youth, whose only defect was that he was deaf and dumb. In the days of his prosperity Crœsus had done the utmost that he could for him, and among other plans which he had devised, had sent to Delphi to consult the oracle on his behalf. The answer which he had received from the Pythoness ran thus:—

Lydian, wide-ruling monarch, thou wondrous simple Crœsus,
Wish not ever to hear in thy palace the voice thou hast prayed for
Uttering intelligent sounds. Far better thy son should be silent!
Ah! woe worth the day when thine ear shall first list to his accents.

When the town was taken, one of the Persians was just going to kill Crœsus, not knowing who he was. Crœsus saw the man coming, but under the pressure of his affliction, did not care to avoid the blow, not minding whether or no he died beneath the stroke. Then this son of his, who was voiceless, beholding the Persian as he rushed towards Crœsus, in the agony of his fear and grief burst into speech, and said, "Man, do not kill Crœsus." This was the first time that he had ever spoken a word, but afterwards he retained the power of speech for the remainder of his life.

86. Thus was Sardis taken by the Persians, and Crœsus himself fell into their hands, after having reigned fourteen years, and been besieged in his capital fourteen days; thus too did Crœsus fulfill the oracle, which said that he should destroy a mighty empire—by destroying his own. Then the Persians who had made Crœsus prisoner brought him before Cyrus. Now a vast pile had been raised by his orders, and Crœsus, laden with fetters, was placed upon it, and with him twice seven of the sons of the Lydians. I know not whether Cyrus was minded to make an offering of the first-fruits to some god or other, or whether he had vowed a vow and was performing it, or whether, as may well be, he had heard that Crœsus was a holy man, and so wished to see if any of the heavenly powers would appear to save him from being burnt alive. However it might be, Cyrus was thus engaged, and Crœsus was already on the pile, when it entered his mind in the depth of his woe that there was a divine warning in the words which had come to him from the lips of Solon, "No one while he lives is happy." When this thought smote him he fetched a long breath, and breaking his deep silence, groaned out aloud, thrice uttering the name of Solon. Cyrus caught the sounds, and bade the interpreters inquire of Crœsus who it was he called on. They drew near and asked him, but he held his peace, and for a long time made no answer to their questionings, until at length, forced to say something, he exclaimed, "One I would give much to see converse with every monarch." Not knowing what he meant by this reply, the interpreters begged him to explain himself; and as they pressed for an answer, and grew to be troublesome, he told them how, a long time before, Solon, an Athenian, had come and seen all his splendour, and made light of it; and how whatever he had said to him had fallen out exactly as he foreshowed, although it was nothing that especially concerned him, but applied to all mankind alike, and most to those who seemed to themselves happy. Meanwhile, as he thus spoke, the pile was lighted, and the outer portion began to blaze. Then Cyrus, hearing from the interpreters what Crœsus had said, relented, bethinking himself that he too was a man, and that it was a fellow-man, and one who had once been as blessed by fortune as himself, that he was burning alive; afraid, moreover, of retribution, and full of the thought that whatever is human is insecure. So he bade them quench the blazing fire as quickly as they could, and take down Crœsus and the other Lydians, which they tried to do, but the flames were not to be mastered.

87. Then, the Lydians say that Crœsus, perceiving by the efforts made to quench the fire that Cyrus had relented, and seeing also that all was in vain, and that the men could not get the fire under, called with a loud voice upon the god Apollo, and prayed him, if he ever received at his hands any acceptable gift, to come to his aid, and deliver him from his present danger. As thus with tears he besought the god, suddenly, though up to that time the sky had been clear and the day without a breath of wind, dark clouds gathered, and the storm burst over their heads with rain of such violence, that the flames were speedily extin-

guished. Cyrus, convinced by this that Crœsus was a good man and a favourite of heaven, asked him after he was taken off the pile, "Who it was that had persuaded him to lead an army into his country, and so become his foe rather than continue his friend?" to which Crœsus made answer as follows: "What I did, oh! king, was to thy advantage and to my own loss. If there be blame, it rests with the god of the Greeks, who encouraged me to begin the war. No one is so foolish as to prefer war to peace, in which, instead of sons burying their fathers, fathers bury their sons. But the gods willed it so."

88. Thus did Crœsus speak. Cyrus then ordered his fetters to be taken off, and made him sit down near himself, and paid him much respect, looking upon him, as did also the courtiers, with a sort of wonder. Crœsus, wrapped in thought, uttered no word. After a while, happening to turn and perceive the Persian soldiers engaged in plundering the town, he said to Cyrus, "May I now tell thee, oh! king, what I have in my mind, or is silence best?" Cyrus bade him speak his mind boldly. Then he put this question: "What is it, oh! Cyrus, which those men yonder are doing so busily?" "Plundering thy city," Cyrus answered, "and carrying off thy riches." "Not my city," rejoined the other, "nor my riches. They are not mine any more. It is thy wealth which they are pillaging."

89. Cyrus, struck by what Crœsus had said, bade all the court to withdraw, and then asked Crœsus what he thought it best for him to do as regarded the plundering. Crœsus answered, "Now that the gods have made me thy slave, oh! Cyrus, it seems to me that it is my part, if I see anything to thy advantage, to show it to thee. Thy subjects, the Persians, are a poor people with a proud spirit. If then thou lettest them pillage and possess themselves of great wealth, I will tell thee what thou hast to expect at their hands. The man who gets the most, look to having him rebel against thee. Now then, if my words please thee, do thus, oh! king:—Let some of thy bodyguards be placed as sentinels at each of the city gates, and let them take their booty from the soldiers as they leave the town, and tell them that they do so because the tenths are due to Jupiter. So wilt thou escape the hatred they would feel if the plunder were taken away from them by force; and they, seeing that what is proposed is just, will do it willingly."

90. Cyrus was beyond measure pleased with this advice, so excellent did it seem to him. He praised Crœsus highly, and gave orders to his bodyguard to do as he had suggested. Then, turning to Crœsus, he said, "Oh! Crœsus, I see that thou art resolved both in speech and act to show thyself a virtuous prince: ask me, therefore, whatever thou wilt as a gift at this moment." Crœsus replied, "Oh! my lord, if thou wilt suffer me to send these fetters to the god of the Greeks, whom I once honoured above all other gods, and ask him if it is his wont to deceive his benefactors—that will be the highest favour thou canst confer on me." Cyrus upon this inquired what charge he had to make against the god. Then Crœsus gave him a full account of all his projects, and of the answers of the oracle, and of the offerings which he had sent, on which he dwelt especially, and told him how it was the encouragement given him by the oracle which had led him to make war upon Persia. All this he related, and at the end again besought permission to reproach the god with his behaviour. Cyrus answered with a laugh, "This I readily grant thee, and whatever else thou shalt at any time ask at my hands." Crœsus, finding his request allowed, sent certain Lydians to Delphi, enjoining them to lay his fetters upon the threshold of the temple, and ask the god, "If he were not ashamed of having encouraged him, as the destined destroyer of the empire of Cyrus, to begin a war with Persia, of which such were the first-fruits?" As they said this they were to point to the fetters; and further they were to inquire, "If it was the wont of the Greek gods to be ungrateful?"

91. The Lydians went to Delphi and delivered their message, on which the Pythoness is said to have replied—"It is not possible even for a god to escape the decree of destiny. Crœsus has been punished for the sin of his fifth ancestor, who, when he was one of the bodyguard of the Heraclides, joined in a woman's fraud, and, slaying his master, wrongfully seized the throne. Apollo was anxious that the fall of Sardis should not happen in the lifetime of Crœsus, but be delayed to his son's days; he could not, however, persuade the Fates. All that they were willing to allow he took and gave to Crœsus. Let Crœsus know that Apollo delayed the taking of Sardis three full years, and that he is thus a prisoner three years later than was his destiny. Moreover it was Apollo who saved him from the burning pile. Nor has Crœsus any right to complain with respect to the oracular answer which he received. For

when the god told him that, if he attacked the Persians, he would destroy a mighty empire, he ought, if he had been wise, to have sent again and inquired which empire was meant, that of Cyrus or his own; but if he neither understood what was said, nor took the trouble to seek for enlightenment, he has only himself to blame for the result. Besides, he had misunderstood the last answer which had been given him about the mule. Cyrus was that mule. For the parents of Cyrus were of different races, and of different conditions—his mother a Median princess, daughter of King Astyages, and his father a Persian and a subject, who, though so far beneath her in all respects, had married his royal mistress."

Such was the answer of the Pythoness. The Lydians returned to Sardis and communicated it to Crœsus, who confessed, on hearing it, that the fault was his, not the god's. Such was the way in which Ionia was first conquered, and so was the empire of Crœsus brought to a close.

92. Besides the offerings which have been already mentioned, there are many others in various parts of Greece presented by Crœsus; as at Thebes in Bœotia, where there is a golden tripod, dedicated by him to Ismenian Apollo; at Ephesus, where the golden heifers, and most of the columns are his gift; and at Delphi, in the temple of Pronaia, where there is a huge shield in gold, which he gave. All these offerings were still in existence in my day; many others have perished: among them those which he dedicated at Branchidæ in Milesia, equal in weight, as I am informed, and in all respects like to those at Delphi. The Delphian presents, and those sent to Amphiaraüs, came from his own private property, being the first-fruits of the fortune which he inherited from his father; his other offerings came from the riches of an enemy, who, before he mounted the throne, headed a party against him, with the view of obtaining the crown of Lydia for Pantaleon. This Pantaleon was a son of Alyattes, but by a different mother from Crœsus; for the mother of Crœsus was a Carian woman, but the mother of Pantaleon an Ionian. When, by the appointment of his father, Crœsus obtained the kingly dignity, he seized the man who had plotted against him, and broke him upon the wheel. His property, which he had previously devoted to the service of the gods, Crœsus applied in the way mentioned above. This is all I shal' say about his offerings.

93. Lydia, 'unlike most other countries,

scarcely offers any wonders for the historian to describe, except the gold-dust which is washed down from the range of Tmolus. It has, however, one structure of enormous size, only inferior to the monuments of Egypt and Babylon. This is the tomb of Alyattes, the father of Crœsus, the base of which is formed of immense blocks of stone, the rest being a vast mound of earth. It was raised by the joint labour of the tradesmen, handicraftsmen, and courtesans of Sardis, and had at the top five stone pillars, which remained to my day, with inscriptions cut on them, showing how much of the work was done by each class of workpeople. It appeared on measurement that the portion of the courtesans was the largest. The daughters of the common people in Lydia, one and all, pursue this traffic, wishing to collect money for their portions. They continue the practice till they marry; and are wont to contract themselves in marriage. The tomb is six stades and two plethra in circumference; its breadth is thirteen plethra. Close to the tomb is a large lake, which the Lydians say is never dry. They call it the Lake Gygæa.

94. The Lydians have very nearly the same customs as the Greeks, with the exception that these last do not bring up their girls in the same way. So far as we have any knowledge, they were the first nation to introduce the use of gold and silver coin, and the first who sold goods by retail. They claim also the invention of all the games which are common to them with the Greeks. These they declare that they invented about the time when they colonised Tyrrhenia, an event of which they give the following account. In the days of Atys, the son of Manes, there was great scarcity through the whole land of Lydia. For some time the Lydians bore the affliction patiently, but finding that it did not pass away, they set to work to devise remedies for the evil. Various expedients were discovered by various persons; dice, and huckle-bones, and ball, and all such games were invented, except tables, the invention of which they do not claim as theirs. The plan adopted against the famine was to engage in games one day so entirely as not to feel any craving for food, and the next day to eat and abstain from games. In this way they passed eighteen years. Still the affliction continued and even became more grievous. So the king determined to divide the nation in half, and to make the two portions draw lots, the one to stay, the other to leave the land. He would continue to reign over those whose lot it should

be to remain behind; the emigrants should have his son Tyrrhênus for their leader. The lot was cast, and they who had to emigrate went down to Smyrna, and built themselves ships, in which, after they had put on board all needful stores, they sailed away in search of new homes and better sustenance. After sailing past many countries they came to Umbria, where they built cities for themselves, and fixed their residence. Their former name of Lydians they laid aside, and called themselves after the name of the king's son, who led the colony, Tyrrhenians.

95. Thus far I have been engaged in showing how the Lydians were brought under the Persian yoke. The course of my history now compels me to inquire who this Cyrus was by whom the Lydian empire was destroyed, and by what means the Persians had become the lords paramount of Asia. And herein I shall follow those Persian authorities whose object it appears to be not to magnify the exploits of Cyrus, but to relate the simple truth. I know besides three ways in which the story of Cyrus is told, all differing from my own narrative.

The Assyrians had held the Empire of Upper Asia for the space of five hundred and twenty years, when the Medes set the example of revolt from their authority. They took arms for the recovery of their freedom, and fought a battle with the Assyrians, in which they behaved with such gallantry as to shake off the yoke of servitude, and to become a free people. Upon their success the other nations also revolted and regained their independence.

96. Thus the nations over that whole extent of country obtained the blessing of self-government, but they fell again under the sway of kings, in the manner which I will now relate. There was a certain Mede named Deioces, son of Phraortes, a man of much wisdom, who had conceived the desire of obtaining to himself the sovereign power. In furtherance of his ambition, therefore, he formed and carried into execution the following scheme. As the Medes at that time dwelt in scattered villages without any central authority, and lawlessness in consequence prevailed throughout the land, Deioces, who was already a man of mark in his own village, applied himself with greater zeal and earnestness than ever before to the practice of justice among his fellows. It was his conviction that justice and injustice are engaged in perpetual war with one another. He therefore began his course of conduct, and presently the men of his village, observing his integrity,

chose him to be the arbiter of all their disputes. Bent on obtaining the sovereign power, he showed himself an honest and an upright judge, and by these means gained such credit with his fellow-citizens as to attract the attention of those who lived in the surrounding villages. They had long been suffering from unjust and oppressive judgments; so that, when they heard of the singular uprightness of Deioces, and of the equity of his decisions, they joyfully had recourse to him in the various quarrels and suits that arose, until at last they came to put confidence in no one else.

97. The number of complaints brought before him continually increasing, as people learnt more and more the fairness of his judgments, Deioces, feeling himself now all important, announced that he did not intend any longer to hear causes, and appeared no more in the seat in which he had been accustomed to sit and administer justice. "It did not square with his interests," he said, "to spend the whole day in regulating other men's affairs to the neglect of his own." Hereupon robbery and lawlessness broke out afresh, and prevailed through the country even more than heretofore; wherefore the Medes assembled from all quarters, and held a consultation on the state of affairs. The speakers, as I think, were chiefly friends of Deioces. "We cannot possibly," they said, "go on living in this country if things continue as they now are; let us therefore set a king over us, that so the land may be well governed, and we ourselves may be able to attend to our own affairs, and not be forced to quit our country on account of anarchy." The assembly was persuaded by these arguments, and resolved to appoint a king.

98. It followed to determine who should be chosen to the office. When this debate began the claims of Deioces and his praises were at once in every mouth; so that presently all agreed that he should be king. Upon this he required a palace to be built for him suitable to his rank, and a guard to be given him for his person. The Medes complied, and built him a strong and large palace, on a spot which he himself pointed out, and likewise gave him liberty to choose himself a bodyguard from the whole nation. Thus settled upon the throne, he further required them to build a single great city, and, disregarding the petty towns in which they had formerly dwelt, make the new capital the object of their chief attention. The Medes were again obedient, and built the city now called Agbatana, the walls of which are of

great size and strength, rising in circles one within the other. The plan of the place is that each of the walls should out-top the one beyond it by the battlements. The nature of the ground, which is a gentle hill, favours this arrangement in some degree, but it was mainly effected by art. The number of the circles is seven, the royal palace and the treasuries standing within the last. The circuit of the outer wall is very nearly the same with that of Athens. Of this wall the battlements are white, of the next black, of the third scarlet, of the fourth blue, of the fifth orange; all these are coloured with paint. The two last have their battlements coated respectively with silver and gold.

99. All these fortifications Deioces caused to be raised for himself and his own palace. The people were required to build their dwellings outside the circuit of the walls. When the town was finished, he proceeded to arrange the ceremonial. He allowed no one to have direct access to the person of the king, but made all communication pass through the hands of messengers, and forbade the king to be seen by his subjects. He also made it an offence for any one whatsoever to laugh or spit in the royal presence. This ceremonial, of which he was the first inventor, Deioces established for his own security, fearing that his compeers, who were brought up together with him, and were of as good family as he, and no whit inferior to him in manly qualities, if they saw him frequently would be pained at the sight, and would therefore be likely to conspire against him; whereas if they did not see him, they would think him quite a different sort of being from themselves.

100. After completing these arrangements, and firmly settling himself upon the throne, Deioces continued to administer justice with the same strictness as before. Causes were stated in writing, and sent in to the king, who passed his judgment upon the contents, and transmitted his decisions to the parties concerned: besides which he had spies and eavesdroppers in all parts of his dominions, and if he heard of any act of oppression, he sent for the guilty party, and awarded him the punishment meet for his offence.

101. Thus Deioces collected the Medes into a nation, and ruled over them alone. Now these are the tribes of which they consist: the Busæ, the Parêtacêni, the Struchates, the Arizanti, the Budii, and the Magi.

102. Having reigned three-and-fifty years, Deioces was at his death succeeded by his son Phraortes. This prince, not satisfied with a dominion which did not extend beyond the single nation of the Medes, began by attacking the Persians; and marching an army into their country, brought them under the Median yoke before any other people. After this success, being now at the head of two nations, both of them powerful, he proceeded to conquer Asia, overrunning province after province. At last he engaged in war with the Assyrians—those Assyrians, I mean, to whom Nineveh belonged, who were formerly the lords of Asia. At present they stood alone by the revolt and desertion of their allies, yet still their internal condition was as flourishing as ever. Phraortes attacked them, but perished in the expedition with the greater part of his army, after having reigned over the Medes two-and-twenty years.

103. On the death of Phraortes his son Cyaxares ascended the throne. Of him it is reported that he was still more war-like than any of his ancestors, and that he was the first who gave organisation to an Asiatic army, dividing the troops into companies, and forming distinct bodies of the spearmen, the archers, and the cavalry, who before his time had been mingled in one mass, and confused together. He it was who fought against the Lydians on the occasion when the day was changed suddenly into night, and who brought under his dominion the whole of Asia beyond the Halys. This prince, collecting together all the nations which owned his sway, marched against Nineveh, resolved to avenge his father, and cherishing a hope that he might succeed in taking the town. A battle was fought, in which the Assyrians suffered a defeat, and Cyaxares had already begun the siege of the place, when a numerous horde of Scyths, under their king Madyes, son of Prtôtohyes, burst into Asia in pursuit of the Cimmerians whom they had driven out of Europe, and entered the Median territory.

104. The distance from the Palus Mæôtis to the river Phasis and the Colchians is thirty days' journey for a lightly-equipped traveller. From Colchis to cross into Media does not take long—there is only a single intervening nation, the Saspirians, passing whom you find yourself in Media. This however was not the road followed by the Scythians, who turned out of the straight course, and took the upper route, which is much longer, keeping the Caucasus upon their right. The Scythians, having thus invaded Media, were opposed by the Medes, who gave them battle, but, being defeated, lost their empire. The Scythians became masters of Asia.

105. After this they marched forward with the design of invading Egypt. When they had reached Palestine, however, Psammetichus the Egyptian king met them with gifts and prayers, and prevailed on them to advance no further. On their return, passing through Ascalon, a city of Syria, the greater part of them went their way without doing any damage; but some few who lagged behind pillaged the temple of Celestial Venus. I have inquired and find that the temple at Ascalon is the most ancient of all the temples to this goddess; for the one in Cyprus, as the Cyprians themselves admit, was built in imitation of it; and that in Cythêra was erected by the Phœnicians, who belong to this part of Syria. The Scythians who plundered the temple were punished by the goddess with the female sickness, which still attaches to their posterity. They themselves confess that they are afflicted with the disease for this reason, and travellers who visit Scythia can see what sort of a disease it is. Those who suffer from it are called Enarees.

106. The dominion of the Scythians over Asia lasted eight-and-twenty years, during which time their insolence and oppression spread ruin on every side. For besides the regular tribute, they exacted from the several nations additional imposts, which they fixed at pleasure; and further, they scoured the country and plundered every one of whatever they could. At length Cyaxares and the Medes invited the greater part of them to a banquet, and made them drunk with wine, after which they were all massacred. The Medes then recovered their empire, and had the same extent of dominion as before. They took Nineveh—I will relate how in another history—and conquered all Assyria except the district of Babylonia. After this Cyaxares died, having reigned over the Medes, if we include the time of the Scythian rule, forty years.

107. Astyages, the son of Cyaxares, succeeded to the throne. He had a daughter who was named Mandané concerning whom he had a wonderful dream. He dreamt that from her such a stream of water flowed forth as not only to fill his capital, but to flood the whole of Asia. This vision he laid before such of the Magi as had the gift of interpreting dreams, who expounded its meaning to him in full, whereat he was greatly terrified. On this account, when his daughter was now of ripe age, he would not give her in marriage to any of the Medes who were of suitable rank, lest the dream should be accomplished; but he married her to a Persian of good family indeed, but of a quiet temper, whom he looked on as much inferior to a Mede of even middle condition.

108. Thus Cambyses (for so was the Persian called) wedded Mandané, and took her to his home, after which, in the very first year, Astyages saw another vision. He fancied that a vine grew from the womb of his daughter, and overshadowed the whole of Asia. After this dream, which he submitted also to the interpreters, he sent to Persia and fetched away Mandané, who was now with child, and was not far from her time. On her arrival he set a watch over her, intending to destroy the child to which she should give birth; for the Magian interpreters had expounded the vision to foreshow that the offspring of his daughter would reign over Asia in his stead. To guard against this, Astyages, as soon as Cyrus was born, sent for Harpagus, a man of his own house and the most faithful of the Medes, to whom he was wont to entrust all his affairs, and addressed him thus—"Harpagus, I beseech thee neglect not the business with which I am about to charge thee; neither betray thou the interests of thy lord for others' sake, lest thou bring destruction on thine own head at some future time. Take the child born of Mandané my daughter; carry him with thee to thy home and slay him there. Then bury him as thou wilt." "Oh! king," replied the other, "never in time past did Harpagus disoblige thee in anything, and be sure that through all future time he will be careful in nothing to offend. If therefore it be thy will that this thing be done, it is for me to serve thee with all diligence."

109. When Harpagus had thus answered, the child was given into his hands, clothed in the garb of death, and he hastened weeping to his home. There on his arrival he found his wife, to whom he told all that Astyages had said. "What then," said she, "is it now in thy heart to do?" "Not what Astyages requires," he answered; "no, he may be madder and more frantic still than he is now, but I will not be the man to work his will, or lend a helping hand to such a murder as this. Many things forbid my slaying him. In the first place the boy is my own kith and kin; and next Astyages is old, and has no son. If then when he dies the crown should go to his daughter—that daughter whose child he now wishes to slay by my hand—what remains for me but danger of the fearfullest kind? For my own safety, indeed, the child must die; but some one belonging to Astyages must take his life, not I or mine."

110. So saying he sent off a messenger to fetch a certain Mitradates, one of the herdsmen of Astyages, whose pasturages he knew to be the fittest for his purpose, lying as they did among mountains infested with wild beasts. This man was married to one of the king's female slaves, whose Median name was Spaco, which is in Greek Cyno, since in the Median tongue the word "Spaca" means a bitch. The mountains, on the skirts of which his cattle grazed, lie to the north of Agbatana, towards the Euxine. That part of Media which borders on the Saspirians is an elevated tract, very mountainous, and covered with forests, while the rest of the Median territory is entirely level ground. On the arrival of the herdsman, who came at the hasty summons, Harpagus said to him—"Astyages requires thee to take this child and lay him in the wildest part of the hills, where he will be sure to die speedily. And he bade me tell thee, that if thou dost not kill the boy, but anyhow allowest him to escape, he will put thee to the most painful of deaths. I myself am appointed to see the child exposed."

111. The herdsman on hearing this took the child in his arms, and went back the way he had come till he reached the folds. There, providentially, his wife, who had been expecting daily to be put to bed, had just, during the absence of her husband, been delivered of a child. Both the herdsman and his wife were uneasy on each other's account, the former fearful because his wife was so near her time, the woman alarmed because it was a new thing for her husband to be sent for by Harpagus. When therefore he came into the house upon his return, his wife, seeing him arrive so unexpectedly, was the first to speak, and begged to know why Harpagus had sent for him in such a hurry. "Wife," said he, "when I got to the town I saw and heard such things as I would to heaven I had never seen—such things as I would to heaven had never happened to our masters. Every one was weeping in Harpagus's house. It quite frightened me, but I went in. The moment I stepped inside, what should I see but a baby lying on the floor, panting and whimpering, and all covered with gold, and wrapped in clothes of such beautiful colours. Harpagus saw me, and directly ordered me to take the child in my arms and carry him off, and what was I to do with him, think you? Why, to lay him in the mountains, where the wild beasts are most plentiful. And he told me it was the king himself that ordered it to be done, and he threatened me with such dreadful things if I

failed. So I took the child up in my arms, and carried him along. I thought it might be the son of one of the household slaves. I did wonder certainly to see the gold and the beautiful baby-clothes, and I could not think why there was such a weeping in Harpagus's house. Well, very soon, as I came along, I got at the truth. They sent a servant with me to show me the way out of the town, and to leave the baby in my hands; and he told me that the child's mother is the king's daughter Mandané, and his father Cambyses, the son of Cyrus; and that the king orders him to be killed; and look, here the child is."

112. With this the herdsman uncovered the infant, and showed him to his wife, who, when she saw him, and observed how fine a child and how beautiful he was, burst into tears, and clinging to the knees of her husband, besought him on no account to expose the babe; to which he answered, that it was not possible for him to do otherwise, as Harpagus would be sure to send persons to see and report to him, and he was to suffer a most cruel death if he disobeyed. Failing thus in her first attempt to persuade her husband, the woman spoke a second time, saying, "If then there is no persuading thee, and a child must needs be seen exposed upon the mountains, at least do thus. The child of which I have just been delivered is stillborn; take it and lay it on the hills, and let us bring up as our own the child of the daughter of Astyages. So shalt thou not be charged with unfaithfulness to thy lord, nor shall we have managed badly for ourselves. Our dead babe will have a royal funeral, and this living child will not be deprived of life."

113. It seemed to the herdsman that this advice was the best under the circumstances. He therefore followed it without loss of time. The child which he had intended to put to death he gave over to his wife, and his own dead child he put in the cradle wherein he had carried the other, clothing it first in all the other's costly attire, and taking it in his arms he laid it in the wildest place of all the mountain-range. When the child had been three days exposed, leaving one of his helpers to watch the body, he started off for the city, and going straight to Harpagus's house, declared himself ready to show the corpse of the boy. Harpagus sent certain of his bodyguard, on whom he had the firmest reliance, to view the body for him, and, satisfied with their seeing it, gave orders for the funeral. Thus was the herdsman's child buried, and the other child, who was after-

wards known by the name of Cyrus, was taken by the herdsman's wife, and brought up under a different name.

114. When the boy was in his tenth year, an accident which I will now relate, caused it to be discovered who he was. He was at play one day in the village where the folds of the cattle were, along with the boys of his own age, in the street. The other boys who were playing with him chose the cowherd's son, as he was called, to be their king. He then proceeded to order them about—some he set to build him houses, others he made his guards, one of them was to be the king's eye, another had the office of carrying his messages; all had some task or other. Among the boys there was one, the son of Artembares, a Mede of distinction, who refused to do what Cyrus had set him. Cyrus told the other boys to take him into custody, and when his orders were obeyed, he chastised him most severely with the whip. The son of Artembares, as soon as he was let go, full of rage at treatment so little befitting his rank, hastened to the city and complained bitterly to his father of what had been done to him by Cyrus. He did not, of course, say "Cyrus," by which name the boy was not yet known, but called him the son of the king's cowherd. Artembares, in the heat of his passion, went to Astyages, accompanied by his son, and made complaint of the gross injury which had been done him. Pointing to the boy's shoulders, he exclaimed, "Thus, oh! king, has thy slave, the son of a cowherd, heaped insult upon us."

115. At this sight and these words Astyages, wishing to avenge the son of Artembares for his father's sake, sent for the cowherd and his boy. When they came together into his presence, fixing his eyes on Cyrus, Astyages said, "Hast thou then, the son of so mean a fellow as that, dared to behave thus rudely to the son of yonder noble, one of the first in my court?" "My lord," replied the boy, "I only treated him as he deserved. I was chosen king in play by the boys of our village, because they thought me the best for it. He himself was one of the boys who chose me. All the others did according to my orders; but he refused, and made light of them, until at last he got his due reward. If for this I deserve to suffer punishment, here I am ready to submit to it."

116. While the boy was yet speaking Astyages was struck with a suspicion who he was. He thought he saw something in the character of his face like his own, and there was a nobleness about the answer he had made; besides

which his age seemed to tally with the time when his grandchild was exposed. Astonished at all this, Astyages could not speak for a while. At last, recovering himself with difficulty, and wishing to be quit of Artembares, that he might examine the herdsman alone, he said to the former, "I promise thee, Artembares, so to settle this business that neither thou nor thy son shall have any cause to complain." Artembares retired from his presence, and the attendants, at the bidding of the king, led Cyrus into an inner apartment. Astyages then being left alone with the herdsman, inquired of him where he had got the boy, and who had given him to him; to which he made answer that the lad was his own child, begotten by himself, and that the mother who bore him was still alive with him in his house. Astyages remarked that he was very ill-advised to bring himself into such great trouble, and at the same time signed to his bodyguard to lay hold of him. Then the herdsman, as they were dragging him to the rack, began at the beginning, and told the whole story exactly as it happened, without concealing anything, ending with entreaties and prayers to the king to grant him forgiveness.

117. Astyages, having got the truth of the matter from the herdsman, was very little further concerned about him, but with Harpagus he was exceedingly enraged. The guards were bidden to summon him into the presence, and on his appearance Astyages asked him, "By what death was it, Harpagus, that thou slewest the child of my daughter whom I gave into thy hands?" Harpagus, seeing the cowherd in the room, did not betake himself to lies, lest he should be confuted and proved false, but replied as follows:—"Sire, when thou gavest the child into my hands I instantly considered with myself how I could contrive to execute thy wishes, and yet, while guiltless of any unfaithfulness towards thee, avoid imbruing my hands in blood which was in truth thy daughter's and thine own. And this was how I contrived it. I sent for this cowherd, and gave the child over to him, telling him that by the king's orders it was to be put to death. And in this I told no lie, for thou hadst so commanded. Moreover, when I gave him the child, I enjoined him to lay it somewhere in the wilds of the mountains, and to stay near and watch till it was dead; and I threatened him with all manner of punishment if he failed. Afterwards, when he had done according to all that I commanded him, and the child had died, I

sent some of the most trustworthy of my eunuchs, who viewed the body for me, and then I had the child buried. This, sire, is the simple truth, and this is the death by which the child died."

118. Thus Harpagus related the whole story in a plain, straightforward way; upon which Astyages, letting no sign escape him of the anger that he felt, began by repeating to him all that he had just heard from the cowherd, and then concluded with saying, "So the boy is alive, and it is best as it is. For the child's fate was a great sorrow to me, and the reproaches of my daughter went to my heart. Truly fortune has played us a good turn in this. Go thou home then, and send thy son to be with the new comer, and to-night, as I mean to sacrifice thank-offerings for the child's safety to the gods to whom such honour is due, I look to have thee a guest at the banquet."

119. Harpagus, on hearing this, made obeisance, and went home rejoicing to find that his disobedience had turned out so fortunately, and that, instead of being punished, he was invited to a banquet given in honour of the happy occasion. The moment he reached home he called for his son, a youth of about thirteen, the only child of his parents, and bade him go to the palace, and do whatever Astyages should direct. Then, in the gladness of his heart, he went to his wife and told her all that had happened. Astyages, meanwhile, took the son of Harpagus, and slew him, after which he cut him in pieces, and roasted some portions before the fire, and boiled others; and when all were duly prepared, he kept them ready for use. The hour for the banquet came, and Harpagus appeared, and with him the other guests, and all sat down to the feast. Astyages and the rest of the guests had joints of meat served up to them; but on the table of Harpagus, nothing was placed except the flesh of his own son. This was all put before him, except the hands and feet and head, which were laid by themselves in a covered basket. When Harpagus seemed to have eaten his fill, Astyages called out to him to know how he had enjoyed the repast. On his reply that he had enjoyed it excessively, they whose business it was brought him the basket, in which were the hands and feet and head of his son, and bade him open it, and take out what he pleased. Harpagus accordingly uncovered the basket, and saw within it the remains of his son. The sight, however, did not scare him, or rob him of his self-possession. Being asked by Astyages if he knew what beast's

flesh it was that he had been eating, he answered that he knew very well, and that whatever the king did was agreeable. After this reply, he took with him such morsels of the flesh as were uneaten, and went home, intending, as I conceive, to collect the remains and bury them.

120. Such was the mode in which Astyages punished Harpagus: afterwards, proceeding to consider what he should do with Cyrus, his grandchild, he sent for the Magi, who formerly interpreted his dream in the way which alarmed him so much, and asked them how they had expounded it. They answered, without varying from what they had said before, that "the boy must needs be a king if he grew up, and did not die too soon." Then Astyages addressed them thus: "The boy has escaped, and lives; he has been brought up in the country, and the lads of the village where he lives have made him their king. All that kings commonly do he has done. He has had his guards, and his doorkeepers, and his messengers, and all the other usual officers. Tell me, then, to what, think you, does all this tend?" The Magi answered, "If the boy survives, and has ruled as a king without any craft or contrivance, in that case we bid thee cheer up, and feel no more alarm on his account. He will not reign a second time. For we have found even oracles sometimes fulfilled in an unimportant way; and dreams, still oftener, have wondrously mean accomplishments." "It is what I myself most incline to think," Astyages rejoined; "the boy having been already king, the dream is out, and I have nothing more to fear from him. Nevertheless, take good heed and counsel me the best you can for the safety of my house and your own interests." "Truly," said the Magi in reply, "it very much concerns our interests that thy kingdom be firmly established; for if it went to this boy it would pass into foreign hands, since he is a Persian: and then we Medes should lose our freedom, and be quite despised by the Persians, as being foreigners. But so long as thou, our fellow-countryman, art on the throne, all manner of honours are ours, and we are even not without some share in the government. Much reason therefore have we to forecast well for thee and for thy sovereignty. If then we saw any cause for present fear, be sure we would not keep it back from thee. But truly we are persuaded that the dream has had its accomplishment in this harmless way; and so our own fears being at rest, we recommend thee to banish thine. As

for the boy, our advice is that thou send him away to Persia, to his father and mother."

121. Astyages heard their answer with pleasure, and calling Cyrus into his presence, said to him, "My child, I was led to do thee a wrong by a dream which has come to nothing: from that wrong thou wert saved by thy own good fortune. Go now with a light heart to Persia; I will provide thy escort. Go, and when thou gettest to thy journey's end, thou wilt behold thy father and thy mother, quite other people from Mitradates the cowherd and his wife."

122. With these words Astyages dismissed his grandchild. On his arrival at the house of Cambyses, he was received by his parents, who, when they learnt who he was, embraced him heartily, having always been convinced that he died almost as soon as he was born. So they asked him by what means he had chanced to escape; and he told them how that till lately he had known nothing at all about the matter, but had been mistaken—oh! so widely!—and how that he had learnt his history by the way, as he came from Media. He had been quite sure that he was the son of the king's cowherd, but on the road the king's escort had told him all the truth; and then he spoke of the cowherd's wife who had brought him up, and filled his whole talk with her praises; in all that he had to tell them about himself, it was always Cyno— Cyno was everything. So it happened that his parents, catching the name at his mouth, and wishing to persuade the Persians that there was a special providence in his preservation, spread the report that Cyrus, when he was exposed, was suckled by a bitch. This was the sole origin of the rumour.

123. Afterwards, when Cyrus grew to manhood, and became known as the bravest and most popular of all his compeers, Harpagus, who was bent on revenging himself upon Astyages, began to pay him court by gifts and messages. His own rank was too humble for him to hope to obtain vengeance without some foreign help. When therefore he saw Cyrus, whose wrongs were so similar to his own, growing up expressly (as it were) to be the avenger whom he needed, he set to work to procure his support and aid in the matter. He had already paved the way for his designs, by persuading, severally, the great Median nobles, whom the harsh rule of their monarch had offended, that the best plan would be to put Cyrus at their head, and dethrone Astyages. These preparations made, Harpagus, being now ready for revolt, was anxious to make

known his wishes to Cyrus, who still lived in Persia; but as the roads between Media and Persia were guarded, he had to contrive a means of sending word secretly, which he did in the following way. He took a hare, and cutting open its belly without hurting the fur, he slipped in a letter containing what he wanted to say, and then carefully sewing up the paunch, he gave the hare to one of his most faithful slaves, disguising him as a hunter with nets, and sent him off to Persia to take the game as a present to Cyrus, bidding him tell Cyrus, by word of mouth, to paunch the animal himself, and let no one be present at the time.

124. All was done as he wished, and Cyrus, on cutting the hare open, found the letter inside, and read as follows:—"Son of Cambyses, the gods assuredly watch over thee, or never wouldst thou have passed through thy many wonderful adventures—now is the time when thou mayst avenge thyself upon Astyages, thy murderer. He willed thy death, remember; to the gods and to me thou owest that thou art still alive. I think thou art not ignorant of what he did to thee, nor of what I suffered at his hands because I committed thee to the cowherd, and did not put thee to death. Listen now to me, and obey my words, and all the empire of Astyages shall be thine. Raise the standard of revolt in Persia, and then march straight on Media. Whether Astyages appoint me to command his forces against thee, or whether he appoint any other of the princes of the Medes, all will go as thou couldst wish. They will be the first to fall away from him, and joining thy side, exert themselves to overturn his power. Be sure that on our part all is ready; wherefore do thou thy part, and that speedily."

125. Cyrus, on receiving the tidings contained in this letter, set himself to consider how he might best persuade the Persians to revolt. After much thought, he hit on the following as the most expedient course: he wrote what he thought proper upon a roll, and then calling an assembly of the Persians, he unfolded the roll, and read out of it that Astyages appointed him their general. "And now," said he, "since it is so, I command you to go and bring each man his reaping-hook." With these words he dismissed the assembly.

Now the Persian nation is made up of many tribes. Those which Cyrus assembled and persuaded to revolt from the Medes were the principal ones on which all the others are dependent. These are the Pasargadæ, the Maraphians, and the Maspians, of whom the Pasargadæ are the noblest. The Achæmenidæ, from which spring all the Perseid kings, is one of their clans. The rest of the Persian tribes are the following: the Panthialæans, the Derusiæans, the Germanians, who are engaged in husbandry; the Daans, the Mardians, the Dropicans, and the Sagartians, who are nomads.

126. When, in obedience to the orders which they had received, the Persians came with their reaping-hooks, Cyrus led them to a tract of ground, about eighteen or twenty furlongs each way, covered with thorns, and ordered them to clear it before the day was out. They accomplished their task; upon which he issued a second order to them, to take the bath the day following, and again come to him. Meanwhile he collected together all his father's flocks, both sheep and goats, and all his oxen, and slaughtered them, and made ready to give an entertainment to the entire Persian army. Wine, too, and bread of the choicest kinds were prepared for the occasion. When the morrow came, and the Persians appeared, he bade them recline upon the grass, and enjoy themselves. After the feast was over, he requested them to tell him "which they liked best, to-day's work, or yesterday's?" They answered that "the contrast was indeed strong: yesterday brought them nothing but what was bad, to-day everything that was good." Cyrus instantly seized on their reply, and laid bare his purpose in these words: "Ye men of Persia, thus do matters stand with you. If you choose to hearken to my words, you may enjoy these and ten thousand similar delights, and never condescend to any slavish toil; but if you will not hearken, prepare yourselves for unnumbered toils as hard as yesterday's. Now therefore follow my bidding, and be free. For myself I feel that I am destined by Providence to undertake your liberation; and you, I am sure, are no whit inferior to the Medes in anything, least of all in bravery. Revolt, therefore, from Astyages, without a moment's delay."

127. The Persians, who had long been impatient of the Median dominion, now that they had found a leader, were delighted to shake off the yoke. Meanwhile Astyages, informed of the doings of Cyrus, sent a messenger to summon him to his presence. Cyrus replied, "Tell Astyages that I shall appear in his presence sooner than he will like." Astyages, when he received this message, instantly armed all his subjects, and, as if God had deprived him of his senses, appointed Harpagus to be their general, forgetting how greatly he had injured him. So when the two armies met and engaged, only a few of the Medes, who were not in the secret, fought; others deserted openly to the Persians; while the greater number counterfeited fear, and fled.

128. Astyages, on learning the shameful flight and dispersion of his army, broke out into threats against Cyrus, saying, "Cyrus shall nevertheless have no reason to rejoice"; and directly he seized the Magian interpreters, who had persuaded him to allow Cyrus to escape, and impaled them; after which, he armed all the Medes who had remained in the city, both young and old; and leading them against the Persians, fought a battle, in which he was utterly defeated, his army being destroyed, and he himself falling into the enemy's hands.

129. Harpagus then, seeing him a prisoner, came near, and exulted over him with many jibes and jeers. Among other cutting speeches which he made, he alluded to the supper where the flesh of his son was given him to eat, and asked Astyages to answer *him* now, how he enjoyed being a slave instead of a king? Astyages looked in his face, and asked him in return, why he claimed as his own the achievements of Cyrus? "Because," said Harpagus, "it was my letter which made him revolt, and so I am entitled to all the credit of the enterprise." Then Astyages declared that "in that case he was at once the silliest and the most unjust of men: the silliest, if when it was in his power to put the crown on his own head, as it must assuredly have been, if the revolt was entirely his doing, he had placed it on the head of another; the most unjust, if on account of that supper he had brought slavery on the Medes. For, supposing that he was obliged to invest another with the kingly power, and not retain it himself, yet justice required that a Mede, rather than a Persian, should receive the dignity. Now, however, the Medes, who had been no parties to the wrong of which he complained, were made slaves instead of lords, and slaves moreover of those who till recently had been their subjects."

130. Thus after a reign of thirty-five years, Astyages lost his crown, and the Medes, in consequence of his cruelty, were brought under the rule of the Persians. Their empire over the parts of Asia beyond the Halys had lasted one hundred and twenty-eight years, except during the time when the Scythians had the dominion. Afterwards the Medes repented of their submission, and revolted from Darius,

but were defeated in battle, and again reduced to subjection. Now, however, in the time of Astyages, it was the Persians who under Cyrus revolted from the Medes, and became thenceforth the rulers of Asia. Cyrus kept Astyages at his court during the remainder of his life, without doing him any further injury. Such then were the circumstances of the birth and bringing up of Cyrus, and such were the steps by which he mounted the throne. It was at a later date that he was attacked by Crœsus, and overthrew him, as I have related in an earlier portion of this history. The overthrow of Crœsus made him master of the whole of Asia.

131. The customs which I know the Persians to observe are the following: they have no images of the gods, no temples nor altars, and consider the use of them a sign of folly. This comes, I think, from their not believing the gods to have the same nature with men, as the Greeks imagine. Their wont, however, is to ascend the summits of the loftiest mountains, and there to offer sacrifice to Jupiter, which is the name they give to the whole circuit of the firmament. They likewise offer to the sun and moon, to the earth, to fire, to water, and to the winds. These are the only gods whose worship has come down to them from ancient times. At a later period they began the worship of Urania, which they borrowed from the Arabians and Assyrians. Mylitta is the name by which the Assyrians know this goddess, whom the Arabians call Alitta, and the Persians Mitra.[1]

132. To these gods the Persians offer sacrifice in the following manner: they raise no altar, light no fire, pour no libations; there is no sound of the flute, no putting on of chaplets, no consecrated barley-cake; but the man who wishes to sacrifice brings his victim to a spot of ground which is pure from pollution, and there calls upon the name of the god to whom he intends to offer. It is usual to have the turban encircled with a wreath, most commonly of myrtle. The sacrificer is not allowed to pray for blessings on himself alone, but he prays for the welfare of the king, and of the whole Persian people, among whom he is of necessity included. He cuts the victim in pieces, and having boiled the flesh, he lays it out upon the tenderest herbage that he can find, trefoil especially. When all is ready, one of the Magi comes forward and chants a hymn, which they

say recounts the origin of the gods. It is not lawful to offer sacrifice unless there is a Magus present. After waiting a short time the sacrificer carries the flesh of the victim away with him, and makes whatever use of it he may please.

133. Of all the days in the year, the one which they celebrate most is their birthday. It is customary to have the board furnished on that day with an ampler supply than common. The richer Persians cause an ox, a horse, a camel, and an ass to be baked whole and so served up to them: the poorer classes use instead the smaller kinds of cattle. They eat little solid food but abundance of dessert, which is set on table a few dishes at a time; this it is which makes them say that "the Greeks, when they eat, leave off hungry, having nothing worth mention served up to them after the meats; whereas, if they had more put before them, they would not stop eating." They are very fond of wine, and drink it in large quantities. To vomit or obey natural calls in the presence of another is forbidden among them. Such are their customs in these matters.

It is also their general practice to deliberate upon affairs of weight when they are drunk; and then on the morrow, when they are sober, the decision to which they came the night before is put before them by the master of the house in which it was made; and if it is then approved of, they act on it; if not, they set it aside. Sometimes, however, they are sober at their first deliberation, but in this case they always reconsider the matter under the influence of wine.

134. When they meet each other in the streets, you may know if the persons meeting are of equal rank by the following token: if they are, instead of speaking, they kiss each other on the lips. In the case where one is a little inferior to the other, the kiss is given on the cheek; where the difference of rank is great, the inferior prostrates himself upon the ground. Of nations, they honour most their nearest neighbours, whom they esteem next to themselves; those who live beyond these they honour in the second degree; and so with the remainder, the further they are removed, the less the esteem in which they hold them. The reason is that they look upon themselves as very greatly superior in all respects to the rest of mankind, regarding others as approaching to excellence in proportion as they dwell nearer to them; whence it comes to pass that those who are the farthest off must be the most de-

[1] This identification is altogether a mistake. The Persians, like their Vedic brethren, worshipped the sun under the name of Mithra.

graded of mankind.[1] Under the dominion of the Medes, the several nations of the empire exercised authority over each other in this order. The Medes were lords over all, and governed the nations upon their borders, who in their turn governed the States beyond, who likewise bore rule over the nations which adjoined on them.[2] And this is the order which the Persians also follow in their distribution of honour; for that people, like the Medes, has a progressive scale of administration and government.

135. There is no nation which so readily adopts foreign customs as the Persians. Thus, they have taken the dress of the Medes, considering it superior to their own; and in war they wear the Egyptian breastplate. As soon as they hear of any luxury, they instantly make it their own: and hence, among other novelties, they have learnt unnatural lust from the Greeks. Each of them has several wives, and a still larger number of concubines.

136. Next to prowess in arms, it is regarded as the greatest proof of manly excellence to be the father of many sons. Every year the king sends rich gifts to the man who can show the largest number: for they hold that number is strength. Their sons are carefully instructed from their fifth to their twentieth year, in three things alone,—to ride, to draw the bow, and to speak the truth. Until their fifth year they are not allowed to come into the sight of their father, but pass their lives with the women. This is done that, if the child die young, the father may not be afflicted by its loss.

137. To my mind it is a wise rule, as also is the following—that the king shall not put any one to death for a single fault, and that none of the Persians shall visit a single fault in a slave with any extreme penalty; but in every case the services of the offender shall be set against his misdoings; and, if the latter be found to outweigh the former, the aggrieved party shall then proceed to punishment.

138. The Persians maintain that never yet did any one kill his own father or mother; but in all such cases they are quite sure that, if matters were sifted to the bottom, it would be found that the child was either a changeling or else the fruit of adultery; for it is not likely, they say, that the real father should perish by the hands of his child.

139. They hold it unlawful to talk of anything which it is unlawful to do. The most disgraceful thing in the world, they think, is to tell a lie; the next worst, to owe a debt: because, among other reasons, the debtor is obliged to tell lies. If a Persian has the leprosy he is not allowed to enter into a city, or to have any dealings with the other Persians; he must, they say, have sinned against the sun. Foreigners attacked by this disorder, are forced to leave the country: even white pigeons are often driven away, as guilty of the same offence. They never defile a river with the secretions of their bodies, nor even wash their hands in one; nor will they allow others to do so, as they have a great reverence for rivers. There is another peculiarity, which the Persians themselves have never noticed, but which has not escaped my observation. Their names, which are expressive of some bodily or mental excellence, all end with the same letter—the letter which is called San by the Dorians, and Sigma by the Ionians. Any one who examines will find that the Persian names, one and all without exception, end with this letter.[3]

140. Thus much I can declare of the Persians with entire certainty, from my own actual knowledge. There is another custom which is spoken of with reserve, and not openly, concerning their dead. It is said that the body of a male Persian is never buried, until it has been torn either by a dog or a bird of prey. That the Magi have this custom is beyond a doubt, for they practise it without any concealment. The dead bodies are covered with wax, and then buried in the ground.

[1] In an early stage of geographical knowledge each nation regards itself as occupying the centre of the earth. Herodotus tacitly assumes that Greece is the centre.

[2] It is quite inconceivable that there should have been any such system of government either in Media or Persia, as Herodotus here indicates. With respect to Persia, we know that the most distant satrapies were held as directly of the crown as the nearest. The utmost that can be said with truth is that in the Persian and Median, as in the Roman empire, there were *three* grades; first, the ruling nation; secondly, the conquered provinces; thirdly, the nations on the frontier, governed by their own laws and princes, but owning the supremacy of the imperial power, and reckoned among its tributaries.

[3] Here Herodotus was again mistaken. The Persian names of men which terminate with a consonant end indeed invariably with the letter *s*, or rather *sh*, as *Kurúsh* (Cyrus), *Dáryavush* (Darius). But a large number of Persian names of men were pronounced with a vowel termination, not expressed in writing, and in these the last consonant might be almost any letter.

The Magi are a very peculiar race, different entirely from the Egyptian priests, and indeed from all other men whatsoever. The Egyptian priests make it a point of religion not to kill any live animals except those which they offer in sacrifice. The Magi, on the contrary, kill animals of all kinds with their own hands, excepting dogs and men. They even seem to take a delight in the employment, and kill, as readily as they do other animals, ants and snakes, and such like flying or creeping things. However, since this has always been their custom, let them keep to it. I return to my former narrative.

141. Immediately after the conquest of Lydia by the Persians, the Ionian and Æolian Greeks sent ambassadors to Cyrus at Sardis, and prayed to become his lieges on the footing which they had occupied under Crœsus. Cyrus listened attentively to their proposals, and answered them by a fable. "There was a certain piper," he said, "who was walking one day by the seaside, when he espied some fish; so he began to pipe to them, imagining they would come out to him upon the land. But as he found at last that his hope was vain, he took a net, and enclosing a great draught of fishes, drew them ashore. The fish then began to leap and dance; but the piper said, 'Cease your dancing now, as you did not choose to come and dance when I piped to you.'" Cyrus gave this answer to the Ionians and Æolians, because, when he urged them by his messengers to revolt from Crœsus, they refused; but now, when his work was done, they came to offer their allegiance. It was in anger, therefore, that he made them this reply. The Ionians, on hearing it, set to work to fortify their towns, and held meetings at the Panionium, which were attended by all excepting the Milesians, with whom Cyrus had concluded a separate treaty, by which he allowed them the terms they had formerly obtained from Crœsus. The other Ionians resolved, with one accord, to send ambassadors to Sparta to implore assistance.

142. Now the Ionians of Asia, who meet at the Panionium, have built their cities in a region where the air and climate are the most beautiful in the whole world: for no other region is equally blessed with Ionia, neither above it nor below it, nor east nor west of it. For in other countries either the climate is over cold and damp, or else the heat and drought are sorely oppressive. The Ionians do not all speak the same language, but use in different places four different dialects. Towards the

south their first city is Miletus, next to which lie Myus and Priêné; all these three are in Caria and have the same dialect. Their cities in Lydia are the following: Ephesus, Colophon, Lebedus, Teos, Clazomenæ, and Phocæa. The inhabitants of these towns have none of the peculiarities of speech which belong to the three first-named cities, but use a dialect of their own. There remain three other Ionian towns, two situate in isles, namely, Samos and Chios; and one upon the mainland, which is Erythræ. Of these Chios and Erythræ have the same dialect, while Samos possesses a language peculiar to itself. Such are the four varieties of which I spoke.

143. Of the Ionians at this period, one people, the Milesians, were in no danger of attack, as Cyrus had received them into alliance. The islanders also had as yet nothing to fear, since Phœnicia was still independent of Persia, and the Persians themselves were not a seafaring people. The Milesians had separated from the common cause solely on account of the extreme weakness of the Ionians: for, feeble as the power of the entire Hellenic race was at that time, of all its tribes the Ionic was by far the feeblest and least esteemed, not possessing a single State of any mark excepting Athens. The Athenians and most of the other Ionic States over the world, went so far in their dislike of the name as actually to lay it aside; and even at the present day the greater number of them seem to me to be ashamed of it. But the twelve cities in Asia have always gloried in the appellation; they gave the temple which they built for themselves the name of the Panionium, and decreed that it should not be open to any of the other Ionic States; no State, however, except Smyrna, has craved admission to it.

144. In the same way the Dorians of the region which is now called the Pentapolis, but which was formerly known as the Doric Hexapolis, exclude all their Dorian neighbours from their temple, the Triopium: nay, they have even gone so far as to shut out from it certain of their own body who were guilty of an offence against the customs of the place. In the games which were anciently celebrated in honour of the Triopian Apollo, the prizes given to the victors were tripods of brass; and the rule was that these tripods should not be carried away from the temple, but should then and there be dedicated to the god. Now a man of Halicarnassus, whose name was Agasicles, being declared victor in the games, in open contempt of

the law, took the tripod home to his own house and there hung it against the wall. As a punishment for this fault, the five other cities, Lindus, Ialyssus, Cameirus, Cos, and Cnidus, deprived the sixth city, Halicarnassus, of the right of entering the temple.

145. The Ionians founded twelve cities in Asia, and refused to enlarge the number, on account (as I imagine) of their having been divided into twelve States when they lived in the Peloponnese; just as the Achæans, who drove them out, are at the present day. The first city of the Achæans after Sicyon, is Pellênê, next to which are Ægeira, Ægæ upon the Crathis, a stream which is never dry, and from which the Italian Crathis received its name,—Bura, Helicé—where the Ionians took refuge on their defeat by the Achæan invaders—Ægium, Rhypes, Patreis, Phareis, Olenus on the Peirus, which is a large river—Dymé and Tritæeis, all sea-port towns except the last two, which lie up the country.

146. These are the twelve divisions of what is now Achæa, and was formerly Ionia; and it was owing to their coming from a country so divided that the Ionians, on reaching Asia, founded their twelve States: for it is the height of folly to maintain that these Ionians are more Ionian than the rest, or in any respect better born, since the truth is that no small portion of them were Abantians from Eubœa, who are not even Ionians in name; and, besides, there were mixed up with the emigration Minyæ from Orchomenus, Cadmeians, Dryopians, Phocians from the several cities of Phocis, Molossians, Arcadian Pelasgi, Dorians from Epidaurus, and many other distinct tribes. Even those who came from the Prytanêum of Athens, and reckon themselves the purest Ionians of all, brought no wives with them to the new country, but married Carian girls, whose fathers they had slain. Hence these women made a law, which they bound themselves by an oath to observe, and which they handed down to their daughters after them, "That none should ever sit at meat with her husband, or call him by his name"; because the invaders slew their fathers, their husbands, and their sons, and then forced them to become their wives. It was at Miletus that these events took place.

147. The kings, too, whom they set over them, were either Lycians, of the blood of Glaucus, son of Hippolochus, or Pylian Caucons of the blood of Codrus, son of Melanthus; or else from both those families. But since these Ionians set more store by the name than any of the others, let them pass for the pure-bred Ionians; though truly all are Ionians who have their origin from Athens, and keep the Apaturia. This is a festival which all the Ionians celebrate, except the Ephesians and the Colophonians, whom a certain act of bloodshed excludes from it.

148. The Panionium is a place in Mycalé, facing the north, which was chosen by the common voice of the Ionians and made sacred to Heliconian Neptune. Mycalé itself is a promontory of the mainland, stretching out westward towards Samos, in which the Ionians assemble from all their States to keep the feast of the Panionia. The names of festivals, not only among the Ionians but among all the Greeks, end, like the Persian proper names, in one and the same letter.

149. The above-mentioned, then, are the twelve towns of the Ionians. The Æolic cities are the following:—Cymé, called also Phricônis, Larissa, Neonteichus, Temnus, Cilla, Notium, Ægiroëssa, Pitané, Ægææ, Myrina, and Gryneia. These are the eleven ancient cities of the Æolians. Originally, indeed, they had twelve cities upon the mainland, like the Ionians, but the Ionians deprived them of Smyrna, one of the number. The soil of Æolis is better than that of Ionia, but the climate is less agreeable.

150. The following is the way in which the loss of Smyrna happened. Certain men of Colophon had been engaged in a sedition there, and being the weaker party, were driven by the others into banishment. The Smyrnæans received the fugitives, who, after a time, watching their opportunity, while the inhabitants were celebrating a feast to Bacchus outside the walls, shut to the gates, and so got possession of the town. The Æolians of the other States came to their aid, and terms were agreed on between the parties, the Ionians consenting to give up all the moveables, and the Æolians making a surrender of the place. The expelled Smyrnæans were distributed among the other States of the Æolians, and were everywhere admitted to citizenship.

151. These, then, were all the Æolic cities upon the mainland, with the exception of those about Mount Ida, which made no part of this confederacy. As for the islands, Lesbos contains five cities. Arisba, the sixth, was taken by the Methymnæans, their kinsmen, and the inhabitants reduced to slavery. Tenedos contains one city, and there is another which is built on what are called the Hundred Isles. The Æolians of

Lesbos and Tenedos, like the Ionian islanders, had at this time nothing to fear. The other Æolians decided in their common assembly to follow the Ionians, whatever course they should pursue.

152. When the deputies of the Ionians and Æolians, who had journeyed with all speed to Sparta, reached the city, they chose one of their number, Pythermus, a Phocæan, to be their spokesman. In order to draw together as large an audience as possible, he clothed himself in a purple garment, and so attired stood forth to speak. In a long discourse he besought the Spartans to come to the assistance of his countrymen, but they were not to be persuaded, and voted against sending any succour. The deputies accordingly went their way, while the Lacedæmonians, notwithstanding the refusal which they had given to the prayer of the deputation, despatched a penteconter to the Asiatic coast with certain Spartans on board, for the purpose, as I think, of watching Cyrus and Ionia. These men, on their arrival at Phocæa, sent to Sardis Lacrines, the most distinguished of their number, to prohibit Cyrus, in the name of the Lacedæmonians, from offering molestation to any city of Greece, since they would not allow it.

153. Cyrus is said, on hearing the speech of the herald, to have asked some Greeks who were standing by, "Who these Lacedæmonians were, and what was their number, that they dared to send him such a notice?" When he had received their reply, he turned to the Spartan herald and said, "I have never yet been afraid of any men, who have a set place in the middle of their city, where they come together to cheat each other and forswear themselves. If I live, the Spartans shall have troubles enough of their own to talk of, without concerning themselves about the Ionians." Cyrus intended these words as a reproach against all the Greeks, because of their having market-places where they buy and sell, which is a custom unknown to the Persians, who never make purchases in open marts, and indeed have not in their whole country a single market-place.

After this interview Cyrus quitted Sardis, leaving the city under the charge of Tabalus, a Persian, but appointing Pactyas, a native, to collect the treasure belonging to Crœsus and the other Lydians, and bring it after him. Cyrus himself proceeded towards Agbatana, carrying Crœsus along with him, not regarding the Ionians as important enough to be his immediate object. Larger designs were in his mind. He wished to war in person against Babylon, the Bactrians, the Sacæ, and Egypt; he therefore determined to assign to one of his generals the task of conquering the Ionians.

154. No sooner, however, was Cyrus gone from Sardis than Pactyas induced his countrymen to rise in open revolt against him and his deputy Tabalus. With the vast treasures at his disposal he then went down to the sea, and employed them in hiring mercenary troops, while at the same time he engaged the people of the coast to enrol themselves in his army. He then marched upon Sardis, where he besieged Tabalus, who shut himself up in the citadel.

155. When Cyrus, on his way to Agbatana, received these tidings, he returned to Crœsus and said, "Where will all this end, Crœsus, thinkest thou? It seemeth that these Lydians will not cease to cause trouble both to themselves and others. I doubt me if it were not best to sell them all for slaves. Methinks what I have now done is as if a man were to 'kill the father and then spare the child.' Thou, who wert something more than a father to thy people, I have seized and carried off, and to that people I have entrusted their city. Can I then feel surprise at their rebellion?" Thus did Cyrus open to Crœsus his thoughts; whereat the latter, full of alarm lest Cyrus should lay Sardis in ruins, replied as follows: "Oh! my king, thy words are reasonable; but do not, I beseech thee, give full vent to thy anger, nor doom to destruction an ancient city, guiltless alike of the past and of the present trouble. I caused the one, and in my own person now pay the forfeit. Pactyas has caused the other, he to whom thou gavest Sardis in charge; let him bear the punishment. Grant, then, forgiveness to the Lydians, and to make sure of their never rebelling against thee, or alarming thee more, send and forbid them to keep any weapons of war, command them to wear tunics under their cloaks, and to put buskins upon their legs, and make them bring up their sons to cithern-playing, harping, and shop-keeping. So wilt thou soon see them become women instead of men, and there will be no more fear of their revolting from thee."

156. Crœsus thought the Lydians would even so be better off than if they were sold for slaves, and therefore gave the above advice to Cyrus, knowing that, unless he brought forward some notable suggestion, he would not be able to persuade him to alter his mind. He was likewise afraid lest, after escaping the danger which now pressed, the Lydians at some fu-

ture time might revolt from the Persians and so bring themselves to ruin. The advice pleased Cyrus, who consented to forego his anger and do as Crœsus had said. Thereupon he summoned to his presence a certain Mede, Mazares by name, and charged him to issue orders to the Lydians in accordance with the terms of Crœsus' discourse. Further, he commanded him to sell for slaves all who had joined the Lydians in their attack upon Sardis, and above aught else to be sure that he brought Pactyas with him alive on his return. Having given these orders Cyrus continued his journey towards the Persian territory.

157. Pactyas, when news came of the near approach of the army sent against him, fled in terror to Cymé. Mazares, therefore, the Median general, who had marched on Sardis with a detachment of the army of Cyrus, finding on his arrival that Pactyas and his troops were gone, immediately entered the town. And first of all he forced the Lydians to obey the orders of his master, and change (as they did from that time) their entire manner of living. Next, he despatched messengers to Cymé, and required to have Pactyas delivered up to him. On this the Cymæans resolved to send to Branchidæ and ask the advice of the god. Branchidæ is situated in the territory of Miletus, above the port of Panormus. There was an oracle there, established in very ancient times, which both the Ionians and Æolians were wont often to consult.

158. Hither therefore the Cymæans sent their deputies to make inquiry at the shrine, "What the gods would like them to do with the Lydian, Pactyas?" The oracle told them, in reply, to give him up to the Persians. With this answer the messengers returned, and the people of Cymé were ready to surrender him accordingly; but as they were preparing to do so, Aristodicus, son of Heraclides, a citizen of distinction, hindered them. He declared that he distrusted the response, and believed that the messengers had reported it falsely; until at last another embassy, of which Aristodicus himself made part, was despatched, to repeat the former inquiry concerning Pactyas.

159. On their arrival at the shrine of the god, Aristodicus, speaking on behalf of the whole body, thus addressed the oracle: "Oh! king, Pactyas the Lydian, threatened by the Persians with a violent death, has come to us for sanctuary, and lo, they ask him at our hands, calling upon our nation to deliver him up. Now, though we greatly dread the Persian power, yet have we not been bold to give up our suppliant, till we have certain knowledge of thy mind, what thou wouldst have us to do." The oracle thus questioned gave the same answer as before, bidding them surrender Pactyas to the Persians; whereupon Aristodicus, who had come prepared for such an answer, proceeded to make the circuit of the temple, and to take all the nests of young sparrows and other birds that he could find about the building. As he was thus employed, a voice, it is said, came forth from the inner sanctuary, addressing Aristodicus in these words: "Most impious of men, what is this thou hast the face to do? Dost thou tear my suppliants from my temple?" Aristodicus, at no loss for a reply, rejoined, "Oh, king, art thou so ready to protect thy suppliants, and dost thou command the Cymæans to give up a suppliant?" "Yes," returned the god, "I do command it, that so for the impiety you may the sooner perish, and not come here again to consult my oracle about the surrender of suppliants."

160. On the receipt of this answer the Cymæans, unwilling to bring the threatened destruction on themselves by giving up the man, and afraid of having to endure a siege if they continued to harbour him, sent Pactyas away to Mytilêné. On this Mazares despatched envoys to the Mytilenæans to demand the fugitive of them, and they were preparing to give him up for a reward (I cannot say with certainty how large, as the bargain was not completed), when the Cymæans, hearing what the Mytilenæans were about, sent a vessel to Lesbos, and conveyed away Pactyas to Chios. From hence it was that he was surrendered. The Chians dragged him from the temple of Minerva Poliuchus and gave him up to the Persians, on condition of receiving the district of Atarneus, a tract of Mysia opposite to Lesbos, as the price of the surrender. Thus did Pactyas fall into the hands of his pursuers, who kept a strict watch upon him that they might be able to produce him before Cyrus. For a long time afterwards none of the Chians would use the barley of Atarneus to place on the heads of victims, or make sacrificial cakes of the corn grown there, but the whole produce of the land was excluded from all their temples.

161. Meanwhile Mazares, after he had recovered Pactyas from the Chians, made war upon those who had taken part in the attack on Tabalus, and in the first place took Priêné and sold the inhabitants for slaves, after which he overran the whole plain of the Mæander and

the district of Magnesia, both of which he gave up for pillage to the soldiery. He then suddenly sickened and died.

162. Upon his death Harpagus was sent down to the coast to succeed to his command. He also was of the race of the Medes, being the man whom the Median king, Astyages, feasted at the unholy banquet, and who lent his aid to place Cyrus upon the throne. Appointed by Cyrus to conduct the war in these parts, he entered Ionia, and took the cities by means of mounds. Forcing the enemy to shut themselves up within their defences, he heaped mounds of earth against their walls, and thus carried the towns. Phocæa was the city against which he directed his first attack.

163. Now the Phocæans were the first of the Greeks who performed long voyages, and it was they who made the Greeks acquainted with the Adriatic and with Tyrrhenia, with Iberia, and the city of Tartessus. The vessel which they used in their voyages was not the round-built merchant-ship, but the long penteconter. On their arrival at Tartessus, the king of the country, whose name was Arganthônius, took a liking to them. This monarch reigned over the Tartessians for eighty years, and lived to be a hundred and twenty years old. He regarded the Phocæans with so much favour as, at first, to beg them to quit Ionia and settle in whatever part of his country they liked. Afterwards, finding that he could not prevail upon them to agree to this, and hearing that the Mede was growing great in their neighbourhood, he gave them money to build a wall about their town, and certainly he must have given it with a bountiful hand, for the town is many furlongs in circuit, and the wall is built entirely of great blocks of stone skilfully fitted together. The wall, then, was built by his aid.

164. Harpagus, having advanced against the Phocæans with his army, laid siege to their city, first, however, offering them terms. "It would content him," he said, "if the Phocæans would agree to throw down one of their battlements, and dedicate one dwelling-house to the king." The Phocæans, sorely vexed at the thought of becoming slaves, asked a single day to deliberate on the answer they should return, and besought Harpagus during that day to draw off his forces from the walls. Harpagus replied, "that he understood well enough what they were about to do, but nevertheless he would grant their request." Accordingly the troops were withdrawn, and the Phocæans forthwith took advantage of their absence to launch their penteconters, and put on board their wives and children, their household goods, and even the images of their gods, with all the votive offerings from the fanes, except the paintings and the works in stone or brass, which were left behind. With the rest they embarked, and putting to sea, set sail for Chios. The Persians, on their return, took possession of an empty town.

165. Arrived at Chios, the Phocæans made offers for the purchase of the islands called the Œnussæ, but the Chians refused to part with them, fearing lest the Phocæans should establish a factory there, and exclude their merchants from the commerce of those seas. On their refusal, the Phocæans, as Arganthônius was now dead, made up their minds to sail to Cyrnus (Corsica), where, twenty years before, following the direction of an oracle, they had founded a city, which was called Alalia. Before they set out, however, on this voyage, they sailed once more to Phocæa, and surprising the Persian troops appointed by Harpagus to garrison the town, put them all to the sword. After this they laid the heaviest curses on the man who should draw back and forsake the armament; and having dropped a heavy mass of iron into the sea, swore never to return to Phocæa till that mass reappeared upon the surface. Nevertheless, as they were preparing to depart for Cyrnus, more than half of their number were seized with such sadness and so great a longing to see once more their city and their ancient homes, that they broke the oath by which they had bound themselves and sailed back to Phocæa.

166. The rest of the Phocæans, who kept their oath, proceeded without stopping upon their voyage, and when they came to Cyrnus established themselves along with the earlier settlers at Alalia and built temples in the place. For five years they annoyed their neighbours by plundering and pillaging on all sides, until at length the Carthaginians and Tyrrhenians leagued against them, and sent each a fleet of sixty ships to attack the town. The Phocæans, on their part, manned all their vessels, sixty in number, and met their enemy on the Sardinian sea. In the engagement which followed the Phocæans were victorious, but their success was only a sort of Cadmeian victory.[1] They lost forty ships in the battle, and the twenty which remained came out of the engagement with beaks so bent and blunted as to be no

[1] A Cadmeian victory was one from which the victor received more hurt than profit.

longer serviceable. The Phocæans therefore sailed back again to Alalia, and taking their wives and children on board, with such portion of their goods and chattels as the vessels could bear, bade adieu to Cyrnus and sailed to Rhegium.

167. The Carthaginians and Tyrrhenians, who had got into their hands many more than the Phocæans from among the crews of the forty vessels that were destroyed, landed their captives upon the coast after the fight, and stoned them all to death. Afterwards, when sheep, or oxen, or even men of the district of Agylla passed by the spot where the murdered Phocæans lay, their bodies became distorted, or they were seized with palsy, or they lost the use of some of their limbs. On this the people of Agylla sent to Delphi to ask the oracle how they might expiate their sin. The answer of the Pythoness required them to institute the custom, which they still observe, of honouring the dead Phocæans with magnificent funeral rites, and solemn games, both gymnic and equestrian. Such, then, was the fate that befell the Phocæan prisoners. The other Phocæans, who had fled to Rhegium, became after a while the founders of the city called Vela, in the district of Œnotria. This city they colonised, upon the showing of a man of Posidonia, who suggested that the oracle had not meant to bid them set up a town in Cyrnus the island, but set up the worship of Cyrnus the hero.

168. Thus fared it with the men of the city of Phocæa in Ionia. They of Teos did and suffered almost the same; for they too, when Harpagus had raised his mound to the height of their defences, took ship, one and all, and sailing across the sea to Thrace, founded there the city of Abdêra. The site was one which Timêsius of Clazomenæ had previously tried to colonise, but without any lasting success, for he was expelled by the Thracians. Still the Teians of Abdêra worship him to this day as a hero.

169. Of all the Ionians these two states alone, rather than submit to slavery, forsook their fatherland. The others (I except Miletus) resisted Harpagus no less bravely than those who fled their country, and performed many feats of arms, each fighting in their own defence, but one after another they suffered defeat; the cities were taken, and the inhabitants submitted, remaining in their respective countries, and obeying the behests of their new lords. Miletus, as I have already mentioned, had made terms with Cyrus, and so continued at peace. Thus was continental Ionia once more reduced to servitude; and when the Ionians of the islands saw their brethren upon the mainland subjugated, they also, dreading the like, gave themselves up to Cyrus.

170. It was while the Ionians were in this distress, but still, amid it all, held their meetings, as of old, at the Panionium, that Bias of Priêné, who was present at the festival, recommended (as I am informed) a project of the very highest wisdom, which would, had it been embraced, have enabled the Ionians to become the happiest and most flourishing of the Greeks. He exhorted them "to join in one body, set sail for Sardinia, and there found a single Pan-Ionic city; so they would escape from slavery and rise to great fortune, being masters of the largest island in the world, exercising dominion even beyond its bounds; whereas if they stayed in Ionia, he saw no prospect of their ever recovering their lost freedom." Such was the counsel which Bias gave the Ionians in their affliction. Before their misfortunes began, Thales, a man of Miletus, of Phœnician descent, had recommended a different plan. He counselled them to establish a single seat of government, and pointed out Teos as the fittest place for it; "for that," he said, "was the centre of Ionia. Their other cities might still continue to enjoy their own laws, just as if they were independent states." This also was good advice.

171. After conquering the Ionians, Harpagus proceeded to attack the Carians, the Caunians, and the Lycians. The Ionians and Æolians were forced to serve in his army. Now, of the above nations the Carians are a race who came into the mainland from the islands. In ancient times they were subjects of king Minos, and went by the name of Leleges, dwelling among the isles, and, so far as I have been able to push my inquiries, never liable to give tribute to any man. They served on board the ships of king Minos whenever he required; and thus, as he was a great conqueror and prospered in his wars, the Carians were in his day the most famous by far of all the nations of the earth. They likewise were the inventors of three things, the use of which was borrowed from them by the Greeks; they were the first to fasten crests on helmets and to put devices on shields, and they also invented handles for shields. In the earlier times shields were without handles, and their wearers managed them by the aid of a leathern thong, by which they were slung round the neck and left shoulder. Long after the time of Minos, the Carians were driven from the islands by the Ionians and

Dorians, and so settled upon the mainland. The above is the account which the Cretans give of the Carians: the Carians themselves say very differently. They maintain that they are the aboriginal inhabitants of the part of the mainland where they now dwell, and never had any other name than that which they still bear; and in proof of this they show an ancient temple of Carian Jove in the country of the Mylasians, in which the Mysians and Lydians have the right of worshipping, as brother races to the Carians: for Lydus and Mysus, they say, were brothers of Car. These nations, therefore, have the aforesaid right; but such as are of a different race, even though they have come to use the Carian tongue, are excluded from this temple.

172. The Caunians, in my judgment, are aboriginals; but by their own account they came from Crete. In their language, either they have approximated to the Carians, or the Carians to them—on this point I cannot speak with certainty. In their customs, however, they differ greatly from the Carians, and not only so, but from all other men. They think it a most honourable practice for friends or persons of the same age, whether they be men, women, or children, to meet together in large companies, for the purpose of drinking wine. Again, on one occasion they determined that they would no longer make use of the foreign temples which had been long established among them, but would worship their own old ancestral gods alone. Then their whole youth took arms, and striking the air with their spears, marched to the Calyndic frontier, declaring that they were driving out the foreign gods.

173. The Lycians are in good truth anciently from Crete; which island, in former days, was wholly peopled with barbarians. A quarrel arising there between the two sons of Europa, Sarpedon and Minos, as to which of them should be king, Minos, whose party prevailed, drove Sarpedon and his followers into banishment. The exiles sailed to Asia, and landed on the Milyan territory. Milyas was the ancient name of the country now inhabited by the Lycians: the Milyæ of the present day were, in those times, called Solymi. So long as Sarpedon reigned, his followers kept the name which they brought with them from Crete, and were called Termilæ, as the Lycians still are by those who live in their neighbourhood. But after Lycus, the son of Pandion, banished from Athens by his brother Ægeus, had found a refuge with Sarpedon in the country of these Termilæ, they

came, in course of time, to be called from him Lycians. Their customs are partly Cretan, partly Carian. They have, however, one singular custom in which they differ from every other nation in the world. They take the mother's and not the father's name. Ask a Lycian who he is, and he answers by giving his own name, that of his mother, and so on in the female line. Moreover, if a free woman marry a man who is a slave, their children are full citizens; but if a free man marry a foreign woman, or live with a concubine, even though he be the first person in the State, the children forfeit all the rights of citizenship.

174. Of these nations, the Carians submitted to Harpagus without performing any brilliant exploits. Nor did the Greeks who dwelt in Caria behave with any greater gallantry. Among them were the Cnidians, colonists from Lacedæmon, who occupy a district facing the sea, which is called Triopium. This region adjoins upon the Bybassian Chersonese; and, except a very small space, is surrounded by the sea, being bounded on the north by the Ceramic Gulf, and on the south by the channel towards the islands of Symé and Rhodes. While Harpagus was engaged in the conquest of Ionia, the Cnidians, wishing to make their country an island, attempted to cut through this narrow neck of land, which was no more than five furlongs across from sea to sea. Their whole territory lay inside the isthmus; for where Cnidia ends towards the mainland, the isthmus begins which they were now seeking to cut through. The work had been commenced, and many hands were employed upon it, when it was observed that there seemed to be something unusual and unnatural in the number of wounds that the workmen received, especially about their eyes, from the splintering of the rock. The Cnidians, therefore, sent to Delphi, to inquire what it was that hindered their efforts; and received, according to their own account, the following answer from the oracle:—

Fence not the isthmus off, nor dig it through—
Jove would have made an island, had he wished.

So the Cnidians ceased digging, and when Harpagus advanced with his army, they gave themselves up to him without striking a blow.

175. Above Halicarnassus, and further from the coast, were the Pedasians. With this people, when any evil is about to befall either themselves or their neighbours, the priestess of Minerva grows an ample beard. Three times has this marvel happened. They alone, of all the

dwellers in Caria, resisted Harpagus for a while, and gave him much trouble, maintaining themselves in a certain mountain called Lida, which they had fortified; but in course of time they also were forced to submit.

176. When Harpagus, after these successes, led his forces into the Xanthian plain, the Lycians of Xanthus went out to meet him in the field: though but a small band against a numerous host, they engaged in battle, and performed many glorious exploits. Overpowered at last, and forced within their walls, they collected into the citadel their wives and children, all their treasures, and their slaves; and having so done, fired the building, and burnt it to the ground. After this, they bound themselves together by dreadful oaths, and sallying forth against the enemy, died sword in hand, not one escaping. Those Lycians who now claim to be Xanthians, are foreign immigrants, except eighty families, who happened to be absent from the country, and so survived the others. Thus was Xanthus taken by Harpagus, and Caunus fell in like manner into his hands; for the Caunians in the main followed the example of the Lycians.

177. While the lower parts of Asia were in this way brought under by Harpagus, Cyrus in person subjected the upper regions, conquering every nation, and not suffering one to escape. Of these conquests I shall pass by the greater portion, and give an account of those only which gave him the most trouble, and are the worthiest of mention. When he had brought all the rest of the continent under his sway, he made war on the Assyrians.

178. Assyria possesses a vast number of great cities, whereof the most renowned and strongest at this time was Babylon, whither, after the fall of Nineveh, the seat of government had been removed. The following is a description of the place:— The city stands on a broad plain, and is an exact square, a hundred and twenty furlongs in length each way, so that the entire circuit is four hundred and eighty furlongs. While such is its size, in magnificence there is no other city that approaches to it. It is surrounded, in the first place, by a broad and deep moat, full of water, behind which rises a wall fifty royal cubits in width, and two hundred in height. (The royal cubit is longer by three fingers' breadth than the common cubit.)

179. And here I may not omit to tell the use to which the mould dug out of the great moat was turned, nor the manner wherein the wall was wrought. As fast as they dug the moat the soil which they got from the cutting was made into bricks, and when a sufficient number were completed they baked the bricks in kilns. Then they set to building, and began with bricking the borders of the moat, after which they proceeded to construct the wall itself, using throughout for their cement hot bitumen, and interposing a layer of wattled reeds at every thirtieth course of the bricks. On the top, along the edges of the wall, they constructed buildings of a single chamber facing one another, leaving between them room for a four-horse chariot to turn. In the circuit of the wall are a hundred gates, all of brass, with brazen lintels and side-posts. The bitumen used in the work was brought to Babylon from the Is, a small stream which flows into the Euphrates at the point where the city of the same name stands, eight days' journey from Babylon. Lumps of bitumen are found in great abundance in this river.

180. The city is divided into two portions by the river which runs through the midst of it. This river is the Euphrates, a broad, deep, swift stream, which rises in Armenia, and empties itself into the Erythræan sea. The city wall is brought down on both sides to the edge of the stream: thence, from the corners of the wall, there is carried along each bank of the river a fence of burnt bricks. The houses are mostly three and four stories high; the streets all run in straight lines, not only those parallel to the river, but also the cross streets which lead down to the water-side. At the river end of these cross streets are low gates in the fence that skirts the stream, which are, like the great gates in the outer wall, of brass, and open on the water.

181. The outer wall is the main defence of the city. There is, however, a second inner wall, of less thickness than the first, but very little inferior to it in strength. The centre of each division of the town was occupied by a fortress. In the one stood the palace of the kings, surrounded by a wall of great strength and size: in the other was the sacred precinct of Jupiter Belus, a square enclosure two furlongs each way, with gates of solid brass; which was also remaining in my time. In the middle of the precinct there was a tower of solid masonry, a furlong in length and breadth, upon which was raised a second tower, and on that a third, and so on up to eight. The ascent to the top is on the outside, by a path which winds round all the towers. When one is about half-way up, one finds a resting-place and seats,

where persons are wont to sit some time on their way to the summit. On the topmost tower there is a spacious temple, and inside the temple stands a couch of unusual size, richly adorned, with a golden table by its side. There is no statue of any kind set up in the place, nor is the chamber occupied of nights by any one but a single native woman, who, as the Chaldæans, the priests of this god, affirm, is chosen for himself by the deity out of all the women of the land.

182. They also declare—but I for my part do not credit it—that the god comes down in person into this chamber, and sleeps upon the couch. This is like the story told by the Egyptians of what takes place in their city of Thebes, where a woman always passes the night in the temple of the Theban Jupiter.[1] In each case the woman is said to be debarred all intercourse with men. It is also like the custom of Patara, in Lycia, where the priestess who delivers the oracles, during the time that she is so employed—for at Patara there is not always an oracle—is shut up in the temple every night.

183. Below, in the same precinct, there is a second temple, in which is a sitting figure of Jupiter, all of gold. Before the figure stands a large golden table, and the throne whereon it sits, and the base on which the throne is placed, are likewise of gold. The Chaldæans told me that all the gold together was eight hundred talents' weight. Outside the temple are two altars, one of solid gold, on which it is only lawful to offer sucklings; the other a common altar, but of great size, on which the full-grown animals are sacrificed. It is also on the great altar that the Chaldæans burn the frankincense, which is offered to the amount of a thousand talents' weight, every year, at the festival of the God. In the time of Cyrus there was likewise in this temple a figure of a man, twelve cubits high, entirely of solid gold. I myself did not see this figure, but I relate what the Chaldæans report concerning it. Darius, the son of Hystaspes, plotted to carry the statue off, but had not the hardihood to lay his hands upon it. Xerxes, however, the son of Darius, killed the priest who forbade him to move the statue, and took it away. Besides the ornaments which I have mentioned, there are a large number of private offerings in this holy precinct.

184. Many sovereigns have ruled over this city of Babylon, and lent their aid to the build-

ing of its walls and the adornment of its temples, of whom I shall make mention in my Assyrian history. Among them two were women. Of these, the earlier, called Semiramis, held the throne five generations before the later princess. She raised certain embankments well worthy of inspection, in the plain near Babylon, to control the river, which, till then, used to overflow, and flood the whole country round about.

185. The later of the two queens, whose name was Nitocris, a wiser princess than her predecessor, not only left behind her, as memorials of her occupancy of the throne, the works which I shall presently describe, but also, observing the great power and restless enterprise of the Medes, who had taken so large a number of cities, and among them Nineveh, and expecting to be attacked in her turn, made all possible exertions to increase the defences of her empire. And first, whereas the river Euphrates, which traverses the city, ran formerly with a straight course to Babylon, she, by certain excavations which she made at some distance up the stream, rendered it so winding that it comes three several times in sight of the same village, a village in Assyria, which is called Ardericca; and to this day, they who would go from our sea to Babylon, on descending to the river touch three times, and on three different days, at this very place. She also made an embankment along each side of the Euphrates, wonderful both for breadth and height, and dug a basin for a lake a great way above Babylon, close alongside of the stream, which was sunk everywhere to the point where they came to water, and was of such breadth that the whole circuit measured four hundred and twenty furlongs. The soil dug out of this basin was made use of in the embankments along the waterside. When the excavation was finished, she had stones brought, and bordered with them the entire margin of the reservoir. These two things were done, the river made to wind, and the lake excavated, that the stream might be slacker by reason of the number of curves, and the voyage be rendered circuitous, and that at the end of the voyage it might be necessary to skirt the lake and so make a long round. All these works were on that side of Babylon where the passes lay, and the roads into Media were the straightest, and the aim of the queen in making them was to prevent the Medes from holding intercourse with the Babylonians, and so to keep them in ignorance of her affairs.

[1] The *Theban* Jupiter, or god worshipped as the Supreme Being in the city of Thebes, was Ammon (Amun).

186. While the soil from the excavation was being thus used for the defence of the city, Nitocris engaged also in another undertaking, a mere by-work compared with those we have already mentioned. The city, as I said, was divided by the river into two distinct portions. Under the former kings, if a man wanted to pass from one of these divisions to the other, he had to cross in a boat; which must, it seems to me, have been very troublesome. Accordingly, while she was digging the lake, Nitocris bethought herself of turning it to a use which should at once remove this inconvenience, and enable her to leave another monument of her reign over Babylon. She gave orders for the hewing of immense blocks of stone, and when they were ready and the basin was excavated, she turned the entire stream of the Euphrates into the cutting, and thus for a time, while the basin was filling, the natural channel of the river was left dry. Forthwith she set to work, and in the first place lined the banks of the stream within the city with quays of burnt brick, and also bricked the landing-places opposite the river-gates, adopting throughout the same fashion of brickwork which had been used in the town wall; after which, with the materials which had been prepared, she built, as near the middle of the town as possible, a stone bridge, the blocks whereof were bound together with iron and lead. In the daytime square wooden platforms were laid along from pier to pier, on which the inhabitants crossed the stream; but at night they were withdrawn, to prevent people passing from side to side in the dark to commit robberies. When the river had filled the cutting, and the bridge was finished, the Euphrates was turned back again into its ancient bed; and thus the basin, transformed suddenly into a lake, was seen to answer the purpose for which it was made, and the inhabitants, by help of the basin, obtained the advantage of a bridge.

187. It was this same princess by whom a remarkable deception was planned. She had her tomb constructed in the upper part of one of the principal gateways of the city, high above the heads of the passers by, with this inscription cut upon it:—"If there be one among my successors on the throne of Babylon who is in want of treasure, let him open my tomb, and take as much as he chooses—not, however, unless he be truly in want, for it will not be for his good." This tomb continued untouched until Darius came to the kingdom. To him it seemed a monstrous thing that he should be un-able to use one of the gates of the town, and that a sum of money should be lying idle, and moreover inviting his grasp, and he not seize upon it. Now he could not use the gate, because, as he drove through, the dead body would have been over his head. Accordingly he opened the tomb; but instead of money, found only the dead body, and a writing which said—"Hadst thou not been insatiate of pelf, and careless how thou gottest it, thou wouldst not have broken open the sepulchres of the dead."

188. The expedition of Cyrus was undertaken against the son of this princess, who bore the same name as his father Labynetus, and was king of the Assyrians. The Great King, when he goes to the wars, is always supplied with provisions carefully prepared at home, and with cattle of his own. Water too from the river Choaspes, which flows by Susa, is taken with him for his drink, as that is the only water which the kings of Persia taste. Wherever he travels, he is attended by a number of four-wheeled cars drawn by mules, in which the Choaspes water, ready boiled for use, and stored in flagons of silver, is moved with him from place to place.

189. Cyrus on his way to Babylon came to the banks of the Gyndes, a stream which, rising in the Matienian mountains, runs through the country of the Dardanians, and empties itself into the river Tigris. The Tigris, after receiving the Gyndes, flows on by the city of Opis, and discharges its waters into the Erythræan sea. When Cyrus reached this stream, which could only be passed in boats, one of the sacred white horses accompanying his march, full of spirit and high mettle, walked into the water, and tried to cross by himself; but the current seized him, swept him along with it, and drowned him in its depths. Cyrus, enraged at the insolence of the river, threatened so to break its strength that in future even women should cross it easily without wetting their knees. Accordingly he put off for a time his attack on Babylon, and, dividing his army into two parts, he marked out by ropes one hundred and eighty trenches on each side of the Gyndes, leading off from it in all directions, and setting his army to dig, some on one side of the river, some on the other, he accomplished his threat by the aid of so great a number of hands, but not without losing thereby the whole summer season.

190. Having, however, thus wreaked his vengeance on the Gyndes, by dispersing it through three hundred and sixty channels, Cy-

rus, with the first approach of the ensuing spring, marched forward against Babylon. The Babylonians, encamped without their walls, awaited his coming. A battle was fought at a short distance from the city, in which the Babylonians were defeated by the Persian king, whereupon they withdrew within their defences. Here they shut themselves up, and made light of his siege, having laid in a store of provisions for many years in preparation against this attack; for when they saw Cyrus conquering nation after nation, they were convinced that he would never stop, and that their turn would come at last.

191. Cyrus was now reduced to great perplexity, as time went on and he made no progress against the place. In this distress either some one made the suggestion to him, or he bethought himself of a plan, which he proceeded to put in execution. He placed a portion of his army at the point where the river enters the city, and another body at the back of the place where it issues forth, with orders to march into the town by the bed of the stream, as soon as the water became shallow enough: he then himself drew off with the unwarlike portion of his host, and made for the place where Nitocris dug the basin for the river, where he did exactly what she had done formerly: he turned the Euphrates by a canal into the basin, which was then a marsh, on which the river sank to such an extent that the natural bed of the stream became fordable. Hereupon the Persians who had been left for the purpose at Babylon by the river-side, entered the stream, which had now sunk so as to reach about midway up a man's thigh, and thus got into the town. Had the Babylonians been apprised of what Cyrus was about, or had they noticed their danger, they would never have allowed the Persians to enter the city, but would have destroyed them utterly; for they would have made fast all the street-gates which gave upon the river, and mounting upon the walls along both sides of the stream, would so have caught the enemy, as it were, in a trap. But, as it was, the Persians came upon them by surprise and so took the city. Owing to the vast size of the place, the inhabitants of the central parts (as the residents at Babylon declare) long after the outer portions of the town were taken, knew nothing of what had chanced, but as they were engaged in a festival, continued dancing and revelling until they learnt the capture but too certainly. Such, then, were the circumstances of the first taking of Babylon.

192. Among many proofs which I shall bring forward of the power and resources of the Babylonians, the following is of special account. The whole country under the dominion of the Persians, besides paying a fixed tribute, is parcelled out into divisions, which have to supply food to the Great King and his army during different portions of the year. Now out of the twelve months which go to a year, the district of Babylon furnishes food during four, the other regions of Asia during eight; by which it appears that Assyria, in respect of resources, is one-third of the whole of Asia. Of all the Persian governments, or satrapies as they are called by the natives, this is by far the best. When Tritantæchmes, son of Artabazus, held it of the king, it brought him in an artaba of silver every day. The artaba is a Persian measure, and holds three chœnixes more than the medimnus of the Athenians. He also had, belonging to his own private stud, besides warhorses, eight hundred stallions and sixteen thousand mares, twenty to each stallion. Besides which he kept so great a number of Indian hounds, that four large villages of the plain were exempted from all other charges on condition of finding them in food.

193. But little rain falls in Assyria, enough, however, to make the corn begin to sprout, after which the plant is nourished and the ears formed by means of irrigation from the river. For the river does not, as in Egypt, overflow the corn-lands of its own accord, but is spread over them by the hand, or by the help of engines. The whole of Babylonia is, like Egypt, intersected with canals. The largest of them all, which runs towards the winter sun, and is impassable except in boats, is carried from the Euphrates into another stream, called the Tigris, the river upon which the town of Nineveh formerly stood. Of all the countries that we know there is none which is so fruitful in grain. It makes no pretension indeed of growing the fig, the olive, the vine, or any other tree of the kind; but in grain it is so fruitful as to yield commonly two-hundred-fold, and when the production is the greatest, even three-hundred-fold. The blade of the wheat-plant and barley-plant is often four fingers in breadth. As for the millet and the sesame, I shall not say to what height they grow, though within my own knowledge; for I am not ignorant that what I have already written concerning the fruitfulness of Babylonia must seem incredible to those who have never visited the country. The only oil they use is made from

the sesame-plant. Palm-trees grow in great numbers over the whole of the flat country, mostly of the kind which bears fruit, and this fruit supplies them with bread, wine, and honey. They are cultivated like the fig-tree in all respects, among others in this. The natives tie the fruit of the male-palms, as they are called by the Greeks, to the branches of the date-bearing palm, to let the gall-fly enter the dates and ripen them, and to prevent the fruit from falling off. The male-palms, like the wild fig-trees, have usually the gall-fly in their fruit.

194. But that which surprises me most in the land, after the city itself, I will now proceed to mention. The boats which come down the river to Babylon are circular, and made of skins. The frames, which are of willow, are cut in the country of the Armenians above Assyria, and on these, which serve for hulls, a covering of skins is stretched outside, and thus the boats are made, without either stem or stern, quite round like a shield. They are then entirely filled with straw, and their cargo is put on board, after which they are suffered to float down the stream. Their chief freight is wine, stored in casks made of the wood of the palm-tree. They are managed by two men who stand upright in them, each plying an oar, one pulling and the other pushing. The boats are of various sizes, some larger, some smaller; the biggest reach as high as five thousand talents' burthen. Each vessel has a live ass on board; those of larger size have more than one. When they reach Babylon, the cargo is landed and offered for sale; after which the men break up their boats, sell the straw and the frames, and loading their asses with the skins, set off on their way back to Armenia. The current is too strong to allow a boat to return upstream, for which reason they make their boats of skins rather than wood. On their return to Armenia they build fresh boats for the next voyage.

195. The dress of the Babylonians is a linen tunic reaching to the feet, and above it another tunic made in wool, besides which they have a short white cloak thrown round them, and shoes of a peculiar fashion, not unlike those worn by the Bœotians. They have long hair, wear turbans on their heads, and anoint their whole body with perfumes. Every one carries a seal, and a walking-stick, carved at the top into the form of an apple, a rose, a lily, an eagle, or something similar; for it is not their habit to use a stick without an ornament.

196. Of their customs, whereof I shall now proceed to give an account, the following (which I understand belongs to them in common with the Illyrian tribe of the Eneti) is the wisest in my judgment. Once a year in each village the maidens of age to marry were collected all together into one place; while the men stood round them in a circle. Then a herald called up the damsels one by one, and offered them for sale. He began with the most beautiful. When she was sold for no small sum of money, he offered for sale the one who came next to her in beauty. All of them were sold to be wives. The richest of the Babylonians who wished to wed bid against each other for the loveliest maidens, while the humbler wife-seekers, who were indifferent about beauty, took the more homely damsels with marriage-portions. For the custom was that when the herald had gone through the whole number of the beautiful damsels, he should then call up the ugliest—a cripple, if there chanced to be one—and offer her to the men, asking who would agree to take her with the smallest marriage-portion. And the man who offered to take the smallest sum had her assigned to him. The marriage-portions were furnished by the money paid for the beautiful damsels, and thus the fairer maidens portioned out the uglier. No one was allowed to give his daughter in marriage to the man of his choice, nor might any one carry away the damsel whom he had purchased without finding bail really and truly to make her his wife; if, however, it turned out that they did not agree, the money might be paid back. All who liked might come even from distant villages and bid for the women. This was the best of all their customs, but it has now fallen into disuse. They have lately hit upon a very different plan to save their maidens from violence, and prevent their being torn from them and carried to distant cities, which is to bring up their daughters to be courtesans. This is now done by all the poorer of the common people, who since the conquest have been maltreated by their lords, and have had ruin brought upon their families.

197. The following custom seems to me the wisest of their institutions next to the one lately praised. They have no physicians, but when a man is ill, they lay him in the public square, and the passers-by come up to him, and if they have ever had his disease themselves or have known any one who has suffered from it, they give him advice, recommending him to do whatever they found good in their own case, or in the case known to them; and no one is al-

lowed to pass the sick man in silence without asking him what his ailment is.

198. They bury their dead in honey, and have funeral lamentations like the Egyptians. When a Babylonian has consorted with his wife, he sits down before a censer of burning incense, and the woman sits opposite to him. At dawn of day they wash; for till they are washed they will not touch any of their common vessels. This practice is observed also by the Arabians.

199. The Babylonians have one most shameful custom. Every woman born in the country must once in her life go and sit down in the precinct of Venus, and there consort with a stranger. Many of the wealthier sort, who are too proud to mix with the others, drive in covered carriages to the precinct, followed by a goodly train of attendants, and there take their station. But the larger number seat themselves within the holy enclosure with wreaths of string about their heads—and here there is always a great crowd, some coming and others going; lines of cord mark out paths in all directions among the women, and the strangers pass along them to make their choice. A woman who has once taken her seat is not allowed to return home till one of the strangers throws a silver coin into her lap, and takes her with him beyond the holy ground. When he throws the coin he says these words—"The goddess Mylitta prosper thee." (Venus is called Mylitta by the Assyrians.) The silver coin may be of any size; it cannot be refused, for that is forbidden by the law, since once thrown it is sacred. The woman goes with the first man who throws her money, and rejects no one. When she has gone with him, and so satisfied the goddess, she returns home, and from that time forth no gift however great will prevail with her. Such of the women as are tall and beautiful are soon released, but others who are ugly have to stay a long time before they can fulfil the law. Some have waited three or four years in the precinct. A custom very much like this is found also in certain parts of the island of Cyprus.

200. Such are the customs of the Babylonians generally. There are likewise three tribes among them who eat nothing but fish. These are caught and dried in the sun, after which they are brayed in a mortar, and strained through a linen sieve. Some prefer to make cakes of this material, while others bake it into a kind of bread.

201. When Cyrus had achieved the conquest of the Babylonians, he conceived the desire of bringing the Massagetæ under his dominion. Now the Massagetæ are said to be a great and warlike nation, dwelling eastward, toward the rising of the sun, beyond the river Araxes, and opposite the Issedonians. By many they are regarded as a Scythian race.

202. As for the Araxes, it is, according to some accounts, larger, according to others smaller than the Ister (Danube). It has islands in it, many of which are said to be equal in size to Lesbos. The men who inhabit them feed during the summer on roots of all kinds, which they dig out of the ground, while they store up the fruits, which they gather from the trees at the fitting season, to serve them as food in the winter-time. Besides the trees whose fruit they gather for this purpose, they have also a tree which bears the strangest produce. When they are met together in companies they throw some of it upon the fire round which they are sitting, and presently, by the mere smell of the fumes which it gives out in burning, they grow drunk, as the Greeks do with wine. More of the fruit is then thrown on the fire, and, their drunkenness increasing, they often jump up and begin to dance and sing. Such is the account which I have heard of this people.

The river Araxes, like the Gyndes, which Cyrus dispersed into three hundred and sixty channels, has its source in the country of the Matienians. It has forty mouths, whereof all, except one, end in bogs and swamps. These bogs and swamps are said to be inhabited by a race of men who feed on raw fish, and clothe themselves with the skins of seals. The other mouth of the river flows with a clear course into the Caspian Sea.[1]

203. The Caspian is a sea by itself, having no connection with any other. The sea frequented by the Greeks, that beyond the Pillars of Hercules, which is called the Atlantic, and also the Erythræan, are all one and the same sea. But the Caspian is a distinct sea, lying by itself, in length fifteen days' voyage with a row-boat, in breadth, at the broadest part, eight days' voyage. Along its western shore runs the chain of the Caucasus, the most extensive and loftiest of all mountain-ranges. Many and various are the tribes by which it is inhabited, most of whom live entirely on the wild fruits of the forest. In these forests certain trees are said to grow, from the leaves of which, pounded and

[1] Herodotus appears to have confused together the information which had reached him concerning two or three distinct streams.

mixed with water, the inhabitants make a dye, wherewith they paint upon their clothes the figures of animals; and the figures so impressed never wash out, but last as though they had been inwoven in the cloth from the first, and wear as long as the garment.

204. On the west then, as I have said, the Caspian Sea is bounded by the range of Caucasus. On the east it is followed by a vast plain, stretching out interminably before the eye, the greater portion of which is possessed by those Massagetæ, against whom Cyrus was now so anxious to make an expedition. Many strong motives weighed with him and urged him on —his birth especially, which seemed something more than human, and his good fortune in all his former wars, wherein he had always found that against what country soever he turned his arms, it was impossible for that people to escape.

205. At this time the Massagetæ were ruled by a queen, named Tomyris, who at the death of her husband, the late king, had mounted the throne. To her Cyrus sent ambassadors, with instructions to court her on his part, pretending that he wished to take her to wife. Tomyris, however, aware that it was her kingdom, and not herself, that he courted, forbade the men to approach. Cyrus, therefore, finding that he did not advance his designs by this deceit, marched towards the Araxes, and openly displaying his hostile intentions, set to work to construct a bridge on which his army might cross the river, and began building towers upon the boats which were to be used in the passage.

206. While the Persian leader was occupied in these labours, Tomyris sent a herald to him, who said, "King of the Medes, cease to press this enterprise, for thou canst not know if what thou art doing will be of real advantage to thee. Be content to rule in peace thy own kingdom, and bear to see us reign over the countries that are ours to govern. As, however, I know thou wilt not choose to hearken to this counsel, since there is nothing thou less desirest than peace and quietness, come now, if thou art so mightily desirous of meeting the Massagetæ in arms, leave thy useless toil of bridge-making; let us retire three days' march from the river bank, and do thou come across with thy soldiers; or, if thou likest better to give us battle on thy side the stream, retire thyself an equal distance." Cyrus, on this offer, called together the chiefs of the Persians, and laid the matter before them, requesting them to advise him what he should do. All the votes were in favour of his letting Tomyris cross the stream, and giving battle on Persian ground.

207. But Crœsus the Lydian, who was present at the meeting of the chiefs, disapproved of this advice; he therefore rose, and thus delivered his sentiments in opposition to it: "Oh! my king! I promised thee long since, that, as Jove had given me into thy hands, I would, to the best of my power, avert impending danger from thy house. Alas! my own sufferings, by their very bitterness, have taught me to be keen-sighted of dangers. If thou deemest thyself an immortal, and thine army an army of immortals, my counsel will doubtless be thrown away upon thee. But if thou feelest thyself to be a man, and a ruler of men, lay this first to heart, that there is a wheel on which the affairs of men revolve, and that its movement forbids the same man to be always fortunate. Now concerning the matter in hand, my judgment runs counter to the judgment of thy other counsellors. For if thou agreest to give the enemy entrance into thy country, consider what risk is run! Lose the battle, and therewith thy whole kingdom is lost. For assuredly, the Massagetæ, if they win the fight, will not return to their homes, but will push forward against the states of thy empire. Or if thou gainest the battle, why, then thou gainest far less than if thou wert across the stream, where thou mightest follow up thy victory. For against thy loss, if they defeat thee on thine own ground, must be set theirs in like case. Rout their army on the other side of the river, and thou mayest push at once into the heart of their country. Moreover, were it not disgrace intolerable for Cyrus the son of Cambyses to retire before and yield ground to a woman? My counsel, therefore, is that we cross the stream, and pushing forward as far as they shall fall back, then seek to get the better of them by stratagem. I am told they are unacquainted with the good things on which the Persians live, and have never tasted the great delights of life. Let us then prepare a feast for them in our camp; let sheep be slaughtered without stint, and the winecups be filled full of noble liquor, and let all manner of dishes be prepared: then leaving behind us our worst troops, let us fall back towards the river. Unless I very much mistake, when they see the good fare set out, they will forget all else and fall to. Then it will remain for us to do our parts manfully."

208. Cyrus, when the two plans were thus placed in contrast before him, changed his mind, and preferring the advice which Crœsus

had given, returned for answer to Tomyris that she should retire, and that he would cross the stream. She therefore retired, as she had engaged; and Cyrus, giving Crœsus into the care of his son Cambyses (whom he had appointed to succeed him on the throne), with strict charge to pay him all respect and treat him well, if the expedition failed of success; and sending them both back to Persia, crossed the river with his army.

209. The first night after the passage, as he slept in the enemy's country, a vision appeared to him. He seemed to see in his sleep the eldest of the sons of Hystaspes, with wings upon his shoulders, shadowing with the one wing Asia, and Europe with the other. Now Hystaspes, the son of Arsames, was of the race of the Achæmenidæ, and his eldest son, Darius, was at that time scarce twenty years old; wherefore, not being of age to go to the wars, he had remained behind in Persia. When Cyrus woke from his sleep, and turned the vision over in his mind, it seemed to him no light matter. He therefore sent for Hystaspes, and taking him aside said, "Hystaspes, thy son is discovered to be plotting against me and my crown. I will tell thee how I know it so certainly. The gods watch over my safety, and warn me beforehand of every danger. Now last night, as I lay in my bed, I saw in a vision the eldest of thy sons with wings upon his shoulders, shadowing with the one wing Asia, and Europe with the other. From this it is certain, beyond all possible doubt, that he is engaged in some plot against me. Return thou then at once to Persia, and be sure, when I come back from conquering the Massagetæ, to have thy son ready to produce before me, that I may examine him."

210. Thus Cyrus spoke, in the belief that he was plotted against by Darius; but he missed the true meaning of the dream, which was sent by God to forewarn him, that he was to die then and there, and that his kingdom was to fall at last to Darius.

Hystaspes made answer to Cyrus in these words:—"Heaven forbid, sire, that there should be a Persian living who would plot against thee! If such an one there be, may a speedy death overtake him! Thou foundest the Persians a race of slaves, thou hast made them free men: thou foundest them subject to others, thou hast made them lords of all. If a vision has announced that my son is practising against thee, lo, I resign him into thy hands to deal with as thou wilt." Hystaspes, when he had thus answered, recrossed the Araxes and has-

tened back to Persia, to keep a watch on his son Darius.

211. Meanwhile Cyrus, having advanced a day's march from the river, did as Crœsus had advised him, and, leaving the worthless portion of his army in the camp, drew off with his good troops towards the river. Soon afterwards, a detachment of the Massagetæ, one-third of their entire army, led by Spargapises, son of the queen Tomyris, coming up, fell upon the body which had been left behind by Cyrus, and on their resistance put them to the sword. Then, seeing the banquet prepared, they sat down and began to feast. When they had eaten and drunk their fill, and were now sunk in sleep, the Persians under Cyrus arrived, slaughtered a great multitude, and made even a larger number prisoners. Among these last was Spargapises himself.

212. When Tomyris heard what had befallen her son and her army, she sent a herald to Cyrus, who thus addressed the conqueror:—"Thou bloodthirsty Cyrus, pride not thyself on this poor success: it was the grape-juice—which, when ye drink it, makes you so mad, and as ye swallow it down brings up to your lips such bold and wicked words—it was this poison wherewith thou didst ensnare my child, and so overcamest him, not in fair open fight. Now hearken what I advise, and be sure I advise thee for thy good. Restore my son to me and get thee from the land unharmed, triumphant over a third part of the host of the Massagetæ. Refuse, and I swear by the sun, the sovereign lord of the Massagetæ, bloodthirsty as thou art, I will give thee thy fill of blood."

213. To the words of this message Cyrus paid no manner of regard. As for Spargapises, the son of the queen, when the wine went off, and he saw the extent of his calamity, he made request to Cyrus to release him from his bonds; then, when his prayer was granted, and the fetters were taken from his limbs, as soon as his hands were free, he destroyed himself.

214. Tomyris, when she found that Cyrus paid no heed to her advice, collected all the forces of her kingdom, and gave him battle. Of all the combats in which the barbarians have engaged among themselves, I reckon this to have been the fiercest. The following, as I understand, was the manner of it:—First, the two armies stood apart and shot their arrows at each other; then, when their quivers were empty, they closed and fought hand-to-hand with lances and daggers; and thus they continued fighting for a length of time, neither

choosing to give ground. At length the Massagetæ prevailed. The greater part of the army of the Persians was destroyed and Cyrus himself fell, after reigning nine and twenty years. Search was made among the slain by order of the queen for the body of Cyrus, and when it was found she took a skin, and, filling it full of human blood, she dipped the head of Cyrus in the gore, saying, as she thus insulted the corse, "I live and have conquered thee in fight, and yet by thee am I ruined, for thou tookest my son with guile; but thus I make good my threat, and give thee thy fill of blood." Of the many different accounts which are given of the death of Cyrus, this which I have followed appears to me most worthy of credit.

215. In their dress and mode of living the Massagetæ resemble the Scythians. They fight both on horseback and on foot, neither method is strange to them: they use bows and lances, but their favourite weapon is the battle-axe. Their arms are all either of gold or brass. For their spear-points, and arrow-heads, and for their battle-axes, they make use of brass; for head-gear, belts, and girdles, of gold. So too with the caparison of their horses, they give them breastplates of brass, but employ gold about the reins, the bit, and the cheek-plates. They use neither iron nor silver, having none in their country; but they have brass and gold in abundance.

216. The following are some of their customs;—Each man has but one wife, yet all the wives are held in common; for this is a custom of the Massagetæ and not of the Scythians, as the Greeks wrongly say. Human life does not come to its natural close with this people; but when a man grows very old, all his kinsfolk collect together and offer him up in sacrifice; offering at the same time some cattle also. After the sacrifice they boil the flesh and feast on it; and those who thus end their days are reckoned the happiest. If a man dies of disease they do not eat him, but bury him in the ground, bewailing his ill-fortune that he did not come to be sacrificed. They sow no grain, but live on their herds, and on fish, of which there is great plenty in the Araxes. Milk is what they chiefly drink. The only god they worship is the sun, and to him they offer the horse in sacrifice; under the notion of giving to the swiftest of the gods the swiftest of all mortal creatures.

The Second Book, Entitled
EUTERPÉ

1. On the death of Cyrus, Cambyses his son by Cassandané daughter of Pharnaspes took the kingdom. Cassandané had died in the lifetime of Cyrus, who had made a great mourning for her at her death, and had commanded all the subjects of his empire to observe the like. Cambyses, the son of this lady and of Cyrus, regarding the Ionian and Æolian Greeks as vassals of his father, took them with him in his expedition against Egypt among the other nations which owned his sway.

2. Now the Egyptians, before the reign of their king Psammetichus, believed themselves to be the most ancient of mankind. Since Psammetichus, however, made an attempt to discover who were actually the primitive race, they have been of opinion that while they surpass all other nations, the Phrygians surpass them in antiquity. This king, finding it impossible to make out by dint of inquiry what men were the most ancient, contrived the following method of discovery:—He took two children of the common sort, and gave them over to a herdsman to bring up at his folds, strictly charging him to let no one utter a word in their presence, but to keep them in a sequestered cottage, and from time to time introduce goats to their apartment, see that they got their fill of milk, and in all other respects look after them. His object herein was to know, after the indistinct babblings of infancy were over, what word they would first articulate. It happened as he had anticipated. The herdsman obeyed his orders for two years, and at the end of that time, on his one day opening the door of their room and going in, the children both ran up to him with outstretched arms, and distinctly said "Becos." When this first happened the herdsman took no notice; but afterwards when he observed, on coming often to see after them, that the word was constantly in their mouths, he informed his lord, and by his command brought the children into his presence. Psammetichus then himself heard them say the word, upon which he proceeded to make inquiry what people there was who called anything "becos," and hereupon he learnt that "becos" was the Phrygian name for bread. In consideration of this circumstance the Egyptians yielded their claims, and admitted the greater antiquity of the Phrygians.

3. That these were the real facts I learnt at Memphis from the priests of Vulcan. The Greeks, among other foolish tales, relate that Psammetichus had the children brought up by women whose tongues he had previously cut out; but the priests said their bringing up was such as I have stated above. I got much other information also from conversation with these priests while I was at Memphis, and I even went to Heliopolis and to Thebes, expressly to try whether the priests of those places would agree in their accounts with the priests at Memphis. The Heliopolitans have the reputation of being the best skilled in history of all the Egyptians. What they told me concerning their religion it is not my intention to repeat, except the names of their deities, which I believe all men know equally. If I relate anything else concerning these matters, it will only be when compelled to do so by the course of my narrative.

4. Now with regard to mere human matters, the accounts which they gave, and in which all agreed, were the following. The Egyptians, they said, were the first to discover the solar year, and to portion out its course into twelve parts. They obtained this knowledge from the stars. (To my mind they contrive their year much more cleverly than the Greeks, for these last every other year intercalate a whole month, but the Egyptians, dividing the year into twelve months of thirty days each, add every year a space of five days besides, whereby the

circuit of the seasons is made to return with uniformity.) The Egyptians, they went on to affirm, first brought into use the names of the twelve gods, which the Greeks adopted from them; and first erected altars, images, and temples to the gods; and also first engraved upon stone the figures of animals. In most of these cases they proved to me that what they said was true. And they told me that the first man who ruled over Egypt was Mên, and that in his time all Egypt, except the Thebaic canton, was a marsh, none of the land below Lake Mœris then showing itself above the surface of the water. This is a distance of seven days' sail from the sea up the river.

5. What they said of their country seemed to me very reasonable. For any one who sees Egypt, without having heard a word about it before, must perceive, if he has only common powers of observation, that the Egypt to which the Greeks go in their ships is an acquired country, the gift of the river. The same is true of the land above the lake, to the distance of three days' voyage, concerning which the Egyptians say nothing, but which is exactly the same kind of country.

The following is the general character of the region. In the first place, on approaching it by sea, when you are still a day's sail from the land, if you let down a sounding-line you will bring up mud, and find yourself in eleven fathoms' water, which shows that the soil washed down by the stream extends to that distance.

6. The length of the country along shore, according to the bounds that we assign to Egypt, namely from the Plinthinêtic gulf to Lake Serbônis, which extends along the base of Mount Casius, is sixty schœnes. The nations whose territories are scanty measure them by the fathom; those whose bounds are less confined, by the furlong; those who have an ample territory, by the parasang; but if men have a country which is very vast, they measure it by the schœne. Now the length of the parasang is thirty furlongs, but the schœne, which is an Egyptian measure, is sixty furlongs. Thus the coastline of Egypt would extend a length of three thousand six hundred furlongs.

7. From the coast inland as far as Heliopolis the breadth of Egypt is considerable, the country is flat, without springs, and full of swamps. The length of the route from the sea up to Heliopolis is almost exactly the same as that of the road which runs from the altar of the twelve gods at Athens to the temple of Olympian Jove at Pisa. If a person made a calculation he would find but a very little difference between the two routes, not more than about fifteen furlongs; for the road from Athens to Pisa falls short of fifteen hundred furlongs by exactly fifteen, whereas the distance of Heliopolis from the sea is just the round number.

8. As one proceeds beyond Heliopolis up the country, Egypt becomes narrow, the Arabian range of hills, which has a direction from north to south, shutting it in upon the one side, and the Libyan range upon the other. The former ridge runs on without a break, and stretches away to the sea called the Erythræan; it contains the quarries whence the stone was cut for the pyramids of Memphis: and this is the point where it ceases its first direction, and bends away in the manner above indicated. In its greatest length from east to west it is, as I have been informed, a distance of two months' journey; towards the extreme east its skirts produce frankincense. Such are the chief features of this range. On the Libyan side, the other ridge whereon the pyramids stand is rocky and covered with sand; its direction is the same as that of the Arabian ridge in the first part of its course. Above Heliopolis, then, there is no great breadth of territory for such a country as Egypt, but during four days' sail Egypt is narrow; the valley between the two ranges is a level plain, and seemed to me to be, at the narrowest point, not more than two hundred furlongs across from the Arabian to the Libyan hills. Above this point Egypt again widens.

9. From Heliopolis to Thebes is nine days' sail up the river; the distance is eighty-one schœnes, or 4860 furlongs. If we now put together the several measurements of the country we shall find that the distance along shore is, as I stated above, 3600 furlongs, and the distance from the sea inland to Thebes 6120 furlongs. Further, it is a distance of eighteen hundred furlongs from Thebes to the place called Elephantiné.

10. The greater portion of the country above described seemed to me to be, as the priests declared, a tract gained by the inhabitants. For the whole region above Memphis, lying between the two ranges of hills that have been spoken of, appeared evidently to have formed at one time a gulf of the sea. It resembles (to compare small things with great) the parts about Ilium and Teuthrania, Ephesus, and the plain of the Mæander. In all these regions the land has been formed by rivers, whereof the greatest is not to compare for size with any one

of the five mouths of the Nile. I could mention other rivers also, far inferior to the Nile in magnitude, that have effected very great changes. Among these not the least is the Acheloüs, which, after passing through Acarnania, empties itself into the sea opposite the islands called Echinades, and has already joined one-half of them to the continent.

11. In Arabia, not far from Egypt, there is a long and narrow gulf running inland from the sea called the Erythræan, of which I will here set down the dimensions. Starting from its innermost recess, and using a row-boat, you take forty days to reach the open main, while you may cross the gulf at its widest part in the space of half a day. In this sea there is an ebb and flow of the tide every day. My opinion is that Egypt was formerly very much such a gulf as this—one gulf penetrated from the sea that washes Egypt on the north, and extended itself towards Ethiopia; another entered from the southern ocean, and stretched towards Syria; the two gulfs ran into the land so as almost to meet each other, and left between them only a very narrow tract of country. Now if the Nile should choose to divert his waters from their present bed into this Arabian gulf, what is there to hinder it from being filled up by the stream within, at the utmost, twenty thousand years? For my part, I think it would be filled in half the time. How then should not a gulf, even of much greater size, have been filled up in the ages that passed before I was born, by a river that is at once so large and so given to working changes?

12. Thus I give credit to those from whom I received this account of Egypt, and am myself, moreover, strongly of the same opinion, since I remarked that the country projects into the sea further than the neighbouring shores, and I observed that there were shells upon the hills, and that salt exuded from the soil to such an extent as even to injure the pyramids; and I noticed also that there is but a single hill in all Egypt where sand is found, namely, the hill above Memphis; and further, I found the country to bear no resemblance either to its borderland Arabia, or to Libya—nay, nor even to Syria, which forms the seaboard of Arabia; but whereas the soil of Libya is, we know, sandy and of a reddish hue, and that of Arabia and Syria inclines to stone and clay, Egypt has a soil that is black and crumbly, as being alluvial and formed of the deposits brought down by the river from Ethiopia.

13. One fact which I learnt of the priests is to me a strong evidence of the origin of the country. They said that when Mœris was king, the Nile overflowed all Egypt below Memphis, as soon as it rose so little as eight cubits. Now Mœris had not been dead 900 years at the time when I heard this of the priests; yet at the present day, unless the river rise sixteen, or, at the very least, fifteen cubits, it does not overflow the lands. It seems to me, therefore, that if the land goes on rising and growing at this rate, the Egyptians who dwell below Lake Mœris, in the Delta (as it is called) and elsewhere, will one day, by the stoppage of the inundations, suffer permanently the fate which they told me they expected would some time or other befall the Greeks. On hearing that the whole land of Greece is watered by rain from heaven, and not, like their own, inundated by rivers, they observed—"Some day the Greeks will be disappointed of their grand hope, and then they will be wretchedly hungry"; which was as much as to say, "If God shall some day see fit not to grant the Greeks rain, but shall afflict them with a long drought, the Greeks will be swept away by a famine, since they have nothing to rely on but rain from Jove, and have no other resource for water."

14. And certes, in thus speaking of the Greeks the Egyptians say nothing but what is true. But now let me tell the Egyptians how the case stands with themselves. If, as I said before, the country below Memphis, which is the land that is always rising, continues to increase in height at the rate at which it has risen in times gone by, how will it be possible for the inhabitants of that region to avoid hunger, when they will certainly have no rain, and the river will not be able to overflow their corn-lands? At present, it must be confessed, they obtain the fruits of the field with less trouble than any other people in the world, the rest of the Egyptians included, since they have no need to break up the ground with the plough, nor to use the hoe, nor to do any of the work which the rest of mankind find necessary if they are to get a crop; but the husbandman waits till the river has of its own accord spread itself over the fields and withdrawn again to its bed, and then sows his plot of ground, and after sowing turns his swine into it—the swine tread in the corn—after which he has only to await the harvest. The swine serve him also to thrash the grain, which is then carried to the garner.

15. If then we choose to adopt the views of the Ionians concerning Egypt, we must come

to the conclusion that the Egyptians had formerly no country at all. For the Ionians say that
nothing is really Egypt but the Delta, which
extends along shore from the Watch-tower of
Perseus, as it is called, to the Pelusiac Salt-Pans,
a distance of forty schœnes, and stretches inland as far as the city of Cercasôrus, where the
Nile divides into the two streams which reach
the sea at Pelusium and Canôbus respectively.
The rest of what is accounted Egypt belongs,
they say, either to Arabia or Libya. But the
Delta, as the Egyptians affirm, and as I myself
am persuaded, is formed of the deposits of the
river, and has only recently, if I may use the
expression, come to light. If, then, they had
formerly no territory at all, how came they to
be so extravagant as to fancy themselves the
most ancient race in the world? Surely there
was no need of their making the experiment
with the children to see what language they
would first speak. But in truth I do not believe
that the Egyptians came into being at the same
time with the Delta, as the Ionians call it; I
think they have always existed ever since the
human race began; as the land went on increasing, part of the population came down
into the new country, part remained in their
old settlements. In ancient times the Thebaïs
bore the name of Egypt, a district of which the
entire circumference is but 6120 furlongs.

16. If, then, my judgment on these matters
be right, the Ionians are mistaken in what they
say of Egypt. If, on the contrary, it is they who
are right, then I undertake to show that neither
the Ionians nor any of the other Greeks know
how to count. For they all say that the earth is
divided into three parts, Europe, Asia, and
Libya, whereas they ought to add a fourth part,
the Delta of Egypt, since they do not include it
either in Asia or Libya. For is it not their
theory that the Nile separates Asia from Libya? As the Nile, therefore, splits in two at the
apex of the Delta, the Delta itself must be a
separate country, not contained in either Asia
or Libya.

17. Here I take my leave of the opinions of
the Ionians, and proceed to deliver my own
sentiments on these subjects. I consider Egypt
to be the whole country inhabited by the Egyptians, just as Cilicia is the tract occupied by the
Cilicians, and Assyria that possessed by the Assyrians. And I regard the only proper boundary-line between Libya and Asia to be that
which is marked out by the Egyptian frontier.
For if we take the boundary-line commonly received by the Greeks, we must regard Egypt

as divided, along its whole length from Elephantiné and the Cataracts to Cercasôrus, into
two parts, each belonging to a different portion of the world, one to Asia, the other to Libya; since the Nile divides Egypt in two from
the Cataracts to the sea, running as far as the
city of Cercasôrus in a single stream, but at that
point separating into three branches, whereof
the one which bends eastward is called the Pelusiac mouth, and that which slants to the west,
the Canobic. Meanwhile the straight course of
the stream, which comes down from the upper
country and meets the apex of the Delta, continues on, dividing the Delta down the middle,
and empties itself into the sea by a mouth,
which is as celebrated, and carries as large a
body of water, as most of the others, the mouth
called the Sebennytic. Besides these there are
two other mouths which run out of the Sebennytic called respectively the Saitic and the Mendesian. The Bolbitine mouth, and the Bucolic,
are not natural branches, but channels made by
excavation.

18. My judgment as to the extent of Egypt
is confirmed by an oracle delivered at the
shrine of Ammon, of which I had no knowledge at all until after I had formed my opinion. It happened that the people of the cities
Marea and Apis, who live in the part of Egypt
that borders on Libya, took a dislike to the religious usages of the country concerning sacrificial animals, and wished no longer to be re-
stricted from eating the flesh of cows. So, as
they believed themselves to be Libyans and not
Egyptians, they sent to the shrine to say that,
having nothing in common with the Egyptians, neither inhabiting the Delta nor using
the Egyptian tongue, they claimed to be allowed to eat whatever they pleased. Their request, however, was refused by the god, who
declared in reply that Egypt was the entire
tract of country which the Nile overspreads
and irrigates, and the Egyptians were the people who lived below Elephantiné, and drank
the waters of that river.

19. So said the oracle. Now the Nile, when
it overflows, floods not only the Delta, but also
the tracts of country on both sides the stream
which are thought to belong to Libya and Arabia, in some places reaching to the extent of
two days' journey from its banks, in some even
exceeding that distance, but in others falling
short of it.

Concerning the nature of the river, I was not
able to gain any information either from the
priests or from others. I was particularly anx-

ious to learn from them why the Nile, at the commencement of the summer solstice, begins to rise, and continues to increase for a hundred days—and why, as soon as that number is past, it forthwith retires and contracts its stream, continuing low during the whole of the winter until the summer solstice comes round again. On none of these points could I obtain any explanation from the inhabitants, though I made every inquiry, wishing to know what was commonly reported—they could neither tell me what special virtue the Nile has which makes it so opposite in its nature to all other streams, nor why, unlike every other river, it gives forth no breezes from its surface.

20. Some of the Greeks, however, wishing to get a reputation for cleverness, have offered explanations of the phenomena of the river, for which they have accounted in three different ways. Two of these I do not think it worth while to speak of, further than simply to mention what they are. One pretends that the Etesian winds cause the rise of the river by preventing the Nile-water from running off into the sea. But in the first place it has often happened, when the Etesian winds did not blow, that the Nile has risen according to its usual wont; and further, if the Etesian winds produced the effect, the other rivers which flow in a direction opposite to those winds ought to present the same phenomena as the Nile, and the more so as they are all smaller streams, and have a weaker current. But these rivers, of which there are many both in Syria and Libya, are entirely unlike the Nile in this respect.

21. The second opinion is even more unscientific than the one just mentioned, and also, if I may so say, more marvellous. It is that the Nile acts so strangely, because it flows from the ocean, and that the ocean flows all round the earth.

22. The third explanation, which is very much more plausible than either of the others, is positively the furthest from the truth; for there is really nothing in what it says, any more than in the other theories. It is, that the inundation of the Nile is caused by the melting of snows.[1] Now, as the Nile flows out of Libya, through Ethiopia, into Egypt, how is it possible that it can be formed of melted snow, running,

as it does, from the hottest regions of the world into cooler countries? Many are the proofs whereby any one capable of reasoning on the subject may be convinced that it is most unlikely this should be the case. The first and strongest argument is furnished by the winds, which always blow hot from these regions. The second is that rain and frost are unknown there.[2] Now whenever snow falls, it must of necessity rain within five days; so that, if there were snow, there must be rain also in those parts. Thirdly, it is certain that the natives of the country are black with the heat, that the kites and the swallows remain there the whole year, and that the cranes, when they fly from the rigours of a Scythian winter, flock thither to pass the cold season. If then, in the country whence the Nile has its source, or in that through which it flows, there fell ever so little snow, it is absolutely impossible that any of these circumstances could take place.

23. As for the writer[3] who attributes the phenomenon to the ocean, his account is involved in such obscurity that it is impossible to disprove it by argument. For my part I know of no river called Ocean, and I think that Homer, or one of the earlier poets, invented the name, and introduced it into his poetry.

24. Perhaps, after censuring all the opinions that have been put forward on this obscure subject, one ought to propose some theory of one's own. I will therefore proceed to explain what I think to be the reason of the Nile's swelling in the summer time. During the winter, the sun is driven out of his usual course by the storms, and removes to the upper parts of Libya. This is the whole secret in the fewest possible words; for it stands to reason that the country to which the Sun-god approaches the nearest, and which he passes most directly over, will be scantest of water, and that there the streams which feed the rivers will shrink the most.

25. To explain, however, more at length, the case is this. The sun, in his passage across the upper parts of Libya, affects them in the following way. As the air in those regions is constantly clear, and the country warm through the absence of cold winds, the sun in his passage across them acts upon them exactly as he is wont to act elsewhere in summer, when his path is in the middle of heaven—that

[1] Herodotus is wrong in supposing snow could not be found on mountains in the hot climate of Africa; perpetual snow is not confined to certain latitudes; and ancient and modern discoveries prove that it is found in the ranges S. of Abyssinia.

[2] Herodotus was not aware of the rainy season in Sennár and the S.S.W. of Abyssinia, nor did he know of the Abyssinian snow.
[3] Hecatæus.

is, he attracts the water. After attracting it, he again repels it into the upper regions, where the winds lay hold of it, scatter it, and reduce it to a vapour, whence it naturally enough comes to pass that the winds which blow from this quarter—the south and south-west—are of all winds the most rainy. And my own opinion is that the sun does not get rid of all the water which he draws year by year from the Nile, but retains some about him. When the winter begins to soften, the sun goes back again to his old place in the middle of the heaven, and proceeds to attract water equally from all countries. Till then the other rivers run big, from the quantity of rain-water which they bring down from countries where so much moisture falls that all the land is cut into gullies; but in summer, when the showers fail, and the sun attracts their water, they become low. The Nile, on the contrary, not deriving any of its bulk from rains, and being in winter subject to the attraction of the sun, naturally runs at that season, unlike all other streams, with a less burthen of water than in the summer time. For in summer it is exposed to attraction equally with all other rivers, but in winter it suffers alone. The sun, therefore, I regard as the sole cause of the phenomenon.

26. It is the sun also, in my opinion, which, by heating the space through which it passes, makes the air in Egypt so dry. There is thus perpetual summer in the upper parts of Libya. Were the position of the heavenly regions reversed, so that the place where now the north wind and the winter have their dwelling became the station of the south wind and of the noon-day, while, on the other hand, the station of the south wind became that of the north, the consequence would be that the sun, driven from the mid-heaven by the winter and the northern gales, would betake himself to the upper parts of Europe, as he now does to those of Libya, and then I believe his passage across Europe would affect the Ister exactly as the Nile is affected at the present day.

27. And with respect to the fact that no breeze blows from the Nile, I am of opinion that no wind is likely to arise in very hot countries, for breezes love to blow from some cold quarter.

28. Let us leave these things, however, to their natural course, to continue as they are and have been from the beginning. With regard to the *sources* of the Nile, I have found no one among all those with whom I have conversed, whether Egyptians, Libyans, or Greeks, who professed to have any knowledge, except a single person. He was the scribe who kept the register of the sacred treasures of Minerva in the city of Saïs, and he did not seem to me to be in earnest when he said that he knew them perfectly well. His story was as follows:—"Between Syêné, a city of the Thebaïs, and Elephantiné, there are" (he said) "two hills with sharp conical tops; the name of the one is Crophi, of the other, Mophi. Midway between them are the fountains of the Nile, fountains which it is impossible to fathom. Half the water runs northward into Egypt, half to the south towards Ethiopia." The fountains were known to be unfathomable, he declared, because Psammetichus, an Egyptian king, had made trial of them. He had caused a rope to be made, many thousand fathoms in length, and had sounded the fountain with it, but could find no bottom. By this the scribe gave me to understand, if there was any truth at all in what he said, that in this fountain there are certain strong eddies, and a regurgitation, owing to the force wherewith the water dashes against the mountains, and hence a sounding-line cannot be got to reach the bottom of the spring.

29. No other information on this head could I obtain from any quarter. All that I succeeded in learning further of the more distant portions of the Nile, by ascending myself as high as Elephantiné, and making inquiries concerning the parts beyond, was the following:—As one advances beyond Elephantiné, the land rises. Hence it is necessary in this part of the river to attach a rope to the boat on each side, as men harness an ox, and so proceed on the journey. If the rope snaps, the vessel is borne away down stream by the force of the current. The navigation continues the same for four days, the river winding greatly, like the Mæander, and the distance traversed amounting to twelve schœnes. Here you come upon a smooth and level plain, where the Nile flows in two branches, round an island called Tachompso. The country above Elephantiné is inhabited by the Ethiopians, who possess one-half of this island, the Egyptians occupying the other. Above the island there is a great lake, the shores of which are inhabited by Ethiopian nomads; after passing it, you come again to the stream of the Nile, which runs into the lake. Here you land, and travel for forty days along the banks of the river, since it is impossible to proceed further in a boat on account of the sharp peaks which jut out from the water, and

the sunken rocks which abound in that part of the stream. When you have passed this portion of the river in the space of forty days, you go on board another boat and proceed by water for twelve days more, at the end of which time you reach a great city called Meroë, which is said to be the capital of the other Ethiopians. The only gods worshipped by the inhabitants are Jupiter and Bacchus, to whom great honours are paid. There is an oracle of Jupiter in the city, which directs the warlike expeditions of the Ethiopians; when it commands they go to war, and in whatever direction it bids them march, thither straightway they carry their arms.

30. On leaving this city, and again mounting the stream, in the same space of time which it took you to reach the capital from Elephantiné, you come to the Deserters, who bear the name of Asmach. This word, translated into our language, means "the men who stand on the left hand of the king." These Deserters are Egyptians of the warrior caste, who, to the number of two hundred and forty thousand, went over to the Ethiopians in the reign of king Psammetichus. The cause of their desertion was the following:—Three garrisons were maintained in Egypt at that time, one in the city of Elephantiné against the Ethiopians, another in the Pelusiac Daphnæ, against the Syrians and Arabians, and a third, against the Libyans, in Marea. (The very same posts are to this day occupied by the Persians, whose forces are in garrison both in Daphnæ and in Elephantiné.) Now it happened, that on one occasion the garrisons were not relieved during the space of three years; the soldiers, therefore, at the end of that time, consulted together, and having determined by common consent to revolt, marched away towards Ethiopia. Psammetichus, informed of the movement, set out in pursuit, and coming up with them, besought them with many words not to desert the gods of their country, nor abandon their wives and children. "Nay, but," said one of the deserters with an unseemly gesture, "wherever we go, we are sure enough of finding wives and children." Arrived in Ethiopia, they placed themselves at the disposal of the king. In return, he made them a present of a tract of land which belonged to certain Ethiopians with whom he was at feud, bidding them expel the inhabitants and take possession of their territory. From the time that this settlement was formed, their acquaintance with Egyptian manners has tended to civilise the Ethiopians.

31. Thus the course of the Nile is known, not only throughout Egypt, but to the extent of four months' journey either by land or water above the Egyptian boundary; for on calculation it will be found that it takes that length of time to travel from Elephantiné to the country of the Deserters. There the direction of the river is from west to east. Beyond, no one has any certain knowledge of its course, since the country is uninhabited by reason of the excessive heat.

32. I did hear, indeed, what I will now relate, from certain natives of Cyrênê. Once upon a time, they said, they were on a visit to the oracular shrine of Ammon, when it chanced that in the course of conversation with Etearchus, the Ammonian king, the talk fell upon the Nile, how that its sources were unknown to all men. Etearchus upon this mentioned that some Nasamonians had once come to his court, and when asked if they could give any information concerning the uninhabited parts of Libya, had told the following tale. (The Nasamonians are a Libyan race who occupy the Syrtis, and a tract of no great size towards the east.) They said there had grown up among them some wild young men, the sons of certain chiefs, who, when they came to man's estate, indulged in all manner of extravagancies, and among other things drew lots for five of their number to go and explore the desert parts of Libya, and try if they could not penetrate further than any had done previously. The coast of Libya along the sea which washes it to the north, throughout its entire length from Egypt to Cape Soloeis,[1] which is its furthest point, is inhabited by Libyans of many distinct tribes who possess the whole tract except certain portions which belong to the Phœnicians and the Greeks. Above the coast-line and the country inhabited by the maritime tribes, Libya is full of wild beasts; while beyond the wild beast region there is a tract which is wholly sand, very scant of water, and utterly and entirely a desert. The young men therefore, despatched on this errand by their comrades with a plentiful supply of water and provisions, travelled at first through the inhabited region, passing which they came to the wild beast tract, whence they finally entered upon the desert, which they proceeded to cross in a direction from east to west. After journeying for many days over a wide extent of sand, they came at last to a plain where they observed trees growing; approaching them, and seeing fruit on

[1] Cape *Spartel,* near Tangier.

them, they proceeded to gather it. While they were thus engaged, there came upon them some dwarfish men, under the middle height, who seized them and carried them off. The Nasamonians could not understand a word of their language, nor had they any acquaintance with the language of the Nasamonians. They were led across extensive marshes, and finally came to a town, where all the men were of the height of their conductors, and black-complexioned. A great river flowed by the town, running from west to east, and containing crocodiles.

33. Here let me dismiss Etearchus the Ammonian, and his story, only adding that (according to the Cyrenæans) he declared that the Nasamonians got safe back to their country, and that the men whose city they had reached were a nation of sorcerers. With respect to the river which ran by their town, Etearchus conjectured it to be the Nile; and reason favours that view. For the Nile certainly flows out of Libya, dividing it down the middle, and as I conceive, judging the unknown from the known, rises at the same distance from its mouth as the Ister. This latter river has its source in the country of the Celts near the city Pyrêné, and runs through the middle of Europe, dividing it into two portions. The Celts live beyond the pillars of Hercules, and border on the Cynesians, who dwell at the extreme west of Europe. Thus the Ister flows through the whole of Europe before it finally empties itself into the Euxine at Istria, one of the colonies of the Milesians.

34. Now as this river flows through regions that are inhabited, its course is perfectly well known; but of the sources of the Nile no one can give any account, since Libya, the country through which it passes, is desert and without inhabitants. As far as it was possible to get information by inquiry, I have given a description of the stream. It enters Egypt from the parts beyond. Egypt lies almost exactly opposite the mountainous portion of Cilicia, whence a lightly-equipped traveller may reach Sinôpé on the Euxine in five days by the direct route. Sinôpé lies opposite the place where the Ister falls into the sea.[1] My opinion therefore is that the Nile, as it traverses the whole of Libya, is of equal length with the Ister. And here I take my leave of this subject.

[1] This of course is neither true, nor near the truth; and it is difficult to make out in what sense Herodotus meant to assert it. Perhaps he attached no very distinct geographical meaning to the word "opposite."

35. Concerning Egypt itself I shall extend my remarks to a great length, because there is no country that possesses so many wonders, nor any that has such a number of works which defy description. Not only is the climate different from that of the rest of the world, and the rivers unlike any other rivers, but the people also, in most of their manners and customs, exactly reverse the common practice of mankind. The women attend the markets and trade, while the men sit at home at the loom; and here, while the rest of the world works the woof up the warp, the Egyptians work it down; the women likewise carry burthens upon their shoulders, while the men carry them upon their heads. They eat their food out of doors in the streets, but retire for private purposes to their houses, giving as a reason that what is unseemly, but necessary, ought to be done in secret, but what has nothing unseemly about it, should be done openly. A woman cannot serve the priestly office, either for god or goddess, but men are priests to both; sons need not support their parents unless they choose, but daughters must, whether they choose or no.

36. In other countries the priests have long hair, in Egypt their heads are shaven; elsewhere it is customary, in mourning, for near relations to cut their hair close: the Egyptians, who wear no hair at any other time, when they lose a relative, let their beards and the hair of their heads grow long. All other men pass their lives separate from animals, the Egyptians have animals always living with them; others make barley and wheat their food; it is a disgrace to do so in Egypt,[2] where the grain they live on is spelt, which some call zea. Dough they knead with their feet; but they mix mud, and even take up dirt, with their hands. They are the only people in the world—they at least, and such as have learnt the practice from them—who use circumcision. Their men wear two garments apiece, their women but one. They put on the rings and fasten the ropes to sails inside; others put them outside. When they write or calculate, instead of going, like the Greeks, from left to right, they move their hand from right to left; and they insist, notwithstanding, that it is they who go to the right, and the Greeks who go to the left. They have two quite different kinds of writing, one of which is called sacred, the other common.

37. They are religious to excess, far beyond any other race of men, and use the following ceremonies:—They drink out of brazen cups,

[2] This statement is contrary to fact.

which they scour every day: there is no exception to this practice. They wear linen garments, which they are specially careful to have always fresh washed. They practise circumcision for the sake of cleanliness, considering it better to be cleanly than comely. The priests shave their whole body every other day, that no lice or other impure thing may adhere to them when they are engaged in the service of the gods. Their dress is entirely of linen, and their shoes of the papyrus plant: it is not lawful for them to wear either dress or shoes of any other material. They bathe twice every day in cold water, and twice each night; besides which they observe, so to speak, thousands of ceremonies. They enjoy, however, not a few advantages. They consume none of their own property, and are at no expense for anything; but every day bread is baked for them of the sacred corn, and a plentiful supply of beef and of goose's flesh is assigned to each, and also a portion of wine made from the grape. Fish they are not allowed to eat; and beans—which none of the Egyptians ever sow, or eat, if they come up of their own accord, either raw or boiled—the priests will not even endure to look on, since they consider it an unclean kind of pulse. Instead of a single priest, each god has the attendance of a college, at the head of which is a chief priest; when one of these dies, his son is appointed in his room.

38. Male kine are reckoned to belong to Epaphus, and are therefore tested in the following manner:—One of the priests appointed for the purpose searches to see if there is a single black hair on the whole body, since in that case the beast is unclean. He examines him all over, standing on his legs, and again laid upon his back; after which he takes the tongue out of his mouth, to see if it be clean in respect of the prescribed marks (what they are I will mention elsewhere); he also inspects the hairs of the tail, to observe if they grow naturally. If the animal is pronounced clean in all these various points, the priest marks him by twisting a piece of papyrus round his horns, and attaching thereto some sealing-clay, which he then stamps with his own signet-ring. After this the beast is led away; and it is forbidden, under the penalty of death, to sacrifice an animal which has not been marked in this way.

39. The following is their manner of sacrifice:—They lead the victim, marked with their signet, to the altar where they are about to offer it, and setting the wood alight, pour a libation of wine upon the altar in front of the victim, and at the same time invoke the god. Then they slay the animal, and cutting off his head, proceed to flay the body. Next they take the head, and heaping imprecations on it, if there is a market-place and a body of Greek traders in the city, they carry it there and sell it instantly; if, however, there are no Greeks among them, they throw the head into the river. The imprecation is to this effect:—They pray that if any evil is impending either over those who sacrifice, or over universal Egypt, it may be made to fall upon that head. These practices, the imprecations upon the heads, and the libations of wine, prevail all over Egypt, and extend to victims of all sorts; and hence the Egyptians will never eat the head of any animal.

40. The disembowelling and burning are, however, different in different sacrifices. I will mention the mode in use with respect to the goddess whom they regard as the greatest, and honour with the chiefest festival. When they have flayed their steer they pray, and when their prayer is ended they take the paunch of the animal out entire, leaving the intestines and the fat inside the body; they then cut off the legs, the ends of the loins, the shoulders, and the neck; and having so done, they fill the body of the steer with clean bread, honey, raisins, figs, frankincense, myrrh, and other aromatics. Thus filled, they burn the body, pouring over it great quantities of oil. Before offering the sacrifice they fast, and while the bodies of the victims are being consumed they beat themselves. Afterwards, when they have concluded this part of the ceremony, they have the other parts of the victim served up to them for a repast.

41. The male kine, therefore, if clean, and the male calves, are used for sacrifice by the Egyptians universally; but the females they are not allowed to sacrifice, since they are sacred to Isis. The statue of this goddess has the form of a woman but with horns like a cow, resembling thus the Greek representations of Io; and the Egyptians, one and all, venerate cows much more highly than any other animal. This is the reason why no native of Egypt, whether man or woman, will give a Greek a kiss, or use the knife of a Greek, or his spit, or his cauldron, or taste the flesh of an ox, known to be pure, if it has been cut with a Greek knife. When kine die, the following is the manner of their sepulture:—The females are thrown into the river; the males are buried in the suburbs of the towns, with one or both of their horns appear-

ing above the surface of the ground to mark the place. When the bodies are decayed, a boat comes, at an appointed time, from the island called Prosôpitis,—which is a portion of the Delta, nine schœnes in circumference,—and calls at the several cities in turn to collect the bones of the oxen. Prosôpitis is a district containing several cities; the name of that from which the boats come is Atarbêchis. Venus has a temple there of much sanctity. Great numbers of men go forth from this city and proceed to the other towns, where they dig up the bones, which they take away with them and bury together in one place. The same practice prevails with respect to the interment of all other cattle—the law so determining; they do not slaughter any of them.

42. Such Egyptians as possess a temple of the Theban Jove, or live in the Thebaïc canton, offer no sheep in sacrifice, but only goats; for the Egyptians do not all worship the same gods, excepting Isis and Osiris, the latter of whom they say is the Grecian Bacchus. Those, on the contrary, who possess a temple dedicated to Mendes, or belong to the Mendesian canton, abstain from offering goats, and sacrifice sheep instead. The Thebans, and such as imitate them in their practice, give the following account of the origin of the custom:—"Hercules," they say, "wished of all things to see Jove, but Jove did not choose to be seen of him. At length, when Hercules persisted, Jove hit on a device—to flay a ram, and, cutting off his head, hold the head before him, and cover himself with the fleece. In this guise he showed himself to Hercules." Therefore the Egyptians give their statues of Jupiter the face of a ram: and from them the practice has passed to the Ammonians, who are a joint colony of Egyptians and Ethiopians, speaking a language between the two; hence also, in my opinion, the latter people took their name of Ammonians, since the Egyptian name for Jupiter is Amun. Such, then, is the reason why the Thebans do not sacrifice rams, but consider them sacred animals. Upon one day in the year, however, at the festival of Jupiter, they slay a single ram, and stripping off the fleece, cover with it the statue of that god, as he once covered himself, and then bring up to the statue of Jove an image of Hercules. When this has been done, the whole assembly beat their breasts in mourning for the ram, and afterwards bury him in a holy sepulchre.

43. The account which I received of this Hercules makes him one of the twelve gods. Of the other Hercules, with whom the Greeks are familiar, I could hear nothing in any part of Egypt. That the Greeks, however (those I mean who gave the son of Amphitryon that name), took the name[1] from the Egyptians, and not the Egyptians from the Greeks, is I think clearly proved, among other arguments, by the fact that both the parents of Hercules, Amphitryon as well as Alcmêna, were of Egyptian origin. Again, the Egyptians disclaim all knowledge of the names of Neptune and the Dioscûri, and do not include them in the number of their gods; but had they adopted the name of any god from the Greeks, these would have been the likeliest to obtain notice, since the Egyptians, as I am well convinced, practised navigation at that time, and the Greeks also were some of them mariners, so that they would have been more likely to know the names of these gods than that of Hercules. But the Egyptian Hercules is one of their ancient gods. Seventeen thousand years before the reign of Amasis, the twelve gods were, they affirm, produced from the eight: and of these twelve, Hercules is one.

44. In the wish to get the best information that I could on these matters, I made a voyage to Tyre in Phœnicia, hearing there was a temple of Hercules at that place, very highly venerated. I visited the temple, and found it richly adorned with a number of offerings, among which were two pillars, one of pure gold, the other of emerald, shining with great brilliancy at night. In a conversation which I held with the priests, I inquired how long their temple had been built, and found by their answer that they, too, differed from the Greeks. They said that the temple was built at the same time that the city was founded, and that the foundation of the city took place two thousand three hundred years ago. In Tyre I remarked another temple where the same god was worshipped as the Thasian Hercules. So I went on to Thasos, where I found a temple of Hercules which had been built by the Phœnicians who colonised that island when they sailed in search of Europa. Even this was five generations earlier than the time when Hercules, son of Amphitryon, was born in Greece. These researches show plainly that there is an ancient god Hercules; and my own opinion is that those Greeks act most wisely who build and maintain two temples of Hercules, in the one of

[1] It is scarcely necessary to say that no Egyptian god has a name from which that of Hercules can by any possibility have been formed.

which the Hercules worshipped is known by the name of Olympian, and has sacrifice offered to him as an immortal, while in the other the honours paid are such as are due to a hero.

45. The Greeks tell many tales without due investigation, and among them the following silly fable respecting Hercules:—"Hercules," they say, "went once to Egypt, and there the inhabitants took him, and putting a chaplet on his head, led him out in solemn procession, intending to offer him a sacrifice to Jupiter. For a while he submitted quietly; but when they led him up to the altar and began the ceremonies, he put forth his strength and slew them all." Now to me it seems that such a story proves the Greeks to be utterly ignorant of the character and customs of the people. The Egyptians do not think it allowable even to sacrifice cattle, excepting sheep, and the male kine and calves, provided they be pure, and also geese. How, then, can it be believed that they would sacrifice men? And again, how would it have been possible for Hercules alone, and, as they confess, a mere mortal, to destroy so many thousands? In saying thus much concerning these matters, may I incur no displeasure either of god or hero!

46. I mentioned above that some of the Egyptians abstain from sacrificing goats, either male or female. The reason is the following:— These Egyptians, who are the Mendesians, consider Pan to be one of the eight gods who existed before the twelve, and Pan is represented in Egypt by the painters and the sculptors, just as he is in Greece, with the face and legs of a goat. They do not, however, believe this to be his shape, or consider him in any respect unlike the other gods; but they represent him thus for a reason which I prefer not to relate. The Mendesians hold all goats in veneration, but the male more than the female, giving the goatherds of the males especial honour. One is venerated more highly than all the rest, and when he dies there is a great mourning throughout all the Mendesian canton. In Egyptian, the goat and Pan are both called Mendes.

47. The pig is regarded among them as an unclean animal, so much so that if a man in passing accidentally touch a pig, he instantly hurries to the river, and plunges in with all his clothes on. Hence, too, the swineherds, notwithstanding that they are of pure Egyptian blood, are forbidden to enter into any of the temples, which are open to all other Egyptians; and further, no one will give his daughter in marriage to a swineherd, or take a wife from among them,

so that the swineherds are forced to intermarry among themselves. They do not offer swine in sacrifice to any of their gods, excepting Bacchus and the Moon, whom they honour in this way at the same time, sacrificing pigs to both of them at the same full moon, and afterwards eating of the flesh. There is a reason alleged by them for their detestation of swine at all other seasons, and their use of them at this festival, with which I am well acquainted, but which I do not think it proper to mention. The following is the mode in which they sacrifice the swine to the Moon:—As soon as the victim is slain, the tip of the tail, the spleen, and the caul are put together, and having been covered with all the fat that has been found in the animal's belly, are straightway burnt. The remainder of the flesh is eaten on the same day that the sacrifice is offered, which is the day of the full moon: at any other time they would not so much as taste it. The poorer sort, who cannot afford live pigs, form pigs of dough, which they bake and offer in sacrifice.

48. To Bacchus, on the eve of his feast, every Egyptian sacrifices a hog before the door of his house, which is then given back to the swineherd by whom it was furnished, and by him carried away. In other respects the festival is celebrated almost exactly as Bacchic festivals are in Greece, excepting that the Egyptians have no choral dances. They also use instead of phalli another invention, consisting of images a cubit high, pulled by strings, which the women carry round to the villages. A piper goes in front, and the women follow, singing hymns in honour of Bacchus. They give a religious reason for the peculiarities of the image.

49. Melampus, the son of Amytheon, cannot (I think) have been ignorant of this ceremony —nay, he must, I should conceive, have been well acquainted with it. He it was who introduced into Greece the name of Bacchus, the ceremonial of his worship, and the procession of the phallus. He did not, however, so completely apprehend the whole doctrine as to be able to communicate it entirely, but various sages since his time have carried out his teaching to greater perfection. Still it is certain that Melampus introduced the phallus, and that the Greeks learnt from him the ceremonies which they now practise. I therefore maintain that Melampus, who was a wise man, and had acquired the art of divination, having become acquainted with the worship of Bacchus through knowledge derived from Egypt, introduced it into Greece, with a few slight changes,

at the same time that he brought in various other practices. For I can by no means allow that it is by mere coincidence that the Bacchic ceremonies in Greece are so nearly the same as the Egyptian—they would then have been more Greek in their character, and less recent in their origin. Much less can I admit that the Egyptians borrowed these customs, or any other, from the Greeks. My belief is that Melampus got his knowledge of them from Cadmus the Tyrian, and the followers whom he brought from Phœnicia into the country which is now called Bœotia.

50. Almost all the names of the gods came into Greece from Egypt. My inquiries prove that they were all derived from a foreign source, and my opinion is that Egypt furnished the greater number. For with the exception of Neptune and the Dioscûri, whom I mentioned above, and Juno, Vesta, Themis, the Graces, and the Nereids, the other gods have been known from time immemorial in Egypt. This I assert on the authority of the Egyptians themselves. The gods, with whose names they profess themselves unacquainted, the Greeks received, I believe, from the Pelasgi, except Neptune. Of him they got their knowledge from the Libyans, by whom he has been always honoured, and who were anciently the only people that had a god of the name. The Egyptians differ from the Greeks also in paying no divine honours to heroes.

51. Besides these which have been here mentioned, there are many other practices whereof I shall speak hereafter, which the Greeks have borrowed from Egypt. The peculiarity, however, which they observe in their statues of Mercury they did not derive from the Egyptians, but from the Pelasgi; from them the Athenians first adopted it, and afterwards it passed from the Athenians to the other Greeks. For just at the time when the Athenians were entering into the Hellenic body, the Pelasgi came to live with them in their country, whence it was that the latter came first to be regarded as Greeks. Whoever has been initiated into the mysteries of the Cabiri will understand what I mean. The Samothracians received these mysteries from the Pelasgi, who, before they went to live in Attica, were dwellers in Samothrace, and imparted their religious ceremonies to the inhabitants. The Athenians, then, who were the first of all the Greeks to make their statues of Mercury in this way, learnt the practice from the Pelasgians; and by this people a religious account of the matter is given, which is explained in the Samothracian mysteries.

52. In early times the Pelasgi, as I know by information which I got at Dodôna, offered sacrifices of all kinds, and prayed to the gods, but had no distinct names or appellations for them, since they had never heard of any. They called them gods (Θεοι, disposers), because they had disposed and arranged all things in such a beautiful order. After a long lapse of time the names of the gods came to Greece from Egypt, and the Pelasgi learnt them, only as yet they knew nothing of Bacchus, of whom they first heard at a much later date. Not long after the arrival of the names they sent to consult the oracle at Dodôna about them. This is the most ancient oracle in Greece, and at that time there was no other. To their question, "Whether they should adopt the names that had been imported from the foreigners?" the oracle replied by recommending their use. Thenceforth in their sacrifices the Pelasgi made use of the names of the gods, and from them the names passed afterwards to the Greeks.

53. Whence the gods severally sprang, whether or no they had all existed from eternity, what forms they bore—these are questions of which the Greeks knew nothing until the other day, so to speak. For Homer and Hesiod were the first to compose Theogonies, and give the gods their epithets, to allot them their several offices and occupations, and describe their forms; and they lived but four hundred years before my time, as I believe. As for the poets who are thought by some to be earlier than these, they are, in my judgment, decidedly later writers. In these matters I have the authority of the priestesses of Dodôna for the former portion of my statements; what I have said of Homer and Hesiod is my own opinion.

54. The following tale is commonly told in Egypt concerning the oracle of Dodôna in Greece, and that of Ammon in Libya. My informants on the point were the priests of Jupiter at Thebes. They said "that two of the sacred women were once carried off from Thebes by the Phœnicians, and that the story went that one of them was sold into Libya, and the other into Greece, and these women were the first founders of the oracles in the two countries." On my inquiring how they came to know so exactly what became of the women, they answered, "that diligent search had been made after them at the time, but that it had not been found possible to discover where they were; afterwards, however, they

received the information which they had given me."

55. This was what I heard from the priests at Thebes; at Dodôna, however, the women who deliver the oracles relate the matter as follows:—"Two black doves flew away from Egyptian Thebes, and while one directed its flight to Libya, the other came to them. She alighted on an oak, and sitting there began to speak with a human voice, and told them that on the spot where she was, there should henceforth be an oracle of Jove. They understood the announcement to be from heaven, so they set to work at once and erected the shrine. The dove which flew to Libya bade the Libyans to establish there the oracle of Ammon." This likewise is an oracle of Jupiter. The persons from whom I received these particulars were three priestesses of the Dodonæans, the eldest Promeneia, the next Timareté, and the youngest Nicandra—what they said was confirmed by the other Dodonæans who dwell around the temple.

56. My own opinion of these matters is as follows:—I think that, if it be true that the Phœnicians carried off the holy women, and sold them for slaves, the one into Libya and the other into Greece, or Pelasgia (as it was then called), this last must have been sold to the Thesprotians. Afterwards, while undergoing servitude in those parts, she built under a real oak a temple to Jupiter, her thoughts in her new abode reverting—as it was likely they would do, if she had been an attendant in a temple of Jupiter at Thebes—to that particular god. Then, having acquired a knowledge of the Greek tongue, she set up an oracle. She also mentioned that her sister had been sold for a slave into Libya by the same persons as herself.

57. The Dodonæans called the women doves because they were foreigners, and seemed to them to make a noise like birds. After a while the dove spoke with a human voice, because the woman, whose foreign talk had previously sounded to them like the chattering of a bird, acquired the power of speaking what they could understand. For how can it be conceived possible that a dove should really speak with the voice of a man? Lastly, by calling the dove black the Dodonæans indicated that the woman was an Egyptian. And certainly the character of the oracles at Thebes and Dodôna is very similar. Besides this form of divination, the Greeks learnt also divination by means of victims from the Egyptians.

58. The Egyptians were also the first to in-troduce solemn assemblies, processions, and litanies to the gods; of all which the Greeks were taught the use by them. It seems to me a sufficient proof of this that in Egypt these practices have been established from remote antiquity, while in Greece they are only recently known.

59. The Egyptians do not hold a single solemn assembly, but several in the course of the year. Of these the chief, which is better attended than any other, is held at the city of Bubastis in honour of Diana. The next in importance is that which takes place at Busiris, a city situated in the very middle of the Delta; it is in honour of Isis, who is called in the Greek tongue Demêter (Ceres). There is a third great festival in Saïs to Minerva, a fourth in Heliopolis to the Sun, a fifth in Buto to Latona, and a sixth in Paprêmis to Mars.

60. The following are the proceedings on occasion of the assembly at Bubastis:—Men and women come sailing all together, vast numbers in each boat, many of the women with castanets, which they strike, while some of the men pipe during the whole time of the voyage; the remainder of the voyagers, male and female, sing the while, and make a clapping with their hands. When they arrive opposite any of the towns upon the banks of the stream, they approach the shore, and, while some of the women continue to play and sing, others call aloud to the females of the place and load them with abuse, while a certain number dance, and some standing up uncover themselves. After proceeding in this way all along the river-course, they reach Bubastis, where they celebrate the feast with abundant sacrifices. More grape-wine is consumed at this festival than in all the rest of the year besides. The number of those who attend, counting only the men and women and omitting the children, amounts, according to the native reports, to seven hundred thousand.

61. The ceremonies at the feast of Isis in the city of Busiris have been already spoken of. It is there that the whole multitude, both of men and women, many thousands in number, beat themselves at the close of the sacrifice, in honour of a god, whose name a religious scruple forbids me to mention.[1] The Carian dwellers in Egypt proceed on this occasion to still greater lengths, even cutting their faces with their knives, whereby they let it been seen that they are not Egyptians but foreigners.

62. At Saïs, when the assembly takes place

[1] Osiris.

for the sacrifices, there is one night on which the inhabitants all burn a multitude of lights in the open air round their houses. They use lamps in the shape of flat saucers filled with a mixture of oil and salt, on the top of which the wick floats. These burn the whole night, and give to the festival the name of the Feast of Lamps. The Egyptians who are absent from the festival observe the night of the sacrifice, no less than the rest, by a general lighting of lamps; so that the illumination is not confined to the city of Saïs, but extends over the whole of Egypt. And there is a religious reason assigned for the special honour paid to this night, as well as for the illumination which acccompanies it.

63. At Heliopolis and Buto the assemblies are merely for the purpose of sacrifice; but at Paprêmis, besides the sacrifices and other rites which are performed there as elsewhere, the following custom is observed:—When the sun is getting low, a few only of the priests continue occupied about the image of the god, while the greater number, armed with wooden clubs, take their station at the portal of the temple. Opposite to them is drawn up a body of men, in number above a thousand, armed, like the others, with clubs, consisting of persons engaged in the performance of their vows. The image of the god, which is kept in a small wooden shrine covered with plates of gold, is conveyed from the temple into a second sacred building the day before the festival begins. The few priests still in attendance upon the image place it, together with the shrine containing it, on a four-wheeled car, and begin to drag it along; the others stationed at the gateway of the temple, oppose its admission. Then the votaries come forward to espouse the quarrel of the god, and set upon the opponents, who are sure to offer resistance. A sharp fight with clubs ensues, in which heads are commonly broken on both sides. Many, I am convinced, die of the wounds that they receive, though the Egyptians insist that no one is ever killed.

64. The natives give the subjoined account of this festival. They say that the mother of the god Mars once dwelt in the temple. Brought up at a distance from his parent, when he grew to man's estate he conceived a wish to visit her. Accordingly he came, but the attendants, who had never seen him before, refused him entrance, and succeeded in keeping him out. So he went to another city and collected a body of men, with whose aid he handled the attendants very roughly, and forced his way in to his mother. Hence they say arose the custom of a fight with sticks in honour of Mars at this festival.

The Egyptians first made it a point of religion to have no converse with women in the sacred places, and not to enter them without washing, after such converse. Almost all other nations, except the Greeks and the Egyptians, act differently, regarding man as in this matter under no other law than the brutes. Many animals, they say, and various kinds of birds, may be seen to couple in the temples and the sacred precincts, which would certainly not happen if the gods were displeased at it. Such are the arguments by which they defend their practice, but I nevertheless can by no means approve of it. In these points the Egyptians are specially careful, as they are indeed in everything which concerns their sacred edifices.

65. Egypt, though it borders upon Libya, is not a region abounding in wild animals. The animals that do exist in the country, whether domesticated or otherwise, are all regarded as sacred. If I were to explain why they are consecrated to the several gods, I should be led to speak of religious matters, which I particularly shrink from mentioning; the points whereon I have touched slightly hitherto have all been introduced from sheer necessity. Their custom with respect to animals is as follows:—For every kind there are appointed certain guardians, some male, some female, whose business it is to look after them; and this honour is made to descend from father to son. The inhabitants of the various cities, when they have made a vow to any god, pay it to his animals in the way which I will now explain. At the time of making the vow they shave the head of the child, cutting off all the hair, or else half, or sometimes a third part, which they then weigh in a balance against a sum of silver; and whatever sum the hair weighs is presented to the guardian of the animals, who thereupon cuts up some fish, and gives it to them for food— such being the stuff whereon they are fed. When a man has killed one of the sacred animals, if he did it with *malice prepense,* he is punished with death; if unwittingly, he has to pay such a fine as the priests choose to impose. When an ibis, however, or a hawk is killed, whether it was done by accident or on purpose, the man must needs die.

66. The number of domestic animals in Egypt is very great, and would be still greater were it not for what befalls the cats. As the females, when they have kittened, no longer seek

the company of the males, these last, to obtain once more their companionship, practise a curious artifice. They seize the kittens, carry them off, and kill them, but do not eat them afterwards. Upon this the females, being deprived of their young, and longing to supply their place, seek the males once more, since they are particularly fond of their offspring. On every occasion of a fire in Egypt the strangest prodigy occurs with the cats. The inhabitants allow the fire to rage as it pleases, while they stand about at intervals and watch these animals, which, slipping by the men or else leaping over them, rush headlong into the flames. When this happens, the Egyptians are in deep affliction. If a cat dies in a private house by a natural death, all the inmates of the house shave their eyebrows; on the death of a dog they shave the head and the whole of the body.

67. The cats on their decease are taken to the city of Bubastis, where they are embalmed, after which they are buried in certain sacred repositories. The dogs are interred in the cities to which they belong, also in sacred burial-places. The same practice obtains with respect to the ichneumons; the hawks and shrew-mice, on the contrary, are conveyed to the city of Buto for burial, and the ibises to Hermopolis. The bears, which are scarce in Egypt, and the wolves, which are not much bigger than foxes, they bury wherever they happen to find them lying.

68. The following are the peculiarities of the crocodile:—During the four winter months they eat nothing; they are four-footed, and live indifferently on land or in the water. The female lays and hatches her eggs ashore, passing the greater portion of the day on dry land, but at night retiring to the river, the water of which is warmer than the night-air and the dew. Of all known animals this is the one which from the smallest size grows to be the greatest: for the egg of the crocodile is but little bigger than that of the goose, and the young crocodile is in proportion to the egg; yet when it is full grown, the animal measures frequently seventeen cubits and even more. It has the eyes of a pig, teeth large and tusk-like, of a size proportioned to its frame; unlike any other animal, it is without a tongue; it cannot move its under-jaw, and in this respect too it is singular, being the only animal in the world which moves the upper-jaw but not the under. It has strong claws and a scaly skin, impenetrable upon the back. In the water it is blind, but on land it is very keen of sight. As it lives chiefly in the river, it has the inside of its mouth constantly covered with leeches; hence it happens that, while all the other birds and beasts avoid it, with the trochilus it lives at peace, since it owes much to that bird: for the crocodile, when he leaves the water and comes out upon the land, is in the habit of lying with his mouth wide open, facing the western breeze: at such times the trochilus goes into his mouth and devours the leeches. This benefits the crocodile, who is pleased, and takes care not to hurt the trochilus.

69. The crocodile is esteemed sacred by some of the Egyptians, by others he is treated as an enemy. Those who live near Thebes, and those who dwell around Lake Mœris, regard them with especial veneration. In each of these places they keep one crocodile in particular, who is taught to be tame and tractable. They adorn his ears with ear-rings of molten stone or gold, and put bracelets on his fore-paws, giving him daily a set portion of bread, with a certain number of victims; and, after having thus treated him with the greatest possible attention while alive, they embalm him when he dies and bury him in a sacred repository. The people of Elephantiné on the other hand, are so far from considering these animals as sacred that they even eat their flesh. In the Egyptian language they are not called crocodiles, but Champsæ. The name of crocodiles was given them by the Ionians, who remarked their resemblance to the lizards, which in Ionia live in the walls and are called crocodiles.

70. The modes of catching the crocodile are many and various. I shall only describe the one which seems to me most worthy of mention. They bait a hook with a chine of pork and let the meat be carried out into the middle of the stream, while the hunter upon the bank holds a living pig, which he belabours. The crocodile hears its cries, and making for the sound, encounters the pork, which he instantly swallows down. The men on the shore haul, and when they have got him to land, the first thing the hunter does is to plaster his eyes with mud. This once accomplished, the animal is despatched with ease, otherwise he gives great trouble.

71. The hippopotamus, in the canton of Paprêmis, is a sacred animal, but not in any other part of Egypt. It may be thus described:—It is a quadruped, cloven-footed, with hoofs like an ox, and a flat nose. It has the mane and tail of a horse, huge tusks which are very conspicuous, and a voice like a horse's neigh. In size

it equals the biggest oxen, and its skin is so tough that when dried it is made into javelins.

72. Otters also are found in the Nile, and are considered sacred. Only two sorts of fish are venerated, that called the lepidôtus and the eel. These are regarded as sacred to the Nile, as likewise among birds is the vulpanser, or fox-goose.

73. They have also another sacred bird called the phœnix, which I myself have never seen, except in pictures. Indeed it is a great rarity, even in Egypt, only coming there (according to the accounts of the people of Heliopolis) once in five hundred years, when the old phœnix dies. Its size and appearance, if it is like the pictures, are as follow:—The plumage is partly red, partly golden, while the general make and size are almost exactly that of the eagle. They tell a story of what this bird does, which does not seem to me to be credible: that he comes all the way from Arabia, and brings the parent bird, all plastered over with myrrh, to the temple of the Sun, and there buries the body. In order to bring him, they say, he first forms a ball of myrrh as big as he finds that he can carry; then he hollows out the ball, and puts his parent inside, after which he covers over the opening with fresh myrrh, and the ball is then of exactly the same weight as at first; so he brings it to Egypt, plastered over as I have said, and deposits it in the temple of the Sun. Such is the story they tell of the doings of this bird.

74. In the neighbourhood of Thebes there are some sacred serpents which are perfectly harmless. They are of small size, and have two horns growing out of the top of the head. These snakes, when they die, are buried in the temple of Jupiter, the god to whom they are sacred.

75. I went once to a certain place in Arabia, almost exactly opposite the city of Buto, to make inquiries concerning the winged serpents. On my arrival I saw the back-bones and ribs of serpents in such numbers as it is impossible to describe: of the ribs there were a multitude of heaps, some great, some small, some middle-sized. The place where the bones lie is at the entrance of a narrow gorge between steep mountains, which there open upon a spacious plain communicating with the great plain of Egypt. The story goes that with the spring the winged snakes come flying from Arabia towards Egypt, but are met in this gorge by the birds called ibises, who forbid their entrance and destroy them all. The Arabians assert, and the Egyptians also admit, that

it is on account of the service thus rendered that the Egyptians hold the ibis in so much reverence.

76. The ibis is a bird of a deep-black colour, with legs like a crane; its beak is strongly hooked, and its size is about that of the land-rail. This is a description of the black ibis which contends with the serpents. The commoner sort, for there are two quite distinct species, has the head and the whole throat bare of feathers; its general plumage is white, but the head and neck are jet black, as also are the tips of the wings and the extremity of the tail; in its beak and legs it resembles the other species. The winged serpent is shaped like the water-snake. Its wings are not feathered, but resemble very closely those of the bat. And thus I conclude the subject of the sacred animals.

77. With respect to the Egyptians themselves, it is to be remarked that those who live in the corn country, devoting themselves, as they do, far more than any other people in the world, to the preservation of the memory of past actions, are the best skilled in history of any men that I have ever met. The following is the mode of life habitual to them:—For three successive days in each month they purge the body by means of emetics and clysters, which is done out of a regard for their health, since they have a persuasion that every disease to which men are liable is occasioned by the substances whereon they feed. Apart from any such precautions, they are, I believe, next to the Libyans, the healthiest people in the world —an effect of their climate, in my opinion, which has no sudden changes. Diseases almost always attack men when they are exposed to a change, and never more than during changes of the weather. They live on bread made of spelt, which they form into loaves called in their own tongue *cyllêstis*. Their drink is a wine which they obtain from barley, as they have no vines in their country. Many kinds of fish they eat raw, either salted or dried in the sun. Quails also, and ducks and small birds, they eat uncooked, merely first salting them. All other birds and fishes, excepting those which are set apart as sacred, are eaten either roasted or boiled.

78. In social meetings among the rich, when the banquet is ended, a servant carries round to the several guests a coffin, in which there is a wooden image of a corpse, carved and painted to resemble nature as nearly as possible, about a cubit or two cubits in length. As he shows it to each guest in turn, the servant says,

"Gaze here, and drink and be merry; for when you die, such will you be."

79. The Egyptians adhere to their own national customs, and adopt no foreign usages. Many of these customs are worthy of note: among others their song, the Linus, which is sung under various names not only in Egypt but in Phœnicia, in Cyprus, and in other places; and which seems to be exactly the same as that in use among the Greeks, and by them called Linus. There were very many things in Egypt which filled me with astonishment, and this was one of them. Whence could the Egyptians have got the Linus? It appears to have been sung by them from the very earliest times. For the Linus in Egyptian is called Manerôs; and they told me that Manerôs was the only son of their first king, and that on his untimely death he was honoured by the Egyptians with these dirgelike strains, and in this way they got their first and only melody.

80. There is another custom in which the Egyptians resemble a particular Greek people, namely the Lacedæmonians. Their young men, when they meet their elders in the streets, give way to them and step aside; and if an elder come in where young men are present, these latter rise from their seats. In a third point they differ entirely from all the nations of Greece. Instead of speaking to each other when they meet in the streets, they make an obeisance, sinking the hand to the knee.

81. They wear a linen tunic fringed about the legs, and called *calasiris;* over this they have a white woollen garment thrown on afterwards. Nothing of woollen, however, is taken into their temples or buried with them, as their religion forbids it. Here their practice resembles the rites called Orphic and Bacchic, but which are in reality Egyptian and Pythagorean; for no one initiated in these mysteries can be buried in a woollen shroud, a religious reason being assigned for the observance.

82. The Egyptians likewise discovered to which of the gods each month and day is sacred; and found out from the day of a man's birth what he will meet with in the course of his life, and how he will end his days, and what sort of man he will be—discoveries whereof the Greeks engaged in poetry have made a use. The Egyptians have also discovered more prognostics than all the rest of mankind besides. Whenever a prodigy takes place, they watch and record the result; then, if anything similar ever happens again, they expect the same consequences.

83. With respect to divination, they hold that it is a gift which no mortal possesses, but only certain of the gods: thus they have an oracle of Hercules, one of Apollo, of Minerva, of Diana, of Mars, and of Jupiter. Besides these, there is the oracle of Latona at Buto, which is held in much higher repute than any of the rest. The mode of delivering the oracles is not uniform, but varies at the different shrines.

84. Medicine is practised among them on a plan of separation; each physician treats a single disorder, and no more: thus the country swarms with medical practitioners, some undertaking to cure diseases of the eye, others of the head, others again of the teeth, others of the intestines, and some those which are not local.

85. The following is the way in which they conduct their mournings and their funerals:—On the death in any house of a man of consequence, forthwith the women of the family beplaster their heads, and sometimes even their faces, with mud; and then, leaving the body indoors, sally forth and wander through the city, with their dress fastened by a band, and their bosoms bare, beating themselves as they walk. All the female relations join them and do the same. The men too, similarly begirt, beat their breasts separately. When these ceremonies are over, the body is carried away to be embalmed.

86. There are a set of men in Egypt who practice the art of embalming, and make it their proper business. These persons, when a body is brought to them, show the bearers various models of corpses, made in wood, and painted so as to resemble nature. The most perfect is said to be after the manner of him whom I do not think it religious to name in connection with such a matter; the second sort is inferior to the first, and less costly; the third is the cheapest of all. All this the embalmers explain, and then ask in which way it is wished that the corpse should be prepared. The bearers tell them, and having concluded their bargain, take their departure, while the embalmers, left to themselves, proceed to their task. The mode of embalming, according to the most perfect process, is the following:—They take first a crooked piece of iron, and with it draw out the brain through the nostrils, thus getting rid of a portion, while the skull is cleared of the rest by rinsing with drugs; next they make a cut along the flank with a sharp Ethiopian stone, and take out the whole contents of the abdo-

men, which they then cleanse, washing it thoroughly with palm wine, and again frequently with an infusion of pounded aromatics. After this they fill the cavity with the purest bruised myrrh, with cassia, and every other sort of spicery except frankincense, and sew up the opening. Then the body is placed in natrum for seventy days, and covered entirely over. After the expiration of that space of time, which must not be exceeded, the body is washed, and wrapped round, from head to foot, with bandages of fine linen cloth, smeared over with gum, which is used generally by the Egyptians in the place of glue, and in this state it is given back to the relations, who enclose it in a wooden case which they have had made for the purpose, shaped into the figure of a man. Then fastening the case, they place it in a sepulchral chamber, upright against the wall. Such is the most costly way of embalming the dead.

87. If persons wish to avoid expense, and choose the second process, the following is the method pursued:—Syringes are filled with oil made from the cedar-tree, which is then, without any incision or disembowelling, injected into the abdomen. The passage by which it might be likely to return is stopped, and the body laid in natrum the prescribed number of days. At the end of the time the cedar-oil is allowed to make its escape; and such is its power that it brings with it the whole stomach and intestines in a liquid state. The natrum meanwhile has dissolved the flesh, and so nothing is left of the dead body but the skin and the bones. It is returned in this condition to the relatives, without any further trouble being bestowed upon it.

88. The third method of embalming, which is practised in the case of the poorer classes, is to clear out the intestines with a clyster, and let the body lie in natrum the seventy days, after which it is at once given to those who come to fetch it away.

89. The wives of men of rank are not given to be embalmed immediately after death, nor indeed are any of the more beautiful and valued women. It is not till they have been dead three or four days that they are carried to the embalmers. This is done to prevent indignities from being offered them. It is said that once a case of this kind occurred: the man was detected by the information of his fellow-workman.

90. Whensoever any one, Egyptian or foreigner, has lost his life by falling a prey to a crocodile, or by drowning in the river, the law compels the inhabitants of the city near which the body is cast up to have it embalmed, and to bury it in one of the sacred repositories with all possible magnificence. No one may touch the corpse, not even any of the friends or relatives, but only the priests of the Nile, who prepare it for burial with their own hands—regarding it as something more than the mere body of a man—and themselves lay it in the tomb.

91. The Egyptians are averse to adopt Greek customs, or, in a word, those of any other nation. This feeling is almost universal among them. At Chemmis, however, which is a large city in the Thebaïc canton, near Neapolis, there is a square enclosure sacred to Perseus, son of Danaë. Palm trees grow all round the place, which has a stone gateway of an unusual size, surmounted by two colossal statues, also in stone. Inside this precinct is a temple, and in the temple an image of Perseus. The people of Chemmis say that Perseus often appears to them, sometimes within the sacred enclosure, sometimes in the open country: one of the sandals which he has worn is frequently found —two cubits in length, as they affirm—and then all Egypt flourishes greatly. In the worship of Perseus Greek ceremonies are used; gymnastic games are celebrated in his honour, comprising every kind of contest, with prizes of cattle, cloaks, and skins. I made inquiries of the Chemmites why it was that Perseus appeared to them and not elsewhere in Egypt, and how they came to celebrate gymnastic contests unlike the rest of the Egyptians: to which they answered, "that Perseus belonged to their city by descent. Danaüs and Lynceus were Chemmites before they set sail for Greece, and from them Perseus was descended," they said, tracing the genealogy; "and he, when he came to Egypt for the purpose" (which the Greeks also assign) "of bringing away from Libya the Gorgon's head, paid them a visit, and acknowledged them for his kinsmen—he had heard the name of their city from his mother before he left Greece—he bade them institute a gymnastic contest in his honour, and that was the reason why they observed the practice."

92. The customs hitherto described are those of the Egyptians who live above the marsh-country. The inhabitants of the marshes have the same customs as the rest, as well in those matters which have been mentioned above as in respect of marriage, each Egyptian taking to himself, like the Greeks, a single wife; but for greater cheapness of living the marsh-men practise certain peculiar customs, such as these

following. They gather the blossoms of a certain water-lily, which grows in great abundance all over the flat country at the time when the Nile rises and floods the regions along its banks—the Egyptians call it the lotus—they gather, I say, the blossoms of this plant and dry them in the sun, after which they extract from the centre of each blossom a substance like the head of a poppy, which they crush and make into bread. The root of the lotus is likewise eatable, and has a pleasant sweet taste: it is round, and about the size of an apple. There is also another species of the lily in Egypt, which grows, like the lotus, in the river, and resembles the rose. The fruit springs up side by side with the blossom, on a separate stalk, and has almost exactly the look of the comb made by wasps. It contains a number of seeds, about the size of an olive-stone, which are good to eat: and these are eaten both green and dried. The byblus (papyrus), which grows year after year in the marshes, they pull up, and, cutting the plant in two, reserve the upper portion for other purposes, but take the lower, which is about a cubit long, and either eat it or else sell it. Such as wish to enjoy the byblus in full perfection bake it first in a closed vessel, heated to a glow. Some of these folk, however, live entirely on fish, which are gutted as soon as caught, and then hung up in the sun: when dry, they are used as food.

93. Gregarious fish are not found in any numbers in the rivers; they frequent the lagunes, whence, at the season of breeding, they proceed in shoals towards the sea. The males lead the way, and drop their milt as they go, while the females, following close behind, eagerly swallow it down. From this they conceive,[1] and when, after passing some time in the sea, they begin to be in spawn, the whole shoal sets off on its return to its ancient haunts. Now, however, it is no longer the males, but the females, who take the lead: they swim in front in a body, and do exactly as the males did before, dropping, little by little, their grains of spawn as they go, while the males in the rear devour the grains, each one of which is a fish. A portion of the spawn escapes and is not swallowed by the males, and hence come the fishes which grow afterwards to maturity. When any of this sort of fish are taken on their passage to the sea, they are found to have the left side of the head scarred and bruised; while if taken on their return, the marks appear on the right. The reason is that as they swim

[1] Aristotle shows the absurdity of this statement.

down the Nile seaward, they keep close to the bank of the river upon their left, and returning again up stream they still cling to the same side, hugging it and brushing against it constantly, to be sure that they miss not their road through the great force of the current. When the Nile begins to rise, the hollows in the land and the marshy spots near the river are flooded before any other places by the percolation of the water through the riverbanks; and these, almost as soon as they become pools, are found to be full of numbers of little fishes. I think that I understand how it is this comes to pass. On the subsidence of the Nile the year before, though the fish retired with the retreating waters, they had first deposited their spawn in the mud upon the banks; and so, when at the usual season the water returns, small fry are rapidly engendered out of the spawn of the preceding year. So much concerning the fish.

94. The Egyptians who live in the marshes use for the anointing of their bodies an oil made from the fruit of the sillicyprium, which is known among them by the name of "kiki." To obtain this they plant the sillicyprium (which grows wild in Greece) along the banks of the rivers and by the sides of the lakes, where it produces fruit in great abundance, but with a very disagreeable smell. This fruit is gathered, and then bruised and pressed, or else boiled down after roasting: the liquid which comes from it is collected and is found to be unctuous, and as well suited as olive-oil for lamps, only that it gives out an unpleasant odour.

95. The contrivances which they use against gnats, wherewith the country swarms, are the following. In the parts of Egypt above the marshes the inhabitants pass the night upon lofty towers, which are of great service, as the gnats are unable to fly to any height on account of the winds. In the marsh-country, where there are no towers, each man possesses a net instead. By day it serves him to catch fish, while at night he spreads it over the bed in which he is to rest, and creeping in, goes to sleep underneath. The gnats, which, if he rolls himself up in his dress or in a piece of muslin, are sure to bite through the covering, do not so much as attempt to pass the net.

96. The vessels used in Egypt for the transport of merchandise are made of the Acantha (Thorn), a tree which in its growth is very like the Cyrenaïc lotus, and from which there exudes a gum. They cut a quantity of planks about two cubits in length from this tree, and

then proceed to their ship-building, arranging the planks like bricks, and attaching them by ties to a number of long stakes or poles till the hull is complete, when they lay the cross-planks on the top from side to side. They give the boats no ribs, but caulk the seams with papyrus on the inside. Each has a single rudder, which is driven straight through the keel. The mast is a piece of acantha-wood, and the sails are made of papyrus. These boats cannot make way against the current unless there is a brisk breeze; they are, therefore, towed up-stream from the shore: down-stream they are managed as follows: There is a raft belonging to each, made of the wood of the tamarisk, fastened together with a wattling of reeds; and also a stone bored through the middle about two talents in weight. The raft is fastened to the vessel by a rope, and allowed to float down the stream in front, while the stone is attached by another rope astern. The result is that the raft, hurried forward by the current, goes rapidly down the river, and drags the "baris" (for so they call this sort of boat) after it; while the stone, which is pulled along in the wake of the vessel, and lies deep in the water, keeps the boat straight. There are a vast number of these vessels in Egypt, and some of them are of many thousand talents' burthen.

97. When the Nile overflows, the country is converted into a sea, and nothing appears but the cities, which look like the islands in the Egean. At this season boats no longer keep the course of the river, but sail right across the plain. On the voyage from Naucratis to Memphis at this season, you pass close to the pyramids, whereas the usual course is by the apex of the Delta, and the city of Cercasôrus. You can sail also from the maritime town of Canôbus across the flat to Naucratis, passing by the cities of Anthylla and Archandropolis.

98. The former of these cities, which is a place of note, is assigned expressly to the wife of the ruler of Egypt for the time being, to keep her in shoes. Such has been the custom ever since Egypt fell under the Persian yoke. The other city seems to me to have got its name of Archandropolis from Archander the Phthian, son of Achæus, and son-in-law of Danaus. There might certainly have been another Archander; but, at any rate, the name is not Egyptian.

99. Thus far I have spoken of Egypt from my own observation, relating what I myself saw, the ideas that I formed, and the results of my own researches. What follows rests on the accounts given me by the Egyptians, which I shall now repeat, adding thereto some particulars which fell under by own notice.

The priests said that Mên was the first king of Egypt, and that it was he who raised the dyke which protects Memphis from the inundations of the Nile. Before his time the river flowed entirely along the sandy range of hills which skirts Egypt on the side of Libya. He, however, by banking up the river at the bend which it forms about a hundred furlongs south of Memphis, laid the ancient channel dry, while he dug a new course for the stream halfway between the two lines of hills. To this day, the elbow which the Nile forms at the point where it is forced aside into the new channel is guarded with the greatest care by the Persians, and strengthened every year; for if the river were to burst out at this place, and pour over the mound, there would be danger of Memphis being completely overwhelmed by the flood. Mên, the first king, having thus, by turning the river, made the tract where it used to run, dry land, proceeded in the first place to build the city now called Memphis, which lies in the narrow part of Egypt; after which he further excavated a lake outside the town, to the north and west, communicating with the river, which was itself the eastern boundary. Besides these works, he also, the priests said, built the temple of Vulcan which stands within the city, a vast edifice, very worthy of mention.

100. Next, they read me from a papyrus the names of three hundred and thirty monarchs, who (they said) were his successors upon the throne. In this number of generations there were eighteen Ethiopian kings, and one queen who was a native; all the rest were kings and Egyptians. The queen bore the same name as the Babylonian princess, namely, Nitocris. They said that she succeeded her brother; he had been king of Egypt, and was put to death by his subjects, who then placed her upon the throne. Bent on avenging his death, she devised a cunning scheme by which she destroyed a vast number of Egyptians. She constructed a spacious underground chamber, and, on pretence of inaugurating it, contrived the following:—Inviting to a banquet those of the Egyptians whom she knew to have had the chief share in the murder of her brother, she suddenly, as they were feasting, let the river in upon them, by means of a secret duct of large size. This, and this only, did they tell me of her, except that, when she had done as I have said, she threw herself into an apartment full

of ashes, that she might escape the vengeance whereto she would otherwise have been exposed.

101. The other kings, they said, were personages of no note or distinction, and left no monuments of any account, with the exception of the last, who was named Mœris. He left several memorials of his reign—the northern gateway of the temple of Vulcan, the lake excavated by his orders, whose dimensions I shall give presently, and the pyramids built by him in the lake, the size of which will be stated when I describe the lake itself wherein they stand. Such were his works: the other kings left absolutely nothing.

102. Passing over these monarchs, therefore, I shall speak of the king who reigned next, whose name was Sesostris. He, the priests said, first of all proceeded in a fleet of ships of war from the Arabian gulf along the shores of the Erythræan sea, subduing the nations as he went, until he finally reached a sea which could not be navigated by reason of the shoals. Hence he returned to Egypt, where, they told me, he collected a vast armament, and made a progress by land across the continent, conquering every people which fell in his way. In the countries where the natives withstood his attack, and fought gallantly for their liberties, he erected pillars, on which he inscribed his own name and country, and how that he had here reduced the inhabitants to subjection by the might of his arms: where, on the contrary, they submitted readily and without a struggle, he inscribed on the pillars, in addition to these particulars, an emblem to mark that they were a nation of women, that is, unwarlike and effeminate.

103. In this way he traversed the whole continent of Asia, whence he passed on into Europe, and made himself master of Scythia and of Thrace, beyond which countries I do not think that his army extended its march. For thus far the pillars which he erected are still visible, but in the remoter regions they are no longer found. Returning to Egypt from Thrace, he came, on his way, to the banks of the river Phasis. Here I cannot say with any certainty what took place. Either he of his own accord detached a body of troops from his main army and left them to colonise the country, or else a certain number of his soldiers, wearied with their long wanderings, deserted, and established themselves on the banks of this stream.

104. There can be no doubt that the Colchians are an Egyptian race. Before I heard any mention of the fact from others, I had remarked it myself. After the thought had struck me, I made inquiries on the subject both in Colchis and in Egypt, and I found that the Colchians had a more distinct recollection of the Egyptians, than the Egyptians had of them. Still the Egyptians said that they believed the Colchians to be descended from the army of Sesostris. My own conjectures were founded, first, on the fact that they are black-skinned and have woolly hair, which certainly amounts to but little, since several other nations are so too; but further and more especially, on the circumstance that the Colchians, the Egyptians, and the Ethiopians, are the only nations who have practised circumcision from the earliest times. The Phœnicians and the Syrians of Palestine themselves confess that they learnt the custom of the Egyptians; and the Syrians who dwell about the rivers Thermôdon and Parthenius, as well as their neighbours the Macronians, say that they have recently adopted it from the Colchians. Now these are the only nations who use circumcision, and it is plain that they all imitate herein the Egyptians. With respect to the Ethiopians, indeed, I cannot decide whether they learnt the practice of the Egyptians, or the Egyptians of them—it is undoubtedly of very ancient date in Ethiopia—but that the others derived their knowledge of it from Egypt is clear to me from the fact that the Phœnicians, when they come to have commerce with the Greeks, cease to follow the Egyptians in this custom, and allow their children to remain uncircumcised.

105. I will add a further proof to the identity of the Egyptians and the Colchians. These two nations weave their linen in exactly the same way, and this is a way entirely unknown to the rest of the world; they also in their whole mode of life and in their language resemble one another. The Colchian linen is called by the Greeks Sardinian, while that which comes from Egypt is known as Egyptian.

106. The pillars which Sesostris erected in the conquered countries have for the most part disappeared; but in the part of Syria called Palestine, I myself saw them still standing, with the writing above-mentioned, and the emblem distinctly visible. In Ionia also, there are two representations of this prince engraved upon rocks, one on the road from Ephesus to Phocæa, the other between Sardis and Smyrna. In each case the figure is that of a man, four cubits and a span high, with a spear in his

right hand and a bow in his left, the rest of his costume being likewise half Egyptian, half Ethiopian. There is an inscription across the breast from shoulder to shoulder, in the sacred character of Egypt, which says, "With my own shoulders I conquered this land." The conqueror does not tell who he is, or whence he comes, though elsewhere Sesostris records these facts. Hence it has been imagined by some of those who have seen these forms, that they are figures of Memnon; but such as think so err very widely from the truth.

107. This Sesostris, the priests went on to say, upon his return home, accompanied by vast multitudes of the people whose countries he had subdued, was received by his brother, whom he had made viceroy of Egypt on his departure, at Daphnæ near Pelusium, and invited by him to a banquet, which he attended, together with his sons. Then his brother piled a quantity of wood all round the building, and having so done set it alight. Sesostris, discovering what had happened, took counsel instantly with his wife, who had accompanied him to the feast, and was advised by her to lay two of their six sons upon the fire, and so make a bridge across the flames, whereby the rest might effect their escape. Sesostris did as she recommended, and thus while two of his sons were burnt to death, he himself and his other children were saved.

108. The king then returned to his own land and took vengeance upon his brother, after which he proceeded to make use of the multitudes whom he had brought with him from the conquered countries, partly to drag the huge masses of stone which were moved in the course of his reign to the temple of Vulcan— partly to dig the numerous canals with which the whole of Egypt is intersected. By these forced labours the entire face of the country was changed; for whereas Egypt had formerly been a region suited both for horses and carriages, henceforth it became entirely unfit for either. Though a flat country throughout its whole extent, it is now unfit for either horse or carriage, being cut up by the canals, which are extremely numerous and run in all directions. The king's object was to supply Nile water to the inhabitants of the towns situated in the mid-country, and not lying upon the river; for previously they had been obliged, after the subsidence of the floods, to drink a brackish water which they obtained from wells.

109. Sesostris also, they declared, made a division of the soil of Egypt among the inhabitants, assigning square plots of ground of equal size to all, and obtaining his chief revenue from the rent which the holders were required to pay him year by year. If the river carried away any portion of a man's lot, he appeared before the king, and related what had happened; upon which the king sent persons to examine, and determine by measurement the exact extent of the loss; and thenceforth only such a rent was demanded of him as was proportionate to the reduced size of his land. From this practice, I think, geometry first came to be known in Egypt, whence it passed into Greece. The sun-dial, however, and the gnomon with the division of the day into twelve parts, were received by the Greeks from the Babylonians.

110. Sesostris was king not only of Egypt, but also of Ethiopia. He was the only Egyptian monarch who ever ruled over the latter country. He left, as memorials of his reign, the stone statues which stand in front of the temple of Vulcan, two of which, representing himself and his wife, are thirty cubits in height, while the remaining four, which represent his sons, are twenty cubits. These are the statues, in front of which the priest of Vulcan, very many years afterwards, would not allow Darius the Persian to place a statue of himself; "because," he said, "Darius had not equalled the achievements of Sesostris the Egyptian: for while Sesostris had subdued to the full as many nations as ever Darius had brought under, he had likewise conquered the Scythians, whom Darius had failed to master. It was not fair, therefore, that he should erect his statue in front of the offerings of a king, whose deeds he had been unable to surpass." Darius, they say, pardoned the freedom of this speech.

111. On the death of Sesostris, his son Pheron, the priests said, mounted the throne. He undertook no warlike expeditions; being struck with blindness, owing to the following circumstance. The river had swollen to the unusual height of eighteen cubits, and had overflowed all the fields, when, a sudden wind arising, the water rose in great waves. Then the king, in a spirit of impious violence, seized his spear, and hurled it into the strong eddies of the stream. Instantly he was smitten with disease of the eyes, from which after a little while he became blind, continuing without the power of vision for ten years. At last, in the eleventh year, an oracular announcement reached him from the city of Buto, to the effect, that "the time of his punishment had run out,

and he should recover his sight by washing his eyes with urine. He must find a woman who had been faithful to her husband, and had never preferred to him another man." The king, therefore, first of all made trial of his wife, but to no purpose—he continued as blind as before. So he made the experiment with other women, until at length he succeeded, and in this way recovered his sight. Hereupon he assembled all the women, except the last, and bringing them to the city which now bears the name of Erythrabôlus (Red-soil), he there burnt them all, together with the place itself. The woman to whom he owed his cure, he married, and after his recovery was complete, he presented offerings to all the temples of any note, among which the best worthy of mention are the two stone obelisks which he gave to the temple of the Sun. These are magnificent works; each is made of a single stone, eight cubits broad, and a hundred cubits in height.

112. Pheron, they said, was succeeded by a man of Memphis, whose name, in the language of the Greeks, was Proteus. There is a sacred precinct of this king in Memphis, which is very beautiful, and richly adorned, situated south of the great temple of Vulcan. Phœnicians from the city of Tyre dwell all round this precinct, and the whole place is known by the name of "the camp of the Tyrians." Within the enclosure stands a temple, which is called that of Venus *the Stranger*. I conjecture the building to have been erected to Helen, the daughter of Tyndarus; first, because she, as I have heard say, passed some time at the court of Proteus; and secondly, because the temple is dedicated to Venus *the Stranger;* for among all the many temples of Venus there is no other where the goddess bears this title.

113. The priests, in answer to my inquiries on the subject of Helen, informed me of the following particulars. When Alexander had carried off Helen from Sparta, he took ship and sailed homewards. On his way across the Egean a gale arose, which drove him from his course and took him down to the sea of Egypt; hence, as the wind did not abate, he was carried on to the coast, when he went ashore, landing at the Salt-Pans, in that mouth of the Nile which is now called the Canobic. At this place there stood upon the shore a temple, which still exists, dedicated to Hercules. If a slave runs away from his master, and taking sanctuary at this shrine gives himself up to the god, and receives certain sacred marks upon his person, whosoever his master may be, he cannot lay hand on

him. This law still remained unchanged to my time. Hearing, therefore, of the custom of the place, the attendants of Alexander deserted him, and fled to the temple, where they sat as suppliants. While there, wishing to damage their master, they accused him to the Egyptians, narrating all the circumstances of the rape of Helen and the wrong done to Menelaus. These charges they brought, not only before the priests, but also before the warden of that mouth of the river, whose name was Thônis.

114. As soon as he received the intelligence, Thônis sent a message to Proteus, who was at Memphis, to this effect: "A stranger is arrived from Greece; he is by race a Teucrian, and has done a wicked deed in the country from which he is come. Having beguiled the wife of the man whose guest he was, he carried her away with him, and much treasure also. Compelled by stress of weather, he has now put in here. Are we to let him depart as he came, or shall we seize what he has brought?" Proteus replied, "Seize the man, be he who he may, that has dealt thus wickedly with his friend, and bring him before me, that I may hear what he will say for himself."

115. Thônis, on receiving these orders, arrested Alexander, and stopped the departure of his ships; then, taking with him Alexander, Helen, the treasures, and also the fugitive slaves, he went up to Memphis. When all were arrived, Proteus asked Alexander, "who he was, and whence he had come?" Alexander replied by giving his descent, the name of his country, and a true account of his late voyage. Then Proteus questioned him as to how he got possession of Helen. In his reply Alexander became confused, and diverged from the truth, whereon the slaves interposed, confuted his statements, and told the whole history of the crime. Finally, Proteus delivered judgment as follows: "Did I not regard it as a matter of the utmost consequence that no stranger driven to my country by adverse winds should ever be put to death, I would certainly have avenged the Greek by slaying thee. Thou basest of men, —after accepting hospitality, to do so wicked a deed! First, thou didst seduce the wife of thy own host—then, not content therewith, thou must violently excite her mind, and steal her away from her husband. Nay, even so thou wert not satisfied, but on leaving, thou must plunder the house in which thou hadst been a guest. Now then, as I think it of the greatest importance to put no stranger to death, I suffer

thee to depart; but the woman and the treasures I shall not permit to be carried away. Here they must stay, till the Greek stranger comes in person and takes them back with him. For thyself and thy companions, I command thee to begone from my land within the space of three days—and I warn you, that otherwise at the end of that time you will be treated as enemies."

116. Such was the tale told me by the priests concerning the arrival of Helen at the court of Proteus. It seems to me that Homer was acquainted with this story, and while discarding it, because he thought it less adapted for epic poetry than the version which he followed, showed that it was not unknown to him. This is evident from the travels which he assigns to Alexander in the *Iliad*—and let it be borne in mind that he has nowhere else contradicted himself—making him be carried out of his course on his return with Helen, and after divers wanderings come at last to Sidon in Phœnicia. The passage is in the Bravery of Diomed,[1] and the words are as follows:—

There were the robes, many-coloured, the work of Sidonian women:
They from Sidon had come, what time god-shaped Alexander
Over the broad sea brought, that way, the high-born Helen.

In the *Odyssey* also the same fact is alluded to, in these words:[2]—

Such, so wisely prepared, were the drugs that her stores afforded,
Excellent; gift which once Polydamna, partner of Thônis,
Gave her in Egypt, where many the simples that grow in the meadows,
Potent to cure in part, in part as potent to injure.

Menelaus too, in the same poem, thus addresses Telemachus:[3]—

Much did I long to return, but the Gods still kept me in Egypt—
Angry because I had failed to pay them their hecatombs duly.

In these places Homer shows himself acquainted with the voyage of Alexander to Egypt, for Syria borders on Egypt, and the Phœnicians, to whom Sidon belongs, dwell in Syria.

117. From these various passages, and from that about Sidon especially, it is clear that Homer did not write the *Cypria*. For there it is

[1] *Iliad*, Bk vi. 290-292.
[2] *Odyssey*, Bk iv. 227-230.
[3] *Ibid.*, Bk iv. 351-352.

said that Alexander arrived at Ilium with Helen on the third day after he left Sparta, the wind having been favourable, and the sea smooth; whereas in the *Iliad,* the poet makes him wander before he brings her home. Enough, however, for the present of Homer and the *Cypria.*

118. I made inquiry of the priests whether the story which the Greeks tell about Ilium is a fable, or no. In reply they related the following particulars, of which they declared that Menelaus had himself informed them. After the rape of Helen, a vast army of Greeks, wishing to render help to Menelaus, set sail for the Teucrian territory; on their arrival they disembarked, and formed their camp, after which they sent ambassadors to Ilium, of whom Menelaus was one. The embassy was received within the walls, and demanded the restoration of Helen with the treasures which Alexander had carried off, and likewise required satisfaction for the wrong done. The Teucrians gave at once the answer in which they persisted ever afterwards, backing their assertions sometimes even with oaths, to wit, that neither Helen, nor the treasures claimed, were in their possession, —both the one and the other had remained, they said, in Egypt; and it was not just to come upon them for what Proteus, king of Egypt, was detaining. The Greeks, imagining that the Teucrians were merely laughing at them, laid siege to the town, and never rested until they finally took it. As, however, no Helen was found, and they were still told the same story, they at length believed in its truth, and despatched Menelaus to the court of Proteus.

119. So Menelaus travelled to Egypt, and on his arrival sailed up the river as far as Memphis, and related all that had happened. He met with the utmost hospitality, received Helen back unharmed, and recovered all his treasures. After this friendly treatment Menelaus, they said, behaved most unjustly towards the Egyptians; for as it happened that at the time when he wanted to take his departure, he was detained by the wind being contrary, and as he found this obstruction continue, he had recourse to a most wicked expedient. He seized, they said, two children of the people of the country, and offered them up in sacrifice. When this became known, the indignation of the people was stirred, and they went in pursuit of Menelaus, who, however, escaped with his ships to Libya, after which the Egyptians could not say whither he went. The rest they knew full well, partly by the inquiries which

they had made, and partly from the circumstances having taken place in their own land, and therefore not admitting of doubt.

120. Such is the account given by the Egyptian priests, and I am myself inclined to regard as true all that they say of Helen from the following considerations:—If Helen had been at Troy, the inhabitants would, I think, have given her up to the Greeks, whether Alexander consented to it or no. For surely neither Priam, nor his family, could have been so infatuated as to endanger their own persons, their children, and their city, merely that Alexander might possess Helen. At any rate, if they determined to refuse at first, yet afterwards when so many of the Trojans fell on every encounter with the Greeks, and Priam too in each battle lost a son, or sometimes two, or three, or even more, if we may credit the epic poets, I do not believe that even if Priam himself had been married to her he would have declined to deliver her up, with the view of bringing the series of calamities to a close. Nor was it as if Alexander had been heir to the crown, in which case he might have had the chief management of affairs, since Priam was already old. Hector, who was his elder brother, and a far braver man, stood before him, and was the heir to the kingdom on the death of their father Priam. And it could not be Hector's interest to uphold his brother in his wrong, when it brought such dire calamities upon himself and the other Trojans. But the fact was that they had no Helen to deliver, and so they told the Greeks, but the Greeks would not believe what they said—Divine Providence, as I think, so willing, that by their utter destruction it might be made evident to all men that when great wrongs are done, the gods will surely visit them with great punishments. Such, at least, is my view of the matter.

121. (1.) When Proteus died, Rhampsinitus, the priests informed me, succeeded to the throne. His monuments were the western gateway of the temple of Vulcan, and the two statues which stand in front of this gateway, called by the Egyptians, the one Summer, the other Winter, each twenty-five cubits in height. The statue of Summer, which is the northernmost of the two, is worshipped by the natives, and has offerings made to it; that of Winter, which stands towards the south, is treated in exactly the contrary way. King Rhampsinitus was possessed, they said, of great riches in silver—indeed to such an amount, that none of the princes, his successors, surpassed or even equalled his wealth. For the better custody of this money, he proposed to build a vast chamber of hewn stone, one side of which was to form a part of the outer wall of his palace. The builder, therefore, having designs upon the treasures, contrived, as he was making the building, to insert in this wall a stone, which could easily be removed from its place by two men, or even by one. So the chamber was finished, and the king's money stored away in it. Time passed, and the builder fell sick, when finding his end approaching, he called for his two sons, and related to them the contrivance he had made in the king's treasure-chamber, telling them it was for their sakes he had done it, that so they might always live in affluence. Then he gave them clear directions concerning the mode of removing the stone, and communicated the measurements, bidding them carefully keep the secret, whereby they would be Comptrollers of the Royal Exchequer so long as they lived. Then the father died, and the sons were not slow in setting to work: they went by night to the palace, found the stone in the wall of the building, and having removed it with ease, plundered the treasury of a round sum.

(2.) When the king next paid a visit to the apartment, he was astonished to see that the money was sunk in some of the vessels wherein it was stored away. Whom to accuse, however, he knew not, as the seals were all perfect, and the fastenings of the room secure. Still each time that he repeated his visits, he found that more money was gone. The thieves in truth never stopped, but plundered the treasury ever more and more. At last the king determined to have some traps made, and set near the vessels which contained his wealth. This was done, and when the thieves came, as usual, to the treasure-chamber, and one of them entering through the aperture, made straight for the jars, suddenly he found himself caught in one of the traps. Perceiving that he was lost, he instantly called his brother, and telling him what had happened, entreated him to enter as quickly as possible and cut off his head, that when his body should be discovered it might not be recognised, which would have the effect of bringing ruin upon both. The other thief thought the advice good, and was persuaded to follow it—then, fitting the stone into its place, he went home, taking with him his brother's head.

(3.) When day dawned, the king came into the room, and marvelled greatly to see the body of the thief in the trap without a head, while the building was still whole, and neither entrance nor exit was to be seen anywhere. In this perplexity he commanded the body of the dead man to be hung up outside the palace wall, and set a guard to watch it, with orders that if any persons were seen weeping or lamenting near the place, they should be seized and brought before him. When the mother heard of this exposure of the corpse of her son, she took it sorely to heart, and spoke to her surviving child, bidding him devise some plan or other to get back the body, and threatening, that if he did not exert himself, she would go herself to the king, and denounce him as the robber.

(4.) The son said all he could to persuade her to let the matter rest, but in vain; she still continued to trouble him, until at last he yielded to her importunity, and contrived as follows:—Filling some skins with wine, he loaded them on donkeys, which he drove before him till he came to the place where the guards were watching the dead body, when pulling two or three of the skins towards him, he untied some of the necks which dangled by the asses' sides. The wine poured freely out, whereupon he began to beat his head, and shout with all his might, seeming not to know which of the donkeys he should turn to first. When the guards saw the wine running, delighted to profit by the occasion, they rushed one and all into the road, each with some vessel or other, and caught the liquor as it was spilling. The driver pretended anger, and loaded them with abuse; whereon they did their best to pacify him, until at last he appeared to soften, and recover his good humour, drove his asses aside out of the road, and set to work to rearrange their burthens; meanwhile, as he talked and chatted with the guards, one of them began to rally him, and make him laugh, whereupon he gave them one of the skins as a gift. They now made up their minds to sit down and have a drinking-bout where they were, so they begged him to remain and drink with them. Then the man let himself be persuaded, and stayed. As the drinking went on, they grew very friendly together, so presently he gave them another skin, upon which they drank so copiously that they were all overcome with the liquor, and growing drowsy lay down, and fell asleep on the spot. The thief waited till it was the dead of the night, and then took down the body of his brother; after which, in mockery, he shaved off the right side of all the soldiers'

beards,[1] and so left them. Laying his brother's body upon the asses, he carried it home to his mother, having thus accomplished the thing that she had required of him.

(5.) When it came to the king's ears that the thief's body was stolen away, he was sorely vexed. Wishing, therefore, whatever it might cost, to catch the man who had contrived the trick, he had recourse (the priests said) to an expedient, which I can scarcely credit. He sent his own daughter to the common stews, with orders to admit all comers, but to require every man to tell her what was the cleverest and wickedest thing he had done in the whole course of his life. If any one in reply told her the story of the thief, she was to lay hold of him and not allow him to get away. The daughter did as her father willed, whereon the thief, who was well aware of the king's motive, felt a desire to outdo him in craft and cunning. Accordingly he contrived the following plan:— He procured the corpse of a man lately dead, and cutting off one of the arms at the shoulder, put it under his dress, and so went to the king's daughter. When she put the question to him as she had done to all the rest, he replied that the wickedest thing he had ever done was cutting off the head of his brother when he was caught in a trap in the king's treasury, and the cleverest was making the guards drunk and carrying off the body. As he spoke, the princess caught at him, but the thief took advantage of the darkness to hold out to her the hand of the corpse. Imagining it to be his own hand, she seized and held it fast; while the thief, leaving it in her grasp, made his escape by the door.

(6.) The king, when word was brought him of this fresh success, amazed at the sagacity and boldness of the man, sent messengers to all the towns in his dominions to proclaim a free pardon for the thief, and to promise him a rich reward, if he came and made himself known. The thief took the king at his word, and came boldly into his presence; whereupon Rhampsinitus, greatly admiring him, and looking on him as the most knowing of men, gave him his daughter in marriage. "The Egyptians," he said, "excelled all the rest of the world in wisdom, and this man excelled all other Egyptians."

[1] This is a curious mistake for any one to make who had been in Egypt, since the soldiers had no beards, and it was the custom of all classes to shave. Herodotus could not have learnt this story from the Egyptians, and it is evidently from a Greek source.

122. The same king, I was also informed by the priests, afterwards descended alive into the region which the Greeks call Hades, and there played at dice with Ceres, sometimes winning and sometimes suffering defeat. After a while he returned to earth, and brought with him a golden napkin, a gift which he had received from the goddess. From this descent of Rhampsinitus into Hades, and return to earth again, the Egyptians, I was told, instituted a festival, which they certainly celebrated in my day. On what occasion it was that they instituted it, whether upon this or upon any other, I cannot determine. The following are the ceremonies: —On a certain day in the year the priests weave a mantle, and binding the eyes of one of their number with a fillet, they put the mantle upon him, and take him with them into the roadway conducting to the temple of Ceres, when they depart and leave him to himself. Then the priest, thus blindfolded, is led (they say) by two wolves to the temple of Ceres, distant twenty furlongs from the city, where he stays awhile, after which he is brought back from the temple by the wolves, and left upon the spot where they first joined him.

123. Such as think the tales told by the Egyptians credible are free to accept them for history. For my own part, I propose to myself throughout my whole work faithfully to record the traditions of the several nations. The Egyptians maintain that Ceres and Bacchus preside in the realms below. They were also the first to broach the opinion that the soul of man is immortal, and that, when the body dies, it enters into the form of an animal which is born at the moment, thence passing on from one animal into another, until it has circled through the forms of all the creatures which tenant the earth, the water, and the air, after which it enters again into a human frame, and is born anew. The whole period of the transmigration is (they say) three thousand years. There are Greek writers, some of an earlier, some of a later date, who have borrowed this doctrine from the Egyptians, and put it forward as their own. I could mention their names, but I abstain from doing so.

124. Till the death of Rhampsinitus, the priests said, Egypt was excellently governed, and flourished greatly; but after him Cheops succeeded to the throne, and plunged into all manner of wickedness. He closed the temples, and forbade the Egyptians to offer sacrifice, compelling them instead to labour, one and all, in his service. Some were required to drag blocks of stone down to the Nile from the quarries in the Arabian range of hills; others received the blocks after they had been conveyed in boats across the river, and drew them to the range of hills called the Libyan. A hundred thousand men laboured constantly, and were relieved every three months by a fresh lot. It took ten years' oppression of the people to make the causeway for the conveyance of the stones, a work not much inferior, in my judgment, to the pyramid itself. This causeway is five furlongs in length, ten fathoms wide, and in height, at the highest part, eight fathoms. It is built of polished stone, and is covered with carvings of animals. To make it took ten years, as I said—or rather to make the causeway, the works on the mound where the pyramid stands, and the underground chambers, which Cheops intended as vaults for his own use: these last were built on a sort of island, surrounded by water introduced from the Nile by a canal. The pyramid itself was twenty years in building. It is a square, eight hundred feet each way, and the height the same, built entirely of polished stone, fitted together with the utmost care. The stones of which it is composed are none of them less than thirty feet in length.

125. The pyramid was built in steps, battlement-wise, as it is called, or, according to others, altar-wise. After laying the stones for the base, they raised the remaining stones to their places by means of machines formed of short wooden planks. The first machine raised them from the ground to the top of the first step. On this there was another machine, which received the stone upon its arrival, and conveyed it to the second step, whence a third machine advanced it still higher. Either they had as many machines as there were steps in the pyramid, or possibly they had but a single machine, which, being easily moved, was transferred from tier to tier as the stone rose—both accounts are given, and therefore I mention both. The upper portion of the pyramid was finished first, then the middle, and finally the part which was lowest and nearest the ground. There is an inscription in Egyptian characters on the pyramid which records the quantity of radishes, onions, and garlic consumed by the labourers who constructed it; and I perfectly well remember that the interpreter who read the writing to me said that the money expended in this way was 1600 talents of silver. If this then is a true record, what a vast sum must have been spent on the iron tools used in

the work, and on the feeding and clothing of the labourers, considering the length of time the work lasted, which has already been stated, and the additional time—no small space, I imagine—which must have been occupied by the quarrying of the stones, their conveyance, and the formation of the underground apartments.

126. The wickedness of Cheops reached to such a pitch that, when he had spent all his treasures and wanted more, he sent his daughter to the stews, with orders to procure him a certain sum—how much I cannot say, for I was not told; she procured it, however, and at the same time, bent on leaving a monument which should perpetuate her own memory, she required each man to make her a present of a stone towards the works which she contemplated. With these stones she built the pyramid which stands midmost of the three that are in front of the great pyramid, measuring along each side a hundred and fifty feet.

127. Cheops reigned, the Egyptians said, fifty years, and was succeeded at his demise by Chephren, his brother.

Chephren imitated the conduct of his predecessor, and, like him, built a pyramid, which did not, however, equal the dimensions of his brother's. Of this I am certain, for I measured them both myself. It has no subterraneous apartments, nor any canal from the Nile to supply it with water, as the other pyramid has. In that, the Nile water, introduced through an artificial duct, surrounds an island, where the body of Cheops is said to lie. Chephren built his pyramid close to the great pyramid of Cheops, and of the same dimensions, except that he lowered the height forty feet. For the basement he employed the many-coloured stone of Ethiopia. These two pyramids stand both on the same hill, an elevation not far short of a hundred feet in height. The reign of Chephren lasted fifty-six years.

128. Thus the affliction of Egypt endured for the space of one hundred and six years, during the whole of which time the temples were shut up and never opened. The Egyptians so detest the memory of these kings that they do not much like even to mention their names. Hence they commonly call the pyramids after Philition, a shepherd who at that time fed his flocks about the place.

129. After Chephren, Mycerinus (they said), son of Cheops, ascended the throne. This prince disapproved the conduct of his father, re-opened the temples, and allowed the people, who were ground down to the lowest point of misery, to return to their occupations, and to resume the practice of sacrifice. His justice in the decision of causes was beyond that of all the former kings. The Egyptians praise him in this respect more highly than any of their other monarchs, declaring that he not only gave his judgments with fairness, but also, when any one was dissatisfied with his sentence, made compensation to him out of his own purse, and thus pacified his anger. Mycerinus had established his character for mildness, and was acting as I have described, when the stroke of calamity fell on him. First of all his daughter died, the only child that he possessed. Experiencing a bitter grief at this visitation, in his sorrow he conceived the wish to entomb his child in some unusual way. He therefore caused a cow to be made of wood, and after the interior had been hollowed out, he had the whole surface coated with gold; and in this novel tomb laid the dead body of his daughter.

130. The cow was not placed under ground, but continued visible to my times: it was at Saïs, in the royal palace, where it occupied a chamber richly adorned. Every day there are burnt before it aromatics of every kind; and all night long a lamp is kept burning in the apartment. In an adjoining chamber are statues which the priests at Saïs declared to represent the various concubines of Mycerinus. They are colossal figures in wood, of the number of about twenty, and are represented naked. Whose images they really are, I cannot say —I can only repeat the account which was given to me.

131. Concerning these colossal figures and the sacred cow, there is also another tale narrated, which runs thus: "Mycerinus was enamoured of his daughter, and offered her violence—the damsel for grief hanged herself, and Mycerinus entombed her in the cow. Then her mother cut off the hands of all her tiring-maids, because they had sided with the father, and betrayed the child; and so the statues of the maids have no hands." All this is mere fable in my judgment, especially what is said about the hands of the colossal statues. I could plainly see that the figures had only lost their hands through the effect of time. They had dropped off, and were still lying on the ground about the feet of the statues.

132. As for the cow, the greater portion of it is hidden by a scarlet coverture; the head and neck, however, which are visible, are coated very thickly with gold, and between the horns

there is a representation in gold of the orb of the sun. The figure is not erect, but lying down, with the limbs under the body; the dimensions being fully those of a large animal of the kind. Every year it is taken from the apartment where it is kept, and exposed to the light of day—this is done at the season when the Egyptians beat themselves in honour of one of their gods, whose name I am unwilling to mention in connection with such a matter.[1] They say that the daughter of Mycerinus requested her father in her dying moments to allow her once a year to see the sun.

133. After the death of his daughter, Mycerinus was visited with a second calamity, of which I shall now proceed to give an account. An oracle reached him from the town of Buto, which said, "Six years only shalt thou live upon the earth, and in the seventh thou shalt end thy days." Mycerinus, indignant, sent an angry message to the oracle, reproaching the god with his injustice—"My father and uncle," he said, "though they shut up the temples, took no thought of the gods, and destroyed multitudes of men, nevertheless enjoyed a long life; I, who am pious, am to die so soon!" There came in reply a second message from the oracle—"For this very reason is thy life brought so quickly to a close—thou hast not done as it behoved thee. Egypt was fated to suffer affliction one hundred and fifty years—the two kings who preceded thee upon the throne understood this—thou hast not understood it." Mycerinus, when this answer reached him, perceiving that his doom was fixed, had lamps prepared, which he lighted every day at eventime, and feasted and enjoyed himself unceasingly both day and night, moving about in the marsh-country and the woods, and visiting all the places that he heard were agreeable sojourns. His wish was to prove the oracle false, by turning the nights into days, and so living twelve years in the space of six.

134. He too left a pyramid, but much inferior in size to his father's. It is a square, each side of which falls short of three plethra by twenty feet, and is built for half its height of the stone of Ethiopia. Some of the Greeks call it the work of Rhodôpis the courtesan, but they report falsely. It seems to me that these persons cannot have any real knowledge who Rhodôpis was; otherwise they would scarcely have ascribed to her a work on which uncounted treasures, so to speak, must have been expended. Rhodôpis also lived during the reign of Ama-

[1] Osiris.

sis, not of Mycerinus, and was thus very many years later than the time of the kings who built the pyramids. She was a Thracian by birth, and was the slave of Iadmon, son of Hephæstopolis, a Samian. Æsop, the fable-writer, was one of her fellow-slaves. That Æsop belonged to Iadmon is proved by many facts—among others, by this. When the Delphians, in obedience to the command of the oracle, made proclamation that if any one claimed compensation for the murder of Æsop he should receive it, the person who at last came forward was Iadmon, grandson of the former Iadmon, and he received the compensation. Æsop therefore must certainly have been the former Iadmon's slave.

135. Rhodôpis really arrived in Egypt under the conduct of Xantheus the Samian; she was brought there to exercise her trade, but was redeemed for a vast sum by Charaxus, a Mytilenæan, the son of Scamandrônymus, and brother of Sappho the poetess. After thus obtaining her freedom, she remained in Egypt, and, as she was very beautiful, amassed great wealth, for a person in her condition; not, however, enough to enable her to erect such a work as this pyramid. Any one who likes may go and see to what the tenth part of her wealth amounted, and he will thereby learn that her riches must not be imagined to have been very wonderfully great. Wishing to leave a memorial of herself in Greece, she determined to have something made the like of which was not to be found in any temple, and to offer it at the shrine at Delphi. So she set apart a tenth of her possessions, and purchased with the money a quantity of iron spits, such as are fit for roasting oxen whole, whereof she made a present to the oracle. They are still to be seen there, lying of a heap, behind the altar which the Chians dedicated, opposite the sanctuary. Naucratis seems somehow to be the place where such women are most attractive. First there was this Rhodôpis of whom we have been speaking, so celebrated a person that her name came to be familiar to all the Greeks; and, afterwards, there was another, called Archidicé, notorious throughout Greece, though not so much talked of as her predecessor. Charaxus, after ransoming Rhodôpis, returned to Mytilene, and was often lashed by Sappho in her poetry. But enough has been said on the subject of this courtesan.

136. After Mycerinus, the priests said, Asychis ascended the throne. He built the eastern gateway of the temple of Vulcan, which in size and beauty far surpasses the other three.

All the four gateways have figures graven on them, and a vast amount of architectural ornament, but the gateway of Asychis is by far the most richly adorned. In the reign of this king, money being scarce and commercial dealings straitened, a law was passed that the borrower might pledge his father's body to raise the sum whereof he had need. A proviso was appended to this law, giving the lender authority over the entire sepulchre of the borrower, so that a man who took up money under this pledge, if he died without paying the debt, could not obtain burial either in his own ancestral tomb, or in any other, nor could he during his lifetime bury in his own tomb any member of his family. The same king, desirous of eclipsing all his predecessors upon the throne, left as a monument of his reign a pyramid of brick. It bears an inscription, cut in stone, which runs thus:—"Despise me not in comparison with the stone pyramids; for I surpass them all, as much as Jove surpasses the other gods. A pole was plunged into a lake, and the mud which clave thereto was gathered; and bricks were made of the mud, and so I was formed." Such were the chief actions of this prince.

137. He was succeeded on the throne, they said, by a blind man, a native of Anysis, whose own name also was Anysis. Under him Egypt was invaded by a vast army of Ethiopians, led by Sabacôs, their king. The blind Anysis fled away to the marsh-country, and the Ethiopian was lord of the land for fifty years, during which his mode of rule was the following:—When an Egyptian was guilty of an offence, his plan was not to punish him with death: instead of so doing, he sentenced him, according to the nature of his crime, to raise the ground to a greater or a less extent in the neighbourhood of the city to which he belonged. Thus the cities came to be even more elevated than they were before. As early as the time of Sesostris, they had been raised by those who dug the canals in his reign; this second elevation of the soil under the Ethiopian king gave them a very lofty position. Among the many cities which thus attained to a great elevation, none (I think) was raised so much as the town called Bubastis, where there is a temple of the goddess Bubastis, which well deserves to be described. Other temples may be grander, and may have cost more in the building, but there is none so pleasant to the eye as this of Bubastis. The Bubastis of the Egyptians is the same as the Artemis (Diana) of the Greeks.

138. The following is a description of this edifice:—Excepting the entrance, the whole forms an island. Two artificial channels from the Nile, one on either side of the temple, encompass the building, leaving only a narrow passage by which it is approached. These channels are each a hundred feet wide, and are thickly shaded with trees. The gateway is sixty feet in height, and is ornamented with figures cut upon the stone, six cubits high and well worthy of notice. The temple stands in the middle of the city, and is visible on all sides as one walks round it; for as the city has been raised up by embankment, while the temple has been left untouched in its original condition, you look down upon it wheresoever you are. A low wall runs round the enclosure, having figures engraved upon it, and inside there is a grove of beautiful tall trees growing round the shrine, which contains the image of the goddess. The enclosure is a furlong in length, and the same in breadth. The entrance to it is by a road paved with stone for a distance of about three furlongs, which passes straight through the market-place with an easterly direction, and is about four hundred feet in width. Trees of an extraordinary height grow on each side the road, which conducts from the temple of Bubastis to that of Mercury.

139. The Ethiopian finally quitted Egypt, the priests said, by a hasty flight under the following circumstances. He saw in his sleep a vision:—a man stood by his side, and counselled him to gather together all the priests of Egypt and cut every one of them asunder. On this, according to the account which he himself gave, it came into his mind that the gods intended hereby to lead him to commit an act of sacrilege, which would be sure to draw down upon him some punishment either at the hands of gods or men. So he resolved not to do the deed suggested to him, but rather to retire from Egypt, as the time during which it was fated that he should hold the country had now (he thought) expired. For before he left Ethiopia he had been told by the oracles which are venerated there, that he was to reign fifty years over Egypt. The years were now fled, and the dream had come to trouble him; he therefore of his own accord withdrew from the land.

140. As soon as Sabacôs was gone, the blind king left the marshes, and resumed the government. He had lived in the marsh-region the whole time, having formed for himself an island there by a mixture of earth and ashes. While he remained, the natives had orders to

bring him food unbeknown to the Ethiopian, and latterly, at his request, each man had brought him, with the food, a certain quantity of ashes. Before Amyrtæus, no one was able to discover the site of this island, which continued unknown to the kings of Egypt who preceded him on the throne for the space of seven hundred years and more. The name which it bears is Elbo. It is about ten furlongs across in each direction.

141. The next king, I was told, was a priest of Vulcan, called Sethôs. This monarch despised and neglected the warrior class of the Egyptians, as though he did not need their services. Among other indignities which he offered them, he took from them the lands which they had possessed under all the previous kings, consisting of twelve acres of choice land for each warrior. Afterwards, therefore, when Sanacharib, king of the Arabians[1] and Assyrians, marched his vast army into Egypt, the warriors one and all refused to come to his aid. On this the monarch, greatly distressed, entered into the inner sanctuary, and, before the image of the god, bewailed the fate which impended over him. As he wept he ꞏcll asleep, and dreamed that the god came and stood at his side, bidding him be of good cheer, and go boldly forth to meet the Arabian host, which would do him no hurt, as he himself would send those who should help him. Sethôs, then, relying on the dream, collected such of the Egyptians as were willing to follow him, who were none of them warriors, but traders, artisans, and market people; and with these marched to Pelusium, which commands the entrance into Egypt, and there pitched his camp. As the two armies lay here opposite one another, there came in the night, a multitude of field-mice, which devoured all the quivers and bowstrings of the enemy, and ate the thongs by which they managed their shields. Next morning they commenced their fight, and great multitudes fell, as they had no arms

[1] It is curious to find Sennacherib called the "king of *the Arabians* and Assyrians"—an order of words which seems even to regard him as *rather* an Arabian than an Assyrian king. In the same spirit his army is termed afterwards "the Arabian host." It is impossible altogether to defend the view which Herodotus here discloses, but we may understand how such a mistake was possible, if we remember how Arabians were mixed up with other races in Lower Mesopotamia and what an extensive influence a great Assyrian king would exercise over the tribes of the desert, especially those bordering on Mesopotamia.

with which to defend themselves. There stands to this day in the temple of Vulcan, a stone statue of Sethôs, with a mouse in his hand, and an inscription to this effect—"Look on me, and learn to reverence the gods."

142. Thus far I have spoken on the authority of the Egyptians and their priests. They declare that from their first king to this last-mentioned monarch, the priest of Vulcan, was a period of three hundred and forty-one generations; such, at least, they say, was the number both of their kings, and of their high-priests, during this interval. Now three hundred generations of men make ten thousand years, three generations filling up the century; and the remaining forty-one generations make thirteen hundred and forty years. Thus the whole number of years is eleven thousand, three hundred and forty; in which entire space, they said, no god had ever appeared in a human form; nothing of this kind had happened either under the former or under the later Egyptian kings. The sun, however, had within this period of time, on four several occasions, moved from his wonted course, twice rising where he now sets, and twice setting where he now rises. Egypt was in no degree affected by these changes; the productions of the land, and of the river, remained the same; nor was there anything unusual either in the diseases or the deaths.

143. When Hecatæus the historian was at Thebes, and, discoursing of his genealogy, traced his descent to a god in the person of his sixteenth ancestor, the priests of Jupiter did to him exactly as they afterwards did to me, though I made no boast of my family. They led me into the inner sanctuary, which is a spacious chamber, and showed me a multitude of colossal statues, in wood, which they counted up, and found to amount to the exact number they had said; the custom being for every high-priest during his lifetime to set up his statue in the temple. As they showed me the figures and reckoned them up, they assured me that each was the son of the one preceding him; and this they repeated throughout the whole line, beginning with the representation of the priest last deceased, and continuing till they had completed the series. When Hecatæus, in giving his genealogy, mentioned a god as his sixteenth ancestor, the priests opposed their genealogy to his, going through this list, and refusing to allow that any man was ever born of a god. Their colossal figures were each, they said, a Pirômis, born of a Pirômis, and the number of them was three hundred and forty-five; through

the whole series Pirômis followed Pirômis, and the line did not run up either to a god or a hero. The word *Pirômis* may be rendered "gentleman."

144. Of such a nature were, they said, the beings represented by these images—they were very far indeed from being gods. However, in the times anterior to them it was otherwise; then Egypt had gods for its rulers, who dwelt upon the earth with men, one being always supreme above the rest. The last of these was Horus, the son of Osiris, called by the Greeks Apollo. He deposed Typhon, and ruled over Egypt as its last god-king. Osiris is named Dionysus (Bacchus) by the Greeks.

145. The Greeks regard Hercules, Bacchus, and Pan as the youngest of the gods. With the Egyptians, contrariwise, Pan is exceedingly ancient, and belongs to those whom they call "the eight gods," who existed before the rest. Hercules is one of the gods of the second order, who are known as "the twelve"; and Bacchus belongs to the gods of the third order, whom the twelve produced. I have already mentioned how many years intervened according to the Egyptians between the birth of Hercules and the reign of Amasis. From Pan to this period they count a still longer time; and even from Bacchus, who is the youngest of the three, they reckon fifteen thousand years to the reign of that king. In these matters they say they cannot be mistaken, as they have always kept count of the years, and noted them in their registers. But from the present day to the time of Bacchus, the reputed son of Semelé, daughter of Cadmus, is a period of not more than sixteen hundred years; to that of Hercules, son of Alcmêna, is about nine hundred; while to the time of Pan, son of Penelopé (Pan, according to the Greeks, was her child by Mercury), is a shorter space than to the Trojan war, eight hundred years or thereabouts.

146. It is open to all to receive whichever he may prefer of these two traditions; my own opinion about them has been already declared. If indeed these gods had been publicly known, and had grown old in Greece, as was the case with Hercules, son of Amphitryon, Bacchus, son of Semelé, and Pan, son of Penelopé, it might have been said that the last-mentioned personages were men who bore the names of certain previously existing deities. But Bacchus, according to the Greek tradition, was no sooner born than he was sewn up in Jupiter's thigh, and carried off to Nysa, above Egypt, in Ethiopia; and as to Pan, they do not even profess to know what happened to him after his birth. To me, therefore, it is quite manifest that the names of these gods became known to the Greeks after those of their other deities, and that they count their birth from the time when they first acquired a knowledge of them. Thus far my narrative rests on the accounts given by the Egyptians.

147. In what follows I have the authority, not of the Egyptians only, but of others also who agree with them. I shall speak likewise in part from my own observation. When the Egyptians regained their liberty after the reign of the priest of Vulcan, unable to continue any while without a king, they divided Egypt into twelve districts, and set twelve kings over them. These twelve kings, united together by intermarriages, ruled Egypt in peace, having entered into engagements with one another not to depose any of their number, nor to aim at any aggrandisement of one above the rest, but to dwell together in perfect amity. Now the reason why they made these stipulations, and guarded with care against their infraction, was because at the very first establishment of the twelve kingdoms an oracle had declared—"That he among them who should pour in Vulcan's temple a libation from a cup of bronze would become monarch of the whole land of Egypt." Now the twelve held their meetings at all the temples.

148. To bind themselves yet more closely together, it seemed good to them to leave a common monument. In pursuance of this resolution they made the Labyrinth which lies a little above Lake Mœris, in the neighbourhood of the place called the city of Crocodiles. I visited this place, and found it to surpass description; for if all the walls and other great works of the Greeks could be put together in one, they would not equal, either for labour or expense, this Labyrinth; and yet the temple of Ephesus is a building worthy of note, and so is the temple of Samos. The pyramids likewise surpass description, and are severally equal to a number of the greatest works of the Greeks, but the Labyrinth surpasses the pyramids. It has twelve courts, all of them roofed, with gates exactly opposite one another, six looking to the north, and six to the south. A single wall surrounds the entire building. There are two different sorts of chambers throughout—half under ground, half above ground, the latter built upon the former; the whole number of these chambers is three thousand, fifteen hundred of each kind. The upper chambers I myself passed

through and saw, and what I say concerning them is from my own observation; of the underground chambers I can only speak from report: for the keepers of the building could not be got to show them, since they contained (as they said) the sepulchres of the kings who built the Labyrinth, and also those of the sacred crocodiles. Thus it is from hearsay only that I can speak of the lower chambers. The upper chambers, however, I saw with my own eyes, and found them to excel all other human productions; for the passages through the houses, and the varied windings of the paths across the courts excited in me infinite admiration as I passed from the courts into chambers, and from the chambers into colonnades, and from the colonnades into fresh houses, and again from these into courts unseen before. The roof was throughout of stone, like the walls; and the walls were carved all over with figures; every court was surrounded with a colonnade which was built of white stones exquisitely fitted together. At the corner of the Labyrinth stands a pyramid, forty fathoms high, with large figures engraved on it, which is entered by a subterranean passage.

149. Wonderful as is the Labyrinth, the work called the Lake of Mœris, which is close by the Labyrinth, is yet more astonishing. The measure of its circumference is sixty schœnes, or three thousand six hundred furlongs, which is equal to the entire length of Egypt along the sea-coast. The lake stretches in its longest direction from north to south, and in its deepest parts is of the depth of fifty fathoms. It is manifestly an artificial excavation, for nearly in the centre there stand two pyramids, rising to the height of fifty fathoms above the surface of the water, and extending as far beneath, crowned each of them with a colossal statue sitting upon a throne. Thus these pyramids are one hundred fathoms high, which is exactly a furlong (stadium) of six hundred feet: the fathom being six feet in length, or four cubits, which is the same thing, since a cubit measures six, and a foot four, palms. The water of the lake does not come out of the ground, which is here excessively dry, but is introduced by a canal from the Nile. The current sets for six months into the lake from the river, and for the next six months into the river from the lake. While it runs outward it returns a talent of silver daily to the royal treasury from the fish that are taken, but when the current is the other way the return sinks to one-third of that sum.

150. The natives told me that there was a subterranean passage from this lake to the Libyan Syrtis, running westward into the interior by the hills above Memphis. As I could not anywhere see the earth which had been taken out when the excavation was made, and I was curious to know what had become of it, I asked the Egyptians who live closest to the lake where the earth had been put. The answer that they gave me I readily accepted as true, since I had heard of the same thing being done at Nineveh of the Assyrians. There, once upon a time, certain thieves, having formed a plan to get into their possession the vast treasures of Sardanapalus, the Ninevite king, which were laid up in subterranean treasuries, proceeded to tunnel a passage from the house where they lived into the royal palace, calculating the distance and the direction. At nightfall they took the earth from the excavation and carried it to the river Tigris, which ran by Nineveh, continuing to get rid of it in this manner until they had accomplished their purpose. It was exactly in the same way that the Egyptians disposed of the mould from their excavation, except that they did it by day and not by night; for as fast as the earth was dug, they carried it to the Nile, which they knew would disperse it far and wide. Such was the account which I received of the formation of this lake.

151. The twelve kings for some time dealt honourably by one another, but at length it happened that on a certain occasion, when they had met to worship in the temple of Vulcan, the high-priest on the last day of the festival, in bringing forth the golden goblets from which they were wont to pour the libations, mistook the number and brought eleven goblets only for the twelve princes. Psammetichus was standing last, and, being left without a cup, he took his helmet, which was of bronze, from off his head, stretched it out to receive the liquor, and so made his libation. All the kings were accustomed to wear helmets, and all indeed wore them at this very time. Nor was there any crafty design in the action of Psammetichus. The eleven, however, when they came to consider what had been done, and bethought them of the oracle which had declared "that he who, of the twelve, should pour a libation from a cup of bronze, the same would be king of the whole land of Egypt," doubted at first if they should not put Psammetichus to death. Finding, however, upon examination, that he had acted in the matter without any guilty intent, they did not think it would be just to kill him; but determined, instead, to

strip him of the chief part of his power and to banish him to the marshes, forbidding him to leave them or to hold any communication with the rest of Egypt.

152. This was the second time that Psammetichus had been driven into banishment. On a former occasion he had fled from Sabacôs the Ethiopian, who had put his father Necôs to death; and had taken refuge in Syria from whence, after the retirement of the Ethiop in consequence of his dream, he was brought back by the Egyptians of the Saïtic canton. Now it was his ill-fortune to be banished a second time by the eleven kings, on account of the libation which he had poured from his helmet; on this occasion he fled to the marshes. Feeling that he was an injured man, and designing to avenge himself upon his persecutors, Psammetichus sent to the city of Buto, where there is an oracle of Latona, the most veracious of all the oracles of the Egyptians, and having inquired concerning means of vengeance, received for answer that "Vengeance would come from the sea, when brazen men should appear." Great was his incredulity when this answer arrived, for never, he thought, would brazen men arrive to be his helpers. However, not long afterwards certain Carians and Ionians, who had left their country on a voyage of plunder, were carried by stress of weather to Egypt where they disembarked, all equipped in their brazen armour, and were seen by the natives, one of whom carried the tidings to Psammetichus, and, as he had never before seen men clad in brass, he reported that brazen men had come from the sea and were plundering the plain. Psammetichus, perceiving at once that the oracle was accomplished, made friendly advances to the strangers, and engaged them, by splendid promises, to enter into his service. He then, with their aid and that of the Egyptians who espoused his cause, attacked the eleven and vanquished them.

153. When Psammetichus had thus become sole monarch of Egypt, he built the southern gateway of the temple of Vulcan in Memphis, and also a court for Apis, in which Apis is kept whenever he makes his appearance in Egypt. This court is opposite the gateway of Psammetichus, and is surrounded with a colonnade and adorned with a multitude of figures. Instead of pillars, the colonnade rests upon colossal statues, twelve cubits in height. The Greek name for Apis is Epaphus.

154. To the Ionians and Carians who had lent him their assistance Psammetichus assigned as abodes two places opposite to each other, one on either side of the Nile, which received the name of "the Camps." He also made good all the splendid promises by which he had gained their support; and further, he intrusted to their care certain Egyptian children whom they were to teach the language of the Greeks. These children, thus instructed, became the parents of the entire class of interpreters in Egypt. The Ionians and Carians occupied for many years the places assigned them by Psammetichus, which lay near the sea, a little below the city of Bubastis, on the Pelusiac mouth of the Nile. King Amasis long afterwards removed the Greeks hence, and settled them at Memphis to guard him against the native Egyptians. From the date of the original settlement of these persons in Egypt, we Greeks, through our intercourse with them, have acquired an accurate knowledge of the several events in Egyptian history, from the reign of Psammetichus downwards; but before his time no foreigners had ever taken up their residence in that land. The docks where their vessels were laid up and the ruins of their habitations were still to be seen in my day at the place where they dwelt originally, before they were removed by Amasis. Such was the mode by which Psammetichus became master of Egypt.

155. I have already made mention more than once of the Egyptian oracle, and, as it well deserves notice, I shall now proceed to give an account of it more at length. It is a temple of Latona, situated in the midst of a great city on the Sebennytic mouth of the Nile, at some distance up the river from the sea. The name of the city, as I have before observed, is Buto; and in it are two other temples also, one of Apollo and one of Diana. Latona's temple, which contains the oracle, is a spacious building with a gateway ten fathoms in height. The most wonderful thing that was actually to be seen about this temple was a chapel in the enclosure made of a single stone, the length and height of which were the same, each wall being forty cubits square, and the whole a single block! Another block of stone formed the roof and projected at the eaves to the extent of four cubits.

156. This, as I have said, was what astonished me the most, of all the things that were actually to be seen about the temple. The next greatest marvel was the island called Chemmis. This island lies in the middle of a broad and deep lake close by the temple, and the

natives declare that it floats. For my own part I did not see it float, or even move; and I wondered greatly, when they told me concerning it, whether there be really such a thing as a floating island. It has a grand temple of Apollo built upon it, in which are three distinct altars. Palm trees grow on it in great abundance, and many other trees, some of which bear fruit, while others are barren. The Egyptians tell the following story in connection with this island, to explain the way in which it first came to float:—"In former times, when the isle was still fixed and motionless, Latona, one of the eight gods of the first order, who dwelt in the city of Buto, where now she has her oracle, received Apollo as a sacred charge from Isis, and saved him by hiding him in what is now called the floating island. Typhon meanwhile was searching everywhere in hopes of finding the child of Osiris." (According to the Egyptians, Apollo and Diana are the children of Bacchus and Isis, while Latona is their nurse and their preserver. They call Apollo, in their language, Horus; Ceres they call Isis; Diana, Bubastis. From this Egyptian tradition, and from no other, it must have been that Æschylus, the son of Euphorion, took the idea, which is found in none of the earlier poets, of making Diana the daughter of Ceres.) The island, therefore, in consequence of this event, was first made to float. Such at least is the account which the Egyptians give.

157. Psammetichus ruled Egypt for fifty-four years, during twenty-nine of which he pressed the siege of Azôtus without intermission, till finally he took the place. Azôtus is a great town in Syria. Of all the cities that we know, none ever stood so long a siege.

158. Psammetichus left a son called Necôs, who succeeded him upon the throne. This prince was the first to attempt the construction of the canal to the Red Sea—a work completed afterwards by Darius the Persian—the length of which is four days' journey, and the width such as to admit of two triremes being rowed along it abreast. The water is derived from the Nile, which the canal leaves a little above the city of Bubastis, near Patûmus, the Arabian town, being continued thence until it joins the Red Sea. At first it is carried along the Arabian side of the Egyptian plain, as far as the chain of hills opposite Memphis, whereby the plain is bounded, and in which lie the great stone quarries; here it skirts the base of the hills running in a direction from west to east, after which it turns and enters a narrow pass, trend-

ing southwards from this point until it enters the Arabian Gulf. From the northern sea to that which is called the southern or Erythræan, the shortest and quickest passage, which is from Mount Casius, the boundary between Egypt and Syria, to the Gulf of Arabia, is a distance of exactly one thousand furlongs. But the way by the canal is very much longer on account of the crookedness of its course. A hundred and twenty thousand of the Egyptians, employed upon the work in the reign of Necôs, lost their lives in making the excavation. He at length desisted from his undertaking, in consequence of an oracle which warned him "that he was labouring for the barbarian." The Egyptians call by the name of barbarians all such as speak a language different from their own.

159. Necôs, when he gave up the construction of the canal, turned all his thoughts to war, and set to work to build a fleet of triremes, some intended for service in the northern sea, and some for the navigation of the Erythræan. These last were built in the Arabian Gulf where the dry docks in which they lay are still visible. These fleets he employed wherever he had occasion, while he also made war by land upon the Syrians and defeated them in a pitched battle at Magdolus, after which he made himself master of Cadytis, a large city of Syria. The dress which he wore on these occasions he sent to Branchidæ in Milesia, as an offering to Apollo. After having reigned in all sixteen years, Necôs died, and at his death bequeathed the throne to his son Psammis.

160. In the reign of Psammis, ambassadors from Elis arrived in Egypt, boasting that their arrangements for the conduct of the Olympic Games were the best and fairest that could be devised, and fancying that not even the Egyptians, who surpassed all other nations in wisdom, could add anything to their perfection. When these persons reached Egypt, and explained the reason of their visit, the king summoned an assembly of all the wisest of the Egyptians. They met, and the Eleans having given them a full account of all their rules and regulations with respect to the contests said that they had come to Egypt for the express purpose of learning whether the Egyptians could improve the fairness of their regulations in any particular. The Egyptians considered awhile and then made inquiry, "If they allowed their own citizens to enter the lists?" The Eleans answered, "That the lists were open to all Greeks, whether they belonged to

Elis or to any other state." Hereupon the Egyptians observed, "That if this were so, they departed from justice very widely, since it was impossible but that they would favour their own countrymen and deal unfairly by foreigners. If therefore they really wished to manage the games with fairness, and if this was the object of their coming to Egypt, they advised them to confine the contests to strangers, and allow no native of Elis to be a candidate." Such was the advice which the Egyptians gave to the Eleans.

161. Psammis reigned only six years. He attacked Ethiopia, and died almost directly afterwards. Apries, his son, succeeded him upon the throne, who, excepting Psammetichus, his great-grandfather, was the most prosperous of all the kings that ever ruled over Egypt. The length of his reign was twenty-five years, and in the course of it he marched an army to attack Sidon, and fought a battle with the king of Tyre by sea. When at length the time came that was fated to bring him woe, an occasion arose which I shall describe more fully in my Libyan history, only touching it very briefly here. An army despatched by Apries to attack Cyrêné, having met with a terrible reverse, the Egyptians laid the blame on him, imagining that he had, of *malice prepense,* sent the troops into the jaws of destruction. They believed he had wished a vast number of them to be slain in order that he himself might reign with more security over the rest of the Egyptians. Indignant therefore at this usage, the soldiers who returned and the friends of the slain broke instantly into revolt.

162. Apries, on learning these circumstances, sent Amasis to the rebels to appease the tumult by persuasion. Upon his arrival, as he was seeking to restrain the malcontents by his exhortations, one of them, coming behind him, put a helmet on his head, saying, as he put it on, that he thereby crowned him king. Amasis was not altogether displeased at the action, as his conduct soon made manifest; for no sooner had the insurgents agreed to make him actually their king than he prepared to march with them against Apries. That monarch, on tidings of these events reaching him, sent Patarbêmis, one of his courtiers, a man of high rank, to Amasis with orders to bring him alive into his presence. Patarbêmis, on arriving at the place where Amasis was, called on him to come back with him to the king, whereupon Amasis broke a coarse jest, and said, "Prythee take that back to thy master." When the envoy, notwithstanding this reply, persisted in his request, exhorting Amasis to obey the summons of the king, he made answer "that this was exactly what he had long been intending to do; Apries would have no reason to complain of him on the score of delay; he would shortly come himself to the king, and bring others with him." Patarbêmis, upon this, comprehending the intention of Amasis, partly from his replies and partly from the preparations which he saw in progress, departed hastily, wishing to inform the king with all speed of what was going on. Apries, however, when he saw him approaching without Amasis, fell into a paroxysm of rage, and not giving himself time for reflection, commanded the nose and ears of Patarbêmis to be cut off. Then the rest of the Egyptians, who had hitherto espoused the cause of Apries, when they saw a man of such note among them so shamefully outraged, without a moment's hesitation went over to the rebels, and put themselves at the disposal of Amasis.

163. Apries, informed of this new calamity, armed his mercenaries, and led them against the Egyptians: this was a body of Carians and Ionians, numbering thirty thousand men, which was now with him at Saïs, where his palace stood—a vast building, well worthy of notice. The army of Apries marched out to attack the host of the Egyptians, while that of Amasis went forth to fight the strangers; and now both armies drew near the city of Momemphis and prepared for the coming fight.

164. The Egyptians are divided into seven distinct classes—these are, the priests, the warriors, the cowherds, the swineherds, the tradesmen, the interpreters, and the boatmen. Their titles indicate their occupations. The warriors consist of Hermotybians and Calasirians, who come from different cantons, the whole of Egypt being parcelled out into districts bearing this name.

165. The following cantons furnish the Hermotybians:—The cantons of Busiris, Saïs, Chemmis, Paprêmis, that of the island called Prosôpitis, and half of Natho. They number, when most numerous, a hundred and sixty thousand. None of them ever practices a trade, but all are given wholly to war.

166. The cantons of the Calasirians are different—they include the following:—The cantons of Thebes, Bubastis, Aphthis, Tanis, Mendes, Sebennytus, Athribis, Pharbæthus, Thmuis, Onuphis, Anysis, and Myecphoris—this last canton consists of an island which lies over

against the town of Bubastis. The Calasirians, when at their greatest number, have amounted to two hundred and fifty thousand. Like the Hermotybians, they are forbidden to pursue any trade, and devote themselves entirely to warlike exercises, the son following the father's calling.

167. Whether the Greeks borrowed from the Egyptians their notions about trade, like so many others, I cannot say for certain. I have remarked that the Thracians, the Scyths, the Persians, the Lydians, and almost all other barbarians, hold the citizens who practice trades, and their children, in less repute than the rest, while they esteem as noble those who keep aloof from handicrafts, and especially honour such as are given wholly to war. These ideas prevail throughout the whole of Greece, particularly among the Lacedæmonians. Corinth is the place where mechanics are least despised.

168. The warrior class in Egypt had certain special privileges in which none of the rest of the Egyptians participated, except the priests. In the first place each man had twelve arurae[1] of land assigned him free from tax. (The arura is a square of a hundred Egyptian cubits, the Egyptian cubit being of the same length as the Samian.) All the warriors enjoyed this privilege together, but there were other advantages which came to each in rotation, the same man never obtaining them twice. A thousand Calasirians, and the same number of Hermotybians, formed in alternate years the body-guard of the king; and during their year of service these persons, besides their arurae, received a daily portion of meat and drink, consisting of five pounds of baked bread, two pounds of beef, and four cups of wine.

169. When Apries, at the head of his mercenaries, and Amasis, in command of the whole native force of the Egyptians, encountered one another near the city of Momemphis, an engagement presently took place. The foreign troops fought bravely, but were overpowered by numbers, in which they fell very far short of their adversaries. It is said that Apries believed that there was not a god who could cast him down from his eminence, so firmly did he think that he had established himself in his kingdom. But at this time the battle went against him, and his army being worsted, he fell into the enemy's hands and was brought back a prisoner to Saïs, where he was lodged in what had been his own house,

but was now the palace of Amasis. Amasis treated him with kindness, and kept him in the palace for a while; but finding his conduct blamed by the Egyptians, who charged him with acting unjustly in preserving a man who had shown himself so bitter an enemy both to them and him, he gave Apries over into the hands of his former subjects, to deal with as they chose. Then the Egyptians took him and strangled him, but having so done they buried him in the sepulchre of his fathers. This tomb is in the temple of Minerva, very near the sanctuary, on the left hand as one enters. The Saïtes buried all the kings who belonged to their canton inside this temple; and thus it even contains the tomb of Amasis, as well as that of Apries and his family. The latter is not so close to the sanctuary as the former, but still it is within the temple. It stands in the court, and is a spacious cloister built of stone and adorned with pillars carved so as to resemble palm trees, and with other sumptuous ornaments. Within the cloister is a chamber with folding doors, behind which lies the sepulchre of the king.

170. Here too, in this same precinct of Minerva at Saïs, is the burial-place of one whom I think it not right to mention in such a connection.[2] It stands behind the temple, against the backwall, which it entirely covers. There are also some large stone obelisks in the enclosure, and there is a lake near them, adorned with an edging of stone. In form it is circular, and in size, as it seemed to me, about equal to the lake in Delos called "the Hoop."

171. On this lake it is that the Egyptians represent by night his sufferings whose name I refrain from mentioning, and this representation they call their Mysteries. I know well the whole course of the proceedings in these ceremonies, but they shall not pass my lips. So too, with regard to the mysteries of Ceres, which the Greeks term "the Thesmophoria," I know them, but I shall not mention them, except so far as may be done without impiety. The daughters of Danaus brought these rites from Egypt, and taught them to the Pelasgic women of the Peloponnese. Afterwards, when the inhabitants of the peninsula were driven from their homes by the Dorians, the rites perished. Only in Arcadia, where the natives remained and were not compelled to migrate, their observance continued.

172. After Apries had been put to death in the way that I have described above, Amasis reigned over Egypt. He belonged to the can-

[1] The arura was a little more than three-fourths of an English acre, and was only a land measure.

[2] Osiris.

ton of Saïs, being a native of the town called Siouph. At first his subjects looked down on him and held him in small esteem, because he had been a mere private person, and of a house of no great distinction; but after a time Amasis succeeded in reconciling them to his rule, not by severity, but by cleverness. Among his other splendour he had a golden foot-pan, in which his guests and himself were wont upon occasion to wash their feet. This vessel he caused to be broken in pieces, and made of the gold an image of one of the gods, which he set up in the most public place in the whole city; upon which the Egyptians flocked to the image, and worshipped it with the utmost reverence. Amasis, finding this was so, called an assembly, and opened the matter to them, explaining how the image had been made of the foot-pan, wherein they had been wont formerly to wash their feet and to put all manner of filth, yet now it was greatly reverenced. "And truly," he went on to say, "it had gone with him as with the foot-pan. If he was a private person formerly, yet now he had come to be their king. And so he bade them honour and reverence him." Such was the mode in which he won over the Egyptians, and brought them to be content to do him service.

173. The following was the general habit of his life:—from early dawn to the time when the forum is wont to fill, he sedulously transacted all the business that was brought before him; during the remainder of the day he drank and joked with his guests, passing the time in witty and, sometimes, scarce seemly conversation. It grieved his friends that he should thus demean himself, and accordingly some of them chid him on the subject, saying to him—"Oh! king, thou dost but ill guard thy royal dignity whilst thou allowest thyself in such levities. Thou shouldest sit in state upon a stately throne, and busy thyself with affairs the whole day long. So would the Egyptians feel that a great man rules them, and thou wouldst be better spoken of. But now thou conductest thyself in no kingly fashion." Amasis answered them thus:—"Bowmen bend their bows when they wish to shoot; unbrace them when the shooting is over. Were they kept always strung they would break, and fail the archer in time of need. So it is with men. If they give themselves constantly to serious work, and never indulge awhile in pastime or sport, they lose their senses, and become mad or moody. Knowing this, I divide my life between pastime and business." Thus he answered his friends.

174. It is said that Amasis, even while he was a private man, had the same tastes for drinking and jesting, and was averse to engaging in any serious employment. He lived in constant feasts and revelries, and whenever his means failed him, he roamed about and robbed people. On such occasions the persons from whom he had stolen would bring him, if he denied the charge, before the nearest oracle; sometimes the oracle would pronounce him guilty of the theft, at other times it would acquit him. When afterwards he came to be king, he neglected the temples of such gods as had declared that he was not a thief, and neither contributed to their adornment nor frequented them for sacrifice, since he regarded them as utterly worthless and their oracles as wholly false: but the gods who had detected his guilt he considered to be true gods whose oracles did not deceive, and these he honoured exceedingly.

175. First of all, therefore, he built the gateway of the temple of Minerva at Saïs, which is an astonishing work, far surpassing all other buildings of the same kind both in extent and height, and built with stones of rare size and excellency. In the next place, he presented to the temple a number of large colossal statues and several prodigious andro-sphinxes, besides certain stones for the repairs, of a most extraordinary size. Some of these he got from the quarries over against Memphis, but the largest were brought from Elephantiné, which is twenty days' voyage from Saïs. Of all these wonderful masses that which I most admire is a chamber made of a single stone, which was quarried at Elephantiné. It took three years to convey this block from the quarry to Saïs; and in the conveyance were employed no fewer than two thousand labourers, who were all from the class of boatmen. The length of this chamber on the outside is twenty-one cubits, its breadth fourteen cubits, and its height, eight. The measurements inside are the following:—the length, eighteen cubits and five-sixths; the breadth, twelve cubits; and the height, five. It lies near the entrance of the temple, where it was left in consequence of the following circumstance:—it happened that the architect, just as the stone had reached the spot where it now stands, heaved a sigh, considering the length of time that the removal had taken, and feeling wearied with the heavy toil. The sigh was heard by Amasis who, regarding it as an omen, would not allow the chamber to be moved forward any farther. Some, however,

say that one of the workmen engaged at the levers was crushed and killed by the mass, and that this was the reason of its being left where it now stands.

176. To the other temples of much note Amasis also made magnificent offerings—at Memphis, for instance, he gave the recumbent colossus in front of the temple of Vulcan, which is seventy-five feet long. Two other co-lossal statues stand on the same base, each twenty feet high, carved in the stone of Ethi-opia, one on either side of the temple. There is also a stone colossus of the same size at Saïs, recumbent like that at Memphis. Amasis final-ly built the temple of Isis at Memphis, a vast structure, well worth seeing.

177. It is said that the reign of Amasis was the most prosperous time that Egypt ever saw, —the river was more liberal to the land, and the land brought forth more abundantly for the service of man than had ever been known before; while the number of inhabited cities was not less than twenty thousand. It was this king Amasis who established the law that every Egyptian should appear once a year before the governor of his canton, and show his means of living; or, failing to do so, and to prove that he got an honest livelihood, should be put to death. Solon the Athenian borrowed this law from the Egyptians, and imposed it on his countrymen, who have ob-served it ever since. It is indeed an excellent custom.

178. Amasis was partial to the Greeks, and among other favours which he granted them, gave to such as liked to settle in Egypt the city of Naucratis for their residence. To those who only wished to trade upon the coast, and did not want to fix their abode in the country, he granted certain lands where they might set up altars and erect temples to the gods. Of these temples the grandest and most famous, which is also the most frequented, is that called "the Hellenium." It was built conjointly by the Io-nians, Dorians, and Æolians, the following cities taking part in the work:—the Ionian states of Chios, Teos, Phocæa, and Clazomenæ; Rhodes, Cnidus, Halicarnassus, and Phasêlis of the Dorians; and Mytilêne of the Æolians. These are the states to whom the temple be-longs, and they have the right of appointing the governors of the factory; the other cities which claim a share in the building, claim what in no sense belongs to them. Three na-tions, however, consecrated for themselves sep-arate temples—the Eginetans one to Jupiter,

the Samians to Juno, and the Milesians to Apollo.

179. In ancient times there was no factory but Naucratis in the whole of Egypt; and if a person entered one of the other mouths of the Nile, he was obliged to swear that he had not come there of his own free will. Having so done, he was bound to sail in his ship to the Canobic mouth, or were that impossible ow-ing to contrary winds, he must take his wares by boat all round the Delta, and so bring them to Naucratis, which had an exclusive privilege.

180. It happened in the reign of Amasis that the temple of Delphi had been accidentally burnt, and the Amphictyons had contracted to have it rebuilt for three hundred talents, of which sum one-fourth was to be furnished by the Delphians. Under these circumstances the Delphians went from city to city begging con-tributions, and among their other wanderings came to Egypt and asked for help. From few other places did they obtain so much—Amasis gave them a thousand talents of alum, and the Greek settlers twenty minæ.[1]

181. A league was concluded by Amasis with the Cyrenæans, by which Cyrêné and Egypt became close friends and allies. He like-wise took a wife from that city, either as a sign of his friendly feeling, or because he had a fancy to marry a Greek woman. However this may be, certain it is that he espoused a lady of Cyrêné, by name Ladicé, daughter, some say, of Battus or Arcesilaüs, the king—others, of Critobûlus, one of the chief citizens. When the time came to complete the contract, Amasis was struck with weakness. Astonished hereat —for he was not wont to be so afflicted—the king thus addressed his bride: "Woman, thou hast certainly bewitched me—now therefore be sure thou shalt perish more miserably than ever woman perished yet." Ladicé protested her innocence, but in vain; Amasis was not softened. Hereupon she made a vow internal-ly, that if he recovered within the day (for no longer time was allowed her), she would pre-sent a statue to the temple of Venus at Cyrêné. Immediately she obtained her wish, and the king's weakness disappeared. Amasis loved her greatly ever after, and Ladicé performed her vow. The statue which she caused to be made, and sent to Cyrêné, continued there to my day, standing with its face looking out-wards from the city. Ladicé herself, when Cam-

[1] Twenty minæ would be somewhat more than £80. The entire sum which the Delphians had to collect exceeded £18,000.

byses conquered Egypt, suffered no wrong; for Cambyses, on learning of her who she was, sent her back unharmed to her country.

182. Besides the marks of favour already mentioned, Amasis also enriched with offerings many of the Greek temples. He sent to Cyrênê a statue of Minerva covered with plates of gold, and a painted likeness of himself. To the Minerva of Lindus he gave two statues in stone, and a linen corslet well worth inspection. To the Samian Juno he presented two statues of himself, made in wood, which stood in the great temple to my day, behind the doors. Samos was honoured with these gifts on account of the bond of friendship subsisting between Amasis and Polycrates, the son of Æaces: Lindus, for no such reason, but because of the tradition that the daughters of Danaus touched there in their flight from the sons of Ægyptus, and built the temple of Minerva. Such were the offerings of Amasis. He likewise took Cyprus, which no man had ever done before, and compelled it to pay him a tribute.

The Third Book, Entitled
THALIA

❯❯ ❯❯ ❯❯ ❯❯ ❯❯ ❯❯ ❯❯ ❯❯ ❯❯ ❯❯ ❯❯ ❯❯ ❯❯ ❯❯ ❯❯ ❮❮ ❮❮ ❮❮ ❮❮ ❮❮ ❮❮ ❮❮ ❮❮ ❮❮ ❮❮ ❮❮ ❮❮ ❮❮ ❮❮ ❮❮

1. The above-mentioned Amasis was the Egyptian king against whom Cambyses, son of Cyrus, made his expedition; and with him went an army composed of the many nations under his rule, among them being included both Ionic and Æolic Greeks. The reason of the invasion was the following. Cambyses, by the advice of a certain Egyptian, who was angry with Amasis for having torn him from his wife and children and given him over to the Persians, had sent a herald to Amasis to ask his daughter in marriage. His adviser was a physician, whom Amasis, when Cyrus had requested that he would send him the most skilful of all the Egyptian eye-doctors, singled out as the best from the whole number. Therefore the Egyptian bore Amasis a grudge, and his reason for urging Cambyses to ask the hand of the king's daughter was, that if he complied, it might cause him annoyance; if he refused, it might make Cambyses his enemy. When the message came, Amasis, who much dreaded the power of the Persians, was greatly perplexed whether to give his daughter or no; for that Cambyses did not intend to make her his wife, but would only receive her as his concubine, he knew for certain. He therefore cast the matter in his mind, and finally resolved what he would do. There was a daughter of the late king Apries, named Nitêtis, a tall and beautiful woman, the last survivor of that royal house. Amasis took this woman, and decking her out with gold and costly garments, sent her to Persia as if she had been his own child. Some time afterwards, Cambyses, as he gave her an embrace, happened to call her by her father's name, whereupon she said to him, "I see, O king, thou knowest not how thou has been cheated by Amasis; who took me, and, tricking me out with gauds, sent me to thee as his own daughter. But I am in truth the child of Apries, who was his lord and master, until he

rebelled against him, together with the rest of the Egyptians, and put him to death." It was this speech, and the cause of quarrel it disclosed, which roused the anger of Cambyses, son of Cyrus, and brought his arms upon Egypt. Such is the Persian story.

2. The Egyptians, however, claim Cambyses as belonging to them, declaring that he was the son of this Nitêtis. It was Cyrus, they say, and not Cambyses, who sent to Amasis for his daughter. But here they mis-state the truth. Acquainted as they are beyond all other men with the laws and customs of the Persians, they cannot but be well aware, first, that it is not the Persian wont to allow a bastard to reign when there is a legitimate heir; and next, that Cambyses was the son of Cassandané, the daughter of Pharnaspes, an Achæmenian, and not of this Egyptian. But the fact is that they pervert history in order to claim relationship with the house of Cyrus. Such is the truth of this matter.

3. I have also heard another account, which I do not at all believe: that a Persian lady came to visit the wives of Cyrus, and seeing how tall and beautiful were the children of Cassandané, then standing by, broke out into loud praise of them, and admired them exceedingly. But Cassandané, wife of Cyrus, answered, "Though such the children I have borne him, yet Cyrus slights me and gives all his regard to the new-comer from Egypt." Thus did she express her vexation on account of Nitêtis: whereupon Cambyses, the eldest of her boys, exclaimed, "Mother, when I am a man, I will turn Egypt upside down for you." He was but ten years old, as the tale runs, when he said this, and astonished all the women, yet he never forgot it afterwards; and on this account, they say, when he came to be a man, and mounted the throne, he made his expedition against Egypt.

4. There was another matter, quite distinct, which helped to bring about the expedition. One of the mercenaries of Amasis, a Halicarnassian, Phanes by name, a man of good judgment, and a brave warrior, dissatisfied for some reason or other with his master, deserted the service, and taking ship, fled to Cambyses, wishing to get speech with him. As he was a person of no small account among the mercenaries, and one who could give very exact intelligence about Egypt, Amasis, anxious to recover him, ordered that he should be pursued. He gave the matter in charge to one of the most trusty of the eunuchs, who went in quest of the Halicarnassian in a vessel of war. The eunuch caught him in Lycia, but did not contrive to bring him back to Egypt, for Phanes outwitted him by making his guards drunk, and then escaping into Persia. Now it happened that Cambyses was meditating his attack on Egypt, and doubting how he might best pass the desert, when Phanes arrived, and not only told him all the secrets of Amasis, but advised him also how the desert might be crossed. He counselled him to send an ambassador to the king of the Arabs, and ask him for safe-conduct through the region.

5. Now the only entrance into Egypt is by this desert: the country from Phœnicia to the borders of the city Cadytis belongs to the people called the Palæstine Syrians; from Cadytis, which it appears to me is a city almost as large as Sardis, the marts upon the coast till you reach Jenysus are the Arabian king's; after Jenysus the Syrians again come in, and extend to Lake Serbônis, near the place where Mount Casius juts out into the sea. At Lake Serbônis, where the tale goes that Typhon hid himself, Egypt begins. Now the whole tract between Jenysus on the one side, and Lake Serbônis and Mount Casius on the other, and this is no small space, being as much as three days' journey, is a dry desert without a drop of water.

6. I shall now mention a thing of which few of those who sail to Egypt are aware. Twice a year wine is brought into Egypt from every part of Greece, as well as from Phœnicia, in earthen jars; and yet in the whole country you will nowhere see, as I may say, a single jar. What then, every one will ask, becomes of the jars? This, too, I will clear up. The burgomaster of each town has to collect the wine-jars within his district, and to carry them to Memphis, where they are all filled with water by the Memphians, who then convey them to this desert tract of Syria. And so it comes to pass

that all the jars which enter Egypt year by year, and are there put up to sale, find their way into Syria, whither all the old jars have gone before them.

7. This way of keeping the passage into Egypt fit for use by storing water there, was begun by the Persians so soon as they became masters of that country. As, however, at the time of which we speak the tract had not yet been so supplied, Cambyses took the advice of his Halicarnassian guest, and sent messengers to the Arabian to beg a safe-conduct through the region. The Arabian granted his prayer, and each pledged faith to the other.

8. The Arabs keep such pledges more religiously than almost any other people. They plight faith with the forms following. When two men would swear a friendship, they stand on each side of a third: he with a sharp stone makes a cut on the inside of the hand of each near the middle finger, and, taking a piece from their dress, dips it in the blood of each, and moistens therewith seven stones lying in the midst, calling the while on Bacchus and Urania. After this, the man who makes the pledge commends the stranger (or the citizen, if citizen he be) to all his friends, and they deem themselves bound to stand to the engagement. They have but these two gods, to wit, Bacchus and Urania; and they say that in their mode of cutting the hair, they follow Bacchus. Now their practice is to cut it in a ring, away from the temples. Bacchus they call in their language Orotal, and Urania, Alilat.

9. When, therefore, the Arabian had pledged his faith to the messengers of Cambyses, he straightway contrived as follows:—he filled a number of camels' skins with water, and loading therewith all the live camels that he possessed, drove them into the desert, and awaited the coming of the army. This is the more likely of the two tales that are told. The other is an improbable story, but, as it is related, I think that I ought not to pass it by. There is a great river in Arabia, called the Corys, which empties itself into the Erythræan sea. The Arabian king, they say, made a pipe of the skins of oxen and other beasts, reaching from this river all the way to the desert, and so brought the water to certain cisterns which he had had dug in the desert to receive it. It is a twelve days' journey from the river to this desert tract. And the water, they say, was brought through three different pipes to three separate places.

10. Psammenitus, son of Amasis, lay encamped at the mouth of the Nile, called the

Pelusiac, awaiting Cambyses. For Cambyses, when he went up against Egypt, found Amasis no longer in life: he had died after ruling Egypt forty and four years, during all which time no great misfortune had befallen him. When he died, his body was embalmed, and buried in the tomb which he had himself caused to be made in the temple. After his son Psammenitus had mounted the throne, a strange prodigy occurred in Egypt—rain fell at Egyptian Thebes, a thing which never happened before, and which, to the present time, has never happened again, as the Thebans themselves testify. In Upper Egypt it does not usually rain at all; but on this occasion, rain fell at Thebes in small drops.

11. The Persians crossed the desert, and, pitching their camp close to the Egyptians, made ready for battle. Hereupon the mercenaries in the pay of Psammenitus, who were Greeks and Carians, full of anger against Phanes for having brought a foreign army upon Egypt, bethought themselves of a mode whereby they might be revenged on him. Phanes had left sons in Egypt. The mercenaries took these, and leading them to the camp, displayed them before the eyes of their father; after which they brought out a bowl, and, placing it in the space between the two hosts, they led the sons of Phanes, one by one, to the vessel, and slew them over it. When the last was dead, water and wine were poured into the bowl, and all the soldiers tasted of the blood, and so they went to the battle. Stubborn was the fight which followed, and it was not till vast numbers had been slain upon both sides, that the Egyptians turned and fled.

12. On the field where this battle was fought I saw a very wonderful thing which the natives pointed out to me. The bones of the slain lie scattered upon the field in two lots, those of the Persians in one place by themselves, as the bodies lay at the first—those of the Egyptians in another place apart from them. If, then, you strike the Persian skulls, even with a pebble, they are so weak, that you break a hole in them; but the Egyptian skulls are so strong, that you may smite them with a stone and you will scarcely break them in. They gave me the following reason for this difference, which seemed to me likely enough:—The Egyptians (they said) from early childhood have the head shaved, and so by the action of the sun the skull becomes thick and hard. The same cause prevents baldness in Egypt, where you see fewer bald men than in any other land.

Such, then, is the reason why the skulls of the Egyptians are so strong. The Persians, on the other hand, have feeble skulls, because they keep themselves shaded from the first, wearing turbans upon their heads. What I have here mentioned I saw with my own eyes, and I observed also the like at Paprêmis, in the case of the Persians who were killed with Achæmenes, the son of Darius, by Inarus the Libyan.

13. The Egyptians who fought in the battle, no sooner turned their backs upon the enemy, than they fled away in complete disorder to Memphis, where they shut themselves up within the walls. Hereupon Cambyses sent a Mytilenæan vessel, with a Persian herald on board, who was to sail up the Nile to Memphis, and invite the Egyptians to a surrender. They, however, when they saw the vessel entering the town, poured forth in crowds from the castle, destroyed the ship, and, tearing the crew limb from limb, so bore them into the fortress. After this Memphis was besieged, and in due time surrendered. Hereon the Libyans who bordered upon Egypt, fearing the fate of that country, gave themselves up to Cambyses without a battle, made an agreement to pay tribute to him, and forthwith sent him gifts. The Cyrenæans too, and the Barcæans, having the same fear as the Libyans, immediately did the like. Cambyses received the Libyan presents very graciously, but not so the gifts of the Cyrenæans. They had sent no more than five hundred minæ of silver, which Cambyses, I imagine, thought too little. He therefore snatched the money from them, and with his own hands scattered it among his soldiers.

14. Ten days after the fort had fallen, Cambyses resolved to try the spirit of Psammenitus, the Egyptian king, whose whole reign had been but six months. He therefore had him set in one of the suburbs, and many other Egyptians with him, and there subjected him to insult. First of all he sent his daughter out from the city, clothed in the garb of a slave, with a pitcher to draw water. Many virgins, the daughters of the chief nobles, accompanied her, wearing the same dress. When the damsels came opposite the place where their fathers sate, shedding tears and uttering cries of woe, the fathers, all but Psammenitus, wept and wailed in return, grieving to see their children in so sad a plight; but he, when he had looked and seen, bent his head towards the ground. In this way passed by the water-carriers. Next to them came Psammenitus' son, and two thousand Egyptians of the same age with him—all

of them having ropes round their necks and bridles in their mouths—and they too passed by on their way to suffer death for the murder of the Mytilenæans who were destroyed, with their vessel, in Memphis. For so had the royal judges given their sentence—"for each Mytilenæan ten of the noblest Egyptians must forfeit life." King Psammenitus saw the train pass on, and knew his son was being led to death, but while the other Egyptians who sate around him wept and were sorely troubled, he showed no further sign than when he saw his daughter. And now, when they too were gone, it chanced that one of his former boon-companions, a man advanced in years, who had been stripped of all that he had and was a beggar, came where Psammenitus, son of Amasis, and the rest of the Egyptians were, asking alms from the soldiers. At this sight the king burst into tears, and weeping out aloud, called his friend by his name, and smote himself on the head. Now there were some who had been set to watch Psammenitus and see what he would do as each train went by; so these persons went and told Cambyses of his behaviour. Then he, astonished at what was done, sent a messenger to Psammenitus, and questioned him, saying, "Psammenitus, thy lord Cambyses asketh thee why, when thou sawest thy daughter brought to shame, and thy son on his way to death, thou didst neither utter cry nor shed tear, while to a beggar, who is, he hears, a stranger to thy race, thou gavest those marks of honour." To this question Psammenitus made answer, "O son of Cyrus, my own misfortunes were too great for tears; but the woe of my friend deserved them. When a man falls from splendour and plenty into beggary at the threshold of old age, one may well weep for him." When the messenger brought back this answer, Cambyses owned it was just; Crœsus, likewise, the Egyptians say, burst into tears—for he too had come into Egypt with Cambyses—and the Persians who were present wept. Even Cambyses himself was touched with pity, and he forthwith gave an order that the son of Psammenitus should be spared from the number of those appointed to die, and Psammenitus himself brought from the suburb into his presence.

15. The messengers were too late to save the life of Psammenitus' son, who had been cut in pieces the first of all; but they took Psammenitus himself and brought him before the king. Cambyses allowed him to live with him, and gave him no more harsh treatment; nay, could he have kept from intermeddling with

affairs, he might have recovered Egypt, and ruled it as governor. For the Persian wont is to treat the sons of kings with honour, and even to give their fathers' kingdoms to the children of such as revolt from them. There are many cases from which one may collect that this is the Persian rule, and especially those of Pausiris and Thannyras. Thannyras was son of Inarus the Libyan, and was allowed to succeed his father, as was also Pausiris, son of Amyrtæus; yet certainly no two persons ever did the Persians more damage than Amyrtæus and Inarus. In this case Psammenitus plotted evil, and received his reward accordingly. He was discovered to be stirring up revolt in Egypt, wherefore Cambyses, when his guilt clearly appeared, compelled him to drink bull's blood, which presently caused his death. Such was the end of Psammenitus.

16. After this Cambyses left Memphis, and went to Saïs, wishing to do that which he actually did on his arrival there. He entered the palace of Amasis, and straightway commanded that the body of the king should be brought forth from the sepulchre. When the attendants did according to his commandment, he further bade them scourge the body, and prick it with goads, and pluck the hair from it,[1] and heap upon it all manner of insults. The body, however, having been embalmed, resisted, and refused to come apart, do what they would to it; so the attendants grew weary of their work; whereupon Cambyses bade them take the corpse and burn it. This was truly an impious command to give, for the Persians hold fire to be a god, and never by any chance burn their dead. Indeed this practice is unlawful, both with them and with the Egyptians—with them for the reason above mentioned, since they deem it wrong to give the corpse of a man to a god; and with the Egyptians, because they believe fire to be a live animal, which eats whatever it can seize, and then, glutted with the food, dies with the matter which it feeds upon. Now to give a man's body to be devoured by beasts is in no wise agreeable to their customs, and indeed this is the very reason why they embalm their dead; namely, to prevent them from being eaten in the grave by worms. Thus Cambyses commanded what both nations accounted unlawful. According to the Egyptians,

[1] This is evidently a Greek statement, and not derived from the Egyptian priests. There was no hair to pluck out, the "head and all the body" of the kings and priests being shaved. The whole story may be doubted.

it was not Amasis who was thus treated, but another of their nation who was of about the same height. The Persians, believing this man's body to be the king's, abused it in the fashion described above. Amasis, they say, was warned by an oracle of what would happen to him after his death: in order, therefore, to prevent the impending fate, he buried the body, which afterwards received the blows, inside his own tomb near the entrance, commanding his son to bury him, when he died, in the furthest recess of the same sepulchre. For my own part I do not believe that these orders were ever given by Amasis; the Egyptians, as it seems to me, falsely assert it, to save their own dignity.

17. After this Cambyses took counsel with himself, and planned three expeditions. One was against the Carthaginians, another against the Ammonians, and a third against the long-lived Ethiopians, who dwelt in that part of Libya which borders upon the southern sea. He judged it best to despatch his fleet against Carthage and to send some portion of his land army to act against the Ammonians, while his spies went into Ethiopia, under the pretence of carrying presents to the king, but in reality to take note of all they saw, and especially to observe whether there was really what is called "the table of the Sun" in Ethiopia.

18. Now the table of the Sun according to the accounts given of it may be thus described:—It is a meadow in the skirts of their city full of the boiled flesh of all manner of beasts, which the magistrates are careful to store with meat every night, and where whoever likes may come and eat during the day. The people of the land say that the earth itself brings forth the food. Such is the description which is given of this table.

19. When Cambyses had made up his mind that the spies should go, he forthwith sent to Elephantiné for certain of the Icthyophagi who were acquainted with the Ethiopian tongue; and, while they were being fetched, issued orders to his fleet to sail against Carthage. But the Phœnicians said they would not go, since they were bound to the Carthaginians by solemn oaths, and since besides it would be wicked in them to make war on their own children. Now when the Phœnicians refused, the rest of the fleet was unequal to the undertaking; and so it was that the Carthaginians escaped, and were not enslaved by the Persians. Cambyses thought it not right to force the war upon the Phœnicians, because they had yielded themselves to the Persians, and because upon the

Phœnicians all his sea-service depended. The Cyprians had also joined the Persians of their own accord, and took part with them in the expedition against Egypt.

20. As soon as the Icthyophagi arrived from Elephantiné, Cambyses, having told them what they were to say, forthwith despatched them into Ethiopia with these following gifts: to wit, a purple robe, a gold chain for the neck, armlets, an alabaster box of myrrh, and a cask of palm wine. The Ethiopians to whom this embassy was sent are said to be the tallest and handsomest men in the whole world. In their customs they differ greatly from the rest of mankind, and particularly in the way they choose their kings; for they find out the man who is the tallest of all the citizens, and of strength equal to his height, and appoint him to rule over them.

21. The Icthyophagi on reaching this people, delivered the gifts to the king of the country, and spoke as follows:—"Cambyses, king of the Persians, anxious to become thy ally and sworn friend, has sent us to hold converse with thee, and to bear thee the gifts thou seest, which are the things wherein he himself delights the most." Hereon the Ethiopian, who knew they came as spies, made answer:—"The king of the Persians sent you not with these gifts because he much desired to become my sworn friend—nor is the account which ye give of yourselves true, for ye are come to search out my kingdom. Also your king is not a just man—for were he so, he had not coveted a land which is not his own, nor brought slavery on a people who never did him any wrong. Bear him this bow, and say—'The king of the Ethiops thus advises the king of the Persians—when the Persians can pull a bow of this strength thus easily, then let him come with an army of superior strength against the long-lived Ethiopians—till then, let him thank the gods that they have not put it into the heart of the sons of the Ethiops to covet countries which do not belong to them.'"

22. So speaking, he unstrung the bow, and gave it into the hands of the messengers. Then, taking the purple robe, he asked them what it was, and how it had been made. They answered truly, telling him concerning the purple, and the art of the dyer—whereat he observed "that the men were deceitful, and their garments also." Next he took the neck-chain and the armlets, and asked about them. So the Icthyophagi explained their use as ornaments. Then the king laughed, and fancying they

were fetters, said, "the Ethiopians had much stronger ones." Thirdly, he inquired about the myrrh, and when they told him how it was made and rubbed upon the limbs, he said the same as he had said about the robe. Last of all he came to the wine, and having learnt their way of making it, he drank a draught, which greatly delighted him; whereupon he asked what the Persian king was wont to eat, and to what age the longest-lived of the Persians had been known to attain. They told him that the king ate bread, and described the nature of wheat—adding that eighty years was the longest term of man's life among the Persians. Hereat he remarked, "It did not surprise him, if they fed on dirt, that they died so soon; indeed he was sure they never would have lived so long as eighty years, except for the refreshment they got from that drink (meaning the wine), wherein he confessed the Persians surpassed the Ethiopians."

23. The Icthyophagi then in their turn questioned the king concerning the term of life, and diet of his people, and were told that most of them lived to be a hundred and twenty years old, while some even went beyond that age—they ate boiled flesh, and had for their drink nothing but milk. When the Icthyophagi showed wonder at the number of the years, he led them to a fountain, wherein when they had washed, they found their flesh all glossy and sleek, as if they had bathed in oil—and a scent came from the spring like that of violets. The water was so weak, they said, that nothing would float in it, neither wood, nor any lighter substance, but all went to the bottom. If the account of this fountain be true, it would be their constant use of the water from it which makes them so long-lived. When they quitted the fountain the king led them to a prison, where the prisoners were all of them bound with fetters of gold. Among these Ethiopians copper is of all metals the most scarce and valuable. After they had seen the prison, they were likewise shown what is called "the table of the Sun."

24. Also, last of all, they were allowed to behold the coffins of the Ethiopians, which are made (according to report) of crystal, after the following fashion:—When the dead body has been dried, either in the Egyptian, or in some other manner, they cover the whole with gypsum, and adorn it with painting until it is as like the living man as possible. Then they place the body in a crystal pillar which has been hollowed out to receive it, crystal being dug up

in great abundance in their country, and of a kind very easy to work. You may see the corpse through the pillar within which it lies; and it neither gives out any unpleasant odour, nor is it in any respect unseemly; yet there is no part that is not as plainly visible as if the body were bare. The next of kin keep the crystal pillar in their houses for a full year from the time of the death, and give it the first fruits continually, and honour it with sacrifice. After the year is out they bear the pillar forth, and set it up near the town.

25. When the spies had now seen everything, they returned back to Egypt, and made report to Cambyses, who was stirred to anger by their words. Forthwith he set out on his march against the Ethiopians without having made any provision for the sustenance of his army, or reflected that he was about to wage war in the uttermost parts of the earth. Like a senseless madman as he was, no sooner did he receive the report of the Icthyophagi than he began his march, bidding the Greeks who were with his army remain where they were, and taking only his land force with him. At Thebes, which he passed through on his way, he detached from his main body some fifty thousand men, and sent them against the Ammonians with orders to carry the people into captivity, and burn the oracle of Jupiter. Meanwhile he himself went on with the rest of his forces against the Ethiopians. Before, however, he had accomplished one-fifth part of the distance, all that the army had in the way of provisions failed; whereupon the men began to eat the sumpter beasts, which shortly failed also. If then, at this time, Cambyses, seeing what was happening, had confessed himself in the wrong, and led his army back, he would have done the wisest thing that he could after the mistake made at the outset; but as it was, he took no manner of heed, but continued to march forwards. So long as the earth gave them anything, the soldiers sustained life by eating the grass and herbs; but when they came to the bare sand, a portion of them were guilty of a horrid deed: by tens they cast lots for a man, who was slain to be the food of the others. When Cambyses heard of these doings, alarmed at such cannibalism, he gave up his attack on Ethiopia, and retreating by the way he had come, reached Thebes, after he had lost vast numbers of his soldiers. From Thebes he marched down to Memphis, where he dismissed the Greeks, allowing them to sail home. And so ended the expedition against Ethiopia.

26. The men sent to attack the Ammonians, started from Thebes, having guides with them, and may be clearly traced as far as the city Oasis, which is inhabited by Samians, said to be of the tribe Æschrionia. The place is distant from Thebes seven days' journey across the sand, and is called in our tongue "the Island of the Blessed." Thus far the army is known to have made its way; but thenceforth nothing is to be heard of them, except what the Ammonians, and those who get their knowledge from them, report. It is certain they neither reached the Ammonians, nor even came back to Egypt. Further than this, the Ammonians relate as follows:—That the Persians set forth from Oasis across the sand, and had reached about half way between that place and themselves when, as they were at their midday meal, a wind arose from the south, strong and deadly, bringing with it vast columns of whirling sand, which entirely covered up the troops and caused them wholly to disappear. Thus, according to the Ammonians, did it fare with this army.

27. About the time when Cambyses arrived at Memphis, Apis appeared to the Egyptians. Now Apis is the god whom the Greeks call Epaphus. As soon as he appeared, straightway all the Egyptians arrayed themselves in their gayest garments, and fell to feasting and jollity: which when Cambyses saw, making sure that these rejoicings were on account of his own ill success, he called before him the officers who had charge of Memphis, and demanded of them—"Why, when he was in Memphis before, the Egyptians had done nothing of this kind, but waited until now, when he had returned with the loss of so many of his troops?" The officers made answer, "That one of their gods had appeared to them, a god who at long intervals of time had been accustomed to show himself in Egypt—and that always on his appearance the whole of Egypt feasted and kept jubilee." When Cambyses heard this, he told them that they lied, and as liars he condemned them all to suffer death.

28. When they were dead, he called the priests to his presence, and questioning them received the same answer; whereupon he observed, "That he would soon know whether a tame god had really come to dwell in Egypt" —and straightway, without another word, he bade them bring Apis to him. So they went out from his presence to fetch the god. Now this Apis, or Epaphus, is the calf of a cow which is never afterwards able to bear young. The Egyptians say that fire comes down from heaven upon the cow, which thereupon conceives Apis. The calf which is so called has the following marks:—He is black, with a square spot of white upon his forehead, and on his back the figure of an eagle; the hairs in his tail are double, and there is a beetle upon his tongue.

29. When the priests returned bringing Apis with them, Cambyses, like the harebrained person that he was, drew his dagger, and aimed at the belly of the animal, but missed his mark, and stabbed him in the thigh. Then he laughed, and said thus to the priests:—"Oh! blockheads, and think ye that gods become like this, of flesh and blood, and sensible to steel? A fit god indeed for Egyptians, such an one! But it shall cost you dear that you have made me your laughing-stock." When he had so spoken, he ordered those whose business it was to scourge the priests, and if they found any of the Egyptians keeping festival to put them to death. Thus was the feast stopped throughout the land of Egypt, and the priests suffered punishment. Apis, wounded in the thigh, lay some time pining in the temple; at last he died of his wound, and the priests buried him secretly without the knowledge of Cambyses.

30. And now Cambyses, who even before had not been quite in his right mind, was forthwith, as the Egyptians say, smitten with madness for this crime. The first of his outrages was the slaying of Smerdis, his full brother, whom he had sent back to Persia from Egypt out of envy, because he drew the bow brought from the Ethiopians by the Icthyophagi (which none of the other Persians were able to bend) the distance of two fingers' breadth. When Smerdis was departed into Persia, Cambyses had a vision in his sleep—he thought a messenger from Persia came to him with tidings that Smerdis sat upon the royal throne and with his head touched the heavens. Fearing therefore for himself, and thinking it likely that his brother would kill him and rule in his stead, Cambyses sent into Persia Prexaspes, whom he trusted beyond all the other Persians, bidding him put Smerdis to death. So this Prexaspes went up to Susa and slew Smerdis. Some say he killed him as they hunted together, others, that he took him down to the Erythræan Sea, and there drowned him.

31. This, it is said, was the first outrage which Cambyses committed. The second was

the slaying of his sister, who had accompanied him into Egypt, and lived with him as his wife, though she was his full sister, the daughter both of his father and his mother. The way wherein he had made her his wife was the following:—It was not the custom of the Persians, before his time, to marry their sisters—but Cambyses, happening to fall in love with one of his and wishing to take her to wife, as he knew that it was an uncommon thing, called together the royal judges, and put it to them, "whether there was any law which allowed a brother, if he wished, to marry his sister?" Now the royal judges are certain picked men among the Persians, who hold their office for life, or until they are found guilty of some misconduct. By them justice is administered in Persia, and they are the interpreters of the old laws, all disputes being referred to their decision. When Cambyses, therefore, put his question to these judges, they gave him an answer which was at once true and safe—"they did not find any law," they said, "allowing a brother to take his sister to wife, but they found a law, that the king of the Persians might do whatever he pleased." And so they neither warped the law through fear of Cambyses, nor ruined themselves by over stiffly maintaining the law; but they brought another quite distinct law to the king's help, which allowed him to have his wish. Cambyses, therefore, married the object of his love, and no long time afterwards he took to wife another sister. It was the younger of these who went with him into Egypt, and there suffered death at his hands.

32. Concerning the manner of her death, as concerning that of Smerdis, two different accounts are given. The story which the Greeks tell is that Cambyses had set a young dog to fight the cub of a lioness—his wife looking on at the time. Now the dog was getting the worse, when a pup of the same litter broke his chain, and came to his brother's aid—then the two dogs together fought the lion, and conquered him. The thing greatly pleased Cambyses, but his sister who was sitting by shed tears. When Cambyses saw this, he asked her why she wept: whereon she told him, that seeing the young dog come to his brother's aid made her think of Smerdis, whom there was none to help. For this speech, the Greeks say, Cambyses put her to death. But the Egyptians tell the story thus:—The two were sitting at table, when the sister took a lettuce, and stripping the leaves off, asked her brother "when he thought the lettuce looked the prettiest—when it had all its leaves on, or now that it was stripped?" He answered, "When the leaves were on." "But thou," she rejoined, "hast done as I did to the lettuce, and made bare the house of Cyrus." Then Cambyses was wroth, and sprang fiercely upon her, though she was with child at the time. And so it came to pass that she miscarried and died.

33. Thus mad was Cambyses upon his own kindred, and this either from his usage of Apis, or from some other among the many causes from which calamities are wont to arise. They say that from his birth he was afflicted with a dreadful disease, the disorder which some call "the sacred sickness."[1] It would be by no means strange, therefore, if his mind were affected in some degree, seeing that his body laboured under so sore a malady.

34. He was mad also upon others besides his kindred; among the rest, upon Prexaspes, the man whom he esteemed beyond all the rest of the Persians, who carried his messages, and whose son held the office—an honour of no small account in Persia—of his cupbearer. Him Cambyses is said to have once addressed as follows:—"What sort of man, Prexaspes, do the Persians think me? What do they say of me?" Prexaspes answered, "Oh! sire, they praise thee greatly in all things but one—they say thou art too much given to love of wine." Such Prexaspes told him was the judgment of the Persians; whereupon Cambyses, full of rage, made answer, "What? they say now that I drink too much wine, and so have lost my senses, and am gone out of my mind! Then their former speeches about me were untrue." For once, when the Persians were sitting with him, and Crœsus was by, he had asked them, "What sort of man they thought him compared to his father Cyrus?" Hereon they had answered, "That he surpassed his father, for he was lord of all that his father ever ruled, and further had made himself master of Egypt, and the sea." Then Crœsus, who was standing near, and misliked the comparison, spoke thus to Cambyses: "In my judgment, O son of Cyrus, thou art not equal to thy father, for thou hast not yet left behind thee such a son as he." Cambyses was delighted when he heard this reply, and praised the judgment of Crœsus.

35. Recollecting these answers, Cambyses spoke fiercely to Prexaspes, saying, "Judge now thyself, Prexaspes, whether the Persians tell the truth, or whether it is not they who are mad for speaking as they do. Look there now

[1] Epilepsy.

at thy son standing in the vestibule—if I shoot and hit him right in the middle of the heart, it will be plain the Persians have no grounds for what they say: if I miss him, then I allow that the Persians are right, and that I am out of my mind." So speaking he drew his bow to the full, and struck the boy, who straightway fell down dead. Then Cambyses ordered the body to be opened, and the wound examined; and when the arrow was found to have entered the heart, the king was quite overjoyed, and said to the father with a laugh, "Now thou seest plainly, Prexaspes, that it is not I who am mad, but the Persians who have lost their senses. I pray thee tell me, sawest thou ever mortal man send an arrow with a better aim?" Prexaspes, seeing that the king was not in his right mind, and fearing for himself, replied, "Oh! my lord, I do not think that God himself could shoot so dexterously." Such was the outrage which Cambyses committed at this time: at another, he took twelve of the noblest Persians, and, without bringing any charge worthy of death against them, buried them all up to the neck.

36. Hereupon Crœsus the Lydian thought it right to admonish Cambyses, which he did in these words following:—"Oh! king, allow not thyself to give way entirely to thy youth, and the heat of thy temper, but check and control thyself. It is well to look to consequences, and in forethought is true wisdom. Thou layest hold of men, who are thy fellow-citizens, and, without cause of complaint, slayest them —thou even puttest children to death—bethink thee now, if thou shalt often do things like these, will not the Persians rise in revolt against thee? It is by thy father's wish that I offer thee advice; he charged me strictly to give thee such counsel as I might see to be most for thy good." In thus advising Cambyses, Crœsus meant nothing but what was friendly. But Cambyses answered him, "Dost thou presume to offer me advice? Right well thou ruledst thy own country when thou wert a king, and right sage advice thou gavest thy father Cyrus, bidding him cross the Araxes and fight the Massagetæ in their own land, when they were willing to have passed over into ours. By thy misdirection of thine own affairs thou broughtest ruin upon thyself, and by thy bad counsel, which he followed, thou broughtest ruin upon Cyrus, my father. But thou shalt not escape punishment now, for I have long been seeking to find some occasion against thee." As he thus spoke, Cambyses took up his bow to shoot at

Crœsus; but Crœsus ran hastily out, and escaped. So when Cambyses found that he could not kill him with his bow, he bade his servants seize him, and put him to death. The servants, however, who knew their master's humour, thought it best to hide Crœsus; that so, if Cambyses relented, and asked for him, they might bring him out, and get a reward for having saved his life—if, on the other hand, he did not relent, or regret the loss, they might then despatch him. Not long afterwards, Cambyses did in fact regret the loss of Crœsus, and the servants, perceiving it, let him know that he was still alive. "I am glad," said he, "that Crœsus lives, but as for you who saved him, ye shall not escape my vengeance, but shall all of you be put to death." And he did even as he had said.

37. Many other wild outrages of this sort did Cambyses commit, both upon the Persians and the allies, while he still stayed at Memphis; among the rest he opened the ancient sepulchres, and examined the bodies that were buried in them. He likewise went into the temple of Vulcan, and made great sport of the image. For the image of Vulcan is very like the Patæci of the Phœnicians, wherewith they ornament the prows of their ships of war. If persons have not seen these, I will explain in a different way—it is a figure resembling that of a pigmy. He went also into the temple of the Cabiri, which it is unlawful for any one to enter except the priests, and not only made sport of the images, but even burnt them. They are made like the statue of Vulcan, who is said to have been their father.

38. Thus it appears certain to me, by a great variety of proofs, that Cambyses was raving mad; he would not else have set himself to make a mock of holy rites and long-established usages. For if one were to offer men to choose out of all the customs in the world such as seemed to them the best, they would examine the whole number, and end by preferring their own; so convinced are they that their own usages far surpass those of all others. Unless, therefore, a man was mad, it is not likely that he would make sport of such matters. That people have this feeling about their laws may be seen by very many proofs: among others, by the following. Darius, after he had got the kingdom, called into his presence certain Greeks who were at hand, and asked—"What he should pay them to eat the bodies of their fathers when they died?" To which they answered, that there was no sum that would

tempt them to do such a thing. He then sent
for certain Indians, of the race called Callati-
ans, men who eat their fathers, and asked
them, while the Greeks stood by, and knew
by the help of an interpreter all that was said
—"What he should give them to burn the bodies of their fathers at their decease?" The Indians exclaimed aloud, and bade him forbear
such language. Such is men's wont herein; and
Pindar was right, in my judgment, when he
said, "Law is the king o'er all."

39. While Cambyses was carrying on this
war in Egypt, the Lacedæmonians likewise
sent a force to Samos against Polycrates, the
son of Æaces, who had by insurrection made
himself master of that island. At the outset he
divided the state into three parts, and shared
the kingdom with his brothers, Pantagnôtus
and Syloson; but later, having killed the former and banished the latter, who was the
younger of the two, he held the whole island.
Hereupon he made a contract of friendship
with Amasis the Egyptian king, sending him
gifts, and receiving from him others in return.
In a little while his power so greatly increased,
that the fame of it went abroad throughout Ionia and the rest of Greece. Wherever he turned
his arms, success waited on him. He had a fleet
of a hundred penteconters, and bowmen to the
number of a thousand. Herewith he plundered
all, without distinction of friend or foe; for he
argued that a friend was better pleased if you
gave him back what you had taken from him,
than if you spared him at the first. He captured many of the islands, and several towns
upon the mainland. Among his other doings
he overcame the Lesbians in a sea-fight, when
they came with all their forces to the help of
Miletus, and made a number of them prisoners. These persons, laden with fetters, dug the
moat which surrounds the castle at Samos.

40. The exceeding good fortune of Polycrates did not escape the notice of Amasis, who
was much disturbed thereat. When therefore
his successes continued increasing, Amasis
wrote him the following letter, and sent it to
Samos. "Amasis to Polycrates thus sayeth: It
is a pleasure to hear of a friend and ally pros-
pering, but thy exceeding prosperity does not
cause me joy, forasmuch as I know that the gods
are envious. My wish for myself and for those
whom I love is to be now successful, and now
to meet with a check; thus passing through life
amid alternate good and ill, rather than with
perpetual good fortune. For never yet did I
hear tell of any one succeeding in all his under-

takings, who did not meet with calamity at
last, and come to utter ruin. Now, therefore,
give ear to my words, and meet thy good luck
in this way: bethink thee which of all thy treasures thou valuest most and canst least bear to
part with; take it, whatsoever it be, and throw
it away, so that it may be sure never to come
any more into the sight of man. Then, if thy
good fortune be not thenceforth chequered
with ill, save thyself from harm by again doing
as I have counselled."

41. When Polycrates read this letter, and
perceived that the advice of Amasis was good,
he considered carefully with himself which of
the treasures that he had in store it would
grieve him most to lose. After much thought
he made up his mind that it was a signet-ring
which he was wont to wear, an emerald set in
gold, the workmanship of Theodore, son of
Têlecles, a Samian. So he determined to throw
this away; and, manning a penteconter, he
went on board, and bade the sailors put out
into the open sea. When he was now a long
way from the island, he took the ring from his
finger, and, in the sight of all those who were
on board, flung it into the deep. This done, he
returned home, and gave vent to his sorrow.

42. Now it happened five or six days afterwards that a fisherman caught a fish so large
and beautiful that he thought it well deserved
to be made a present of to the king. So he took
it with him to the gate of the palace, and said
that he wanted to see Polycrates. Then Polycrates allowed him to come in, and the fisherman gave him the fish with these words following—"Sir king, when I took this prize, I
thought I would not carry it to market, though
I am a poor man who live by my trade. I said
to myself, it is worthy of Polycrates and his
greatness; and so I brought it here to give it to
you." The speech pleased the king, who thus
spoke in reply:—"Thou didst right well,
friend, and I am doubly indebted, both for the
gift, and for the speech. Come now, and sup
with me." So the fisherman went home, es-
teeming it a high honour that he had been
asked to sup with the king. Meanwhile the
servants, on cutting open the fish, found the
signet of their master in its belly. No sooner
did they see it than they seized upon it, and
hastening to Polycrates with great joy, restored
it to him, and told him in what way it had
been found. The king, who saw something
providential in the matter, forthwith wrote a
letter to Amasis, telling him all that had happened, what he had himself done, and what

had been the upshot—and despatched the letter to Egypt.

43. When Amasis had read the letter of Polycrates, he perceived that it does not belong to man to save his fellow-man from the fate which is in store for him; likewise he felt certain that Polycrates would end ill, as he prospered in everything, even finding what he had thrown away. So he sent a herald to Samos, and dissolved the contract of friendship. This he did, that when the great and heavy misfortune came, he might escape the grief which he would have felt if the sufferer had been his bond-friend.

44. It was with this Polycrates, so fortunate in every undertaking, that the Lacedæmonians now went to war. Certain Samians, the same who afterwards founded the city of Cydonia in Crete, had earnestly intreated their help. For Polycrates, at the time when Cambyses, son of Cyrus, was gathering together an armament against Egypt, had sent to beg him not to omit to ask aid from Samos; whereupon Cambyses with much readiness despatched a messenger to the island, and made request that Polycrates would give some ships to the naval force which he was collecting against Egypt. Polycrates straightway picked out from among the citizens such as he thought most likely to stir revolt against him, and manned with them forty triremes, which he sent to Cambyses, bidding him keep the men safe, and never allow them to return home.

45. Now some accounts say that these Samians did not reach Egypt; for that when they were off Carpathus, they took counsel together and resolved to sail no further. But others maintain that they did go to Egypt, and, finding themselves watched, deserted, and sailed back to Samos. There Polycrates went out against them with his fleet, and a battle was fought and gained by the exiles; after which they disembarked upon the island and engaged the land forces of Polycrates, but were defeated, and so sailed off to Lacedæmon. Some relate that the Samians from Egypt overcame Polycrates, but it seems to me untruly; for had the Samians been strong enough to conquer Polycrates by themselves, they would not have needed to call in the aid of the Lacedæmonians. And moreover, it is not likely that a king who had in his pay so large a body of foreign mercenaries, and maintained likewise such a force of native bowmen, would have been worsted by an army so small as that of the returned Samians. As for his own subjects, to

hinder them from betraying him and joining the exiles, Polycrates shut up their wives and children in the sheds built to shelter his ships, and was ready to burn sheds and all in case of need.

46. When the banished Samians reached Sparta, they had audience of the magistrates, before whom they made a long speech, as was natural with persons greatly in want of aid. Accordingly at this first sitting the Spartans answered them that they had forgotten the first half of their speech, and could make nothing of the remainder. Afterwards the Samians had another audience, whereat they simply said, showing a bag which they had brought with them, "The bag wants flour." The Spartans answered that they did not need to have said "the bag"; however, they resolved to give them aid.

47. Then the Lacedæmonians made ready and set forth to the attack of Samos, from a motive of gratitude, if we may believe the Samians, because the Samians had once sent ships to their aid against the Messenians; but as the Spartans themselves say, not so much from any wish to assist the Samians who begged their help, as from a desire to punish the people who had seized the bowl which they sent to Crœsus, and the corselet which Amasis, king of Egypt, sent as a present to them. The Samians made prize of this corselet the year before they took the bowl—it was of linen, and had a vast number of figures of animals inwoven into its fabric, and was likewise embroidered with gold and tree-wool. What is most worthy of admiration in it is that each of the twists, although of fine texture, contains within it three hundred and sixty threads, all of them clearly visible. The corselet which Amasis gave to the temple of Minerva in Lindus is just such another.

48. The Corinthians likewise right willingly lent a helping hand towards the expedition against Samos; for a generation earlier, about the time of the seizure of the wine-bowl, they too had suffered insult at the hands of the Samians. It happened that Periander, son of Cypselus, had taken three hundred boys, children of the chief nobles among the Corcyræans, and sent them to Alyattes for eunuchs; the men who had them in charge touched at Samos on their way to Sardis; whereupon the Samians, having found out what was to become of the boys when they reached that city, first prompted them to take sanctuary at the temple of Diana; and after

this, when the Corinthians, as they were for-bidden to tear the suppliants from the holy place, sought to cut off from them all supplies of food, invented a festival in their behalf, which they celebrate to this day with the self-same rites. Each evening, as night closed in, during the whole time that the boys continued there, choirs of youths and virgins were placed about the temple, carrying in their hands cakes made of sesame and honey, in order that the Corcyræan boys might snatch the cakes, and so get enough to live upon.

49. And this went on for so long, that at last the Corinthians who had charge of the boys gave them up, and took their departure, upon which the Samians conveyed them back to Corcyra. If now, after the death of Periander, the Corinthians and Corcyræans had been good friends, it is not to be imagined that the former would ever have taken part in the expedition against Samos for such a reason as this; but as, in fact, the two people have always, ever since the first settlement of the island, been enemies to one another, this outrage was remembered, and the Corinthians bore the Samians a grudge for it. Periander had chosen the youths from among the first families in Corcyra, and sent them a present to Alyattes, to avenge a wrong which he had received. For it was the Cor-cyræans who began the quarrel and injured Periander by an outrage of a horrid nature.

50. After Periander had put to death his wife Melissa, it chanced that on this first afflic-tion a second followed of a different kind. His wife had borne him two sons, and one of them had now reached the age of seventeen, the other of eighteen years, when their mother's father, Procles, tyrant of Epidaurus, asked them to his court. They went, and Procles treated them with much kindness, as was nat-ural, considering they were his own daughter's children. At length, when the time for parting came, Procles, as he was sending them on their way, said, "Know you now, my children, who it was that caused your mother's death?" The elder son took no account of this speech, but the younger, whose name was Lycophron, was sorely troubled at it—so much so, that when he got back to Corinth, looking upon his father as his mother's murderer, he would neither speak to him, nor answer when spoken to, nor utter a word in reply to all his questionings. So Periander at last, growing furious at such be-haviour, banished him from his house.

51. The younger son gone, he turned to the elder and asked him, "what it was that their grandfather had said to them?" Then he re-lated in how kind and friendly a fashion he had received them; but, not having taken any notice of the speech which Procles had uttered at parting, he quite forgot to mention it. Peri-ander insisted that it was not possible this should be all—their grandfather must have given them some hint or other—and he went on pressing him, till at last the lad remembered the parting speech and told it. Periander, after he had turned the whole matter over in his thoughts, and felt unwilling to give way at all, sent a messenger to the persons who had opened their houses to his outcast son, and for-bade them to harbour him. Then the boy, when he was chased from one friend, sought refuge with another, but was driven from shelter to shelter by the threats of his father, who men-aced all those that took him in, and command-ed them to shut their doors against him. Still, as fast as he was forced to leave one house he went to another, and was received by the inmates; for his acquaintance, although in no small alarm, yet gave him shelter, as he was Periander's son.

52. At last Periander made proclamation that whoever harboured his son or even spoke to him, should forfeit a certain sum of money to Apollo. On hearing this no one any longer liked to take him in, or even to hold converse with him, and he himself did not think it right to seek to do what was forbidden; so, abiding by his resolve, he made his lodging in the pub-lic porticos. When four days had passed in this way, Periander, seeing how wretched his son was, that he neither washed nor took any food, felt moved with compassion towards him; wherefore, foregoing his anger, he approached him, and said, "Which is better, oh! my son, to fare as now thou farest, or to receive my crown and all the good things that I possess, on the one condition of submitting thyself to thy fa-ther? See, now, though my own child, and lord of this wealthy Corinth, thou hast brought thyself to a beggar's life, because thou must re-sist and treat with anger him whom it least be-hoves thee to oppose. If there has been a calam-ity, and thou bearest me ill will on that ac-count, bethink thee that I too feel it, and am the greatest sufferer, in as much as it was by me that the deed was done. For thyself, now that thou knowest how much better a thing it is to be envied than pitied, and how dangerous it is to indulge anger against parents and su-periors, come back with me to thy home." With such words as these did Periander chide his son; but the son made no reply, except to re-

mind his father that he was indebted to the god in the penalty for coming and holding converse with him. Then Periander knew that there was no cure for the youth's malady, nor means of overcoming it; so he prepared a ship and sent him away out of his sight to Corcyra, which island at that time belonged to him. As for Procles, Periander, regarding him as the true author of all his present troubles, went to war with him as soon as his son was gone, and not only made himself master of his kingdom Epidaurus, but also took Procles himself, and carried him into captivity.

53. As time went on, and Periander came to be old, he found himself no longer equal to the oversight and management of affairs. Seeing, therefore, in his eldest son no manner of ability, but knowing him to be dull and blockish, he sent to Corcyra and recalled Lycophron to take the kingdom. Lycophron, however, did not even deign to ask the bearer of this message a question. But Periander's heart was set upon the youth, so he sent again to him, this time by his own daughter, the sister of Lycophron, who would, he thought, have more power to persuade him than any other person. Then she, when she reached Corcyra, spoke thus with her brother:—"Dost thou wish the kingdom, brother, to pass into strange hands, and our father's wealth to be made a prey, rather than thyself return to enjoy it? Come back home with me, and cease to punish thyself. It is scant gain, this obstinacy. Why seek to cure evil by evil? Mercy, remember, is by many set above justice. Many, also, while pushing their mother's claims have forfeited their father's fortune. Power is a slippery thing—it has many suitors; and he is old and stricken in years—let not thy own inheritance go to another." Thus did the sister, who had been tutored by Periander what to say, urge all the arguments most likely to have weight with her brother. He however made answer, "That so long as he knew his father to be still alive, he would never go back to Corinth." When the sister brought Periander this reply, he sent to his son a third time by a herald, and said he would come himself to Corcyra, and let his son take his place at Corinth as heir to his kingdom. To these terms Lycophron agreed; and Periander was making ready to pass into Corcyra and his son to return to Corinth, when the Corcyræans, being informed of what was taking place, to keep Periander away, put the young man to death. For this reason it was that Periander took vengeance on the Corcyræans.

54. The Lacedæmonians arrived before Samos with a mighty armament, and forthwith laid siege to the place. In one of the assaults upon the walls, they forced their way to the top of the tower which stands by the sea on the side where the suburb is, but Polycrates came in person to the rescue with a strong force, and beat them back. Meanwhile at the upper tower, which stood on the ridge of the hill, the besieged, both mercenaries and Samians, made a sally; but after they had withstood the Lacedæmonians a short time, they fled backwards, and the Lacedæmonians, pressing upon them, slew numbers.

55. If now all who were present had behaved that day like Archias and Lycôpas, two of the Lacedæmonians, Samos might have been taken. For these two heroes, following hard upon the flying Samians, entered the city along with them, and, being all alone, and their retreat cut off, were slain within the walls of the place. I myself once fell in with the grandson of this Archias, a man named Archias like his grandsire, and the son of Samius, whom I met at Pitana, to which canton he belonged. He respected the Samians beyond all other foreigners, and he told me that his father was called Samius, because his grandfather Archias died in Samos so gloriously, and that the reason why he respected the Samians so greatly was that his grandsire was buried with public honours by the Samian people.

56. The Lacedæmonians besieged Samos during forty days, but not making any progress before the place, they raised the siege at the end of that time, and returned home to the Peloponnese. There is a silly tale told that Polycrates struck a quantity of the coin of his country in lead, and, coating it with gold, gave it to the Lacedæmonians, who on receiving it took their departure.

This was the first expedition into Asia of the Lacedæmonian Dorians.

57. The Samians who had fought against Polycrates, when they knew that the Lacedæmonians were about to forsake them, left Samos themselves, and sailed to Siphnos. They happened to be in want of money; and the Siphnians at that time were at the height of their greatness, no islanders having so much wealth as they. There were mines of gold and silver in their country, and of so rich a yield, that from a tithe of the ores the Siphnians furnished out a treasury at Delphi which was on a par with the grandest there. What the mines yielded was divided year by year among

the citizens. At the time when they formed the treasury, the Siphnians consulted the oracle, and asked whether their good things would remain to them many years. The Pythoness made answer as follows:—

When the Prytanies' seat shines white in the island of Siphnos,
White-browed all the forum—need then of a true seer's wisdom—
Danger will threat from a wooden host, and a herald in scarlet.

Now about this time the forum of the Siphnians and their townhall or prytaneum had been adorned with Parian marble.

58. The Siphnians, however, were unable to understand the oracle, either at the time when it was given, or afterwards on the arrival of the Samians. For these last no sooner came to anchor off the island than they sent one of their vessels, with an ambassage on board, to the city. All ships in these early times were painted with vermilion; and this was what the Pythoness had meant when she told them to beware of danger "from a wooden host, and a herald in scarlet." So the ambassadors came ashore and besought the Siphnians to lend them ten talents; but the Siphnians refused, whereupon the Samians began to plunder their lands. Tidings of this reached the Siphnians, who straightway sallied forth to save their crops; then a battle was fought, in which the Siphnians suffered defeat, and many of their number were cut off from the city by the Samians, after which these latter forced the Siphnians to give them a hundred talents.

59. With this money they bought of the Hermionians the island of Hydrea, off the coast of the Peloponnese, and this they gave in trust to the Trœzenians, to keep for them, while they themselves went on to Crete, and founded the city of Cydonia. They had not meant, when they set sail, to settle there, but only to drive out the Zacynthians from the island. However they rested at Cydonia, where they flourished greatly for five years. It was they who built the various temples that may still be seen at that place, and among them the fane of Dictyna. But in the sixth year they were attacked by the Eginetans, who beat them in a sea-fight, and, with the help of the Cretans, reduced them all to slavery. The beaks of their ships, which carried the figure of a wild boar, they sawed off, and laid them up in the temple of Minerva in Egina. The Eginetans took part against the Samians on account of an ancient grudge, since the Samians had

first, when Amphicrates was king of Samos, made war on them and done great harm to their island, suffering, however, much damage also themselves. Such was the reason which moved the Eginetans to make this attack.

60. I have dwelt the longer on the affairs of the Samians, because three of the greatest works in all Greece were made by them. One is a tunnel, under a hill one hundred and fifty fathoms high, carried entirely through the base of the hill, with a mouth at either end. The length of the cutting is seven furlongs—the height and width are each eight feet. Along the whole course there is a second cutting, twenty cubits deep and three feet broad, whereby water is brought, through pipes, from an abundant source into the city. The architect of this tunnel was Eupalinus, son of Naustrophus, a Megarian. Such is the first of their great works; the second is a mole in the sea, which goes all round the harbour, near twenty fathoms deep, and in length above two furlongs. The third is a temple; the largest of all the temples known to us, whereof Rhœcus, son of Phileus, a Samian, was first architect. Because of these works I have dwelt the longer on the affairs of Samos.

61. While Cambyses, son of Cyrus, after losing his senses, still lingered in Egypt, two Magi, brothers, revolted against him. One of them had been left in Persia by Cambyses as comptroller of his household; and it was he who began the revolt. Aware that Smerdis was dead, and that his death was hid and known to few of the Persians, while most believed that he was still alive, he laid his plan, and made a bold stroke for the crown. He had a brother—the same of whom I spoke before as his partner in the revolt—who happened greatly to resemble Smerdis the son of Cyrus, whom Cambyses his brother had put to death. And not only was this brother of his like Smerdis in person, but he also bore the selfsame name, to wit Smerdis. Patizeithes, the other Magus, having persuaded him that he would carry the whole business through, took him and made him sit upon the royal throne. Having so done, he sent heralds through all the land, to Egypt and elsewhere, to make proclamation to the troops that henceforth they were to obey Smerdis the son of Cyrus, and not Cambyses.

62. The other heralds therefore made proclamation as they were ordered, and likewise the herald whose place it was to proceed into Egypt. He, when he reached Agbatana in

Syria, finding Cambyses and his army there, went straight into the middle of the host, and standing forth before them all, made the proclamation which Patizeithes the Magus had commanded. Cambyses no sooner heard him, than believing that what the herald said was true, and imagining that he had been betrayed by Prexaspes (who, he supposed, had not put Smerdis to death when sent into Persia for that purpose), he turned his eyes full upon Prexaspes, and said, "Is this the way, Prexaspes, that thou didst my errand?" "Oh! my liege," answered the other, "there is no truth in the tidings that Smerdis thy brother has revolted against thee, nor hast thou to fear in time to come any quarrel, great or small, with that man. With my own hands I wrought thy will on him, and with my own hands I buried him. If of a truth the dead can leave their graves, expect Astyages the Mede to rise and fight against thee; but if the course of nature be the same as formerly, then be sure no ill will ever come upon thee from this quarter. Now, therefore, my counsel is that we send in pursuit of the herald, and strictly question him who it was that charged him to bid us obey king Smerdis."

63. When Prexaspes had so spoken, and Cambyses had approved his words, the herald was forthwith pursued, and brought back to the king. Then Prexaspes said to him, "Sirrah, thou bear'st us a message, sayst thou, from Smerdis, son of Cyrus. Now answer truly, and go thy way scathless. Did Smerdis have thee to his presence and give thee thy orders, or hadst thou them from one of his officers?" The herald answered, "Truly I have not set eyes on Smerdis son of Cyrus, since the day when king Cambyses led the Persians into Egypt. The man who gave me my orders was the Magus that Cambyses left in charge of the household; but he said that Smerdis son of Cyrus sent you the message." In all this the herald spoke nothing but the strict truth. Then Cambyses said thus to Prexaspes:—"Thou art free from all blame, Prexaspes, since, as a right good man, thou hast not failed to do the thing which I commanded. But tell me now, which of the Persians can have taken the name of Smerdis, and revolted from me?" "I think, my liege," he answered, "that I apprehend the whole business. The men who have risen in revolt against thee are the two Magi, Patizeithes, who was left comptroller of thy household, and his brother, who is named Smerdis."

64. Cambyses no sooner heard the name of

Smerdis than he was struck with the truth of Prexaspes' words, and the fulfilment of his own dream—the dream, I mean, which he had in former days, when one appeared to him in his sleep and told him that Smerdis sate upon the royal throne, and with his head touched the heavens. So when he saw that he had needlessly slain his brother Smerdis, he wept and bewailed his loss: after which, smarting with vexation as he thought of all his ill luck, he sprang hastily upon his steed, meaning to march his army with all haste to Susa against the Magus. As he made his spring, the button of his sword-sheath fell off, and the bared point entered his thigh, wounding him exactly where he had himself once wounded the Egyptian god Apis. Then Cambyses, feeling that he had got his death-wound, inquired the name of the place where he was, and was answered, "Agbatana." Now before this it had been told him by the oracle at Buto that he should end his days at Agbatana. He, however, had understood the Median Agbatana, where all his treasures were, and had thought that he should die there in a good old age; but the oracle meant Agbatana in Syria. So when Cambyses heard the name of the place, the double shock that he had received, from the revolt of the Magus and from his wound, brought him back to his senses. And he understood now the true meaning of the oracle, and said, "Here then Cambyses, son of Cyrus, is doomed to die."

65. At this time he said no more; but twenty days afterwards he called to his presence all the chief Persians who were with the army, and addressed them as follows:—"Persians, needs must I tell you now what hitherto I have striven with the greatest care to keep concealed. When I was in Egypt I saw in my sleep a vision, which would that I had never beheld! I thought a messenger came to me from my home, and told me that Smerdis sate upon the royal throne, and with his head touched the heavens. Then I feared to be cast from my throne by Smerdis my brother, and I did what was more hasty than wise. Ah! truly, do what they may, it is impossible for men to turn aside the coming fate. I, in my folly, sent Prexaspes to Susa to put my brother to death. So this great woe was accomplished, and I then lived without fear, never imagining that, after Smerdis was dead, I need dread revolt from any other. But herein I had quite mistaken what was about to happen, and so I slew my brother without any need, and nevertheless have lost my crown. For it was Smerdis the Magus, and

not Smerdis my brother, of whose rebellion God forewarned me by the vision. The deed is done, however, and Smerdis, son of Cyrus, be sure is lost to you. The Magi have the royal power—Patizeithes, whom I left at Susa to overlook my household, and Smerdis his brother. There was one who would have been bound beyond all others to avenge the wrongs I have suffered from these Magians, but he, alas! has perished by a horrid fate, deprived of life by those nearest and dearest to him. In his default, nothing now remains for me but to tell you, O Persians, what I would wish to have done after I have breathed my last. Therefore, in the name of the gods that watch over our royal house, I charge you all, and specially such of you as are Achæmenids, that ye do not tamely allow the kingdom to go back to the Medes. Recover it one way or another, by force or fraud; by fraud, if it is by fraud that they have seized on it; by force, if force has helped them in their enterprise. Do this, and then may your land bring you forth fruit abundantly, and your wives bear children, and your herds increase, and freedom be your portion for ever: but do it not—make no brave struggle to regain the kingdom—and then my curse be on you, and may the opposite of all these things happen to you—and not only so, but may you, one and all, perish at the last by such a fate as mine!" Then Cambyses, when he left speaking, bewailed his whole misfortune from beginning to end.

66. Whereupon the Persians, seeing their king weep, rent the garments that they had on, and uttered lamentable cries; after which, as the bone presently grew carious, and the limb gangrened, Cambyses, son of Cyrus, died. He had reigned in all seven years and five months, and left no issue behind him, male or female. The Persians who had heard his words, put no faith in anything that he said concerning the Magi having the royal power; but believed that he spoke out of hatred towards Smerdis, and had invented the tale of his death to cause the whole Persian race to rise up in arms against him. Thus they were convinced that it was Smerdis the son of Cyrus who had rebelled and now sate on the throne. For Prexaspes stoutly denied that he had slain Smerdis, since it was not safe for him, after Cambyses was dead, to allow that a son of Cyrus had met with death at his hands.

67. Thus then Cambyses died, and the Magus now reigned in security, and passed himself off for Smerdis the son of Cyrus. And so went by the seven months which were wanting to complete the eighth year of Cambyses. His subjects, while his reign lasted, received great benefits from him, insomuch that, when he died, all the dwellers in Asia mourned his loss exceedingly, except only the Persians. For no sooner did he come to the throne than forthwith he sent round to every nation under his rule, and granted them freedom from war-service and from taxes for the space of three years.

68. In the eighth month, however, it was discovered who he was in the mode following. There was a man called Otanes, the son of Pharnaspes, who for rank and wealth was equal to the greatest of the Persians. This Otanes was the first to suspect that the Magus was not Smerdis the son of Cyrus, and to surmise moreover who he really was. He was led to guess the truth by the king never quitting the citadel, and never calling before him any of the Persian noblemen. As soon, therefore, as his suspicions were aroused he adopted the following measures:—One of his daughters, who was called Phædima, had been married to Cambyses, and was taken to wife, together with the rest of Cambyses' wives, by the Magus. To this daughter Otanes sent a message, and inquired of her "who it was whose bed she shared,—was it Smerdis the son of Cyrus, or was it some other man?" Phædima in reply declared she did not know—Smerdis the son of Cyrus she had never seen, and so she could not tell whose bed she shared. Upon this Otanes sent a second time, and said, "If thou dost not know Smerdis son of Cyrus thyself, ask queen Atossa who it is with whom ye both live—she cannot fail to know her own brother." To this the daughter made answer, "I can neither get speech with Atossa, nor with any of the women who lodge in the palace. For no sooner did this man, be he who he may, obtain the kingdom, than he parted us from one another, and gave us all separate chambers."

69. This made the matter seem still more plain to Otanes. Nevertheless he sent a third message to his daughter in these words following:—"Daughter, thou art of noble blood—thou wilt not shrink from a risk which thy father bids thee encounter. If this fellow be not Smerdis the son of Cyrus, but the man whom I think him to be, his boldness in taking thee to be his wife, and lording it over the Persians, must not be allowed to pass unpunished. Now therefore do as I command—when next he passes the night with thee, wait till

thou art sure he is fast asleep, and then feel for his ears. If thou findest him to have ears, then believe him to be Smerdis the son of Cyrus, but if he has none, know him for Smerdis the Magian." Phædima returned for answer, "It would be a great risk. If he was without ears, and caught her feeling for them, she well knew he would make away with her—nevertheless she would venture." So Otanes got his daughter's promise that she would do as he desired. Now Smerdis the Magian had had his ears cut off in the lifetime of Cyrus son of Cambyses, as a punishment for a crime of no slight heinousness. Phædima therefore, Otanes' daughter, bent on accomplishing what she had promised her father, when her turn came, and she was taken to the bed of the Magus (in Persia a man's wives sleep with him in their turns), waited till he was sound asleep, and then felt for his ears. She quickly perceived that he had no ears; and of this, as soon as day dawned, she sent word to her father.

70. Then Otanes took to him two of the chief Persians, Aspathines and Gobryas, men whom it was most advisable to trust in such a matter, and told them everything. Now they had already of themselves suspected how the matter stood. When Otanes therefore laid his reasons before them they at once came into his views; and it was agreed that each of the three should take as companion in the work the Persian in whom he placed the greatest confidence. Then Otanes chose Intaphernes, Gobryas Megabyzus, and Aspathines Hydarnes. After the number had thus become six, Darius, the son of Hystaspes, arrived at Susa from Persia, whereof his father was governor. On his coming it seemed good to the six to take him likewise into their counsels.

71. After this, the men, being now seven in all, met together to exchange oaths, and hold discourse with one another. And when it came to the turn of Darius to speak his mind, he said as follows:—"Methought no one but I knew that Smerdis, the son of Cyrus, was not now alive, and that Smerdis the Magian ruled over us; on this account I came hither with speed, to compass the death of the Magian. But as it seems the matter is known to you all, and not to me only, my judgment is that we should act at once, and not any longer delay. For to do so were not well." Otanes spoke upon this:—"Son of Hystaspes," said he, "thou art the child of a brave father, and seemest likely to show thyself as bold a gallant as he. Beware, however, of rash haste in this matter; do not

hurry so, but proceed with soberness. We must add to our number ere we adventure to strike the blow." "Not so," Darius rejoined; "for let all present be well assured that if the advice of Otanes guide our acts, we shall perish most miserably. Some one will betray our plot to the Magians for lucre's sake. Ye ought to have kept the matter to yourselves, and so made the venture; but as ye have chosen to take others into your secret, and have opened the matter to me, take my advice and make the attempt to-day—or if not, if a single day be suffered to pass by, be sure that I will let no one betray me to the Magian. I myself will go to him, and plainly denounce you all."

72. Otanes, when he saw Darius so hot, replied, "But if thou wilt force us to action, and not allow a day's delay, tell us, I pray thee, how we shall get entrance into the palace, so as to set upon them. Guards are placed everywhere, as thou thyself well knowest—for if thou hast not seen, at least thou hast heard tell of them. How are we to pass these guards, I ask thee?" "Otanes," answered Darius, "there are many things easy enough in act, which by speech it is hard to explain. There are also things concerning which speech is easy, but no noble action follows when the speech is done. As for these guards, ye know well that we shall not find it hard to make our way through them. Our rank alone would cause them to allow us to enter—shame and fear alike forbidding them to say us nay. But besides, I have the fairest plea that can be conceived for gaining admission. I can say that I have just come from Persia, and have a message to deliver to the king from my father. An untruth must be spoken, where need requires. For whether men lie, or say true, it is with one and the same object. Men lie, because they think to gain by deceiving others; and speak the truth, because they expect to get something by their true speaking, and to be trusted afterwards in more important matters. Thus, though their conduct is so opposite, the end of both is alike. If there were no gain to be got, your true-speaking man would tell untruths as much as your liar, and your liar would tell the truth as much as your true-speaking man. The doorkeeper, who lets us in readily, shall have his guerdon some day or other; but woe to the man who resists us, he must forthwith be declared an enemy. Forcing our way past him, we will press in and go straight to our work."

73. After Darius had thus said, Gobryas spoke as follows:—"Dear friends, when will

a fitter occasion offer for us to recover the kingdom, or, if we are not strong enough, at least die in the attempt? Consider that we Persians are governed by a Median Magus, and one, too, who has had his ears cut off! Some of you were present when Cambyses lay upon his death-bed—such, doubtless, remember what curses he called down upon the Persians if they made no effort to recover the kingdom. Then, indeed, we paid but little heed to what he said, because we thought he spoke out of hatred to set us against his brother. Now, however, my vote is that we do as Darius has counselled—march straight in a body to the palace from the place where we now are, and forthwith set upon the Magian." So Gobryas spake, and the others all approved.

74. While the seven were thus taking counsel together, it so chanced that the following events were happening:—The Magi had been thinking what they had best do, and had resolved for many reasons to make a friend of Prexaspes. They knew how cruelly he had been outraged by Cambyses, who slew his son with an arrow; they were also aware that it was by his hand that Smerdis the son of Cyrus fell, and that he was the only person privy to that prince's death; and they further found him to be held in the highest esteem by all the Persians. So they called him to them, made him their friend, and bound him by a promise and by oaths to keep silence about the fraud which they were practising upon the Persians, and not discover it to any one; and they pledged themselves that in this case they would give him thousands of gifts of every sort and kind. So Prexaspes agreed, and the Magi, when they found that they had persuaded him so far, went on to another proposal, and said they would assemble the Persians at the foot of the palace wall, and he should mount one of the towers and harangue them from it, assuring them that Smerdis the son of Cyrus, and none but he, ruled the land. This they bade him do, because Prexaspes was a man of great weight with his countrymen, and had often declared in public that Smerdis the son of Cyrus was still alive, and denied being his murderer.

75. Prexaspes said he was quite ready to do their will in the matter; so the Magi assembled the people, and placed Prexaspes upon the top of the tower, and told him to make his speech. Then this man, forgetting of set purpose all that the Magi had intreated him to say, began with Achæmenes, and traced down the descent of Cyrus; after which, when he came to that king, he recounted all the services that had been rendered by him to the Persians, from whence he went on to declare the truth, which hitherto he had concealed, he said, because it would not have been safe for him to make it known, but now necessity was laid on him to disclose the whole. Then he told how, forced to it by Cambyses, he had himself taken the life of Smerdis, son of Cyrus, and how that Persia was now ruled by the Magi. Last of all, with many curses upon the Persians if they did not recover the kingdom, and wreak vengeance on the Magi, he threw himself headlong from the tower into the abyss below. Such was the end of Prexaspes, a man all his life of high repute among the Persians.

76. And now the seven Persians, having resolved that they would attack the Magi without more delay, first offered prayers to the gods and then set off for the palace, quite unacquainted with what had been done by Prexaspes. The news of his doings reached them upon their way, when they had accomplished about half the distance. Hereupon they turned aside out of the road, and consulted together. Otanes and his party said they must certainly put off the business, and not make the attack when affairs were in such a ferment. Darius, on the other hand, and his friends, were against any change of plan, and wished to go straight on, and not lose a moment. Now, as they strove together, suddenly there came in sight two pairs of vultures, and seven pairs of hawks, pursuing them, and the hawks tore the vultures both with their claws and bills. At this sight the seven with one accord came in to the opinion of Darius, and encouraged by the omen hastened on towards the palace.

77. At the gate they were received as Darius had foretold. The guards, who had no suspicion that they came for any ill purpose, and held the chief Persians in much reverence, let them pass without difficulty—it seemed as if they were under the special protection of the gods—none even asked them any question. When they were now in the great court they fell in with certain of the eunuchs, whose business it was to carry the king's messages, who stopped them and asked what they wanted, while at the same time they threatened the doorkeepers for having let them enter. The seven sought to press on, but the eunuchs would not suffer them. Then these men, with cheers encouraging one another, drew their daggers, and stabbing those who strove to

withstand them, rushed forward to the apartment of the males.

78. Now both the Magi were at this time within, holding counsel upon the matter of Prexaspes. So when they heard the stir among the eunuchs, and their loud cries, they ran out themselves, to see what was happening. Instantly perceiving their danger, they both flew to arms; one had just time to seize his bow, the other got hold of his lance; when straightway the fight began. The one whose weapon was the bow found it of no service at all; the foe was too near, and the combat too close to allow of his using it. But the other made a stout defence with his lance, wounding two of the seven, Aspathines in the leg, and Intaphernes in the eye. This wound did not kill Intaphernes, but it cost him the sight of that eye. The other Magus, when he found his bow of no avail, fled into a chamber which opened out into the apartment of the males, intending to shut the doors. But two of the seven entered the room with him, Darius and Gobryas. Gobryas seized the Magus and grappled with him, while Darius stood over them, not knowing what to do; for it was dark, and he was afraid that if he struck a blow he might kill Gobryas. Then Gobryas, when he perceived that Darius stood doing nothing, asked him, "why his hand was idle?" "I fear to hurt thee," he answered. "Fear not," said Gobryas; "strike, though it be through both." Darius did as he desired, drove his dagger home, and by good hap killed the Magus.

79. Thus were the Magi slain; and the seven, cutting off both the heads, and leaving their own wounded in the palace, partly because they were disabled, and partly to guard the citadel, went forth from the gates with the heads in their hands, shouting and making an uproar. They called out to all the Persians whom they met, and told them what had happened, showing them the heads of the Magi, while at the same time they slew every Magus who fell in their way. Then the Persians, when they knew what the seven had done, and understood the fraud of the Magi, thought it but just to follow the example set them, and, drawing their daggers, they killed the Magi wherever they could find any. Such was their fury, that, unless night had closed in, not a single Magus would have been left alive. The Persians observe this day with one accord, and keep it more strictly than any other in the whole year. It is then that they hold the great festival, which they call the Magophonia. No Magus may show himself abroad during the whole time that the feast lasts; but all must remain at home the entire day.

80. And now when five days were gone, and the hubbub had settled down, the conspirators met together to consult about the situation of affairs. At this meeting speeches were made, to which many of the Greeks give no credence, but they were made nevertheless. Otanes recommended that the management of public affairs should be entrusted to the whole nation. "To me," he said, "it seems advisable, that we should no longer have a single man to rule over us—the rule of one is neither good nor pleasant. Ye cannot have forgotten to what lengths Cambyses went in his haughty tyranny, and the haughtiness of the Magi ye have yourselves experienced. How indeed is it possible that monarchy should be a well-adjusted thing, when it allows a man to do as he likes without being answerable? Such licence is enough to stir strange and unwonted thoughts in the heart of the worthiest of men. Give a person this power, and straightway his manifold good things puff him up with pride, while envy is so natural to human kind that it cannot but arise in him. But pride and envy together include all wickedness—both of them leading on to deeds of savage violence. True it is that kings, possessing as they do all that heart can desire, ought to be void of envy; but the contrary is seen in their conduct towards the citizens. They are jealous of the most virtuous among their subjects, and wish their death; while they take delight in the meanest and basest, being ever ready to listen to the tales of slanderers. A king, besides, is beyond all other men inconsistent with himself. Pay him court in moderation, and he is angry because you do not show him more profound respect—show him profound respect, and he is offended again, because (as he says) you fawn on him. But the worst of all is, that he sets aside the laws of the land, puts men to death without trial, and subjects women to violence. The rule of the many, on the other hand, has, in the first place, the fairest of names, to wit, *isonomy;* and further it is free from all those outrages which a king is wont to commit. There, places are given by lot, the magistrate is answerable for what he does, and measures rest with the commonalty. I vote, therefore, that we do away with monarchy, and raise the people to power. For the people are all in all."

81. Such were the sentiments of Otanes. Megabyzus spoke next, and advised the setting

up of an oligarchy:—"In all that Otanes has said to persuade you to put down monarchy," he observed, "I fully concur; but his recommendation that we should call the people to power seems to me not the best advice. For there is nothing so void of understanding, nothing so full of wantonness, as the unwieldy rabble. It were folly not to be borne, for men, while seeking to escape the wantonness of a tyrant, to give themselves up to the wantonness of a rude unbridled mob. The tyrant, in all his doings, at least knows what is he about, but a mob is altogether devoid of knowledge; for how should there be any knowledge in a rabble, untaught, and with no natural sense of what is right and fit? It rushes wildly into state affairs with all the fury of a stream swollen in the winter, and confuses everything. Let the enemies of the Persians be ruled by democracies; but let us choose out from the citizens a certain number of the worthiest, and put the government into their hands. For thus both we ourselves shall be among the governors, and power being entrusted to the best men, it is likely that the best counsels will prevail in the state."

82. This was the advice which Megabyzus gave, and after him Darius came forward, and spoke as follows:—"All that Megabyzus said against democracy was well said, I think; but about oligarchy he did not speak advisedly; for take these three forms of government—democracy, oligarchy, and monarchy—and let them each be at their best, I maintain that monarchy far surpasses the other two. What government can possibly be better than that of the very best man in the whole state? The counsels of such a man are like himself, and so he governs the mass of the people to their heart's content; while at the same time his measures against evil-doers are kept more secret than in other states. Contrariwise, in oligarchies, where men vie with each other in the service of the commonwealth, fierce enmities are apt to arise between man and man, each wishing to be leader, and to carry his own measures; whence violent quarrels come, which lead to open strife, often ending in bloodshed. Then monarchy is sure to follow; and this too shows how far that rule surpasses all others. Again, in a democracy, it is impossible but that there will be malpractices: these malpractices, however, do not lead to enmities, but to close friendships, which are formed among those engaged in them, who must hold well together to carry on their villainies. And so things go on until a man stands forth as champion of the commonalty, and puts down the evil-doers. Straightway the author of so great a service is admired by all, and from being admired soon comes to be appointed king; so that here too it is plain that monarchy is the best government. Lastly, to sum up all in a word, whence, I ask, was it that we got the freedom which we enjoy?— did democracy give it us, or oligarchy, or a monarch? As a single man recovered our freedom for us, my sentence is that we keep to the rule of one. Even apart from this, we ought not to change the laws of our forefathers when they work fairly; for to do so is not well."

83. Such were the three opinions brought forward at this meeting; the four other Persians voted in favour of the last. Otanes, who wished to give his countrymen a democracy, when he found the decision against him, arose a second time, and spoke thus before the assembly:—"Brother conspirators, it is plain that the king who is to be chosen will be one of ourselves, whether we make the choice by casting lots for the prize, or by letting the people decide which of us they will have to rule over them, in or any other way. Now, as I have neither a mind to rule nor to be ruled, I shall not enter the lists with you in this matter. I withdraw, however, on one condition—none of you shall claim to exercise rule over me or my seed for ever." The six agreed to these terms, and Otanes withdrew and stood aloof from the contest. And still to this day the family of Otanes continues to be the only free family in Persia; those who belong to it submit to the rule of the king only so far as they themselves choose; they are bound, however, to observe the laws of the land like the other Persians.

84. After this the six took counsel together, as to the fairest way of setting up a king: and first, with respect to Otanes, they resolved, that if any of their own number got the kingdom, Otanes and his seed after him should receive year by year, as a mark of special honour, a Median robe, and all such other gifts as are accounted the most honourable in Persia. And these they resolved to give him, because he was the man who first planned the outbreak, and who brought the seven together. These privileges, therefore, were assigned specially to Otanes. The following were made common to them all:—It was to be free to each, whenever he pleased, to enter the palace unannounced, unless the king were in the company of one of his wives; and the king was to be bound to marry into no family excepting those of the

conspirators. Concerning the appointment of a king, the resolve to which they came was the following:—They would ride out together next morning into the skirts of the city, and he whose steed first neighed after the sun was up should have the kingdom.

85. Now Darius had a groom, a sharp-witted knave, called Œbares. After the meeting had broken up, Darius sent for him, and said, "Œbares, this is the way in which the king is to be chosen—we are to mount our horses, and the man whose horse first neighs after the sun is up is to have the kingdom. If then you have any cleverness, contrive a plan whereby the prize may fall to us, and not go to another." "Truly, master," Œbares answered, "if it depends on this whether thou shalt be king or no, set thine heart at ease, and fear nothing: I have a charm which is sure not to fail." "If thou hast really aught of the kind," said Darius, "hasten to get it ready. The matter does not brook delay, for the trial is to be to-morrow." So Œbares when he heard that, did as follows:—When night came, he took one of the mares, the chief favourite of the horse which Darius rode, and tethering it in the suburb, brought his master's horse to the place; then, after leading him round and round the mare several times, nearer and nearer at each circuit, he ended by letting them come together.

86. And now, when the morning broke, the six Persians, according to agreement, met together on horseback, and rode out to the suburb. As they went along they neared the spot where the mare was tethered the night before, whereupon the horse of Darius sprang forward and neighed. Just at the same time, though the sky was clear and bright, there was a flash of lightning, followed by a thunderclap. It seemed as if the heavens conspired with Darius, and hereby inaugurated him king: so the five other nobles leaped with one accord from their steeds, and bowed down before him and owned him for their king.

87. This is the account which some of the Persians gave of the contrivance of Œbares; but there are others who relate the matter differently. They say that in the morning he stroked the mare with his hand, which he then hid in his trousers until the sun rose and the horses were about to start, when he suddenly drew his hand forth and put it to the nostrils of his master's horse, which immediately snorted and neighed.

88. Thus was Darius, son of Hystaspes, ap-

pointed king; and, except the Arabians, all they of Asia were subject to him; for Cyrus, and after him Cambyses, had brought them all under. The Arabians were never subject as slaves to the Persians, but had a league of friendship with them from the time when they brought Cambyses on his way as he went into Egypt; for had they been unfriendly the Persians could never have made their invasion.

And now Darius contracted marriages of the first rank, according to the notions of the Persians: to wit, with two daughters of Cyrus, Atossa and Artystône; of whom, Atossa had been twice married before, once to Cambyses, her brother, and once to the Magus, while the other, Artystône, was a virgin. He married also Parmys, daughter of Smerdis, son of Cyrus; and he likewise took to wife the daughter of Otanes, who had made the discovery about the Magus. And now when his power was established firmly throughout all the kingdoms, the first thing that he did was to set up a carving in stone, which showed a man mounted upon a horse, with an inscription in these words following:—"Darius, son of Hystaspes, by aid of his good horse" (here followed the horse's name), "and of his good groom Œbares, got himself the kingdom of the Persians."

89. This he set up in Persia; and afterwards he proceeded to establish twenty governments of the kind which the Persians call satrapies, assigning to each its governor, and fixing the tribute which was to be paid him by the several nations. And generally he joined together in one satrapy the nations that were neighbours, but sometimes he passed over the nearer tribes, and put in their stead those which were more remote. The following is an account of these governments, and of the yearly tribute which they paid to the king:—Such as brought their tribute in silver were ordered to pay according to the Babylonian talent; while the Euboic was the standard measure for such as brought gold. Now the Babylonian talent contains seventy Euboic minæ.[1] During all the reign of Cyrus, and afterwards when Cambyses ruled, there were no fixed tributes, but the nations severally brought gifts to the king. On account of this

---

[1] Standards of weight probably passed into Greece from Asia, when the word mina (μνᾶ) seems certainly to have been derived. That the standard known to the Greeks as the Euboic was an Asiatic one, is plain from this passage. If the (later) Attic talent was worth £243 15s., the Euboic (silver) talent would be £250 8s. 5d., and the Babylonian £292 3s. 3d.

and other like doings, the Persians say that Darius was a huckster, Cambyses a master, and Cyrus a father; for Darius looked to making a gain in everything; Cambyses was harsh and reckless; while Cyrus was gentle, and procured them all manner of goods.

90. The Ionians, the Magnesians of Asia, the Æolians, the Carians, the Lycians, the Milyans, and the Pamphylians, paid their tribute in a single sum, which was fixed at four hundred talents of silver. These formed together the first satrapy.

The Mysians, Lydians, Lasonians, Cabalians, and Hygennians paid the sum of five hundred talents. This was the second satrapy.

The Hellespontians, of the right coast as one enters the straits, the Phrygians, the Asiatic Thracians, the Paphlagonians, the Mariandynians, and the Syrians paid a tribute of three hundred and sixty talents. This was the third satrapy.

The Cilicians gave three hundred and sixty white horses, one for each day in the year, and five hundred talents of silver. Of this sum one hundred and forty talents went to pay the cavalry which guarded the country, while the remaining three hundred and sixty were received by Darius. This was the fourth satrapy.

91. The country reaching from the city of Posideïum (built by Amphilochus, son of Amphiaraüs, on the confines of Syria and Cilicia) to the borders of Egypt, excluding therefrom a district which belonged to Arabia and was free from tax, paid a tribute of three hundred and fifty talents. All Phœnicia, Palestine Syria, and Cyprus, were herein contained. This was the fifth satrapy.

From Egypt, and the neighbouring parts of Libya, together with the towns of Cyrêné and Barca, which belonged to the Egyptian satrapy, the tribute which came in was seven hundred talents. These seven hundred talents did not include the profits of the fisheries of Lake Mœris, nor the corn furnished to the troops at Memphis. Corn was supplied to 120,000 Persians, who dwelt at Memphis in the quarter called the White Castle, and to a number of auxiliaries. This was the sixth satrapy.

The Sattagydians, the Gandarians, the Dadicæ, and the Aparytæ, who were all reckoned together, paid a tribute of a hundred and seventy talents. This was the seventh satrapy.

Susa, and the other parts of Cissia, paid three hundred talents. This was the eighth satrapy.

92. From Babylonia, and the rest of Assyria, were drawn a thousand talents of silver, and five hundred boy-eunuchs. This was the ninth satrapy.

Agbatana, and the other parts of Media, together with the Paricanians and Orthocorybantes, paid in all four hundred and fifty talents. This was the tenth satrapy.

The Caspians, Pausicæ, Pantimathi, and Daritæ, were joined in one government, and paid the sum of two hundred talents. This was the eleventh satrapy.

From the Bactrian tribes as far as the Ægli, the tribute received was three hundred and sixty talents. This was the twelfth satrapy.

93. From Pactyïca, Armenia, and the countries reaching thence to the Euxine, the sum drawn was four hundred talents. This was the thirteenth satrapy.

The Sagartians, Sarangians, Thamanæans, Utians, and Mycians, together with the inhabitants of the islands in the Erythræan sea, where the king sends those whom he banishes, furnished altogether a tribute of six hundred talents. This was the fourteenth satrapy.

The Sacans and Caspians gave two hundred and fifty talents. This was the fifteenth satrapy.

The Parthians, Chorasmians, Sogdians, and Arians, gave three hundred. This was the sixteenth satrapy.

94. The Paricanians and Ethiopians of Asia furnished a tribute of four hundred talents. This was the seventeenth satrapy.

The Matienians, Saspeires, and Alarodians were rated to pay two hundred talents. This was the eighteenth satrapy.

The Moschi, Tibareni, Macrones, Mosynœci, and Mares had to pay three hundred talents. This was the nineteenth satrapy.

The Indians, who are more numerous than any other nation with which we are acquainted, paid a tribute exceeding that of every other people, to wit, three hundred and sixty talents of gold-dust. This was the twentieth satrapy.

95. If the Babylonian money here spoken of be reduced to the Euboic scale, it will make nine thousand five hundred and forty such talents; and if the gold be reckoned at thirteen times the worth of silver, the Indian gold-dust will come to four thousand six hundred and eighty talents. Add these two amounts together and the whole revenue which came in to Darius year by year will be found to be in Euboic money fourteen thousand five hundred and sixty talents, not to mention parts of a talent.

96. Such was the revenue which Darius de-

rived from Asia and a small part of Libya. Later in his reign the sum was increased by the tribute of the islands, and of the nations of Europe as far as Thessaly. The Great King stores away the tribute which he receives after this fashion—he melts it down, and, while it is in a liquid state, runs it into earthen vessels, which are afterwards removed, leaving the metal in a solid mass. When money is wanted, he coins as much of this bullion as the occasion requires.

97. Such then were the governments, and such the amounts of tribute at which they were assessed respectively. Persia alone has not been reckoned among the tributaries—and for this reason, because the country of the Persians is altogether exempt from tax. The following peoples paid no settled tribute, but brought gifts to the king: first, the Ethiopians bordering upon Egypt, who were reduced by Cambyses when he made war on the long-lived Ethiopians, and who dwell about the sacred city of Nysa, and have festivals in honour of Bacchus. The grain on which they and their next neighbours feed is the same as that used by the Calantian Indians. Their dwelling-houses are under ground. Every third year these two nations brought—and they still bring to my day —two chœnices[1] of virgin gold, two hundred logs of ebony, five Ethiopian boys, and twenty elephant tusks. The Colchians, and the neighbouring tribes who dwell between them and the Caucasus—for so far the Persian rule reaches, while north of the Caucasus no one fears them any longer—undertook to furnish a gift, which in my day was still brought every fifth year, consisting of a hundred boys, and the same number of maidens. The Arabs brought every year a thousand talents of frankincense. Such were the gifts which the king received over and above the tribute-money.

98. The way in which the Indians get the plentiful supply of gold which enables them to furnish year by year so vast an amount of gold-dust to the king, is the following:—eastward of India lies a tract which is entirely sand. Indeed of all the inhabitants of Asia, concerning whom anything certain is known, the Indians dwell the nearest to the east, and the rising of the sun. Beyond them the whole country is desert on account of the sand. The tribes of Indians are numerous, and do not all speak the same language—some are wandering tribes, others not. They who dwell in the marshes along the river live on raw fish, which

they take in boats made of reeds, each formed out of a single joint. These Indians wear a dress of sedge, which they cut in the river and bruise; afterwards they weave it into mats, and wear it as we wear a breast-plate.

99. Eastward of these Indians are another tribe, called Padæans, who are wanderers, and live on raw flesh. This tribe is said to have the following customs:—If one of their number be ill, man or woman, they take the sick person, and if he be a man, the men of his acquaintance proceed to put him to death, because, they say, his flesh would be spoilt for them if he pined and wasted away with sickness. The man protests he is not ill in the least; but his friends will not accept his denial—in spite of all he can say, they kill him, and feast themselves on his body. So also if a woman be sick, the women, who are her friends, take her and do with her exactly the same as the men. If one of them reaches to old age, about which there is seldom any question, as commonly before that time they have had some disease or other, and so have been put to death—but if a man, notwithstanding, comes to be old, then they offer him in sacrifice to their gods, and afterwards eat his flesh.

100. There is another set of Indians whose customs are very different. They refuse to put any live animal to death, they sow no corn, and have no dwelling-houses. Vegetables are their only food. There is a plant which grows wild in their country, bearing seed, about the size of millet-seed, in a calyx: their wont is to gather this seed and having boiled it, calyx and all, to use it for food. If one of them is attacked with sickness, he goes forth into the wilderness, and lies down to die; no one has the least concern either for the sick or for the dead.

101. All the tribes which I have mentioned live together like the brute beasts: they have also all the same tint of skin, which approaches that of the Ethiopians. Their country is a long way from Persia towards the south: nor had king Darius ever any authority over them.

102. Besides these, there are Indians of another tribe, who border on the city of Caspatyrus, and the country of Pactyïca; these people dwell northward of all the rest of the Indians, and follow nearly the same mode of life as the Bactrians. They are more warlike than any of the other tribes, and from them the men are sent forth who go to procure the gold. For it is in this part of India that the sandy desert lies. Here, in this desert, there live amid the sand great ants, in size somewhat less than dogs,

[1] About two quarts.

but bigger than foxes. The Persian king has a number of them, which have been caught by the hunters in the land whereof we are speaking. Those ants make their dwellings under ground, and like the Greek ants, which they very much resemble in shape, throw up sand-heaps as they burrow. Now the sand which they throw up is full of gold. The Indians, when they go into the desert to collect this sand, take three camels and harness them together, a female in the middle and a male on either side, in a leading-rein. The rider sits on the female, and they are particular to choose for the purpose one that has but just dropped her young; for their female camels can run as fast as horses, while they bear burthens very much better.

103. As the Greeks are well acquainted with the shape of the camel, I shall not trouble to describe it; but I shall mention what seems to have escaped their notice. The camel has in its hind legs four thigh-bones and four knee-joints.[1]

104. When the Indians therefore have thus equipped themselves they set off in quest of the gold, calculating the time so that they may be engaged in seizing it during the most sultry part of the day, when the ants hide themselves to escape the heat. The sun in those parts shines fiercest in the morning, not, as elsewhere, at noonday; the greatest heat is from the time when he has reached a certain height, until the hour at which the market closes. During this space he burns much more furiously than at midday in Greece, so that the men there are said at that time to drench themselves with water. At noon his heat is much the same in India as in other countries, after which, as the day declines, the warmth is only equal to that of the morning sun elsewhere. Towards evening the coolness increases, till about sunset it becomes very cold.

105. When the Indians reach the place where the gold is, they fill their bags with the sand, and ride away at their best speed: the ants, however, scenting them, as the Persians say, rush forth in pursuit. Now these animals are, they declare, so swift, that there is nothing in the world like them: if it were not, therefore, that the Indians get a start while the ants are mustering, not a single gold-gatherer could

escape. During the flight the male camels, which are not so fleet as the females, grow tired, and begin to drag, first one, and then the other; but the females recollect the young which they have left behind, and never give way or flag. Such, according to the Persians, is the manner in which the Indians get the greater part of their gold; some is dug out of the earth, but of this the supply is more scanty.

106. It seems as if the extreme regions of the earth were blessed by nature with the most excellent productions, just in the same way that Greece enjoys a climate more excellently tempered than any other country. In India, which, as I observed lately, is the furthest region of the inhabited world towards the east, all the four-footed beasts and the birds are very much bigger than those found elsewhere, except only the horses, which are surpassed by the Median breed called the Nisæan. Gold too is produced there in vast abundance, some dug from the earth, some washed down by the rivers, some carried off in the mode which I have but now described. And further, there are trees which grow wild there, the fruit whereof is a wool exceeding in beauty and goodness that of sheep. The natives make their clothes of this tree-wool.

107. Arabia is the last of inhabited lands towards the south, and it is the only country which produces frankincense, myrrh, cassia, cinnamon, and ledanum. The Arabians do not get any of these, except the myrrh, without trouble. The frankincense they procure by means of the gum styrax, which the Greeks obtain from the Phœnicians; this they burn, and thereby obtain the spice. For the trees which bear the frankincense are guarded by winged serpents, small in size, and of varied colours, whereof vast numbers hang about every tree. They are of the same kind as the serpents that invade Egypt; and there is nothing but the smoke of the styrax which will drive them from the trees.

108. The Arabians say that the whole world would swarm with these serpents, if they were not kept in check in the way in which I know that vipers are. Of a truth Divine Providence does appear to be, as indeed one might expect beforehand, a wise contriver. For timid animals which are a prey to others are all made to produce young abundantly, that so the species may not be entirely eaten up and lost; while savage and noxious creatures are made very unfruitful. The hare, for instance, which is hunted alike by beasts, birds, and men,

[1] This is of course untrue, and it is difficult to understand how Herodotus could entertain such a notion. There is no *real* difference, as regards the anatomy of the leg, between the horse and the camel.

breeds so abundantly as even to superfetate, a thing which is true of no other animal. You find in a hare's belly, at one and the same time, some of the young all covered with fur, others quite naked, others again just fully formed in the womb, while the hare perhaps has lately conceived afresh. The lioness, on the other hand, which is one of the strongest and boldest of brutes, brings forth young but once in her lifetime,[1] and then a single cub; she cannot possibly conceive again, since she loses her womb at the same time that she drops her young. The reason of this is that as soon as the cub begins to stir inside the dam, his claws, which are sharper than those of any other animal, scratch the womb; as the time goes on, and he grows bigger, he tears it ever more and more; so that at last, when the birth comes, there is not a morsel in the whole womb that is sound.

109. Now with respect to the vipers and the winged snakes of Arabia, if they increased as fast as their nature would allow, impossible were it for man to maintain himself upon the earth. Accordingly it is found that when the male and female come together, at the very moment of impregnation, the female seizes the male by the neck, and having once fastened, cannot be brought to leave go till she has bit the neck entirely through. And so the male perishes; but after a while he is revenged upon the female by means of the young, which, while still unborn, gnaw a passage through the womb, and then through the belly of their mother, and so make their entrance into the world. Contrariwise, other snakes, which are harmless, lay eggs, and hatch a vast number of young. Vipers are found in all parts of the world, but the winged serpents are nowhere seen except in Arabia, where they are all congregated together. This makes them appear so numerous.

110. Such, then, is the way in which the Arabians obtain their frankincense; their manner of collecting the cassia is the following:— They cover all their body and their face with the hides of oxen and other skins, leaving only holes for the eyes, and thus protected go in search of the cassia, which grows in a lake of no great depth. All round the shores and in the lake itself there dwell a number of winged animals, much resembling bats, which screech horribly, and are very valiant. These creatures they must keep from their eyes all the while that they gather the cassia.

[1] The fabulous character of the whole of this account was known to Aristotle.

111. Still more wonderful is the mode in which they collect the cinnamon. Where the wood grows, and what country produces it, they cannot tell—only some, following probability, relate that it comes from the country in which Bacchus was brought up. Great birds, they say, bring the sticks which we Greeks, taking the word from the Phœnicians, call cinnamon, and carry them up into the air to make their nests. These are fastened with a sort of mud to a sheer face of rock, where no foot of man is able to climb. So the Arabians, to get the cinnamon, use the following artifice. They cut all the oxen and asses and beasts of burthen that die in their land into large pieces, which they carry with them into those regions, and place near the nests: then they withdraw to a distance, and the old birds, swooping down, seize the pieces of meat and fly with them up to their nests; which, not being able to support the weight, break off and fall to the ground. Hereupon the Arabians return and collect the cinnamon, which is afterwards carried from Arabia into other countries.

112. Ledanum, which the Arabs call *ladanum,* is procured in a yet stranger fashion. Found in a most inodorous place, it is the sweetest-scented of all substances. It is gathered from the beards of he-goats, where it is found sticking like gum, having come from the bushes on which they browse. It is used in many sorts of unguents, and is what the Arabs burn chiefly as incense.

113. Concerning the spices of Arabia let no more be said. The whole country is scented with them, and exhales an odour marvellously sweet. There are also in Arabia two kinds of sheep worthy of admiration, the like of which is nowhere else to be seen; the one kind has long tails, not less than three cubits in length, which, if they were allowed to trail on the ground, would be bruised and fall into sores. As it is, all the shepherds know enough of carpentering to make little trucks for their sheep's tails. The trucks are placed under the tails, each sheep having one to himself, and the tails are then tied down upon them. The other kind has a broad tail, which is a cubit across sometimes.

114. Where the south declines towards the setting sun lies the country called Ethiopia, the last inhabited land in that direction. There gold is obtained in great plenty, huge elephants abound, with wild trees of all sorts, and ebony; and the men are taller, handsomer, and longer lived than anywhere else.

115. Now these are the farthest regions of the world in Asia and Libya. Of the extreme tracts of Europe towards the west I cannot speak with any certainty; for I do not allow that there is any river, to which the barbarians give the name of Eridanus, emptying itself into the northern sea, whence (as the tale goes) amber is procured; nor do I know of any islands called the Cassiterides (Tin Islands), whence the tin comes which we use. For in the first place the name Eridanus is manifestly not a barbarian word at all, but a Greek name, invented by some poet or other; and secondly, though I have taken vast pains, I have never been able to get an assurance from an eye-witness that there is any sea on the further side of Europe. Nevertheless, tin and amber do certainly come to us from the ends of the earth.

116. The northern parts of Europe are very much richer in gold than any other region: but how it is procured I have no certain knowledge. The story runs that the one-eyed Arimaspi purloin it from the griffins; but here too I am incredulous, and cannot persuade myself that there is a race of men born with one eye, who in all else resemble the rest of mankind. Nevertheless it seems to be true that the extreme regions of the earth, which surround and shut up within themselves all other countries, produce the things which are the rarest, and which men reckon the most beautiful.

117. There is a plain in Asia which is shut in on all sides by a mountain-range, and in this mountain-range are five openings. The plain lies on the confines of the Chorasmians, Hyrcanians, Parthians, Sarangians, and Thamanæans, and belonged formerly to the first-mentioned of those peoples. Ever since the Persians, however, obtained the mastery of Asia, it has been the property of the Great King. A mighty river, called the Aces, flows from the hills inclosing the plain; and this stream, formerly splitting into five channels, ran through the five openings in the hills, and watered the lands of the five nations which dwell around. The Persian came, however, and conquered the region, and then it went ill with the people of these lands. The Great King blocked up all the passages between the hills with dykes and flood-gates, and so prevented the water from flowing out. Then the plain within the hills became a sea, for the river kept rising, and the water could find no outlet. From that time the five nations which were wont formerly to have the use of the stream, losing their accus-tomed supply of water, have been in great distress. In winter, indeed, they have rain from heaven like the rest of the world, but in summer, after sowing their millet and their sesame, they always stand in need of water from the river. When, therefore, they suffer from this want, hastening to Persia, men and women alike, they take their station at the gate of the king's palace, and wail aloud. Then the king orders the flood-gates to be opened towards the country whose need is greatest, and lets the soil drink until it has had enough; after which the gates on this side are shut, and others are unclosed for the nation which, of the remainder, needs it most. It has been told me that the king never gives the order to open the gates till the suppliants have paid him a large sum of money over and above the tribute.

118. Of the seven Persians who rose up against the Magus, one, Intaphernes, lost his life very shortly after the outbreak, for an act of insolence. He wished to enter the palace and transact a certain business with the king. Now the law was that all those who had taken part in the rising against the Magus might enter unannounced into the king's presence, unless he happened to be in private with his wife. So Intaphernes would not have any one announce him, but, as he belonged to the seven, claimed it as his right to go in. The doorkeeper, however, and the chief usher forbade his entrance, since the king, they said, was with his wife. But Intaphernes thought they told lies; so, drawing his scymitar, he cut off their noses and their ears, and, hanging them on the bridle of his horse, put the bridle round their necks, and so let them go.

119. Then these two men went and showed themselves to the king, and told him how it had come to pass that they were thus treated. Darius trembled lest it was by the common consent of the six that the deed had been done; he therefore sent for them all in turn, and sounded them to know if they approved the conduct of Intaphernes. When he found by their answers that there had been no concert between him and them, he laid hands on Intaphernes, his children, and all his near kindred; strongly suspecting that he and his friends were about to raise a revolt. When all had been seized and put in chains, as malefactors condemned to death, the wife of Intaphernes came and stood continually at the palace-gates, weeping and wailing sore. So Darius after a while, seeing that she never ceased to stand and weep, was touched with pity for her, and bade a mes-

senger go to her and say, "Lady, king Darius gives thee as a boon the life of one of thy kinsmen—choose which thou wilt of the prisoners." Then she pondered awhile before she answered, "If the king grants me the life of one alone, I make choice of my brother." Darius, when he heard the reply, was astonished, and sent again, saying, "Lady, the king bids thee tell him why it is that thou passest by thy husband and thy children, and preferrest to have the life of thy brother spared. He is not so near to thee as thy children, nor so dear as thy husband." She answered, "O king, if the gods will, I may have another husband and other children when these are gone. But as my father and my mother are no more, it is impossible that I should have another brother. This was my thought when I asked to have my brother spared." Then it seemed to Darius that the lady spoke well, and he gave her, besides the life that she had asked, the life also of her eldest son, because he was greatly pleased with her. But he slew all the rest. Thus one of the seven died, in the way I have described, very shortly after the insurrection.

120. About the time of Cambyses' last sickness, the following events happened. There was a certain Orœtes, a Persian, whom Cyrus had made governor of Sardis. This man conceived a most unholy wish. He had never suffered wrong or had an ill word from Polycrates the Samian—nay, he had not so much as seen him in all his life; yet, notwithstanding, he conceived the wish to seize him and put him to death. This wish, according to the account which the most part give, arose from what happened one day as he was sitting with another Persian in the gate of the king's palace. The man's name was Mitrobates, and he was ruler of the satrapy of Dascyleium. He and Orœtes had been talking together, and from talking they fell to quarrelling and comparing their merits; whereupon Mitrobates said to Orœtes reproachfully, "Art thou worthy to be called a man, when, near as Samos lies to thy government, and easy as it is to conquer, thou hast omitted to bring it under the dominion of the king? Easy to conquer, said I? Why, a mere common citizen, with the help of fifteen men-at-arms, mastered the island, and is still king of it." Orœtes, they say, took this reproach greatly to heart; but, instead of seeking to revenge himself on the man by whom it was uttered, he conceived the desire of destroying Polycrates, since it was on Polycrates' account that the reproach had fallen on him.

121. Another less common version of the story is that Orœtes sent a herald to Samos to make a request, the nature of which is not stated; Polycrates was at the time reclining in the apartment of the males, and Anacreon the Teian was with him; when therefore the herald came forward to converse, Polycrates, either out of studied contempt for the power of Orœtes, or it may be merely by chance, was lying with his face turned away towards the wall; and so he lay all the time that the herald spake, and when he ended, did not even vouchsafe him a word.

122. Such are the two reasons alleged for the death of Polycrates; it is open to all to believe which they please. What is certain is that Orœtes, while residing at Magnesia on the Mæander, sent a Lydian, by name Myrsus, the son of Gyges, with a message to Polycrates at Samos, well knowing what that monarch designed. For Polycrates entertained a design which no other Greek, so far as we know, ever formed before him, unless it were Minos the Cnossian, and those (if there were any such) who had the mastery of the Egæan at an earlier time—Polycrates, I say, was the first of mere human birth who conceived the design of gaining the empire of the sea, and aspired to rule over Ionia and the islands. Knowing then that Polycrates was thus minded, Orœtes sent his message, which ran as follows:—

"Orœtes to Polycrates thus sayeth: I hear thou raisest thy thoughts high, but thy means are not equal to thy ambition. Listen then to my words, and learn how thou mayest at once serve thyself and preserve me. King Cambyses is bent on my destruction—of this I have warning from a sure hand. Come thou, therefore, and fetch me away, me and all my wealth—share my wealth with me, and then, so far as money can aid, thou mayest make thyself master of the whole of Greece. But if thou doubtest of my wealth, send the trustiest of thy followers, and I will show my treasures to him."

123. Polycrates, when he heard this message, was full of joy, and straightway approved the terms; but, as money was what he chiefly desired, before stirring in the business he sent his secretary, Mæandrius, son of Mæandrius, a Samian, to look into the matter. This was the man who, not very long afterwards, made an offering at the temple of Juno of all the furniture which had adorned the male apartments in the palace of Polycrates, an offering well worth seeing. Orœtes learning that one was coming to view his treasures, contrived as fol-

lows:—he filled eight great chests almost brim-ful of stones, and then covering over the stones with gold, corded the chests, and so held them in readiness. When Mæandrius arrived, he was shown this as Orœtes' treasure, and having seen it returned to Samos.

124. On hearing his account, Polycrates, notwithstanding many warnings given him by the soothsayers, and much dissuasion of his friends, made ready to go in person. Even the dream which visited his daughter failed to check him. She had dreamed that she saw her father hanging high in air, washed by Jove, and anointed by the sun. Having therefore thus dreamed, she used every effort to prevent her father from going; even as he went on board his penteconter crying after him with words of evil omen. Then Polycrates threatened her that, if he returned in safety, he would keep her unmarried many years. She answered, "Oh! that he might perform his threat; far better for her to remain long unmarried than to be bereft of her father!"

125. Polycrates, however, making light of all the counsel offered him, set sail and went to Orœtes. Many friends accompanied him; among the rest, Democêdes, the son of Calli-phon, a native of Crotona, who was a physi-cian, and the best skilled in his art of all men then living. Polycrates, on his arrival at Mag-nesia, perished miserably, in a way unworthy of his rank and of his lofty schemes. For, if we except the Syracusans, there has never been one of the Greek tyrants who was to be com-pared with Polycrates for magnificence. Orœ-tes, however, slew him in a mode which is not fit to be described, and then hung his dead body upon a cross. His Samian followers Orœ-tes let go free, bidding them thank him that they were allowed their liberty; the rest, who were in part slaves, in part free foreigners, he alike treated as his slaves by conquest. Then was the dream of the daughter of Polycrates fulfilled; for Polycrates, as he hung upon the cross, and rain fell on him, was washed by Ju-piter; and he was anointed by the sun, when his own moisture overspread his body. And so the vast good fortune of Polycrates came at last to the end which Amasis the Egyptian king had prophesied in days gone by.

126. It was not long before retribution for the murder of Polycrates overtook Orœtes. After the death of Cambyses, and during all the time that the Magus sat upon the throne, Orœ-tes remained in Sardis, and brought no help to the Persians, whom the Medes had robbed

of the sovereignty. On the contrary, amid the troubles of this season, he slew Mitrobates, the satrap of Dascyleium, who had cast the re-proach upon him in the matter of Polycrates; and he slew also Mitrobates's son, Cranaspes —both men of high repute among the Per-sians. He was likewise guilty of many other acts of insolence; among the rest, of the follow-ing:—there was a courier sent to him by Da-rius whose message was not to his mind— Orœtes had him waylaid and murdered on his road back to the king; the man and his horse both disappeared, and no traces were left of either.

127. Darius therefore was no sooner settled upon the throne than he longed to take ven-geance upon Orœtes for all his misdoings, and especially for the murder of Mitrobates and his son. To send an armed force openly against him, however, he did not think advisable, as the whole kingdom was still unsettled, and he too was but lately come to the throne, while Orœtes, as he understood, had a great power. In truth a thousand Persians attended on him as a bodyguard, and he held the satrapies of Phrygia, Lydia, and Ionia. Darius therefore proceeded by artifice. He called together a meeting of all the chief of the Persians, and thus addressed them:—"Who among you, O Persians, will undertake to accomplish me a matter by skill without force or tumult? Force is misplaced where the work wants skilful management. Who, then, will undertake to bring me Orœtes alive, or else to kill him? He never did the Persians any good in his life, and he has wrought us abundant injury. Two of our number, Mitrobates and his son, he has slain; and when messengers go to recall him, even though they have their mandate from me, with an insolence which is not to be en-dured, he puts them to death. We must kill this man, therefore, before he does the Persians any greater hurt."

128. Thus spoke Darius; and straightway thirty of those present came forward and of-fered themselves for the work. As they strove together, Darius interfered, and bade them have recourse to the lot. Accordingly lots were cast, and the task fell to Bagæus, son of Ar-tontes. Then Bagæus caused many letters to be written on divers matters, and sealed them all with the king's signet; after which he took the letters with him, and departed for Sardis. On his arrival he was shown into the presence of Orœtes, when he uncovered the letters one by one, and giving them to the king's secretary—

every satrap has with him a king's secretary—commanded him to read their contents. Herein his design was to try the fidelity of the bodyguard, and to see if they would be likely to fall away from Orœtes. When therefore he saw that they showed the letters all due respect, and even more highly reverenced their contents, he gave the secretary a paper in which was written, "Persians, king Darius forbids you to guard Orœtes." The soldiers at these words laid aside their spears. So Bagæus, finding that they obeyed this mandate, took courage, and gave into the secretary's hands the last letter, wherein it was written, "King Darius commands the Persians who are in Sardis to kill Orœtes." Then the guards drew their swords and slew him upon the spot. Thus did retribution for the murder of Polycrates the Samian overtake Orœtes the Persian.

129. Soon after the treasures of Orœtes had been conveyed to Sardis it happened that king Darius, as he leaped from his horse during the chase, sprained his foot. The sprain was one of no common severity, for the ankle-bone was forced quite out of the socket. Now Darius already had at his court certain Egyptians whom he reckoned the best-skilled physicians in all the world; to their aid, therefore, he had recourse; but they twisted the foot so clumsily, and used such violence, that they only made the mischief greater. For seven days and seven nights the king lay without sleep, so grievous was the pain he suffered. On the eighth day of his indisposition, one who had heard before leaving Sardis of the skill of Democêdes the Crotoniat, told Darius, who commanded that he should be brought with all speed into his presence. When, therefore, they had found him among the slaves of Orœtes, quite uncared for by any one, they brought him just as he was, clanking his fetters, and all clothed in rags, before the king.

130. As soon as he was entered into the presence, Darius asked him if he knew medicine—to which he answered "No," for he feared that if he made himself known he would lose all chance of ever again beholding Greece. Darius, however, perceiving that he dealt deceitfully, and really understood the art, bade those who had brought him to the presence go fetch the scourges and the pricking-irons. Upon this Democêdes made confession, but at the same time said, that he had no thorough knowledge of medicine—he had but lived some time with a physician, and in this way had gained a slight smattering of the art.

However, Darius put himself under his care, and Democêdes, by using the remedies customary among the Greeks, and exchanging the violent treatment of the Egyptians for milder means, first enabled him to get some sleep, and then in a very little time restored him altogether, after he had quite lost the hope of ever having the use of his foot. Hereupon the king presented Democêdes with two sets of fetters wrought in gold; so Democêdes asked if he meant to double his sufferings because he had brought him back to health? Darius was pleased at the speech, and bade the eunuchs take Democêdes to see his wives, which they did accordingly, telling them all that this was the man who had saved the king's life. Then each of the wives dipped with a saucer into a chest of gold, and gave so bountifully to Democêdes, that a slave named Sciton, who followed him, and picked up the staters[1] which fell from the saucers, gathered together a great heap of gold.

131. This Democêdes left his country and became attached to Polycrates in the following way:—His father, who dwelt at Crotona, was a man of a savage temper, and treated him cruelly. When, therefore, he could no longer bear such constant ill-usage, Democêdes left his home, and sailed away to Egina. There he set up in business, and succeeded the first year in surpassing all the best-skilled physicians of the place, notwithstanding that he was without instruments, and had with him none of the appliances needful for the practice of his art. In the second year the state of Egina hired his services at the price of a talent; in the third the Athenians engaged him at a hundred minæ; and in the fourth Polycrates at two talents. So he went to Samos, and there took up his abode. It was in no small measure from his success that the Crotoniats came to be reckoned such good physicians; for about this period the physicians of Crotona had the name of being the best, and those of Cyrêné the second best, in all Greece. The Argives, about the same time, were thought to be the first musicians in Greece.

132. After Democêdes had cured Darius at Susa, he dwelt there in a large house, and feasted daily at the king's table, nor did he lack anything that his heart desired, excepting liberty to return to his country. By interceding for them with Darius, he saved the lives of the Egyptian physicians who had had the care of the king before he came, when they were about

[1] A stater was worth $5.72.

to be impaled because they had been surpassed by a Greek; and further, he succeeded in rescuing an Elean soothsayer, who had followed the fortunes of Polycrates, and was lying in utter neglect among his slaves. In short there was no one who stood so high as Democêdes in the favour of the king.

133. Moreover, within a little while it happened that Atossa, the daughter of Cyrus, who was married to Darius, had a boil form upon her breast, which, after it burst, began to spread and increase. Now so long as the sore was of no great size, she hid it through shame and made no mention of it to any one; but when it became worse, she sent at last for Democêdes, and showed it to him. Democêdes said that he would make her well, but she must first promise him with an oath that if he cured her she would grant him whatever request he might prefer; assuring her at the same time that it should be nothing which she could blush to hear.

134. On these terms Democêdes applied his art, and soon cured the abscess; and Atossa, when she had heard his request, spake thus one night to Darius:—

"It seemeth to me strange, my lord, that, with the mighty power which is thine, thou sittest idle, and neither makest any conquest, nor advancest the power of the Persians. Methinks that one who is so young, and so richly endowed with wealth, should perform some noble achievement to prove to the Persians that it is a man who governs them. Another reason, too, should urge thee to attempt some enterprise. Not only does it befit thee to show the Persians that a man rules them, but for thy own peace thou shouldest waste their strength in wars lest idleness breed revolt against thy authority. Now, too, whilst thou art still young, thou mayest well accomplish some exploit; for as the body grows in strength the mind too ripens, and as the body ages, the mind's powers decay, till at last it becomes dulled to everything."

So spake Atossa, as Democêdes had instructed her. Darius answered:—"Dear lady, thou hast uttered the very thoughts that occupy my brain. I am minded to construct a bridge which shall join our continent with the other, and so carry war into Scythia. Yet a brief space and all will be accomplished as thou desirest."

But Atossa rejoined:—"Look now, this war with Scythia were best reserved awhile—for the Scythians may be conquered at any time. Prithee, lead me thy host first into Greece. I long to be served by some of those Lacedæmonian maids of whom I have heard so much. I want also Argive, and Athenian, and Corinthian women. There is now at the court a man who can tell thee better than any one else in the whole world whatever thou wouldst know concerning Greece, and who might serve thee right well as guide; I mean him who performed the cure on thy foot."

"Dear lady," Darius answered, "since it is thy wish that we try first the valour of the Greeks, it were best, methinks, before marching against them, to send some Persians to spy out the land; they may go in company with the man thou mentionest, and when they have seen and learnt all, they can bring us back a full report. Then, having a more perfect knowledge of them, I will begin the war."

135. Darius, having so spoke, put no long distance between the word and the deed, but as soon as day broke he summoned to his presence fifteen Persians of note, and bade them take Democêdes for their guide, and explore the sea-coasts of Greece. Above all, they were to be sure to bring Democêdes back with them, and not suffer him to run away and escape. After he had given these orders, Darius sent for Democêdes, and besought him to serve as guide to the Persians, and when he had shown them the whole of Greece to come back to Persia. He should take, he said, all the valuables he possessed as presents to his father and his brothers, and he should receive on his return a far more abundant store. Moreover, the king added, he would give him, as his contribution towards the presents, a merchantship laden with all manner of precious things, which should accompany him on his voyage. Now I do not believe that Darius, when he made these promises, had any guile in his heart: Democêdes, however, who suspected that the king spoke to try him, took care not to snatch at the offers with any haste; but said, "he would leave his own goods behind to enjoy upon his return—the merchant-ship which the king proposed to grant him to carry gifts to his brothers, that he would accept at the king's hands." So when Darius had laid his orders upon Democêdes, he sent him and the Persians away to the coast.

136. The men went down to Phœnicia, to Sidon, the Phœnician town, where straightway they fitted out two triremes and a trading-vessel, which they loaded with all manner of precious merchandise; and, everything being now ready, they set sail for Greece. When they had

made the land, they kept along the shore and examined it, taking notes of all that they saw; and in this way they explored the greater portion of the country, and all the most famous regions, until at last they reached Tarentum in Italy. There Aristophilides, king of the Tarentines, out of kindness to Democêdes, took the rudders off the Median ships, and detained their crews as spies. Meanwhile Democêdes escaped to Crotona, his native city, whereupon Aristophilides released the Persians from prison, and gave their rudders back to them.

137. The Persians now quitted Tarentum, and sailed to Crotona in pursuit of Democêdes; they found him in the market-place, where they straightway laid violent hands on him. Some of the Crotoniats, who greatly feared the power of the Persians, were willing to give him up; but others resisted, held Democêdes fast, and even struck the Persians with their walking-sticks. They, on their part, kept crying out, "Men of Crotona, beware what you do. It is the king's runaway slave that you are rescuing. Think you Darius will tamely submit to such an insult? Think you, that if you carry off the man from us, it will hereafter go well with you? Will you not rather be the first persons on whom we shall make war? Will not your city be the first we shall seek to lead away captive?" Thus they spake, but the Crotoniats did not heed them; they rescued Democêdes, and seized also the trading-ship which the Persians had brought with them from Phœnicia. Thus robbed, and bereft of their guide, the Persians gave up all hope of exploring the rest of Greece, and set sail for Asia. As they were departing, Democêdes sent to them and begged they would inform Darius that the daughter of Milo was affianced to him as his bride. For the name of Milo the wrestler was in high repute with the king. My belief is, that Democêdes hastened his marriage by the payment of a large sum of money for the purpose of showing Darius that he was a man of mark in his own country.

138. The Persians weighed anchor and left Crotona, but, being wrecked on the coast of Iapygia, were made slaves by the inhabitants. From this condition they were rescued by Gillus, a banished Tarentine, who ransomed them at his own cost, and took them back to Darius. Darius offered to repay this service by granting Gillus whatever boon he chose to ask; whereupon Gillus told the king of his misfortune, and begged to be restored to his country. Fearing, however, that he might bring trouble on Greece if a vast armament were sent to Italy on his account, he added that it would content him if the Cnidians undertook to obtain his recall. Now the Cnidians were close friends of the Tarentines, which made him think there was no likelier means of procuring his return. Darius promised and performed his part; for he sent a messenger to Cnidus, and commanded the Cnidians to restore Gillus. The Cnidians did as he wished, but found themselves unable to persuade the Tarentines, and were too weak to attempt force. Such then was the course which this matter took. These were the first Persians who ever came from Asia to Greece; and they were sent to spy out the land for the reason which I have before mentioned.

139. After this, king Darius besieged and took Samos, which was the first city, Greek or Barbarian, that he conquered. The cause of his making war upon Samos was the following:— at the time when Cambyses, son of Cyrus, marched against Egypt, vast numbers of Greeks flocked thither; some, as might have been looked for, to push their trade; others, to serve in his army; others again, merely to see the land: among these last was Syloson, son of Æaces, and brother of Polycrates, at that time an exile from Samos. This Syloson, during his stay in Egypt, met with a singular piece of good fortune. He happened one day to put on a scarlet cloak, and thus attired to go into the market-place at Memphis, when Darius, who was one of Cambyses' bodyguard, and not at that time a man of any account, saw him, and taking a strong liking to the dress, went up and offered to purchase it. Syloson perceived how anxious he was, and by a lucky inspiration answered: "There is no price at which I would sell my cloak; but I will give it thee for nothing, if it must needs be thine." Darius thanked him, and accepted the garment.

140. Poor Syloson felt at the time that he had fooled away his cloak in a very simple manner; but afterwards, when in the course of years Cambyses died, and the seven Persians rose in revolt against the Magus, and Darius was the man chosen out of the seven to have the kingdom, Syloson learnt that the person to whom the crown had come was the very man who had coveted his cloak in Egypt, and to whom he had freely given it. So he made his way to Susa, and seating himself at the portal of the royal palace, gave out that he was a benefactor of the king. Then the doorkeeper went and told Darius. Amazed at what he heard, the king said thus within himself:—"What Greek

can have been my benefactor, or to which of them do I owe anything, so lately as I have got the kingdom? Scarcely a man of them all has been here, not more than one or two certainly, since I came to the throne. Nor do I remember that I am in the debt of any Greek. However, bring him in, and let me hear what he means by his boast." So the doorkeeper ushered Syloson into the presence, and the interpreters asked him who he was, and what he had done that he should call himself a benefactor of the king. Then Syloson told the whole story of the cloak, and said that it was he who had made Darius the present. Hereupon Darius exclaimed, "Oh! thou most generous of men, art thou indeed he who, when I had no power at all, gavest me something, albeit little? Truly the favour is as great as a very grand present would be nowadays. I will therefore give thee in return gold and silver without stint, that thou mayest never repent of having rendered a service to Darius, son of Hystaspes." "Give me not, O king," replied Syloson, "either silver or gold, but recover me Samos, my native land, and let that be thy gift to me. It belongs now to a slave of ours, who, when Orœtes put my brother Polycrates to death, became its master. Give me Samos, I beg; but give it unharmed, with no bloodshed—no leading into captivity."

141. When he heard this, Darius sent off an army, under Otanes, one of the seven, with orders to accomplish all that Syloson had desired. And Otanes went down to the coast and made ready to cross over.

142. The government of Samos was held at this time by Mæandrius, son of Mæandrius, whom Polycrates had appointed as his deputy. This person conceived the wish to act like the justest of men, but it was not allowed him to do so. On receiving tidings of the death of Polycrates, he forthwith raised an altar to Jove the Protector of Freedom, and assigned it the piece of ground which may still be seen in the suburb. This done, he assembled all the citizens, and spoke to them as follows:—

"Ye know, friends, that the sceptre of Polycrates, and all his power, has passed into my hands, and if I choose I may rule over you. But what I condemn in another I will, if I may, avoid myself. I never approved the ambition of Polycrates to lord it over men as good as himself, nor looked with favour on any of those who have done the like. Now therefore, since he has fulfilled his destiny, I lay down my office, and proclaim equal rights. All that I claim in return is six talents from the treasures of Polycrates, and the priesthood of Jove the Protector of Freedom, for myself and my descendants for ever. Allow me this, as the man by whom his temple has been built, and by whom ye yourselves are now restored to liberty." As soon as Mæandrius had ended, one of the Samians rose up and said, "As if thou wert fit to rule us, base-born and rascal as thou art! Think rather of accounting for the monies which thou hast fingered."

143. The man who thus spoke was a certain Telesarchus, one of the leading citizens. Mæandrius, therefore, feeling sure that if he laid down the sovereign power some one else would become tyrant in his room, gave up the thought of relinquishing it. Withdrawing to the citadel, he sent for the chief men one by one, under pretence of showing them his accounts, and as fast as they came arrested them and put them in irons. So these men were bound; and Mæandrius within a short time fell sick: whereupon Lycarêtus, one of his brothers, thinking that he was going to die, and wishing to make his own accession to the throne the easier, slew all the prisoners. It seemed that the Samians did not choose to be a free people.

144. When the Persians whose business it was to restore Syloson reached Samos, not a man was found to lift up his hand against them. Mæandrius and his partisans expressed themselves willing to quit the island upon certain terms, and these terms were agreed to by Otanes. After the treaty was made, the most distinguished of the Persians had their thrones brought, and seated themselves over against the citadel.

145. Now the king Mæandrius had a light-headed brother—Charilaüs by name—whom for some offence or other he had shut up in prison: this man heard what was going on, and peering through his bars, saw the Persians sitting peacefully upon their seats, whereupon he exclaimed aloud, and said he must speak with Mæandrius. When this was reported to him, Mæandrius gave orders that Charilaüs should be released from prison and brought into his presence. No sooner did he arrive than he began reviling and abusing his brother, and strove to persuade him to attack the Persians. "Thou meanest-spirited of men," he said, "thou canst keep me, thy brother, chained in a dungeon, notwithstanding that I have done nothing worthy of bonds; but when the Persians come and drive thee forth a houseless wanderer from thy native land, thou lookest

on, and hast not the heart to seek revenge, though they might so easily be subdued. If thou, however, art afraid, lend me thy soldiers, and I will make them pay dearly for their coming here. I engage too to send thee first safe out of the island."

146. So spake Charilaüs, and Mæandrius gave consent; not (I believe) that he was so void of sense as to imagine that his own forces could overcome those of the king, but because he was jealous of Syloson, and did not wish him to get so quietly an unharmed city. He desired therefore to rouse the anger of the Persians against Samos, that so he might deliver it up to Syloson with its power at the lowest possible ebb; for he knew well that if the Persians met with a disaster they would be furious against the Samians, while he himself felt secure of a retreat at any time that he liked, since he had a secret passage under ground leading from the citadel to the sea. Mæandrius accordingly took ship and sailed away from Samos; and Charilaüs, having armed all the mercenaries, threw open the gates, and fell upon the Persians, who looked for nothing less, since they supposed that the whole matter had been arranged by treaty. At the first onslaught therefore all the Persians of most note, men who were in the habit of using litters, were slain by the mercenaries; the rest of the army, however, came to the rescue, defeated the mercenaries, and drove them back into the citadel.

147. Then Otanes, the general, when he saw the great calamity which had befallen the Persians, made up his mind to forget the orders which Darius had given him, "not to kill or enslave a single Samian, but to deliver up the island unharmed to Syloson," and gave the word to his army that they should slay the Samians, both men and boys, wherever they could find them. Upon this some of his troops laid siege to the citadel, while others began the massacre, killing all they met, some outside, some inside the temples.

148. Mæandrius fled from Samos to Lacedæmon, and conveyed thither all the riches which he had brought away from the island, after which he acted as follows. Having placed upon his board all the gold and silver vessels that he had, and bade his servants employ themselves in cleaning them, he himself went and entered into conversation with Cleomenes, son of Anaxandridas, king of Sparta, and as they talked brought him along to his house. There Cleomenes, seeing the plate, was filled with wonder

and astonishment; whereon the other begged that he would carry home with him any of the vessels that he liked. Mæandrius said this two or three times; but Cleomenes here displayed surpassing honesty. He refused the gift, and thinking that if Mæandrius made the same offers to others he would get the aid he sought, the Spartan king went straight to the ephors and told them "it would be best for Sparta that the Samian stranger should be sent away from the Peloponnese; for otherwise he might perchance persuade himself or some other Spartan to be base." The ephors took his advice, and let Mæandrius know by a herald that he must leave the city.

149. Meanwhile the Persians netted Samos, and delivered it up to Syloson, stripped of all its men. After some time, however, this same general Otanes was induced to repeople it by a dream which he had, and a loathsome disease that seized on him.

150. After the armament of Otanes had set sail for Samos, the Babylonians revolted, having made every preparation for defence. During all the time that the Magus was king, and while the seven were conspiring, they had profited by the troubles, and had made themselves ready against a siege. And it happened somehow or other that no one perceived what they were doing. At last when the time came for rebelling openly, they did as follows:— having first set apart their mothers, each man chose besides out of his whole household one woman, whomsoever he pleased; these alone were allowed to live, while all the rest were brought to one place and strangled. The women chosen were kept to make bread for the men; while the others were strangled that they might not consume the stores.

151. When tidings reached Darius of what had happened, he drew together all his power, and began the war by marching straight upon Babylon, and laying siege to the place. The Babylonians, however, cared not a whit for his siege. Mounting upon the battlements that crowned their walls, they insulted and jeered at Darius and his mighty host. One even shouted to them and said, "Why sit ye there, Persians? why do ye not go back to your homes? Till mules foal ye will not take our city." This was said by a Babylonian who thought that a mule would never foal.

152. Now when a year and seven months had passed, Darius and his army were quite wearied out, finding that they could not anyhow take the city. All stratagems and all arts

had been used, and yet the king could not prevail—not even when he tried the means by
which Cyrus made himself master of the place.
The Babylonians were ever upon the watch,
and he found no way of conquering them.

153. At last, in the twentieth month, a marvellous thing happened to Zopyrus, son of the
Megabyzus who was among the seven men
that overthrew the Magus. One of his sumpter-
mules gave birth to a foal. Zopyrus, when they
told him, not thinking that it could be true,
went and saw the colt with his own eyes; after
which he commanded his servants to tell no
one what had come to pass, while he himself
pondered the matter. Calling to mind then the
words of the Babylonian at the beginning of
the siege, "Till mules foal ye shall not take our
city"—he thought, as he reflected on this
speech, that Babylon might now be taken. For
it seemed to him that there was a Divine Providence in the man having used the phrase, and
then his mule having foaled.

154. As soon therefore as he felt within himself that Babylon was fated to be taken, he
went to Darius and asked him if he set a very
high value on its conquest. When he found
that Darius did indeed value it highly, he considered further with himself how he might
make the deed his own, and be the man to take
Babylon. Noble exploits in Persia are ever
highly honoured and bring their authors to
greatness. He therefore reviewed all ways of
bringing the city under, but found none by
which he could hope to prevail, unless he
maimed himself and then went over to the
enemy. To do this seeming to him a light matter, he mutilated himself in a way that was
utterly without remedy. For he cut off his own
nose and ears, and then, clipping his hair close
and flogging himself with a scourge, he came
in this plight before Darius.

155. Wrath stirred within the king at the
sight of a man of his lofty rank in such a condition; leaping down from his throne, he exclaimed aloud, and asked Zopyrus who it was
that had disfigured him, and what he had done
to be so treated. Zopyrus answered, "There is
not a man in the world, but thou, O king, that
could reduce me to such a plight—no stranger's hands have wrought this work on me, but
my own only. I maimed myself because I could
not endure that the Assyrians should laugh at
the Persians." "Wretched man," said Darius,
"thou coverest the foulest deed with the fairest
possible name, when thou sayest thy maiming
is to help our siege forward. How will thy dis-

figurement, thou simpleton, induce the enemy
to yield one day the sooner? Surely thou hadst
gone out of thy mind when thou didst so mis-
use thyself." "Had I told thee," rejoined the
other, "what I was bent on doing, thou wouldest not have suffered it; as it is, I kept my own
counsel, and so accomplished my plans. Now,
therefore, if there be no failure on thy part, we
shall take Babylon. I will desert to the enemy
as I am, and when I get into their city I will
tell them that it is by thee I have been thus
treated. I think they will believe my words,
and entrust me with a command of troops.
Thou, on thy part, must wait till the tenth day
after I am entered within the town, and then
place near to the gates of Semiramis a detachment of thy army, troops for whose loss thou
wilt care little, a thousand men. Wait, after
that, seven days, and post me another detachment, two thousand strong, at the Nineveh
gates; then let twenty days pass, and at the end
of that time station near the Chaldæan gates
a body of four thousand. Let neither these nor
the former troops be armed with any weapons
but their swords—those thou mayest leave
them. After the twenty days are over, bid thy
whole army attack the city on every side, and
put me two bodies of Persians, one at the Belian, the other at the Cissian gates; for I expect,
that, on account of my successes, the Babylonians will entrust everything, even the keys
of their gates, to me. Then it will be for me
and my Persians to do the rest."

156. Having left these instructions, Zopyrus
fled towards the gates of the town, often looking back, to give himself the air of a deserter.
The men upon the towers, whose business it
was to keep a lookout, observing him, hastened down, and setting one of the gates slightly ajar, questioned him who he was, and on
what errand he had come. He replied that he
was Zopyrus, and had deserted to them from
the Persians. Then the doorkeepers, when they
heard this, carried him at once before the Magistrates. Introduced into the assembly, he began to bewail his misfortunes, telling them
that Darius had maltreated him in the way
they could see, only because he had given advice that the siege should be raised, since there
seemed no hope of taking the city. "And now,"
he went on to say, "my coming to you, Babylonians, will prove the greatest gain that you
could possibly receive, while to Darius and the
Persians it will be the severest loss. Verily he
by whom I have been so mutilated shall not
escape unpunished. And truly all the paths of

his counsels are known to me." Thus did Zopyrus speak.

157. The Babylonians, seeing a Persian of such exalted rank in so grievous a plight, his nose and ears cut off, his body red with marks of scourging and with blood, had no suspicion but that he spoke the truth, and was really come to be their friend and helper. They were ready, therefore, to grant him anything that he asked; and on his suing for a command, they entrusted to him a body of troops, with the help of which he proceeded to do as he had arranged with Darius. On the tenth day after his flight he led out his detachment, and surrounding the thousand men, whom Darius according to agreement had sent first, he fell upon them and slew them all. Then the Babylonians, seeing that his deeds were as brave as his words, were beyond measure pleased, and set no bounds to their trust. He waited, however, and when the next period agreed on had elapsed, again with a band of picked men he sallied forth, and slaughtered the two thousand. After this second exploit, his praise was in all mouths. Once more, however, he waited till the interval appointed had gone by, and then leading the troops to the place where the four thousand were, he put them also to the sword. This last victory gave the finishing stroke to his power, and made him all in all with the Babylonians: accordingly they committed to him the command of their whole army, and put the keys of their city into his hands.

158. Darius now, still keeping to the plan agreed upon, attacked the walls on every side, whereupon Zopyrus played out the remainder of his stratagem. While the Babylonians, crowding to the walls, did their best to resist the Persian assault, he threw open the Cissian and the Belian gates, and admitted the enemy.

Such of the Babylonians as witnessed the treachery, took refuge in the temple of Jupiter Belus; the rest, who did not see it, kept at their posts, till at last they too learnt that they were betrayed.

159. Thus was Babylon taken for the second time. Darius having become master of the place, destroyed the wall, and tore down all the gates; for Cyrus had done neither the one nor the other when he took Babylon. He then chose out near three thousand of the leading citizens, and caused them to be crucified, while he allowed the remainder still to inhabit the city. Further, wishing to prevent the race of the Babylonians from becoming extinct, he provided wives for them in the room of those whom (as I explained before) they strangled, to save their stores. These he levied from the nations bordering on Babylonia, who were each required to send so large a number to Babylon, that in all there were collected no fewer than fifty thousand. It is from these women that the Babylonians of our times are sprung.

160. As for Zopyrus, he was considered by Darius to have surpassed, in the greatness of his achievements, all other Persians, whether of former or of later times, except only Cyrus—with whom no Persian ever yet thought himself worthy to compare. Darius, as the story goes, would often say that "he had rather Zopyrus were unmaimed, than be master of twenty more Babylons." And he honoured Zopyrus greatly; year by year he presented him with all the gifts which are held in most esteem among the Persians; he gave him likewise the government of Babylon for his life, free from tribute; and he also granted him many other favours. Megabyzus, who held the command in Egypt against the Athenians and their allies, was a son of this Zopyrus. And Zopyrus, who fled from Persia to Athens, was a son of this Megabyzus.

The Fourth Book, Entitled
MELPOMENE

1. After the taking of Babylon, an expedition was led by Darius into Scythia. Asia abounding in men, and vast sums flowing into the treasury, the desire seized him to exact vengeance from the Scyths, who had once in days gone by invaded Media, defeated those who met them in the field, and so begun the quarrel. During the space of eight-and-twenty years, as I have before mentioned, the Scyths continued lords of the whole of Upper Asia. They entered Asia in pursuit of the Cimmerians, and overthrew the empire of the Medes, who till they came possessed the sovereignty. On their return to their homes after the long absence of twenty-eight years, a task awaited them little less troublesome than their struggle with the Medes. They found an army of no small size prepared to oppose their entrance. For the Scythian women, when they saw that time went on, and their husbands did not come back, had intermarried with their slaves.

2. Now the Scythians blind all their slaves, to use them in preparing their milk. The plan they follow is to thrust tubes made of bone, not unlike our musical pipes, up the vulva of the mare, and then to blow into the tubes with their mouths, some milking while the others blow. They say that they do this because when the veins of the animal are full of air, the udder is forced down. The milk thus obtained is poured into deep wooden casks, about which the blind slaves are placed, and then the milk is stirred round. That which rises to the top is drawn off, and considered the best part; the under portion is of less account. Such is the reason why the Scythians blind all those whom they take in war; it arises from their not being tillers of the ground, but a pastoral race.

3. When therefore the children sprung from these slaves and the Scythian women grew to manhood, and understood the circumstances of their birth, they resolved to oppose the army which was returning from Media. And, first of all, they cut off a tract of country from the rest of Scythia by digging a broad dyke from the Tauric mountains to the vast lake of the Mæotis. Afterwards, when the Scythians tried to force an entrance, they marched out and engaged them. Many battles were fought, and the Scythians gained no advantage, until at last one of them thus addressed the remainder: "What are we doing, Scythians? We are fighting our slaves, diminishing our own number when we fall, and the number of those that belong to us when they fall by our hands. Take my advice—lay spear and bow aside, and let each man fetch his horsewhip, and go boldly up to them. So long as they see us with arms in our hands, they imagine themselves our equals in birth and bravery; but let them behold us with no other weapon but the whip, and they will feel that they are our slaves, and flee before us."

4. The Scythians followed this counsel, and the slaves were so astounded, that they forgot to fight, and immediately ran away. Such was the mode in which the Scythians, after being for a time the lords of Asia, and being forced to quit it by the Medes, returned and settled in their own country. This inroad of theirs it was that Darius was anxious to avenge, and such was the purpose for which he was now collecting an army to invade them.

5. According to the account which the Scythians themselves give, they are the youngest of all nations. Their tradition is as follows. A certain Targitaüs was the first man who ever lived in their country, which before his time was a desert without inhabitants. He was a child—I do not believe the tale, but it is told nevertheless—of Jove and a daughter of the Borysthenes. Targitaüs, thus descended, begat three sons, Leipoxais, Arpoxais, and Colaxais, who was the youngest born of the three. While

they still ruled the land, there fell from the sky four implements, all of gold—a plough, a yoke, a battle-axe, and a drinking-cup. The eldest of the brothers perceived them first, and approached to pick them up; when lo! as he came near, the gold took fire, and blazed. He therefore went his way, and the second coming forward made the attempt, but the same thing happened again. The gold rejected both the eldest and the second brother. Last of all the youngest brother approached, and immediately the flames were extinguished; so he picked up the gold, and carried it to his home. Then the two elder agreed together, and made the whole kingdom over to the youngest born.

6. From Leipoxais sprang the Scythians of the race called Auchatæ; from Arpoxais, the middle brother, those known as the Catiari and Traspians; from Colaxais, the youngest, the Royal Scythians, or Paralatæ. All together they are named Scoloti, after one of their kings: the Greeks, however, call them Scythians.

7. Such is the account which the Scythians give of their origin. They add that from the time of Targitaüs, their first king, to the invasion of their country by Darius, is a period of one thousand years, neither less nor more. The Royal Scythians guard the sacred gold with most especial care, and year by year offer great sacrifices in its honour. At this feast, if the man who has the custody of the gold should fall asleep in the open air, he is sure (the Scythians say) not to outlive the year. His pay therefore is as much land as he can ride round on horseback in a day. As the extent of Scythia is very great, Colaxais gave each of his three sons a separate kingdom, one of which was of ampler size than the other two: in this the gold was preserved. Above, to the northward of the farthest dwellers in Scythia, the country is said to be concealed from sight and made impassable by reason of the feathers which are shed abroad abundantly. The earth and air are alike full of them, and this it is which prevents the eye from obtaining any view of the region.

8. Such is the account which the Scythians give of themselves, and of the country which lies above them. The Greeks who dwell about the Pontus tell a different story. According to them, Hercules, when he was carrying off the cows of Geryon, arrived in the region which is now inhabited by the Scyths, but which was then a desert. Geryon lived outside the Pontus, in an island called by the Greeks Erytheia, near Gades, which is beyond the Pillars of Hercules upon the Ocean. Now some say that the Ocean begins in the east, and runs the whole way round the world; but they give no proof that this is really so. Hercules came from thence into the region now called Scythia, and, being overtaken by storm and frost, drew his lion's skin about him, and fell fast asleep. While he slept, his mares, which he had loosed from his chariot to graze, by some wonderful chance disappeared.

9. On waking, he went in quest of them, and, after wandering over the whole country, came at last to the district called "the Woodland," where he found in a cave a strange being, between a maiden and a serpent, whose form from the waist upwards was like that of a woman, while all below was like a snake. He looked at her wonderingly; but nevertheless inquired, whether she had chanced to see his strayed mares anywhere. She answered him, "Yes, and they were now in her keeping; but never would she consent to give them back, unless he took her for his mistress." So Hercules, to get his mares back, agreed; but afterwards she put him off and delayed restoring the mares, since she wished to keep him with her as long as possible. He, on the other hand, was only anxious to secure them and to get away. At last, when she gave them up, she said to him, "When thy mares strayed hither, it was I who saved them for thee: now thou hast paid their salvage; for lo! I bear in my womb three sons of thine. Tell me therefore when thy sons grow up, what must I do with them? Wouldst thou wish that I should settle them here in this land, whereof I am mistress, or shall I send them to thee?" Thus questioned, they say, Hercules answered, "When the lads have grown to manhood, do thus, and assuredly thou wilt not err. Watch them, and when thou seest one of them bend this bow as I now bend it, and gird himself with this girdle thus, choose *him* to remain in the land. Those who fail in the trial, send away. Thus wilt thou at once please thyself and obey me."

10. Hereupon he strung one of his bows—up to that time he had carried two—and showed her how to fasten the belt. Then he gave both bow and belt into her hands. Now the belt had a golden goblet attached to its clasp. So after he had given them to her, he went his way; and the woman, when her children grew to manhood, first gave them severally their names. One she called Agathyrsus, one Gelônus, and the other, who was the youngest, Scythes. Then she remembered the

instructions she had received from Hercules, and, in obedience to his orders, she put her sons to the test. Two of them, Agathyrsus and Gelônus, proving unequal to the task enjoined, their mother sent them out of the land; Scythes, the youngest, succeeded, and so he was allowed to remain. From Scythes, the son of Hercules, were descended the after kings of Scythia; and from the circumstance of the goblet which hung from the belt, the Scythians to this day wear goblets at their girdles. This was the only thing which the mother of Scythes did for him. Such is the tale told by the Greeks who dwell around the Pontus.

11. There is also another different story, now to be related, in which I am more inclined to put faith than in any other. It is that the wandering Scythians once dwelt in Asia, and there warred with the Massagetæ, but with ill success; they therefore quitted their homes, crossed the Araxes, and entered the land of Cimmeria. For the land which is now inhabited by the Scyths was formerly the country of the Cimmerians. On their coming, the natives, who heard how numerous the invading army was, held a council. At this meeting opinion was divided, and both parties stiffly maintained their own view; but the counsel of the Royal tribe was the braver. For the others urged that the best thing to be done was to leave the country, and avoid a contest with so vast a host; but the Royal tribe advised remaining and fighting for the soil to the last. As neither party chose to give way, the one determined to retire without a blow and yield their lands to the invaders; but the other, remembering the good things which they had enjoyed in their homes, and picturing to themselves the evils which they had to expect if they gave them up, resolved not to flee, but rather to die and at least be buried in their fatherland. Having thus decided, they drew apart in two bodies, the one as numerous as the other, and fought together. All of the Royal tribe were slain, and the people buried them near the river Tyras, where their grave is still to be seen. Then the rest of the Cimmerians departed, and the Scythians, on their coming, took possession of a deserted land.

12. Scythia still retains traces of the Cimmerians; there are Cimmerian castles, and a Cimmerian ferry, also a tract called Cimmeria, and a Cimmerian Bosphorus. It appears likewise that the Cimmerians, when they fled into Asia to escape the Scyths, made a settlement in the peninsula where the Greek city of Si-

nôpé was afterwards built. The Scyths, it is plain, pursued them, and missing their road, poured into Media. For the Cimmerians kept the line which led along the sea-shore, but the Scyths in their pursuit held the Caucasus upon their right, thus proceeding inland, and falling upon Media. This account is one which is common both to Greeks and barbarians.

13. Aristeas also, son of Caÿstrobius, a native of Proconnêsus, says in the course of his poem that wrapt in Bacchic fury he went as far as the Issedones. Above them dwelt the Arimaspi, men with one eye; still further, the gold-guarding griffins; and beyond these, the Hyperboreans, who extended to the sea. Except the Hyperboreans, all these nations, beginning with the Arimaspi, were continually encroaching upon their neighbours. Hence it came to pass that the Arimaspi drove the Issedonians from their country, while the Issedonians dispossessed the Scyths; and the Scyths, pressing upon the Cimmerians, who dwelt on the shores of the Southern Sea, forced them to leave their land. Thus even Aristeas does not agree in his account of this region with the Scythians.

14. The birthplace of Aristeas, the poet who sung of these things, I have already mentioned. I will now relate a tale which I heard concerning him both at Proconnêsus and at Cyzicus. Aristeas, they said, who belonged to one of the noblest families in the island, had entered one day into a fuller's shop, when he suddenly dropt down dead. Hereupon the fuller shut up his shop, and went to tell Aristeas' kindred what had happened. The report of the death had just spread through the town, when a certain Cyzicenian, lately arrived from Artaca, contradicted the rumour, affirming that he had met Aristeas on his road to Cyzicus, and had spoken with him. This man, therefore, strenuously denied the rumour; the relations, however, proceeded to the fuller's shop with all things necessary for the funeral, intending to carry the body away. But on the shop being opened, no Aristeas was found, either dead or alive. Seven years afterwards he reappeared, they told me, in Proconnêsus, and wrote the poem called by the Greeks *The Arimaspeia,* after which he disappeared a second time. This is the tale current in the two cities abovementioned.

15. What follows I know to have happened to the Metapontines of Italy, three hundred and forty years[1] after the second disappear-

[1] This date must certainly be wrong. The date usually assigned to Aristeas is about 580 B.C.

ance of Aristeas, as I collect by comparing the accounts given me at Proconnêsus and Metapontum. Aristeas then, as the Metapontines affirm, appeared to them in their own country, and ordered them to set up an altar in honour of Apollo, and to place near it a statue to be called that of Aristeas the Proconnêsian. "Apollo," he told them, "had come to their country once, though he had visited no other Italiots; and he had been with Apollo at the time, not however in his present form, but in the shape of a crow." Having said so much, he vanished. Then the Metapontines, as they relate, sent to Delphi, and inquired of the god in what light they were to regard the appearance of this ghost of a man. The Pythoness, in reply, bade them attend to what the spectre said, "for so it would go best with them." Thus advised, they did as they had been directed: and there is now a statue bearing the name of Aristeas, close by the image of Apollo in the market-place of Metapontum, with bay-trees standing around it. But enough has been said concerning Aristeas.

16. With regard to the regions which lie above the country whereof this portion of my history treats, there is no one who possesses any exact knowledge. Not a single person can I find who professes to be acquainted with them by actual observation. Even Aristeas, the traveller of whom I lately spoke, does not claim— and he is writing poetry—to have reached any farther than the Issedonians. What he relates concerning the regions beyond is, he confesses, mere hearsay, being the account which the Issedonians gave him of those countries. However, I shall proceed to mention all that I have learnt of these parts by the most exact inquiries which I have been able to make concerning them.

17. Above the mart of the Borysthenites, which is situated in the very centre of the whole sea-coast of Scythia, the first people who inhabit the land are the Callipedæ, a Græco-Scythic race. Next to them, as you go inland, dwell the people called the Alazonians. These two nations in other respects resemble the Scythians in their usages, but sow and eat corn, also onions, garlic, lentils, and millet. Beyond the Alazonians reside Scythian cultivators, who grow corn, not for their own use, but for sale. Still higher up are the Neuri. Northwards of the Neuri the continent, as far as it is known to us, is uninhabited. These are the nations along the course of the river Hypanis, west of the Borysthenes.

18. Across the Borysthenes, the first country after you leave the coast is Hylæa (the Woodland). Above this dwell the Scythian Husbandmen, whom the Greeks living near the Hypanis call Borysthenites, while they call themselves Olbiopolites. These Husbandmen extend eastward a distance of three days' journey to a river bearing the name of Panticapes, while northward the country is theirs for eleven days' sail up the course of the Borysthenes. Further inland there is a vast tract which is uninhabited. Above this desolate region dwell the Cannibals, who are a people apart, much unlike the Scythians. Above them the country becomes an utter desert; not a single tribe, so far as we know, inhabits it.

19. Crossing the Panticapes, and proceeding eastward of the Husbandmen, we come upon the wandering Scythians, who neither plough nor sow. Their country, and the whole of this region, except Hylæa, is quite bare of trees. They extend towards the east a distance of fourteen[1] days' journey, occupying a tract which reaches to the river Gerrhus.

20. On the opposite side of the Gerrhus is the Royal district, as it is called: here dwells the largest and bravest of the Scythian tribes, which looks upon all the other tribes in the light of slaves. Its country reaches on the south to Taurica, on the east to the trench dug by the sons of the blind slaves, the mart upon the Palus Mæotis, called Cremni (the Cliffs), and in part to the river Tanais. North of the country of the Royal Scythians are the Melanchlæni (Black-Robes), a people of quite a different race from the Scythians. Beyond them lie marshes and a region without inhabitants, so far as our knowledge reaches.

21. When one crosses the Tanais, one is no longer in Scythia; the first region on crossing is that of the Sauromatæ, who, beginning at the upper end of the Palus Mæotis, stretch northward a distance of fifteen days' journey, inhabiting a country which is entirely bare of trees, whether wild or cultivated. Above them, possessing the second region, dwell the Budini, whose territory is thickly wooded with trees of every kind.

22. Beyond the Budini, as one goes northward, first there is a desert, seven days' journey across; after which, if one inclines somewhat to the east, the Thyssagetæ are reached, a nu-

[1] Rennell proposes to read "four days' journey" —and indeed without some such alteration the geography of this part of Scythia is utterly inexplicable.

merous nation quite distinct from any other, and living by the chase. Adjoining them, and within the limits of the same region, are the people who bear the name of Iyrcæ; they also support themselves by hunting, which they practise in the following manner. The hunter climbs a tree, the whole country abounding in wood, and there sets himself in ambush; he has a dog at hand, and a horse, trained to lie down upon its belly, and thus make itself low; the hunter keeps watch, and when he sees his game, lets fly an arrow; then mounting his horse, he gives the beast chase, his dog following hard all the while. Beyond these people, a little to the east, dwells a distinct tribe of Scyths, who revolted once from the Royal Scythians, and migrated into these parts.

23. As far as their country, the tract of land whereof I have been speaking is all a smooth plain, and the soil deep; beyond you enter on a region which is rugged and stony. Passing over a great extent of this rough country, you come to a people dwelling at the foot of lofty mountains, who are said to be all—both men and women—bald from their birth, to have flat noses, and very long chins. These people speak a language of their own, but the dress which they wear is the same as the Scythian. They live on the fruit of a certain tree, the name of which is Ponticum; in size it is about equal to our fig-tree, and it bears a fruit like a bean, with a stone inside. When the fruit is ripe, they strain it through cloths; the juice which runs off is black and thick, and is called by the natives "aschy." They lap this up with their tongues, and also mix it with milk for a drink; while they make the lees, which are solid, into cakes, and eat them instead of meat; for they have but few sheep in their country, in which there is no good pasturage. Each of them dwells under a tree, and they cover the tree in winter with a cloth of thick white felt, but take off the covering in the summer-time. No one harms these people, for they are looked upon as sacred—they do not even possess any warlike weapons. When their neighbours fall out, they make up the quarrel; and when one flies to them for refuge, he is safe from all hurt. They are called the Argippæans.

24. Up to this point the territory of which we are speaking is very completely explored, and all the nations between the coast and the bald-headed men are well known to us. For some of the Scythians are accustomed to penetrate as far, of whom inquiry may easily be made, and Greeks also go there from the mart

on the Borysthenes, and from the other marts along the Euxine. The Scythians who make this journey communicate with the inhabitants by means of seven interpreters and seven languages.

25. Thus far, therefore, the land is known; but beyond the bald-headed men lies a region of which no one can give any exact account. Lofty and precipitous mountains, which are never crossed, bar further progress. The bald men say, but it does not seem to me credible, that the people who live in these mountains have feet like goats; and that after passing them you find another race of men, who sleep during one half of the year. This latter statement appears to me quite unworthy of credit. The region east of the bald-headed men is well known to be inhabited by the Issedonians, but the tract that lies to the north of these two nations is entirely unknown, except by the accounts which they give of it.

26. The Issedonians are said to have the following customs. When a man's father dies, all the near relatives bring sheep to the house; which are sacrificed, and their flesh cut in pieces, while at the same time the dead body undergoes the like treatment. The two sorts of flesh are afterwards mixed together, and the whole is served up at a banquet. The head of the dead man is treated different'y: it is stripped bare, cleansed, and set in gold. It then becomes an ornament on which they pride themselves, and is brought out year by year at the great festival which sons keep in honour of their fathers' death, just as the Greeks keep their Genesia. In other respects the Issedonians are reputed to be observers of justice: and it is to be remarked that their women have equal authority with the men. Thus our knowledge extends as far as this nation.

27. The regions beyond are known only from the accounts of the Issedonians, by whom the stories are told of the one-eyed race of men and the gold-guarding griffins. These stories are received by the Scythians from the Issedonians, and by them passed on to us Greeks: whence it arises that we give the one-eyed race the Scythian name of Arimaspi, *"arima"* being the Scythic word for "one," and *"spŭ"* for "the eye."

28. The whole district whereof we have here discoursed has winters of exceeding rigour. During eight months the frost is so intense that water poured upon the ground does not form mud, but if a fire be lighted on it mud is produced. The sea freezes, and the Cimmer-

ian Bosphorus is frozen over. At that season the Scythians who dwell inside the trench make warlike expeditions upon the ice, and even drive their waggons across to the country of the Sindians. Such is the intensity of the cold during eight months out of the twelve; and even in the remaining four the climate is still cool. The character of the winter likewise is unlike that of the same season in any other country; for at that time, when the rains ought to fall in Scythia, there is scarcely any rain worth mentioning, while in summer it never gives over raining; and thunder, which elsewhere is frequent then, in Scythia is unknown in that part of the year, coming only in summer, when it is very heavy. Thunder in the winter-time is there accounted a prodigy; as also are earthquakes, whether they happen in winter or summer. Horses bear the winter well, cold as it is, but mules and asses are quite unable to bear it; whereas in other countries mules and asses are found to endure the cold, while horses, if they stand still, are frost-bitten.

29. To me it seems that the cold may likewise be the cause which prevents the oxen in Scythia from having horns. There is a line of Homer's in the *Odyssey* which gives a support to my opinion:—

Libya too, where horns bud quick on the fore-heads of lambkins.[1]

He means to say what is quite true, that in warm countries the horns come early. So too in countries where the cold is severe animals either have no horns, or grow them with difficulty—the cold being the cause in this instance.

30. Here I must express my wonder—additions being what my work always from the very first affected—that in Elis, where the cold is not remarkable, and there is nothing else to account for it, mules are never produced. The Eleans say it is in consequence of a curse; and their habit is, when the breeding-time comes, to take their mares into one of the adjoining countries, and there keep them till they are in foal, when they bring them back again into Elis.

31. With respect to the feathers which are said by the Scythians to fill the air, and to prevent persons from penetrating into the remoter parts of the continent, or even having any view of those regions, my opinion is that in the countries above Scythia it always snows—less, of course, in the summer than in the winter-time. Now snow when it falls looks like feath-

[1] *Odyssey*, Bk. iv. 85.

ers, as every one is aware who has seen it come down close to him. These northern regions, therefore, are uninhabitable by reason of the severity of the winter; and the Scythians, with their neighbours, call the snow-flakes feathers because, I think, of the likeness which they bear to them. I have now related what is said of the most distant parts of this continent whereof any account is given.

32. Of the Hyperboreans nothing is said either by the Scythians or by any of the other dwellers in these regions, unless it be the Issedonians. But in my opinion, even the Issedonians are silent concerning them; otherwise the Scythians would have repeated their statements, as they do those concerning the one-eyed men. Hesiod, however, mentions them, and Homer also in the *Epigoni*, if that be really a work of his.

33. But the persons who have by far the most to say on this subject are the Delians. They declare that certain offerings, packed in wheaten straw, were brought from the country of the Hyperboreans into Scythia, and that the Scythians received them and passed them on to their neighbours upon the west, who continued to pass them on until at last they reached the Adriatic. From hence they were sent southward, and when they came to Greece, were received first of all by the Dodonæans. Thence they descended to the Maliac Gulf, from which they were carried across into Eubœa, where the people handed them on from city to city, till they came at length to Carystus. The Carystians took them over to Tenos, without stopping at Andros; and the Tenians brought them finally to Delos. Such, according to their own account, was the road by which the offerings reached the Delians. Two damsels, they say, named Hyperoché and Laodicé, brought the first offerings from the Hyperboreans; and with them the Hyperboreans sent five men to keep them from all harm by the way; these are the persons whom the Delians call "Perpherees," and to whom great honours are paid at Delos. Afterwards the Hyperboreans, when they found that their messengers did not return, thinking it would be a grievous thing always to be liable to lose the envoys they should send, adopted the following plan:—they wrapped their offerings in the wheaten straw, and bearing them to their borders, charged their neighbours to send them forward from one nation to another, which was done accordingly, and in this way the offerings reached Delos. I myself know of a practice like this,

which obtains with the women of Thrace and Pæonia. They in their sacrifices to the queenly Diana bring wheaten straw always with their offerings. Of my own knowledge I can testify that this is so.

34. The damsels sent by the Hyperboreans died in Delos; and in their honour all the Delian girls and youths are wont to cut off their hair. The girls, before their marriage-day, cut off a curl, and twining it round a distaff, lay it upon the grave of the strangers. This grave is on the left as one enters the precinct of Diana, and has an olive-tree growing on it. The youths wind some of their hair round a kind of grass, and, like the girls, place it upon the tomb. Such are the honours paid to these damsels by the Delians.

35. They add that, once before, there came to Delos by the same road as Hyperoché and Laodicé, two other virgins from the Hyperboreans, whose names were Argé and Opis. Hyperoché and Laodicé came to bring to Ilithyia the offering which they had laid upon themselves, in acknowledgment of their quick labours; but Argé and Opis came at the same time as the gods of Delos,[1] and are honoured by the Delians in a different way. For the Delian women make collections in these maidens' names, and invoke them in the hymn which Olen, a Lycian, composed for them; and the rest of the islanders, and even the Ionians, have been taught by the Delians to do the like. This Olen, who came from Lycia, made the other old hymns also which are sung in Delos. The Delians add that the ashes from the thigh-bones burnt upon the altar are scattered over the tomb of Opis and Argé. Their tomb lies behind the temple of Diana, facing the east, near the banqueting-hall of the Ceians. Thus much then, and no more, concerning the Hyperboreans.

36. As for the tale of Abaris, who is said to have been a Hyperborean, and to have gone with his arrow all round the world without once eating, I shall pass it by in silence. Thus much, however, is clear: if there are Hyperboreans, there must also be Hypernotians. For my part, I cannot but laugh when I see numbers of persons drawing maps of the world without having any reason to guide them; making, as they do, the ocean-stream to run all round the earth, and the earth itself to be an exact circle, as if described by a pair of compasses, with Europe and Asia just of the same size. The truth in this matter I will now proceed to ex-

[1] Apollo and Diana.

plain in a very few words, making it clear what the real size of each region is, and what shape should be given them.

37. The Persians inhabit a country upon the southern or Erythræan sea; above them, to the north, are the Medes; beyond the Medes, the Saspirians; beyond them, the Colchians, reaching to the northern sea, into which the Phasis empties itself. These four nations fill the whole space from one sea to the other.

38. West of these nations there project into the sea two tracts which I will now describe; one, beginning at the river Phasis on the north, stretches along the Euxine and the Hellespont to Sigeum in the Troas; while on the south it reaches from the Myriandrian gulf, which adjoins Phœnicia, to the Triopic promontory. This is one of the tracts, and is inhabited by thirty different nations.

39. The other starts from the country of the Persians, and stretches into the Erythræan sea, containing first Persia, then Assyria, and after Assyria, Arabia. It ends, that is to say, it is considered to end, though it does not really come to a termination, at the Arabian gulf—the gulf whereinto Darius conducted the canal which he made from the Nile. Between Persia and Phœnicia lies a broad and ample tract of country, after which the region I am describing skirts our sea, stretching from Phœnicia along the coast of Palestine-Syria till it comes to Egypt, where it terminates. This entire tract contains but three nations. The whole of Asia west of the country of the Persians is comprised in these two regions.

40. Beyond the tract occupied by the Persians, Medes, Saspirians, and Colchians, towards the east and the region of the sunrise, Asia is bounded on the south by the Erythræan sea, and on the north by the Caspian and the river Araxes, which flows towards the rising sun. Till you reach India the country is peopled; but further east it is void of inhabitants, and no one can say what sort of region it is. Such then is the shape, and such the size of Asia.

41. Libya belongs to one of the above-mentioned tracts, for it adjoins on Egypt. In Egypt the tract is at first a narrow neck, the distance from our sea to the Erythræan not exceeding a hundred thousand fathoms, or, in other words, a thousand furlongs; but from the point where the neck ends, the tract which bears the name of Libya is of very great breadth.

42. For my part I am astonished that men should ever have divided Libya, Asia, and Eu-

rope as they have, for they are exceedingly un-equal. Europe extends the entire length of the other two, and for breadth will not even (as I think) bear to be compared to them. As for Libya, we know it to be washed on all sides by the sea, except where it is attached to Asia. This discovery was first made by Necôs, the Egyptian king, who on desisting from the canal which he had begun between the Nile and the Arabian gulf, sent to sea a number of ships manned by Phœnicians, with orders to make for the Pillars of Hercules, and return to Egypt through them, and by the Mediterran-ean. The Phœnicians took their departure from Egypt by way of the Erythræan sea, and so sailed into the southern ocean. When au-tumn came, they went ashore, wherever they might happen to be, and having sown a tract of land with corn, waited until the grain was fit to cut. Having reaped it, they again set sail; and thus it came to pass that two whole years went by, and it was not till the third year that they doubled the Pillars of Hercules, and made good their voyage home. On their return, they declared—I for my part do not believe them, but perhaps others may—that in sailing round Libya they had the sun upon their right hand. In this way was the extent of Libya first discovered.

43. Next to these Phœnicians the Carthagin-ians, according to their own accounts, made the voyage. For Sataspes, son of Teaspes the Achæmenian, did not circumnavigate Libya, though he was sent to do so; but, fearing the length and desolateness of the journey, he turned back and left unaccomplished the task which had been set him by his mother. This man had used violence towards a maiden, the daughter of Zopyrus, son of Megabyzus, and King Xerxes was about to impale him for the offence, when his mother, who was a sister of Darius, begged him off, undertaking to punish his crime more heavily than the king himself had designed. She would force him, she said, to sail round Libya and return to Egypt by the Arabian gulf. Xerxes gave his consent; and Sataspes went down to Egypt, and there got a ship and crew, with which he set sail for the Pillars of Hercules. Having passed the Straits, he doubled the Libyan headland, known as Cape Soloeis, and proceeded southward. Fol-lowing this course for many months over a vast stretch of sea, and finding that more water than he had crossed still lay ever before him, he put about, and came back to Egypt. Thence proceeding to the court, he made report to Xerxes, that at the farthest point to which he had reached, the coast was occupied by a dwarfish race, who wore a dress made from the palm tree. These people, whenever he landed, left their towns and fled away to the moun-tains; his men, however, did them no wrong, only entering into their cities and taking some of their cattle. The reason why he had not sailed quite round Libya was, he said, because the ship stopped, and would no go any further. Xerxes, however, did not accept this account for true; and so Sataspes, as he had failed to ac-complish the task set him, was impaled by the king's orders in accordance with the former sentence. One of his eunuchs, on hearing of his death, ran away with a great portion of his wealth, and reached Samos, where a certain Samian seized the whole. I know the man's name well, but I shall willingly forget it here.

44. Of the greater part of Asia Darius was the discoverer. Wishing to know where the Indus (which is the only river save one that produces crocodiles) emptied itself into the sea, he sent a number of men, on whose truthful-ness he could rely, and among them Scylax of Caryanda, to sail down the river. They started from the city of Caspatyrus, in the region called Pactyïca, and sailed down the stream in an easterly direction to the sea. Here they turned westward, and, after a voyage of thirty months, reached the place from which the Egyptian king, of whom I spoke above, sent the Phœnicians to sail round Libya. After this voyage was completed, Darius conquered the Indians, and made use of the sea in those parts. Thus all Asia, except the eastern portion, has been found to be similarly circumstanced with Libya.

45. But the boundaries of Europe are quite unknown, and there is not a man who can say whether any sea girds it round either on the north or on the east, while in length it un-doubtedly extends as far as both the other two. For my part I cannot conceive why three names, and women's names especially, should ever have been given to a tract which is in re-ality one, nor why the Egyptian Nile and the Colchian Phasis (or according to others the Mæotic Tanais and Cimmerian ferry) should have been fixed upon for the boundary lines; nor can I even say who gave the three tracts their names, or whence they took the epithets. According to the Greeks in general, Libya was so called after a certain Libya, a native woman, and Asia after the wife of Prometheus. The Lydians, however, put in a claim to the latter name, which, they declare, was not derived

from Asia the wife of Prometheus, but from Asies, the son of Cotys, and grandson of Manes, who also gave name to the tribe Asias at Sardis. As for Europe, no one can say whether it is surrounded by the sea or not, neither is it known whence the name of Europe was derived, nor who gave it name, unless we say that Europe was so called after the Tyrian Europé, and before her time was nameless, like the other divisions. But it is certain that Europé was an Asiatic, and never even set foot on the land which the Greeks now call Europe, only sailing from Phœnicia to Crete, and from Crete to Lycia. However let us quit these matters. We shall ourselves continue to use the names which custom sanctions.

46. The Euxine sea, where Darius now went to war, has nations dwelling around it, with the one exception of the Scythians, more unpolished than those of any other region that we know of. For, setting aside Anacharsis and the Scythian people, there is not within this region a single nation which can be put forward as having any claims to wisdom, or which has produced a single person of any high repute. The Scythians indeed have in one respect, and that the very most important of all those that fall under man's control, shown themselves wiser than any nation upon the face of the earth. Their customs otherwise are not such as I admire. The one thing of which I speak is the contrivance whereby they make it impossible for the enemy who invades them to escape destruction, while they themselves are entirely out of his reach, unless it please them to engage with him. Having neither cities nor forts, and carrying their dwellings with them wherever they go; accustomed, moreover, one and all of them, to shoot from horseback; and living not by husbandry but on their cattle, their waggons the only houses that they possess, how can they fail of being unconquerable, and unassailable even?

47. The nature of their country, and the rivers by which it is intersected, greatly favour this mode of resisting attacks. For the land is level, well watered, and abounding in pasture; while the rivers which traverse it are almost equal in number to the canals of Egypt. Of these I shall only mention the most famous and such as are navigable to some distance from the sea. They are, the Ister, which has five mouths; the Tyras, the Hypanis, the Borysthenes, the Panticapes, the Hypacyris, the Gerrhus, and the Tanais. The courses of these streams I shall now proceed to describe.

48. The Ister is of all the rivers with which we are acquainted the mightiest. It never varies in height, but continues at the same level summer and winter. Counting from the west it is the first of the Scythian rivers, and the reason of its being the greatest is that it receives the water of several tributaries. Now the tributaries which swell its flood are the following: first, on the side of Scythia, these five—the stream called by the Scythians Porata, and by the Greeks Pyretus, the Tiarantus, the Ararus, the Naparis, and the Ordessus. The first mentioned is a great stream, and is the easternmost of the tributaries. The Tiarantus is of less volume, and more to the west. The Ararus, Naparis, and Ordessus fall into the Ister between these two. All the above mentioned are genuine Scythian rivers, and go to swell the current of the Ister.

49. From the country of the Agathyrsi comes down another river, the Maris, which empties itself into the same; and from the heights of Hæmus descend with a northern course three mighty streams, the Atlas, the Auras, and the Tibisis, and pour their waters into it. Thrace gives it three tributaries, the Athrys, the Noës, and the Artanes, which all pass through the country of the Crobyzian Thracians. Another tributary is furnished by Pæonia, namely, the Scius; this river, rising near Mount Rhodopé, forces its way through the chain of Hæmus,[1] and so reaches the Ister. From Illyria comes another stream, the Angrus, which has a course from south to north, and after watering the Triballian plain, falls into the Brongus, which falls into the Ister. So the Ister is augmented by these two streams, both considerable. Besides all these, the Ister receives also the waters of the Carpis and the Alpis, two rivers running in a northerly direction from the country above the Umbrians. For the Ister flows through the whole extent of Europe, rising in the country of the Celts (the most westerly of all the nations of Europe, excepting the Cynetians), and thence running across the continent till it reaches Scythia, whereof it washes the flanks.

50. All these streams, then, and many others, add their waters to swell the flood of the Ister, which thus increased becomes the mightiest of rivers; for undoubtedly if we compare the stream of the Nile with the *single* stream of the Ister, we must give the preference to the Nile, of which no tributary river, nor even rivulet,

---

[1] This is untrue. No stream forces its way through this chain.

augments the volume. The Ister remains at the same level both summer and winter—owing to the following reasons, as I believe. During the winter it runs at its natural height, or a very little higher, because in those countries there is scarcely any rain in winter, but constant snow. When summer comes, this snow, which is of great depth, begins to melt, and flows into the Ister, which is swelled at that season, not only by this cause but also by the rains, which are heavy and frequent at that part of the year. Thus the various streams which go to form the Ister are higher in summer than in winter, and just so much higher as the sun's power and attraction are greater; so that these two causes counteract each other, and the effect is to produce a balance, whereby the Ister remains always at the same level.

51. This, then, is one of the great Scythian rivers; the next to it is the Tyras, which rises from a great lake separating Scythia from the land of the Neuri, and runs with a southerly course to the sea. Greeks dwell at the mouth of the river, who are called Tyritæ.

52. The third river is the Hypanis. This stream rises within the limits of Scythia, and has its source in another vast lake, around which wild white horses graze. The lake is called, properly enough, the Mother of the Hypanis. The Hypanis, rising here, during the distance of five days' navigation is a shallow stream, and the water sweet and pure; thence, however, to the sea, which is a distance of four days, it is exceedingly bitter. This change is caused by its receiving into it at that point a brook the waters of which are so bitter that, although it is but a tiny rivulet, it nevertheless taints the entire Hypanis, which is a large stream among those of the second order. The source of this bitter spring is on the borders of the Scythian Husbandmen, where they adjoin upon the Alazonians; and the place where it rises is called in the Scythic tongue *Exampæus,* which means in our language, "The Sacred Ways." The spring itself bears the same name. The Tyras and the Hypanis approach each other in the country of the Alazonians, but afterwards separate, and leave a wide space between their streams.

53. The fourth of the Scythian rivers is the Borysthenes. Next to the Ister, it is the greatest of them all; and, in my judgment, it is the most productive river, not merely in Scythia, but in the whole world, excepting only the Nile, with which no stream can possibly compare. It has upon its banks the loveliest and most excellent

pasturages for cattle; it contains abundance of the most delicious fish; its water is most pleasant to the taste; its stream is limpid, while all the other rivers near it are muddy; the richest harvests spring up along its course, and where the ground is not sown, the heaviest crops of grass; while salt forms in great plenty about its mouth without human aid, and large fish are taken in it of the sort called Antacæi, without any prickly bones, and good for pickling. Nor are these the whole of its marvels. As far inland as the place named Gerrhus, which is distant forty days' voyage from the sea, its course is known, and its direction is from north to south; but above this no one has traced it, so as to say through what countries it flows. It enters the territory of the Scythian Husbandmen after running for some time across a desert region, and continues for ten days' navigation to pass through the land which they inhabit. It is the only river besides the Nile the sources of which are unknown to me, as they are also (I believe) to all the other Greeks. Not long before it reaches the sea, the Borysthenes is joined by the Hypanis, which pours its waters into the same lake. The land that lies between them, a narrow point like the beak of a ship, is called Cape Hippolaüs. Here is a temple dedicated to Ceres, and opposite the temple upon the Hypanis is the dwelling-place of the Borysthenites. But enough has been said of these streams.

54. Next in succession comes the fifth river, called the Panticapes, which has, like the Borysthenes, a course from north to south, and rises from a lake. The space between this river and the Borysthenes is occupied by the Scythians who are engaged in husbandry. After watering their country, the Panticapes flows through Hylæa, and empties itself into the Borysthenes.

55. The sixth stream is the Hypacyris, a river rising from a lake, and running directly through the middle of the Nomadic Scythians. It falls into the sea near the city of Carcinitis, leaving Hylæa and the course of Achilles to the right.

56. The seventh river is the Gerrhus, which is a branch thrown out by the Borysthenes at the point where the course of that stream first begins to be known, to wit, the region called by the same name as the stream itself, viz. Gerrhus. This river on its passage towards the sea divides the country of the Nomadic from that of the Royal Scyths. It runs into the Hypacyris.

57. The eighth river is the Tanais, a stream which has its source, far up the country, in a

lake of vast size, and which empties itself into another still larger lake, the Palus Mæotis, whereby the country of the Royal Scythians is divided from that of the Sauromatæ. The Tanais receives the waters of a tributary stream, called the Hyrgis.

58. Such then are the rivers of chief note in Scythia. The grass which the land produces is more apt to generate gall in the beasts that feed on it than any other grass which is known to us, as plainly appears on the opening of their carcases.

59. Thus abundantly are the Scythians provided with the most important necessaries. Their manners and customs come now to be described. They worship only the following gods, namely, Vesta, whom they reverence beyond all the rest, Jupiter, and Tellus, whom they consider to be the wife of Jupiter; and after these Apollo, Celestial Venus, Hercules, and Mars. These gods are worshipped by the whole nation: the Royal Scythians offer sacrifice likewise to Neptune. In the Scythic tongue Vesta is called *Tabiti,* Jupiter (very properly, in my judgment) *Papæus,* Tellus *Apia,* Apollo *Œtosyrus,* Celestial Venus *Artimpasa,* and Neptune *Thamimasadas.* They use no images, altars, or temples, except in the worship of Mars; but in his worship they do use them.

60. The manner of their sacrifices is everywhere and in every case the same; the victim stands with its two fore-feet bound together by a cord, and the person who is about to offer, taking his station behind the victim, gives the rope a pull, and thereby throws the animal down; as it falls he invokes the god to whom he is offering; after which he puts a noose round the animal's neck, and, inserting a small stick, twists it round, and so strangles him. No fire is lighted, there is no consecration, and no pouring out of drink-offerings; but directly that the beast is strangled the sacrificer flays him, and then sets to work to boil the flesh.

61. As Scythia, however, is utterly barren of firewood, a plan has had to be contrived for boiling the flesh, which is the following. After flaying the beasts, they take out all the bones, and (if they possess such gear) put the flesh into boilers made in the country, which are very like the cauldrons of the Lesbians, except that they are of a much larger size; then placing the bones of the animals beneath the cauldron, they set them alight, and so boil the meat. If they do not happen to possess a cauldron, they make the animal's paunch hold the flesh, and pouring in at the same time a little

water, lay the bones under and light them. The bones burn beautifully; and the paunch easily contains all the flesh when it is stript from the bones, so that by this plan your ox is made to boil himself, and other victims also to do the like. When the meat is all cooked, the sacrificer offers a portion of the flesh and of the entrails, by casting it on the ground before him. They sacrifice all sorts of cattle, but most commonly horses.

62. Such are the victims offered to the other gods, and such is the mode in which they are sacrificed; but the rites paid to Mars are different. In every district, at the seat of government, there stands a temple of this god, whereof the following is a description. It is a pile of brushwood, made of a vast quantity of fagots, in length and breadth three furlongs; in height somewhat less, having a square platform upon the top, three sides of which are precipitous, while the fourth slopes so that men may walk up it. Each year a hundred and fifty waggon-loads of brushwood are added to the pile, which sinks continually by reason of the rains. An antique iron sword is planted on the top of every such mound, and serves as the image of Mars: yearly sacrifices of cattle and of horses are made to it, and more victims are offered thus than to all the rest of their gods. When prisoners are taken in war, out of every hundred men they sacrifice one, not however with the same rites as the cattle, but with different. Libations of wine are first poured upon their heads, after which they are slaughtered over a vessel; the vessel is then carried up to the top of the pile, and the blood poured upon the scymitar. While this takes place at the top of the mound, below, by the side of the temple, the right hands and arms of the slaughtered prisoners are cut off, and tossed on high into the air. Then the other victims are slain, and those who have offered the sacrifice depart, leaving the hands and arms where they may chance to have fallen, and the bodies also, separate.

63. Such are the observances of the Scythians with respect to sacrifice. They never use swine for the purpose, nor indeed is it their wont to breed them in any part of their country.

64. In what concerns war, their customs are the following. The Scythian soldier drinks the blood of the first man he overthrows in battle. Whatever number he slays, he cuts off all their heads, and carries them to the king; since he is thus entitled to a share of the booty, whereto he forfeits all claim if he does not produce a

head. In order to strip the skull of its covering, he makes a cut round the head above the ears, and, laying hold of the scalp, shakes the skull out; then with the rib of an ox he scrapes the scalp clean of flesh, and softening it by rubbing between the hands, uses it thenceforth as a napkin. The Scyth is proud of these scalps, and hangs them from his bridle-rein; the greater the number of such napkins that a man can show, the more highly is he esteemed among them. Many make themselves cloaks, like the capotes of our peasants, by sewing a quantity of these scalps together. Others flay the right arms of their dead enemies, and make of the skin, which is stripped off with the nails hanging to it, a covering for their quivers. Now the skin of a man is thick and glossy, and would in whiteness surpass almost all other hides. Some even flay the entire body of their enemy, and stretching it upon a frame carry it about with them wherever they ride. Such are the Scythian customs with respect to scalps and skins.

65. The skulls of their enemies, not indeed of all, but of those whom they most detest, they treat as follows. Having sawn off the portion below the eyebrows, and cleaned out the inside, they cover the outside with leather. When a man is poor, this is all that he does; but if he is rich, he also lines the inside with gold: in either case the skull is used as a drinking-cup. They do the same with the skulls of their own kith and kin if they have been at feud with them, and have vanquished them in the presence of the king. When strangers whom they deem of any account come to visit them, these skulls are handed round, and the host tells how that these were his relations who made war upon him, and how that he got the better of them; all this being looked upon as proof of bravery.

66. Once a year the governor of each district, at a set place in his own province, mingles a bowl of wine, of which all Scythians have a right to drink by whom foes have been slain; while they who have slain no enemy are not allowed to taste of the bowl, but sit aloof in disgrace. No greater shame than this can happen to them. Such as have slain a very large number of foes, have two cups instead of one, and drink from both.

67. Scythia has an abundance of soothsayers, who foretell the future by means of a number of willow wands. A large bundle of these wands is brought and laid on the ground. The soothsayer unties the bundle, and places each wand by itself, at the same time uttering his prophecy: then, while he is still speaking, he gathers the rods together again, and makes them up once more into a bundle. This mode of divination is of home growth in Scythia. The Enarees, or woman-like men, have another method, which they say Venus taught them. It is done with the inner bark of the linden-tree. They take a piece of this bark, and, splitting it into three strips, keep twining the strips about their fingers, and untwining them, while they prophesy.

68. Whenever the Scythian king falls sick, he sends for the three soothsayers of most renown at the time, who come and make trial of their art in the mode above described. Generally they say that the king is ill because such or such a person, mentioning his name, has sworn falsely by the royal hearth. This is the usual oath among the Scythians, when they wish to swear with very great solemnity. Then the man accused of having foresworn himself is arrested and brought before the king. The soothsayers tell him that by their art it is clear he has sworn a false oath by the royal hearth, and so caused the illness of the king—he denies the charge, protests that he has sworn no false oath, and loudly complains of the wrong done to him. Upon this the king sends for six new soothsayers, who try the matter by soothsaying. If they too find the man guilty of the offence, straightway he is beheaded by those who first accused him, and his goods are parted among them: if, on the contrary, they acquit him, other soothsayers, and again others, are sent for, to try the case. Should the greater number decide in favour of the man's innocence, then they who first accused him forfeit their lives.

69. The mode of their execution is the following: a waggon is loaded with brushwood, and oxen are harnessed to it; the soothsayers, with their feet tied together, their hands bound behind their backs, and their mouths gagged, are thrust into the midst of the brushwood; finally the wood is set alight, and the oxen, being startled, are made to rush off with the waggon. It often happens that the oxen and the soothsayers are both consumed together, but sometimes the pole of the waggon is burnt through, and the oxen escape with a scorching. Diviners—lying diviners, they call them—are burnt in the way described, for other causes besides the one here spoken of. When the king puts one of them to death, he takes care not to let any of his sons survive: all the male off-

spring are slain with the father, only the females being allowed to live.

70. Oaths among the Scyths are accompanied with the following ceremonies: a large earthern bowl is filled with wine, and the parties to the oath, wounding themselves slightly with a knife or an awl, drop some of their blood into the wine; then they plunge into the mixture a scymitar, some arrows, a battle-axe, and a javelin, all the while repeating prayers; lastly the two contracting parties drink each a draught from the bowl, as do also the chief men among their followers.

71. The tombs of their kings are in the land of the Gerrhi, who dwell at the point where the Borysthenes is first navigable. Here, when the king dies, they dig a grave, which is square in shape, and of great size. When it is ready, they take the king's corpse, and, having opened the belly, and cleaned out the inside, fill the cavity with a preparation of chopped cypress, frankincense, parsley-seed, and anise-seed, after which they sew up the opening, enclose the body in wax, and, placing it on a waggon, carry it about through all the different tribes. On this procession each tribe, when it receives the corpse, imitates the example which is first set by the Royal Scythians; every man chops off a piece of his ear, crops his hair close, and makes a cut all round his arm, lacerates his forehead and his nose, and thrusts an arrow through his left hand. Then they who have the care of the corpse carry it with them to another of the tribes which are under the Scythian rule, followed by those whom they first visited. On completing the circuit of all the tribes under their sway, they find themselves in the country of the Gerrhi, who are the most remote of all, and so they come to the tombs of the kings. There the body of the dead king is laid in the grave prepared for it, stretched upon a mattress; spears are fixed in the ground on either side of the corpse, and beams stretched across above it to form a roof, which is covered with a thatching of osier twigs. In the open space around the body of the king they bury one of his concubines, first killing her by strangling, and also his cup-bearer, his cook, his groom, his lacquey, his messenger, some of his horses, firstlings of all his other possessions, and some golden cups; for they use neither silver nor brass. After this they set to work, and raise a vast mound above the grave, all of them vying with each other and seeking to make it as tall as possible.

72. When a year is gone by, further ceremonies take place. Fifty of the best of the late king's attendants are taken, all native Scythians —for, as bought slaves are unknown in the country, the Scythian kings choose any of their subjects that they like, to wait on them—fifty of these are taken and strangled, with fifty of the most beautiful horses. When they are dead, their bowels are taken out, and the cavity cleaned, filled full of chaff, and straightway sewn up again. This done, a number of posts are driven into the ground, in sets of two pairs each, and on every pair half the felly of a wheel is placed archwise; then strong stakes are run lengthways through the bodies of the horses from tail to neck, and they are mounted up upon the fellies, so that the felly in front supports the shoulders of the horse, while that behind sustains the belly and quarters, the legs dangling in mid-air; each horse is furnished with a bit and bridle, which latter is stretched out in front of the horse, and fastened to a peg. The fifty strangled youths are then mounted severally on the fifty horses. To effect this, a second stake is passed through their bodies along the course of the spine to the neck; the lower end of which projects from the body, and is fixed into a socket, made in the stake that runs lengthwise down the horse. The fifty riders are thus ranged in a circle round the tomb, and so left.

73. Such, then, is the mode in which the kings are buried: as for the people, when any one dies, his nearest of kin lay him upon a waggon and take him round to all his friends in succession: each receives them in turn and entertains them with a banquet, whereat the dead man is served with a portion of all that is set before the others; this is done for forty days, at the end of which time the burial takes place. After the burial, those engaged in it have to purify themselves, which they do in the following way. First they well soap and wash their heads; then, in order to cleanse their bodies, they act as follows: they make a booth by fixing in the ground three sticks inclined towards one another, and stretching around them woollen felts, which they arrange so as to fit as close as possible: inside the booth a dish is placed upon the ground, into which they put a number of red-hot stones, and then add some hemp-seed.

74. Hemp grows in Scythia: it is very like flax; only that it is a much coarser and taller plant: some grows wild about the country, some is produced by cultivation: the Thracians make garments of it which closely resemble

linen; so much so, indeed, that if a person has never seen hemp he is sure to think they are linen, and if he has, unless he is very experienced in such matters, he will not know of which material they are.

75. The Scythians, as I said, take some of this hemp-seed, and, creeping under the felt coverings, throw it upon the red-hot stones; immediately it smokes, and gives out such a vapour as no Grecian vapour-bath can exceed; the Scyths, delighted, shout for joy, and this vapour serves them instead of a water-bath; for they never by any chance wash their bodies with water. Their women make a mixture of cypress, cedar, and frankincense wood, which they pound into a paste upon a rough piece of stone, adding a little water to it. With this substance, which is of a thick consistency, they plaster their faces all over, and indeed their whole bodies. A sweet odour is thereby imparted to them, and when they take off the plaster on the day following, their skin is clean and glossy.

76. The Scythians have an extreme hatred of all foreign customs, particularly of those in use among the Greeks, as the instances of Anacharsis, and, more lately, of Scylas, have fully shown. The former, after he had travelled over a great portion of the world, and displayed wherever he went many proofs of wisdom, as he sailed through the Hellespont on his return to Scythia touched at Cyzicus. There he found the inhabitants celebrating with much pomp and magnificence a festival to the Mother of the Gods,[1] and was himself induced to make a vow to the goddess, whereby he engaged, if he got back safe and sound to his home, that he would give her a festival and a night-procession in all respects like those which he had seen in Cyzicus. When, therefore, he arrived in Scythia, he betook himself to the district called the Woodland, which lies opposite the course of Achilles, and is covered with trees of all manner of different kinds, and there went through all the sacred rites with the tabour in his hand, and the images tied to him. While thus employed, he was noticed by one of the Scythians, who went and told king Saulius what he had seen. Then king Saulius came in person, and when he perceived what Anacharsis was about, he shot at him with an arrow and killed him. To this day, if you ask the Scyths about Anacharsis, they pretend ignorance of him, because of his Grecian travels and adoption of the customs of foreigners. I

[1] Cybelé or Rhea.

learnt, however, from Timnes, the steward of Ariapithes, that Anacharsis was paternal uncle to the Scythian king Idanthyrsus, being the son of Gnurus, who was the son of Lycus and the grandson of Spargapithes. If Anacharsis were really of this house, it must have been by his own brother that he was slain, for Idanthyrsus was a son of the Saulius who put Anacharsis to death.

77. I have heard, however, another tale, very different from this, which is told by the Peloponnesians: they say, that Anacharsis was sent by the king of the Scyths to make acquaintance with Greece—that he went, and on his return home reported that the Greeks were all occupied in the pursuit of every kind of knowledge, except the Lacedæmonians; who, however, alone knew how to converse sensibly. A silly tale this, which the Greeks have invented for their amusement! There is no doubt that Anacharsis suffered death in the mode already related, on account of his attachment to foreign customs, and the intercourse which he held with the Greeks.

78. Scylas, likewise, the son of Ariapithes, many years later, met with almost the very same fate. Ariapithes, the Scythian king, had several sons, among them this Scylas, who was the child, not of a native Scyth, but of a woman of Istria. Bred up by her, Scylas gained an acquaintance with the Greek language and letters. Some time afterwards, Ariapithes was treacherously slain by Spargapithes, king of the Agathyrsi; whereupon Scylas succeeded to the throne, and married one of his father's wives, a woman named Opœa. This Opœa was a Scythian by birth, and had brought Ariapithes a son called Oricus. Now when Scylas found himself king of Scythia, as he disliked the Scythic mode of life, and was attached, by his bringing up, to the manners of the Greeks, he made it his usual practice, whenever he came with his army to the town of the Borysthenites, who, according to their own account, are colonists of the Milesians—he made it his practice, I say, to leave the army before the city, and, having entered within the walls by himself, and carefully closed the gates, to exchange his Scythian dress for Grecian garments, and in this attire to walk about the forum, without guards or retinue. The Borysthenites kept watch at the gates, that no Scythian might see the king thus apparelled. Scylas, meanwhile, lived exactly as the Greeks, and even offered sacrifices to the gods according to the Grecian rites. In this way he would pass a month, or

more, with the Borysthenites, after which he would clothe himself again in his Scythian dress, and so take his departure. This he did repeatedly, and even built himself a house in Borysthenes, and married a wife there who was a native of the place.

79. But when the time came that was ordained to bring him woe, the occasion of his ruin was the following. He wanted to be initiated in the Bacchic mysteries, and was on the point of obtaining admission to the rites, when a most strange prodigy occurred to him. The house which he possessed, as I mentioned a short time back, in the city of the Borysthenites, a building of great extent and erected at a vast cost, round which there stood a number of sphinxes and griffins carved in white marble, was struck by lightning from on high, and burnt to the ground. Scylas, nevertheless, went on and received the initiation. Now the Scythians are wont to reproach the Greeks with their Bacchanal rage, and to say that it is not reasonable to imagine there is a god who impels men to madness. No sooner, therefore, was Scylas initiated in the Bacchic mysteries than one of the Borysthenites went and carried the news to the Scythians—"You Scyths laugh at us," he said, "because we rave when the god seizes us. But now our god has seized upon your king, who raves like us, and is maddened by the influence. If you think I do not tell you true, come with me, and I will show him to you." The chiefs of the Scythians went with the man accordingly, and the Borysthenite, conducting them into the city, placed them secretly on one of the towers. Presently Scylas passed by with the band of revellers, raving like the rest, and was seen by the watchers. Regarding the matter as a very great misfortune they instantly departed, and came and told the army what they had witnessed.

80. When, therefore, Scylas, after leaving Borysthenes, was about returning home, the Scythians broke out into revolt. They put at their head Octamasadas, grandson (on the mother's side) of Teres. Then Scylas, when he learned the danger with which he was threatened, and the reason of the disturbance, made his escape to Thrace. Octamasadas, discovering whither he had fled, marched after him, and had reached the Ister, when he was met by the forces of the Thracians. The two armies were about to engage, but before they joined battle, Sitalces sent a message to Octamasadas to this effect—"Why should there be trial of arms betwixt thee and me? Thou art my own

sister's son, and thou hast in thy keeping my brother. Surrender him into my hands, and I will give thy Scylas back to thee. So neither thou nor I will risk our armies." Sitalces sent this message to Octamasadas, by a herald, and Octamasadas, with whom a brother of Sitalces had formerly taken refuge, accepted the terms. He surrendered his own uncle to Sitalces, and obtained in exchange his brother Scylas. Sitalces took his brother with him and withdrew; but Octamasadas beheaded Scylas upon the spot. Thus rigidly do the Scythians maintain their own customs, and thus severely do they punish such as adopt foreign usages.

81. What the population of Scythia is I was not able to learn with certainty; the accounts which I received varied from one another. I heard from some that they were very numerous indeed; others made their numbers but scanty for such a nation as the Scyths. Thus much, however, I witnessed with my own eyes. There is a tract called Exampæus between the Borysthenes and the Hypanis. I made some mention of it in a former place, where I spoke of the bitter stream which rising there flows into the Hypanis, and renders the water of that river undrinkable. Here then stands a brazen bowl, six times as big as that at the entrance of the Euxine, which Pausanias, the son of Cleombrotus, set up. Such as have never seen that vessel may understand me better if I say that the Scythian bowl holds with ease six hundred amphoræ,[1] and is of the thickness of six fingers' breadth. The natives gave me the following account of the manner in which it was made. One of their kings, by name Ariantas, wishing to know the number of his subjects, ordered them all to bring him, on pain of death, the point off one of their arrows. They obeyed; and he collected thereby a vast heap of arrow-heads, which he resolved to form into a memorial that might go down to posterity. Accordingly he made of them this bowl, and dedicated it at Exampæus. This was all that I could learn concerning the number of the Scythians.

82. The country has no marvels except its rivers, which are larger and more numerous than those of any other land. These, and the vastness of the great plain, are worthy of note, and one thing besides, which I am about to mention. They show a footmark of Hercules,

[1] The Greek *amphora* (ἀμφορεύς) contained nearly nine of our gallons; whence it appears that this bowl would have held about 5400 gallons, or above 85 hogsheads.

impressed on a rock, in shape like the print of a man's foot, but two cubits in length. It is in the neighbourhood of the Tyras. Having described this, I return to the subject on which I originally proposed to discourse.

83. The preparations of Darius against the Scythians had begun, messengers had been despatched on all sides with the king's commands, some being required to furnish troops, others to supply ships, others again to bridge the Thracian Bosphorus, when Artabanus, son of Hystaspes and brother of Darius, entreated the king to desist from his expedition, urging on him the great difficulty of attacking Scythia. Good, however, as the advice of Artabanus was, it failed to persuade Darius. He therefore ceased his reasonings; and Darius, when his preparations were complete, led his army forth from Susa.

84. It was then that a certain Persian, by name Œobazus, the father of three sons, all of whom were to accompany the army, came and prayed the king that he would allow one of his sons to remain with him. Darius made answer, as if he regarded him in the light of a friend who had urged a moderate request, "that he would allow them all to remain." Œobazus was overjoyed, expecting that all his children would be excused from serving; the king, however, bade his attendants take the three sons of Œobazus and forthwith put them to death. Thus they were all left behind, but not till they had been deprived of life.

85. When Darius, on his march from Susa, reached the territory of Chalcedon on the shores of the Bosphorus, where the bridge had been made, he took ship and sailed thence to the Cyanean islands, which, according to the Greeks, once floated. He took his seat also in the temple and surveyed the Pontus, which is indeed well worthy of consideration. There is not in the world any other sea so wonderful: it extends in length eleven thousand one hundred furlongs, and its breadth, at the widest part, is three thousand three hundred. The mouth is but four furlongs wide; and this strait, called the Bosphorus, and across which the bridge of Darius had been thrown, is a hundred and twenty furlongs in length, reaching from the Euxine to the Propontis. The Propontis is five hundred furlongs across, and fourteen hundred long. Its waters flow into the Hellespont, the length of which is four hundred furlongs, and the width no more than seven. The Hellespont opens into the wide sea called the Egean.

86. The mode in which these distances have been measured is the following. In a long day a vessel generally accomplishes about seventy thousand fathoms, in the night sixty thousand. Now from the mouth of the Pontus to the river Phasis, which is the extreme length of this sea, is a voyage of nine days and eight nights, which makes the distance one million one hundred and ten thousand fathoms, or eleven thousand one hundred furlongs. Again, from Sindica, to Themiscyra on the river Thermôdon, where the Pontus is wider than at any other place, is a sail of three days and two nights; which makes three hundred and thirty thousand fathoms, or three thousand three hundred furlongs. Such is the plan on which I have measured the Pontus, the Bosphorus, and the Hellespont, and such is the account which I have to give of them. The Pontus has also a lake belonging to it, not very much inferior to itself in size. The waters of this lake run into the Pontus: it is called the Mæotis, and also the Mother of the Pontus.

87. Darius, after he had finished his survey, sailed back to the bridge, which had been constructed for him by Mandrocles a Samian. He likewise surveyed the Bosphorus, and erected upon its shores two pillars of white marble, whereupon he inscribed the names of all the nations which formed his army—on the one pillar in Greek, on the other in Assyrian characters. Now his army was drawn from all the nations under his sway; and the whole amount, without reckoning the naval forces, was seven hundred thousand men, including cavalry. The fleet consisted of six hundred ships. Some time afterwards the Byzantines removed these pillars to their own city, and used them for an altar which they erected to Orthosian Diana. One block remained behind: it lay near the temple of Bacchus at Byzantium, and was covered with Assyrian writing. The spot where Darius bridged the Bosphorus was, I think, but I speak only from conjecture, half-way between the city of Byzantium and the temple at the mouth of the strait.

88. Darius was so pleased with the bridge thrown across the strait by the Samian Mandrocles, that he not only bestowed upon him all the customary presents, but gave him ten of every kind. Mandrocles, by the way of offering first-fruits from these presents, caused a picture to be painted which showed the whole of the bridge, with King Darius sitting in a seat of honour, and his army engaged in the passage. This painting he dedicated in the temple

of Juno at Samos, attaching to it the inscription following:—

The fish-fraught Bosphorus bridged, to Juno's fane
  Did Mandrocles this proud memorial bring;
When for himself a crown he'd skill to gain,
  For Samos praise, contenting the Great King.

Such was the memorial of his work which was left by the architect of the bridge.

89. Darius, after rewarding Mandrocles, passed into Europe, while he ordered the Ionians to enter the Pontus, and sail to the mouth of the Ister. There he bade them throw a bridge across the stream and await his coming. The Ionians, Æolians, and Hellespontians were the nations which furnished the chief strength of his navy. So the fleet, threading the Cyanean Isles, proceeded straight to the Ister, and, mounting the river to the point where its channels separate, a distance of two days' voyage from the sea, yoked the neck of the stream. Meantime Darius, who had crossed the Bosphorus by the bridge over it, marched through Thrace; and happening upon the sources of the Tearus, pitched his camp and made a stay of three days.

90. Now the Tearus is said by those who dwell near it, to be the most healthful of all streams, and to cure, among other diseases, the scab either in man or beast. Its sources, which are eight and thirty in number, all flowing from the same rock, are in part cold, in part hot. They lie at an equal distance from the town of Heræum near Perinthus, and Apollonia on the Euxine, a two days' journey from each. This river, the Tearus, is a tributary of the Contadesdus, which runs into the Agrianes, and that into the Hebrus. The Hebrus empties itself into the sea near the city of Ænus.

91. Here then, on the banks of the Tearus, Darius stopped and pitched his camp. The river charmed him so, that he caused a pillar to be erected in this place also, with an inscription to the following effect: "The fountains of the Tearus afford the best and most beautiful water of all rivers: they were visited, on his march into Scythia, by the best and most beautiful of men, Darius, son of Hystaspes, king of the Persians, and of the whole continent." Such was the inscription which he set up at this place.

92. Marching thence, he came to a second river, called the Artiscus, which flows through the country of the Odrysians. Here he fixed upon a certain spot, where every one of his soldiers should throw a stone as he passed by.

When his orders were obeyed, Darius continued his march, leaving behind him great hills formed of the stones cast by his troops.

93. Before arriving at the Ister, the first people whom he subdued were the Getæ, who believe in their immortality. The Thracians of Salmydessus, and those who dwelt above the cities of Apollonia and Mesembria—the Scyrmiadæ and Nipsæans, as they are called—gave themselves up to Darius without a struggle; but the Getæ obstinately defending themselves, were forthwith enslaved, notwithstanding that they are the noblest as well as the most just of all the Thracian tribes.

94. The belief of the Getæ in respect of immortality is the following. They think that they do not really die, but that when they depart this life they go to Zalmoxis, who is called also Gebeleïzis by some among them. To this god every five years they send a messenger, who is chosen by lot out of the whole nation, and charged to bear him their several requests. Their mode of sending him is this. A number of them stand in order, each holding in his hand three darts; others take the man who is to be sent to Zalmoxis, and swinging him by his hands and feet, toss him into the air so that he falls upon the points of the weapons. If he is pierced and dies, they think that the god is propitious to them; but if not, they lay the fault on the messenger, who (they say) is a wicked man: and so they choose another to send away. The messages are given while the man is still alive. This same people, when it lightens and thunders, aim their arrows at the sky, uttering threats against the god; and they do not believe that there is any god but their own.

95. I am told by the Greeks who dwell on the shores of the Hellespont and the Pontus, that this Zalmoxis was in reality a man, that he lived at Samos, and while there was the slave of Pythagoras son of Mnesarchus. After obtaining his freedom he grew rich, and leaving Samos, returned to his own country. The Thracians at that time lived in a wretched way, and were a poor ignorant race; Zalmoxis, therefore, who by his commerce with the Greeks, and especially with one who was by no means their most contemptible philosopher, Pythagoras to wit, was acquainted with the Ionic mode of life and with manners more refined than those current among his countrymen, had a chamber built, in which from time to time he received and feasted all the principal Thracians, using the occasion to teach them that neither he, nor they, his boon companions,

nor any of their posterity would ever perish, but that they would all go to a place where they would live for aye in the enjoyment of every conceivable good. While he was acting in this way, and holding this kind of discourse, he was constructing an apartment underground, into which, when it was completed, he withdrew, vanishing suddenly from the eyes of the Thracians, who greatly regretted his loss, and mourned over him as one dead. He meanwhile abode in his secret chamber three full years, after which he came forth from his concealment, and showed himself once more to his countrymen, who were thus brought to believe in the truth of what he had taught them. Such is the account of the Greeks.

96. I for my part neither put entire faith in this story of Zalmoxis and his underground chamber, nor do I altogether discredit it: but I believe Zalmoxis to have lived long before the time of Pythagoras. Whether there was ever really a man of the name, or whether Zalmoxis is nothing but a native god of the Getæ, I now bid him farewell. As for the Getæ themselves, the people who observe the practices described above, they were now reduced by the Persians, and accompanied the army of Darius.

97. When Darius, with his land forces, reached the Ister, he made his troops cross the stream, and after all were gone over gave orders to the Ionians to break the bridge, and follow him with the whole naval force in his land march. They were about to obey his command, when the general of the Mytilenæans, Coës son of Erxander, having first asked whether it was agreeable to the king to listen to one who wished to speak his mind, addressed him in the words following:—"Thou art about, Sire, to attack a country no part of which is cultivated, and wherein there is not a single inhabited city. Keep this bridge, then, as it is, and leave those who built it to watch over it. So if we come up with the Scythians and succeed against them as we could wish, we may return by this route; or if we fail of finding them, our retreat will still be secure. For I have no fear lest the Scythians defeat us in battle, but my dread is lest we be unable to discover them, and suffer loss while we wander about their territory. And now, mayhap, it will be said, I advise thee thus in the hope of being myself allowed to remain behind; but in truth I have no other design than to recommend the course which seems to me the best; nor will I consent to be among those left behind, but my resolve is, in any case, to follow

thee." The advice of Coës pleased Darius highly, who thus replied to him:—"Dear Lesbian, when I am safe home again in my palace, be sure thou come to me, and with good deeds will I recompense thy good words of to-day."

98. Having so said, the king took a leathern thong, and tying sixty knots in it, called together the Ionian tyrants, and spoke thus to them:—"Men of Ionia, my former commands to you concerning the bridge are now withdrawn. See, here is a thong: take it, and observe my bidding with respect to it. From the time that I leave you to march forward into Scythia, untie every day one of the knots. If I do not return before the last day to which the knots will hold out, then leave your station, and sail to your several homes. Meanwhile, understand that my resolve is changed, and that you are to guard the bridge with all care, and watch over its safety and preservation. By so doing ye will oblige me greatly." When Darius had thus spoken, he set out on his march with all speed.

99. Before you come to Scythia, on the sea coast, lies Thrace. The land here makes a sweep, and then Scythia begins, the Ister falling into the sea at this point with its mouth facing the east. Starting from the Ister I shall now describe the measurements of the seashore of Scythia. Immediately that the Ister is crossed, Old Scythia begins, and continues as far as the city called Carcinitis, fronting towards the south wind and the mid-day. Here upon the same sea, there lies a mountainous tract projecting into the Pontus, which is inhabited by the Tauri, as far as what is called the Rugged Chersonese, which runs out into the sea upon the east. For the boundaries of Scythia extend on two sides to two different seas, one upon the south, and the other towards the east, as is also the case with Attica. And the Tauri occupy a position in Scythia like that which a people would hold in Attica, who, being foreigners and not Athenians, should inhabit the high land of Sunium, from Thoricus to the township of Anaphlystus, if this tract projected into the sea somewhat further than it does. Such, to compare great things with small, is the Tauric territory. For the sake of those who may not have made the voyage round these parts of Attica, I will illustrate in another way. It is as if in Iapygia a line were drawn from Port Brundusium to Tarentum, and a people different from the Iapygians inhabited the promontory. These two instances may suggest a number of others where the

shape of the land closely resembles that of Taurica.

100. Beyond this tract, we find the Scythians again in possession of the country above the Tauri and the parts bordering on the eastern sea, as also of the whole district lying west of the Cimmerian Bosphorus and the Palus Mæotis, as far as the river Tanais, which empties itself into that lake at its upper end. As for the inland boundaries of Scythia, if we start from the Ister, we find it enclosed by the following tribes, first the Agathyrsi, next the Neuri, then the Androphagi, and last of all, the Melanchlæni.

101. Scythia then, which is square in shape, and has two of its sides reaching down to the sea, extends inland to the same distance that it stretches along the coast, and is equal every way. For it is a ten days' journey from the Ister to the Borysthenes, and ten more from the Borysthenes to the Palus Mæotis, while the distance from the coast inland to the country of the Melanchlæni, who dwell above Scythia, is a journey of twenty days. I reckon the day's journey at two hundred furlongs. Thus the two sides which run straight inland are four thousand furlongs each, and the transverse sides at right angles to these are also of the same length, which gives the full size of Scythia.

102. The Scythians, reflecting on their situation, perceived that they were not strong enough by themselves to contend with the army of Darius in open fight. They, therefore, sent envoys to the neighbouring nations, whose kings had already met, and were in consultation upon the advance of so vast a host. Now they who had come together were the kings of the Tauri, the Agathyrsi, the Neuri, the Androphagi, the Melanchlæni, the Gelôni, the Budini, and the Sauromatæ.

103. The Tauri have the following customs. They offer in sacrifice to the Virgin all shipwrecked persons, and all Greeks compelled to put into their ports by stress of weather. The mode of sacrifice is this. After the preparatory ceremonies, they strike the victim on the head with a club. Then, according to some accounts, they hurl the trunk from the precipice whereon the temple stands, and nail the head to a cross. Others grant that the head is treated in this way, but deny that the body is thrown down the cliff—on the contrary, they say, it is buried. The goddess to whom these sacrifices are offered the Tauri themselves declare to be Iphigenia the daughter of Agamemnon. When they take prisoners in war they treat them in the following way. The man who has taken a captive cuts off his head, and carrying it to his home, fixes it upon a tall pole, which he elevates above his house, most commonly over the chimney. The reason that the heads are set up so high, is (it is said) in order that the whole house may be under their protection. These people live entirely by war and plundering.

104. The Agathyrsi are a race of men very luxurious, and very fond of wearing gold on their persons. They have wives in common, that so they may be all brothers, and, as members of one family, may neither envy nor hate one another. In other respects their customs approach nearly to those of the Thracians.

105. The Neurian customs are like the Scythian. One generation before the attack of Darius they were driven from their land by a huge multitude of serpents which invaded them. Of these some were produced in their own country, while others, and those by far the greater number, came in from the deserts on the north. Suffering grievously beneath this scourge, they quitted their homes, and took refuge with the Budini. It seems that these people are conjurers: for both the Scythians and the Greeks who dwell in Scythia say that every Neurian once a year becomes a wolf for a few days, at the end of which time he is restored to his proper shape. Not that I believe this, but they constantly affirm it to be true, and are even ready to back their assertion with an oath.

106. The manners of the Androphagi[1] are more savage than those of any other race. They neither observe justice, nor are governed by any laws. They are nomads, and their dress is Scythian; but the language which they speak is peculiar to themselves. Unlike any other nation in these parts, they are cannibals.

107. The Melanchlæni[2] wear, all of them, black cloaks, and from this derive the name which they bear. Their customs are Scythic.

108. The Budini are a large and powerful nation: they have all deep blue eyes, and bright red hair. There is a city in their territory, called Gelônus, which is surrounded with a lofty wall, thirty furlongs each way, built entirely of wood. All the houses in the place and all the temples are of the same material. Here are temples built in honour of the Grecian gods, and adorned after the Greek fashion with images, altars, and shrines, all in wood. There is even a festival, held every third year in honour of Bacchus, at which the natives fall into

[1] Or "Men-eaters."
[2] Or "Black-cloaks."

the Bacchic fury. For the fact is that the Gelôni were anciently Greeks, who, being driven out of the factories along the coast, fled to the Budini and took up their abode with them. They still speak a language half Greek, half Scythian.

109. The Budini, however, do not speak the same language as the Gelôni, nor is their mode of life the same. They are the aboriginal people of the country, and are nomads; unlike any of the neighbouring races, they eat lice. The Gelôni, on the contrary, are tillers of the soil, eat bread, have gardens, and both in shape and complexion are quite different from the Budini. The Greeks notwithstanding call these latter Gelôni; but it is a mistake to give them the name. Their country is thickly planted with trees of all manner of kinds. In the very woodiest part is a broad deep lake, surrounded by marshy ground with reeds growing on it. Here otters are caught, and beavers, with another sort of animal which has a square face. With the skins of this last the natives border their capotes: and they also get from them a remedy, which is of virtue in diseases of the womb.

110. It is reported of the Sauromatæ, that when the Greeks fought with the Amazons, whom the Scythians call *Oior-pata* or "man-slayers," as it may be rendered, *Oior* being Scythic for "man," and *pata* for "to slay"—it is reported, I say, that the Greeks after gaining the battle of the Thermôdon, put to sea, taking with them on board three of their vessels all the Amazons whom they had made prisoners; and that these women upon the voyage rose up against the crews, and massacred them to a man. As however they were quite strange to ships, and did not know how to use either rudder, sails, or oars, they were carried, after the death of the men, where the winds and the waves listed. At last they reached the shores of the Palus Mæotis and came to a place called Cremni or "the Cliffs," which is in the country of the free Scythians. Here they went ashore, and proceeded by land towards the inhabited regions; the first herd of horses which they fell in with they seized, and mounting upon their backs, fell to plundering the Scythian territory.

111. The Scyths could not tell what to make of the attack upon them—the dress, the language, the nation itself, were alike unknown —whence the enemy had come even, was a marvel. Imagining, however, that they were all men of about the same age, they went out against them, and fought a battle. Some of the bodies of the slain fell into their hands, whereby they discovered the truth. Hereupon they deliberated, and made a resolve to kill no more of them, but to send against them a detachment of their youngest men, as near as they could guess equal to the women in number, with orders to encamp in their neighbourhood, and do as they saw them do—when the Amazons advanced against them, they were to retire, and avoid a fight—when they halted, the young men were to approach and pitch their camp near the camp of the enemy. All this they did on account of their strong desire to obtain children from so notable a race.

112. So the youths departed, and obeyed the orders which had been given them. The Amazons soon found out that they had not come to do them any harm; and so they on their part ceased to offer the Scythians any molestation. And now day after day the camps approached nearer to one another; both parties led the same life, neither having anything but their arms and horses, so that they were forced to support themselves by hunting and pillage.

113. At last an incident brought two of them together—the man easily gained the good graces of the woman, who bade him by signs (for they did not understand each other's language) to bring a friend the next day to the spot where they had met—promising on her part to bring with her another woman. He did so, and the woman kept her word. When the rest of the youths heard what had taken place, they also sought and gained the favour of the other Amazons.

114. The two camps were then joined in one, the Scythians living with the Amazons as their wives; and the men were unable to learn the tongue of the women, but the women soon caught up the tongue of the men. When they could thus understand one another, the Scyths addressed the Amazons in these words—"We have parents, and properties, let us therefore give up this mode of life, and return to our nation, and live with them. You shall be our wives there no less than here, and we promise you to have no others." But the Amazons said —"We could not live with your women—our customs are quite different from theirs. To draw the bow, to hurl the javelin, to bestride the horse, these are our arts—of womanly employments we know nothing. Your women, on the contrary, do none of these things; but stay at home in their waggons, engaged in womanish tasks, and never go out to hunt, or to do

anything. We should never agree together. But if you truly wish to keep us as your wives, and would conduct yourselves with strict justice towards us, go you home to your parents, bid them give you your inheritance, and then come back to us, and let us and you live together by ourselves."

115. The youths approved of the advice, and followed it. They went and got the portion of goods which fell to them, returned with it, and rejoined their wives, who then addressed them in these words following:—'We are ashamed, and afraid to live in the country where we now are. Not only have we stolen you from your fathers, but we have done great damage to Scythia by our ravages. As you like us for wives, grant the request we make of you. Let us leave this country together, and go and dwell beyond the Tanais." Again the youths complied.

116. Crossing the Tanais they journeyed eastward a distance of three days' march from that stream, and again northward a distance of three days' march from the Palus Mæotis. Here they came to the country where they now live, and took up their abode in it. The women of the Sauromatæ have continued from that day to the present to observe their ancient customs, frequently hunting on horseback with their husbands, sometimes even unaccompanied; in war taking the field; and wearing the very same dress as the men.

117. The Sauromatæ speak the language of Scythia, but have never talked it correctly, because the Amazons learnt it imperfectly at the first. Their marriage-law lays it down that no girl shall wed till she has killed a man in battle. Sometimes it happens that a woman dies unmarried at an advanced age, having never been able in her whole lifetime to fulfil the condition.

118. The envoys of the Scythians, on being introduced into the presence of the kings of these nations, who were assembled to deliberate, made it known to them that the Persian, after subduing the whole of the other continent, had thrown a bridge over the strait of the Bosphorus, and crossed into the continent of Europe, where he had reduced the Thracians, and was now making a bridge over the Ister, his aim being to bring under his sway all Europe also. "Stand ye not aloof then from this contest," they went on to say, "look not on tamely while we are perishing—but make common cause with us, and together let us meet the enemy. If ye refuse, we must yield to the pressure, and either quit our country, or make terms with the invaders. For what else is left for us to do, if your aid be withheld from us? The blow, be sure, will not light on you more gently upon this account. The Persian comes against you no less than against us: and will not be content, after we are conquered, to leave you in peace. We can bring strong proof of what we here advance. Had the Persian leader indeed come to avenge the wrongs which he suffered at our hands when we enslaved his people, and to war on us only, he would have been bound to march straight upon Scythia, without molesting any nation by the way. Then it would have been plain to all that Scythia alone was aimed at. But now, what has his conduct been? From the moment of his entrance into Europe, he has subjugated without exception every nation that lay in his path. All the tribes of the Thracians have been brought under his sway, and among them even our next neighbours, the Getæ."

119. The assembled princes of the nations, after hearing all that the Scythians had to say, deliberated. At the end opinion was divided —the kings of the Gelôni, Budini, and Sauromatæ were of accord, and pledged themselves to give assistance to the Scythians; but the Agathyrsian and Neurian princes, together with the sovereigns of the Androphagi, the Melanchlæni, and the Tauri, replied to their request as follows:—"If you had not been the first to wrong the Persians, and begin the war, we should have thought the request you make just; we should then have complied with your wishes, and joined our arms with yours. Now, however, the case stands thus—you, independently of us, invaded the land of the Persians, and so long as God gave you the power, lorded it over them: raised up now by the same God, they are come to do to you the like. We, on our part, did no wrong to these men in the former war, and will not be the first to commit wrong now. If they invade our land, and begin aggressions upon us, we will not suffer them; but, till we see this come to pass, we will remain at home. For we believe that the Persians are not come to attack us, but to punish those who are guilty of first injuring them."

120. When this reply reached the Scythians, they resolved, as the neighbouring nations refused their alliance, that they would not openly venture on any pitched battle with the enemy, but would retire before them, driving off their herds, choking up all the wells and springs as they retreated, and leaving the whole country

bare of forage. They divided themselves into three bands, one of which, namely, that commanded by Scopasis, it was agreed should be joined by the Sauromatæ, and if the Persians advanced in the direction of the Tanais, should retreat along the shores of the Palus Mæotis and make for that river; while if the Persians retired, they should at once pursue and harass them. The two other divisions, the principal one under the command of Idanthyrsus, and the third, of which Taxacis was king, were to unite in one, and, joined by the detachments of the Gelôni and Budini, were, like the others, to keep at the distance of a day's march from the Persians, falling back as they advanced, and doing the same as the others. And first, they were to take the direction of the nations which had refused to join the alliance, and were to draw the war upon them: that so, if they would not of their own free will engage in the contest, they might by these means be forced into it. Afterwards, it was agreed that they should retire into their own land, and, should it on deliberation appear to them expedient, join battle with the enemy.

121. When these measures had been determined on, the Scythians went out to meet the army of Darius, sending on in front as scouts the fleetest of their horsemen. Their waggons, wherein their women and their children lived, and all their cattle, except such a number as was wanted for food, which they kept with them, were made to precede them in their retreat, and departed, with orders to keep marching, without change of course, to the north.

122. The scouts of the Scythians found the Persian host advanced three days' march from the Ister, and immediately took the lead of them at the distance of a day's march, encamping from time to time, and destroying all that grew on the ground. The Persians no sooner caught sight of the Scythian horse than they pursued upon their track, while the enemy retired before them. The pursuit of the Persians was directed towards the single division of the Scythian army, and thus their line of march was eastward toward the Tanais. The Scyths crossed the river, and the Persians after them, still in pursuit. In this way they passed through the country of the Sauromatæ, and entered that of the Budini.

123. As long as the march of the Persian army lay through the countries of the Scythians and Sauromatæ, there was nothing which they could damage, the land being waste and barren; but on entering the territories of the Bu-

dini, they came upon the wooden fortress above mentioned, which was deserted by its inhabitants and left quite empty of everything. This place they burnt to the ground; and having so done, again pressed forward on the track of the retreating Scythians, till, having passed through the entire country of the Budini, they reached the desert, which has no inhabitants, and extends a distance of seven days' journey above the Budinian territory. Beyond this desert dwell the Thyssagetæ, out of whose land four great streams flow. These rivers all traverse the country of the Mæotians, and fall into the Palus Mæotis. Their names are the Lycus, the Oarus, the Tanais, and the Syrgis.

124. When Darius reached the desert, he paused from his pursuit, and halted his army upon the Oarus. Here he built eight large forts, at an equal distance from one another, sixty furlongs apart or thereabouts, the ruins of which were still remaining in my day. During the time that he was so occupied, the Scythians whom he had been following made a circuit by the higher regions, and re-entered Scythia. On their complete disappearance, Darius, seeing nothing more of them, left his forts half finished, and returned towards the west. He imagined that the Scythians whom he had seen were the entire nation, and that they had fled in that direction.

125. He now quickened his march, and entering Scythia, fell in with the two combined divisions of the Scythian army, and instantly gave them chase. They kept to their plan of retreating before him at the distance of a day's march; and, he still following them hotly, they led him, as had been previously settled, into the territories of the nations that had refused to become their allies, and first of all into the country of the Melanchlæni. Great disturbance was caused among this people by the invasion of the Scyths first, and then of the Persians. So, having harassed them after this sort, the Scythians led the way into the land of the Androphagi, with the same result as before; and thence passed onwards into Neuris, where their coming likewise spread dismay among the inhabitants. Still retreating they approached the Agathyrsi; but this people, which had witnessed the flight and terror of their neighbours, did not wait for the Scyths to invade them, but sent a herald to forbid them to cross their borders, and to forewarn them, that, if they made the attempt, it would be resisted by force of arms. The Agathyrsi then proceeded to the frontier, to defend their coun-

try against the invaders. As for the other nations, the Melanchlæni, the Androphagi, and the Neuri, instead of defending themselves, when the Scyths and Persians overran their lands, they forgot their threats and fled away in confusion to the deserts lying towards the north. The Scythians, when the Agathyrsi forbade them to enter their country, refrained; and led the Persians back from the Neurian district into their own land.

126. This had gone on so long, and seemed so interminable, that Darius at last sent a horseman to Idanthyrsus, the Scythian king, with the following message:—"Thou strange man, why dost thou keep on flying before me, when there are two things thou mightest do so easily? If thou deemest thyself able to resist my arms, cease thy wanderings and come, let us engage in battle. Or if thou art conscious that my strength is greater than thine—even so thou shouldest cease to run away—thou hast but to bring thy lord earth and water, and to come at once to a conference."

127. To this message Idanthyrsus, the Scythian king, replied:—"This is my way, Persian. I never fear men or fly from them. I have not done so in times past, nor do I now fly from thee. There is nothing new or strange in what I do; I only follow my common mode of life in peaceful years. Now I will tell thee why I do not at once join battle with thee. We Scythians have neither towns nor cultivated lands, which might induce us, through fear of their being taken or ravaged, to be in any hurry to fight with you. If, however, you must needs come to blows with us speedily, look you now, there are our fathers' tombs—seek them out, and attempt to meddle with them—then ye shall see whether or no we will fight with you. Till ye do this, be sure we shall not join battle, unless it pleases us. This is my answer to the challenge to fight. As for lords, I acknowledge only Jove my ancestor, and Vesta, the Scythian queen. Earth and water, the tribute thou askedst, I do not send, but thou shalt soon receive more suitable gifts. Last of all, in return for thy calling thyself my lord, I say to thee, 'Go weep.'" (This is what men mean by the Scythian mode of speech.) So the herald departed, bearing this message to Darius.

128. When the Scythian kings heard the name of slavery they were filled with rage, and despatched the division under Scopasis to which the Sauromatæ were joined, with orders that they should seek a conference with the Ionians, who had been left at the Ister to guard the bridge. Meanwhile the Scythians who remained behind resolved no longer to lead the Persians hither and thither about their country, but to fall upon them whenever they should be at their meals. So they waited till such times, and then did as they had determined. In these combats the Scythian horse always put to flight the horse of the enemy; these last, however, when routed, fell back upon their foot, who never failed to afford them support; while the Scythians, on their side, as soon as they had driven the horse in, retired again, for fear of the foot. By night too the Scythians made many similar attacks.

129. There was one very strange thing which greatly advantaged the Persians, and was of equal disservice to the Scyths, in these assaults on the Persian camp. This was the braying of the asses and the appearance of the mules. For, as I observed before, the land of the Scythians produces neither ass nor mule, and contains no single specimen of either animal, by reason of the cold. So, when the asses brayed, they frightened the Scythian cavalry; and often, in the middle of a charge, the horses, hearing the noise made by the asses, would take fright and wheel round, pricking up their ears, and showing astonishment. This was owing to their having never heard the noise, or seen the form, of the animal before: and it was not without some little influence on the progress of the war.

130. The Scythians, when they perceived signs that the Persians were becoming alarmed, took steps to induce them not to quit Scythia, in the hope, if they stayed, of inflicting on them the greater injury, when their supplies should altogether fail. To effect this, they would leave some of their cattle exposed with the herdsmen, while they themselves moved away to a distance: the Persians would make a foray, and take the beasts, whereupon they would be highly elated.

131. This they did several times, until at last Darius was at his wits' end; hereon the Scythian princes, understanding how matters stood, despatched a herald to the Persian camp with presents for the king: these were, a bird, a mouse, a frog, and five arrows. The Persians asked the bearer to tell them what these gifts might mean, but he made answer that he had no orders except to deliver them, and return again with all speed. If the Persians were wise, he added, they would find out the meaning for themselves. So when they heard this, they held a council to consider the matter.

132. Darius gave it as his opinion that the Scyths intended a surrender of themselves and their country, both land and water, into his hands. This he conceived to be the meaning of the gifts, because the mouse is an inhabitant of the earth, and eats the same food as man, while the frog passes his life in the water; the bird bears a great resemblance to the horse, and the arrows might signify the surrender of all their power. To the explanation of Darius, Gobryas, one of the seven conspirators against the Magus, opposed another which was as follows:—"Unless, Persians, ye can turn into birds and fly up into the sky, or become mice and burrow under the ground, or make yourselves frogs, and take refuge in the fens, ye will never make escape from this land, but die pierced by our arrows." Such were the meanings which the Persians assigned to the gifts.

133. The single division of the Scyths, which in the early part of the war had been appointed to keep guard about the Palus Mæotis, and had now been sent to get speech of the Ionians stationed at the Ister, addressed them, on reaching the bridge, in these words—"Men of Ionia, we bring you freedom, if ye will only do as we recommend. Darius, we understand, enjoined you to keep your guard here at this bridge just sixty days; then, if he did not appear, you were to return home. Now, therefore, act so as to be free from blame, alike in his sight, and in ours. Tarry here the appointed time, and at the end go your ways." Having said this, and received a promise from the Ionians to do as they desired, the Scythians hastened back with all possible speed.

134. After the sending of the gifts to Darius, the part of the Scythian army which had not marched to the Ister, drew out in battle array horse and foot against the Persians, and seemed about to come to an engagement. But as they stood in battle array, it chanced that a hare started up between them and the Persians, and set to running; when immediately all the Scyths who saw it, rushed off in pursuit, with great confusion and loud cries and shouts. Darius, hearing the noise, inquired the cause of it, and was told that the Scythians were all engaged in hunting a hare. On this he turned to those with whom he was wont to converse, and said:—"These men do indeed despise us utterly: and now I see that Gobryas was right about the Scythian gifts. As, therefore, his opinion is now mine likewise, it is time we form some wise plan, whereby we may secure ourselves a safe return to our homes." "Ah! sire," Gobryas rejoined, "I was well nigh sure, ere I came here, that this was an impracticable race—since our coming I am yet more convinced of it, especially now that I see them making game of us. My advice is, therefore, that, when night falls, we light our fires as we are wont to do at other times, and leaving behind us on some pretext that portion of our army which is weak and unequal to hardship, taking care also to leave our asses tethered, retreat from Scythia, before our foes march forward to the Ister and destroy the bridge, or the Ionians come to any resolution which may lead to our ruin."

135. So Gobryas advised; and when night came, Darius followed his counsel, and leaving his sick soldiers, and those whose loss would be of least account, with the asses also tethered about the camp, marched away. The asses were left that their noise might be heard: the men, really because they were sick and useless, but under the pretence that he was about to fall upon the Scythians with the flower of his troops, and that they meanwhile were to guard his camp for him. Having thus declared his plans to the men whom he was deserting, and having caused the fires to be lighted, Darius set forth, and marched hastily towards the Ister. The asses, aware of the departure of the host, brayed louder than ever; and the Scythians, hearing the sound, entertained no doubt of the Persians being still in the same place.

136. When day dawned, the men who had been left behind, perceiving that they were betrayed by Darius, stretched out their hands towards the Scythians, and spoke as befitted their situation. The enemy no sooner heard, than they quickly joined all their troops in one, and both portions of the Scythian army—alike that which consisted of a single division, and that made up of two—accompanied by all their allies, the Sauromatæ, the Budini, and the Gelôni, set off in pursuit, and made straight for the Ister. As, however, the Persian army was chiefly foot, and had no knowledge of the routes, which are not cut out in Scythia; while the Scyths were all horsemen and well acquainted with the shortest way; it so happened that the two armies missed one another, and the Scythians, getting far ahead of their adversaries, came first to the bridge. Finding that the Persians were not yet arrived, they addressed the Ionians, who were aboard their ships, in these words:—"Men of Ionia, the number of your days is out, and ye do wrong to remain. Fear doubtless has kept you here hitherto:

now, however, you may safely break the bridge, and hasten back to your homes, rejoicing that you are free, and thanking for it the gods and the Scythians. Your former lord and master we undertake so to handle, that he will never again make war upon any one."

137. The Ionians now held a council. Miltiades the Athenian, who was king of the Chersonesites upon the Hellespont, and their commander at the Ister, recommended the other generals to do as the Scythians wished, and restore freedom to Ionia. But Histiæus the Milesian opposed this advice. "It is through Darius," he said, "that we enjoy our thrones in our several states. If his power be overturned, I cannot continue lord of Miletus, nor ye of your cities. For there is not one of them which will not prefer democracy to kingly rule." Then the other captains, who, till Histiæus spoke, were about to vote with Miltiades, changed their minds, and declared in favour of the last speaker.

138. The following were the voters on this occasion—all of them men who stood high in the esteem of the Persian king: the tyrants of the Hellespont—Daphnis of Abydos, Hippoclus of Lampsacus, Herophantus of Parium, Metrodôrus of Proconnêsus, Aristagoras of Cyzicus, and Ariston of Byzantium; the Ionian princes—Strattis of Chios, Æaces of Samos, Laodamas of Phocæa, and Histiæus of Miletus, the man who had opposed Miltiades. Only one Æolian of note was present, to wit, Aristagoras of Cymé.

139. Having resolved to follow the advice of Histiæus, the Greek leaders further determined to speak and act as follows. In order to appear to the Scythians to be doing something, when in fact they were doing nothing of consequence, and likewise to prevent them from forcing a passage across the Ister by the bridge, they resolved to break up the part of the bridge which abutted on Scythia, to the distance of a bowshot from the river bank; and to assure the Scythians, while the demolition was proceeding, that there was nothing which they would not do to pleasure them. Such were the additions made to the resolution of Histiæus; and then Histiæus himself stood forth and made answer to the Scyths in the name of all the Greeks:—"Good is the advice which ye have brought us, Scythians, and well have ye done to come here with such speed. Your efforts have now put us into the right path; and our efforts shall not be wanting to advance your cause. Your own eyes see that we are en-

gaged in breaking the bridge; and, believe us, we will work zealously to procure our own freedom. Meantime, while we labour here at our task, be it your business to seek them out, and, when found, for our sakes, as well as your own, to visit them with the vengeance which they so well deserve."

140. Again the Scyths put faith in the promises of the Ionian chiefs, and retraced their steps, hoping to fall in with the Persians. They missed, however, the enemy's whole line of march; their own former acts being to blame for it. Had they not ravaged all the pasturages of that region, and filled in all the wells, they would have easily found the Persians whenever they chose. But, as it turned out, the measures which seemed to them so wisely planned were exactly what caused their failure. They took a route where water was to be found and fodder could be got for their horses, and on this track sought their adversaries, expecting that they too would retreat through regions where these things were to be obtained. The Persians, however, kept strictly to the line of their former march, never for a moment departing from it; and even so gained the bridge with difficulty. It was night when they arrived, and their terror, when they found the bridge broken up, was great; for they thought that perhaps the Ionians had deserted them.

141. Now there was in the army of Darius a certain man, an Egyptian, who had a louder voice than any other man in the world. This person was bid by Darius to stand at the water's edge, and call Histiæus the Milesian. The fellow did as he was bid; and Histiæus, hearing him at the very first summons, brought the fleet to assist in conveying the army across, and once more made good the bridge.

142. By these means the Persians escaped from Scythia, while the Scyths sought for them in vain, again missing their track. And hence the Scythians are accustomed to say of the Ionians, by way of reproach, that, if they be looked upon as freemen, they are the basest and most dastardly of all mankind—but if they be considered as under servitude, they are the faithfullest of slaves, and the most fondly attached to their lords.

143. Darius, having passed through Thrace, reached Sestos in the Chersonese, whence he crossed by the help of his fleet into Asia, leaving a Persian, named Megabazus, commander on the European side. This was the man on whom Darius once conferred special honour by a compliment which he paid him before all

the Persians. He was about to eat some pomegranates, and had opened the first, when his brother Artabanus asked him "what he would like to have in as great plenty as the seeds of the pomegranate?" Darius answered—"Had I as many men like Megabazus as there are seeds here, it would please me better than to be lord of Greece." Such was the compliment wherewith Darius honoured the general to whom at this time he gave the command of the troops left in Europe, amounting in all to some eighty thousand men.

144. This same Megabazus got himself an undying remembrance among the Hellespontians, by a certain speech which he made. It came to his knowledge, while he was staying at Byzantium, that the Chalcedonians made their settlement seventeen years earlier than the Byzantines. "Then," said he, "the Chalcedonians must at that time have been labouring under blindness—otherwise, when so far more excellent a site was open to them, they would never have chosen one so greatly inferior." Megabazus now, having been appointed to take the command upon the Hellespont, employed himself in the reduction of all those states which had not of their own accord joined the Medes.

145. About this very time another great expedition was undertaken against Libya, on a pretext which I will relate when I have premised certain particulars. The descendants of the Argonauts in the third generation, driven out of Lemnos by the Pelasgi who carried off the Athenian women from Brauron, took ship and went to Lacedæmon, where, seating themselves on Mount Taÿgetum, they proceeded to kindle their fires. The Lacedæmonians, seeing this, sent a herald to inquire of them "who they were, and from what region they had come"; whereupon they made answer, "that they were Minyæ, sons of the heroes by whom the ship Argo was manned; for these persons had stayed awhile in Lemnos, and had there become their progenitors." On hearing this account of their descent, the Lacedæmonians sent to them a second time, and asked "what was their object in coming to Lacedæmon, and there kindling their fires?" They answered, "that, driven from their own land by the Pelasgi, they had come, as was most reasonable, to their fathers; and their wish was to dwell with them in their country, partake their privileges, and obtain allotments of land. It seemed good to the Lacedæmonians to receive the Minyæ among them on their own terms; to assign

them lands, and enrol them in their tribes. What chiefly moved them to this was the consideration that the sons of Tyndarus had sailed on board the Argo. The Minyæ, on their part, forthwith married Spartan wives, and gave the wives, whom they had married in Lemnos, to Spartan husbands.

146. However, before much time had elapsed, the Minyæ began to wax wanton, demanded to share the throne, and committed other impieties: whereupon the Lacedæmonians passed on them sentence of death, and, seizing them, cast them into prison. Now the Lacedæmonians never put criminals to death in the daytime, but always at night. When the Minyæ, accordingly, were about to suffer, their wives, who were not only citizens, but daughters of the chief men among the Spartans, entreated to be allowed to enter the prison, and have some talk with their lords; and the Spartans, not expecting any fraud from such a quarter, granted their request. The women entered the prison, gave their own clothes to their husbands, and received theirs in exchange: after which the Minyæ, dressed in their wives' garments, and thus passing for women, went forth. Having effected their escape in this manner, they seated themselves once more upon Taÿgetum.

147. It happened that at this very time Theras, son of Autesion (whose father Tisamenus was the son of Thersander, and grandson of Polynices), was about to lead out a colony from Lacedæmon. This Theras, by birth a Cadmeian, was uncle on the mother's side to the two sons of Aristodêmus, Procles and Eurysthenes, and, during their infancy, administered in their right the royal power. When his nephews, however, on attaining to man's estate, took the government, Theras, who could not bear to be under the authority of others after he had wielded authority so long himself, resolved to leave Sparta and cross the sea to join his kindred. There were in the island now called Thera, but at that time Callisté, certain descendants of Membliarus, the son of Pœciles, a Phœnician. (For Cadmus, the son of Agenor, when he was sailing in search of Europé, made a landing on this island; and, either because the country pleased him, or because he had a purpose in so doing, left there a number of Phœnicians, and with them his own kinsman Membliarus. Callisté had been inhabited by this race for eight generations of men, before the arrival of Theras from Lacedæmon.)

148. Theras now, having with him a certain

number of men from each of the tribes, was setting forth on his expedition hitherward. Far from intending to drive out the former inhabitants, he regarded them as his near kin, and meant to settle among them. It happened that just at this time the Minyæ, having escaped from their prison, had taken up their station upon Mount Taÿgetum; and the Lacedæmonians, wishing to destroy them, were considering what was best to be done, when Theras begged their lives, undertaking to remove them from the territory. His prayer being granted, he took ship, and sailed, with three triaconters, to join the descendants of Membliarus. He was not, however, accompanied by all the Minyæ, but only by some few of them. The greater number fled to the land of the Paroreats and Caucons, whom they drove out, themselves occupying the region in six bodies, by which were afterwards built the towns of Lepreum, Macistus, Phryxæ, Pyrgus, Epium, and Nudium; whereof the greater part were in my day demolished by the Eleans.

149. The island was called Thera after the name of its founder. This same Theras had a son, who refused to cross the sea with him; Theras therefore left him behind, "a sheep," as he said, "among wolves." From this speech his son came to be called Œolycus, a name which afterwards grew to be the only one by which he was known. This Œolycus was the father of Ægeus, from whom sprang the Ægîdæ, a great tribe in Sparta. The men of this tribe lost at one time all their children, whereupon they were bidden by an oracle to build a temple to the furies of Laïus and Œdipus; they complied, and the mortality ceased. The same thing happened in Thera to the descendants of these men.

150. Thus far the history is delivered without variation both by the Theræans and the Lacedæmonians; but from this point we have only the Theræan narrative. Grinus (they say), the son of Æsanius, a descendant of Theras, and king of the island of Thera, went to Delphi to offer a hecatomb on behalf of his native city. He was accompanied by a large number of the citizens, and among the rest by Battus, the son of Polymnestus, who belonged to the Minyan family of the Euphemidæ. On Grinus consulting the oracle about sundry matters, the Pythoness gave him for answer, "that he should found a city in Libya." Grinus replied to this: "I, O king! am too far advanced in years, and too inactive, for such a work. Bid one of these youngsters undertake it." As he

spoke, he pointed towards Battus; and thus the matter rested for that time. When the embassy returned to Thera, small account was taken of the oracle by the Theræans, as they were quite ignorant where Libya was, and were not so venturesome as to send out a colony in the dark.

151. Seven years passed from the utterance of the oracle, and not a drop of rain fell in Thera: all the trees in the island, except one, were killed with the drought. The Theræans upon this sent to Delphi, and were reminded reproachfully that they had never colonised Libya. So, as there was no help for it, they sent messengers to Crete, to inquire whether any of the Cretans, or of the strangers sojourning among them, had ever travelled as far as Libya: and these messengers of theirs, in their wanderings about the island, among other places visited Itanus, where they fell in with a man, whose name was Corôbius, a dealer in purple. In answer to their inquiries, he told them that contrary winds had once carried him to Libya, where he had gone ashore on a certain island which was named Platea. So they hired this man's services, and took him back with them to Thera. A few persons then sailed from Thera to reconnoitre. Guided by Corôbius to the island of Platea, they left him there with provisions for a certain number of months, and returned home with all speed to give their countrymen an account of the island.

152. During their absence, which was prolonged beyond the time that had been agreed upon, Corôbius' provisions failed him. He was relieved, however, after a while by a Samian vessel, under the command of a man named Colæus, which, on its way to Egypt, was forced to put in at Platea. The crew, informed by Corôbius of all the circumstances, left him sufficient food for a year. They themselves quitted the island; and, anxious to reach Egypt, made sail in that direction, but were carried out of their course by a gale of wind from the east. The storm not abating, they were driven past the Pillars of Hercules, and at last, by some special guiding providence, reached Tartessus. This trading town was in those days a virgin port, unfrequented by the merchants. The Samians, in consequence, made by the return voyage a profit greater than any Greeks before their day, excepting Sostratus, son of Laodamas, an Eginetan, with whom no one else can compare. From the tenth part of their gains, amounting to six talents, the Samians made a brazen vessel, in shape like an Argive wine-

bowl, adorned with the heads of griffins standing out in high relief. This bowl, supported by three kneeling colossal figures in bronze, of the height of seven cubits, was placed as an offering in the temple of Juno at Samos. The aid given to Corôbius was the original cause of that close friendship which afterwards united the Cyrenæans and Theræans with the Samians.

153. The Theræans who had left Corôbius at Platea, when they reached Thera, told their countrymen that they had colonised an island on the coast of Libya. They of Thera, upon this, resolved that men should be sent to join the colony from each of their seven districts, and that the brothers in every family should draw lots to determine who were to go. Battus was chosen to be king and leader of the colony. So these men departed for Platea on board of two penteconters.

154. Such is the account which the Theræans give. In the sequel of the history their accounts tally with those of the people of Cyrênê; but in what they relate of Battus these two nations differ most widely. The following is the Cyrenaic story. There was once a king named Etearchus, who ruled over Axus, a city in Crete, and had a daughter named Phronima. This girl's mother having died, Etearchus married a second wife; who no sooner took up her abode in his house than she proved a true step-mother to poor Phronima, always vexing her, and contriving against her every sort of mischief. At last she taxed her with light conduct; and Etearchus, persuaded by his wife that the charge was true, bethought himself of a most barbarous mode of punishment. There was a certain Theræan, named Themison, a merchant, living at Axus. This man Etearchus invited to be his friend and guest, and then induced him to swear that he would do him any service he might require. No sooner had he given the promise, than the king fetched Phronima, and, delivering her into his hands, told him to carry her away and throw her into the sea. Hereupon Themison, full of indignation at the fraud whereby his oath had been procured, dissolved forthwith the friendship, and, taking the girl with him, sailed away from Crete. Having reached the open main, to acquit himself of the obligation under which he was laid by his oath to Etearchus, he fastened ropes about the damsel, and, letting her down into the sea, drew her up again, and so made sail for Thera.

155. At Thera, Polymnêstus, one of the chief citizens of the place, took Phronima to be his concubine. The fruit of this union was a son, who stammered and had a lisp in his speech. According to the Cyrenæans and Theræans, the name given to the boy was Battus: in my opinion, however, he was called at the first something else, and only got the name of Battus after his arrival in Libya, assuming it either in consequence of the words addressed to him by the Delphian oracle, or on account of the office which he held. For, in the Libyan tongue, the word "Battus" means "a king." And this, I think, was the reason why the Pythoness addressed him as she did: she knew he was to be a king in Libya, and so she used the Libyan word in speaking to him. For after he had grown to man's estate, he made a journey to Delphi, to consult the oracle about his voice; when, upon his putting his question, the Pythoness thus replied to him:—

Battus, thou camest to ask of thy voice; but Phœbus Apollo
Bids thee establish a city in Libya, abounding in fleeces;

which was as if she had said in her own tongue, "King, thou camest to ask of thy voice." Then he replied, "Mighty lord, I did indeed come hither to consult thee about my voice, but thou speakest to me of quite other matters, bidding me colonise Libya—an impossible thing! what power have I? what followers?" Thus he spake, but he did not persuade the Pythoness to give him any other response; so, when he found that she persisted in her former answer, he left her speaking, and set out on his return to Thera.

156. After a while, everything began to go wrong both with Battus and with the rest of the Theræans, whereupon these last, ignorant of the cause of their sufferings, sent to Delphi to inquire for what reason they were afflicted. The Pythoness in reply told them "that if they and Battus would make a settlement at Cyrênê in Libya, things would go better with them." Upon this the Theræans sent out Battus with two penteconters, and with these he proceeded to Libya, but within a little time, not knowing what else to do, the men returned and arrived off Thera. The Theræans, when they saw the vessels approaching, received them with showers of missiles, would not allow them to come near the shore, and ordered the men to sail back from whence they came. Thus compelled to return, they settled on an island near the Libyan coast, which (as I have already said) was called Platea. In size it is re-

ported to have been about equal to the city of Cyrêné, as it now stands.

157. In this place they continued two years, but at the end of that time, as their ill luck still followed them, they left the island to the care of one of their number, and went in a body to Delphi, where they made complaint at the shrine to the effect that, notwithstanding they had colonised Libya, they prospered as poorly as before. Hereon the Pythoness made them the following answer:—

Knowest thou better than I, fair Libya abounding in fleeces?
Better the stranger than he who has trod it? Oh! clever Theræans!

Battus and his friends, when they heard this, sailed back to Platea: it was plain the god would not hold them acquitted of the colony till they were absolutely in Libya. So, taking with them the man whom they had left upon the island, they made a settlement on the mainland directly opposite Platea, fixing themselves at a place called Aziris, which is closed in on both sides by the most beautiful hills, and on one side is washed by a river.

158. Here they remained six years, at the end of which time the Libyans induced them to move, promising that they would lead them to a better situation. So the Greeks left Aziris and were conducted by the Libyans towards the west, their journey being so arranged, by the calculation of their guides, that they passed in the night the most beautiful district of that whole country, which is the region called Irasa. The Libyans brought them to a spring, which goes by the name of Apollo's fountain, and told them—"Here, Grecians, is the proper place for you to settle; for here the sky leaks."

159. During the lifetime of Battus, the founder of the colony, who reigned forty years, and during that of his son Arcesilaüs, who reigned sixteen, the Cyrenæans continued at the same level, neither more nor fewer in number than they were at the first. But in the reign of the third king, Battus, surnamed the Happy, the advice of the Pythoness brought Greeks from every quarter into Libya, to join the settlement. The Cyrenæans had offered to all comers a share in their lands; and the oracle had spoken as follows:—

He that is backward to share in the pleasant Libyan acres,
Sooner or later, I warn him, will feel regret at his folly.

Thus a great multitude were collected together to Cyrêné, and the Libyans of the neighbour-

hood found themselves stripped of large portions of their lands. So they, and their king Adicran, being robbed and insulted by the Cyrenæans, sent messengers to Egypt, and put themselves under the rule of Apries, the Egyptian monarch; who, upon this, levied a vast army of Egyptians, and sent them against Cyrêné. The inhabitants of that place left their walls and marched out in force to the district of Irasa, where, near the spring called Thesté, they engaged the Egyptian host, and defeated it. The Egyptians, who had never before made trial of the prowess of the Greeks, and so thought but meanly of them, were routed with such slaughter that but a very few of them ever got back home. For this reason, the subjects of Apries, who laid the blame of the defeat on him, revolted from his authority.

160. This Battus left a son called Arcesilaüs, who, when he came to the throne, had dissensions with his brothers, which ended in their quitting him and departing to another region of Libya, where, after consulting among themselves, they founded the city, which is still called by the name then given to it, Barca. At the same time they endeavoured to induce the Libyans to revolt from Cyrêné. Not long afterwards Arcesilaüs made an expedition against the Libyans who had received his brothers and been prevailed upon to revolt; and they, fearing his power, fled to their countrymen who dwelt towards the east. Arcesilaüs pursued, and chased them to a place called Leucon, which is in Libya, where the Libyans resolved to risk a battle. Accordingly they engaged the Cyrenæans, and defeated them so entirely that as many as seven thousand of their heavy-armed were slain in the fight. Arcesilaüs, after this blow, fell sick, and, whilst he was under the influence of a draught which he had taken, was strangled by Learchus, one of his brothers. This Learchus was afterwards entrapped by Eryxo, the widow of Arcesilaüs, and put to death.

161. Battus, Arcesilaüs' son, succeeded to the kingdom, a lame man, who limped in his walk. Their late calamities now induced the Cyrenæans to send to Delphi and inquire of the god what form of government they had best set up to secure themselves prosperity. The Pythoness answered by recommending them to fetch an arbitrator from Mantinea in Arcadia. Accordingly they sent; and the Mantineans gave them a man named Demônax, a person of high repute among the citizens; who, on his arrival at Cyrêné, having first made himself ac-

quainted with all the circumstances, proceeded to enrol the people in three tribes. One he made to consist of the Theræans and their vassals; another of the Peloponnesians and Cretans; and a third of the various islanders. Besides this, he deprived the king Battus of his former privileges, only reserving for him certain sacred lands and offices; while, with respect to the powers which had hitherto been exercised by the king, he gave them all into the hands of the people.

162. Thus matters rested during the lifetime of this Battus, but when his son Arcesilaüs came to the throne, great disturbance arose about the privileges. For Arcesilaüs, son of Battus the lame and Pheretima, refused to submit to the arrangements of Demônax the Mantinean, and claimed all the powers of his forefathers. In the contention which followed Arcesilaüs was worsted, whereupon he fled to Samos, while his mother took refuge at Salamis in the island of Cyprus. Salamis was at that time ruled by Evelthon, the same who offered at Delphi the censer which is in the treasury of the Corinthians, a work deserving of admiration. Of him Pheretima made request that he would give her an army whereby she and her son might regain Cyrêné. But Evelthon, preferring to give her anything rather than an army, made her various presents. Pheretima accepted them all, saying, as she took them: "Good is this too, O king! but better were it to give me the army which I crave at thy hands." Finding that she repeated these words each time that he presented her with a gift, Evelthon at last sent her a golden spindle and distaff, with the wool ready for spinning. Again she uttered the same speech as before, whereupon Evelthon rejoined—"These are the gifts I present to women, not armies."

163. At Samos, meanwhile, Arcesilaüs was collecting troops by the promise of granting them lands. Having in this way drawn together a vast host, he sent to Delphi to consult the oracle about his restoration. The answer of the Pythoness was this: "Loxias grants thy race to rule over Cyrêné, till four kings Battus, four Arcesilaüs by name, have passed away. Beyond this term of eight generations of men, he warns you not to seek to extend your reign. Thou, for thy part, be gentle, when thou art restored. If thou findest the oven full of jars, bake not the jars; but be sure to speed them on their way. If, however, thou heatest the oven, then avoid the island—else thou wilt die thyself, and with thee the most beautiful bull."

164. So spake the Pythoness. Arcesilaüs upon this returned to Cyrêné, taking with him the troops which he had raised in Samos. There he obtained possession of the supreme power; whereupon, forgetful of the oracle, he took proceedings against those who had driven him into banishment. Some of them fled from him and quitted the country for good; others fell into his hands and were sent to suffer death in Cyprus. These last happening on their passage to put in through stress of weather at Cnidus, the Cnidians rescued them, and sent them off to Thera. Another body found a refuge in the great tower of Aglômachus, a private edifice, and were there destroyed by Arcesilaüs, who heaped wood around the place, and burnt them to death. Aware, after the deed was done, that this was what the Pythoness meant when she warned him, if he found the jars in the oven, not to bake them, he withdrew himself of his own accord from the city of Cyrêné, believing that to be the island of the oracle, and fearing to die as had been prophesied. Being married to a relation of his own, a daughter of Alazir, at that time king of the Barcæans, he took up his abode with him. At Barca, however, certain of the citizens, together with a number of Cyrenæan exiles, recognising him as he walked in the forum, killed him; they slew also at the same time Alazir, his father-in-law. So Arcesilaüs, wittingly or unwittingly, disobeyed the oracle, and thereby fulfilled his destiny.

165. Pheretima, the mother of Arcesilaüs, during the time that her son, after working his own ruin, dwelt at Barca, continued to enjoy all his privileges at Cyrêné, managing the government, and taking her seat at the council-board. No sooner, however, did she hear of the death of her son at Barca, than leaving Cyrêné, she fled in haste to Egypt. Arcesilaüs had claims for service done to Cambyses, son of Cyrus; since it was by him that Cyrêné was put under the Persian yoke, and a rate of tribute agreed upon. Pheretima therefore went straight to Egypt, and presenting herself as a suppliant before Aryandes, entreated him to avenge her wrongs. Her son, she said, had met his death on account of his being so well affected towards the Medes.

166. Now Aryandes had been made governor of Egypt by Cambyses. He it was who in after times was punished with death by Darius for seeking to rival him. Aware, by report and also by his own eyesight, that Darius wished to leave a memorial of himself, such as no king

had ever left before, Aryandes resolved to follow his example, and did so, till he got his reward. Darius had refined gold to the last perfection of purity in order to have coins struck of it: Aryandes, in his Egyptian government, did the very same with silver, so that to this day there is no such pure silver anywhere as the Aryandic. Darius, when this came to his ears, brought another charge, a charge of rebellion, against Aryandes, and put him to death.

167. At the time of which we are speaking Aryandes, moved with compassion for Pheretima, granted her all the forces which there were in Egypt, both land and sea. The command of the army he gave to Amasis, a Maraphian; while Badres, one of the tribe of the Pasargadæ, was appointed to lead the fleet. Before the expedition, however, left Egypt, he sent a herald to Barca to inquire who it was that had slain king Arcesilaüs. The Barcæans replied "that they, one and all, acknowledged the deed—Arcesilaüs had done them many and great injuries." After receiving this reply, Aryandes gave the troops orders to march with Pheretima. Such was the cause which served as a pretext for this expedition: its real object was, I believe, the subjugation of Libya. For Libya is inhabited by many and various races, and of these but a very few were subjects of the Persian king, while by far the larger number held Darius in no manner of respect.

168. The Libyans dwell in the order which I will now describe. Beginning on the side of Egypt, the first Libyans are the Adyrmachidæ. These people have, in most points, the same customs as the Egyptians, but use the costume of the Libyans. Their women wear on each leg a ring made of bronze; they let their hair grow long, and when they catch any vermin on their persons, bite it and throw it away. In this they differ from all the other Libyans. They are also the only tribe with whom the custom obtains of bringing all women about to become brides before the king, that he may choose such as are agreeable to him. The Adyrmachidæ extend from the borders of Egypt to the harbour called Port Plynus.

169. Next to the Adyrmachidæ are the Gilligammæ, who inhabit the country westward as far as the island of Aphrodisias. Off this tract is the island of Platea, which the Cyrenæans colonised. Here too, upon the mainland, are Port Menelaüs, and Aziris, where the Cyrenæans once lived. The Silphium begins to grow in this region, extending from the island of Platea on the one side to the mouth of the Syrtis on the other. The customs of the Gilligammæ are like those of the rest of their countrymen.

170. The Asbystæ adjoin the Gilligammæ upon the west. They inhabit the regions above Cyrêné, but do not reach to the coast, which belongs to the Cyrenæans. Four-horse chariots are in more common use among them than among any other Libyans. In most of their customs they ape the manners of the Cyrenæans.

171. Westward of the Asbystæ dwell the Auschisæ, who possess the country above Barca, reaching, however, to the sea at the place called Euesperides. In the middle of their territory is the little tribe of the Cabalians, which touches the coast near Tauchira, a city of the Barcæans. Their customs are like those of the Libyans above Cyrêné.

172. The Nasamonians, a numerous people, are the western neighbours of the Auschisæ. In summer they leave their flocks and herds upon the sea-shore, and go up the country to a place called Augila, where they gather the dates from the palms, which in those parts grow thickly, and are of great size, all of them being of the fruit-bearing kind. They also chase the locusts, and, when caught, dry them in the sun, after which they grind them to powder, and, sprinkling this upon their milk, so drink it. Each man among them has several wives, in their intercourse with whom they resemble the Massagetæ. The following are their customs in the swearing of oaths and the practice of augury. The man, as he swears, lays his hand upon the tomb of some one considered to have been pre-eminently just and good, and so doing swears by his name. For divination they betake themselves to the sepulchres of their own ancestors, and, after praying, lie down to sleep upon their graves; by the dreams which then come to them they guide their conduct. When they pledge their faith to one another, each gives the other to drink out of his hand; if there be no liquid to be had, they take up dust from the ground, and put their tongues to it.

173. On the country of the Nasamonians borders that of the Psylli, who were swept away under the following circumstances. The south-wind had blown for a long time and dried up all the tanks in which their water was stored. Now the whole region within the Syrtis is utterly devoid of springs. Accordingly the Psylli took counsel among themselves, and by common consent made war upon the south-wind—so at least the Libyans say, I do but re-

peat their words—they went forth and reached the desert; but there the south-wind rose and buried them under heaps of sand: whereupon, the Psylli being destroyed, their lands passed to the Nasamonians.

174. Above the Nasamonians, towards the south, in the district where the wild beasts abound, dwell the Garamantians, who avoid all society or intercourse with their fellow-men, have no weapon of war, and do not know how to defend themselves.

175. These border the Nasamonians on the south: westward along the sea-shore their neighbours are the Macæ, who, by letting the locks about the crown of their head grow long, while they clip them close everywhere else, make their hair resemble a crest. In war these people use the skins of ostriches for shields. The river Cinyps rises among them from the height called "the Hill of the Graces," and runs from thence through their country to the sea. The Hill of the Graces is thickly covered with wood, and is thus very unlike the rest of Libya, which is bare. It is distant two hundred furlongs from the sea.

176. Adjoining the Macæ are the Gindanes, whose women wear on their legs anklets of leather. Each lover that a woman has gives her one; and she who can show the most is the best esteemed, as she appears to have been loved by the greatest number of men.

177. A promontory jutting out into the sea from the country of the Gindanes is inhabited by the Lotophagi, who live entirely on the fruit of the lotus-tree. The lotus fruit is about the size of the lentisk berry, and in sweetness resembles the date. The Lotophagi even succeed in obtaining from it a sort of wine.

178. The sea-coast beyond the Lotophagi is occupied by the Machlyans, who use the lotus to some extent, though not so much as the people of whom we last spoke. The Machlyans reach as far as the great river called the Triton, which empties itself into the great lake Tritônis. Here, in this lake, is an island called Phla, which it is said the Lacedæmonians were to have colonised, according to an oracle.

179. The following is the story as it is commonly told. When Jason had finished building the Argo at the foot of Mount Pelion, he took on board the usual hecatomb, and moreover a brazen tripod. Thus equipped, he set sail, intending to coast round the Peloponnese, and so to reach Delphi. The voyage was prosperous as far as Malea; but at that point a gale of wind from the north came on suddenly, and carried

him out of his course to the coast of Libya; where, before he discovered the land, he got among the shallows of Lake Tritônis. As he was turning it in his mind how he should find his way out, Triton (they say) appeared to him, and offered to show him the channel, and secure him a safe retreat, if he would give him the tripod. Jason complying, was shown by Triton the passage through the shallows; after which the god took the tripod, and, carrying it to his own temple, seated himself upon it, and, filled with prophetic fury, delivered to Jason and his companions a long prediction. "When a descendant," he said, "of one of the Argo's crew should seize and carry off the brazen tripod, then by inevitable fate would a hundred Grecian cities be built around Lake Tritônis." The Libyans of that region, when they heard the words of this prophecy, took away the tripod and hid it.

180. The next tribe beyond the Machlyans is the tribe of the Auseans. Both these nations inhabit the borders of Lake Tritônis, being separated from one another by the river Triton. Both also wear their hair long, but the Machlyans let it grow at the back of the head, while the Auseans have it long in front. The Ausean maidens keep year by year a feast in honour of Minerva, whereat their custom is to draw up in two bodies, and fight with stones and clubs. They say that these are rites which have come down to them from their fathers, and that they honour with them their native goddess, who is the same as the Minerva (Athené) of the Grecians. If any of the maidens die of the wounds they receive, the Auseans declare that such are false maidens. Before the fight is suffered to begin, they have another ceremony. One of the virgins, the loveliest of the number, is selected from the rest; a Corinthian helmet and a complete suit of Greek armour are publicly put upon her; and, thus adorned, she is made to mount into a chariot, and led around the whole lake in a procession. What arms they used for the adornment of their damsels before the Greeks came to live in their country, I cannot say. I imagine they dressed them in Egyptian armour, for I maintain that both the shield and the helmet came into Greece from Egypt. The Auseans declare that Minerva is the daughter of Neptune and the Lake Tritônis—they say she quarrelled with her father, and applied to Jupiter, who consented to let her be his child; and so she became his adopted daughter. These people do not marry or live in families, but dwell together like the gregarious beasts.

When their children are full-grown, they are brought before the assembly of the men, which is held every third month, and assigned to those whom they most resemble.

181. Such are the tribes of wandering Libyans dwelling upon the sea-coast. Above them inland is the wild-beast tract: and beyond that, a ridge of sand, reaching from Egyptian Thebes to the Pillars of Hercules. Throughout this ridge, at the distance of about ten days' journey from one another, heaps of salt in large lumps lie upon hills. At the top of every hill there gushes forth from the middle of the salt a stream of water, which is both cold and sweet. Around dwell men who are the last inhabitants of Libya on the side of the desert, living, as they do, more inland than the wild-beast district. Of these nations the first is that of the Ammonians, who dwell at a distance of ten days' journey from Thebes, and have a temple derived from that of the Theban Jupiter. For at Thebes likewise, as I mentioned above, the image of Jupiter has a face like that of a ram. The Ammonians have another spring besides that which rises from the salt. The water of this stream is lukewarm at early dawn; at the time when the market fills it is much cooler; by noon it has grown quite cold; at this time, therefore, they water their gardens. As the afternoon advances the coldness goes off, till, about sunset, the water is once more lukewarm; still the heat increases, and at midnight it boils furiously. After this time it again begins to cool, and grows less and less hot till morning comes. This spring is called "the Fountain of the Sun."

182. Next to the Ammonians, at the distance of ten days' journey along the ridge of sand, there is a second salt-hill like the Ammonian, and a second spring. The country round is inhabited, and the place bears the name of Augila. Hither it is that the Nasamonians come to gather in the dates.

183. Ten days' journey from Augila there is again a salt-hill and a spring; palms of the fruitful kind grow here abundantly, as they do also at the other salt-hills. This region is inhabited by a nation called the Garamantians, a very powerful people, who cover the salt with mould, and then sow their crops. From thence is the shortest road to the Lotophagi, a journey of thirty days. In the Garamantian country are found the oxen which, as they graze, walk backwards. This they do because their horns curve outwards in front of their heads, so that it is not possible for them when grazing to move forwards, since in that case their horns would become fixed in the ground. Only herein do they differ from other oxen, and further in the thickness and hardness of their hides. The Garamantians have four-horse chariots, in which they chase the Troglodyte Ethiopians, who of all the nations whereof any account has reached our ears are by far the swiftest of foot. The Troglodytes feed on serpents, lizards, and other similar reptiles. Their language is unlike that of any other people; it sounds like the screeching of bats.

184. At the distance of ten days' journey from the Garamantians there is again another salt-hill and spring of water; around which dwell a people, called the Atarantians, who alone of all known nations are destitute of names. The title of Atarantians is borne by the whole race in common; but the men have no particular names of their own. The Atarantians, when the sun rises high in the heaven, curse him, and load him with reproaches, because (they say) he burns and wastes both their country and themselves. Once more at the distance of ten days' journey there is a salt-hill, a spring, and an inhabited tract. Near the salt is a mountain called Atlas, very taper and round; so lofty, moreover, that the top (it is said) cannot be seen, the clouds never quitting it either summer or winter. The natives call this mountain "the Pillar of Heaven"; and they themselves take their name from it, being called Atlantes. They are reported not to eat any living thing, and never to have any dreams.

185. As far as the Atlantes the names of the nations inhabiting the sandy ridge are known to me; but beyond them my knowledge fails. The ridge itself extends as far as the Pillars of Hercules, and even further than these; and throughout the whole distance, at the end of every ten days' journey, there is a salt-mine, with people dwelling round it who all of them build their houses with blocks of the salt. No rain falls in these parts of Libya; if it were otherwise, the walls of these houses could not stand. The salt quarried is of two colours, white and purple. Beyond the ridge, southwards, in the direction of the interior, the country is a desert, with no springs, no beasts, no rain, no wood, and altogether destitute of moisture.

186. Thus from Egypt as far as Lake Tritônis Libya is inhabited by wandering tribes, whose drink is milk and their food the flesh of animals. Cow's flesh, however, none of these tribes ever taste, but abstain from it for the

same reason as the Egyptians, neither do they any of them breed swine. Even at Cyrêne, the women think it wrong to eat the flesh of the cow, honouring in this Isis, the Egyptian goddess, whom they worship both with fasts and festivals. The Barcæan women abstain, not from cow's flesh only, but also from the flesh of swine.

187. West of Lake Tritônis the Libyans are no longer wanderers, nor do they practise the same customs as the wandering people, or treat their children in the same way. For the wandering Libyans, many of them at any rate, if not all—concerning which I cannot speak with certainty—when their children come to the age of four years, burn the veins at the top of their heads with a flock from the fleece of a sheep: others burn the veins about the temples. This they do to prevent them from being plagued in their after lives by a flow of rheum from the head; and such they declare is the reason why they are so much more healthy than other men. Certainly the Libyans are the healthiest men that I know; but whether this is what makes them so, or not, I cannot positively say—the healthiest certainly they are. If when the children are being burnt convulsions come on, there is a remedy of which they have made discovery. It is to sprinkle goat's water upon the child, who thus treated, is sure to recover. In all this I only repeat what is said by the Libyans.

188. The rites which the wandering Libyans use in sacrificing are the following. They begin with the ear of the victim, which they cut off and throw over their house: this done, they kill the animal by twisting the neck. They sacrifice to the Sun and Moon, but not to any other god. This worship is common to all the Libyans. The inhabitants of the parts about Lake Tritônis worship in addition Triton, Neptune, and Minerva, the last especially.

189. The dress wherewith Minerva's statues are adorned, and her Ægis, were derived by the Greeks from the women of Libya. For, except that the garments of the Libyan women are of leather, and their fringes made of leathern thongs instead of serpents, in all else the dress of both is exactly alike. The name too itself shows that the mode of dressing the Pallas-statues came from Libya. For the Libyan women wear over their dress goat-skins stript of the hair, fringed at their edges, and coloured with vermilion; and from these goat-skins the Greeks get their word Ægis (goat-harness). I think for my part that the loud cries uttered in our sacred rites came also from thence; for the Libyan women are greatly given to such cries and utter them very sweetly. Likewise the Greeks learnt from the Libyans to yoke four horses to a chariot.

190. All the wandering tribes bury their dead according to the fashion of the Greeks, except the Nasamonians. They bury them sitting, and are right careful when the sick man is at the point of giving up the ghost, to make him sit and not let him die lying down. The dwellings of these people are made of the stems of the asphodel, and of rushes wattled together. They can be carried from place to place. Such are the customs of the afore-mentioned tribes.

191. Westward of the river Triton and adjoining upon the Auseans, are other Libyans who till the ground, and live in houses: these people are named the Maxyans. They let the hair grow long on the right side of their heads, and shave it close on the left; they besmear their bodies with red paint; and they say that they are descended from the men of Troy. Their country and the remainder of Libya towards the west is far fuller of wild beasts and of wood than the country of the wandering people. For the eastern side of Libya, where the wanderers dwell, is low and sandy, as far as the river Triton; but westward of that the land of the husbandmen is very hilly, and abounds with forests and wild beasts. For this is the tract in which the huge serpents are found, and the lions, the elephants, the bears, the aspicks, and the horned asses. Here too are the dog-faced creatures, and the creatures without heads, whom the Libyans declare to have their eyes in their breasts; and also the wild men, and wild women, and many other far less fabulous beasts.

192. Among the wanderers are none of these, but quite other animals; as antelopes, gazelles, buffaloes, and asses, not of the horned sort, but of a kind which does not need to drink; also oryxes, whose horns are used for the curved sides of citherns, and whose size is about that of the ox; foxes, hyænas, porcupines, wild rams, dictyes, jackals, panthers, boryes, land-crocodiles about three cubits in length, very like lizards, ostriches, and little snakes, each with a single horn. All these animals are found here, and likewise those belonging to other countries, except the stag and the wild-boar; but neither stag nor wild-boar are found in any part of Libya. There are, however, three sorts of mice in these parts; the first are called two-footed; the next, zegeries, which is a Libyan word meaning "hills"; and the third,

urchins. Weasels also are found in the Silphium region, much like the Tartessian. So many, therefore, are the animals belonging to the land of the wandering Libyans, in so far at least as my researches have been able to reach.

193. Next to the Maxyan Libyans are the Zavecians, whose wives drive their chariots to battle.

194. On them border the Gyzantians; in whose country a vast deal of honey is made by bees; very much more, however, by the skill of men. The people all paint themselves red, and eat monkeys, whereof there is inexhaustible store in the hills.

195. Off their coast, as the Carthaginians report, lies an island, by name Cyraunis, the length of which is two hundred furlongs, its breadth not great, and which is soon reached from the mainland. Vines and olive trees cover the whole of it, and there is in the island a lake, from which the young maidens of the country draw up gold-dust, by dipping into the mud birds' feathers smeared with pitch. If this be true, I know not; I but write what is said. It may be even so, however; since I myself have seen pitch drawn up out of the water from a lake in Zacynthus. At the place I speak of there are a number of lakes; but one is larger than the rest, being seventy feet every way, and two fathoms in depth. Here they let down a pole into the water, with a bunch of myrtle tied to one end, and when they raise it again, there is pitch sticking to the myrtle, which in smell is like to bitumen, but in all else is better than the pitch of Pieria. This they pour into a trench dug by the lake's side; and when a good deal has thus been got together, they draw it off and put it up in jars. Whatever falls into the lake passes underground, and comes up in the sea, which is no less than four furlongs distant. So then what is said of the island off the Libyan coast is not without likelihood.

196. The Carthaginians also relate the following:—There is a country in Libya, and a nation, beyond the Pillars of Hercules, which they are wont to visit, where they no sooner arrive but forthwith they unlade their wares, and, having disposed them after an orderly fashion along the beach, leave them, and, returning aboard their ships, raise a great smoke. The natives, when they see the smoke, come down to the shore, and, laying out to view so much gold as they think the worth of the wares, withdraw to a distance. The Carthaginians upon this come ashore and look. If they think the gold enough, they take it and go

their way; but if it does not seem to them sufficient, they go aboard ship once more, and wait patiently. Then the others approach and add to their gold, till the Carthaginians are content. Neither party deals unfairly by the other: for they themselves never touch the gold till it comes up to the worth of their goods, nor do the natives ever carry off the goods till the gold is taken away.

197. These be the Libyan tribes whereof I am able to give the names; and most of these cared little then, and indeed care little now, for the king of the Medes. One thing more also I can add concerning this region, namely, that, so far as our knowledge reaches, four nations, and no more, inhabit it; and two of these nations are indigenous, while two are not. The two indigenous are the Libyans and Ethiopians, who dwell respectively in the north and the south of Libya. The Phœnicians and the Greek are in-comers.

198. It seems to me that Libya is not to compare for goodness of soil with either Asia or Europe, except the Cinyps region, which is named after the river that waters it. This piece of land is equal to any country in the world for cereal crops, and is in nothing like the rest of Libya. For the soil here is black, and springs of water abound; so that there is nothing to fear from drought; nor do heavy rains (and it rains in that part of Libya) do any harm when they soak the ground. The returns of the harvest come up to the measure which prevails in Babylonia. The soil is likewise good in the country of the Euesperites; for there the land brings forth in the best years a hundred-fold. But the Cinyps region yields three hundred-fold.

199. The country of the Cyrenæans, which is the highest tract within the part of Libya inhabited by the wandering tribes, has three seasons that deserve remark. First the crops along the sea-coast begin to ripen, and are ready for the harvest and the vintage; after they have been gathered in, the crops of the middle tract above the coast region (the hill-country, as they call it) need harvesting; while about the time when this middle crop is housed, the fruits ripen and are fit for cutting in the highest tract of all. So that the produce of the first tract has been all eaten and drunk by the time that the last harvest comes in. And the harvest-time of the Cyrenæans continues thus for eight full months. So much concerning these matters.

200. When the Persians sent from Egypt by Aryandes to help Pheretima reached Barca,

they laid siege to the town, calling on those within to give up the men who had been guilty of the murder of Arcesilaüs. The townspeople, however, as they had one and all taken part in the deed, refused to entertain the proposition. So the Persians beleaguered Barca for nine months, in the course of which they dug several mines from their own lines to the walls, and likewise made a number of vigorous assaults. But their mines were discovered by a man who was a worker in brass, who went with a brazen shield all round the fortress, and laid it on the ground inside the city. In other places the shield, when he laid it down, was quite dumb; but where the ground was undermined, there the brass of the shield rang. Here, therefore, the Barcæans countermined, and slew the Persian diggers. Such was the way in which the mines were discovered; as for the assaults, the Barcæans beat them back.

201. When much time had been consumed, and great numbers had fallen on both sides, nor had the Persians lost fewer than their adversaries, Amasis, the leader of the land-army, perceiving that, although the Barcæans would never be conquered by force, they might be overcome by fraud, contrived as follows. One night he dug a wide trench, and laid light planks of wood across the opening, after which he brought mould and placed it upon the planks, taking care to make the place level with the surrounding ground. At dawn of day he summoned the Barcæans to a parley: and they gladly hearkening, the terms were at length agreed upon. Oaths were interchanged upon the ground over the hidden trench, and the agreement ran thus—"So long as the ground beneath our feet stands firm, the oath shall abide unchanged; the people of Barca agree to pay a fair sum to the king, and the Persians promise to cause no further trouble to the people of Barca." After the oath, the Barcæans, relying upon its terms, threw open all their gates, went out themselves beyond the walls, and allowed as many of the enemy as chose to enter. Then the Persians broke down their secret bridge, and rushed at speed into the town—their reason for breaking the bridge being that so they might observe what they had sworn; for they had promised the Barcæans that the oath should continue "so long as the ground whereon they stood was firm." When, therefore, the bridge was once broken down, the oath ceased to hold.

202. Such of the Barcæans as were most guilty the Persians gave up to Pheretima, who nailed them to crosses all round the walls of the city. She also cut off the breasts of their wives, and fastened them likewise about the walls. The remainder of the people she gave as booty to the Persians, except only the Battiadæ and those who had taken no part in the murder, to whom she handed over the possession of the town.

203. The Persians now set out on their return home, carrying with them the rest of the Barcæans, whom they had made their slaves. On their way they came to Cyrênê; and the Cyrenæans, out of regard for an oracle, let them pass through the town. During the passage, Bares, the commander of the fleet, advised to seize the place; but Amasis, the leader of the land-force, would not consent; "because," he said, "they had only been charged to attack the one Greek city of Barca." When, however, they had passed through the town, and were encamped upon the hill of Lycæan Jove, it repented them that they had not seized Cyrênê, and they endeavoured to enter it a second time. The Cyrenæans, however, would not suffer this; whereupon, though no one appeared to offer them battle, yet a panic came upon the Persians, and they ran a distance of full sixty furlongs before they pitched their camp. Here as they lay, a messenger came to them from Aryandes, ordering them home. Then the Persians besought the men of Cyrênê to give them provisions for the way, and, these consenting, they set off on their return to Egypt. But the Libyans now beset them, and, for the sake of their clothes and harness, slew all who dropped behind and straggled, during the whole march homewards.

204. The furthest point of Libya reached by this Persian host was the city of Euesperides. The Barcæans carried into slavery were sent from Egypt to the king; and Darius assigned them a village in Bactria for their dwelling-place. To this village they gave the name of Barca, and it was to my time an inhabited place in Bactria.

205. Nor did Pheretima herself end her days happily. For on her return to Egypt from Libya, directly after taking vengeance on the people of Barca, she was overtaken by a most horrid death. Her body swarmed with worms, which ate her flesh while she was still alive. Thus do men, by over-harsh punishments, draw down upon themselves the anger of the gods. Such then, and so fierce, was the vengeance which Pheretima, daughter of Battus, took upon the Barcæans.

The Fifth Book, Entitled
TERPSICHORE

1. The Persians left behind by King Darius in Europe, who had Megabazus for their general, reduced, before any other Hellespontine state, the people of Perinthus, who had no mind to become subjects of the king. Now the Perinthians had ere this been roughly handled by another nation, the Pæonians. For the Pæonians from about the Strymon were once bidden by an oracle to make war upon the Perinthians, and if these latter, when the camps faced one another, challenged them by name to fight, then to venture on a battle, but if otherwise, not to make the hazard. The Pæonians followed the advice. Now the men of Perinthus drew out to meet them in the skirts of their city; and a threefold single combat was fought on challenge given. Man to man, and horse to horse, and dog to dog, was the strife waged; and the Perinthians, winners of two combats out of the three, in their joy had raised the pæan; when the Pæonians, struck by the thought that this was what the oracle had meant, passed the word one to another, saying, "Now of a surety has the oracle been fulfilled for us; now our work begins." Then the Pæonians set upon the Perinthians in the midst of their pæan, and defeated them utterly, leaving but few of them alive.

2. Such was the affair of the Pæonians, which happened a long time previously. At this time the Perinthians, after a brave struggle for freedom, were overcome by numbers, and yielded to Megabazus and his Persians. After Perinthus had been brought under, Megabazus led his host through Thrace, subduing to the dominion of the king all the towns and all the nations of those parts. For the king's command to him was that he should conquer Thrace.

3. The Thracians are the most powerful people in the world, except, of course, the Indians; and if they had one head, or were agreed among themselves, it is my belief that their match could not be found anywhere, and that they would very far surpass all other nations. But such union is impossible for them, and there are no means of ever bringing it about. Herein therefore consists their weakness. The Thracians bear many names in the different regions of their country, but all of them have like usages in every respect, excepting only the Getæ, the Trausi, and those who dwell above the people of Creston.

4. Now the manners and customs of the Getæ, who believe in their immortality, I have already spoken of. The Trausi in all else resemble the other Thracians, but have customs at births and deaths which I will now describe. When a child is born all its kindred sit round about it in a circle and weep for the woes it will have to undergo now that it is come into the world, making mention of every ill that falls to the lot of humankind; when, on the other hand, a man has died, they bury him with laughter and rejoicings, and say that now he is free from a host of sufferings, and enjoys the completest happiness.

5. The Thracians who live above the Crestonæans observe the following customs. Each man among them has several wives; and no sooner does a man die than a sharp contest ensues among the wives upon the question which of them all the husband loved most tenderly; the friends of each eagerly plead on her behalf, and she to whom the honour is adjudged, after receiving the praises both of men and women, is slain over the grave by the hand of her next of kin, and then buried with her husband. The others are sorely grieved, for nothing is considered such a disgrace.

6. The Thracians who do not belong to these tribes have the customs which follow. They sell their children to traders. On their maidens they keep no watch, but leave them

160

altogether free, while on the conduct of their wives they keep a most strict watch. Brides are purchased of their parents for large sums of money. Tattooing among them marks noble birth, and the want of it low birth. To be idle is accounted the most honourable thing, and to be a tiller of the ground the most dishonourable. To live by war and plunder is of all things the most glorious. These are the most remarkable of their customs.

7. The gods which they worship are but three, Mars, Bacchus, and Dian. Their kings, however, unlike the rest of the citizens, worship Mercury more than any other god, always swearing by his name, and declaring that they are themselves sprung from him.

8. Their wealthy ones are buried in the following fashion. The body is laid out for three days; and during this time they kill victims of all kinds, and feast upon them, after first bewailing the departed. Then they either burn the body or else bury it in the ground. Lastly, they raise a mound over the grave, and hold games of all sorts, wherein the single combat is awarded the highest prize. Such is the mode of burial among the Thracians.

9. As regards the region lying north of this country no one can say with any certainty what men inhabit it. It appears that you no sooner cross the Ister than you enter on an interminable wilderness. The only people of whom I can hear as dwelling beyond the Ister are the race named Sigynnæ, who wear, they say, a dress like the Medes, and have horses which are covered entirely with a coat of shaggy hair, five fingers in length. They are a small breed, flat-nosed, and not strong enough to bear men on their backs; but when yoked to chariots, they are among the swiftest known, which is the reason why the people of that country use chariots. Their borders reach down almost to the Eneti upon the Adriatic Sea, and they call themselves colonists of the Medes; but how they can be colonists of the Medes I for my part cannot imagine. Still nothing is impossible in the long lapse of ages. Sigynnæ is the name which the Ligurians who dwell above Massilia give to traders, while among the Cyprians the word means spears.

10. According to the account which the Thracians give, the country beyond the Ister is possessed by bees,[1] on account of which it is impossible to penetrate farther. But in this they seem to me to say what has no likelihood; for it is certain that those creatures are very impatient of cold. I rather believe that it is on account of the cold that the regions which lie under the Bear are without inhabitants. Such then are the accounts given of this country, the sea-coast whereof Megabazus was now employed in subjecting to the Persians.

11. King Darius had no sooner crossed the Hellespont and reached Sardis, than he bethought himself of the good deed of Histiæus the Milesian, and the good counsel of the Mytilenean Coës. He therefore sent for both of them to Sardis, and bade them each crave a boon at his hands. Now Histiæus, as he was already king of Miletus, did not make request for any government besides, but asked Darius to give him Myrcinus of the Edonians, where he wished to build him a city. Such was the choice that Histiæus made. Coës, on the other hand, as he was a mere burgher, and not a king, requested the sovereignty of Mytilêné. Both alike obtained their requests, and straightway betook themselves to the places which they had chosen.

12. It chanced in the meantime that King Darius saw a sight which determined him to bid Megabazus remove the Pæonians from their seats in Europe and transport them to Asia. There were two Pæonians, Pigres and Mantyes, whose ambition it was to obtain the sovereignty over their countrymen. As soon therefore as ever Darius crossed into Asia, these men came to Sardis, and brought with them their sister, who was a tall and beautiful woman. Having so done, they waited till a day came when the king sat in state in the suburb of the Lydians; and then dressing their sister in the richest gear they could, sent her to draw water for them. She bore a pitcher upon her head, and with one arm led a horse, while all the way as she went she span flax. Now as she passed by where the king was, Darius took notice of her; for it was neither like the Persians nor the Lydians, nor any of the dwellers in Asia, to do as she did. Darius accordingly noted her, and ordered some of his guard to follow her steps, and watch to see what she would do with the horse. So the spearmen went; and the woman, when she came to the river, first watered the horse, and then filling the pitcher, came back the same way she had gone, with the pitcher of water upon her head, and the horse dragging upon her arm, while she still kept twirling the spindle.

13. King Darius was full of wonder both at what they who had watched the woman told him, and at what he had himself seen. So he

[1] In reality, mosquitoes.

commanded that she should be brought before him. And the woman came; and with her appeared her brothers, who had been watching everything a little way off. Then Darius asked them of what nation the woman was; and the young men replied that they were Pæonians, and she was their sister. Darius rejoined by asking, "Who the Pæonians were, and in what part of the world they lived? and, further, what business had brought the young men to Sardis?" Then the brothers told him they had come to put themselves under his power, and Pæonia was a country upon the river Strymon, and the Strymon was at no great distance from the Hellespont. The Pæonians, they said, were colonists of the Teucrians from Troy. When they had thus answered his questions, Darius asked if all the women of their country worked so hard? Then the brothers eagerly answered, Yes; for this was the very object with which the whole thing had been done.

14. So Darius wrote letters to Megabazus, the commander whom he had left behind in Thrace, and ordered him to remove the Pæonians from their own land, and bring them into his presence, men, women, and children. And straightway a horseman took the message, and rode at speed to the Hellespont; and, crossing it, gave the paper to Megabazus. Then Megabazus, as soon as he had read it, and procured guides from Thrace, made war upon Pæonia.

15. Now when the Pæonians heard that the Persians were marching against them, they gathered themselves together, and marched down to the sea-coast, since they thought the Persians would endeavour to enter their country on that side. Here then they stood in readiness to oppose the army of Megabazus. But the Persians, who knew that they had collected, and were gone to keep guard at the pass near the sea, got guides, and taking the inland route before the Pæonians were aware, poured down upon their cities, from which the men had all marched out; and finding them empty, easily got possession of them. Then the men, when they heard that all their towns were taken, scattered this way and that to their homes, and gave themselves up to the Persians. And so these tribes of the Pæonians, to wit, the Siropæonians, the Pæoplians, and all the others as far as Lake Prasias, were torn from their seats and led away into Asia.

16. They on the other hand who dwelt about Mount Pangæum and in the country of the Dobêres, the Agrianians, and the Odomantians, and they likewise who inhabited Lake Prasias, were not conquered by Megabazus. He sought indeed to subdue the dwellers upon the lake, but could not effect his purpose. Their manner of living is the following. Platforms supported upon tall piles stand in the middle of the lake, which are approached from the land by a single narrow bridge. At the first the piles which bear up the platforms were fixed in their places by the whole body of the citizens, but since that time the custom which has prevailed about fixing them is this:—they are brought from a hill called Orbêlus, and every man drives in three for each wife that he marries. Now the men have all many wives apiece; and this is the way in which they live. Each has his own hut, wherein he dwells, upon one of the platforms, and each has also a trap-door giving access to the lake beneath; and their wont is to tie their baby children by the foot with a string, to save them from rolling into the water. They feed their horses and their other beasts upon fish, which abound in the lake to such a degree that a man has only to open his trap-door and to let down a basket by a rope into the water, and then to wait a very short time, when he draws it up quite full of them. The fish are of two kinds, which they call the paprax and the tilon.

17. The Pæonians therefore—at least such of them as had been conquered—were led away into Asia. As for Megabazus, he no sooner brought the Pæonians under, than he sent into Macedonia an embassy of Persians, choosing for the purpose the seven men of most note in all the army after himself. These persons were to go to Amyntas, and require him to give earth and water to King Darius. Now there is a very short cut from the Lake Prasias across to Macedonia. Quite close to the lake is the mine which yielded afterwards a talent of silver a day to Alexander; and from this mine you have only to cross the mountain called Dysôrum to find yourself in the Macedonian territory.

18. So the Persians sent upon this errand, when they reached the court, and were brought into the presence of Amyntas, required him to give earth and water to King Darius. And Amyntas not only gave them what they asked, but also invited them to come and feast with him; after which he made ready the board with great magnificence, and entertained the Persians in right friendly fashion. Now when the meal was over, and they were all set to the drinking, the Persians said—

"Dear Macedonian, we Persians have a custom when we make a great feast to bring with us to the board our wives and concubines, and make them sit beside us. Now then, as thou hast received us so kindly, and feasted us so handsomely, and givest moreover earth and water to King Darius, do also after our custom in this matter."

Then Amyntas answered—"O, Persians! we have no such custom as this; but with us men and women are kept apart. Nevertheless, since you, who are our lords, wish it, this also shall be granted to you."

When Amyntas had thus spoken, he bade some go and fetch the women. And the women came at his call and took their seats in a row over against the Persians. Then, when the Persians saw that the women were fair and comely, they spoke again to Amyntas and said, that "what had been done was not wise; for it had been better for the women not to have come at all, than to come in this way, and not sit by their sides, but remain over against them, the torment of their eyes." So Amyntas was forced to bid the women sit side by side with the Persians. The women did as he ordered; and then the Persians, who had drunk more than they ought, began to put their hands on them, and one even tried to give the woman next him a kiss.

19. King Amyntas saw, but he kept silence, although sorely grieved, for he greatly feared the power of the Persians. Alexander, however, Amyntas' son, who was likewise there and witnessed the whole, being a young man and unacquainted with suffering, could not any longer restrain himself. He therefore, full of wrath, spake thus to Amyntas:—"Dear father, thou art old and shouldst spare thyself. Rise up from table and go take thy rest; do not stay out the drinking. I will remain with the guests and give them all that is fitting."

Amyntas, who guessed that Alexander would play some wild prank, made answer:—"Dear son, thy words sound to me as those of one who is well nigh on fire, and I perceive thou sendest me away that thou mayest do some wild deed. I beseech thee make no commotion about these men, lest thou bring us all to ruin, but bear to look calmly on what they do. For myself, I will e'en withdraw as thou biddest me."

20. Amyntas, when he had thus besought his son, went out; and Alexander said to the Persians, "Look on these ladies as your own, dear strangers, all or any of them—only tell us your wishes. But now, as the evening wears, and I see you have all had wine enough, let them, if you please, retire, and when they have bathed they shall come back again." To this the Persians agreed, and Alexander, having got the women away, sent them off to the harem, and made ready in their room an equal number of beardless youths, whom he dressed in the garments of the women, and then, arming them with daggers, brought them in to the Persians, saying as he introduced them, "Methinks, dear Persians, that your entertainment has fallen short in nothing. We have set before you all that we had ourselves in store, and all that we could anywhere find to give you—and now, to crown the whole, we make over to you our sisters and our mothers, that you may perceive yourselves to be entirely honoured by us, even as you deserve to be—and also that you may take back word to the king who sent you here, that there was one man, a Greek, the satrap of Macedonia, by whom you were both feasted and lodged handsomely." So speaking, Alexander set by the side of each Persian one of those whom he had called Macedonian women, but who were in truth men. And these men, when the Persians began to be rude, despatched them with their daggers.

21. So the ambassadors perished by this death, both they and also their followers. For the Persians had brought a great train with them, carriages, and attendants, and baggage of every kind—all of which disappeared at the same time as the men themselves. Not very long afterwards the Persians made strict search for their lost embassy; but Alexander, with much wisdom, hushed up the business, bribing those sent on the errand, partly with money, and partly with the gift of his own sister Gygæa, whom he gave in marriage to Bubares, a Persian, the chief leader of the expedition which came in search of the lost men. Thus the death of these Persians was hushed up, and no more was said of it.

22. Now that the men of this family are Greeks, sprung from Perdiccas, as they themselves affirm, is a thing which I can declare of my own knowledge, and which I will hereafter make plainly evident. That they are so has been already adjudged by those who manage the Pan-Hellenic contest at Olympia. For when Alexander wished to contend in the games, and had come to Olympia with no other view, the Greeks who were about to run against him would have excluded him from the contest—saying that Greeks only were allowed to contend, and not barbarians. But Alexander proved himself to be an Argive, and

was distinctly adjudged a Greek; after which he entered the lists for the foot-race, and was drawn to run in the first pair. Thus was this matter settled.

23. Megabazus, having reached the Hellespont with the Pæonians, crossed it, and went up to Sardis. He had become aware while in Europe that Histiæus the Milesian was raising a wall at Myrcinus—the town upon the Strymon which he had obtained from King Darius as his guerdon for keeping the bridge. No sooner therefore did he reach Sardis with the Pæonians than he said to Darius, "What mad thing is this that thou hast done, sire, to let a Greek, a wise man and a shrewd, get hold of a town in Thrace, a place too where there is abundance of timber fit for shipbuilding, and oars in plenty, and mines of silver, and about which are many dwellers both Greek and barbarian, ready enough to take him for their chief, and by day and night to do his bidding! I pray thee make this man cease his work, if thou wouldest not be entangled in a war with thine own followers. Stop him, but with a gentle message, only bidding him to come to thee. Then when thou once hast him in thy power, be sure thou take good care that he never get back to Greece again."

24. With these words Megabazus easily persuaded Darius, who thought he had shown true foresight in this matter. Darius therefore sent a messenger to Myrcinus, who said, "These be the words of the king to thee, O Histiæus! I have looked to find a man well affectioned towards me and towards my greatness; and I have found none whom I can trust like thee. Thy deeds, and not thy words only, have proved thy love for me. Now then, since I have a mighty enterprise in hand, I pray thee come to me, that I may show thee what I purpose!"

Histiæus, when he heard this, put faith in the words of the messenger; and, as it seemed to him a grand thing to be the king's counsellor, he straightway went up to Sardis. Then Darius, when he was come, said to him, "Dear Histiæus, hear why I have sent for thee. No sooner did I return from Scythia, and lose thee out of my sight, than I longed, as I have never longed for aught else, to behold thee once more, and to interchange speech with thee. Right sure I am there is nothing in all the world so precious as a friend who is at once wise and true: both which thou art, as I have had good proof in what thou hast already done for me. Now then 'tis well thou art come; for look, I have an offer to make to thee. Let go

Miletus and thy newly-founded town in Thrace, and come with me up to Susa; share all that I have; live with me, and be my counsellor.

25. When Darius had thus spoken he made Artaphernes, his brother by the father's side, governor of Sardis, and taking Histiæus with him, went up to Susa. He left as general of all the troops upon the sea-coast Otanes, son of Sisamnes, whose father King Cambyses slew and flayed, because that he, being of the number of the royal judges, had taken money to give an unrighteous sentence. Therefore Cambyses slew and flayed Sisamnes, and cutting his skin into strips, stretched them across the seat of the throne whereon he had been wont to sit when he heard causes. Having so done Cambyses appointed the son of Sisamnes to be judge in his father's room, and bade him never forget in what way his seat was cushioned.

26. Accordingly this Otanes, who had occupied so strange a throne, became the successor of Megabazus in his command, and took first of all Byzantium and Chalcêdon, then Antandrus in the Troas, and next Lampônium. This done, he borrowed ships of the Lesbians, and took Lemnos and Imbrus, which were still inhabited by Pelasgians.

27. Now the Lemnians stood on their defence, and fought gallantly; but they were brought low in course of time. Such as outlived the struggle were placed by the Persians under the government of Lycarêtus, the brother of that Mæandrius who was tyrant of Samos. (This Lycarêtus died afterwards in his government.) The cause which Otanes alleged for conquering and enslaving all these nations was that some had refused to join the king's army against Scythia, while others had molested the host on its return. Such were the exploits which Otanes performed in his command.

28. Afterwards, but for no long time, there was a respite from suffering. Then from Nazos and Miletus troubles gathered anew about Ionia. Now Naxos at this time surpassed all the other islands in prosperity, and Miletus had reached the height of her power, and was the glory of Ionia. But previously for two generations the Milesians had suffered grievously from civil disorders, which were composed by the Parians, whom the Milesians chose before all the rest of the Greeks to rearrange their government.

29. Now the way in which the Parians healed their differences was the following. A

number of the chief Parians came to Miletus, and when they saw in how ruined a condition the Milesians were, they said that they would like first to go over their country. So they went through all Milesia, and on their way, whenever they saw in the waste and desolate country any land that was well farmed, they took down the names of the owners in their tablets; and having thus gone through the whole region, and obtained after all but few names, they called the people together on their return to Miletus, and made proclamation that they gave the government into the hands of those persons whose lands they had found well farmed; for they thought it likely (they said) that the same persons who had managed their own affairs well would likewise conduct aright the business of the state. The other Milesians, who in time past had been at variance, they placed under the rule of these men. Thus was the Milesian government set in order by the Parians.

30. It was, however, from the two cities above mentioned that troubles began now to gather again about Ionia; and this is the way in which they arose. Certain of the rich men had been banished from Naxos by the commonalty, and, upon their banishment, had fled to Miletus. Aristagoras, son of Molpagoras, the nephew and likewise the son-in-law of Histiæus, son of Lysagoras, who was still kept by Darius at Susa, happened to be regent of Miletus at the time of their coming. For the kingly power belonged to Histiæus; but he was at Susa when the Naxians came. Now these Naxians had in times past been bond-friends of Histiæus; and so on their arrival at Miletus they addressed themselves to Aristagoras and begged him to lend them such aid as his ability allowed, in hopes thereby to recover their country. Then Aristagoras, considering with himself that, if the Naxians should be restored by his help, he would be lord of Naxos, put forward the friendship with Histiæus to cloak his views, and spoke as follows:—

"I cannot engage to furnish you with such a power as were needful to force you, against their will, upon the Naxians who hold the city; for I know they can bring into the field eight thousand bucklers, and have also a vast number of ships of war. But I will do all that lies in my power to get you some aid, and I think I can manage it in this way. Artaphernes happens to be my friend. Now he is a son of Hystaspes, and brother to King Darius. All the sea-coast of Asia is under him, and he has a numerous army and numerous ships. I think I can prevail on him to do what we require."

When the Naxians heard this, they empowered Aristagoras to manage the matter for them as well as he could, and told him to promise gifts and pay for the soldiers, which (they said) they would readily furnish, since they had great hope that the Naxians, so soon as they saw them returned, would render them obedience, and likewise the other islanders. For at that time not one of the Cyclades was subject to King Darius.

31. So Aristagoras went to Sardis and told Artaphernes that Naxos was an island of no great size, but a fair land and fertile, lying near Ionia, and containing much treasure and a vast number of slaves. "Make war then upon this land (he said) and reinstate the exiles; for if thou wilt do this, first of all, I have very rich gifts in store for thee (besides the cost of the armament, which it is fair that we who are the authors of the war should pay); and, secondly, thou wilt bring under the power of the king not only Naxos but the other islands which depend on it, as Paros, Andros, and all the rest of the Cyclades. And when thou hast gained these, thou mayest easily go on against Eubœa, which is a large and wealthy island not less in size than Cyprus, and very easy to bring under. A hundred ships were quite enough to subdue the whole." The other answered— "Truly thou art the author of a plan which may much advantage the house of the king, and thy counsel is good in all points except the number of the ships. Instead of a hundred, two hundred shall be at thy disposal when the spring comes. But the king himself must first approve the undertaking."

32. When Aristagoras heard this he was greatly rejoiced, and went home in good heart to Miletus. And Artaphernes, after he had sent a messenger to Susa to lay the plans of Aristagoras before the king, and received his approval of the undertaking, made ready a fleet of two hundred triremes and a vast army of Persians and their confederates. The command of these he gave to a Persian named Megabates, who belonged to the house of the Achæmenids, being nephew both to himself and to King Darius. It was to a daughter of this man that Pausanias the Lacedæmonian, the son of Cleombrotus (if at least there be any truth in the tale), was affianced many years afterwards, when he conceived the desire of becoming tyrant of Greece. Artaphernes now, having named Megabates to the command, sent for-

ward the armament to Aristagoras.

33. Megabates set sail, and, touching at Miletus, took on board Aristagoras with the Ionian troops and the Naxians; after which he steered, as he gave out, for the Hellespont; and when he reached Chios, he brought the fleet to anchor off Caucasa, being minded to wait there for a north wind, and then sail straight to Naxos. The Naxians however were not to perish at this time; and so the following events were brought about. As Megabates went his rounds to visit the watches on board the ships, he found a Myndian vessel upon which there was none set. Full of anger at such carelessness, he bade his guards to seek out the captain, one Scylax by name, and thrusting him through one of the holes in the ship's side, to fasten him there in such a way that his head might show outside the vessel, while his body remained within. When Scylax was thus fastened, one went and informed Aristagoras that Megabates had bound his Myndian friend and was entreating him shamefully. So he came and asked Megabates to let the man off; but the Persian refused him; whereupon Aristagoras went himself and set Scylax free. When Megabates heard this he was still more angry than before, and spoke hotly to Aristagoras. Then the latter said to him—

"What hast thou to do with these matters? Wert thou not sent here by Artaphernes to obey me, and to sail whithersoever I ordered? Why dost meddle so?"

Thus spake Aristagoras. The other, in high dudgeon at such language, waited till the night, and then despatched a boat to Naxos, to warn the Naxians of the coming danger.

34. Now the Naxians up to this time had not had any suspicion that the armament was directed against them; as soon, therefore, as the message reached them, forthwith they brought within their walls all that they had in the open field, and made themselves ready against a siege by provisioning their town both with food and drink. Thus was Naxos placed in a posture of defence; and the Persians, when they crossed the sea from Chios, found the Naxians fully prepared for them. However they sat down before the place, and besieged it for four whole months. When at length all the stores which they had brought with them were exhausted, and Aristagoras had likewise spent upon the siege no small sum from his private means, and more was still needed to insure success, the Persians gave up the attempt, and first building certain forts, wherein they left

the banished Naxians, withdrew to the mainland, having utterly failed in their undertaking.

35. And now Aristagoras found himself quite unable to make good his promises to Artaphernes; nay, he was even hard pressed to meet the claims whereto he was liable for the pay of the troops; and at the same time his fear was great, lest, owing to the failure of the expedition and his own quarrel with Megabates, he should be ousted from the government of Miletus. These manifold alarms had already caused him to contemplate raising a rebellion, when the man with the marked head came from Susa, bringing him instructions on the part of Histiæus to revolt from the king. For Histiæus, when he was anxious to give Aristagoras orders to revolt, could find but one safe way, as the roads were guarded, of making his wishes known; which was by taking the trustiest of his slaves, shaving all the hair from off his head, and then pricking letters upon the skin, and waiting till the hair grew again. Thus accordingly he did; and as soon as ever the hair was grown, he despatched the man to Miletus, giving him no other message than this—"When thou art come to Miletus, bid Aristagoras shave thy head, and look thereon." Now the marks on the head, as I have already mentioned, were a command to revolt. All this Histiæus did because it irked him greatly to be kept at Susa, and because he had strong hopes that, if troubles broke out, he would be sent down to the coast to quell them, whereas, if Miletus made no movement, he did not see a chance of his ever again returning thither.

36. Such, then, were the views which led Histiæus to despatch his messenger; and it so chanced that all these several motives to revolt were brought to bear upon Aristagoras at one and the same time.

Accordingly, at this conjuncture Aristagoras held a council of his trusty friends, and laid the business before them, telling them both what he had himself purposed, and what message had been sent him by Histiæus. At this council all his friends were of the same way of thinking, and recommended revolt, except only Hecatæus the historian. He, first of all, advised them by all means to avoid engaging in war with the king of the Persians, whose might he set forth, and whose subject nations he enumerated. As however he could not induce them to listen to this counsel, he next advised that they should do all that lay in their power to make themselves masters of the sea. "There was one only way," he said, "so far as he could see, of their succeeding in this. Miletus was, he knew, a weak state—but if the treasures in the temple at Branchidæ, which Crœsus the Lydian gave to it, were seized, he had strong hopes that the mastery of the sea might be thereby gained; at least it would give them money to begin the war, and would save the treasures from falling into the hands of the enemy." Now these treasures were of very great value, as I showed in the first part of my History. The assembly, however, rejected the counsel of Hecatæus, while, nevertheless, they resolved upon a revolt. One of their number, it was agreed, should sail to Myus, where the fleet had been lying since its return from Naxos, and endeavour to seize the captains who had gone there with the vessels.

37. Iatragoras accordingly was despatched on this errand, and he took with guile Oliatus the son of Ibanôlis the Mylassian, and Histiæus the son of Tymnes the Termerean—Coës likewise, the son of Erxander, to whom Darius gave Mytilênê, and Aristagoras the son of Heraclides the Cymæan, and also many others. Thus Aristagoras revolted openly from Darius; and now he set to work to scheme against him in every possible way. First of all, in order to induce the Milesians to join heartily in the revolt, he gave out that he laid down his own lordship over Miletus, and in lieu thereof established a commonwealth: after which, throughout all Ionia he did the like; for from some of the cities he drove out their tyrants, and to others, whose goodwill he hoped thereby to gain, he handed theirs over, thus giving up all the men whom he had seized at the Naxian fleet, each to the city whereto he belonged.

38. Now the Mytileneans had no sooner got Coës into their power, than they led him forth from the city and stoned him; the Cymæans, on the other hand, allowed their tyrant to go free; as likewise did most of the others. And so this form of government ceased throughout all the cities. Aristagoras the Milesian, after he had in this way put down the tyrants, and bidden the cities choose themselves captains in their room, sailed away himself on board a trireme to Lacedæmon; for he had great need of obtaining the aid of some powerful ally.

39. At Sparta, Anaxandridas the son of Leo was no longer king: he had died, and his son Cleomenes had mounted the throne, not however by right of merit, but of birth. Anaxandridas took to wife his own sister's daughter,

and was tenderly attached to her; but no children came from the marriage. Hereupon the Ephors called him before them, and said—"If thou hast no care for thine own self, nevertheless *we* cannot allow this, nor suffer the race of Eurysthenes to die out from among us. Come then, as thy present wife bears thee no children, put her away, and wed another. So wilt thou do what is well-pleasing to the Spartans." Anaxandridas however refused to do as they required, and said it was no good advice the Ephors gave, to bid him put away his wife when she had done no wrong, and take to himself another. He therefore declined to obey them.

40. Then the Ephors and Elders took counsel together, and laid this proposal before the king:—"Since thou art so fond, as we see thee to be, of thy present wife, do what we now advise, and gainsay us not, lest the Spartans make some unwonted decree concerning thee. We ask thee not now to put away thy wife to whom thou art married—give her still the same love and honour as ever—but take thee another wife beside, who may bear thee children."

When he heard this offer, Anaxandridas gave way—and henceforth he lived with two wives in two separate houses, quite against all Spartan custom.

41. In a short time, the wife whom he had last married bore him a son, who received the name of Cleomenes; and so the heir to the throne was brought into the world by her. After this, the first wife also, who in time past had been barren, by some strange chance conceived, and came to be with child. Then the friends of the second wife, when they heard a rumour of the truth, made a great stir, and said it was a false boast, and she meant, they were sure, to bring forward as her own a supposititious child. So they raised an outcry against her; and therefore, when her full time was come, the Ephors, who were themselves incredulous, sat round her bed, and kept a strict watch on the labour. At this time then she bore Dorieus, and after him, quickly, Leonidas, and after him, again quickly, Cleombrotus. Some even say that Leonidas and Cleombrotus were twins. On the other hand, the second wife, the mother of Cleomenes (who was a daughter of Prinetadas, the son of Demarmenus), never gave birth to a second child.

42. Now Cleomenes, it is said, was not right in his mind; indeed he verged upon madness;

while Dorieus surpassed all his co-mates, and looked confidently to receiving the kingdom on the score of merit. When, therefore, after the death of Anaxandridas, the Spartans kept to the law, and made Cleomenes, his eldest son, king in his room, Dorieus, who had imagined that he should be chosen, and who could not bear the thought of having such a man as Cleomenes to rule over him, asked the Spartans to give him a body of men, and left Sparta with them in order to found a colony. However, he neither took counsel of the oracle at Delphi as to the place whereto he should go, nor observed any of the customary usages; but left Sparta in dudgeon, and sailed away to Libya, under the guidance of certain men who were Theræans. These men brought him to Cinyps, where he colonised a spot, which has not its equal in all Libya, on the banks of a river: but from this place he was driven in the third year by the Macians, the Libyans, and the Carthaginians.

43. Dorieus returned to the Peloponnese; whereupon Antichares the Eleônian gave him a counsel (which he got from the oracle of Laïus), to "found the city of Heraclea in Sicily; the whole country of Eryx belonged," he said, "to the Heracleids, since Hercules himself conquered it." On receiving this advice, Dorieus went to Delphi to inquire of the oracle whether he would take the place to which he was about to go. The Pythoness prophesied that he would; whereupon Dorieus went back to Libya, took up the men who had sailed with him at the first, and proceeded upon his way along the shores of Italy.

44. Just at this time, the Sybarites say, they and their king Têlys were about to make war upon Crotôna, and the Crotoniats, greatly alarmed, besought Dorieus to lend them aid. Dorieus was prevailed upon, bore part in the war against Sybaris, and had a share in taking the town. Such is the account which the Sybarites give of what was done by Dorieus and his companions. The Crotoniats, on the other hand, maintain that no foreigner lent them aid in their war against the Sybarites, save and except Callias the Elean, a soothsayer of the race of the Iamidæ; and he only forsook Têlys the Sybaritic king, and deserted to their side, when he found on sacrificing that the victims were not favourable to an attack on Crotôna. Such is the account which each party gives of these matters.

45. Both parties likewise adduce testimonies to the truth of what they say. The Sybarites show a temple and sacred precinct near the dry stream of the Crastis, which they declare that Dorieus, after taking their city, dedicated to Minerva Crastias. And further, they bring forward the death of Dorieus as the surest proof; since he fell, they say, because he disobeyed the oracle. For had he in nothing varied from the directions given him, but confined himself to the business on which he was sent, he would assuredly have conquered the Erycian territory, and kept possession of it, instead of perishing with all his followers. The Crotoniats, on the other hand, point to the numerous allotments within their borders which were assigned to Callias the Elean by their countrymen, and which to my day remained in the possession of his family; while Dorieus and his descendants (they remark) possess nothing. Yet if Dorieus had really helped them in the Sybaritic war, he would have received very much more than Callias. Such are the testimonies which are adduced on either side; it is open to every man to adopt whichever view he deems the best.

46. Certain Spartans accompanied Dorieus on his voyage as co-founders, to wit, Thessalus, Paræbates, Celeas, and Euryleon. These men and all the troops under their command reached Sicily; but there they fell in a battle wherein they were defeated by the Egestæans and Phœnicians, only one, Euryleon, surviving the disaster. He then, collecting the remnants of the beaten army, made himself master of Minôa, the Selinusian colony, and helped the Selinusians to throw off the yoke of their tyrant Peithagoras. Having upset Peithagoras, he sought to become tyrant in his room, and he even reigned at Selinus for a brief space—but after a while the Selinusians rose up in revolt against him, and though he fled to the altar of Jupiter Agoræus, they notwithstanding put him to death.

47. Another man who accompanied Dorieus, and died with him, was Philip the son of Butacidas, a man of Crotôna; who, after he had been betrothed to a daughter of Têlys the Sybarite, was banished from Crotôna, whereupon his marriage came to nought; and he in his disappointment took ship and sailed to Cyrêné. From thence he became a follower of Dorieus, furnishing to the fleet a trireme of his own, the crew of which he supported at his own charge. This Philip was an Olympian victor, and the handsomest Greek of his day. His beauty gained him honours at the hands of the Egestæans which they never accorded to any one

else; for they raised a hero-temple over his grave, and they still worship him with sacrifices.

48. Such then was the end of Dorieus, who if he had brooked the rule of Cleomenes, and remained in Sparta, would have been king of Lacedæmon; since Cleomenes, after reigning no great length of time, died without male offspring, leaving behind him an only daughter, by name Gorgo.

49. Cleomenes, however, was still king when Aristagoras, tyrant of Miletus, reached Sparta. At their interview, Aristagoras, according to the report of the Lacedæmonians, produced a bronze tablet, whereupon the whole circuit of the earth was engraved, with all its seas and rivers. Discourse began between the two; and Aristagoras addressed the Spartan king in these words following:—"Think it not strange, O King Cleomenes, that I have been at the pains to sail hither; for the posture of affairs, which I will now recount unto thee, made it fitting. Shame and grief is it indeed to none so much as to us, that the sons of the Ionians should have lost their freedom, and come to be the slaves of others; but yet it touches you likewise, O Spartans, beyond the rest of the Greeks, inasmuch as the pre-eminence over all Greece appertains to you. We beseech you, therefore, by the common gods of the Grecians, deliver the Ionians, who are your own kinsmen, from slavery. Truly the task is not difficult; for the barbarians are an unwarlike people; and you are the best and bravest warriors in the whole world. Their mode of fighting is the following:—they use bows and arrows and a short spear; they wear trousers in the field, and cover their heads with turbans. So easy are they to vanquish! Know too that the dwellers in these parts have more good things than all the rest of the world put together—gold, and silver, and brass, and embroidered garments, beasts of burthen, and bond-servants—all which, if you only wish it, you may soon have for your own. The nations border on one another, in the order which I will now explain. Next to these Ionians" (here he pointed with his finger to the map of the world which was engraved upon the tablet that he had brought with him) "these Lydians dwell; their soil is fertile, and few people are so rich in silver. Next to them," he continued, "come these Phrygians, who have more flocks and herds than any race that I know, and more plentiful harvests. On them border the Cappadocians, whom we Greeks know by the name of Syrians: they are neighbours to the Cilicians, who extend all the way to this sea, where Cyprus (the island which you see here) lies. The Cilicians pay the king a yearly tribute of five hundred talents. Next to them come the Armenians, who live here—they too have numerous flocks and herds. After them come the Matiêni, inhabiting this country; then Cissia, this province, where you see the river Choaspes marked, and likewise the town Susa upon its banks, where the Great King holds his court, and where the treasuries are in which his wealth is stored. Once masters of this city, you may be bold to vie with Jove himself for riches. In the wars which ye wage with your rivals of Messenia, with them of Argos likewise and of Arcadia, about paltry boundaries and strips of land not so remarkably good, ye contend with those who have no gold, nor silver even, which often give men heart to fight and die. Must ye wage such wars, and when ye might so easily be lords of Asia, will ye decide otherwise?" Thus spoke Aristagoras; and Cleomenes replied to him,—"Milesian stranger, three days hence I will give thee an answer."

50. So they proceeded no further at that time. When, however, the day appointed for the answer came, and the two once more met, Cleomenes asked Aristagoras, "how many days' journey it was from the sea of the Ionians to the king's residence?" Hereupon Aristagoras, who had managed the rest so cleverly, and succeeded in deceiving the king, tripped in his speech and blundered; for instead of concealing the truth, as he ought to have done if he wanted to induce the Spartans to cross into Asia, he said plainly that it was a journey of three months. Cleomenes caught at the words, and, preventing Aristagoras from finishing what he had begun to say concerning the road, addressed him thus:—"Milesian stranger, quit Sparta before sunset. This is no good proposal that thou makest to the Lacedæmonians, to conduct them a distance of three months' journey from the sea." When he had thus spoken, Cleomenes went to his home.

51. But Aristagoras took an olive-bough in his hand, and hastened to the king's house, where he was admitted by reason of his suppliant's guise. Gorgo, the daughter of Cleomenes, and his only child, a girl of about eight or nine years of age, happened to be there, standing by her father's side. Aristagoras, seeing her, requested Cleomenes to send her out of the room before he began to speak with

him; but Cleomenes told him to say on, and not mind the child. So Aristagoras began with a promise of ten talents if the king would grant him his request, and when Cleomenes shook his head, contined to raise his offer till it reached fifty talents; whereupon the child spoke:—"Father," she said, "get up and go, or the stranger will certainly corrupt thee." Then Cleomenes, pleased at the warning of his child, withdrew and went into another room. Aristagoras quitted Sparta for good, not being able to discourse any more concerning the road which led up to the king.

52. Now the true account of the road in question is the following:—Royal stations exist along its whole length, and excellent caravanserais; and throughout, it traverses an inhabited tract, and is free from danger. In Lydia and Phrygia there are twenty stations within a distance of 94½ parasangs. On leaving Phrygia the Halys has to be crossed; and here are gates through which you must needs pass ere you can traverse the stream. A strong force guards this post. When you have made the passage, and are come into Cappadocia, 28 stations and 104 parasangs bring you to the borders of Cilicia, where the road passes through two sets of gates, at each of which there is a guard posted. Leaving these behind, you go on through Cilicia, where you find three stations in a distance of 15½ parasangs. The boundary between Cilicia and Armenia is the river Euphrates, which it is necessary to cross in boats. In Armenia the resting-places are 15 in number, and the distance is 56½ parasangs. There is one place where a guard is posted. Four large streams intersect this district, all of which have to be crossed by means of boats. The first of these is the Tigris; the second and the third have both of them the same name, though they are not only different rivers, but do not even run from the same place. For the one which I have called the first of the two has its source in Armenia, while the other flows afterwards out of the country of the Matienians. The fourth of the streams is called the Gyndes, and this is the river which Cyrus dispersed by digging for it three hundred and sixty channels. Leaving Armenia and entering the Matienian country, you have four stations; these passed you find yourself in Cissia, where eleven stations and 42½ parasangs bring you to another navigable stream, the Choaspes, on the banks of which the city of Susa is built. Thus the entire number of the stations is raised to one hundred and eleven;

and so many are in fact the resting-places that one finds between Sardis and Susa.

53. If then the royal road be measured aright, and the parasang equals, as it does, thirty furlongs, the whole distance from Sardis to the palace of Memnon (as it is called), amounting thus to 450 parasangs, would be 13,500 furlongs. Travelling then at the rate of 150 furlongs a day, one will take exactly ninety days to perform the journey.

54. Thus when Aristagoras the Milesian told Cleomenes the Lacedæmonian that it was a three months' journey from the sea up to the king, he said no more than the truth. The exact distance (if any one desires still greater accuracy) is somewhat more; for the journey from Ephesus to Sardis must be added to the foregoing account; and this will make the whole distance between the Greek Sea and Susa (or the city of Memnon, as it is called) 14,040 furlongs; since Ephesus is distant from Sardis 540 furlongs. This would add three days to the three months' journey.

55. When Aristagoras left Sparta he hastened to Athens, which had got quit of its tyrants in the way that I will now describe. After the death of Hipparchus (the son of Pisistratus, and brother of the tyrant Hippias), who, in spite of the clear warning he had received concerning his fate in a dream, was slain by Harmodius and Aristogeiton (men both of the race of the Gephyræans), the oppression of the Athenians continued by the space of four years; and they gained nothing, but were worse used than before.

56. Now the dream of Hipparchus was the following:—The night before the Panathenaic festival, he thought he saw in his sleep a tall and beautiful man, who stood over him, and read him the following riddle:—

Bear thou unbearable woes with the all-bearing heart of a lion;
Never, be sure, shall wrong-doer escape the reward of wrong-doing.

As soon as day dawned he sent and submitted his dream to the interpreters, after which he offered the averting sacrifices, and then went and led the procession in which he perished.

57. The family of the Gephyræans, to which the murderers of Hipparchus belonged, according to their own account, came originally from Eretria. My inquiries, however, have made it clear to me that they are in reality Phœnicians, descendants of those who came with Cadmus into the country now called Bœotia. Here they received for their portion the

district of Tanagra, in which they afterwards dwelt. On their expulsion from this country by the Bœotians (which happened some time after that of the Cadmeians from the same parts by the Argives) they took refuge at Athens. The Athenians received them among their citizens upon set terms, whereby they were excluded from a number of privileges which are not worth mentioning.

58. Now the Phœnicians who came with Cadmus, and to whom the Gephyræi belonged, introduced into Greece upon their arrival a great variety of arts, among the rest that of writing, whereof the Greeks till then had, as I think, been ignorant. And originally they shaped their letters exactly like all the other Phœnicians, but afterwards, in course of time, they changed by degrees their language, and together with it the form likewise of their characters. Now the Greeks who dwelt about those parts at that time were chiefly the Ionians. The Phœnician letters were accordingly adopted by them, but with some variation in the shape of a few, and so they arrived at the present use, still calling the letters Phœnician, as justice required, after the name of those who were the first to introduce them into Greece. Paper rolls also were called from of old "parchments" by the Ionians, because formerly when paper was scarce they used, instead, the skins of sheep and goats—on which material many of the barbarians are even now wont to write.

59. I myself saw Cadmeian characters engraved upon some tripods in the temple of Apollo Ismenias in Bœotian Thebes, most of them shaped like the Ionian. One of the tripods has the inscription following:—

Me did Amphitryon place, from the far Teleboans coming.

This would be about the age of Laïus, the son of Labdacus, the son of Polydorus, the son of Cadmus.

60. Another of the tripods has this legend in the hexameter measure:—

I to far-shooting Phœbus was offered by Scæus the boxer,
When he had won at the games—a wondrous beautiful offering.

This might be Scæus, the son of Hippocoön; and the tripod, if dedicated by him, and not by another of the same name, would belong to the time of Œdipus, the son of Laïus.

61. The third tripod has also an inscription in hexameters, which runs thus:—

King Laodamas gave this tripod to far-seeing Phœbus,
When he was set on the throne—a wondrous beautiful offering.

It was in the reign of this Laodamas, the son of Eteocles, that the Cadmeians were driven by the Argives out of their country, and found a shelter with the Encheleans. The Gephyræans at that time remained in the country, but afterwards they retired before the Bœotians, and took refuge at Athens, where they have a number of temples for their separate use, which the other Athenians are not allowed to enter—among the rest, one of Achæan Ceres, in whose honour they likewise celebrate special orgies.

62. Having thus related the dream which Hipparchus saw, and traced the descent of the Gephyræans, the family whereto his murderers belonged, I must proceed with the matter whereof I was intending before to speak; to wit, the way in which the Athenians got quit of their tyrants. Upon the death of Hipparchus, Hippias, who was king, grew harsh towards the Athenians; and the Alcmæonidæ, an Athenian family which had been banished by the Pisistratidæ, joined the other exiles, and endeavoured to procure their own return, and to free Athens, by force. They seized and fortified Leipsydrium above Pæonia, and tried to gain their object by arms; but great disasters befell them, and their purpose remained unaccomplished. They therefore resolved to shrink from no contrivance that might bring them success; and accordingly they contracted with the Amphictyons to build the temple which now stands at Delphi, but which in those days did not exist. Having done this, they proceeded, being men of great wealth and members of an ancient and distinguished family, to build the temple much more magnificently than the plan obliged them. Besides other improvements, instead of the coarse stone whereof by the contract the temple was to have been constructed, they made the facings of Parian marble.

63. These same men, if we may believe the Athenians, during their stay at Delphi persuaded the Pythoness by a bribe to tell the Spartans, whenever any of them came to consult the oracle, either on their own private affairs or on the business of the state, that they must free Athens. So the Lacedæmonians, when they found no answer ever returned to them but this, sent at last Anchimolius, the son of Aster—a man of note among their citizens —at the head of an army against Athens, with

orders to drive out the Pisistratidæ, albeit they were bound to them by the closest ties of friendship. For they esteemed the things of heaven more highly than the things of men. The troops went by sea and were conveyed in transports. Anchimolius brought them to an anchorage at Phalerum; and there the men disembarked. But the Pisistratidæ, who had previous knowledge of their intentions, had sent to Thessaly, between which country and Athens there was an alliance, with a request for aid. The Thessalians, in reply to their entreaties, sent them by a public vote 1000 horsemen, under the command of their king, Cineas, who was a Coniæan. When this help came, the Pisistratidæ laid their plan accordingly: they cleared the whole plain about Phalerum so as to make it fit for the movements of cavalry, and then charged the enemy's camp with their horse, which fell with such fury upon the Lacedæmonians as to kill numbers, among the rest Anchimolius, the general, and to drive the remainder to their ships. Such was the fate of the first army sent from Lacedæmon, and the tomb of Anchimolius may be seen to this day in Attica; it is at Alopecæ (Foxtown), near the temple of Hercules in Cynosargos.

64. Afterwards, the Lacedæmonians despatched a larger force against Athens, which they put under the command of Cleomenes, son of Anaxandridas, one of their kings. These troops were not sent by sea, but marched by the mainland. When they were come into Attica, their first encounter was with the Thessalian horse, which they shortly put to flight, killing above forty men; the remainder made good their escape, and fled straight to Thessaly. Cleomenes proceeded to the city, and, with the aid of such of the Athenians as wished for freedom, besieged the tyrants, who had shut themselves up in the Pelasgic fortress.

65. And now there had been small chance of the Pisistratidæ falling into the hands of the Spartans, who did not even design to sit down before the place, which had moreover been well provisioned beforehand with stores both of meat and drink,—nay, it is likely that after a few days' blockade the Lacedæmonians would have quitted Attica altogether, and gone back to Sparta—had not an event occurred most unlucky for the besieged, and most advantageous for the besiegers. The children of the Pisistratidæ were made prisoners, as they were being removed out of the country. By this calamity all their plans were deranged, and— as the ransom of their children—they con-sented to the demands of the Athenians, and agreed within five days' time to quit Attica. Accordingly they soon afterwards left the country, and withdrew to Sigeum on the Scamander, after reigning thirty-six years over the Athenians. By descent they were Pylians, of the family of the Neleids, to which Codrus and Melanthus likewise belonged, men who in former times from foreign settlers became kings of Athens. And hence it was that Hippocrates came to think of calling his son Pisistratus: he named him after the Pisistratus who was a son of Nestor. Such then was the mode in which the Athenians got quit of their tyrants. What they did and suffered worthy of note from the time when they gained their freedom until the revolt of Ionia from King Darius, and the coming of Aristagoras to Athens with a request that the Athenians would lend the Ionians aid, I shall now proceed to relate.

66. The power of Athens had been great before; but, now that the tyrants were gone, it became greater than ever. The chief authority was lodged with two persons, Clisthenes, of the family of the Alcmæonids, who is said to have been the persuader of the Pythoness, and Isagoras, the son of Tisander, who belonged to a noble house, but whose pedigree I am not able to trace further. Howbeit his kinsmen offer sacrifice to the Carian Jupiter. These two men strove together for the mastery; and Clisthenes, finding himself the weaker, called to his aid the common people. Hereupon, instead of the four tribes among which the Athenians had been divided hitherto, Clisthenes made ten tribes, and parcelled out the Athenians among them. He likewise changed the names of the tribes; for whereas they had till now been called after Geleon, Ægicores, Argades, and Hoples, the four sons of Ion, Clisthenes set these names aside, and called his tribes after certain other heroes, all of whom were native, except Ajax. Ajax was associated because, although a foreigner, he was a neighbour and an ally of Athens.

67. My belief is that in acting thus he did but imitate his maternal grandfather, Clisthenes, king of Sicyon. This king, when he was at war with Argos, put an end to the contests of the rhapsodists at Sicyon, because in the Homeric poems Argos and the Argives were so constantly the theme of song. He likewise conceived the wish to drive Adrastus, the son of Talaüs, out of his country, seeing that he was an Argive hero. For Adrastus had a

shrine at Sicyon, which yet stands in the market-place of the town. Clisthenes therefore went to Delphi, and asked the oracle if he might expel Adrastus. To this the Pythoness is reported to have answered—"Adrastus is the Sicyonians' king, but thou art only a robber." So when the god would not grant his request, he went home and began to think how he might contrive to make Adrastus withdraw of his own accord. After a while he hit upon a plan which he thought would succeed. He sent envoys to Thebes in Bœotia, and informed the Thebans that he wished to bring Melanippus, the son of Astacus, to Sicyon. The Thebans consenting, Clisthenes carried Melanippus back with him, assigned him a precinct within the government-house, and built him a shrine there in the safest and strongest part. The reason for his so doing (which I must not forbear to mention) was because Melanippus was Adrastus' great enemy, having slain both his brother Mecistes and his son-in-law Tydeus. Clisthenes, after assigning the precinct to Melanippus, took away from Adrastus the sacrifices and festivals wherewith he had till then been honoured, and transferred them to his adversary. Hitherto the Sicyonians had paid extraordinary honours to Adrastus, because the country had belonged to Polybus, and Adrastus was Polybus' daughter's son; whence it came to pass that Polybus, dying childless, left Adrastus his kingdom. Besides other ceremonies, it had been their wont to honour Adrastus with tragic choruses, which they assigned to him rather than Bacchus, on account of his calamities. Clisthenes now gave the choruses to Bacchus, transferring to Melanippus the rest of the sacred rites.

68. Such were his doings in the matter of Adrastus. With respect to the Dorian tribes, not choosing the Sicyonians to have the same tribes as the Argives, he changed all the old names for new ones; and here he took special occasion to mock the Sicyonians, for he drew his new names from the words "pig," and "ass," adding thereto the usual tribe-endings; only in the case of his own tribe he did nothing of the sort, but gave them a name drawn from his own kingly office. For he called his own tribe the Archelaï, or Rulers, while the others he named Hyatæ, or Pig-folk, Oneatæ, or Ass-folk, and Chœreatæ, or Swine-folk. The Sicyonians kept these names, not only during the reign of Clisthenes, but even after his death, by the space of sixty years: then, however, they took counsel together, and changed to the well-

known names of Hyllæans, Pamphylians, and Dymanatæ, taking at the same time, as a fourth name, the title of Ægialeans, from Ægialeus the son of Adrastus.

69. Thus had Clisthenes the Sicyonian done. The Athenian Clisthenes, who was grandson by the mother's side of the other, and had been named after him, resolved, from contempt (as I believe) of the Ionians, that his tribes should not be the same as theirs; and so followed the pattern set him by his namesake of Sicyon. Having brought entirely over to his own side the common people of Athens, whom he had before disdained, he gave all the tribes new names, and made the number greater than formerly; instead of the four phylarchs he established ten; he likewise placed ten demes in each of the tribes; and he was, now that the common people took his part, very much more powerful than his adversaries.

70. Isagoras in his turn lost ground; and therefore, to counter-plot his enemy, he called in Cleomenes the Lacedæmonian, who had already, at the time when he was besieging the Pisistratidæ, made a contract of friendship with him. A charge is even brought against Cleomenes that he was on terms of too great familiarity with Isagoras's wife. At this time the first thing that he did was to send a herald and require that Clisthenes, and a large number of Athenians besides, whom he called "The Accursed," should leave Athens. This message he sent at the suggestion of Isagoras: for in the affair referred to, the blood-guiltiness lay on the Alcmæonidæ and their partisans, while he and his friends were quite clear of it.

71. The way in which "The Accursed" at Athens got their name, was the following. There was a certain Athenian called Cylon, a victor at the Olympic Games, who aspired to the sovereignty, and aided by a number of his companions, who were of the same age with himself, made an attempt to seize the citadel. But the attack failed; and Cylon became a suppliant at the image. Hereupon the Heads of the Naucraries, who at that time bore rule in Athens, induced the fugitives to remove by a promise to spare their lives. Nevertheless they were all slain; and the blame was laid on the Alcmæonidæ. All this happened before the time of Pisistratus.

72. When the message of Cleomenes arrived, requiring Clisthenes and "The Accursed" to quit the city, Clisthenes departed of his own accord. Cleomenes, however, notwithstanding his departure, came to Athens, with

a small band of followers; and on his arrival sent into banishment seven hundred Athenian families, which were pointed out to him by Isagoras. Succeeding here, he next endeavoured to dissolve the council, and to put the government into the hands of three hundred of the partisans of that leader. But the council resisted, and refused to obey his orders; whereupon Cleomenes, Isagoras, and their followers took possession of the citadel. Here they were attacked by the rest of the Athenians, who took the side of the council, and were besieged for the space of two days: on the third day they accepted terms, being allowed—at least such of them as were Lacedæmonians—to quit the country. And so the word which came to Cleomenes received its fulfilment. For when he first went up into the citadel, meaning to seize it, just as he was entering the sanctuary of the goddess, in order to question her, the priestess arose from her throne, before he had passed the doors, and said—"Stranger from Lacedæmon, depart hence, and presume not to enter the holy place—it is not lawful for a Dorian to set foot there." But he answered, "Oh! woman, I am not a Dorian, but an Achæan." Slighting this warning, Cleomenes made his attempt, and so he was forced to retire, together with his Lacedæmonians. The rest were cast into prison by the Athenians, and condemned to die—among them Timasitheüs the Delphian, of whose prowess and courage I have great things which I could tell.

73. So these men died in prison. The Athenians directly afterwards recalled Clisthenes, and the seven hundred families which Cleomenes had driven out; and, further, they sent envoys to Sardis, to make an alliance with the Persians, for they knew that war would follow with Cleomenes and the Lacedæmonians. When the ambassadors reached Sardis and delivered their message, Artaphernes, son of Hystaspes, who was at that time governor of the place, inquired of them "who they were, and in what part of the world they dwelt, that they wanted to become allies of the Persians?" The messengers told him; upon which he answered them shortly—that "if the Athenians chose to give earth and water to King Darius, he would conclude an alliance with them; but if not, they might go home again." After consulting together, the envoys, anxious to form the alliance, accepted the terms; but on their return to Athens, they fell into deep disgrace on account of their compliance.

74. Meanwhile Cleomenes, who considered himself to have been insulted by the Athenians both in word and deed, was drawing a force together from all parts of the Peloponnese, without informing any one of his object; which was to revenge himself on the Athenians, and to establish Isagoras, who had escaped with him from the citadel, as despot of Athens. Accordingly, with a large army, he invaded the district of Eleusis, while the Bœotians, who had concerted measures with him, took Œnoë and Hysiæ, two country towns upon the frontier; and at the same time the Chalcideans, on another side, plundered divers places in Attica. The Athenians, notwithstanding that danger threatened them from every quarter, put off all thought of the Bœotians and Chalcideans till a future time, and marched against the Peloponnesians, who were at Eleusis.

75. As the two hosts were about to engage, first of all the Corinthians, bethinking themselves that they were perpetrating a wrong, changed their minds, and drew off from the main army. Then Demaratus, son of Ariston, who was himself king of Sparta and jointleader of the expedition, and who till now had had no sort of quarrel with Cleomenes, followed their example. On account of this rupture between the kings, a law was passed at Sparta, forbidding both monarchs to go out together with the army, as had been the custom hitherto. The law also provided, that, as one of the kings was to be left behind, one of the Tyndaridæ should also remain at home; whereas hitherto both had accompanied the expeditions, as auxiliaries. So when the rest of the allies saw that the Lacedæmonian kings were not of one mind, and that the Corinthian troops had quitted their post, they likewise drew off and departed.

76. This was the fourth time that the Dorians had invaded Attica: twice they came as enemies, and twice they came to do good service to the Athenian people. Their first invasion took place at the period when they founded Megara, and is rightly placed in the reign of Codrus at Athens; the second and third occasions were when they came from Sparta to drive out the Pisistratidæ; the fourth was the present attack, when Cleomenes, at the head of a Peloponnesian army, entered at Eleusis. Thus the Dorians had now four times invaded Attica.

77. So when the Spartan army had broken up from its quarters thus ingloriously, the Athenians, wishing to revenge themselves,

marched first against the Chalcideans. The Bœotians, however, advancing to the aid of the latter as far as the Euripus, the Athenians thought it best to attack them first. A battle was fought accordingly; and the Athenians gained a very complete victory, killing a vast number of the enemy, and taking seven hundred of them alive. After this, on the very same day, they crossed into Eubœa, and engaged the Chalcideans with the like success; whereupon they left four thousand settlers[1] upon the lands of the Hippobotæ,[2]—which is the name the Chalcideans give to their rich men. All the Chalcidean prisoners whom they took were put in irons, and kept for a long time in close confinement, as likewise were the Bœotians, until the ransom asked for them was paid; and this the Athenians fixed at two minæ the man. The chains wherewith they were fettered the Athenians suspended in their citadel; where they were still to be seen in my day, hanging against the wall scorched by the Median flames, opposite the chapel which faces the west. The Athenians made an offering of the tenth part of the ransom-money: and expended it on the brazen chariot drawn by four steeds, which stands on the left hand immediately that one enters the gateway of the citadel. The inscription runs as follows:—

When Chalcis and Bœotia dared her might,
Athens subdued their pride in valorous fight;
Gave bonds for insults; and, the ransom paid,
From the full tenths these steeds for Pallas made.

78. Thus did the Athenians increase in strength. And it is plain enough, not from this instance only, but from many everywhere, that freedom is an excellent thing; since even the Athenians, who, while they continued under the rule of tyrants, were not a whit more valiant than any of their neighbours, no sooner shook off the yoke than they became decidedly the first of all. These things show that, while undergoing oppression, they let themselves be beaten, since then they worked for a master; but so soon as they got their freedom, each man was eager to do the best he could for himself. So fared it now with the Athenians.

79. Meanwhile the Thebans, who longed to be revenged on the Athenians, had sent to the oracle, and been told by the Pythoness that of their own strength they would be unable to

[1] Literally, "allotment-holders" (κληροῦχοι).
[2] The Chalcidean Hippobotæ, or "horse-keepers," were a wealthy aristocracy and correspond to the knights (ἱππεῖς) of most Grecian states, and the "equites," or "celeres," of the Romans.

accomplish their wish: "they must lay the matter," she said, "before the many-voiced, and ask the aid of those nearest them." The messengers, therefore, on their return, called a meeting, and laid the answer of the oracle before the people, who no sooner heard the advice to "ask the aid of those nearest them" than they exclaimed—"What! are not they who dwell the nearest to us the men of Tanagra, of Coronæa, and Thespiæ? Yet these men always fight on our side, and have aided us with a good heart all through the war. Of what use is it to ask them? But maybe this is not the true meaning of the oracle."

80. As they were thus discoursing one with another, a certain man, informed of the debate, cried out—"Methinks that I understand what course the oracle would recommend to us. Asôpus, they say, had two daughters, Thêbé and Egina. The god means that, as these two were sisters, we ought to ask the Eginetans to lend us aid." As no one was able to hit on any better explanation, the Thebans forthwith sent messengers to Egina, and, according to the advice of the oracle, asked their aid, as the people "nearest to them." In answer to this petition the Eginetans said that they would give them the Æacidæ for helpers.

81. The Thebans now, relying on the assistance of the Æacidæ, ventured to renew the war; but they met with so rough a reception, that they resolved to send to the Eginetans again, returning the Æacidæ, and beseeching them to send some men instead. The Eginetans, who were at that time a most flourishing people, elated with their greatness, and at the same time calling to mind their ancient feud with Athens, agreed to lend the Thebans aid, and forthwith went to war with the Athenians, without even giving them notice by a herald. The attention of these latter being engaged by the struggle with the Bœotians, the Eginetans in their ships of war made descents upon Attica, plundered Phalerum, and ravaged a vast number of the townships upon the sea-board, whereby the Athenians suffered very grievous damage.

82. The ancient feud between the Eginetans and Athenians arose out of the following circumstances. Once upon a time the land of Epidaurus would bear no crops; and the Epidaurians sent to consult the oracle of Delphi concerning their affliction. The answer bade them set up the images of Damia and Auxesia, and promised them better fortune when that should be done. "Shall the images be made of

bronze or stone?" the Epidaurians asked; but the Pythoness replied, "Of neither: but let them be made of the garden olive." Then the Epidaurians sent to Athens and asked leave to cut olive wood in Attica, believing the Athenian olives to be the holiest; or, according to others, because there were no olives at that time anywhere else in all the world but at Athens.[1] The Athenians answered that they would give them leave, but on condition of their bringing offerings year by year to Minerva Polias and to Erechtheus. The Epidaurians agreed, and having obtained what they wanted, made the images of olive wood, and set them up in their own country. Henceforth their land bore its crops; and they duly paid the Athenians what had been agreed upon.

83. Anciently, and even down to the time when this took place, the Eginetans were in all things subject to the Epidaurians, and had to cross over to Epidaurus for the trial of all suits in which they were engaged one with another. After this, however, the Eginetans built themselves ships, and, growing proud, revolted from the Epidaurians. Having thus come to be at enmity with them, the Eginetans, who were masters of the sea, ravaged Epidaurus, and even carried off these very images of Damia and Auxesia, which they set up in their own country, in the interior, at a place called Œa, about twenty furlongs from their city. This done, they fixed a worship for the images, which consisted in part of sacrifices, in part of female satiric choruses; while at the same time they appointed certain men to furnish the choruses, ten for each goddess. These choruses did not abuse men, but only the women of the country. Holy orgies of a similar kind were in use also among the Epidaurians, and likewise another sort of holy orgies, whereof it is not lawful to speak.

84. After the robbery of the images the Epidaurians ceased to make the stipulated payments to the Athenians, wherefore the Athenians sent to Epidaurus to remonstrate. But the Epidaurians proved to them that they were not guilty of any wrong:—"While the images continued in their country," they said, "they had duly paid the offerings according to the agreement; now that the images had been taken from them, they were no longer under any obligation to pay: the Athenians should make their demand of the Eginetans, in whose pos-

session the figures now were." Upon this the Athenians sent to Egina, and demanded the images back; but the Eginetans answered that the Athenians had nothing whatever to do with them.

85. After this the Athenians relate that they sent a trireme to Egina with certain citizens on board, and that these men, who bore commission from the state, landed in Egina, and sought to take the images away, considering them to be their own, inasmuch as they were made of their wood. And first they endeavoured to wrench them from their pedestals, and so carry them off; but failing herein, they in the next place tied ropes to them, and set to work to try if they could haul them down. In the midst of their hauling suddenly there was a thunderclap, and with the thunderclap an earthquake; and the crew of the trireme were forthwith seized with madness, and, like enemies, began to kill one another; until at last there was but one left, who returned alone to Phalerum.

86. Such is the account given by the Athenians. The Eginetans deny that there was only a single vessel:—"Had there been only one," they say, "or no more than a few, they would easily have repulsed the attack, even if they had had no fleet at all; but the Athenians came against them with a large number of ships, wherefore they gave way, and did not hazard a battle." They do not however explain clearly whether it was from a conviction of their own inferiority at sea that they yielded, or whether it was for the purpose of doing that which in fact they did. Their account is that the Athenians, disembarking from their ships, when they found that no resistance was offered, made for the statues, and failing to wrench them from their pedestals, tied ropes to them and began to haul. Then, they say—and some people will perhaps believe them, though I for my part do not—the two statues, as they were being dragged and hauled, fell down both upon their knees; in which attitude they still remain. Such, according to them, was the conduct of the Athenians; they meanwhile, having learnt beforehand what was intended, had prevailed on the Argives to hold themselves in readiness; and the Athenians accordingly were but just landed on their coasts when the Argives came to their aid. Secretly and silently they crossed over from Epidaurus, and, before the Athenians were aware, cut off their retreat to their ships, and fell upon them; and the thunder came exactly at that moment, and the earthquake with it.

[1] This is, of course, not true, for the olive had been cultivated in the east from a very remote antiquity.

87. The Argives and the Eginetans both agree in giving this account; and the Athenians themselves acknowledge that but one of their men returned alive to Attica. According to the Argives, he escaped from the battle in which the rest of the Athenian troops were destroyed by them. According to the Athenians, it was the god who destroyed their troops; and even this one man did not escape, for he perished in the following manner. When he came back to Athens, bringing word of the calamity, the wives of those who had been sent out on the expedition took it sorely to heart that he alone should have survived the slaughter of all the rest;—they therefore crowded round the man, and struck him with the brooches by which their dresses were fastened —each, as she struck, asking him where she had left her husband. And the man died in this way. The Athenians thought the deed of the women more horrible even than the fate of the troops; as however they did not know how else to punish them, they changed their dress and compelled them to wear the costume of the Ionians. Till this time the Athenian women had worn a Dorian dress, shaped nearly like that which prevails at Corinth. Henceforth they were made to wear the linen tunic, which does not require brooches.

88. In very truth, however, this dress is not originally Ionian, but Carian; for anciently the Greek women all wore the costume which is now called the Dorian. It is said further that the Argives and Eginetans made it a custom, on this same account, for their women to wear brooches half as large again as formerly, and to offer brooches rather than anything else in the temple of these goddesses. They also forbade the bringing of anything Attic into the temple, were it even a jar of earthenware, and made a law that none but native drinking vessels should be used there in time to come. From this early age to my own day the Argive and Eginetan women have always continued to wear their brooches larger than formerly, through hatred of the Athenians.

89. Such then was the origin of the feud which existed between the Eginetans and the Athenians. Hence, when the Thebans made their application for succour, the Eginetans, calling to mind the matter of images, gladly lent their aid to the Bœotians. They ravaged all the sea-coast of Attica; and the Athenians were about to attack them in return, when they were stopped by the oracle of Delphi, which bade them wait till thirty years had passed from the time that the Eginetans did the wrong, and in the thirty-first year, having first set apart a precinct for Æacus, then to begin the war. "So should they succeed to their wish," the oracle said; "but if they went to war at once, though they would still conquer the island in the end, yet they must go through much suffering and much exertion before taking it." On receiving this warning the Athenians set apart a precinct for Æacus—the same which still remains dedicated to him in their market-place—but they could not hear with any patience of waiting thirty years, after they had suffered such grievous wrong at the hands of the Eginetans.

90. Accordingly they were making ready to take their revenge when a fresh stir on the part of the Lacedæmonians hindered their projects. These last had become aware of the truth—how that the Alcmæonidæ had practised on the Pythoness, and the Pythoness had schemed against themselves, and against the Pisistratidæ; and the discovery was a double grief to them, for while they had driven their own sworn friends into exile, they found that they had not gained thereby a particle of good will from Athens. They were also moved by certain prophecies, which declared that many dire calamities should befall them at the hands of the Athenians. Of these in times past they had been ignorant; but now they had become acquainted with them by means of Cleomenes, who had brought them with him to Sparta, having found them in the Athenian citadel, where they had been left by the Pisistratidæ when they were driven from Athens: they were in the temple, and Cleomenes having discovered them, carried them off.

91. So when the Lacedæmonians obtained possession of the prophecies, and saw that the Athenians were growing in strength, and had no mind to acknowledge any subjection to their control, it occurred to them that, if the people of Attica were free, they would be likely to be as powerful as themselves, but if they were oppressed by a tyranny, they would be weak and submissive. Under this feeling they sent and recalled Hippias, the son of Pisistratus, from Sigeum upon the Hellespont, where the Pisistratidæ had taken shelter. Hippias came at their bidding, and the Spartans on his arrival summoned deputies from all their other allies, and thus addressed the assembly:—

"Friends and brothers in arms, we are free to confess that we did lately a thing which was not right. Misled by counterfeit oracles, we drove from their country those who were our sworn and true friends, and who had, moreover, engaged to keep Athens in dependence upon us; and we delivered the government into the hands of an unthankful people—a people who no sooner got their freedom by our means, and grew in power, than they turned us and our king, with every token of insult, out of their city. Since then they have gone on continually raising their thoughts higher, as their neighbours of Bœotia and Chalcis have already discovered to their cost, and as others too will presently discover if they shall offend them. Having thus erred, we will endeavour now, with your help, to remedy the evils we have caused, and to obtain vengeance on the Athenians. For this cause we have sent for Hippias to come here, and have summoned you likewise from your several states, that we may all now with heart and hand unite to restore him to Athens, and thereby give him back that which we took from him formerly."

92. (§ 1.) Such was the address of the Spartans. The greater number of the allies listened without being persuaded. None however broke silence but Sosicles the Corinthian, who exclaimed—

"Surely the heaven will soon be below, and the earth above, and men will henceforth live in the sea, and fish take their place upon the dry land, since you, Lacedæmonians, propose to put down free governments in the cities of Greece, and to set up tyrannies in their room. There is nothing in the whole world so unjust, nothing so bloody, as a tyranny. If, however, it seems to you a desirable thing to have the cities under despotic rule, begin by putting a tyrant over yourselves, and then establish despots in the other states. While you continue yourselves, as you have always been, unacquainted with tyranny, and take such excellent care that Sparta may not suffer from it, to act as you are now doing is to treat your allies unworthily. If you knew what tyranny was as well as ourselves, you would be better advised than you now are in regard to it. (§ 2.) The government at Corinth was once an oligarchy —a single race, called Bacchiadæ, who intermarried only among themselves, held the management of affairs. Now it happened that Amphion, one of these, had a daughter, named Labda, who was lame, and whom therefore none of the Bacchiadæ would consent to marry; so she was taken to wife by Aëtion, son of Echecrates, a man of the township of Petra, who was, however, by descent of the race of the Lapithæ, and of the house of Cæneus. Aëtion, as he had no child, either by this wife or by any other, went to Delphi to consult the oracle concerning the matter. Scarcely had he entered the temple when the Pythoness saluted him in these words—

No one honours thee now, Aëtion, worthy of honour—
Labda shall soon be a mother—her offspring a rock, that will one day
Fall on the kingly race, and right the city of Corinth.

By some chance this address of the oracle to Aëtion came to the ears of the Bacchiadæ, who till then had been unable to perceive the meaning of another earlier prophecy which likewise bore upon Corinth, and pointed to the same event as Aëtion's prediction. It was the following:—

When mid the rocks an eagle shall bear a carnivorous lion,
Mighty and fierce, he shall loosen the limbs of many beneath them—
Brood ye well upon this, all ye Corinthian people,
Ye who dwell by fair Peirênê, and beetling Corinth.

(§ 3.) The Bacchiadæ had possessed this oracle for some time; but they were quite at a loss to know what it meant until they heard the response given to Aëtion; then however they at once perceived its meaning, since the two agreed so well together. Nevertheless, though the bearing of the first prophecy was now clear to them, they remained quiet, being minded to put to death the child which Aëtion was expecting. As soon, therefore, as his wife was delivered, they sent ten of their number to the township where Aëtion lived, with orders to make away with the baby. So the men came to Petra, and went into Aëtion's house, and there asked if they might see the child; and Labda, who knew nothing of their purpose, but thought their inquiries arose from a kindly feeling towards her husband, brought the child, and laid him in the arms of one of them. Now they had agreed by the way that whoever first got hold of the child should dash it against the ground. It happened, however, by a providential chance, that the babe, just as Labda put him into the man's arms, smiled in his face. The man saw the smile, and was touched with pity, so that he could not kill it; he therefore passed it on to his next neighbour, who gave it to a third; and so it went through all the ten without any one choosing to be the murderer. The mother received her child back; and the men went out of the house, and stood near the door, and there blamed and reproached one another; chiefly however accusing the man who had first had the child in his arms, because he had not done as had been agreed upon. At last, after much time had been thus spent, they resolved to go into the house again and all take part in the murder. (§ 4.) But it was fated that evil should come upon Corinth from the progeny of Aëtion; and so it chanced that Labda, as she stood near the door, heard all that the men said to one another, and fearful of their changing their mind, and returning to destroy her baby, she carried him off and hid him in what seemed to her the most unlikely place to be suspected, viz., a 'cypsel' or corn-bin. She knew that if they came back to look for the child, they would search all her house; and so indeed they did, but not finding the child after looking everywhere, they thought it best to go away, and declare to those by whom they had been sent that they had done their bidding. And thus they reported on their return home. (§ 5.) Aëtion's son grew up, and, in remembrance of the danger from which he had escaped, was named Cypselus, after the corn-bin. When he reached to man's estate, he went to Delphi, and on consulting the oracle, received a response which was two-sided. It was the following:—

See there comes to my dwelling a man much favour'd of fortune,
Cypselus, son of Aëtion, and king of the glorious Corinth—
He and his children too, but not his children's children.

Such was the oracle; and Cypselus put so much faith in it that he forthwith made his attempt, and thereby became master of Corinth. Having thus got the tyranny, he showed himself a harsh ruler—many of the Corinthians he drove into banishment, many he deprived of their fortunes, and a still greater number of their lives. (§ 6.) His reign lasted thirty years, and was prosperous to its close; insomuch that he left the government to Periander, his son. This prince at the beginning of his reign was of a milder temper than his father; but after he corresponded by means of messengers with Thrasybulus, tyrant of Miletus, he became even more sanguinary. On one occasion he sent a herald to ask Thrasybulus what mode of government it was safest to set up in order to rule with honour. Thrasybulus led the messenger without the city, and took him into a field of corn, through which he began to walk, while he asked him again and again concerning his coming from Corinth, ever as he went breaking off and throwing away all such ears of corn as over-topped the rest. In this way he went through the whole field, and destroyed all the best and richest part of the crop; then, without a word, he sent the messenger back. On the return of the man to Corinth, Periander was eager to know what Thrasybulus had counselled, but the messenger reported that he had said nothing; and he wondered that Periander had sent him to so strange a man, who seemed to have lost his senses, since he did nothing but destroy his own property. And upon this he told how Thrasybulus had behaved at the interview. (§ 7.) Periander, perceiving what the action meant, and knowing that Thrasybulus advised the destruction of all the leading citizens, treated his subjects from this time forward with the very greatest cruelty. Where Cypselus had spared any, and had neither put them to death nor banished them, Periander completed what his father had left unfinished. One day he stripped all the women of Corinth stark naked, for the sake of his own wife Melissa. He had sent messengers into Thesprotia to consult the oracle of the dead upon the Acheron concerning a pledge which had been given into his charge by a stranger. and Melissa appeared, but refused to speak or tell where the pledge was—'she was chill,' she said, 'having no clothes; the garments buried with her were of no manner of use, since they had not been burnt. And this should be her token to Periander, that what she said was true —the oven was cold when he baked his loaves in it.' When this message was brought him, Periander knew the token; wherefore he straightway made proclamation, that all the wives of the Corinthians should go forth to the temple of Juno. So the women apparelled themselves in their bravest, and went forth, as if to a festival. Then, with the help of his guards, whom he had placed for the purpose, he stripped them one and all, making no difference between the free women and the slaves; and, taking their clothes to a pit, he called on the name of Melissa, and burnt the whole heap. This done, he sent a second time to the oracle; and Melissa's ghost told him where he would find the stranger's pledge. Such, O Lacedæmonians! is tyranny, and such are the deeds which spring from it. We Corinthians marvelled greatly when we first knew of your having sent for Hippias; and now it surprises us still more to hear you speak as you do. We adjure you, by the common gods of Greece, plant not despots in her cities. If however you are determined, if you persist, against all justice, in seeking to restore Hippias—know, at least, that the Corinthians will not approve your conduct."

93. When Sosicles, the deputy from Corinth, had thus spoken, Hippias replied, and, invoking the same gods, he said—"Of a surety the Corinthians will, beyond all others, regret the Pisistratidæ, when the fated days come for them to be distressed by the Athenians." Hippias spoke thus because he knew the prophecies better than any man living. But the rest of the allies, who till Sosicles spoke had remained quiet, when they heard him utter his thoughts thus boldly, all together broke silence, and declared themselves of the same mind; and withal, they conjured the Lacedæmonians "not to revolutionise a Grecian city." And in this way the enterprise came to nought.

94. Hippias hereupon withdrew; and Amyntas the Macedonian offered him the city of Anthemûs, while the Thessalians were willing to give him Iolcôs: but he would accept neither the one nor the other, preferring to go back to Sigêum, which city Pisistratus had taken by force of arms from the Mytilenæans. Pisistratus, when he became master of the place, established there as tyrant his own natural son, Hegesistratus, whose mother was an Argive woman. But this prince was not allowed to enjoy peaceably what his father had made over to him; for during very many years there had been war between the Athenians of Sigêum and the Mytilenæans of the city called Achilleum. They of Mytilênê insisted on having the place restored to them: but the Athenians refused, since they argued that the Æolians had no better claim to the Trojan territory than themselves, or than any of the other Greeks who helped Menelaüs on occasion of the rape of Helen.

95. War accordingly continued, with many and various incidents, whereof the following was one. In a battle which was gained by the Athenians, the poet Alcæus took to flight, and saved himself, but lost his arms, which fell into the hands of the conquerors. They hung them up in the temple of Minerva at Sigêum; and Alcæus made a poem, describing his misadventure to his friend Melanippus, and sent it to him at Mytilênê. The Mytilenæans and Athenians were reconciled by Periander, the son of Cypselus, who was chosen by both parties as

arbiter—he decided that they should each retain that of which they were at the time possessed; and Sigêum passed in this way under the dominion of Athens.

96. On the return of Hippias to Asia from Lacedæmon, he moved heaven and earth to set Artaphernes against the Athenians, and did all that lay in his power to bring Athens into subjection to himself and Darius. So when the Athenians learnt what he was about, they sent envoys to Sardis, and exhorted the Persians not to lend an ear to the Athenian exiles. Artaphernes told them in reply, "that if they wished to remain safe, they must receive back Hippias." The Athenians, when this answer was reported to them, determined not to consent, and therefore made up their minds to be at open enmity with the Persians.

97. The Athenians had come to this decision, and were already in bad odour with the Persians, when Aristagoras the Milesian, dismissed from Sparta by Cleomenes the Lacedæmonian, arrived at Athens. He knew that, after Sparta, Athens was the most powerful of the Grecian states. Accordingly he appeared before the people, and, as he had done at Sparta, spoke to them of the good things which there were in Asia, and of the Persian mode of fight—how they used neither shield nor spear, and were very easy to conquer. All this he urged, and reminded them also that Miletus was a colony from Athens, and therefore ought to receive their succour, since they were so powerful—and in the earnestness of his entreaties, he cared little what he promised—till, at the last, he prevailed and won them over. It seems indeed to be easier to deceive a multitude than one man—for Aristagoras, though he failed to impose on Cleomenes the Lacedæmonian, succeeded with the Athenians, who were thirty thousand. Won by his persuasions, they voted that twenty ships should be sent to the aid of the Ionians, under the command of Melanthius, one of the citizens, a man of mark in every way. These ships were the beginning of mischief both to the Greeks and to the barbarians.

98. Aristagoras sailed away in advance, and when he reached Miletus, devised a plan, from which no manner of advantage could possibly accrue to the Ionians;—indeed, in forming it, he did not aim at their benefit, but his sole wish was to annoy King Darius. He sent a messenger into Phrygia to those Pæonians who had been led away captive by Megabazus from the river Strymon, and who now dwelt by

themselves in Phrygia, having a tract of land and a hamlet of their own. This man, when he reached the Pæonians, spoke thus to them:—

"Men of Pæonia, Aristagoras, king of Miletus, has sent me to you, to inform you that you may now escape, if you choose to follow the advice he proffers. All Ionia has revolted from the king; and the way is open to you to return to your own land. You have only to contrive to reach the sea-coast; the rest shall be our business."

When the Pæonians heard this, they were exceedingly rejoiced, and, taking with them their wives and children, they made all speed to the coast; a few only remaining in Phrygia through fear. The rest, having reached the sea, crossed over to Chios, where they had just landed, when a great troop of Persian horse came following upon their heels, and seeking to overtake them. Not succeeding, however, they sent a message across to Chios, and begged the Pæonians to come back again. These last refused, and were conveyed by the Chians from Chios to Lesbos, and by the Lesbians thence to Doriscus; from which place they made their way on foot to Pæonia.

99. The Athenians now arrived with a fleet of twenty sail, and brought also in their company five triremes of the Eretrians; which had joined the expedition, not so much out of goodwill towards Athens, as to pay a debt which they already owed to the people of Miletus. For in the old war between the Chalcideans and Eretrians, the Milesians fought on the Eretrian side throughout, while the Chalcideans had the help of the Samian people. Aristagoras, on their arrival, assembled the rest of his allies, and proceeded to attack Sardis, not however leading the army in person, but appointing to the command his own brother Charopinus and Hermophantus, one of the citizens, while he himself remained behind in Miletus.

100. The Ionians sailed with this fleet to Ephesus, and, leaving their ships at Coressus in the Ephesian territory, took guides from the city, and went up the country with a great host. They marched along the course of the river Caÿster, and, crossing over the ridge of Tmôlus, came down upon Sardis and took it, no man opposing them;—the whole city fell into their hands, except only the citadel, which Artaphernes defended in person, having with him no contemptible force.

101. Though, however, they took the city, they did not succeed in plundering it; for, as the houses in Sardis were most of them built of reeds, and even the few which were of brick had a reed thatching for their roof, one of them was no sooner fired by a soldier than the flames ran speedily from house to house, and spread over the whole place. As the fire raged, the Lydians and such Persians as were in the city, inclosed on every side by the flames, which had seized all the skirts of the town, and finding themselves unable to get out, came in crowds into the market-place, and gathered themselves upon the banks of the Pactôlus. This stream, which comes down from Mount Tmôlus, and brings the Sardians a quantity of gold-dust, runs directly through the market place of Sardis, and joins the Hermus, before that river reaches the sea. So the Lydians and Persians, brought together in this way in the market-place and about the Pactôlus, were forced to stand on their defence; and the Ionians, when they saw the enemy in part resisting, in part pouring towards them in dense crowds, took fright, and drawing off to the ridge which is called Tmôlus, when night came, went back to their ships.

102. Sardis however was burnt, and, among other buildings, a temple of the native goddess Cybelé was destroyed; which was the reason afterwards alleged by the Persians for setting on fire the temples of the Greeks. As soon as what had happened was known, all the Persians who were stationed on this side the Halys drew together, and brought help to the Lydians. Finding however, when they arrived, that the Ionians had already withdrawn from Sardis, they set off, and, following close upon their track, came up with them at Ephesus. The Ionians drew out against them in battle array; and a fight ensued, wherein the Greeks had very greatly the worse. Vast numbers were slain by the Persians: among other men of note, they killed the captain of the Eretrians, a certain Eualcidas, a man who had gained crowns at the Games, and received much praise from Simonides the Cean. Such as made their escape from the battle, dispersed among the several cities.

103. So ended this encounter. Afterwards the Athenians quite forsook the Ionians, and, though Aristagoras besought them much by his ambassadors, refused to give him any further help. Still the Ionians, notwithstanding this desertion, continued unceasingly their preparations to carry on the war against the Persian king, which their late conduct towards him

had rendered unavoidable. Sailing into the Hellespont, they brought Byzantium, and all the other cities in that quarter, under their sway. Again, quitting the Hellespont, they went to Caria, and won the greater part of the Carians to their side; while Caunus, which had formerly refused to join with them, after the burning of Sardis, came over likewise.

104. All the Cyprians too, excepting those of Amathûs, of their own proper motion espoused the Ionian cause. The occasion of their revolting from the Medes was the following. There was a certain Onesilus, younger brother of Gorgus, king of Salamis, and son of Chersis, who was son of Siromus, and grandson of Evelthon. This man had often in former times entreated Gorgus to rebel against the king; but, when he heard of the revolt of the Ionians, he left him no peace with his importunity. As, however, Gorgus would not hearken to him, he watched his occasion, and when his brother had gone outside the town, he with his partisans closed the gates upon him. Gorgus, thus deprived of his city, fled to the Medes; and Onesilus, being now king of Salamis, sought to bring about a revolt of the whole of Cyprus. All were prevailed on except the Amathusians, who refused to listen to him; whereupon Onesilus sate down before Amathûs, and laid siege to it.

105. While Onesilus was engaged in the siege of Amathûs, King Darius received tidings of the taking and burning of Sardis by the Athenians and Ionians; and at the same time he learnt that the author of the league, the man by whom the whole matter had been planned and contrived, was Aristagoras the Milesian. It is said that he no sooner understood what had happened, than, laying aside all thought concerning the Ionians, who would, he was sure, pay dear for their rebellion, he asked, "Who the Athenians were?" and, being informed, called for his bow, and placing an arrow on the string, shot upward into the sky, saying, as he let fly the shaft—"Grant me, Jupiter, to revenge myself on the Athenians!" After this speech, he bade one of his servants every day, when his dinner was spread, three times repeat these words to him—"Master, remember the Athenians."

106. Then he summoned into his presence Histiæus of Miletus, whom he had kept at his court for so long a time; and on his appearance addressed him thus—"I am told, O Histiæus, that thy lieutenant, to whom thou hast given Miletus in charge, has raised a rebellion against me. He has brought men from the other continent to contend with me, and, prevailing on the Ionians—whose conduct I shall know how to recompense—to join with this force, he has robbed me of Sardis! Is this as it should be, thinkest thou? Or can it have been done without thy knowledge and advice? Beware lest it be found hereafter that the blame of these acts is thine."

Histiæus answered—"What words are these, O king, to which thou hast given utterance? I advise aught from which unpleasantness of any kind, little or great, should come to thee! What could I gain by so doing? Or what is there that I lack now? Have I not all that thou hast, and am I not thought worthy to partake all thy counsels? If my lieutenant has indeed done as thou sayest, be sure he has done it all of his own head. For my part, I do not think it can really be that the Milesians and my lieutenant have raised a rebellion against thee. But if they have indeed committed aught to thy hurt, and the tidings are true which have come to thee, judge thou how ill-advised thou wert to remove me from the sea-coast. The Ionians, it seems, have waited till I was no longer in sight, and then sought to execute that which they long ago desired; whereas, if I had been there, not a single city would have stirred. Suffer me then to hasten at my best speed to Ionia, that I may place matters there upon their former footing, and deliver up to thee the deputy of Miletus, who has caused all the troubles. Having managed this business to thy heart's content, I swear by all the gods of thy royal house, I will not put off the clothes in which I reach Ionia till I have made Sardinia, the biggest island in the world, thy tributary."

107. Histiæus spoke thus, wishing to deceive the king; and Darius, persuaded by his words, let him go; only bidding him be sure to do as he had promised, and afterwards come back to Susa.

108. In the meantime—while the tidings of the burning of Sardis were reaching the king, and Darius was shooting the arrow and having the conference with Histiæus, and the latter, by permission of Darius, was hastening down to the sea—in Cyprus the following events took place. Tidings came to Onesilus, the Salaminian, who was still besieging Amathûs, that a certain Artybius, a Persian, was looked for to arrive in Cyprus with a great Persian armament. So Onesilus, when the news reached him, sent off heralds to all parts of Ionia, and besought the Ionians to give him

aid. After brief deliberation, these last in full force passed over into the island; and the Persians about the same time crossed in their ships from Cilicia, and proceeded by land to attack Salamis; while the Phœnicians, with the fleet, sailed round the promontory which goes by the name of "the Keys of Cyprus."

109. In this posture of affairs the princes of Cyprus called together the captains of the Ionians, and thus addressed them:—

"Men of Ionia, we Cyprians leave it to you to choose whether you will fight with the Persians or with the Phœnicians. If it be your pleasure to try your strength on land against the Persians, come on shore at once, and array yourselves for the battle; we will then embark aboard your ships and engage the Phœnicians by sea. If, on the other hand, ye prefer to encounter the Phœnicians, let that be your task: only be sure, whichever part you choose, to acquit yourselves so that Ionia and Cyprus, so far as depends on you, may preserve their freedom."

The Ionians made answer—"The commonwealth of Ionia sent us here to guard the sea, not to make over our ships to you, and engage with the Persians on shore. We will therefore keep the post which has been assigned to us, and seek therein to be of some service. Do you, remembering what you suffered when you were the slaves of the Medes, behave like brave warriors."

110. Such was the reply of the Ionians. Not long afterwards the Persians advanced into the plain before Salamis, and the Cyprian kings ranged their troops in order of battle against them, placing them so that while the rest of the Cyprians were drawn up against the auxiliaries of the enemy, the choicest troops of the Salaminians and the Solians were set to oppose the Persians. At the same time Onesilus, of his own accord, took post opposite to Artybius, the Persian general.

111. Now Artybius rode a horse which had been trained to rear up against a foot-soldier. Onesilus, informed of this, called to him his shieldbearer, who was a Carian by nation, a man well skilled in war, and of daring courage; and thus addressed him:—"I hear," he said, "that the horse which Artybius rides, rears up and attacks with his fore legs and teeth the man against whom his rider urges him. Consider quickly therefore and tell me which wilt thou undertake to encounter, the steed or the rider?" Then the squire answered him, "Both, my liege, or either, am I ready to un-

dertake, and there is nothing that I will shrink from at thy bidding. But I will tell thee what seems to me to make most for thy interests. As thou art a prince and a general, I think thou shouldest engage with one who is himself both a prince and also a general. For then, if thou slayest thine adversary, 'twill redound to thine honour, and if he slays thee (which may Heaven forefend!), yet to fall by the hand of a worthy foe makes death lose half its horror. To us, thy followers, leave his war-horse and his retinue. And have thou no fear of the horse's tricks. I warrant that this is the last time he will stand up against any one."

112. Thus spake the Carian; and shortly after, the two hosts joined battle both by sea and land. And here it chanced that by sea the Ionians, who that day fought as they have never done either before or since, defeated the Phœnicians, the Samians especially distinguishing themselves. Meanwhile the combat had begun on land, and the two armies were engaged in a sharp struggle, when thus it fell out in the matter of the generals. Artybius, astride upon his horse, charged down upon Onesilus, who, as he had agreed with his shieldbearer, aimed his blow at the rider; the horse reared and placed his fore feet upon the shield of Onesilus, when the Carian cut at him with a reaping-hook, and severed the two legs from the body. The horse fell upon the spot, and Artybius, the Persian general, with him.

113. In the thick of the fight, Stesanor, tyrant of Curium, who commanded no inconsiderable body of troops, went over with them to the enemy. On this desertion of the Curians —Argive colonists, if report says true—forthwith the war-chariots of the Salaminians followed the example set them, and went over likewise; whereupon victory declared in favour of the Persians; and the army of the Cyprians being routed, vast numbers were slain, and among them Onesilus, the son of Chersis, who was the author of the revolt, and Aristocyprus, king of the Solians. This Aristocyprus was son of Philocyprus, whom Solon the Athenian, when he visited Cyprus, praised in his poems beyond all other sovereigns.

114. The Amathusians, because Onesilus had laid siege to their town, cut the head off his corpse, and took it with them to Amathûs, where it was set up over the gates. Here it hung till it became hollow; whereupon a swarm of bees took possession of it, and filled it with a honeycomb. On seeing this the Amathusians consulted the oracle, and were com-

manded "to take down the head and bury it, and thenceforth to regard Onesilus as a hero, and offer sacrifice to him year by year; so it would go the better with them." And to this day the Amathusians do as they were then bidden.

115. As for the Ionians who had gained the sea-fight, when they found that the affairs of Onesilus were utterly lost and ruined, and that siege was laid to all the cities of Cyprus excepting Salamis, which the inhabitants had surrendered to Gorgus, the former king— forthwith they left Cyprus, and sailed away home. Of the cities which were besieged, Soli held out the longest: the Persians took it by undermining the wall in the fifth month from the beginning of the siege.

116. Thus, after enjoying a year of freedom, the Cyprians were enslaved for the second time. Meanwhile Daurises, who was married to one of the daughters of Darius, together with Hymeas, Otanes, and other Persian captains, who were likewise married to daughters of the king, after pursuing the Ionians who had fought at Sardis, defeating them, and driving them to their ships, divided their efforts against the different cities, and proceeded in succession to take and sack each one of them.

117. Daurises attacked the towns upon the Hellespont, and took in as many days the five cities of Dardanus, Abydos, Percôté, Lampsacus, and Pæsus. From Pæsus he marched against Parium; but on his way receiving intelligence that the Carians had made common cause with the Ionians, and thrown off the Persian yoke, he turned round, and, leaving the Hellespont, marched away towards Caria.

118. The Carians by some chance got information of this movement before Daurises arrived, and drew together their strength to a place called "the White Columns," which is on the river Marsyas, a stream running from the Idrian country, and emptying itself into the Mæander. Here when they were met, many plans were put forth; but the best, in my judgment, was that of Pixodarus, the son of Mausôlus, a Cindyan, who was married to a daughter of Syennesis, the Cilician king. His advice was that the Carians should cross the Mæander, and fight with the river at their back; that so, all chance of flight being cut off, they might be forced to stand their ground, and have their natural courage raised to a still higher pitch. His opinion, however, did not prevail; it was thought best to make the enemy have the Mæander behind them; that so, if they were defeated in the battle and put

to flight, they might have no retreat open, but be driven headlong into the river.

119. The Persians soon afterwards approached, and, crossing the Mæander, engaged the Carians upon the banks of the Marsyas; where for a long time the battle was stoutly contested, but at last the Carians were defeated, being overpowered by numbers. On the side of the Persians there fell 2000, while the Carians had not fewer than 10,000 slain. Such as escaped from the field of battle collected together at Labranda, in the vast precinct of Jupiter Stratius—a deity worshipped only by the Carians—and in the sacred grove of planetrees. Here they deliberated as to the best means of saving themselves, doubting whether they would fare better if they gave themselves up to the Persians, or if they abandoned Asia for ever.

120. As they were debating these matters a body of Milesians and allies came to their assistance; whereupon the Carians, dismissing their former thoughts, prepared themselves afresh for war, and on the approach of the Persians gave them battle a second time. They were defeated, however, with still greater loss than before; and while all the troops engaged suffered severely, the blow fell with most force on the Milesians.

121. The Carians, some while after, repaired their ill fortune in another action. Understanding that the Persians were about to attack their cities, they laid an ambush for them on the road which leads to Pedasus; the Persians, who were making a night-march, fell into the trap, and the whole army was destroyed, together with the generals, Daurises, Amorges, and Sisimaces: Myrsus too, the son of Gyges, was killed at the same time. The leader of the ambush was Heraclides, the son of Ibanôlis, a man of Mylasa. Such was the way in which these Persians perished.

122. In the meantime Hymeas, who was likewise one of those by whom the Ionians were pursued after their attack on Sardis, directing his course towards the Propontis, took Cius, a city of Mysia. Learning, however, that Daurises had left the Hellespont, and was gone into Caria, he in his turn quitted the Propontis, and marching with the army under his command to the Hellespont, reduced all the Æolians of the Troad, and likewise conquered the Gergithæ, a remnant of the ancient Teucrians: He did not, however, quit the Troad, but, after gaining these successes, was himself carried off by disease.

123. After his death, which happened as I have related, Artaphernes, the satrap of Sardis, and Otanes, the third general, were directed to undertake the conduct of the war against Ionia and the neighbouring Æolis. By them Clazomenæ in the former, and Cymé in the latter, were recovered.

124. As the cities fell one after another, Aristagoras the Milesian (who was in truth, as he now plainly showed, a man of but little courage), notwithstanding that it was he who had caused the disturbances in Ionia and made so great a commotion, began, seeing his danger, to look about for means of escape. Being convinced that it was in vain to endeavour to overcome King Darius, he called his brothers-in-arms together, and laid before them the following project:—" 'Twould be well," he said, "to have some place of refuge, in case they were driven out of Miletus. Should he go out at the head of a colony to Sardinia, or should he sail to Myrcinus in Edonia, which Histiæus had received as a gift from King Darius, and had begun to fortify?"

125. To this question of Aristagoras, Hecatæus, the historian, son of Hegesander, made answer that in his judgment neither place was suitable. "Aristagoras should build a fort," he said, "in the island of Leros, and, if driven from Miletus, should go there and bide his time; from Leros attacks might readily be made, and he might re-establish himself in Miletus." Such was the advice given by Hecatæus.

126. Aristagoras, however, was bent on retiring to Myrcinus. Accordingly, he put the government of Miletus into the hands of one of the chief citizens, named Pythagoras, and, taking with him all who liked to go, sailed to Thrace, and there made himself master of the place in question. From thence he proceeded to attack the Thracians; but here he was cut off with his whole army, while besieging a city whose defenders were anxious to accept terms of surrender.

The Sixth Book, Entitled
ERATO

1. ARISTAGORAS, the author of the Ionian revolt, perished in the way which I have described. Meanwhile Histiæus, tyrant of Miletus, who had been allowed by Darius to leave Susa, came down to Sardis. On his arrival, being asked by Artaphernes, the Sardian satrap, what he thought was the reason that the Ionians had rebelled, he made answer that he could not conceive, and it had astonished him greatly, pretending to be quite unconscious of the whole business. Artaphernes, however, who perceived that he was dealing dishonestly, and who had in fact full knowledge of the whole history of the outbreak, said to him, "I will tell thee how the case stands, Histiæus: this shoe is of thy stitching; Aristagoras has but put it on."

2. Such was the remark made by Artaphernes concerning the rebellion. Histiæus, alarmed at the knowledge which he displayed, so soon as night fell, fled away to the coast. Thus he forfeited his word to Darius; for though he had pledged himself to bring Sardinia, the biggest island in the whole world, under the Persian yoke, he in reality sought to obtain the direction of the war against the king. Crossing over to Chios, he was there laid in bonds by the inhabitants, who accused him of intending some mischief against them in the interest of Darius. However, when the whole truth was laid before them, and they found that Histiæus was in reality a foe to the king, they forthwith set him at large again.

3. After this the Ionians inquired of him for what reason he had so strongly urged Aristagoras to revolt from the king, thereby doing their nation so ill a service. In reply, he took good care not to disclose to them the real cause, but told them that King Darius had intended to remove the Phœnicians from their own country, and place them in Ionia, while he planted the Ionians in Phœnicia, and that it was for this reason he sent Aristagoras the order. Now it was not true that the king had entertained any such intention, but Histiæus succeeded hereby in arousing the fears of the Ionians.

4. After this, Histiæus, by means of a certain Hermippus, a native of Atarneus, sent letters to many of the Persians in Sardis, who had before held some discourse with him concerning a revolt. Hermippus, however, instead of conveying them to the persons to whom they were addressed, delivered them into the hands of Artaphernes, who, perceiving what was on foot, commanded Hermippus to deliver the letters according to their addresses, and then bring him back the answers which were sent to Histiæus. The traitors being in this way discovered, Artaphernes put a number of Persians to death, and caused a commotion in Sardis.

5. As for Histiæus, when his hopes in this matter were disappointed, he persuaded the Chians to carry him back to Miletus; but the Milesians were too well pleased at having got quit of Aristagoras to be anxious to receive another tyrant into their country; besides which they had now tasted liberty. They therefore opposed his return; and when he endeavoured to force an entrance during the night, one of the inhabitants even wounded him in the thigh. Having been thus rejected from his country, he went back to Chios; whence, after failing in an attempt to induce the Chians to give him ships, he crossed over to Mytilênê, where he succeeded in obtaining vessels from the Lesbians. They fitted out a squadron of eight triremes, and sailed with him to the Hellespont, where they took up their station, and proceeded to seize all the vessels which passed out from the Euxine, unless the crews declared themselves ready to obey his orders.

6. While Histiæus and the Mytilenæans were thus employed, Miletus was expecting an attack from a vast armament, which comprised both a fleet and also a land force. The Persian captains had drawn their several detachments together, and formed them into a single army; and had resolved to pass over all the other cities, which they regarded as of lesser account, and to march straight on Miletus. Of the naval states, Phœnicia showed the greatest zeal; but the fleet was composed likewise of the Cyprians (who had so lately been brought under), the Cilicians, and also the Egyptians.

7. While the Persians were thus making preparations against Miletus and Ionia, the Ionians, informed of their intent, sent their deputies to the Panionium, and held a council upon the posture of their affairs. Hereat it was determined that no land force should be collected to oppose the Persians, but that the Milesians should be left to defend their own walls as they could; at the same time they agreed that the whole naval force of the states, not excepting a single ship, should be equipped, and should muster at Ladé, a small island lying off Miletus—to give battle on behalf of the place.

8. Presently the Ionians began to assemble in their ships, and with them came the Æolians of Lesbos; and in this way they marshalled their line:—The wing towards the east was formed of the Milesians themselves, who furnished eighty ships; next to them came the Prienians with twelve, and the Myusians with three ships; after the Myusians were stationed the Teians, whose ships were seventeen; then the Chians, who furnished a hundred. The Erythræans and Phocæans followed, the former with eight, the latter with three ships; beyond the Phocæans were the Lesbians, furnishing seventy; last of all came the Samians, forming the western wing, and furnishing sixty vessels. The fleet amounted in all to three hundred and fifty-three triremes. Such was the number on the Ionian side.

9. On the side of the barbarians the number of vessels was six hundred. These assembled off the coast of Milesia, while the land army collected upon the shore; but the leaders, learning the strength of the Ionian fleet, began to fear lest they might fail to defeat them, in which case, not having the mastery at sea, they would be unable to reduce Miletus, and might in consequence receive rough treatment at the hands of Darius. So when they thought of all these things, they resolved on the following course:—Calling together the Ionian tyrants, who had fled to the Medes for refuge when Aristagoras deposed them from their governments, and who were now in camp, having joined in the expedition against Miletus, the Persians addressed them thus: "Men of Ionia, now is the fit time to show your zeal for the house of the king. Use your best efforts, every one of you, to detach your fellow-countrymen from the general body. Hold forth to them the promise that, if they submit, no harm shall happen to them on account of their rebellion; their temples shall not be burnt, nor any of their private buildings; neither shall they be treated with greater harshness than before the outbreak. But if they refuse to yield, and determine to try the chance of a battle, threaten them with the fate which shall assuredly overtake them in that case. Tell them, when they are vanquished in fight, they shall be enslaved; their boys shall be made eunuchs, and their maidens transported to Bactra; while their country shall be delivered into the hands of foreigners."

10. Thus spake the Persians. The Ionian tyrants sent accordingly by night to their respective citizens, and reported the words of the Persians; but the people were all staunch, and refused to betray their countrymen, those of each state thinking that they alone had had overtures made to them. Now these events happened on the first appearance of the Persians before Miletus.

11. Afterwards, while the Ionian fleet was still assembled at Ladé, councils were held, and speeches made by divers persons—among the rest by Dionysius, the Phocæan captain, who thus expressed himself:—"Our affairs hang on the razor's edge, men of Ionia, either to be free or to be slaves; and slaves, too, who have shown themselves runaways. Now then you have to choose whether you will endure hardships, and so for the present lead a life of toil, but thereby gain ability to overcome your enemies and establish your own freedom; or whether you will persist in this slothfulness and disorder, in which case I see no hope of your escaping the king's vengeance for your rebellion. I beseech you, be persuaded by me, and trust yourselves to my guidance. Then, if the gods only hold the balance fairly between us, I undertake to say that our foes will either decline a battle, or, if they fight, suffer complete discomfiture."

12. These words prevailed with the Ionians,

and forthwith they committed themselves to Dionysius; whereupon he proceeded every day to make the ships move in column, and the rowers ply their oars, and exercise themselves in breaking the line; while the marines were held under arms, and the vessels were kept, till evening fell, upon their anchors, so that the men had nothing but toil from morning even to night. Seven days did the Ionians continue obedient, and do whatsoever he bade them; but on the eighth day, worn out by the hardness of the work and the heat of the sun, and quite unaccustomed to such fatigues, they began to confer together, and to say one to another, "What god have we offended to bring upon ourselves such a punishment as this? Fools and distracted that we were, to put ourselves into the hands of this Phocæan braggart, who does but furnish three ships to the fleet! He, now that he has got us, plagues us in the most desperate fashion; many of us, in consequence, have fallen sick already—many more expect to follow. We had better suffer anything rather than these hardships; even the slavery with which we are threatened, however harsh, can be no worse than our present thraldom. Come, let us refuse him obedience." So saying, they forthwith ceased to obey his orders, and pitched their tents, as if they had been soldiers, upon the island, where they reposed under the shade all day, and refused to go aboard the ships and train themselves.

13. Now when the Samian captains perceived what was taking place, they were more inclined than before to accept the terms which Æaces, the son of Syloson, had been authorised by the Persians to offer them, on condition of their deserting from the confederacy. For they saw that all was disorder among the Ionians, and they felt also that it was hopeless to contend with the power of the king; since if they defeated the fleet which had been sent against them, they knew that another would come five times as great. So they took advantage of the occasion which now offered, and as soon as ever they saw the Ionians refuse to work, hastened gladly to provide for the safety of their temples and their properties. This Æaces, who made the overtures to the Samians, was the son of Syloson, and grandson of the earlier Æaces. He had formerly been tyrant of Samos, but was ousted from his government by Aristagoras the Milesian, at the same time with the other tyrants of the Ionians.

14. The Phœnicians soon afterwards sailed to the attack; and the Ionians likewise put themselves in line, and went out to meet them. When they had now neared one another, and joined battle, which of the Ionians fought like brave men and which like cowards, I cannot declare with any certainty, for charges are brought on all sides; but the tale goes that the Samians, according to the agreement which they had made with Æaces, hoisted sail, and quitting their post bore away for Samos, except eleven ships, whose captains gave no heed to the orders of the commanders, but remained and took part in the battle. The state of Samos, in consideration of this action, granted to these men, as an acknowledgment of their bravery, the honour of having their names, and the names of their fathers, inscribed upon a pillar, which still stands in the market-place. The Lesbians also, when they saw the Samians, who were drawn up next them, begin to flee, themselves did the like; and the example, once set, was followed by the greater number of the Ionians.

15. Of those who remained and fought, none were so rudely handled as the Chians, who displayed prodigies of valour, and disdained to play the part of cowards. They furnished to the common fleet, as I mentioned above, one hundred ships, having each of them forty armed citizens, and those picked men, on board; and when they saw the greater portion of the allies betraying the common cause, they for their part, scorning to imitate the base conduct of these traitors, although they were left almost alone and unsupported, a very few friends continuing to stand by them, notwithstanding went on with the fight, and ofttimes cut the line of the enemy, until at last, after they had taken very many of their adversaries' ships, they ended by losing more than half of their own. Hereupon, with the remainder of their vessels, the Chians fled away to their own country.

16. As for such of their ships as were damaged and disabled, these, being pursued by the enemy, made straight for Mycalé, where the crews ran them ashore, and abandoning them began their march along the continent. Happening in their way upon the territory of Ephesus, they essayed to cross it; but here a dire misfortune befell them. It was night, and the Ephesian women chanced to be engaged in celebrating the Thesmophoria—the previous calamity of the Chians had not been heard of —so when the Ephesians saw their country invaded by an armed band, they made no question of the new-comers being robbers who pur-

posed to carry off their women; and accordingly they marched out against them in full force, and slew them all. Such were the misfortunes which befell them of Chios.

17. Dionysius, the Phocæan, when he perceived that all was lost, having first captured three ships from the enemy, himself took to flight. He would not, however, return to Phocæa, which he well knew must fall again, like the rest of Ionia, under the Persian yoke; but straightway, as he was, he set sail for Phœnicia, and there sunk a number of merchantmen, and gained a great booty; after which he directed his course to Sicily, where he established himself as a corsair, and plundered the Carthaginians and Tyrrhenians, but did no harm to the Greeks.

18. The Persians, when they had vanquished the Ionians in the sea-fight, besieged Miletus both by land and sea, driving mines under the walls, and making use of every known device, until at length they took both the citadel and the town, six years from the time when the revolt first broke out under Aristagoras. All the inhabitants of the city they reduced to slavery, and thus the event tallied with the announcement which had been made by the oracle.

19. For once upon a time, when the Argives had sent to Delphi to consult the god about the safety of their own city, a prophecy was given them, in which others besides themselves were interested; for while it bore in part upon the fortunes of Argos, it touched in a by-clause the fate of the men of Miletus. I shall set down the portion which concerned the Argives when I come to that part of my History, mentioning at present only the passage in which the absent Milesians were spoken of. This passage was as follows:—

Then shalt thou, Miletus, so oft the contriver of evil,
Be, thyself, to many a feast and an excellent booty:
Then shall thy matrons wash the feet of long-haired masters—
Others shall then possess our lov'd Didymian temple.

Such a fate now befell the Milesians; for the Persians, who wore their hair long, after killing most of the men, made the women and children slaves; and the sanctuary at Didyma, the oracle no less than the temple was plundered and burnt; of the riches whereof I have made frequent mention in other parts of my History.

20. Those of the Milesians whose lives were spared, being carried prisoners to Susa, received no ill treatment at the hands of King Darius, but were established by him in Ampé, a city on the shores of the Erythræan sea, near the spot where the Tigris flows into it. Miletus itself, and the plain about the city, were kept by the Persians for themselves, while the hill-country was assigned to the Carians of Pedasus.

21. And now the Sybarites, who after the loss of their city occupied Laüs and Scidrus, failed duly to return the former kindness of the Milesians. For these last, when Sybaris was taken by the Crotoniats, made a great mourning, all of them, youths as well as men, shaving their heads; since Miletus and Sybaris were, of all the cities whereof we have any knowledge, the two most closely united to one another. The Athenians, on the other hand, showed themselves beyond measure afflicted at the fall of Miletus, in many ways expressing their sympathy, and especially by their treatment of Phrynichus. For when this poet brought out upon the stage his drama of the Capture of Miletus, the whole theatre burst into tears; and the people sentenced him to pay a fine of a thousand drachms, for recalling to them their own misfortunes. They likewise made a law that no one should ever again exhibit that piece.

22. Thus was Miletus bereft of its inhabitants. In Samos the people of the richer sort were much displeased with the doings of the captains, and the dealings they had had with the Medes; they therefore held a council, very shortly after the sea-fight, and resolved that they would not remain to become the slaves of Æaces and the Persians, but before the tyrant set foot in their country, would sail away and found a colony in another land. Now it chanced that about this time the Zanclæans of Sicily had sent ambassadors to the Ionians, and invited them to Kalé-Acté, where they wished an Ionian city to be founded. This place, Kalé-Acté (or the Fair Strand) as it is called, is in the country of the Sicilians, and is situated in the part of Sicily which looks towards Tyrrhenia. The offer thus made to all the Ionians was embraced only by the Samians, and by such of the Milesians as had contrived to effect their escape.

23. Hereupon this is what ensued. The Samians on their voyage reached the country of the Epizephyrian Locrians, at a time when the Zanclæans and their king Scythas were engaged in the siege of a Sicilian town which they hoped to take. Anaxilaüs, tyrant of Rhe-

gium, who was on ill terms with the Zanclæans, knowing how matters stood, made application to the Samians, and persuaded them
to give up the thought of Kalé-Acté, the place
to which they were bound, and to seize Zanclé
itself, which was left without men. The Samians followed this counsel and possessed
themselves of the town; which the Zanclæans
no sooner heard than they hurried to the rescue, calling to their aid Hippocrates, tyrant of
Gela, who was one of their allies. Hippocrates
came with his army to their assistance; but on
his arrival he seized Scythas, the Zanclæan
king, who had just lost his city, and sent him
away in chains, together with his brother
Pythogenes, to the town of Inycus; after which
he came to an understanding with the Samians, exchanged oaths with them, and agreed
to betray the people of Zanclé. The reward of
his treachery was to be one-half of the goods
and chattels, including slaves, which the town
contained, and all that he could find in the
open country. Upon this Hippocrates seized
and bound the greater number of the Zanclæans as slaves; delivering, however, into the
hands of the Samians three hundred of the
principal citizens, to be slaughtered; but the
Samians spared the lives of these persons.

24. Scythas, the king of the Zanclæans, made
his escape from Inycus, and fled to Himera;
whence he passed into Asia, and went up to
the court of Darius. Darius thought him the
most upright of all the Greeks to whom he
afforded a refuge; for with the king's leave he
paid a visit to Sicily, and thence returned back
to Persia, where he lived in great comfort, and
died by a natural death at an advanced age.

25. Thus did the Samians escape the yoke
of the Medes, and possess themselves without
any trouble of Zanclé, a most beautiful city. At
Samos itself the Phœnicians, after the fight
which had Miletus for its prize was over, re-
established Æaces, the son of Syloson, upon his
throne. This they did by the command of the
Persians, who looked upon Æaces as one who
had rendered them a high service and therefore deserved well at their hands. They likewise spared the Samians, on account of the
desertion of their vessels, and did not burn
either their city or their temples, as they did
those of the other rebels. Immediately after the
fall of Miletus the Persians recovered Caria,
bringing some of the cities over by force, while
others submitted of their own accord.

26. Meanwhile tidings of what had befallen
Miletus reached Histiæus the Milesian, who
was still at Byzantium, employed in intercept-
ing the Ionian merchantmen as they issued
from the Euxine. Histiæus had no sooner heard
the news than he gave the Hellespont in charge
to Bisaltes, son of Apollophanes, a native of
Abydos, and himself, at the head of his Lesbians, set sail for Chios. One of the Chian garrisons which opposed him he engaged at a
place called "The Hollows," situated in the
Chian territory, and of these he slaughtered a
vast number; afterwards, by the help of his
Lesbians, he reduced all the rest of the Chians,
who were weakened by their losses in the sea-
fight, Polichné, a city of Chios, serving him as
head-quarters.

27. It mostly happens that there is some
warning when great misfortunes are about to
befall a state or nation; and so it was in this
instance, for the Chians had previously had
some strange tokens sent to them. A choir of
a hundred of their youths had been despatched
to Delphi; and of these only two had returned;
the remaining ninety-eight having been carried off by a pestilence. Likewise, about the
same time, and very shortly before the sea-
fight, the roof of a school-house had fallen in
upon a number of their boys, who were at
lessons; and out of a hundred and twenty
children there was but one left alive. Such were
the signs which God sent to warn them. It
was very shortly afterwards that the sea-fight
happened, which brought the city down upon
its knees; and after the sea-fight came the
attack of Histiæus and his Lesbians, to whom
the Chians, weakened as they were, furnished
an easy conquest.

28. Histiæus now led a numerous army,
composed of Ionians and Æolians, against
Thasos, and had laid siege to the place when
news arrived that the Phœnicians were about
to quit Miletus and attack the other cities of
Ionia. On hearing this, Histiæus raised the
siege of Thasos, and hastened to Lesbos with
all his forces. There his army was in great
straits for want of food; whereupon Histiæus
left Lesbos and went across to the mainland,
intending to cut the crops which were growing
in the Atarnean territory, and likewise in the
plain of the Caïcus, which belonged to Mysia.
Now it chanced that a certain Persian named
Harpagus was in these regions at the head of
an army of no little strength. He, when Histiæus landed, marched out to meet him, and
engaging with his forces destroyed the greater number of them, and took Histiæus himself
prisoner.

29. Histiæus fell into the hands of the Persians in the following manner. The Greeks and Persians engaged at Malêna, in the region of Atarneus; and the battle was for a long time stoutly contested, till at length the cavalry came up, and, charging the Greeks, decided the conflict. The Greeks fled; and Histiæus, who thought that Darius would not punish his fault with death, showed how he loved his life by the following conduct. Overtaken in his flight by one of the Persians, who was about to run him through, he cried aloud in the Persian tongue that he was Histiæus the Milesian.

30. Now, had he been taken straightway before King Darius, I verily believe that he would have received no hurt, but the king would have freely forgiven him. Artaphernes, however, satrap of Sardis, and his captor Harpagus, on this very account—because they were afraid that, if he escaped, he would be again received into high favour by the king—put him to death as soon as he arrived at Sardis. His body they impaled at that place, while they embalmed his head and sent it up to Susa to the king. Darius, when he learnt what had taken place, found great fault with the men engaged in this business for not bringing Histiæus alive into his presence, and commanded his servants to wash and dress the head with all care, and then bury it, as the head of a man who had been a great benefactor to himself and the Persians. Such was the sequel of the history of Histiæus.

31. The naval armament of the Persians wintered at Miletus, and in the following year proceeded to attack the islands off the coast, Chios, Lesbos, and Tenedos, which were reduced without difficulty. Whenever they became masters of an island, the barbarians, in every single instance, netted the inhabitants. Now the mode in which they practise this netting is the following. Men join hands, so as to form a line across from the north coast to the south, and then march through the island from end to end and hunt out the inhabitants. In like manner the Persians took also the Ionian towns upon the mainland, not however netting the inhabitants, as it was not possible.

32. And now their generals made good all the threats wherewith they had menaced the Ionians before the battle. For no sooner did they get possession of the towns than they choose out all the best favoured boys and made them eunuchs, while the most beautiful of the girls they tore from their homes and sent as presents to the king, at the same time burning the cities themselves, with their temples. Thus were the Ionians for the third time reduced to slavery; once by the Lydians, and a second, and now a third time, by the Persians.

33. The sea force, after quitting Ionia, proceeded to the Hellespont, and took all the towns which lie on the left shore as one sails into the straits. For the cities on the right bank had already been reduced by the land force of the Persians. Now these are the places which border the Hellespont on the European side; the Chersonese, which contains a number of cities, Perinthus, the forts in Thrace, Selybria, and Byzantium. The Byzantines at this time, and their opposite neighbours, the Chalcedonians, instead of awaiting the coming of the Phœnicians, quitted their country, and sailing into the Euxine, took up their abode at the city of Mesêmbria. The Phœnicians, after burning all the places above mentioned, proceeded to Proconnêsus and Artaca, which they likewise delivered to the flames; this done, they returned to the Chersonese, being minded to reduce those cities which they had not ravaged in their former cruise. Upon Cyzicus they made no attack at all, as before their coming the inhabitants had made terms with Œbares, the son of Megabazus, and satrap of Dascyleium, and had submitted themselves to the king. In the Chersonese the Phœnicians subdued all the cities, excepting Cardia.

34. Up to this time the cities of the Chersonese had been under the government of Miltiades, the son of Cimon, and grandson of Stesagoras, to whom they had descended from Miltiades, the son of Cypselus, who obtained possession of them in the following manner. The Dolonci, a Thracian tribe, to whom the Chersonese at that time belonged, being harassed by a war in which they were engaged with the Apsinthians, sent their princes to Delphi to consult the oracle about the matter. The reply of the Pythoness bade them "take back with them as a colonist into their country the man who should first offer them hospitality after they quitted the temple." The Dolonci, following the Sacred Road, passed through the regions of Phocis and Bœotia; after which, as still no one invited them in, they turned aside, and travelled to Athens.

35. Now Pisistratus was at this time sole lord of Athens; but Miltiades, the son of Cypselus, was likewise a person of much distinction. He belonged to a family which was wont to contend in the four-horse-chariot races,

and traced its descent to Æacus and Egina, but which, from the time of Philæas, the son of Ajax, who was the first Athenian citizen of the house, had been naturalised at Athens. It happened that as the Dolonci passed his door Miltiades was sitting in his vestibule, which caused him to remark them, dressed as they were in outlandish garments, and armed moreover with lances. He therefore called to them, and, on their approach, invited them in, offering them lodging and entertainment. The strangers accepted his hospitality, and, after the banquet was over, they laid before him in full the directions of the oracle and besought him on their own part to yield obedience to the god. Miltiades was persuaded ere they had done speaking; for the government of Pisistratus was irksome to him, and he wanted to be beyond the tyrant's reach. He therefore went straightway to Delphi, and inquired of the oracle whether he should do as the Dolonci desired.

36. As the Pythoness backed their request, Miltiades, son of Cypselus who had already won the four-horse chariot-race at Olympia, left Athens, taking with him as many of the Athenians as liked to join in the enterprise, and sailed away with the Dolonci. On his arrival at the Chersonese, he was made king by those who had invited him. After this his first act was to build a wall across the neck of the Chersonese from the city of Cardia to Pactya, to protect the country from the incursions and ravages of the Apsinthians. The breadth of the isthmus at this part is thirty-six furlongs, the whole length of the peninsula within the isthmus being four hundred and twenty furlongs.

37. When he had finished carrying the wall across the isthmus, and had thus secured the Chersonese against the Apsinthians, Miltiades proceeded to engage in other wars, and first of all attacked the Lampsacenians; but falling into an ambush which they had laid he had the misfortune to be taken prisoner. Now it happened that Miltiades stood high in the favour of Crœsus, king of Lydia. When Crœsus therefore heard of his calamity, he sent and commanded the men of Lampsacus to give Miltiades his freedom; "if they refused," he said, "he would destroy them like a fir." Then the Lampsacenians were somewhile in doubt about this speech of Crœsus, and could not tell how to construe his threat "that he would destroy them like a fir"; but at last one of their elders divined the true sense, and told them that the fir is the only tree which, when cut down,

makes no fresh shoots, but forthwith dies outright. So the Lampsacenians, being greatly afraid of Crœsus, released Miltiades, and let him go free.

38. Thus did Miltiades, by the help of Crœsus, escape this danger. Some time afterwards he died childless, leaving his kingdom and his riches to Stesagoras, who was the son of Cimon, his half-brother. Ever since his death the people of the Chersonese have offered him the customary sacrifices of a founder; and they have further established in his honour a gymnic contest and a chariot-race, in neither of which is it lawful for any Lampsacenian to contend. Before the war with Lampsacus was ended Stesagoras too died childless: he was sitting in the hall of justice when he was struck upon the head with a hatchet by a man who pretended to be a deserter, but was in good sooth an enemy, and a bitter one.

39. Thus died Stesagoras; and upon his death the Pisistratidæ fitted out a trireme, and sent Miltiades, the son of Cimon, and brother of the deceased, to the Chersonese, that he might undertake the management of affairs in that quarter. They had already shown him much favour at Athens, as if, forsooth, they had been no parties to the death of his father Cimon—a matter whereof I will give an account in another place. He upon his arrival remained shut up within the house, pretending to do honour to the memory of his dead brother; whereupon the chief people of the Chersonese gathered themselves together from all the cities of the land, and came in a procession to the place where Miltiades was, to condole with him upon his misfortune. Miltiades commanded them to be seized and thrown into prison; after which he made himself master of the Chersonese, maintained a body of five hundred mercenaries, and married Hegesipyla, daughter of the Thracian king Olorus.

40. This Miltiades, the son of Cimon, had not been long in the country when a calamity befell him yet more grievous than those in which he was now involved: for three years earlier he had had to fly before an incursion of the Scyths. These nomads, angered by the attack of Darius, collected in a body and marched as far as the Chersonese. Miltiades did not await their coming, but fled, and remained away until the Scyths retired, when the Dolonci sent and fetched him back. All this happened three years before the events which befell Miltiades at the present time.

41. He now no sooner heard that the Phœ-

nicians were attacking Tenedos than he loaded five triremes with his goods and chattels, and set sail for Athens. Cardia was the point from which he took his departure; and as he sailed down the gulf of Melas, along the shore of the Chersonese, he came suddenly upon the whole Phœnician fleet. However he himself escaped, with four of his vessels, and got into Imbrus, one trireme only falling into the hands of his pursuers. This vessel was under the command of his eldest son Metiochus, whose mother was not the daughter of the Thracian king Olorus, but a different woman. Metiochus and his ship were taken; and when the Phœnicians found out that he was a son of Miltiades they resolved to convey him to the king, expecting thereby to rise high in the royal favour. For they remembered that it was Miltiades who counselled the Ionians to hearken when the Scyths prayed them to break up the bridge and return home. Darius, however, when the Phœnicians brought Metiochus into his presence, was so far from doing him any hurt, that he loaded him with benefits. He gave him a house and estate, and also a Persian wife, by whom there were children born to him who were accounted Persians. As for Miltiades himself, from Imbrus he made his way in safety to Athens.

42. At this time the Persians did no more hurt to the Ionians; but on the contrary, before the year was out, they carried into effect the following measures, which were greatly to their advantage. Artaphernes, satrap of Sardis, summoned deputies from all the Ionian cities, and forced them to enter into agreements with one another, not to harass each other by force of arms, but to settle their disputes by reference. He likewise took the measurement of their whole country in parasangs—such is the name which the Persians give to a distance of thirty furlongs—and settled the tributes which the several cities were to pay, at a rate that has continued unaltered from the time when Artaphernes fixed it down to the present day. The rate was very nearly the same as that which had been paid before the revolt. Such were the peaceful dealings of the Persians with the Ionians.

43. The next spring Darius superseded all the other generals, and sent down Mardonius, the son of Gobryas, to the coast, and with him a vast body of men, some fit for sea, others for land service. Mardonius was a youth at this time, and had only lately married Artazôstra, the king's daughter. When Mardonius, accompanied by this numerous host, reached Cilicia, he took ship and proceeded along shore with his fleet, while the land army marched under other leaders towards the Hellespont. In the course of his voyage along the coast of Asia he came to Ionia; and here I have a marvel to relate which will greatly surprise those Greeks who cannot believe that Otanes advised the seven conspirators to make Persia a commonwealth. Mardonius put down all the despots throughout Ionia, and in lieu of them established democracies. Having so done, he hastened to the Hellespont, and when a vast multitude of ships had been brought together, and likewise a powerful land force, he conveyed his troops across the strait by means of his vessels, and proceeded through Europe against Eretria and Athens.

44. At least these towns served as a pretext for the expedition, the real purpose of which was to subjugate as great a number as possible of the Grecian cities; and this became plain when the Thasians, who did not even lift a hand in their defence, were reduced by the sea force, while the land army added the Macedonians to the former slaves of the king. All the tribes on the hither side of Macedonia had been reduced previously. From Thasos the fleet stood across to the mainland, and sailed along shore to Acanthus, whence an attempt was made to double Mount Athos. But here a violent north wind sprang up, against which nothing could contend, and handled a large number of the ships with much rudeness, shattering them and driving them aground upon Athos. 'Tis said the number of the ships destroyed was little short of three hundred; and the men who perished were more than twenty thousand. For the sea about Athos abounds in monsters beyond all others; and so a portion were seized and devoured by these animals, while others were dashed violently against the rocks; some, who did not know how to swim, were engulfed; and some died of the cold.

45. While thus it fared with the fleet, on land Mardonius and his army were attacked in their camp during the night by the Brygi, a tribe of Thracians; and here vast numbers of the Persians were slain, and even Mardonius himself received a wound. The Brygi, nevertheless, did not succeed in maintaining their own freedom: for Mardonius would not leave the country till he had subdued them and made them subjects of Persia. Still, though he brought them under the yoke, the blow which his land force had received at their hands, and

the great damage done to his fleet off Athos, induced him to set out upon his retreat; and so this armament, having failed disgracefully, returned to Asia.

46. The year after these events, Darius received information from certain neighbours of the Thasians that those islanders were making preparations for revolt; he therefore sent a herald, and bade them dismantle their walls, and bring all their ships to Abdêra. The Thasians, at the time when Histiæus the Milesian made his attack upon them, had resolved that, as their income was very great, they would apply their wealth to building ships of war, and surrounding their city with another and a stronger wall. Their revenue was derived partly from their possessions upon the mainland, partly from the mines which they owned. They were masters of the gold mines at Scapté-Hylé, the yearly produce of which amounted in all to eighty talents. Their mines in Thasos yielded less, but still were so far prolific that, besides being entirely free from land-tax, they had a surplus income, derived from the two sources of their territory on the main and their mines, in common years of two hundred, and in the best years of three hundred talents.

47. I myself have seen the mines in question: by far the most curious of them are those which the Phœnicians discovered at the time when they went with Thasus and colonised the island, which afterwards took its name from him. These Phœnician workings are in Thasos itself, between Cœnyra and a place called Ænyra, over against Samothrace: a huge mountain has been turned upside down in the search for ores. Such then was the source of their wealth. On this occasion no sooner did the Great King issue his commands than straightway the Thasians dismantled their wall, and took their whole fleet to Abdêra.

48. After this Darius resolved to prove the Greeks, and try the bent of their minds, whether they were inclined to resist him in arms or prepared to make their submission. He therefore sent out heralds in divers directions round about Greece, with orders to demand everywhere earth and water for the king. At the same time he sent other heralds to the various seaport towns which paid him tribute, and required them to provide a number of ships of war and horse-transports.

49. These towns accordingly began their preparations; and the heralds who had been sent into Greece obtained what the king had bid them ask from a large number of the states

upon the mainland, and likewise from all the islanders whom they visited. Among these last were included the Eginetans, who, equally with the rest, consented to give earth and water to the Persian king.

When the Athenians heard what the Eginetans had done, believing that it was from enmity to themselves that they had given consent, and that the Eginetans intended to join the Persian in his attack upon Athens, they straightway took the matter in hand. In good truth it greatly rejoiced them to have so fair a pretext; and accordingly they sent frequent embassies to Sparta, and made it a charge against the Eginetans that their conduct in this matter proved them to be traitors to Greece.

50. Hereupon Cleomenes, the son of Anaxandridas, who was then king of the Spartans, went in person to Egina, intending to seize those whose guilt was the greatest. As soon however as he tried to arrest them, a number of the Eginetans made resistance; a certain Crius, son of Polycritus, being the foremost in violence. This person told him "he should not carry off a single Eginetan without it costing him dear—the Athenians had bribed him to make this attack, for which he had no warrant from his own government—otherwise *both* the kings would have come together to make the seizure." This he said in consequence of instructions which he had received from Demaratus. Hereupon Cleomenes, finding that he must quit Egina, asked Crius his name; and when Crius told him, "Get thy horns tipped with brass with all speed, O Crius!" he said, "for thou wilt have to struggle with a great danger."

51. Meanwhile Demaratus, son of Ariston, was bringing charges against Cleomenes at Sparta. He too, like Cleomenes, was king of the Spartans, but he belonged to the lower house—not indeed that his house was of any lower origin than the other, for both houses are of one blood—but the house of Eurysthenes is the more honoured of the two, inasmuch as it is the elder branch.

52. The Lacedæmonians declare, contradicting therein all the poets, that it was king Aristodemus himself, son of Aristomachus, grandson of Cleodæus, and great-grandson of Hyllus, who conducted them to the land which they now possess, and not the sons of Aristodemus. The wife of Aristodemus, whose name (they say) was Argeia, and who was daughter of Autesion, son of Tisamenus, grandson of Thersander, and great-grandson of Polynices,

within a little while after their coming into the country, gave birth to twins. Aristodemus just lived to see his children, but died soon afterwards of a disease. The Lacedæmonians of that day determined, according to custom, to take for their king the elder of the two children; but they were so alike, and so exactly of one size, that they could not possibly tell which of the two to choose: so when they found themselves unable to make a choice, or haply even earlier, they went to the mother and asked her to tell them which was the elder, whereupon she declared that "she herself did not know the children apart"; although in good truth she knew them very well, and only feigned ignorance in order that, if it were possible, both of them might be made kings of Sparta. The Lacedæmonians were now in a great strait; so they sent to Delphi and inquired of the oracle how they should deal with the matter. The Pythoness made answer, "Let both be taken to be kings; but let the elder have the greater honour." So the Lacedæmonians were in as great a strait as before, and could not conceive how they were to discover which was the first-born, till at length a certain Messenian, by name Panites, suggested to them to watch and see which of the two the mother washed and fed first; if they found she always gave one the preference, that fact would tell them all they wanted to know; if, on the contrary, she herself varied, and sometimes took the one first, sometimes the other, it would be plain that she knew as little as they; in which case they must try some other plan. The Lacedæmonians did according to the advice of the Messenian, and, without letting her know why, kept a watch upon the mother; by which means they discovered that, whenever she either washed or fed her children, she always gave the same child the preference. So they took the boy whom the mother honoured the most, and regarding him as the first-born, brought him up in the palace; and the name which they gave to the elder boy was Eurysthenes, while his brother they called Procles. When the brothers grew up, there was always, so long as they lived, enmity between them; and the houses sprung from their loins have continued the feud to this day.

53. Thus much is related by the Lacedæmonians, but not by any of the other Greeks; in what follows I give the tradition of the Greeks generally. The kings of the Dorians (they say)—counting up to Perseus, son of Danaë, and so omitting the god— are rightly given in the common Greek lists, and rightly considered to have been Greeks themselves; for even at this early time they ranked among that people. I say "up to Perseus," and not further, because Perseus has no mortal father by whose name he is called, as Hercules has in Amphitryon; whereby it appears that I have reason on my side, and am right in saying, "up to Perseus." If we follow the line of Danaë, daughter of Acrisius, and trace her progenitors, we shall find that the chiefs of the Dorians are really genuine Egyptians. In the genealogies here given I have followed the common Greek accounts.

54. According to the Persian story, Perseus was an Assyrian who became a Greek; his ancestors, therefore, according to them, were not Greeks. They do not admit that the forefathers of Acrisius were in any way related to Perseus, but say they were Egyptians, as the Greeks likewise testify.

55. Enough however of this subject. How it came to pass that Egyptians obtained the kingdoms of the Dorians, and what they did to raise themselves to such a position, these are questions concerning which, as they have been treated by others, I shall say nothing. I proceed to speak of points on which no other writer has touched.

56. The prerogatives which the Spartans have allowed their kings are the following. In the first place, two priesthoods, those (namely) of Lacedæmonian and of Celestial Jupiter; also the right of making war on what country soever they please, without hindrance from any of the other Spartans, under pain of outlawry; on service the privilege of marching first in the advance and last in the retreat, and of having a hundred picked men for their bodyguard while with the army; likewise the liberty of sacrificing as many cattle in their expeditions as it seems them good, and the right of having the skins and the chines of the slaughtered animals for their own use.

57. Such are their privileges in war; in peace their rights are as follows. When a citizen makes a public sacrifice the kings are given the first seats at the banquet; they are served before any of the other guests, and have a double portion of everything; they take the lead in the libations; and the hides of the sacrificed beasts belong to them. Every month, on the first day, and again on the seventh of the first decade,[1] each king receives a beast without

[1] The division of the Greek month was into decades.

blemish at the public cost, which he offers up to Apollo; likewise a *medimnus* of meal,[1] and of wine a Laconian quart. In the contests of the Games they have always the seat of honour; they appoint the citizens who have to entertain foreigners; they also nominate, each of them, two of the Pythians, officers whose business it is to consult the oracle at Delphi, who eat with the kings, and, like them, live at the public charge. If the kings do not come to the public supper, each of them must have two *chœnixes* of meal and a *cotylè* of wine sent home to him at his house; if they come, they are given a double quantity of each, and the same when any private man invites them to his table. They have the custody of all the oracles which are pronounced; but the Pythians must likewise have knowledge of them. They have the whole decision of certain causes, which are these, and these only:—When a maiden is left the heiress of her father's estate, and has not been betrothed by him to any one, they decide who is to marry her; in all matters concerning the public highways they judge; and if a person wants to adopt a child, he must do it before the kings. They likewise have the right of sitting in council with the eight-and-twenty senators; and if they are not present, then the senators nearest of kin to them have their privileges, and give two votes as the royal proxies, besides a third vote, which is their own.

58. Such are the honours which the Spartan people have allowed their kings during their lifetime; after they are dead other honours await them. Horsemen carry the news of their death through all Laconia, while in the city the women go hither and thither drumming upon a kettle. At this signal, in every house two free persons, a man and a woman, must put on mourning, or else be subject to a heavy fine. The Lacedæmonians have likewise a custom at the demise of their kings which is common to them with the barbarians of Asia—indeed with the greater number of the barbarians everywhere—namely, that when one of their kings dies, not only the Spartans, but a certain number of the country people from every part of Laconia are forced, whether they will or no, to attend the funeral. So these persons and the helots, and likewise the Spartans themselves, flock together to the number of several thousands, men and women intermingled; and all

of them smite their foreheads violently, and weep and wail without stint, saying always that their last king was the best. If a king dies in battle, then they make a statue of him, and placing it upon a couch right bravely decked, so carry it to the grave. After the burial, by the space of ten days there is no assembly, nor do they elect magistrates, but continue mourning the whole time.

59. They hold with the Persians also in another custom. When a king dies, and another comes to the throne, the newly-made monarch forgives all the Spartans the debts which they owe either to the king or to the public treasury. And in like manner among the Persians each king when he begins to reign remits the tribute due from the provinces.

60. In one respect the Lacedæmonians resemble the Egyptians. Their heralds and flute-players, and likewise their cooks, take their trades by succession from their fathers. A flute-player must be the son of a flute-player, a cook of a cook, a herald of a herald; and other people cannot take advantage of the loudness of their voice to come into the profession and shut out the heralds' sons; but each follows his father's business. Such are the customs of the Lacedæmonians.

61. At the time of which we are speaking, while Cleomenes in Egina was labouring for the general good of Greece, Demaratus at Sparta continued to bring charges against him, moved not so much by love of the Eginetans as by jealousy and hatred of his colleague. Cleomenes therefore was no sooner returned from Egina than he considered with himself how he might deprive Demaratus of his kingly office; and here the following circumstance furnished a ground for him to proceed upon. Ariston, king of Sparta, had been married to two wives, but neither of them had borne him any children; as however he still thought it was possible he might have offspring, he resolved to wed a third; and this was how the wedding was brought about. He had a certain friend, a Spartan, with whom he was more intimate than with any other citizen. This friend was married to a wife whose beauty far surpassed that of all the other women in Sparta; and what was still more strange, she had once been as ugly as she now was beautiful. For her nurse, seeing how ill-favoured she was, and how sadly her parents, who were wealthy people, took her bad looks to heart, bethought herself of a plan, which was to carry the child every day to the temple of Helen at Therapna,

---

[1] The *medimnus* was about 12 gallons, the *chœnix* somewhat less than a quart, and a *cotylè* half a pint.

which stands above the Phœbeum, and there to place her before the image, and beseech the goddess to take away the child's ugliness. One day, as she left the temple, a woman appeared to her, and begged to know what it was she held in her arms. The nurse told her it was a child, on which she asked to see it; but the nurse refused; the parents, she said, had forbidden her to show the child to any one. However the woman would not take a denial; and the nurse, seeing how highly she prized a look, at last let her see the child. Then the woman gently stroked its head, and said, "One day this child shall be the fairest dame in Sparta." And her looks began to change from that very day. When she was of marriageable age, Agêtus, son of Alcides, the same whom I have mentioned above as the friend of Ariston, made her his wife.

62. Now it chanced that Ariston fell in love with this person; and his love so preyed upon his mind that at last he devised as follows. He went to his friend, the lady's husband, and proposed to him that they should exchange gifts, each taking that which pleased him best out of all the possessions of the other. His friend, who felt no alarm about his wife, since Ariston was also married, consented readily; and so the matter was confirmed between them by an oath. Then Ariston gave Agêtus the present, whatever it was, of which he had made choice, and when it came to his turn to name the present which he was to receive in exchange, required to be allowed to carry home with him Agêtus's wife. But the other demurred, and said, "except his wife, he might have anything else": however, as he could not resist the oath which he had sworn, or the trickery which had been practised on him, at last he suffered Ariston to carry her away to his house.

63. Ariston hereupon put away his second wife and took for his third this woman; and she, in less than the due time—when she had not yet reached her full term of ten months— gave birth to a child, the Demaratus of whom we have spoken. Then one of his servants came and told him the news, as he sat in council with the Ephors; whereat, remembering when it was that the woman became his wife, he counted the months upon his fingers, and having so done, cried out with an oath, "The boy cannot be mine." This was said in the hearing of the Ephors; but they made no account of it at the time. The boy grew up; and Ariston repented of what he had said; for he be-

came altogether convinced that Demaratus was truly his son. The reason why he named him Demaratus was the following. Some time before these events the whole Spartan people, looking upon Ariston as a man of mark beyond all the kings that had reigned at Sparta before him, had offered up a prayer that he might have a son. On this account, therefore, the name Demaratus was given.

64. In course of time Ariston died; and Demaratus received the kingdom: but it was fated, as it seems, that these words, when bruited abroad, should strip him of his sovereignty. This was brought about by means of Cleomenes, whom he had twice sorely vexed, once when he led the army home from Eleusis, and a second time when Cleomenes was gone across to Egina against such as had espoused the side of the Medes.

65. Cleomenes now, being resolved to have his revenge upon Demaratus, went to Leotychides, the son of Menares, and grandson of Agis, who was of the same family as Demaratus, and made agreement with him to this tenor following. Cleomenes was to lend his aid to make Leotychides king in the room of Demaratus; and then Leotychides was to take part with Cleomenes against the Eginetans. Now Leotychides hated Demaratus chiefly on account of Percalus, the daughter of Chilon, son of Demarmenus: this lady had been betrothed to Leotychides; but Demaratus laid a plot, and robbed him of his bride, forestalling him in carrying her off, and marrying her. Such was the origin of the enmity. At the time of which we speak, Leotychides was prevailed upon by the earnest desire of Cleomenes to come forward against Demaratus and make oath "that Demaratus was not rightful king of Sparta, since he was not the true son of Ariston." After he had thus sworn, Leotychides sued Demaratus, and brought up against him the phrase which Ariston had let drop when, on the coming of his servant to announce to him the birth of his son, he counted the months, and cried out with an oath that the child was not his. It was on this speech of Ariston's that Leotychides relied to prove that Demaratus was not his son, and therefore not rightful king of Sparta; and he produced as witnesses the Ephors who were sitting with Ariston at the time and heard what he said.

66. At last, as there came to be much strife concerning this matter, the Spartans made a decree that the Delphic oracle should be asked to say whether Demaratus were Ariston's son

or no. Cleomenes set them upon this plan; and no sooner was the decree passed than he made a friend of Cobon, the son of Aristophantus, a man of the greatest weight among the Delphians; and this Cobon prevailed upon Perialla, the prophetess, to give the answer which Cleomenes wished. Accordingly, when the sacred messengers came and put their question, the Pythoness returned for answer "that Demaratus was not Ariston's son." Some time afterwards all this became known; and Cobon was forced to fly from Delphi; while Perialla the prophetess was deprived of her office.

67. Such were the means whereby the deposition of Demaratus was brought about; but his flying from Sparta to the Medes was by reason of an affront which was put upon him. On losing his kingdom he had been made a magistrate; and in that office soon afterwards, when the feast of the Gymnopædiæ came around, he took his station among the lookers-on; whereupon Leotychides, who was now king in his room, sent a servant to him and asked him, by way of insult and mockery, "how it felt to be a magistrate after one had been a king?" Demaratus, who was hurt at the question, made answer—"Tell him I have tried them both, but he has not. Howbeit this speech will be the cause to Sparta of infinite blessings or else of infinite woes." Having thus spoken he wrapped his head in his robe, and, leaving the theatre, went home to his own house, where he prepared an ox for sacrifice, and offered it to Jupiter, after which he called for his mother.

68. When she appeared, he took of the entrails, and placing them in her hand, besought her in these words following:—

"Dear mother, I beseech you, by all the gods, and chiefly by our own hearth-god Jupiter, tell me the very truth, who was really my father. For Leotychides, in the suit which we had together, declared that when thou becamest Ariston's wife thou didst already bear in thy womb a child by thy former husband, and others repeat a yet more disgraceful tale, that our groom found favour in thine eyes, and that I am his son. I entreat thee therefore by the gods to tell me the truth. For if thou hast gone astray, thou hast done no more than many a woman; and the Spartans remark it as strange, if I am Ariston's son, that he had no children by his other wives."

69. Thus spake Demaratus; and his mother replied as follows: "Dear son, since thou entreatest so earnestly for the truth, it shall in-deed be fully told to thee. When Ariston brought me to his house, on the third night after my coming, there appeared to me one like to Ariston, who, after staying with me a while, rose, and taking the garlands from his own brows placed them upon my head, and so went away. Presently after Ariston entered, and when he saw the garlands which I still wore, asked me who gave them to me. I said, 'twas he; but this he stoutly denied; whereupon I solemnly swore that it was none other, and told him he did not do well to dissemble when he had so lately risen from my side and left the garlands with me. Then Ariston, when he heard my oath, understood that there was something beyond nature in what had taken place. And indeed it appeared that the garlands had come from the hero-temple which stands by our court gates—the temple of him they call Astrabacus—and the soothsayers, moreover, declared that the apparition was that very person. And now, my son, I have told thee all thou wouldest fain know. Either thou art the son of that hero—either thou mayest call Astrabacus sire; or else Ariston was thy father. As for that matter which they who hate thee urge the most, the words of Ariston, who, when the messenger told him of thy birth, declared before many witnesses that 'thou wert not his son, forasmuch as the ten months were not fully out,' it was a random speech, uttered from mere ignorance. The truth is, children are born not only at ten months, but at nine, and even at seven. Thou wert thyself, my son, a seven months' child. Ariston acknowledged, no long time afterwards, that his speech sprang from thoughtlessness. Hearken not then to other tales concerning thy birth, my son: for be assured thou hast the whole truth. As for grooms, pray Heaven Leotychides and all who speak as he does may suffer wrong from them!" Such was the mother's answer.

70. Demaratus, having learnt all that he wished to know, took with him provision for the journey, and went into Elis, pretending that he purposed to proceed to Delphi, and there consult the oracle. The Lacedæmonians, however, suspecting that he meant to fly his country, sent men in pursuit of him; but Demaratus hastened, and leaving Elis before they arrived, sailed across to Zacynthus. The Lacedæmonians followed, and sought to lay hands upon him, and to separate him from his retinue; but the Zacynthians would not give him up to them: so he escaping, made his way afterwards by sea to Asia, and presented him-

self before King Darius, who received him generously, and gave him both lands and cities. Such was the chance which drove Demaratus to Asia, a man distinguished among the Lacedæmonians for many noble deeds and wise counsels, and who alone of all the Spartan kings brought honour to his country by winning at Olympia the prize in the four-horse chariot-race.

71. After Demaratus was deposed, Leotychides, the son of Menares, received the kingdom. He had a son, Zeuxidamus, called Cyniscus by many of the Spartans. This Zeuxidamus did not reign at Sparta, but died before his father, leaving a son, Archidamus. Leotychides, when Zeuxidamus was taken from him, married a second wife, named Eurydamé, the sister of Menius and daughter of Diactorides. By her he had no male offspring, but only a daughter called Lampito, whom he gave in marriage to Archidamus, Zeuxidamus' son.

72. Even Leotychides, however, did not spend his old age in Sparta, but suffered a punishment whereby Demaratus was fully avenged. He commanded the Lacedæmonians when they made war against Thessaly, and might have conquered the whole of it, but was bribed by a large sum of money. It chanced that he was caught in the fact, being found sitting in his tent on a gauntlet, quite full of silver. Upon this he was brought to trial and banished from Sparta; his house was razed to the ground; and he himself fled to Tegea, where he ended his days. But these events took place long afterwards.

73. At the time of which we are speaking, Cleomenes, having carried his proceedings in the matter of Demaratus to a prosperous issue, forthwith took Leotychides with him, and crossed over to attack the Eginetans; for his anger was hot against them on account of the affront which they had formerly put upon him. Hereupon the Eginetans, seeing that both the kings were come against them, thought it best to make no further resistance. So the two kings picked out from all Egina the ten men who for wealth and birth stood the highest, among whom were Crius, son of Polycritus, and Casambus, son of Aristocrates, who wielded the chief power; and these men they carried with them to Attica, and there deposited them in the hands of the Athenians, the great enemies of the Eginetans.

74. Afterwards, when it came to be known what evil arts had been used against Demara-

tus, Cleomenes was seized with fear of his own countrymen, and fled into Thessaly. From thence he passed into Arcadia, where he began to stir up troubles, and endeavoured to unite the Arcadians against Sparta. He bound them by various oaths to follow him whithersover he should lead, and was even desirous of taking their chief leaders with him to the city of Nonacris, that he might swear them to his cause by the waters of the Styx. For the waters of Styx, as the Arcadians say, are in that city, and this is the appearance they present: you see a little water, dripping from a rock into a basin, which is fenced round by a low wall. Nonacris, where this fountain is to be seen, is a city of Arcadia near Pheneus.

75. When the Lacedæmonians heard how Cleomenes was engaged, they were afraid, and agreed with him that he should come back to Sparta and be king as before. So Cleomenes came back; but had no sooner returned than he, who had never been altogether of sound mind, was smitten with downright madness. This he showed by striking every Spartan he met upon the face with his sceptre. On his behaving thus, and showing that he was gone quite out of his mind, his kindred imprisoned him, and even put his feet in the stocks. While so bound, finding himself left alone with a single keeper, he asked the man for a knife. The keeper at first refused, whereupon Cleomenes began to threaten him, until at last he was afraid, being only a helot, and gave him what he required. Cleomenes had no sooner got the steel than, beginning at his legs, he horribly disfigured himself, cutting gashes in his flesh, along his legs, thighs, hips, and loins, until at last he reached his belly, which he likewise began to gash, whereupon in a little time he died. The Greeks generally think that this fate came upon him because he induced the Pythoness to pronounce against Demaratus; the Athenians differ from all others in saying that it was because he cut down the sacred grove of the goddesses when he made his invasion by Eleusis; while the Argives ascribe it to his having taken from their refuge and cut to pieces certain Argives who had fled from battle into a precinct sacred to Argus, where Cleomenes slew them, burning likewise at the same time, through irreverence, the grove itself.

76. For once, when Cleomenes had sent to Delphi to consult the oracle, it was prophesied to him that he should take Argos; upon which he went out at the head of the Spartans, and led them to the river Erasinus. This stream is

reported to flow from the Stymphalian lake, the waters of which empty themselves into a pitch-dark chasm, and then (as they say) re-appear in Argos, where the Argives call them the Erasinus. Cleomenes, having arrived upon the banks of this river, proceeded to offer sac-rifice to it, but, in spite of all that he could do, the victims were not favourable to his crossing. So he said that he admired the god for refus-ing to betray his countrymen, but still the Ar-gives should not escape him for all that. He then withdrew his troops, and led them down to Thyrea, where he sacrificed a bull to the sea, and conveyed his men on shipboard to Nauplia in the Tirynthian territory.

77. The Argives, when they heard of this, marched down to the sea to defend their country; and arriving in the neighbourhood of Tiryns, at the place which bears the name of Sêpeia, they pitched their camp opposite to the Lacedæmonians, leaving no great space be-tween the hosts. And now their fear was not so much lest they should be worsted in open fight as lest some trick should be practised on them; for such was the danger which the ora-cle given to them in common with the Milesi-ans seemed to intimate. The oracle ran as fol-lows:—

*Time shall be when the female shall conquer the
    male, and shall chase him
Far away—gaining so great praise and honour in
    Argos;
Then full many an Argive woman her cheeks
    shall mangle—
Hence, in the times to come 'twill be said by the
    men who are unborn,
"Tamed by the spear expired the coilèd terrible
    serpent."*

At the coincidence of all these things the Ar-gives were greatly cast down; and so they re-solved that they would follow the signals of the enemy's herald. Having made this resolve, they proceeded to act as follows: whenever the herald of the Lacedæmonians gave an order to the soldiers of his own army, the Argives did the like on their side.

78. Now when Cleomenes heard that the Argives were acting thus, he commanded his troops that, so soon as the herald gave the word for the soldiers to go to dinner, they should instantly seize their arms and charge the host of the enemy. Which the Lacedæmonians did accordingly, and fell upon the Argives just as, following the signal, they had begun their re-past; whereby it came to pass that vast num-bers of the Argives were slain, while the rest, who were more than they which died in the fight, were driven to take refuge in the grove of Argus hard by, where they were surround-ed, and watch kept upon them.

79. When things were at this pass Cleo-menes acted as follows: Having learnt the names of the Argives who were shut up in the sacred precinct from certain deserters who had come over to him, he sent a herald to summon them one by one, on pretence of having re-ceived their ransoms. Now the ransom of pris-oners among the Peloponnesians is fixed at two minæ the man. So Cleomenes had these persons called forth severally, to the number of fifty, or thereabouts, and massacred them. All this while they who remained in the en-closure knew nothing of what was happening; for the grove was so thick that the people in-side were unable to see what was taking place without. But at last one of their number climbed up into a tree and spied the treachery; after which none of those who were sum-moned would go forth.

80. Then Cleomenes ordered all the helots to bring brushwood, and heap it around the grove; which was done accordingly; and Cleo-menes set the grove on fire. As the flames spread he asked a deserter "Who was the god of the grove?" whereto the other made answer, "Argus." So he, when he heard that, uttered a loud groan, and said:—

"Greatly hast thou deceived me, Apollo, god of prophecy, in saying that I should take Ar-gos. I fear me thy oracle has now got its ac-complishment."

81. Cleomenes now sent home the greater part of his army, while with a thousand of his best troops he proceeded to the temple of Juno, to offer sacrifice. When however he would have slain the victim on the altar himself, the priest forbade him, as it was not lawful (he said) for a foreigner to sacrifice in that temple. At this Cleomenes ordered his helots to drag the priest from the altar and scourge him, while he performed the sacrifice himself, after which he went back to Sparta.

82. Thereupon his enemies brought him up before the Ephors, and made it a charge against him that he had allowed himself to be bribed, and on that account had not taken Ar-gos when he might have captured it easily. To this he answered—whether truly or falsely I cannot say with certainty—but at any rate his answer to the charge was that "so soon as he discovered the sacred precinct which he had taken to belong to Argos, he directly imagined

that the oracle had received its accomplishment; he therefore thought it not good to attempt the town, at the least until he had inquired by sacrifice, and ascertained if the god meant to grant him the place, or was determined to oppose his taking it. So he offered in the temple of Juno, and when the omens were propitious, immediately there flashed forth a flame of fire from the breast of the image; whereby he knew of a surety that he was not to take Argos. For if the flash had come from the head, he would have gained the town, citadel and all; but as it shone from the breast, he had done so much as the god intended." And his words seemed to the Spartans so true and reasonable, that he came clear off from his adversaries.

83. Argos however was left so bare of men that the slaves managed the state, filled the offices, and administered everything until the sons of those who were slain by Cleomenes grew up. Then these latter cast out the slaves, and got the city back under their own rule; while the slaves who had been driven out fought a battle and won Tiryns. After this for a time there was peace between the two; but a certain man, a soothsayer, named Cleander, who was by race a Phigalean from Arcadia, joined himself to the slaves, and stirred them up to make a fresh attack upon their lords. Then were they at war with one another by the space of many years; but at length the Argives with much trouble gained the upper hand.

84. The Argives say that Cleomenes lost his senses, and died so miserably, on account of these doings. But his own countrymen declare that his madness proceeded not from any supernatural cause whatever, but only from the habit of drinking wine unmixed with water, which he learnt of the Scyths. These nomads, from the time that Darius made his inroad into their country, had always had a wish for revenge. They therefore sent ambassadors to Sparta to conclude a league, proposing to endeavour themselves to enter Media by the Phasis, while the Spartans should march inland from Ephesus, and then the two armies should join together in one. When the Scyths came to Sparta on this errand Cleomenes was with them continually; and growing somewhat too familiar, learnt of them to drink his wine without water, a practice which is thought by the Spartans to have caused his madness. From this distance of time the Spartans, according to their own account, have been accustomed, when they want to drink purer

wine than common, to give the order to fill "Scythian fashion." The Spartans then speak thus concerning Cleomenes; but for my own part I think his death was a judgment on him for wronging Demaratus.

85. No sooner did the news of Cleomenes' death reach Egina than straightway the Eginetans sent ambassadors to Sparta to complain of the conduct of Leotychides in respect of their hostages, who were still kept at Athens. So they of Lacedæmon assembled a court of justice and gave sentence upon Leotychides, that whereas he had grossly affronted the people of Egina, he should be given up to the ambassadors, to be led away in place of the men whom the Athenians had in their keeping. Then the ambassadors were about to lead him away; but Theasides, the son of Leoprepes, who was a man greatly esteemed in Sparta, interfered, and said to them:—

"What are ye minded to do, ye men of Egina? To lead away captive the king of the Spartans, whom his countrymen have given into your hands? Though now in their anger they have passed this sentence, yet belike the time will come when they will punish you, if you act thus, by bringing utter destruction upon your country."

The Eginetans, when they heard this, changed their plan, and, instead of leading Leotychides away captive, agreed with him that he should come with them to Athens, and give them back their men.

86. When however he reached that city, and demanded the restoration of his pledge, the Athenians, being unwilling to comply, proceeded to make excuses, saying "that two kings had come and left the men with them, and they did not think it right to give them back to the one without the other." So when the Athenians refused plainly to restore the men, Leotychides said to them:—

"Men of Athens, act which way you choose —give me up the hostages, and be righteous, or keep them, and be the contrary. I wish, however, to tell you what happened once in Sparta about a pledge. The story goes among us that three generations back there lived in Lacedæmon one Glaucus, the son of Epicydes, a man who in every other respect was on a par with the first in the kingdom, and whose character for justice was such as to place him above all the other Spartans. Now to this man at the appointed season the following events happened. A certain Milesian came to Sparta and, having desired to speak with him, said—

'I am of Miletus, and I have come hither, Glaucus, in the hope of profiting by thy honesty. For when I heard much talk thereof in Ionia and through all the rest of Greece, and when I observed that whereas Ionia is always insecure, the Peloponnese stands firm and unshaken, and noted likewise how wealth is continually changing hands in our country, I took counsel with myself and resolved to turn one-half of my substance into money, and place it in thy hands, since I am well assured that it will be safe in thy keeping. Here then is the silver—take it—and take likewise these tallies, and be careful of them; remember thou art to give back the money to the person who shall bring you their fellows.' Such were the words of the Milesian stranger; and Glaucus took the deposit on the terms expressed to him. Many years had gone by when the sons of the man by whom the money was left came to Sparta, and had an interview with Glaucus, whereat they produced the tallies, and asked to have the money returned to them. But Glaucus sought to refuse, and answered them: 'I have no recollection of the matter; nor can I bring to mind any of those particulars whereof ye speak. When I remember, I will certainly do what is just. If I had the money, you have a right to receive it back; but if it was never given to me, I shall put the Greek law in force against you. For the present I give you no answer; but four months hence I will settle the business.' So the Milesians went away sorrowful, considering that their money was utterly lost to them. As for Glaucus, he made a journey to Delphi, and there consulted the oracle. To his question if he should swear, and so make prize of the money, the Pythoness returned for answer these lines following:—

Best for the present it were, O Glaucus, to do as
  thou wishest,
Swearing an oath to prevail, and so to make prize
  of the money.
Swear then—death is the lot e'en of those who
  never swear falsely.
Yet hath the Oath-God a son who is nameless,
  footless, and handless;
Mighty in strength he approaches to vengeance,
  and whelms in destruction
All who belong to the race, or the house of the
  man who is perjured.
But oath-keeping men leave behind them a flourishing offspring.

Glaucus when he heard these words earnestly besought the god to pardon his question; but the Pythoness replied that it was as bad to have

tempted the god as it would have been to have done the deed. Glaucus, however, sent for the Milesian strangers, and gave them back their money. And now I will tell you, Athenians, what my purpose has been in recounting to you this history. Glaucus at the present time has not a single descendant; nor is there any family known as his—root and branch has he been removed from Sparta. It is a good thing, therefore, when a pledge has been left with one, not even in thought to doubt about restoring it."

Thus spake Leotychides; but, as he found that the Athenians would not hearken to him, he left them and went his way.

87. The Eginetans had never been punished for the wrongs which, to pleasure the Thebans, they had committed upon Athens. Now, however, conceiving that they were themselves wronged, and had a fair ground of complaint against the Athenians, they instantly prepared to revenge themselves. As it chanced that the Athenian *theôris*, which was a vessel of five banks of oars, lay at Sunium, the Eginetans contrived an ambush, and made themselves masters of the holy vessel, on board of which were a number of Athenians of the highest rank, whom they took and threw into prison.

88. At this outrage the Athenians no longer delayed, but set to work to scheme their worst against the Eginetans; and, as there was in Egina at that time a man of mark, Nicodromus by name, the son of Cnœthus, who was on ill terms with his countrymen because on a former occasion they had driven him into banishment, they listened to overtures from this man, who had heard how determined they were to do the Eginetans a mischief, and agreed with him that on a certain day he should be ready to betray the island into their hands, and they would come with a body of troops to his assistance. And Nicodromus, some time after, holding to the agreement, made himself master of what is called the old town.

89. The Athenians, however, did not come to the day; for their own fleet was not of force sufficient to engage the Eginetans, and while they were begging the Corinthians to lend them some ships, the failure of the enterprise took place. In those days the Corinthians were on the best of terms with the Athenians; and accordingly they now yielded to their request, and furnished them with twenty ships; but, as their law did not allow the ships to be given for nothing, they sold them to the Athenians

for five drachms apiece. As soon then as the Athenians had obtained this aid, and, by manning also their own ships, had equipped a fleet of seventy sail, they crossed over to Egina, but arrived a day later than the time agreed upon.

90. Meanwhile Nicodromus, when he found the Athenians did not come to the time appointed, took ship and made his escape from the island. The Eginetans who accompanied him were settled by the Athenians at Sunium, whence they were wont to issue forth and plunder the Eginetans of the island. But this took place at a later date.

91. When the wealthier Eginetans had thus obtained the victory over the common people who had revolted with Nicodromus, they laid hands on a certain number of them, and led them out to death. But here they were guilty of a sacrilege, which, notwithstanding all their efforts, they were never able to atone, being driven from the island before they had appeased the goddess whom they now provoked. Seven hundred of the common people had fallen alive into their hands; and they were all being led out to death, when one of them escaped from his chains, and flying to the gateway of the temple of Ceres the Lawgiver, laid hold of the door-handles, and clung to them. The others sought to drag him from his refuge; but, finding themselves unable to tear him away, they cut off his hands, and so took him, leaving the hands still tightly grasping the handles.

92. Such were the doings of the Eginetans among themselves. When the Athenians arrived, they went out to meet them with seventy ships; and a battle took place, wherein the Eginetans suffered a defeat. Hereupon they had recourse again to their old allies, the Argives; but these latter refused now to lend them any aid, being angry because some Eginetan ships, which Cleomenes had taken by force, accompanied him in his invasion of Argolis, and joined in the disembarkation. The same thing had happened at the same time with certain vessels of the Sicyonians; and the Argives had laid a fine of a thousand talents upon the misdoers, five hundred upon each: whereupon they of Sicyon acknowledged themselves to have sinned, and agreed with the Argives to pay them a hundred talents, and so be quit of the debt; but the Eginetans would make no acknowledgment at all, and showed themselves proud and stiff-necked. For this reason, when they now prayed the Argives for aid, the state refused to send them a single

soldier. Notwithstanding, volunteers joined them from Argos to the number of a thousand, under a captain, Eurybates, a man skilled in the pentathlic contests. Of these men the greater part never returned, but were slain by the Athenians in Egina. Eurybates, their captain, fought a number of single combats, and, after killing three men in this way, was himself slain by the fourth, who was a Decelean, named Sôphanes.

93. Afterwards the Eginetans fell upon the Athenian fleet when it was in some disorder and beat it, capturing four ships with their crews.

94. Thus did war rage between the Eginetans and Athenians. Meantime the Persian pursued his own design, from day to day exhorted by his servant to "remember the Athenians," and likewise urged continually by the Pisistratidæ, who were ever accusing their countrymen. Moreover it pleased him well to have a pretext for carrying war into Greece, that so he might reduce all those who had refused to give him earth and water. As for Mardonius, since his expedition had succeeded so ill, Darius took the command of the troops from him, and appointed other generals in his stead, who were to lead the host against Eretria and Athens; to wit, Datis, who was by descent a Mede, and Artaphernes, the son of Artaphernes, his own nephew. These men received orders to carry Athens and Eretria away captive, and to bring the prisoners into his presence.

95. So the new commanders took their departure from the court and went down to Cilicia, to the Aleïan plain, having with them a numerous and well-appointed land army. Encamping here, they were joined by the sea force which had been required of the several states, and at the same time by the horse-transports which Darius had, the year before, commanded his tributaries to make ready. Aboard these the horses were embarked; and the troops were received by the ships of war; after which the whole fleet, amounting in all to six hundred triremes, made sail for Ionia. Thence, instead of proceeding with a straight course along the shore to the Hellespont and to Thrace, they loosed from Samos and voyaged across the Icarian sea through the midst of the islands; mainly, as I believe, because they feared the danger of doubling Mount Athos, where the year before they had suffered so grievously on their passage; but a constraining cause also was their former failure to take Naxos.

96. When the Persians, therefore, approaching from the Icarian Sea, cast anchor at Naxos, which, recollecting what there befell them formerly, they had determined to attack before any other state, the Naxians, instead of encountering them, took to flight, and hurried off to the hills. The Persians however succeeded in laying hands on some, and them they carried away captive, while at the same time they burnt all the temples together with the town. This done, they left Naxos, and sailed away to the other islands.

97. While the Persians were thus employed, the Delians likewise quitted Delos, and took refuge in Tenos. And now the expedition drew near, when Datis sailed forward in advance of the other ships; commanding them, instead of anchoring at Delos, to rendezvous at Rhênea, over against Delos, while he himself proceeded to discover whither the Delians had fled; after which he sent a herald to them with this message:—

"Why are ye fled, O holy men? Why have ye judged me so harshly and so wrongfully? I have surely sense enough, even had not the king so ordered, to spare the country which gave birth to the two gods—to spare, I say, both the country and its inhabitants. Come back therefore to your dwellings; and once more inhabit your island."

Such was the message which Datis sent by his herald to the Delians. He likewise placed upon the altar three hundred talents' weight of frankincense, and offered it.

98. After this he sailed with his whole host against Eretria, taking with him both Ionians and Æolians. When he was departed, Delos (as the Delians told me) was shaken by an earthquake, the first and last shock that has been felt to this day. And truly this was a prodigy whereby the god warned men of the evils that were coming upon them. For in the three following generations of Darius the son of Hystaspes, Xerxes the son of Darius, and Artaxerxes the son of Xerxes, more woes befell Greece than in the twenty generations preceding Darius—woes caused in part by the Persians, but in part arising from the contentions among their own chief men respecting the supreme power. Wherefore it is not surprising that Delos, though it had never before been shaken, should at that time have felt the shock of an earthquake. And indeed there was an oracle, which said of Delos—

Delos' self will I shake, which never yet has been shaken.

Of the above names Darius may be rendered "Worker," Xerxes "Warrior," and Artaxerxes "Great Warrior." And so might we call these kings in our own language with propriety.

99. The barbarians, after loosing from Delos, proceeded to touch at the other islands, and took troops from each, and likewise carried off a number of the children as hostages. Going thus from one to another, they came at last to Carystus; but here the hostages were refused by the Carystians, who said they would neither give any, nor consent to bear arms against the cities of their neighbours, meaning Athens and Eretria. Hereupon the Persians laid siege to Carystus, and wasted the country round, until at length the inhabitants were brought over and agreed to do what was required of them.

100. Meanwhile the Eretrians, understanding that the Persian armament was coming against them, besought the Athenians for assistance. Nor did the Athenians refuse their aid, but assigned to them as auxiliaries the four thousand landholders to whom they had allotted the estates of the Chalcidean Hippobatæ. At Eretria, however, things were in no healthy state; for though they had called in the aid of the Athenians, yet they were not agreed among themselves how they should act; some of them were minded to leave the city and to take refuge in the heights of Eubœa, while others, who looked to receiving a reward from the Persians, were making ready to betray their country. So when these things came to the ears of Æschines, the son of Nothon, one of the first men in Eretria, he made known the whole state of affairs to the Athenians who were already arrived, and besought them to return home to their own land, and not perish with his countrymen. And the Athenians hearkened to his counsel, and, crossing over to Orôpus, in this way escaped the danger.

101. The Persian fleet now drew near and anchored at Tamynæ, Chœreæ, and Ægilia, three places in the territory of Eretria. Once masters of these posts, they proceeded forthwith to disembark their horses, and made ready to attack the enemy. But the Eretrians were not minded to sally forth and offer battle; their only care, after it had been resolved not to quit the city, was, if possible, to defend their walls. And now the fortress was assaulted in good earnest, and for six days there fell on both sides vast numbers, but on the seventh day Euphorbus, the son of Alcimachus, and Philagrus, the son of Cyneas, who were both

citizens of good repute, betrayed the place to the Persians. These were no sooner entered within the walls than they plundered and burnt all the temples that there were in the town, in revenge for the burning of their own temples at Sardis; moreover, they did according to the orders of Darius, and carried away captive all the inhabitants.

102. The Persians, having thus brought Eretria into subjection after waiting a few days, made sail for Attica, greatly straitening the Athenians as they approached, and thinking to deal with them as they had dealt with the people of Eretria. And, because there was no place in all Attica so convenient for their horse as Marathon, and it lay moreover quite close to Eretria, therefore Hippias, the son of Pisistratus, conducted them thither.

103. When intelligence of this reached the Athenians, they likewise marched their troops to Marathon, and there stood on the defensive, having at their head ten generals, of whom one was Miltiades.

Now this man's father, Cimon, the son of Stesagoras, was banished from Athens by Pisistratus, the son of Hippocrates. In his banishment it was his fortune to win the four-horse chariot-race at Olympia, whereby he gained the very same honour which had before been carried off by Miltiades, his half-brother on the mother's side. At the next Olympiad he won the prize again with the same mares; upon which he caused Pisistratus to be proclaimed the winner, having made an agreement with him that on yielding him this honour he should be allowed to come back to his country. Afterwards, still with the same mares, he won the prize a third time; whereupon he was put to death by the sons of Pisistratus, whose father was no longer living. They set men to lie in wait for him secretly; and these men slew him near the government-house in the night-time. He was buried outside the city, beyond what is called the Valley Road; and right opposite his tomb were buried the mares which had won the three prizes. The same success had likewise been achieved once previously, to wit, by the mares of Evagoras the Lacedæmonian, but never except by them. At the time of Cimon's death Stesagoras, the elder of his two sons, was in the Chersonese, where he lived with Miltiades his uncle; the younger, who was called Miltiades after the founder of the Chersonesite colony, was with his father in Athens.

104. It was this Miltiades who now commanded the Athenians, after escaping from the Chersonese, and twice nearly losing his life. First he was chased as far as Imbrus by the Phœnicians, who had a great desire to take him and carry him up to the king; and when he had avoided this danger, and, having reached his own country, thought himself to be altogether in safety, he found his enemies waiting for him, and was cited by them before a court and impeached for his tyranny in the Chersonese. But he came off victorious here likewise, and was thereupon made general of the Athenians by the free choice of the people.

105. And first, before they left the city, the generals sent off to Sparta a herald, one Pheidippides, who was by birth an Athenian, and by profession and practice a trained runner. This man, according to the account which he gave to the Athenians on his return, when he was near Mount Parthenium, above Tegea, fell in with the god Pan, who called him by his name, and bade him ask the Athenians "wherefore they neglected him so entirely, when he was kindly disposed towards them, and had often helped them in times past, and would do so again in time to come?" The Athenians, entirely believing in the truth of this report, as soon as their affairs were once more in good order, set up a temple to Pan under the Acropolis, and, in return for the message which I have recorded, established in his honour yearly sacrifices and a torch-race.

106. On the occasion of which we speak when Pheidippides was sent by the Athenian generals, and, according to his own account, saw Pan on his journey, he reached Sparta on the very next day after quitting the city of Athens. Upon his arrival he went before the rulers, and said to them:—

"Men of Lacedæmon, the Athenians beseech you to hasten to their aid, and not allow that state, which is the most ancient in all Greece, to be enslaved by the barbarians. Eretria, look you, is already carried away captive; and Greece weakened by the loss of no mean city."

Thus did Pheidippides deliver the message committed to him. And the Spartans wished to help the Athenians, but were unable to give them any present succour, as they did not like to break their established law. It was then the ninth day of the first decade; and they could not march out of Sparta on the ninth, when the moon had not reached the full. So they waited for the full of the moon.

107. The barbarians were conducted to Marathon by Hippias, the son of Pisistratus, who

the night before had seen a strange vision in his sleep. He dreamt of lying in his mother's arms, and conjectured the dream to mean that he would be restored to Athens, recover the power which he had lost, and afterwards live to a good old age in his native country. Such was the sense in which he interpreted the vision. He now proceeded to act as guide to the Persians; and, in the first place, he landed the prisoners taken from Eretria upon the island that is called Ægileia, a tract belonging to the Styreans, after which he brought the fleet to anchor off Marathon, and marshalled the bands of the barbarians as they disembarked. As he was thus employed it chanced that he sneezed and at the same time coughed with more violence than was his wont. Now, as he was a man advanced in years, and the greater number of his teeth were loose, it so happened that one of them was driven out with the force of the cough, and fell down into the sand. Hippias took all the pains he could to find it; but the tooth was nowhere to be seen: whereupon he fetched a deep sigh, and said to the bystanders:—

"After all, the land is not ours; and we shall never be able to bring it under. All my share in it is the portion of which my tooth has possession."

So Hippias believed that in this way his dream was fulfilled.

108. The Athenians were drawn up in order of battle in a sacred close belonging to Hercules, when they were joined by the Platæans, who came in full force to their aid. Some time before, the Platæans had put themselves under the rule of the Athenians; and these last had already undertaken many labours on their behalf. The occasion of the surrender was the following. The Platæans suffered grievous things at the hands of the men of Thebes; so, as it chanced that Cleomenes, the son of Anaxandridas, and the Lacedæmonians were in their neighbourhood, they first of all offered to surrender themselves to them. But the Lacedæmonians refused to receive them, and said:—

"We dwell too far off from you, and ours would be but chill succour. Ye might oftentimes be carried into slavery before one of us heard of it. We counsel you rather to give yourselves up to the Athenians, who are your next neighbours, and well able to shelter you."

This they said, not so much out of good will towards the Platæans as because they wished to involve the Athenians in trouble by engaging them in wars with the Bœotians. The Platæans, however, when the Lacedæmonians gave them this counsel, complied at once; and when the sacrifice to the Twelve Gods was being offered at Athens, they came and sat as suppliants about the altar, and gave themselves up to the Athenians. The Thebans no sooner learnt what the Platæans had done than instantly they marched out against them, while the Athenians sent troops to their aid. As the two armies were about to join battle, the Corinthians, who chanced to be at hand, would not allow them to engage; both sides consented to take them for arbitrators, whereupon they made up the quarrel, and fixed the boundary-line between the two states upon this condition: to wit, that if any of the Bœotians wished no longer to belong to Bœotia, the Thebans should allow them to follow their own inclinations. The Corinthians, when they had thus decreed, forthwith departed to their homes: the Athenians likewise set off on their return; but the Bœotians fell upon them during the march, and a battle was fought wherein they were worsted by the Athenians. Hereupon these last would not be bound by the line which the Corinthians had fixed, but advanced beyond those limits, and made the Asôpus the boundary-line between the country of the Thebans and that of the Platæans and Hysians. Under such circumstances did the Platæans give themselves up to Athens; and now they were come to Marathon to bear the Athenians aid.

109. The Athenian generals were divided in their opinions; and some advised not to risk a battle, because they were too few to engage such a host as that of the Medes, while others were for fighting at once; and among these last was Miltiades. He therefore, seeing that opinions were thus divided, and that the less worthy counsel appeared likely to prevail, resolved to go to the Polemarch, and have a conference with him. For the man on whom the lot fell to be Polemarch at Athens was entitled to give his vote with the ten generals, since anciently the Athenians allowed him an equal right of voting with them. The Polemarch at this juncture was Callimachus of Aphidnæ; to him therefore Miltiades went, and said:—

"With thee it rests, Callimachus, either to bring Athens to slavery, or, by securing her freedom, to leave behind thee to all future generations a memory beyond even Harmodius and Aristogeiton. For never since the time that the Athenians became a people were they in so great a danger as now. If they bow their necks beneath the yoke of the Medes, the woes which they will have to suffer when given into the power of Hippias are already determined on; if, on the other hand, they fight and overcome, Athens may rise to be the very first city in Greece. How it comes to pass that these things are likely to happen, and how the determining of them in some sort rests with thee, I will now proceed to make clear. We generals are ten in number, and our votes are divided; half of us wish to engage, half to avoid a combat. Now, if we do not fight, I look to see a great disturbance at Athens which will shake men's resolutions, and then I fear they will submit themselves; but if we fight the battle before any unsoundness show itself among our citizens, let the gods but give us fair play, and we are well able to overcome the enemy. On thee therefore we depend in this matter, which lies wholly in thine own power. Thou hast only to add thy vote to my side and thy country will be free, and not free only, but the first state in Greece. Or, if thou preferrest to give thy vote to them who would decline the combat, then the reverse will follow."

110. Miltiades by these words gained Callimachus; and the addition of the Polemarch's vote caused the decision to be in favour of fighting. Hereupon all those generals who had been desirous of hazarding a battle, when their turn came to command the army, gave up their right to Miltiades. He however, though he accepted their offers, nevertheless waited, and would not fight until his own day of command arrived in due course.

111. Then at length, when his own turn was come, the Athenian battle was set in array, and this was the order of it. Callimachus the Polemarch led the right wing; for it was at that time a rule with the Athenians to give the right wing to the Polemarch. After this followed the tribes, according as they were numbered, in an unbroken line; while last of all came the Platæans, forming the left wing. And ever since that day it has been a custom with the Athenians, in the sacrifices and assemblies held each fifth year at Athens, for the Athenian herald to implore the blessing of the gods on the Platæans conjointly with the Athenians. Now, as they marshalled the host upon the field of Marathon, in order that the Athenian front might be of equal length with the Median, the ranks of the centre were diminished, and it became the weakest part of the line, while the wings were both made strong with a depth of many ranks.

112. So when the battle was set in array, and the victims showed themselves favourable, instantly the Athenians, so soon as they were let go, charged the barbarians at a run. Now the distance between the two armies was little short of eight furlongs. The Persians, therefore, when they saw the Greeks coming on at speed, made ready to receive them, although it seemed to them that the Athenians were bereft of their senses, and bent upon their own destruction; for they saw a mere handful of men coming on at a run without either horsemen or archers. Such was the opinion of the barbarians; but the Athenians in close array fell upon them, and fought in a manner worthy of being recorded. They were the first of the Greeks, so far as I know, who introduced the custom of charging the enemy at a run, and they were likewise the first who dared to look upon the Median garb, and to face men clad in that fashion. Until this time the very name of the Medes had been a terror to the Greeks to hear.

113. The two armies fought together on the plain of Marathon for a length of time; and in the mid battle, where the Persians themselves and the Sacæ had their place, the barbarians were victorious, and broke and pursued the Greeks into the inner country; but on the two wings the Athenians and the Platæans defeated the enemy. Having so done, they suffered the routed barbarians to fly at their ease, and joining the two wings in one, fell upon those who had broken their own centre, and fought and conquered them. These likewise fled, and now the Athenians hung upon the runaways and cut them down, chasing them all the way to the shore, on reaching which they laid hold of the ships and called aloud for fire.

114. It was in the struggle here that Callimachus the Polemarch, after greatly distinguishing himself, lost his life; Stesilaüs too, the son of Thrasilaüs, one of the generals, was slain; and Cynægirus, the son of Euphorion, having seized on a vessel of the enemy's by the ornament at the stern, had his hand cut off by the blow of an axe, and so perished; as likewise did many other Athenians of note and name.

115. Nevertheless the Athenians secured in this way seven of the vessels; while with the remainder the barbarians pushed off, and taking aboard their Eretrian prisoners from the island where they had left them, doubled Cape Sunium, hoping to reach Athens before the return of the Athenians. The Alcmæonidæ were ac-

cused by their countrymen of suggesting this course to them; they had, it was said, an understanding with the Persians, and made a signal to them, by raising a shield, after they were embarked in their ships.

116. The Persians accordingly sailed round Sunium. But the Athenians with all possible speed marched away to the defence of their city, and succeeded in reaching Athens before the appearance of the barbarians: and as their camp at Marathon had been pitched in a precinct of Hercules, so now they encamped in another precinct of the same god at Cynosarges. The barbarian fleet arrived, and lay to off Phalerum, which was at that time the haven of Athens; but after resting awhile upon their oars, they departed and sailed away to Asia.

117. There fell in this battle of Marathon, on the side of the barbarians, about six thousand and four hundred men; on that of the Athenians, one hundred and ninety-two. Such was the number of the slain on the one side and the other. A strange prodigy likewise happened at this fight. Epizêlus, the son of Cuphagoras, an Athenian, was in the thick of the fray, and behaving himself as a brave man should, when suddenly he was stricken with blindness, without blow of sword or dart; and this blindness continued thenceforth during the whole of his after life. The following is the account which he himself, as I have heard, gave of the matter: he said that a gigantic warrior, with a huge beard, which shaded all his shield, stood over against him; but the ghostly semblance passed him by, and slew the man at his side. Such, as I understand, was the tale which Epizêlus told.

118. Datis meanwhile was on his way back to Asia, and had reached Myconus, when he saw in his sleep a vision. What it was is not known; but no sooner was day come than he caused strict search to be made throughout the whole fleet, and finding on board a Phœnician vessel an image of Apollo overlaid with gold, he inquired from whence it had been taken, and learning to what temple it belonged, he took it with him in his own ship to Delos, and placed it in the temple there, enjoining the Delians, who had now come back to their island, to restore the image to the Theban Delium, which lies on the coast over against Chalcis. Having left these injunctions, he sailed away; but the Delians failed to restore the statue; and it was not till twenty years afterwards that the Thebans, warned by an oracle, themselves brought it back to Delium.

119. As for the Eretrians, whom Datis and Artaphernes had carried away captive, when the fleet reached Asia, they were taken up to Susa. Now King Darius, before they were made his prisoners, nourished a fierce anger against these men for having injured him without provocation; but now that he saw them brought into his presence, and become his subjects, he did them no other harm, but only settled them at one of his own stations in Cissia—a place called Ardericca—two hundred and ten furlongs distant from Susa, and forty from the well which yields produce of three different kinds. For from this well they get bitumen, salt, and oil, procuring it in the way that I will now describe: they draw with a swipe, and instead of a bucket make use of the half of a wine-skin; with this the man dips, and after drawing, pours the liquid into a reservoir, wherefrom it passes into another, and there takes three different shapes. The salt and the bitumen forthwith collect and harden, while the oil is drawn off into casks. It is called by the Persians "rhadinacé," is black, and has an unpleasant smell. Here then King Darius established the Eretrians; and here they continued to my time, and still spoke their old language. So thus it fared with the Eretrians.

120. After the full of the moon two thousand Lacedæmonians came to Athens. So eager had they been to arrive in time, that they took but three days to reach Attica from Sparta. They came, however, too late for the battle; yet, as they had a longing to behold the Medes, they continued their march to Marathon and there viewed the slain. Then, after giving the Athenians all praise for their achievement, they departed and returned home.

121. But it fills me with wonderment, and I can in no wise believe the report, that the Alcmæonidæ had an understanding with the Persians, and held them up a shield as a signal, wishing Athens to be brought under the yoke of the barbarians and of Hippias—the Alcmæonidæ, who have shown themselves at least as bitter haters of tyrants as was Callias, the son of Phænippus, and father of Hipponicus. This Callias was the only person at Athens who, when the Pisistratidæ were driven out, and their goods were exposed for sale by the vote of the people, had the courage to make purchases, and likewise in many other ways to display the strongest hostility.

122. He was a man very worthy to be had in remembrance by all, on several accounts. For not only did he thus distinguish himself be-

yond others in the cause of his country's freedom; but likewise, by the honours which he gained at the Olympic Games, where he carried off the prize in the horse-race, and was second in the four-horse chariot-race, and by his victory at an earlier period in the Pythian Games, he showed himself in the eyes of all the Greeks a man most unsparing in his expenditure. He was remarkable too for his conduct in respect of his daughters, three in number; for when they came to be of marriageable age, he gave to each of them a most ample dowry, and placed it at their own disposal, allowing them to choose their husbands from among all the citizens of Athens, and giving each in marriage to the man of her own choice.[1]

123. Now the Alcmæonidæ fell not a whit short of this person in their hatred of tyrants, so that I am astonished at the charge made against them, and cannot bring myself to believe that they held up a shield; for they were men who had remained in exile during the whole time that the tyranny lasted, and they even contrived the trick by which the Pisistratidæ were deprived of their throne. Indeed I look upon them as the persons who in good truth gave Athens her freedom far more than Harmodius and Aristogeiton. For these last did but exasperate the other Pisistratidæ by slaying Hipparchus, and were far from doing anything towards putting down the tyranny; whereas the Alcmæonidæ were manifestly the actual deliverers of Athens, if at least it be true that the Pythoness was prevailed upon by them to bid the Lacedæmonians set Athens free, as I have already related.

124. But perhaps they were offended with the people of Athens; and therefore betrayed their country. Nay, but on the contrary there were none of the Athenians who were held in such general esteem, or who were so laden with honours. So that it is not even reasonable to suppose that a shield was held up by them on this account. A shield was shown, no doubt; that cannot be gainsaid; but who it was that showed it I cannot any further determine.

125. Now the Alcmæonidæ were, even in days of yore, a family of note at Athens; but from the time of Alcmæon, and again of Megacles, they rose to special eminence. The former of these two personages, to wit, Alcmæon, the son of Megacles, when Crœsus the Lydian sent men from Sardis to consult the Delphic

[1] This chapter is generally regarded as an interpolation. It is wanting in several of the best MSS.

oracle, gave aid gladly to his messengers, and assisted them to accomplish their task. Crœsus, informed of Alcmæon's kindnesses by the Lydians who from time to time conveyed his messages to the god, sent for him to Sardis, and when he arrived, made him a present of as much gold as he should be able to carry at one time about his person. Finding that this was the gift assigned him, Alcmæon took his measures, and prepared himself to receive it in the following way. He clothed himself in a loose tunic, which he made to bag greatly at the waist, and placing upon his feet the widest buskins that he could anywhere find, followed his guides into the treasure-house. Here he fell to upon a heap of gold-dust, and in the first place packed as much as he could inside his buskins, between them and his legs; after which he filled the breast of his tunic quite full of gold, and then sprinkling some among his hair, and taking some likewise in his mouth, he came forth from the treasure-house, scarcely able to drag his legs along, like anything rather than a man, with his mouth crammed full, and his bulk increased every way. On seeing him, Crœsus burst into a laugh, and not only let him have all that he had taken, but gave him presents besides of fully equal worth. Thus this house became one of great wealth; and Alcmæon was able to keep horses for the chariot-race, and won the prize at Olympia.

126. Afterwards, in the generation which followed, Clisthenes, king of Sicyon, raised the family to still greater eminence among the Greeks than even that to which it had attained before. For this Clisthenes, who was the son of Aristonymus, the grandson of Myron, and the great-grandson of Andreas, had a daughter, called Agarista, whom he wished to marry to the best husband that he could find in the whole of Greece. At the Olympic Games, therefore, having gained the prize in the chariot-race, he caused public proclamation to be made to the following effect:—"Whoever among the Greeks deems himself worthy to become the son-in-law of Clisthenes, let him come, sixty days hence, or, if he will, sooner, to Sicyon; for within a year's time, counting from the end of the sixty days, Clisthenes will decide on the man to whom he shall contract his daughter." So all the Greeks who were proud of their own merit or of their country flocked to Sicyon as suitors; and Clisthenes had a foot-course and a wrestling-ground made ready, to try their powers.

127. From Italy there came Smindyrides,

the son of Hippocrates, a native of Sybaris—which city about that time was at the very height of its prosperity. He was a man who in luxuriousness of living exceeded all other persons. Likewise there came Damasus, the son of Amyris, surnamed the Wise, a native of Siris. These two were the only suitors from Italy. From the Ionian Gulf appeared Amphimnestus, the son of Epistrophus, an Epidamnian; from Ætolia Males, the brother of that Titormus who excelled all the Greeks in strength, and who wishing to avoid his fellow-men, withdrew himself into the remotest parts of the Ætolian territory. From the Peloponnese came several—Leocêdes, son of that Pheidon, king of the Argives, who established weights and measures throughout the Peloponnese, and was the most insolent of all the Grecians—the same who drove out the Elean directors of the Games, and himself presided over the contests at Olympia—Leocêdes, I say, appeared, this Pheidon's son; and likewise Amiantus, son of Lycurgus, an Arcadian of the city of Trapezus; Laphanes, an Azenian of Pæus, whose father, Euphorion, as the story goes in Arcadia, entertained the Dioscuri at his residence, and thenceforth kept open house for all comers; and lastly, Onomastus, the son of Agæus, a native of Elis. These four came from the Peloponnese. From Athens there arrived Megacles, the son of that Alcmæon who visited Crœsus, and Tisander's son, Hippoclides, the wealthiest and handsomest of the Athenians. There was likewise one Eubœan, Lysanias, who came from Eretria, then a flourishing city. From Thessaly came Diactorides, a Cranonian, of the race of the Scopadæ; and Alcon arrived from the Molossians. This was the list of the suitors.

128. Now when they were all come, and the day appointed had arrived, Clisthenes first of all inquired of each concerning his country and his family; after which he kept them with him a year, and made trial of their manly bearing, their temper, their accomplishments, and their disposition, sometimes drawing them apart for converse, sometimes bringing them all together. Such as were still youths he took with him from time to time to the gymnasia; but the greatest trial of all was at the banquet-table. During the whole period of their stay he lived with them as I have said; and, further, from first to last he entertained them sumptuously. Somehow or other the suitors who came from Athens pleased him the best of all; and of these Hippoclides, Tisander's son, was specially in favour, partly on account of his manly bearing, and partly also because his ancestors were of kin to the Corinthian Cypselids.

129. When at length the day arrived which had been fixed for the espousals, and Clisthenes had to speak out and declare his choice, he first of all made a sacrifice of a hundred oxen, and held a banquet, whereat he entertained all the suitors and the whole people of Sicyon. After the feast was ended, the suitors vied with each other in music and in speaking on a given subject. Presently, as the drinking advanced, Hippoclides, who quite dumbfoundered the rest, called aloud to the flute-player, and bade him strike up a dance; which the man did, and Hippoclides danced to it. And he fancied that he was dancing excellently well; but Clisthenes, who was observing him, began to misdoubt the whole business. Then Hippoclides, after a pause, told an attendant to bring in a table; and when it was brought, he mounted upon it and danced first of all some Laconian figures, then some Attic ones; after which he stood on his head upon the table, and began to toss his legs about. Clisthenes, notwithstanding that he now loathed Hippoclides for a son-in-law, by reason of his dancing and his shamelessness, still, as he wished to avoid an outbreak, had restrained himself during the first and likewise during the second dance; when, however, he saw him tossing his legs in the air, he could no longer contain himself, but cried out, "Son of Tisander, thou hast danced thy wife away!" "What does Hippoclides care?" was the other's answer. And hence the proverb arose.

130. Then Clisthenes commanded silence, and spake thus before the assembled company:—

"Suitors of my daughter, well pleased am I with you all; and right willingly, if it were possible, would I content you all, and not by making choice of one appear to put a slight upon the rest. But as it is out of my power, seeing that I have but one daughter, to grant to all their wishes, I will present to each of you whom I must needs dismiss a talent of silver, for the honour that you have done me in seeking to ally yourselves with my house, and for your long absence from your homes. But my daughter, Agarista, I betroth to Megacles, the son of Alcmæon, to be his wife, according to the usage and wont of Athens."

Then Megacles expressed his readiness; and Clisthenes had the marriage solemnised.

131. Thus ended the affair of the suitors; and thus the Alcmæonidæ came to be famous throughout the whole of Greece. The issue of this marriage was the Clisthenes—so named after his grandfather the Sicyonian—who made the tribes at Athens, and set up the popular government. Megacles had likewise another son, called Hippocrates, whose children were a Megacles and an Agarista, the latter named after Agarista the daughter of Clisthenes. She married Xanthippus, the son of Ariphron; and when she was with child by him had a dream, wherein she fancied that she was delivered of a lion; after which, within a few days, she bore Xanthippus a son, to wit, Pericles.

132. After the blow struck at Marathon, Miltiades, who was previously held in high esteem by his countrymen, increased yet more in influence. Hence, when he told them that he wanted a fleet of seventy ships, with an armed force, and money, without informing them what country he was going to attack, but only promising to enrich them if they would accompany him, seeing that it was a right wealthy land, where they might easily get as much gold as they cared to have—when he told them this, they were quite carried away, and gave him the whole armament which he required.

133. So Miltiades, having got the armament, sailed against Paros, with the object, as he alleged, of punishing the Parians for having gone to war with Athens, inasmuch as a trireme of theirs had come with the Persian fleet to Marathon. This, however, was a mere pretence; the truth was, that Miltiades owed the Parians a grudge, because Lysagoras, the son of Tisias, who was a Parian by birth, had told tales against him to Hydarnes the Persian. Arrived before the place against which his expedition was designed, he drove the Parians within their walls, and forthwith laid siege to the city. At the same time he sent a herald to the inhabitants, and required of them a hundred talents, threatening that, if they refused, he would press the siege, and never give it over till the town was taken. But the Parians, without giving his demand a thought, proceeded to use every means that they could devise for the defence of their city, and even invented new plans for the purpose, one of which was, by working at night, to raise such parts of the wall as were likely to be carried by assault to double their former height.

134. Thus far all the Greeks agree in their accounts of this business; what follows is related upon the testimony of the Parians only. Miltiades had come to his wit's end, when one of the prisoners, a woman named Timo, who was by birth a Parian, and had held the office of under-priestess in the temple of the infernal goddesses, came and conferred with him. This woman, they say, being introduced into the presence of Miltiades, advised him, if he set great store by the capture of the place, to do something which she could suggest to him. When therefore she had told him what it was she meant, he betook himself to the hill which lies in front of the city, and there leapt the fence enclosing the precinct of Ceres Thesmophorus, since he was not able to open the door. After leaping into the place he went straight to the sanctuary, intending to do something within it—either to remove some of the holy things which it was not lawful to stir, or to perform some act or other, I cannot say what—and had just reached the door, when suddenly a feeling of horror came upon him, and he returned back the way he had come; but in jumping down from the outer wall, he strained his thigh, or, as some say, struck the ground with his knee.

135. So Miltiades returned home sick, without bringing the Athenians any money, and without conquering Paros, having done no more than to besiege the town for six-and-twenty days, and ravage the remainder of the island. The Parians, however, when it came to their knowledge that Timo, the under-priestess of the goddesses, had advised Miltiades what he should do, were minded to punish her for her crime; they therefore sent messengers to Delphi, as soon as the siege was at an end, and asked the god if they should put the under-priestess to death. "She had discovered," they said, "to the enemies of her country how they might bring it into subjection, and had exhibited to Miltiades mysteries which it was not lawful for a man to know." But the Pythoness forbade them, and said, "Timo was not in fault; 'twas decreed that Miltiades should come to an unhappy end; and she was sent to lure him to his destruction." Such was the answer given to the Parians by the Pythoness.

136. The Athenians, upon the return of Miltiades from Paros, had much debate concerning him; and Xanthippus, the son of Ariphron, who spoke more freely against him than all the rest, impleaded him before the people, and brought him to trial for his life, on the charge of having dealt deceitfully with the

Athenians. Miltiades, though he was present in court, did not speak in his own defence; for his thigh had begun to mortify, and disabled him from pleading his cause. He was forced to lie on a couch while his defence was made by his friends, who dwelt at most length on the fight at Marathon, while they made mention also of the capture of Lemnos, telling how Miltiades took the island, and, after executing vengeance on the Pelasgians, gave up his conquest to Athens. The judgment of the people was in his favour so far as to spare his life; but for the wrong he had done them they fined him fifty talents. Soon afterwards his thigh completely gangrened and mortified: and so Miltiades died; and the fifty talents were paid by his son Cimon.

137. Now the way in which Miltiades had made himself master of Lemnos was the following. There were certain Pelasgians whom the Athenians once drove out of Attica; whether they did it justly or unjustly I cannot say, since I only know what is reported concerning it, which is the following: Hecatæus, the son of Hegesander, says in his *History* that it was unjustly. "The Athenians," according to him, "had given to the Pelasgi a tract of land at the foot of Hymettus as payment for the wall with which the Pelasgians had surrounded their citadel. This land was barren, and little worth at the time; but the Pelasgians brought it into good condition; whereupon the Athenians begrudged them the tract, and desired to recover it. And so, without any better excuse, they took arms and drove out the Pelasgians." But the Athenians maintain that they were justified in what they did. "The Pelasgians," they say, "while they lived at the foot of Hymettus, were wont to sally forth from that region and commit outrages on their children. For the Athenians used at that time to send their sons and daughters to draw water at the fountain called 'the Nine Springs,' inasmuch as neither they nor the other Greeks had any household slaves in those days; and the maidens, whenever they came, were used rudely and insolently by the Pelasgians. Nor were they even content thus; but at the last they laid a plot, and were caught by the Athenians in the act of making an attempt upon their city. Then did the Athenians give a proof how much better men they were than the Pelasgians; for whereas they might justly have killed them all, having caught them in the very act of rebelling, they spared their lives, and only required that they should leave the coun-

try. Hereupon the Pelasgians quitted Attica, and settled in Lemnos and other places." Such are the accounts respectively of Hecatæus and the Athenians.

138. These same Pelasgians, after they were settled in Lemnos, conceived the wish to be revenged on the Athenians. So, as they were well acquainted with the Athenian festivals, they manned some penteconters, and having laid an ambush to catch the Athenian women as they kept the festival of Diana at Brauron, they succeeded in carrying off a large number, whom they took to Lemnos and there kept as concubines. After a while the women bore children, whom they taught to speak the language of Attica and observe the manners of the Athenians. These boys refused to have any commerce with the sons of the Pelasgian women; and if a Pelasgian boy struck one of their number, they all made common cause, and joined in avenging their comrade; nay, the Greek boys even set up a claim to exercise lordship over the others, and succeeded in gaining the upper hand. When these things came to the ears of the Pelasgians, they took counsel together, and, on considering the matter, they grew frightened, and said one to another, "If these boys even now are resolved to make common cause against the sons of our lawful wives, and seek to exercise lordship over them, what may we expect when they grow up to be men?" Then it seemed good to the Pelasgians to kill all the sons of the Attic women; which they did accordingly, and at the same time slew likewise their mothers. From this deed, and that former crime of the Lemnian women, when they slew their husbands in the days of Thoas, it has come to be usual throughout Greece to call wicked actions by the name of "Lemnian deeds."

139. When the Pelasgians had thus slain their children and their women, the earth refused to bring forth its fruits for them, and their wives bore fewer children, and their flocks and herds increased more slowly than before, till at last, sore pressed by famine and bereavement, they sent men to Delphi, and begged the god to tell them how they might obtain deliverance from their sufferings. The Pythoness answered that "they must give the Athenians whatever satisfaction they might demand." Then the Pelasgians went to Athens and declared their wish to give the Athenians satisfaction for the wrong which they had done to them. So the Athenians had a couch prepared in their townhall, and adorned it

with the fairest coverlets, and set by its side a table laden with all manner of good things, and then told the Pelasgians they must deliver up their country to them in a similar condition. The Pelasgians answered and said, "When a ship comes with a north wind from your country to ours in a single day, then will we give it up to you." This they said because they knew that what they required was impossible, for Attica lies a long way to the south of Lemnos.

140. No more passed at that time. But very many years afterwards, when the Hellespontian Chersonese had been brought under the power of Athens, Miltiades, the son of Cimon, sailed, during the prevalence of the Etesian winds, from Elæus in the Chersonese to Lemnos, and called on the Pelasgians to quit their island, reminding them of the prophecy which they had supposed it impossible to fulfil. The people of Hephæstia obeyed the call; but they of Myrina, not acknowledging the Chersonese to be any part of Attica, refused and were besieged and brought over by force. Thus was Lemnos gained by the Athenians and Miltiades.

The Seventh Book, Entitled
POLYMNIA

1. Now when tidings of the battle that had been fought at Marathon reached the ears of King Darius, the son of Hystaspes, his anger against the Athenians, which had been already roused by their attack upon Sardis, waxed still fiercer, and he became more than ever eager to lead an army against Greece. Instantly he sent off messengers to make proclamation through the several states that fresh levies were to be raised, and these at an increased rate; while ships, horses, provisions, and transports were likewise to be furnished. So the men published his commands; and now all Asia was in commotion by the space of three years, while everywhere, as Greece was to be attacked, the best and bravest were enrolled for the service, and had to make their preparations accordingly.

After this, in the fourth year, the Egyptians whom Cambyses had enslaved revolted from the Persians; whereupon Darius was more hot for war than ever, and earnestly desired to march an army against both adversaries.

2. Now, as he was about to lead forth his levies against Egypt and Athens, a fierce contention for the sovereign power arose among his sons; since the law of the Persians was that a king must not go out with his army, until he has appointed one to succeed him upon the throne. Darius, before he obtained the kingdom, had had three sons born to him from his former wife, who was a daughter of Gobryas; while, since he began to reign, Atossa, the daughter of Cyrus, had borne him four. Artabazanes was the eldest of the first family, and Xerxes of the second. These two, therefore, being the sons of different mothers, were now at variance. Artabazanes claimed the crown as the eldest of all the children, because it was an established custom all over the world for the eldest to have the pre-eminence; while Xerxes, on the other hand, urged that he was sprung

from Atossa, the daughter of Cyrus, and that it was Cyrus who had won the Persians their freedom.

3. Before Darius had pronounced on the matter, it happened that Demaratus, the son of Ariston, who had been deprived of his crown at Sparta, and had afterwards, of his own accord, gone into banishment, came up to Susa, and there heard of the quarrel of the princes. Hereupon, as report says, he went to Xerxes, and advised him, in addition to all that he had urged before, to plead—that at the time when he was born Darius was already king, and bore rule over the Persians; but when Artabazanes came into the world, he was a mere private person. It would therefore be neither right nor seemly that the crown should go to another in preference to himself. "For at Sparta," said Demaratus, by way of suggestion, "the law is that if a king has sons before he comes to the throne, and another son is born to him afterwards, the child so born is heir to his father's kingdom." Xerxes followed this counsel, and Darius, persuaded that he had justice on his side, appointed him his successor. For my own part I believe that, even without this, the crown would have gone to Xerxes; for Atossa was all-powerful.

4. Darius, when he had thus appointed Xerxes his heir, was minded to lead forth his armies; but he was prevented by death while his preparations were still proceeding. He died in the year following the revolt of Egypt and the matters here related, after having reigned in all six-and-thirty years, leaving the revolted Egyptians and the Athenians alike unpunished. At his death the kingdom passed to his son Xerxes.

5. Now Xerxes, on first mounting the throne, was coldly disposed towards the Grecian war, and made it his business to collect an army against Egypt. But Mardonius, the

son of Gobryas, who was at the court, and had more influence with him than any of the other Persians, being his own cousin, the child of a sister of Darius, plied him with discourses like the following:—

"Master, it is not fitting that they of Athens escape scot-free, after doing the Persians such great injury. Complete the work which thou hast now in hand, and then, when the pride of Egypt is brought low, lead an army against Athens. So shalt thou thyself have good report among men, and others shall fear hereafter to attack thy country."

Thus far it was of vengeance that he spoke; but sometimes he would vary the theme, and observe by the way, "that Europe was a wondrous beautiful region, rich in all kinds of cultivated trees, and the soil excellent: no one, save the king, was worthy to own such a land."

6. All this he said, because he longed for adventures, and hoped to become satrap of Greece under the king; and after a while he had his way, and persuaded Xerxes to do according to his desires. Other things, however, occurring about the same time, helped his persuasions. For, in the first place, it chanced that messengers arrived from Thessaly, sent by the Aleuadæ, Thessalian kings, to invite Xerxes into Greece, and to promise him all the assistance which it was in their power to give. And further, the Pisistratidæ, who had come up to Susa, held the same language as the Aleuadæ, and worked upon him even more than they, by means of Onomacritus of Athens, an oracle-monger, and the same who set forth the prophecies of Musæus in their order. The Pisistratidæ had previously been at enmity with this man, but made up the quarrel before they removed to Susa. He was banished from Athens by Hipparchus, the son of Pisistratus, because he foisted into the writings of Musæus a prophecy that the islands which lie off Lemnos would one day disappear in the sea. Lasus of Hermioné caught him in the act of so doing. For this cause Hipparchus banished him, though till then they had been the closest of friends. Now, however, he went up to Susa with the sons of Pisistratus, and they talked very grandly of him to the king; while he, for his part, whenever he was in the king's company, repeated to him certain of the oracles; and while he took care to pass over all that spoke of disaster to the barbarians, brought forward the passages which promised them the greatest success. " 'Twas fated," he told Xerxes, "that a Persian should bridge the Hel-

lespont, and march an army from Asia into Greece." While Onomacritus thus plied Xerxes with his oracles, the Pisistratidæ and Aleuadæ did not cease to press on him their advice, till at last the king yielded, and agreed to lead forth an expedition.

7. First, however, in the year following the death of Darius, he marched against those who had revolted from him; and having reduced them, and laid all Egypt under a far harder yoke than ever his father had put upon it, he gave the government to Achæmenes, who was his own brother, and son to Darius. This Achæmenes was afterwards slain in his government by Inarôs, the son of Psammetichus, a Libyan.

8. (§ 1.) After Egypt was subdued, Xerxes, being about to take in hand the expedition against Athens, called together an assembly of the noblest Persians to learn their opinions, and to lay before them his own designs. So, when the men were met, the king spake thus to them:—

"Persians, I shall not be the first to bring in among you a new custom—I shall but follow one which has come down to us from our forefathers. Never yet, as our old men assure me, has our race reposed itself, since the time when Cyrus overcame Astyages, and so we Persians wrested the sceptre from the Medes. Now in all this God guides us; and we, obeying his guidance, prosper greatly. What need have I to tell you of the deeds of Cyrus and Cambyses, and my own father Darius, how many nations they conquered, and added to our dominions? Ye know right well what great things they achieved. But for myself, I will say that, from the day on which I mounted the throne, I have not ceased to consider by what means I may rival those who have preceded me in this post of honour, and increase the power of Persia as much as any of them. And truly I have pondered upon this, until at last I have found out a way whereby we may at once win glory, and likewise get possession of a land which is as large and as rich as our own —nay, which is even more varied in the fruits it bears—while at the same time we obtain satisfaction and revenge. For this cause I have now called you together, that I may make known to you what I design to do. (§ 2.) My intent is to throw a bridge over the Hellespont and march an army through Europe against Greece, that thereby I may obtain vengeance from the Athenians for the wrongs committed by them against the Persians and against my father. Your own eyes saw the preparations of Darius against these men; but death came upon him, and balked his hopes of revenge. In his behalf, therefore, and in behalf of all the Persians, I undertake the war, and pledge myself not to rest till I have taken and burnt Athens, which has dared, unprovoked, to injure me and my father. Long since they came to Asia with Aristagoras of Miletus, who was one of our slaves, and, entering Sardis, burnt its temples and its sacred groves; again, more lately, when we made a landing upon their coast under Datis and Artaphernes, how roughly they handled us ye do not need to be told. (§ 3.) For these reasons, therefore, I am bent upon this war; and I see likewise therewith united no few advantages. Once let us subdue this people, and those neighbours of theirs who hold the land of Pelops the Phrygian, and we shall extend the Persian territory as far as God's heaven reaches. The sun will then shine on no land beyond our borders; for I will pass through Europe from one end to the other, and with your aid make of all the lands which it contains one country. For thus, if what I hear be true, affairs stand: the nations whereof I have spoken, once swept away, there is no city, no country left in all the world, which will venture so much as to withstand us in arms. By this course then we shall bring all mankind under our yoke, alike those who are guilty and those who are innocent of doing us wrong. (§ 4.) For yourselves, if you wish to please me, do as follows: when I announce the time for the army to meet together, hasten to the muster with a good will, every one of you; and know that to the man who brings with him the most gallant array I will give the gifts which our people consider the most honourable. This then is what ye have to do. But to show that I am not self-willed in this matter, I lay the business before you, and give you full leave to speak your minds upon it openly."

Xerxes, having so spoken, held his peace.

9. (§ 1.) Whereupon Mardonius took the word, and said:—

"Of a truth, my lord, thou dost surpass, not only all living Persians, but likewise those yet unborn. Most true and right is each word that thou hast now uttered; but best of all thy resolve not to let the Ionians who live in Europe —a worthless crew—mock us any more. It were indeed a monstrous thing if, after conquering and enslaving the Sacæ, the Indians, the Ethiopians, the Assyrians, and many other mighty nations, not for any wrong that they had done

us, but only to increase our empire, we should then allow the Greeks, who have done us such wanton injury, to escape our vengeance. What is it that we fear in them?—not surely their numbers?—not the greatness of their wealth? We know the manner of their battle—we know how weak their power is; already have we subdued their children who dwell in our country, the Ionians, Æolians, and Dorians. I myself have had experience of these men when I marched against them by the orders of thy father; and though I went as far as Macedonia, and came but a little short of reaching Athens itself, yet not a soul ventured to come out against me to battle. (§ 2.) And yet, I am told, these very Greeks are wont to wage wars against one another in the most foolish way, through sheer perversity and doltishness. For no sooner is war proclaimed than they search out the smoothest and fairest plain that is to be found in all the land, and there they assemble and fight; whence it comes to pass that even the conquerors depart with great loss: I say nothing of the conquered, for they are destroyed altogether. Now surely, as they are all of one speech, they ought to interchange heralds and messengers, and make up their differences by any means rather than battle; or, at the worst, if they must needs fight one against another, they ought to post themselves as strongly as possible, and so try their quarrels. But, notwithstanding that they have so foolish a manner of warfare, yet these Greeks, when I led my army against them to the very borders of Macedonia, did not so much as think of offering me battle. (§ 3.) Who then will dare, O king! to meet thee in arms, when thou comest with all Asia's warriors at thy back, and with all her ships? For my part I do not believe the Greek people will be so foolhardy. Grant, however, that I am mistaken herein, and that they are foolish enough to meet us in open fight; in that case they will learn that there are no such soldiers in the whole world as we. Nevertheless let us spare no pains; for nothing comes without trouble; but all that men acquire is got by painstaking."

When Mardonius had in this way softened the harsh speech of Xerxes, he too held his peace.

10. [§ 1.] The other Persians were silent; all feared to raise their voice against the plan proposed to them. But Artabanus, the son of Hystaspes, and uncle of Xerxes, trusting to his relationship, was bold to speak:—"O king!" he

said, "it is impossible, if no more than one opinion is uttered, to make choice of the best: a man is forced then to follow whatever advice may have been given him; but if opposite speeches are delivered, then choice can be exercised. In like manner pure gold is not recognised by itself; but when we test it along with baser ore, we perceive which is the better. I counselled thy father, Darius, who was my own brother, not to attack the Scyths, a race of people who had no town in their whole land. He thought however to subdue those wandering tribes, and would not listen to me, but marched an army against them, and ere he returned home lost many of his bravest warriors. Thou art about, O king! to attack a people far superior to the Scyths, a people distinguished above others both by land and sea. 'Tis fit therefore that I should tell thee what danger thou incurrest hereby. (§ 2.) Thou sayest that thou wilt bridge the Hellespont, and lead thy troops through Europe against Greece. Now suppose some disaster befall thee by land or sea, or by both. It may be even so; for the men are reputed valiant. Indeed one may measure their prowess from what they have already done; for when Datis and Artaphernes led their huge army against Attica, the Athenians singly defeated them. But grant they are not successful on both elements. Still, if they man their ships, and, defeating us by sea, sail to the Hellespont, and there destroy our bridge—that, sire, were a fearful hazard. (§ 3.) And here 'tis not by my own mother wit alone that I conjecture what will happen; but I remember how narrowly we escaped disaster once, when thy father, after throwing bridges over the Thracian Bosphorus and the Ister, marched against the Scythians, and they tried every sort of prayer to induce the Ionians, who had charge of the bridge over the Ister, to break the passage. On that day, if Histiæus, the king of Miletus, had sided with the other princes, and not set himself to oppose their views, the empire of the Persians would have come to nought. Surely a dreadful thing is this even to hear said, that the king's fortunes depended wholly on one man.

(§ 4.) "Think then no more of incurring so great a danger when no need presses, but follow the advice I tender. Break up this meeting, and when thou hast well considered the matter with thyself, and settled what thou wilt do, declare to us thy resolve. I know not of aught in the world that so profits a man as taking good counsel with himself; for even if things

fall out against one's hopes, still one has counselled well, though fortune has made the counsel of none effect: whereas if a man counsels ill and luck follows, he has gotten a windfall, but his counsel is none the less silly. (§ 5.) Seest thou how God with his lightning smites always the bigger animals, and will not suffer them to wax insolent, while those of a lesser bulk chafe him not? How likewise his bolts fall ever on the highest houses and the tallest trees? So plainly does He love to bring down everything that exalts itself. Thus ofttimes a mighty host is discomfited by a few men, when God in his jealousy sends fear or storm from heaven, and they perish in a way unworthy of them. For God allows no one to have high thoughts but Himself. (§ 6.) Again, hurry always brings about disasters, from which huge sufferings are wont to arise; but in delay lie many advantages, not apparent (it may be) at first sight, but such as in course of time are seen of all. Such then is my counsel to thee, O king!

(§ 7.) "And thou, Mardonius, son of Gobryas, forbear to speak foolishly concerning the Greeks, who are men that ought not to be lightly esteemed by us. For while thou revilest the Greeks, thou dost encourage the king to lead his own troops against them; and this, as it seems to me, is what thou art specially striving to accomplish. Heaven send thou succeed not to thy wish! For slander is of all evils the most terrible. In it two men do wrong, and one man has wrong done to him. The slanderer does wrong, forasmuch as he abuses a man behind his back; and the hearer, forasmuch as he believes what he has not searched into thoroughly. The man slandered in his absence suffers wrong at the hands of both: for one brings against him a false charge; and the other thinks him an evildoer. (§ 8.) If, however, it must needs be that we go to war with this people, at least allow the king to abide at home in Persia. Then let thee and me both stake our children on the issue, and do thou choose out thy men, and, taking with thee whatever number of troops thou likest, lead forth our armies to battle. If things go well for the king, as thou sayest they will, let me and my children be put to death; but if they fall out as I prophesy, let thy children suffer, and thyself too, if thou shalt come back alive. But shouldest thou refuse this wager, and still resolve to march an army against Greece, sure I am that some of those whom thou leavest behind thee here will one day receive the sad tidings that Mardonius has brought a great disaster upon the Persian people, and lies a prey to dogs and birds somewhere in the land of the Athenians, or else in that of the Lacedæmonians; unless indeed thou shalt have perished sooner by the way, experiencing in thy own person the might of those men on whom thou wouldest fain induce the king to make war."

11. Thus spake Artabanus. But Xerxes, full of wrath, replied to him:—

"Artabanus, thou art my father's brother—that shall save thee from receiving the due meed of thy silly words. One shame however I will lay upon thee, coward and faint-hearted as thou art—thou shalt not come with me to fight these Greeks, but shalt tarry here with the women. Without thy aid I will accomplish all of which I spake. For let me not be thought the child of Darius, the son of Hystaspes, the son of Arsames, the son of Ariaramnes, the son of Teispes, the son of Cyrus, the son of Cambyses, the son of Teispes, the son of Achæmenes, if I take not vengeance on the Athenians. Full well I know that, were we to remain at rest, yet would not they, but would most certainly invade our country, if at least it be right to judge from what they have already done; for, remember, it was they who fired Sardis and attacked Asia. So now retreat is on both sides impossible, and the choice lies between doing and suffering injury; either our empire must pass under the dominion of the Greeks, or their land become the prey of the Persians; for there is no middle course left in this quarrel. It is right then that we, who have in times past received wrong, should now avenge it, and that I should thereby discover what that great risk is which I run in marching against these men—men whom Pelops the Phrygian, a vassal of my forefathers, subdued so utterly, that to this day both the land, and the people who dwell therein, alike bear the name of the conqueror!"

12. Thus far did the speaking proceed. Afterwards evening fell; and Xerxes began to find the advice of Artabanus greatly disquiet him. So he thought upon it during the night, and concluded at last that it was not for his advantage to lead an army into Greece. When he had thus made up his mind anew, he fell asleep. And now he saw in the night, as the Persians declare, a vision of this nature—he thought a tall and beautiful man stood over him and said, "Hast thou then changed thy mind, Persian, and wilt thou not lead forth thy host against the Greeks, after commanding

the Persians to gather together their levies? Be sure thou doest not well to change; nor is there a man here who will approve thy conduct. The course that thou didst determine on during the day, let that be followed." After thus speaking the man seemed to Xerxes to fly away.

13. Day dawned; and the king made no account of this dream, but called together the same Persians as before, and spake to them as follows:—

"Men of Persia, forgive me if I alter the resolve to which I came so lately. Consider that I have not yet reached to the full growth of my wisdom, and that they who urge me to engage in this war leave me not to myself for a moment. When I heard the advice of Artabanus, my young blood suddenly boiled; and I spake words against him little befitting his years: now however I confess my fault, and am resolved to follow his counsel. Understand then that I have changed my intent with respect to carrying war into Greece, and cease to trouble yourselves."

When they heard these words, the Persians were full of joy, and, falling down at the feet of Xerxes, made obeisance to him.

14. But when night came, again the same vision stood over Xerxes as he slept, and said, "Son of Darius, it seems thou hast openly before all the Persians renounced the expedition, making light of my words, as though thou hadst not heard them spoken. Know therefore and be well assured, that unless thou go forth to the war, this thing shall happen unto thee—as thou art grown mighty and puissant in a short space, so likewise shalt thou within a little time be brought low indeed."

15. Then Xerxes, greatly frightened at the vision which he had seen, sprang from his couch, and sent a messenger to call Artabanus, who came at the summons, when Xerxes spoke to him in these words:—

"Artabanus, at the moment I acted foolishly, when I gave thee ill words in return for thy good advice. However it was not long ere I repented, and was convinced that thy counsel was such as I ought to follow. But I may not now act in this way, greatly as I desire to do so. For ever since I repented and changed my mind a dream has haunted me, which disapproves my intentions, and has now just gone from me with threats. Now if this dream is sent to me from God, and if it is indeed his will that our troops should march against Greece, thou too wilt have the same dream come to thee and receive the same commands as myself. And this will be most sure to happen, I think, if thou puttest on the dress which I am wont to wear, and then, after taking thy seat upon my throne, liest down to sleep on my bed."

16. Such were the words of Xerxes. Artabanus would not at first yield to the command of the king; for he deemed himself unworthy to sit upon the royal throne. At the last however he was forced to give way, and did as Xerxes bade him; but first he spake thus to the king [§ 1.]:—

"To me, sire, it seems to matter little whether a man is wise himself or willing to hearken to such as give good advice. In thee truly are found both tempers; but the counsels of evil men lead thee astray: they are like the gales of wind which vex the sea—else the most useful thing for man in the whole world—and suffer it not to follow the bent of its own nature. For myself, it irked me not so much to be reproached by thee, as to observe that when two courses were placed before the Persian people, one of a nature to increase their pride, the other to humble it, by showing them how hurtful it is to allow one's heart always to covet more than one at present possesses, thou madest choice of that which was the worse both for thyself and for the Persians. (§ 2.) Now thou sayest that from the time when thou didst approve the better course, and give up the thought of warring against Greece, a dream has haunted thee, sent by some god or other, which will not suffer thee to lay aside the expedition. But such things, my son, have of a truth nothing divine in them. The dreams that wander to and fro among mankind, I will tell thee of what nature they are—I who have seen so many more years than thou. Whatever a man has been thinking of during the day is wont to hover round him in the visions of his dreams at night. Now we during these many days past have had our hands full of this enterprise. (§ 3.) If however the matter be not as I suppose, but God has indeed some part therein, thou hast in brief declared the whole that can be said concerning it—let it e'en appear to me as it has to thee, and lay on me the same injunctions. But it ought not to appear to me any the more if I put on thy clothes than if I wear my own, nor if I go to sleep in thy bed than if I do so in mine—supposing, I mean, that it is about to appear at all. For this thing, be it what it may, that visits thee in thy sleep, surely is not so far gone in

folly as to see me, and because I am dressed in thy clothes, straightway to mistake me for thee. Now however our business is to see if it will regard me as of small account, and not vouchsafe to appear to me, whether I wear mine own clothes or thine, while it keeps on haunting thee continually. If it does so, and appears often, I should myself say that it was from God. For the rest, if thy mind is fixed, and it is not possible to turn thee from thy design, but I must needs go and sleep in thy bed, well and good, let it be even so; and when I have done as thou wishest, then let the dream appear to me. Till such time, however, I shall keep to my former opinion."

17. Thus spake Artabanus; and when he had so said, thinking to show Xerxes that his words were nought, he did according to his orders. Having put on the garments which Xerxes was wont to wear and taken his seat upon the royal throne, he lay down to sleep upon the king's own bed. As he slept, there appeared to him the very same dream which had been seen by Xerxes; it came and stood over Artabanus, and said:—

"Thou art the man, then, who, feigning to be tender of Xerxes, seekest to dissuade him from leading his armies against the Greeks! But thou shalt not escape scathless, either now or in time to come, because thou hast sought to prevent that which is fated to happen. As for Xerxes, it has been plainly told to himself what will befall him, if he refuses to perform my bidding."

18. In such words, as Artabanus thought, the vision threatened him, and then endeavoured to burn out his eyes with red-hot irons. At this he shrieked, and, leaping from his couch, hurried to Xerxes, and, sitting down at his side, gave him a full account of the vision; after which he went on to speak in the words which follow:—

"I, O King! am a man who have seen many mighty empires overthrown by weaker ones; and therefore it was that I sought to hinder thee from being quite carried away by thy youth; since I knew how evil a thing it is to covet more than one possesses. I could remember the expedition of Cyrus against the Massagetæ, and what was the issue of it; I could recollect the march of Cambyses against the Ethiops; I had taken part in the attack of Darius upon the Scyths—bearing therefore all these things in mind, I thought with myself that if thou shouldst remain at peace, all men would deem thee fortunate. But as this impulse has plainly come from above, and a heaven-sent destruction seems about to overtake the Greeks, behold, I change to another mind, and alter my thoughts upon the matter. Do thou therefore make known to the Persians what the god has declared, and bid them follow the orders which were first given, and prepare their levies. Be careful to act so that the bounty of the god may not be hindered by slackness on thy part."

Thus spake these two together; and Xerxes, being in good heart on account of the vision, when day broke, laid all before the Persians; while Artabanus, who had formerly been the only person openly to oppose the expedition, now showed as openly that he favoured it.

19. After Xerxes had thus determined to go forth to the war, there appeared to him in his sleep yet a third vision. The Magi were consulted upon it, and said that its meaning reached to the whole earth, and that all mankind would become his servants. Now the vision which the king saw was this: he dreamt that he was crowned with a branch of an olive tree, and that boughs spread out from the olive branch and covered the whole earth; then suddenly the garland, as it lay upon his brow, vanished. So when the Magi had thus interpreted the vision, straightway all the Persians who were come together departed to their several governments, where each displayed the greatest zeal, on the faith of the king's offers. For all hoped to obtain for themselves the gifts which had been promised. And so Xerxes gathered together his host, ransacking every corner of the continent.

20. Reckoning from the recovery of Egypt, Xerxes spent four full years in collecting his host, and making ready all things that were needful for his soldiers. It was not till the close of the fifth year that he set forth on his march, accompanied by a mighty multitude. For of all the armaments whereof any mention has reached us, this was by far the greatest; insomuch that no other expedition compared to this seems of any account, neither that which Darius undertook against the Scythians, nor the expedition of the Scythians (which the attack of Darius was designed to avenge), when they, being in pursuit of the Cimmerians, fell upon the Median territory, and subdued and held for a time almost the whole of Upper Asia; nor, again, that of the Atridæ against Troy, of which we hear in story; nor that of the Mysians and Teucrians, which was still earlier, wherein these nations crossed the Bosphorus into Europe, and, after conquering all Thrace, pressed forward till they came to the Ionian Sea, while southward they reached as far as the river Peneus.

21. All these expeditions, and others, if such there were, are as nothing compared with this. For was there a nation in all Asia which Xerxes did not bring with him against Greece? Or was there a river, except those of unusual size, which sufficed for his troops to drink? One nation furnished ships; another was arrayed among the foot-soldiers; a third had to supply horses; a fourth, transports for the horse and men likewise for the transport service; a fifth, ships of war towards the bridges; a sixth, ships and provisions.

22. And in the first place, because the former fleet had met with so great a disaster about Athos, preparations were made, by the space of about three years, in that quarter. A fleet of triremes lay at Elæus in the Chersonese; and from this station detachments were sent by the various nations whereof the army was composed, which relieved one another at intervals, and worked at a trench beneath the lash of taskmasters; while the people dwelling about Athos bore likewise a part in the labour. Two Persians, Bubares, the son of Megabazus, and Artachæes, the son of Artæus, superintended the undertaking.

Athos is a great and famous mountain, inhabited by men, and stretching far out into the sea. Where the mountain ends towards the mainland it forms a peninsula; and in this place there is a neck of land about twelve furlongs across, the whole extent whereof, from the sea of the Acanthians to that over against Torôné, is a level plain, broken only by a few low hills. Here, upon this isthmus where Athos ends, is Sané, a Greek city. Inside of Sané, and upon Athos itself, are a number of towns, which Xerxes was now employed in disjoining from the continent: these are Dium, Olophyxus, Acrothôum, Thyssus, and Cleônæ. Among these cities Athos was divided.

23. Now the manner in which they dug was the following: a line was drawn across by the city of Sané; and along this the various nations parcelled out among themselves the work to be done. When the trench grew deep, the workmen at the bottom continued to dig, while others handed the earth, as it was dug out, to labourers placed higher up upon ladders, and these taking it, passed it on farther, till it came at last to those at the top, who carried it off and emptied it away. All the

other nations, therefore, except the Phœnicians, had double labour; for the sides of the trench fell in continually, as could not but happen, since they made the width no greater at the top than it was required to be at the bottom. But the Phœnicians showed in this the skill which they are wont to exhibit in all their undertakings. For in the portion of the work which was allotted to them they began by making the trench at the top twice as wide as the prescribed measure, and then as they dug downwards approached the sides nearer and nearer together, so that when they reached the bottom their part of the work was of the same width as the rest. In a meadow near, there was a place of assembly and a market; and hither great quantities of corn, ready ground, were brought from Asia.

24. It seems to me, when I consider this work, that Xerxes, in making it, was actuated by a feeling of pride, wishing to display the extent of his power, and to leave a memorial behind him to posterity. For notwithstanding that it was open to him, with no trouble at all, to have had his ships drawn across the isthmus, yet he issued orders that a canal should be made through which the sea might flow, and that it should be of such a width as would allow of two triremes passing through it abreast with the oars in action. He likewise gave to the same persons who were set over the digging of the trench, the task of making a bridge across the river Strymon.

25. While these things were in progress, he was having cables prepared for his bridges, some of papyrus and some of white flax, a business which he entrusted to the Phœnicians and the Egyptians. He likewise laid up stores of provisions in divers places, to save the army and the beasts of burthen from suffering want upon their march into Greece. He inquired carefully about all the sites, and had the stores laid up in such as were most convenient, causing them to be brought across from various parts of Asia and in various ways, some in transports and others in merchantmen. The greater portion was carried to Leucé-Acté, upon the Thracian coast; some part, however, was conveyed to Tyrodiza, in the country of the Perinthians, some to Doriscus, some to Eïon upon the Strymon, and some to Macedonia.

26. During the time that all these labours were in progress, the land army which had been collected was marching with Xerxes towards Sardis, having started from Critalla in Cappadocia. At this spot all the host which was about to accompany the king in his passage across the continent had been bidden to assemble. And here I have it not in my power to mention which of the satraps was adjudged to have brought his troops in the most gallant array, and on that account rewarded by the king according to his promise; for I do not know whether this matter ever came to a judgment. But it is certain that the host of Xerxes, after crossing the river Halys, marched through Phrygia till it reached the city of Celænæ. Here are the sources of the river Mæander, and likewise of another stream of no less size, which bears the name of Catarrhactes (or the Cataract); the last-named river has its rise in the market-place of Celænæ, and empties itself into the Mæander. Here, too, in this market-place, is hung up to view the skin of the Silênus Marsyas, which Apollo, as the Phrygian story goes, stripped off and placed there.

27. Now there lived in this city a certain Pythius, the son of Atys, a Lydian. This man entertained Xerxes and his whole army in a most magnificent fashion, offering at the same time to give him a sum of money for the war. Xerxes, upon the mention of money, turned to the Persians who stood by, and asked of them, "Who is this Pythius, and what wealth has he, that he should venture on such an offer as this?" They answered him, "This is the man, O king! who gave thy father Darius the golden plane-tree, and likewise the golden vine; and he is still the wealthiest man we know of in all the world, excepting thee."

28. Xerxes marvelled at these last words; and now, addressing Pythius with his own lips, he asked him what the amount of his wealth really was. Pythius answered as follows:—

"O king! I will not hide this matter from thee, nor make pretence that I do not know how rich I am; but as I know perfectly, I will declare all fully before thee. For when thy journey was noised abroad, and I heard thou wert coming down to the Grecian coast, straightway, as I wished to give thee a sum of money for the war, I made count of my stores, and found them to be two thousand talents of silver, and of gold four millions of Daric staters, wanting seven thousand. All this I willingly make over to thee as a gift; and when it is gone, my slaves and my estates in land will be wealth enough for my wants."

29. This speech charmed Xerxes, and he re-

plied, "Dear Lydian, since I left Persia there is no man but thou who has either desired to entertain my army, or come forward of his own free will to offer me a sum of money for the war. Thou hast done both the one and the other, feasting my troops magnificently, and now making offer of a right noble sum. In return, this is what I will bestow on thee. Thou shalt be my sworn friend from this day; and the seven thousand staters which are wanting to make up thy four millions I will supply, so that the full tale may be no longer lacking, and that thou mayest owe the completion of the round sum to me. Continue to enjoy all that thou hast acquired hitherto; and be sure to remain ever such as thou now art. If thou dost, thou wilt not repent of it so long as thy life endures."

30. When Xerxes had so spoken and had made good his promises to Pythius, he pressed forward upon his march; and passing Anaua, a Phrygian city, and a lake from which salt is gathered, he came to Colossæ, a Phrygian city of great size, situated at a spot where the river Lycus plunges into a chasm and disappears. This river, after running under ground a distance of about five furlongs, reappears once more, and empties itself, like the stream above mentioned, into the Mæander. Leaving Colossæ, the army approached the borders of Phrygia where it abuts on Lydia; and here they came to a city called Cydrara, where was a pillar set up by Crœsus, having an inscription on it, showing the boundaries of the two countries.

31. Where it quits Phrygia and enters Lydia the road separates; the way on the left leads into Caria, while that on the right conducts to Sardis. If you follow this route, you must cross the Mæander, and then pass by the city Callatêbus, where the men live who make honey out of wheat and the fruit of the tamarisk Xerxes, who chose this way, found here a plane-tree so beautiful, that he presented it with golden ornaments, and put it under the care of one of his Immortals. The day after, he entered the Lydian capital.

32. Here his first care was to send off heralds into Greece, who were to prefer a demand for earth and water, and to require that preparations should be made everywhere to feast the king. To Athens indeed and to Sparta he sent no such demand; but these cities excepted, his messengers went everywhere. Now the reason why he sent for earth and water to states which had already refused was this: he thought that

although they had refused when Darius made the demand, they would now be too frightened to venture to say him nay. So he sent his heralds, wishing to know for certain how it would be.

33. Xerxes, after this, made preparations to advance to Abydos, where the bridge across the Hellespont from Asia to Europe was lately finished. Midway between Sestos and Madytus in the Hellespontine Chersonese, and right over against Abydos, there is a rocky tongue of land which runs out for some distance into the sea. This is the place where no long time afterwards the Greeks under Xanthippus, the son of Ariphron, took Artaÿctes the Persian, who was at that time governor of Sestos, and nailed him living to a plank. He was the Artaÿctes who brought women into the temple of Protesilaüs at Elæus, and there was guilty of most unholy deeds.

34. Towards this tongue of land then, the men to whom the business was assigned carried out a double bridge from Abydos; and while the Phœnicians constructed one line with cables of white flax, the Egyptians in the other used ropes made of papyrus. Now it is seven furlongs across from Abydos to the opposite coast. When, therefore, the channel had been bridged successfully, it happened that a great storm arising broke the whole work to pieces, and destroyed all that had been done.

35. So when Xerxes heard of it he was full of wrath, and straightway gave orders that the Hellespont should receive three hundred lashes, and that a pair of fetters should be cast into it. Nay, I have even heard it said that he bade the branders take their irons and therewith brand the Hellespont. It is certain that he commanded those who scourged the waters to utter, as they lashed them, these barbarian and wicked words: "Thou bitter water, thy lord lays on thee this punishment because thou hast wronged him without a cause, having suffered no evil at his hands. Verily King Xerxes will cross thee, whether thou wilt or no. Well dost thou deserve that no man should honour thee with sacrifice; for thou art of a truth a treacherous and unsavoury river." While the sea was thus punished by his orders, he likewise commanded that the overseers of the work should lose their heads.

36. Then they, whose business it was, executed the unpleasing task laid upon them; and other master-builders were set over the work, who accomplished it in the way which I will now describe.

They joined together triremes and pente-conters, 360 to support the bridge on the side of the Euxine Sea, and 314 to sustain the other; and these they placed at right angles to the sea, and in the direction of the current of the Hellespont, relieving by these means the tension of the shore cables. Having joined the vessels, they moored them with anchors of unusual size, that the vessels of the bridge towards the Euxine might resist the winds which blow from within the straits, and that those of the more western bridge facing the Egean might withstand the winds which set in from the south and from the south-east. A gap was left in the penteconters in no fewer than three places, to afford a passage for such light craft as chose to enter or leave the Eux-ine. When all this was done, they made the cables taut from the shore by the help of wood-en capstans. This time, moreover, instead of using the two materials separately, they as-signed to each bridge six cables, two of which were of white flax, while four were of papyrus. Both cables were of the same size and quality; but the flaxen were the heavier, weighing not less than a talent the cubit. When the bridge across the channel was thus complete, trunks of trees were sawn into planks, which were cut to the width of the bridge, and these were laid side by side upon the tightened cables, and then fastened on the top. This done, brushwood was brought, and arranged upon the planks, after which earth was heaped upon the brushwood, and the whole trodden down into a solid mass. Lastly a bulwark was set up on either side of this causeway, of such a height as to prevent the sumpter-beasts and the horses from seeing over it and taking fright at the water.

37. And now when all was prepared—the bridges, and the works at Athos, the break-waters about the mouths of the cutting, which were made to hinder the surf from blocking up the entrances, and the cutting itself; and when the news came to Xerxes that this last was completely finished—then at length the host, having first wintered at Sardis, began its march towards Abydos, fully equipped, on the first approach of spring. At the moment of departure, the sun suddenly quitted his seat in the heavens, and disappeared, though there were no clouds in sight, but the sky was clear and serene. Day was thus turned into night; whereupon Xerxes, who saw and remarked the prodigy, was seized with alarm, and send-ing at once for the Magians, inquired of them

the meaning of the portent. They replied—"God is foreshowing to the Greeks the destruc-tion of their cities; for the sun foretells for them, and the moon for us." So Xerxes, thus instructed, proceeded on his way with great gladness of heart.

38. The army had begun its march, when Pythius the Lydian, affrighted at the heaven-ly portent, and emboldened by his gifts, came to Xerxes and said—"Grant me, O my lord! a favour which is to thee a light matter, but to me of vast account." Then Xerxes, who looked for nothing less than such a prayer as Pythius in fact preferred, engaged to grant him whatever he wished, and commanded him to tell his wish freely. So Pythius, full of bold-ness, went on to say:—

"O my lord! thy servant has five sons; and it chances that all are called upon to join thee in this march against Greece. I beseech thee, have compassion upon my years; and let one of my sons, the eldest, remain behind, to be my prop and stay, and the guardian of my wealth. Take with thee the other four; and when thou hast done all that is in thy heart, mayest thou come back in safety."

39. But Xerxes was greatly angered, and re-plied to him: "Thou wretch! darest thou speak to me of thy son, when I am myself on the march against Greece, with sons, and brothers, and kinsfolk, and friends? Thou, who art my bond-slave, and art in duty bound to follow me with all thy household, not excepting thy wife! Know that man's spirit dwelleth in his ears, and when it hears good things, straight-way it fills all his body with delight; but no sooner does it hear the contrary than it heaves and swells with passion. As when thou didst good deeds and madest good offers to me, thou wert not able to boast of having outdone the king in bountifulness, so now when thou art changed and grown impudent, thou shalt not receive all thy deserts, but less. For thyself and four of thy five sons, the entertainment which I had of thee shall gain protection; but as for him to whom thou clingest above the rest, the forfeit of his life shall be thy punish-ment." Having thus spoken, forthwith he com-manded those to whom such tasks were as-signed to seek out the eldest of the sons of Pythius, and having cut his body asunder, to place the two halves, one on the right, the other on the left, of the great road, so that the army might march out between them.

40. Then the king's orders were obeyed; and the army marched out between the two

halves of the carcase. First of all went the baggage-bearers, and the sumpter-beasts, and then a vast crowd of many nations mingled together without any intervals, amounting to more than one half of the army. After these troops an empty space was left, to separate between them and the king. In front of the king went first a thousand horsemen, picked men of the Persian nation—then spearmen a thousand, likewise chosen troops, with their spear-heads pointing towards the ground—next ten of the sacred horses called Nisæan, all daintily caparisoned. (Now these horses are called Nisæan, because they come from the Nisæan plain, a vast flat in Media, producing horses of unusual size.) After the ten sacred horses came the holy chariot of Jupiter, drawn by eight milk-white steeds, with the charioteer on foot behind them holding the reins; for no mortal is ever allowed to mount into the car. Next to this came Xerxes himself, riding in a chariot drawn by Nisæan horses, with his charioteer, Patiramphes, the son of Otanes, a Persian, standing by his side.

41. Thus rode forth Xerxes from Sardis—but he was accustomed every now and then, when the fancy took him, to alight from his chariot and travel in a litter. Immediately behind the king there followed a body of a thousand spearmen, the noblest and bravest of the Persians, holding their lances in the usual manner—then came a thousand Persian horse, picked men—then ten thousand, picked also after the rest, and serving on foot. Of these last one thousand carried spears with golden pomegranates at their lower end instead of spikes; and these encircled the other nine thousand, who bore on their spears pomegranates of silver. The spearmen too who pointed their lances towards the ground had golden pomegranates; and the thousand Persians who followed close after Xerxes had golden apples. Behind the ten thousand footmen came a body of Persian cavalry, likewise ten thousand; after which there was again a void space for as much as two furlongs; and then the rest of the army followed in a confused crowd.

42. The march of the army, after leaving Lydia, was directed upon the river Caïcus and the land of Mysia. Beyond the Caïcus the road, leaving Mount Cana upon the left, passed through the Atarnean plain, to the city of Carina. Quitting this, the troops advanced across the plain of Thebé, passing Adramyttium, and Antandrus, the Pelasgic city; then, holding Mount Ida upon the left hand, it entered the Trojan territory. On this march the Persians suffered some loss; for as they bivouacked during the night at the foot of Ida, a storm of thunder and lightning burst upon them, and killed no small number.

43. On reaching the Scamander, which was the first stream, of all that they had crossed since they left Sardis, whose water failed them and did not suffice to satisfy the thirst of men and cattle, Xerxes ascended into the Pergamus of Priam, since he had a longing to behold the place. When he had seen everything, and inquired into all particulars, he made an offering of a thousand oxen to the Trojan Minerva, while the Magians poured libations to the heroes who were slain at Troy. The night after, a panic fell upon the camp: but in the morning they set off with daylight, and skirting on the left hand the towns Rhœteum, Ophryneum, and Dardanus (which borders on Abydos), on the right the Teucrians of Gergis, so reached Abydos.

44. Arrived here, Xerxes wished to look upon all his host; so as there was a throne of white marble upon a hill near the city, which they of Abydos had prepared beforehand, by the king's bidding, for his especial use, Xerxes took his seat on it, and, gazing thence upon the shore below, beheld at one view all his land forces and all his ships. While thus employed, he felt a desire to behold a sailing-match among his ships, which accordingly took place, and was won by the Phœnicians of Sidon, much to the joy of Xerxes, who was delighted alike with the race and with his army.

45. And now, as he looked and saw the whole Hellespont covered with the vessels of his fleet, and all the shore and every plain about Abydos as full as possible of men, Xerxes congratulated himself on his good fortune; but after a little while he wept.

46. Then Artabanus, the king's uncle (the same who at the first so freely spake his mind to the king, and advised him not to lead his army against Greece), when he heard that Xerxes was in tears, went to him, and said:—

"How different, sire, is what thou art now doing, from what thou didst a little while ago! Then thou didst congratulate thyself; and now, behold! thou weepest."

"There came upon me," replied he, "a sudden pity, when I thought of the shortness of man's life, and considered that of all this host, so numerous as it is, not one will be alive when a hundred years are gone by."

"And yet there are sadder things in life than

that," returned the other. "Short as our time is, there is no man, whether it be here among this multitude or elsewhere, who is so happy, as not to have felt the wish—I will not say once, but full many a time—that he were dead rather than alive. Calamities fall upon us; sicknesses vex and harass us, and make life, short though it be, to appear long. So death, through the wretchedness of our life, is a most sweet refuge to our race: and God, who gives us the tastes that we enjoy of pleasant times, is seen, in his very gift, to be envious."

47. "True," said Xerxes; "human life is even such as thou hast painted it, O Artabanus! But for this very reason let us turn our thoughts from it, and not dwell on what is so sad, when pleasant things are in hand. Tell me rather, if the vision which we saw had not appeared so plainly to thyself, wouldst thou have been still of the same mind as formerly, and have continued to dissuade me from warring against Greece, or wouldst thou at this time think differently? Come now, tell me this honestly."

"O king!" replied the other, "may the dream which hath appeared to us have such issue as we both desire! For my own part, I am still full of fear, and have scarcely power to control myself, when I consider all our dangers, and especially when I see that the two things which are of most consequence are alike opposed to thee."

48. "Thou strange man!" said Xerxes in reply—"what, I pray thee, are the two things thou speakest of? Does my land army seem to thee too small in number, and will the Greeks, thinkest thou, bring into the field a more numerous host? Or is it our fleet which thou deemest weaker than theirs? Or art thou fearful on both accounts? If in thy judgment we fall short in either respect, it were easy to bring together with all speed another armament."

49. "O king!" said Artabanus, "it is not possible that a man of understanding should find fault with the size of thy army or the number of thy ships. The more thou addest to these, the more hostile will those two things, whereof I spake, become. Those two things are the land and the sea. In all the wide sea there is not, I imagine, anywhere a harbour large enough to receive thy vessels, in case a storm arise, and afford them a sure protection. And yet thou wilt want, not one such harbour only, but many in succession, along the entire coast by which thou art about to make thy advance. In default then of such harbours, it is well to bear in mind that chances rule men,

and not men chances. Such is the first of the two dangers; and now I will speak to thee of the second. The land will also be thine enemy; for if no one resists thy advance, as thou proceedest farther and farther, insensibly allured onwards (for who is ever sated with success?), thou wilt find it more and more hostile. I mean this, that, should nothing else withstand thee, yet the mere distance, becoming greater as time goes on, will at last produce a famine. Methinks it is best for men, when they take counsel, to be timorous, and imagine all possible calamities, but when the time for action comes, then to deal boldly."

50. Whereto Xerxes answered—"There is reason, O Artabanus! in everything which thou hast said; but I pray thee, fear not all things alike, nor count up every risk. For if in each matter that comes before us thou wilt look to all possible chances, never wilt thou achieve anything. Far better is it to have a stout heart always, and suffer one's share of evils, than to be ever fearing what may happen, and never incur a mischance. Moreover, if thou wilt oppose whatever is said by others, without thyself showing us the sure course which we ought to take, thou art as likely to lead us into failure as they who advise differently; for thou art but on a par with them. And as for that sure course, how canst thou show it us when thou art but a man? I do not believe thou canst. Success for the most part attends those who act boldly, not those who weigh everything, and are slack to venture. Thou seest to how great a height the power of Persia has now reached—never would it have grown to this point if they who sate upon the throne before me had been like-minded with thee, or even, though not like-minded, had listened to councillors of such a spirit. 'Twas by brave ventures that they extended their sway; for great empires can only be conquered by great risks. We follow then the example of our fathers in making this march; and we set forward at the best season of the year; so, when we have brought Europe under us, we shall return, without suffering from want or experiencing any other calamity. For while on the one hand we carry vast stores of provisions with us, on the other we shall have the grain of all the countries and nations that we attack; since our march is not directed against a pastoral people, but against men who are tillers of the ground."

51. Then said Artabanus—"If, sire, thou art determined that we shall not fear anything, at least hearken to a counsel which I wish to

offer; for when the matters in hand are so many, one cannot but have much to say. Thou knowest that Cyrus the son of Cambyses reduced and made tributary to the Persians all the race of the Ionians, except only those of Attica.[1] Now my advice is that thou on no account lead forth these men against their fathers; since we are well able to overcome them without such aid. Their choice, if we take them with us to the war, lies between showing themselves the most wicked of men by helping to enslave their fatherland, or the most righteous by joining in the struggle to keep it free. If then they choose the side of injustice, they will do us but scant good; while if they determine to act justly, they may greatly injure our host. Lay thou to heart the old proverb, which says truly, 'The beginning and end of a matter are not always seen at once.' "

52. "Artabanus," answered Xerxes, "there is nothing in all that thou hast said, wherein thou art so wholly wrong as in this, that thou suspectest the faith of the Ionians. Have they not given us the surest proof of their attachment—a proof which thou didst thyself witness, and likewise all those who fought with Darius against the Scythians? When it lay wholly with them to save or to destroy the entire Persian army, they dealt by us honourably and with good faith, and did us no hurt at all. Besides, they will leave behind them in our country their wives, their children, and their properties—can it then be conceived that they will attempt rebellion? Have no fear, therefore, on this score; but keep a brave heart and uphold my house and empire. To thee, and thee only, do I intrust my sovereignty."

53. After Xerxes had thus spoken, and had sent Artabanus away to return to Susa, he summoned before him all the Persians of most repute, and when they appeared, addressed them in these words:—

"Persians, I have brought you together because I wished to exhort you to behave bravely, and not to sully with disgrace the former achievements of the Persian people, which are very great and famous. Rather let us one and all, singly and jointly, exert ourselves to the uttermost; for the matter wherein we are engaged concerns the common weal. Strain every nerve, then, I beseech you, in this war. Brave warriors are the men we march against, if report says true; and such that, if we con-

quer them, there is not a people in all the world which will venture thereafter to withstand our arms. And now let us offer prayers to the gods who watch over the welfare of Persia, and then cross the channel."

54. All that day the preparations for the passage continued; and on the morrow they burnt all kinds of spices upon the bridges, and strewed the way with myrtle boughs, while they waited anxiously for the sun, which they hoped to see as he rose. And now the sun appeared; and Xerxes took a golden goblet and poured from it a libation into the sea, praying the while with his face turned to the sun "that no misfortune might befall him such as to hinder his conquest of Europe, until he had penetrated to its uttermost boundaries." After he had prayed, he cast the golden cup into the Hellespont, and with it a golden bowl, and a Persian sword of the kind which they call *acinaces*. I cannot say for certain whether it was as an offering to the sun-god that he threw these things into the deep, or whether he had repented of having scourged the Hellespont, and thought by his gifts to make amends to the sea for what he had done.

55. When, however, his offerings were made, the army began to cross; and the foot-soldiers, with the horsemen, passed over by one of the bridges—that (namely) which lay towards the Euxine—while the sumpter-beasts and the camp-followers passed by the other, which looked on the Egean. Foremost went the Ten Thousand Persians, all wearing garlands upon their heads; and after them a mixed multitude of many nations. These crossed upon the first day.

On the next day the horsemen began the passage; and with them went the soldiers who carried their spears with the point downwards, garlanded, like the Ten Thousand;—then came the sacred horses and the sacred chariot; next Xerxes with his lancers and the thousand horse; then the rest of the army. At the same time the ships sailed over to the opposite shore. According, however, to another account which I have heard, the king crossed the last.

56. As soon as Xerxes had reached the European side, he stood to contemplate his army as they crossed under the lash. And the crossing continued during seven days and seven nights, without rest or pause. 'Tis said that here, after Xerxes had made the passage, a Hellespontian exclaimed—

"Why, O Jove, dost thou, in the likeness of a Persian man, and with the name of Xerxes

[1] This, of course, was not true; but the Persians might not unnaturally be supposed ignorant of all the Ionians of Europe except the Athenians.

instead of thine own, lead the whole race of mankind to the destruction of Greece? It would have been as easy for thee to destroy it without their aid!"

57. When the whole army had crossed, and the troops were now upon their march, a strange prodigy appeared to them, whereof the king made no account, though its meaning was not difficult to conjecture. Now the prodigy was this:—a mare brought forth a hare. Hereby it was shown plainly enough, that Xerxes would lead forth his host against Greece with mighty pomp and splendour, but, in order to reach again the spot from which he set out, would have to run for his life. There had also been another portent, while Xerxes was still at Sardis—a mule dropped a foal, neither male nor female; but this likewise was disregarded.

58. So Xerxes, despising the omens, marched forwards; and his land army accompanied him. But the fleet held an opposite course, and, sailing to the mouth of the Hellespont, made its way along the shore. Thus the fleet proceeded westward, making for Cape Sarpêdon, where the orders were that it should await the coming up of the troops; but the land army marched eastward along the Chersonese, leaving on the right the tomb of Hellé, the daughter of Athamas, and on the left the city of Cardia. Having passed through the town which is called Agora, they skirted the shores of the Gulf of Melas, and then crossed the river Melas, whence the gulf takes its name, the waters of which they found too scanty to supply the host. From this point their march was to the west; and after passing Ænos, an Æolian settlement, and likewise Lake Stentoris, they came to Doriscus.

59. The name Doriscus is given to a beach and a vast plain upon the coast of Thrace, through the middle of which flows the strong stream of the Hebrus. Here was the royal fort which is likewise called Doriscus, where Darius had maintained a Persian garrison ever since the time when he attacked the Scythians. This place seemed to Xerxes a convenient spot for reviewing and numbering his soldiers; which things accordingly he proceeded to do. The sea-captains, who had brought the fleet to Doriscus, were ordered to take the vessels to the beach adjoining, where Salé stands, a city of the Samothracians, and Zôné, another city. The beach extends to Serrhêum, the well-known promontory; the whole district in former times was inhabited by the Ciconians.

Here then the captains were to bring their ships, and to haul them ashore for refitting, while Xerxes at Doriscus was employed in numbering the soldiers.

60. What the exact number of the troops of each nation was I cannot say with certainty—for it is not mentioned by any one—but the whole land army together was found to amount to one million seven hundred thousand men. The manner in which the numbering took place was the following. A body of ten thousand men was brought to a certain place, and the men were made to stand as close together as possible; after which a circle was drawn around them, and the men were let go: then where the circle had been, a fence was built about the height of a man's middle; and the enclosure was filled continually with fresh troops, till the whole army had in this way been numbered. When the numbering was over, the troops were drawn up according to their several nations.

61. Now these were the nations that took part in this expedition. The Persians, who wore on their heads the soft hat called the tiara, and about their bodies, tunics with sleeves of divers colours, having iron scales upon them like the scales of a fish. Their legs were protected by trousers; and they bore wicker shields for bucklers; their quivers hanging at their backs, and their arms being a short spear, a bow of uncommon size, and arrows of reed. They had likewise daggers suspended from their girdles along their right thighs. Otanes, the father of Xerxes' wife, Amestris, was their leader. This people was known to the Greeks in ancient times by the name of Cephenians; but they called themselves and were called by their neighbours, Artæans. It was not till Perseus, the son of Jove and Danaë, visited Cepheus the son of Belus, and, marrying his daughter Andromeda, had by her a son called Perses (whom he left behind him in the country because Cepheus had no male offspring), that the nation took from this Perses the name of Persians.

62. The Medes had exactly the same equipment as the Persians; and indeed the dress common to both is not so much Persian as Median. They had for commander Tigranes, of the race of the Achæmenids. These Medes were called anciently by all people Arians; but when Medêa, the Colchian, came to them from Athens, they changed their name. Such is the account which they themselves give.

The Cissians were equipped in the Persian

fashion, except in one respect:—they wore on their heads, instead of hats, fillets. Anaphes, the son of Otanes, commanded them.

The Hyrcanians were likewise armed in the same way as the Persians. Their leader was Megapanus, the same who was afterwards satrap of Babylon.

63. The Assyrians went to the war with helmets upon their heads made of brass, and plaited in a strange fashion which it is not easy to describe. They carried shields, lances, and daggers very like the Egyptian; but in addition, they had wooden clubs knotted with iron, and linen corselets. This people, whom the Greeks call Syrians, are called Assyrians by the barbarians. The Chaldæans served in their ranks, and they had for commander Otaspes, the son of Artachæus.

64. The Bactrians went to the war wearing a head-dress very like the Median, but armed with bows of cane, after the custom of their country, and with short spears.

The Sacæ, or Scyths, were clad in trousers, and had on their heads tall stiff caps rising to a point. They bore the bow of their country and the dagger; besides which they carried the battle-axe, or *sagaris*. They were in truth Amyrgian Scythians, but the Persians called them Sacæ, since that is the name which they give to all Scythians. The Bactrians and the Sacæ had for leader Hystaspes, the son of Darius and of Atossa, the daughter of Cyrus.

65. The Indians wore cotton dresses, and carried bows of cane, and arrows also of cane with iron at the point. Such was the equipment of the Indians, and they marched under the command of Pharnazathres the son of Artabates.

66. The Arians carried Median bows, but in other respects were equipped like the Bactrians. Their commander was Sisamnes the son of Hydarnes.

The Parthians and Chorasmians, with the Sogdians, the Gandarians, and the Dadicæ, had the Bactrian equipment in all respects. The Parthians and Chorasmians were commanded by Artabazus the son of Pharnaces, the Sogdians by Azanes the son of Artæus, and the Gandarians and Dadicæ by Artyphius the son of Artabanus.

67. The Caspians were clad in cloaks of skin, and carried the cane bow of their country and the scymitar. So equipped they went to the war; and they had for commander Ariomardus the brother of Artyphius.

The Sarangians had dyed garments which showed brightly, and buskins which reached to the knee: they bore Median bows, and lances. Their leader was Pherendates, the son of Megabazus.

The Pactyans wore cloaks of skin, and carried the bow of their country and the dagger. Their commander was Artyntes, the son of Ithamatres.

68. The Utians, the Mycians, and the Paricanians were all equipped like the Pactyans. They had for leaders, Arsamenes, the son of Darius, who commanded the Utians and Mycians; and Siromitres, the son of Œobazus, who commanded the Paricanians.

69. The Arabians wore the *zeira,* or long cloak, fastened about them with a girdle; and carried at their right side long bows, which when unstrung bent backwards.

The Ethiopians were clothed in the skins of leopards and lions, and had long bows made of the stem of the palm-leaf, not less than four cubits in length. On these they laid short arrows made of reed, and armed at the tip, not with iron, but with a piece of stone, sharpened to a point, of the kind used in engraving seals. They carried likewise spears, the head of which was the sharpened horn of an antelope; and in addition they had knotted clubs. When they went into battle they painted their bodies, half with chalk, and half with vermilion. The Arabians, and the Ethiopians who came from the region above Egypt, were commanded by Arsames, the son of Darius and of Artystônê daughter of Cyrus. This Artystônê was the best-beloved of all the wives of Darius; and it was she whose statue he caused to be made of gold wrought with the hammer. Her son Arsames commanded these two nations.

70. The eastern Ethiopians—for two nations of this name served in the army—were marshalled with the Indians. They differed in nothing from the other Ethiopians, save in their language, and the character of their hair. For the eastern Ethiopians have straight hair, while they of Libya are more woolly-haired than any other people in the world. Their equipment was in most points like that of the Indians; but they wore upon their heads the scalps of horses, with the ears and mane attached; the ears were made to stand upright, and the mane served as a crest. For shields this people made use of the skins of cranes.

71. The Libyans wore a dress of leather, and carried javelins made hard in the fire. They had for commander Massages, the son of Oarizus.

72. The Paphlagonians went to the war with plaited helmets upon their heads, and carrying small shields and spears of no great size. They had also javelins and daggers, and wore on their feet the buskin of their country, which reached half way up the shank. In the same fashion were equipped the Ligyans, the Matienians, the Mariandynians, and the Syrians (or Cappadocians, as they are called by the Persians). The Paphlagonians and Matienians were under the command of Dôtus the son of Megasidrus; while the Mariandynians, the Ligyans, and the Syrians had for leader Gobryas, the son of Darius and Artystôné.

73. The dress of the Phrygians closely resembled the Paphlagonian, only in a very few points differing from it. According to the Macedonian account, the Phrygians, during the time that they had their abode in Europe and dwelt with them in Macedonia, bore the name of Brigians; but on their removal to Asia they changed their designation at the same time with their dwelling-place.

The Armenians, who are Phrygian colonists, were armed in the Phrygian fashion. Both nations were under the command of Artochmes, who was married to one of the daughters of Darius.

74. The Lydians were armed very nearly in the Grecian manner. These Lydians in ancient times were called Mæonians, but changed their name, and took their present title from Lydus the son of Atys.

The Mysians wore upon their heads a helmet made after the fashion of their country, and carried a small buckler; they used as javelins staves with one end hardened in the fire. The Mysians are Lydian colonists, and from the mountain-chain of Olympus, are called Olympiêni. Both the Lydians and the Mysians were under the command of Artaphernes, the son of that Artaphernes who, with Datis, made the landing at Marathon.

75. The Thracians went to the war wearing the skins of foxes upon their heads, and about their bodies tunics, over which was thrown a long cloak of many colours. Their legs and feet were clad in buskins made from the skins of fawns; and they had for arms javelins, with light targes, and short dirks. This people, after crossing into Asia, took the name of Bithynians; before, they had been called Strymonians, while they dwelt upon the Strymon; whence, according to their own account, they had been driven out by the Mysians and Teucrians. The commander of these Asiatic Thracians was Bassaces the son of Artabanus.

76. [1] . . . had small shields made of the hide of the ox, and carried each of them two spears such as are used in wolf-hunting. Brazen helmets protected their heads; and above these they wore the ears and horns of an ox fashioned in brass. They had also crests on their helms; and their legs were bound round with purple bands. There is an oracle of Mars in the country of this people.

77. The Cabalians, who are Mæonians, but are called Lasonians, had the same equipment as the Cilicians—an equipment which I shall describe when I come in due course to the Cilician contingent.

The Milyans bore short spears, and had their garments fastened with buckles. Some of their number carried Lycian bows. They wore about their heads skull-caps made of leather. Badres the son of Hystanes led both nations to battle.

78. The Moschians wore helmets made of wood, and carried shields and spears of a small size: their spear-heads, however, were long. The Moschian equipment was that likewise of the Tibarenians, the Macronians, and the Mosynœcians. The leaders of these nations were the following: the Moschians and Tibarenians were under the command of Ariomardus, who was the son of Darius and of Parmys, daughter of Smerdis son of Cyrus; while the Macronians and Mosynœcians had for leader Artaÿctes, the son of Cherasmis, the governor of Sestos upon the Hellespont.

79. The Mares wore on their heads the plaited helmet peculiar to their country, and used small leathern bucklers, and javelins.

The Colchians wore wooden helmets, and carried small shields of raw hide, and short spears; besides which they had swords. Both Mares and Colchians were under the command of Pharandates, the son of Teaspes.

The Alarodians and Saspirians were armed like the Colchians; their leader was Masistes, the son of Siromitras.

80. The Islanders who came from the Erythræan Sea, where they inhabited the islands to which the king sends those whom he banishes, wore a dress and arms almost exactly like the Median. Their leader was Mardontes the son of Bagæus, who the year after perished in the battle of Mycalé, where he was one of the captains.

81. Such were the nations who fought upon

[1] There is a defect here in the text of Herodotus; the name of the nation has been lost and cannot be satisfactorily supplied.

the dry land, and made up the infantry of the Persians. And they were commanded by the captains whose names have been above recorded. The marshalling and numbering of the troops had been committed to them; and by them were appointed the captains over a thousand, and the captains over ten thousand; but the leaders of ten men, or a hundred, were named by the captains over ten thousand. There were other officers also, who gave the orders to the various ranks and nations; but those whom I have mentioned above were the commanders.

82. Over these commanders themselves, and over the whole of the infantry, there were set six generals—namely, Mardonius, son of Gobryas; Tritantæchmes, son of the Artabanus who gave his advice against the war with Greece; Smerdomenes, son of Otanes—these two were the sons of Darius' brothers, and thus were cousins of Xerxes—Masistes, son of Darius and Atossa; Gergis, son of Arizus; and Megabyzus, son of Zopyrus.

83. The whole of the infantry was under the command of these generals, excepting the Ten Thousand. The Ten Thousand, who were all Persians and all picked men, were led by Hydarnes, the son of Hydarnes. They were called "the Immortals," for the following reason. If one of their body failed either by the stroke of death or of disease, forthwith his place was filled up by another man, so that their number was at no time either greater or less than 10,000.

Of all the troops the Persians were adorned with the greatest magnificence, and they were likewise the most valiant. Besides their arms, which have been already described, they glittered all over with gold, vast quantities of which they wore about their persons. They were followed by litters, wherein rode their concubines, and by a numerous train of attendants handsomely dressed. Camels and sumpter-beasts carried their provision, apart from that of the other soldiers.

84. All these various nations fight on horseback; they did not, however, at this time all furnish horsemen, but only the following:—

(i.) The Persians, who were armed in the same way as their own footmen, excepting that some of them wore upon their heads devices fashioned with the hammer in brass or steel.

85. (ii.) The wandering tribe known by the name of Sagartians—a people Persian in language, and in dress half Persian, half Pac-

tyan, who furnished to the army as many as eight thousand horse. It is not the wont of this people to carry arms, either of bronze or steel, except only a dirk; but they use lassoes made of thongs plaited together, and trust to these whenever they go to the wars. Now the manner in which they fight is the following: when they meet their enemy, straightway they discharge their lassoes, which end in a noose; then, whatever the noose encircles, be it man or be it horse, they drag towards them; and the foe, entangled in the toils, is forthwith slain. Such is the manner in which this people fight; and now their horsemen were drawn up with the Persians.

86. (iii.) The Medes, and Cissians, who had the same equipment as their foot-soldiers.

(iv.) The Indians, equipped as their footmen, but some on horseback and some in chariots—the chariots drawn either by horses, or by wild asses.

(v.) The Bactrians and Caspians, arrayed as their foot-soldiers.

(vi.) The Libyans, equipped as their foot-soldiers, like the rest; but all riding in chariots.

(vii.) The Caspeirians and Paricanians, equipped as their foot-soldiers.

(viii.) The Arabians, in the same array as their footmen, but all riding on camels, not inferior in fleetness to horses.

87. These nations, and these only, furnished horse to the army: and the number of the horse was eighty thousand, without counting camels or chariots. All were marshalled in squadrons, excepting the Arabians; who were placed last, to avoid frightening the horses, which cannot endure the sight of the camel.

88. The horse was commanded by Armamithras and Tithæus, sons of Datis. The other commander, Pharnuches, who was to have been their colleague, had been left sick at Sardis; since at the moment that he was leaving the city, a sad mischance befell him:—a dog ran under the feet of the horse upon which he was mounted; and the horse, not seeing it coming, was startled, and, rearing bolt upright, threw his rider. After this fall Pharnuches spat blood, and fell into a consumption. As for the horse, he was treated at once as Pharnuches ordered: the attendants took him to the spot where he had thrown his master, and there cut off his four legs at the hough. Thus Pharnuches lost his command.

89. The triremes amounted in all to twelve hundred and seven; and were furnished by the following nations:—

(i.) The Phœnicians, with the Syrians of Palestine, furnished three hundred vessels, the crews of which were thus accoutred: upon their heads they wore helmets made nearly in the Grecian manner; about their bodies they had breastplates of linen; they carried shields without rims; and were armed with javelins. This nation, according to their own account, dwelt anciently upon the Erythræan Sea, but crossing thence, fixed themselves on the sea-coast of Syria, where they still inhabit. This part of Syria, and all the region extending from hence to Egypt, is known by the name of Palestine.

(ii.) The Egyptians furnished two hundred ships. Their crews had plaited helmets upon their heads, and bore concave shields with rims of unusual size. They were armed with spears suited for a sea-fight, and with huge pole-axes. The greater part of them wore breastplates; and all had long cutlasses.

90. (iii.) The Cyprians furnished a hundred and fifty ships, and were equipped in the following fashion. Their kings had turbans bound about their heads, while the people wore tunics; in other respects they were clad like the Greeks. They are of various races; some are sprung from Athens and Salamis, some from Arcadia, some from Cythnus, some from Phœnicia, and a portion, according to their own account, from Ethiopia.

91. (iv.) The Cilicians furnished a hundred ships. The crews wore upon their heads the helmet of their country, and carried instead of shields light targes made of raw hide; they were clad in woollen tunics, and were each armed with two javelins, and a sword closely resembling the cutlass of the Egyptians. This people bore anciently the name of Hypachæans, but took their present title from Cilix, the son of Agenor, a Phœnician.

(v.) The Pamphylians furnished thirty ships, the crews of which were armed exactly as the Greeks. This nation is descended from those who on the return from Troy were dispersed with Amphilochus and Calchas.

92. (vi.) The Lycians furnished fifty ships. Their crews wore greaves and breastplates, while for arms they had bows of cornel wood, reed arrows without feathers, and javelins. Their outer garment was the skin of a goat, which hung from their shoulders; their head-dress a hat encircled with plumes; and besides their other weapons they carried daggers and falchions. This people came from Crete, and were once called Termilæ; they got the name

which they now bear from Lycus, the son of Pandion, an Athenian.

93. (vii.) The Dorians of Asia furnished thirty ships. They were armed in the Grecian fashion, inasmuch as their forefathers came from the Peloponnese.

(viii.) The Carians furnished seventy ships, and were equipped like the Greeks, but carried, in addition, falchions and daggers. What name the Carians bore anciently was declared in the first part of this History.

94. (ix.) The Ionians furnished a hundred ships, and were armed like the Greeks. Now these Ionians, during the time that they dwelt in the Peloponnese and inhabited the land now called Achæa (which was before the arrival of Danaüs and Xuthus in the Peloponnese), were called, according to the Greek account, Ægialean Pelasgi, or "Pelasgi of the Sea-shore"; but afterwards, from Ion the son of Xuthus, they were called Ionians.

95. The Islanders furnished seventeen ships, and wore arms like the Greeks. They too were a Pelasgian race, who in later times took the name of Ionians for the same reason as those who inhabited the twelve cities founded from Athens.

The Æolians furnished sixty ships, and were equipped in the Grecian fashion. They too were anciently called Pelasgians, as the Greeks declare.

The Hellespontians from the Pontus, who are colonists of the Ionians and Dorians, furnished a hundred ships, the crews of which wore the Grecian armour. This did not include the Abydenians, who stayed in their own country, because the king had assigned them the special duty of guarding the bridges.

96. On board of every ship was a band of soldiers, Persians, Medes, or Sacans. The Phœnician ships were the best sailers in the fleet, and the Sidonian the best among the Phœnicians. The contingent of each nation, whether to the fleet or to the land army, had at its head a native leader; but the names of these leaders I shall not mention, as it is not necessary for the course of my History. For the leaders of some nations were not worthy to have their names recorded; and besides, there were in each nation as many leaders as there were cities. And it was not really as commanders that they accompanied the army, but as mere slaves, like the rest of the host. For I have already mentioned the Persian generals who had the actual command, and were at the head of the several nations which composed the army.

97. The fleet was commanded by the following—Ariabignes, the son of Darius, Prêxaspes, the son of Aspathines, Megabazus, the son of Megabates, and Achæmenes, the son of Darius. Ariabignes, who was the child of Darius by a daughter of Gobryas, was leader of the Ionian and Carian ships; Achæmenes, who was own brother to Xerxes, of the Egyptian; the rest of the fleet was commanded by the other two. Besides the triremes, there was an assemblage of thirty-oared and fifty-oared galleys, of cercuri, and transports for conveying horses, amounting in all to three thousand.

98. Next to the commanders, the following were the most renowned of those who sailed aboard the fleet:—Tetramnêstus, the son of Anysus, the Sidonian; Mapên, the son of Sirom, the Tyrian; Merbal, the son of Agbal, the Aradian; Syennesis, the son of Oromedon, the Cilician; Cyberniscus, the son of Sicas, the Lycian; Gorgus, the son of Chersis, and Timônax, the son of Timagoras, the Cyprians; and Histiæus, the son of Timnes, Pigres, the son of Seldômus, and Damasithymus, the son of Candaules, the Carians.

99. Of the other lower officers I shall make no mention, since no necessity is laid on me; but I must speak of a certain leader named Artemisia, whose participation in the attack upon Greece, notwithstanding that she was a woman, moves my special wonder. She had obtained the sovereign power after the death of her husband; and, though she had now a son grown up, yet her brave spirit and manly daring sent her forth to the war, when no need required her to adventure. Her name, as I said, was Artemisia, and she was the daughter of Lygdamis; by race she was on his side a Halicarnassian, though by her mother a Cretan. She ruled over the Halicarnassians, the men of Cos, of Nisyrus, and of Calydna; and the five triremes which she furnished to the Persians were, next to the Sidonian, the most famous ships in the fleet. She likewise gave to Xerxes sounder counsel than any of his other allies. Now the cities over which I have mentioned that she bore sway were one and all Dorian; for the Halicarnassians were colonists from Trœzen, while the remainder were from Epidaurus. Thus much concerning the sea-force.

100. Now when the numbering and marshalling of the host was ended, Xerxes conceived a wish to go himself throughout the forces, and with his own eyes behold everything. Accordingly he traversed the ranks seated in his chariot, and, going from nation to nation, made manifold inquiries, while his scribes wrote down the answers; till at last he had passed from end to end of the whole land army, both the horsemen and likewise the foot. This done, he exchanged his chariot for a Sidonian galley, and, seated beneath a golden awning, sailed along the prows of all his vessels (the vessels having now been hauled down and launched into the sea), while he made inquiries again, as he had done when he reviewed the land-force, and caused the answers to be recorded by his scribes. The captains took their ships to the distance of about four hundred feet from the shore, and there lay to, with their vessels in a single row, the prows facing the land, and with the fighting-men upon the decks accoutred as if for war, while the king sailed along in the open space between the ships and the shore, and so reviewed the fleet.

101. Now after Xerxes had sailed down the whole line and was gone ashore, he sent for Demaratus the son of Ariston, who had accompanied him in his march upon Greece, and bespake him thus:—

"Demaratus, it is my pleasure at this time to ask thee certain things which I wish to know. Thou art a Greek, and, as I hear from the other Greeks with whom I converse, no less than from thine own lips, thou art a native of a city which is not the meanest or the weakest in their land. Tell me, therefore, what thinkest thou? Will the Greeks lift a hand against us? Mine own judgment is, that even if all the Greeks and all the barbarians of the West were gathered together in one place, they would not be able to abide my onset, not being really of one mind. But I would fain know what thou thinkest hereon."

Thus Xerxes questioned; and the other replied in his turn,—"O king! is it thy will that I give thee a true answer, or dost thou wish for a pleasant one?"

Then the king bade him speak the plain truth, and promised that he would not on that account hold him in less favour than heretofore.

102. So Demaratus, when he heard the promise, spake as follows:—

"O king! since thou biddest me at all risks speak the truth, and not say what will one day prove me to have lied to thee, thus I answer. Want has at all times been a fellow-dweller with us in our land, while Valour is an ally whom we have gained by dint of wisdom and strict laws. Her aid enables us to drive out want and escape thraldom. Brave are all the Greeks who dwell in any Dorian land; but what I am about to say does not concern all, but only the Lacedæmonians. First then, come what may, they will never accept thy terms, which would reduce Greece to slavery; and further, they are sure to join battle with thee, though all the rest of the Greeks should submit to thy will. As for their numbers, do not ask how many they are, that their resistance should be a possible thing; for if a thousand of them should take the field, they will meet thee in battle, and so will any number, be it less than this, or be it more."

103. When Xerxes heard this answer of Demaratus, he laughed and answered:—

"What wild words, Demaratus! A thousand men join battle with such an army as this! Come then, wilt thou—who wert once, as thou sayest, their king—engage to fight this very day with ten men? I trow not. And yet, if all thy fellow-citizens be indeed such as thou sayest they are, thou oughtest, as their king, by thine own country's usages, to be ready to fight with twice the number. If then each one of them be a match for ten of my soldiers, I may well call upon thee to be a match for twenty. So wouldest thou assure the truth of what thou hast now said. If, however, you Greeks, who vaunt yourselves so much, are of a truth men like those whom I have seen about my court, as thyself, Demaratus, and the others with whom I am wont to converse—if, I say, you are really men of this sort and size, how is the speech that thou hast uttered more than a mere empty boast? For, to go to the very verge of likelihood—how could a thousand men, or ten thousand, or even fifty thousand, particularly if they were all alike free, and not under one lord—how could such a force, I say, stand against an army like mine? Let them be five thousand, and we shall have more than a thousand men to each one of theirs. If, indeed, like our troops, they had a single master, their fear of him might make them courageous beyond their natural bent; or they might be urged by lashes against an enemy which far outnumbered them. But left to their own free choice, assuredly they will act differently. For mine own part, I believe, that if the Greeks had to contend with the Persians only, and the numbers were equal on both sides, the Greeks would find it hard to stand their ground. We too have among us such men as those of whom thou spakest—not many indeed, but still we possess a few. For instance, some of my body-

guard would be willing to engage singly with three Greeks. But this thou didst not know; and therefore it was thou talkedst so foolishly."

104. Demaratus answered him—"I knew, O king! at the outset, that if I told thee the truth, my speech would displease thine ears. But as thou didst require me to answer thee with all possible truthfulness, I informed thee what the Spartans will do. And in this I spake not from any love that I bear them—for none knows better than thou what my love towards them is likely to be at the present time, when they have robbed me of my rank and my ancestral honours, and made me a homeless exile, whom thy father did receive, bestowing on me both shelter and sustenance. What likelihood is there that a man of understanding should be unthankful for kindness shown him, and not cherish it in his heart? For mine own self, I pretend not to cope with ten men, nor with two—nay, had I the choice, I would rather not fight even with one. But, if need appeared, or if there were any great cause urging me on, I would contend with right good will against one of those persons who boast themselves a match for any three Greeks. So likewise the Lacedæmonians, when they fight singly, are as good men as any in the world, and when they fight in a body, are the bravest of all. For though they be freemen, they are not in all respects free; Law is the master whom they own; and this master they fear more than thy subjects fear thee. Whatever he commands they do; and his commandment is always the same: it forbids them to flee in battle, whatever the number of their foes, and requires them to stand firm, and either to conquer or die. If in these words, O king! I seem to thee to speak foolishly, I am content from this time forward evermore to hold my peace. I had not now spoken unless compelled by thee. Certes, I pray that all may turn out according to thy wishes."

105. Such was the answer of Demaratus; and Xerxes was not angry with him at all, but only laughed, and sent him away with words of kindness.

After this interview, and after he had made Mascames the son of Megadostes governor of Doriscus, setting aside the governor appointed by Darius, Xerxes started with his army, and marched upon Greece through Thrace.

106. This man, Mascames, whom he left behind him, was a person of such merit that gifts were sent him yearly by the king as a special favour, because he excelled all the other gov-

ernors that had been appointed either by Xer-xes or by Darius. In like manner, Artaxerxes, the son of Xerxes, sent gifts yearly to the de-scendants of Mascames. Persian governors had been established in Thrace and about the Hel-lespont before the march of Xerxes began; but these persons, after the expedition was over, were all driven from their towns by the Greeks, except the governor of Doriscus: no one succeeded in driving out Mascames, though many made the attempt. For this rea-son the gifts are sent him every year by the king who reigns over the Persians.

107. Of the other governors whom the Greeks drove out, there was not one who, in the judgment of Xerxes, showed himself a brave man, excepting Boges, the governor of Eïon. Him Xerxes never could praise enough; and such of his sons as were left in Persia, and survived their father, he very specially hon-oured. And of a truth this Boges was worthy of great commendation; for when he was be-sieged by the Athenians under Cimon, the son of Miltiades, and it was open to him to retire from the city upon terms, and return to Asia, he refused, because he feared the king might think he had played the coward to save his own life, wherefore, instead of surrendering, he held out to the last extremity. When all the food in the fortress was gone, he raised a vast funeral pile, slew his children, his wife, his concubines, and his household slaves, and cast them all into the flames. Then, collecting what-ever gold and silver there was in the place, he flung it from the walls into the Strymon; and, when that was done, to crown all, he himself leaped into the fire. For this action Boges is with reason praised by the Persians even at the present day.

108. Xerxes, as I have said, pursued his march from Doriscus against Greece; and on his way he forced all the nations through which he passed to take part in the expedition. For the whole country as far as the frontiers of Thessaly had been (as I have already shown) enslaved and made tributary to the king by the conquests of Megabazus, and, more lately, of Mardonius. And first, after leaving Doris-cus, Xerxes passed the Samothracian fortresses, whereof Mesambria is the farthermost as one goes toward the west. The next city is Strymé, which belongs to Thasos. Midway between it and Mesambria flows the river Lissus, which did not suffice to furnish water for the army, but was drunk up and failed. This region was formerly called Gallaïca; now it bears the

name of Briantica; but in strict truth it like-wise is really Ciconian.

109. After crossing the dry channel of the Lissus, Xerxes passed the Grecian cities of Marôneia, Dicæa, and Abdêra, and likewise the famous lakes which are in their neighbour-hood, Lake Ismaris between Marôneia and Strymé, and Lake Bistonis near Dicæa, which receives the waters of two rivers, the Travus and the Compsatus. Near Abdêra there was no famous lake for him to pass; but he crossed the river Nestus, which there reaches the sea. Proceeding further upon his way, he passed by several continental cities, one of them pos-sessing a lake nearly thirty furlongs in circuit, full of fish, and very salt, of which the sump-ter-beasts only drank, and which they drained dry. The name of this city was Pistyrus. All these towns, which were Grecian, and lay upon the coast, Xerxes kept upon his left hand as he passed along.

110. The following are the Thracian tribes through whose country he marched: the Pæti, the Ciconians, the Bistonians, the Sapæans, the Dersæans, the Edonians, and the Satræ. Some of these dwelt by the sea, and furnished ships to the king's fleet; while others lived in the more inland parts, and of these all the tribes which I have mentioned, except the Satræ, were forced to serve on foot.

111. The Satræ, so far as our knowledge goes, have never yet been brought under by any one, but continue to this day a free and unconquered people, unlike the other Thraci-ans. They dwell amid lofty mountains clothed with forests of different trees and capped with snow, and are very valiant in fight. They are the Thracians who have an oracle of Bacchus in their country, which is situated upon their highest mountain-range. The Bessi, a Satrian race, deliver the oracles; but the prophet, as at Delphi, is a woman; and her answers are not harder to read.

112. When Xerxes had passed through the region mentioned above, he came next to the Pierian fortresses, one of which is called Pha-gres, and another Pergamus. Here his line of march lay close by the walls, with the long high range of Pangæum upon his right, a tract in which there are mines both of gold and sil-ver, some worked by the Pierians and Odo-mantians, but the greater part by the Satræ.

113. Xerxes then marched through the country of the Pæonian tribes—the Doberians and the Pæoplæ—which lay to the north of Pangæum, and, advancing westward, reached

the river Strymon and the city Eïon, whereof Boges, of whom I spoke a short time ago, and who was then still alive, was governor. The tract of land lying about Mount Pangæum is called Phyllis; on the west it reaches to the river Angites, which flows into the Strymon, and on the south to the Strymon itself, where at this time the Magi were sacrificing white horses to make the stream favourable.

114. After propitiating the stream by these and many other magical ceremonies, the Persians crossed the Strymon, by bridges made before their arrival, at a place called "The Nine Ways," which was in the territory of the Edonians. And when they learnt that the name of the place was "The Nine Ways," they took nine of the youths of the land and as many of their maidens, and buried them alive on the spot. Burying alive is a Persian custom. I have heard that Amestris, the wife of Xerxes, in her old age buried alive seven pairs of Persian youths, sons of illustrious men, as a thank-offering to the god who is supposed to dwell underneath the earth.

115. From the Strymon the army, proceeding westward, came to a strip of shore, on which there stands the Grecian town of Argilus. This shore, and the whole tract above it, is called Bisaltia. Passing this, and keeping on the left hand the Gulf of Posideium, Xerxes crossed the Sylean plain, as it is called, and passing by Stagirus, a Greek city, came to Acanthus. The inhabitants of these parts, as well as those who dwelt about Mount Pangæum, were forced to join the armament, like those others of whom I spoke before; the dwellers along the coast being made to serve in the fleet, while those who lived more inland had to follow with the land forces. The road which the army of Xerxes took remains to this day untouched: the Thracians neither plough nor sow it, but hold it in great honour.

116. On reaching Acanthus, the Persian king, seeing the great zeal of the Acanthians for his service, and hearing what had been done about the cutting, took them into the number of his sworn friends, sent them as a present a Median dress, and besides commended them highly.

117. It was while he remained here that Artachæes, who presided over the canal, a man in high repute with Xerxes, and by birth an Achæmenid, who was moreover the tallest of all the Persians, being only four fingers short of five cubits, royal measure, and who had a stronger voice than any other man in the world, fell sick and died. Xerxes therefore, who was greatly afflicted at the mischance, carried him to the tomb and buried him with all magnificence; while the whole army helped to raise a mound over his grave. The Acanthians, in obedience to an oracle, offer sacrifice to this Artachæes as a hero, invoking him in their prayers by name. But King Xerxes sorrowed greatly over his death.

118. Now the Greeks who had to feed the army, and to entertain Xerxes, were brought thereby to the very extremity of distress, insomuch that some of them were forced even to forsake house and home. When the Thasians received and feasted the host, on account of their possessions upon the mainland, Antipater, the son of Orges, one of the citizens of best repute, and the man to whom the business was assigned, proved that the cost of the meal was four hundred talents of silver.

119. And estimates almost to the same amount were made by the superintendents in other cities. For the entertainment, which had been ordered long beforehand and was reckoned to be of much consequence, was, in the manner of it, such as I will now describe. No sooner did the heralds who brought the orders give their message, than in every city the inhabitants made a division of their stores of corn, and proceeded to grind flour of wheat and of barley for many months together. Besides this, they purchased the best cattle that they could find, and fattened them; and fed poultry and water-fowl in ponds and buildings, to be in readiness for the army; while they likewise prepared gold and silver vases and drinking-cups, and whatsoever else is needed for the service of the table. These last preparations were made for the king only, and those who sat at meat with him; for the rest of the army nothing was made ready beyond the food for which orders had been given. On the arrival of the Persians, a tent ready pitched for the purpose received Xerxes, who took his rest therein, while the soldiers remained under the open heaven. When the dinner hour came, great was the toil of those who entertained the army; while the guests ate their fill, and then, after passing the night at the place, tore down the royal tent next morning, and seizing its contents, carried them all off, leaving nothing behind.

120. On one of these occasions Megacreon of Abdêra wittily recommended his countrymen "to go to the temples in a body, men and women alike, and there take their station as

suppliants, and beseech the gods that they would in future always spare them one-half of the woes which might threaten their peace— thanking them at the same time very warmly for their past goodness in that they had caused Xerxes to be content with one meal in the day." For had the order been to provide breakfast for the king as well as dinner, the Abderites must either have fled before Xerxes came, or, if they awaited his coming, have been brought to absolute ruin. As it was, the nations, though suffering heavy pressure, complied nevertheless with the directions that had been given.

121. At Acanthus Xerxes separated from his fleet, bidding the captains sail on ahead and await his coming at Therma, on the Thermaic Gulf, the place from which the bay takes its name. Through this town lay, he understood, his shortest road. Previously, his order of march had been the following:—from Doriscus to Acanthus his land force had proceeded in three bodies, one of which took the way along the sea-shore in company with the fleet, and was commanded by Mardonius and Masistes, while another pursued an inland track under Tritantæchmes and Gergis; the third, with which was Xerxes himself marching midway between the other two, and having for its leaders Smerdomenes and Megabyzus.

122. The fleet, therefore, after leaving the king, sailed through the channel which had been cut for it by Mount Athos, and came into the bay whereon lie the cities of Assa, Pilôrus, Singus, and Sarta; from all which it received contingents. Thence it stood on for the Thermaic Gulf, and rounding Cape Ampelus, the promontory of the Torônæans, passed the Grecian cities Torôné, Galepsus, Sermyla, Mecyberna, and Olynthus, receiving from each a number of ships and men. This region is called Sithonia.

123. From Cape Ampelus the fleet stretched across by a short course to Cape Canastræum, which is the point of the peninsula of Pallêné that runs out farthest into the sea, and gathered fresh supplies of ships and men from Potidæa, Aphytis, Neapolis, Æga, Therambus, Sciôné, Mendé, and Sané. These are the cities of the tract called anciently Phlegra, but now Pallêné. Hence they again followed the coast, still advancing towards the place appointed by the king, and had accessions from all the cities that lie near Pallêné, and border on the Thermaic Gulf, whereof the names are Lipaxus, Cômbreia, Lisæ, Gigônus, Campsa, Smila,

and Ænêa. The tract where these towns lie still retains its old name of Crossæa. After passing Ænêa, the city which I last named, the fleet found itself arrived in the Thermaic Gulf, off the land of Mygdonia. And so at length they reached Therma, the appointed place, and came likewise to Sindus and Chalestra upon the river Axius, which separates Bottiæa from Mygdonia. Bottiæa has a scanty sea-board, which is occupied by the two cities Ichnæ and Pella.

124. So the fleet anchored off the Axius, and off Therma, and the towns that lay between, waiting the king's coming. Xerxes meanwhile with his land force left Acanthus, and started for Therma, taking his way across the land. This road led him through Pæonia and Crestonia to the river Echeidôrus, which rising in the country of the Crestonians, flows through Mygdonia, and reaches the sea near the marsh upon the Axius.

125. Upon this march the camels that carried the provisions of the army were set upon by lions, which left their lairs and came down by night, but spared the men and the sumpter-beasts, while they made the camels their prey. I marvel what may have been the cause which compelled the lions to leave the other animals untouched and attack the camels, when they had never seen that beast before, nor had any experience of it.

126. That whole region is full of lions and wild bulls, with gigantic horns, which are brought into Greece. The lions are confined within the tract lying between the river Nestus (which flows through Abdêra) on the one side, and the Acheloüs (which waters Acarnania) on the other. No one ever sees a lion in the fore part of Europe east of the Nestus, nor through the entire continent west of the Acheloüs; but in the space between these bounds lions are found.

127. On reaching Therma Xerxes halted his army, which encamped along the coast, beginning at the city of Therma in Mygdonia, and stretching out as far as the rivers Lydias and Haliacmon, two streams which, mingling their waters in one, form the boundary between Bottiæa and Macedonia. Such was the extent of country through which the barbarians encamped. The rivers here mentioned were all of them sufficient to supply the troops, except the Echeidôrus, which was drunk dry.

128. From Therma Xerxes beheld the Thessalian mountains, Olympus and Ossa, which are of a wonderful height. Here, learning that

there lay between these mountains a narrow gorge through which the river Peneus ran, and where there was a road that gave an entrance into Thessaly, he formed the wish to go by sea himself, and examine the mouth of the river. His design was to lead his army by the upper road through the country of the inland Macedonians, and so to enter Perrhæbia, and come down by the city of Gonnus; for he was told that that way was the most secure. No sooner therefore had he formed this wish than he acted accordingly. Embarking, as was his wont on all such occasions, aboard a Sidonian vessel, he gave the signal to the rest of the fleet to get under weigh, and quitting his land army, set sail and proceeded to the Peneus. Here the view of the mouth caused him to wonder greatly; and sending for his guides, he asked them whether it were possible to turn the course of the stream, and make it reach the sea at any other point.

129. Now there is a tradition that Thessaly was in ancient times a lake, shut in on every side by huge hills. Ossa and Pelion—ranges which join at the foot—do in fact inclose it upon the east, while Olympus forms a barrier upon the north, Pindus upon the west, and Othrys towards the south. The tract contained within these mountains, which is a deep basin, is called Thessaly. Many rivers pour their waters into it; but five of them are of more note than the rest, namely, the Peneus, the Apidanus, the Onochônus, the Enipeus, and the Pamisus. These streams flow down from the mountains which surround Thessaly, and, meeting in the plain, mingle their waters together, and discharge themselves into the sea by a single outlet, which is a gorge of extreme narrowness. After the junction all the other names disappear, and the river is known as the Peneus. It is said that of old the gorge which allows the waters an outlet did not exist; accordingly the rivers, which were then, as well as the Lake Bœbêïs, without names, but flowed with as much water as at present, made Thessaly a sea. The Thessalians tell us that the gorge through which the water escapes was caused by Neptune; and this is likely enough; at least any man who believes that Neptune causes earthquakes, and that chasms so produced are his handiwork, would say, upon seeing this rent, that Neptune did it. For it plainly appeared to me that the hills had been torn asunder by an earthquake.

130. When Xerxes therefore asked the guides if there were any other outlet by which the waters could reach the sea, they, being men well acquainted with the nature of their country, made answer:—

"O king! there is no other passage by which this stream can empty itself into the sea save that which thine eye beholds. For Thessaly is girt about with a circlet of hills."

Xerxes is said to have observed upon this—

"Wise men truly are they of Thessaly, and good reason had they to change their minds in time and consult for their own safety. For, to pass by others matters, they must have felt that they lived in a country which may easily be brought under and subdued. Nothing more is needed than to turn the river upon their lands by an embankment which should fill up the gorge and force the stream from its present channel, and lo! all Thessaly, except the mountains, would at once be laid under water."

The king aimed in this speech at the sons of Aleuas, who were Thessalians, and had been the first of all the Greeks to make submission to him. He thought that they had made their friendly offers in the name of the whole people. So Xerxes, when he had viewed the place, and made the above speech, went back to Therma.

131. The stay of Xerxes in Pieria lasted for several days, during which a third part of his army was employed in cutting down the woods on the Macedonian mountain-range to give his forces free passage into Perrhæbia. At this time the heralds who had been sent into Greece to require earth for the king returned to the camp, some of them empty-handed, others with earth and water.

132. Among the number of those from whom earth and water were brought were the Thessalians, Dolopians, Enianians, Perrhæbians, Locrians, Magnetians, Malians, Achæans of Phthiôtis, Thebans, and Bœotians generally, except those of Platæa and Thespiæ. These are the nations against whom the Greeks that had taken up arms to resist the barbarians swore the oath, which ran thus— "From all those of Greek blood who delivered themselves up to the Persians without necessity, when their affairs were in good condition, we will take a tithe of their goods, and give it to the god at Delphi." So ran the words of the Greek oath.

133. King Xerxes had sent no heralds either to Athens or Sparta to ask earth and water, for a reason which I will now relate. When Darius some time before sent messengers for the same purpose, they were thrown, at Athens, into

the pit of punishment, at Sparta into a well, and bidden to take therefrom earth and water for themselves, and carry it to their king. On this account Xerxes did not send to ask them. What calamity came upon the Athenians to punish them for their treatment of the heralds I cannot say, unless it were the laying waste of their city and territory; but that I believe was not on account of this crime.

134. On the Lacedæmonians, however, the wrath of Talthybius, Agamemnon's herald, fell with violence. Talthybius has a temple at Sparta; and his descendants, who are called Talthybiadæ, still live there, and have the privilege of being the only persons who discharge the office of herald. When therefore the Spartans had done the deed of which we speak, the victims at their sacrifices failed to give good tokens; and this failure lasted for a very long time. Then the Spartans were troubled; and, regarding what had befallen them as a grievous calamity, they held frequent assemblies of the people, and made proclamation through the town, "Was any Lacedæmonian willing to give his life for Sparta?" Upon this two Spartans, Sperthias, the son of Anêristus, and Bulis, the son of Nicolaüs, both men of noble birth, and among the wealthiest in the place, came forward and freely offered themselves as an atonement to Xerxes for the heralds of Darius slain at Sparta. So the Spartans sent them away to the Medes to undergo death.

135. Nor is the courage which these men hereby displayed alone worthy of wonder; but so likewise are the following speeches which were made by them. On their road to Susa they presented themselves before Hydarnes. This Hydarnes was a Persian by birth, and had the command of all the nations that dwelt along the sea-coast of Asia. He accordingly showed them hospitality, and invited them to a banquet, where, as they feasted, he said to them:—

"Men of Lacedæmon, why will ye not consent to be friends with the king? Ye have but to look at me and my fortune to see that the king knows well how to honour merit. In like manner ye yourselves, were ye to make your submission to him, would receive at his hands, seeing that he deems you men of merit, some government in Greece."

"Hydarnes," they answered, "thou art a one-sided counsellor. Thou hast experience of half the matter; but the other half is beyond thy knowledge. A slave's life thou understand-

est; but, never having tasted liberty, thou canst not tell whether it be sweet or no. Ah! hadst thou known what freedom is, thou wouldst have bidden us fight for it, not with the spear only, but with the battle-axe."

So they answered Hydarnes.

136. And afterwards, when they were come to Susa into the king's presence, and the guards ordered them to fall down and do obeisance, and went so far as to use force to compel them, they refused, and said they would never do any such thing, even were their heads thrust down to the ground; for it was not their custom to worship men, and they had not come to Persia for that purpose. So they fought off the ceremony; and having done so, addressed the king in words much like the following:—

"O king of the Medes! the Lacedæmonians have sent us hither, in the place of those heralds of thine who were slain in Sparta, to make atonement to thee on their account."

Then Xerxes answered with true greatness of soul "that he would not act like the Lacedæmonians, who, by killing the heralds, had broken the laws which all men hold in common. As he had blamed such conduct in them, he would never be guilty of it himself. And besides, he did not wish, by putting the two men to death, to free the Lacedæmonians from the stain of their former outrage."

137. This conduct on the part of the Spartans caused the anger of Talthybius to cease for a while, notwithstanding that Sperthias and Bulis returned home alive. But many years afterwards it awoke once more, as the Lacedæmonians themselves declare, during the war between the Peloponnesians and the Athenians.

In my judgment this was a case wherein the hand of Heaven was most plainly manifest. That the wrath of Talthybius should have fallen upon ambassadors and not slacked till it had full vent, so much justice required; but that it should have come upon the sons of the very men who were sent up to the Persian king on its account—upon Nicolaüs, the son of Bulis, and Anêristus, the son of Sperthias (the same who carried off fishermen from Tiryns, when cruising in a well-manned merchant-ship)—this does seem to me to be plainly a supernatural circumstance. Yet certain it is that these two men, having been sent to Asia as ambassadors by the Lacedæmonians, were betrayed by Sitalces, the son of Teres, king of Thrace, and Nymphodôrus, the son of Pythes, a native of Abdêra, and being made prisoners at Bisanthé, upon the Hellespont, were conveyed to Attica, and there put to death by the Athenians, at the same time as Aristeas, the son of Adeimantus, the Corinthian. All this happened, however, very many years after the expedition of Xerxes.

138. To return, however, to my main subject—the expedition of the Persian king, though it was in name directed against Athens, threatened really the whole of Greece. And of this the Greeks were aware some time before; but they did not all view the matter in the same light. Some of them had given the Persian earth and water, and were bold on this account, deeming themselves thereby secured against suffering hurt from the barbarian army; while others, who had refused compliance, were thrown into extreme alarm. For whereas they considered all the ships in Greece too few to engage the enemy, it was plain that the greater number of states would take no part in the war, but warmly favoured the Medes.

139. And here I feel constrained to deliver an opinion, which most men, I know, will mislike, but which, as it seems to me to be true, I am determined not to withhold. Had the Athenians, from fear of the approaching danger, quitted their country, or had they without quitting it submitted to the power of Xerxes, there would certainly have been no attempt to resist the Persians by sea; in which case the course of events by land would have been the following. Though the Peloponnesians might have carried ever so many breastworks across the Isthmus, yet their allies would have fallen off from the Lacedæmonians, not by voluntary desertion, but because town after town must have been taken by the fleet of the barbarians; and so the Lacedæmonians would at last have stood alone, and, standing alone, would have displayed prodigies of valour and died nobly. Either they would have done thus, or else, before it came to that extremity, seeing one Greek state after another embrace the cause of the Medes, they would have come to terms with King Xerxes—and thus, either way Greece would have been brought under Persia. For I cannot understand of what possible use the walls across the Isthmus could have been, if the king had had the mastery of the sea. If then a man should now say that the Athenians were the saviours of Greece, he would not exceed the truth. For they truly held the scales; and whichever side they espoused must have carried the day. They too it was

who, when they had determined to maintain the freedom of Greece, roused up that portion of the Greek nation which had not gone over to the Medes; and so, next to the gods, *they* repulsed the invader. Even the terrible oracles which reached them from Delphi, and struck fear into their hearts, failed to persuade them to fly from Greece. They had the courage to remain faithful to their land, and await the coming of the foe.

140. When the Athenians, anxious to consult the oracle, sent their messengers to Delphi, hardly had the envoys completed the customary rites about the sacred precinct, and taken their seats inside the sanctuary of the god, when the Pythoness, Aristonicé by name, thus prophesied:—

Wretches, why sit ye here? Fly, fly to the ends of creation,
Quitting your homes, and the crags which your city crowns with her circlet.
Neither the head, nor the body is firm in its place, nor at bottom
Firm the feet, nor the hands; nor resteth the middle uninjur'd.
All—all ruined and lost. Since fire, and impetuous Ares,
Speeding along in a Syrian chariot, hastes to destroy her.
Not alone shalt thou suffer; full many the towers he will level,
Many the shrines of the gods he will give to a fiery destruction.
Even now they stand with dark sweat horribly dripping,
Trembling and quaking for fear; and lo! from the high roofs trickleth
Black blood, sign prophetic of hard distresses impending.
Get ye away from the temple; and brood on the ills that await ye!

141. When the Athenian messengers heard this reply, they were filled with the deepest affliction: whereupon Timon, the son of Androbûlus, one of the men of most mark among the Delphians, seeing how utterly cast down they were at the gloomy prophecy, advised them to take an olive-branch, and entering the sanctuary again, consult the oracle as suppliants. The Athenians followed this advice, and going in once more, said—"O king! we pray thee reverence these boughs of supplication which we bear in our hands, and deliver to us something more comforting concerning our country. Else we will not leave thy sanctuary, but will stay here till we die." Upon this the priestess gave them a second answer, which was the following:—

*Pallas has not been able to soften the lord of
Olympus,
Though she has often prayed him, and urged him
with excellent counsel.
Yet once more I address thee in words than ada-
mant firmer.
When the foe shall have taken whatever the limit
of Cecrops
Holds within it, and all which divine Cithæron
shelters,
Then far-seeing Jove grants this to the prayers of
Athenê;
Safe shall the wooden wall continue for thee and
thy children.
Wait not the tramp of the horse, nor the footmen
mightily moving
Over the land, but turn your back to the foe, and
retire ye.
Yet shall a day arrive when ye shall meet him in
battle.
Holy Salamis, thou shalt destroy the offspring of
women,
When men scatter the seed, or when they gather
the harvest.*

142. This answer seemed, as indeed it was,
gentler than the former one; so the envoys
wrote it down, and went back with it to Athens. When, however, upon their arrival, they
produced it before the people, and inquiry began to be made into its true meaning, many
and various were the interpretations which
men put on it; two, more especially, seemed to
be directly opposed to one another. Certain of
the old men were of opinion that the god
meant to tell them the citadel would escape;
for this was anciently defended by a palisade;
and they supposed that barrier to be the
"wooden wall" of the oracle. Others maintained that the fleet was what the god pointed
at; and their advice was that nothing should
be thought of except the ships, which had best
be at once got ready. Still such as said the
"wooden wall" meant the fleet, were perplexed
by the last two lines of the oracle—

*Holy Salamis, thou shalt destroy the offspring of
women,
When men scatter the seed, or when they gather
the harvest.*

These words caused great disturbance among
those who took the wooden wall to be the
ships; since the interpreters understood them
to mean that, if they made preparations for a
sea-fight, they would suffer a defeat off Salamis.

143. Now there was at Athens a man who
had lately made his way into the first rank of
citizens: his true name was Themistocles; but
he was known more generally as the son of
Neocles. This man came forward and said
that the interpreters had not explained the oracle altogether aright—"for if," he argued,
"the clause in question had really respected the
Athenians, it would not have been expressed
so mildly; the phrase used would have been
'Luckless Salamis,' rather than 'Holy Salamis,'
had those to whom the island belonged been
about to perish in its neighbourhood. Rightly
taken, the response of the god threatened the
enemy, much more than the Athenians." He
therefore counselled his countrymen to make
ready to fight on board their ships, since *they*
were the wooden wall in which the god told
them to trust. When Themistocles had thus
cleared the matter, the Athenians embraced his
view, preferring it to that of the interpreters.
The advice of these last had been against engaging in a sea-fight; "all the Athenians could
do," they said, "was, without lifting a hand in
their defence, to quit Attica, and make a settlement in some other country."

144. Themistocles had before this given a
counsel which prevailed very seasonably. The
Athenians, having a large sum of money in
their treasury, the produce of the mines at
Laureium, were about to share it among the
full-grown citizens, who would have received
ten drachmas apiece, when Themistocles persuaded them to forbear the distribution, and
build with the money two hundred ships, to
help them in their war against the Eginetans.
It was the breaking out of the Eginetan war
which was at this time the saving of Greece;
for hereby were the Athenians forced to become a maritime power. The new ships were
not used for the purpose for which they had
been built, but became a help to Greece in her
hour of need. And the Athenians had not only
these vessels ready before the war, but they
likewise set to work to build more; while they
determined, in a council which was held after
the debate upon the oracle, that, according to
the advice of the god, they would embark their
whole force aboard their ships, and, with such
Greeks as chose to join them, give battle to
the barbarian invader. Such, then, were the
oracles which had been received by the Athenians.

145. The Greeks who were well affected to
the Grecian cause, having assembled in one
place, and there consulted together, and interchanged pledges with each other, agreed that,
before any other step was taken, the feuds and
enmities which existed between the different
nations should first of all be appeased. Many

such there were; but one was of more importance than the rest, namely, the war which was still going on between the Athenians and the Eginetans. When this business was concluded, understanding that Xerxes had reached Sardis with his army, they resolved to despatch spies into Asia to take note of the king's affairs. At the same time they determined to send ambassadors to the Argives, and conclude a league with them against the Persians; while they likewise despatched messengers to Gelo, the son of Deinomenes, in Sicily, to the people of Corcyra, and to those of Crete, exhorting them to send help to Greece. Their wish was to unite, if possible, the entire Greek name in one, and so to bring all to join in the same plan of defence, inasmuch as the approaching dangers threatened all alike. Now the power of Gelo was said to be very great, far greater than that of any single Grecian people.

146. So when these resolutions had been agreed upon, and the quarrels between the states made up, first of all they sent into Asia three men as spies. These men reached Sardis, and took note of the king's forces, but, being discovered, were examined by order of the generals who commanded the land army, and, having been condemned to suffer death, were led out to execution. Xerxes, however, when the news reached him, disapproving the sentence of the generals, sent some of his body-guard with instructions, if they found the spies still alive, to bring them into his presence. The messengers found the spies alive, and brought them before the king, who, when he heard the purpose for which they had come, gave orders to his guards to take them round the camp, and show them all the footmen and all the horse, letting them gaze at everything to their hearts' content; then, when they were satisfied, to send them away unharmed to whatever country they desired.

147. For these orders Xerxes gave afterwards the following reasons. "Had the spies been put to death," he said, "the Greeks would have continued ignorant of the vastness of his army, which surpassed the common report of it; while he would have done them a very small injury by killing three of their men. On the other hand, by the return of the spies to Greece, his power would become known; and the Greeks," he expected, "would make surrender of their freedom before he began his march, by which means his troops would be saved all the trouble of an expedition." This reasoning was like to that which he used upon another occasion. While he was staying at Abydos, he saw some corn-ships, which were passing through the Hellespont from the Euxine, on their way to Egina and the Peloponnese. His attendants, hearing that they were the enemy's, were ready to capture them, and looked to see when Xerxes would give the signal. He, however, merely asked "whither the ships were bound?" and when they answered, "For thy foes, master, with corn on board,"— "We too are bound thither," he rejoined, "laden, among other things, with corn. What harm is it, if they carry our provisions for us?"

So the spies, when they had seen everything, were dismissed, and came back to Europe.

148. The Greeks who had banded themselves together against the Persian king, after despatching the spies into Asia, sent next ambassadors to Argos. The account which the Argives give of their own proceedings is the following. They say that they had information from the very first of the preparations which the barbarians were making against Greece. So, as they expected that the Greeks would come upon them for aid against the assailant, they sent envoys to Delphi to inquire of the god what it would be best for them to do in the matter. They had lost, not long before, six thousand citizens, who had been slain by the Lacedæmonians under Cleomenes the son of Anaxandridas; which was the reason why they now sent to Delphi. When the Pythoness heard their question, she replied—

Hated of all thy neighbors, beloved of the blessed
  Immortals,
Sit thou still, with thy lance drawn inward, patiently watching;
Warily guard thine head, and the head will take
  care of the body.

This prophecy had been given them some time before the envoys came; but still, when they afterwards arrived, it was permitted them to enter the council-house, and there deliver their message. And this answer was returned to their demands—"Argos is ready to do as ye require, if the Lacedæmonians will first make a truce for thirty years, and will further divide with Argos the leadership of the allied army. Although in strict right the whole command should be hers, she will be content to have the leadership divided equally."

149. Such, they say, was the reply made by the council, in spite of the oracle which forbade them to enter into a league with the Greeks. For, while not without fear of disobeying the oracle, they were greatly desirous of

obtaining a thirty years' truce, to give time for their sons to grow to man's estate. They reflected, that if no such truce were concluded, and it should be their lot to suffer a second calamity at the hands of the Persians, it was likely they would fall hopelessly under the power of Sparta. But to the demands of the Argive council the Lacedæmonian envoys made answer—"They would bring before the people the question of concluding a truce. With regard to the leadership, they had received orders what to say, and the reply was that Sparta had two kings, Argos but one—it was not possible that either of the two Spartans should be stripped of his dignity—but they did not oppose the Argive king having one vote like each of them." The Argives say that they could not brook this arrogance on the part of Sparta, and rather than yield one jot to it, they preferred to be under the rule of the barbarians. So they told the envoys to be gone, before sunset, from their territory, or they should be treated as enemies.

150. Such is the account which is given of these matters by the Argives themselves. There is another story, which is told generally through Greece, of a different tenor. Xerxes, it is said, before he set forth on his expedition against Greece, sent a herald to Argos, who on his arrival spoke as follows:—

"Men of Argos, King Xerxes speaks thus to you. We Persians deem that the Perses from whom we descend was the child of Perseus the son of Danaë, and of Andromeda the daughter of Cepheus. Hereby it would seem that we come of your stock and lineage. So then it neither befits us to make war upon those from whom we spring; nor can it be right for you to fight, on behalf of others, against us. Your place is to keep quiet and hold yourself aloof. Only let matters proceed as I wish, and there is no people whom I shall have in higher esteem than you."

This address, says the story, was highly valued by the Argives, who therefore at the first neither gave a promise to the Greeks nor yet put forward a demand. Afterwards, however, when the Greeks called upon them to give their aid, they made the claim which has been mentioned, because they knew well that the Lacedæmonians would never yield it, and so they would have a pretext for taking no part in the war.

151. Some of the Greeks say that this account agrees remarkably with what happened many years afterwards. Callias, the son of Hipponicus, and certain others with him, had gone up to Susa, the city of Memnon, as ambassadors of the Athenians, upon a business quite distinct from this. While they were there, it happened that the Argives likewise sent ambassadors to Susa, to ask Artaxerxes, the son of Xerxes, "if the friendship which they had formed with his father still continued, or if he looked upon them as his enemies?"—to which King Artaxerxes replied, "Most certainly it continues; and there is no city which I reckon more my friend than Argos."

152. For my own part I cannot positively say whether Xerxes did send the herald to Argos or not; nor whether Argive ambassadors at Susa did really put this question to Artaxerxes about the friendship between them and him; neither do I deliver any opinion hereupon other than that of the Argives themselves. This, however, I know—that if every nation were to bring all its evil deeds to a given place, in order to make an exchange with some other nation, when they had all looked carefully at their neighbours' faults, they would be truly glad to carry their own back again. So, after all, the conduct of the Argives was not perhaps more disgraceful than that of others. For myself, my duty is to report all that is said; but I am not obliged to believe it all alike—a remark which may be understood to apply to my whole History. Some even go so far as to say that the Argives first invited the Persians to invade Greece, because of their ill success in the war with Lacedæmon, since they preferred anything to the smart of their actual sufferings. Thus much concerning the Argives.

153. Other ambassadors, among whom was Syagrus from Lacedæmon, were sent by the allies into Sicily, with instructions to confer with Gelo.

The ancestor of this Gelo, who first settled at Gela, was a native of the isle of Telos, which lies off Triopium. When Gela was colonised by Antiphêmus and the Lindians of Rhodes, he likewise took part in the expedition. In course of time his descendants became the high-priests of the gods who dwell below—an office which they held continually, from the time that Têlines, one of Gelo's ancestors, obtained it in the way which I will now mention. Certain citizens of Gela, worsted in a sedition, had found a refuge at Mactôrium, a town situated on the heights above Gela. Têlines reinstated these men, without any human help, solely by means of the sacred rites of these deities. From whom he received them, or how he himself acquired them, I cannot say; but certain it is that relying on their power he brought the exiles back. For this his reward was to be the office of high-priest of those gods for himself and his seed for ever. It surprises me especially that such a feat should have been performed by Têlines; for I have always looked upon acts of this nature as beyond the abilities of common men, and only to be achieved by such as are of a bold and manly spirit; whereas Têlines is said by those who dwell about Sicily to have been a soft-hearted and womanish person. He however obtained this office in the manner above described.

154. Afterwards, on the death of Cleander the son of Pantares, who was slain by Sabyllus, a citizen of Gela, after he had held the tyranny for seven years, Hippocrates, Cleander's brother, mounted the throne. During his reign, Gelo, a descendant of the high-priest Têlines, served with many others—of whom Ænesidê-mus, son of Pataïcus, was one—in the king's bodyguard. Within a little time his merit caused him to be raised to the command of all the horse. For when Hippocrates laid siege to Callipolis, and afterwards to Naxos, to Zanclé, to Leontini, and moreover to Syracuse, and many cities of the barbarians, Gelo in every war distinguished himself above all the combatants. Of the various cities above named, there was none but Syracuse which was not reduced to slavery. The Syracusans were saved from this fate, after they had suffered defeat on the river Elôrus, by the Corinthians and Corcyræans, who made peace between them and Hippocrates, on condition of their ceding Camarina to him; for that city anciently belonged to Syracuse.

155. When, however, Hippocrates, after a reign of the same length as that of Cleander his brother, perished near the city Hybla, as he was warring with the native Sicilians, then Gelo, pretending to espouse the cause of the two sons of Hippocrates, Eucleides and Cleander, defeated the citizens who were seeking to recover their freedom, and having so done, set aside the children, and himself took the kingly power. After this piece of good fortune, Gelo likewise became master of Syracuse, in the following manner. The Syracusan landholders, as they were called, had been driven from their city by the common people assisted by their own slaves, the Cyllyrians, and had fled to Casmenæ. Gelo brought them back to

Syracuse, and so got possession of the town; for the people surrendered themselves, and gave up their city on his approach.

156. Being now master of Syracuse, Gelo cared less to govern Gela, which he therefore entrusted to his brother Hiero, while he strengthened the defences of his new city, which indeed was now all in all to him. And Syracuse sprang up rapidly to power and became a flourishing place. For Gelo razed Camarina to the ground, and brought all the inhabitants to Syracuse, and made them citizens; he also brought thither more than half the citizens of Gela, and gave them the same rights as the Camarinæans. So likewise with the Megarians of Sicily—after besieging their town and forcing them to surrender, he took the rich men, who, having made the war, looked now for nothing less than death at his hands, and carrying them to Syracuse, established them there as citizens; while the common people, who, as they had not taken any share in the struggle, felt secure that no harm would be done to them, he carried likewise to Syracuse, where he sold them all as slaves to be conveyed abroad. He did the like also by the Eubœans of Sicily, making the same difference. His conduct towards both nations arose from his belief that a "people" was a most unpleasant companion. In this way Gelo became a great king.

157. When the Greek envoys reached Syracuse, and were admitted to an audience, they spoke as follows—

"We have been sent hither by the Lacedæmonians and Athenians, with their respective allies, to ask thee to join us against the barbarian. Doubtless thou hast heard of his invasion, and art aware that a Persian is about to throw a bridge over the Hellespont, and, bringing with him out of Asia all the forces of the East, to carry war into Greece—professing indeed that he only seeks to attack Athens, but really bent on bringing all the Greeks into subjection. Do thou therefore, we beseech thee, aid those who would maintain the freedom of Greece, and thyself assist to free her; since the power which thou wieldest is great, and thy portion in Greece, as lord of Sicily, is no small one. For if all Greece join together in one, there will be a mighty host collected, and we shall be a match for our assailants; but if some turn traitors, and others refuse their aid, and only a small part of the whole body remains sound, then there is reason to fear that all Greece may perish. For do not thou cherish a hope that the Persian, when he has conquered our country, will be content and not advance against thee. Rather take thy measures beforehand, and consider that thou defendest thyself when thou givest aid to us. Wise counsels, be sure, for the most part have prosperous issues."

158. Thus spake the envoys; and Gelo replied with vehemence:—

"Greeks, ye have had the face to come here with selfish words, and exhort me to join in league with you against the barbarian. Yet when I erewhile asked you to join with me in fighting barbarians, what time the quarrel broke out between me and Carthage; and when I earnestly besought you to revenge on the men of Egesta their murder of Dorieus, the son of Anaxandridas, promising to assist you in setting free the trading places from which you receive great profits and advantages, you neither came hither to give me succour, nor yet to revenge Dorieus; but, for any efforts on your part to hinder it, these countries might at this time have been entirely under the barbarians. Now, however, that matters have prospered and gone well with me, while the danger has shifted its ground and at present threatens yourselves, lo! you call Gelo to mind. But though ye slighted me then, I will not imitate you now: I am ready to give you aid, and to furnish as my contribution two hundred triremes, twenty thousand men-at-arms, two thousand cavalry, and an equal number of archers, slingers, and light horsemen, together with corn for the whole Grecian army so long as the war shall last. These services, however, I promise on one condition—that ye appoint me chief captain and commander of the Grecian forces during the war with the barbarian. Unless ye agree to this, I will neither send succours, nor come myself."

159. Syagrus, when he heard these words, was unable to contain himself, and exclaimed:—

"Surely a groan would burst from Pelops' son, Agamemnon, did he hear that her leadership was snatched from Sparta by Gelo and the men of Syracuse. Speak then no more of any such condition, as that we should yield thee the chief command; but if thou art minded to come to the aid of Greece, prepare to serve under Lacedæmonian generals. Wilt thou not serve under a leader?—then, prithee, withhold thy succours."

160. Hereupon Gelo, seeing the indignation which showed itself in the wolds of Syagrus, delivered to the envoys his final offer:—"Spartan stranger," he said, "reproaches cast forth against a man are wont to provoke him to anger; but the insults which thou hast uttered in thy speech shall not persuade me to outstep good breeding in my answer. Surely if you maintain so stoutly your right to the command, it is reasonable that I should be still more stiff in maintaining mine, forasmuch as I am at the head of a far larger fleet and army. Since, however, the claim which I have put forward is so displeasing to you, I will yield, and be content with less. Take, if it please you, the command of the land-force, and I will be admiral of the fleet; or assume, if you prefer it, the command by sea, and I will be leader upon the land. Unless you are satisfied with these terms, you must return home by yourselves, and lose this great alliance." Such was the offer which Gelo made.

161. Hereat broke in the Athenian envoy, before the Spartan could answer, and thus addressed Gelo—

"King of the Syracusans! Greece sent us here to thee to ask for an army, and not to ask for a general. Thou, however, dost not promise to send us any army at all, if thou art not made leader of the Greeks; and this command is what alone thou sticklest for. Now when thy request was to have the whole command, we were content to keep silence; for well we knew that we might trust the Spartan envoy to make answer for us both. But since, after failing in thy claim to lead the whole armament, thou hast now put forward a request to have the command of the fleet, know that, even should the Spartan envoy consent to this, we will not consent. The command by sea, if the Lacedæmonians do not wish for it, belongs to us. While they like to keep this command, we shall raise no dispute; but we will not yield our right to it in favour of any one else. Where would be the advantage of our having raised up a naval force greater than that of any other Greek people, if nevertheless we should suffer Syracusans to take the command away from us?—from us, I say, who are Athenians, the most ancient nation in Greece, the only Greeks who have never changed their abode—the people who are said by the poet Homer to have sent to Troy the man best able of all the Greeks to array and marshal an army—so that we may be allowed to boast somewhat."

162. Gelo replied—"Athenian stranger, ye have, it seems, no lack of commanders; but ye are likely to lack men to receive their orders. As ye are resolved to yield nothing and claim

everything, ye had best make haste back to Greece, and say that the spring of her year is lost to her." The meaning of this expression was the following: as the spring is manifestly the finest season of the year, so (he meant to say) were his troops the finest of the Greek army—Greece, therefore, deprived of his alliance, would be like a year with the spring taken from it.

163. Then the Greek envoys, without having any further dealings with Gelo, sailed away home. And Gelo, who feared that the Greeks would be too weak to withstand the barbarians, and yet could not any how bring himself to go to the Peloponnese, and there, though king of Sicily, serve under the Lacedæmonians, left off altogether to contemplate that course of action, and betook himself to quite a different plan. As soon as ever tidings reached him of the passage of the Hellespont by the Persians, he sent off three penteconters, under the command of Cadmus, the son of Scythas, a native of Cos, who was to go to Delphi, taking with him a large sum of money and a stock of friendly words: there he was to watch the war, and see what turn it would take: if the barbarians prevailed, he was to give Xerxes the treasure, and with it earth and water for the lands which Gelo ruled—if the Greeks won the day, he was to convey the treasure back.

164. This Cadmus had at an earlier time received from his father the kingly power at Cos in a right good condition, and had of his own free will and without the approach of any danger, from pure love of justice, given up his power into the hands of the people at large, and departed to Sicily; where he assisted in the Samian seizure and settlement of Zanclé, or Messana, as it was afterwards called. Upon this occasion Gelo chose him to send into Greece, because he was acquainted with the proofs of honesty which he had given. And now he added to his former honourable deeds an action which is not the least of his merits. With a vast sum entrusted to him and completely in his power, so that he might have kept it for his own use if he had liked, he did not touch it; but when the Greeks gained the sea-fight and Xerxes fled away with his army, he brought the whole treasure back with him to Sicily.

165. They, however, who dwell in Sicily, say that Gelo, though he knew that he must serve under the Lacedæmonians, would nevertheless have come to the aid of the Greeks, had

not it been for Têrillus, the son of Crinippus, king of Himera; who, driven from his city by Thero, the son of Ænesidêmus, king of Agrigentum, brought into Sicily at this very time an army of three hundred thousand men, Phœnicians, Libyans, Iberians, Ligurians, Helisycians, Sardinians, and Corsicans, under the command of Hamilcar the son of Hanno, king of the Carthaginians. Têrillus prevailed upon Hamilcar, partly as his sworn friend, but more through the zealous aid of Anaxilaüs the son of Cretines, king of Rhegium; who, by giving his own sons to Hamilcar as hostages, induced him to make the expedition. Anaxilaüs herein served his own father-in-law; for he was married to a daughter of Têrillus, by name Cydippé. So, as Gelo could not give the Greeks any aid, he sent (they say) the sum of money to Delphi.

166. They say too, that the victory of Gelo and Thero in Sicily over Hamilcar the Carthaginian fell out upon the very day that the Greeks defeated the Persians at Salamis. Hamilcar, who was a Carthaginian on his father's side only, but on his mother's a Syracusan, and who had been raised by his merit to the throne of Carthage, after the battle and the defeat, as I am informed, disappeared from sight: Gelo made the strictest search for him, but he could not be found anywhere, either dead or alive.

167. The Carthaginians, who take probability for their guide, give the following account of this matter:—Hamilcar, they say, during all the time that the battle raged between the Greeks and the barbarians, which was from early dawn till evening, remained in the camp, sacrificing and seeking favourable omens, while he burned on a huge pyre the entire bodies of the victims which he offered. Here, as he poured libations upon the sacrifices, he saw the rout of his army; whereupon he cast himself headlong into the flames, and so was consumed and disappeared. But whether Hamilcar's disappearance happened, as the Phœnicians tell us, in this way, or, as the Syracusans maintain, in some other, certain it is that the Carthaginians offer him sacrifice, and in all their colonies have monuments erected to his honour, as well as one, which is the grandest of all, at Carthage. Thus much concerning the affairs of Sicily.

168. As for the Corcyræans, whom the envoys that visited Sicily took in their way, and to whom they delivered the same message as to Gelo—their answers and actions were the following. With great readiness they promised

to come and give their help to the Greeks; declaring that "the ruin of Greece was a thing which they could not tamely stand by to see; for should she fall, they must the very next day submit to slavery; so that they were bound to assist her to the very uttermost of their power." But notwithstanding that they answered so smoothly, yet when the time came for the succours to be sent, they were of quite a different mind; and though they manned sixty ships, it was long ere they put to sea with them; and when they had so done, they went no further than the Peloponnese, where they lay to with their fleet, off the Lacedæmonian coast, about Pylos and Tænarum—like Gelo, watching to see what turn the war would take. For they despaired altogether of the Greeks gaining the day, and expected that the Persian would win a great battle, and then be master of the whole of Greece. They therefore acted as I have said, in order that they might be able to address Xerxes in words like these: "O king! though the Greeks sought to obtain our aid in their war with thee, and though we had a force of no small size, and could have furnished a greater number of ships than any Greek state except Athens, yet we refused, since we would not fight against thee, nor do aught to cause thee annoyance." The Corcyræans hoped that a speech like this would gain them better treatment from the Persians than the rest of the Greeks; and it would have done so, in my judgment. At the same time, they had an excuse ready to give their countrymen, which they used when the time came. Reproached by them for sending no succours, they replied "that they had fitted out a fleet of sixty triremes, but that the Etesian winds did not allow them to double Cape Malea, and this hindered them from reaching Salamis—it was not from any bad motive that they had missed the sea-fight." In this way the Corcyræans eluded the reproaches of the Greeks.

169. The Cretans, when the envoys sent to ask aid from them came and made their request, acted as follows. They despatched messengers in the name of their state to Delphi, and asked the god, whether it would make for their welfare if they should lend succour to Greece. "Fools!" replied the Pythoness, "do ye not still complain of the woes which the assisting of Menelaüs cost you at the hands of angry Minos? How wroth was he, when, in spite of their having lent you no aid towards avenging his death at Camicus, you helped them to avenge the carrying off by a barbarian of a woman from Sparta!" When this answer was brought from Delphi to the Cretans, they thought no more of assisting the Greeks.

170. Minos, according to tradition, went to Sicania, or Sicily, as it is now called, in search of Dædalus, and there perished by a violent death. After a while the Cretans, warned by some god or other, made a great expedition into Sicania, all except the Polichnites and the Præsians, and besieged Camicus (which in my time belonged to Agrigentum) by the space of five years. At last, however, failing in their efforts to take the place, and unable to carry on the siege any longer from the pressure of hunger, they departed and went their way. Voyaging homewards they had reached Iapygia, when a furious storm arose and threw them upon the coast. All their vessels were broken in pieces; and so, as they saw no means of returning to Crete, they founded the town of Hyria, where they took up their abode, changing their name from Cretans to Messapian Iapygians, and at the same time becoming inhabitants of the mainland instead of islanders. From Hyria they afterwards founded those other towns which the Tarentines at a much later period endeavoured to take, but could not, being defeated signally. Indeed so dreadful a slaughter of Greeks never happened at any other time, so far as my knowledge extends: nor was it only the Tarentines who suffered; but the men of Rhegium too, who had been forced to go to the aid of the Tarentines by Micythus the son of Chœrus, lost here three thousand of their citizens; while the number of the Tarentines who fell was beyond all count. This Micythus had been a household slave of Anaxilaüs, and was by him left in charge of Rhegium: he is the same man who was afterwards forced to leave Rhegium, when he settled at Tegea in Arcadia, from which place he made his many offerings of statues to the shrine at Olympia.

171. This account of the Rhegians and the Tarentines is a digression from the story which I was relating. To return—the Præsians say that men of various nations now flocked to Crete, which was stript of its inhabitants; but none came in such numbers as the Grecians. Three generations after the death of Minos the Trojan war took place; and the Cretans were not the least distinguished among the helpers of Menelaüs. But on this account, when they came back from Troy, famine and pestilence fell upon them, and destroyed both the men and the cattle. Crete was a second time stript

of its inhabitants, a remnant only being left; who form, together with fresh settlers, the third "Cretan" people by whom the island has been inhabited. These were the events of which the Pythoness now reminded the men of Crete; and thereby she prevented them from giving the Greeks aid, though they wished to have gone to their assistance.

172. The Thessalians did not embrace the cause of the Medes until they were forced to do so; for they gave plain proof that the intrigues of the Aleuadæ were not at all to their liking. No sooner did they hear that the Persian was about to cross over into Europe than they despatched envoys to the Greeks who were met to consult together at the Isthmus, whither all the states which were well inclined to the Grecian cause had sent their delegates. These envoys on their arrival thus addressed their countrymen:—

"Men of Greece, it behoves you to guard the pass of Olympus; for thus will Thessaly be placed in safety, as well as the rest of Greece. We for our parts are quite ready to take our share in this work; but you must likewise send us a strong force: otherwise we give you fair warning that we shall make terms with the Persians. For we ought not to be left, exposed as we are in front of all the rest of Greece, to die in your defence alone and unassisted. If however you do not choose to send us aid, you cannot force us to resist the enemy; for there is no force so strong as inability. We shall therefore do our best to secure our own safety."

Such was the declaration of the Thessalians.

173. Hereupon the Greeks determined to send a body of foot to Thessaly by sea, which should defend the pass of Olympus. Accordingly a force was collected, which passed up the Euripus, and disembarking at Alus, on the coast of Achæa, left the ships there, and marched by land into Thessaly. Here they occupied the defile of Tempé; which leads from Lower Macedonia into Thessaly along the course of the Peneus, having the range of Olympus on the one hand and Ossa upon the other. In this place the Greek force that had been collected, amounting to about 10,000 heavy-armed men, pitched their camp; and here they were joined by the Thessalian cavalry. The commanders were, on the part of the Lacedæmonians, Evænetus, the son of Carênus, who had been chosen out of the Polemarchs, but did not belong to the blood royal; and on the part of the Athenians, Themistocles, the son of Neocles. They did not however maintain their station for more than a few days; since envoys came from Alexander, the son of Amyntas, the Macedonian, and counselled them to decamp from Tempé, telling them that if they remained in the pass they would be trodden under foot by the invading army, whose numbers they recounted, and likewise the multitude of their ships. So when the envoys thus counselled them, and the counsel seemed to be good, and the Macedonian who sent it friendly, they did even as he advised. In my opinion what chiefly wrought on them was the fear that the Persians might enter by another pass, whereof they now heard, which led from Upper Macedonia into Thessaly through the territory of the Perrhæbi, and by the town of Gonnus—the pass by which soon afterwards the army of Xerxes actually made its entrance. The Greeks therefore went back to their ships and sailed away to the Isthmus.

174. Such were the circumstances of the expedition into Thessaly; they took place when the king was at Abydos, preparing to pass from Asia into Europe. The Thessalians, when their allies forsook them, no longer wavered, but warmly espoused the side of the Medes; and afterwards, in the course of the war, they were of the very greatest service to Xerxes.

175. The Greeks, on their return to the Isthmus, took counsel together concerning the words of Alexander, and considered where they should fix the war, and what places they should occupy. The opinion which prevailed was that they should guard the pass of Thermopylæ; since it was narrower than the Thessalian defile, and at the same time nearer to them. Of the pathway, by which the Greeks who fell at Thermopylæ were intercepted, they had no knowledge, until, on their arrival at Thermopylæ, it was discovered to them by the Trachinians. This pass then it was determined that they should guard, in order to prevent the barbarians from penetrating into Greece through it; and at the same time it was resolved that the fleet should proceed to Artemisium, in the region of Histiæôtis, for, as those places are near to one another, it would be easy for the fleet and army to hold communication. The two places may be thus described.

176. Artemisium is where the sea of Thrace contracts into a narrow channel, running between the isle of Sciathus and the mainland of Magnesia. When this narrow strait is passed you come to the line of coast called Artemisium; which is a portion of Eubœa, and contains

a temple of Artemis (Diana). As for the entrance into Greece by Trachis, it is, at its narrowest point, about fifty feet wide. This however is not the place where the passage is most contracted; for it is still narrower a little above and a little below Thermopylæ. At Alpêni, which is lower down than that place, it is only wide enough for a single carriage; and up above, at the river Phœnix, near the town called Anthêla, it is the same. West of Thermopylæ rises a lofty and precipitous hill, impossible to climb, which runs up into the chain of Œta; while to the east the road is shut in by the sea and by marshes. In this place are the warm springs, which the natives call "The Cauldrons"; and above them stands an altar sacred to Hercules. A wall had once been carried across the opening; and in this there had of old times been a gateway. These works were made by the Phocians, through fear of the Thessalians, at the time when the latter came from Thesprôtia to establish themselves in the land of Æolis, which they still occupy. As the Thessalians strove to reduce Phocis, the Phocians raised the wall to protect themselves, and likewise turned the hot springs upon the pass, that so the ground might be broken up by watercourses, using thus all possible means to hinder the Thessalians from invading their country. The old wall had been built in very remote times; and the greater part of it had gone to decay through age. Now however the Greeks resolved to repair its breaches, and here make their stand against the barbarian. At this point there is a village very nigh the road, Alpêni by name, from which the Greeks reckoned on getting corn for their troops.

177. These places, therefore, seemed to the Greeks fit for their purpose. Weighing well all that was likely to happen, and considering that in this region the barbarians could make no use of their vast numbers, nor of their cavalry, they resolved to await here the invader of Greece. And when news reached them of the Persians being in Pieria, straightway they broke up from the Isthmus, and proceeded, some on foot to Thermopylæ, others by sea to Artemisium.

178. The Greeks now made all speed to reach the two stations; and about the same time the Delphians, alarmed both for themselves and for their country, consulted the god, and received for answer a command to "pray to the winds, for the winds would do Greece good service." So when this answer was given them, forthwith the Delphians sent word of

the prophecy to those Greeks who were zealous for freedom, and, cheering them thereby amid the fears which they entertained with respect to the barbarian, earned their everlasting gratitude. This done, they raised an altar to the winds at Thyia (where Thyia, the daughter of Cephissus, from whom the region takes its name, has a precinct), and worshipped them with sacrifices. And even to the present day the Delphians sacrifice to the winds, because of this oracle.

179. The fleet of Xerxes now departed from Therma; and ten of the swiftest sailing ships ventured to stretch across direct for Sciathus, at which place there were upon the look-out three vessels belonging to the Greeks, one a ship of Trœzen, another of Egina, and the third from Athens. These vessels no sooner saw from a distance the barbarians approaching than they all hurriedly took to flight.

180. The barbarians at once pursued, and the Trœzenian ship, which was commanded by Prexînus, fell into their hands. Hereupon the Persians took the handsomest of the men-at-arms, and drew him to the prow of the vessel, where they sacrificed him; for they thought the man a good omen to their cause, seeing that he was at once so beautiful, and likewise the first captive they had made. The man who was slain in this way was called Leo; and it may be that the name he bore helped him to his fate in some measure.

181. The Eginetan trireme, under its captain, Asônides, gave the Persians no little trouble, one of the men-at-arms, Pythes, the son of Ischenoüs, distinguishing himself beyond all the others who fought on that day. After the ship was taken this man continued to resist, and did not cease fighting till he fell quite covered with wounds. The Persians who served as men-at-arms in the squadron, finding that he was not dead, but still breathed, and being very anxious to save his life, since he had behaved so valiantly, dressed his wounds with myrrh, and bound them up with bandages of cotton. Then, when they were returned to their own station, they displayed their prisoner admiringly to the whole host, and behaved towards him with much kindness; but all the rest of the ship's crew were treated merely as slaves.

182. Thus did the Persians succeed in taking two of the vessels. The third, a trireme commanded by Phormus of Athens, took to flight and ran aground at the mouth of the river Peneus. The barbarians got possession of

the bark, but not of the men. For the Athenians had no sooner run their vessel aground than they leapt out, and made their way through Thessaly back to Athens.

When the Greeks stationed at Artemisium learnt what had happened by fire-signals from Sciathus, so terrified were they, that, quitting their anchorage-ground at Artemisium, and leaving scouts to watch the foe on the highlands of Euboea, they removed to Chalcis, intending to guard the Euripus.

183. Meantime three of the ten vessels sent forward by the barbarians advanced as far as the sunken rock between Sciathus and Magnesia, which is called "The Ant," and there set up a stone pillar which they had brought with them for that purpose. After this, their course being now clear, the barbarians set sail with all their ships from Therma, eleven days from the time that the king quitted the town. The rock, which lay directly in their course, had been made known to them by Pammon of Scyros. A day's voyage without a stop brought them to Sepias in Magnesia, and to the strip of coast which lies between the town of Casthanæa and the promontory of Sepias.

184. As far as this point then, and on land, as far as Thermopylæ, the armament of Xerxes had been free from mischance; and the numbers were still, according to my reckoning, of the following amount. First there was the ancient complement of the twelve hundred and seven vessels which came with the king from Asia—the contingents of the nations severally —amounting, if we allow to each ship a crew of two hundred men, to 241,400. Each of these vessels had on board, besides native soldiers, thirty fighting men, who were either Persians, Medes, or Sacans; which gives an addition of 36,210. To these two numbers I shall further add the crews of the penteconters; which may be reckoned, one with another, at fourscore men each. Of such vessels there were (as I said before) three thousand; and the men on board them accordingly would be 240,000. This was the sea force brought by the king from Asia; and it amounted in all to 517,610 men. The number of the foot soldiers was 1,700,000; that of the horsemen 80,000; to which must be added the Arabs who rode on camels, and the Libyans who fought in chariots, whom I reckon at 20,000. The whole number, therefore, of the land and sea forces added together amounts to 2,317,610 men. Such was the force brought from Asia, without including the camp followers, or taking any account

of the provision-ships and the men whom they had on board.

185. To the amount thus reached we have still to add the forces gathered in Europe, concerning which I can only speak from conjecture. The Greeks dwelling in Thrace, and in the islands off the coast of Thrace, furnished to the fleet one hundred and twenty ships; the crews of which would amount to 24,000 men. Besides these, footmen were furnished by the Thracians, the Pæonians, the Eordians, the Bottiæans, by the Chalcidean tribes, by the Brygians, the Pierians, the Macedonians, the Perrhæbians, the Enianians, the Dolopians, the Magnesians, the Achæans, and by all the dwellers upon the Thracian sea-board; and the forces of these nations amounted, I believe, to three hundred thousand men. These numbers, added to those of the force which came out of Asia, make the sum of the fighting men 2,641,610.

186. Such then being the number of the fighting men, it is my belief that the attendants who followed the camp, together with the crews of the corn-barks, and of the other craft accompanying the army, made up an amount rather above than below that of the fighting men. However I will not reckon them as either fewer or more, but take them at an equal number. We have therefore to add to the sum already reached an exactly equal amount. This will give 5,283,220 as the whole number of men brought by Xerxes, the son of Darius, as far as Sepias and Thermopylæ.

187. Such then was the amount of the entire host of Xerxes. As for the number of the women who ground the corn, of the concubines, and the eunuchs, no one can give any sure account of it; nor can the baggage-horses and other sumpter-beasts, nor the Indian hounds which followed the army, be calculated, by reason of their multitude. Hence I am not at all surprised that the water of the rivers was found too scant for the army in some instances; rather it is a marvel to me how the provisions did not fail, when the numbers were so great. For I find on calculation that if each man consumed no more than a *chœnix* of corn a day, there must have been used daily by the army 110,340 *medimni,* and this without counting what was eaten by the women, the eunuchs, the sumpter-beasts, and the hounds. Among all this multitude of men there was not one who, for beauty and stature, deserved more than Xerxes himself to wield so vast a power.

188. The fleet then, as I said, on leaving Therma, sailed to the Magnesian territory, and there occupied the strip of coast between the city of Casthanæa and Cape Sepias. The ships of the first row were moored to the land, while the remainder swung at anchor further off. The beach extended but a very little way, so that they had to anchor off the shore, row upon row, eight deep. In this manner they passed the night. But at dawn of day calm and stillness gave place to a raging sea, and a violent storm, which fell upon them with a strong gale from the east—a wind which the people in those parts call Hellespontias. Such of them as perceived the wind rising, and were so moored as to allow of it, forestalled the tempest by dragging their ships up on the beach, and in this way saved both themselves and their vessels. But the ships which the storm caught out at sea were driven ashore, some of them near the place called Ipni, or "The Ovens," at the foot of Pelion; others on the strand itself; others again about Cape Sepias; while a portion were dashed to pieces near the cities of Melibœa and Casthanæa. There was no resisting the tempest.

189. It is said that the Athenians had called upon Boreas to aid the Greeks, on account of a fresh oracle which had reached them, commanding them to "seek help from their son-in-law." For Boreas, according to the tradition of the Greeks, took to wife a woman of Attica, viz., Orithyia, the daughter of Erechtheus. So the Athenians, as the tale goes, considering that this marriage made Boreas their son-in-law, and perceiving, while they lay with their ships at Chalcis of Eubœa, that the wind was rising, or, it may be, even before it freshened, offered sacrifice both to Boreas and likewise to Orithyia, entreating them to come to their aid and to destroy the ships of the barbarians, as they did once before off Mount Athos. Whether it was owing to this that Boreas fell with violence on the barbarians at their anchorage I cannot say; but the Athenians declare that they had received aid from Boreas before, and that it was he who now caused all these disasters. They therefore, on their return home, built a temple to this god on the banks of the Ilissus.

190. Such as put the loss of the Persian fleet in this storm at the lowest say that four hundred of their ships were destroyed, that a countless multitude of men were slain, and a vast treasure engulfed. Ameinocles, the son of Crêtines, a Magnesian, who farmed land near Cape Sepias, found the wreck of these vessels a source of great gain to him; many were the gold and silver drinking-cups, cast up long afterwards by the surf, which he gathered; while treasure-boxes too which had belonged to the Persians, and golden articles of all kinds and beyond count, came into his possession. Ameinocles grew to be a man of great wealth in this way; but in other respects things did not go over well with him: he too, like other men, had his own grief—the calamity of losing his offspring.

191. As for the number of the provision craft and other merchant ships which perished, it was beyond count. Indeed, such was the loss, that the commanders of the sea force, fearing lest in their shattered condition the Thessalians should venture on an attack, raised a lofty barricade around their station out of the wreck of the vessels cast ashore. The storm lasted three days. At length the Magians, by offering victims to the Winds, and charming them with the help of conjurers, while at the same time they sacrificed to Thetis and the Nereids, succeeded in laying the storm four days after it first began; or perhaps it ceased of itself. The reason of their offering sacrifice to Thetis was this: they were told by the Ionians that here was the place whence Peleus carried her off, and that the whole promontory was sacred to her and to her sister Nereids. So the storm lulled upon the fourth day.

192. The scouts left by the Greeks about the highlands of Eubœa hastened down from their stations on the day following that whereon the storm began, and acquainted their countrymen with all that had befallen the Persian fleet. These no sooner heard what had happened than straightway they returned thanks to Neptune the Saviour, and poured libations in his honour; after which they hastened back with all speed to Artemisium, expecting to find a very few ships left to oppose them, and arriving there for the second time, took up their station on that strip of coast: nor from that day to the present have they ceased to address Neptune by the name then given him, of "Saviour."

193. The barbarians, when the wind lulled and the sea grew smooth, drew their ships down to the water, and proceeded to coast along the mainland. Having then rounded the extreme point of Magnesia, they sailed straight into the bay that runs up to Pagasæ. There is a place in this bay, belonging to Magnesia, where Hercules is said to have been put ashore

to fetch water by Jason and his companions; who then deserted him and went on their way to Æa in Colchis, on board the ship Argo, in quest of the golden fleece. From the circumstance that they intended, after watering their vessel at this place, to quit the shore and launch forth into the deep, it received the name of Aphetæ. Here then it was that the fleet of Xerxes came to an anchor.

194. Fifteen ships, which had lagged greatly behind the rest, happening to catch sight of the Greek fleet at Artemisium, mistook it for their own, and sailing down into the midst of it, fell into the hands of the enemy. The commander of this squadron was Sandôces, the son of Thamasius, governor of Cymé, in Æolis. He was of the number of the royal judges, and had been crucified by Darius some time before, on the charge of taking a bribe to determine a cause wrongly; but while he yet hung on the cross, Darius bethought him that the good deeds of Sandôces towards the king's house were more numerous than his evil deeds; and so, confessing that he had acted with more haste than wisdom, he ordered him to be taken down and set at large. Thus Sandôces escaped destruction at the hands of Darius, and was alive at this time; but he was not fated to come off so cheaply from his second peril; for as soon as the Greeks saw the ships making towards them, they guessed their mistake, and putting to sea, took them without difficulty.

195. Aridôlis, tyrant of Alabanda in Caria, was on board one of the ships, and was made prisoner; as also was the Paphian general, Penthylus, the son of Demonoüs, who was on board another. This person had brought with him twelve ships from Paphos, and, after losing eleven in the storm off Sepias, was taken in the remaining one as he sailed towards Artemisium. The Greeks, after questioning their prisoners as much as they wished concerning the forces of Xerxes, sent them away in chains to the Isthmus of Corinth.

196. The sea force of the barbarians, with the exception of the fifteen ships commanded (as I said) by Sandôces, came safe to Aphetæ. Xerxes meanwhile, with the land army, had proceeded through Thessaly and Achæa, and three days earlier, had entered the territory of the Malians. In Thessaly, he matched his own horses against the Thessalian, which he heard were the best in Greece, but the Greek coursers were left far behind in the race. All the rivers in this region had water enough to supply his army, except only the Onochônus; but in Ach-æa, the largest of the streams, the Apidanus, barely held out.

197. On his arrival at Alus in Achæa, his guides, wishing to inform him of everything, told him the tale known to the dwellers in those parts concerning the temple of the Laphystian Jupiter—how that Athamas the son of Æolus took counsel with Ino and plotted the death of Phrixus; and how that afterwards the Achæans, warned by an oracle, laid a forfeit upon his posterity, forbidding the eldest of the race ever to enter into the court-house (which they call the people's house), and keeping watch themselves to see the law obeyed. If one comes within the doors, he can never go out again except to be sacrificed. Further, they told him how that many persons, when on the point of being slain, are seized with such fear that they flee away and take refuge in some other country; and that these, if they come back long afterwards, and are found to be the persons who entered the court-house, are led forth covered with chaplets, and in a grand procession, and are sacrificed. This forfeit is paid by the descendants of Cytissorus the son of Phrixus, because, when the Achæans, in obedience to an oracle, made Athamas the son of Æolus their sin-offering, and were about to slay him, Cytissorus came from Æa in Colchis and rescued Athamus; by which deed he brought the anger of the god upon his own posterity. Xerxes, therefore, having heard this story, when he reached the grove of the god, avoided it, and commanded his army to do the like. He also paid the same respect to the house and precinct of the descendants of Athamas.

198. Such were the doing of Xerxes in Thessaly and in Achæa. From hence he passed on into Malis, along the shores of a bay, in which there is an ebb and flow of the tide daily. By the side of this bay lies a piece of flat land, in one part broad, but in another very narrow indeed, around which runs a range of lofty hills, impossible to climb, enclosing all Malis within them, and called the Trachinian cliffs. The first city upon the bay, as you come from Achæa, is Anticyra, near which the river Spercheius, flowing down from the country of the Enianians, empties itself into the sea. About twenty furlongs from this stream there is a second river, called the Dyras, which is said to have appeared first to help Hercules when he was burning. Again, at the distance of twenty furlongs, there is a stream called the Melas, near which, within about five furlongs, stands the city of Trachis.

199. At the point where this city is built, the plain between the hills and the sea is broader than at any other, for it there measures 22,000 plethra.[1] South of Trachis there is a cleft in the mountain-range which shuts in the territory of Trachinia; and the river Asôpus issuing from this cleft flows for a while along the foot of the hills.

200. Further to the south, another river, called the Phœnix, which has no great body of water, flows from the same hills, and falls into the Asôpus. Here is the narrowest place of all; for in this part there is only a causeway wide enough for a single carriage. From the river Phœnix to Thermopylæ is a distance of fifteen furlongs; and in this space is situate the village called Anthêla, which the river Asôpus passes ere it reaches the sea. The space about Anthêla is of some width, and contains a temple of Amphictyonian Ceres, as well as the seats of the Amphictyonic deputies, and a temple of Amphictyon himself.

201. King Xerxes pitched his camp in the region of Malis called Trachinia, while on their side the Greeks occupied the straits. These straits the Greeks in general call Thermopylæ (the Hot Gates); but the natives, and those who dwell in the neighbourhood, call them Pylæ (the Gates). Here then the two armies took their stand; the one master of all the region lying north of Trachis, the other of the country extending southward of that place to the verge of the continent.

202. The Greeks who at this spot awaited the coming of Xerxes were the following:— From Sparta, three hundred men-at-arms; from Arcadia, a thousand Tegeans and Mantineans, five hundred of each people; a hundred and twenty Orchomenians, from the Arcadian Orchomenus; and a thousand from other cities: from Corinth, four hundred men; from Phlius, two hundred; and from Mycenæ eighty. Such was the number from the Peloponnese. There were also present, from Bœotia, seven hundred Thespians and four hundred Thebans.

203. Besides these troops, the Locrians of Opus and the Phocians had obeyed the call of their countrymen, and sent, the former all the force they had, the latter a thousand men. For envoys had gone from the Greeks at Thermopylæ among the Locrians and Phocians, to call on them for assistance, and to say—"They

were themselves but the vanguard of the host, sent to precede the main body, which might every day be expected to follow them. The sea was in good keeping, watched by the Athenians, the Eginetans, and the rest of the fleet. There was no cause why they should fear; for after all the invader was not a god but a man; and there never had been, and never would be, a man who was not liable to misfortunes from the very day of his birth, and those misfortunes greater in proportion to his own greatness. The assailant therefore, being only a mortal, must needs fall from his glory." Thus urged, the Locrians and the Phocians had come with their troops to Trachis.

204. The various nations had each captains of their own under whom they served; but the one to whom all especially looked up, and who had the command of the entire force, was the Lacedæmonian, Leonidas. Now Leonidas was the son of Anaxandridas, who was the son of Leo, who was the son of Eurycratidas, who was the son of Anaxander, who was the son of Eurycrates, who was the son of Polydôrus, who was the son of Alcamenes, who was the son of Têlecles, who was the son of Archelaüs, who was the son of Agesilaüs, who was the son of Doryssus, who was the son of Labôtas, who was the son of Echestratus, who was the son of Agis, who was the son of Eurysthenes, who was the son of Aristodêmus, who was the son of Aristomachus, who was the son of Cleodæus, who was the son of Hyllus, who was the son of Hercules.

Leonidas had come to be king of Sparta quite unexpectedly.

205. Having two elder brothers, Cleomenes and Dorieus, he had no thought of ever mounting the throne. However, when Cleomenes died without male offspring, as Dorieus was likewise deceased, having perished in Sicily, the crown fell to Leonidas, who was older than Cleombrotus, the youngest of the sons of Anaxandridas, and, moreover, was married to the daughter of Cleomenes. He had now come to Thermopylæ, accompanied by the three hundred men which the law assigned him, whom he had himself chosen from among the citizens, and who were all of them fathers with sons living. On his way he had taken the troops from Thebes, whose number I have already mentioned, and who were under the command of Leontiades the son of Eurymachus. The reason why he made a point of taking troops from Thebes, and Thebes only, was that the Thebans were strongly suspected of

[1]Herodotus is probably using the plethron as a square measure, making here a total of about 5,000 acres.

being well inclined to the Medes. Leonidas therefore called on them to come with him to the war, wishing to see whether they would comply with his demand, or openly refuse, and disclaim the Greek alliance. They, however, though their wishes leant the other way, nevertheless sent the men.

206. The force with Leonidas was sent forward by the Spartans in advance of their main body, that the sight of them might encourage the allies to fight, and hinder them from going over to the Medes, as it was likely they might have done had they seen that Sparta was backward. They intended presently, when they had celebrated the Carneian festival, which was what now kept them at home, to leave a garrison in Sparta, and hasten in full force to join the army. The rest of the allies also intended to act similarly; for it happened that the Olympic festival fell exactly at this same period. None of them looked to see the contest at Thermopylæ decided so speedily; wherefore they were content to send forward a mere advanced guard. Such accordingly were the intentions of the allies.

207. The Greek forces at Thermopylæ, when the Persian army drew near to the entrance of the pass, were seized with fear; and a council was held to consider about a retreat. It was the wish of the Peloponnesians generally that the army should fall back upon the Peloponnese, and there guard the Isthmus. But Leonidas, who saw with what indignation the Phocians and Locrians heard of this plan, gave his voice for remaining where they were, while they sent envoys to the several cities to ask for help, since they were too few to make a stand against an army like that of the Medes.

208. While this debate was going on, Xerxes sent a mounted spy to observe the Greeks, and note how many they were, and see what they were doing. He had heard, before he came out of Thessaly, that a few men were assembled at this place, and that at their head were certain Lacedæmonians, under Leonidas, a descendant of Hercules. The horseman rode up to the camp, and looked about him, but did not see the whole army; for such as were on the further side of the wall (which had been rebuilt and was now carefully guarded) it was not possible for him to behold; but he observed those on the outside, who were encamped in front of the rampart. It chanced that at this time the Lacedæmonians held the outer guard, and were seen by the spy, some of them engaged in gymnastic exercises, others combing their long hair. At this the spy greatly marvelled, but he counted their number, and when he had taken accurate note of everything, he rode back quietly; for no one pursued after him, nor paid any heed to his visit. So he returned, and told Xerxes all that he had seen.

209. Upon this, Xerxes, who had no means of surmising the truth—namely, that the Spartans were preparing to do or die manfully—but thought it laughable that they should be engaged in such employments, sent and called to his presence Demaratus the son of Ariston, who still remained with the army. When he appeared, Xerxes told him all that he had heard, and questioned him concerning the news, since he was anxious to understand the meaning of such behaviour on the part of the Spartans. Then Demaratus said—

"I spake to thee, O king! concerning these men long since, when we had but just begun our march upon Greece; thou, however, didst only laugh at my words, when I told thee of all this, which I saw would come to pass. Earnestly do I struggle at all times to speak truth to thee, sire; and now listen to it once more. These men have come to dispute the pass with us; and it is for this that they are now making ready. 'Tis their custom, when they are about to hazard their lives, to adorn their heads with care. Be assured, however, that if thou canst subdue the men who are here and the Lacedæmonians who remain in Sparta, there is no other nation in all the world which will venture to lift a hand in their defence. Thou hast now to deal with the first kingdom and town in Greece, and with the bravest men."

Then Xerxes, to whom what Demaratus said seemed altogether to surpass belief, asked further "how it was possible for so small an army to contend with his?"

"O king!" Demaratus answered, "let me be treated as a liar, if matters fall not out as I say."

210. But Xerxes was not persuaded any the more. Four whole days he suffered to go by, expecting that the Greeks would run away. When, however, he found on the fifth that they were not gone, thinking that their firm stand was mere impudence and recklessness, he grew wroth, and sent against them the Medes and Cissians, with orders to take them alive and bring them into his presence. Then the Medes rushed forward and charged the Greeks, but fell in vast numbers: others however took the places of the slain, and would not be beaten off, though they suffered terrible

losses. In this way it became clear to all, and especially to the king, that though he had plenty of combatants, he had but very few warriors. The struggle, however, continued during the whole day.

211. Then the Medes, having met so rough a reception, withdrew from the fight; and their place was taken by the band of Persians under Hydarnes, whom the king called his "Immortals": they, it was thought, would soon finish the business. But when they joined battle with the Greeks, 'twas with no better success than the Median detachment—things went much as before—the two armies fighting in a narrow space, and the barbarians using shorter spears than the Greeks, and having no advantage from their numbers. The Lacedæmonians fought in a way worthy of note, and showed themselves far more skilful in fight than their adversaries, often turning their backs, and making as though they were all flying away, on which the barbarians would rush after them with much noise and shouting, when the Spartans at their approach would wheel round and face their pursuers, in this way destroying vast numbers of the enemy. Some Spartans likewise fell in these encounters, but only a very few. At last the Persians, finding that all their efforts to gain the pass availed nothing, and that, whether they attacked by divisions or in any other way, it was to no purpose, withdrew to their own quarters.

212. During these assaults, it is said that Xerxes, who was watching the battle, thrice leaped from the throne on which he sate, in terror for his army.

Next day the combat was renewed, but with no better success on the part of the barbarians. The Greeks were so few that the barbarians hoped to find them disabled, by reason of their wounds, from offering any further resistance; and so they once more attacked them. But the Greeks were drawn up in detachments according to their cities, and bore the brunt of the battle in turns—all except the Phocians, who had been stationed on the mountain to guard the pathway. So, when the Persians found no difference between that day and the preceding, they again retired to their quarters.

213. Now, as the king was in great strait, and knew not how he should deal with the emergency, Ephialtes, the son of Eurydêmus, a man of Malis, came to him and was admitted to a conference. Stirred by the hope of receiving a rich reward at the king's hands, he had come to tell him of the pathway which led across the mountain to Thermopylæ; by which disclosure he brought destruction on the band of Greeks who had there withstood the barbarians. This Ephialtes afterwards, from fear of the Lacedæmonians, fled into Thessaly; and during his exile, in an assembly of the Amphictyons held at Pylæ, a price was set upon his head by the Pylagoræ. When some time had gone by, he returned from exile, and went to Anticyra, where he was slain by Athênades, a native of Trachis. Athênades did not slay him for his treachery, but for another reason, which I shall mention in a later part of my history: yet still the Lacedæmonians honoured him none the less. Thus then did Ephialtes perish a long time afterwards.

214. Besides this there is another story told, which I do not at all believe—to wit, that Onêtas the son of Phanagoras, a native of Carystus, and Corydallus, a man of Anticyra, were the persons who spoke on this matter to the king, and took the Persians across the mountain. One may guess which story is true, from the fact that the deputies of the Greeks, the Pylagoræ, who must have had the best means of ascertaining the truth, did not offer the reward for the heads of Onêtas and Corydallus, but for that of Ephialtes of Trachis; and again from the flight of Ephialtes, which we know to have been on this account. Onêtas, I allow, although he was not a Malian, might have been acquainted with the path, if he had lived much in that part of the country; but as Ephialtes was the person who actually led the Persians round the mountain by the pathway, I leave his name on record as that of the man who did the deed.

215. Great was the joy of Xerxes on this occasion; and as he approved highly of the enterprise which Ephialtes undertook to accomplish, he forthwith sent upon the errand Hydarnes, and the Persians under him. The troops left the camp about the time of the lighting of the lamps. The pathway along which they went was first discovered by the Malians of these parts, who soon afterwards led the Thessalians by it to attack the Phocians, at the time when the Phocians fortified the pass with a wall, and so put themselves under covert from danger. And ever since, the path has always been put to an ill use by the Malians.

216. The course which it takes is the following:—Beginning at the Asôpus, where that stream flows through the cleft in the hills, it runs along the ridge of the mountain (which

is called, like the pathway over it, Anopæa), and ends at the city of Alpênus—the first Locrian town as you come from Malis—by the stone called Melampygus and the seats of the Cercopians. Here it is as narrow as at any other point.

217. The Persians took this path, and, crossing the Asôpus, continued their march through the whole of the night, having the mountains of Œta on their right hand, and on their left those of Trachis. At dawn of day they found themselves close to the summit. Now the hill was guarded, as I have already said, by a thousand Phocian men-at-arms, who were placed there to defend the pathway, and at the same time to secure their own country. They had been given the guard of the mountain path, while the other Greeks defended the pass below, because they had volunteered for the service, and had pledged themselves to Leonidas to maintain the post.

218. The ascent of the Persians became known to the Phocians in the following manner:—During all the time that they were making their way up, the Greeks remained unconscious of it, inasmuch as the whole mountain was covered with groves of oak; but it happened that the air was very still, and the leaves which the Persians stirred with their feet made, as it was likely they would, a loud rustling, whereupon the Phocians jumped up and flew to seize their arms. In a moment the barbarians came in sight, and, perceiving men arming themselves, were greatly amazed; for they had fallen in with an enemy when they expected no opposition. Hydarnes, alarmed at the sight, and fearing lest the Phocians might be Lacedæmonians, inquired of Ephialtes to what nation these troops belonged. Ephialtes told him the exact truth, whereupon he arrayed his Persians for battle. The Phocians, galled by the showers of arrows to which they were exposed, and imagining themselves the special object of the Persian attack, fled hastily to the crest of the mountain, and there made ready to meet death; but while their mistake continued, the Persians, with Ephialtes and Hydarnes, not thinking it worth their while to delay on account of Phocians, passed on and descended the mountain with all possible speed.

219. The Greeks at Thermopylæ received the first warning of the destruction which the dawn would bring on them from the seer Megistias, who read their fate in the victims as he was sacrificing. After this deserters came in, and brought the news that the Persians were marching round by the hills: it was still night when these men arrived. Last of all, the scouts came running down from the heights, and brought in the same accounts, when the day was just beginning to break. Then the Greeks held a council to consider what they should do, and here opinions were divided: some were strong against quitting their post, while others contended to the contrary. So when the council had broken up, part of the troops departed and went their ways homeward to their several states; part however resolved to remain, and to stand by Leonidas to the last.

220. It is said that Leonidas himself sent away the troops who departed, because he tendered their safety, but thought it unseemly that either he or his Spartans should quit the post which they had been especially sent to guard. For my own part, I incline to think that Leonidas gave the order, because he perceived the allies to be out of heart and unwilling to encounter the danger to which his own mind was made up. He therefore commanded them to retreat, but said that he himself could not draw back with honour; knowing that, if he stayed, glory awaited him, and that Sparta in that case would not lose her prosperity. For when the Spartans, at the very beginning of the war, sent to consult the oracle concerning it, the answer which they received from the Pythoness was "that either Sparta must be overthrown by the barbarians, or one of her kings must perish." The prophecy was delivered in hexameter verse, and ran thus:—

O ye men who dwell in the streets of broad Lace-
  dæmon!
Either your glorious town shall be sacked by the
  children of Perseus,
Or, in exchange, must all through the whole Lac-
  onian country
Mourn for the loss of a king, descendant of great
  Hêrácles.
He cannot be withstood by the courage of bulls
  nor of lions,
Strive as they may; he is mighty as Jove; there is
  nought that shall stay him,
Till he have got for his prey your king, or your
  glorious city.

The remembrance of this answer, I think, and the wish to secure the whole glory for the Spartans, caused Leonidas to send the allies away. This is more likely than that they quarrelled with him, and took their departure in such unruly fashion.

221. To me it seems no small argument in

favour of this view, that the seer also who accompanied the army, Megistias, the Acarnanian—said to have been of the blood of Melampus, and the same who was led by the appearance of the victims to warn the Greeks of the danger which threatened them—received orders to retire (as it is certain he did) from Leonidas, that he might escape the coming destruction. Megistias, however, though bidden to depart, refused, and stayed with the army; but he had an only son present with the expedition, whom he now sent away.

222. So the allies, when Leonidas ordered them to retire, obeyed him and forthwith departed. Only the Thespians and the Thebans remained with the Spartans; and of these the Thebans were kept back by Leonidas as hostages, very much against their will. The Thespians, on the contrary, stayed entirely of their own accord, refusing to retreat, and declaring that they would not forsake Leonidas and his followers. So they abode with the Spartans, and died with them. Their leader was Demophilus, the son of Diadromes.

223. At sunrise Xerxes made libations, after which he waited until the time when the forum is wont to fill, and then began his advance. Ephialtes had instructed him thus, as the descent of the mountain is much quicker, and the distance much shorter, than the way round the hills, and the ascent. So the barbarians under Xerxes began to draw nigh; and the Greeks under Leonidas, as they now went forth determined to die, advanced much further than on previous days, until they reached the more open portion of the pass. Hitherto they had held their station within the wall, and from this had gone forth to fight at the point where the pass was the narrowest. Now they joined battle beyond the defile, and carried slaughter among the barbarians, who fell in heaps. Behind them the captains of the squadrons, armed with whips, urged their men forward with continual blows. Many were thrust into the sea, and there perished; a still greater number were trampled to death by their own soldiers; no one heeded the dying. For the Greeks, reckless of their own safety and desperate, since they knew that, as the mountain had been crossed, their destruction was nigh at hand, exerted themselves with the most furious valour against the barbarians.

224. By this time the spears of the greater number were all shivered, and with their swords they hewed down the ranks of the Persians; and here, as they strove, Leonidas fell fighting bravely, together with many other famous Spartans, whose names I have taken care to learn on account of their great worthiness, as indeed I have those of all the three hundred. There fell too at the same time very many famous Persians: among them, two sons of Darius, Abrocomes and Hyperanthes, his children by Phrataguné, the daughter of Artanes. Artanes was brother of King Darius, being a son of Hystaspes, the son of Arsames; and when he gave his daughter to the king, he made him heir likewise of all his substance; for she was his only child.

225. Thus two brothers of Xerxes here fought and fell. And now there arose a fierce struggle between the Persians and the Lacedæmonians over the body of Leonidas, in which the Greeks four times drove back the enemy, and at last by their great bravery succeeded in bearing off the body. This combat was scarcely ended when the Persians with Ephialtes approached; and the Greeks, informed that they drew nigh, made a change in the manner of their fighting. Drawing back into the narrowest part of the pass, and retreating even behind the cross wall, they posted themselves upon a hillock, where they stood all drawn up together in one close body, except only the Thebans. The hillock whereof I speak is at the entrance of the straits, where the stone lion stands which was set up in honour of Leonidas. Here they defended themselves to the last, such as still had swords using them, and the others resisting with their hands and teeth; till the barbarians, who in part had pulled down the wall and attacked them in front, in part had gone round and now encircled them upon every side, overwhelmed and buried the remnant which was left beneath showers of missile weapons.

226. Thus nobly did the whole body of Lacedæmonians and Thespians behave; but nevertheless one man is said to have distinguished himself above all the rest, to wit, Diêneces the Spartan. A speech which he made before the Greeks engaged the Medes, remains on record. One of the Trachinians told him, "Such was the number of the barbarians, that when they shot forth their arrows the sun would be darkened by their multitude." Diêneces, not at all frightened at these words, but making light of the Median numbers, answered, "Our Trachinian friend brings us excellent tidings. If the Medes darken the sun, we shall have our fight in the shade." Other sayings too of a like nature are reported to have been left on record by this same person.

227. Next to him two brothers, Lacedæmonians, are reputed to have made themselves conspicuous: they were named Alpheus and Maro, and were the sons of Orsiphantus. There was also a Thespian who gained greater glory than any of his countrymen: he was a man called Dithyrambus, the son of Harmatidas.

228. The slain were buried where they fell; and in their honour, nor less in honour of those who died before Leonidas sent the allies away, an inscription was set up, which said:—

Here did four thousand men from Pelops' land
Against three hundred myriads bravely stand.

This was in honour of all. Another was for the Spartans alone:—

Go, stranger, and to Lacedæmon tell
That here, obeying her behests, we fell.

This was for the Lacedæmonians. The seer had the following:—

The great Megistias' tomb you here may view,
Whom slew the Medes, fresh from Spercheius'
fords.
Well the wise seer the coming death foreknew,
Yet scorned he to forsake his Spartan lords.

These inscriptions, and the pillars likewise, were all set up by the Amphictyons, except that in honour of Megistias, which was inscribed to him (on account of their sworn friendship) by Simônides, the son of Leôprepes.

229. Two of the three hundred, it is said, Aristodêmus and Eurytus, having been attacked by a disease of the eyes, had received orders from Leonidas to quit the camp; and both lay at Alpêni in the worst stage of the malady. These two men might, had they been so minded, have agreed together to return alive to Sparta; or if they did not like to return, they might have gone both to the field and fallen with their countrymen. But at this time, when either way was open to them, unhappily they could not agree, but took contrary courses. Eurytus no sooner heard that the Persians had come round the mountain than straightway he called for his armour, and having buckled it on, bade his helot lead him to the place where his friends were fighting. The helot did so, and then turned and fled; but Eurytus plunged into the thick of the battle, and so perished. Aristodêmus, on the other hand, was faint of heart, and remained at Alpêni. It is my belief that if Aristodêmus only had been sick and returned, or if both had come back together, the Spartans would have been content and felt no anger; but when there were two men with the very same excuse, and one of them was chary of his life, while the other freely gave it, they could not but be very wroth with the former.

230. This is the account which some give of the escape of Aristodêmus. Others say that he, with another, had been sent on a message from the army, and, having it in his power to return in time for the battle, purposely loitered on the road, and so survived his comrades; while his fellow-messenger came back in time, and fell in the battle.

231. When Aristodêmus returned to Lacedæmon, reproach and disgrace awaited him; disgrace, inasmuch as no Spartan would give him a light to kindle his fire, or so much as address a word to him; and reproach, since all spoke of him as "the craven." However he wiped away all his shame afterwards at the battle of Platæa.

232. Another of the three hundred is likewise said to have survived the battle, a man named Pantites, whom Leonidas had sent on an embassy into Thessaly. He, they say, on his return to Sparta, found himself in such disesteem that he hanged himself.

233. The Thebans under the command of Leontiades remained with the Greeks, and fought against the barbarians, only so long as necessity compelled them. No sooner did they see victory inclining to the Persians, and the Greeks under Leonidas hurrying with all speed towards the hillock, than they moved away from their companions, and with hands upraised advanced towards the barbarians, exclaiming, as was indeed most true—"that they for their part wished well to the Medes, and had been among the first to give earth and water to the king; force alone had brought them to Thermopylæ; and so they must not be blamed for the slaughter which had befallen the king's army." These words, the truth of which was attested by the Thessalians, sufficed to obtain the Thebans the grant of their lives. However, their good fortune was not without some drawback; for several of them were slain by the barbarians on their first approach; and the rest, who were the greater number, had the royal mark branded upon their bodies by the command of Xerxes—Leontiades, their captain, being the first to suffer. (This man's son, Eurymachus, was afterwards slain by the Platæans, when he came with a band of 400 Thebans, and seized their city.)

234. Thus fought the Greeks at Thermopylæ. And Xerxes, after the fight was over, called

for Demaratus to question him; and began as follows:—

"Demaratus, thou art a worthy man; thy true-speaking proves it. All has happened as thou didst forewarn. Now then, tell me, how many Lacedæmonians are there left, and of those left how many are such brave warriors as these? Or are they all alike?"

"O king!" replied the other, "the whole number of the Lacedæmonians is very great; and many are the cities which they inhabit. But I will tell thee what thou really wishest to learn. There is a town of Lacedæmon called Sparta, which contains within it about eight thousand full-grown men. *They* are, one and all, equal to those who have fought here. The other Lacedæmonians are brave men, but not such warriors as these."

"Tell me now, Demaratus," rejoined Xerxes, "how we may with least trouble subdue these men. Thou must know all the paths of their counsels, as thou wert once their king."

235. Then Demaratus answered—"O king! since thou askest my advice so earnestly, it is fitting that I should inform thee what I consider to be the best course. Detach three hundred vessels from the body of thy fleet, and send them to attack the shores of Laconia. There is an island called Cythera in those parts, not far from the coast, concerning which Chilon, one of our wisest men, made the remark that Sparta would gain if it were sunk to the bottom of the sea—so constantly did he expect that it would give occasion to some project like that which I now recommend to thee. I mean not to say that he had a foreknowledge of thy attack upon Greece; but in truth he feared all armaments. Send thy ships then to this island, and thence affright the Spartans. If once they have a war of their own close to their doors, fear not their giving any help to the rest of the Greeks while thy land force is engaged in conquering them. In this way may all Greece be subdued; and then Sparta, left to herself, will be powerless. But if thou wilt not take this advice, I will tell thee what thou mayest look to see. When thou comest to the Peloponnese, thou wilt find a narrow neck of land, where all the Peloponnesians who are leagued against thee will be gathered together; and there thou wilt have to fight bloodier battles than any which thou hast yet witnessed. If, however, thou wilt follow my plan, the Isthmus and the cities of Peloponnese will yield to thee without a battle."

236. Achæmenes, who was present, now took the word, and spoke—he was brother to Xerxes, and, having the command of the fleet, feared lest Xerxes might be prevailed upon to do as Demaratus advised—

"I perceive, O king" (he said), "that thou art listening to the words of a man who is envious of thy good fortune, and seeks to betray thy cause. This is indeed the common temper of the Grecian people—they envy good fortune, and hate power greater than their own. If in this posture of our affairs, after we have lost four hundred vessels by shipwreck, three hundred more be sent away to make a voyage round the Peloponnese, our enemies will become a match for us. But let us keep our whole fleet in one body, and it will be dangerous for them to venture on an attack, as they will certainly be no match for us then. Besides, while our sea and land forces advance together, the fleet and army can each help the other; but if they be parted, no aid will come either from thee to the fleet, or from the fleet to thee. Only order thy own matters well, and trouble not thyself to inquire concerning the enemy—where they will fight, or what they will do, or how many they are. Surely they can manage their own concerns without us, as we can ours without them. If the Lacedæmonians come out against the Persians to battle, they will scarce repair the disaster which has befallen them now."

237. Xerxes replied—"Achæmenes, thy counsel pleases me well, and I will do as thou sayest. But Demaratus advised what he thought best—only his judgment was not so good as thine. Never will I believe that he does not wish well to my cause; for that is disproved both by his former counsels, and also by the circumstances of the case. A citizen does indeed envy any fellow-citizen who is more lucky than himself, and often hates him secretly; if such a man be called on for counsel, he will not give his best thoughts, unless indeed he be a man of very exalted virtue; and such are but rarely found. But a friend of another country delights in the good fortune of his foreign bond-friend, and will give him, when asked, the best advice in his power. Therefore I warn all men to abstain henceforth from speaking ill of Demaratus, who is my bond-friend."

238. When Xerxes had thus spoken, he proceeded to pass through the slain; and finding the body of Leonidas, whom he knew to have been the Lacedæmonian king and captain, he ordered that the head should be struck off,

and the trunk fastened to a cross. This proves to me most clearly, what is plain also in many other ways—namely, that King Xerxes was more angry with Leonidas, while he was still in life, than with any other mortal. Certes, he would not else have used his body so shamefully. For the Persians are wont to honour those who show themselves valiant in fight more highly than any nation that I know. They, however, to whom the orders were given, did according to the commands of the king.

239. I return now to a point in my History, which at the time I left incomplete. The Lacedæmonians were the first of the Greeks to hear of the king's design against their country; and it was at this time that they sent to consult the Delphic oracle, and received the answer of which I spoke a while ago. The discovery was made to them in a very strange way. Demaratus, the son of Ariston, after he took refuge with the Medes, was not, in my judgment, which is supported by probability, a well-wisher to the Lacedæmonians. It may be questioned, therefore, whether he did what I am about to mention from good-will or from insolent triumph. It happened that he was at Susa at the time when Xerxes determined to lead his army into Greece; and in this way becoming acquainted with his design, he resolved to send tidings of it to Sparta. So as there was no other way of effecting his purpose, since the danger of being discovered was great, Demaratus framed the following contrivance. He took a pair of tablets, and, clearing the wax away from them, wrote what the king was purposing to do upon the wood whereof the tablets were made; having done this, he spread the wax once more over the writing, and so sent it. By these means, the guards placed to watch the roads, observing nothing but a blank tablet, were sure to give no trouble to the bearer. When the tablet reached Lacedæmon, there was no one, I understand, who could find out the secret, till Gorgo, the daughter of Cleomenes and wife of Leonidas, discovered it, and told the others. "If they would scrape the wax off the tablet," she said, "they would be sure to find the writing upon the wood." The Lacedæmonians took her advice, found the writing, and read it; after which they sent it round to the other Greeks. Such then is the account which is given of this matter.

The Eighth Book, Entitled
URANIA

1. THE Greeks engaged in the sea-service were the following. The Athenians furnished a hundred and twenty-seven vessels to the fleet, which were manned in part by the Platæans, who, though unskilled in such matters, were led by their active and daring spirit to undertake this duty; the Corinthians furnished a contingent of forty vessels; the Megarians sent twenty; the Chalcideans also manned twenty, which had been furnished to them by the Athenians; the Eginetans came with eighteen; the Sicyonians with twelve; the Lacedæmonians with ten; the Epidaurians with eight; the Eretrians with seven; the Trœzenians with five; the Styreans with two; and the Cêans with two triremes and two penteconters. Last of all, the Locrians of Opus came in aid with a squadron of seven penteconters.

2. Such were the nations which furnished vessels to the fleet now at Artemisium; and in mentioning them I have given the number of ships furnished by each. The total number of the ships thus brought together, without counting the penteconters, was two hundred and seventy-one; and the captain, who had the chief command over the whole fleet, was Eurybiades the son of Eurycleides. He was furnished by Sparta, since the allies had said that "if a Lacedæmonian did not take the command, they would break up the fleet, for never would they serve under the Athenians."

3. From the first, even earlier than the time when the embassy went to Sicily to solicit alliance, there had been a talk of intrusting the Athenians with the command at sea; but the allies were averse to the plan, wherefore the Athenians did not press it; for there was nothing they had so much at heart as the salvation of Greece, and they knew that, if they quarrelled among themselves about the command, Greece would be brought to ruin. Herein they judged rightly; for internal strife is a thing as much worse than war carried on by a united people, as war itself is worse than peace. The Athenians therefore, being so persuaded, did not push their claims, but waived them, so long as they were in such great need of aid from the other Greeks. And they afterwards showed their motive; for at the time when the Persians had been driven from Greece, and were now threatened by the Greeks in their own country, they took occasion of the insolence of Pausanias to deprive the Lacedæmonians of their leadership. This, however, happened afterwards.

4. At the present time the Greeks, on their arrival at Artemisium, when they saw the number of the ships which lay at anchor near Aphetæ, and the abundance of troops everywhere, feeling disappointed that matters had gone with the barbarians so far otherwise than they had expected, and full of alarm at what they saw, began to speak of drawing back from Artemisium towards the inner parts of their country. So when the Eubœans heard what was in debate, they went to Eurybiades, and besought him to wait a few days, while they removed their children and their slaves to a place of safety. But, as they found that they prevailed nothing, they left him and went to Themistocles, the Athenian commander, to whom they gave a bribe of thirty talents, on his promise that the fleet should remain and risk a battle in defence of Eubœa.

5. And Themistocles succeeded in detaining the fleet in the way which I will now relate. He made over to Eurybiades five talents out of the thirty paid him, which he gave as if they came from himself; and having in this way gained over the admiral, he addressed himself to Adeimantus, the son of Ocytus, the Corinthian leader, who was the only remonstrant now, and who still threatened to sail away from Artemisium and not wait for the other

260

captains. Addressing himself to this man, Themistocles said with an oath—"Thou forsake us? By no means! I will pay thee better for remaining than the Mede would for leaving thy friends"—and straightway he sent on board the ship of Adeimantus a present of three talents of silver. So these two captains were won by gifts, and came over to the views of Themistocles, who was thereby enabled to gratify the wishes of the Eubœans. He likewise made his own gain on the occasion; for he kept the rest of the money, and no one knew of it. The commanders who took the gifts thought that the sums were furnished by Athens, and had been sent to be used in this way.

6. Thus it came to pass that the Greeks stayed at Eubœa and there gave battle to the enemy.

Now the battle was on this wise. The barbarians reached Aphetæ early in the afternoon, and then saw (as they had previously heard reported) that a fleet of Greek ships, weak in number, lay at Artemisium. At once they were eager to engage, fearing that the Greeks would fly, and hoping to capture them before they should get away. They did not however think it wise to make straight for the Greek station, lest the enemy should see them as they bore down, and betake themselves to flight immediately; in which case night might close in before they came up with the fugitives, and so they might get clean off and make their escape from them; whereas the Persians were minded not to let a single soul slip through their hands.

7. They therefore contrived a plan, which was the following:—They detached two hundred of their ships from the rest, and—to prevent the enemy from seeing them start—sent them round outside the island of Sciathos, to make the circuit of Eubœa by Caphareus and Geræstus, and so to reach the Euripus. By this plan they thought to enclose the Greeks on every side; for the ships detached would block up the only way by which they could retreat, while the others would press upon them in front. With these designs therefore they dispatched the two hundred ships, while they themselves waited—since they did not mean to attack the Greeks upon that day, or until they knew, by signal, of the arrival of the detachment which had been ordered to sail round Eubœa. Meanwhile they made a muster of the other ships at Aphetæ.

8. Now the Persians had with them a man named Scyllias, a native of Sciôné, who was the most expert diver of his day. At the time of the shipwreck off Mount Pelion he had recovered for the Persians a great part of what they lost; and at the same time he had taken care to obtain for himself a good share of the treasure. He had for some time been wishing to go over to the Greeks; but no good opportunity had offered till now, when the Persians were making the muster of their ships. In what way he contrived to reach the Greeks I am not able to say for certain: I marvel much if the tale that is commonly told be true. 'Tis said he dived into the sea at Aphetæ, and did not once come to the surface till he reached Artemisium, a distance of nearly eighty furlongs. Now many things are related of this man which are plainly false; but some of the stories seem to be true. My own opinion is that on this occasion he made the passage to Artemisium in a boat.

However this might be, Scyllias no sooner reached Artemisium than he gave the Greek captains a full account of the damage done by the storm, and likewise told them of the ships sent to make the circuit of Eubœa.

9. So the Greeks on receiving these tidings held a council, whereat, after much debate, it was resolved that they should stay quiet for the present where they were, and remain at their moorings, but that after midnight they should put out to sea, and encounter the ships which were on their way round the island. Later in the day, when they found that no one meddled with them, they formed a new plan, which was to wait till near evening, and then sail out against the main body of the barbarians, for the purpose of trying their mode of fight and skill in manœuvring.

10. When the Persian commanders and crews saw the Greeks thus boldly sailing towards them with their few ships, they thought them possessed with madness, and went out to meet them, expecting (as indeed seemed likely enough) that they would take all their vessels with the greatest ease. The Greek ships were so few, and their own so far outnumbered them, and sailed so much better, that they resolved, seeing their advantage, to encompass their foe on every side. And now such of the Ionians as wished well to the Grecian cause and served in the Persian fleet unwillingly, seeing their countrymen surrounded, were sorely distressed; for they felt sure that not one of them would ever make his escape, so poor an opinion had they of the strength of the Greeks. On the other hand, such as saw with pleasure the attack on Greece, now vied eagerly with

each other which should be the first to make prize of an Athenian ship, and thereby to secure himself a rich reward from the king. For through both the hosts none were so much accounted of as the Athenians.

11. The Greeks, at a signal, brought the sterns of their ships together into a small compass, and turned their prows on every side towards the barbarians; after which, at a second signal, although inclosed within a narrow space, and closely pressed upon by the foe, yet they fell bravely to work, and captured thirty ships of the barbarians, at the same time taking prisoner Philaon, the son of Chersis, and brother of Gorgus king of Salamis, a man of much repute in the fleet. The first who made prize of a ship of the enemy was Lycomêdes the son of Æschreas, an Athenian, who was afterwards adjudged the meed of valour. Victory however was still doubtful when night came on, and put a stop to the combat. The Greeks sailed back to Artemisium; and the barbarians returned to Aphetæ, much surprised at the result, which was far other than they had looked for. In this battle only one of the Greeks who fought on the side of the king deserted and joined his countrymen. This was Antidôrus of Lemnos, whom the Athenians rewarded for his desertion by the present of a piece of land in Salamis.

12. Evening had barely closed in when a heavy rain—it was about midsummer—began to fall, which continued the whole night, with terrible thunderings and lightnings from Mount Pelion: the bodies of the slain and the broken pieces of the damaged ships were drifted in the direction of Aphetæ, and floated about the prows of the vessels there, disturbing the action of the oars. The barbarians, hearing the storm, were greatly dismayed, expecting certainly to perish, as they had fallen into such a multitude of misfortunes. For before they were well recovered from the tempest and the wreck of their vessels off Mount Pelion, they had been surprised by a sea-fight which had taxed all their strength, and now the sea-fight was scarcely over when they were exposed to floods of rain, and the rush of swollen streams into the sea, and violent thunderings.

13. If, however, they who lay at Aphetæ passed a comfortless night, far worse were the sufferings of those who had been sent to make the circuit of Eubœa; inasmuch as the storm fell on them out at sea, whereby the issue was indeed calamitous. They were sailing along near the Hollows of Eubœa, when the wind began to rise and the rain to pour: overpowered by the force of the gale, and driven they knew not whither, at the last they fell upon rocks—Heaven so contriving, in order that the Persian fleet might not greatly exceed the Greek, but be brought nearly to its level. This squadron, therefore, was entirely lost about the Hollows of Eubœa.

14. The barbarians at Aphetæ were glad when day dawned, and remained in quiet at their station, content if they might enjoy a little peace after so many sufferings. Meanwhile there came to the aid of the Greeks a reinforcement of fifty-three ships from Attica. Their arrival, and the news (which reached Artemisium about the same time) of the complete destruction by the storm of the ships sent to sail round Eubœa, greatly cheered the spirits of the Greek sailors. So they waited again till the same hour as the day before, and, once more putting out to sea, attacked the enemy. This time they fell in with some Cilician vessels, which they sank; when night came on, they withdrew to Artemisium.

15. The third day was now come, and the captains of the barbarians, ashamed that so small a number of ships should harass their fleet, and afraid of the anger of Xerxes, instead of waiting for the others to begin the battle, weighed anchor themselves, and advanced against the Greeks about the hour of noon, with shouts encouraging one another. Now it happened that these sea-fights took place on the very same days with the combats at Thermopylæ; and as the aim of the struggle was in the one case to maintain the pass, so in the other it was to defend the Euripus. While the Greeks, therefore, exhorted one another not to let the barbarians burst in upon Greece, these latter shouted to their fellows to destroy the Grecian fleet, and get possession of the channel.

16. And now the fleet of Xerxes advanced in good order to the attack, while the Greeks on their side remained quite motionless at Artemisium. The Persians therefore spread themselves, and came forward in a half-moon, seeking to encircle the Greeks on all sides, and thereby prevent them from escaping. The Greeks, when they saw this, sailed out to meet their assailants; and the battle forthwith began. In this engagement the two fleets contended with no clear advantage to either—for the armament of Xerxes injured itself by its own greatness, the vessels falling into disorder, and oft-times running foul of one another; yet still they did not give way, but made a stout fight,

since the crews felt it would indeed be a disgrace to turn and fly from a fleet so inferior in number. The Greeks therefore suffered much, both in ships and men; but the barbarians experienced a far larger loss of each. So the fleets separated after such a combat as I have described.

17. On the side of Xerxes the Egyptians distinguished themselves above all the combatants; for besides performing many other noble deeds, they took five vessels from the Greeks with their crews on board. On the side of the Greeks the Athenians bore off the meed of valour; and among them the most distinguished was Clinias, the son of Alcibiades, who served at his own charge with two hundred men, on board a vessel which he had himself furnished.

18. The two fleets, on separating, hastened very gladly to their anchorage-grounds. The Greeks, indeed, when the battle was over, became masters of the bodies of the slain and the wrecks of the vessels; but they had been so roughly handled, especially the Athenians, one-half of whose vessels had suffered damage, that they determined to break up from their station, and withdraw to the inner parts of their country.

19. Then Themistocles, who thought that if the Ionian and Carian ships could be detached from the barbarian fleet, the Greeks might be well able to defeat the rest, called the captains together. They met upon the seashore, where the Eubœans were now assembling their flocks and herds; and here Themistocles told them he thought that he knew of a plan whereby he could detach from the king those who were of most worth among his allies. This was all that he disclosed to them of his plan at that time. Meanwhile, looking to the circumstances in which they were, he advised them to slaughter as many of the Eubœan cattle as they liked—for it was better (he said) that their own troops should enjoy them than the enemy—and to give orders to their men to kindle the fires as usual. With regard to the retreat, he said that he would take upon himself to watch the proper moment, and would manage matters so that they should return to Greece without loss. These words pleased the captains; so they had the fires lighted, and began the slaughter of the cattle.

20. The Eubœans, until now, had made light of the oracle of Bacis, as though it had been void of all significancy, and had neither removed their goods from the island, nor yet taken them into their strong places; as they would most certainly have done if they had believed that war was approaching. By this neglect they had brought their affairs into the very greatest danger. Now the oracle of which I speak ran as follows:—

When o'er the main shall be thrown a byblus yoke
  by a stranger,
Be thou ware, and drive from Eubœa the goats'
  loud-bleating.

So, as the Eubœans had paid no regard to this oracle when the evils approached and impended, now that they had arrived, the worst was likely to befall them.

21. While the Greeks were employed in the way described above, the scout who had been on the watch at Trachis arrived at Artemisium. For the Greeks had employed two watchers: —Polyas, a native of Anticyra, had been stationed off Artemisium, with a row-boat at his command ready to sail at any moment, his orders being that, if an engagement took place by sea, he should convey the news at once to the Greeks at Thermopylæ; and in like manner Abrônychus, the son of Lysicles, an Athenian, had been stationed with a triaconter near Leonidas, to be ready, in case of disaster befalling the land force, to carry tidings of it to Artemisium. It was this Abrônychus who now arrived with news of what had befallen Leonidas and those who were with him. When the Greeks heard the tidings they no longer delayed to retreat, but withdrew in the order wherein they had been stationed, the Corinthians leading, and the Athenians sailing last of all.

22. And now Themistocles chose out the swiftest sailers from among the Athenian vessels, and, proceeding to the various watering-places along the coast, cut inscriptions on the rocks, which were read by the Ionians the day following, on their arrival at Artemisium. The inscriptions ran thus:—"Men of Ionia, ye do wrong to fight against your own fathers, and to give your help to enslave Greece. We beseech you therefore to come over, if possible, to our side: if you cannot do this, then, we pray you, stand aloof from the contest yourselves, and persuade the Carians to do the like. If neither of these things be possible, and you are hindered, by a force too strong to resist, from venturing upon desertion, at least when we come to blows fight backwardly, remembering that you are sprung from us, and that it was through you we first provoked the hatred of the barbarian." Themistocles, in putting up

these inscriptions, looked, I believe, to two chances—either Xerxes would not discover them, in which case they might bring over the Ionians to the side of the Greeks; or they would be reported to him and made a ground of accusation against the Ionians, who would thereupon be distrusted, and would not be allowed to take part in the sea-fights.

23. Shortly after the cutting of the inscriptions, a man of Histiæa went in a merchant-ship to Aphetæ, and told the Persians that the Greeks had fled from Artemisium. Disbelieving his report, the Persians kept the man a prisoner, while they sent some of their fastest vessels to see what had happened. These brought back word how matters stood; wherupon at sunrise the whole fleet advanced together in a body, and sailed to Artemisium, where they remained till mid-day; after which they went on to Histiæa. That city fell into their hands immediately; and they shortly overran the various villages upon the coast in the district of Hellopia, which was part of the Histiæan territory.

24. It was while they were at this station that a herald reached them from Xerxes, whom he had sent after making the following dispositions with respect to the bodies of those who fell at Thermopylæ. Of the twenty thousand who had been slain on the Persian side, he left one thousand upon the field while he buried the rest in trenches; and these he carefully filled up with earth, and hid with foliage, that the sailors might not see any signs of them. The herald, on reaching Histiæa, caused the whole force to be collected together, and spake thus to them:

"Comrades, King Xerxes gives permission to all who please, to quit their posts, and see how he fights with the senseless men who think to overthrow his armies."

25. No sooner had these words been uttered, than it became difficult to get a boat, so great was the number of those who desired to see the sight. Such as went crossed the strait, and passing among the heaps of dead, in this way viewed the spectacle. Many helots were included in the slain, but every one imagined that the bodies were all either Lacedæmonians or Thespians. However, no one was deceived by what Xerxes had done with his own dead. It was indeed most truly a laughable device— on the one side a thousand men were seen lying about the field, on the other four thousand crowded together into one spot. This day then was given up to sight-seeing; on the next

the seamen embarked on board their ships and sailed back to Histiæa, while Xerxes and his army proceeded upon their march.

26. There came now a few deserters from Arcadia to join the Persians—poor men who had nothing to live on, and were in want of employment. The Persians brought them into the king's presence, and there inquired of them, by a man who acted as their spokesman, "what the Greeks were doing?" The Arcadians answered—"They are holding the Olympic Games, seeing the athletic sports and the chariot-races." "And what," said the man, "is the prize for which they contend?" "An olive-wreath," returned the others, "which is given to the man who wins." On hearing this, Tritantæchmes, the son of Artabanus, uttered a speech which was in truth most noble, but which caused him to be taxed with cowardice by King Xerxes. Hearing the men say that the prize was not money but a wreath of olive, he could not forbear from exclaiming before them all: "Good heavens! Mardonius, what manner of men are these against whom thou hast brought us to fight?—men who contend with one another, not for money, but for honour!"

27. A little before this, and just after the blow had been struck at Thermopylæ, a herald was sent into Phôcis by the Thessalians, who had always been on bad terms with the Phocians, and especially since their last overthrow. For it was not many years previous to this invasion of Greece by the king, that the Thessalians, with their allies, entered Phôcis in full force, but were defeated by the Phocians in an engagement wherein they were very roughly handled. The Phocians, who had with them as soothsayer Tellias of Elis, were blocked up in the mountain of Parnassus, when the following stratagem was contrived for them by their Elean ally. He took six hundred of their bravest men, and whitened their bodies and their arms with chalk; then instructing them to slay every one whom they should meet that was not whitened like themselves, he made a night attack upon the Thessalians. No sooner did the Thessalian sentries, who were the first to see them, behold this strange sight, than, imagining it to be a prodigy, they were all filled with affright. From the sentries the alarm spread to the army, which was seized with such a panic that the Phocians killed four thousand of them, and became masters of their dead bodies and shields. Of the shields one half were sent as an offering to

the temple at Abæ, the other half were deposited at Delphi; while from the tenth part of the booty gained in the battle, were made the gigantic figures which stand round the tripod in front of the Delphic shrine, and likewise the figures of the same size and character at Abæ.

28. Besides this slaughter of the Thessalian foot when it was blockading them, the Phocians had dealt a blow to their horse upon its invading their territory, from which they had never recovered. There is a pass near the city of Hyampolis, where the Phocians, having dug a broad trench, filled up the void with empty wine-jars, after which they covered the place with mould, so that the ground all looked alike, and then awaited the coming of the Thessalians. These, thinking to destroy the Phocians at one sweep, rushed rapidly forward, and became entangled in the wine-jars, which broke the legs of their horses.

29. The Thessalians had therefore a double cause of quarrel with the Phocians, when they dispatched the herald above mentioned, who thus delivered his message:—

"At length acknowledge, ye men of Phôcis, that ye may not think to match with us. In times past, when it pleased us to hold with the Greeks, we had always the vantage over you; and now our influence is such with the barbarian, that, if we choose it, you will lose your country, and (what is even worse) you will be sold as slaves. However, though we can now do with you exactly as we like, we are willing to forget our wrongs. Quit them with a payment of fifty talents of silver, and we undertake to ward off the evils which threaten your country."

30. Such was the message which the Thessalians sent. The Phocians were the only people in these parts who had not espoused the cause of the Medes; and it is my deliberate opinion that the motive which swayed them was none other—neither more nor less—than their hatred of the Thessalians: for had the Thessalians declared in favour of the Greeks, I believe that the men of Phôcis would have joined the Median side. As it was, when the message arrived, the Phocians made answer, that "they would not pay anything—it was open to them, equally with the Thessalians, to make common cause with the Medes, if they only chose so to do—but they would never of their own free will become traitors to Greece."

31. On the return of this answer, the Thessalians, full of wrath against the Phocians,

offered themselves as guides to the barbarian army, and led them forth from Trachinia into Dôris. In this place there is a narrow tongue of Dorian territory, not more than thirty furlongs across, interposed between Malis and Phôcis; it is the tract in ancient times called Dryopis; and the land, of which it is a part, is the mother-country of the Dorians in the Peloponnese. This territory the barbarians did not plunder, for the inhabitants had espoused their side; and besides, the Thessalians wished that they should be spared.

32. From Dôris they marched forward into Phôcis; but here the inhabitants did not fall into their power: for some of them had taken refuge in the high grounds of Parnassus—one summit of which, called Tithorea, standing quite by itself, not far from the city of Neon, is well fitted to give shelter to a large body of men, and had now received a number of the Phocians with their movables; while the greater portion had fled to the country of the Ozolian Locrians, and placed their goods in the city called Amphissa, which lies above the Crissæan plain. The land of Phôcis, however, was entirely overrun, for the Thessalians led the Persian army through the whole of it; and wherever they went, the country was wasted with fire and sword, the cities and even the temples being wilfully set alight by the troops.

33. The march of the army lay along the valley of the Cephissus; and here they ravaged far and wide, burning the towns of Drymus, Charadra, Erôchus, Tethrônium, Amphicæa, Neon, Pedieis, Triteis, Elateia, Hyampolis, Parapotamii, and Abæ. At the last-named place there was a temple of Apollo, very rich, and adorned with a vast number of treasures and offerings. There was likewise an oracle there in those days, as indeed there is at the present time. This temple the Persians plundered and burnt; and here they captured a number of the Phocians before they could reach the hills, and caused the death of some of their women by ill-usage.

34. After passing Parapotamii, the barbarians marched to Panopeis; and now the army separated into two bodies, whereof one, which was the more numerous and the stronger of the two, marched, under Xerxes himself, towards Athens, entering Bœotia by the country of the Orchomenians. The Bœotians had one and all embraced the cause of the Medes; and their towns were in the possession of Macedonian garrisons, whom Alexander had sent there, to make it manifest to Xerxes that the

Bœotians were on the Median side. Such then was the road followed by one division of the barbarians.

35. The other division took guides, and proceeded towards the temple of Delphi, keeping Mount Parnassus on their right hand. They too laid waste such parts of Phôcis as they passed through, burning the city of the Panopeans, together with those of the Daulians and of the Æolidæ. This body had been detached from the rest of the army, and made to march in this direction, for the purpose of plundering the Delphian temple and conveying to King Xerxes the riches which were there laid up. For Xerxes, as I am informed, was better acquainted with what there was worthy of note at Delphi, than even with what he had left in his own house; so many of those about him were continually describing the treasures—more especially the offerings made by Crœsus the son of Alyattes.

36. Now when the Delphians heard what danger they were in, great fear fell on them. In their terror they consulted the oracle concerning the holy treasures, and inquired if they should bury them in the ground, or carry them away to some other country. The god, in reply, bade them leave the treasures untouched—"He was able," he said, "without help to protect his own." So the Delphians, when they received this answer, began to think about saving themselves. And first of all they sent their women and children across the gulf into Achæa; after which the greater number of them climbed up into the tops of Parnassus, and placed their goods for safety in the Corycian cave; while some effected their escape to Amphissa in Locris. In this way all the Delphians quitted the city, except sixty men, and the Prophet.

37. When the barbarian assailants drew near and were in sight of the place, the Prophet, who was named Acêratus, beheld, in front of the temple, a portion of the sacred armour, which it was not lawful for any mortal hand to touch, lying upon the ground, removed from the inner shrine where it was wont to hang. Then went he and told the prodigy to the Delphians who had remained behind. Meanwhile the enemy pressed forward briskly, and had reached the shrine of Minerva Pronaia, when they were overtaken by other prodigies still more wonderful than the first. Truly it was marvel enough, when warlike harness was seen lying outside the temple, removed there by no power but its own; what followed,

however, exceeded in strangeness all prodigies that had ever before been seen. The barbarians had just reached in their advance the chapel of Minerva Pronaia, when a storm of thunder burst suddenly over their heads—at the same time two crags split off from Mount Parnassus, and rolled down upon them with a loud noise, crushing vast numbers beneath their weight—while from the temple of Minerva there went up the war-cry and the shout of victory.

38. All these things together struck terror into the barbarians, who forthwith turned and fled. The Delphians, seeing this, came down from their hiding-places, and smote them with a great slaughter, from which such as escaped fled straight into Bœotia. These men, on their return, declared (as I am told) that besides the marvels mentioned above, they witnessed also other supernatural sights. Two armed warriors, they said, of a stature more than human, pursued after their flying ranks, pressing them close and slaying them.

39. These men, the Delphians maintain, were two Heroes belonging to the place—by name Phylacus and Autonoüs—each of whom has a sacred precinct near the temple; one, that of Phylacus, hard by the road which runs above the temple of Pronaia; the other, that of Autonoüs, near the Castalian spring, at the foot of the peak called Hyampeia. The blocks of stone which fell from Parnassus might still be seen in my day; they lay in the precinct of Pronaia, where they stopped, after rolling through the host of the barbarians. Thus was this body of men forced to retire from the temple.

40. Meanwhile, the Grecian fleet, which had left Artemisium, proceeded to Salamis, at the request of the Athenians, and there cast anchor. The Athenians had begged them to take up this position, in order that they might convey their women and children out of Attica, and further might deliberate upon the course which it now behoved them to follow. Disappointed in the hopes which they had previously entertained, they were about to hold a council concerning the present posture of their affairs. For they had looked to see the Peloponnesians drawn up in full force to resist the enemy in Bœotia, but found nothing of what they had expected; nay, they learnt that the Greeks of those parts, only concerning themselves about their own safety, were building a wall across the Isthmus, and intended to guard the Peloponnese, and let the rest of Greece take its chance. These tidings caused them to make

the request whereof I spoke, that the combined fleet should anchor at Salamis.

41. So while the rest of the fleet lay to off this island, the Athenians cast anchor along their own coast. Immediately upon their arrival, proclamation was made that every Athenian should save his children and household as he best could; whereupon some sent their families to Egina, some to Salamis, but the greater number to Trœzen. This removal was made with all possible haste, partly from a desire to obey the advice of the oracle, but still more for another reason. The Athenians say that they have in their Acropolis a huge serpent, which lives in the temple, and is the guardian of the whole place. Nor do they only say this, but, as if the serpent really dwelt there, every month they lay out its food, which consists of a honey-cake. Up to this time the honey-cake had always been consumed; but now it remained untouched. So the priestess told the people what had happened; whereupon they left Athens the more readily, since they believed that the goddess had already abandoned the citadel. As soon as all was removed, the Athenians sailed back to their station.

42. And now, the remainder of the Grecian sea-force, hearing that the fleet which had been at Artemisium, was come to Salamis, joined it at that island from Trœzen—orders having been issued previously that the ships should muster at Pôgon, the port of the Trœzenians. The vessels collected were many more in number than those which had fought at Artemisium, and were furnished by more cities. The admiral was the same who had commanded before, to wit, Eurybiades, the son of Eurycleides, who was a Spartan, but not of the family of the kings: the city, however, which sent by far the greatest number of ships, and the best sailers, was Athens.

43. Now these were the nations who composed the Grecian fleet. From the Peloponnese, the following—the Lacedæmonians with sixteen ships; the Corinthians with the same number as at Artemisium; the Sicyonians with fifteen; the Epidaurians with ten; the Trœzenians with five; and the Hermionians with three. These were Dorians and Macedonians all of them (except those from Hermioné), and had emigrated last from Erineus, Pindus, and Dryopis. The Hermionians were Dryopians, of the race which Hercules and the Malians drove out of the land now called Dôris. Such were the Peloponnesian nations.

44. From the mainland of Greece beyond the Peloponnese, came the Athenians with a hundred and eighty ships, a greater number than that furnished by any other people; and these were now manned wholly by themselves; for the Platæans did not serve aboard the Athenian ships at Salamis, owing to the following reason. When the Greeks, on their withdrawal from Artemisium, arrived off Chalcis, the Platæans disembarked upon the opposite shore of Bœotia, and set to work to remove their households, whereby it happened that they were left behind. (The Athenians, when the region which is now called Greece was held by the Pelasgi, were Pelasgians, and bore the name of Cranaans; but under their king Cecrops, they were called Cecropidæ; when Erechtheus got the sovereignty, they changed their name to Athenians; and when Ion, the son of Xuthus, became their general, they were named after him Ionians.)

45. The Megarians served with the same number of ships as at Artemisium; the Ambraciots came with seven; the Leucadians (who were Dorians from Corinth) with three.

46. Of the islanders, the Eginetans furnished thirty ships—they had a larger number equipped; but some were kept back to guard their own coasts, and only thirty, which however were their best sailers, took part in the fight at Salamis. (The Eginetans are Dorians from Epidaurus; their island was called formerly Œnôné). The Chalcideans came next in order; they furnished the twenty ships with which they had served at Artemisium. The Eretrians likewise furnished their seven. These races are Ionian. Cêos gave its old number—the Ceans are Ionians from Attica. Naxos furnished four: this detachment, like those from the other islands, had been sent by the citizens at home to join the Medes; but they made light of the orders given them, and joined the Greeks, at the instigation of Democritus, a citizen of good report, who was at that time captain of a trireme. The Naxians are Ionians, of the Athenian stock. The Styreans served with the same ships as before; the Cythnians contributed one, and likewise a penteconter —these two nations are Dryopians: the Seriphians, Siphnians, and Melians, also served; they were the only islanders who had not given earth and water to the barbarian.

47. All these nations dwelt inside the river Acheron and the country inhabited by the Thesprotians; for that people borders on the Ambraciots and Leucadians, who are the most

remote of all those by whom the fleet was furnished. From the countries beyond, there was only one people which gave help to the Greeks in their danger. This was the people of Crotôna, who contributed a single ship, under the command of Phaÿllus, a man who had thrice carried off the prize at the Pythian Games. The Crotoniats are, by descent, Achæans.

48. Most of the allies came with triremes; but the Melians, Siphnians, and Seriphians, brought penteconters. The Melians, who draw their race from Lacedæmon, furnished two; the Siphnians and Seriphians, who are Ionians of the Athenian stock, one each. The whole number of the ships, without counting the penteconters, was three hundred and seventy-eight.

49. When the captains from these various nations were come together at Salamis, a council of war was summoned; and Eurybiades proposed that any one who liked to advise, should say which place seemed to him the fittest, among those still in the possession of the Greeks, to be the scene of a naval combat. Attica, he said, was not to be thought of now; but he desired their counsel as to the remainder. The speakers mostly advised that the fleet should sail away to the Isthmus, and there give battle in defence of the Peloponnese; and they urged as a reason for this, that if they were worsted in a sea-fight at Salamis, they would be shut up in an island where they could get no help; but if they were beaten near the Isthmus, they could escape to their homes.

50. As the captains from the Peloponnese were thus advising, there came an Athenian to the camp, who brought word that the barbarians had entered Attica, and were ravaging and burning everything. For the division of the army under Xerxes was just arrived at Athens from its march through Bœotia, where it had burnt Thespiæ and Platæa—both which cities were forsaken by their inhabitants, who had fled to the Peloponnese—and now it was laying waste all the possessions of the Athenians. Thespiæ and Platæa had been burnt by the Persians, because they knew from the Thebans that neither of those cities had espoused their side.

51. Since the passage of the Hellespont and the commencement of the march upon Greece, a space of four months had gone by; one, while the army made the crossing, and delayed about the region of the Hellespont; and three while they proceeded thence to Attica, which they entered in the archonship of Calliades. They found the city forsaken; a few people only remained in the temple, either keepers of the treasures, or men of the poorer sort. These persons having fortified the citadel with planks and boards, held out against the enemy. It was in some measure their poverty which had prevented them from seeking shelter in Salamis; but there was likewise another reason which in part induced them to remain. They imagined themselves to have discovered the true meaning of the oracle uttered by the Pythoness, which promised that "the wooden wall" should never be taken—the wooden wall, they thought, did not mean the ships, but the place where they had taken refuge.

52. The Persians encamped upon the hill over against the citadel, which is called Mars' hill by the Athenians, and began the siege of the place, attacking the Greeks with arrows whereto pieces of lighted tow were attached, which they shot at the barricade. And now those who were within the citadel found themselves in a most woeful case; for their wooden rampart betrayed them; still, however, they continued to resist. It was in vain that the Pisistratidæ came to them and offered terms of surrender—they stoutly refused all parley, and among their other modes of defence, rolled down huge masses of stone upon the barbarians as they were mounting up to the gates: so that Xerxes was for a long time very greatly perplexed, and could not contrive any way to take them.

53. At last, however, in the midst of these many difficulties, the barbarians made discovery of an access. For verily the oracle had spoken truth; and it was fated that the whole mainland of Attica should fall beneath the sway of the Persians. Right in front of the citadel, but behind the gates and the common ascent —where no watch was kept, and no one would have thought it possible that any foot of man could climb—a few soldiers mounted from the sanctuary of Aglaurus, Cecrops' daughter, notwithstanding the steepness of the precipice. As soon as the Athenians saw them upon the summit, some threw themselves headlong from the wall, and so perished; while others fled for refuge to the inner part of the temple. The Persians rushed to the gates and opened them, after which they massacred the suppliants. When all were slain, they plundered the temple, and fired every part of the citadel.

54. Xerxes, thus completely master of Athens, despatched a horseman to Susa, with a message to Artabanus, informing him of his

success hitherto. The day after, he collected together all the Athenian exiles who had come into Greece in his train, and bade them go up into the citadel, and there offer sacrifice after their own fashion. I know not whether he had had a dream which made him give this order, or whether he felt some remorse on account of having set the temple on fire. However this may have been, the exiles were not slow to obey the command given them.

55. I will now explain why I have made mention of this circumstance: there is a temple of Erechtheus the Earth-born, as he is called, in this citadel, containing within it an olive-tree and a sea. The tale goes among the Athenians, that they were placed there as witnesses by Neptune and Minerva, when they had their contention about the country. Now this olive-tree had been burnt with the rest of the temple when the barbarians took the place. But when the Athenians, whom the king had commanded to offer sacrifice, went up into the temple for the purpose, they found a fresh shoot, as much as a cubit in length, thrown out from the old trunk. Such at least was the account which these persons gave.

56. Meanwhile, at Salamis, the Greeks no sooner heard what had befallen the Athenian citadel, than they fell into such alarm that some of the captains did not even wait for the council to come to a vote, but embarked hastily on board their vessels, and hoisted sail as though they would take to flight immediately. The rest, who stayed at the council board, came to a vote that the fleet should give battle at the Isthmus. Night now drew on; and the captains, dispersing from the meeting, proceeded on board their respective ships.

57. Themistocles, as he entered his own vessel, was met by Mnesiphilus, an Athenian, who asked him what the council had resolved to do. On learning that the resolve was to stand away for the Isthmus, and there give battle on behalf of the Peloponnese, Mnesiphilus exclaimed:—

"If these men sail away from Salamis, thou wilt have no fight at all for the one fatherland; for they will all scatter themselves to their own homes; and neither Eurybiades nor any one else will be able to hinder them, nor to stop the breaking up of the armament. Thus will Greece be brought to ruin through evil counsels. But haste thee now; and, if there be any possible way, seek to unsettle these resolves— mayhap thou mightest persuade Eurybiades to change his mind, and continue here."

58. The suggestion greatly pleased Themistocles; and without answering a word, he went straight to the vessel of Eurybiades. Arrived there, he let him know that he wanted to speak with him on a matter touching the public service. So Eurybiades bade him come on board, and say whatever he wished. Then Themistocles, seating himself at his side, went over all the arguments which he had heard from Mnesiphilus, pretending as if they were his own, and added to them many new ones besides; until at last he persuaded Eurybiades, by his importunity, to quit his ship and again collect the captains to council.

59. As soon as they were come, and before Eurybiades had opened to them his purpose in assembling them together, Themistocles, as men are wont to do when they are very anxious, spoke much to divers of them; whereupon the Corinthian captain, Adeimantus, the son of Ocytus, observed—"Themistocles, at the Games they who start too soon are scourged." "True," rejoined the other in his excuse, "but they who wait too late are not crowned."

60. Thus he gave the Corinthian at this time a mild answer; and towards Eurybiades himself he did not now use any of those arguments which he had urged before, or say aught of the allies betaking themselves to flight if once they broke up from Salamis; it would have been ungraceful for him, when the confederates were present, to make accusation against any: but he had recourse to quite a new sort of reasoning, and addressed him as follows:—

"With thee it rests, O Eurybiades! to save Greece, if thou wilt only hearken unto me, and give the enemy battle here, rather than yield to the advice of those among us, who would have the fleet withdrawn to the Isthmus. Hear now, I beseech thee, and judge between the two courses. At the Isthmus thou wilt fight in an open sea, which is greatly to our disadvantage, since our ships are heavier and fewer in number than the enemy's; and further, thou wilt in any case lose Salamis, Megara, and Egina, even if all the rest goes well with us. The land and sea force of the Persians will advance together; and thy retreat will but draw them towards the Peloponnese, and so bring all Greece into peril. If, on the other hand, thou doest as I advise, these are the advantages which thou wilt so secure: in the first place, as we shall fight in a narrow sea with few ships against many, if the war follows the common course, we shall gain a great victory; for to fight in a narrow space is favourable to us—in an open sea, to them. Again, Salamis will in this case be preserved, where we have placed our wives and children. Nay, that very point by which ye set most store, is secured as much by this course as by the other; for whether we fight here or at the Isthmus, we shall equally give battle in defence of the Peloponnese. Assuredly ye will not do wisely to draw the Persians upon that region. For if things turn out as I anticipate, and we beat them by sea, then we shall have kept your Isthmus free from the barbarians, and they will have advanced no further than Attica, but from thence have fled back in disorder; and we shall, moreover, have saved Megara, Egina, and Salamis itself, where an oracle has said that we are to overcome our enemies. When men counsel reasonably, reasonable success ensues; but when in their counsels they reject reason, God does not choose to follow the wanderings of human fancies."

61. When Themistocles had thus spoken, Adeimantus the Corinthian again attacked him, and bade him be silent, since he was a man without a city; at the same time he called on Eurybiades not to put the question at the instance of one who had no country, and urged that Themistocles should show of what state he was envoy, before he gave his voice with the rest. This reproach he made, because the city of Athens had been taken, and was in the hands of the barbarians. Hereupon Themistocles spake many bitter things against Adeimantus and the Corinthians generally; and for proof that he had a country, reminded the captains, that with two hundred ships at his command, all fully manned for battle, he had both city and territory as good as theirs; since there was no Grecian state which could resist his men if they were to make a descent.

62. After this declaration, he turned to Eurybiades, and addressing him with still greater warmth and earnestness—"If thou wilt stay here," he said, "and behave like a brave man, all will be well—if not, thou wilt bring Greece to ruin. For the whole fortune of the war depends on our ships. Be thou persuaded by my words. If not, we will take our families on board, and go, just as we are, to Siris, in Italy, which is ours from of old, and which the prophecies declare we are to colonise some day or other. You then, when you have lost allies like us, will hereafter call to mind what I have now said."

63. At these words of Themistocles, Eurybiades changed his determination; principally,

as I believe, because he feared that if he withdrew the fleet to the Isthmus, the Athenians would sail away, and knew that without the Athenians, the rest of their ships could be no match for the fleet of the enemy. He therefore decided to remain, and give battle at Salamis.

64. And now, the different chiefs, notwithstanding their skirmish of words, on learning the decision of Eurybiades, at once made ready for the fight. Morning broke; and, just as the sun rose, the shock of an earthquake was felt both on shore and at sea: whereupon the Greeks resolved to approach the gods with prayer, and likewise to send and invite the Æacids to their aid. And this they did, with as much speed as they had resolved on it. Prayers were offered to all the gods; and Telamon and Ajax were invoked at once from Salamis, while a ship was sent to Egina to fetch Æacus himself, and the other Æacids.

65. The following is a tale which was told by Dicæus, the son of Theocydes, an Athenian, who was at this time an exile, and had gained a good report among the Medes. He declared that after the army of Xerxes had, in the absence of the Athenians, wasted Attica, he chanced to be with Demaratus the Lacedæmonian in the Thriasian plain, and that while there, he saw a cloud of dust advancing from Eleusis, such as a host of thirty thousand men might raise. As he and his companion were wondering who the men, from whom the dust arose, could possibly be, a sound of voices reached his ear, and he thought that he recognised the mystic hymn to Bacchus. Now Demaratus was unacquainted with the rites of Eleusis, and so he inquired of Dicæus what the voices were saying. Dicæus made answer—"O Demaratus! beyond a doubt some mighty calamity is about to befall the king's army! For it is manifest, inasmuch as Attica is deserted by its inhabitants, that the sound which we have heard is an unearthly one, and is now upon its way from Eleusis to aid the Athenians and their confederates. If it descends upon the Peloponnese, danger will threaten the king himself and his land army—if it moves towards the ships at Salamis, 'twill go hard but the king's fleet there suffers destruction. Every year the Athenians celebrate this feast to the Mother and the Daughter; and all who wish, whether they be Athenians or any other Greeks, are initiated. The sound thou hearest is the Bacchic song, which is wont to be sung at that festival." "Hush now," rejoined the

other; "and see thou tell no man of this matter. For if thy words be brought to the king's ear, thou wilt assuredly lose thy head because of them; neither I nor any man living can then save thee. Hold thy peace therefore. The gods will see to the king's army." Thus Demaratus counselled him; and they looked, and saw the dust, from which the sound arose, become a cloud, and the cloud rise up into the air and sail away to Salamis, making for the station of the Grecian fleet. Then they knew that it was the fleet of Xerxes which would suffer destruction. Such was the tale told by Dicæus the son of Theocŷdes; and he appealed for its truth to Demaratus and other eye-witnesses.

66. The men belonging to the fleet of Xerxes, after they had seen the Spartan dead at Thermopylæ, and crossed the channel from Trachis to Histiæa, waited there by the space of three days, and then sailing down through the Euripus, in three more came to Phalêrum. In my judgment, the Persian forces both by land and sea when they invaded Attica were not less numerous than they had been on their arrival at Sêpias and Thermopylæ. For against the Persian loss in the storm and at Thermopylæ, and again in the sea-fights off Artemisium, I set the various nations which had since joined the king—as the Malians, the Dorians, the Locrians, and the Bœotians—each serving in full force in his army except the last, who did not number in their ranks either the Thespians or the Platæans; and together with these, the Carystians, the Andrians, the Tenians, and the other people of the islands, who all fought on this side except the five states already mentioned. For as the Persians penetrated further into Greece, they were joined continually by fresh nations.

67. Reinforced by the contingents of all these various states, except Paros, the barbarians reached Athens. As for the Parians, they tarried at Cythnus, waiting to see how the war would go. The rest of the sea forces came safe to Phalêrum; where they were visited by Xerxes, who had conceived a desire to go aboard and learn the wishes of the fleet. So he came and sate in a seat of honour; and the sovereigns of the nations, and the captains of the ships, were sent for, to appear before him, and as they arrived took their seats according to the rank assigned them by the king. In the first seat sate the king of Sidon; after him, the king of Tyre; then the rest in their order. When the whole had taken their places, one after another, and were set down in orderly array, Xerxes,

to try them, sent Mardonius and questioned each, whether a sea-fight should be risked or no.

68. Mardonius accordingly went round the entire assemblage, beginning with the Sidonian monarch, and asked this question; to which all gave the same answer, advising to engage the Greeks, except only Artemisia, who spake as follows (§ 1.):—

"Say to the king, Mardonius, that these are my words to him: I was not the least brave of those who fought at Eubœa, nor were my achievements there among the meanest; it is my right, therefore, O my lord, to tell thee plainly what I think to be most for thy advantage now. This then is my advice. Spare thy ships, and do not risk a battle; for these people are as much superior to thy people in seamanship, as men to women. What so great need is there for thee to incur hazard at sea? Art thou not master of Athens, for which thou didst undertake thy expedition? Is not Greece subject to thee? Not a soul now resists thy advance. They who once resisted, were handled even as they deserved. (§ 2.) Now learn how I expect that affairs will go with thy adversaries. If thou art not over-hasty to engage with them by sea, but wilt keep thy fleet near the land, then whether thou abidest as thou art, or marchest forward towards the Peloponnese, thou wilt easily accomplish all for which thou art come hither. The Greeks cannot hold out against thee very long; thou wilt soon part them asunder, and scatter them to their several homes. In the island where they lie, I hear they have no food in store; nor is it likely, if thy land force begins its march towards the Peloponnese, that they will remain quietly where they are—at least such as come from that region. Of a surety *they* will not greatly trouble themselves to give battle on behalf of the Athenians. (§ 3.) On the other hand, if thou art hasty to fight, I tremble lest the defeat of thy sea force bring harm likewise to thy land army. This, too, thou shouldst remember, O king; good masters are apt to have bad servants, and bad masters good ones. Now, as thou art the best of men, thy servants must needs be a sorry set. These Egyptians, Cyprians, Cilicians, and Pamphylians, who are counted in the number of thy subject-allies, of how little service are they to thee!"

69. As Artemisia spake, they who wished her well were greatly troubled concerning her words, thinking that she would suffer some hurt at the king's hands, because she exhorted

him not to risk a battle; they, on the other hand, who disliked and envied her, favoured as she was by the king above all the rest of the allies, rejoiced at her declaration, expecting that her life would be the forfeit. But Xerxes, when the words of the several speakers were reported to him, was pleased beyond all others with the reply of Artemisia; and whereas, even before this, he had always esteemed her much, he now praised her more than ever. Nevertheless, he gave orders that the advice of the greater number should be followed; for he thought that at Eubœa the fleet had not done its best, because he himself was not there to see—whereas this time he resolved that he would be an eye-witness of the combat.

70. Orders were now given to stand out to sea; and the ships proceeded towards Salamis, and took up the stations to which they were directed, without let or hindrance from the enemy. The day, however, was too far spent for them to begin the battle, since night already approached: so they prepared to engage upon the morrow. The Greeks, meanwhile, were in great distress and alarm, more especially those of the Peloponnese, who were troubled that they had been kept at Salamis to fight on behalf of the Athenian territory, and feared that, if they should suffer defeat, they would be pent up and besieged in an island, while their own country was left unprotected.

71. The same night the land army of the barbarians began its march towards the Peloponnese, where, however, all that was possible had been done to prevent the enemy from forcing an entrance by land. As soon as ever news reached the Peloponnese of the death of Leonidas and his companions at Thermopylæ, the inhabitants flocked together from the various cities, and encamped at the Isthmus, under the command of Cleombrotus, son of Anaxandridas, and brother of Leonidas. Here their first care was to block up the Scironian Way; after which it was determined in council to build a wall across the Isthmus. As the number assembled amounted to many tens of thousands, and there was not one who did not give himself to the work, it was soon finished. Stones, bricks, timber, baskets filled full of sand, were used in the building; and not a moment was lost by those who gave their aid; for they laboured without ceasing either by night or day.

72. Now the nations who gave their aid, and who had flocked in full force to the Isthmus, were the following: the Lacedæmonians, all the tribes of the Arcadians, the Eleans, the Corinthians, the Sicyonians, the Epidaurians, the Phliasians, the Trœzenians, and the Hermionians. These all gave their aid, being greatly alarmed at the danger which threatened Greece. But the other inhabitants of the Peloponnese took no part in the matter; though the Olympic and Carneian festivals were now over.

73. Seven nations inhabit the Peloponnese. Two of them are aboriginal, and still continue in the regions where they dwelt at the first—to wit, the Arcadians and the Cynurians. A third, that of the Achæans, has never left the Peloponnese, but has been dislodged from its own proper country, and inhabits a district which once belonged to others. The remaining nations, four out of the seven, are all immigrants—namely, the Dorians, the Ætolians, the Dryopians, and the Lemnians. To the Dorians belong several very famous cities; to the Ætolians one only, that is, Elis; to the Dryopians, Hermioné and that Asiné which lies over against Cardamylé in Laconia; to the Lemnians, all the towns of the Paroreats. The aboriginal Cynurians alone seem to be Ionians; even they, however, have, in course of time, grown to be Dorians, under the government of the Argives, whose Orneats and vassals they were. All the cities of these seven nations, except those mentioned above, stood aloof from the war; and by so doing, if I may speak freely, they in fact took part with the Medes.

74. So the Greeks at the Isthmus toiled unceasingly, as though in the greatest peril; since they never imagined that any great success would be gained by the fleet. The Greeks at Salamis, on the other hand, when they heard what the rest were about, felt greatly alarmed; but their fear was not so much for themselves as for the Peloponnese. At first they conversed together in low tones, each man with his fellow, secretly, and marvelled at the folly shown by Eurybiades; but presently the smothered feeling broke out, and another assembly was held; whereat the old subjects provoked much talk from the speakers, one side maintaining that it was best to sail to the Peloponnese and risk battle for that, instead of abiding at Salamis and fighting for a land already taken by the enemy; while the other, which consisted of the Athenians, Eginetans, and Megarians, was urgent to remain and have the battle fought where they were.

75. Then Themistocles, when he saw that the Peloponnesians would carry the vote against him, went out secretly from the coun-

cil, and, instructing a certain man what he should say, sent him on board a merchant ship to the fleet of the Medes. The man's name was Sicinnus; he was one of Themistocles' household slaves, and acted as tutor to his sons; in after times, when the Thespians were admitting persons to citizenship, Themistocles made him a Thespian, and a rich man to boot. The ship brought Sicinnus to the Persian fleet, and there he delivered his message to the leaders in these words:—

"The Athenian commander has sent me to you privily, without the knowledge of the other Greeks. He is a well-wisher to the king's cause, and would rather success should attend on you than on his countrymen; wherefore he bids me tell you that fear has seized the Greeks and they are meditating a hasty flight. Now then it is open to you to achieve the best work that ever ye wrought, if only ye will hinder their escaping. They no longer agree among themselves, so that they will not now make any resistance—nay, 'tis likely ye may see a fight already begun between such as favour and such as oppose your cause." The messenger, when he had thus expressed himself, departed and was seen no more.

76. Then the captains, believing all that the messenger had said, proceeded to land a large body of Persian troops on the islet of Psyttaleia, which lies between Salamis and the mainland; after which, about the hour of midnight, they advanced their western wing towards Salamis, so as to inclose the Greeks. At the same time the force stationed about Ceos and Cynosura moved forward, and filled the whole strait as far as Munychia with their ships. This advance was made to prevent the Greeks from escaping by flight, and to block them up in Salamis, where it was thought that vengeance might be taken upon them for the battles fought near Artemisium. The Persian troops were landed on the islet of Psyttaleia, because, as soon as the battle began, the men and wrecks were likely to be drifted thither, as the isle lay in the very path of the coming fight—and they would thus be able to save their own men and destroy those of the enemy. All these movements were made in silence, that the Greeks might have no knowledge of them; and they occupied the whole night, so that the men had no time to get their sleep.

77. I cannot say that there is no truth in prophecies, or feel inclined to call in question those which speak with clearness, when I think of the following:—

When they shall bridge with their ships to the sacred strand of Diana
Girt with the golden falchion, and eke to marine Cynosura,
Mad hope swelling their hearts at the downfall of beautiful Athens
Then shall godlike Right extinguish haughty Presumption,
Insult's furious offspring, who thinketh to overthrow all things.
Brass with brass shall mingle, and Mars with blood shall empurple
Ocean's waves. Then—then shall the day of Grecia's freedom
Come from Victory fair, and Saturn's son all-seeing.

When I look to this, and perceive how clearly Bacis spoke, I neither venture myself to say anything against prophecies, nor do I approve of others impugning them.

78. Meanwhile, among the captains at Salamis, the strife of words grew fierce. As yet they did not know that they were encompassed, but imagined that the barbarians remained in the same places where they had seen them the day before.

79. In the midst of their contention, Aristides, the son of Lysimachus, who had crossed from Egina, arrived in Salamis. He was an Athenian, and had been ostracised by the commonalty; yet I believe, from what I have heard concerning his character, that there was not in all Athens a man so worthy or so just as he. He now came to the council, and, standing outside, called for Themistocles. Now Themistocles was not his friend, but his most determined enemy. However, under the pressure of the great dangers impending, Aristides forgot their feud, and called Themistocles out of the council, since he wished to confer with him. He had heard before his arrival of the impatience of the Peloponnesians to withdraw the fleet to the Isthmus. As soon therefore as Themistocles came forth, Aristides addressed him in these words:—

"Our rivalry at all times, and especially at the present season, ought to be a struggle, which of us shall most advantage our country. Let me then say to thee, that so far as regards the departure of the Peloponnesians from this place, much talk and little will be found precisely alike. I have seen with my own eyes that which I now report: that, however much the Corinthians or Eurybiades himself may wish it, they cannot now retreat; for we are enclosed on every side by the enemy. Go in to them, and make this known."

80. "Thy advice is excellent," answered the other; "and thy tidings are also good. That which I earnestly desired to happen, thine eyes have beheld accomplished. Know that what the Medes have now done was at my instance; for it was necessary, as our men would not fight here of their own free will, to make them fight whether they would or no. But come now, as thou hast brought the good news, go in and tell it. For if I speak to them, they will think it a feigned tale, and will not believe that the barbarians have inclosed us around. Therefore do thou go to them, and inform them how matters stand. If they believe thee, 'twill be for the best; but if otherwise, it will not harm. For it is impossible that they should now flee away, if we are indeed shut in on all sides, as thou sayest."

81. Then Aristides entered the assembly, and spoke to the captains: he had come, he told them, from Egina, and had but barely escaped the blockading vessels—the Greek fleet was entirely inclosed by the ships of Xerxes—and he advised them to get themselves in readiness to resist the foe. Having said so much, he withdrew. And now another contest arose; for the greater part of the captains would not believe the tidings.

82. But while they still doubted, a Tenian trireme, commanded by Panætius the son of Sôsimenes, deserted from the Persians and joined the Greeks, bringing full intelligence. For this reason the Tenians were inscribed upon the tripod at Delphi among those who overthrew the barbarians. With this ship, which deserted to their side at Salamis, and the Lemnian vessel which came over before at Artemisium, the Greek fleet was brought to the full number of 380 ships; otherwise it fell short by two of that amount.

83. The Greeks now, not doubting what the Tenians told them, made ready for the coming fight. At the dawn of day, all the men-at-arms were assembled together, and speeches were made to them, of which the best was that of Themistocles; who throughout contrasted what was noble with what was base, and bade them, in all that came within the range of man's nature and constitution, *always* to make choice of the nobler part. Having thus wound up his discourse, he told them to go at once on board their ships, which they accordingly did; and about his time the trireme, that had been sent to Egina for the Æacidæ, returned; whereupon the Greeks put to sea with all their fleet.

84. The fleet had scarce left the land when they were attacked by the barbarians. At once most of the Greeks began to back water, and were about touching the shore, when Ameinias of Pallênê, one of the Athenian captains, darted forth in front of the line, and charged a ship of the enemy. The two vessels became entangled, and could not separate, whereupon the rest of the fleet came up to help Ameinias, and engaged with the Persians. Such is the account which the Athenians give of the way in which the battle began; but the Eginetans maintain that the vessel which had been to Egina for the Æacidæ, was the one that brought on the fight. It is also reported, that a phantom in the form of a woman appeared to the Greeks, and, in a voice that was heard from end to end of the fleet, cheered them on to the fight; first, however, rebuking them, and saying— "Strange men, how long are ye going to back water?"

85. Against the Athenians, who held the western extremity of the line towards Eleusis, were placed the Phœnicians; against the Lacedæmonians, whose station was eastward towards the Piræus, the Ionians. Of these last a few only followed the advice of Themistocles, to fight backwardly; the greater number did far otherwise. I could mention here the names of many trierarchs who took vessels from the Greeks, but I shall pass over all excepting Theomêstor, the son of Androdamas, and Phylacus, the son of Histiæus, both Samians. I show this preference to them, inasmuch as for this service Theomêstor was made tyrant of Samos by the Persians, which Phylacus was enrolled among the king's benefactors, and presented with a large estate in land. In the Persian tongue the king's benefactors are called *Orosangs*.

86. Far the greater number of the Persian ships engaged in this battle were disabled, either by the Athenians or by the Eginetans. For as the Greeks fought in order and kept their line, while the barbarians were in confusion and had no plan in anything that they did, the issue of the battle could scarce be other than it was. Yet the Persians fought far more bravely here than at Eubœa, and indeed surpassed themselves; each did his utmost through fear of Xerxes, for each thought that the king's eye was upon himself.

87. What part the several nations, whether Greek or barbarian, took in the combat, I am not able to say for certain; Artemisia, however, I know, distinguished herself in such a way as raised her even higher than she stood before

in the esteem of the king. For after confusion had spread throughout the whole of the king's fleet, and her ship was closely pursued by an Athenian trireme, she, having no way to fly, since in front of her were a number of friendly vessels, and she was nearest of all the Persians to the enemy, resolved on a measure which in fact proved her safety. Pressed by the Athenian pursuer, she bore straight against one of the ships of her own party, a Calyndian, which had Damasithymus, the Calyndian king, himself on board. I cannot say whether she had had any quarrel with the man while the fleet was at the Hellespont, or no—neither can I decide whether she of set purpose attacked his vessel, or whether it merely chanced that the Calyndian ship came in her way—but certain it is that she bore down upon his vessel and sank it, and that thereby she had the good fortune to procure herself a double advantage. For the commander of the Athenian trireme, when he saw her bear down on one of the enemy's fleet, thought immediately that her vessel was a Greek, or else had deserted from the Persians, and was now fighting on the Greek side; he therefore gave up the chase, and turned away to attack others.

88. Thus in the first place she saved her life by the action, and was enabled to get clear off from the battle; while further, it fell out that in the very act of doing the king an injury she raised herself to a greater height than ever in his esteem. For as Xerxes beheld the fight, he remarked (it is said) the destruction of the vessel, whereupon the bystanders observed to him—"Seest thou, master, how well Artemisia fights, and how she has just sunk a ship of the enemy?" Then Xerxes asked if it were really Artemisia's doing; and they answered, "Certainly; for they knew her ensign": while all made sure that the sunken vessel belonged to the opposite side. Everything, it is said, conspired to prosper the queen—it was especially fortunate for her that not one of those on board the Calyndian ship survived to become her accuser. Xerxes, they say, in reply to the remarks made to him, observed—"My men have behaved like women, my women like men!"

89. There fell in this combat Ariabignes, one of the chief commanders of the fleet, who was son of Darius and brother of Xerxes; and with him perished a vast number of men of high repute, Persians, Medes, and allies. Of the Greeks there died only a few; for, as they were able to swim, all those that were not slain outright by the enemy escaped from the sinking vessels and swam across to Salamis. But on the side of the barbarians more perished by drowning than in any other way, since they did not know how to swim. The great destruction took place when the ships which had been first engaged began to fly; for they who were stationed in the rear, anxious to display their valour before the eyes of the king, made every effort to force their way to the front, and thus became entangled with such of their own vessels as were retreating.

90. In this confusion the following event occurred: certain Phœnicians belonging to the ships which had thus perished made their appearance before the king, and laid the blame of their loss on the Ionians, declaring that they were traitors, and had wilfully destroyed the vessels. But the upshot of this complaint was that the Ionian captains escaped the death which threatened them, while their Phœnician accusers received death as their reward. For it happened that, exactly as they spoke, a Samothracian vessel bore down on an Athenian and sank it, but was attacked and crippled immediately by one of the Eginetan squadron. Now the Samothracians were expert with the javelin, and aimed their weapons so well, that they cleared the deck of the vessel which had disabled their own, after which they sprang on board, and took it. This saved the Ionians. Xerxes, when he saw the exploit, turned fiercely on the Phœnicians—(he was ready, in his extreme vexation, to find fault with any one) —and ordered their heads to be cut off, to prevent them, he said, from casting the blame of their own misconduct upon braver men. During the whole time of the battle Xerxes sate at the base of the hill called Ægaleôs, over against Salamis; and whenever he saw any of his own captains perform any worthy exploit he inquired concerning him; and the man's name was taken down by his scribes, together with the names of his father and his city. Ariaramnes too, a Persian, who was a friend of the Ionians, and present at the time whereof I speak, had a share in bringing about the punishment of the Phœnicians.

91. When the rout of the barbarians began, and they sought to make their escape to Phalêrum, the Eginetans, awaiting them in the channel, performed exploits worthy to be recorded. Through the whole of the confused struggle the Athenians employed themselves in destroying such ships as either made resistance or fled to shore, while the Eginetans dealt with those which endeavoured to escape

down the strait; so that the Persian vessels were no sooner clear of the Athenians than forthwith they fell into the hands of the Eginetan squadron.

92. It chanced here that there was a meeting between the ship of Themistocles, which was hasting in pursuit of the enemy, and that of Polycritus, son of Crius the Eginetan, which had just charged a Sidonian trireme. The Sidonian vessel was the same that captured the Eginetan guard-ship off Sciathus, which had Pytheas, the son of Ischenoüs, on board—that Pytheas, I mean, who fell covered with wounds, and whom the Sidonians kept on board their ship, from admiration of his gallantry. This man afterwards returned in safety to Egina; for when the Sidonian vessel with its Persian crew fell into the hands of the Greeks, he was still found on board. Polycritus no sooner saw the Athenian trireme than, knowing at once whose vessel it was, as he observed that it bore the ensign of the admiral, he shouted to Themistocles jeeringly, and asked him, in a tone of reproach, if the Eginetans did not show themselves rare friends to the Medes. At the same time, while he thus reproached Themistocles, Polycritus bore straight down on the Sidonian. Such of the barbarian vessels as escaped from the battle fled to Phalêrum, and there sheltered themselves under the protection of the land army.

93. The Greeks who gained the greatest glory of all in the sea-fight off Salamis were the Eginetans, and after them the Athenians. The individuals of most distinction were Polycritus the Eginetan, and two Athenians, Eumenes of Anagyrus, and Ameinias of Pallênê; the latter of whom had pressed Artemisia so hard. And assuredly, if he had known that the vessel carried Artemisia on board, he would never have given over the chase till he had either succeeded in taking her, or else been taken himself. For the Athenian captains had received special orders touching the queen; and moreover a reward of ten thousand drachmas had been proclaimed for any one who should make her prisoner; since there was great indignation felt that a woman should appear in arms against Athens. However, as I said before, she escaped; and so did some others whose ships survived the engagement; and these were all now assembled at the port of Phalêrum.

94. The Athenians say that Adeimantus, the Corinthian commander, at the moment when the two fleets joined battle, was seized with fear, and being beyond measure alarmed, spread his sails, and hasted to fly away; on which the other Corinthians, seeing their leader's ship in full flight, sailed off likewise. They had reached in their flight that part of the coast of Salamis where stands the temple of Minerva Sciras, when they met a light bark, a very strange apparition: it was never discovered that any one had sent it to them; and till it appeared they were altogether ignorant how the battle was going. That there was something beyond nature in the matter they judged from this—that when the men in the bark drew near to their ships they addressed them, saying—"Adeimantus, while thou playest the traitor's part, by withdrawing all these ships, and flying away from the fight, the Greeks whom thou hast deserted are defeating their foes as completely as they ever wished in their prayers." Adeimantus, however, would not believe what the men said; whereupon they told him "he might take them with him as hostages, and put them to death if he did not find the Greeks winning." Then Adeimantus put about, both he and those who were with him; and they re-joined the fleet when the victory was already gained. Such is the tale which the Athenians tell concerning them of Corinth; these latter however do not allow its truth. On the contrary, they declare that they were among those who distinguished themselves most in the fight. And the rest of Greece bears witness in their favour.

95. In the midst of the confusion Aristides, the son of Lysimachus, the Athenian, of whom I lately spoke as a man of the greatest excellence, performed the following service. He took a number of the Athenian heavy-armed troops, who had previously been stationed along the shore of Salamis, and, landing with them on the islet of Psyttaleia, slew all the Persians by whom it was occupied.

96. As soon as the sea-fight was ended, the Greeks drew together to Salamis all the wrecks that were to be found in that quarter, and prepared themselves for another engagement, supposing that the king would renew the fight with the vessels which still remained to him. Many of the wrecks had been carried away by a westerly wind to the coast of Attica, where they were thrown upon the strip of shore called Côlias. Thus not only were the prophecies of Bacis and Musæus concerning this battle fulfilled completely, but likewise, by the place to which the wrecks were drifted, the prediction of Lysistratus, an Athenian sooth-

sayer, uttered many years before these events, and quite forgotten at the time by all the Greeks, was fully accomplished. The words were—

Then shall the sight of the oars fill Colian dames with amazement.

Now this must have happened as soon as the king was departed.

97. Xerxes, when he saw the extent of his loss, began to be afraid lest the Greeks might be counselled by the Ionians, or without their advice might determine to sail straight to the Hellespont and break down the bridges there; in which case he would be blocked up in Europe, and run great risk of perishing. He therefore made up his mind to fly; but, as he wished to hide his purpose alike from the Greeks and from his own people, he set to work to carry a mound across the channel to Salamis, and at the same time began fastening a number of Phœnician merchant ships together, to serve at once for a bridge and a wall. He likewise made many warlike preparations, as if he were about to engage the Greeks once more at sea. Now, when these things were seen, all grew fully persuaded that the king was bent on remaining, and intended to push the war in good earnest. Mardonius, however, was in no respect deceived; for long acquaintance enabled him to read all the king's thoughts. Meanwhile, Xerxes, though engaged in this way, sent off a messenger to carry intelligence of his misfortune to Persia.

98. Nothing mortal travels so fast as these Persian messengers. The entire plan is a Persian invention; and this is the method of it. Along the whole line of road there are men (they say) stationed with horses, in number equal to the number of days which the journey takes, allowing a man and horse to each day; and these men will not be hindered from accomplishing at their best speed the distance which they have to go, either by snow, or rain, or heat, or by the darkness of night. The first rider delivers his despatch to the second, and the second passes it to the third; and so it is borne from hand to hand along the whole line, like the light in the torch-race, which the Greeks celebrate to Vulcan. The Persians give the riding post in this manner, the name of "Angarum."

99. At Susa, on the arrival of the first message, which said that Xerxes was master of Athens, such was the delight of the Persians who had remained behind, that they forthwith strewed all the streets with myrtle boughs, and burnt incense, and fell to feasting and merriment. In like manner, when the second message reached them, so sore was their dismay, that they all with one accord rent their garments, and cried aloud, and wept and wailed without stint. They laid the blame of the disaster on Mardonius; and their grief on the occasion was less on account of the damage done to their ships, than owing to the alarm which they felt about the safety of the king. Hence their trouble did not cease till Xerxes himself, by his arrival, put an end to their fears.

100. And now Mardonius, perceiving that Xerxes took the defeat of his fleet greatly to heart, and suspecting that he had made up his mind to leave Athens and fly away, began to think of the likelihood of his being visited with punishment for having persuaded the king to undertake the war. He therefore considered that it would be the best thing for him to adventure further, and either become the conqueror of Greece—which was the result he rather expected—or else die gloriously after aspiring to a noble achievement. So with these thoughts in his mind, he said one day to the king:—

"Do not grieve, master, or take so greatly to heart thy late loss. Our hopes hang not altogether on the fate of a few planks, but on our brave steeds and horsemen. These fellows, whom thou imaginest to have quite conquered us, will not venture—no, not one of them—to come ashore and contend with our land army; nor will the Greeks who are upon the mainland fight our troops; such as did so have received their punishment. If thou so pleasest, we may at once attack the Peloponnese; if thou wouldst rather wait a while, that too is in our power. Only be not disheartened. For it is not possible that the Greeks can avoid being brought to account, alike for this and for their former injuries; nor can they anyhow escape being thy slaves. Thou shouldst therefore do as I have said. If, however, thy mind is made up, and thou art resolved to retreat and lead away thy army, listen to the counsel which, in that case, I have to offer. Make not the Persians, O king! a laughing-stock to the Greeks. If thy affairs have succeeded ill, it has not been by their fault; thou canst not say that thy Persians have ever shown themselves cowards. What matters it if Phœnicians and Egyptians, Cyprians and Cilicians, have misbehaved?— their misconduct touches not us. Since then thy Persians are without fault, be advised by me. Depart home, if thou art so minded, and take with thee the bulk of thy army; but first let me choose out 300,000 troops, and let it be my task to bring Greece beneath thy sway."

101. Xerxes, when he heard these words, felt a sense of joy and delight, like a man who is relieved from care. Answering Mardonius, therefore, "that he would consider his counsel, and let him know which course he might prefer," Xerxes proceeded to consult with the chief men among the Persians; and because Artemisia on the former occasion had shown herself the only person who knew what was best to be done, he was pleased to summon her to advise him now. As soon as she arrived, he put forth all the rest, both councillors and bodyguards, and said to her:—

"Mardonius wishes me to stay and attack the Peloponnese. My Persians, he says, and my other land forces, are not to blame for the disasters which have befallen our arms; and of this he declares they would very gladly give me the proof. He therefore exhorts me, either to stay and act as I have said, or to let him choose out 300,000 of my troops—wherewith he undertakes to reduce Greece beneath my sway—while I myself retire with the rest of my forces, and withdraw into my own country. Do thou, therefore, as thou didst counsel me so wisely to decline the sea-fight, now also advise me in this matter, and say, which course of the twain I ought to take for my own good."

102. Thus did the king ask Artemisia's counsel; and the following are the words wherewith she answered him:—

" 'Tis a hard thing, O king! to give the best possible advice to one who asks our counsel. Nevertheless, as thy affairs now stand, it seemeth to me that thou wilt do right to return home. As for Mardonius, if he prefers to remain, and undertakes to do as he has said, leave him behind by all means, with the troops which he desires. If his design succeeds, and he subdues the Greeks, as he promises, thine is the conquest, master; for thy slaves will have accomplished it. If, on the other hand, affairs run counter to his wishes, we can suffer no great loss, so long as thou art safe, and thy house is in no danger. The Greeks, too, while thou livest, and thy house flourishes, must be prepared to fight full many a battle for their freedom; whereas if Mardonius fall, it matters nothing —they will have gained but a poor triumph— a victory over one of thy slaves! Remember also, thou goest home having gained the purpose of thy expedition; for thou hast burnt Athens!"

103. The advice of Artemesia pleased Xerxes well; for she had exactly uttered his own thoughts. I, for my part, do not believe that he would have remained had all his counsellors, both men and women, united to urge his stay, so great was the alarm that he felt. As it was, he gave praise to Artemisia, and entrusted certain of his children to her care, ordering her to convey them to Ephesus; for he had been accompanied on the expedition by some of his natural sons.

104. He likewise sent away at this time one of the principal of his eunuchs, a man named Hermotimus, a Pedasian, who was bidden to take charge of these sons. Now the Pedasians inhabit the region above Halicarnassus; and it is related of them, that in their country the following circumstance happens: when a mischance is about to befall any of their neighbours within a certain time, the priestess of Minerva in their city grows a long beard. This has already taken place on two occasions.

105. The Hermotimus of whom I spoke above was, as I said, a Pedasian; and he, of all men whom we know, took the most cruel vengeance on the person who had done him an injury. He had been made a prisoner of war, and when his captors sold him, he was bought by a certain Panionius, a native of Chios, who made his living by a most nefarious traffic. Whenever he could get any boys of unusual beauty, he made them eunuchs, and, carrying them to Sardis or Ephesus, sold them for large sums of money. For the barbarians value eunuchs more than others, since they regard them as more trustworthy. Many were the slaves that Panionius, who made his living by the practice, had thus treated; and among them was this Hermotimus of whom I have here made mention. However, he was not without his share of good fortune; for after a while he was sent from Sardis, together with other gifts, as a present to the king. Nor was it long before he came to be esteemed by Xerxes more highly than all his eunuchs.

106. When the king was on his way to Athens with the Persian army, and abode for a time at Sardis, Hermotimus happened to make a journey upon business into Mysia; and there, in a district which is called Atarneus, but belongs to Chios, he chanced to fall in with Panionius. Recognising him at once, he entered into a long and friendly talk with him, wherein he counted up the numerous blessings he enjoyed through his means, and promised him all manner of favours in return, if he would

bring his household to Sardis and live there. Panionius was overjoyed, and, accepting the offer made him, came presently, and brought with him his wife and children. Then Hermotimus, when he had got Panionius and all his family into his power, addressed him in these words:—

"Thou man, who gettest a living by viler deeds than any one else in the whole world, what wrong to thee or thine had I or any of mine done, that thou shouldst have made me the *nothing* that I now am? Ah! surely thou thoughtest that the gods took no note of thy crimes. But they in their justice have delivered thee, the doer of unrighteousness, into my hands; and now thou canst not complain of the vengeance which I am resolved to take on thee."

After these reproaches, Hermotimus commanded the four sons of Panionius to be brought, and forced the father to make them eunuchs with his own hand. Unable to resist, he did as Hermotimus required; and then his sons were made to treat him in the self-same way. So in this way there came to Panionius requital at the hands of Hermotimus.

107. Xerxes, after charging Artemesia to convey his sons safe to Ephesus, sent for Mardonius, and bade him choose from all his army such men as he wished, and see that he made his achievements answer to his promises. During this day he did no more; but no sooner was night come, than he issued his orders, and at once the captains of the ships left Phalêrum, and bore away for the Hellespont, each making all the speed he could, and hasting to guard the bridges against the king's return. On their way, as they sailed by Zôster, where certain narrow points of land project into the sea, they took the cliffs for vessels, and fled far away in alarm. Discovering their mistake, however, after a time, they joined company once more, and proceeded upon their voyage.

108. Next day the Greeks, seeing the land force of the barbarians encamped in the same place, thought that their ships must still be lying at Phalêrum; and, expecting another attack from that quarter, made preparations to defend themselves. Soon however news came that the ships were all departed and gone away; whereupon it was instantly resolved to make sail in pursuit. They went as far as Andros; but, seeing nothing of the Persian fleet, they stopped at that place, and held a council of war. At this council Themistocles advised that the Greeks should follow on through the islands, still pressing the pursuit, and making all haste to the Hellespont, there to break down the bridges. Eurybiades, however, delivered a contrary opinion. "If," he said, "the Greeks should break down the bridges, it would be the worst thing that could possibly happen for Greece. The Persian, supposing that his retreat were cut off, and he compelled to remain in Europe, would be sure never to give them any peace. Inaction on his part would ruin all his affairs, and leave him no chance of ever getting back to Asia—nay, would even cause his army to perish by famine: whereas, if he bestirred himself, and acted vigorously, it was likely that the whole of Europe would in course of time become subject to him; since, by degrees, the various towns and tribes would either fall before his arms, or else agree to terms of submission; and in this way, his troops would find food sufficient for them, since each year the Greek harvest would be theirs. As it was, the Persian, because he had lost the sea-fight, intended evidently to remain no longer in Europe. The Greeks ought to let him depart; and when he was gone from among them, and had returned into his own country, then would be the time for them to contend with him for the possession of *that*."

The other captains of the Peloponnesians declared themselves of the same mind.

109. Whereupon Themistocles, finding that the majority was against him, and that he could not persuade them to push on to the Hellespont, changed round, and addressing himself to the Athenians, who of all the allies were the most nettled at the enemy's escape, and who eagerly desired, if the other Greeks would not stir, to sail on by themselves to the Hellespont and break the bridges, spake as follows:—

"I have often myself witnessed occasions, and I have heard of many more from others, where men who had been conquered by an enemy, having been driven quite to desperation, have renewed the fight, and retrieved their former disasters. We have now had the great good luck to save both ourselves and all Greece by the repulse of this vast cloud of men; let us then be content and not press them too hard, now that they have begun to fly. Be sure we have not done this by our own might. It is the work of gods and heroes, who were jealous that one man should be king at once of Europe and of Asia—more especially a man like this, unholy and presumptuous—a man who esteems alike things sacred and things profane; who has cast down and burnt the very images of the gods themselves; who even caused the sea to be scourged with rods and commanded fetters to be thrown into it. At present all is well with us—let us then abide in Greece, and look to ourselves and to our families. The barbarian is clean gone—we have driven him off—let each now repair his own house, and sow his land diligently. In the spring we will take ship and sail to the Hellespont and to Ionia!"

All this Themistocles said in the hope of establishing a claim upon the king; for he wanted to have a safe retreat in case any mischance should befall him at Athens—which indeed came to pass afterwards.

110. At present, however, he dissembled; and the Athenians were persuaded by his words. For they were ready now to do whatever he advised; since they had always esteemed him a wise man, and he had lately proved himself most truly wise and well-judging. Accordingly, they came in to his views; whereupon he lost no time in sending messengers, on board a light bark, to the king, choosing for this purpose men whom he could trust to keep his instructions secret, even although they should be put to every kind of torture. Among them was the house-slave Sicinnus, the same whom he had made use of previously. When the men reached Attica, all the others stayed with the boat; but Sicinnus went up to the king, and spake to him as follows:—

"I am sent to thee by Themistocles, the son of Neocles, who is the leader of the Athenians, and the wisest and bravest man of all the allies, to bear thee this message: 'Themistocles the Athenian, anxious to render thee a service, has restrained the Greeks, who were impatient to pursue thy ships, and to break up the bridges at the Hellespont. Now, therefore, return home at thy leisure.'"

The messengers, when they had performed their errand, sailed back to the fleet.

111. And the Greeks, having resolved that they would neither proceed further in pursuit of the barbarians, nor push forward to the Hellespont and destroy the passage, laid siege to Andros, intending to take the town by storm. For Themistocles had required the Andrians to pay down a sum of money; and they had refused, being the first of all the islanders who did so. To his declaration, "that the money must needs be paid, as the Athenians had brought with him two mighty gods—Persuasion and Necessity," they made reply, that "Athens might well be a great and glorious city, since she was blest with such excellent gods; but *they* were wretchedly poor, stinted for land, and cursed with two unprofitable gods, who always dwelt with them and would never quit their island—to wit, Poverty and Helplessness. These were the gods of the Andrians, and therefore they would not pay the money. For the power of Athens could not possibly be stronger than their inability." This reply, coupled with the refusal to pay the sum required, caused their city to be besieged by the Greeks.

112. Meanwhile Themistocles, who never ceased his pursuit of gain, sent threatening messages to the other islanders with demands for different sums, employing the same messengers and the same words as he had used towards the Andrians. "If," he said, "they did not send him the amount required, he would bring the Greek fleet upon them, and besiege them till he took their cities." By these means he collected large sums from the Carystians and the Parians, who, when they heard that Andros was already besieged, and that Themistocles was the best esteemed of all the captains, sent the money through fear. Whether any of the other islanders did the like, I cannot say for certain; but I think some did besides those I have mentioned. However, the Carystians, though they complied, were not spared any the more; but Themistocles was softened by the Parians' gift, and therefore they received no visit from the army. In this way it was that Themistocles, during his stay at Andros, obtained money from the islanders, unbeknown to the other captains.

113. King Xerxes and his army waited but a few days after the sea-fight, and then withdrew into Bœotia by the road which they had followed on their advance. It was the wish of Mardonius to escort the king a part of the way; and as the time of year was no longer suitable for carrying on war, he thought it best to winter in Thessaly, and wait for the spring before he attempted the Peloponnese. After the army was come into Thessaly, Mardonius made choice of the troops that were to stay with him; and, first of all, he took the whole body called the "Immortals," except only their leader, Hydarnes, who refused to quit the person of the king. Next, he chose the Persians who wore breastplates, and the thousand picked horse; likewise the Medes, the Sacans, the Bactrians, and the Indians, foot and horse equally. These nations he took entire: from the rest of the allies he culled a few men, taking either such as were remarkable for their appearance, or else

such as had performed, to his knowledge, some valiant deed. The Persians furnished him with the greatest number of troops, men who were adorned with chains and armlets. Next to them were the Medes, who in number equalled the Persians, but in valour fell short of them. The whole army, reckoning the horsemen with the rest, amounted to 300,000 men.

114. At the time when Mardonius was making choice of his troops, and Xerxes still continued in Thessaly, the Lacedæmonians received a message from the Delphic oracle, bidding them seek satisfaction at the hands of Xerxes for the death of Leonidas, and take whatever he chose to give them. So the Spartans sent a herald with all speed into Thessaly, who arrived while the entire Persian army was still there. This man, being brought before the king, spake as follows:—

"King of the Medes, the Lacedæmonians and the Heracleids of Sparta require of thee the satisfaction due for bloodshed, because thou slewest their king, who fell fighting for Greece."

Xerxes laughed, and for a long time spake not a word. At last, however, he pointed to Mardonius, who was standing by him, and said:—"Mardonius here shall give them the satisfaction they deserve to get." And the herald accepted the answer, and forthwith went his way.

115. Xerxes, after this, left Mardonius in Thessaly, and marched away himself, at his best speed, toward the Hellespont. In five-and-forty days he reached the place of passage, where he arrived with scarce a fraction, so to speak, of his former army. All along their line of march, in every country where they chanced to be, his soldiers seized and devoured whatever corn they could find belonging to the inhabitants; while, if no corn was to be found, they gathered the grass that grew in the fields, and stripped the trees, whether cultivated or wild, alike of their bark and of their leaves, and so fed themselves. They left nothing anywhere, so hard were they pressed by hunger. Plague too and dysentery attacked the troops while still upon their march, and greatly thinned their ranks. Many died; others fell sick and were left behind in the different cities that lay upon the route, the inhabitants being strictly charged by Xerxes to tend and feed them. Of these some remained in Thessaly, others in Siris of Pæonia, others again in Macedon. Here Xerxes, on his march into Greece, had left the sacred car and steeds of Jove; which upon his return he was unable to recover; for the Pæonians had disposed of them to the Thracians, and, when Xerxes demanded them back, they said that the Thracian tribes who dwelt about the sources of the Strymon had stolen the mares as they pastured.

116. Here too a Thracian chieftain, king of the Bisaltians and of Crestonia, did a deed which went beyond nature. He had refused to become the willing slave of Xerxes, and had fled before him into the heights of Rhodopé, at the same time forbidding his sons to take part in the expedition against Greece. But they, either because they cared little for his orders, or because they wished greatly to see the war, joined the army of Xerxes. At this time they had all returned home to him—the number of the men was six—quite safe and sound. But their father took them, and punished their offence by plucking out their eyes from the sockets. Such was the treatment which these men received.

117. The Persians, having journeyed through Thrace and reached the passage, entered their ships hastily and crossed the Hellespont to Abydos. The bridges were not found stretched across the strait; since a storm had broken and dispersed them. At Abydos the troops halted, and, obtaining more abundant provision than they had yet got upon their march, they fed without stint; from which cause, added to the change in their water, great numbers of those who had hitherto escaped perished. The remainder, together with Xerxes himself, came safe to Sardis.

118. There is likewise another account given of the return of the king. It is said that when Xerxes on his way from Athens arrived at Eïon upon the Strymon, he gave up travelling by land, and, intrusting Hydarnes with the conduct of his forces to the Hellespont, embarked himself on board a Phœnician ship, and so crossed into Asia. On his voyage the ship was assailed by a strong wind blowing from the mouth of the Strymon, which caused the sea to run high. As the storm increased, and the ship laboured heavily, because of the number of the Persians who had come in the king's train, and who now crowded the deck, Xerxes was seized with fear, and called out to the helmsman in a loud voice, asking him, if there were any means whereby they might escape the danger. "No means, master," the helmsman answered, "unless we could be quit of these too numerous passengers." Xerxes, they say, on hearing this, addressed the Persians as

follows: "Men of Persia," he said, "now is the time for you to show what love ye bear your king. My safety, as it seems, depends wholly upon you." So spake the king; and the Persians instantly made obeisance, and then leapt over into the sea. Thus was the ship lightened, and Xerxes got safe to Asia. As soon as he had reached the shore, he sent for the helmsman, and gave him a golden crown because he had preserved the life of the king,—but because he had caused the death of a number of Persians, he ordered his head to be struck from his shoulders.

119. Such is the other account which is given of the return of Xerxes; but to me it seems quite unworthy of belief, alike in other respects, and in what relates to the Persians. For had the helmsman made any such speech to Xerxes, I suppose there is not one man in ten thousand who will doubt that this is the course which the king would have followed:—he would have made the men upon the ship's deck, who were not only Persians, but Persians of the very highest rank, quit their place and go down below; and would have cast into the sea an equal number of the rowers, who were Phœnicians. But the truth is, that the king, as I have already said, returned into Asia by the same road as the rest of the army.

120. I will add a strong proof of this. It is certain that Xerxes on his way back from Greece passed through Abdêra, where he made a contract of friendship with the inhabitants, and presented them with a golden scymitar, and a tiara broidered with gold. The Abderites declare—but I put no faith in this part of their story—that from the time of the king's leaving Athens, he never once loosed his girdle till he came to their city, since it was not till then that he felt himself in safety. Now Abdêra is nearer to the Hellespont than Eïon and the Strymon, where Xerxes, according to the other tale, took ship.

121. Meanwhile the Greeks, finding that they could not capture Andros, sailed away to Carystus, and wasted the lands of the Carystians, after which they returned to Salamis. Arrived here, they proceeded, before entering on any other matter, to make choice of the first-fruits which should be set apart as offerings to the gods. These consisted of divers gifts; among them were three Phœnician triremes, one of which was dedicated at the Isthmus, where it continued to my day; another at Sunium; and the third, at Salamis itself, which was devoted to Ajax. This done, they made a divi-sion of the booty, and sent away the first-fruits to Delphi. Thereof was made the statue, holding in its hand the beak of a ship, which is twelve cubits high, and which stands in the same place with the golden one of Alexander the Macedonian.

122. After the first-fruits had been sent to Delphi, the Greeks made inquiry of the god, in the name of their whole body, if he had received his full share of the spoils and was satisfied therewith. The god made answer that all the other Greeks had paid him his full due, except only the Eginetans; on them he had still a claim for the prize of valour which they had gained at Salamis. So the Eginetans, when they heard this, dedicated the three golden stars which stand on the top of a bronze mast in the corner near the bowl offered by Crœsus.

123. When the spoils had been divided, the Greeks sailed to the Isthmus, where a prize of valour was to be awarded to the man who, of all the Greeks, had shown the most merit during the war. When the chiefs were all come, they met at the altar of Neptune, and took the ballots wherewith they were to give their votes for the first and for the second in merit. Then each man gave himself the first vote, since each considered that he was himself the worthiest; but the second votes were given chiefly to Themistocles. In this way, while the others received but one vote apiece, Themistocles had for the second prize a large majority of the suffrages.

124. Envy, however, hindered the chiefs from coming to a decision, and they all sailed away to their homes without making any award. Nevertheless Themistocles was regarded everywhere as by far the wisest man of all the Greeks; and the whole country rang with his fame. As the chiefs who fought at Salamis, notwithstanding that he was really entitled to the prize, had withheld his honour from him, he went without delay to Lacedæmon, in the hope that he would be honoured there. And the Lacedæmonians received him handsomely, and paid him great respect. The prize of valour indeed, which was a crown of olive, they gave to Eurybiades; but Themistocles was given a crown of olive too, as the prize of wisdom and dexterity. He was likewise presented with the most beautiful chariot that could be found in Sparta; and after receiving abundant praises, was, upon his departure, escorted as far as the borders of Tegea, by the three hundred picked Spartans, who are called the Knights. Never was it known, either before or since, that the

Spartans escorted a man out of their city.

125. On the return of Themistocles to Athens, Timodêmus of Aphidnæ, who was one of his enemies, but otherwise a man of no repute, became so maddened with envy that he openly railed against him, and, reproaching him with his journey to Sparta, said—" 'Twas not his own merit that had won him honour from the men of Lacedæmon, but the fame of Athens, his country." Then Themistocles, seeing that Timodêmus repeated this phrase unceasingly, replied—

"Thus stands the case, friend. I had never got this honour from the Spartans, had I been a Belbinite—nor thou, hadst thou been an Athenian!"

126. Artabazus, the son of Pharnaces, a man whom the Persians had always held in much esteem, but who, after the affair of Platæa, rose still higher in their opinion, escorted King Xerxes as far as the strait, with sixty thousand of the chosen troops of Mardonius. When the king was safe in Asia, Artabazus set out upon his return; and on arriving near Pallêné, and finding that Mardonius had gone into winterquarters in Thessaly and Macedonia, and was in no hurry for him to join the camp, he thought it his bounden duty, as the Potidæans had just revolted, to occupy himself in reducing them to slavery. For as soon as the king had passed beyond their territory, and the Persian fleet had made its hasty flight from Salamis, the Potidæans revolted from the barbarians openly; as likewise did all the other inhabitants of that peninsula.

127. Artabazus, therefore, laid siege to Potidæa; and having a suspicion that the Olynthians were likely to revolt shortly, he besieged their city also. Now Olynthus was at that time held by the Bottiæans, who had been driven from the parts about the Thermaic Gulf by the Macedonians. Artabazus took the city, and, having so done, led out all the inhabitants to a marsh in the neighbourhood, and there slew them. After this he delivered the place into the hands of the people called Chalcideans, having first appointed Critobûlus of Torône to be governor. Such was the way in which the Chalcideans got Olynthus.

128. When this town had fallen, Artabazus pressed the siege of Potidæa all the more unremittingly; and was pushing his operations with vigour, when Timoxenus, captain of the Scionæans, entered into a plot to betray the town to him. How the matter was managed at first, I cannot pretend to say, for no account

has come down to us: but at the last this is what happened. Whenever Timoxenus wished to send a letter to Artabazus, or Artabazus to send one to Timoxenus, the letter was written on a strip of paper, and rolled round the notched end of an arrow-shaft; the feathers were then put on over the paper, and the arrow thus prepared was shot to some place agreed upon. But after a while the plot of Timoxenus to betray Potidæa was discovered in this way. Artabazus, on one occasion, shot off his arrow, intending to send it to the accustomed place, but, missing his mark, hit one of the Potidæans in the shoulder. A crowd gathered about the wounded man, as commonly happens in war; and when the arrow was pulled out, they noticed the paper, and straightway carried it to the captains who were present from the various cities of the peninsula. The captains read the letter, and, finding who the traitor was, nevertheless resolved, out of regard for the city of Siône, that as they did not wish the Scionæans to be thenceforth branded with the name of traitors, they would not bring against him any charge of treachery. Such accordingly was the mode in which this plot was discovered.

129. After Artabazus had continued the siege by the space of three months, it happened that there was an unusual ebb of the tide, which lasted a long while. So when the barbarians saw that what had been sea was now no more than a swamp, they determined to push across it into Pallêné. And now the troops had already made good two-fifths of their passage, and three-fifths still remained before they could reach Pallêné, when the tide came in with a very high flood, higher than had ever been seen before, as the inhabitants of those parts declare, though high floods are by no means uncommon. All who were not able to swim perished immediately; the rest were slain by the Potidæans, who bore down upon them in their sailing vessels. The Potidæans say that what caused this swell and flood, and so brought about the disaster of the Persians which ensued therefrom, was the profanation, by the very men now destroyed in the sea, of the temple and image of Neptune, situated in their suburb. And in this they seem to me to say well. Artabazus afterwards led away the remainder of his army, and joined Mardonius in Thessaly. Thus fared it with the Persians who escorted the king to the strait.

130. As for that part of the fleet of Xerxes which had survived the battle, when it had

made good its escape from Salamis to the coast of Asia, and conveyed the king with his army across the strait from the Chersonese to Abydos, it passed the winter at Cymé. On the first approach of spring, there was an early muster of the ships at Samos, where some of them indeed had remained throughout the winter. Most of the men-at-arms who served on board were Persians, or else Medes; and the command of the fleet had been taken by Mardontes, the son of Bagæus, and Artaÿntes, the son of Artachæus; while there was likewise a third commander, Ithamitres, the nephew of Artaÿntes, whom his uncle had advanced to the post. Further west than Samos, however, they did not venture to proceed; for they remembered what a defeat they had suffered, and there was no one to compel them to approach any nearer to Greece. They therefore remained at Samos, and kept watch over Ionia, to hinder it from breaking into revolt. The whole number of their ships, including those furnished by the Ionians, was three hundred. It did not enter into their thoughts that the Greeks would proceed against Ionia; on the contrary, they supposed that the defence of their own country would content them, more especially as they had not pursued the Persian fleet when it fled from Salamis, but had so readily given up the chase. They despaired, however, altogether of gaining any success by sea themselves, though by land they thought that Mardonius was quite sure of victory. So they remained at Samos, and took counsel together, if by any means they might harass the enemy, at the same time that they waited eagerly to hear how matters would proceed with Mardonius.

131. The approach of spring, and the knowledge that Mardonius was in Thessaly, roused the Greeks from inaction. Their land force indeed was not yet come together; but the fleet, consisting of one hundred and ten ships, proceeded to Egina, under the command of Leotychides. This Leotychides, who was both general and admiral, was the son of Menares, the son of Agesilaüs, the son of Hippocratides, the son of Leotychides, the son of Anaxilaüs, the son of Archidamus, the son of Anaxandrides, the son of Theopompus, the son of Nicander, the son of Charillus, the son of Eunomus, the son of Polydectes, the son of Prytanis, the son of Euryphon, the son of Procles, the son of Aristodêmus, the son of Aristomachus, the son of Cleodæus, the son of Hyllus, the son of Hercules. He belonged to the younger branch

of the royal house. All his ancestors, except the two next in the above list to himself, had been kings of Sparta. The Athenian vessels were commanded by Xanthippus, the son of Ariphron.

132. When the whole fleet was collected together at Egina, ambassadors from Ionia arrived at the Greek station; they had but just come from paying a visit to Sparta, where they had been intreating the Lacedæmonians to undertake the deliverance of their native land. One of these ambassadors was Herodotus, the son of Basileides. Originally they were seven in number; and the whole seven had conspired to slay Strattis the tyrant of Chios; one, however, of those engaged in the plot betrayed the enterprise; and the conspiracy being in this way discovered, Herodotus, and the remaining five, quitted Chios, and went straight to Sparta, whence they had now proceeded to Egina, their object being to beseech the Greeks that they would pass over to Ionia. It was not, however, without difficulty that they were induced to advance even so far as Delos. All beyond that seemed to the Greeks full of danger; the places were quite unknown to them, and to their fancy swarmed with Persian troops; as for Samos, it appeared to them as far off as the Pillars of Hercules. Thus it came to pass, that at the very same time the barbarians were hindered by their fears from venturing any further west than Samos, and the prayers of the Chians failed to induce the Greeks to advance any further east than Delos. Terror guarded the mid region.

133. The Greek fleet was now on its way to Delos; but Mardonius still abode in his winter-quarters in Thessaly. When he was about to leave them, he despatched a man named Mys, a Europian by birth, to go and consult the different oracles, giving him orders to put questions everywhere to all the oracles whereof he found it possible to make trial. What it was that he wanted to know, when he gave Mys these orders, I am not able to say, for no account has reached me of the matter; but for my own part, I suppose that he sent to inquire concerning the business which he had in hand, and not for any other purpose.

134. Mys, it is certain, went to Lebadeia, and, by the payment of a sum of money, induced one of the inhabitants to go down to Trophônius; he likewise visited Abæ of the Phocians, and there consulted the god; while at Thebes, to which place he went first of all, he not only got access to Apollo Ismenius (of

whom inquiry is made by means of victims, according to the custom practised also at Olympia), but likewise prevailed on a man, who was not a Theban but a foreigner, to pass the night in the temple of Amphiaraüs. No Theban can lawfully consult this oracle, for the following reason: Amphiaraüs by an oracle gave the Thebans their choice, to have him for their prophet or for their helper in war; he bade them elect between the two, and forego either one or the other; so they chose rather to have him for their helper. On this account it is unlawful for a Theban to sleep in his temple.

135. One thing which the Thebans declare to have happened at this time is to me very surprising. Mys, the Europian, they say, after he had gone about to all the oracles, came at last to the sacred precinct of Apollo Ptoüs. The place itself bears the name of Ptôüm; it is in the country of the Thebans, and is situated on the mountain side overlooking Lake Copaïs, only a very little way from the town called Acræphia. Here Mys arrived, and entered the temple, followed by three Theban citizens—picked men whom the state had appointed to take down whatever answer the god might give. No sooner was he entered than the prophet delivered him an oracle, but in a foreign tongue; so that his Theban attendants were astonished, hearing a strange language when they expected Greek, and did not know what to do. Mys, however, the Europian, snatched from their hands the tablet which they had brought with them, and wrote down what the prophet uttered. The reply, he told them, was in the Carian dialect. After this, Mys departed and returned to Thessaly.

136. Mardonius, when he had read the answers given by the oracles, sent next an envoy to Athens. This was Alexander, the son of Amyntas, a Macedonian, of whom he made choice for two reasons. Alexander was connected with the Persians by family ties; for Gygæa, who was the daughter of Amyntas, and sister to Alexander himself, was married to Bubares, a Persian, and by him had a son, to wit, Amyntas of Asia; who was named after his mother's father, and enjoyed the revenues of Alabanda, a large city of Phrygia, which had been assigned him by the king. Alexander was likewise (and of this too Mardonius was well aware), both by services which he had rendered, and by formal compact of friendship, connected with Athens. Mardonius therefore thought that, by sending him, he would be most likely to gain over the Athenians to the Persian side. He had heard that they were a numerous and a warlike people, and he knew that the disasters which had befallen the Persians by sea were mainly their work; he therefore expected that, if he could form alliance with them, he would easily get the mastery of the sea (as indeed he would have done, beyond a doubt), while by land he believed that he was already greatly superior; and so he thought by this alliance to make sure of overcoming the Greeks. Perhaps, too, the oracles leant this way, and counselled him to make Athens his friend: so that it may have been in obedience to them that he sent the embassy.

137. This Alexander was descended in the seventh degree from Perdiccas, who obtained the sovereignty over the Macedonians in the way which I will now relate. Three brothers, descendants of Têmenus, fled from Argos to the Illyrians; their names were Gauanes, Aëropus, and Perdiccas. From Illyria they went across to Upper Macedonia, where they came to a certain town called Lebæa. There they hired themselves out to serve the king in different employs; one tended the horses; another looked after the cows; while Perdiccas, who was the youngest, took charge of the smaller cattle. In those early times poverty was not confined to the people: kings themselves were poor, and so here it was the king's wife who cooked the victuals. Now, whenever she baked the bread, she always observed that the loaf of the labouring boy Perdiccas swelled to double its natural size. So the queen, finding this never fail, spoke of it to her husband. Directly that it came to his ears, the thought struck him that it was a miracle, and boded something of no small moment. He therefore sent for the three labourers, and told them to begone out of his dominions. They answered, "they had a right to their wages; if he would pay them what was due, they were quite willing to go." Now it happened that the sun was shining down the chimney into the room where they were; and the king, hearing them talk of wages, lost his wits, and said, "There are the wages which you deserve; take that—I give it you!" and pointed, as he spoke, to the sunshine. The two elder brothers, Gauanes and Aëropus, stood aghast at the reply, and did nothing; but the boy, who had a knife in his hand, made a mark with it round the sunshine on the floor of the room, and said, "O king! we accept your payment." Then he received the light of the sun three times into his bosom,

and so went away; and his brothers went with him.

138. When they were gone, one of those who sat by told the king what the youngest of the three had done, and hinted that he must have had some meaning in accepting the wages given. Then the king, when he heard what had happened, was angry, and sent horsemen after the youths to slay them. Now there is a river in Macedonia to which the descendants of these Argives offer sacrifice as their saviour. This stream swelled so much, as soon as the sons of Têmenus were safe across, that the horsemen found it impossible to follow. So the brothers escaped into another part of Macedonia, and took up their abode near the place called "the Gardens of Midas, son of Gordias." In these gardens there are roses which grow of themselves, so sweet that no others can come near them, and with blossoms that have as many as sixty petals apiece. It was here, according to the Macedonians, that Silenus was made a prisoner. Above the gardens stands a mountain called Bermius, which is so cold that none can reach the top. Here the brothers made their abode; and from this place by degrees they conquered all Macedonia.

139. From the Perdiccas of whom we have here spoken, Alexander was descended in the following way:—Alexander was the son of Amyntas, Amyntas of Alcetas; the father of Alcetas was Aëropus; of Aëropus, Philip; of Philip, Argæus; of Argæus, Perdiccas, the first sovereign. Such was the descent of Alexander.

140. (§ 1.) When Alexander reached Athens as the ambassador of Mardonius, he spoke as follows:—

"O men of Athens, these be the words of Mardonius. 'The king has sent a message to me, saying, "All the trespasses which the Athenians have committed against me I freely forgive. Now then, Mardonius, thus shalt thou act towards them. Restore to them their territory; and let them choose for themselves whatever land they like besides, and let them dwell therein as a free people. Build up likewise all their temples which I burned, if on these terms they will consent to enter into a league with me." Such are the orders which I have received, and which I must needs obey, unless there be a hindrance on your part. And now I say unto you,—why are ye so mad as to levy war against the king, whom ye cannot possibly overcome, or even resist for ever? Ye have seen the multitude and the bravery of the host of Xerxes; ye know also how large a power remains with me in your land; suppose then ye should get the better of us, and defeat this army—a thing whereof ye will not, if ye be wise, entertain the least hope—what follows even then but a contest with a still greater force? Do not, because you would fain match yourselves with the king, consent to lose your country and live in constant danger of your lives. Rather agree to make peace; which ye can now do without any tarnish to your honour, since the king invites you to it. Continue free, and make an alliance with us, without fraud or deceit.'

(§ 2.) "These are the words, O Athenians! which Mardonius had bid me speak to you. For my own part, I will say nothing of the good will I bear your nation, since ye have not now for the first time to become acquainted with it. But I will add my intreaties also, and beseech you to give ear to Mardonius; for I see clearly that it is impossible for you to go on for ever contending against Xerxes. If that had appeared to me possible, I would not now have come hither the bearer of such a message. But the king's power surpasses that of man, and his arm reaches far. If then ye do not hasten to conclude a peace, when such fair terms are offered you, I tremble to think of what you will have to endure—you, who of all the allies lie most directly in the path of danger, whose land will always be the chief battleground of the contending powers, and who will therefore constantly have to suffer alone. Hearken then, I pray you, to Mardonius! Surely it is no small matter that the Great King chooses you out from all the rest of the Greeks, to offer you forgiveness of the wrongs you have done him, and to propose himself as your friend and ally!"

141. Such were the words of Alexander. Now the Lacedæmonians, when tidings reached them that Alexander was gone to Athens to bring about a league between the Athenians and the barbarians, and when at the same time they called to mind the prophecies which declared that the Dorian race should one day be driven from the Peloponnese by the Medes and the Athenians, were exceedingly afraid lest the Athenians might consent to the alliance with Persia. They therefore lost no time in sending envoys to Athens; and it so happened that these envoys were given their audience at the same time with Alexander: for the Athenians had waited and made delays, because they felt sure that the Lacedæmonians would hear that an ambassador was

come to them from the Persians, and as soon as they heard it would with all speed send an embassy. They contrived matters therefore of set purpose, so that the Lacedæmonians might hear them deliver their sentiments on the occasion.

142. As soon as Alexander had finished speaking, the ambassadors from Sparta took the word and said,—

"We are sent here by the Lacedæmonians to entreat of you that ye will not do a new thing in Greece, nor agree to the terms which are offered you by the barbarian. Such conduct on the part of any of the Greeks were alike unjust and dishonourable; but in you 'twould be worse than in others, for divers reasons. 'Twas by you that this war was kindled at the first among us—our wishes were in no way considered; the contest began by your seeking to extend your empire—now the fate of Greece is involved in it. Besides it was surely an intolerable thing that the Athenians, who have always hitherto been known as a nation to which many men owed their freedom, should now become the means of bringing all other Greeks into slavery. We feel, however, for the heavy calamities which press on you—the loss of your harvest these two years, and the ruin in which your homes have lain for so long a time. We offer you, therefore, on the part of the Lacedæmonians and the allies, sustenance for your women and for the unwarlike portion of your households, so long as the war endures. Be ye not seduced by Alexander the Macedonian, who softens down the rough words of Mardonius. He does as is natural for him to do—a tyrant himself, he helps forward a tyrant's cause. But ye, Athenians, should do differently, at least if ye be truly wise; for ye should know that with barbarians there is neither faith nor truth."

143. Thus spake the envoys. After which the Athenians returned this answer to Alexander:—

"We know, as well as thou dost, that the power of the Mede is many times greater than our own: we did not need to have *that* cast in our teeth. Nevertheless we cling so to freedom that we shall offer what resistance we may. Seek not to persuade us into making terms with the barbarian—say what thou wilt, thou wilt never gain our assent. Return rather at once, and tell Mardonius that our answer to him is this:—'So long as the sun keeps his present course, we will never join alliance with

Xerxes. Nay, we shall oppose him unceasingly, trusting in the aid of those gods and heroes whom he has lightly esteemed, whose houses and whose images he has burnt with fire.' And come not thou again to us with words like these; nor, thinking to do us a service, persuade us to unholy actions. Thou art the guest and friend of our nation—we would not that thou shouldst receive hurt at our hands."

144. Such was the answer which the Athenians gave to Alexander. To the Spartan envoys they said:—

"'Twas natural no doubt that the Lacedæmonians should be afraid we might make terms with the barbarian; but nevertheless 'twas a base fear in men who knew so well of what temper and spirit we are. Not all the gold that the whole earth contains—not the fairest and most fertile of all lands—would bribe us to take part with the Medes and help them to enslave our countrymen. Even could we anyhow have brought ourselves to such a thing, there are many very powerful motives which would now make it impossible. The first and chief of these is the burning and destruction of our temples and the images of our gods, which forces us to make no terms with their destroyer, but rather to pursue him with our resentment to the uttermost. Again, there is our common brotherhood with the Greeks: our common language, the altars and the sacrifices of which we all partake, the common character which we bear—did the Athenians betray all these, of a truth it would not be well. Know then now, if ye have not known it before, that while one Athenian remains alive, we will never join alliance with Xerxes. We thank you, however, for your forethought on our behalf, and for your wish to give our families sustenance, now that ruin has fallen on us—the kindness is complete on your part; but for ourselves, we will endure as we may, and not be burdensome to you. Such then is our resolve. Be it your care with all speed to lead out your troops; for if we surmise aright, the barbarian will not wait long ere he invade our territory, but will set out so soon as he learns our answer to be, that we will do none of those things which he requires of us. Now then is the time for us, before he enters Attica, to go forth ourselves into Bœotia, and give him battle."

When the Athenians had thus spoken, the ambassadors from Sparta departed, and returned back to their own country.

The Ninth Book, Entitled
CALLIOPÉ

⋙ ⋙ ⋙ ⋙ ⋙ ⋙ ⋙ ⋙ ⋙ ⋙ ⋙ ⋙ ⋙ ⋙ ⋙ ⋘ ⋘ ⋘ ⋘ ⋘ ⋘ ⋘ ⋘ ⋘ ⋘ ⋘ ⋘ ⋘ ⋘ ⋘

1. Mardonius, when Alexander upon his return made known to him the answer of the Athenians, forthwith broke up from Thessaly, and led his army with all speed against Athens; forcing the several nations through whose land he passed to furnish him with additional troops. The chief men of Thessaly, far from repenting of the part which they had taken in the war hitherto, urged on the Persians to the attack more earnestly than ever. Thorax of Larissa in particular, who had helped to escort Xerxes on his flight to Asia, now openly encouraged Mardonius in his march upon Greece.

2. When the army reached Bœotia, the Thebans sought to induce Mardonius to make a halt: "He would not," they told him, "find anywhere a more convenient place in which to pitch his camp; and their advice to him was, that he should go no further, but fix himself there, and thence take measures to subdue all Greece without striking a blow. If the Greeks, who had held together hitherto, still continued united among themselves, it would be difficult for the whole world to overcome them by force of arms. But if thou wilt do as we advise," they went on to say, "thou mayest easily obtain the direction of all their counsels. Send presents to the men of most weight in the several states, and by so doing thou wilt sow division among them. After that, it will be a light task, with the help of such as side with thee, to bring under all thy adversaries."

3. Such was the advice of the Thebans: but Mardonius did not follow it. A strong desire of taking Athens a second time possessed him, in part arising from his inborn stubbornness, in part from a wish to inform the king at Sardis, by fire-signals along the islands, that he was master of the place. However, he did not on his arrival in Attica find the Athenians in their country—they had again withdrawn, some to their ships, but the greater part to Salamis—and he only gained possession of a deserted town. It was ten months after the taking of the city by the king that Mardonius came against it for the second time.

4. Mardonius, being now in Athens, sent an envoy to Salamis, one Murychides, a Hellespontine Greek, to offer the Athenians once more the same terms which had been conveyed to them by Alexander. The reason for his sending a second time, though he knew beforehand their unfriendly feelings towards him, was,—that he hoped, when they saw the whole land of Attica conquered and in his power, their stubbornness would begin to give way. On this account, therefore, he dispatched Murychides to Salamis.

5. Now, when Murychides came before the council, and delivered his message, one of the councillors, named Lycidas, gave it as his opinion—"that the best course would be, to admit the proposals brought by Murychides, and lay them before the assembly of the people." This he stated to be his opinion, perhaps because he had been bribed by Mardonius, or it may be because that course really appeared to him the most expedient. However, the Athenians—both those in the council, and those who stood without, when they heard of the advice—were full of wrath, and forthwith surrounded Lycidas, and stoned him to death. As for Murychides, the Hellespontine Greek, him they sent away unharmed. Now there was a stir in the island about Lycidas, and the Athenian women learnt what had happened. Then each exhorted her fellow, and one brought another to take part in the deed; and they all flocked of their own accord to the house of Lycidas, and stoned to death his wife and his children.

6. The circumstances under which the Athenians had sought refuge in Salamis were the following. So long as any hope remained that

a Peloponnesian army would come to give them aid, they abode still in Attica; but when it appeared that the allies were slack and slow to move, while the invader was reported to be pressing forward and to have already entered Bœotia, then they proceeded to remove their goods and chattels from the mainland, and themselves again crossed the strait to Salamis. At the same time they sent ambassadors to Lacedæmon, who were to reproach the Lacedæmonians for having allowed the barbarian to advance into Attica, instead of joining them and going out to meet him in Bœotia. They were likewise to remind the Lacedæmonians of the offers by which the Persian had sought to win Athens over to his side, and to warn them, that if no aid came from Sparta, the Athenians must consult for their own safety.

7. The truth was, the Lacedæmonians were keeping holiday at that time; for it was the feast of the Hyacinthia, and they thought nothing of so much moment as to perform the service of the god. They were also engaged in building their wall across the Isthmus, which was now so far advanced that the battlements had begun to be placed upon it.

When the envoys of the Athenians, accompanied by ambassadors from Megara and Platæa, reached Lacedæmon, they came before the Ephors, and spoke as follows:—

"The Athenians have sent us to you to say, —the king of the Medes offers to give us back our country, and wishes to conclude an alliance with us on fair and equal terms, without fraud or deceit. He is willing likewise to bestow on us another country besides our own, and bids us choose any land that we like. But we, because we reverenced Hellenic Jupiter, and thought it a shameful act to betray Greece, instead of consenting to these terms, refused them; notwithstanding that we have been wronged and deserted by the other Greeks, and are fully aware that it is far more for our advantage to make peace with the Persian than to prolong the war with him. Still we shall not, of our own free will, consent to any terms of peace. Thus do we, in all our dealings with the Greeks, avoid what is base and counterfeit: while contrariwise, ye, who were but now so full of fear least we should make terms with the enemy, having learnt of what temper we are, and assured yourselves that we shall not prove traitors to our country—having brought moreover your wall across the Isthmus to an advanced state—cease altogether to have any care for us. Ye covenanted with us to go out

and meet the Persian in Bœotia; but when the time came, ye were false to your word, and looked on while the barbarian host advanced into Attica. At this time, therefore, the Athenians are angered with you; and justly,—for ye have not done what was right. They bid you, however, make haste to send forth your army, that we may even yet meet Mardonius in Attica. Now that Bœotia is lost to us, the best place for the fight within our country, will be the plain of Thria."

8. The Ephors, when they had heard this speech, delayed their answer till the morrow; and when the morrow came, till the day following. And thus they acted for ten days, continually putting off the ambassadors from one day to the next. Meanwhile the Peloponnesians generally were labouring with great zeal at the wall, and the work nearly approached completion. I can give no other reason for the conduct of the Lacedæmonians in showing themselves so anxious, at the time when Alexander came, that the Athenians should not join the Medes, and now being quite careless about it, except that at the former time the wall across the Isthmus was not complete, and they worked at it in great fear of the Persians, whereas now the bulwark had been raised, and so they imagined that they had no further need of the Athenians.

9. At last the ambassadors got an answer, and the troops marched forth from Sparta, under the following circumstances. The last audience had been fixed for the ambassadors, when, the very day before it was to be given, a certain Tegean, named Chileüs, a man who had more influence at Sparta than any other foreigner, learning from the Ephors exactly what the Athenians had said, addressed these words to them—"The case stands thus, O ye Ephors! If the Athenians are not our friends, but league themselves with the barbarians, however strong our wall across the Isthmus may be, there will be doors enough, and wide enough open too, by which the Persian may gain entrance to the Peloponnese. Grant their request then, before they make any fresh resolve, which may bring Greece to ruin."

10. Such was the counsel which Chileüs gave: and the Ephors, taking the advice into consideration, determined forthwith, without speaking a word to the ambassadors from the three cities, to despatch to the Isthmus a body of five thousand Spartans; and accordingly they sent them forth the same night, appointing to each Spartan a retinue of seven Helots,

and giving the command of the expedition to
Pausanias the son of Cleombrotus. The chief
power belonged of right at this time to Pleis-
tarchus, the son of Leonidas; but as he was
still a child Pausanias, his cousin, was regent
in his room. For the father of Pausanias, Cleombrotus, the son of Anaxandridas, no longer
lived; he had died a short time after bringing
back from the Isthmus the troops who had
been employed in building the wall. A prodigy
had caused him to bring his army home; for
while he was offering sacrifice to know if he
should march out against the Persian, the sun
was suddenly darkened in mid sky. Pausanias
took with him, as joint-leader of the army, Euryanax, the son of Dorieus, a member of his
own family.

11. The army accordingly had marched out
from Sparta with Pausanias: while the ambassadors, when day came, appeared before the
Ephors, knowing nothing of the march of the
troops, and purposing themselves to leave Sparta forthwith, and return each man to his own
country. They therefore addressed the Ephors
in these words:—"Lacedæmonians, as you do
not stir from home, but keep the Hyacinthian
festival, and amuse yourselves, deserting the
cause of your confederates, the Athenians,
whom your behaviour wrongs, and who have
no other allies, will make such terms with the
Persians as they shall find possible. Now when
terms are once made, it is plain that, having
become the king's allies, we shall march with
the barbarians whithersoever they choose to
lead. Then at length you will perceive what
the consequences will be to yourselves." When
the envoys had spoken, the Ephors declared to
them with an oath:—"Our troops must be at
Orestêum by this time, on their march against
the strangers." (The Spartans say "strangers"
for "barbarians.") At this the ambassadors,
quite ignorant of what had happened, questioned them concerning their meaning; and
when, by much questioning, they had discovered the truth, they were greatly astonished
thereat, and forthwith set off, at their best
speed, to overtake the Spartan army. At the
same time a body of five thousand Lacedæmonian Periœci, all picked men and fully
armed, set forth from Sparta, in the company
of the ambassadors.

12. So these troops marched in haste towards the Isthmus. Meanwhile the Argives,
who had promised Mardonius that they would
stop the Spartans from crossing their borders,
as soon as they learnt that Pausanias with his
army had started from Sparta, took the swiftest courier they could find, and sent him off
to Attica. The message which he delivered, on
his arrival at Athens, was the following: "Mardonius," he said, "the Argives have sent me to
tell thee that the Lacedæmonian youth are
gone forth from their city, and that the Argives
are too weak to hinder them. Take good heed
therefore to thyself at this time." After thus
speaking, without a word more, he returned
home.

13. When Mardonius learnt that the Spartans were on their march, he no longer cared
to remain in Attica. Hitherto he had kept
quiet, wishing to see what the Athenians
would do, and had neither ravaged their territory, nor done it any the least harm; for till
now he had cherished the hope that the Athenians would come to terms with him. As, however, he found that his persuasions were of no
avail, and as their whole policy was now clear
to him, he determined to withdraw from Attica before Pausanias with his army reached
the Isthmus; first, however, he resolved to burn
Athens, and to cast down and level with the
ground whatever remained standing of the
walls, temples, and other buildings. His reason for retreating was, that Attica was not a
country where horse could act with advantage;
and further, that if he suffered defeat in a battle, no way of escape was open to him, except
through defiles, where a handful of troops
might stop all his army. So he determined to
withdraw to Thebes, and give the Greeks battle in the neighbourhood of a friendly city,
and on ground well suited for cavalry.

14. After he had quitted Attica and was already upon his march, news reached him that
a body of a thousand Lacedæmonians, distinct
from the army of Pausanias, and sent on in
advance, had arrived in the Megarid. When he
heard it, wishing, if possible, to destroy this detachment first, Mardonius considered with
himself how he might compass their ruin.
With a sudden change of march he made for
Megara, while the horse, pushing on in advance, entered and ravaged the Megarid.
(Here was the furthest point in Europe towards the setting sun to which this Persian
army ever penetrated.)

15. After this, Mardonius received another
message, whereby he learnt that the forces of
the Greeks were collected together at the Isthmus; which tidings caused him to draw back,
and leave Attica by the way of Deceleia. The
Bœotarchs had sent for some of the neighbours

of the Asopians; and these persons served as guides to the army, and led them first to Sphendalé, and from thence to Tanagra, where Mardonius rested a night; after which, upon the morrow, he bent his course to Scôlus, which brought him into the territory of the Thebans. And now, although the Thebans had espoused the cause of the Medes, yet Mardonius cut down all the trees in these parts; not however from any enmity towards the Thebans, but on account of his own urgent needs; for he wanted a rampart to protect his army from attack, and he likewise desired to have a place of refuge, whither his troops might flee, in case the battle should go contrary to his wishes. His army at this time lay on the Asôpus, and stretched from Erythræ, along by Hysiæ, to the territory of the Platæans. The wall, however, was not made to extend so far, but formed a square of about ten furlongs each way.

While the barbarians were employed in this work, a certain citizen of Thebes, Attagînus by name, the son of Phrynon, having made great preparations, gave a banquet, and invited Mardonius thereto, together with fifty of the noblest Persians. Now the banquet was held at Thebes; and all the guests who were invited came to it.

16. What follows was recounted to me by Thersander, a native of Orchomenus, a man of the first rank in that city. Thersander told me that he was himself among those invited to the feast, and that besides the Persians fifty Thebans were asked; and the two nations were not arranged separately, but a Persian and a Theban were set side by side upon each couch. After the feast was ended, and the drinking had begun, the Persian who shared Thersander's couch addressed him in the Greek tongue, and inquired of him from what city he came. He answered, that he was of Orchomenus; whereupon the other said—

"Since thou hast eaten with me at one table, and poured libation from one cup, I would fain leave with thee a memorial of the belief I hold—the rather that thou mayest have timely warning thyself, and so be able to provide for thy own safety. Seest thou these Persians here feasting, and the army which we left encamped yonder by the river-side? Yet a little while, and of all this number thou wilt behold but a few surviving!"

As he spake, the Persian let fall a flood of tears: whereon Thersander, who was astonished at his words, replied—"Surely thou shouldest say all this to Mardonius, and the Persians who are next him in honour"—but the other rejoined—"Dear friend, it is not possible for man to avert that which God has decreed shall happen. No one believes warnings, however true. Many of us Persians know our danger, but we are constrained by necessity to do as our leader bids us. Verily 'tis the sorest of all human ills, to abound in knowledge and yet have no power over action." All this I heard myself from Thersander the Orchomenian; who told me further, that he mentioned what had happened to divers persons, before the battle was fought at Platæa.

17. When Mardonius formerly held his camp in Bœotia, all the Greeks of those parts who were friendly to the Medes sent troops to join his army, and these troops accompanied him in his attack upon Athens. The Phocians alone abstained, and took no part in the invasion; for, though they had espoused the Median cause warmly, it was very much against their will, and only because they were compelled so to do. However, a few days after the arrival of the Persian army at Thebes, a thousand of their heavy-armed soldiers came up, under the command of Harmocŷdes, one of their most distinguished citizens. No sooner had these troops reached Thebes, than some horsemen came to them from Mardonius, with orders that they should take up a position upon the plain, away from the rest of the army. The Phocians did so, and forthwith the entire Persian cavalry drew nigh to them: whereupon there went a rumour through the whole of the Greek force encamped with the Medes, that Mardonius was about to destroy the Phocians with missiles. The same conviction ran through the Phocian troops themselves; and Harmocŷdes, their leader, addressed them thus with words of encouragement—"Phocians" said he, " 'tis plain that these men have resolved beforehand to take our lives, because of the accusations of the Thessalians, as I imagine. Now, then, is the time for you all to show yourselves brave men. 'Tis better to die fighting and defending our lives, than tamely to allow them to slay us in this shameful fashion. Let them learn that they are barbarians, and that the men whose death they have plotted are Greeks!"

18. Thus spake Harmocŷdes; and the Persian horse, having encircled the Phocians, charged towards them, as if about to deal out death, with bows bent, and arrows ready to be let fly; nay, here and there some did even discharge their weapons. But the Phocians stood

firm, keeping close one to another, and serrying their ranks as much as possible: whereupon the horse suddenly wheeled round and rode off. I cannot say with certainty whether they came, at the prayer of the Thessalians, to destroy the Phocians, but seeing them prepared to stand on their defence, and fearing to suffer damage at their hands, on that account beat a retreat, having orders from Mardonius so to act; or whether his sole intent was to try the temper of the Phocians and see whether they had any courage or no. However this may have been, when the horsemen retired, Mardonius sent a herald to the Phocians, saying—"Fear not, Phocians—ye have shown yourselves valiant men—much unlike the report I had heard of you. Now therefore be forward in the coming war. Ye will not readily outdo either the king or myself in services." Thus ended the affair of the Phocians.

19. The Lacedæmonians, when they reached the Isthmus, pitched their camp there; and the other Peloponnesians who had embraced the good side, hearing or else seeing that they were upon the march, thought it not right to remain behind when the Spartans were going forth to the war. So the Peloponnesians went out in one body from the Isthmus, the victims being favourable for setting forth; and marched as far as Eleusis, where again they offered sacrifices, and, finding the omens still encouraging, advanced further. At Eleusis they were joined by the Athenians, who had come across from Salamis, and now accompanied the main army. On reaching Erythræ in Bœotia, they learnt that the barbarians were encamped upon the Asôpus; wherefore they themselves, after considering how they should act, disposed their forces opposite to the enemy upon the slopes of Mount Cithæron.

20. Mardonius, when he saw that the Greeks would not come down into the plain, sent all his cavalry, under Masistius (or Macistius, as the Greeks call him), to attack them where they were. Now Masistius was a man of much repute among the Persians, and rode a Nisæan charger with a golden bit, and otherwise magnificently caparisoned. So the horse advanced against the Greeks, and made attacks upon them in divisions, doing them great damage at each charge, and insulting them by calling them women.

21. It chanced that the Megarians were drawn up in the position most open to attack, and where the ground offered the best approach to the cavalry. Finding themselves therefore hard pressed by the assaults upon their ranks, they sent a herald to the Greek leaders, who came and said to them, "This is the message of the Megarians—We cannot, brothers-in-arms, continue to resist the Persian horse in that post which we have occupied from the first, if we are left without succours. Hitherto, although hard pressed, we have held out against them firmly and courageously. Now, however, if you do not send others to take our place, we warn you that we shall quit our post." Such were the words of the herald. Pausanias, when he heard them, inquired among his troops if there were any who would volunteer to take the post, and so relieve the Megarians. Of the rest none were willing to go, whereupon the Athenians offered themselves; and a body of picked men, three hundred in number, commanded by Olympiodôrus, the son of Lampo, undertook the service.

22. Selecting, to accompany them, the whole body of archers, these men relieved the Megarians, and occupied a post which all the other Greeks collected at Erythræ had shrunk from holding. After the struggle had continued for a while, it came to an end on this wise. As the barbarians continued charging in divisions, the horse of Masistius, which was in front of the others, received an arrow in his flank, the pain of which caused him to rear and throw his rider. Immediately the Athenians rushed upon Masistius as he lay, caught his horse, and when he himself made resistance, slew him. At first, however, they were not able to take his life; for his armour hindered them. He had on a breastplate formed of golden scales, with a scarlet tunic covering it. Thus the blows, all falling upon his breastplate, took no effect, till one of the soldiers, perceiving the reason, drove his weapon into his eye and so slew him. All this took place without any of the other horsemen seeing it: they had neither observed their leader fall from his horse, nor beheld him slain; for he fell as they wheeled round and prepared for another charge, so that they were quite ignorant of what had happened. When, however, they halted, and found that there was no one to marshal their line, Masistius was missed; and instantly his soldiers, understanding what must have befallen him, with loud cheers charged the enemy in one mass, hoping to recover the dead body.

23. So when the Athenians saw that, instead of coming up in squadrons, the whole mass of

the horse was about to charge them at once, they called out to the other troops to make haste to their aid. While the rest of the infantry, however, was moving to their assistance, the contest waxed fierce about the dead body of Masistius. The three hundred, so long as they fought by themselves, had greatly the worse of the encounter, and were forced to retire and yield up the body to the enemy; but when the other troops approached, the Persian horse could no longer hold their ground, but fled without carrying off the body, having incurred in the attempt a further loss of several of their number. They therefore retired about two furlongs, and consulted with each other what was best to be done. Being without a leader, it seemed to them the fittest course to return to Mardonius.

24. When the horse reached the camp, Mardonius and all the Persian army made great lamentation for Masistius. They shaved off all the hair from their own heads, and cut the manes from their war-horses and their sumpter-beasts, while they vented their grief in such loud cries that all Bœotia resounded with the clamour, because they had lost the man who, next to Mardonius, was held in the greatest esteem, both by the king and by the Persians generally. So the barbarians, after their own fashion, paid honours to the dead Masistius.

25. The Greeks, on the other hand, were greatly emboldened by what had happened, seeing that they had not only stood their ground against the attacks of the horse, but had even compelled them to beat a retreat. They therefore placed the dead body of Masistius upon a cart, and paraded it along the ranks of the army. Now the body was a sight which well deserved to be gazed upon, being remarkable both for stature and for beauty; and it was to stop the soldiers from leaving their ranks to look at it, that they resolved to carry it round. After this the Greeks determined to quit the high ground and go nearer Platæa, as the land there seemed far more suitable for an encampment than the country about Erythræ, particularly because it was better supplied with water. To this place therefore, and more especially to a spring-head which was called Gargaphia, they considered that it would be best for them to remove, after which they might once more encamp in their order. So they took their arms, and proceeded along the slopes of Cithæron, past Hysiæ, to the territory of the Platæans; and here they drew themselves up, nation by nation, close by the fountain Gargaphia, and the sacred precinct of the Hero Androcrates, partly along some hillocks of no great height, and partly upon the level of the plain.

26. Here, in the marshalling of the nations, a fierce battle of words arose between the Athenians and the Tegeans, both of whom claimed to have one of the wings assigned to them. On each side were brought forward the deeds which they had done, whether in earlier or in later times; and first the Tegeans urged their claim as follows:—

"This post has been always considered our right, and not the right of any of the other allies, in all the expeditions which have been entered into conjointly by the Peloponnesians, both anciently and in later times. Ever since the Heraclidæ made their attempt, after the death of Eurystheus, to return by force of arms into the Peloponnese, this custom has been observed. It was then that the right became ours, and this was the way in which we gained it:— When, in company with the Achæans and Ionians who then dwelt in the Peloponnese, we marched out to the Isthmus, and pitched our camp over against the invaders, then, as the tale goes, that Hyllus made proclamation, saying—'It needs not to imperil two armies in a general battle; rather let one be chosen from the Peloponnesian ranks, whomsoever they deem the bravest, and let him engage with me in single combat, on such terms as shall be agreed upon.' The saying pleased the Peloponnesians, and oaths were sworn to the effect following:—'If Hyllus conquer the Peloponnesian champion, the Heraclidæ shall return to their inheritance; if, on the other hand, he be conquered, the Heraclidæ shall withdraw, lead back their army, and engage for the next hundred years to make no further endeavours to force their return." Hereupon Echemus, the son of Aëropus and grandson of Phêgeus, who was our leader and king, offered himself, and was preferred before all his brothers-in-arms as champion, engaged in single combat with Hyllus, and slew him upon the spot. For this exploit we were rewarded by the Peloponnesians of that day with many goodly privileges, which we have ever since enjoyed; and, among the rest, we obtained the right of holding the leading post in one wing, whenever a joint expedition goes forth beyond our borders. With you then, O Lacedæmonians, we do not claim to compete; choose you which wing ye please; we yield and grant you the preference: but we maintain that the command of the other wing belongs of right to us, now no less than formerly. Moreover, set aside this exploit which we have related, and still our title to the chief post is better than that of the Athenians: witness the many glorious fights in which we have been engaged against yourselves, O Spartans! as well as those which we have maintained with others. We have therefore more right to this place than they; for they have performed no exploits to be compared to ours, whether we look to earlier or to later times."

27. Thus spake the Tegeans; and the Athenians made reply as follows:—"We are not ignorant that our forces were gathered here, not for the purpose of speech-making, but for battle against the barbarian. Yet as the Tegeans have been pleased to bring into debate the exploits performed by our two nations, alike in earlier and in later times, we have no choice but to set before you the grounds on which we claim it as our heritage, deserved by our unchanging bravery, to be preferred above Arcadians. In the first place, then, those very Heraclidæ, whose leader they boast to have slain at the Isthmus, and whom the other Greeks would not receive when they asked a refuge from the bondage wherewith they were threatened by the people of Mycênæ, were given a shelter by us; and we brought down the insolence of Eurystheus, and helped to gain the victory over those who were at that time lords of the Peloponnese. Again, when the Argives led their troops with Polynices against Thebes, and were slain and refused burial, it is our boast that we went out against the Cadmeians, recovered the bodies, and buried them at Eleusis in our own territory. Another noble deed of ours was that against the Amazons, when they came from their seats upon the Thermôdon, and poured their hosts into Attica; and in the Trojan war too we were not a whit behind any of the Greeks. But what boots it to speak of these ancient matters? A nation which was brave in those days might have grown cowardly since, and a nation of cowards then might now be valiant. Enough therefore of our ancient achievements. Had we performed no other exploit than that at Marathon —though in truth we have performed exploits as many and as noble as any of the Greeks— yet had we performed no other, we should deserve this privilege, and many a one beside. There we stood alone, and singly fought with the Persians; nay, and venturing on so dangerous a cast, we overcame the enemy, and conquered on that day forty and six nations!

Does not this one achievement suffice to make good our title to the post we claim? Nevertheless, Lacedæmonians, as to strive concerning place at such a time as this is not right, we are ready to do as ye command, and to take our station at whatever part of the line, and face whatever nation ye think most expedient. Wheresoever ye place us, 'twill be our endeavour to behave as brave men. Only declare your will, and we shall at once obey you."

28. Such was the reply of the Athenians; and forthwith all the Lacedæmonian troops cried out with one voice, that the Athenians were worthier to have the left wing than the Arcadians. In this way were the Tegeans overcome; and the post was assigned to the Athenians.

When this matter had been arranged, the Greek army, which was in part composed of those who came at the first, in part of such as had flocked in from day to day, drew up in the following order:—Ten thousand Lacedæmonian troops held the right wing, five thousand of whom were Spartans; and these five thousand were attended by a body of thirty-five thousand Helots, who were only lightly armed— seven Helots to each Spartan. The place next to themselves the Spartans gave to the Tegeans, on account of their courage and of the esteem in which they held them. They were all fully armed, and numbered fifteen hundred men. Next in order came the Corinthians, five thousand strong; and with them Pausanias had placed, at their request, the band of three hundred which had come from Potidæa in Pallêné. The Arcadians of Orchomenus, in number six hundred, came next; then the Sicyonians, three thousand; then the Epidaurians, eight hundred; then the Trœzenians, one thousand; then the Lepreats, two hundred; the Mycenæans and Tirynthians, four hundred; the Phliasians, one thousand; the Hermionians, three hundred; the Eretrians and Styreans, six hundred; the Chalcideans, four hundred; and the Ambraciots, five hundred. After these came the Leucadians and Anactorians, who numbered eight hundred; the Paleans of Cephallênia, two hundred; the Eginetans, five hundred; the Megarians, three thousand; and the Platæans, six hundred. Last of all, but first at their extremity of the line, were the Athenians, who, to the number of eight thousand, occupied the left wing, under the command of Aristides, the son of Lysimachus.

29. All these, except the Helots—seven of whom, as I said, attended each Spartan—were

heavy-armed troops; and they amounted to thirty-eight thousand seven hundred men. This was the number of Hoplites, or heavy-armed soldiers, which was brought together against the barbarian. The light-armed troops consisted of the thirty-five thousand ranged with the Spartans, seven in attendance upon each, who were all well equipped for war; and of thirty-four thousand five hundred others, belonging to the Lacedæmonians and the rest of the Greeks, at the rate (nearly) of one light to one heavy armed. Thus the entire number of the light-armed was sixty-nine thousand five hundred.

30. The Greek army, therefore, which mustered at Platæa, counting light-armed as well as heavy-armed, was but eighteen hundred men short of one hundred and ten thousand; and this amount was exactly made up by the Thespians who were present in the camp; for eighteen hundred Thespians, being the whole number left, were likewise with the army; but these men were without arms. Such was the array of the Greek troops when they took post on the Asôpus.

31. The barbarians under Mardonius, when the mourning for Masistius was at an end, and they learnt that the Greeks were in the Platæan territory, moved likewise towards the river Asôpus, which flows in those parts. On their arrival Mardonius marshalled them against the Greeks in the following order:—Against the Lacedæmonians he posted his Persians; and as the Persians were far more numerous he drew them up with their ranks deeper than common, and also extended their front so that part faced the Tegeans; and here he took care to choose out the best troops to face the Lacedæmonians, whilst against the Tegeans he arrayed those on whom he could not so much depend. This was done at the suggestion and by the advice of the Thebans. Next to the Persians he placed the Medes, facing the Corinthians, Potidæans, Orchomenians, and Sicyonians; then the Bactrians, facing the Epidaurians, Trœzenians, Lepreats, Tirynthians, Mycenæans, and Phliasians; after them the Indians, facing the Hermionians, Eretrians, Styreans, and Chalcidians; then the Sacans, facing the Ambraciots, Anactorians, Leucadians, Paleans, and Eginetans; last of all, facing the Athenians, the Platæans, and the Megarians, he placed the troops of the Bœotians, Locrians, Malians, and Thessalians, and also the thousand Phocians. The whole nation of the Phocians had not joined the Medes; on the con-trary, there were some who had gathered themselves into bands about Parnassus, and made expeditions from thence, whereby they distressed Mardonius and the Greeks who sided with him, and so did good service to the Grecian cause. Besides those mentioned above, Mardonius likewise arrayed against the Athenians the Macedonians and the tribes dwelling about Thessaly.

32. I have named here the greatest of the nations which were marshalled by Mardonius on this occasion, to wit, all those of most renown and account. Mixed with these, however, were men of divers other peoples, as Phrygians, Thracians, Mysians, Pæonians, and the like; Ethiopians again, and Egyptians, both of the Hermotybian and Calasirian races, whose weapon is the sword, and who are the only fighting men in that country. These persons had formerly served on board the fleet of Xerxes, but Mardonius disembarked them before he left Phalerum; in the land force which Xerxes brought to Athens there were no Egyptians. The number of the barbarians, as I have already mentioned, was three hundred thousand; that of the Greeks who had made alliance with Mardonius is known to none, for they were never counted: I should guess that they mustered near fifty thousand strong. The troops thus marshalled were all foot soldiers. As for the horse, it was drawn up by itself.

33. When the marshalling of Mardonius' troops by nations and by maniples was ended, the two armies proceeded on the next day to offer sacrifice. The Grecian sacrifice was offered by Tisamenus, the son of Antiochus, who accompanied the army as soothsayer: he was an Elean, and belonged to the Clytiad branch of the Iamidæ, but had been admitted among their own citizens by the Lacedæmonians. Now his admission among them was on this wise:—Tisamenus had gone to Delphi to consult the god concerning his lack of offspring, when it was declared to him by the Pythoness that he would win five very glorious combats. Misunderstanding the oracle, and imagining that he was to win combats in the games, Tisamenus at once applied himself to the practice of gymnastics. He trained himself for the Pentathlum, and, on contending at Olympia, came within a little of winning it; for he was successful in everything, except the wrestling-match, which was carried off by Hieronymus the Andrian. Hereon the Lacedæmonians perceived that the combats of which the oracle spoke were not combats in the games, but bat-

tles: they therefore sought to induce Tisamenus to hire out his services to them, in order that they might join him with their Heracleid kings in the conduct of their wars. He however, when he saw that they set great store by his friendship, forthwith raised his price, and told them, "If they would receive him among their citizens, and give him equal rights with the rest, he was willing to do as they desired, but on no other terms would they ever gain his consent." The Spartans, when they heard this, at first thought it monstrous, and ceased to implore his aid. Afterwards, however, when the fearful danger of the Persian war hung over their heads, they sent for him and agreed to his terms; but Tisamenus now, perceiving them so changed, declared, "He could no longer be content with what he had asked before: they must likewise make his brother Hagias a Spartan, with the same rights as himself."

34. In acting thus he did but follow the example once set by Melampus, at least if kingship may be compared with citizenship. For when the women of Argos were seized with madness, and the Argives would have hired Melampus to come from Pylos and heal them of their disease, he demanded as his reward one-half of the kingdom; but as the Argives disdained to stoop to this, they left him and went their way. Afterwards, however, when many more of their women were seized, they brought themselves to agree to his terms; and accordingly they went again to him, and said they were content to give what he required. Hereon Melampus, seeing them so changed, raised his demand, and told them, "Except they would give his brother Bias one-third of the kingdom likewise, he would not do as they wished." So, as the Argives were in a strait, they consented even to this.

35. In like manner the Spartans, as they were in great need of Tisamenus, yielded everything: and Tisamenus the Elean, having in this way become a Spartan citizen, afterwards, in the capacity of soothsayer, helped the Spartans to gain five very glorious combats. He and his brother were the only men whom the Spartans ever admitted to citizenship. The five combats were these following:—The first was the combat at Platæa; the second, that near Tegea, against the Tegeans and the Argives; the third, that at Dipæeis, against all the Arcadians excepting those of Mantinea; the fourth, that at the Isthmus, against the Messenians; and the fifth, that at Tanagra, against the Athenians and the Argives. The battle here fought was the last of all the five.

36. The Spartans had now brought Tisamenus with them to the Platæan territory, where he acted as soothsayer for the Greeks. He found the victims favourable, if the Greeks stood on the defensive, but not if they began the battle or crossed the river Asôpus.

37. With Mardonius also, who was very eager to begin the battle, the victims were not favourable for so doing; but he likewise found them bode him well, if he was content to stand on his defence. He too had made use of the Grecian rites; for Hêgêsistratus, an Elean, and the most renowned of the Telliads, was his soothsayer. This man had once been taken captive by the Spartans, who, considering that he had done them many grievous injuries, laid him in bonds, with the intent to put him to death. Thereupon Hêgêsistratus, finding himself in so sore a case, since not only was his life in danger, but he knew that he would have to suffer torments of many kinds before his death, —Hêgêsistratus, I say, did a deed for which no words suffice. He had been set with one foot in the stocks, which were of wood but bound with iron bands; and in this condition received from without an iron implement, wherewith he contrived to accomplish the most courageous deed upon record. Calculating how much of his foot he would be able to draw through the hole, he cut off the front portion with his own hand; and then, as he was guarded by watchmen, forced a way through the wall of his prison, and made his escape to Tegea, travelling during the night, but in the daytime stealing into the woods, and staying there. In this way, though the Lacedæmonians went out in full force to search for him, he nevertheless escaped, and arrived the third evening at Tegea. So the Spartans were amazed at the man's endurance, when they saw on the ground the piece which he had cut off his foot, and yet for all their seeking could not find him anywhere. Hêgêsistratus, having thus escaped the Lacedæmonians, took refuge in Tegea; for the Tegeans at that time were ill friends with the Lacedæmonians. When his wound was healed, he procured himself a wooden foot, and became an open enemy to Sparta. At the last, however, this enmity brought him to trouble; for the Spartans took him captive as he was exercising his office in Zacynthus, and forthwith put him to death. But these things happened some while after the fight at Platæa. At present he was serving Mardonius on the Asô-

pus, having been hired at no inconsiderable price; and here he offered sacrifice with a right good will, in part from his hatred of the Lacedæmonians, in part for lucre's sake.

38. So when the victims did not allow either the Persians or their Greek allies to begin the battle—these Greeks had their own soothsayer in the person of Hippomachus, a Leucadian—and when soldiers continued to pour into the opposite camp and the numbers on the Greek side to increase continually, Timagenidas, the son of Herpys, a Theban, advised Mardonius to keep a watch on the passes of Cithæron, telling him how supplies of men kept flocking in day after day, and assuring him that he might cut off large numbers.

39. It was eight days after the two armies first encamped opposite to one another when this advice was given by Timagenidas. Mardonius, seeing it to be good, as soon as evening came, sent his cavalry to that pass of Mount Cithæron which opens out upon Platæa, a pass called by the Bœotians the "Three Heads," but called the "Oak-Heads" by the Athenians. The horse sent on this errand did not make the movement in vain. They came upon a body of five hundred sumpter-beasts which were just entering the plain, bringing provisions to the Greek camp from the Peloponnese, with a number of men driving them. Seeing this prey in their power, the Persians set upon them and slaughtered them, sparing none, neither man nor beast; till at last, when they had had enough of slaying, they secured such as were left, and bore them off to the camp to Mardonius.

40. After this they waited again for two days more, neither army wishing to begin the fight. The barbarians indeed advanced as far as the Asôpus, and endeavoured to tempt the Greeks to cross; but neither side actually passed the stream. Still the cavalry of Mardonius harassed and annoyed the Greeks incessantly; for the Thebans, who were zealous in the cause of the Medes, pressed the war forward with all eagerness, and often led the charge till the lines met, when the Medes and Persians took their place, and displayed, many of them, uncommon valour.

41. For ten days nothing was done more than this; but on the eleventh day from the time when the two hosts first took station, one over against the other, near Platæa—the number of the Greeks being now much greater than it was at the first, and Mardonius being impatient of the delay—there was a conference held between Mardonius, son of Gobryas, and Artabazus, son of Pharnaces, a man who was esteemed by Xerxes more than almost any of the Persians. At this consultation the following were the opinions delivered:—Artabazus thought it would be best for them to break up from their quarters as soon as possible, and withdraw the whole army to the fortified town of Thebes, where they had abundant stores of corn for themselves, and of fodder for the sumpter-beasts. There, he said, they had only to sit quiet, and the war might be brought to an end on this wise:—Coined gold was plentiful in the camp, and uncoined gold too; they had silver moreover in great abundance, and drinking-cups. Let them not spare to take of these, and distribute them among the Greeks, especially among the leaders in the several cities; 'twould not be long before the Greeks gave up their liberty, without risking another battle for it. Thus the opinion of Artabazus agreed with that of the Thebans; for he too had more foresight than some. Mardonius, on the other hand, expressed himself with more fierceness and obstinacy, and was utterly disinclined to yield. "Their army," he said, "was vastly superior to that of the Greeks; and they had best engage at once, and not wait till greater numbers were gathered against them. As for Hêgêsistratus and his victims, they should let them pass unheeded, not seeking to force them to be favourable, but, according to the old Persian custom, hasting to join battle."

42. When Mardonius had thus declared his sentiments, no one ventured to say him nay; and accordingly his opinion prevailed, for it was to him, and not to Artabazus, that the king had given the command of the army.

Mardonius now sent for the captains of the squadrons, and the leaders of the Greeks in his service, and questioned them:—"Did they know of any prophecy which said that the Persians were to be destroyed in Greece?" All were silent; some because they did not know the prophecies, but others, who knew them full well, because they did not think it safe to speak out. So Mardonius, when none answered, said, "Since ye know of no such oracle, or do not dare to speak of it, I, who know it well, will myself declare it to you. There is an oracle which says that the Persians shall come into Greece, sack the temple at Delphi, and when they have so done, perish one and all. Now we, as we are aware of the prediction, will neither go against the temple nor make any attempt to sack it: we therefore shall not perish for this trespass. Rejoice then thus far, all ye who are well-wishers to the Persians, and doubt not we shall get the better of the Greeks." When he had so spoken, he further ordered them to prepare themselves, and to put all in readiness for a battle upon the morrow.

43. As for the oracle of which Mardonius spoke, and which he referred to the Persians, it did not, I am well assured, mean them, but the Illyrians and the Enchelean host. There are, however, some verses of Bacis which did speak of this battle:—

By Thermôdon's stream, and the grass-clad banks of Asôpus,
See where gather the Grecians, and hark to the foreigners' war-shout—
There in death shall lie, ere fate or Lachesis doomed him,
Many a bow-bearing Mede, when the day of calamity cometh.

These verses, and some others like them which Musæus wrote, referred, I well know, to the Persians. The river Thermôdon flows between Tanagra and Glisas.

44. After Mardonius had put his question about the prophecies, and spoken the above words of encouragement, night drew on apace, and on both sides the watches were set. As soon then as there was silence throughout the camp,—the night being now well advanced, and the men seeming to be in their deepest sleep,—Alexander, the son of Amyntas, king and leader of the Macedonians, rode up on horseback to the Athenian outposts, and desired to speak with the generals. Hereupon, while the greater part continued on guard, some of the watch ran to the chiefs, and told them, "There had come a horseman from the Median camp who would not say a word, except that he wished to speak with the generals, of whom he mentioned the names."

45. They at once, hearing this, made haste to the outpost, where they found Alexander, who addressed them as follows:—

"Men of Athens, that which I am about to say I trust to your honour; and I charge you to keep it secret from all excepting Pausanias, if you would not bring me to destruction. Had I not greatly at heart the common welfare of Greece, I should not have come to tell you; but I am myself a Greek by descent, and I would not willingly see Greece exchange freedom for slavery. Know then that Mardonius and his army cannot obtain favourable omens; had it not been for this, they would have fought with you long ago. Now, however, they

have determined to let the victims pass unheeded, and, as soon as day dawns, to engage in battle. Mardonius, I imagine, is afraid that, if he delays, you will increase in number. Make ready then to receive him. Should he however still defer the combat, do you abide where you are; for his provisions will not hold out many more days. If ye prosper in this war, forget not to do something for my freedom; consider the risk I have run, out of zeal for the Greek cause, to acquaint you with what Mardonius intends, and to save you from being surprised by the barbarians. I am Alexander of Macedon."

As soon as he had said this, Alexander rode back to the camp, and returned to the station assigned him.

46. Meanwhile the Athenian generals hastened to the right wing, and told Pausanias all that they had learnt from Alexander. Hereupon Pausanias, who no sooner heard the intention of the Persians than he was struck with fear, addressed the generals, and said,—

"Since the battle is to come with to-morrow's dawn, it were well that you Athenians should stand opposed to the Persians, and we Spartans to the Bœotians and the other Greeks; for ye know the Medes and their manner of fight, since ye have already fought with them once at Marathon, but we are quite ignorant and without any experience of their warfare. While, however, there is not a Spartan present who has ever fought against a Mede, of the Bœotians and Thessalians we have had experience. Take then your arms, and march over to our post upon the right, while we supply your place in the left wing."

Hereto the Athenians replied—"We, too, long ago, when we saw that the Persians were drawn up to face you, were minded to suggest to you the very course which you have now been the first to bring forward. We feared, however, that perhaps our words might not be pleasing to you. But, as you have now spoken of these things yourselves, we gladly give our consent, and are ready to do as ye have said."

47. Both sides agreeing hereto, at the dawn of day the Spartans and Athenians changed places. But the movement was perceived by the Bœotians, and they gave notice of it to Mardonius; who at once, on hearing what had been done, made a change in the disposition of his own forces, and brought the Persians to face the Lacedæmonians. Then Pausanias, finding that his design was discovered, led back his Spartans to the right wing; and Mardonius,

seeing this, replaced his Persians upon the left of his army.

48. When the troops again occupied their former posts, Mardonius sent a herald to the Spartans, who spoke as follows:—

"Lacedæmonians, in these parts the men say that you are the bravest of mankind, and admire you because you never turn your backs in flight nor quit your ranks, but always stand firm, and either die at your posts or else destroy your adversaries. But in all this which they say concerning you there is not one word of truth; for now have we seen you, before battle was joined or our two hosts had come to blows, flying and leaving your posts, wishing the Athenians to make the first trial of our arms, and taking your own station against our slaves. Surely these are not the deeds of brave men. Much do we find ourselves deceived in you; for we believed the reports of you that reached our ears, and expected that you would send a herald with a challenge to us, proposing to fight by yourselves against our division of native Persians. We for our part were ready to have agreed to this; but ye have made us no such offer—nay! ye seem rather to shrink from meeting us. However, as no challenge of this kind comes from you to us, lo! we send a challenge to you. Why should not you on the part of the Greeks, as you are thought to be the bravest of all, and we on the part of the barbarians, fight a battle with equal numbers on both sides? Then, if it seems good to the others to fight likewise, let them engage afterwards—but if not,—if they are content that we should fight on behalf of all, let us so do—and whichever side wins the battle, let them win it for their whole army."

49. When the herald had thus spoken, he waited a while, but, as no one made him any answer, he went back, and told Mardonius what had happened. Mardonius was full of joy thereat, and so puffed up by the empty victory, that he at once gave orders to his horse to charge the Greek line. Then the horsemen drew near, and with their javelins and their arrows—for though horsemen they used the bow —sorely distressed the Greek troops, which could not bring them to close combat. The fountain of Gargaphia, whence the whole Greek army drew its water, they at this time choked up and spoiled. The Lacedæmonians were the only troops who had their station near this fountain; the other Greeks were more or less distant from it, according to their place in the line; they however were not far from the

Asôpus. Still, as the Persian horse with their missile weapons did not allow them to approach, and so they could not get their water from the river, these Greeks, no less than the Lacedæmonians, resorted at this time to the fountain.

50. When the fountain was choked, the Grecian captains, seeing that the army had no longer a water-place, and observing moreover that the cavalry greatly harassed them, held a meeting on these and other matters at the headquarters of Pausanias upon the right. For besides the above-named difficulties, which were great enough, other circumstances added to their distress. All the provisions that they had brought with them were gone; and the attendants who had been sent to fetch supplies from the Peloponnese, were prevented from returning to camp by the Persian horse, which had now closed the passage.

51. The captains therefore held a council, whereat it was agreed, that if the Persians did not give battle that day, the Greeks should move to the Island—a tract of ground which lies in front of Platæa, at the distance of ten furlongs from the Asôpus and fount Gargaphia, where the army was encamped at that time. This tract was a sort of island in the continent: for there is a river which, dividing near its source, runs down from Mount Cithæron into the plain below in two streams, flowing in channels about three furlongs apart, which after a while unite and become one. The name of this river is Oëroë, and the dwellers in those parts call it, the daughter of the Asôpus. This was the place to which the Greeks resolved to remove; and they chose it, first because they would there have no lack of water, and secondly, because the horse could not harass them as when it was drawn up right in their front. They thought it best to begin their march at the second watch of the night, lest the Persians should see them as they left their station, and should follow and harass them with their cavalry. It was agreed likewise, that after they had reached the place, which the Asôpus-born Oëroë surrounds, as it flows down from Cithæron, they should despatch, the very same night, one half of their army towards that mountain-range, to relieve those whom they had sent to procure provisions, and who were now blocked up in that region.

52. Having made these resolves, they continued during that whole day to suffer beyond measure from the attacks of the enemy's

horse. At length when towards dusk the attacks of the horse ceased, and, night having closed in, the hour arrived at which the army was to commence its retreat, the greater number struck their tents and began the march towards the rear. They were not minded, however, to make for the place agreed upon; but in their anxiety to escape from the Persian horse, no sooner had they begun to move than they fled straight to Platæa; where they took post at the temple of Juno, which lies outside the city, at the distance of about twenty furlongs from Gargaphia; and here they pitched their camp in front of the sacred building.

53. As soon as Pausanias saw a portion of the troops in motion, he issued orders to the Lacedæmonians to strike their tents and follow those who had been the first to depart, supposing that they were on their march to the place agreed upon. All the captains but one were ready to obey his orders: Amompharetus, however, the son of Poliadas, who was leader of the Pitanate cohort, refused to move, saying, "He for one would not fly from the strangers, or of his own will bring disgrace upon Sparta." It had happened that he was absent from the former conference of the captains; and so what was now taking place astonished him. Pausanias and Euryanax thought it a monstrous thing that Amompharetus would not hearken to them; but considered that it would be yet more monstrous, if, when he was so minded, they were to leave the Pitanates to their fate; seeing that, if they forsook them to keep their agreement with the other Greeks, Amompharetus and those with him might perish. On this account, therefore, they kept the Lacedæmonian force in its place, and made every endeavour to persuade Amompharetus that he was wrong to act as he was doing.

54. While the Spartans were engaged in these efforts to turn Amompharetus—the only man unwilling to retreat either in their own army or in that of the Tegeans—the Athenians on their side did as follows. Knowing that it was the Spartan temper to say one thing and do another, they remained quiet in their station until the army began to retreat, when they despatched a horseman to see whether the Spartans really meant to set forth, or whether after all they had no intention of moving. The horseman was also to ask Pausanias what he wished the Athenians to do.

55. The herald on his arrival found the Lacedæmonians drawn up in their old position, and their leaders quarrelling with one another. Pausanias and Euryanax had gone on urging Amompharetus not to endanger the lives of his men by staying behind while the others drew off, but without succeeding in persuading him; until at last the dispute had waxed hot between them just at the moment when the Athenian herald arrived. At this point Amompharetus, who was still disputing, took up with both his hands a vast rock, and placed it at the feet of Pausanias, saying— "With this pebble I give my vote not to run away from the strangers." (By "strangers" he meant barbarians.) Pausanias, in reply, called him a fool and a madman, and, turning to the Athenian herald, who had made the inquiries with which he was charged, bade him tell his countrymen how he was occupied, and ask them to approach nearer, and retreat or not according to the movements of the Spartans.

56. So the herald went back to the Athenians; and the Spartans continued to dispute till morning began to dawn upon them. Then Pausanias, who as yet had not moved, gave the signal for retreat—expecting (and rightly, as the event proved) that Amompharetus, when he saw the rest of the Lacedæmonians in motion, would be unwilling to be left behind. No sooner was the signal given, than all the army except the Pitanates began their march, and retreated along the line of the hills; the Tegeans accompanying them. The Athenians likewise set off in good order, but proceeded by a different way from the Lacedæmonians. For while the latter clung to the hilly ground and the skirts of Mount Cithæron, on account of the fear which they entertained of the enemy's horse, the former betook themselves to the low country and marched through the plain.

57. As for Amompharetus, at first he did not believe that Pausanias would really dare to leave him behind; he therefore remained firm in his resolve to keep his men at their post; when, however, Pausanias and his troops were now some way off, Amompharetus, thinking himself forsaken in good earnest, ordered his band to take their arms, and led them at a walk towards the main army. Now the army was waiting for them at a distance of about ten furlongs, having halted upon the river Moloeis at a place called Argiopius, where stands a temple dedicated to Eleusinian Ceres. They had stopped here, that, in case Amompharetus and his band should refuse to quit the spot where they were drawn up, and should really not stir from it, they might have it in their power to move back and lend them

assistance. Amompharetus, however, and his companions rejoined the main body; and at the same time the whole mass of the barbarian cavalry arrived and began to press hard upon them. The horsemen had followed their usual practice and ridden up to the Greek camp, when they discovered that the place where the Greeks had been posted hitherto was deserted. Hereupon they pushed forward without stopping, and, as soon as they overtook the enemy, pressed heavily on them.

58. Mardonius, when he heard that the Greeks had retired under cover of the night, and beheld the place, where they had been stationed, empty, called to him Thorax of Larissa, and his brethren, Eurypylus and Thrasideius, and said:—

"O sons of Aleuas! what will ye say now, when ye see yonder place empty? Why, you, who dwell in their neighbourhood, told me the Lacedæmonians never fled from battle, but were brave beyond all the rest of mankind. Lately, however, you yourselves beheld them change their place in the line; and here, as all may see, they have run away during the night. Verily, when their turn came to fight with those who are of a truth the bravest warriors in all the world, they showed plainly enough that they are men of no worth, who have distinguished themselves among *Greeks*—men likewise of no worth at all. However, I can readily excuse you, who, knowing nothing of the Persians, praised these men from your acquaintance with certain exploits of theirs; but I marvel all the more at Artabazus, that *he* should have been afraid of the Lacedæmonians, and have therefore given us so dastardly a counsel,—bidding us, as he did, break up our camp, and remove to Thebes, and there allow ourselves to be besieged by the Greeks—advice whereof I shall take care to inform the king. But of this hereafter. Now we must not allow them to escape us, but must pursue after them till we overtake them; and then we must exact vengeance for all the wrongs which have been suffered at their hands by the Persians."

59. When he had so spoken, he crossed the Asôpus, and led the Persians forward at a run directly upon the track of the Greeks, whom he believed to be in actual flight. He could not see the Athenians; for, as they had taken the way of the plain, they were hidden from his sight by the hills; he therefore led on his troops against the Lacedæmonians and the Tegeans only. When the commanders of the other divisions of the barbarians saw the Persians pursuing the Greeks so hastily, they all forthwith seized their standards, and hurried after at their best speed in great disorder and disarray. On they went with loud shouts and in a wild rout, thinking to swallow up the runaways.

60. Meanwhile Pausanias had sent a horseman to the Athenians, at the time when the cavalry first fell upon him, with this message:—

"Men of Athens! now that the great struggle has come, which is to decide the freedom or the slavery of Greece, we twain, Lacedæmonians and Athenians, are deserted by all the other allies, who have fled away from us during the past night. Nevertheless, we are resolved what to do—we must endeavour, as best we may, to defend ourselves and to succour one another. Now, had the horse fallen upon you first, we ourselves with the Tegeans (who remain faithful to the Greek cause) would have been bound to render you assistance against them. As, however, the entire body has advanced upon us, 'tis your place to come to our aid, sore pressed as we are by the enemy. Should you yourselves be so straitened that you cannot come, at least send us your archers, and be sure you will earn our gratitude. We acknowledge that throughout this whole war there has been no zeal to be compared to yours—we therefore doubt not that you will do us this service."

61. The Athenians, as soon as they received this message, were anxious to go to the aid of the Spartans, and to help them to the uttermost of their power; but, as they were upon the march, the Greeks on the king's side, whose place in the line had been opposite theirs, fell upon them, and so harassed them by their attacks that it was not possible for them to give the succour they desired. Accordingly the Lacedæmonians, and the Tegeans—whom nothing could induce to quit their side—were left alone to resist the Persians. Including the light-armed, the number of the former was 50,000; while that of the Tegeans was 3000. Now, therefore, as they were about to engage with Mardonius and the troops under him, they made ready to offer sacrifice. The victims, however, for some time were not favourable; and, during the delay, many fell on the Spartan side, and a still greater number were wounded. For the Persians had made a rampart of their wicker shields, and shot from behind them such clouds of arrows, that the Spartans were sorely distressed. The victims continued unpropitious; till at last Pausanias

raised his eyes to the Heræum of the Platæans, and calling the goddess to his aid, besought her not to disappoint the hopes of the Greeks.

62. As he offered his prayer, the Tegeans, advancing before the rest, rushed forward against the enemy; and the Lacedæmonians, who had obtained favourable omens the moment that Pausanias prayed, at length, after their long delay, advanced to the attack; while the Persians, on their side, left shooting, and prepared to meet them. And first the combat was at the wicker shields. Afterwards, when these were swept down, a fierce contest took place by the side of the temple of Ceres, which lasted long, and ended in a hand-to-hand struggle. The barbarians many times seized hold of the Greek spears and brake them; for in boldness and warlike spirit the Persians were not a whit inferior to the Greeks; but they were without bucklers, untrained, and far below the enemy in respect of skill in arms. Sometimes singly, sometimes in bodies of ten, now fewer and now more in number, they dashed upon the Spartan ranks, and so perished.

63. The fight went most against the Greeks, where Mardonius, mounted upon a white horse, and surrounded by the bravest of all the Persians, the thousand picked men, fought in person. So long as Mardonius was alive, this body resisted all attacks, and, while they defended their own lives, struck down no small number of Spartans; but after Mardonius fell, and the troops with him, which were the main strength of the army, perished, the remainder yielded to the Lacedæmonians, and took to flight. Their light clothing, and want of bucklers, were of the greatest hurt to them: for they had to contend against men heavily armed, while they themselves were without any such defence.

64. Then was the warning of the oracle fulfilled; and the vengeance which was due to the Spartans for the slaughter of Leonidas was paid them by Mardonius—then too did Pausanias, the son of Cleombrotus, and grandson of Anaxandridas (I omit to recount his other ancestors, since they are the same with those of Leonidas), win a victory exceeding in glory all those to which our knowledge extends. Mardonius was slain by Aeimnêstus, a man famous in Sparta—the same who in the Messenian war, which came after the struggle against the Medes, fought a battle near Stenyclêrus with but three hundred men against the whole force of the Messenians, and himself

perished, and the three hundred with him.

65. The Persians, as soon as they were put to flight by the Lacedæmonians, ran hastily away, without preserving any order, and took refuge in their own camp, within the wooden defence which they had raised in the Theban territory. It is a marvel to me how it came to pass, that although the battle was fought quite close to the grove of Ceres, yet not a single Persian appears to have died on the sacred soil, nor even to have set foot upon it, while round about the precinct, in the unconsecrated ground, great numbers perished. I imagine—if it is lawful, in matters which concern the gods, to imagine anything—that the goddess herself kept them out, because they had burnt her dwelling at Eleusis. Such, then, was the issue of this battle.

66. Artabazus, the son of Pharnaces, who had disapproved from the first of the king's leaving Mardonius behind him, and had made great endeavours, but all in vain, to dissuade Mardonius from risking a battle, when he found that the latter was bent on acting otherwise than he wished, did as follows. He had a force under his orders which was far from inconsiderable, amounting, as it did, to near forty thousand men. Being well aware, therefore, how the battle was likely to go, as soon as the two armies began to fight, he led his soldiers forward in an orderly array, bidding them one and all proceed at the same pace, and follow him with such celerity as they should observe him to use. Having issued these commands, he pretended to lead them to the battle. But when, advancing before his army, he saw that the Persians were already in flight, instead of keeping the same order, he wheeled his troops suddenly round, and beat a retreat; nor did he even seek shelter within the palisade or behind the walls of Thebes, but hurried on into Phocis, wishing to make his way to the Hellespont with all possible speed. Such accordingly was the course which these Persians took.

67. As for the Greeks upon the king's side, while most of them played the coward purposely, the Bœotians, on the contrary, had a long struggle with the Athenians. Those of the Thebans who were attached to the Medes, displayed especially no little zeal; far from playing the coward, they fought with such fury that three hundred of the best and bravest among them were slain by the Athenians in this passage of arms. But at last they too were routed, and fled away—not, however, in the same direction as the Persians and the crowd

of allies, who, having taken no part in the battle, ran off without striking a blow—but to the city of Thebes.

68. To me it shows very clearly how completely the rest of the barbarians were dependent upon the Persian troops, that here they all fled at once, without ever coming to blows with the enemy, merely because they saw the Persians running away. And so it came to pass that the whole army took to flight, except only the horse, both Persian and Bœotian. These did good service to the flying foot-men, by advancing close to the enemy, and separating between the Greeks and their own fugitives.

69. The victors however pressed on, pursuing and slaying the remnant of the king's army.

Meantime, while the flight continued, tidings reached the Greeks who were drawn up round the Heræum, and so were absent from the battle, that the fight was begun, and that Pausanias was gaining the victory. Hearing this, they rushed forward without any order, the Corinthians taking the upper road across the skirts of Cithæron and the hills, which led straight to the temple of Ceres; while the Megarians and Phliasians followed the level route through the plain. These last had almost reached the enemy, when the Theban horse espied them, and, observing their disarray, despatched against them the squadron of which Asôpodôrus, the son of Timander, was captain. Asôpodôrus charged them with such effect that the left six hundred of their number dead upon the plain, and, pursuing the rest, compelled them to seek shelter in Cithæron. So these men perished without honour.

70. The Persians, and the multitude with them, who fled to the wooden fortress, were able to ascend into the towers before the Lacedæmonians came up. Thus placed, they proceeded to strengthen the defences as well as they could; and when the Lacedæmonians arrived, a sharp fight took place at the rampart. So long as the Athenians were away, the barbarians kept off their assailants, and had much the best of the combat, since the Lacedæmonians were unskilled in the attack of walled places: but on the arrival of the Athenians, a more violent assault was made, and the wall was for a long time attacked with fury. In the end the valour of the Athenians and their perseverance prevailed—they gained the top of the wall, and, breaking a breach through it, enabled the Greeks to pour in. The first to enter here were the Tegeans, and they it was who

plundered the tent of Mardonius; where among other booty the found the manger from which his horses ate, all made of solid brass, and well worth looking at. This manger was given by the Tegeans to the temple of Minerva Alea, while the remainder of their booty was brought into the common stock of the Greeks. As soon as the wall was broken down, the barbarians no longer kept together in any array, nor was there one among them who thought of making further resistance—in good truth, they were all half dead with fright, huddled as so many thousands were into so narrow and confined a space. With such tameness did they submit to be slaughtered by the Greeks, that of the 300,000 men who composed the army—omitting the 40,000 by whom Artabazus was accompanied in his flight—no more than 3000 outlived the battle. Of the Lacedæmonians from Sparta there perished in this combat ninety-one; of the Tegeans, sixteen; of the Athenians, fifty-two.

71. On the side of the barbarians, the greatest courage was manifested, among the foot-soldiers, by the Persians; among the horse, by the Sacæ; while Mardonius himself, as a man, bore off the palm from the rest. Among the Greeks, the Athenians and the Tegeans fought well; but the prowess shown by the Lacedæmonians was beyond either. Of this I have but one proof to offer—since all the three nations overthrew the force opposed to them—and that is, that the Lacedæmonians fought and conquered the best troops. The bravest man by far on that day was, in my judgment, Aristodêmus—the same who alone escaped from the slaughter of the three hundred at Thermopylæ, and who on that account had endured disgrace and reproach: next to him were Posidônius, Philocyon, and Amompharetus the Spartan. The Spartans, however, who took part in the fight, when the question of "who had distinguished himself most," came to be talked over among them, decided—"that Aristodêmus, who, on account of the blame which attached to him, had manifestly courted death, and had therefore left his place in the line and behaved like a madman, had done of a truth very notable deeds; but that Posidônius, who, with no such desire to lose his life, had quitted himself no less gallantly, was by so much a braver man than he." Perchance, however, it was envy that made them speak after this sort. Of those whom I have named above as slain in this battle, all, save and except Aristodêmus, received public honours: Aristodêmus alone

had no honours, because he courted death for the reason which I have mentioned.

72. These then were the most distinguished of those who fought at Platæa. As for Callicrates,—the most beautiful man, not among the Spartans only, but in the whole Greek camp,—he was not killed in the battle; for it was while Pausanias was still consulting the victims, that as he sat in his proper place in the line, an arrow struck him on the side. While his comrades advanced to the fight, he was borne out of the ranks, very loath to die, as he showed by the words which he addressed to Arimnestus, one of the Platæans;—"I grieve," said he, "not because I have to die for my country, but because I have not lifted my arm against the enemy, nor done any deed worthy of me, much as I have desired to achieve something."

73. The Athenian who is said to have distinguished himself the most was Sôphanes, the son of Eutychides, of the Deceleian canton. The men of this canton, once upon a time, did a deed, which (as the Athenians themselves confess) has ever since been serviceable to them. When the Tyndaridæ, in days of yore, invaded Attica with a mighty army to recover Helen, and, not being able to find out whither she had been carried, desolated the cantons,— at this time, they say, the Deceleians (or Decelus himself, according to some), displeased at the rudeness of Theseus, and fearing that the whole territory would suffer, discovered everything to the enemy, and even showed them the way to Aphidnæ, which Titacus, a native of the place, betrayed into their hands. As a reward for this action, Sparta has always, from that time to the present, allowed the Deceleians to be free from all dues, and to have seats of honour at their festivals; and hence too, in the war which took place many years after these events between the Peloponnesians and the Athenians, the Lacedæmonians, while they laid waste all the rest of Attica, spared the lands of the Deceleians.

74. Of this canton was Sôphanes, the Athenian, who most distinguished himself in the battle. Two stories are told concerning him: according to the one, he wore an iron anchor, fastened to the belt which secured his breastplate by a brazen chain; and this, when he came near the enemy, he threw out; to the intent that, when they made their charge, it might be impossible for him to be driven from his post: as soon, however, as the enemy fled, his wont was to take up his anchor and join the pursuit. Such, then, is one of the said stories. The other, which is contradictory to the first, relates that Sôphanes, instead of having an iron anchor fastened to his breastplate, bore the device of an anchor upon his shield, which he never allowed to rest, but made to run round continually.

75. Another glorious deed was likewise performed by this same Sôphanes. At the time when the Athenians were laying siege to Egina, he took up the challenge of Eurybates the Argive, a winner of the Pentathlum, and slew him. The fate of Sôphanes in after times was the following: he was leader of an Athenian army in conjunction with Leagrus, the son of Glaucon, and in a battle with the Edonians near Datum, about the gold-mines there, he was slain, after displaying uncommon bravery.

76. As soon as the Greeks at Platæa had overthrown the barbarians, a woman came over to them from the enemy. She was one of the concubines of Pharandates, the son of Teäspes, a Persian; and when she heard that the Persians were all slain and that the Greeks had carried the day, forthwith she adorned herself and her maids with many golden ornaments, and with the bravest of the apparel that she had brought with her, and, alighting from her litter, came forward to the Lacedæmonians, ere the work of slaughter was well over. When she saw that all the orders were given by Pausanias, with whose name and country she was well acquainted, as she had oftentimes heard tell of them, she knew who he must be; wherefore she embraced his knees, and said—

"O king of Sparta! save thy suppliant from the slavery that awaits the captive. Already I am beholden to thee for one service—the slaughter of these men, wretches who had no regard either for gods or angels. I am by birth a Coan, the daughter of Hêgêtoridas, son of Antagoras. The Persian seized me by force in Cos, and kept me against my will."

"Lady," answered Pausanias, "fear nothing: as a suppliant thou art safe—and still more, if thou hast spoken truth, and Hêgêtoridas of Cos is thy father—for he is bound to me by closer ties of friendship than any other man in those regions."

When he had thus spoken, Pausanias placed the woman in the charge of some of the Ephors who were present, and afterwards sent her to Egina, whither she had a desire to go.

77. About the time of this woman's coming, the Mantineans arrived upon the field, and found that all was over, and that it was too late

to take any part in the battle. Greatly distressed hereat, they declared themselves to deserve a fine, as laggarts; after which, learning that a portion of the Medes had fled away under Artabazus, they were anxious to go after them as far as Thessaly. The Lacedæmonians however would not suffer the pursuit; so they returned again to their own land, and sent the leaders of their army into banishment. Soon after the Mantineans, the Eleans likewise arrived, and showed the same sorrow; after which they too returned home, and banished their leaders. But enough concerning these nations.

78. There was a man at Platæa among the troops of the Eginetans, whose name was Lampon; he was the son of Pytheas, and a person of the first rank among his countrymen. Now this Lampon went about this same time to Pausanias, and counselled him to do a deed of exceeding wickedness. "Son of Cleombrotus," he said very earnestly, "what thou hast already done is passing great and glorious. By the favour of Heaven thou hast saved Greece, and gained a renown beyond all the Greeks of whom we have any knowledge. Now then so finish thy work, that thine own fame may be increased thereby, and that henceforth barbarians may fear to commit outrages on the Grecians. When Leonidas was slain at Thermopylæ, Xerxes and Mardonius commanded that he should be beheaded and crucified. Do thou the like at this time by Mardonius, and thou wilt have glory in Sparta, and likewise through the whole of Greece. For, by hanging him upon a cross, thou wilt avenge Leonidas, who was thy father's brother."

79. Thus spake Lampon, thinking to please Pausanias; but Pausanias answered him—"My Eginetan friend, for thy foresight and thy friendliness I am much beholden to thee: but the counsel which thou hast offered is not good. First hast thou lifted me up to the skies, by thy praise of my country and my achievement; and then thou hast cast me down to the ground, by bidding me maltreat the dead, and saying that thus I shall raise myself in men's esteem. Such doings befit barbarians rather than Greeks; and even in barbarians we detest them. On such terms then I could not wish to please the Eginetans, nor those who think as they think— enough for me to gain the approval of my own countrymen, by righteous deeds as well as by righteous words. Leonidas, whom thou wouldst have me avenge, is, I maintain, abundantly avenged already. Surely the countless

lives here taken are enough to avenge not him only, but all those who fell at Thermopylæ. Come not thou before me again with such a speech, nor with such counsel; and thank my forbearance that thou art not now punished." Then Lampon, having received this answer, departed, and went his way.

80. After this Pausanias caused proclamation to be made, that no one should lay hands on the booty, but that the Helots should collect it and bring it all to one place. So the Helots went and spread themselves through the camp, wherein were found many tents richly adorned with furniture of gold and silver, many couches covered with plates of the same, and many golden bowls, goblets, and other drinking-vessels. On the carriages were bags containing silver and golden kettles; and the bodies of the slain furnished bracelets and chains, and scymitars with golden ornaments—not to mention embroidered apparel, of which no one made any account. The Helots at this time stole many things of much value, which they sold in after times to the Eginetans; however, they brought in likewise no small quantity, chiefly such things as it was not possible for them to hide. And this was the beginning of the great wealth of the Eginetans, who bought the gold of the Helots as if it had been mere brass.

81. When all the booty had been brought together, a tenth of the whole was set apart for the Delphian god; and hence was made the golden tripod which stands on the bronze serpent with the three heads, quite close to the altar. Portions were also set apart for the gods of Olympia, and of the Isthmus; from which were made, in the one case, a bronze Jupiter ten cubits high; and in the other, a bronze Neptune of seven cubits. After this, the rest of the spoil was divided among the soldiers, each of whom received less or more according to his deserts; and in this way was a distribution made of the Persian concubines, of the gold, the silver, the beasts of burthen, and all the other valuables. What special gifts were presented to those who had most distinguished themselves in the battle, I do not find mentioned by any one; but I should suppose that they must have had some gifts beyond the others. As for Pausanias, the portion which was set apart for him consisted of ten specimens of each kind of thing—women, horses, talents, camels, or whatever else there was in the spoil.

82. It is said that the following circumstance happened likewise at this time. Xerxes, when

he fled away out of Greece, left his war-tent with Mardonius: when Pausanias, therefore, saw the tent with its adornments of gold and silver, and its hangings of divers colours, he gave commandment to the bakers and the cooks to make him ready a banquet in such fashion as was their wont for Mardonius. Then they made ready as they were bidden; and Pausanius, beholding the couches of gold and silver daintily decked out with their rich covertures, and the tables of gold and silver laid, and the feast itself prepared with all magnificence, was astonished at the good things which were set before him, and, being in a pleasant mood, gave commandment to his own followers to make ready a Spartan supper. When the suppers were both served, and it was apparent how vast a difference lay between the two, Pausanias laughed, and sent his servants to call to him the Greek generals. On their coming, he pointed to the two boards, and said:—

"I sent for you, O Greeks, to show you the folly of this Median captain, who, when he enjoyed such fare as this, must needs come here to rob us of our penury."

Such, it is said, were the words of Pausanias to the Grecian generals.

83. During many years afterwards, the Platæans used often to find upon the field of battle concealed treasures of gold, and silver, and other valuables. More recently they likewise made discovery of the following: the flesh having all fallen away from the bodies of the dead, and their bones having been gathered together into one place, the Platæans found a skull without any seam, made entirely of a single bone; likewise a jaw, both the upper bone and the under, wherein all the teeth, front and back, were joined together and made of one bone; also, the skeleton of a man not less than five cubits in height.

84. The body of Mardonius disappeared the day after the battle; but who it was that stole it away I cannot say with certainty. I have heard tell of a number of persons, and those too of many different nations, who are said to have given him burial; and I know that many have received large sums on this score from Artontes the son of Mardonius: but I cannot discover with any certainty which of them it was who really took the body away, and buried it. Among others, Dionysophanes, an Ephesian, is rumoured to have been the actual person.

85. The Greeks, after sharing the booty upon the field of Platæa, proceeded to bury their own dead, each nation apart from the rest. The Lacedæmonians made three graves; in one they buried their youths, among whom were Posidônius, Amompharetus, Philocyon, and Callicrates;—in another, the rest of the Spartans; and in the third, the Helots. Such was their mode of burial. The Tegeans buried all their dead in a single grave; as likewise did the Athenians theirs, and the Megarians and Phliasians those who were slain by the horse. These graves, then, had bodies buried in them: as for the other tombs which are to be seen at Platæa, they were raised, as I understand, by the Greeks whose troops took no part in the battle; and who, being ashamed of themselves, erected empty barrows upon the field, to obtain credit with those who should come after them. Among others, the Eginetans have a grave there, which goes by their name; but which, as I learn, was made ten years later by Cleades, the son of Autodicus, a Platæan, at the request of the Eginetans, whose agent he was.

86. After the Greeks had buried their dead at Platæa, they presently held a council, whereat it was resolved to make war upon Thebes, and to require that those who had joined the Medes should be delivered into their hands. Two men, who had been the chief leaders on the occasion, were especially named—to wit, Timagenidas and Attagînus. If the Thebans should refuse to give these men up, it was determined to lay siege to their city, and never stir from before it till it should surrender. After this resolve, the army marched upon Thebes; and having demanded the men, and been refused, began the siege, laying waste the country all around, and making assaults upon the wall in divers places.

87. When twenty days were gone by, and the violence of the Greeks did not slacken, Timagenidas thus bespake his countrymen—

"Ye men of Thebes, since the Greeks have so decreed, that they will never desist from the siege till either they take Thebes or we are delivered to them, we would not that the land of Bœotia should suffer any longer on our behalf. If it be money that they in truth desire, and their demand of us be no more than a pretext, let money from the treasury of the state be given them; for the state, and not we alone, embraced the cause of the Medes. If, however, they really want our persons, and on that account press this siege, we are ready to be delivered to them and to stand our trial."

The Thebans thought this offer very right and seasonable; wherefore, they despatched a herald without any delay to Pausanias, and told him they were willing to deliver up the men.

88. As soon as an agreement had been concluded upon these terms, Attagînus made his escape from the city; his sons, however, were surrendered in his place; but Pausanias refused to hold them guilty, since children (he said) could have had no part in such an offence. The rest of those whom the Thebans gave up had expected to obtain a trial, and in that case their trust was to escape by means of bribery; but Pausanias, afraid of this, dismissed at once the whole army of allies, and took the men with him to Corinth, where he slew them all. Such were the events which happened at Platæa and at Thebes.

89. Artabazus, the son of Pharnaces, who fled away from Platæa, was soon far sped on his journey. When he reached Thessaly, the inhabitants received him hospitably, and made inquiries of him concerning the rest of the army, since they were still altogether ignorant of what had taken place at Platæa: whereupon the Persian, knowing well that, if he told them the truth, he would run great risk of perishing himself, together with his whole army—for if the facts were once blazoned abroad, all who learnt them would be sure to fall upon him— the Persian, I say, considering this, as he had before kept all secret from the Phocians, so now answered the Thessalians after the following fashion:—

"I myself, Thessalians, am hastening, as ye see, into Thrace; and I am fain to use all possible despatch, as I am sent with this force on special business from the main army. Mardonius and his host are close behind me, and may be looked for shortly. When he comes, receive him as ye have received me, and show him every kindness. Be sure ye will never hereafter regret it, if ye so do."

With these words he took his departure, and marched his troops at their best speed through Thessaly and Macedon straight upon Thrace, following the inland route, which was the shortest, and, in good truth, using all possible despatch. He himself succeeded in reaching Byzantium; but a great part of his army perished upon the road—many being cut to pieces by the Thracians, and others dying from hunger and excess of toil. From Byzantium Artabazus set sail, and crossed the strait; returning into Asia in the manner which has been here described.

90. On the same day that the blow was struck at Platæa, another defeat befell the Persians at Mycalé in Ionia. While the Greek fleet under Leotychides the Lacedæmonian was still lying inactive at Delos, there arrived at that place an embassy from Samos, consisting of three men, Lampon the son of Thrascycles, Athenagoras the son of Archestratidas, and Hêgêsistratus the son of Aristagoras. The Samians had sent them secretly, concealing their departure both from the Persians and from their own tyrant Theomestor, the son of Androdamas, whom the Persians had made ruler of Samos. When the ambassadors came before the Greek captains Hêgêsistratus took the word, and urged them with many and various arguments, saying, "that the Ionians only needed to see them arrive in order to revolt from the Persians; and that the Persians would never abide their coming; or if they did, 'twould be to offer them the finest booty that they could anywhere expect to gain;" while at the same time he made appeal to the gods of their common worship, and besought them to deliver from bondage a Grecian race, and withal to drive back the barbarians. "This," he said, "might very easily be done, for the Persian ships were bad sailers, and far from a match for theirs;" adding, moreover, "that if there was any suspicion lest the Samians intended to deal treacherously, they were themselves ready to become hostages, and to return on board the ships of their allies to Asia."

91. When the Samian stranger continued importunately beseeching him, Leotychides, either because he wanted an omen, or by a mere chance, as God guided him, asked the man—"Samian stranger! prithee, tell me thy name?" "Hêgêsistratus (army-leader)," answered the other, and might have said more, but Leotychides stopped him by exclaiming— "I accept, O Samian! the omen which thy name affords. Only, before thou goest back, swear to us, thyself and thy brother-envoys, that the Samians will indeed be our warm friends and allies."

92. No sooner had he thus spoken than he proceeded to hurry forward the business. The Samians pledged their faith upon the spot; and oaths of alliance were exchanged between them and the Greeks. This done, two of the ambassadors forthwith sailed away; as for Hêgêsistratus, Leotychides kept him to accompany his own fleet, for he considered his name to be a good omen. The Greeks abode where they were that day, and on the morrow sacrificed, and found the victims favourable. Their soothsayer was Deïphonus, the son of Evênius,

a man of Apollonia—I mean the Apollonia which lies upon the Ionian Gulf.

93. A strange thing happened to this man's father, Evênius. The Apolloniats have a flock of sheep sacred to the sun. During the day-time these sheep graze along the banks of the river which flows from Mount Lacmon through their territory and empties itself into the sea by the port of Oricus; while at night they are guarded by the richest and noblest of the citizens, who are chosen to serve the office, and who keep the watch each for one year. Now the Apolloniats set great store by these sheep, on account of an oracle which they received concerning them. The place where they are folded at night is a cavern, a long way from the town. Here it happened that Evênius, when he was chosen to keep the watch, by some accident fell asleep upon his guard; and while he slept, the cave was entered by wolves, which destroyed some sixty of the flock under his care. Evênius, when he woke and found what had occurred, kept silence about it and told no one; for he thought to buy other sheep and put them in the place of the slain. But the matter came to the ears of the Apolloniats, who forthwith brought Evênius to trial, and condemned him to lose his eyes, because he had gone to sleep upon his post. Now when Evênius was blinded, straightway the sheep had no young, and the land ceased to bear its wonted harvests. Then the Apolloniats sent to Do-dôna, and to Delphi, and asked the prophets, what had caused the woes which so afflicted them. The answer which they received was this—"The woes were come for Evênius, the guardian of the sacred sheep, whom the Apolloniats had wrongfully deprived of sight. They (the gods) had themselves sent the wolves; nor would they ever cease to exact vengeance for Evênius, till the Apolloniats made him whatever atonement he liked to ask. When this was paid, *they* would likewise give him a gift, which would make many men call him blessed."

94. Such was the tenor of the prophecies. The Apolloniats kept them close, but charged some of their citizens to go and make terms with Evênius; and these men managed the business for them in the way which I will now describe. They found Evênius sitting upon a bench, and, approaching him, they sat down by his side, and began to talk: at first they spoke of quite other matters, but in the end they mentioned his misfortune, and offered him their condolence. Having thus beguiled him, at last they put the question—"What atonement would he desire, if the Apolloniats were willing to make him satisfaction for the wrong which they had done to him?" Hereupon Evênius, who had not heard of the oracle, made answer—"If I were given the lands of this man and that—" (here he named the two men whom he knew to have the finest farms in Apollonia), "and likewise the house of this other"—(and here he mentioned the house which he knew to be the handsomest in the town), "I would, when master of these, be quite content, and my wrath would cease altogether." As soon as Evênius had thus spoken, the men who sat by him rejoined—"Evênius, the Apolloniats give thee the atonement which thou hast desired, according to the bidding of the oracles." Then Evênius understood the whole matter, and was enraged that they had deceived him so; but the Apolloniats bought the farms from their owners, and gave Evênius what he had chosen. After this was done, straightway Evênius had the gift of prophecy, insomuch that he became a famous man in Greece.

95. Deïphonus, the son of this Evênius, had accompanied the Corinthians, and was soothsayer, as I said before, to the Greek armament. One account, however, which I have heard, declares that he was not really the son of this man, but only took the name, and then went about Greece and let out his services for hire.

96. The Greeks, as soon as the victims were favourable, put to sea, and sailed across from Delos to Samos. Arriving off Calami, a place upon the Samian coast, they brought the fleet to an anchor near the temple of Juno which stands there, and prepared to engage the Persians by sea. These latter, however, no sooner heard of the approach of the Greeks, than, dismissing the Phœnician ships, they sailed away with the remainder to the mainland. For it had been resolved in council not to risk a battle, since the Persian fleet was thought to be no match for that of the enemy. They fled, therefore, to the main, to be under the protection of their land army, which now lay at Mycalé, and consisted of the troops left behind by Xerxes to keep guard over Ionia. This was an army of sixty thousand men, under the command of Tigranes, a Persian of more than common beauty and stature. The captains resolved therefore to betake themselves to these troops for defence, to drag their ships ashore, and to build a rampart around them, which might at once protect the fleet, and serve likewise as

a place of refuge for themselves.

97. Having so resolved, the commanders put out to sea; and passing the temple of the Eumenides, arrived at Gæson and Scolopoeis, which are in the territory of Mycalé. Here is a temple of Eleusinian Ceres, built by Philistus the son of Pasicles who came to Asia with Neileus the son of Codrus, what time he founded Miletus. At this place they drew the ships up on the beach, and surrounded them with a rampart made of stones and trunks of trees, cutting down for this purpose all the fruit-trees which grew near, and defending the barrier by means of stakes firmly planted in the ground. Here they were prepared either to win a battle, or undergo a siege—their thoughts embracing both chances.

98. The Greeks, when they understood that the barbarians had fled to the mainland, were sorely vexed at their escape: nor could they determine at first what they should do, whether they should return home, or proceed to the Hellespont. In the end, however, they resolved to do neither, but to make sail for the continent. So they made themselves ready for a sea-fight by the preparation of boarding-bridges, and what else was necessary; provided with which they sailed to Mycalé. Now when they came to the place where the camp was, they found no one venture out to meet them, but observed the ships all dragged ashore within the barrier, and a strong land-force drawn up in battle array upon the beach; Leotychides therefore sailed along the shore in his ship, keeping as close hauled to the land as possible, and by the voice of a herald thus addressed the Ionians:—

"Men of Ionia—ye who can hear me speak—do ye take heed to what I say; for the Persians will not understand a word that I utter. When we join battle with them, before aught else, remember Freedom—and next, recollect our watchword, which is Hêbé. If there be any who hear me not, let those who hear report my words to the others."

In all this Leotychides had the very same design which Themistocles entertained at Artemisium. Either the barbarians would not know what he had said, and the Ionians would be persuaded to revolt from them; or if his words were reported to the former, they would mistrust their Greek soldiers.

99. After Leotychides had made this address, the Greeks brought their ships to the land, and, having disembarked, arrayed themselves for the battle. When the Persians saw them marshalling their array, and bethought themselves of the advice which had been offered to the Ionians, their first act was to disarm the Samians, whom they suspected of complicity with the enemy. For it had happened lately that a number of the Athenians who lingered in Attica, having been made prisoners by the troops of Xerxes, were brought to Asia on board the barbarian fleet; and these men had been ransomed, one and all, by the Samians, who sent them back to Athens, well furnished with provisions for the way. On this account, as much as on any other, the Samians were suspected, as men who had paid the ransom of five hundred of the king's enemies. After disarming them, the Persians next despatched the Milesians to guard the paths which lead up into the heights of Mycalé, because (they said) the Milesians were well acquainted with that region: their true object, however, was to remove them to a distance from the camp. In this way the Persians sought to secure themselves against such of the Ionians as they thought likely, if occasion offered, to make rebellion. They then joined shield to shield, and so made themselves a breastwork against the enemy.

100. The Greeks now, having finished their preparations, began to move towards the barbarians; when, lo! as they advanced, a rumour flew through the host from one end to the other—that the Greeks had fought and conquered the army of Mardonius in Bœotia. At the same time a herald's wand was observed lying upon the beach. Many things prove to me that the gods take part in the affairs of man. How else, when the battles of Mycalé and Platæa were about to happen on the self same day, should such a rumour have reached the Greeks in that region, greatly cheering the whole army, and making them more eager than before to risk their lives.

101. A strange coincidence too it was, that both the battles should have been fought near a precinct of Eleusinian Ceres. The fight at Platæa took place, as I said before, quite close to one of Ceres' temples; and now the battle at Mycalé was to be fought hard by another. Rightly, too, did the rumour run, that the Greeks with Pausanias *had gained* their victory; for the fight at Platæa fell early in the day, whereas that at Mycalé was towards evening. That the two battles were really fought on the same day of the same month became apparent when inquiries were made a short time afterwards. Before the rumour reached them,

the Greeks were full of fear, not so much on their own account, as for their countrymen, and for Greece herself, lest she should be worsted in her struggle with Mardonius. But when the voice fell on them, their fear vanished, and they charged more vigorously and at a quicker pace. So the Greeks and the barbarians rushed with like eagerness to the fray; for the Hellespont and the Islands formed the prize for which they were about to fight.

102. The Athenians, and the force drawn up with them, who formed one half of the army, marched along the shore, where the country was low and level; but the way for the Lacedæmonians, and the troops with them, lay across hills and a torrent-course. Hence, while the Lacedæmonians were effecting their passage round, the Athenians on the other wing had already closed with the enemy. So long as the wicker bucklers of the Persians continued standing, they made a stout defence, and had not even the worst of the battle; but when the Athenians, and the allies with them, wishing to make the victory their own, and not share it with the Lacedæmonians, cheered each other on with shouts, and attacked them with the utmost fierceness, then at last the face of things became changed. For, bursting through the line of shields, and rushing forwards in a body, the Greeks fell upon the Persians; who, though they bore the charge and for a long time maintained their ground, yet at length took refuge in their intrenchment. Here the Athenians themselves, together with those who followed them in the line of battle, the Corinthians, the Sicyonians, and the Trœzenians, pressed so closely on the steps of their flying foes, that they entered along with them into the fortress. And now, when even their fortress was taken, the barbarians no longer offered resistance, but fled hastily away, all save only the Persians. *They* still continued to fight in knots of a few men against the Greeks, who kept pouring into the intrenchment. And here, while two of the Persian commanders fled, two fell upon the field: Artaÿntes and Ithamitres, who were leaders of the fleet, escaped; Mardontes, and the commander of the land force, Tigranes, died fighting.

103. The Persians still held out, when the Lacedæmonians, and their part of the army, reached the camp, and joined in the remainder of the battle. The number of Greeks who fell in the struggle here was not small; the Sicyonians especially lost many, and, among the rest, Perilaüs their general.

The Samians, who served with the Medes, and who, although disarmed, still remained in the camp, seeing from the very beginning of the fight that the victory was doubtful, did all that lay in their power to render help to the Greeks. And the other Ionians likewise, beholding their example, revolted and attacked the Persians.

104. As for the Milesians, who had been ordered, for the better security of the Persians, to guard the mountain-paths,—that, in case any accident befell them such as had now happened, they might not lack guides to conduct them into the high tracts of Mycalé,—and who had also been removed to hinder them from making an outbreak in the Persian camp; they, instead of obeying their orders, broke them in every respect. For they guided the flying Persians by wrong roads, which brought them into the presence of the enemy; and at last they set upon them with their own hands, and showed themselves the hottest of their adversaries. Ionia, therefore, on this day revolted a second time from the Persians.

105. In this battle the Greeks who behaved with the greatest bravery were the Athenians; and among them the palm was borne off by Hermolycus, the son of Euthynus, a man accomplished in the Pancratium. This Hermolycus was afterwards slain in the war between the Athenians and Carystians. He fell in the fight near Cyrnus in the Carystian territory, and was buried in the neighbourhood of Geræstus. After the Athenians, the most distinguished on the Greek side were the Corinthians, the Trœzenians, and the Sicyonians.

106. The Greeks, when they had slaughtered the greater portion of the barbarians, either in the battle or in the rout, set fire to their ships and burnt them, together with the bulwark which had been raised for their defence, first however removing therefrom all the booty, and carrying it down to the beach. Besides other plunder, they found here many caskets of money. When they had burnt the rampart and the vessels, the Greeks sailed away to Samos, and there took counsel together concerning the Ionians, whom they thought of removing out of Asia. Ionia they proposed to abandon to the barbarians; and their doubt was, in what part of their own possessions in Greece they should settle its inhabitants. For it seemed to them a thing impossible that they should be ever on the watch to guard and protect Ionia; and yet otherwise there could be no hope that the Ionians would escape

the vengeance of the Persians. Hereupon the Peloponnesian leaders proposed that the seaport towns of such Greeks as had sided with the Medes should be taken away from them, and made over to the Ionians. The Athenians, on the other hand, were very unwilling that any removal at all should take place, and disliked the Peloponnesians holding councils concerning their colonists. So, as they set themselves against the change, the Peloponnesians yielded with a good will. Hereupon the Samians, Chians, Lesbians, and other islanders, who had helped the Greeks at this time, were received into the league of the allies; and took the oaths, binding themselves to be faithful, and not desert the common cause. Then the Greeks sailed away to the Hellespont, where they meant to break down the bridges, which they supposed to be still extended across the strait.

107. The barbarians who escaped from the battle—a scanty remnant—took refuge in the heights of Mycalé, whence they made good their retreat to Sardis. During the march, Masistes, the son of Darius, who had been present at the disaster, had words with Artaÿntes, the general, on whom he showered many reproaches. He called him, among other things, "worse than a woman," for the way in which he had exercised his command, and said there was no punishment which he did not deserve to suffer for doing the king's house such grievous hurt. Now with the Persians there is no greater insult than to call a man "worse than a woman." So when Artaÿntes had borne the reproaches for some while, at last he fell in a rage, and drew his scymitar upon Masistes, being fain to kill him. But a certain Halicarnassian, Xenagoras by name, the son of Praxilaüs, who stood behind Artaÿntes at the time, seeing him in the act of rushing forward, seized him suddenly round the waist, and, lifting him from his feet, dashed him down upon the ground; which gave time for the spearmen who guarded Masistes to come to his aid. By his conduct here Xenagoras gained the favour, not of Masistes only, but likewise of Xerxes himself, whose brother he had preserved from death; and the king rewarded his action by setting him over the whole land of Cilicia. Except this, nothing happened upon the road; and the men continued their march and came all safe to Sardis. At Sardis they found the king, who had been there ever since he lost the sea-fight and fled from Athens to Asia.

108. During the time that Xerxes abode at this place, he fell in love with the wife of Masistes, who was likewise staying in the city. He therefore sent her messages, but failed to win her consent; and he could not dare to use violence, out of regard to Masistes, his brother. This the woman knew well enough, and hence it was that she had the boldness to resist him. So Xerxes, finding no other way open, devised a marriage between his own son Darius and a daughter of this woman and Masistes—thinking that he might better obtain his ends if he effected this union. Accordingly he betrothed these two persons to one another, and, after the usual ceremonies were completed, took his departure for Susa. When he was come there, and had received the woman into his palace as his son's bride, a change came over him, and losing all love for the wife of Masistes, he conceived a passion for his son's bride, Masistes' daughter. And Artaÿnta—for so was she called —very soon returned his love.

109. After a while the thing was discovered in the way which I will now relate. Amestris, the wife of Xerxes, had woven with her own hands a long robe, of many colours, and very curious, which she presented to her husband as a gift. Xerxes, who was greatly pleased with it, forthwith put it on; and went in it to visit Artaÿnta, who happened likewise on this day to please him greatly. He therefore bade her ask him whatever boon she liked, and promised that, whatever it was, he would assuredly grant her request. Then Artaÿnta, who was doomed to suffer calamity together with her whole house, said to him—"Wilt thou indeed give me whatever I like to ask?" So the king, suspecting nothing less than that her choice would fall where it did, pledged his word, and swore to her. She then, as soon as she heard his oath, asked boldly for the robe. Hereupon Xerxes tried all possible means to avoid the gift; not that he grudged to give it, but because he dreaded Amestris, who already suspected, and would now, he feared, detect his love. So he offered her cities instead, and heaps of gold, and an army which should obey no other leader. (The last of these is a thoroughly Persian gift.) But, as nothing could prevail on Artaÿnta to change her mind, at the last he gave her the robe. Then Artaÿnta was very greatly rejoiced, and she often wore the garment and was proud of it. And so it came to the ears of Amestris that the robe had been given to her.

110. Now when Amestris learnt the whole matter, she felt no anger against Artaÿnta; but, looking upon her mother, the wife of Masistes, as the cause of all the mischief, she determined

to compass her death. She waited, therefore, till her husband gave the great royal banquet, a feast which takes place once every year, in celebration of the king's birthday—"Tykta" the feast is called in the Persian tongue, which in our language may be rendered "perfect".—and this is the only day in all the year on which the king soaps his head, and distributes gifts to the Persians. Amestris waited, accordingly, for this day, and then made request of Xerxes, that he would please to give her, as her present, the wife of Masistes. But he refused; for it seemed to him shocking and monstrous to give into the power of another a woman who was not only his brother's wife, but was likewise wholly guiltless of what had happened—the more especially as he knew well enough with what intent Amestris had preferred her request.

111. At length, however, wearied by her importunity, and constrained moreover by the law of the feast, which required that no one who asked a boon that day at the king's board should be denied his request, he yielded, but with a very ill will, and gave the woman into her power. Having so done, and told Amestris she might deal with her as she chose, the king called his brother into his presence, and said—

"Masistes, thou art my brother, the son of my father Darius; and, what is more, thou art a good man. I pray thee, live no longer with the wife whom thou now hast. Behold, I will give thee instead my own daughter in marriage; take her to live with thee. But part first with the wife thou now hast—I like not that thou keep to her."

To this Masistes, greatly astonished, answered—

"My lord and master, how strange a speech hast thou uttered! Thou biddest me put away my wife, who has borne me three goodly youths, and daughters besides, whereof thou hast taken one and espoused her to a son of thine own—thou biddest me put away this wife, notwithstanding that she pleases me greatly, and marry a daughter of thine! In truth, O king! that I am accounted worthy to wed thy daughter, is an honour which I mightily esteem; but yet to do as thou sayest am I in no wise willing. I pray thee, use not force to compel me to yield to thy prayer. Be sure thy daughter will find a husband to the full as worthy as myself. Suffer me then to live on with my own wife."

Thus did Masistes answer; and Xerxes, in wrath, replied—"I will tell thee, Masistes, what thou hast gained by these words. I will

not give thee my daughter; nor shalt thou live any longer with thy own wife. So mayest thou learn, in time to come, to take what is offered thee." Masistes, when he heard this, withdrew, only saying—"Master, thou hast not yet taken my life."

112. While these things were passing between Xerxes and his brother Masistes, Amestris sent for the spearmen of the royal bodyguard, and caused the wife of Masistes to be mutilated in a horrible fashion. Her two breasts, her nose, ears, and lips were cut off and thrown to the dogs; her tongue was torn out by the roots, and thus disfigured she was sent back to her home.

113. Masistes, who knew nothing of what had happened, but was fearful that some calamity had befallen him, ran hastily to his house. There, finding his wife so savagely used, he forthwith took counsel with his sons, and, accompanied by them and certain others also, set forth on his way to Bactria, intending to stir up revolt in that province, and hoping to do great hurt to Xerxes: all which, I believe, he would have accomplished, if he had once reached the Bactrian and Sacan people; for he was greatly beloved by them both, and was moreover satrap of Bactria. But Xerxes, hearing of his designs, sent an armed force upon his track, and slew him while he was still upon the road, with his sons and his whole army. Such is the tale of King Xerxes' love and of the death of his brother Masistes.

114. Meanwhile the Greeks, who had left Mycalé, and sailed for the Hellespont, were forced by contrary winds to anchor near Lectum; from which place they afterwards sailed on to Abydos. On arriving here, they discovered that the bridges, which they had thought to find standing, and which had been the chief cause of their proceeding to the Hellespont, were already broken up and destroyed. Upon this discovery, Leotychides, and the Peloponnesians under him, were anxious to sail back to Greece; but the Athenians, with Xanthippus their captain, thought good to remain, and resolved to make an attempt upon the Chersonese. So, while the Peloponnesians sailed away to their homes, the Athenians crossed over from Abydos to the Chersonese, and there laid siege to Sestos.

115. Now, as Sestos was the strongest fortress in all that region, the rumour had no sooner gone forth that the Greeks were arrived at the Hellespont, than great numbers flocked thither from all the towns in the neighbour-

hood. Among the rest there came a certain Œobazus, a Persian, from the city of Cardia, where he had laid up the shore-cables which had been used in the construction of the bridges. The town was guarded by its own Æolian inhabitants, but contained also some Persians, and a great multitude of their allies.

116. The whole district was under the rule of Artaÿctes, one of the king's satraps; who was a Persian, but a wicked and cruel man. At the time when Xerxes was marching against Athens, he had craftily possessed himself of the treasures belonging to Protesilaüs the son of Iphiclus, which were at Elæsûs in the Chersonese. For at this place is the tomb of Protesilaüs, surrounded by a sacred precinct; and here there was great store of wealth, vases of gold and silver, works in brass, garments, and other offerings, all which Artaÿctes made his prey, having got the king's consent by thus cunningly addressing him—

"Master, there is in this region the house of a Greek, who, when he attacked thy territory, met his due reward, and perished. Give me his house, I pray thee, that hereafter men may fear to carry arms against *thy* land."

By these words he easily persuaded Xerxes to give him the man's house; for there was no suspicion of his design in the king's mind. And he could say in a certain sense that Protesilaüs had borne arms against the land of the king; because the Persians consider all Asia to belong to them, and to their king for the time being. So when Xerxes allowed his request, he brought all the treasures from Elæsûs to Sestos, and made the sacred land into cornfields and pasture land; nay, more, whenever he paid a visit to Elæûs, he polluted the shrine itself by vile uses. It was this Artaÿctes who was now besieged by the Athenians—and he was but ill prepared for defence; since the Greeks had fallen upon him quite unawares, nor had he in the least expected their coming.

117. When it was now late in the autumn, and the siege still continued, the Athenians began to murmur that they were kept abroad so long; and, seeing that they were not able to take the place, besought their captains to lead them back to their own country. But the captains refused to move, till either the city had fallen, or the Athenian people ordered them to return home. So the soldiers patiently bore up against their sufferings.

118. Meanwhile those within the walls were reduced to the last straits, and forced even to boil the very thongs of their beds for food. At last, when these too failed them, Artaÿctes and Œobazus, with the native Persians, fled away from the place by night, having let themselves down from the wall at the back of the town, where the blockading force was scantiest. As soon as day dawned, they of the Chersonese made signals to the Greeks from the walls, and let them know what had happened, at the same time throwing open the gates of their city. Hereupon, while some of the Greeks entered the town, others, and those the more numerous body, set out in pursuit of the enemy.

119. Œobazus fled into Thrace; but there the Apsinthian Thracians seized him, and offered him, after their wonted fashion, to Pleistôrus, one of the gods of their country. His companions they likewise put to death, but in a different manner. As for Artaÿctes and the troops with him, who had been the last to leave the town, they were overtaken by the Greeks, not far from Ægospotami, and defended themselves stoutly for a time, but were at last either killed or taken prisoners. Those whom they made prisoners the Greeks bound with chains, and brought with them to Sestos. Artaÿctes and his son were among the number.

120. Now the Chersonesites relate that the following prodigy befell one of the Greeks who guarded the captives. He was broiling upon a fire some salted fish, when of a sudden they began to leap and quiver, as if they had been only just caught. Hereat, the rest of the guards hurried round to look, and were greatly amazed at the sight. Artaÿctes, however, beholding the prodigy, called the man to him, and said—

"Fear not, Athenian stranger, because of this marvel. It has not appeared on thy account, but on mine. Protesilaüs of Elæûs has sent it to show me, that albeit he is dead and embalmed with salt, he has power from the gods to chastise his injurer. Now then I would fain acquit my debt to him thus. For the riches which I took from his temple, I will fix my fine at one hundred talents—while for myself and this boy of mine, I will give the Athenians two hundred talents, on condition that they will spare our lives."

Such were the promises of Artaÿctes; but they failed to persuade Xanthippus. For the men of Elæûs, who wished to avenge Protesilaüs, entreated that he might be put to death; and Xanthippus himself was of the same mind. So they led Artaÿctes to the tongue of land where the bridges of Xerxes had been fixed—or, according to others, to the knoll above the town of Madytus; and, having nailed him to a board, they left him hanging thereupon. As for the son of Artaÿctes, him they stoned to death before his eyes.

121. This done, they sailed back to Greece, carrying with them, besides other treasures, the shore cables from the bridges of Xerxes, which they wished to dedicate in their temples. And this was all that took place that year.

122. It was the grandfather of the Artaÿctes, one Artembares by name, who suggested to the Persians a proposal which they readily embraced, and thus urged upon Cyrus:—"Since Jove," they said, "has overthrown Astyages, and given the rule to the Persians, and to thee chiefly, O Cyrus! come now, let us quit this land wherein we dwell—for it is a scant land and a rugged—and let us choose ourselves some other better country. Many such lie around us, some nearer, some further off: if we take one of these, men will admire us far more than they do now. Who that had the power would not so act? And when shall we have a fairer time than now, when we are lords of so many nations, and rule all Asia?" Then Cyrus, who did not greatly esteem the counsel, told them,—"they might do so, if they liked—but he warned them not to expect in that case to continue rulers, but to prepare for being ruled by others—soft countries gave birth to soft men—there was no region which produced very delightful fruits, and at the same time men of a warlike spirit." So the Persians departed with altered minds, confessing that Cyrus was wiser than they; and chose rather to dwell in a churlish land, and exercise lordship, than to cultivate plains, and be the slaves of others.

MAPS: HERODOTUS

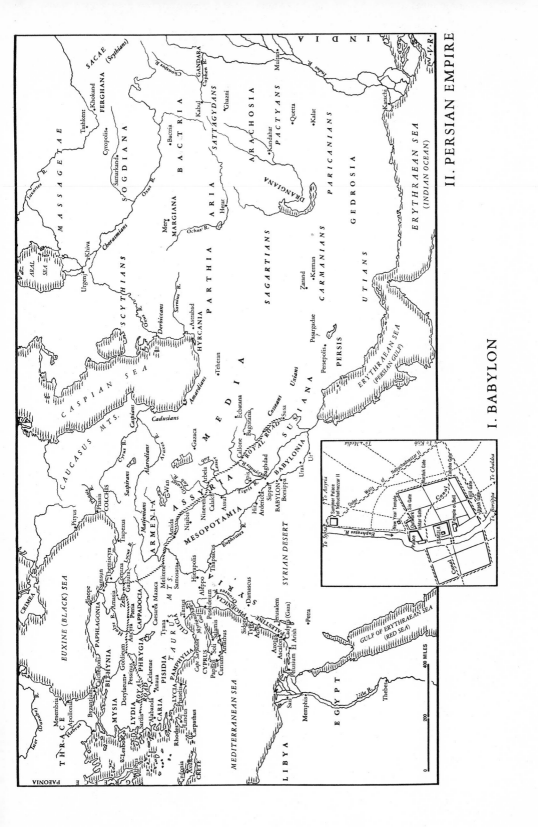

II. PERSIAN EMPIRE

I. BABYLON

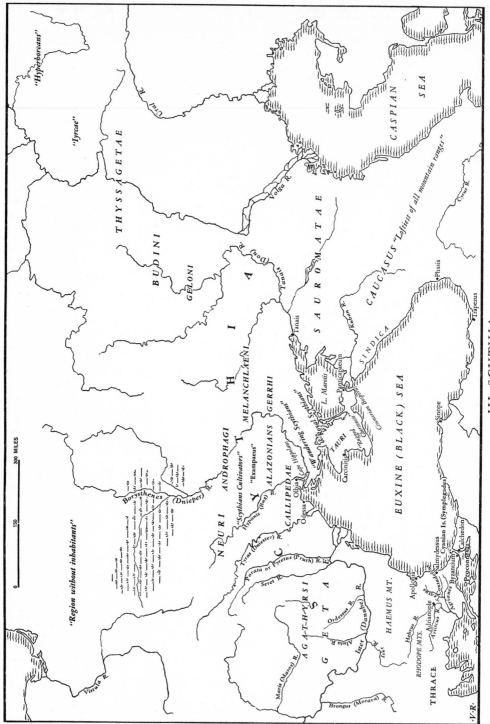

"Hyperboreans"

"Iyrcae"

Ural R.

THYSSAGETAE

BUDINI

GELONI

H   I   A

Volga R.

Tanais (Don) R.

Tanais R.

SAUROMATAE

CASPIAN SEA

Cyrus R.

CAUCASUS "Loftiest of all mountain ranges"

Phasis

Trapezus

SINDICA

Kuban R.

L. Maeotis

Pantacapaeum

Cimmerian Bosphorus

Cimmerian Bosphorus

Tanais

"Region without inhabitants"

300 MILES

150

0

Borysthenes (Dnieper) R.

NEURI

ANDROPHAGI

MELANCHLAENI

"Scythians Cultivators"

"Exampaeus"

V

ALAZONIANS

GERRHI

Hypanis (Bug) R.

Olbia

Odessa

Cape Hippolaus

"Wandering Scythians"

"Royal Scythians"

TAURI

Carcinitis

"Rugged Peninsula"

EUXINE (BLACK) SEA

Sinope

CALLIPEDAE

Tyras (Dniester) R.

C

Porata or Pyretus (Pruth) R. E.

Seret R.

Vistula R.

AG-A-T-H-Y-R-S I

GETA

Maris (Maros) R.

Aluta R.

Ordessus R.

Ister (Danube) R.

HAEMUS MT.

Brongus (Morava) R.

Hebrus R.

RHODOPE MTS.

Artiscus R.

Adrianople

Apollonia

Salmydessus

Cyanian Is. (Symplegades)

Astacus R.

Byzantium

Calchedon

Proconnesus

THRACE

V.R.

III. SCYTHIA

V.R.

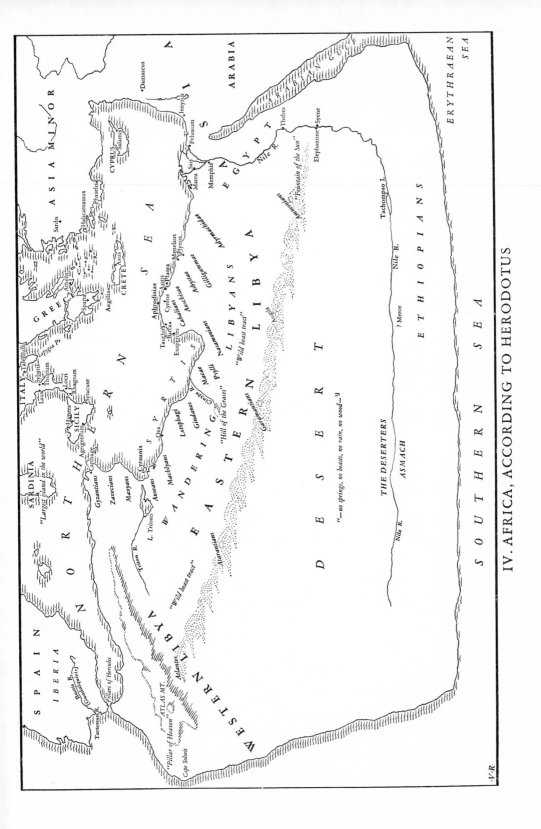

IV. AFRICA, ACCORDING TO HERODOTUS

ILLYRIS
MACEDONIA
L. Lychnites
Nestus R.
Axius R.
Strymon R.
Siris
L. Cercinitis
Crenides
Myrcinus
Abdera
CRESTONIA
Aegae
Amphipolis
PIERIA
Neapolis
Pella Ichnae
Pergamus
THASOS
Echedorus R.
Argilus
Eion Phagres
L. Bolbe
Sindus
Apollonia
L. Bigorritis
Chalastra
Therma
Stagirus
Oresticum
Aenea
Anthemus
CHALCIDICE
Acanthus
Olophyxus
Campsa
Apollonia
Sane
THRACIAN SEA
Pydna
Gigonus
Olynthus
Mecyberna
Thyssus
Haliacmon R.
PIERIA
Combraea
Potidaea
Sermyle
Pilorus
Singus
Cleonae
Petra
Dium
Mt. Athos
Acrothoum
EPIRUS
Mt. Olympus
Aphytis
Dium
Galepsus
Torone
Ilium
Gonnus
Neapolis
PALLENE
Therambus
Dodona
Ossa Mt.
Mende
Scione
Canastraeum Pr.
Ampelus Pr.
PINDUS MTS.
Meliboea
Aous R.
Peneus R.
Larissa
THESSALY
L. Boebeis
Mt. Pelion
Casthanaea
Sepias Pr.
Icos
THESSALIOTIS
Iolcus
Pagasae
Sciathos
AMBRACIA
Apidanus
PHTHIOTIS
Pagasaean Gulf
Artemisium Pr.
Peparethos
Charadra
Onochonus
ACHAIA
Halus
Aphetae
Thyrea
DOLOPIA
PHTHIOTIS
SCYROS
Acheron R.
ACARNANIA
MALIS
Histiaea
Spercheius R.
Pindus
Thermopylae
Cytinium
Drymus
LEUCAS
Stratus
AETOLIA
DORIS
Tithronium
Erochus
Achelous R.
Thermum
Amphicaea
Neon
Elatea
Hyampolis
Chersonesus Pr.
Ithaca
Mt. Parnassus
Parapotamii
Abae
Opus
Elaeus
Amphissa
Delphi
Fanopeus
Orchomenus
Chalcis
Eretria
Tamynae
CEPHALLENIA
Echinades Is.
LOCRIS
Lebadeia
Thebes
Tanagra
Amphiaraus
Opus
Anticyra
Glisas
Rhium Pr.
Rhypes
Aegium
Thespiae
Scolus
Chaeroneia
Patrae
Helice
Plataea
Asopus R.
AEGILIA
Olenus
Bura
ATTICA
Dyme
ACHAIA
Aegae
Aegira
GULF OF CORINTH
Eleusis
Marathon
Pallene
Styra
Capbereus Pr.
Tritaea
Nonacris
Sicyon
Isthmus of Megara
Nisaea
Carystus
Pheneus
Corinth
ATHENS
Geraestus Pr.
Zacynthus
Paeus
L. Stymphalus
Phlius
Posidium
Phalerum
ELIS
Stymphalus
Mt. Hymettus
ANDROS
ZACYNTHUS
Olympia
ARCADIA
Mycenae
Aegina
Aegilia
Alpheus R.
ARGOLIS
Epidaurus
Laurium Mt.
Ceos
Mantinea
Argos Tiryns
Aegina
Sunium Pr.
Phigalia
Hysiae
Nauplia
Tegea
Troezen
IONIAN SEA
Megalopolis
Thyrea
Hermione
Cythnos
Syros
Messene
Thornax Mt.
Hydrea
Pityussa
MYRTOUM
MESSENIA
Pylos
SPARTA
Therapna
SEA
Seriphos
Phareis
Methone
LACONIA
Cardamyle
Siphnos
Asine
Oenussae Is.
MELOS
Pholegandros
Taenarum
Malea Pr.

| 0 | 25 | 50 | 100 MILES |

·V·R·

CYTHERA

V. THE REGION

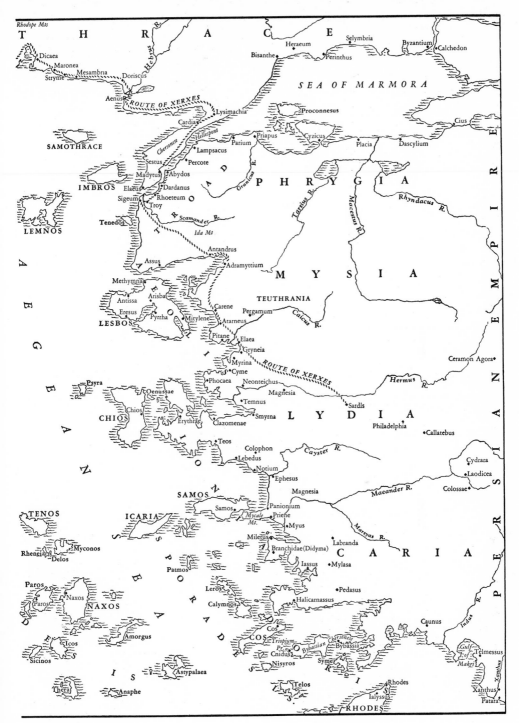

OF THE ÆGEAN

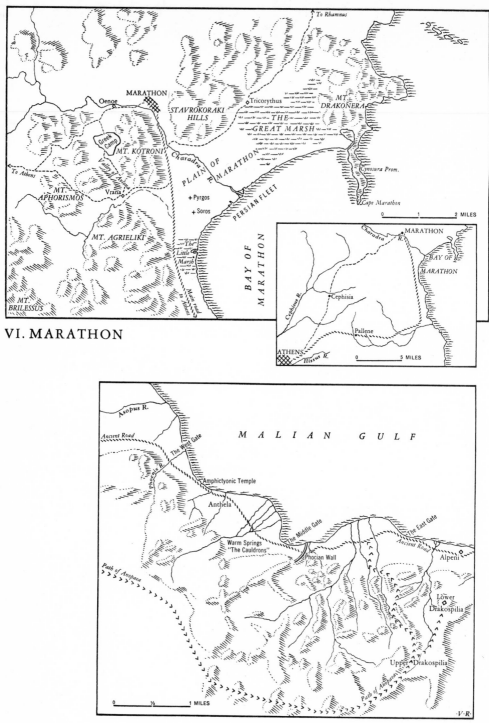

VI. MARATHON

To Rhamnus

MARATHON

Oenoe

STAVROKORAKI
HILLS

Tricorythus

MT.
DRAKONERA

THE

GREAT MARSH

Charadra R.

Greek
Camp

MT. KOTRONI

PLAIN OF MARATHON

Cynosura Prom.

To Athens

Valley of Avlona

MT.
APHORISMOS

Vrana

PERSIAN FLEET

Cape Marathon

+ Pyrgos

+ Soros

MT. AGRIELIKI

"The
Little
Marsh"

BAY OF MARATHON

0   1   2 MILES

Main road to Athens

MT.
BRILESSUS

Charadra R.

MARATHON

Cephisia R.

Cephisia

BAY OF
MARATHON

Pallene

ATHENS

Ilissus R.

0   5 MILES

MALIAN GULF

Asopus R.

Ancient Road

The West Gate

Phoenix R.

Amphictyonic Temple

Anthela

The Middle Gate

The East Gate

Warm Springs
"The Cauldrons"

Ancient Road

Phocian Wall

Alpeni

Path of Anopaea

Lower
Drakospilia

Upper Drakospilia

Path of Anopaea

0   ½   1 MILES

·V·R·

VII. THERMOPYLÆ

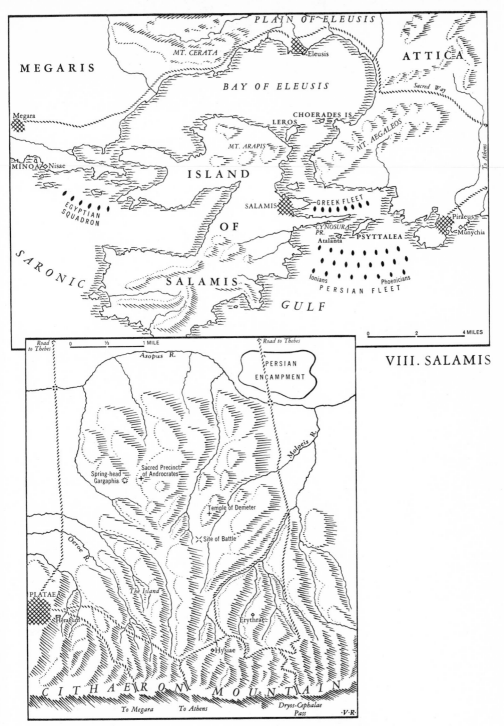

VIII. SALAMIS

IX. PLATÆA

Index

THUCYDIDES: THE HISTORY OF
THE PELOPONNESIAN WAR

BIOGRAPHICAL NOTE
THUCYDIDES, c.460–c.400 B.C.

THUCYDIDES records that he began writing his *History of the Peloponnesian War* "at the moment that it broke out" and that he was then "of an age to comprehend events." From this it is inferred he was somewhere between twenty-five and forty years of age at that time, which would place his birth between 471 and 455 B.C.

His father, Olorus, was an Athenian citizen and perhaps related to the Thracian prince, Cimon, son of Miltiades. He derived considerable wealth from the possession of the gold mines on the coast opposite Thasos. Thucydides by birth thus enjoyed two homes, one in Athens and the other in Thrace, and a position in society which gave him access to the leading figures of his time.

It is uncertain how much of his youth was passed in Athens, but, according to the ancient biographers, he studied philosophy with Anaxagoras and rhetoric with Antiphon, the oligarch famous for his oratory, whom Thucydides praised as "one of the best men of his day in Athens." During his youth Athenian power was at its height, and he was presumably a member of the brilliant circle about Pericles.

Thucydides was in Athens when the Peloponnesian war broke out in 431 B.C. and also the following year during the great plague, when, as he records, "I had the disease myself and watched its operation in the case of others." The turning-point in his career came six years later, in 424. He had attained a position of sufficient importance to have been appointed one of the two generals assigned to guard the Athenian interests in "the regions towards Thrace." His colleague, Eucles, commanded the land forces while he had charge of the navy. The town of Amphipolis was the Athenian stronghold in that region, and to guard it was then a matter of particular urgency since the ablest of the Spartan leaders, Brasidas, was then making rapid gains in the vicinity. Thucydides with the seven ships under his command was anchored at the isle of Thasos, half a day's sail away. He records that "Brasidas, afraid of help arriving by sea from Thasos, and learning that Thucydides possessed the right of working the gold mines in that part of Thrace, and had thus great influence with the inhabitants of the continent, hastened to gain the town." By the offer of generous terms and the aid of the disaffected part of the population, he succeeded in his object before Thucydides could bring relief. "The news that Amphipolis was in the hands of the enemy caused great alarm at Athens," and Thucydides for his share in the disaster was relieved of his command and exiled.

His exile from Athens lasted for twenty years and is supposed to have been passed for the most part at his property in Thrace. He probably took advantage of his position as an Athenian exile to visit the countries of the Peloponnesian allies, including Sparta and perhaps Sicily. The main purpose of such travels was undoubtedly to gather material for his *History,* for, as he noted, "being present with both parties, and more especially with the Peloponnesians by reason of my exile, I had leisure to observe affairs somewhat particularly."

His own words make it clear that he returned to Athens, at least for a time, in 404. The general amnesty of that year would have made it possible if he had not already received a special pardon, as is sometimes claimed. According to ancient testimony, he soon afterwards met his death at the hands of an assassin. Plutarch declares that he was killed at his home in Thrace and buried at Athens in the vault of Cimon's family.

CONTENTS

MAPS, p. 596

INDEX, p. 603

The First Book

CHAPTER I

*The State of Greece from the earliest Times to the
Commencement of the Peloponnesian War*

[*1*] THUCYDIDES, an Athenian, wrote the history of the war between the Peloponnesians and the Athenians, beginning at the moment that it broke out, and believing that it would be a great war and more worthy of relation than any that had preceded it. This belief was not without its grounds. The preparations of both the combatants were in every department in the last state of perfection; and he could see the rest of the Hellenic race taking sides in the quarrel; those who delayed doing so at once having it in contemplation. Indeed this was the greatest movement yet known in history, not only of the Hellenes, but of a large part of the barbarian world—I had almost said of mankind. For though the events of remote antiquity, and even those that more immediately preceded the war, could not from lapse of time be clearly ascertained, yet the evidences which an inquiry carried as far back as was practicable leads me to trust, all point to the conclusion that there was nothing on a great scale, either in war or in other matters.

[*2*] For instance, it is evident that the country now called Hellas had in ancient times no settled population; on the contrary, migrations were of frequent occurrence, the several tribes readily abandoning their homes under the pressure of superior numbers. Without commerce, without freedom of communication either by land or sea, cultivating no more of their territory than the exigencies of life required, destitute of capital, never planting their land (for they could not tell when an invader might not come and take it all away, and when he did come they had no walls to stop

[GENERAL NOTE: The bracketed italic numbers indicate the usual chapter divisions. The twenty-six chapter headings are arbitrary subdivisions devised by the translator.]

him), thinking that the necessities of daily sustenance could be supplied at one place as well as another, they cared little for shifting their habitation, and consequently neither built large cities nor attained to any other form of greatness. The richest soils were always most subject to this change of masters; such as the district now called Thessaly, Boeotia, most of the Peloponnese, Arcadia excepted, and the most fertile parts of the rest of Hellas. The goodness of the land favoured the aggrandizement of particular individuals, and thus created faction which proved a fertile source of ruin. It also invited invasion. Accordingly Attica, from the poverty of its soil enjoying from a very remote period freedom from faction, never changed its inhabitants. And here is no inconsiderable exemplification of my assertion that the migrations were the cause of there being no correspondent growth in other parts. The most powerful victims of war or faction from the rest of Hellas took refuge with the Athenians as a safe retreat; and at an early period, becoming naturalized, swelled the already large population of the city to such a height that Attica became at last too small to hold them, and they had to send out colonies to Ionia.

[*3*] There is also another circumstance that contributes not a little to my conviction of the weakness of ancient times. Before the Trojan war there is no indication of any common action in Hellas, nor indeed of the universal prevalence of the name; on the contrary, before the time of Hellen, son of Deucalion, no such appellation existed, but the country went by the names of the different tribes, in particular of the Pelasgian. It was not till Hellen and his sons grew strong in Phthiotis, and were invited as allies into the other cities, that one by one they gradually acquired from the connection the name of Hellenes; though a long time elapsed before that name could fasten itself upon all. The best proof of this is furnished by Homer. Born long after the Trojan War, he

nowhere calls all of them by that name, nor indeed any of them except the followers of Achilles from Phthiotis, who were the original Hellenes: in his poems they are called Danaans, Argives, and Achaeans. He does not even use the term barbarian, probably because the Hellenes had not yet been marked off from the rest of the world by one distinctive appellation. It appears therefore that the several Hellenic communities, comprising not only those who first acquired the name, city by city, as they came to understand each other, but also those who assumed it afterwards as the name of the whole people, were before the Trojan war prevented by their want of strength and the absence of mutual intercourse from displaying any collective action.

[4] Indeed, they could not unite for this expedition till they had gained increased familiarity with the sea. And the first person known to us by tradition as having established a navy is Minos. He made himself master of what is now called the Hellenic sea, and ruled over the Cyclades, into most of which he sent the first colonies, expelling the Carians and appointing his own sons governors; and thus did his best to put down piracy in those waters, a necessary step to secure the revenues for his own use.

[5] For in early times the Hellenes and the barbarians of the coast and islands, as communication by sea became more common, were tempted to turn pirates, under the conduct of their most powerful men; the motives being to serve their own cupidity and to support the needy. They would fall upon a town unprotected by walls, and consisting of a mere collection of villages, and would plunder it; indeed, this came to be the main source of their livelihood, no disgrace being yet attached to such an achievement, but even some glory. An illustration of this is furnished by the honour with which some of the inhabitants of the continent still regard a successful marauder, and by the question we find the old poets everywhere representing the people as asking of voyagers—"Are they pirates?"—as if those who are asked the question would have no idea of disclaiming the imputation, or their interrogators of reproaching them for it. The same rapine prevailed also by land.

[6] And even at the present day many parts of Hellas still follow the old fashion, the Ozolian Locrians for instance, the Aetolians, the Acarnanians, and that region of the continent; and the custom of carrying arms is still kept up among these continentals, from the old piratical habits. The whole of Hellas used once to carry arms, their habitations being unprotected and their communication with each other unsafe; indeed, to wear arms was as much a part of everyday life with them as with the barbarians. And the fact that the people in these parts of Hellas are still living in the old way points to a time when the same mode of life was once equally common to all. The Athenians were the first to lay aside their weapons, and to adopt an easier and more luxurious mode of life; indeed, it is only lately that their rich old men left off the luxury of wearing undergarments of linen, and fastening a knot of their hair with a tie of golden grasshoppers, a fashion which spread to their Ionian kindred and long prevailed among the old men there. On the contrary, a modest style of dressing, more in conformity with modern ideas, was first adopted by the Lacedaemonians, the rich doing their best to assimilate their way of life to that of the common people. They also set the example of contending naked, publicly stripping and anointing themselves with oil in their gymnastic exercises. Formerly, even in the Olympic contests, the athletes who contended wore belts across their middles; and it is but a few years since that the practice ceased. To this day among some of the barbarians, especially in Asia, when prizes for boxing and wrestling are offered, belts are worn by the combatants. And there are many other points in which a likeness might be shown between the life of the Hellenic world of old and the barbarian of to-day.

[7] With respect to their towns, later on, at an era of increased facilities of navigation and a greater supply of capital, we find the shores becoming the site of walled towns, and the isthmuses being occupied for the purposes of commerce and defence against a neighbour. But the old towns, on account of the great prevalence of piracy, were built away from the sea, whether on the islands or the continent, and still remain in their old sites. For the pirates used to plunder one another, and indeed all coast populations, whether seafaring or not.

[8] The islanders, too, were great pirates. These islanders were Carians and Phoenicians, by whom most of the islands were colonized, as was proved by the following fact. During the purification of Delos by Athens in this war all the graves in the island were taken up, and it was found that above half their inmates were Carians: they were identified by the fashion of the arms buried with them, and by the method

of interment, which was the same as the Carians still follow. But as soon as Minos had formed his navy, communication by sea became easier, as he colonized most of the islands, and thus expelled the malefactors. The coast population now began to apply themselves more closely to the acquisition of wealth, and their life became more settled; some even began to build themselves walls on the strength of their newly acquired riches. For the love of gain would reconcile the weaker to the dominion of the stronger, and the possession of capital enabled the more powerful to reduce the smaller towns to subjection. And it was at a somewhat later stage of this development that they went on the expedition against Troy.

[9] What enabled Agamemnon to raise the armament was more, in my opinion, his superiority in strength, than the oaths of Tyndareus, which bound the suitors to follow him. Indeed, the account given by those Peloponnesians who have been the recipients of the most credible tradition is this. First of all Pelops, arriving among a needy population from Asia with vast wealth, acquired such power that, stranger though he was, the country was called after him; and this power fortune saw fit materially to increase in the hands of his descendants. Eurystheus had been killed in Attica by the Heraclids. Atreus was his mother's brother; and to the hands of his relation, who had left his father on account of the death of Chrysippus, Eurystheus, when he set out on his expedition, had committed Mycenae and the government. As time went on and Eurystheus did not return, Atreus complied with the wishes of the Mycenaeans, who were influenced by fear of the Heraclids—besides, his power seemed considerable, and he had not neglected to court the favour of the populace —and assumed the sceptre of Mycenae and the rest of the dominions of Eurystheus. And so the power of the descendants of Pelops came to be greater than that of the descendants of Perseus. To all this Agamemnon succeeded. He had also a navy far stronger than his contemporaries, so that, in my opinion, fear was quite as strong an element as love in the formation of the confederate expedition. The strength of his navy is shown by the fact that his own was the largest contingent, and that of the Arcadians was furnished by him; this at least is what Homer says, if his testimony is deemed sufficient. Besides, in his account of the transmission of the sceptre, he calls him

Of many an isle, and of all Argos king.

Now Agamemnon's was a continental power; and he could not have been master of any except the adjacent islands (and these would not be many), but through the possession of a fleet.

[10] And from this expedition we may infer the character of earlier enterprises. Now Mycenae may have been a small place, and many of the towns of that age may appear comparatively insignificant, but no exact observer would therefore feel justified in rejecting the estimate given by the poets and by tradition of the magnitude of the armament. For I suppose if Lacedaemon were to become desolate, and the temples and the foundations of the public buildings were left, that as time went on there would be a strong disposition with posterity to refuse to accept her fame as a true exponent of her power. And yet they occupy two-fifths of Peloponnese and lead the whole, not to speak of their numerous allies without. Still, as the city is neither built in a compact form nor adorned with magnificent temples and public edifices, but composed of villages after the old fashion of Hellas, there would be an impression of inadequacy. Whereas, if Athens were to suffer the same misfortune, I suppose that any inference from the appearance presented to the eye would make her power to have been twice as great as it is. We have therefore no right to be sceptical, nor to content ourselves with an inspection of a town to the exclusion of a consideration of its power; but we may safely conclude that the armament in question surpassed all before it, as it fell short of modern efforts; if we can here also accept the testimony of Homer's poems, in which, without allowing for the exaggeration which a poet would feel himself licensed to employ, we can see that it was far from equalling ours. He has represented it as consisting of twelve hundred vessels; the Boeotian complement of each ship being a hundred and twenty men, that of the ships of Philoctetes fifty. By this, I conceive, he meant to convey the maximum and the minimum complement: at any rate, he does not specify the amount of any others in his catalogue of the ships. That they were all rowers as well as warriors we see from his account of the ships of Philoctetes, in which all the men at the oar are bowmen. Now it is improbable that many supernumeraries sailed, if we except the kings and high officers; especially as they had to cross the open sea with munitions of war, in ships, moreover, that had no decks, but were equipped in the old piratical fashion. So that if we strike the average of

the largest and smallest ships, the number of those who sailed will appear inconsiderable, representing, as they did, the whole force of Hellas. *[11]* And this was due not so much to scarcity of men as of money. Difficulty of subsistence made the invaders reduce the numbers of the army to a point at which it might live on the country during the prosecution of the war. Even after the victory they obtained on their arrival—and a victory there must have been, or the fortifications of the naval camp could never have been built—there is no indication of their whole force having been employed; on the contrary, they seem to have turned to cultivation of the Chersonese and to piracy from want of supplies. This was what really enabled the Trojans to keep the field for ten years against them; the dispersion of the enemy making them always a match for the detachment left behind. If they had brought plenty of supplies with them, and had persevered in the war without scattering for piracy and agriculture, they would have easily defeated the Trojans in the field, since they could hold their own against them with the division on service. In short, if they had stuck to the siege, the capture of Troy would have cost them less time and less trouble. But as want of money proved the weakness of earlier expeditions, so from the same cause even the one in question, more famous than its predecessors, may be pronounced on the evidence of what it effected to have been inferior to its renown and to the current opinion about it formed under the tuition of the poets.

[12] Even after the Trojan War, Hellas was still engaged in removing and settling, and thus could not attain to the quiet which must precede growth. The late return of the Hellenes from Ilium caused many revolutions, and factions ensued almost everywhere; and it was the citizens thus driven into exile who founded the cities. Sixty years after the capture of Ilium, the modern Boeotians were driven out of Arne by the Thessalians, and settled in the present Boeotia, the former Cadmeis; though there was a division of them there before, some of whom joined the expedition to Ilium. Twenty years later, the Dorians and the Heraclids became masters of Peloponnese; so that much had to be done and many years had to elapse before Hellas could attain to a durable tranquillity undisturbed by removals, and could begin to send out colonies, as Athens did to Ionia and most of the islands, and the Peloponnesians to most of Italy and Sicily and some places in the rest

of Hellas. All these places were founded subsequently to the war with Troy.

[13] But as the power of Hellas grew, and the acquisition of wealth became more an object, the revenues of the states increasing, tyrannies were by their means established almost everywhere—the old form of government being hereditary monarchy with definite prerogatives—and Hellas began to fit out fleets and apply herself more closely to the sea. It is said that the Corinthians were the first to approach the modern style of naval architecture, and that Corinth was the first place in Hellas where galleys were built; and we have Ameinocles, a Corinthian shipwright, making four ships for the Samians. Dating from the end of this war, it is nearly three hundred years ago that Ameinocles went to Samos. Again, the earliest sea-fight in history was between the Corinthians and Corcyraeans; this was about two hundred and sixty years ago, dating from the same time. Planted on an isthmus, Corinth had from time out of mind been a commercial emporium; as formerly almost all communication between the Hellenes within and without Peloponnese was carried on overland, and the Corinthian territory was the highway through which it travelled. She had consequently great money resources, as is shown by the epithet "wealthy" bestowed by the old poets on the place, and this enabled her, when traffic by sea became more common, to procure her navy and put down piracy; and as she could offer a mart for both branches of the trade, she acquired for herself all the power which a large revenue affords. Subsequently the Ionians attained to great naval strength in the reign of Cyrus, the first king of the Persians, and of his son Cambyses, and while they were at war with the former commanded for a while the Ionian sea. Polycrates also, the tyrant of Samos, had a powerful navy in the reign of Cambyses, with which he reduced many of the islands, and among them Rhenea, which he consecrated to the Delian Apollo. About this time also the Phocaeans, while they were founding Marseilles, defeated the Carthaginians in a sea-fight. *[14]* These were the most powerful navies. And even these, although so many generations had elapsed since the Trojan war, seem to have been principally composed of the old fifty-oars and long-boats, and to have counted few galleys among their ranks. Indeed it was only shortly before the Persian war, and the death of Darius the successor of Cambyses, that the Sicilian tyrants and the Corcyraeans acquired

any large number of galleys. For after these there were no navies of any account in Hellas till the expedition of Xerxes; Aegina, Athens, and others may have possessed a few vessels, but they were principally fifty-oars. It was quite at the end of this period that the war with Aegina and the prospect of the barbarian invasion enabled Themistocles to persuade the Athenians to build the fleet with which they fought at Salamis; and even these vessels had not complete decks.

[15] The navies, then, of the Hellenes during the period we have traversed were what I have described. All their insignificance did not prevent their being an element of the greatest power to those who cultivated them, alike in revenue and in dominion. They were the means by which the islands were reached and reduced, those of the smallest area falling the easiest prey. Wars by land there were none, none at least by which power was acquired; we have the usual border contests, but of distant expeditions with conquest for object we hear nothing among the Hellenes. There was no union of subject cities round a great state, no spontaneous combination of equals for confederate expeditions; what fighting there was consisted merely of local warfare between rival neighbours. The nearest approach to a coalition took place in the old war between Chalcis and Eretria; this was a quarrel in which the rest of the Hellenic name did to some extent take sides.

[16] Various, too, were the obstacles which the national growth encountered in various localities. The power of the Ionians was advancing with rapid strides, when it came into collision with Persia, under King Cyrus, who, after having dethroned Croesus and overrun everything between the Halys and the sea, stopped not till he had reduced the cities of the coast; the islands being only left to be subdued by Darius and the Phoenician navy.

[17] Again, wherever there were tyrants, their habit of providing simply for themselves, of looking solely to their personal comfort and family aggrandizement, made safety the great aim of their policy, and prevented anything great proceeding from them; though they would each have their affairs with their immediate neighbours. All this is only true of the mother country, for in Sicily they attained to very great power. Thus for a long time everywhere in Hellas do we find causes which make the states alike incapable of combination for great and national ends, or of any vigorous action of their own.

[18] But at last a time came when the tyrants of Athens and the far older tyrannies of the rest of Hellas were, with the exception of those in Sicily, once and for all put down by Lacedaemon; for this city, though after the settlement of the Dorians, its present inhabitants, it suffered from factions for an unparalleled length of time, still at a very early period obtained good laws, and enjoyed a freedom from tyrants which was unbroken; it has possessed the same form of government for more than four hundred years, reckoning to the end of the late war, and has thus been in a position to arrange the affairs of the other states. Not many years after the deposition of the tyrants, the battle of Marathon was fought between the Medes and the Athenians. Ten years afterwards, the barbarian returned with the armada for the subjugation of Hellas. In the face of this great danger, the command of the confederate Hellenes was assumed by the Lacedaemonians in virtue of their superior power; and the Athenians, having made up their minds to abandon their city, broke up their homes, threw themselves into their ships, and became a naval people. This coalition, after repulsing the barbarian, soon afterwards split into two sections, which included the Hellenes who had revolted from the King, as well as those who had aided him in the war. At the end of the one stood Athens, at the head of the other Lacedaemon, one the first naval, the other the first military power in Hellas. For a short time the league held together, till the Lacedaemonians and Athenians quarrelled and made war upon each other with their allies, a duel into which all the Hellenes sooner or later were drawn, though some might at first remain neutral. So that the whole period from the Median war to this, with some peaceful intervals, was spent by each power in war, either with its rival, or with its own revolted allies, and consequently afforded them constant practice in military matters, and that experience which is learnt in the school of danger.

[19] The policy of Lacedaemon was not to exact tribute from her allies, but merely to secure their subservience to her interests by establishing oligarchies among them; Athens, on the contrary, had by degrees deprived hers of their ships, and imposed instead contributions in money on all except Chios and Lesbos. Both found their resources for this war separately to exceed the sum of their strength when the alliance flourished intact.

[20] Having now given the result of my in-

quiries into early times, I grant that there will be a difficulty in believing every particular detail. The way that most men deal with traditions, even traditions of their own country, is to receive them all alike as they are delivered, without applying any critical test whatever. The general Athenian public fancy that Hipparchus was tyrant when he fell by the hands of Harmodius and Aristogiton, not knowing that Hippias, the eldest of the sons of Pisistratus, was really supreme, and that Hipparchus and Thessalus were his brothers; and that Harmodius and Aristogiton suspecting, on the very day, nay at the very moment fixed on for the deed, that information had been conveyed to Hippias by their accomplices, concluded that he had been warned, and did not attack him, yet, not liking to be apprehended and risk their lives for nothing, fell upon Hipparchus near the temple of the daughters of Leos, and slew him as he was arranging the Panathenaic procession.

There are many other unfounded ideas current among the rest of the Hellenes, even on matters of contemporary history, which have not been obscured by time. For instance, there is the notion that the Lacedaemonian kings have two votes each, the fact being that they have only one; and that there is a company of Pitane, there being simply no such thing. So little pains do the vulgar take in the investigation of truth, accepting readily the first story that comes to hand. *[21]* On the whole, however, the conclusions I have drawn from the proofs quoted may, I believe, safely be relied on. Assuredly they will not be disturbed either by the lays of a poet displaying the exaggeration of his craft, or by the compositions of the chroniclers that are attractive at truth's expense; the subjects they treat of being out of the reach of evidence, and time having robbed most of them of historical value by enthroning them in the region of legend. Turning from these, we can rest satisfied with having proceeded upon the clearest data, and having arrived at conclusions as exact as can be expected in matters of such antiquity. To come to this war: despite the known disposition of the actors in a struggle to overrate its importance, and when it is over to return to their admiration of earlier events, yet an examination of the facts will show that it was much greater than the wars which preceded it.

[22] With reference to the speeches in this history, some were delivered before the war began, others while it was going on; some I heard myself, others I got from various quarters; it was in all cases difficult to carry them word for word in one's memory, so my habit has been to make the speakers say what was in my opinion demanded of them by the various occasions, of course adhering as closely as possible to the general sense of what they really said. And with reference to the narrative of events, far from permitting myself to derive it from the first source that came to hand, I did not even trust my own impressions, but it rests partly on what I saw myself, partly on what others saw for me, the accuracy of the report being always tried by the most severe and detailed tests possible. My conclusions have cost me some labour from the want of coincidence between accounts of the same occurrences by different eye-witnesses, arising sometimes from imperfect memory, sometimes from undue partiality for one side or the other. The absence of romance in my history will, I fear, detract somewhat from its interest; but if it be judged useful by those inquirers who desire an exact knowledge of the past as an aid to the interpretation of the future, which in the course of human things must resemble if it does not reflect it, I shall be content. In fine, I have written my work, not as an essay which is to win the applause of the moment, but as a possession for all time.

[23] The Median War, the greatest achievement of past times, yet found a speedy decision in two actions by sea and two by land. The Peloponnesian War was prolonged to an immense length, and, long as it was, it was short without parallel for the misfortunes that it brought upon Hellas. Never had so many cities been taken and laid desolate, here by the barbarians, here by the parties contending (the old inhabitants being sometimes removed to make room for others); never was there so much banishing and blood-shedding, now on the field of battle, now in the strife of faction. Old stories of occurrences handed down by tradition, but scantily confirmed by experience, suddenly ceased to be incredible; there were earthquakes of unparalleled extent and violence; eclipses of the sun occurred with a frequency unrecorded in previous history; there were great droughts in sundry places and consequent famines, and that most calamitous and awfully fatal visitation, the plague. All this came upon them with the late war, which was begun by the Athenians and Peloponnesians by the dissolution of the thirty years' truce made after the conquest of Euboea. To the question why they broke the

treaty, I answer by placing first an account of their grounds of complaint and points of difference, that no one may ever have to ask the immediate cause which plunged the Hellenes into a war of such magnitude. The real cause I consider to be the one which was formally most kept out of sight. The growth of the power of Athens, and the alarm which this inspired in Lacedaemon, made war inevitable. Still it is well to give the grounds alleged by either side which led to the dissolution of the treaty and the breaking out of the war.

CHAPTER II

Causes of the War—The Affair of Epidamnus—
The Affair of Potidaea

[24] THE city of Epidamnus stands on the right of the entrance of the Ionic Gulf. Its vicinity is inhabited by the Taulantians, an Illyrian people. The place is a colony from Corcyra, founded by Phalius, son of Eratocleides, of the family of the Heraclids, who had according to ancient usage been summoned for the purpose from Corinth, the mother country. The colonists were joined by some Corinthians, and others of the Dorian race. Now, as time went on, the city of Epidamnus became great and populous; but falling a prey to factions arising, it is said, from a war with her neighbours the barbarians, she became much enfeebled, and lost a considerable amount of her power. The last act before the war was the expulsion of the nobles by the people. The exiled party joined the barbarians, and proceeded to plunder those in the city by sea and land; and the Epidamnians, finding themselves hard pressed, sent ambassadors to Corcyra beseeching their mother country not to allow them to perish, but to make up matters between them and the exiles, and to rid them of the war with the barbarians. The ambassadors seated themselves in the temple of Hera as suppliants, and made the above requests to the Corcyraeans. But the Corcyraeans refused to accept their supplication, and they were dismissed without having effected anything.

[25] When the Epidamnians found that no help could be expected from Corcyra, they were in a strait what to do next. So they sent to Delphi and inquired of the God whether they should deliver their city to the Corinthians and endeavour to obtain some assistance from their founders. The answer he gave them was to deliver the city and place themselves under Corinthian protection. So the Epidamnians went to Corinth and delivered over the colony in obedience to the commands of the oracle. They showed that their founder came from Corinth, and revealed the answer of the god; and they begged them not to allow them to perish, but to assist them. This the Corinthians consented to do. Believing the colony to belong as much to themselves as to the Corcyraeans, they felt it to be a kind of duty to undertake their protection. Besides, they hated the Corcyraeans for their contempt of the mother country. Instead of meeting with the usual honours accorded to the parent city by every other colony at public assemblies, such as precedence at sacrifices, Corinth found herself treated with contempt by a power which in point of wealth could stand comparison with any even of the richest communities in Hellas, which possessed great military strength, and which sometimes could not repress a pride in the high naval position of an island whose nautical renown dated from the days of its old inhabitants, the Phaeacians. This was one reason of the care that they lavished on their fleet, which became very efficient; indeed they began the war with a force of a hundred and twenty galleys.

[26] All these grievances made Corinth eager to send the promised aid to Epidamnus. Advertisement was made for volunteer settlers, and a force of Ambraciots, Leucadians, and Corinthians was dispatched. They marched by land to Apollonia, a Corinthian colony, the route by sea being avoided from fear of Corcyraean interruption. When the Corcyraeans heard of the arrival of the settlers and troops in Epidamnus, and the surrender of the colony to Corinth, they took fire. Instantly putting to sea with five-and-twenty ships, which were quickly followed by others, they insolently commanded the Epidamnians to receive back the banished nobles—(it must be premised that the Epidamnian exiles had come to Corcyra and, pointing to the sepulchres of their ancestors, had appealed to their kindred to restore them)—and to dismiss the Corinthian garrison and settlers. But to all this the Epidamnians turned a deaf ear. Upon this the Corcyraeans commenced operations against them with a fleet of forty sail. They took with them the exiles, with a view to their restoration, and also secured the services of the Illyrians. Sitting down before the city, they issued a proclamation to the effect that any of the natives that chose, and the foreigners, might depart unharmed, with the alterna-

tive of being treated as enemies. On their refusal the Corcyraeans proceeded to besiege the
city, which stands on an isthmus; [27] and the
Corinthians, receiving intelligence of the investment of Epidamnus, got together an armament and proclaimed a colony to Epidamnus,
perfect political equality being guaranteed to
all who chose to go. Any who were not prepared to sail at once might, by paying down
the sum of fifty Corinthian drachmae, have a
share in the colony without leaving Corinth.
Great numbers took advantage of this proclamation, some being ready to start directly,
others paying the requisite forfeit. In case of
their passage being disputed by the Corcyraeans, several cities were asked to lend them a
convoy. Megara prepared to accompany them
with eight ships, Pale in Cephallonia with
four; Epidaurus furnished five, Hermione one,
Troezen two, Leucas ten, and Ambracia eight.
The Thebans and Phliasians were asked for
money, the Eleans for hulls as well; while Corinth herself furnished thirty ships and three
thousand heavy infantry.

[28] When the Corcyraeans heard of their
preparations they came to Corinth with envoys
from Lacedaemon and Sicyon, whom they persuaded to accompany them, and bade her recall the garrison and settlers, as she had nothing to do with Epidamnus. If, however, she
had any claims to make, they were willing to
submit the matter to the arbitration of such of
the cities in Peloponnese as should be chosen
by mutual agreement, and that the colony
should remain with the city to whom the arbitrators might assign it. They were also willing
to refer the matter to the oracle at Delphi. If, in
defiance of their protestations, war was appealed to, they should be themselves compelled
by this violence to seek friends in quarters
where they had no desire to seek them, and to
make even old ties give way to the necessity of
assistance. The answer they got from Corinth
was that, if they would withdraw their fleet
and the barbarians from Epidamnus, negotiation might be possible; but, while the town
was still being besieged, going before arbitrators was out of the question. The Corcyraeans
retorted that if Corinth would withdraw her
troops from Epidamnus they would withdraw
theirs, or they were ready to let both parties remain *in statu quo,* an armistice being concluded till judgment could be given.

[29] Turning a deaf ear to all these proposals, when their ships were manned and
their allies had come in, the Corinthians sent a

herald before them to declare war and, getting
under way with seventy-five ships and two
thousand heavy infantry, sailed for Epidamnus
to give battle to the Corcyraeans. The fleet was
under the command of Aristeus, son of Pel-
lichas, Callicrates, son of Callias, and Tima-
nor, son of Timanthes; the troops under that of
Archetimus, son of Eurytimus, and Isarchidas,
son of Isarchus. When they had reached Actium in the territory of Anactorium, at the
mouth of the Gulf of Ambracia, where the
temple of Apollo stands, the Corcyraeans sent
on a herald in a light boat to warn them not to
sail against them. Meanwhile they proceeded
to man their ships, all of which had been
equipped for action, the old vessels being un-
dergirded to make them seaworthy. On the return of the herald without any peaceful answer
from the Corinthians, their ships being now
manned, they put out to sea to meet the enemy
with a fleet of eighty sail (forty were engaged
in the siege of Epidamnus), formed line, and
went into action, and gained a decisive victory,
and destroyed fifteen of the Corinthian vessels.
The same day had seen Epidamnus compelled
by its besiegers to capitulate; the conditions being that the foreigners should be sold, and the
Corinthians kept as prisoners of war, till their
fate should be otherwise decided.

[30] After the engagement the Corcyraeans
set up a trophy on Leukimme, a headland of
Corcyra, and slew all their captives except the
Corinthians, whom they kept as prisoners of
war. Defeated at sea, the Corinthians and their
allies repaired home, and left the Corcyraeans
masters of all the sea about those parts. Sailing
to Leucas, a Corinthian colony, they ravaged
their territory, and burnt Cyllene, the harbour
of the Eleans, because they had furnished ships
and money to Corinth. For almost the whole
of the period that followed the battle they remained masters of the sea, and the allies of
Corinth were harassed by Corcyraean cruisers.
At last Corinth, roused by the sufferings of her
allies, sent out ships and troops in the fall of
the summer, who formed an encampment at
Actium and about Chimerium, in Thesprotis,
for the protection of Leucas and the rest of the
friendly cities. The Corcyraeans on their part
formed a similar station on Leukimme. Neither party made any movement, but they remained confronting each other till the end of
the summer, and winter was at hand before
either of them returned home.

[31] Corinth, exasperated by the war with
the Corcyraeans, spent the whole of the year

after the engagement and that succeeding it in building ships, and in straining every nerve to form an efficient fleet; rowers being drawn from Peloponnese and the rest of Hellas by the inducement of large bounties. The Corcyraeans, alarmed at the news of their preparations, being without a single ally in Hellas (for they had not enrolled themselves either in the Athenian or in the Lacedaemonian confederacy), decided to repair to Athens in order to enter into alliance and to endeavour to procure support from her. Corinth also, hearing of their intentions, sent an embassy to Athens to prevent the Corcyraean navy being joined by the Athenian, and her prospect of ordering the war according to her wishes being thus impeded. An assembly was convoked, and the rival advocates appeared: the Corcyraeans spoke as follows:

[32] "Athenians! when a people that have not rendered any important service or support to their neighbours in times past, for which they might claim to be repaid, appear before them as we now appear before you to solicit their assistance, they may fairly be required to satisfy certain preliminary conditions. They should show, first, that it is expedient or at least safe to grant their request; next, that they will retain a lasting sense of the kindness. But if they cannot clearly establish any of these points, they must not be annoyed if they meet with a rebuff. Now the Corcyraeans believe that with their petition for assistance they can also give you a satisfactory answer on these points, and they have therefore dispatched us hither. It has so happened that our policy as regards you with respect to this request, turns out to be inconsistent, and as regards our interests, to be at the present crisis inexpedient. We say inconsistent, because a power which has never in the whole of her past history been willing to ally herself with any of her neighbours, is now found asking them to ally themselves with her. And we say inexpedient, because in our present war with Corinth it has left us in a position of entire isolation, and what once seemed the wise precaution of refusing to involve ourselves in alliances with other powers, lest we should also involve ourselves in risks of their choosing, has now proved to be folly and weakness. It is true that in the late naval engagement we drove back the Corinthians from our shores single-handed. But they have now got together a still larger armament from Peloponnese and the rest of Hellas; and we, seeing our utter inability to cope with them without foreign aid, and the magnitude of the danger which subjection to them implies, find it necessary to ask help from you and from every other power. And we hope to be excused if we forswear our old principle of complete political isolation, a principle which was not adopted with any sinister intention, but was rather the consequence of an error in judgment.

[33] "Now there are many reasons why in the event of your compliance you will congratulate yourselves on this request having been made to you. First, because your assistance will be rendered to a power which, herself inoffensive, is a victim to the injustice of others. Secondly, because all that we most value is at stake in the present contest, and your welcome of us under these circumstances will be a proof of goodwill which will ever keep alive the gratitude you will lay up in our hearts. Thirdly, yourselves excepted, we are the greatest naval power in Hellas. Moreover, can you conceive a stroke of good fortune more rare in itself, or more disheartening to your enemies, than that the power whose adhesion you would have valued above much material and moral strength should present herself self-invited, should deliver herself into your hands without danger and without expense, and should lastly put you in the way of gaining a high character in the eyes of the world, the gratitude of those whom you shall assist, and a great accession of strength for yourselves? You may search all history without finding many instances of a people gaining all these advantages at once, or many instances of a power that comes in quest of assistance being in a position to give to the people whose alliance she solicits as much safety and honour as she will receive. But it will be urged that it is only in the case of a war that we shall be found useful. To this we answer that if any of you imagine that that war is far off, he is grievously mistaken, and is blind to the fact that Lacedaemon regards you with jealousy and desires war, and that Corinth is powerful there—the same, remember, that is your enemy, and is even now trying to subdue us as a preliminary to attacking you. And this she does to prevent our becoming united by a common enmity, and her having us both on her hands, and also to ensure getting the start of you in one of two ways, either by crippling our power or by making its strength her own. Now it is our policy to be beforehand with her—that is, for Corcyra to make an offer of alliance and for you to ac-

cept it; in fact, we ought to form plans against her instead of waiting to defeat the plans she forms against us.

[*34*] "If she asserts that for you to receive a colony of hers into alliance is not right, let her know that every colony that is well treated honours its parent state, but becomes estranged from it by injustice. For colonists are not sent forth on the understanding that they are to be the slaves of those that remain behind, but that they are to be their equals. And that Corinth was injuring us is clear. Invited to refer the dispute about Epidamnus to arbitration, they chose to prosecute their complaints by war rather than by a fair trial. And let their conduct towards us who are their kindred be a warning to you not to be misled by their deceit, nor to yield to their direct requests; concessions to adversaries only end in self-reproach, and the more strictly they are avoided the greater will be the chance of security.

[*35*] "If it be urged that your reception of us will be a breach of the treaty existing between you and Lacedaemon, the answer is that we are a neutral state, and that one of the express provisions of that treaty is that it shall be competent for any Hellenic state that is neutral to join whichever side it pleases. And it is intolerable for Corinth to be allowed to obtain men for her navy not only from her allies, but also from the rest of Hellas, no small number being furnished by your own subjects; while we are to be excluded both from the alliance left open to us by treaty, and from any assistance that we might get from other quarters, and you are to be accused of political immorality if you comply with our request. On the other hand, we shall have much greater cause to complain of you, if you do not comply with it; if we, who are in peril and are no enemies of yours, meet with a repulse at your hands, while Corinth, who is the aggressor and your enemy, not only meets with no hindrance from you, but is even allowed to draw material for war from your dependencies. This ought not to be, but you should either forbid her enlisting men in your dominions, or you should lend us too what help you may think advisable.

[*36*] "But your real policy is to afford us avowed countenance and support. The advantages of this course, as we premised in the beginning of our speech, are many. We mention one that is perhaps the chief. Could there be a clearer guarantee of our good faith than is offered by the fact that the power which is at enmity with you is also at enmity with us, and

that that power is fully able to punish defection? And there is a wide difference between declining the alliance of an inland and of a maritime power. For your first endeavour should be to prevent, if possible, the existence of any naval power except your own; failing this, to secure the friendship of the strongest that does exist. And if any of you believe that what we urge is expedient, but fear to act upon this belief, lest it should lead to a breach of the treaty, you must remember that on the one hand, whatever your fears, your strength will be formidable to your antagonists; on the other, whatever the confidence you derive from refusing to receive us, your weakness will have no terrors for a strong enemy. You must also remember that your decision is for Athens no less than Corcyra, and that you are not making the best provision for her interests, if at a time when you are anxiously scanning the horizon that you may be in readiness for the breaking out of the war which is all but upon you, you hesitate to attach to your side a place whose adhesion or estrangement is alike pregnant with the most vital consequences. For it lies conveniently for the coast-navigation in the direction of Italy and Sicily, being able to bar the passage of naval reinforcements from thence to Peloponnese, and from Peloponnese thither; and it is in other respects a most desirable station. To sum up as shortly as possible, embracing both general and particular considerations, let this show you the folly of sacrificing us. Remember that there are but three considerable naval powers in Hellas—Athens, Corcyra, and Corinth—and that if you allow two of these three to become one, and Corinth to secure us for herself, you will have to hold the sea against the united fleets of Corcyra and Peloponnese. But if you receive us, you will have our ships to reinforce you in the struggle."

Such were the words of the Corcyraeans. After they had finished, the Corinthians spoke as follows:

[*37*] "These Corcyraeans in the speech we have just heard do not confine themselves to the question of their reception into your alliance. They also talk of our being guilty of injustice, and their being the victims of an unjustifiable war. It becomes necessary for us to touch upon both these points before we proceed to the rest of what we have to say, that you may have a more correct idea of the grounds of our claim, and have good cause to reject their petition. According to them, their old policy of refusing all offers of alliance was

a policy of moderation. It was in fact adopted for bad ends, not for good; indeed their conduct is such as to make them by no means desirous of having allies present to witness it, or of having the shame of asking their concurrence. Besides, their geographical situation makes them independent of others, and consequently the decision in cases where they injure any lies not with judges appointed by mutual agreement, but with themselves, because, while they seldom make voyages to their neighbours, they are constantly being visited by foreign vessels which are compelled to put in to Corcyra. In short, the object that they propose to themselves, in their specious policy of complete isolation, is not to avoid sharing in the crimes of others, but to secure monopoly of crime to themselves—the licence of outrage wherever they can compel, of fraud wherever they can elude, and the enjoyment of their gains without shame. And yet if they were the honest men they pretend to be, the less hold that others had upon them, the stronger would be the light in which they might have put their honesty by giving and taking what was just.

[38] "But such has not been their conduct either towards others or towards us. The attitude of our colony towards us has always been one of estrangement and is now one of hostility; for, say they: 'We were not sent out to be ill-treated.' We rejoin that we did not found the colony to be insulted by them, but to be their head and to be regarded with a proper respect. At any rate our other colonies honour us, and we are much beloved by our colonists; and clearly, if the majority are satisfied with us, these can have no good reason for a dissatisfaction in which they stand alone, and we are not acting improperly in making war against them, nor are we making war against them without having received signal provocation. Besides, if we were in the wrong, it would be honourable in them to give way to our wishes, and disgraceful for us to trample on their moderation; but in the pride and licence of wealth they have sinned again and again against us, and never more deeply than when Epidamnus, our dependency, which they took no steps to claim in its distress upon our coming to relieve it, was by them seized, and is now held by force of arms.

[39] "As to their allegation that they wished the question to be first submitted to arbitration, it is obvious that a challenge coming from the party who is safe in a commanding position cannot gain the credit due only to him

who, before appealing to arms, in deeds as well as words, places himself on a level with his adversary. In their case, it was not before they laid siege to the place, but after they at length understood that we should not tamely suffer it, that they thought of the specious word *arbitration*. And not satisfied with their own misconduct there, they appear here now requiring you to join with them not in alliance but in crime, and to receive them in spite of their being at enmity with us. But it was when they stood firmest that they should have made overtures to you, and not at a time when we have been wronged and they are in peril; nor yet at a time when you will be admitting to a share in your protection those who never admitted you to a share in their power, and will be incurring an equal amount of blame from us with those in whose offences you had no hand. No, they should have shared their power with you before they asked you to share your fortunes with them.

[40] "So then the reality of the grievances we come to complain of, and the violence and rapacity of our opponents, have both been proved. But that you cannot equitably receive them, this you have still to learn. It may be true that one of the provisions of the treaty is that it shall be competent for any state, whose name was not down on the list, to join whichever side it pleases. But this agreement is not meant for those whose object in joining is the injury of other powers, but for those whose need of support does not arise from the fact of defection, and whose adhesion will not bring to the power that is mad enough to receive them war instead of peace; which will be the case with you, if you refuse to listen to us. For you cannot become their auxiliary and remain our friend; if you join in their attack, you must share the punishment which the defenders inflict on them. And yet you have the best possible right to be neutral, or, failing this, you should on the contrary join us against them. Corinth is at least in treaty with you; with Corcyra you were never even in truce. But do not lay down the principle that defection is to be patronized. Did we on the defection of the Samians record our vote against you, when the rest of the Peloponnesian powers were equally divided on the question whether they should assist them? No, we told them to their face that every power has a right to punish its own allies. Why, if you make it your policy to receive and assist all offenders, you will find that just as many of your dependencies will come

over to us, and the principle that you establish will press less heavily on us than on yourselves.

[41] "This then is what Hellenic law entitles us to demand as a right. But we have also advice to offer and claims on your gratitude, which, since there is no danger of our injuring you, as we are not enemies, and since our friendship does not amount to very frequent intercourse, we say ought to be liquidated at the present juncture. When you were in want of ships of war for the war against the Aeginetans, before the Persian invasion, Corinth supplied you with twenty vessels. That good turn, and the line we took on the Samian question, when we were the cause of the Peloponnesians refusing to assist them, enabled you to conquer Aegina and to punish Samos. And we acted thus at crises when, if ever, men are wont in their efforts against their enemies to forget everything for the sake of victory, regarding him who assists them then as a friend, even if thus far he has been a foe, and him who opposes them then as a foe, even if he has thus far been a friend; indeed they allow their real interests to suffer from their absorbing preoccupation in the struggle.

[42] "Weigh well these considerations, and let your youth learn what they are from their elders, and let them determine to do unto us as we have done unto you. And let them not acknowledge the justice of what we say, but dispute its wisdom in the contingency of war. Not only is the straightest path generally speaking the wisest; but the coming of the war, which the Corcyraeans have used as a bugbear to persuade you to do wrong, is still uncertain, and it is not worth while to be carried away by it into gaining the instant and declared enmity of Corinth. It were, rather, wise to try and counteract the unfavourable impression which your conduct to Megara has created. For kindness opportunely shown has a greater power of removing old grievances than the facts of the case may warrant. And do not be seduced by the prospect of a great naval alliance. Abstinence from all injustice to other first-rate powers is a greater tower of strength than anything that can be gained by the sacrifice of permanent tranquillity for an apparent temporary advantage. [43] It is now our turn to benefit by the principle that we laid down at Lacedaemon, that every power has a right to punish her own allies. We now claim to receive the same from you, and protest against your rewarding us for benefiting you by our vote by injuring us by yours. On the contrary, return

us like for like, remembering that this is that very crisis in which he who lends aid is most a friend, and he who opposes is most a foe. And for these Corcyraeans—neither receive them into alliance in our despite, nor be their abettors in crime. So do, and you will act as we have a right to expect of you, and at the same time best consult your own interests."

[44] Such were the words of the Corinthians.

When the Athenians had heard both out, two assemblies were held. In the first there was a manifest disposition to listen to the representations of Corinth; in the second, public feeling had changed and an alliance with Corcyra was decided on, with certain reservations. It was to be a defensive, not an offensive alliance. It did not involve a breach of the treaty with Peloponnese: Athens could not be required to join Corcyra in any attack upon Corinth. But each of the contracting parties had a right to the other's assistance against invasion, whether of his own territory or that of an ally. For it began now to be felt that the coming of the Peloponnesian war was only a question of time, and no one was willing to see a naval power of such magnitude as Corcyra sacrificed to Corinth; though if they could let them weaken each other by mutual conflict, it would be no bad preparation for the struggle which Athens might one day have to wage with Corinth and the other naval powers. At the same time the island seemed to lie conveniently on the coasting passage to Italy and Sicily. [45] With these views, Athens received Corcyra into alliance and, on the departure of the Corinthians not long afterwards, sent ten ships to their assistance. They were commanded by Lacedaemonius, the son of Cimon, Diotimus, the son of Strombichus, and Proteas, the son of Epicles. Their instructions were to avoid collision with the Corinthian fleet except under certain circumstances. If it sailed to Corcyra and threatened a landing on her coast, or in any of her possessions, they were to do their utmost to prevent it. These instructions were prompted by an anxiety to avoid a breach of the treaty.

[46] Meanwhile the Corinthians completed their preparations, and sailed for Corcyra with a hundred and fifty ships. Of these Elis furnished ten, Megara twelve, Leucas ten, Ambracia twenty-seven, Anactorium one, and Corinth herself ninety. Each of these contingents had its own admiral, the Corinthian being under the command of Xenoclides, son of Euthycles, with four colleagues. Sailing from

Leucas, they made land at the part of the continent opposite Corcyra. They anchored in the harbour of Chimerium, in the territory of Thesprotis, above which, at some distance from the sea, lies the city of Ephyre, in the Elean district. By this city the Acherusian lake pours its waters into the sea. It gets its name from the river Acheron, which flows through Thesprotis and falls into the lake. There also the river Thyamis flows, forming the boundary between Thesprotis and Kestrine; and between these rivers rises the point of Chimerium. In this part of the continent the Corinthians now came to anchor, and formed an encampment. [47] When the Corcyraeans saw them coming, they manned a hundred and ten ships, commanded by Meikiades, Aisimides, and Eurybatus, and stationed themselves at one of the Sybota isles; the ten Athenian ships being present. On Point Leukimme they posted their land forces, and a thousand heavy infantry who had come from Zacynthus to their assistance. Nor were the Corinthians on the mainland without their allies. The barbarians flocked in large numbers to their assistance, the inhabitants of this part of the continent being old allies of theirs.

[48] When the Corinthian preparations were completed, they took three days' provisions and put out from Chimerium by night, ready for action. Sailing with the dawn, they sighted the Corcyraean fleet out at sea and coming towards them. When they perceived each other, both sides formed in order of battle. On the Corcyraean right wing lay the Athenian ships, the rest of the line being occupied by their own vessels formed in three squadrons, each of which was commanded by one of the three admirals. Such was the Corcyraean formation. The Corinthian was as follows: on the right wing lay the Megarian and Ambraciot ships, in the centre the rest of the allies in order. But the left was composed of the best sailers in the Corinthian navy, to encounter the Athenians and the right wing of the Corcyraeans. [49] As soon as the signals were raised on either side, they joined battle. Both sides had a large number of heavy infantry on their decks, and a large number of archers and darters, the old imperfect armament still prevailing. The sea-fight was an obstinate one, though not remarkable for its science; indeed it was more like a battle by land. Whenever they charged each other, the multitude and crush of the vessels made it by no means easy to get loose; besides, their hopes of victory lay principally in the heavy infantry on the decks, who stood and fought in order, the ships remaining stationary. The manœuvre of breaking the line was not tried; in short, strength and pluck had more share in the fight than science. Everywhere tumult reigned, the battle being one scene of confusion; meanwhile the Athenian ships, by coming up to the Corcyraeans whenever they were pressed, served to alarm the enemy, though their commanders could not join in the battle from fear of their instructions. The right wing of the Corinthians suffered most. The Corcyraeans routed it, and chased them in disorder to the continent with twenty ships, sailed up to their camp, and burnt the tents which they found empty, and plundered the stuff. So in this quarter the Corinthians and their allies were defeated, and the Corcyraeans were victorious. But where the Corinthians themselves were, on the left, they gained a decided success; the scanty forces of the Corcyraeans being further weakened by the want of the twenty ships absent on the pursuit. Seeing the Corcyraeans hard pressed, the Athenians began at length to assist them more unequivocally. At first, it is true, they refrained from charging any ships; but when the rout was becoming patent, and the Corinthians were pressing on, the time at last came when every one set to, and all distinction was laid aside, and it came to this point, that the Corinthians and Athenians raised their hands against each other.

[50] After the rout, the Corinthians, instead of employing themselves in lashing fast and hauling after them the hulls of the vessels which they had disabled, turned their attention to the men, whom they butchered as they sailed through, not caring so much to make prisoners. Some even of their own friends were slain by them, by mistake, in their ignorance of the defeat of the right wing. For the number of the ships on both sides, and the distance to which they covered the sea, made it difficult, after they had once joined, to distinguish between the conquering and the conquered; this battle proving far greater than any before it, any at least between Hellenes, for the number of vessels engaged. After the Corinthians had chased the Corcyraeans to the land, they turned to the wrecks and their dead, most of whom they succeeded in getting hold of and conveying to Sybota, the rendezvous of the land forces furnished by their barbarian allies. Sybota, it must be known, is a desert harbour of Thesprotis. This task over, they mustered anew, and sailed

against the Corcyraeans, who on their part advanced to meet them with all their ships that were fit for service and remaining to them, accompanied by the Athenian vessels, fearing that they might attempt a landing in their territory. It was by this time getting late, and the paean had been sung for the attack, when the Corinthians suddenly began to back water. They had observed twenty Athenian ships sailing up, which had been sent out afterwards to reinforce the ten vessels by the Athenians, who feared, as it turned out justly, the defeat of the Corcyraeans and the inability of their handful of ships to protect them. [51] These ships were thus seen by the Corinthians first. They suspected that they were from Athens, and that those which they saw were not all, but that there were more behind; they accordingly began to retire. The Corcyraeans meanwhile had not sighted them, as they were advancing from a point which they could not so well see, and were wondering why the Corinthians were backing water, when some caught sight of them, and cried out that there were ships in sight ahead. Upon this they also retired; for it was now getting dark, and the retreat of the Corinthians had suspended hostilities. Thus they parted from each other, and the battle ceased with night. The Corcyraeans were in their camp at Leukimme, when these twenty ships from Athens, under the command of Glaucon, the son of Leagrus, and Andocides, son of Leogoras, bore on through the corpses and the wrecks, and sailed up to the camp, not long after they were sighted. It was now night, and the Corcyraeans feared that they might be hostile vessels; but they soon knew them, and the ships came to anchor.

[52] The next day the thirty Athenian vessels put out to sea, accompanied by all the Corcyraean ships that were seaworthy, and sailed to the harbour at Sybota, where the Corinthians lay, to see if they would engage. The Corinthians put out from the land and formed a line in the open sea, but beyond this made no further movement, having no intention of assuming the offensive. For they saw reinforcements arrived fresh from Athens, and themselves confronted by numerous difficulties, such as the necessity of guarding the prisoners whom they had on board and the want of all means of refitting their ships in a desert place. What they were thinking more about was how their voyage home was to be effected; they feared that the Athenians might consider that the treaty was dissolved by the collision which

had occurred, and forbid their departure.

[53] Accordingly they resolved to put some men on board a boat, and send them without a herald's wand to the Athenians, as an experiment. Having done so, they spoke as follows: "You do wrong, Athenians, to begin war and break the treaty. Engaged in chastising our enemies, we find you placing yourselves in our path in arms against us. Now if your intentions are to prevent us sailing to Corcyra, or anywhere else that we may wish, and if you are for breaking the treaty, first take us that are here and treat us as enemies." Such was what they said, and all the Corcyraean armament that were within hearing immediately called out to take them and kill them. But the Athenians answered as follows: "Neither are we beginning war, Peloponnesians, nor are we breaking the treaty; but these Corcyraeans are our allies, and we are come to help them. So if you want to sail anywhere else, we place no obstacle in your way; but if you are going to sail against Corcyra, or any of her possessions, we shall do our best to stop you."

[54] Receiving this answer from the Athenians, the Corinthians commenced preparations for their voyage home, and set up a trophy in Sybota, on the continent; while the Corcyraeans took up the wrecks and dead that had been carried out to them by the current, and by a wind which rose in the night and scattered them in all directions, and set up their trophy in Sybota, on the island, as victors. The reasons each side had for claiming the victory were these. The Corinthians had been victorious in the sea-fight until night; and having thus been enabled to carry off most wrecks and dead, they were in possession of no fewer than a thousand prisoners of war, and had sunk close upon seventy vessels. The Corcyraeans had destroyed about thirty ships, and after the arrival of the Athenians had taken up the wrecks and dead on their side; they had besides seen the Corinthians retire before them, backing water on sight of the Athenian vessels, and upon the arrival of the Athenians refuse to sail out against them from Sybota. Thus both sides claimed the victory.

[55] The Corinthians on the voyage home took Anactorium, which stands at the mouth of the Ambracian gulf. The place was taken by treachery, being common ground to the Corcyraeans and Corinthians. After establishing Corinthian settlers there, they retired home. Eight hundred of the Corcyraeans were slaves; these they sold; two hundred and fifty they re-

tained in captivity, and treated with great attention, in the hope that they might bring over their country to Corinth on their return; most of them being, as it happened, men of very high position in Corcyra. In this way Corcyra maintained her political existence in the war with Corinth, and the Athenian vessels left the island. This was the first cause of the war that Corinth had against the Athenians, viz., that they had fought against them with the Corcyraeans in time of treaty.

[56] Almost immediately after this, fresh differences arose between the Athenians and Peloponnesians, and contributed their share to the war. Corinth was forming schemes for retaliation, and Athens suspected her hostility. The Potidaeans, who inhabit the isthmus of Pallene, being a Corinthian colony, but tributary allies of Athens, were ordered to raze the wall looking towards Pallene, to give hostages, to dismiss the Corinthian magistrates, and in future not to receive the persons sent from Corinth annually to succeed them. It was feared that they might be persuaded by Perdiccas and the Corinthians to revolt, and might draw the rest of the allies in the direction of Thrace to revolt with them. [57] These precautions against the Potidaeans were taken by the Athenians immediately after the battle at Corcyra. Not only was Corinth at length openly hostile, but Perdiccas, son of Alexander, king of the Macedonians, had from an old friend and ally been made an enemy. He had been made an enemy by the Athenians entering into alliance with his brother Philip and Derdas, who were in league against him. In his alarm he had sent to Lacedaemon to try and involve the Athenians in a war with the Peloponnesians, and was endeavouring to win over Corinth in order to bring about the revolt of Potidaea. He also made overtures to the Chalcidians in the direction of Thrace, and to the Bottiaeans, to persuade them to join in the revolt; for he thought that if these places on the border could be made his allies, it would be easier to carry on the war with their co-operation. Alive to all this, and wishing to anticipate the revolt of the cities, the Athenians acted as follows. They were just then sending off thirty ships and a thousand heavy infantry for his country under the command of Archestratus, son of Lycomedes, with four colleagues. They instructed the captains to take hostages of the Potidaeans, to raze the wall, and to be on their guard against the revolt of the neighbouring cities.

[58] Meanwhile the Potidaeans sent envoys to Athens on the chance of persuading them to take no new steps in their matters; they also went to Lacedaemon with the Corinthians to secure support in case of need. Failing after prolonged negotiation to obtain anything satisfactory from the Athenians; being unable, for all they could say, to prevent the vessels that were destined for Macedonia from also sailing against them; and receiving from the Lacedaemonian government a promise to invade Attica, if the Athenians should attack Potidaea, the Potidaeans, thus favoured by the moment, at last entered into league with the Chalcidians and Bottiaeans, and revolted. And Perdiccas induced the Chalcidians to abandon and demolish their towns on the seaboard and, settling inland at Olynthus, to make that one city a strong place: meanwhile to those who followed his advice he gave a part of his territory in Mygdonia round Lake Bolbe as a place of abode while the war against the Athenians should last. They accordingly demolished their towns, removed inland, and prepared for war.

[59] The thirty ships of the Athenians, arriving before the Thracian places, found Potidaea and the rest in revolt. Their commanders, considering it to be quite impossible with their present force to carry on war with Perdiccas and with the confederate towns as well, turned to Macedonia, their original destination, and, having established themselves there, carried on war in co-operation with Philip, and the brothers of Derdas, who had invaded the country from the interior.

[60] Meanwhile the Corinthians, with Potidaea in revolt and the Athenian ships on the coast of Macedonia, alarmed for the safety of the place and thinking its danger theirs, sent volunteers from Corinth, and mercenaries from the rest of Peloponnese, to the number of sixteen hundred heavy infantry in all, and four hundred light troops. Aristeus, son of Adimantus, who was always a steady friend to the Potidaeans, took command of the expedition, and it was principally for love of him that most of the men from Corinth volunteered. They arrived in Thrace forty days after the revolt of Potidaea.

[61] The Athenians also immediately received the news of the revolt of the cities. On being informed that Aristeus and his reinforcements were on their way, they sent two thousand heavy infantry of their own citizens and forty ships against the places in revolt, under the command of Callias, son of Calliades, and four colleagues. They arrived in Macedonia

first, and found the force of a thousand men that had been first sent out, just become masters of Therme and besieging Pydna. Accordingly they also joined in the investment, and besieged Pydna for a while. Subsequently they came to terms and concluded a forced alliance with Perdiccas, hastened by the calls of Potidaea and by the arrival of Aristeus at that place. They withdrew from Macedonia, going to Beroea and thence to Strepsa, and, after a futile attempt on the latter place, they pursued by land their march to Potidaea with three thousand heavy infantry of their own citizens, besides a number of their allies, and six hundred Macedonian horsemen, the followers of Philip and Pausanias. With these sailed seventy ships along the coast. Advancing by short marches, on the third day they arrived at Gigonus, where they encamped.

[62] Meanwhile the Potidaeans and the Peloponnesians with Aristeus were encamped on the side looking towards Olynthus on the isthmus, in expectation of the Athenians, and had established their market outside the city. The allies had chosen Aristeus general of all the infantry; while the command of the cavalry was given to Perdiccas, who had at once left the alliance of the Athenians and gone back to that of the Potidaeans, having deputed Iolaus as his general. The plan of Aristeus was to keep his own force on the isthmus, and await the attack of the Athenians; leaving the Chalcidians and the allies outside the isthmus, and the two hundred cavalry from Perdiccas in Olynthus to act upon the Athenian rear, on the occasion of their advancing against him; and thus to place the enemy between two fires. While Callias the Athenian general and his colleagues dispatched the Macedonian horse and a few of the allies to Olynthus, to prevent any movement being made from that quarter, the Athenians themselves broke up their camp and marched against Potidaea. After they had arrived at the isthmus, and saw the enemy preparing for battle, they formed against him, and soon afterwards engaged. The wing of Aristeus, with the Corinthians and other picked troops round him, routed the wing opposed to it, and followed for a considerable distance in pursuit. But the rest of the army of the Potidaeans and of the Peloponnesians was defeated by the Athenians, and took refuge within the fortifications. *[63]* Returning from the pursuit, Aristeus perceived the defeat of the rest of the army. Being at a loss which of the two risks to choose, whether to go to Olynthus or to Potidaea, he at last determined to draw his men into as small a space as possible, and force his way with a run into Potidaea. Not without difficulty, through a storm of missiles, he passed along by the breakwater through the sea, and brought off most of his men safe, though a few were lost. Meanwhile the auxiliaries of the Potidaeans from Olynthus, which is about seven miles off and in sight of Potidaea, when the battle began and the signals were raised, advanced a little way to render assistance; and the Macedonian horse formed against them to prevent it. But on victory speedily declaring for the Athenians and the signals being taken down, they retired back within the wall; and the Macedonians returned to the Athenians. Thus there were no cavalry present on either side. After the battle the Athenians set up a trophy, and gave back their dead to the Potidaeans under truce. The Potidaeans and their allies had close upon three hundred killed; the Athenians a hundred and fifty of their own citizens, and Callias their general.

[64] The wall on the side of the isthmus had now works at once raised against it, and manned by the Athenians. That on the side of Pallene had no works raised against it. They did not think themselves strong enough at once to keep a garrison in the isthmus and to cross over to Pallene and raise works there; they were afraid that the Potidaeans and their allies might take advantage of their division to attack them. Meanwhile the Athenians at home learning that there were no works at Pallene, some time afterwards sent off sixteen hundred heavy infantry of their own citizens under the command of Phormio, son of Asopius. Arrived at Pallene, he fixed his headquarters at Aphytis, and led his army against Potidaea by short marches, ravaging the country as he advanced. No one venturing to meet him in the field, he raised works against the wall on the side of Pallene. So at length Potidaea was strongly invested on either side, and from the sea by the ships co-operating in the blockade. *[65]* Aristeus, seeing its investment complete, and having no hope of its salvation, except in the event of some movement from the Peloponnese, or of some other improbable contingency, advised all except five hundred to watch for a wind and sail out of the place, in order that their provisions might last the longer. He was willing to be himself one of those who remained. Unable to persuade them, and desirous of acting on the next alternative, and of having

things outside in the best posture possible, he eluded the guardships of the Athenians and sailed out. Remaining among the Chalcidians, he continued to carry on the war; in particular he laid an ambuscade near the city of the Sermylians, and cut off many of them; he also communicated with Peloponnese, and tried to contrive some method by which help might be brought. Meanwhile, after the completion of the investment of Potidaea, Phormio next employed his sixteen hundred men in ravaging Chalcidice and Bottica: some of the towns also were taken by him.

CHAPTER III

Congress of the Peloponnesian Confederacy at Lacedaemon

[66] THE Athenians and Peloponnesians had these antecedent grounds of complaint against each other: the complaint of Corinth was that her colony of Potidaea, and Corinthian and Peloponnesian citizens within it, were being besieged; that of Athens against the Peloponnesians that they had incited a town of hers, a member of her alliance and a contributor to her revenue, to revolt, and had come and were openly fighting against her on the side of the Potidaeans. For all this, war had not yet broken out: there was still truce for a while; for this was a private enterprise on the part of Corinth.

[67] But the siege of Potidaea put an end to her inaction; she had men inside it: besides, she feared for the place. Immediately summoning the allies to Lacedaemon, she came and loudly accused Athens of breach of the treaty and aggression on the rights of Peloponnese. With her, the Aeginetans, formally unrepresented from fear of Athens, in secret proved not the least urgent of the advocates for war, asserting that they had not the independence guaranteed to them by the treaty. After extending the summons to any of their allies and others who might have complaints to make of Athenian aggression, the Lacedaemonians held their ordinary assembly, and invited them to speak. There were many who came forward and made their several accusations; among them the Megarians, in a long list of grievances, called special attention to the fact of their exclusion from the ports of the Athenian empire and the market of Athens, in defiance of the treaty. Last of all the Corinthians came forward, and having let those who preceded them inflame the Lacedaemonians,

now followed with a speech to this effect:

[68] "Lacedaemonians! the confidence which you feel in your constitution and social order, inclines you to receive any reflections of ours on other powers with a certain scepticism. Hence springs your moderation, but hence also the rather limited knowledge which you betray in dealing with foreign politics. Time after time was our voice raised to warn you of the blows about to be dealt us by Athens, and time after time, instead of taking the trouble to ascertain the worth of our communications, you contented yourselves with suspecting the speakers of being inspired by private interest. And so, instead of calling these allies together before the blow fell, you have delayed to do so till we are smarting under it; allies among whom we have not the worst title to speak, as having the greatest complaints to make, complaints of Athenian outrage and Lacedaemonian neglect. Now if these assaults on the rights of Hellas had been made in the dark, you might be unacquainted with the facts, and it would be our duty to enlighten you. As it is, long speeches are not needed where you see servitude accomplished for some of us, meditated for others—in particular for our allies—and prolonged preparations in the aggressor against the hour of war. Or what, pray, is the meaning of their reception of Corcyra by fraud, and their holding it against us by force? what of the siege of Potidaea?—places one of which lies most conveniently for any action against the Thracian towns; while the other would have contributed a very large navy to the Peloponnesians?

[69] "For all this you are responsible. You it was who first allowed them to fortify their city after the Median war, and afterwards to erect the long walls—you who, then and now, are always depriving of freedom not only those whom they have enslaved, but also those who have as yet been your allies. For the true author of the subjugation of a people is not so much the immediate agent, as the power which permits it having the means to prevent it; particularly if that power aspires to the glory of being the liberator of Hellas. We are at last assembled. It has not been easy to assemble, nor even now are our objects defined. We ought not to be still inquiring into the fact of our wrongs, but into the means of our defence. For the aggressors with matured plans to oppose to our indecision have cast threats aside and betaken themselves to action. And we know what are the paths by which Atheni-

ian aggression travels, and how insidious is its progress. A degree of confidence she may feel from the idea that your bluntness of perception prevents your noticing her; but it is nothing to the impulse which her advance will receive from the knowledge that you see, but do not care to interfere. You, Lacedaemonians, of all the Hellenes are alone inactive, and defend yourselves not by doing anything but by looking as if you would do something; you alone wait till the power of an enemy is becoming twice its original size, instead of crushing it in its infancy. And yet the world used to say that you were to be depended upon; but in your case, we fear, it said more than the truth. The Mede, we ourselves know, had time to come from the ends of the earth to Peloponnese, without any force of yours worthy of the name advancing to meet him. But this was a distant enemy. Well, Athens at all events is a near neighbour, and yet Athens you utterly disregard; against Athens you prefer to act on the defensive instead of on the offensive, and to make it an affair of chances by deferring the struggle till she has grown far stronger than at first. And yet you know that on the whole the rock on which the barbarian was wrecked was himself, and that if our present enemy Athens has not again and again annihilated us, we owe it more to her blunders than to your protection. Indeed, expectations from you have before now been the ruin of some, whose faith induced them to omit preparation.

[70] "We hope that none of you will consider these words of remonstrance to be rather words of hostility; men remonstrate with friends who are in error, accusations they reserve for enemies who have wronged them. Besides, we consider that we have as good a right as any one to point out a neighbour's faults, particularly when we contemplate the great contrast between the two national characters; a contrast of which, as far as we can see, you have little perception, having never yet considered what sort of antagonists you will encounter in the Athenians, how widely, how absolutely different from yourselves. The Athenians are addicted to innovation, and their designs are characterized by swiftness alike in conception and execution; you have a genius for keeping what you have got, accompanied by a total want of invention, and when forced to act you never go far enough. Again, they are adventurous beyond their power, and daring beyond their judgment, and in danger they are sanguine; your wont is

to attempt less than is justified by your power, to mistrust even what is sanctioned by your judgment, and to fancy that from danger there is no release. Further, there is promptitude on their side against procrastination on yours; they are never at home, you are never from it: for they hope by their absence to extend their acquisitions, you fear by your advance to endanger what you have left behind. They are swift to follow up a success, and slow to recoil from a reverse. Their bodies they spend ungrudgingly in their country's cause; their intellect they jealously husband to be employed in her service. A scheme unexecuted is with them a positive loss, a successful enterprise a comparative failure. The deficiency created by the miscarriage of an undertaking is soon filled up by fresh hopes; for they alone are enabled to call a thing hoped for a thing got, by the speed with which they act upon their resolutions. Thus they toil on in trouble and danger all the days of their life, with little opportunity for enjoying, being ever engaged in getting: their only idea of a holiday is to do what the occasion demands, and to them laborious occupation is less of a misfortune than the peace of a quiet life. To describe their character in a word, one might truly say that they were born into the world to take no rest themselves and to give none to others.

[71] "Such is Athens, your antagonist. And yet, Lacedaemonians, you still delay, and fail to see that peace stays longest with those, who are not more careful to use their power justly than to show their determination not to submit to injustice. On the contrary, your ideal of fair dealing is based on the principle that, if you do not injure others, you need not risk your own fortunes in preventing others from injuring you. Now you could scarcely have succeeded in such a policy even with a neighbour like yourselves; but in the present instance, as we have just shown, your habits are old-fashioned as compared with theirs. It is the law as in art, so in politics, that improvements ever prevail; and though fixed usages may be best for undisturbed communities, constant necessities of action must be accompanied by the constant improvement of methods. Thus it happens that the vast experience of Athens has carried her further than you on the path of innovation.

"Here, at least, let your procrastination end. For the present, assist your allies and Potidaea in particular, as you promised, by a speedy invasion of Attica, and do not sacrifice friends and kindred to their bitterest enemies, and drive the rest of us in despair to some other alliance. Such a step would not be condemned either by the Gods who received our oaths, or by the men who witnessed them. The breach of a treaty cannot be laid to the people whom desertion compels to seek new relations, but to the power that fails to assist its confederate. But if you will only act, we will stand by you; it would be unnatural for us to change, and never should we meet with such a congenial ally. For these reasons choose the right course, and endeavour not to let Peloponnese under your supremacy degenerate from the prestige that it enjoyed under that of your ancestors."

[72] Such were the words of the Corinthians. There happened to be Athenian envoys present at Lacedaemon on other business. On hearing the speeches they thought themselves called upon to come before the Lacedaemonians. Their intention was not to offer a defence on any of the charges which the cities brought against them, but to show on a comprehensive view that it was not a matter to be hastily decided on, but one that demanded further consideration. There was also a wish to call attention to the great power of Athens, and to refresh the memory of the old and enlighten the ignorance of the young, from a notion that their words might have the effect of inducing them to prefer tranquillity to war. So they came to the Lacedaemonians and said that they too, if there was no objection, wished to speak to their assembly. They replied by inviting them to come forward. The Athenians advanced, and spoke as follows:

[73] "The object of our mission here was not to argue with your allies, but to attend to the matters on which our state dispatched us. However, the vehemence of the outcry that we hear against us has prevailed on us to come forward. It is not to combat the accusations of the cities (indeed you are not the judges before whom either we or they can plead), but to prevent your taking the wrong course on matters of great importance by yielding too readily to the persuasions of your allies. We also wish to show on a review of the whole indictment that we have a fair title to our possessions, and that our country has claims to consideration. We need not refer to remote antiquity: there we could appeal to the voice of tradition, but not to the experience of our audience. But to the Median War and contemporary history we must refer, although we are rather tired of continually bringing this subject forward. In

our action during that war we ran great risk to obtain certain advantages: you had your share in the solid results, do not try to rob us of all share in the good that the glory may do us. However, the story shall be told not so much to deprecate hostility as to testify against it, and to show, if you are so ill advised as to enter into a struggle with Athens, what sort of an antagonist she is likely to prove. We assert that at Marathon we were at the front, and faced the barbarian single-handed. That when he came the second time, unable to cope with him by land we went on board our ships with all our people, and joined in the action at Salamis. This prevented his taking the Peloponnesian states in detail, and ravaging them with his fleet; when the multitude of his vessels would have made any combination for self-defence impossible. The best proof of this was furnished by the invader himself. Defeated at sea, he considered his power to be no longer what it had been, and retired as speedily as possible with the greater part of his army.

[74] "Such, then, was the result of the matter, and it was clearly proved that it was on the fleet of Hellas that her cause depended. Well, to this result we contributed three very useful elements, viz., the largest number of ships, the ablest commander, and the most unhesitating patriotism. Our contingent of ships was little less than two-thirds of the whole four hundred; the commander was Themistocles, through whom chiefly it was that the battle took place in the straits, the acknowledged salvation of our cause. Indeed, this was the reason of your receiving him with honours such as had never been accorded to any foreign visitor. While for daring patriotism we had no competitors. Receiving no reinforcements from behind, seeing everything in front of us already subjugated, we had the spirit, after abandoning our city, after sacrificing our property (instead of deserting the remainder of the league or depriving them of our services by dispersing), to throw ourselves into our ships and meet the danger, without a thought of resenting your neglect to assist us. We assert, therefore, that we conferred on you quite as much as we received. For you had a stake to fight for; the cities which you had left were still filled with your homes, and you had the prospect of enjoying them again; and your coming was prompted quite as much by fear for yourselves as for us; at all events, you never appeared till we had nothing left to lose. But we left behind us a city that was a city no

longer, and staked our lives for a city that had an existence only in desperate hope, and so bore our full share in your deliverance and in ours. But if we had copied others, and allowed fears for our territory to make us give in our adhesion to the Mede before you came, or if we had suffered our ruin to break our spirit and prevent us embarking in our ships, your naval inferiority would have made a sea-fight unnecessary, and his objects would have been peaceably attained.

[75] "Surely, Lacedaemonians, neither by the patriotism that we displayed at that crisis, nor by the wisdom of our counsels, do we merit our extreme unpopularity with the Hellenes, not at least unpopularity for our empire. That empire we acquired by no violent means, but because you were unwilling to prosecute to its conclusion the war against the barbarian, and because the allies attached themselves to us and spontaneously asked us to assume the command. And the nature of the case first compelled us to advance our empire to its present height; fear being our principal motive, though honour and interest afterwards came in. And at last, when almost all hated us, when some had already revolted and had been subdued, when you had ceased to be the friends that you once were, and had become objects of suspicion and dislike, it appeared no longer safe to give up our empire; especially as all who left us would fall to you. And no one can quarrel with a people for making, in matters of tremendous risk, the best provision that it can for its interest.

[76] "You, at all events, Lacedaemonians, have used your supremacy to settle the states in Peloponnese as is agreeable to you. And if at the period of which we were speaking you had persevered to the end of the matter, and had incurred hatred in your command, we are sure that you would have made yourselves just as galling to the allies, and would have been forced to choose between a strong government and danger to yourselves. It follows that it was not a very wonderful action, or contrary to the common practice of mankind, if we did accept an empire that was offered to us, and refused to give it up under the pressure of three of the strongest motives, fear, honour, and interest. And it was not we who set the example, for it has always been the law that the weaker should be subject to the stronger. Besides, we believed ourselves to be worthy of our position, and so you thought us till now, when calculations of interest have made you take up the cry of justice—a consideration which no one ever yet brought forward to hinder his ambition when he had a chance of gaining anything by might. And praise is due to all who, if not so superior to human nature as to refuse dominion, yet respect justice more than their position compels them to do.

[77] "We imagine that our moderation would be best demonstrated by the conduct of others who should be placed in our position; but even our equity has very unreasonably subjected us to condemnation instead of approval. Our abatement of our rights in the contract trials with our allies, and our causing them to be decided by impartial laws at Athens, have gained us the character of being litigious. And none care to inquire why this reproach is not brought against other imperial powers, who treat their subjects with less moderation than we do; the secret being that where force can be used, law is not needed. But our subjects are so habituated to associate with us as equals that any defeat whatever that clashes with their notions of justice, whether it proceeds from a legal judgment or from the power which our empire gives us, makes them forget to be grateful for being allowed to retain most of their possessions, and more vexed at a part being taken, than if we had from the first cast law aside and openly gratified our covetousness. If we had done so, not even would they have disputed that the weaker must give way to the stronger. Men's indignation, it seems, is more excited by legal wrong than by violent wrong; the first looks like being cheated by an equal, the second like being compelled by a superior. At all events they contrived to put up with much worse treatment than this from the Mede, yet they think our rule severe, and this is to be expected, for the present always weighs heavy on the conquered. This at least is certain. If you were to succeed in overthrowing us and in taking our place, you would speedily lose the popularity with which fear of us has invested you, if your policy of to-day is at all to tally with the sample that you gave of it during the brief period of your command against the Mede. Not only is your life at home regulated by rules and institutions incompatible with those of others, but your citizens abroad act neither on these rules nor on those which are recognized by the rest of Hellas.

[78] "Take time then in forming your resolution, as the matter is of great importance; and do not be persuaded by the opinions and complaints of others to bring trouble on your-

selves, but consider the vast influence of accident in war, before you are engaged in it. As it continues, it generally becomes an affair of chances, chances from which neither of us is exempt, and whose event we must risk in the dark. It is a common mistake in going to war to begin at the wrong end, to act first, and wait for disaster to discuss the matter. But we are not yet by any means so misguided, nor, so far as we can see, are you; accordingly, while it is still open to us both to choose aright, we bid you not to dissolve the treaty, or to break your oaths, but to have our differences settled by arbitration according to our agreement. Or else we take the gods who heard the oaths to witness, and if you begin hostilities, whatever line of action you choose, we will try not to be behindhand in repelling you."

[79] Such were the words of the Athenians. After the Lacedaemonians had heard the complaints of the allies against the Athenians, and the observations of the latter, they made all withdraw, and consulted by themselves on the question before them. The opinions of the majority all led to the same conclusion; the Athenians were open aggressors, and war must be declared at once. But Archidamus, the Lacedaemonian king, came forward, who had the reputation of being at once a wise and a moderate man, and made the following speech:

[80] "I have not lived so long, Lacedaemonians, without having had the experience of many wars, and I see those among you of the same age as myself, who will not fall into the common misfortune of longing for war from inexperience or from a belief in its advantage and its safety. This, the war on which you are now debating, would be one of the greatest magnitude, on a sober consideration of the matter. In a struggle with Peloponnesians and neighbours our strength is of the same character, and it is possible to move swiftly on the different points. But a struggle with a people who live in a distant land, who have also an extraordinary familiarity with the sea, and who are in the highest state of preparation in every other department; with wealth private and public, with ships, and horses, and heavy infantry, and a population such as no one other Hellenic place can equal, and lastly a number of tributary allies—what can justify us in rashly beginning such a struggle? wherein is our trust that we should rush on it unprepared? Is it in our ships? There we are inferior; while if we are to practise and become a match for them, time must intervene. Is it in

our money? There we have a far greater deficiency. We neither have it in our treasury, nor are we ready to contribute it from our private funds. [81] Confidence might possibly be felt in our superiority in heavy infantry and population, which will enable us to invade and devastate their lands. But the Athenians have plenty of other land in their empire, and can import what they want by sea. Again, if we are to attempt an insurrection of their allies, these will have to be supported with a fleet, most of them being islanders. What then is to be our war? For unless we can either beat them at sea, or deprive them of the revenues which feed their navy, we shall meet with little but disaster. Meanwhile our honour will be pledged to keeping on, particularly if it be the opinion that we began the quarrel. For let us never be elated by the fatal hope of the war being quickly ended by the devastation of their lands. I fear rather that we may leave it as a legacy to our children; so improbable is it that the Athenian spirit will be the slave of their land, or Athenian experience be cowed by war.

[82] "Not that I would bid you be so unfeeling as to suffer them to injure your allies, and to refrain from unmasking their intrigues; but I do bid you not to take up arms at once, but to send and remonstrate with them in a tone not too suggestive of war, nor again too suggestive of submission, and to employ the interval in perfecting our own preparations. The means will be, first, the acquisition of allies, Hellenic or barbarian it matters not, so long as they are an accession to our strength naval or pecuniary—I say Hellenic or barbarian, because the odium of such an accession to all who like us are the objects of the designs of the Athenians is taken away by the law of self-preservation—and secondly the development of our home resources. If they listen to our embassy, so much the better; but if not, after the lapse of two or three years our position will have become materially strengthened, and we can then attack them if we think proper. Perhaps by that time the sight of our preparations, backed by language equally significant, will have disposed them to submission, while their land is still untouched, and while their counsels may be directed to the retention of advantages as yet undestroyed. For the only light in which you can view their land is that of a hostage in your hands, a hostage the more valuable the better it is cultivated. This you ought to spare as long as possible, and not make them desperate, and so increase the diffi-

culty of dealing with them. For if while still unprepared, hurried away by the complaints of our allies, we are induced to lay it waste, have a care that we do not bring deep disgrace and deep perplexity upon Peloponnese. Complaints, whether of communities or individuals, it is possible to adjust; but war undertaken by a coalition for sectional interests, whose progress there is no means of foreseeing, does not easily admit of creditable settlement.

[83] "And none need think it cowardice for a number of confederates to pause before they attack a single city. The Athenians have allies as numerous as our own, and allies that pay tribute, and war is a matter not so much of arms as of money, which makes arms of use. And this is more than ever true in a struggle between a continental and a maritime power. First, then, let us provide money, and not allow ourselves to be carried away by the talk of our allies before we have done so: as we shall have the largest share of responsibility for the consequences be they good or bad, we have also a right to a tranquil inquiry respecting them.

[84] "And the slowness and procrastination, the parts of our character that are most assailed by their criticism, need not make you blush. If we undertake the war without preparation, we should by hastening its commencement only delay its conclusion: further, a free and a famous city has through all time been ours. The quality which they condemn is really nothing but a wise moderation; thanks to its possession, we alone do not become insolent in success and give way less than others in misfortune; we are not carried away by the pleasure of hearing ourselves cheered on to risks which our judgment condemns; nor, if annoyed, are we any the more convinced by attempts to exasperate us by accusation. We are both warlike and wise, and it is our sense of order that makes us so. We are warlike, because self-control contains honour as a chief constituent, and honour bravery. And we are wise, because we are educated with too little learning to despise the laws, and with too severe a self-control to disobey them, and are brought up not to be too knowing in useless matters—such as the knowledge which can give a specious criticism of an enemy's plans in theory, but fails to assail them with equal success in practice—but are taught to consider that the schemes of our enemies are not dissimilar to our own, and that the freaks of chance are not determinable by calculation. In prac-

tice we always base our preparations against an enemy on the assumption that his plans are good; indeed, it is right to rest our hopes not on a belief in his blunders, but on the soundness of our provisions. Nor ought we to believe that there is much difference between man and man, but to think that the superiority lies with him who is reared in the severest school. [85] These practices, then, which our ancestors have delivered to us, and by whose maintenance we have always profited, must not be given up. And we must not be hurried into deciding in a day's brief space a question which concerns many lives and fortunes and many cities, and in which honour is deeply involved—but we must decide calmly. This our strength peculiarly enables us to do. As for the Athenians, send to them on the matter of Potidaea, send on the matter of the alleged wrongs of the allies, particularly as they are prepared with legal satisfaction; and to proceed against one who offers arbitration as against a wrongdoer, law forbids. Meanwhile do not omit preparation for war. This decision will be the best for yourselves, the most terrible to your opponents."

Such were the words of Archidamus. Last came forward Sthenelaidas, one of the ephors for that year, and spoke to the Lacedaemonians as follows:

[86] "The long speech of the Athenians I do not pretend to understand. They said a good deal in praise of themselves, but nowhere denied that they are injuring our allies and Peloponnese. And yet if they behaved well against the Mede then, but ill towards us now, they deserve double punishment for having ceased to be good and for having become bad. We meanwhile are the same then and now, and shall not, if we are wise, disregard the wrongs of our allies, or put off till to-morrow the duty of assisting those who must suffer today. Others have much money and ships and horses, but we have good allies whom we must not give up to the Athenians, nor by lawsuits and words decide the matter, as it is anything but in word that we are harmed, but render instant and powerful help. And let us not be told that it is fitting for us to deliberate under injustice; long deliberation is rather fitting for those who have injustice in contemplation. Vote therefore, Lacedaemonians, for war, as the honour of Sparta demands, and neither allow the further aggrandizement of Athens, nor betray our allies to ruin, but with the gods let us advance against the aggressors."

[87] With these words he, as ephor, himself put the question to the assembly of the Lacedaemonians. He said that he could not determine which was the loudest acclamation (their mode of decision is by acclamation not by voting); the fact being that he wished to make them declare their opinion openly and thus to increase their ardour for war. Accordingly he said: "All Lacedaemonians who are of opinion that the treaty has been broken, and that Athens is guilty, leave your seats and go there," pointing out a certain place; "all who are of the opposite opinion, there." They accordingly stood up and divided; and those who held that the treaty had been broken were in a decided majority. Summoning the allies, they told them that their opinion was that Athens had been guilty of injustice, but that they wished to convoke all the allies and put it to the vote; in order that they might make war, if they decided to do so, on a common resolution. Having thus gained their point, the delegates returned home at once; the Athenian envoys a little later, when they had dispatched the objects of their mission. This decision of the assembly, judging that the treaty had been broken, was made in the fourteenth year of the thirty years' truce, which was entered into after the affair of Euboea.

[88] The Lacedaemonians voted that the treaty had been broken, and that the war must be declared, not so much because they were persuaded by the arguments of the allies, as because they feared the growth of the power of the Athenians, seeing most of Hellas already subject to them.

CHAPTER IV

From the end of the Persian to the beginning of the Peloponnesian War—The Progress from Supremacy to Empire

[89] THE way in which Athens came to be placed in the circumstances under which her power grew was this. After the Medes had returned from Europe, defeated by sea and land by the Hellenes, and after those of them who had fled with their ships to Mycale had been destroyed, Leotychides, king of the Lacedaemonians, the commander of the Hellenes at Mycale, departed home with the allies from Peloponnese. But the Athenians and the allies from Ionia and Hellespont, who had now revolted from the King, remained and laid siege to Sestos, which was still held by the Medes. After wintering before it, they became masters of the place on its evacuation by the barbarians; and after this they sailed away from Hellespont to their respective cities. Meanwhile the Athenian people, after the departure of the barbarian from their country, at once proceeded to carry over their children and wives, and such property as they had left, from the places where they had deposited them, and prepared to rebuild their city and their walls. For only isolated portions of the circumference had been left standing, and most of the houses were in ruins; though a few remained, in which the Persian grandees had taken up their quarters.

[90] Perceiving what they were going to do, the Lacedaemonians sent an embassy to Athens. They would have themselves preferred to see neither her nor any other city in possession of a wall; though here they acted principally at the instigation of their allies, who were alarmed at the strength of her newly acquired navy and the valour which she had displayed in the war with the Medes. They begged her not only to abstain from building walls for herself, but also to join them in throwing down the walls that still held together of the ultra-Peloponnesian cities. The real meaning of their advice, the suspicion that it contained against the Athenians, was not proclaimed; it was urged that so the barbarian, in the event of a third invasion, would not have any strong place, such as he now had in Thebes, for his base of operations; and that Peloponnese would suffice for all as a base both for retreat and offence. After the Lacedaemonians had thus spoken, they were, on the advice of Themistocles, immediately dismissed by the Athenians, with the answer that ambassadors should be sent to Sparta to discuss the question. Themistocles told the Athenians to send him off with all speed to Lacedaemon, but not to dispatch his colleagues as soon as they had selected them, but to wait until they had raised their wall to the height from which defence was possible. Meanwhile the whole population in the city was to labour at the wall, the Athenians, their wives, and their children, sparing no edifice, private or public, which might be of any use to the work, but throwing all down. After giving these instructions, and adding that he would be responsible for all other matters there, he departed. Arrived at Lacedaemon he did not seek an audience with the authorities, but tried to gain time and made excuses. When any of the government asked him why he did not appear in the assembly, he

would say that he was waiting for his colleagues, who had been detained in Athens by some engagement; however, that he expected their speedy arrival, and wondered that they were not yet there. [91] At first the Lacedaemonians trusted the words of Themistocles, through their friendship for him; but when others arrived, all distinctly declaring that the work was going on and already attaining some elevation, they did not know how to disbelieve it. Aware of this, he told them that rumours are deceptive, and should not be trusted; they should send some reputable persons from Sparta to inspect, whose report might be trusted. They dispatched them accordingly. Concerning these Themistocles secretly sent word to the Athenians to detain them as far as possible without putting them under open constraint, and not to let them go until they had themselves returned. For his colleagues had now joined him, Abronichus, son of Lysicles, and Aristides, son of Lysimachus, with the news that the wall was sufficiently advanced; and he feared that when the Lacedaemonians heard the facts, they might refuse to let them go. So the Athenians detained the envoys according to his message, and Themistocles had an audience with the Lacedaemonians, and at last openly told them that Athens was now fortified sufficiently to protect its inhabitants; that any embassy which the Lacedaemonians or their allies might wish to send to them should in future proceed on the assumption that the people to whom they were going was able to distinguish both its own and the general interests. That when the Athenians thought fit to abandon their city and to embark in their ships, they ventured on that perilous step without consulting them; and that on the other hand, wherever they had deliberated with the Lacedaemonians, they had proved themselves to be in judgment second to none. That they now thought it fit that their city should have a wall, and that this would be more for the advantage of both the citizens of Athens and the Hellenic confederacy; for without equal military strength it was impossible to contribute equal or fair counsel to the common interest. It followed, he observed, either that all the members of the confederacy should be without walls, or that the present step should be considered a right one. [92] The Lacedaemonians did not betray any open signs of anger against the Athenians at what they heard. The embassy, it seems, was prompted not by a desire to obstruct, but to guide the counsels of their government: besides, Spartan feeling was at that time very friendly towards Athens on account of the patriotism which she had displayed in the struggle with the Mede. Still the defeat of their wishes could not but cause them secret annoyance. The envoys of each state departed home without complaint.

[93] In this way the Athenians walled their city in a little while. To this day the building shows signs of the haste of its execution; the foundations are laid of stones of all kinds, and in some places not wrought or fitted, but placed just in the order in which they were brought by the different hands; and many columns, too, from tombs, and sculptured stones were put in with the rest. For the bounds of the city were extended at every point of the circumference; and so they laid hands on everything without exception in their haste. Themistocles also persuaded them to finish the walls of Piraeus, which had been begun before, in his year of office as archon; being influenced alike by the fineness of a locality that has three natural harbours, and by the great start which the Athenians would gain in the acquisition of power by becoming a naval people. For he first ventured to tell them to stick to the sea and forthwith began to lay the foundations of the empire. It was by his advice, too, that they built the walls of that thickness which can still be discerned round Piraeus, the stones being brought up by two wagons meeting each other. Between the walls thus formed there was neither rubble nor mortar, but great stones hewn square and fitted together, cramped to each other on the outside with iron and lead. About half the height that he intended was finished. His idea was by their size and thickness to keep off the attacks of an enemy; he thought that they might be adequately defended by a small garrison of invalids, and the rest be freed for service in the fleet. For the fleet claimed most of his attention. He saw, as I think, that the approach by sea was easier for the king's army than that by land: he also thought Piraeus more valuable than the upper city; indeed, he was always advising the Athenians, if a day should come when they were hard pressed by land, to go down into Piraeus, and defy the world with their fleet. Thus, therefore, the Athenians completed their wall, and commenced their other buildings immediately after the retreat of the Mede. [94] Meanwhile Pausanias, son of Cleombrotus, was sent out from Lacedaemon as

commander-in-chief of the Hellenes, with twenty ships from Peloponnese. With him sailed the Athenians with thirty ships, and a number of the other allies. They made an expedition against Cyprus and subdued most of the island, and afterwards against Byzantium, which was in the hands of the Medes, and compelled it to surrender. This event took place while the Spartans were still supreme. [95] But the violence of Pausanias had already begun to be disagreeable to the Hellenes, particularly to the Ionians and the newly liberated populations. These resorted to the Athenians and requested them as their kinsmen to become their leaders, and to stop any attempt at violence on the part of Pausanias. The Athenians accepted their overtures, and determined to put down any attempt of the kind and to settle everything else as their interests might seem to demand. In the meantime the Lacedaemonians recalled Pausanias for an investigation of the reports which had reached them. Manifold and grave accusations had been brought against him by Hellenes arriving in Sparta; and, to all appearance, there had been in him more of the mimicry of a despot than of the attitude of a general. As it happened, his recall came just at the time when the hatred which he had inspired had induced the allies to desert him, the soldiers from Peloponnese excepted, and to range themselves by the side of the Athenians. On his arrival at Lacedaemon, he was censured for his private acts of oppression, but was acquitted on the heaviest counts and pronounced not guilty; it must be known that the charge of Medism formed one of the principal, and to all appearance one of the best founded, articles against him. The Lacedaemonians did not, however, restore him to his command, but sent out Dorkis and certain others with a small force; who found the allies no longer inclined to concede to them the supremacy. Perceiving this they departed, and the Lacedaemonians did not send out any to succeed them. They feared for those who went out a deterioration similar to that observable in Pausanias; besides, they desired to be rid of the Median War, and were satisfied of the competency of the Athenians for the position, and of their friendship at the time towards themselves.
[96] The Athenians, having thus succeeded to the supremacy by the voluntary act of the allies through their hatred of Pausanias, fixed which cities were to contribute money against the barbarian, which ships; their professed object being to retaliate for their sufferings by ravaging the King's country. Now was the time that the office of "Treasurers for Hellas" was first instituted by the Athenians. These officers received the tribute, as the money contributed was called. The tribute was first fixed at four hundred and sixty talents. The common treasury was at Delos, and the congresses were held in the temple. [97] Their supremacy commenced with independent allies who acted on the resolutions of a common congress. It was marked by the following undertakings in war and in administration during the interval between the Median and the present war, against the barbarian, against their own rebel allies, and against the Peloponnesian powers which would come in contact with them on various occasions. My excuse for relating these events, and for venturing on this digression, is that this passage of history has been omitted by all my predecessors, who have confined themselves either to Hellenic history before the Median War, or the Median War itself. Hellanicus, it is true, did touch on these events in his Athenian history; but he is somewhat concise and not accurate in his dates. Besides, the history of these events contains an explanation of the growth of the Athenian empire.
[98] First the Athenians besieged and captured Eion on the Strymon from the Medes, and made slaves of the inhabitants, being under the command of Cimon, son of Miltiades. Next they enslaved Scyros, the island in the Aegean, containing a Dolopian population, and colonized it themselves. This was followed by a war against Carystus, in which the rest of Euboea remained neutral, and which was ended by surrender on conditions. After this Naxos left the confederacy, and a war ensued, and she had to return after a siege; this was the first instance of the engagement being broken by the subjugation of an allied city, a precedent which was followed by that of the rest in the order which circumstances prescribed. [99] Of all the causes of defection, that connected with arrears of tribute and vessels, and with failure of service, was the chief; for the Athenians were very severe and exacting, and made themselves offensive by applying the screw of necessity to men who were not used to and in fact not disposed for any continuous labour. In some other respects the Athenians were not the old popular rulers they had been at first; and if they had more than their fair share of service, it was correspondingly easy for them to reduce any that tried to leave

the confederacy. For this the allies had themselves to blame; the wish to get off service making most of them arrange to pay their share of the expense in money instead of in ships, and so to avoid having to leave their homes. Thus while Athens was increasing her navy with the funds which they contributed, a revolt always found them without resources or experience for war.

[*100*] Next we come to the actions by land and by sea at the river Eurymedon, between the Athenians with their allies, and the Medes, when the Athenians won both battles on the same day under the conduct of Cimon, son of Miltiades, and captured and destroyed the whole Phoenician fleet, consisting of two hundred vessels. Some time afterwards occurred the defection of the Thasians, caused by disagreements about the marts on the opposite coast of Thrace, and about the mine in their possession. Sailing with a fleet to Thasos, the Athenians defeated them at sea and effected a landing on the island. About the same time they sent ten thousand settlers of their own citizens and the allies to settle the place then called Ennea Hodoi or Nine Ways, now Amphipolis. They succeeded in gaining possession of Ennea Hodoi from the Edonians, but on advancing into the interior of Thrace were cut off in Drabescus, a town of the Edonians, by the assembled Thracians, who regarded the settlement of the place Ennea Hodoi as an act of hostility. [*101*] Meanwhile the Thasians being defeated in the field and suffering siege, appealed to Lacedaemon, and desired her to assist them by an invasion of Attica. Without informing Athens, she promised and intended to do so, but was prevented by the occurrence of the earthquake, accompanied by the secession of the Helots and the Thuriats and Aethaeans of the Perioeci to Ithome. Most of the Helots were the descendants of the old Messenians that were enslaved in the famous war; and so all of them came to be called Messenians. So the Lacedaemonians being engaged in a war with the rebels in Ithome, the Thasians in the third year of the siege obtained terms from the Athenians by razing their walls, delivering up their ships, and arranging to pay the moneys demanded at once, and tribute in future; giving up their possessions on the continent together with the mine.

[*102*] The Lacedaemonians, meanwhile, finding the war against the rebels in Ithome likely to last, invoked the aid of their allies, and especially of the Athenians, who came in some force under the command of Cimon. The reason for this pressing summons lay in their reputed skill in siege operations; a long siege had taught the Lacedaemonians their own deficiency in this art, else they would have taken the place by assault. The first open quarrel between the Lacedaemonians and Athenians arose out of this expedition. The Lacedaemonians, when assault failed to take the place, apprehensive of the enterprising and revolutionary character of the Athenians, and further looking upon them as of alien extraction, began to fear that, if they remained, they might be tempted by the besieged in Ithome to attempt some political changes. They accordingly dismissed them alone of the allies, without declaring their suspicions, but merely saying that they had now no need of them. But the Athenians, aware that their dismissal did not proceed from the more honourable reason of the two, but from suspicions which had been conceived, went away deeply offended, and conscious of having done nothing to merit such treatment from the Lacedaemonians; and the instant that they returned home they broke off the alliance which had been made against the Mede, and allied themselves with Sparta's enemy Argos; each of the contracting parties taking the same oaths and making the same alliance with the Thessalians.

[*103*] Meanwhile the rebels in Ithome, unable to prolong further a ten years' resistance, surrendered to Lacedaemon; the conditions being that they should depart from Peloponnese under safe conduct, and should never set foot in it again: any one who might hereafter be found there was to be the slave of his captor. It must be known that the Lacedaemonians had an old oracle from Delphi, to the effect that they should let go the suppliant of Zeus at Ithome. So they went forth with their children and their wives, and being received by Athens from the hatred that she now felt for the Lacedaemonians, were located at Naupactus, which she had lately taken from the Ozolian Locrians. The Athenians received another addition to their confederacy in the Megarians; who left the Lacedaemonian alliance, annoyed by a war about boundaries forced on them by Corinth. The Athenians occupied Megara and Pegae, and built the Megarians their long walls from the city to Nisaea, in which they placed an Athenian garrison. This was the principal cause of the Corinthians conceiving such a deadly hatred against Athens.

[*104*] Meanwhile Inaros, son of Psammeti-

chus, a Libyan king of the Libyans on the Egyptian border, having his headquarters at Marea, the town above Pharos, caused a revolt of almost the whole of Egypt from King Artaxerxes and, placing himself at its head, invited the Athenians to his assistance. Abandoning a Cyprian expedition upon which they happened to be engaged with two hundred ships of their own and their allies, they arrived in Egypt and sailed from the sea into the Nile, and making themselves masters of the river and two-thirds of Memphis, addressed themselves to the attack of the remaining third, which is called White Castle. Within it were Persians and Medes who had taken refuge there, and Egyptians who had not joined the rebellion.

[105] Meanwhile the Athenians, making a descent from their fleet upon Haliae, were engaged by a force of Corinthians and Epidaurians; and the Corinthians were victorious. Afterwards the Athenians engaged the Peloponnesian fleet off Cecruphalia; and the Athenians were victorious. Subsequently war broke out between Aegina and Athens, and there was a great battle at sea off Aegina between the Athenians and Aeginetans, each being aided by their allies; in which victory remained with the Athenians, who took seventy of the enemy's ships, and landed in the country and commenced a siege under the command of Leocrates, son of Stroebus. Upon this the Peloponnesians, desirous of aiding the Aeginetans, threw into Aegina a force of three hundred heavy infantry, who had before been serving with the Corinthians and Epidaurians. Meanwhile the Corinthians and their allies occupied the heights of Geraneia, and marched down into the Megarid, in the belief that, with a large force absent in Aegina and Egypt, Athens would be unable to help the Megarians without raising the siege of Aegina. But the Athenians, instead of moving the army of Aegina, raised a force of the old and young men that had been left in the city, and marched into the Megarid under the command of Myronides. After a drawn battle with the Corinthians, the rival hosts parted, each with the impression that they had gained the victory. The Athenians, however, if anything, had rather the advantage, and on the departure of the Corinthians set up a trophy. Urged by the taunts of the elders in their city, the Corinthians made their preparations, and about twelve days afterwards came and set up their trophy as victors. Sallying out from Megara, the Athe-

nians cut off the party that was employed in erecting the trophy, and engaged and defeated the rest. [106] In the retreat of the vanquished army, a considerable division, pressed by the pursuers and mistaking the road, dashed into a field on some private property, with a deep trench all round it, and no way out. Being acquainted with the place, the Athenians hemmed their front with heavy infantry and, placing the light troops round in a circle, stoned all who had gone in. Corinth here suffered a severe blow. The bulk of her army continued its retreat home.

[107] About this time the Athenians began to build the long walls to the sea, that towards Phalerum and that towards Piraeus. Meanwhile the Phocians made an expedition against Doris, the old home of the Lacedaemonians, containing the towns of Boeum, Kitinium, and Erineum. They had taken one of these towns, when the Lacedaemonians under Nicomedes, son of Cleombrotus, commanding for King Pleistoanax, son of Pausanias, who was still a minor, came to the aid of the Dorians with fifteen hundred heavy infantry of their own, and ten thousand of their allies. After compelling the Phocians to restore the town on conditions, they began their retreat. The route by sea, across the Crissaean Gulf, exposed them to the risk of being stopped by the Athenian fleet; that across Geraneia seemed scarcely safe, the Athenians holding Megara and Pegae. For the pass was a difficult one, and was always guarded by the Athenians; and, in the present instance, the Lacedaemonians had information that they meant to dispute their passage. So they resolved to remain in Boeotia, and to consider which would be the safest line of march. They had also another reason for this resolve. Secret encouragement had been given them by a party in Athens, who hoped to put an end to the reign of democracy and the building of the Long Walls. Meanwhile the Athenians marched against them with their whole levy and a thousand Argives and the respective contingents of the rest of their allies. Altogether they were fourteen thousand strong. The march was prompted by the notion that the Lacedaemonians were at a loss how to effect their passage, and also by suspicions of an attempt to overthrow the democracy. Some cavalry also joined the Athenians from their Thessalian allies; but these went over to the Lacedaemonians during the battle.

[108] The battle was fought at Tanagra in

Boeotia. After heavy loss on both sides, victory declared for the Lacedaemonians and their allies. After entering the Megarid and cutting down the fruit trees, the Lacedaemonians returned home across Geraneia and the isthmus. Sixty-two days after the battle the Athenians marched into Boeotia under the command of Myronides, defeated the Boeotians in battle at Oenophyta, and became masters of Boeotia and Phocis. They dismantled the walls of the Tanagraeans, took a hundred of the richest men of the Opuntian Locrians as hostages, and finished their own long walls. This was followed by the surrender of the Aeginetans to Athens on conditions; they pulled down their walls, gave up their ships, and agreed to pay tribute in future. The Athenians sailed round Peloponnese under Tolmides, son of Tolmaeus, burnt the arsenal of Lacedaemon, took Chalcis, a town of the Corinthians, and in a descent upon Sicyon defeated the Sicyonians in battle.

[109] Meanwhile the Athenians in Egypt and their allies were still there, and encountered all the vicissitudes of war. First the Athenians were masters of Egypt, and the King sent Megabazus a Persian to Lacedaemon with money to bribe the Peloponnesians to invade Attica and so draw off the Athenians from Egypt. Finding that the matter made no progress, and that the money was only being wasted, he recalled Megabazus with the remainder of the money, and sent Megabuzus, son of Zopyrus, a Persian, with a large army to Egypt. Arriving by land he defeated the Egyptians and their allies in a battle, and drove the Hellenes out of Memphis, and at length shut them up in the island of Prosopitis, where he besieged them for a year and six months. At last, draining the canal of its waters, which he diverted into another channel, he left their ships high and dry and joined most of the island to the mainland, and then marched over on foot and captured it. [110] Thus the enterprise of the Hellenes came to ruin after six years of war. Of all that large host a few travelling through Libya reached Cyrene in safety, but most of them perished. And thus Egypt returned to its subjection to the King, except Amyrtaeus, the king in the marshes, whom they were unable to capture from the extent of the marsh; the marshmen being also the most warlike of the Egyptians. Inaros, the Libyan king, the sole author of the Egyptian revolt, was betrayed, taken, and crucified. Meanwhile a relieving squadron of fifty vessels had sailed

from Athens and the rest of the confederacy for Egypt. They put in to shore at the Mendesian mouth of the Nile, in total ignorance of what had occurred. Attacked on the land side by the troops, and from the sea by the Phoenician navy, most of the ships were destroyed; the few remaining being saved by retreat. Such was the end of the great expedition of the Athenians and their allies to Egypt.

[111] Meanwhile Orestes, son of Echecratidas, the Thessalian king, being an exile from Thessaly, persuaded the Athenians to restore him. Taking with them the Boeotians and Phocians their allies, the Athenians marched to Pharsalus in Thessaly. They became masters of the country, though only in the immediate vicinity of the camp; beyond which they could not go for fear of the Thessalian cavalry. But they failed to take the city or to attain any of the other objects of their expedition, and returned home with Orestes without having effected anything. Not long after this a thousand of the Athenians embarked in the vessels that were at Pegae (Pegae, it must be remembered, was now theirs), and sailed along the coast to Sicyon under the command of Pericles, son of Xanthippus. Landing in Sicyon and defeating the Sicyonians who engaged them, they immediately took with them the Achaeans and, sailing across, marched against and laid siege to Oeniadae in Acarnania. Failing however to take it, they returned home.

[112] Three years afterwards a truce was made between the Peloponnesians and Athenians for five years. Released from Hellenic war, the Athenians made an expedition to Cyprus with two hundred vessels of their own and their allies, under the command of Cimon. Sixty of these were detached to Egypt at the instance of Amyrtaeus, the king in the marshes; the rest laid siege to Kitium, from which, however, they were compelled to retire by the death of Cimon and by scarcity of provisions. Sailing off Salamis in Cyprus, they fought with the Phoenicians, Cyprians, and Cilicians by land and sea and, being victorious on both elements departed home, and with them the returned squadron from Egypt. After this the Lacedaemonians marched out on a sacred war, and, becoming masters of the temple at Delphi, placed it in the hands of the Delphians. Immediately after their retreat, the Athenians marched out, became masters of the temple, and placed it in the hands of the Phocians.

[113] Some time after this, Orchomenus, Chaeronea, and some other places in Boeotia

being in the hands of the Boeotian exiles, the Athenians marched against the above-mentioned hostile places with a thousand Athenian heavy infantry and the allied contingents, under the command of Tolmides, son of Tolmaeus. They took Chaeronea, and made slaves of the inhabitants, and, leaving a garrison, commenced their return. On their road they were attacked at Coronea by the Boeotian exiles from Orchomenus, with some Locrians and Euboean exiles, and others who were of the same way of thinking, were defeated in battle, and some killed, others taken captive. The Athenians evacuated all Boeotia by a treaty providing for the recovery of the men; and the exiled Boeotians returned, and with all the rest regained their independence.

[114] This was soon afterwards followed by the revolt of Euboea from Athens. Pericles had already crossed over with an army of Athenians to the island, when news was brought to him that Megara had revolted, that the Peloponnesians were on the point of invading Attica, and that the Athenian garrison had been cut off by the Megarians, with the exception of a few who had taken refuge in Nisaea. The Megarians had introduced the Corinthians, Sicyonians, and Epidaurians into the town before they revolted. Meanwhile Pericles brought his army back in all haste from Euboea. After this the Peloponnesians marched into Attica as far as Eleusis and Thrius, ravaging the country under the conduct of King Pleistoanax, the son of Pausanias, and without advancing further returned home. The Athenians then crossed over again to Euboea under the command of Pericles, and subdued the whole of the island: all but Histiaea was settled by convention; the Histiaeans they expelled from their homes, and occupied their territory themselves.

[115] Not long after their return from Euboea, they made a truce with the Lacedaemonians and their allies for thirty years, giving up the posts which they occupied in Peloponnese—Nisaea, Pegae, Troezen, and Achaia. In the sixth year of the truce, war broke out between the Samians and Milesians about Priene. Worsted in the war, the Milesians came to Athens with loud complaints against the Samians. In this they were joined by certain private persons from Samos itself, who wished to revolutionize the government. Accordingly the Athenians sailed to Samos with forty ships and set up a democracy; took hostages from the Samians, fifty boys and as many men, lodged them in Lemnos, and after leaving a garrison in the island returned home. But some of the Samians had not remained in the island, but had fled to the continent. Making an agreement with the most powerful of those in the city, and an alliance with Pissuthnes, son of Hystaspes, the then satrap of Sardis, they got together a force of seven hundred mercenaries, and under cover of night crossed over to Samos. Their first step was to rise on the commons, most of whom they secured; their next to steal their hostages from Lemnos; after which they revolted, gave up the Athenian garrison left with them and its commanders to Pissuthnes, and instantly prepared for an expedition against Miletus. The Byzantines also revolted with them.

[116] As soon as the Athenians heard the news, they sailed with sixty ships against Samos. Sixteen of these went to Caria to look out for the Phoenician fleet, and to Chios and Lesbos carrying round orders for reinforcements, and so never engaged; but forty-four ships under the command of Pericles with nine colleagues gave battle, off the island of Tragia, to seventy Samian vessels, of which twenty were transports, as they were sailing from Miletus. Victory remained with the Athenians. Reinforced afterwards by forty ships from Athens, and twenty-five Chian and Lesbian vessels, the Athenians landed, and having the superiority by land invested the city with three walls; it was also invested from the sea. Meanwhile Pericles took sixty ships from the blockading squadron, and departed in haste for Caunus and Caria, intelligence having been brought in of the approach of the Phoenician fleet to the aid of the Samians; indeed Stesagoras and others had left the island with five ships to bring them. [117] But in the meantime the Samians made a sudden sally, and fell on the camp, which they found unfortified. Destroying the look-out vessels, and engaging and defeating such as were being launched to meet them, they remained masters of their own seas for fourteen days, and carried in and carried out what they pleased. But on the arrival of Pericles, they were once more shut up. Fresh reinforcements afterwards arrived—forty ships from Athens with Thucydides, Hagnon, and Phormio; twenty with Tlepolemus and Anticles, and thirty vessels from Chios and Lesbos. After a brief attempt at fighting, the Samians, unable to hold out, were reduced after a nine months' siege and surrendered on conditions; they razed their walls, gave hostages, delivered up their ships, and arranged to pay the ex-

penses of the war by instalments. The Byzantines also agreed to be subject as before.

CHAPTER V

Second Congress at Lacedaemon—Preparations for War and Diplomatic Skirmishes—Cylon—Pausanias—Themistocles

[*118*] AFTER this, though not many years later, we at length come to what has been already related, the affairs of Corcyra and Potidaea, and the events that served as a pretext for the present war. All these actions of the Hellenes against each other and the barbarian occurred in the fifty years' interval between the retreat of Xerxes and the beginning of the present war. During this interval the Athenians succeeded in placing their empire on a firmer basis, and advanced their own home power to a very great height. The Lacedaemonians, though fully aware of it, opposed it only for a little while, but remained inactive during most of the period, being of old slow to go to war except under the pressure of necessity, and in the present instance being hampered by wars at home; until the growth of the Athenian power could be no longer ignored, and their own confederacy became the object of its encroachments. They then felt that they could endure it no longer, but that the time had come for them to throw themselves heart and soul upon the hostile power, and break it, if they could, by commencing the present war. And though the Lacedaemonians had made up their own minds on the fact of the breach of the treaty and the guilt of the Athenians, yet they sent to Delphi and inquired of the God whether it would be well with them if they went to war; and, as it is reported, received from him the answer that if they put their whole strength into the war, victory would be theirs, and the promise that he himself would be with them, whether invoked or uninvoked. [*119*] Still they wished to summon their allies again, and to take their vote on the propriety of making war. After the ambassadors from the confederates had arrived and a congress had been convened, they all spoke their minds, most of them denouncing the Athenians and demanding that the war should begin. In particular the Corinthians. They had before on their own account canvassed the cities in detail to induce them to vote for the war, in the fear that it might come too late to save Potidaea; they were present also on this occasion, and came forward the last, and made the following speech:

[*120*] "Fellow allies, we can no longer accuse the Lacedaemonians of having failed in their duty: they have not only voted for war themselves, but have assembled us here for that purpose. We say their duty, for supremacy has its duties. Besides equitably administering private interests, leaders are required to show a special care for the common welfare in return for the special honours accorded to them by all in other ways. For ourselves, all who have already had dealings with the Athenians require no warning to be on their guard against them. The states more inland and out of the highway of communication should understand that, if they omit to support the coast powers, the result will be to injure the transit of their produce for exportation and the reception in exchange of their imports from the sea; and they must not be careless judges of what is now said, as if it had nothing to do with them, but must expect that the sacrifice of the powers on the coast will one day be followed by the extension of the danger to the interior, and must recognize that their own interests are deeply involved in this discussion. For these reasons they should not hesitate to exchange peace for war. If wise men remain quiet, while they are not injured, brave men abandon peace for war when they are injured, returning to an understanding on a favourable opportunity: in fact, they are neither intoxicated by their success in war, nor disposed to take an injury for the sake of the delightful tranquillity of peace. Indeed, to falter for the sake of such delights is, if you remain inactive, the quickest way of losing the sweets of repose to which you cling; while to conceive extravagant pretensions from success in war is to forget how hollow is the confidence by which you are elated. For if many ill-conceived plans have succeeded through the still greater fatuity of an opponent, many more, apparently well laid, have on the contrary ended in disgrace. The confidence with which we form our schemes is never completely justified in their execution; speculation is carried on in safety, but, when it comes to action, fear causes failure.

[*121*] "To apply these rules to ourselves, if we are now kindling war it is under the pressure of injury, and with adequate grounds of complaint; and after we have chastised the Athenians we will in season desist. We have many reasons to expect success—first, superiority in numbers and in military experience, and secondly our general and unvarying obedi-

ence in the execution of orders. The naval strength which they possess shall be raised by us from our respective antecedent resources, and from the moneys at Olympia and Delphi. A loan from these enables us to seduce their foreign sailors by the offer of higher pay. For the power of Athens is more mercenary than national; while ours will not be exposed to the same risk, as its strength lies more in men than in money. A single defeat at sea is in all likelihood their ruin: should they hold out, in that case there will be the more time for us to exercise ourselves in naval matters; and as soon as we have arrived at an equality in science, we need scarcely ask whether we shall be their superiors in courage. For the advantages that we have by nature they cannot acquire by education; while their superiority in science must be removed by our practice. The money required for these objects shall be provided by our contributions: nothing indeed could be more monstrous than the suggestion that, while their allies never tire of contributing for their own servitude, we should refuse to spend for vengeance and self-preservation the treasure which by such refusal we shall forfeit to Athenian rapacity and see employed for our own ruin.

[122] "We have also other ways of carrying on the war, such as revolt of their allies, the surest method of depriving them of their revenues, which are the source of their strength, and establishment of fortified positions in their country, and various operations which cannot be foreseen at present. For war of all things proceeds least upon definite rules, but draws principally upon itself for contrivances to meet an emergency; and in such cases the party who faces the struggle and keeps his temper best meets with most security, and he who loses his temper about it with correspondent disaster. Let us also reflect that if it was merely a number of disputes of territory between rival neighbours, it might be borne; but here we have an enemy in Athens that is a match for our whole coalition, and more than a match for any of its members; so that unless as a body and as individual nationalities and individual cities we make an unanimous stand against her, she will easily conquer us divided and in detail. That conquest, terrible as it may sound, would, it must be known, have no other end than slavery pure and simple; a word which Peloponnese cannot even hear whispered without disgrace, or without disgrace see so many states abused by one. Meanwhile the opinion would

be either that we were justly so used, or that we put up with it from cowardice, and were proving degenerate sons in not even securing for ourselves the freedom which our fathers gave to Hellas; and in allowing the establishment in Hellas of a tyrant state, though in individual states we think it our duty to put down sole rulers. And we do not know how this conduct can be held free from three of the gravest failings, want of sense, of courage, or of vigilance. For we do not suppose that you have taken refuge in that contempt of an enemy which has proved so fatal in so many instances—a feeling which from the numbers that it has ruined has come to be called not contemptuous but contemptible.

[123] "There is, however, no advantage in reflections on the past further than may be of service to the present. For the future we must provide by maintaining what the present gives us and redoubling our efforts; it is hereditary to us to win virtue as the fruit of labour, and you must not change the habit, even though you should have a slight advantage in wealth and resources; for it is not right that what was won in want should be lost in plenty; no, we must boldly advance to the war for many reasons; the god has commanded it and promised to be with us, and the rest of Hellas will all join in the struggle, part from fear, part from interest. You will be the first to break a treaty which the god, in advising us to go to war, judges to be violated already, but rather to support a treaty that has been outraged: indeed, treaties are broken not by resistance but by aggression.

[124] "Your position, therefore, from whatever quarter you may view it, will amply justify you in going to war; and this step we recommend in the interests of all, bearing in mind that identity of interest is the surest of bonds, whether between states or individuals. Delay not, therefore, to assist Potidaea, a Dorian city besieged by Ionians, which is quite a reversal of the order of things; nor to assert the freedom of the rest. It is impossible for us to wait any longer when waiting can only mean immediate disaster for some of us, and, if it comes to be known that we have conferred but do not venture to protect ourselves, like disaster in the near future for the rest. Delay not, fellow allies, but, convinced of the necessity of the crisis and the wisdom of this counsel, vote for the war, undeterred by its immediate terrors, but looking beyond to the lasting peace by which it will be succeeded. Out of war peace gains

fresh stability, but to refuse to abandon repose for war is not so sure a method of avoiding danger. We must believe that the tyrant city that has been established in Hellas has been established against all alike, with a programme of universal empire, part fulfilled, part in contemplation; let us then attack and reduce it, and win future security for ourselves and freedom for the Hellenes who are now enslaved."

[125] Such were the words of the Corinthians. The Lacedaemonians, having now heard all, give their opinion, took the vote of all the allied states present in order, great and small alike; and the majority voted for war. This decided, it was still impossible for them to commence at once, from their want of preparation; but it was resolved that the means requisite were to be procured by the different states, and that there was to be no delay. And indeed, in spite of the time occupied with the necessary arrangements, less than a year elapsed before Attica was invaded, and the war openly begun.

[126] This interval was spent in sending embassies to Athens charged with complaints, in order to obtain as good a pretext for war as possible, in the event of her paying no attention to them. The first Lacedaemonian embassy was to order the Athenians to drive out the curse of the goddess; the history of which is as follows. In former generations there was an Athenian of the name of Cylon, a victor at the Olympic games, of good birth and powerful position, who had married a daughter of Theagenes, a Megarian, at that time tyrant of Megara. Now this Cylon was inquiring at Delphi, when he was told by the god to seize the Acropolis of Athens on the grand festival of Zeus. Accordingly, procuring a force from Theagenes and persuading his friends to join him, when the Olympic festival in Peloponnese came, he seized the Acropolis, with the intention of making himself tyrant, thinking that this was the grand festival of Zeus, and also an occasion appropriate for a victor at the Olympic games. Whether the grand festival that was meant was in Attica or elsewhere was a question which he never thought of, and which the oracle did not offer to solve. For the Athenians also have a festival which is called the grand festival of Zeus Meilichios or Gracious, viz., the Diasia. It is celebrated outside the city, and the whole people sacrifice not real victims but a number of bloodless offerings peculiar to the country. However, fancying he had chosen the right time, he made the attempt. As soon as the Athenians perceived it,

they flocked in, one and all, from the country, and sat down, and laid siege to the citadel. But as time went on, weary of the labour of blockade, most of them departed; the responsibility of keeping guard being left to the nine archons, with plenary powers to arrange everything according to their good judgment. It must be known that at that time most political functions were discharged by the nine archons. Meanwhile Cylon and his besieged companions were distressed for want of food and water. Accordingly Cylon and his brother made their escape; but the rest being hard pressed, and some even dying of famine, seated themselves as suppliants at the altar in the Acropolis. The Athenians who were charged with the duty of keeping guard, when they saw them at the point of death in the temple, raised them up on the understanding that no harm should be done to them, led them out, and slew them. Some who as they passed by took refuge at the altars of the awful goddesses were dispatched on the spot. From this deed the men who killed them were called accursed and guilty against the goddess, they and their descendants. Accordingly these cursed ones were driven out by the Athenians, driven out again by Cleomenes of Lacedaemon and an Athenian faction; the living were driven out, and the bones of the dead were taken up; thus they were cast out. For all that, they came back afterwards, and their descendants are still in the city.

[127] This, then was the curse that the Lacedaemonians ordered them to drive out. They were actuated primarily, as they pretended, by a care for the honour of the gods; but they also know that Pericles, son of Xanthippus, was connected with the curse on his mother's side, and they thought that his banishment would materially advance their designs on Athens. Not that they really hoped to succeed in procuring this; they rather thought to create a prejudice against him in the eyes of his countrymen from the feeling that the war would be partly caused by his misfortune. For being the most powerful man of his time, and the leading Athenian statesman, he opposed the Lacedaemonians in everything, and would have no concessions, but ever urged the Athenians on to war.

[128] The Athenians retorted by ordering the Lacedaemonians to drive out the curse of Taenarus. The Lacedaemonians had once raised up some Helot suppliants from the temple of Poseidon at Taenarus, led them away

and slain them; for which they believe the great earthquake at Sparta to have been a retribution. The Athenians also ordered them to drive out the curse of the goddess of the Brazen House; the history of which is as follows. After Pausanias the Lacedaemonian had been recalled by the Spartans from his command in the Hellespont (this is his first recall), and had been tried by them and acquitted, not being again sent out in a public capacity, he took a galley of Hermione on his own responsibility, without the authority of the Lacedaemonians, and arrived as a private person in the Hellespont. He came ostensibly for the Hellenic war, really to carry on his intrigues with the King, which he had begun before his recall, being ambitious of reigning over Hellas. The circumstance which first enabled him to lay the King under an obligation, and to make a beginning of the whole design, was this. Some connections and kinsmen of the King had been taken in Byzantium, on its capture from the Medes, when he was first there, after the return from Cyprus. These captives he sent off to the King without the knowledge of the rest of the allies, the account being that they had escaped from him. He managed this with the help of Gongylus, an Eretrian, whom he had placed in charge of Byzantium and the prisoners. He also gave Gongylus a letter for the King, the contents of which were as follows, as was afterwards discovered: "Pausanias, the general of Sparta, anxious to do you a favour, sends you these his prisoners of war. I propose also, with your approval, to marry your daughter, and to make Sparta and the rest of Hellas subject to you. I may say that I think I am able to do this, with your co-operation. Accordingly if any of this please you, send a safe man to the sea through whom we may in future conduct our correspondence."

[129] This was all that was revealed in the writing, and Xerxes was pleased with the letter. He sent off Artabazus, son of Pharnaces, to the sea with orders to supersede Megabates, the previous governor in the satrapy of Daskylion, and to send over as quickly as possible to Pausanias at Byzantium a letter which he entrusted to him; to show him the royal signet, and to execute any commission which he might receive from Pausanias on the King's matters with all care and fidelity. Artabazus on his arrival carried the King's orders into effect, and sent over the letter, which contained the following answer: "Thus saith King Xerxes to Pausanias. For the men whom you have saved for me across sea from Byzantium, an obligation is laid up for you in our house, recorded for ever; and with your proposals I am well pleased. Let neither night nor day stop you from diligently performing any of your promises to me; neither for cost of gold nor of silver let them be hindered, nor yet for number of troops, wherever it may be that their presence is needed; but with Artabazus, an honourable man whom I send you, boldly advance my objects and yours, as may be most for the honour and interest of us both."

[130] Before held in high honour by the Hellenes as the hero of Plataea, Pausanias, after the receipt of this letter, became prouder than ever, and could no longer live in the usual style, but went out of Byzantium in a Median dress, was attended on his march through Thrace by a bodyguard of Medes and Egyptians, kept a Persian table, and was quite unable to contain his intentions, but betrayed by his conduct in trifles what his ambition looked one day to enact on a grander scale. He also made himself difficult of access, and displayed so violent a temper to every one without exception that no one could come near him. Indeed, this was the principal reason why the confederacy went over to the Athenians.

[131] The above-mentioned conduct, coming to the ears of the Lacedaemonians, occasioned his first recall. And after his second voyage out in the ship of Hermione, without their orders, he gave proofs of similar behaviour. Besieged and expelled from Byzantium by the Athenians, he did not return to Sparta; but news came that he had settled at Colonae in the Troad, and was intriguing with the barbarians, and that his stay there was for no good purpose; and the ephors, now no longer hesitating, sent him a herald and a scytale with orders to accompany the herald or be declared a public enemy. Anxious above everything to avoid suspicion, and confident that he could quash the charge by means of money, he returned a second time to Sparta. At first thrown into prison by the ephors (whose powers enable them to do this to the King), he soon compromised the matter and came out again, and offered himself for trial to any who wished to institute an inquiry concerning him.

[132] Now the Spartans had no tangible proof against him—neither his enemies nor the nation—of that indubitable kind required for the punishment of a member of the royal family, and at that moment in high office; he being regent for his first cousin King Pleistar-

chus, Leonidas's son, who was still a minor. But by his contempt of the laws and imitation of the barbarians, he gave grounds for much suspicion of his being discontented with things established; all the occasions on which he had in any way departed from the regular customs were passed in review, and it was remembered that he had taken upon himself to have inscribed on the tripod at Delphi, which was dedicated by the Hellenes as the first-fruits of the spoil of the Medes, the following couplet:

The Mede defeated, great Pausanias raised
This monument, that Phoebus might be praised.

At the time the Lacedaemonians had at once erased the couplet, and inscribed the names of the cities that had aided in the overthrow of the barbarian and dedicated the offering. Yet it was considered that Pausanias had here been guilty of a grave offence, which, interpreted by the light of the attitude which he had since assumed, gained a new significance, and seemed to be quite in keeping with his present schemes. Besides, they were informed that he was even intriguing with the Helots; and such indeed was the fact, for he promised them freedom and citizenship if they would join him in insurrection and would help him to carry out his plans to the end. Even now, mistrusting the evidence even of the Helots themselves, the ephors would not consent to take any decided step against him; in accordance with their regular custom towards themselves, namely, to be slow in taking any irrevocable resolve in the matter of a Spartan citizen without indisputable proof. At last, it is said, the person who was going to carry to Artabazus the last letter for the King, a man of Argilus, once the favourite and most trusty servant of Pausanias, turned informer. Alarmed by the reflection that none of the previous messengers had ever returned, having counterfeited the seal, in order that, if he found himself mistaken in his surmises, or if Pausanias should ask to make some correction, he might not be discovered, he undid the letter, and found the postscript that he had suspected, viz., an order to put him to death.

[*133*] On being shown the letter, the ephors now felt more certain. Still, they wished to hear Pausanias commit himself with their own ears. Accordingly the man went by appointment to Taenarus as a suppliant, and there built himself a hut divided into two by a partition; within which he concealed some of the ephors and let them hear the whole matter plainly. For Pausanias came to him and asked him the reason of his suppliant position; and the man reproached him with the order that he had written concerning him, and one by one declared all the rest of the circumstances, how he who had never yet brought him into any danger, while employed as agent between him and the King, was yet just like the mass of his servants to be rewarded with death. Admitting all this, and telling him not to be angry about the matter, Pausanias gave him the pledge of raising him up from the temple, and begged him to set off as quickly as possible, and not to hinder the business in hand.

[*134*] The ephors listened carefully, and then departed, taking no action for the moment, but, having at last attained to certainty, were preparing to arrest him in the city. It is reported that, as he was about to be arrested in the street, he saw from the face of one of the ephors what he was coming for; another, too, made him a secret signal, and betrayed it to him from kindness. Setting off with a run for the temple of the goddess of the Brazen House, the enclosure of which was near at hand, he succeeded in taking sanctuary before they took him, and entering into a small chamber, which formed part of the temple, to avoid being exposed to the weather, lay still there. The ephors, for the moment distanced in the pursuit, afterwards took off the roof of the chamber, and having made sure that he was inside, shut him in, barricaded the doors, and staying before the place, reduced him by starvation. When they found that he was on the point of expiring, just as he was, in the chamber, they brought him out of the temple, while the breath was still in him, and as soon as he was brought out he died. They were going to throw him into the Kaiadas, where they cast criminals, but finally decided to inter him somewhere near. But the god at Delphi afterwards ordered the Lacedaemonians to remove the tomb to the place of his death—where he now lies in the consecrated ground, as an inscription on a monument declares—and, as what had been done was a curse to them, to give back two bodies instead of one to the goddess of the Brazen House. So they had two brazen statues made, and dedicated them as a substitute for Pausanias. Accordingly the Athenians retorted by telling the Lacedaemonians to drive out what the god himself had pronounced to be a curse.

[*135*] To return to the Medism of Pausanias. Matter was found in the course of the in-

quiry to implicate Themistocles; and the Lacedaemonians accordingly sent envoys to the Athenians, and required them to punish him as they had punished Pausanias. The Athenians consented to do so. But he had, as it happened, been ostracized, and, with a residence at Argos, was in the habit of visiting other parts of Peloponnese. So they sent with the Lacedaemonians, who were ready to join in the pursuit, persons with instructions to take him wherever they found him. *[136]* But Themistocles got scent of their intentions, and fled from Peloponnese to Corcyra, which was under obligations towards him. But the Corcyraeans alleged that they could not venture to shelter him at the cost of offending Athens and Lacedaemon, and they conveyed him over to the continent opposite. Pursued by the officers who hung on the report of his movements, at a loss where to turn, he was compelled to stop at the house of Admetus, the Molossian king, though they were not on friendly terms. Admetus happened not to be indoors, but his wife, to whom he made himself a suppliant, instructed him to take their child in his arms and sit down by the hearth. Soon afterwards Admetus came in, and Themistocles told him who he was, and begged him not to revenge on Themistocles in exile any opposition which his requests might have experienced from Themistocles at Athens. Indeed, he was now far too low for his revenge; retaliation was only honourable between equals. Besides, his opposition to the king had only affected the success of a request, not the safety of his person; if the king were to give him up to the pursuers that he mentioned, and the fate which they intended for him, he would just be consigning him to certain death.

[137] The King listened to him and raised him up with his son, as he was sitting with him in his arms after the most effectual method of supplication, and on the arrival of the Lacedaemonians not long afterwards, refused to give him up for anything they could say, but sent him off by land to the other sea to Pydna in Alexander's dominions, as he wished to go to the Persian king. There he met with a merchantman on the point of starting for Ionia. Going on board, he was carried by a storm to the Athenian squadron which was blockading Naxos. In his alarm—he was luckily unknown to the people in the vessel—he told the master who he was and what he was flying for, and said that, if he refused to save him, he would declare that he was taking him for a bribe.

Meanwhile their safety consisted in letting no one leave the ship until a favourable time for sailing should arise. If he complied with his wishes, he promised him a proper recompense. The master acted as he desired, and, after lying to for a day and a night out of reach of the squadron, at length arrived at Ephesus.

After having rewarded him with a present of money, as soon as he received some from his friends at Athens and from his secret hoards at Argos, Themistocles started inland with one of the coast Persians, and sent a letter to King Artaxerxes, Xerxes's son, who had just come to the throne. Its contents were as follows: "I, Themistocles, am come to you, who did your house more harm than any of the Hellenes, when I was compelled to defend myself against your father's invasion—harm, however, far surpassed by the good that I did him during his retreat, which brought no danger for me but much for him. For the past, you are a good turn in my debt"—here he mentioned the warning sent to Xerxes from Salamis to retreat, as well as his finding the bridges unbroken, which, as he falsely pretended, was due to him—"for the present, able to do you great service, I am here, pursued by the Hellenes for my friendship for you. However, I desire a year's grace, when I shall be able to declare in person the objects of my coming."

[138] It is said that the King approved his intention, and told him to do as he said. He employed the interval in making what progress he could in the study of the Persian tongue, and of the customs of the country. Arrived at court at the end of the year, he attained to very high consideration there, such as no Hellene has ever possessed before or since; partly from his splendid antecedents, partly from the hopes which he held out of effecting for him the subjugation of Hellas, but principally by the proof which experience daily gave of his capacity. For Themistocles was a man who exhibited the most indubitable signs of genius; indeed, in this particular he has a claim on our admiration quite extraordinary and unparalleled. By his own native capacity, alike unformed and unsupplemented by study, he was at once the best judge in those sudden crises which admit of little or of no deliberation, and the best prophet of the future, even to its most distant possibilities. An able theoretical expositor of all that came within the sphere of his practice, he was not without the power of passing an adequate judgment in matters in which he had no experience. He

could also excellently divine the good and evil which lay hid in the unseen future. In fine, whether we consider the extent of his natural powers, or the slightness of his application, this extraordinary man must be allowed to have surpassed all others in the faculty of intuitively meeting an emergency. Disease was the real cause of his death; though there is a story of his having ended his life by poison, on finding himself unable to fulfil his promises to the king. However this may be, there is a monument to him in the marketplace of Asiatic Magnesia. He was governor of the district, the King having given him Magnesia, which brought in fifty talents a year, for bread, Lampsacus, which was considered to be the richest wine country, for wine, and Myos for other provisions. His bones, it is said, were conveyed home by his relatives in accordance with his wishes, and interred in Attic ground. This was done without the knowledge of the Athenians; as it is against the law to bury in Attica an outlaw for treason. So ends the history of Pausanias and Themistocles, the Lacedaemonian and the Athenian, the most famous men of their time in Hellas.

[*139*] To return to the Lacedaemonians. The history of their first embassy, the injunctions which it conveyed, and the rejoinder which it provoked, concerning the expulsion of the accursed persons, have been related already. It was followed by a second, which ordered Athens to raise the siege of Potidaea, and to respect the independence of Aegina. Above all, it gave her most distinctly to understand that war might be prevented by the revocation of the Megara decree, excluding the Megarians from the use of Athenian harbours and of the market of Athens. But Athens was not inclined either to revoke the decree, or to entertain their other proposals; she accused the Megarians of pushing their cultivation into the consecrated ground and the unenclosed land on the border, and of harbouring her runaway slaves. At last an embassy arrived with the Lacedaemonian ultimatum. The ambassadors were Ramphias, Melesippus, and Agesander. Not a word was said on any of the old subjects; there was simply this: "Lacedaemon wishes the peace to continue, and there is no reason why it should not, if you would leave the Hellenes independent." Upon this the Athenians held an assembly, and laid the matter before their consideration. It was resolved to deliberate once for all on all their demands, and to give them an answer. There were many

speakers who came forward and gave their support to one side or the other, urging the necessity of war, or the revocation of the decree and the folly of allowing it to stand in the way of peace. Among them came forward Pericles, son of Xanthippus, the first man of his time at Athens, ablest alike in counsel and in action, and gave the following advice:

[*140*] "There is one principle, Athenians, which I hold to through everything, and that is the principle of no concession to the Peloponnesians. I know that the spirit which inspires men while they are being persuaded to make war is not always retained in action; that as circumstances change, resolutions change. Yet I see that now as before the same, almost literally the same, counsel is demanded of me; and I put it to those of you who are allowing yourselves to be persuaded, to support the national resolves even in the case of reverses, or to forfeit all credit for their wisdom in the event of success. For sometimes the course of things is as arbitrary as the plans of man; indeed this is why we usually blame chance for whatever does not happen as we expected. Now it was clear before that Lacedaemon entertained designs against us; it is still more clear now. The treaty provides that we shall mutually submit our differences to legal settlement, and that we shall meanwhile each keep what we have. Yet the Lacedaemonians never yet made us any such offer, never yet would accept from us any such offer; on the contrary, they wish complaints to be settled by war instead of by negotiation; and in the end we find them here dropping the tone of expostulation and adopting that of command. They order us to raise the siege of Potidaea, to let Aegina be independent, to revoke the Megara decree; and they conclude with an ultimatum warning us to leave the Hellenes independent. I hope that you will none of you think that we shall be going to war for a trifle if we refuse to revoke the Megara decree, which appears in front of their complaints, and the revocation of which is to save us from war, or let any feeling of self-reproach linger in your minds, as if you went to war for slight cause. Why, this trifle contains the whole seal and trial of your resolution. If you give way, you will instantly have to meet some greater demand, as having been frightened into obedience in the first instance; while a firm refusal will make them clearly understand that they must treat you more as equals. [*141*] Make your decision therefore at once, either to submit before you are harmed, or if

we are to go to war, as I for one think we ought, to do so without caring whether the ostensible cause be great or small, resolved against making concessions or consenting to a precarious tenure of our possessions. For all claims from an equal, urged upon a neighbour as commands before any attempt at legal settlement, be they great or be they small, have only one meaning, and that is slavery.

"As to the war and the resources of either party, a detailed comparison will not show you the inferiority of Athens. Personally engaged in the cultivation of their land, without funds either private or public, the Peloponnesians are also without experience in long wars across sea, from the strict limit which poverty imposes on their attacks upon each other. Powers of this description are quite incapable of often manning a fleet or often sending out an army: they cannot afford the absence from their homes, the expenditure from their own funds; and besides, they have not command of the sea. Capital, it must be remembered, maintains a war more than forced contributions. Farmers are a class of men that are always more ready to serve in person than in purse. Confident that the former will survive the dangers, they are by no means so sure that the latter will not be prematurely exhausted, especially if the war last longer than they expect, which it very likely will. In a single battle the Peloponnesians and their allies may be able to defy all Hellas, but they are incapacitated from carrying on a war against a power different in character from their own, by the want of the single council-chamber requisite to prompt and vigorous action, and the substitution of a diet composed of various races, in which every state possesses an equal vote, and each presses its own ends, a condition of things which generally results in no action at all. The great wish of some is to avenge themselves on some particular enemy, the great wish of others to save their own pocket. Slow in assembling, they devote a very small fraction of the time to the consideration of any public object, most of it to the prosecution of their own objects. Meanwhile each fancies that no harm will come of his neglect, that it is the business of somebody else to look after this or that for him; and so, by the same notion being entertained by all separately, the common cause imperceptibly decays.

[142] "But the principal point is the hindrance that they will experience from want of money. The slowness with which it comes in will cause delay; but the opportunities of war wait for no man. Again, we need not be alarmed either at the possibility of their raising fortifications in Attica, or at their navy. It would be difficult for any system of fortifications to establish a rival city, even in time of peace, much more, surely, in an enemy's country, with Athens just as much fortified against it as it against Athens; while a mere post might be able to do some harm to the country by incursions and by the facilities which it would afford for desertion, but can never prevent our sailing into their country and raising fortifications there, and making reprisals with our powerful fleet. For our naval skill is of more use to us for service on land, than their military skill for service at sea. Familiarity with the sea they will not find an easy acquisition. If you who have been practising at it ever since the Median invasion have not yet brought it to perfection, is there any chance of anything considerable being effected by an agricultural, unseafaring population, who will besides be prevented from practising by the constant presence of strong squadrons of observation from Athens? With a small squadron they might hazard an engagement, encouraging their ignorance by numbers; but the restraint of a strong force will prevent their moving, and through want of practice they will grow more clumsy, and consequently more timid. It must be kept in mind that seamanship, just like anything else, is a matter of art, and will not admit of being taken up occasionally as an occupation for times of leisure; on the contrary, it is so exacting as to leave leisure for nothing else.

[143] "Even if they were to touch the moneys at Olympia or Delphi, and try to seduce our foreign sailors by the temptation of higher pay, that would only be a serious danger if we could not still be a match for them by embarking our own citizens and the aliens resident among us. But in fact by this means we are always a match for them; and, best of all, we have a larger and higher class of native coxswains and sailors among our own citizens than all the rest of Hellas. And to say nothing of the danger of such a step, none of our foreign sailors would consent to become an outlaw from his country, and to take service with them and their hopes, for the sake of a few days' high pay.

"This, I think, is a tolerably fair account of the position of the Peloponnesians; that of Athens is free from the defects that I have criticized in them, and has other advantages of its own, which they can show nothing to equal. If they march against our country we will sail against theirs, and it will then be found that the desolation of the whole of Attica is not the same as that of even a fraction of Peloponnese; for they will not be able to supply the deficiency except by a battle, while we have plenty of land both on the islands and the continent. The rule of the sea is indeed a great matter. Consider for a moment. Suppose that we were islanders; can you conceive a more impregnable position? Well, this in future should, as far as possible, be our conception of our position. Dismissing all thought of our land and houses, we must vigilantly guard the sea and the city. No irritation that we may feel for the former must provoke us to a battle with the numerical superiority of the Peloponnesians. A victory would only be succeeded by another battle against the same superiority: a reverse involves the loss of our allies, the source of our strength, who will not remain quiet a day after we become unable to march against them. We must cry not over the loss of houses and land but of men's lives; since houses and land do not gain men, but men them. And if I had thought that I could persuade you, I would have bid you go out and lay them waste with your own hands, and show the Peloponnesians that this at any rate will not make you submit.

[144] "I have many other reasons to hope for a favourable issue, if you can consent not to combine schemes of fresh conquest with the conduct of the war, and will abstain from wilfully involving yourselves in other dangers; indeed, I am more afraid of our own blunders than of the enemy's devices. But these matters shall be explained in another speech, as events require; for the present dismiss these men with the answer that we will allow Megara the use of our market and harbours, when the Lacedaemonians suspend their alien acts in favour of us and our allies, there being nothing in the treaty to prevent either one or the other:

that we will leave the cities independent, if independent we found them when we made the treaty, and when the Lacedaemonians grant to their cities an independence not involving subservience to Lacedaemonian interests, but such as each severally may desire: that we are willing to give the legal satisfaction which our agreements specify, and that we shall not commence hostilities, but shall resist those who do commence them. This is an answer agreeable at once to the rights and the dignity of Athens. It must be thoroughly understood that war is a necessity; but that the more readily we accept it, the less will be the ardour of our opponents, and that out of the greatest dangers communities and individuals acquire the greatest glory. Did not our fathers resist the Medes not only with resources far different from ours, but even when those resources had been abandoned; and more by wisdom than by fortune, more by daring than by strength, did not they beat off the barbarian and advance their affairs to their present height? We must not fall behind them, but must resist our enemies in any way and in every way, and attempt to hand down our power to our posterity unimpaired."

[145] Such were the words of Pericles. The Athenians, persuaded of the wisdom of his advice, voted as he desired, and answered the Lacedaemonians as he recommended, both on the separate points and in the general; they would do nothing on dictation, but were ready to have the complaints settled in a fair and impartial manner by the legal method, which the terms of the truce prescribed. So the envoys departed home and did not return again.

[146] These were the charges and differences existing between the rival powers before the war, arising immediately from the affair at Epidamnus and Corcyra. Still intercourse continued in spite of them, and mutual communication. It was carried on without heralds, but not without suspicion, as events were occurring which were equivalent to a breach of the treaty and matter for war.

The Second Book

⇛ ⇛ ⇛ ⇛ ⇛ ⇛ ⇛ ⇛ ⇛ ⇛ ⇛ ⇛ ⇛ ⇛ ⇛ ⇚ ⇚ ⇚ ⇚ ⇚ ⇚ ⇚ ⇚ ⇚ ⇚ ⇚ ⇚ ⇚ ⇚ ⇚

CHAPTER VI

Beginning of the Peloponnesian War—First Invasion of Attica—Funeral Oration of Pericles

[1] THE war between the Athenians and Peloponnesians and the allies on either side now really begins. For now all intercourse except through the medium of heralds ceased, and hostilities were commenced and prosecuted without intermission. The history follows the chronological order of events by summers and winters.

[2] The thirty years' truce which was entered into after the conquest of Euboea lasted fourteen years. In the fifteenth, in the forty-eighth year of the priestess-ship of Chrysis at Argos, in the ephorate of Aenesias at Sparta, in the last month but two of the archonship of Pythodorus at Athens, and six months after the battle of Potidaea, just at the beginning of spring, a Theban force a little over three hundred strong, under the command of their Boeotarchs, Pythangelus, son of Phyleides, and Diemporus, son of Onetorides, about the first watch of the night, made an armed entry into Plataea, a town of Boeotia in alliance with Athens. The gates were opened to them by a Plataean called Naucleides, who, with his party, had invited them in, meaning to put to death the citizens of the opposite party, bring over the city to Thebes, and thus obtain power for themselves. This was arranged through Eurymachus, son of Leontiades, a person of great influence at Thebes. For Plataea had always been at variance with Thebes; and the latter, foreseeing that war was at hand, wished to surprise her old enemy in time of peace, before hostilities had actually broken out. Indeed this was how they got in so easily without being observed, as no guard had been posted. After the soldiers had grounded arms in the market-place, those who had invited them in wished them to set to work at once and go to their enemies' houses. This, however, the Thebans refused to do, but determined to make a conciliatory proclamation, and if possible to come to a friendly understanding with the citizens. Their herald accordingly invited any who wished to resume their old place in the confederacy of their countrymen to ground arms with them, for they thought that in this way the city would readily join them.

[3] On becoming aware of the presence of the Thebans within their gates, and of the sudden occupation of the town, the Plataeans concluded in their alarm that more had entered than was really the case, the night preventing their seeing them. They accordingly came to terms and, accepting the proposal, made no movement; especially as the Thebans offered none of them any violence. But somehow or other, during the negotiations, they discovered the scanty numbers of the Thebans, and decided that they could easily attack and overpower them; the mass of the Plataeans being averse to revolting from Athens. At all events they resolved to attempt it. Digging through the party walls of the houses, they thus managed to join each other without being seen going through the streets, in which they placed wagons without the beasts in them, to serve as a barricade, and arranged everything else as seemed convenient for the occasion. When everything had been done that circumstances permitted, they watched their opportunity and went out of their houses against the enemy. It was still night, though daybreak was at hand: in daylight it was thought that their attack would be met by men full of courage and on equal terms with their assailants, while in darkness it would fall upon panic-stricken troops, who would also be at a disadvantage from their enemy's knowledge of the locality. So they made their assault at once, and came to

close quarters as quickly as they could.

[4] The Thebans, finding themselves out-witted, immediately closed up to repel all attacks made upon them. Twice or thrice they beat back their assailants. But the men shouted and charged them, the women and slaves screamed and yelled from the houses and pelt-ed them with stones and tiles; besides, it had been raining hard all night; and so at last their courage gave way, and they turned and fled through the town. Most of the fugitives were quite ignorant of the right ways out, and this, with the mud, and the darkness caused by the moon being in her last quarter, and the fact that their pursuers knew their way about and could easily stop their escape, proved fatal to many. The only gate open was the one by which they had entered, and this was shut by one of the Plataeans driving the spike of a javelin into the bar instead of the bolt; so that even here there was no longer any means of exit. They were now chased all over the town. Some got on the wall and threw themselves over, in most cases with a fatal result. One party managed to find a deserted gate, and ob-taining an axe from a woman, cut through the bar; but as they were soon observed only a few succeeded in getting out. Others were cut off in detail in different parts of the city. The most numerous and compact body rushed into a large building next to the city wall: the doors on the side of the street happened to be open, and the Thebans fancied that they were the gates of the town, and that there was a pass-age right through to the outside. The Pla-taeans, seeing their enemies in a trap, now con-sulted whether they should set fire to the build-ing and burn them just as they were, or whether there was anything else that they could do with them; until at length these and the rest of the Theban survivors found wander-ing about the town agreed to an uncondi-tional surrender of themselves and their arms to the Plataeans.

[5] While such was the fate of the party in Plataea, the rest of the Thebans who were to have joined them with all their forces before daybreak, in case of anything miscarrying with the body that had entered, received the news of the affair on the road, and pressed forward to their succour. Now Plataea is nearly eight miles from Thebes, and their march was de-layed by the rain that had fallen in the night, for the river Asopus had risen and was not easy of passage; and so, having to march in the rain, and being hindered in crossing the river,

they arrived too late, and found the whole party either slain or captive. When they learned what had happened, they at once formed a design against the Plataeans outside the city. As the attack had been made in time of peace, and was perfectly unexpected, there were of course men and stock in the fields; and the Thebans wished if possible to have some prisoners to exchange against their country-men in the town, should any chance to have been taken alive. Such was their plan. But the Plataeans suspected their intention almost be-fore it was formed, and becoming alarmed for their fellow citizens outside the town, sent a herald to the Thebans, reproaching them for their unscrupulous attempt to seize their city in time of peace, and warning them against any outrage on those outside. Should the warning be disregarded, they threatened to put to death the men they had in their hands, but added that, on the Thebans retiring from their territory, they would surrender the pris-oners to their friends. This is the Theban ac-count of the matter, and they say that they had an oath given them. The Plataeans, on the other hand, do not admit any promise of an immediate surrender, but make it contingent upon subsequent negotiation: the oath they deny altogether. Be this as it may, upon the Thebans retiring from their territory without committing any injury, the Plataeans hastily got in whatever they had in the country and immediately put the men to death. The pris-oners were a hundred and eighty in number; Eurymachus, the person with whom the trai-tors had negotiated, being one.

[6] This done, the Plataeans sent a mes-senger to Athens, gave back the dead to the Thebans under a truce, and arranged things in the city as seemed best to meet the present emergency. The Athenians meanwhile, hav-ing had word of the affair sent them im-mediately after its occurrence, had instantly seized all the Boeotians in Attica, and sent a herald to the Plataeans to forbid their pro-ceeding to extremities with their Theban pris-oners without instructions from Athens. The news of the men's death had of course not arrived; the first messenger having left Plataea just when the Thebans entered it, the second just after their defeat and capture; so there was no later news. Thus the Athenians sent their orders in ignorance of the facts; and the herald on his arrival found the men slain. After this the Athenians marched to Plataea and brought in provisions, and left a garrison in the place,

also taking away the women and children and such of the men as were least efficient.

[7] After the affair at Plataea, the treaty had been broken by an overt act, and Athens at once prepared for war, as did also Lacedaemon and her allies. They resolved to send embassies to the King and to such other of the barbarian powers as either party could look to for assistance, and tried to ally themselves with the independent states at home. Lacedaemon, in addition to the existing marine, gave orders to the states that had declared for her in Italy and Sicily to build vessels up to a grand total of five hundred, the quota of each city being determined by its size, and also to provide a specified sum of money. Till these were ready they were to remain neutral and to admit single Athenian ships into their harbours. Athens on her part reviewed her existing confederacy, and sent embassies to the places more immediately round Peloponnese—Corcyra, Cephallenia, Acarnania, and Zacynthus—perceiving that if these could be relied on she could carry the war all round Peloponnese.

[8] And if both sides nourished the boldest hopes and put forth their utmost strength for the war, this was only natural. Zeal is always at its height at the commencement of an undertaking; and on this particular occasion Peloponnese and Athens were both full of young men whose inexperience made them eager to take up arms, while the rest of Hellas stood straining with excitement at the conflict of its leading cities. Everywhere predictions were being recited and oracles being chanted by such persons as collect them, and this not only in the contending cities. Further, some while before this, there was an earthquake at Delos, for the first time in the memory of the Hellenes. This was said and thought to be ominous of the events impending; indeed, nothing of the kind that happened was allowed to pass without remark. The good wishes of men made greatly for the Lacedaemonians, especially as they proclaimed themselves the liberators of Hellas. No private or public effort that could help them in speech or action was omitted; each thinking that the cause suffered wherever he could not himself see to it. So general was the indignation felt against Athens, whether by those who wished to escape from her empire, or were apprehensive of being absorbed by it. [9] Such were the preparations and such the feelings with which the contest opened.

The allies of the two belligerents were the following. These were the allies of Lacedaemon: all the Peloponnesians within the Isthmus except the Argives and Achaeans, who were neutral; Pellene being the only Achaean city that first joined in the war, though her example was afterwards followed by the rest. Outside Peloponnese the Megarians, Locrians, Boeotians, Phocians, Ambraciots, Leucadians, and Anactorians. Of these, ships were furnished by the Corinthians, Megarians, Sicyonians, Pellenians, Eleans, Ambraciots, and Leucadians; and cavalry by the Boeotians, Phocians, and Locrians. The other states sent infantry. This was the Lacedaemonian confederacy. That of Athens comprised the Chians, Lesbians, Plataeans, the Messenians in Naupactus, most of the Acarnanians, the Corcyraeans, Zacynthians, and some tributary cities in the following countries, viz., Caria upon the sea with her Dorian neighbours, Ionia, the Hellespont, the Thracian towns, the islands lying between Peloponnese and Crete towards the east, and all the Cyclades except Melos and Thera. Of these, ships were furnished by Chios, Lesbos, and Corcyra, infantry and money by the rest. Such were the allies of either party and their resources for the war.

[10] Immediately after the affair at Plataea, Lacedaemon sent round orders to the cities in Peloponnese and the rest of her confederacy to prepare troops and the provisions requisite for a foreign campaign, in order to invade Attica. The several states were ready at the time appointed and assembled at the Isthmus: the contingent of each city being two-thirds of its whole force. After the whole army had mustered, the Lacedaemonian king, Archidamus, the leader of the expedition, called together the generals of all the states and the principal persons and officers, and exhorted them as follows:

[11] "Peloponnesians and allies, our fathers made many campaigns both within and without Peloponnese, and the elder men among us here are not without experience in war. Yet we have never set out with a larger force than the present; and if our numbers and efficiency are remarkable, so also is the power of the state against which we march. We ought not then to show ourselves inferior to our ancestors, or unequal to our own reputation. For the hopes and attention of all Hellas are bent upon the present effort, and its sympathy is with the enemy of the hated Athens. Therefore, numerous as the invading army may appear to be, and certain as some may think it that our ad-

versary will not meet us in the field, this is no sort of justification for the least negligence upon the march; but the officers and men of each particular city should always be prepared for the advent of danger in their own quarters. The course of war cannot be foreseen, and its attacks are generally dictated by the impulse of the moment; and where overweening self-confidence has despised preparation, a wise apprehension has often been able to make head against superior numbers. Not that confidence is out of place in an army of invasion, but in an enemy's country it should also be accompanied by the precautions of apprehension: troops will by this combination be best inspired for dealing a blow, and best secured against receiving one. In the present instance, the city against which we are going, far from being so impotent for defence, is on the contrary most excellently equipped at all points; so that we have every reason to expect that they will take the field against us, and that if they have not set out already before we are there, they will certainly do so when they see us in their territory wasting and destroying their property. For men are always exasperated at suffering injuries to which they are not accustomed, and on seeing them inflicted before their very eyes; and where least inclined for reflection, rush with the greatest heat to action. The Athenians are the very people of all others to do this, as they aspire to rule the rest of the world, and are more in the habit of invading and ravaging their neighbours' territory, than of seeing their own treated in the like fashion. Considering, therefore, the power of the state against which we are marching, and the greatness of the reputation which, according to the event, we shall win or lose for our ancestors and ourselves, remember as you follow where you may be led to regard discipline and vigilance as of the first importance, and to obey with alacrity the orders transmitted to you; as nothing contributes so much to the credit and safety of an army as the union of large bodies by a single discipline."

[12] With this brief speech dismissing the assembly, Archidamus first sent off Melesippus, son of Diacritus, a Spartan, to Athens, in case she should be more inclined to submit on seeing the Peloponnesians actually on the march. But the Athenians did not admit him into the city or to their assembly, Pericles having already carried a motion against admitting either herald or embassy from the Lacedaemonians after they had once marched out.

The herald was accordingly sent away without an audience, and ordered to be beyond the frontier that same day; in future, if those who sent him had a proposition to make, they must retire to their own territory before they dispatched embassies to Athens. An escort was sent with Melesippus to prevent his holding communication with any one. When he reached the frontier and was just going to be dismissed, he departed with these words: "This day will be the beginning of great misfortunes to the Hellenes." As soon as he arrived at the camp, and Archidamus learnt that the Athenians had still no thoughts of submitting, he at length began his march, and advanced with his army into their territory. Meanwhile the Boeotians, sending their contingent and cavalry to join the Peloponnesian expedition, went to Plataea with the remainder and laid waste the country.

[13] While the Peloponnesians were still mustering at the Isthmus, or on the march before they invaded Attica, Pericles, son of Xanthippus, one of the ten generals of the Athenians, finding that the invasion was to take place, conceived the idea that Archidamus, who happened to be his friend, might possibly pass by his estate without ravaging it. This he might do, either from a personal wish to oblige him, or acting under instructions from Lacedaemon for the purpose of creating a prejudice against him, as had been before attempted in the demand for the expulsion of the accursed family. He accordingly took the precaution of announcing to the Athenians in the assembly that, although Archidamus was his friend, yet this friendship should not extend to the detriment of the state, and that in case the enemy should make his houses and lands an exception to the rest and not pillage them, he at once gave them up to be public property, so that they should not bring him into suspicion. He also gave the citizens some advice on their present affairs in the same strain as before. They were to prepare for the war, and to carry in their property from the country. They were not to go out to battle, but to come into the city and guard it, and get ready their fleet, in which their real strength lay. They were also to keep a tight rein on their allies—the strength of Athens being derived from the money brought in by their payments, and success in war depending principally upon conduct and capital. Here they had no reason to despond. Apart from other sources of income, an average revenue of six hundred tal-

ents of silver was drawn from the tribute of the allies; and there were still six thousand talents of coined silver in the Acropolis, out of nine thousand seven hundred that had once been there, from which the money had been taken for the porch of the Acropolis, the other public buildings, and for Potidaea. This did not include the uncoined gold and silver in public and private offerings, the sacred vessels for the processions and games, the Median spoils, and similar resources to the amount of five hundred talents. To this he added the treasures of the other temples. These were by no means inconsiderable, and might fairly be used. Nay, if they were ever absolutely driven to it, they might take even the gold ornaments of Athene herself; for the statue contained forty talents of pure gold and it was all removable. This might be used for self-preservation, and must every penny of it be restored. Such were their financial position—surely a satisfactory one. Then they had an army of thirteen thousand heavy infantry, besides sixteen thousand more in the garrisons and on home duty at Athens. This was at first the number of men on guard in the event of an invasion: it was composed of the oldest and youngest levies and the resident aliens who had heavy armour. The Phaleric wall ran for four miles, before it joined that round the city; and of this last nearly five had a guard, although part of it was left without one, viz., that between the Long Wall and the Phaleric. Then there were the Long Walls to Piraeus, a distance of some four miles and a half, the outer of which was manned. Lastly, the circumference of Piraeus with Munychia was nearly seven miles and a half; only half of this, however, was guarded. Pericles also showed them that they had twelve hundred horse including mounted archers, with sixteen hundred archers unmounted, and three hundred galleys fit for service. Such were the resources of Athens in the different departments when the Peloponnesian invasion was impending and hostilities were being commenced. Pericles also urged his usual arguments for expecting a favourable issue to the war.

[14] The Athenians listened to his advice, and began to carry in their wives and children from the country, and all their household furniture, even to the woodwork of their houses which they took down. Their sheep and cattle they sent over to Euboea and the adjacent islands. But they found it hard to move, as most of them had been always used to live in the country.

[15] From very early times this had been more the case with the Athenians than with others. Under Cecrops and the first kings, down to the reign of Theseus, Attica had always consisted of a number of independent townships, each with its own town hall and magistrates. Except in times of danger the king at Athens was not consulted; in ordinary seasons they carried on their government and settled their affairs without his interference; sometimes even they waged war against him, as in the case of the Eleusinians with Eumolpus against Erechtheus. In Theseus, however, they had a king of equal intelligence and power; and one of the chief features in his organization of the country was to abolish the council-chambers and magistrates of the petty cities, and to merge them in the single council-chamber and town hall of the present capital. Individuals might still enjoy their private property just as before, but they were henceforth compelled to have only one political centre, viz., Athens; which thus counted all the inhabitants of Attica among her citizens, so that when Theseus died he left a great state behind him. Indeed, from him dates the Synoecia, or Feast of Union; which is paid for by the state, and which the Athenians still keep in honour of the goddess. Before this the city consisted of the present citadel and the district beneath it looking rather towards the south. This is shown by the fact that the temples of the other deities, besides that of Athene, are in the citadel; and even those that are outside it are mostly situated in this quarter of the city, as that of the Olympian Zeus, of the Pythian Apollo, of Earth, and of Dionysus in the Marshes, the same in whose honour the older Dionysia are to this day celebrated in the month of Anthesterion not only by the Athenians but also by their Ionian descendants. There are also other ancient temples in this quarter. The fountain too, which, since the alteration made by the tyrants, has been called Enneacrounos, or Nine Pipes, but which, when the spring was open, went by the name of Callirhoe, or Fairwater, was in those days, from being so near, used for the most important offices. Indeed, the old fashion of using the water before marriage and for other sacred purposes is still kept up. Again, from their old residence in that quarter, the citadel is still known among Athenians as the *city*.

[16] The Athenians thus long lived scattered over Attica in independent townships.

Even after the centralization of Theseus, old habit still prevailed; and from the early times down to the present war most Athenians still lived in the country with their families and households, and were consequently not at all inclined to move now, especially as they had only just restored their establishments after the Median invasion. Deep was their trouble and discontent at abandoning their houses and the hereditary temples of the ancient constitution, and at having to change their habits of life and to bid farewell to what each regarded as his native city.

[17] When they arrived at Athens, though a few had houses of their own to go to, or could find an asylum with friends or relatives, by far the greater number had to take up their dwelling in the parts of the city that were not built over and in the temples and chapels of the heroes, except the Acropolis and the temple of the Eleusinian Demeter and such other places as were always kept closed. The occupation of the plot of ground lying below the citadel called the Pelasgian had been forbidden by a curse; and there was also an ominous fragment of a Pythian oracle which said:

Leave the Pelasgian parcel desolate,
Woe worth the day that men inhabit it!

Yet this too was now built over in the necessity of the moment. And in my opinion, if the oracle proved true, it was in the opposite sense to what was expected. For the misfortunes of the state did not arise from the unlawful occupation, but the necessity of the occupation from the war; and though the god did not mention this, he foresaw that it would be an evil day for Athens in which the plot came to be inhabited. Many also took up their quarters in the towers of the walls or wherever else they could. For when they were all come in, the city proved too small to hold them; though afterwards they divided the Long Walls and a great part of Piraeus into lots and settled there. All this while great attention was being given to the war; the allies were being mustered, and an armament of a hundred ships equipped for Peloponnese. Such was the state of preparation at Athens.

[18] Meanwhile the army of the Peloponnesians was advancing. The first town they came to in Attica was Oenoe, where they were to enter the country. Sitting down before it, they prepared to assault the wall with engines and otherwise. Oenoe, standing upon the Athenian and Boeotian border, was of course a walled town, and was used as a fortress by the Athenians in time of war. So the Peloponnesians prepared for their assault, and wasted some valuable time before the place. This delay brought the gravest censure upon Archidamus. Even during the levying of the war he had gained credit for weakness and Athenian sympathies by the half measures he had advocated; and after the army had assembled he had further injured himself in public estimation by his loitering at the Isthmus and the slowness with which the rest of the march had been conducted. But all this was as nothing to the delay at Oenoe. During this interval the Athenians were carrying in their property; and it was the belief of the Peloponnesians that a quick advance would have found everything still out, had it not been for his procrastination. Such was the feeling of the army towards Archidamus during the siege. But he, it is said, expected that the Athenians would shrink from letting their land be wasted, and would make their submission while it was still uninjured; and this was why he waited.

[19] But after he had assaulted Oenoe, and every possible attempt to take it had failed, as no herald came from Athens, he at last broke up his camp and invaded Attica. This was about eighty days after the Theban attempt upon Plataea, just in the middle of summer, when the corn was ripe, and Archidamus, son of Zeuxis, king of Lacedaemon, was in command. Encamping in Eleusis and the Thriasian plain, they began their ravages, and putting to flight some Athenian horse at a place called Rheiti, or the Brooks, they then advanced, keeping Mount Aegaleus on their right, through Cropia, until they reached Acharnae, the largest of the Athenian demes or townships. Sitting down before it, they formed a camp there, and continued their ravages for a long while.

[20] The reason why Archidamus remained in order of battle at Acharnae during this incursion, instead of descending into the plain, is said to have been this. He hoped that the Athenians might possibly be tempted by the multitude of their youth and the unprecedented efficiency of their service to come out to battle and attempt to stop the devastation of their lands. Accordingly, as they had not met him at Eleusis or the Thriasian plain, he tried if they could be provoked to a sally by the spectacle of a camp at Acharnae. He thought the place itself a good position for encamping; and it seemed likely that such an important

part of the state as the three thousand heavy infantry of the Acharnians would refuse to submit to the ruin of their property, and would force a battle on the rest of the citizens. On the other hand, should the Athenians not take the field during this incursion, he could then fearlessly ravage the plain in future invasions, and extend his advance up to the very walls of Athens. After the Acharnians had lost their own property they would be less willing to risk themselves for that of their neighbours; and so there would be division in the Athenian counsels. These were the motives of Archidamus for remaining at Acharnae.

[21] In the meanwhile, as long as the army was at Eleusis and the Thriasian plain, hopes were still entertained of its not advancing any nearer. It was remembered that Pleistoanax, son of Pausanias, king of Lacedaemon, had invaded Attica with a Peloponnesian army fourteen years before, but had retreated without advancing farther than Eleusis and Thria, which indeed proved the cause of his exile from Sparta, as it was thought he had been bribed to retreat. But when they saw the army at Acharnae, barely seven miles from Athens, they lost all patience. The territory of Athens was being ravaged before the very eyes of the Athenians, a sight which the young men had never seen before and the old only in the Median wars; and it was naturally thought a grievous insult, and the determination was universal, especially among the young men, to sally forth and stop it. Knots were formed in the streets and engaged in hot discussion; for if the proposed sally was warmly recommended, it was also in some cases opposed. Oracles of the most various import were recited by the collectors, and found eager listeners in one or other of the disputants. Foremost in pressing for the sally were the Acharnians, as constituting no small part of the army of the state, and as it was their land that was being ravaged. In short, the whole city was in a most excited state; Pericles was the object of general indignation; his previous counsels were totally forgotten; he was abused for not leading out the army which he commanded, and was made responsible for the whole of the public suffering.

[22] He, meanwhile, seeing anger and infatuation just now in the ascendant, and confident of his wisdom in refusing a sally, would not call either assembly or meeting of the people, fearing the fatal results of a debate inspired by passion and not by prudence. Accordingly he addressed himself to the defence of the city,

and kept it as quiet as possible, though he constantly sent out cavalry to prevent raids on the lands near the city from flying parties of the enemy. There was a trifling affair at Phrygia between a squadron of the Athenian horse with the Thessalians and the Boeotian cavalry; in which the former had rather the best of it, until the heavy infantry advanced to the support of the Boeotians, when the Thessalians and Athenians were routed and lost a few men, whose bodies, however, were recovered the same day without a truce. The next day the Peloponnesians set up a trophy. Ancient alliance brought the Thessalians to the aid of Athens; those who came being the Larisaeans, Pharsalians, Cranonians, Pyrasians, Gyrtonians, and Pheraeans. The Larisaean commanders were Polymedes and Aristonus, two party leaders in Larisa; the Pharsalian general was Menon; each of the other cities had also its own commander.

[23] In the meantime the Peloponnesians, as the Athenians did not come out to engage them, broke up from Acharnae and ravaged some of the demes between Mount Parnes and Brilessus. While they were in Attica the Athenians sent off the hundred ships which they had been preparing round Peloponnese, with a thousand heavy infantry and four hundred archers on board, under the command of Carcinus, son of Xenotimus, Proteas, son of Epicles, and Socrates, son of Antigenes. This armament weighed anchor and started on its cruise, and the Peloponnesians, after remaining in Attica as long as their provisions lasted, retired through Boeotia by a different road to that by which they had entered. As they passed Oropus they ravaged the territory of Graea, which is held by the Oropians from Athens, and reaching Peloponnese broke up to their respective cities.

[24] After they had retired the Athenians set guards by land and sea at the points at which they intended to have regular stations during the war. They also resolved to set apart a special fund of a thousand talents from the moneys in the Acropolis. This was not to be spent, but the current expenses of the war were to be otherwise provided for. If any one should move or put to the vote a proposition for using the money for any purpose whatever except that of defending the city in the event of the enemy bringing a fleet to make an attack by sea, it should be a capital offence. With this sum of money they also set aside a special fleet of one hundred galleys, the best ships of each

year, with their captains. None of these were to be used except with the money and against the same peril, should such peril arise.

[25] Meanwhile the Athenians in the hundred ships round Peloponnese, reinforced by a Corcyraean squadron of fifty vessels and some others of the allies in those parts, cruised about the coasts and ravaged the country. Among other places they landed in Laconia and made an assault upon Methone; there being no garrison in the place, and the wall being weak. But it so happened that Brasidas, son of Tellis, a Spartan, was in command of a guard for the defence of the district. Hearing of the attack, he hurried with a hundred heavy infantry to the assistance of the besieged, and dashing through the army of the Athenians, which was scattered over the country and had its attention turned to the wall, threw himself into Methone. He lost a few men in making good his entrance, but saved the place and won the thanks of Sparta by his exploit, being thus the first officer who obtained this notice during the war. The Athenians at once weighed anchor and continued their cruise. Touching at Pheia in Elis, they ravaged the country for two days and defeated a picked force of three hundred men that had come from the vale of Elis and the immediate neighbourhood to the rescue. But a stiff squall came down upon them, and, not liking to face it in a place where there was no harbour, most of them got on board their ships, and doubling Point Ichthys sailed into the port of Pheia. In the meantime the Messenians, and some others who could not get on board, marched over by land and took Pheia. The fleet afterwards sailed round and picked them up and then put to sea; Pheia being evacuated, as the main army of the Eleans had now come up. The Athenians continued their cruise, and ravaged other places on the coast.

[26] About the same time the Athenians sent thirty ships to cruise round Locris and also to guard Euboea; Cleopompus, son of Clinias, being in command. Making descents from the fleet he ravaged certain places on the sea-coast, and captured Thronium and took hostages from it. He also defeated at Alope the Locrians that had assembled to resist him.

[27] During the summer the Athenians also expelled the Aeginetans with their wives and children from Aegina, on the ground of their having been the chief agents in bringing the war upon them. Besides, Aegina lies so near Peloponnese that it seemed safer to send colonists of their own to hold it, and shortly afterwards the settlers were sent out. The banished Aeginetans found an asylum in Thyrea, which was given to them by Lacedaemon, not only on account of her quarrel with Athens, but also because the Aeginetans had laid her under obligations at the time of the earthquake and the revolt of the Helots. The territory of Thyrea is on the frontier of Argolis and Laconia, reaching down to the sea. Those of the Aeginetans who did not settle here were scattered over the rest of Hellas.

[28] The same summer, at the beginning of a new lunar month, the only time by the way at which it appears possible, the sun was eclipsed after noon. After it had assumed the form of a crescent and some of the stars had come out, it returned to its natural shape.

[29] During the same summer Nymphodorus, son of Pythes, an Abderite, whose sister Sitalces had married, was made their *proxenus* by the Athenians and sent for to Athens. They had hitherto considered him their enemy; but he had great influence with Sitalces, and they wished this prince to become their ally. Sitalces was the son of Teres and King of the Thracians. Teres, the father of Sitalces, was the first to establish the great kingdom of the Odrysians on a scale quite unknown to the rest of Thrace, a large portion of the Thracians being independent. This Teres is in no way related to Tereus who married Pandion's daughter Procne from Athens; nor indeed did they belong to the same part of Thrace. Tereus lived in Daulis, part of what is now called Phocis, but which at that time was inhabited by Thracians. It was in this land that the women perpetrated the outrage upon Itys; and many of the poets when they mention the nightingale call it the Daulian bird. Besides, Pandion in contracting an alliance for his daughter would consider the advantages of mutual assistance, and would naturally prefer a match at the above moderate distance to the journey of many days which separates Athens from the Odrysians. Again the names are different; and this Teres was king of the Odrysians, the first by the way who attained to any power. Sitalces, his son, was now sought as an ally by the Athenians, who desired his aid in the reduction of the Thracian towns and of Perdiccas. Coming to Athens, Nymphodorus concluded the alliance with Sitalces and made his son Sadocus an Athenian citizen, and promised to finish the war in Thrace by persuading Sitalces to send the Athenians a force of Thracian horse and targeteers. He also reconciled

them with Perdiccas, and induced them to restore Therme to him; upon which Perdiccas at once joined the Athenians and Phormio in an expedition against the Chalcidians. Thus Sitalces, son of Teres, King of the Thracians, and Perdiccas, son of Alexander, King of the Macedonians, became allies of Athens.

[30] Meanwhile the Athenians in the hundred vessels were still cruising round Peloponnese. After taking Sollium, a town belonging to Corinth, and presenting the city and territory to the Acarnanians of Palaira, they stormed Astacus, expelled its tyrant Evarchus, and gained the place for their confederacy. Next they sailed to the island of Cephallenia and brought it over without using force. Cephallenia lies off Acarnania and Leucas, and consists of four states, the Paleans, Cranians, Samaeans, and Pronaeans. Not long afterwards the fleet returned to Athens. [31] Towards the autumn of this year the Athenians invaded the Megarid with their whole levy, resident aliens included, under the command of Pericles, son of Xanthippus. The Athenians in the hundred ships round Peloponnese on their journey home had just reached Aegina, and hearing that the citizens at home were in full force at Megara, now sailed over and joined them. This was without doubt the largest army of Athenians ever assembled, the state being still in the flower of her strength and yet unvisited by the plague. Full ten thousand heavy infantry were in the field, all Athenian citizens, besides the three thousand before Potidaea. Then the resident aliens who joined in the incursion were at least three thousand strong; besides which there was a multitude of light troops. They ravaged the greater part of the territory, and then retired. Other incursions into the Megarid were afterwards made by the Athenians annually during the war, sometimes only with cavalry, sometimes with all their forces. This went on until the capture of Nisaea. [32] Atalanta also, the desert island off the Opuntian coast, was towards the end of this summer converted into a fortified post by the Athenians, in order to prevent privateers issuing from Opus and the rest of Locris and plundering Euboea. Such were the events of this summer after the return of the Peloponnesians from Attica.

[33] In the ensuing winter the Acarnanian Evarchus, wishing to return to Astacus, persuaded the Corinthians to sail over with forty ships and fifteen hundred heavy infantry and restore him; himself also hiring some merce-naries. In command of the force were Euphamidas, son of Aristonymus, Timoxenus, son of Timocrates, and Eumachus, son of Chrysis, who sailed over and restored him and, after failing in an attempt on some places on the Acarnanian coast which they were desirous of gaining, began their voyage home. Coasting along shore they touched at Cephallenia and made a descent on the Cranian territory, and losing some men by the treachery of the Cranians, who fell suddenly upon them after having agreed to treat, put to sea somewhat hurriedly and returned home.

[34] In the same winter the Athenians gave a funeral at the public cost to those who had first fallen in this war. It was a custom of their ancestors, and the manner of it is as follows. Three days before the ceremony, the bones of the dead are laid out in a tent which has been erected; and their friends bring to their relatives such offerings as they please. In the funeral procession cypress coffins are borne in cars, one for each tribe; the bones of the deceased being placed in the coffin of their tribe. Among these is carried one empty bier decked for the missing, that is, for those whose bodies could not be recovered. Any citizen or stranger who pleases, joins in the procession: and the female relatives are there to wail at the burial. The dead are laid in the public sepulchre in the Beautiful suburb of the city, in which those who fall in war are always buried; with the exception of those slain at Marathon, who for their singular and extraordinary valour were interred on the spot where they fell. After the bodies have been laid in the earth, a man chosen by the state, of approved wisdom and eminent reputation, pronounces over them an appropriate panegyric; after which all retire. Such is the manner of the burying; and throughout the whole of the war, whenever the occasion arose, the established custom was observed. Meanwhile these were the first that had fallen, and Pericles, son of Xanthippus, was chosen to pronounce their eulogium. When the proper time arrived, he advanced from the sepulchre to an elevated platform in order to be heard by as many of the crowd as possible, and spoke as follows:

[35] "Most of my predecessors in this place have commended him who made this speech part of the law, telling us that it is well that it should be delivered at the burial of those who fall in battle. For myself, I should have thought that the worth which had displayed itself in deeds would be sufficiently rewarded by hon-

ours also shown by deeds; such as you now see in this funeral prepared at the people's cost. And I could have wished that the reputations of many brave men were not to be imperilled in the mouth of a single individual, to stand or fall according as he spoke well or ill. For it is hard to speak properly upon a subject where it is even difficult to convince your hearers that you are speaking the truth. On the one hand, the friend who is familiar with every fact of the story may think that some point has not been set forth with that fullness which he wishes and knows it to deserve; on the other, he who is a stranger to the matter may be led by envy to suspect exaggeration if he hears anything above his own nature. For men can endure to hear others praised only so long as they can severally persuade themselves of their own ability to equal the actions recounted: when this point is passed, envy comes in and with it incredulity. However, since our ancestors have stamped this custom with their approval, it becomes my duty to obey the law and to try to satisfy your several wishes and opinions as best I may.

[36] "I shall begin with our ancestors: it is both just and proper that they should have the honour of the first mention on an occasion like the present. They dwelt in the country without break in the succession from generation to generation, and handed it down free to the present time by their valour. And if our more remote ancestors deserve praise, much more do our own fathers, who added to their inheritance the empire which we now possess, and spared no pains to be able to leave their acquisitions to us of the present generation. Lastly, there are few parts of our dominions that have not been augmented by those of us here, who are still more or less in the vigour of life; while the mother country has been furnished by us with everything that can enable her to depend on her own resources whether for war or for peace. That part of our history which tells of the military achievements which gave us our several possessions, or of the ready valour with which either we or our fathers stemmed the tide of Hellenic or foreign aggression, is a theme too familiar to my hearers for me to dilate on, and I shall therefore pass it by. But what was the road by which we reached our position, what the form of government under which our greatness grew, what the national habits out of which it sprang; these are questions which I may try to solve before I proceed to my panegyric upon these

men; since I think this to be a subject upon which on the present occasion a speaker may properly dwell, and to which the whole assemblage, whether citizens or foreigners, may listen with advantage.

[37] "Our constitution does not copy the laws of neighbouring states; we are rather a pattern to others than imitators ourselves. Its administration favours the many instead of the few; this is why it is called a democracy. If we look to the laws, they afford equal justice to all in their private differences; if no social standing, advancement in public life falls to reputation for capacity, class considerations not being allowed to interfere with merit; nor again does poverty bar the way, if a man is able to serve the state, he is not hindered by the obscurity of his condition. The freedom which we enjoy in our government extends also to our ordinary life. There, far from exercising a jealous surveillance over each other, we do not feel called upon to be angry with our neighbour for doing what he likes, or even to indulge in those injurious looks which cannot fail to be offensive, although they inflict no positive penalty. But all this ease in our private relations does not make us lawless as citizens. Against this fear is our chief safeguard, teaching us to obey the magistrates and the laws, particularly such as regard the protection of the injured, whether they are actually on the statute book, or belong to that code which, although unwritten, yet cannot be broken without acknowledged disgrace.

[38] "Further, we provide plenty of means for the mind to refresh itself from business. We celebrate games and sacrifices all the year round, and the elegance of our private establishments forms a daily source of pleasure and helps to banish the spleen; while the magnitude of our city draws the produce of the world into our harbour, so that to the Athenian the fruits of other countries are as familiar a luxury as those of his own.

[39] "If we turn to our military policy, there also we differ from our antagonists. We throw open our city to the world, and never by alien acts exclude foreigners from any opportunity of learning or observing, although the eyes of an enemy may occasionally profit by our liberality; trusting less in system and policy than to the native spirit of our citizens; while in education, where our rivals from their very cradles by a painful discipline seek after manliness, at Athens we live exactly as we please, and yet are just as ready to encounter every

legitimate danger. In proof of this it may be noticed that the Lacedaemonians do not invade our country alone, but bring with them all their confederates; while we Athenians advance unsupported into the territory of a neighbour, and fighting upon a foreign soil usually vanquish with ease men who are defending their homes. Our united force was never yet encountered by any enemy, because we have at once to attend to our marine and to dispatch our citizens by land upon a hundred different services; so that, wherever they engage with some such fraction of our strength, a success against a detachment is magnified into a victory over the nation, and a defeat into a reverse suffered at the hands of our entire people. And yet if with habits not of labour but of ease, and courage not of art but of nature, we are still willing to encounter danger, we have the double advantage of escaping the experience of hardships in anticipation and of facing them in the hour of need as fearlessly as those who are never free from them.

"Nor are these the only points in which our city is worthy of admiration. [40] We cultivate refinement without extravagance and knowledge without effeminacy; wealth we employ more for use than for show, and place the real disgrace of poverty not in owning to the fact but in declining the struggle against it. Our public men have, besides politics, their private affairs to attend to, and our ordinary citizens, though occupied with the pursuits of industry, are still fair judges of public matters; for, unlike any other nation, regarding him who takes no part in these duties not as unambitious but as useless, we Athenians are able to judge at all events if we cannot originate, and, instead of looking on discussion as a stumbling-block in the way of action, we think it an indispensable preliminary to any wise action at all. Again, in our enterprises we present the singular spectacle of daring and deliberation, each carried to its highest point, and both united in the same persons; although usually decision is the fruit of ignorance, hesitation of reflection. But the palm of courage will surely be adjudged most justly to those, who best know the difference between hardship and pleasure and yet are never tempted to shrink from danger. In generosity we are equally singular, acquiring our friends by conferring, not by receiving, favours. Yet, of course, the doer of the favour is the firmer friend of the two, in order by continued kind-

ness to keep the recipient in his debt; while the debtor feels less keenly from the very consciousness that the return he makes will be a payment, not a free gift. And it is only the Athenians, who, fearless of consequences, confer their benefits not from calculations of expediency, but in the confidence of liberality.

[41] "In short, I say that as a city we are the school of Hellas; while I doubt if the world can produce a man who, where he has only himself to depend upon, is equal to so many emergencies, and graced by so happy a versatility, as the Athenian. And that this is no mere boast thrown out for the occasion, but plain matter of fact, the power of the state acquired by these habits proves. For Athens alone of her contemporaries is found when tested to be greater than her reputation, and alone gives no occasion to her assailants to blush at the antagonist by whom they have been worsted, or to her subjects to question her title by merit to rule. Rather, the admiration of the present and succeeding ages will be ours, since we have not left our power without witness, but have shown it by mighty proofs; and far from needing a Homer for our panegyrist, or other of his craft whose verses might charm for the moment only for the impression which they gave to melt at the touch of fact, we have forced every sea and land to be the highway of our daring, and everywhere, whether for evil or for good, have left imperishable monuments behind us. Such is the Athens for which these men, in the assertion of their resolve not to lose her, nobly fought and died; and well may every one of their survivors be ready to suffer in her cause.

[42] "Indeed if I have dwelt at some length upon the character of our country, it has been to show that our stake in the struggle is not the same as theirs who have no such blessings to lose, and also that the panegyric of the men over whom I am now speaking might be by definite proofs established. That panegyric is now in a great measure complete; for the Athens that I have celebrated is only what the heroism of these and their like have made her, men whose fame, unlike that of most Hellenes, will be found to be only commensurate with their deserts. And if a test of worth be wanted, it is to be found in their closing scene, and this not only in the cases in which it set the final seal upon their merit, but also in those in which it gave the first intimation of their having any. For there is justice in the claim that steadfastness in his country's battles should be as a cloak

to cover a man's other imperfections; since the good action has blotted out the bad, and his merit as a citizen more than outweighed his demerits as an individual. But none of these allowed either wealth with its prospect of future enjoyment to unnerve his spirit, or poverty with its hope of a day of freedom and riches to tempt him to shrink from danger. No, holding that vengeance upon their enemies was more to be desired than any personal blessings, and reckoning this to be the most glorious of hazards, they joyfully determined to accept the risk, to make sure of their vengeance, and to let their wishes wait; and while committing to hope the uncertainty of final success, in the business before them they thought fit to act boldly and trust in themselves. Thus choosing to die resisting, rather than to live submitting, they fled only from dishonour, but met danger face to face, and after one brief moment, while at the summit of their fortune, escaped, not from their fear, but from their glory.

[43] "So died these men as became Athenians. You, their survivors, must determine to have as unfaltering a resolution in the field, though you may pray that it may have a happier issue. And not contented with ideas derived only from words of the advantages which are bound up with the defence of your country, though these would furnish a valuable text to a speaker even before an audience so alive to them as the present, you must yourselves realize the power of Athens, and feed your eyes upon her from day to day, till love of her fills your hearts; and then, when all her greatness shall break upon you, you must reflect that it was by courage, sense of duty, and a keen feeling of honour in action that men were enabled to win all this, and that no personal failure in an enterprise could make them consent to deprive their country of their valour, but they laid it at her feet as the most glorious contribution that they could offer. For this offering of their lives made in common by them all they each of them individually received that renown which never grows old, and for a sepulchre, not so much that in which their bones have been deposited, but that noblest of shrines wherein their glory is laid up to be eternally remembered upon every occasion on which deed or story shall call for its commemoration. For heroes have the whole earth for their tomb; and in lands far from their own, where the column with its epitaph declares it, there is enshrined in every breast a record unwritten with no tablet to preserve it, except that of the heart. These take as your model and, judging happiness to be the fruit of freedom and freedom of valour, never decline the dangers of war. For it is not the miserable that would most justly be unsparing of their lives; these have nothing to hope for: it is rather they to whom continued life may bring reverses as yet unknown, and to whom a fall, if it came, would be most tremendous in its consequences. And surely, to a man of spirit, the degradation of cowardice must be immeasurably more grievous than the unfelt death which strikes him in the midst of his strength and patriotism!

[44] "Comfort, therefore, not condolence, is what I have to offer to the parents of the dead who may be here. Numberless are the chances to which, as they know, the life of man is subject; but fortunate indeed are they who draw for their lot a death so glorious as that which has caused your mourning, and to whom life has been so exactly measured as to terminate in the happiness in which it has been passed. Still I know that this is a hard saying, especially when those are in question of whom you will constantly be reminded by seeing in the homes of others blessings of which once you also boasted: for grief is felt not so much for the want of what we have never known, as for the loss of that to which we have been long accustomed. Yet you who are still of an age to beget children must bear up in the hope of having others in their stead; not only will they help you to forget those whom you have lost, but will be to the state at once a reinforcement and a security; for never can a fair or just policy be expected of the citizen who does not, like his fellows, bring to the decision the interests and apprehensions of a father. While those of you who have passed your prime must congratulate yourselves with the thought that the best part of your life was fortunate, and that the brief span that remains will be cheered by the fame of the departed. For it is only the love of honour that never grows old; and honour it is, not gain, as some would have it, that rejoices the heart of age and helplessness.

[45] "Turning to the sons or brothers of the dead, I see an arduous struggle before you. When a man is gone, all are wont to praise him, and should your merit be ever so transcendent, you will still find it difficult not merely to overtake, but even to approach their renown. The living have envy to contend with,

while those who are no longer in our path are honoured with a goodwill into which rivalry does not enter. On the other hand, if I must say anything on the subject of female excellence to those of you who will now be in widowhood, it will be all comprised in this brief exhortation. Great will be your glory in not falling short of your natural character; and greatest will be hers who is least talked of among the men, whether for good or for bad.

[46] "My task is now finished. I have performed it to the best of my ability, and in word, at least, the requirements of the law are now satisfied. If deeds be in question, those who are here interred have received part of their honours already, and for the rest, their children will be brought up till manhood at the public expense: the state thus offers a valuable prize, as the garland of victory in this race of valour, for the reward both of those who have fallen and their survivors. And where the rewards for merit are greatest, there are found the best citizens.

"And now that you have brought to a close your lamentations for your relatives, you may depart."

CHAPTER VII

Second Year of the War—The Plague of Athens —Position and Policy of Pericles—Fall of Potidaea

[47] SUCH was the funeral that took place during this winter, with which the first year of the war came to an end. In the first days of summer the Lacedaemonians and their allies, with two-thirds of their forces as before, invaded Attica, under the command of Archidamus, son of Zeuxidamus, King of Lacedaemon, and sat down and laid waste the country. Not many days after their arrival in Attica the plague first began to show itself among the Athenians. It was said that it had broken out in many places previously in the neighbourhood of Lemnos and elsewhere; but a pestilence of such extent and mortality was nowhere remembered. Neither were the physicians at first of any service, ignorant as they were of the proper way to treat it, but they died themselves the most thickly, as they visited the sick most often; nor did any human art succeed any better. Supplications in the temples, divinations, and so forth were found equally futile, till the overwhelming nature of the disaster at last put a stop to them altogether.

[48] It first began, it is said, in the parts of Ethiopia above Egypt, and thence descended into Egypt and Libya and into most of the King's country. Suddenly falling upon Athens, it first attacked the population in Piraeus—which was the occasion of their saying that the Peloponnesians had poisoned the reservoirs, there being as yet no wells there—and afterwards appeared in the upper city, when the deaths became much more frequent. All speculation as to its origin and its causes, if causes can be found adequate to produce so great a disturbance, I leave to other writers, whether lay or professional; for myself, I shall simply set down its nature, and explain the symptoms by which perhaps it may be recognized by the student, if it should ever break out again. This I can the better do, as I had the disease myself, and watched its operation in the case of others.

[49] That year then is admitted to have been otherwise unprecedentedly free from sickness; and such few cases as occurred all determined in this. As a rule, however, there was no ostensible cause; but people in good health were all of a sudden attacked by violent heats in the head, and redness and inflammation in the eyes, the inward parts, such as the throat or tongue, becoming bloody and emitting an unnatural and fetid breath. These symptoms were followed by sneezing and hoarseness, after which the pain soon reached the chest, and produced a hard cough. When it fixed in the stomach, it upset it; and discharges of bile of every kind named by physicians ensued, accompanied by very great distress. In most cases also an ineffectual retching followed, producing violent spasms, which in some cases ceased soon after, in others much later. Externally the body was not very hot to the touch, nor pale in its appearance, but reddish, livid, and breaking out into small pustules and ulcers. But internally it burned so that the patient could not bear to have on him clothing or linen even of the very lightest description; or indeed to be otherwise than stark naked. What they would have liked best would have been to throw themselves into cold water; as indeed was done by some of the neglected sick, who plunged into the rain-tanks in their agonies of unquenchable thirst; though it made no difference whether they drank little or much. Besides this, the miserable feeling of not being able to rest or sleep never ceased to torment them. The body meanwhile did not waste away so long as the distemper was at its height, but held out to a marvel against its ravages; so that

when they succumbed, as in most cases, on the seventh or eighth day to the internal inflammation, they had still some strength in them. But if they passed this stage, and the disease descended further into the bowels, inducing a violent ulceration there accompanied by severe diarrhoea, this brought on a weakness which was generally fatal. For the disorder first settled in the head, ran its course from thence through the whole of the body, and, even where it did not prove mortal, it still left its mark on the extremities; for it settled in the privy parts, the fingers and the toes, and many escaped with the loss of these, some too with that of their eyes. Others again were seized with an entire loss of memory on their first recovery, and did not know either themselves or their friends.

[50] But while the nature of the distemper was such as to baffle all description, and its attacks almost too grievous for human nature to endure, it was still in the following circumstance that its difference from all ordinary disorders was most clearly shown. All the birds and beasts that prey upon human bodies, either abstained from touching them (though there were many lying unburied), or died after tasting them. In proof of this, it was noticed that birds of this kind actually disappeared; they were not about the bodies, or indeed to be seen at all. But of course the effects which I have mentioned could best be studied in a domestic animal like the dog.

[51] Such then, if we pass over the varieties of particular cases which were many and peculiar, were the general features of the distemper. Meanwhile the town enjoyed an immunity from all the ordinary disorders; or if any case occurred, it ended in this. Some died in neglect, others in the midst of every attention. No remedy was found that could be used as a specific; for what did good in one case, did harm in another. Strong and weak constitutions proved equally incapable of resistance, all alike being swept away, although dieted with the utmost precaution. By far the most terrible feature in the malady was the dejection which ensued when any one felt himself sickening, for the despair into which they instantly fell took away their power of resistance, and left them a much easier prey to the disorder; besides which, there was the awful spectacle of men dying like sheep, through having caught the infection in nursing each other. This caused the greatest mortality. On the one hand, if they were afraid to visit each other, they

perished from neglect; indeed many houses were emptied of their inmates for want of a nurse: on the other, if they ventured to do so, death was the consequence. This was especially the case with such as made any pretensions to goodness: honour made them unsparing of themselves in their attendance in their friends' houses, where even the members of the family were at last worn out by the moans of the dying, and succumbed to the force of the disaster. Yet it was with those who had recovered from the disease that the sick and the dying found most compassion. These knew what it was from experience, and had now no fear for themselves; for the same man was never attacked twice—never at least fatally. And such persons not only received the congratulations of others, but themselves also, in the elation of the moment, half entertained the vain hope that they were for the future safe from any disease whatsoever.

[52] An aggravation of the existing calamity was the influx from the country into the city, and this was especially felt by the new arrivals. As there were no houses to receive them, they had to be lodged at the hot season of the year in stifling cabins, where the mortality raged without restraint. The bodies of dying men lay one upon another, and half-dead creatures reeled about the streets and gathered round all the fountains in their longing for water. The sacred places also in which they had quartered themselves were full of corpses of persons that had died there, just as they were; for as the disaster passed all bounds, men, not knowing what was to become of them, became utterly careless of everything, whether sacred or profane. All the burial rites before in use were entirely upset, and they buried the bodies as best they could. Many from want of the proper appliances, through so many of their friends having died already, had recourse to the most shameless sepultures: sometimes getting the start of those who had raised a pile, they threw their own dead body upon the stranger's pyre and ignited it; sometimes they tossed the corpse which they were carrying on the top of another that was burning, and so went off.

[53] Nor was this the only form of lawless extravagance which owed its origin to the plague. Men now coolly ventured on what they had formerly done in a corner, and not just as they pleased, seeing the rapid transitions produced by persons in prosperity suddenly dying and those who before had nothing succeeding

to their property. So they resolved to spend quickly and enjoy themselves, regarding their lives and riches as alike things of a day. Perseverance in what men called honour was popular with none, it was so uncertain whether they would be spared to attain the object; but it was settled that present enjoyment, and all that contributed to it, was both honourable and useful. Fear of gods or law of man there was none to restrain them. As for the first, they judged it to be just the same whether they worshipped them or not, as they saw all alike perishing; and for the last, no one expected to live to be brought to trial for his offences, but each felt that a far severer sentence had been already passed upon them all and hung ever over their heads, and before this fell it was only reasonable to enjoy life a little.

[54] Such was the nature of the calamity, and heavily did it weigh on the Athenians; death raging within the city and devastation without. Among other things which they remembered in their distress was, very naturally, the following verse which the old men said had long ago been uttered:

A Dorian war shall come and with it death.

So a dispute arose as to whether *dearth* and not *death* had not been the word in the verse; but at the present juncture, it was of course decided in favour of the latter; for the people made their recollection fit in with their sufferings. I fancy, however, that if another Dorian war should ever afterwards come upon us, and a dearth should happen to accompany it, the verse will probably be read accordingly. The oracle also which had been given to the Lacedaemonians was now remembered by those who knew of it. When the god was asked whether they should go to war, he answered that if they put their might into it, victory would be theirs, and that he would himself be with them. With this oracle events were supposed to tally. For the plague broke out as soon as the Peloponnesians invaded Attica, and never entering Peloponnese (not at least to an extent worth noticing), committed its worst ravages at Athens, and next to Athens, at the most populous of the other towns. Such was the history of the plague.

[55] After ravaging the plain, the Peloponnesians advanced into the Paralian region as far as Laurium, where the Athenian silver mines are, and first laid waste the side looking towards Peloponnese, next that which faces Euboea and Andros. But Pericles, who was

still general, held the same opinion as in the former invasion, and would not let the Athenians march out against them.

[56] However, while they were still in the plain, and had not yet entered the Paralian land, he had prepared an armament of a hundred ships for Peloponnese, and when all was ready put out to sea. On board the ships he took four thousand Athenian heavy infantry, and three hundred cavalry in horse transports, and then for the first time made out of old galleys; fifty Chian and Lesbian vessels also joining in the expedition. When this Athenian armament put out to sea, they left the Peloponnesians in Attica in the Paralian region. Arriving at Epidaurus in Peloponnese they ravaged most of the territory, and even had hopes of taking the town by an assault: in this however they were not successful. Putting out from Epidaurus, they laid waste the territory of Troezen, Halieis, and Hermione, all towns on the coast of Peloponnese, and thence sailing to Prasiai, a maritime town in Laconia, ravaged part of its territory, and took and sacked the place itself; after which they returned home, but found the Peloponnesians gone and no longer in Attica.

[57] During the whole time that the Peloponnesians were in Attica and the Athenians on the expedition in their ships, men kept dying of the plague both in the armament and in Athens. Indeed it was actually asserted that the departure of the Peloponnesians was hastened by fear of the disorder; as they heard from deserters that it was in the city, and also could see the burials going on. Yet in this invasion they remained longer than in any other, and ravaged the whole country, for they were about forty days in Attica.

[58] The same summer Hagnon, son of Nicias, and Cleopompus, son of Clinias, the colleagues of Pericles, took the armament of which he had lately made use, and went off upon an expedition against the Chalcidians in the direction of Thrace and Potidaea, which was still under siege. As soon as they arrived, they brought up their engines against Potidaea and tried every means of taking it, but did not succeed either in capturing the city or in doing anything else worthy of their preparations. For the plague attacked them here also, and committed such havoc as to cripple them completely, even the previously healthy soldiers of the former expedition catching the infection from Hagnon's troops; while Phormio and the sixteen hundred men whom he commanded

only escaped by being no longer in the neighbourhood of the Chalcidians. The end of it was that Hagnon returned with his ships to Athens, having lost one thousand and fifty out of four thousand heavy infantry in about forty days; though the soldiers stationed there before remained in the country and carried on the siege of Potidaea.

[59] After the second invasion of the Peloponnesians a change came over the spirit of the Athenians. Their land had now been twice laid waste; and war and pestilence at once pressed heavy upon them. They began to find fault with Pericles, as the author of the war and the cause of all their misfortunes, and became eager to come to terms with Lacedaemon, and actually sent ambassadors thither, who did not however succeed in their mission. Their despair was now complete and all vented itself upon Pericles. When he saw them exasperated at the present turn of affairs and acting exactly as he had anticipated, he called an assembly, being (it must be remembered) still general, with the double object of restoring confidence and of leading them from these angry feelings to a calmer and more hopeful state of mind. He accordingly came forward and spoke as follows:

[60] "I was not unprepared for the indignation of which I have been the object, as I know its causes; and I have called an assembly for the purpose of reminding you upon certain points, and of protesting against your being unreasonably irritated with me, or cowed by your sufferings. I am of opinion that national greatness is more for the advantage of private citizens, than any individual well-being coupled with public humiliation. A man may be personally ever so well off, and yet if his country be ruined he must be ruined with it; whereas a flourishing commonwealth always affords chances of salvation to unfortunate individuals. Since then a state can support the misfortunes of private citizens, while they cannot support hers, it is surely the duty of every one to be forward in her defence, and not like you to be so confounded with your domestic afflictions as to give up all thoughts of the common safety, and to blame me for having counselled war and yourselves for having voted it. And yet if you are angry with me, it is with one who, as I believe, is second to no man either in knowledge of the proper policy, or in the ability to expound it, and who is moreover not only a patriot but an honest one. A man possessing that knowledge without that faculty

of exposition might as well have no idea at all on the matter: if he had both these gifts, but no love for his country, he would be but a cold advocate for her interests; while were his patriotism not proof against bribery, everything would go for a price. So that if you thought that I was even moderately distinguished for these qualities when you took my advice and went to war, there is certainly no reason now why I should be charged with having done wrong.

[61] "For those of course who have a free choice in the matter and whose fortunes are not at stake, war is the greatest of follies. But if the only choice was between submission with loss of independence, and danger with the hope of preserving that independence, in such a case it is he who will not accept the risk that deserves blame, not he who will. I am the same man and do not alter, it is you who change, since in fact you took my advice while unhurt, and waited for misfortune to repent of it; and the apparent error of my policy lies in the infirmity of your resolution, since the suffering that it entails is being felt by every one among you, while its advantage is still remote and obscure to all, and a great and sudden reverse having befallen you, your mind is too much depressed to persevere in your resolves. For before what is sudden, unexpected, and least within calculation, the spirit quails; and putting all else aside, the plague has certainly been an emergency of this kind. Born, however, as you are, citizens of a great state, and brought up, as you have been, with habits equal to your birth, you should be ready to face the greatest disasters and still to keep unimpaired the lustre of your name. For the judgment of mankind is as relentless to the weakness that falls short of a recognized renown, as it is jealous of the arrogance that aspires higher than its due. Cease then to grieve for your private afflictions, and address yourselves instead to the safety of the commonwealth.

[62] "If you shrink before the exertions which the war makes necessary, and fear that after all they may not have a happy result, you know the reasons by which I have often demonstrated to you the groundlessness of your apprehensions. If those are not enough, I will now reveal an advantage arising from the greatness of your dominion, which I think has never yet suggested itself to you, which I never mentioned in my previous speeches, and which has so bold a sound that I should scarce adven-

ture it now, were it not for the unnatural depression which I see around me. You perhaps think that your empire extends only over your allies; I will declare to you the truth. The visible field of action has two parts, land and sea. In the whole of one of these you are completely supreme, not merely as far as you use it at present, but also to what further extent you may think fit: in fine, your naval resources are such that your vessels may go where they please, without the King or any other nation on earth being able to stop them. So that although you may think it a great privation to lose the use of your land and houses, still you must see that this power is something widely different; and instead of fretting on their account, you should really regard them in the light of the gardens and other accessories that embellish a great fortune, and as, in comparison, of little moment. You should know too that liberty preserved by your efforts will easily recover for us what we have lost, while, the knee once bowed, even what you have will pass from you. Your fathers receiving these possessions not from others, but from themselves, did not let slip what their labour had acquired, but delivered them safe to you; and in this respect at least you must prove yourselves their equals, remembering that to lose what one has got is more disgraceful than to be balked in getting, and you must confront your enemies not merely with spirit but with disdain. Confidence indeed a blissful ignorance can impart, ay, even to a coward's breast, but disdain is the privilege of those who, like us, have been assured by reflection of their superiority to their adversary. And where the chances are the same, knowledge fortifies courage by the contempt which is its consequence, its trust being placed, not in hope, which is the prop of the desperate, but in a judgment grounded upon existing resources, whose anticipations are more to be depended upon.

[63] "Again, your country has a right to your services in sustaining the glories of her position. These are a common source of pride to you all, and you cannot decline the burdens of empire and still expect to share its honours. You should remember also that what you are fighting against is not merely slavery as an exchange for independence, but also loss of empire and danger from the animosities incurred in its exercise. Besides, to recede is no longer possible, if indeed any of you in the alarm of the moment has become enamoured of the honesty of such an unambitious part. For what

you hold is, to speak somewhat plainly, a tyranny; to take it perhaps was wrong, but to let it go is unsafe. And men of these retiring views, making converts of others, would quickly ruin a state; indeed the result would be the same if they could live independent by themselves; for the retiring and unambitious are never secure without vigorous protectors at their side; in fine, such qualities are useless to an imperial city, though they may help a dependency to an unmolested servitude.

[64] "But you must not be seduced by citizens like these or angry with me—who, if I voted for war, only did as you did yourselves—in spite of the enemy having invaded your country and done what you could be certain that he would do, if you refused to comply with his demands; and although besides what we counted for, the plague has come upon us—the only point indeed at which our calculation has been at fault. It is this, I know, that has had a large share in making me more unpopular than I should otherwise have been—quite undeservedly, unless you are also prepared to give me the credit of any success with which chance may present you. Besides, the hand of heaven must be borne with resignation, that of the enemy with fortitude; this was the old way at Athens, and do not you prevent it being so still. Remember, too, that if your country has the greatest name in all the world, it is because she never bent before disaster; because she has expended more life and effort in war than any other city, and has won for herself a power greater than any hitherto known, the memory of which will descend to the latest posterity; even if now, in obedience to the general law of decay, we should ever be forced to yield, still it will be remembered that we held rule over more Hellenes than any other Hellenic state, that we sustained the greatest wars against their united or separate powers, and inhabited a city unrivalled by any other in resources or magnitude. These glories may incur the censure of the slow and unambitious; but in the breast of energy they will awake emulation, and in those who must remain without them an envious regret. Hatred and unpopularity at the moment have fallen to the lot of all who have aspired to rule others; but where odium must be incurred, true wisdom incurs it for the highest objects. Hatred also is short-lived; but that which makes the splendour of the present and the glory of the future remains for ever unforgotten. Make your decision, therefore, for glory then and honour now, and

attain both objects by instant and zealous effort: do not send heralds to Lacedaemon, and do not betray any sign of being oppressed by your present sufferings, since they whose minds are least sensitive to calamity, and whose hands are most quick to meet it, are the greatest men and the greatest communities."

[65] Such were the arguments by which Pericles tried to cure the Athenians of their anger against him and to divert their thoughts from their immediate afflictions. As a community he succeeded in convincing them; they not only gave up all idea of sending to Lacedaemon, but applied themselves with increased energy to the war; still as private individuals they could not help smarting under their sufferings, the common people having been deprived of the little that they were possessed, while the higher orders had lost fine properties with costly establishments and buildings in the country, and, worst of all, had war instead of peace. In fact, the public feeling against him did not subside until he had been fined. Not long afterwards, however, according to the way of the multitude, they again elected him general and committed all their affairs to his hands, having now become less sensitive to their private and domestic afflictions, and understanding that he was the best man of all for the public necessities. For as long as he was at the head of the state during the peace, he pursued a moderate and conservative policy; and in his time its greatness was at its height. When the war broke out, here also he seems to have rightly gauged the power of his country. He outlived its commencement two years and six months, and the correctness of his previsions respecting it became better known by his death. He told them to wait quietly, to pay attention to their marine, to attempt no new conquests, and to expose the city to no hazards during the war, and doing this, promised them a favourable result. What they did was the very contrary, allowing private ambitions and private interests, in matters apparently quite foreign to the war, to lead them into projects unjust both to themselves and to their allies—projects whose success would only conduce to the honour and advantage of private persons, and whose failure entailed certain disaster on the country in the war. The causes of this are not far to seek. Pericles indeed, by his rank, ability, and known integrity, was enabled to exercise an independent control over the multitude—in short, to lead them instead of being led by them; for as he never sought power by improper means, he was never compelled to flatter them, but, on the contrary, enjoyed so high an estimation that he could afford to anger them by contradiction. Whenever he saw them unseasonably and insolently elated, he would with a word reduce them to alarm; on the other hand, if they fell victims to a panic, he could at once restore them to confidence. In short, what was nominally a democracy became in his hands government by the first citizen. With his successors it was different. More on a level with one another, and each grasping at supremacy, they ended by committing even the conduct of state affairs to the whims of the multitude. This, as might have been expected in a great and sovereign state, produced a host of blunders, and amongst them the Sicilian expedition; though this failed not so much through a miscalculation of the power of those against whom it was sent, as through a fault in the senders in not taking the best measures afterwards to assist those who had gone out, but choosing rather to occupy themselves with private cabals for the leadership of the commons, by which they not only paralysed operations in the field, but also first introduced civil discord at home. Yet after losing most of their fleet besides other forces in Sicily, and with faction already dominant in the city, they could still for three years make head against their original adversaries, joined not only by the Sicilians, but also by their own allies nearly all in revolt, and at last by the King's son, Cyrus, who furnished the funds for the Peloponnesian navy. Nor did they finally succumb till they fell the victims of their own intestine disorders. So superfluously abundant were the resources from which the genius of Pericles foresaw an easy triumph in the war over the unaided forces of the Peloponnesians.

[66] During the same summer the Lacedaemonians and their allies made an expedition with a hundred ships against Zacynthus, an island lying off the coast of Elis, peopled by a colony of Achaeans from Peloponnese, and in alliance with Athens. There were a thousand Lacedaemonian heavy infantry on board, and Cnemus, a Spartan, as admiral. They made a descent from their ships, and ravaged most of the country; but as the inhabitants would not submit, they sailed back home.

[67] At the end of the same summer the Corinthian Aristeus, Aneristus, Nicolaus, and Stratodemus, envoys from Lacedaemon, Timagoras, a Tegean, and a private individual

named Pollis from Argos, on their way to Asia to persuade the King to supply funds and join in the war, came to Sitalces, son of Teres in Thrace, with the idea of inducing him, if possible, to forsake the alliance of Athens and to march on Potidaea then besieged by an Athenian force, and also of getting conveyed by his means to their destination across the Hellespont to Pharnabazus, who was to send them up the country to the King. But there chanced to be with Sitalces some Athenian ambassadors—Learchus, son of Callimachus, and Ameiniades, son of Philemon—who persuaded Sitalces' son, Sadocus, the new Athenian citizen, to put the men into their hands and thus prevent their crossing over to the King and doing their part to injure the country of his choice. He accordingly had them seized, as they were travelling through Thrace to the vessel in which they were to cross the Hellespont, by a party whom he had sent on with Learchus and Ameiniades, and gave orders for their delivery to the Athenian ambassadors, by whom they were brought to Athens. On their arrival, the Athenians, afraid that Aristeus, who had been notably the prime mover in the previous affairs of Potidaea and their Thracian possessions, might live to do them still more mischief if he escaped, slew them all the same day, without giving them a trial or hearing the defence which they wished to offer, and cast their bodies into a pit; thinking themselves justified in using in retaliation the same mode of warfare which the Lacedaemonians had begun, when they slew and cast into pits all the Athenian and allied traders whom they caught on board the merchantmen round Peloponnese. Indeed, at the outset of the war, the Lacedaemonians butchered as enemies all whom they took on the sea, whether allies of Athens or neutrals.

[68] About the same time towards the close of the summer, the Ambraciot forces, with a number of barbarians that they had raised, marched against the Amphilochian Argos and the rest of that country. The origin of their enmity against the Argives was this. This Argos and the rest of Amphilochia were colonized by Amphilochus, son of Amphiaraus. Dissatisfied with the state of affairs at home on his return thither after the Trojan War, he built this city in the Ambracian Gulf, and named it Argos after his own country. This was the largest town in Amphilochia, and its inhabitants the most powerful. Under the pressure of misfortune many generations afterwards, they called in the Ambraciots, their neighbours on the

Amphilochian border, to join their colony; and it was by this union with the Ambraciots that they learnt their present Hellenic speech, the rest of the Amphilochians being barbarians. After a time the Ambraciots expelled the Argives and held the city themselves. Upon this the Amphilochians gave themselves over to the Acarnanians; and the two together called the Athenians, who sent them Phormio as general and thirty ships; upon whose arrival they took Argos by storm, and made slaves of the Ambraciots; and the Amphilochians and Acarnanians inhabited the town in common. After this began the alliance between the Athenians and Acarnanians. The enmity of the Ambraciots against the Argives thus commenced with the enslavement of their citizens; and afterwards during the war they collected this armament among themselves and the Chaonians, and other of the neighbouring barbarians. Arrived before Argos, they became masters of the country; but not being successful in their attacks upon the town, returned home and dispersed among their different peoples.

Such were the events of the summer. [69] The ensuing winter the Athenians sent twenty ships round Peloponnese, under the command of Phormio, who stationed himself at Naupactus and kept watch against any one sailing in or out of Corinth and the Crissaean Gulf. Six others went to Caria and Lycia under Melesander, to collect tribute in those parts, and also to prevent the Peloponnesian privateers from taking up their station in those waters and molesting the passage of the merchantmen from Phaselis and Phoenicia and the adjoining continent. However, Melesander, going up the country into Lycia with a force of Athenians from the ships and the allies, was defeated and killed in battle, with the loss of a number of his troops.

[70] The same winter the Potidaeans at length found themselves no longer able to hold out against their besiegers. The inroads of the Peloponnesians into Attica had not had the desired effect of making the Athenians raise the siege. Provisions there were none left; and so far had distress for food gone in Potidaea that, besides a number of other horrors, instances had even occurred of the people having eaten one another. So in this extremity they at last made proposals for capitulating to the Athenian generals in command against them —Xenophon, son of Euripides, Hestiodorus, son of Aristocleides, and Phanomachus, son of Callimachus. The generals accepted their pro-

posals, seeing the sufferings of the army in so exposed a position; besides which the state had already spent two thousand talents upon the siege. The terms of the capitulation were as follows: a free passage out for themselves, their children, wives and auxiliaries, with one garment apiece, the women with two, and a fixed sum of money for their journey. Under this treaty they went out to Chalcidice and other places, according as was their power. The Athenians, however, blamed the generals for granting terms without instructions from home, being of opinion that the place would have had to surrender at discretion. They afterwards sent settlers of their own to Potidaea, and colonized it. Such were the events of the winter, and so ended the second year of this war of which Thucydides was the historian.

CHAPTER VIII

Third Year of the War—Investment of Plataea— Naval Victories of Phormio—Thracian Irruption into Macedonia under Sitalces

[71] THE next summer the Peloponnesians and their allies, instead of invading Attica, marched against Plataea, under the command of Archidamus, son of Zeuxidamus, king of the Lacedaemonians. He had encamped his army and was about to lay waste the country, when the Plataeans hastened to send envoys to him, and spoke as follows: "Archidamus and Lacedaemonians, in invading the Plataean territory, you do what is wrong in itself, and worthy neither of yourselves nor of the fathers who begot you. Pausanias, son of Cleombrotus, your countryman, after freeing Hellas from the Medes with the help of those Hellenes who were willing to undertake the risk of the battle fought near our city, offered sacrifice to Zeus the Liberator in the marketplace of Plataea, and calling all the allies together restored to the Plataeans their city and territory, and declared it independent and inviolate against aggression or conquest. Should any such be attempted, the allies present were to help according to their power. Your fathers rewarded us thus for the courage and patriotism that we displayed at that perilous epoch; but you do just the contrary, coming with our bitterest enemies, the Thebans, to enslave us. We appeal, therefore, to the gods to whom the oaths were then made, to the gods of your ancestors, and lastly to those of our country, and call upon you to refrain from violating our territory or transgressing the oaths, and to let us

live independent, as Pausanias decreed."

[72] The Plataeans had got thus far when they were cut short by Archidamus saying: "There is justice, Plataeans, in what you say, if you act up to your words. According to the grant of Pausanias, continue to be independent yourselves, and join in freeing those of your fellow countrymen who, after sharing in the perils of that period, joined in the oaths to you, and are now subject to the Athenians; for it is to free them and the rest that all this provision and war has been made. I could wish that you would share our labours and abide by the oaths yourselves; if this is impossible, do what we have already required of you—remain neutral, enjoying your own; join neither side, but receive both as friends, neither as allies for the war. With this we shall be satisfied." Such were the words of Archidamus. The Plataeans, after hearing what he had to say, went into the city and acquainted the people with what had passed, and presently returned for answer that it was impossible for them to do what he proposed without consulting the Athenians, with whom their children and wives now were; besides which they had their fears for the town. After his departure, what was to prevent the Athenians from coming and taking it out of their hands, or the Thebans, who would be included in the oaths, from taking advantage of the proposed neutrality to make a second attempt to seize the city? Upon these points he tried to reassure them by saying: "You have only to deliver over the city and houses to us Lacedaemonians, to point out the boundaries of your land, the number of your fruit-trees, and whatever else can be numerically stated, and yourselves to withdraw wherever you like as long as the war shall last. When it is over we will restore to you whatever we received, and in the interim hold it in trust and keep it in cultivation, paying you a sufficient allowance."

[73] When they had heard what he had to say, they re-entered the city, and after consulting with the people said that they wished first to acquaint the Athenians with this proposal, and in the event of their approving to accede to it; in the meantime they asked him to grant them a truce and not to lay waste their territory. He accordingly granted a truce for the number of days requisite for the journey, and meanwhile abstained from ravaging their territory. The Plataean envoys went to Athens, and consulted with the Athenians, and returned with the following message to those in

the city: "The Athenians say, Plataeans, that they never hitherto, since we became their allies, on any occasion abandoned us to an enemy, nor will they now neglect us, but will help us according to their ability; and they adjure you by the oaths which your fathers swore, to keep the alliance unaltered."

[74] On the delivery of this message by the envoys, the Plataeans resolved not to be unfaithful to the Athenians but to endure, if it must be, seeing their lands laid waste and any other trials that might come to them, and not to send out again, but to answer from the wall that it was impossible for them to do as the Lacedaemonians proposed. As soon as he had received this answer, King Archidamus proceeded first to make a solemn appeal to the gods and heroes of the country in words following: "Ye gods and heroes of the Plataean territory, be my witnesses that not as aggressors originally, nor until these had first departed from the common oath, did we invade this land, in which our fathers offered you their prayers before defeating the Medes, and which you made auspicious to the Hellenic arms; nor shall we be aggressors in the measures to which we may now resort, since we have made many fair proposals but have not been successful. Graciously accord that those who were the first to offend may be punished for it, and that vengeance may be attained by those who would righteously inflict it."

[75] After this appeal to the gods Archidamus put his army in motion. First he enclosed the town with a palisade formed of the fruit-trees which they cut down, to prevent further egress from Plataea; next they threw up a mound against the city, hoping that the largeness of the force employed would ensure the speedy reduction of the place. They accordingly cut down timber from Cithaeron, and built it up on either side, laying it like lattice-work to serve as a wall to keep the mound from spreading abroad, and carried to it wood and stones and earth and whatever other material might help to complete it. They continued to work at the mound for seventy days and nights without intermission, being divided into relief parties to allow of some being employed in carrying while others took sleep and refreshment; the Lacedaemonian officer attached to each contingent keeping the men to the work. But the Plataeans, observing the progress of the mound, constructed a wall of wood and fixed it upon that part of the city wall against which the mound was being erected, and built

up bricks inside it which they took from the neighbouring houses. The timbers served to bind the building together, and to prevent its becoming weak as it advanced in height; it had also a covering of skins and hides, which protected the woodwork against the attacks of burning missiles and allowed the men to work in safety. Thus the wall was raised to a great height, and the mound opposite made no less rapid progress. The Plataeans also thought of another expedient; they pulled out part of the wall upon which the mound abutted, and carried the earth into the city.

[76] Discovering this the Peloponnesians twisted up clay in wattles of reed and threw it into the breach formed in the mound, in order to give it consistency and prevent its being carried away like the soil. Stopped in this way the Plataeans changed their mode of operation, and digging a mine from the town calculated their way under the mound, and began to carry off its material as before. This went on for a long while without the enemy outside finding it out, so that for all they threw on the top their mound made no progress in proportion, being carried away from beneath and constantly settling down in the vacuum. But the Plataeans, fearing that even thus they might not be able to hold out against the superior numbers of the enemy, had yet another invention. They stopped working at the large building in front of the mound, and starting at either end of it inside from the old low wall, built a new one in the form of a crescent running in towards the town; in order that in the event of the great wall being taken this might remain, and the enemy have to throw up a fresh mound against it, and as they advanced within might not only have their trouble over again, but also be exposed to missiles on their flanks. While raising the mound the Peloponnesians also brought up engines against the city, one of which was brought up upon the mound against the great building and shook down a good piece of it, to the no small alarm of the Plataeans. Others were advanced against different parts of the wall but were lassoed and broken by the Plataeans; who also hung up great beams by long iron chains from either extremity of two poles laid on the wall and projecting over it, and drew them up at an angle whenever any point was threatened by the engine, and loosing their hold let the beam go with its chains slack, so that it fell with a run and snapped off the nose of the battering ram.

[77] After this the Peloponnesians, finding that their engines effected nothing, and that their mound was met by the counterwork, concluded that their present means of offence were unequal to the taking of the city, and prepared for its circumvallation. First, however, they determined to try the effects of fire and see whether they could not, with the help of a wind, burn the town, as it was not a large one; indeed they thought of every possible expedient by which the place might be reduced without the expense of a blockade. They accordingly brought faggots of brushwood and threw them from the mound, first into the space between it and the wall; and this soon becoming full from the number of hands at work, they next heaped the faggots up as far into the town as they could reach from the top, and then lighted the wood by setting fire to it with sulphur and pitch. The consequence was a fire greater than any one had ever yet seen produced by human agency, though it could not of course be compared to the spontaneous conflagrations sometimes known to occur through the wind rubbing the branches of a mountain forest together. And this fire was not only remarkable for its magnitude, but was also, at the end of so many perils, within an ace of proving fatal to the Plataeans; a great part of the town became entirely inaccessible, and had a wind blown upon it, in accordance with the hopes of the enemy, nothing could have saved them. As it was, there is also a story of heavy rain and thunder having come on by which the fire was put out and the danger averted.

[78] Failing in this last attempt the Peloponnesians left a portion of their forces on the spot, dismissing the rest, and built a wall of circumvallation round the town, dividing the ground among the various cities present; a ditch being made within and without the lines, from which they got their bricks. All being finished by about the rising of Arcturus, they left men enough to man half the wall, the rest being manned by the Boeotians, and drawing off their army dispersed to their several cities. The Plataeans had before sent off their wives and children and oldest men and the mass of the non-combatants to Athens; so that the number of the besieged left in the place comprised four hundred of their own citizens, eighty Athenians, and a hundred and ten women to bake their bread. This was the sum total at the commencement of the siege, and there was no one else within the walls, bond or free. Such were the arrangements made for the blockade of Plataea.

[79] The same summer and simultaneously with the expedition against Plataea, the Athenians marched with two thousand heavy infantry and two hundred horse against the Chalcidians in the direction of Thrace and the Bottiaeans, just as the corn was getting ripe, under the command of Xenophon, son of Euripides, with two colleagues. Arriving before Spartolus in Bottiaea, they destroyed the corn and had some hopes of the city coming over through the intrigues of a faction within. But those of a different way of thinking had sent to Olynthus; and a garrison of heavy infantry and other troops arrived accordingly. These issuing from Spartolus were engaged by the Athenians in front of the town: the Chalcidian heavy infantry, and some auxiliaries with them, were beaten and retreated into Spartolus; but the Chalcidian horse and light troops defeated the horse and light troops of the Athenians. The Chalcidians had already a few targeteers from Crusis, and presently after the battle were joined by some others from Olynthus; upon seeing whom the light troops from Spartolus, emboldened by this accession and by their previous success, with the help of the Chalcidian horse and the reinforcement just arrived again attacked the Athenians, who retired upon the two divisions which they had left with their baggage. Whenever the Athenians advanced, their adversary gave way, pressing them with missiles the instant they began to retire. The Chalcidian horse also, riding up and charging them just as they pleased, at last caused a panic amongst them and routed and pursued them to a great distance. The Athenians took refuge in Potidaea, and afterwards recovered their dead under truce, and returned to Athens with the remnant of their army; four hundred and thirty men and all the generals having fallen. The Chalcidians and Bottiaeans set up a trophy, took up their dead, and dispersed to their several cities.

[80] The same summer, not long after this, the Ambraciots and Chaonians, being desirous of reducing the whole of Acarnania and detaching it from Athens, persuaded the Lacedaemonians to equip a fleet from their confederacy and send a thousand heavy infantry to Acarnania, representing that, if a combined movement were made by land and sea, the coast Acarnanians would be unable to march, and the conquest of Zacynthus and Cephallenia easily following on the possession of Acarnania, the cruise round Peloponnese would be

no longer so convenient for the Athenians. Besides which there was a hope of taking Naupactus. The Lacedaemonians accordingly at once sent off a few vessels with Cnemus, who was still high admiral, and the heavy infantry on board; and sent round orders for the fleet to equip as quickly as possible and sail to Leucas. The Corinthians were the most forward in the business; the Ambraciots being a colony of theirs. While the ships from Corinth, Sicyon, and the neighbourhood were getting ready, and those from Leucas, Anactorium, and Ambracia, which had arrived before, were waiting for them at Leucas, Cnemus and his thousand heavy infantry had run into the gulf, giving the slip to Phormio, the commander of the Athenian squadron stationed off Naupactus, and began at once to prepare for the land expedition. The Hellenic troops with him consisted of the Ambraciots, Leucadians, and Anactorians, and the thousand Peloponnesians with whom he came; the barbarian of a thousand Chaonians, who, belonging to a nation that has no king, were led by Photys and Nicanor, the two members of the royal family to whom the chieftainship for that year had been confided. With the Chaonians came also some Thesprotians, like them without a king, some Molossians and Atintanians led by Sabylinthus, the guardian of King Tharyps who was still a minor, and some Paravaeans, under their king Oroedus, accompanied by a thousand Orestians, subjects of King Antichus and placed by him under the command of Oroedus. There were also a thousand Macedonians sent by Perdiccas without the knowledge of the Athenians, but they arrived too late. With this force Cnemus set out, without waiting for the fleet from Corinth. Passing through the territory of Amphilochian Argos, and sacking the open village of Limnaea, they advanced to Stratus the Acarnanian capital; this once taken, the rest of the country, they felt convinced, would speedily follow.

[81] The Acarnanians, finding themselves invaded by a large army by land, and from the sea threatened by a hostile fleet, made no combined attempt at resistance, but remained to defend their homes, and sent for help to Phormio, who replied that, when a fleet was on the point of sailing from Corinth, it was impossible for him to leave Naupactus unprotected. The Peloponnesians meanwhile and their allies advanced upon Stratus in three divisions, with the intention of encamping near it and attempting the wall by force if they

failed to succeed by negotiation. The order of march was as follows: the centre was occupied by the Chaonians and the rest of the barbarians, with the Leucadians and Anactorians and their followers on the right, and Cnemus with the Peloponnesians and Ambraciots on the left; each division being a long way off from, and sometimes even out of sight of, the others. The Hellenes advanced in good order, keeping a look-out till they encamped in a good position; but the Chaonians, filled with self-confidence, and having the highest character for courage among the tribes of that part of the continent, without waiting to occupy their camp, rushed on with the rest of the barbarians, in the idea that they should take the town by assault and obtain the sole glory of the enterprise. While they were coming on, the Stratians, becoming aware how things stood, and thinking that the defeat of this division would considerably dishearten the Hellenes behind it, occupied the environs of the town with ambuscades, and as soon as they approached engaged them at close quarters from the city and the ambuscades. A panic seizing the Chaonians, great numbers of them were slain; and as soon as they were seen to give way the rest of the barbarians turned and fled. Owing to the distance by which their allies had preceded them, neither of the Hellenic divisions knew anything of the battle, but fancied they were hastening on to encamp. However, when the flying barbarians broke in upon them, they opened their ranks to receive them, brought their divisions together, and stopped quiet where they were for the day; the Stratians not offering to engage them, as the rest of the Acarnanians had not yet arrived, but contenting themselves with slinging at them from a distance, which distressed them greatly, as there was no stirring without their armour. The Acarnanians would seem to excel in this mode of warfare.

[82] As soon as night fell, Cnemus hastily drew off his army to the river Anapus, about nine miles from Stratus, recovering his dead next day under truce, and being there joined by the friendly Oeniadae, fell back upon their city before the enemy's reinforcements came up. From hence each returned home; and the Stratians set up a trophy for the battle with the barbarians.

[83] Meanwhile the fleet from Corinth and the rest of the confederates in the Crissaean Gulf, which was to have co-operated with Cnemus and prevented the coast Acarnanians from joining their countrymen in the interior,

was disabled from doing so by being compelled about the same time as the battle at Stratus to fight with Phormio and the twenty Athenian vessels stationed at Naupactus. For they were watched, as they coasted along out of the gulf, by Phormio, who wished to attack in the open sea. But the Corinthians and allies had started for Acarnania without any idea of fighting at sea, and with vessels more like transports for carrying soldiers; besides which, they never dreamed of the twenty Athenian ships venturing to engage their forty-seven. However, while they were coasting along their own shore, there were the Athenians sailing along in line with them; and when they tried to cross over from Patrae in Achaea to the mainland on the other side, on their way to Acarnania, they saw them again coming out from Chalcis and the river Evenus to meet them. They slipped from their moorings in the night, but were observed, and were at length compelled to fight in mid passage. Each state that contributed to the armament had its own general; the Corinthian commanders were Machaon, Isocrates, and Agatharchidas. The Peloponnesians ranged their vessels in as large a circle as possible without leaving an opening, with the prows outside and the sterns in; and placed within all the small craft in company, and their five best sailers to issue out at a moment's notice and strengthen any point threatened by the enemy.

[84] The Athenians, formed in line, sailed round and round them, and forced them to contract their circle, by continually brushing past and making as though they would attack at once, having been previously cautioned by Phormio not to do so till he gave the signal. His hope was that the Peloponnesians would not retain their order like a force on shore, but that the ships would fall foul of one another and the small craft cause confusion; and if the wind should blow from the gulf (in expectation of which he kept sailing round them, and which usually rose towards morning), they would not, he felt sure, remain steady an instant. He also thought that it rested with him to attack when he pleased, as his ships were better sailers, and that an attack timed by the coming of the wind would tell best. When the wind came down, the enemy's ships were now in a narrow space, and what with the wind and the small craft dashing against them, at once fell into confusion: ship fell foul of ship, while the crews were pushing them off with poles, and by their shouting, swearing, and

struggling with one another, made captains' orders and boatswains' cries alike inaudible, and through being unable for want of practice to clear their oars in the rough water, prevented the vessels from obeying their helmsmen properly. At this moment Phormio gave the signal, and the Athenians attacked. Sinking first one of the admirals, they then disabled all they came across, so that no one thought of resistance for the confusion, but fled for Patrae and Dyme in Achaea. The Athenians gave chase and captured twelve ships, and taking most of the men out of them sailed to Molycrium, and after setting up a trophy on the promontory of Rhium and dedicating a ship to Poseidon, returned to Naupactus. As for the Peloponnesians, they at once sailed with their remaining ships along the coast from Dyme and Patrae to Cyllene, the Eleian arsenal; where Cnemus, and the ships from Leucas that were to have joined them, also arrived after the battle at Stratus.

[85] The Lacedaemonians now sent to the fleet to Cnemus three commissioners—Timocrates, Bradidas, and Lycophron—with orders to prepare to engage again with better fortune, and not to be driven from the sea by a few vessels; for they could not at all account for their discomfiture, the less so as it was their first attempt at sea; and they fancied that it was not that their marine was so inferior, but that there had been misconduct somewhere, not considering the long experience of the Athenians as compared with the little practice which they had had themselves. The commissioners were accordingly sent in anger. As soon as they arrived they set to work with Cnemus to order ships from the different states, and to put those which they already had in fighting order. Meanwhile Phormio sent word to Athens of their preparations and his own victory, and desired as many ships as possible to be speedily sent to him, as he stood in daily expectation of a battle. Twenty were accordingly sent, but instructions were given to their commander to go first to Crete. For Nicias, a Cretan of Gortys, who was *proxenus* of the Athenians, had persuaded them to sail against Cydonia, promising to procure the reduction of that hostile town; his real wish being to oblige the Polichnitans, neighbours of the Cydonians. He accordingly went with the ships to Crete, and, accompanied by the Polichnitans, laid waste the lands of the Cydonians; and, what with adverse winds and stress of weather, wasted no little time there.

[86] While the Athenians were thus detained in Crete, the Peloponnesians in Cyllene got ready for battle, and coasted along to Panormus in Achaea, where their land army had come to support them. Phormio also coasted along to Molycrian Rhium, and anchored outside it with twenty ships, the same as he had fought with before. This Rhium was friendly to the Athenians. The other, in Peloponnese, lies opposite to it; the sea between them is about three-quarters of a mile broad, and forms the mouth of the Crissaean gulf. At this, the Achaean Rhium, not far off Panormus, where their army lay, the Peloponnesians now cast anchor with seventy-seven ships, when they saw the Athenians do so. For six or seven days they remained opposite each other, practising and preparing for the battle; the one resolved not to sail out of the Rhia into the open sea, for fear of the disaster which had already happened to them, the other not to sail into the straits, thinking it advantageous to the enemy to fight in the narrows. At last Cnemus and Brasidas and the rest of the Peloponnesian commanders, being desirous of bringing on a battle as soon as possible, before reinforcements should arrive from Athens, and noticing that the men were most of them cowed by the previous defeat and out of heart for the business, first called them together and encouraged them as follows:

[87] "Peloponnesians, the late engagement, which may have made some of you afraid of the one now in prospect, really gives no just ground for apprehension. Preparation for it, as you know, there was little enough; and the object of our voyage was not so much to fight at sea as an expedition by land. Besides this, the chances of war were largely against us; and perhaps also inexperience had something to do with our failure in our first naval action. It was not, therefore, cowardice that produced our defeat, nor ought the determination which force has not quelled, but which still has a word to say with its adversary, to lose its edge from the result of an accident; but admitting the possibility of a chance miscarriage, we should know that brave hearts must be always brave, and while they remain so can never put forward inexperience as an excuse for misconduct. Nor are you so behind the enemy in experience as you are ahead of him in courage; and although the science of your opponents would, if valour accompanied it, have also the presence of mind to carry out at in emergency the lesson it has learnt, yet a faint heart will make all art powerless in the face of danger. For fear takes away presence of mind, and without valour art is useless. Against their superior experience set your superior daring, and against the fear induced by defeat the fact of your having been then unprepared; remember, too, that you have always the advantage of superior numbers, and of engaging off your own coast, supported by your heavy infantry; and as a rule, numbers and equipment give victory. At no point, therefore, is defeat likely; and as for our previous mistakes, the very fact of their occurrence will teach us better for the future. Steersmen and sailors may, therefore, confidently attend to their several duties, none quitting the station assigned to them: as for ourselves, we promise to prepare for the engagement at least as well as your previous commanders, and to give no excuse for any one misconducting himself. Should any insist on doing so, he shall meet with the punishment he deserves, while the brave shall be honoured with the appropriate rewards of valour."

[88] The Peloponnesian commanders encouraged their men after this fashion. Phormio, meanwhile, being himself not without fears for the courage of his men, and noticing that they were forming in groups among themselves and were alarmed at the odds against them, desired to call them together and give them confidence and counsel in the present emergency. He had before continually told them, and had accustomed their minds to the idea, that there was no numerical superiority that they could not face; and the men themselves had long been persuaded that Athenians need never retire before any quantity of Peloponnesian vessels. At the moment, however, he saw that they were dispirited by the sight before them, and wishing to refresh their confidence, called them together and spoke as follows:

[89] "I see, my men, that you are frightened by the number of the enemy, and I have accordingly called you together, not liking you to be afraid of what is not really terrible. In the first place, the Peloponnesians, already defeated, and not even themselves thinking that they are a match for us, have not ventured to meet us on equal terms, but have equipped this multitude of ships against us. Next, as to that upon which they most rely, the courage which they suppose constitutional to them, their confidence here only arises from the success which their experience in land service usually gives them, and which they fancy will do the same

for them at sea. But this advantage will in all justice belong to us on this element, if to them on that; as they are not superior to us in courage, but we are each of us more confident, according to our experience in our particular department. Besides, as the Lacedaemonians use their supremacy over their allies to promote their own glory, they are most of them being brought into danger against their will, or they would never, after such a decided defeat, have ventured upon a fresh engagement. You need not, therefore, be afraid of their dash. You, on the contrary, inspire a much greater and better founded alarm, both because of your late victory and also of their belief that we should not face them unless about to do something worthy of a success so signal. An adversary numerically superior, like the one before us, comes into action trusting more to strength than to resolution; while he who voluntarily confronts tremendous odds must have very great internal resources to draw upon. For these reasons the Peloponnesians fear our irrational audacity more than they would ever have done a more commensurate preparation. Besides, many armaments have before now succumbed to an inferior through want of skill or sometimes of courage; neither of which defects certainly are ours. As to the battle, it shall not be, if I can help it, in the strait, nor will I sail in there at all; seeing that in a contest between a number of clumsily managed vessels and a small, fast, well-handled squadron, want of sea room is an undoubted disadvantage. One cannot run down an enemy properly without having a sight of him a good way off, nor can one retire at need when pressed; one can neither break the line nor return upon his rear, the proper tactics for a fast sailer; but the naval action necessarily becomes a land one, in which numbers must decide the matter. For all this I will provide as far as can be. Do you stay at your posts by your ships, and be sharp at catching the word of command, the more so as we are observing one another from so short a distance; and in action think order and silence all-important—qualities useful in war generally, and in naval engagements in particular; and behave before the enemy in a manner worthy of your past exploits. The issues you will fight for are great—to destroy the naval hopes of the Peloponnesians or to bring nearer to the Athenians their fears for the sea. And I may once more remind you that you have defeated most of them already; and beaten men do not face a danger twice with the same determination."

[90] Such was the exhortation of Phormio. The Peloponnesians finding that the Athenians did not sail into the gulf and the narrows, in order to lead them in whether they wished it or not, put out at dawn, and forming four abreast, sailed inside the gulf in the direction of their own country, the right wing leading as they had lain at anchor. In this wing were placed twenty of their best sailers; so that in the event of Phormio thinking that their object was Naupactus, and coasting along thither to save the place, the Athenians might not be able to escape their onset by getting outside their wing, but might be cut off by the vessels in question. As they expected, Phormio, in alarm for the place at that moment emptied of its garrison, as soon as he saw them put out, reluctantly and hurriedly embarked and sailed along shore; the Messenian land forces moving along also to support him. The Peloponnesians seeing him coasting along with his ships in single file, and by this inside the gulf and close inshore as they so much wished, at one signal tacked suddenly and bore down in line at their best speed on the Athenians, hoping to cut off the whole squadron. The eleven leading vessels, however, escaped the Peloponnesian wing and its sudden movement, and reached the more open water; but the rest were overtaken as they tried to run through, driven ashore and disabled; such of the crews being slain as had not swum out of them. Some of the ships the Peloponnesians lashed to their own, and towed off empty; one they took with the men in it; others were just being towed off, when they were saved by the Messenians dashing into the sea with their armour and fighting from the decks that they had boarded.

[91] Thus far victory was with the Peloponnesians, and the Athenian fleet destroyed; the twenty ships in the right wing being meanwhile in chase of the eleven Athenian vessels that had escaped their sudden movement and reached the more open water. These, with the exception of one ship, all outsailed them and got safe into Naupactus, and forming close inshore opposite the temple of Apollo, with their prows facing the enemy, prepared to defend themselves in case the Peloponnesians should sail inshore against them. After a while the Peloponnesians came up, chanting the paean for their victory as they sailed on; the single Athenian ship remaining being chased by a Leucadian far ahead of the rest. But there happened to be a merchantman lying at anchor

in the roadstead, which the Athenian ship found time to sail round, and struck the Leucadian in chase amidships and sank her. An exploit so sudden and unexpected produced a panic among the Peloponnesians; and having fallen out of order in the excitement of victory, some of them dropped their oars and stopped their way in order to let the main body come up—an unsafe thing to do considering how near they were to the enemy's prows; while others ran aground in the shallows, in their ignorance of the localities.

[92] Elated at this incident, the Athenians at one word gave a cheer, and dashed at the enemy, who, embarrassed by his mistakes and the disorder in which he found himself, only stood for an instant, and then fled for Panormus, whence he had put out. The Athenians following on his heels took the six vessels nearest them, and recovered those of their own which had been disabled close inshore and taken in tow at the beginning of the action; they killed some of the crews and took some prisoners. On board the Leucadian which went down off the merchantman, was the Lacedaemonian Timocrates, who killed himself when the ship was sunk, and was cast up in the harbour of Naupactus. The Athenians on their return set up a trophy on the spot from which they had put out and turned the day, and picking up the wrecks and dead that were on their shore, gave back to the enemy their dead under truce. The Peloponnesians also set up a trophy as victors for the defeat inflicted upon the ships they had disabled in shore, and dedicated the vessel which they had taken at Achaean Rhium, side by side with the trophy. After this, apprehensive of the reinforcement expected from Athens, all except the Leucadians sailed into the Crissaean Gulf for Corinth. Not long after their retreat, the twenty Athenian ships, which were to have joined Phormio before the battle, arrived at Naupactus.

Thus the summer ended. [93] Winter was now at hand; but dispersing the fleet, which had retired to Corinth and the Crissaean Gulf, Cnemus, Brasidas, and the other Peloponnesian captains allowed themselves to be persuaded by the Megarians to make an attempt upon Piraeus, the port of Athens, which from her decided superiority at sea had been naturally left unguarded and open. Their plan was as follows: The men were each to take their oar, cushion, and rowlock thong, and, going overland from Corinth to the sea on the Athenian

side, to get to Megara as quickly as they could, and launching forty vessels, which happened to be in the docks at Nisaea, to sail at once to Piraeus. There was no fleet on the look-out in the harbour, and no one had the least idea of the enemy attempting a surprise; while an open attack would, it was thought, never be deliberately ventured on, or, if in contemplation, would be speedily known at Athens. Their plan formed, the next step was to put it in execution. Arriving by night and launching the vessels from Nisaea, they sailed, not to Piraeus as they had originally intended, being afraid of the risk, besides which there was some talk of a wind having stopped them, but to the point of Salamis that looks towards Megara; where there was a fort and a squadron of three ships to prevent anything sailing in or out of Megara. This fort they assaulted, and towed off the galleys empty, and surprising the inhabitants began to lay waste the rest of the island.

[94] Meanwhile fire signals were raised to alarm Athens, and a panic ensued there as serious as any that occurred during the war. The idea in the city was that the enemy had already sailed into Piraeus: in Piraeus it was thought that they had taken Salamis and might at any moment arrive in the port; as indeed might easily have been done if their hearts had been a little firmer: certainly no wind would have prevented them. As soon as day broke, the Athenians assembled in full force, launched their ships, and embarking in haste and uproar went with the fleet to Salamis, while their soldiery mounted guard in Piraeus. The Peloponnesians, on becoming aware of the coming relief, after they had overrun most of Salamis, hastily sailed off with their plunder and captives and the three ships from Fort Budorum to Nisaea; the state of their ships also causing them some anxiety, as it was a long while since they had been launched, and they were not water-tight. Arrived at Megara, they returned back on foot to Corinth. The Athenians finding them no longer at Salamis, sailed back themselves; and after this made arrangements for guarding Piraeus more diligently in future, by closing the harbours, and by other suitable precautions.

[95] About the same time, at the beginning of this winter, Sitalces, son of Teres, the Odrysian king of Thrace, made an expedition against Perdiccas, son of Alexander, king of Macedonia, and the Chalcidians in the neighbourhood of Thrace; his object being to en-

force one promise and fulfil another. On the one hand Perdiccas had made him a promise, when hard pressed at the commencement of the war, upon condition that Sitalces should reconcile the Athenians to him and not attempt to restore his brother and enemy, the pretender Philip, but had not offered to fulfil his engagement; on the other he, Sitalces, on entering into alliance with the Athenians, had agreed to put an end to the Chalcidian war in Thrace. These were the two objects of his invasion. With him he brought Amyntas, the son of Philip, whom he destined for the throne of Macedonia, and some Athenian envoys then at his court on this business, and Hagnon as general; for the Athenians were to join him against the Chalcidians with a fleet and as many soldiers as they could get together.

[96] Beginning with the Odrysians, he first called out the Thracian tribes subject to him between Mounts Haemus and Rhodope and the Euxine and Hellespont; next the Getae beyond Haemus, and the other hordes settled south of the Danube in the neighbourhood of the Euxine, who, like the Getae, border on the Scythians and are armed in the same manner, being all mounted archers. Besides these he summoned many of the hill Thracian independent swordsmen, called Dii and mostly inhabiting Mount Rhodope, some of whom came as mercenaries, others as volunteers; also the Agrianes and Laeaeans, and the rest of the Paeonian tribes in his empire, at the confines of which these lay, extending up to the Laeaean Paeonians and the river Strymon, which flows from Mount Scombrus through the country of the Agrianes and Laeaeans; there the empire of Sitalces ends and the territory of the independent Paeonians begins. Bordering on the Triballi, also independent, were the Treres and Tilataeans, who dwell to the north of Mount Scombrus and extend towards the setting sun as far as the river Oskius. This river rises in the same mountains as the Nestus and Hebrus, a wild and extensive range connected with Rhodope.

[97] The empire of the Odrysians extended along the seaboard from Abdera to the mouth of the Danube in the Euxine. The navigation of this coast by the shortest route takes a merchantman four days and four nights with a wind astern the whole way: by land an active man, travelling by the shortest road, can get from Abdera to the Danube in eleven days. Such was the length of its coast line. Inland from Byzantium to the Laeaeans and the Stry-

mon, the farthest limit of its extension into the interior, it is a journey of thirteen days for an active man. The tribute from all the barbarian districts and the Hellenic cities, taking what they brought in under Seuthes, the successor of Sitalces, who raised it to its greatest height, amounted to about four hundred talents in gold and silver. There were also presents in gold and silver to a no less amount, besides stuff, plain and embroidered, and other articles, made not only for the king, but also for the Odrysian lords and nobles. For there was here established a custom opposite to that prevailing in the Persian kingdom, namely, of taking rather than giving; more disgrace being attached to not giving when asked than to asking and being refused; and although this prevailed elsewhere in Thrace, it was practised most extensively among the powerful Odrysians, it being impossible to get anything done without a present. It was thus a very powerful kingdom; in revenue and general prosperity surpassing all in Europe between the Ionian Gulf and the Euxine, and in numbers and military resources coming decidedly next to the Scythians, with whom indeed no people in Europe can bear comparison, there not being even in Asia any nation singly a match for them if unanimous, though of course they are not on a level with other races in general intelligence and the arts of civilized life.

[98] It was the master of this empire that now prepared to take the field. When everything was ready, he set out on his march for Macedonia, first through his own dominions, next over the desolate range of Cercine that divides the Sintians and Paeonians, crossing by a road which he had made by felling the timber on a former campaign against the latter people. Passing over these mountains, with the Paeonians on his right and the Sintians and Maedians on the left, he finally arrived at Doberus, in Paeonia, losing none of his army on the march, except perhaps by sickness, but receiving some augmentations, many of the independent Thracians volunteering to join him in the hope of plunder; so that the whole is said to have formed a grand total of a hundred and fifty thousand. Most of this was infantry, though there was about a third cavalry, furnished principally by the Odrysians themselves and next to them by the Getae. The most warlike of the infantry were the independent swordsmen who came down from Rhodope; the rest of the mixed multitude that followed him being chiefly formidable by their numbers.

[99] Assembling in Doberus, they prepared for descending from the heights upon Lower Macedonia, where the dominions of Perdiccas lay; for the Lyncestae, Elimiots, and other tribes more inland, though Macedonians by blood, and allies and dependants of their kindred, still have their own separate governments. The country on the sea coast, now called Macedonia, was first acquired by Alexander, the father of Perdiccas, and his ancestors, originally Temenids from Argos. This was effected by the expulsion from Pieria of the Pierians, who afterwards inhabited Phagres and other places under Mount Pangaeus, beyond the Strymon (indeed the country between Pangaeus and the sea is still called the Pierian Gulf); of the Bottiaeans, at present neighbours of the Chalcidians, from Bottia, and by the acquisition in Paeonia of a narrow strip along the river Axius extending to Pella and the sea; the district of Mygdonia, between the Axius and the Strymon, being also added by the expulsion of the Edonians. From Eordia also were driven the Eordians, most of whom perished, though a few of them still live round Physca, and the Almopians from Almopia. These Macedonians also conquered places belonging to the other tribes, which are still theirs—Anthemus, Crestonia, Bisaltia, and much of Macedonia proper. The whole is now called Macedonia, and at the time of the invasion of Sitalces, Perdiccas, Alexander's son, was the reigning king.

[100] These Macedonians, unable to take the field against so numerous an invader, shut themselves up in such strong places and fortresses as the country possessed. Of these there was no great number, most of those now found in the country having been erected subsequently by Archelaus, the son of Perdiccas, on his accession, who also cut straight roads, and otherwise put the kingdom on a better footing as regards horses, heavy infantry, and other war material than had been done by all the eight kings that preceded him. Advancing from Doberus, the Thracian host first invaded what had been once Philip's government, and took Idomene by assault, Gortynia, Atalanta, and some other places by negotiation, these last coming over for love of Philip's son, Amyntas, then with Sitalces. Laying siege to Europus, and failing to take it, he next advanced into the rest of Macedonia to the left of Pella and Cyrrhus, not proceeding beyond this into Bottiaea and Pieria, but staying to lay waste Mygdonia, Crestonia, and Anthemus.

The Macedonians never even thought of meeting him with infantry; but the Thracian host was, as opportunity offered, attacked by handfuls of their horse, which had been reinforced from their allies in the interior. Armed with cuirasses, and excellent horsemen, wherever these charged they overthrew all before them, but ran considerable risk in entangling themselves in the masses of the enemy, and so finally desisted from these efforts, deciding that they were not strong enough to venture against numbers so superior.

[101] Meanwhile Sitalces opened negotiations with Perdiccas on the objects of his expedition; and finding that the Athenians, not believing that he would come, did not appear with their fleet, though they sent presents and envoys, dispatched a large part of his army against the Chalcidians and Bottiaeans, and shutting them up inside their walls laid waste their country. While he remained in these parts, the people farther south, such as the Thessalians, Magnetes, and the other tribes subject to the Thessalians, and the Hellenes as far as Thermopylae, all feared that the army might advance against them, and prepared accordingly. These fears were shared by the Thracians beyond the Strymon to the north, who inhabited the plains, such as the Panaeans, the Odomanti, the Droi, and the Dersaeans, all of whom are independent. It was even matter of conversation among the Hellenes who were enemies of Athens whether he might not be invited by his ally to advance also against them. Meanwhile he held Chalcidice and Bottice and Macedonia, and was ravaging them all; but finding that he was not succeeding in any of the objects of his invasion, and that his army was without provisions and was suffering from the severity of the season, he listened to the advice of Seuthes, son of Spardacus, his nephew and highest officer, and decided to retreat without delay. This Seuthes had been secretly gained by Perdiccas by the promise of his sister in marriage with a rich dowry. In accordance with this advice, and after a stay of thirty days in all, eight of which were spent in Chalcidice, he retired home as quickly as he could; and Perdiccas afterwards gave his sister Stratonice to Seuthes as he had promised. Such was the history of the expedition of Sitalces.

[102] In the course of this winter, after the dispersion of the Peloponnesian fleet, the Athenians in Naupactus, under Phormio, coasted along to Astacus and disembarked, and

marched into the interior of Acarnania with four hundred Athenian heavy infantry and four hundred Messenians. After expelling some suspected persons from Stratus, Coronta, and other places, and restoring Cynes, son of Theolytus, to Coronta, they returned to their ships, deciding that it was impossible in the winter season to march against Oeniadae, a place which, unlike the rest of Acarnania, had been always hostile to them; for the river Achelous flowing from Mount Pindus through Dolopia and the country of the Agraeans and Amphilochians and the plain of Acarnania, past the town of Stratus in the upper part of its course, forms lakes where it falls into the sea round Oeniadae, and thus makes it impracticable for an army in winter by reason of the water. Opposite to Oeniadae lie most of the islands called Echinades, so close to the mouths of the Achelous that that powerful stream is constantly forming deposits against them, and has already joined some of the islands to the continent, and seems likely in no long while to do the same with the rest. For the current is strong, deep, and turbid, and the islands are so thick together that they serve to imprison the alluvial deposit and prevent its dispersing, lying, as they do, not in one line, but irregularly, so as to leave no direct passage for the water into the open sea. The islands in question are uninhabited and of no great size. There is also a story that Alcmaeon, son of Amphiraus, during his wanderings after the murder of his mother was bidden by Apollo to inhabit this spot, through an oracle which intimated that he would have no release from his terrors until he should find a country to dwell in which had not been seen by the sun, or existed as land at the time he slew his mother; all else being to him polluted ground. Perplexed at this, the story goes on to say, he at last observed this deposit of the Achelous, and considered that a place sufficient to support life upon, might have been thrown up during the long interval that had elapsed since the death of his mother and the beginning of his wanderings. Settling, therefore, in the district round Oeniadae, he founded a dominion, and left the country its name from his son Acarnan. Such is the story we have received concerning Alcmaeon.

[103] The Athenians and Phormio putting back from Acarnania and arriving at Naupactus, sailed home to Athens in the spring, taking with them the ships that they had captured, and such of the prisoners made in the late actions as were freemen; who were exchanged, man for man. And so ended this winter, and the third year of this war, of which Thucydides was the historian.

The Third Book

CHAPTER IX

Fourth and Fifth Years of the War— Revolt of Mitylene

[1] THE next summer, just as the corn was getting ripe, the Peloponnesians and their allies invaded Attica under the command of Archidamus, son of Zeuxidamus, king of the Lacedaemonians, and sat down and ravaged the land; the Athenian horse as usual attacking them, wherever it was practicable, and preventing the mass of the light troops from advancing from their camp and wasting the parts near the city. After staying the time for which they had taken provisions, the invaders retired and dispersed to their several cities.

[2] Immediately after the invasion of the Peloponnesians all Lesbos, except Methymna, revolted from the Athenians. The Lesbians had wished to revolt even before the war, but the Lacedaemonians would not receive them; and yet now when they did revolt, they were compelled to do so sooner than they had intended. While they were waiting until the moles for their harbours and the ships and walls that they had in building should be finished, and for the arrival of archers and corn and other things that they were engaged in fetching from the Pontus, the Tenedians, with whom they were at enmity, and the Methymnians, and some factious persons in Mitylene itself, who were *proxeni* of Athens, informed the Athenians that the Mitylenians were forcibly uniting the island under their sovereignty, and that the preparations about which they were so active, were all concerted with the Boeotians their kindred and the Lacedaemonians with a view to a revolt, and that, unless they were immediately prevented, Athens would lose Lesbos.

[3] However, the Athenians, distressed by the plague, and by the war that had recently broken out and was now raging, thought it a serious matter to add Lesbos with its fleet and untouched resources to the list of their enemies; and at first would not believe the charge, giving too much weight to their wish that it might not be true. But when an embassy which they sent had failed to persuade the Mitylenians to give up the union and preparations complained of, they became alarmed, and resolved to strike the first blow. They accordingly suddenly sent off forty ships that had been got ready to sail round Peloponnese, under the command of Cleippides, son of Deinias, and two others; word having been brought them of a festival in honour of the Malean Apollo outside the town, which is kept by the whole people of Mitylene, and at which, if haste were made, they might hope to take them by surprise. If this plan succeeded, well and good; if not, they were to order the Mitylenians to deliver up their ships and to pull down their walls, and if they did not obey, to declare war. The ships accordingly set out; the ten galleys, forming the contingent of the Mitylenians present with the fleet according to the terms of the alliance, being detained by the Athenians, and their crews placed in custody. However, the Mitylenians were informed of the expedition by a man who crossed from Athens to Euboea, and going overland to Geraestus, sailed from thence by a merchantman which he found on the point of putting to sea, and so arrived at Mitylene the third day after leaving Athens. The Mitylenians accordingly refrained from going out to the temple at Malea, and moreover barricaded and kept guard round the half-finished parts of their walls and harbours.

[4] When the Athenians sailed in not long after and saw how things stood, the generals delivered their orders, and upon the Mitylenians refusing to obey, commenced hostilities. The Mitylenians, thus compelled to go to war

without notice and unprepared, at first sailed out with their fleet and made some show of fighting, a little in front of the harbour; but being driven back by the Athenian ships, immediately offered to treat with the commanders, wishing, if possible, to get the ships away for the present upon any tolerable terms. The Athenian commanders accepted their offers, being themselves fearful that they might not be able to cope with the whole of Lesbos; and an armistice having been concluded, the Mitylenians sent to Athens one of the informers, already repentant of his conduct, and others with him, to try to persuade the Athenians of the innocence of their intentions and to get the fleet recalled. In the meantime, having no great hope of a favourable answer from Athens, they also sent off a galley with envoys to Lacedaemon, unobserved by the Athenian fleet which was anchored at Malea to the north of the town.

While these envoys, reaching Lacedaemon after a difficult journey across the open sea, were negotiating for succours being sent them, [5] the ambassadors from Athens returned without having effected anything; and hostilities were at once begun by the Mitylenians and the rest of Lesbos, with the exception of the Methymnians, who came to the aid of the Athenians with the Imbrians and Lemnians and some few of the other allies. The Mitylenians made a sortie with all their forces against the Athenian camp; and a battle ensued, in which they gained some slight advantage, but retired notwithstanding, not feeling sufficient confidence in themselves to spend the night upon the field. After this they kept quiet, wishing to wait for the chance of reinforcements arriving from Peloponnese before making a second venture, being encouraged by the arrival of Meleas, a Laconian, and Hermaeondas, a Theban, who had been sent off before the insurrection but had been unable to reach Lesbos before the Athenian expedition, and who now stole in in a galley after the battle, and advised them to send another galley and envoys back with them, which the Mitylenians accordingly did.

[6] Meanwhile the Athenians, greatly encouraged by the inaction of the Mitylenians, summoned allies to their aid, who came in all the quicker from seeing so little vigour displayed by the Lesbians, and bringing round their ships to a new station to the south of the town, fortified two camps, one on each side of the city, and instituted a blockade of both the harbours. The sea was thus closed against the Mitylenians, who, however, commanded the whole country, with the rest of the Lesbians who had now joined them; the Athenians only holding a limited area round their camps, and using Malea more as the station for their ships and their market.

[7] While the war went on in this way at Mitylene, the Athenians, about the same time in this summer, also sent thirty ships to Peloponnese under Asopius, son of Phormio; the Acarnanians insisting that the commander sent should be some son or relative of Phormio. As the ships coasted along shore they ravaged the seaboard of Laconia; after which Asopius sent most of the fleet home, and himself went on with twelve vessels to Naupactus, and afterwards raising the whole Acarnanian population made an expedition against Oeniadae, the fleet sailing along the Achelous, while the army laid waste the country. The inhabitants, however, showing no signs of submitting, he dismissed the land forces and himself sailed to Leucas, and making a descent upon Nericus was cut off during his retreat, and most of his troops with him, by the people in those parts aided by some coastguards; after which the Athenians sailed away, recovering their dead from the Leucadians under truce.

[8] Meanwhile the envoys of the Mitylenians sent out in the first ship were told by the Lacedaemonians to come to Olympia, in order that the rest of the allies might hear them and decide upon their matter, and so they journeyed thither. It was the Olympiad in which the Rhodian Dorieus gained his second victory, and the envoys having been introduced to make their speech after the festival, spoke as follows:

[9] "Lacedaemonians and allies, the rule established among the Hellenes is not unknown to us. Those who revolt in war and forsake their former confederacy are favourably regarded by those who receive them, in so far as they are of use to them, but otherwise are thought less well of, through being considered traitors to their former friends. Nor is this an unfair way of judging, where the rebels and the power from whom they secede are at one in policy and sympathy, and a match for each other in resources and power, and where no reasonable ground exists for the rebellion. But with us and the Athenians this was not the case; and no one need think the worse of us for revolting from them in danger, after having been honoured by them in time of peace.

[10] "Justice and honesty will be the first topics of our speech, especially as we are asking for alliance; because we know that there can never be any solid friendship between individuals, or union between communities that is worth the name, unless the parties be persuaded of each other's honesty, and be generally congenial the one to the other; since from difference in feeling springs also difference in conduct. Between ourselves and the Athenians alliance began, when you withdrew from the Median War and they remained to finish the business. But we did not become allies of the Athenians for the subjugation of the Hellenes, but allies of the Hellenes for their liberation from the Mede; and as long as the Athenians led us fairly we followed them loyally; but when we saw them relax their hostility to the Mede, to try to compass the subjection of the allies, then our apprehensions began. Unable, however, to unite and defend themselves, on account of the number of confederates that had votes, all the allies were enslaved, except ourselves and the Chians, who continued to send our contingents as independent and nominally free. Trust in Athens as a leader, however, we could no longer feel, judging by the examples already given; it being unlikely that she would reduce our fellow confederates, and not do the same by us who were left, if ever she had the power.

[11] "Had we all been still independent, we could have had more faith in their not attempting any change; but the greater number being their subjects, while they were treating us as equals, they would naturally chafe under this solitary instance of independence as contrasted with the submission of the majority; particularly as they daily grew more powerful, and we more destitute. Now the only sure basis of an alliance is for each party to be equally afraid of the other; he who would like to encroach is then deterred by the reflection that he will not have odds in his favour. Again, if we were left independent, it was only because they thought they saw their way to empire more clearly by specious language and by the paths of policy than by those of force. Not only were we useful as evidence that powers who had votes, like themselves, would not, surely, join them in their expeditions, against their will, without the party attacked being in the wrong; but the same system also enabled them to lead the stronger states against the weaker first, and so to leave the former to the last, stripped of their natural allies, and less capable of resistance. But if they had begun with us, while all the states still had their resources under their own control, and there was a centre to rally round, the work of subjugation would have been found less easy. Besides this, our navy gave them some apprehension: it was always possible that it might unite with you or with some other power, and become dangerous to Athens. The court which we paid to their commons and its leaders for the time being also helped us to maintain our independence. However, we did not expect to be able to do so much longer, if this war had not broken out, from the examples that we had had of their conduct to the rest.

[12] "How then could we put our trust in such friendship or freedom as we had here? We accepted each other against our inclination; fear made them court us in war, and us them in peace; sympathy, the ordinary basis of confidence, had its place supplied by terror, fear having more share than friendship in detaining us in the alliance; and the first party that should be encouraged by the hope of impunity was certain to break faith with the other. So that to condemn us for being the first to break off, because they delay the blow that we dread, instead of ourselves delaying to know for certain whether it will be dealt or not, is to take a false view of the case. For if we were equally able with them to meet their plots and imitate their delay, we should be their equals and should be under no necessity of being their subjects; but the liberty of offence being always theirs, that of defence ought clearly to be ours.

[13] "Such, Lacedaemonians and allies, are the grounds and the reasons of our revolt; clear enough to convince our hearers of the fairness of our conduct, and sufficient to alarm ourselves, and to make us turn to some means of safety. This we wished to do long ago, when we sent to you on the subject while the peace yet lasted, but were balked by your refusing to receive us; and now, upon the Boeotians inviting us, we at once responded to the call, and decided upon a twofold revolt, from the Hellenes and from the Athenians, not to aid the latter in harming the former, but to join in their liberation, and not to allow the Athenians in the end to destroy us, but to act in time against them. Our revolt, however, has taken place prematurely and without preparation—a fact which makes it all the more incumbent on you to receive us into alliance and to send us speedy relief, in order to show that you

support your friends, and at the same time do harm to your enemies. You have an opportunity such as you never had before. Disease and expenditure have wasted the Athenians: their ships are either cruising round your coasts, or engaged in blockading us; and it is not probable that they will have any to spare, if you invade them a second time this summer by sea and land; but they will either offer no resistance to your vessels, or withdraw from both our shores. Nor must it be thought that this is a case of putting yourselves into danger for a country which is not yours. Lesbos may appear far off, but when help is wanted she will be found near enough. It is not in Attica that the war will be decided, as some imagine, but in the countries by which Attica is supported; and the Athenian revenue is drawn from the allies, and will become still larger if they reduce us; as not only will no other state revolt, but our resources will be added to theirs, and we shall be treated worse than those that were enslaved before. But if you will frankly support us, you will add to your side a state that has a large navy, which is your great want; you will smooth the way to the overthrow of the Athenians by depriving them of their allies, who will be greatly encouraged to come over; and you will free yourselves from the imputation made against you, of not supporting insurrection. In short, only show yourselves as liberators, and you may count upon having the advantage in the war.

[14] "Respect, therefore, the hopes placed in you by the Hellenes, and that Olympian Zeus, in whose temple we stand as very suppliants; become the allies and defenders of the Mitylenians, and do not sacrifice us, who put our lives upon the hazard, in a cause in which general good will result to all from our success, and still more general harm if we fail through your refusing to help us; but be the men that the Hellenes think you, and our fears desire."

[15] Such were the words of the Mitylenians. After hearing them out, the Lacedaemonians and confederates granted what they urged, and took the Lesbians into alliance, and deciding in favour of the invasion of Attica, told the allies present to march as quickly as possible to the Isthmus with two-thirds of their forces; and arriving there first themselves, got ready hauling machines to carry their ships across from Corinth to the sea on the side of Athens, in order to make their attack by sea and land at once. However, the zeal which

they displayed was not imitated by the rest of the confederates, who came in but slowly, being engaged in harvesting their corn and sick of making expeditions.

[16] Meanwhile the Athenians, aware that the preparations of the enemy were due to his conviction of their weakness, and wishing to show him that he was mistaken, and that they were able, without moving the Lesbian fleet, to repel with ease that with which they were menaced from Peloponnese, manned a hundred ships by embarking the citizens of Athens, except the knights and Pentacosiomedimni, and the resident aliens; and putting out to the Isthmus, displayed their power, and made descents upon Peloponnese wherever they pleased. A disappointment so signal made the Lacedaemonians think that the Lesbians had not spoken the truth; and embarrassed by the non-appearance of the confederates, coupled with the news that the thirty ships round Peloponnese were ravaging the lands near Sparta, they went back home. Afterwards, however, they got ready a fleet to send to Lesbos, and ordering a total of forty ships from the different cities in the league, appointed Alcidas to command the expedition in his capacity of high admiral. Meanwhile the Athenians in the hundred ships, upon seeing the Lacedaemonians go home, went home likewise.

[17] If, at the time that this fleet was at sea, Athens had almost the largest number of first-rate ships in commission that she ever possessed at any one moment, she had as many or even more when the war began. At that time one hundred guarded Attica, Euboea, and Salamis; a hundred more were cruising round Peloponnese, besides those employed at Potidaea and in other places; making a grand total of two hundred and fifty vessels employed on active service in a single summer. It was this, with Potidaea, that most exhausted her revenues—Potidaea being blockaded by a force of heavy infantry (each drawing two drachmae a day, one for himself and another for his servant), which amounted to three thousand at first, and was kept at this number down to the end of the siege; besides sixteen hundred with Phormio who went away before it was over; and the ships being all paid at the same rate. In this way her money was wasted at first; and this was the largest number of ships ever manned by her.

[18] About the same time that the Lacedaemonians were at the Isthmus, the Mitylenians marched by land with their mercenaries

against Methymna, which they thought to gain by treachery. After assaulting the town, and not meeting with the success that they anticipated, they withdrew to Antissa, Pyrrha, and Eresus; and taking measures for the better security of these towns and strengthening their walls, hastily returned home. After their departure the Methymnians marched against Antissa, but were defeated in a sortie by the Antissians and their mercenaries, and retreated in haste after losing many of their number. Word of this reaching Athens, and the Athenians learning that the Mitylenians were masters of the country and their own soldiers unable to hold them in check, they sent out about the beginning of autumn Paches, son of Epicurus, to take the command, and a thousand Athenian heavy infantry; who worked their own passage and, arriving at Mitylene, built a single wall all round it, forts being erected at some of the strongest points. Mitylene was thus blockaded strictly on both sides, by land and by sea; and winter now drew near.

[19] The Athenians needing money for the siege, although they had for the first time raised a contribution of two hundred talents from their own citizens, now sent out twelve ships to levy subsidies from their allies, with Lysicles and four others in command. After cruising to different places and laying them under contribution, Lysicles went up the country from Myus, in Caria, across the plain of the Meander, as far as the hill of Sandius; and being attacked by the Carians and the people of Anaia, was slain with many of his soldiers.

[20] The same winter the Plataeans, who were still being besieged by the Peloponnesians and Boeotians, distressed by the failure of their provisions, and seeing no hope of relief from Athens, nor any other means of safety, formed a scheme with the Athenians besieged with them for escaping, if possible, by forcing their way over the enemy's walls; the attempt having been suggested by Theaenetus, son of Tolmides, a soothsayer, and Eupompides, son of Daïmachus, one of their generals. At first all were to join: afterwards, half hung back, thinking the risk great; about two hundred and twenty, however, voluntarily persevered in the attempt, which was carried out in the following way. Ladders were made to match the height of the enemy's wall, which they measured by the layers of bricks, the side turned towards them not being thoroughly whitewashed. These were counted by many persons at once; and though some might miss

the right calculation, most would hit upon it, particularly as they counted over and over again, and were no great way from the wall, but could see it easily enough for their purpose. The length required for the ladders was thus obtained, being calculated from the breadth of the brick.

[21] Now the wall of the Peloponnesians was constructed as follows. It consisted of two lines drawn round the place, one against the Plataeans, the other against any attack on the outside from Athens, about sixteen feet apart. The intermediate space of sixteen feet was occupied by huts portioned out among the soldiers on guard, and built in one block, so as to give the appearance of a single thick wall with battlements on either side. At intervals of every ten battlements were towers of considerable size, and the same breadth as the wall, reaching right across from its inner to its outer face, with no means of passing except through the middle. Accordingly on stormy and wet nights the battlements were deserted, and guard kept from the towers, which were not far apart and roofed in above.

Such being the structure of the wall by which the Plataeans were blockaded, [22] when their preparations were completed, they waited for a stormy night of wind and rain and without any moon, and then set out, guided by the authors of the enterprise. Crossing first the ditch that ran round the town, they next gained the wall of the enemy unperceived by the sentinels, who did not see them in the darkness, or hear them, as the wind drowned with its roar the noise of their approach; besides which they kept a good way off from each other, that they might not be betrayed by the clash of their weapons. They were also lightly equipped, and had only the left foot shod to preserve them from slipping in the mire. They came up to the battlements at one of the intermediate spaces where they knew them to be unguarded: those who carried the ladders went first and planted them; next twelve light-armed soldiers with only a dagger and a breastplate mounted, led by Ammias, son of Coroebus, who was the first on the wall; his followers getting up after him and going six to each of the towers. After these came another party of light troops armed with spears, whose shields, that they might advance the easier, were carried by men behind, who were to hand them to them when they found themselves in presence of the enemy. After a good many had mounted they were discovered by the sentinels in the towers, by the noise made by a tile which was knocked down by one of the Plataeans as he was laying hold of the battlements. The alarm was instantly given, and the troops rushed to the wall, not knowing the nature of the danger, owing to the dark night and stormy weather; the Plataeans in the town having also chosen that moment to make a sortie against the wall of the Peloponnesians upon the side opposite to that on which their men were getting over, in order to divert the attention of the besiegers. Accordingly they remained distracted at their several posts, without any venturing to stir to give help from his own station, and at a loss to guess what was going on. Meanwhile the three hundred set aside for service on emergencies went outside the wall in the direction of the alarm. Fire-signals of an attack were also raised towards Thebes; but the Plataeans in the town at once displayed a number of others, prepared beforehand for this very purpose, in order to render the enemy's signals unintelligible, and to prevent his friends getting a true idea of what was passing and coming to his aid before their comrades who had gone out should have made good their escape and be in safety.

[23] Meanwhile the first of the scaling party that had got up, after carrying both the towers and putting the sentinels to the sword, posted themselves inside to prevent any one coming through against them; and rearing ladders from the wall, sent several men up on the towers, and from their summit and base kept in check all of the enemy that came up, with their missiles, while their main body planted a number of ladders against the wall, and knocking down the battlements, passed over between the towers; each as soon as he had got over taking up his station at the edge of the ditch, and plying from thence with arrows and darts any who came along the wall to stop the passage of his comrades. When all were over, the party on the towers came down, the last of them not without difficulty, and proceeded to the ditch, just as the three hundred came up carrying torches. The Plataeans, standing on the edge of the ditch in the dark, had a good view of their opponents, and discharged their arrows and darts upon the unarmed parts of their bodies, while they themselves could not be so well seen in the obscurity for the torches; and thus even the last of them got over the ditch, though not without effort and difficulty; as ice had formed in it, not strong enough to walk upon, but of that watery kind which gen-

erally comes with a wind more east than north, and the snow which this wind had caused to fall during the night had made the water in the ditch rise, so that they could scarcely breast it as they crossed. However, it was mainly the violence of the storm that enabled them to effect their escape at all.

[24] Starting from the ditch, the Plataeans went all together along the road leading to Thebes, keeping the chapel of the hero Androcrates upon their right; considering that the last road which the Peloponnesians would suspect them of having taken would be that towards their enemies' country. Indeed they could see them pursuing with torches upon the Athens road towards Cithaeron and Druoskephalai or Oakheads. After going for rather more than half a mile upon the road to Thebes, the Plataeans turned off and took that leading to the mountain, to Erythrae and Hysiae, and reaching the hills, made good their escape to Athens, two hundred and twelve men in all; some of their number having turned back into the town before getting over the wall, and one archer having been taken prisoner at the outer ditch. Meanwhile the Peloponnesians gave up the pursuit and returned to their posts; and the Plataeans in the town, knowing nothing of what had passed, and informed by those who had turned back that not a man had escaped, sent out a herald as soon as it was day to make a truce for the recovery of the dead bodies, and then, learning the truth, desisted. In this way the Plataean party got over and were saved.

[25] Towards the close of the same winter, Salaethus, a Lacedaemonian, was sent out in a galley from Lacedaemon to Mitylene. Going by sea to Pyrrha, and from thence overland, he passed along the bed of a torrent, where the line of circumvallation was passable, and thus entering unperceived into Mitylene told the magistrates that Attica would certainly be invaded, and the forty ships destined to relieve them arrive, and that he had been sent on to announce this and to superintend matters generally. The Mitylenians upon this took courage, and laid aside the idea of treating with the Athenians; and now this winter ended, and with it ended the fourth year of the war of which Thucydides was the historian.

[26] The next summer the Peloponnesians sent off the forty-two ships for Mitylene, under Alcidas, their high admiral, and themselves and their allies invaded Attica, their object being to distract the Athenians by a double

movement, and thus to make it less easy for them to act against the fleet sailing to Mitylene. The commander in this invasion was Cleomenes, in the place of King Pausanias, son of Pleistoanax, his nephew, who was still a minor. Not content with laying waste whatever had shot up in the parts which they had before devastated, the invaders now extended their ravages to lands passed over in their previous incursions; so that this invasion was more severely felt by the Athenians than any except the second; the enemy staying on and on until they had overrun most of the country, in the expectation of hearing from Lesbos of something having been achieved by their fleet, which they thought must now have got over. However, as they did not obtain any of the results expected, and their provisions began to run short, they retreated and dispersed to their different cities.

[27] In the meantime the Mitylenians, finding their provisions failing, while the fleet from Peloponnese was loitering on the way instead of appearing at Mitylene, were compelled to come to terms with the Athenians in the following manner. Salaethus having himself ceased to expect the fleet to arrive, now armed the commons with heavy armour, which they had not before possessed, with the intention of making a sortie against the Athenians. The commons, however, no sooner found themselves possessed of arms than they refused any longer to obey their officers; and forming in knots together, told the authorities to bring out in public the provisions and divide them amongst them all, or they would themselves come to terms with the Athenians and deliver up the city.

[28] The government, aware of their inability to prevent this, and of the danger they would be in, if left out of the capitulation, publicly agreed with Paches and the army to surrender Mitylene at discretion and to admit the troops into the town; upon the understanding that the Mitylenians should be allowed to send an embassy to Athens to plead their cause, and that Paches should not imprison, make slaves of, or put to death any of the citizens until its return. Such were the terms of the capitulation; in spite of which the chief authors of the negotiation with Lacedaemon were so completely overcome by terror when the army entered that they went and seated themselves by the altars, from which they were raised up by Paches under promise that he would do them no wrong, and lodged by him in Tenedos, until

he should learn the pleasure of the Athenians concerning them. Paches also sent some galleys and seized Antissa, and took such other military measures as he thought advisable.

[29] Meanwhile the Peloponnesians in the forty ships, who ought to have made all haste to relieve Mitylene, lost time in coming round Peloponnese itself, and proceeding leisurely on the remainder of the voyage, made Delos without having been seen by the Athenians at Athens, and from thence arriving at Icarus and Myconus, there first heard of the fall of Mitylene. Wishing to know the truth, they put into Embatum, in the Erythraeid, about seven days after the capture of the town. Here they learned the truth, and began to consider what they were to do; and Teutiaplus, an Elean, addressed them as follows:

[30] "Alcidas and Peloponnesians who share with me the command of this armament, my advice is to sail just as we are to Mitylene, before we have been heard of. We may expect to find the Athenians as much off their guard as men generally are who have just taken a city: this will certainly be so by sea, where they have no idea of any enemy attacking them, and where our strength, as it happens, mainly lies; while even their land forces are probably scattered about the houses in the carelessness of victory. If therefore we were to fall upon them suddenly and in the night, I have hopes, with the help of the well-wishers that we may have left inside the town, that we shall become masters of the place. Let us not shrink from the risk, but let us remember that this is just the occasion for one of the baseless panics common in war: and that to be able to guard against these in one's own case, and to detect the moment when an attack will find an enemy at this disadvantage, is what makes a successful general."

[31] These words of Teutiaplus failing to move Alcidas, some of the Ionian exiles and the Lesbians with the expedition began to urge him, since this seemed too dangerous, to seize one of the Ionian cities or the Aeolic town of Cyme, to use as a base for effecting the revolt of Ionia. This was by no means a hopeless enterprise, as their coming was welcome everywhere; their object would be by this move to deprive Athens of her chief source of revenue, and at the same time to saddle her with expense, if she chose to blockade them; and they would probably induce Pissuthnes to join them in the war. However, Alcidas gave this proposal as bad a reception as the other, being eager, since he had come too late for Mitylene,

to find himself back in Peloponnese as soon as possible.

[*32*] Accordingly he put out from Embatum and proceeded along shore; and touching at the Teian town, Myonnesus, there butchered most of the prisoners that he had taken on his passage. Upon his coming to anchor at Ephesus, envoys came to him from the Samians at Anaia, and told him that he was not going the right way to free Hellas in massacring men who had never raised a hand against him, and who were not enemies of his, but allies of Athens against their will, and that if he did not stop he would turn many more friends into enemies than enemies into friends. Alcidas agreed to this, and let go all the Chians still in his hands and some of the others that he had taken; the inhabitants, instead of flying at the sight of his vessels, rather coming up to them, taking them for Athenian, having no sort of expectation that while the Athenians commanded the sea Peloponnesian ships would venture over to Ionia.

[*33*] From Ephesus Alcidas set sail in haste and fled. He had been seen by the Salaminian and Paralian galleys, which happened to be sailing from Athens, while still at anchor off Clarus; and fearing pursuit he now made across the open sea, fully determined to touch nowhere, if he could help it, until he got to Peloponnese. Meanwhile news of him had come in to Paches from the Erythraeid, and indeed from all quarters. As Ionia was unfortified, great fears were felt that the Peloponnesians coasting along shore, even if they did not intend to stay, might make descents in passing and plunder the towns; and now the Paralian and Salaminian, having seen him at Clarus, themselves brought intelligence of the fact. Paches accordingly gave hot chase, and continued the pursuit as far as the isle of Patmos, and then finding that Alcidas had got on too far to be overtaken, came back again. Meanwhile he thought it fortunate that, as he had not fallen in with them out at sea, he had not overtaken them anywhere where they would have been forced to encamp, and so give him the trouble of blockading them.

[*34*] On his return along shore he touched, among other places, at Notium, the port of Colophon, where the Colophonians had settled after the capture of the upper town by Itamenes and the barbarians, who had been called in by certain individuals in a party quarrel. The capture of the town took place about the time of the second Peloponnesian invasion of Attica. However, the refugees, after settling at Notium, again split up into factions, one of which called in Arcadian and barbarian mercenaries from Pissuthnes and, entrenching these in a quarter apart, formed a new community with the Median party of the Colophonians who joined them from the upper town. Their opponents had retired into exile, and now called in Paches, who invited Hippias, the commander of the Arcadians in the fortified quarter, to a parley, upon condition that, if they could not agree, he was to be put back safe and sound in the fortification. However, upon his coming out to him, he put him into custody, though not in chains, and attacked suddenly and took by surprise the fortification, and putting the Arcadians and the barbarians found in it to the sword, afterwards took Hippias into it as he had promised, and, as soon as he was inside, seized him and shot him down. Paches then gave up Notium to the Colophonians not of the Median party; and settlers were afterwards sent out from Athens, and the place colonized according to Athenian laws, after collecting all the Colophonians found in any of the cities.

[*35*] Arrived at Mitylene, Paches reduced Pyrrha and Eresus; and finding the Lacedaemonian, Salaethus, in hiding in the town, sent him off to Athens, together with the Mitylenians that he had placed in Tenedos, and any other persons that he thought concerned in the revolt. He also sent back the greater part of his forces, remaining with the rest to settle Mitylene and the rest of Lesbos as he thought best.

[*36*] Upon the arrival of the prisoners with Salaethus, the Athenians at once put the latter to death, although he offered, among other things, to procure the withdrawal of the Peloponnesians from Plataea, which was still under siege; and after deliberating as to what they should do with the former, in the fury of the moment determined to put to death not only the prisoners at Athens, but the whole adult male population of Mitylene, and to make slaves of the women and children. It was remarked that Mitylene had revolted without being, like the rest, subjected to the empire; and what above all swelled the wrath of the Athenians was the fact of the Peloponnesian fleet having ventured over to Ionia to her support, a fact which was held to argue a long meditated rebellion. They accordingly sent a galley to communicate the decree to Paches, commanding him to lose no time in dispatching the Mitylenians. The morrow brought re-

penitance with it and reflection on the horrid cruelty of a decree, which condemned a whole city to the fate merited only by the guilty. This was no sooner perceived by the Mitylenian ambassadors at Athens and their Athenian supporters, than they moved the authorities to put the question again to the vote; which they the more easily consented to do, as they themselves plainly saw that most of the citizens wished some one to give them an opportunity for reconsidering the matter. An assembly was therefore at once called, and after much expression of opinion upon both sides, Cleon, son of Cleaenetus, the same who had carried the former motion of putting the Mitylenians to death, the most violent man at Athens, and at that time by far the most powerful with the commons, came forward again and spoke as follows:

[37] "I have often before now been convinced that a democracy is incapable of empire, and never more so than by your present change of mind in the matter of Mitylene. Fears or plots being unknown to you in your daily relations with each other, you feel just the same with regard to your allies, and never reflect that the mistakes into which you may be led by listening to their appeals, or by giving way to your own compassion, are full of danger to yourselves, and bring you no thanks for your weakness from your allies; entirely forgetting that your empire is a despotism and your subjects disaffected conspirators, whose obedience is ensured not by your suicidal concessions, but by the superiority given you by your own strength and not their loyalty. The most alarming feature in the case is the constant change of measures with which we appear to be threatened, and our seeming ignorance of the fact that bad laws which are never changed are better for a city than good ones that have no authority; that unlearned loyalty is more serviceable than quick-witted insubordination; and that ordinary men usually manage public affairs better than their more gifted fellows. The latter are always wanting to appear wiser than the laws, and to overrule every proposition brought forward, thinking that they cannot show their wit in more important matters, and by such behaviour too often ruin their country; while those who mistrust their own cleverness are content to be less learned than the laws, and less able to pick holes in the speech of a good speaker; and being fair judges rather than rival athletes, generally conduct affairs successfully. These we

ought to imitate, instead of being led on by cleverness and intellectual rivalry to advise your people against our real opinions.

[38] "For myself, I adhere to my former opinion, and wonder at those who have proposed to reopen the case of the Mitylenians, and who are thus causing a delay which is all in favour of the guilty, by making the sufferer proceed against the offender with the edge of his anger blunted; although where vengeance follows most closely upon the wrong, it best equals it and most amply requites it. I wonder also who will be the man who will maintain the contrary, and will pretend to show that the crimes of the Mitylenians are of service to us, and our misfortunes injurious to the allies. Such a man must plainly either have such confidence in his rhetoric as to adventure to prove that what has been once for all decided is still undetermined, or be bribed to try to delude us by elaborate sophisms. In such contests the state gives the rewards to others, and takes the dangers for herself. The persons to blame are you who are so foolish as to institute these contests; who go to see an oration as you would to see a sight, take your facts on hearsay, judge of the practicability of a project by the wit of its advocates, and trust for the truth as to past events not to the fact which you saw more than to the clever strictures which you heard; the easy victims of new-fangled arguments, unwilling to follow received conclusions; slaves to every new paradox, despisers of the commonplace; the first wish of every man being that he could speak himself, the next to rival those who can speak by seeming to be quite up with their ideas by applauding every hit almost before it is made, and by being as quick in catching an argument as you are slow in foreseeing its consequences; asking, if I may so say, for something different from the conditions under which we live, and yet comprehending inadequately those very conditions; very slaves to the pleasure of the ear, and more like the audience of a rhetorician than the council of a city.

[39] "In order to keep you from this, I proceed to show that no one state has ever injured you as much as Mitylene. I can make allowance for those who revolt because they cannot bear our empire, or who have been forced to do so by the enemy. But for those who possessed an island with fortifications; who could fear our enemies only by sea, and there had their own force of galleys to protect them; who were independent and held in the highest honour by you—to act as these have

done, this is not revolt—revolt implies oppression; it is deliberate and wanton aggression; an attempt to ruin us by siding with our bitterest enemies; a worse offence than a war undertaken on their own account in the acquisition of power. The fate of those of their neighbours who had already rebelled and had been subdued was no lesson to them; their own prosperity could not dissuade them from affronting danger; but blindly confident in the future, and full of hopes beyond their power though not beyond their ambition, they declared war and made their decision to prefer might to right, their attack being determined not by provocation but by the moment which seemed propitious. The truth is that great good fortune coming suddenly and unexpectedly tends to make a people insolent; in most cases it is safer for mankind to have success in reason than out of reason; and it is easier for them, one may say, to stave off adversity than to preserve prosperity. Our mistake has been to distinguish the Mitylenians as we have done: had they been long ago treated like the rest, they never would have so far forgotten themselves, human nature being as surely made arrogant by consideration as it is awed by firmness. Let them now therefore be punished as their crime requires, and do not, while you condemn the aristocracy, absolve the people. This is certain, that all attacked you without distinction, although they might have come over to us and been now again in possession of their city. But no, they thought it safer to throw in their lot with the aristocracy and so joined their rebellion! Consider therefore: if you subject to the same punishment the ally who is forced to rebel by the enemy, and him who does so by his own free choice, which of them, think you, is there that will not rebel upon the slightest pretext; when the reward of success is freedom, and the penalty of failure nothing so very terrible? We meanwhile shall have to risk our money and our lives against one state after another; and if successful, shall receive a ruined town from which we can no longer draw the revenue upon which our strength depends; while if unsuccessful, we shall have an enemy the more upon our hands, and shall spend the time that might be employed in combating our existing foes in warring with our own allies.

[40] "No hope, therefore, that rhetoric may instil or money purchase, of the mercy due to human infirmity must be held out to the Mitylenians. Their offence was not involuntary, but of malice and deliberate; and mercy is only for

unwilling offenders. I therefore, now as before, persist against your reversing your first decision, or giving way to the three failings most fatal to empire—pity, sentiment, and indulgence. Compassion is due to those who can reciprocate the feeling, not to those who will never pity us in return, but are our natural and necessary foes: the orators who charm us with sentiment may find other less important arenas for their talents, in the place of one where the city pays a heavy penalty for a momentary pleasure, themselves receiving fine acknowledgments for their fine phrases; while indulgence should be shown towards those who will be our friends in future, instead of towards men who will remain just what they were, and as much our enemies as before. To sum up shortly, I say that if you follow my advice you will do what is just towards the Mitylenians, and at the same time expedient; while by a different decision you will not oblige them so much as pass sentence upon yourselves. For if they were right in rebelling, you must be wrong in ruling. However, if, right or wrong, you determine to rule, you must carry out your principle and punish the Mitylenians as your interest requires; or else you must give up your empire and cultivate honesty without danger. Make up your minds, therefore, to give them like for like; and do not let the victims who escaped the plot be more insensible than the conspirators who hatched it; but reflect what they would have done if victorious over you, especially as they were the aggressors. It is they who wrong their neighbour without a cause, that pursue their victim to the death, on account of the danger which they foresee in letting their enemy survive; since the object of a wanton wrong is more dangerous, if he escape, than an enemy who has not this to complain of. Do not, therefore, be traitors to yourselves, but recall as nearly as possible the moment of suffering and the supreme importance which you then attached to their reduction; and now pay them back in their turn, without yielding to present weakness or forgetting the peril that once hung over you. Punish them as they deserve, and teach your other allies by a striking example that the penalty of rebellion is death. Let them once understand this and you will not have so often to neglect your enemies while you are fighting with your own confederates."

[41] Such were the words of Cleon. After him Diodotus, son of Eucrates, who had also in the previous assembly spoken most strongly against putting the Mitylenians to

death, came forward and spoke as follows:

[42] "I do not blame the persons who have reopened the case of the Mitylenians, nor do I approve the protests which we have heard against important questions being frequently debated. I think the two things most opposed to good counsel are haste and passion; haste usually goes hand in hand with folly, passion with coarseness and narrowness of mind. As for the argument that speech ought not to be the exponent of action, the man who uses it must be either senseless or interested: senseless if he believes it possible to treat of the uncertain future through any other medium; interested if, wishing to carry a disgraceful measure and doubting his ability to speak well in a bad cause, he thinks to frighten opponents and hearers by well-aimed calumny. What is still more intolerable is to accuse a speaker of making a display in order to be paid for it. If ignorance only were imputed, an unsuccessful speaker might retire with a reputation for honesty, if not for wisdom; while the charge of dishonesty makes him suspected, if successful, and thought, if defeated, not only a fool but a rogue. The city is no gainer by such a system, since fear deprives it of its advisers; although in truth, if our speakers are to make such assertions, it would be better for the country if they could not speak at all, as we should then make fewer blunders. The good citizen ought to triumph not by frightening his opponents but by beating them fairly in argument; and a wise city, without over-distinguishing its best advisers, will nevertheless not deprive them of their due, and, far from punishing an unlucky counsellor, will not even regard him as disgraced. In this way successful orators would be least tempted to sacrifice their convictions to popularity, in the hope of still higher honours, and unsuccessful speakers to resort to the same popular arts in order to win over the multitude.

[43] "This is not our way; and, besides, the moment that a man is suspected of giving advice, however good, from corrupt motives, we feel such a grudge against him for the gain which after all we are not certain he will receive, that we deprive the city of its certain benefit. Plain good advice has thus come to be no less suspected than bad; and the advocate of the most monstrous measures is not more obliged to use deceit to gain the people, than the best counsellor is to lie in order to be believed. The city and the city only, owing to these refinements, can never be served openly and without disguise; he who does serve it

openly being always suspected of serving himself in some secret way in return. Still, considering the magnitude of the interests involved, and the position of affairs, we orators must make it our business to look a little farther than you who judge offhand; especially as we, your advisers, are responsible, while you, our audience, are not so. For if those who gave the advice, and those who took it, suffered equally, you would judge more calmly; as it is, you visit the disasters into which the whim of the moment may have led you upon the single person of your adviser, not upon yourselves, his numerous companions in error.

[44] "However, I have not come forward either to oppose or to accuse in the matter of Mitylene; indeed, the question before us as sensible men is not their guilt, but our interests. Though I prove them ever so guilty, I shall not, therefore, advise their death, unless it be expedient; nor though they should have claims to indulgence, shall I recommend it, unless it be clearly for the good of the country. I consider that we are deliberating for the future more than for the present; and where Cleon is so positive as to the useful deterrent effects that will follow from making rebellion capital, I, who consider the interests of the future quite as much as he, as positively maintain the contrary. And I require you not to reject my useful considerations for his specious ones: his speech may have the attraction of seeming the more just in your present temper against Mitylene; but we are not in a court of justice, but in a political assembly; and the question is not justice, but how to make the Mitylenians useful to Athens.

[45] "Now of course communities have enacted the penalty of death for many offences far lighter than this: still hope leads men to venture, and no one ever yet put himself in peril without the inward conviction that he would succeed in his design. Again, was there ever city rebelling that did not believe that it possessed either in itself or in its alliances resources adequate to the enterprise? All, states and individuals, are alike prone to err, and there is no law that will prevent them; or why should men have exhausted the list of punishments in search of enactments to protect them from evildoers? It is probable that in early times the penalties for the greatest offences were less severe, and that, as these were disregarded, the penalty of death has been by degrees in most cases arrived at, which is itself disregarded in like manner. Either then some means of terror

more terrible than this must be discovered, or it must be owned that this restraint is useless; and that as long as poverty gives men the courage of necessity, or plenty fills them with the ambition which belongs to insolence and pride, and the other conditions of life remain each under the thraldom of some fatal and master passion, so long will the impulse never be wanting to drive men into danger. Hope also and cupidity, the one leading and the other following, the one conceiving the attempt, the other suggesting the facility of succeeding, cause the widest ruin, and, although invisible agents, are far stronger than the dangers that are seen. Fortune, too, powerfully helps the delusion and, by the unexpected aid that she sometimes lends, tempts men to venture with inferior means; and this is especially the case with communities, because the stakes played for are the highest, freedom or empire, and, when all are acting together, each man irrationally magnifies his own capacity. In fine, it is impossible to prevent, and only great simplicity can hope to prevent, human nature doing what it has once set its mind upon, by force of law or by any other deterrent force whatsoever.

[46] "We must not, therefore, commit ourselves to a false policy through a belief in the efficacy of the punishment of death, or exclude rebels from the hope of repentance and an early atonement of their error. Consider a moment. At present, if a city that has already revolted perceive that it cannot succeed, it will come to terms while it is still able to refund expenses, and pay tribute afterwards. In the other case, what city, think you, would not prepare better than is now done, and hold out to the last against its besiegers, if it is all one whether it surrender late or soon? And how can it be otherwise than hurtful to us to be put to the expense of a siege, because surrender is out of the question; and if we take the city, to receive a ruined town from which we can no longer draw the revenue which forms our real strength against the enemy? We must not, therefore, sit as strict judges of the offenders to our own prejudice, but rather see how by moderate chastisements we may be enabled to benefit in future by the revenue-producing powers of our dependencies; and we must make up our minds to look for our protection not to legal terrors but to careful administration. At present we do exactly the opposite. When a free community, held in subjection by force, rises, as is only natural, and asserts its independence,

it is no sooner reduced than we fancy ourselves obliged to punish it severely; although the right course with freemen is not to chastise them rigorously when they do rise, but rigorously to watch them before they rise, and to prevent their ever entertaining the idea, and, the insurrection suppressed, to make as few responsible for it as possible.

[47] "Only consider what a blunder you would commit in doing as Cleon recommends. As things are at present, in all the cities the people is your friend, and either does not revolt with the oligarchy, or, if forced to do so, becomes at once the enemy of the insurgents; so that in the war with the hostile city you have the masses on your side. But if you butcher the people of Mitylene, who had nothing to do with the revolt, and who, as soon as they got arms, of their own motion surrendered the town, first you will commit the crime of killing your benefactors; and next you will play directly into the hands of the higher classes, who when they induce their cities to rise, will immediately have the people on their side, through your having announced in advance the same punishment for those who are guilty and for those who are not. On the contrary, even if they were guilty, you ought to seem not to notice it, in order to avoid alienating the only class still friendly to us. In short, I consider it far more useful for the preservation of our empire voluntarily to put up with injustice, than to put to death, however justly, those whom it is our interest to keep alive. As for Cleon's idea that in punishment the claims of justice and expediency can both be satisfied, facts do not confirm the possibility of such a combination.

[48] "Confess, therefore, that this is the wisest course, and without conceding too much either to pity or to indulgence, by neither of which motives do I any more than Cleon wish you to be influenced, upon the plain merits of the case before you, be persuaded by me to try calmly those of the Mitylenians whom Paches sent off as guilty, and to leave the rest undisturbed. This is at once best for the future, and most terrible to your enemies at the present moment; inasmuch as good policy against an adversary is superior to the blind attacks of brute force."

[49] Such were the words of Diodotus. The two opinions thus expressed were the ones that most directly contradicted each other; and the Athenians, notwithstanding their change of feeling, now proceeded to a division, in which the show of hands was almost equal, although

the motion of Diodotus carried the day. Another galley was at once sent off in haste, for fear that the first might reach Lesbos in the interval, and the city be found destroyed; the first ship having about a day and a night's start. Wine and barley-cakes were provided for the vessel by the Mitylenian ambassadors, and great promises made if they arrived in time; which caused the men to use such diligence upon the voyage that they took their meals of barley-cakes kneaded with oil and wine as they rowed, and only slept by turns while the others were at the oar. Luckily they met with no contrary wind, and the first ship making no haste upon so horrid an errand, while the second pressed on in the manner described, the first arrived so little before them, that Paches had only just had time to read the decree, and to prepare to execute the sentence, when the second put into port and prevented the massacre. The danger of Mitylene had indeed been great.

[50] The other party whom Paches had sent off as the prime movers in the rebellion, were upon Cleon's motion put to death by the Athenians, the number being rather more than a thousand. The Athenians also demolished the walls of the Mitylenians, and took possession of their ships. Afterwards tribute was not imposed upon the Lesbians; but all their land, except that of the Methymnians, was divided into three thousand allotments, three hundred of which were reserved as sacred for the gods, and the rest assigned by lot to Athenian shareholders, who were sent out to the island. With these the Lesbians agreed to pay a rent of two minae a year for each allotment, and cultivated the land themselves. The Athenians also took possession of the towns on the continent belonging to the Mitylenians, which thus became for the future subject to Athens. Such were the events that took place at Lesbos.

CHAPTER X

Fifth Year of the War—Trial and Execution of the Plataeans—Corcyraean Revolution

[51] DURING the same summer, after the reduction of Lesbos, the Athenians under Nicias, son of Niceratus, made an expedition against the island of Minoa, which lies off Megara and was used as a fortified post by the Megarians, who had built a tower upon it. Nicias wished to enable the Athenians to maintain their blockade from this nearer station instead of from Budorum and Salamis; to stop the Peloponnesian galleys and privateers sailing out unobserved from the island, as they had been in the habit of doing; and at the same time prevent anything from coming into Megara. Accordingly, after taking two towers projecting on the side of Nisaea, by engines from the sea, and clearing the entrance into the channel between the island and the shore, he next proceeded to cut off all communication by building a wall on the mainland at the point where a bridge across a morass enabled succours to be thrown into the island, which was not far off from the continent. A few days sufficing to accomplish this, he afterwards raised some works in the island also, and leaving a garrison there, departed with his forces.

[52] About the same time in this summer, the Plataeans, being now without provisions and unable to support the siege, surrendered to the Peloponnesians in the following manner. An assault had been made upon the wall, which the Plataeans were unable to repel. The Lacedaemonian commander, perceiving their weakness, wished to avoid taking the place by storm; his instructions from Lacedaemon having been so conceived, in order that if at any future time peace should be made with Athens, and they should agree each to restore the places that they had taken in the war, Plataea might be held to have come over voluntarily, and not be included in the list. He accordingly sent a herald to them to ask if they were willing voluntarily to surrender the town to the Lacedaemonians, and accept them as their judges, upon the understanding that the guilty should be punished, but no one without form of law. The Plataeans were now in the last state of weakness, and the herald had no sooner delivered his message than they surrendered the town. The Peloponnesians fed them for some days until the judges from Lacedaemon, who were five in number, arrived. Upon their arrival no charge was preferred; they simply called up the Plataeans, and asked them whether they had done the Lacedaemonians and allies any service in the war then raging. The Plataeans asked leave to speak at greater length, and deputed two of their number to represent them: Astymachus, son of Asopolaus, and Lacon, son of Aeimnestus, *proxenus* of the Lacedaemonians, who came forward and spoke as follows:

[53] "Lacedaemonians, when we surrendered our city we trusted in you, and looked forward to a trial more agreeable to the forms of law than the present, to which we had no idea of being subjected; the judges also in whose hands we consented to place ourselves

were you, and you only (from whom we thought we were most likely to obtain justice), and not other persons, as is now the case. As matters stand, we are afraid that we have been doubly deceived. We have good reason to suspect, not only that the issue to be tried is the most terrible of all, but that you will not prove impartial; if we may argue from the fact that no accusation was first brought forward for us to answer, but we had ourselves to ask leave to speak, and from the question being put so shortly, that a true answer to it tells against us, while a false one can be contradicted. In this dilemma, our safest, and indeed our only course, seems to be to say something at all risks: placed as we are, we could scarcely be silent without being tormented by the damning thought that speaking might have saved us. Another difficulty that we have to encounter is the difficulty of convincing you. Were we unknown to each other we might profit by bringing forward new matter with which you were unacquainted: as it is, we can tell you nothing that you do not know already, and we fear, not that you have condemned us in your own minds of having failed in our duty towards you, and make this our crime, but that to please a third party we have to submit to a trial the result of which is already decided. [54] Nevertheless, we will place before you what we can justly urge, not only on the question of the quarrel which the Thebans have against us, but also as addressing you and the rest of the Hellenes; and we will remind you of our good services, and endeavour to prevail with you.

"To your short question, whether we have done the Lacedaemonians and allies any service in this war, we say, if you ask us as enemies, that to refrain from serving you was not to do you injury; if as friends, that you are more in fault for having marched against us. During the peace, and against the Mede, we acted well: we have not now been the first to break the peace, and we were the only Boeotians who then joined in defending against the Mede the liberty of Hellas. Although an inland people, we were present at the action at Artemisium; in the battle that took place in our territory we fought by the side of yourselves and Pausanias; and in all the other Hellenic exploits of the time we took a part quite out of proportion to our strength. Besides, you, as Lacedaemonians, ought not to forget that at the time of the great panic at Sparta, after the earthquake, caused by the secession of the Helots to Ithomé, we

sent the third part of our citizens to assist you.

[55] "On these great and historical occasions such was the part that we chose, although afterwards we became your enemies. For this you were to blame. When we asked for your alliance against our Theban oppressors, you rejected our petition, and told us to go to the Athenians who were our neighbours, as you lived too far off. In the war we never have done to you, and never should have done to you, anything unreasonable. If we refused to desert the Athenians when you asked us, we did no wrong; they had helped us against the Thebans when you drew back, and we could no longer give them up with honour; especially as we had obtained their alliance and had been admitted to their citizenship at our own request, and after receiving benefits at their hands; but it was plainly our duty loyally to obey their orders. Besides, the faults that either of you may commit in your supremacy must be laid, not upon the followers, but on the chiefs that lead them astray.

[56] "With regard to the Thebans, they have wronged us repeatedly, and their last aggression, which has been the means of bringing us into our present position, is within your own knowledge. In seizing our city in time of peace, and what is more at a holy time in the month, they justly encountered our vengeance, in accordance with the universal law which sanctions resistance to an invader; and it cannot now be right that we should suffer on their account. By taking your own immediate interest and their animosity as the test of justice, you will prove yourselves to be rather waiters on expediency than judges of right; although if they seem useful to you now, we and the rest of the Hellenes gave you much more valuable help at a time of greater need. Now you are the assailants, and others fear you; but at the crisis to which we allude, when the barbarian threatened all with slavery, the Thebans were on his side. It is just, therefore, to put our patriotism then against our error now, if error there has been; and you will find the merit outweighing the fault, and displayed at a juncture when there were few Hellenes who would set their valour against the strength of Xerxes, and when greater praise was theirs who preferred the dangerous path of honour to the safe course of consulting their own interest with respect to the invasion. To these few we belonged, and highly were we honoured for it; and yet we now fear to perish by having again

acted on the same principles, and chosen to act well with Athens sooner than wisely with Sparta. Yet in justice the same cases should be decided in the same way, and policy should not mean anything else than lasting gratitude for the service of a good ally combined with a proper attention to one's own immediate interest.

[57] "Consider also that at present the Hellenes generally regard you as a pattern of worth and honour; and if you pass an unjust sentence upon us in this which is no obscure cause, but one in which you, the judges, are as illustrious as we, the prisoners, are blameless, take care that displeasure be not felt at an unworthy decision in the matter of honourable men made by men yet more honourable than they, and at the consecration in the national temples of spoils taken from the Plataeans, the benefactors of Hellas. Shocking indeed will it seem for Lacedaemonians to destroy Plataea, and for the city whose name your fathers inscribed upon the tripod at Delphi for its good service, to be by you blotted out from the map of Hellas, to please the Thebans. To such a depth of misfortune have we fallen that, while the Medes' success had been our ruin, Thebans now supplant us in your once fond regards; and we have been subjected to two dangers, the greatest of any—that of dying of starvation then, if we had not surrendered our town, and now of being tried for our lives. So that we Plataeans, after exertions beyond our power in the cause of the Hellenes, are rejected by all, forsaken and unassisted; helped by none of our allies, and reduced to doubt the stability of our only hope, yourselves.

[58] "Still, in the name of the gods who once presided over our confederacy, and of our own good service in the Hellenic cause, we adjure you to relent; to recall the decision which we fear that the Thebans may have obtained from you; to ask back the gift that you have given them, that they disgrace not you by slaying us; to gain a pure instead of a guilty gratitude, and not to gratify others to be yourselves rewarded with shame. Our lives may be quickly taken, but it will be a heavy task to wipe away the infamy of the deed; as we are no enemies whom you might justly punish, but friends forced into taking arms against you. To grant us our lives would be, therefore, a righteous judgment; if you consider also that we are prisoners who surrendered of their own accord, stretching out our hands for quarter, whose slaughter Hellenic law forbids, and who besides were always your benefactors. Look at the sepulchres of your fathers, slain by the Medes and buried in our country, whom year by year we honoured with garments and all other dues, and the first-fruits of all that our land produced in their season, as friends from a friendly country and allies to our old companions in arms. Should you not decide aright, your conduct would be the very opposite to ours. Consider only: Pausanias buried them thinking that he was laying them in friendly ground and among men as friendly; but you, if you kill us and make the Plataean territory Theban, will leave your fathers and kinsmen in a hostile soil and among their murderers, deprived of the honours which they now enjoy. What is more, you will enslave the land in which the freedom of the Hellenes was won, make desolate the temples of the gods to whom they prayed before they overcame the Medes, and take away your ancestral sacrifices from those who founded and instituted them.

[59] "It were not to your glory, Lacedaemonians, either to offend in this way against the common law of the Hellenes and against your own ancestors, or to kill us your benefactors to gratify another's hatred without having been wronged yourselves: it were more so to spare us and to yield to the impressions of a reasonable compassion; reflecting not merely on the awful fate in store for us, but also on the character of the sufferers, and on the impossibility of predicting how soon misfortune may fall even upon those who deserve it not. We, as we have a right to do and as our need impels us, entreat you, calling aloud upon the gods at whose common altar all the Hellenes worship, to hear our request, to be not unmindful of the oaths which your fathers swore, and which we now plead—we supplicate you by the tombs of your fathers, and appeal to those that are gone to save us from falling into the hands of the Thebans and their dearest friends from being given up to their most detested foes. We also remind you of that day on which we did the most glorious deeds, by your fathers' sides, we who now on this are like to suffer the most dreadful fate. Finally, to do what is necessary and yet most difficult for men in our situation—that is, to make an end of speaking, since with that ending the peril of our lives draws near—in conclusion we say that we did not surrender our city to the Thebans (to that we would have preferred inglorious starvation), but trusted in and capitu-

lated to you; and it would be just, if we fail to persuade you, to put us back in the same position and let us take the chance that falls to us. And at the same time we adjure you not to give us up—your suppliants, Lacedaemonians, out of your hands and faith, Plataeans foremost of the Hellenic patriots, to Thebans, our most hated enemies—but to be our saviours, and not, while you free the rest of the Hellenes, to bring us to destruction."

[60] Such were the words of the Plataeans. The Thebans, afraid that the Lacedaemonians might be moved by what they had heard, came forward and said that they too desired to address them, since the Plataeans had, against their wish, been allowed to speak at length instead of being confined to a simple answer to the question. Leave being granted, the Thebans spoke as follows:

[61] "We should never have asked to make this speech if the Plataeans on their side had contented themselves with shortly answering the question, and had not turned round and made charges against us, coupled with a long defence of themselves upon matters outside the present inquiry and not even the subject of accusation, and with praise of what no one finds fault with. However, since they have done so, we must answer their charges and refute their self-praise, in order that neither our bad name nor their good may help them, but that you may hear the real truth on both points, and so decide.

"The origin of our quarrel was this. We settled Plataea some time after the rest of Boeotia, together with other places out of which we had driven the mixed population. The Plataeans not choosing to recognize our supremacy, as had been first arranged, but separating themselves from the rest of the Boeotians, and proving traitors to their nationality, we used compulsion; upon which they went over to the Athenians, and with them did as much harm, for which we retaliated.

[62] "Next, when the barbarian invaded Hellas, they say that they were the only Boeotians who did not Medize; and this is where they most glorify themselves and abuse us. We say that if they did not Medize, it was because the Athenians did not do so either; just as afterwards when the Athenians attacked the Hellenes they, the Plataeans, were again the only Boeotians who Atticized. And yet consider the forms of our respective governments when we so acted. Our city at that juncture had neither an oligarchical constitution in which all the nobles enjoyed equal rights, nor a democracy, but that which is most opposed to law and good government and nearest a tyranny—the rule of a close cabal. These, hoping to strengthen their individual power by the success of the Mede, kept down by force the people, and brought him into the town. The city as a whole was not its own mistress when it so acted, and ought not to be reproached for the errors that it committed while deprived of its constitution. Examine only how we acted after the departure of the Mede and the recovery of the constitution; when the Athenians attacked the rest of Hellas and endeavoured to subjugate our country, of the greater part of which faction had already made them masters. Did not we fight and conquer at Coronea and liberate Boeotia, and do we not now actively contribute to the liberation of the rest, providing horses to the cause and a force unequalled by that of any other state in the confederacy?

"Let this suffice to excuse us for our Medism. [63] We will now endeavour to show that you have injured the Hellenes more than we, and are more deserving of condign punishment. It was in defence against us, say you, that you became allies and citizens of Athens. If so, you ought only to have called in the Athenians against us, instead of joining them in attacking others: it was open to you to do this if you ever felt that they were leading you where you did not wish to follow, as Lacedaemon was already your ally against the Mede, as you so much insist; and this was surely sufficient to keep us off, and above all to allow you to deliberate in security. Nevertheless, of your own choice and without compulsion you chose to throw your lot in with Athens. And you say that it had been base for you to betray your benefactors; but it was surely far baser and more iniquitous to sacrifice the whole body of the Hellenes, your fellow confederates, who were liberating Hellas, than the Athenians only, who were enslaving it. The return that you made them was therefore neither equal nor honourable, since you called them in, as you say, because you were being oppressed yourselves, and then became their accomplices in oppressing others; although baseness rather consists in not returning like for like than in not returning what is justly due but must be unjustly paid.

[64] "Meanwhile, after thus plainly showing that it was not for the sake of the Hellenes

that you alone then did not Medize, but because the Athenians did not do so either, and you wished to side with them and to be against the rest; you now claim the benefit of good deeds done to please your neighbours. This cannot be admitted: you chose the Athenians, and with them you must stand or fall. Nor can you plead the league then made and claim that it should now protect you. You abandoned that league, and offended against it by helping instead of hindering the subjugation of the Aeginetans and others of its members, and that not under compulsion, but while in enjoyment of the same institutions that you enjoy to the present hour, and no one forcing you as in our case. Lastly, an invitation was addressed to you before you were blockaded to be neutral and join neither party: this you did not accept. Who then merit the detestation of the Hellenes more justly than you, you who sought their ruin under the mask of honour? The former virtues that you allege you now show not to be proper to your character; the real bent of your nature has been at length damningly proved: when the Athenians took the path of injustice you followed them.

"Of our unwilling Medism and your wilful Atticizing this then is our explanation. [65] The last wrong of which you complain consists in our having, as you say, lawlessly invaded your town in time of peace and festival. Here again we cannot think that we were more in fault than yourselves. If of our own proper motion we made an armed attack upon your city and ravaged your territory, we are guilty; but if the first men among you in estate and family, wishing to put an end to the foreign connection and to restore you to the common Boeotian country, of their own free will invited us, wherein is our crime? Where wrong is done, those who lead, as you say, are more to blame than those who follow. Not that, in our judgment, wrong was done either by them or by us. Citizens like yourselves, and with more at stake than you, they opened their own walls and introduced us into their own city, not as foes but as friends, to prevent the bad among you from becoming worse; to give honest men their due; to reform principles without attacking persons, since you were not to be banished from your city, but brought home to your kindred, nor to be made enemies to any, but friends alike to all.

[66] "That our intention was not hostile is proved by our behaviour. We did no harm to any one, but publicly invited those who wished to live under a national, Boeotian government to come over to us; which as first you gladly did, and made an agreement with us and remained tranquil, until you became aware of the smallness of our numbers. Now it is possible that there may have been something not quite fair in our entering without the consent of your commons. At any rate you did not repay us in kind. Instead of refraining, as we had done, from violence, and inducing us to retire by negotiation, you fell upon us in violation of your agreement, and slew some of us in fight, of which we do not so much complain, for in that there was a certain justice; but others who held out their hands and received quarter, and whose lives you subsequently promised us, you lawlessly butchered. If this was not abominable, what is? And after these three crimes committed one after the other—the violation of your agreement, the murder of the men afterwards, and the lying breach of your promise not to kill them, if we refrained from injuring your property in the country—you still affirm that we are the criminals and yourselves pretend to escape justice. Not so, if these your judges decide aright, but you will be punished for all together.

[67] "Such, Lacedaemonians, are the facts. We have gone into them at some length both on your account and on our own, that you may feel that you will justly condemn the prisoners, and we, that we have given an additional sanction to our vengeance. We would also prevent you from being melted by hearing of their past virtues, if any such they had: these may be fairly appealed to by the victims of injustice, but only aggravate the guilt of criminals, since they offend against their better nature. Nor let them gain anything by crying and wailing, by calling upon your fathers' tombs and their own desolate condition. Against this we point to the far more dreadful fate of our youth, butchered at their hands; the fathers of whom either fell at Coronea, bringing Boeotia over to you, or seated, forlorn old men by desolate hearths, with far more reason implore your justice upon the prisoners. The pity which they appeal to is rather due to men who suffer unworthily; those who suffer justly as they do are on the contrary subjects for triumph. For their present desolate condition they have themselves to blame, since they wilfully rejected the better alliance. Their lawless act was not provoked by any action of ours: hate, not justice, inspired their decision; and even now the satisfaction which they afford us is not

adequate; they will suffer by a legal sentence, not as they pretend as suppliants asking for quarter in battle, but as prisoners who have surrendered upon agreement to take their trial. Vindicate, therefore, Lacedaemonians, the Hellenic law which they have broken; and to us, the victims of its violation, grant the reward merited by our zeal. Nor let us be supplanted in your favour by their harangues, but offer an example to the Hellenes, that the contests to which you invite them are of deeds, not words: good deeds can be shortly stated, but where wrong is done a wealth of language is needed to veil its deformity. However, if leading powers were to do what you are now doing, and putting one short question to all alike were to decide accordingly, men would be less tempted to seek fine phrases to cover bad actions."

[68] Such were the words of the Thebans. The Lacedaemonian judges decided that the question whether they had received any service from the Plataeans in the war, was a fair one for them to put; as they had always invited them to be neutral, agreeably to the original covenant of Pausanias after the defeat of the Mede, and had again definitely offered them the same conditions before the blockade. This offer having been refused, they were now, they conceived, by the loyalty of their intention released from their covenant; and having, as they considered, suffered evil at the hands of the Plataeans, they brought them in again one by one and asked each of them the same question, that is to say, whether they had done the Lacedaemonians and allies any service in the war; and upon their saying that they had not, took them out and slew them, all without exception. The number of Plataeans thus massacred was not less than two hundred, with twenty-five Athenians who had shared in the siege. The women were taken as slaves. The city the Thebans gave for about a year to some political emigrants from Megara and to the surviving Plataeans of their own party to inhabit, and afterwards razed it to the ground from the very foundations, and built on to the precinct of Hera an inn two hundred feet square, with rooms all round above and below, making use for this purpose of the roofs and doors of the Plataeans: of the rest of the materials in the wall, the brass and the iron, they made couches which they dedicated to Hera, for whom they also built a stone chapel of a hundred feet square. The land they confiscated and let out on a ten years' lease to

Theban occupiers. The adverse attitude of the Lacedaemonians in the whole Plataean affair was mainly adopted to please the Thebans, who were thought to be useful in the war at that moment raging. Such was the end of Plataea, in the ninety-third year after she became the ally of Athens.

[69] Meanwhile, the forty ships of the Peloponnesians that had gone to the relief of the Lesbians, and which we left flying across the open sea, pursued by the Athenians, were caught in a storm off Crete, and scattering from thence made their way to Peloponnese, where they found at Cyllene thirteen Leucadian and Ambraciot galleys, with Brasidas, son of Tellis, lately arrived as counsellor to Alcidas; the Lacedaemonians, upon the failure of the Lesbian expedition, having resolved to strengthen their fleet and sail to Corcyra, where a revolution had broken out, so as to arrive there before the twelve Athenian ships at Naupactus could be reinforced from Athens. Brasidas and Alcidas began to prepare accordingly.

[70] The Corcyraean revolution began with the return of the prisoners taken in the seafights off Epidamnus. These the Corinthians had released, nominally upon the security of eight hundred talents given by their *proxeni,* but in reality upon their engagement to bring over Corcyra to Corinth. These men proceeded to canvass each of the citizens, and to intrigue with the view of detaching the city from Athens. Upon the arrival of an Athenian and a Corinthian vessel, with envoys on board, a conference was held in which the Corcyraeans voted to remain allies of the Athenians according to their agreement, but to be friends of the Peloponnesians as they had been formerly. Meanwhile, the returned prisoners brought Peithias, a volunteer *proxenus* of the Athenians and leader of the commons, to trial, upon the charge of enslaving Corcyra to Athens. He, being acquitted, retorted by accusing five of the richest of their number of cutting stakes in the ground sacred to Zeus and Alcinous; the legal penalty being a stater for each stake. Upon their conviction, the amount of the penalty being very large, they seated themselves as suppliants in the temples to be allowed to pay it by instalments; but Peithias, who was one of the senate, prevailed upon that body to enforce the law; upon which the accused, rendered desperate by the law, and also learning that Peithias had the intention, while still a member of the senate, to persuade the people to con-

clude a defensive and offensive alliance with Athens, banded together armed with daggers, and suddenly bursting into the senate killed Peithias and sixty others, senators and private persons; some few only of the party of Peithias taking refuge in the Athenian galley, which had not yet departed.

[71] After this outrage, the conspirators summoned the Corcyraeans to an assembly, and said that this would turn out for the best, and would save them from being enslaved by Athens: for the future, they moved to receive neither party unless they came peacefully in a single ship, treating any larger number as enemies. This motion made, they compelled it to be adopted, and instantly sent off envoys to Athens to justify what had been done and to dissuade the refugees there from any hostile proceedings which might lead to a reaction.

[72] Upon the arrival of the embassy, the Athenians arrested the envoys and all who listened to them, as revolutionists, and lodged them in Aegina. Meanwhile a Corinthian galley arriving in the island with Lacedaemonian envoys, the dominant Corcyraean party attacked the commons and defeated them in battle. Night coming on, the commons took refuge in the Acropolis and the higher parts of the city, and concentrated themselves there, having also possession of the Hyllaic harbour; their adversaries occupying the market-place, where most of them lived, and the harbour adjoining, looking towards the mainland.

[73] The next day passed in skirmishes of little importance, each party sending into the country to offer freedom to the slaves and to invite them to join them. The mass of the slaves answered the appeal of the commons; their antagonists being reinforced by eight hundred mercenaries from the continent.

[74] After a day's interval hostilities recommenced, victory remaining with the commons, who had the advantage in numbers and position, the women also valiantly assisting them, pelting with tiles from the houses, and supporting the mêlée with a fortitude beyond their sex. Towards dusk, the oligarchs in full rout, fearing that the victorious commons might assault and carry the arsenal and put them to the sword, fired the houses round the market-place and the lodging-houses, in order to bar their advance; sparing neither their own, nor those of their neighbours; by which much stuff of the merchants was consumed and the city risked total destruction, if a wind had come to help the flame by blowing on it. Hostilities

now ceasing, both sides kept quiet, passing the night on guard, while the Corinthian ship stole out to sea upon the victory of the commons, and most of the mercenaries passed over secretly to the continent.

[75] The next day the Athenian general, Nicostratus, son of Diitrephes, came up from Naupactus with twelve ships and five hundred Messenian heavy infantry. He at once endeavoured to bring about a settlement, and persuaded the two parties to agree together to bring to trial ten of the ringleaders, who presently fled, while the rest were to live in peace, making terms with each other, and entering into a defensive and offensive alliance with the Athenians. This arranged, he was about to sail away, when the leaders of the commons induced him to leave them five of his ships to make their adversaries less disposed to move, while they manned and sent with him an equal number of their own. He had no sooner consented, than they began to enroll their enemies for the ships; and these, fearing that they might be sent off to Athens, seated themselves as suppliants in the temple of the Dioscuri. An attempt on the part of Nicostratus to reassure them and to persuade them to rise proving unsuccessful, the commons armed upon this pretext, alleging the refusal of their adversaries to sail with them as a proof of the hollowness of their intentions, and took their arms out of their houses, and would have dispatched some whom they fell in with, if Nicostratus had not prevented it. The rest of the party, seeing what was going on, seated themselves as suppliants in the temple of Hera, being not less than four hundred in number; until the commons, fearing that they might adopt some desperate resolution, induced them to rise, and conveyed them over to the island in front of the temple, where provisions were sent across to them.

[76] At this stage in the revolution, on the fourth or fifth day after the removal of the men to the island, the Peloponnesian ships arrived from Cyllene where they had been stationed since their return from Ionia, fifty-three in number, still under the command of Alcidas, but with Brasidas also on board as his adviser; and dropping anchor at Sybota, a harbour on the mainland, at daybreak made sail for Corcyra.

[77] The Corcyraeans in great confusion and alarm at the state of things in the city and at the approach of the invader, at once proceeded to equip sixty vessels, which they sent out, as fast as they were manned, against the en-

emy, in spite of the Athenians recommending them to let them sail out first, and to follow themselves afterwards with all their ships together. Upon their vessels coming up to the enemy in this straggling fashion, two immediately deserted: in others the crews were fighting among themselves, and there was no order in anything that was done; so that the Peloponnesians, seeing their confusion, placed twenty ships to oppose the Corcyraeans, and ranged the rest against the twelve Athenian ships, amongst which were the two vessels *Salaminia* and *Paralus*.

[78] While the Corcyraeans, attacking without judgment and in small detachments, were already crippled by their own misconduct, the Athenians, afraid of the numbers of the enemy and of being surrounded, did not venture to attack the main body or even the centre of the division opposed to them, but fell upon its wing and sank one vessel; after which the Peloponnesians formed in a circle, and the Athenians rowed round them and tried to throw them into disorder. Perceiving this, the division opposed to the Corcyraeans, fearing a repetition of the disaster of Naupactus, came to support their friends, and the whole fleet now bore down, united, upon the Athenians, who retired before it, backing water, retiring as leisurely as possible in order to give the Corcyraeans time to escape, while the enemy was thus kept occupied. Such was the character of this sea-fight, which lasted until sunset.

[79] The Corcyraeans now feared that the enemy would follow up their victory and sail against the town and rescue the men in the island, or strike some other blow equally decisive, and accordingly carried the men over again to the temple of Hera, and kept guard over the city. The Peloponnesians, however, although victorious in the sea-fight, did not venture to attack the town, but took the thirteen Corcyraean vessels which they had captured, and with them sailed back to the continent from whence they had put out. The next day equally they refrained from attacking the city, although the disorder and panic were at their height, and though Brasidas, it is said, urged Alcidas, his superior officer, to do so, but they landed upon the promontory of Leukimme and laid waste the country.

[80] Meanwhile the commons in Corcyra, being still in great fear of the fleet attacking them, came to a parley with the suppliants and their friends, in order to save the town; and prevailed upon some of them to go on board

the ships, of which they still manned thirty, against the expected attack. But the Peloponnesians after ravaging the country until midday sailed away, and towards nightfall were informed by beacon signals of the approach of sixty Athenian vessels from Leucas, under the command of Eurymedon, son of Thucles; which had been sent off by the Athenians upon the news of the revolution and of the fleet with Alcidas being about to sail for Corcyra.

[81] The Peloponnesians accordingly at once set off in haste by night for home, coasting along shore; and hauling their ships across the Isthmus of Leucas, in order not to be seen doubling it, so departed. The Corcyraeans, made aware of the approach of the Athenian fleet and of the departure of the enemy, brought the Messenians from outside the walls into the town, and ordered the fleet which they had manned to sail round into the Hyllaic harbour; and while it was so doing, slew such of their enemies as they laid hands on, dispatching afterwards, as they landed them, those whom they had persuaded to go on board the ships. Next they went to the sanctuary of Hera and persuaded about fifty men to take their trial, and condemned them all to death. The mass of the suppliants who had refused to do so, on seeing what was taking place, slew each other there in the consecrated ground; while some hanged themselves upon the trees, and others destroyed themselves as they were severally able. During seven days that Eurymedon stayed with his sixty ships, the Corcyraeans were engaged in butchering those of their fellow citizens whom they regarded as their enemies: and although the crime imputed was that of attempting to put down the democracy, some were slain also for private hatred, others by their debtors because of the moneys owed to them. Death thus raged in every shape; and, as usually happens at such times, there was no length to which violence did not go; sons were killed by their fathers, and suppliants dragged from the altar or slain upon it; while some were even walled up in the temple of Dionysus and died there.

[82] So bloody was the march of the revolution, and the impression which it made was the greater as it was one of the first to occur. Later on, one may say, the whole Hellenic world was convulsed; struggles being everywhere made by the popular chiefs to bring in the Athenians, and by the oligarchs to introduce the Lacedaemonians. In peace there would have been neither the pretext nor the

wish to make such an invitation; but in war, with an alliance always at the command of either faction for the hurt of their adversaries and their own corresponding advantage, opportunities for bringing in the foreigner were never wanting to the revolutionary parties. The sufferings which revolution entailed upon the cities were many and terrible, such as have occurred and always will occur, as long as the nature of mankind remains the same; though in a severer or milder form, and varying in their symptoms, according to the variety of the particular cases. In peace and prosperity, states and individuals have better sentiments, because they do not find themselves suddenly confronted with imperious necessities; but war takes away the easy supply of daily wants, and so proves a rough master, that brings most men's characters to a level with their fortunes. Revolution thus ran its course from city to city, and the places which it arrived at last, from having heard what had been done before, carried to a still greater excess the refinement of their inventions, as manifested in the cunning of their enterprises and the atrocity of their reprisals. Words had to change their ordinary meaning and to take that which was now given them. Reckless audacity came to be considered the courage of a loyal ally; prudent hesitation, specious cowardice; moderation was held to be a cloak for unmanliness; ability to see all sides of a question, inaptness to act on any. Frantic violence became the attribute of manliness; cautious plotting, a justifiable means of self-defence. The advocate of extreme measures was always trustworthy; his opponent a man to be suspected. To succeed in a plot was to have a shrewd head, to divine a plot a still shrewder; but to try to provide against having to do either was to break up your party and to be afraid of your adversaries. In fine, to forestall an intending criminal, or to suggest the idea of a crime where it was wanting, was equally commended, until even blood became a weaker tie than party, from the superior readiness of those united by the latter to dare everything without reserve; for such associations had not in view the blessings derivable from established institutions but were formed by ambition for their overthrow; and the confidence of their members in each other rested less on any religious sanction than upon complicity in crime. The fair proposals of an adversary were met with jealous precautions by the stronger of the two, and not with a generous confidence. Revenge also was held of more account than

self-preservation. Oaths of reconciliation, being only proffered on either side to meet an immediate difficulty, only held good so long as no other weapon was at hand; but when opportunity offered, he who first ventured to seize it and to take his enemy off his guard, thought this perfidious vengeance sweeter than an open one, since, considerations of safety apart, success by treachery won him the palm of superior intelligence. Indeed it is generally the case that men are readier to call rogues clever than simpletons honest, and are as ashamed of being the second as they are proud of being the first. The cause of all these evils was the lust for power arising from greed and ambition; and from these passions proceeded the violence of parties once engaged in contention. The leaders in the cities, each provided with the fairest professions, on the one side with the cry of political equality of the people, on the other of a moderate aristocracy, sought prizes for themselves in those public interests which they pretended to cherish, and, recoiling from no means in their struggles for ascendancy, engaged in the direst excesses; in their acts of vengeance they went to even greater lengths, not stopping at what justice or the good of the state demanded, but making the party caprice of the moment their only standard, and invoking with equal readiness the condemnation of an unjust verdict or the authority of the strong arm to glut the animosities of the hour. Thus religion was in honour with neither party; but the use of fair phrases to arrive at guilty ends was in high reputation. Meanwhile the moderate part of the citizens perished between the two, either for not joining in the quarrel, or because envy would not suffer them to escape.

[83] Thus every form of iniquity took root in the Hellenic countries by reason of the troubles. The ancient simplicity into which honour so largely entered was laughed down and disappeared; and society became divided into camps in which no man trusted his fellow. To put an end to this, there was neither promise to be depended upon, nor oath that could command respect; but all parties dwelling rather in their calculation upon the hopelessness of a permanent state of things, were more intent upon self-defence than capable of confidence. In this contest the blunter wits were most successful. Apprehensive of their own deficiencies and of the cleverness of their antagonists, they feared to be worsted in debate and to be surprised by the combinations of their more versa-

tile opponents, and so at once boldly had recourse to action: while their adversaries, arrogantly thinking that they should know in time, and that it was unnecessary to secure by action what policy afforded, often fell victims to their want of precaution.

[84] Meanwhile Corcyra gave the first example of most of the crimes alluded to; of the reprisals exacted by the governed who had never experienced equitable treatment or indeed aught but insolence from their rulers—when their hour came; of the iniquitous resolves of those who desired to get rid of their accustomed poverty, and ardently coveted their neighbours' goods; and lastly, of the savage and pitiless excesses into which men who had begun the struggle, not in a class but in a party spirit, were hurried by their ungovernable passions. In the confusion into which life was now thrown in the cities, human nature, always rebelling against the law and now its master, gladly showed itself ungoverned in passion, above respect for justice, and the enemy of all superiority; since revenge would not have been set above religion, and gain above justice, had it not been for the fatal power of envy. Indeed men too often take upon themselves in the prosecution of their revenge to set the example of doing away with those general laws to which all alike can look for salvation in adversity, instead of allowing them to subsist against the day of danger when their aid may be required.

[85] While the revolutionary passions thus for the first time displayed themselves in the factions of Corcyra, Eurymedon and the Athenian fleet sailed away; after which some five hundred Corcyraean exiles who had succeeded in escaping, took some forts on the mainland, and becoming masters of the Corcyraean territory over the water, made this their base to plunder their countrymen in the island, and did so much damage as to cause a severe famine in the town. They also sent envoys to Lacedaemon and Corinth to negotiate their restoration; but meeting with no success, afterwards got together boats and mercenaries and crossed over to the island, being about six hundred in all; and burning their boats so as to have no hope except in becoming masters of the country, went up to Mount Istone, and fortifying themselves there, began to annoy those in the city and obtained command of the country.

[86] At the close of the same summer the Athenians sent twenty ships under the command of Laches, son of Melanopus, and Charoeades, son of Euphiletus, to Sicily, where the Syracusans and Leontines were at war. The Syracusans had for allies all the Dorian cities except Camarina—these had been included in the Lacedaemonian confederacy from the commencement of the war, though they had not taken any active part in it—the Leontines had Camarina and the Chalcidian cities. In Italy the Locrians were for the Syracusans, the Rhegians for their Leontine kinsmen. The allies of the Leontines now sent to Athens and appealed to their ancient alliance and to their Ionian origin, to persuade the Athenians to send them a fleet, as the Syracusans were blockading them by land and sea. The Athenians sent it upon the plea of their common descent, but in reality to prevent the exportation of Sicilian corn to Peloponnese and to test the possibility of bringing Sicily into subjection. Accordingly they established themselves at Rhegium in Italy, and from thence carried on the war in concert with their allies.

CHAPTER XI

Sixth Year of the War—Campaigns of Demosthenes in Western Greece—Ruin of Ambracia

SUMMER was now over. [87] The winter following, the plague a second time attacked the Athenians; for although it had never entirely left them, still there had been a notable abatement in its ravages. The second visit lasted no less than a year, the first having lasted two; and nothing distressed the Athenians and reduced their power more than this. No less than four thousand four hundred heavy infantry in the ranks died of it and three hundred cavalry, besides a number of the multitude that was never ascertained. At the same time took place the numerous earthquakes in Athens, Euboea, and Boeotia, particularly at Orchomenus in the last-named country.

[88] The same winter the Athenians in Sicily and the Rhegians, with thirty ships, made an expedition against the islands of Aeolus; being impossible to invade them in summer, owing to the want of water. These islands are occupied by the Liparaeans, a Cnidian colony, who live in one of them of no great size called Lipara; and from this as their headquarters cultivate the rest, Didyme, Strongyle, and Hiera. In Hiera the people in those parts believe that Hephaestus has his forge, from the quantity of flame which they see it send out by night, and of smoke by day. These islands lie

off the coast of the Sicels and Messinese, and were allies of the Syracusans. The Athenians laid waste their land, and as the inhabitants did not submit, sailed back to Rhegium. Thus the winter ended, and with it ended the fifth year of this war, of which Thucydides was the historian.

[89] The next summer the Peloponnesians and their allies set out to invade Attica under the command of Agis, son of Archidamus, and went as far as the Isthmus, but numerous earthquakes occurring, turned back again without the invasion taking place. About the same time that these earthquakes were so common, the sea at Orobiae, in Euboea, retiring from the then line of coast, returned in a huge wave and invaded a great part of the town, and retreated leaving some of it still under water; so that what was once land is now sea; such of the inhabitants perishing as could not run up to the higher ground in time. A similar inundation also occurred at Atalanta, the island off the Opuntian Locrian coast, carrying away part of the Athenian fort and wrecking one of two ships which were drawn up on the beach. At Peparethus also the sea retreated a little, without however any inundation following; and an earthquake threw down part of the wall, the town hall, and a few other buildings. The cause, in my opinion, of this phenomenon must be sought in the earthquake. At the point where its shock has been the most violent, the sea is driven back and, suddenly recoiling with redoubled force, causes the inundation. Without an earthquake I do not see how such an accident could happen.

[90] During the same summer different operations were carried on by the different belligerents in Sicily; by the Siceliots themselves against each other, and by the Athenians and their allies: I shall however confine myself to the actions in which the Athenians took part, choosing the most important. The death of the Athenian general Charoeades, killed by the Syracusans in battle, left Laches in the sole command of the fleet, which he now directed in concert with the allies against Mylae, a place belonging to the Messinese. Two Messinese battalions in garrison at Mylae laid an ambush for the party landing from the ships, but were routed with great slaughter by the Athenians and their allies, who thereupon assaulted the fortification and compelled them to surrender the Acropolis and to march with them upon Messina. This town afterwards also submitted upon the approach of the Athenians and their allies, and gave hostages and all other securities required.

[91] The same summer the Athenians sent thirty ships round Peloponnese under Demosthenes, son of Alcisthenes, and Procles, son of Theodorus, and sixty others, with two thousand heavy infantry, against Melos, under Nicias, son of Niceratus; wishing to reduce the Melians, who, although islanders, refused to be subjects of Athens or even to join her confederacy. The devastation of their land not procuring their submission, the fleet, weighing from Melos, sailed to Oropus in the territory of Graea, and landing at nightfall, the heavy infantry started at once from the ships by land for Tanagra in Boeotia, where they were met by the whole levy from Athens, agreeably to a concerted signal, under the command of Hipponicus, son of Callias, and Eurymedon, son of Thucles. They encamped, and passing that day in ravaging the Tanagraean territory, remained there for the night; and next day, after defeating those of the Tanagraeans who sailed out against them and some Thebans who had come up to help the Tanagraeans, took some arms, set up a trophy, and retired, the troops to the city and the others to the ships. Nicias with his sixty ships coasted alongshore and ravaged the Locrian seaboard, and so returned home.

[92] About this time the Lacedaemonians founded their colony of Heraclea in Trachis, their object being the following: the Malians form in all three tribes, the Paralians, the Hiereans, and the Trachinians. The last of these having suffered severely in a war with their neighbours the Oetaeans, at first intended to give themselves up to Athens; but afterwards fearing not to find in her the security that they sought, sent to Lacedaemon, having chosen Tisamenus for their ambassador. In this embassy joined also the Dorians from the mother country of the Lacedaemonians, with the same request, as they themselves also suffered from the same enemy. After hearing them, the Lacedaemonians determined to send out the colony, wishing to assist the Trachinians and Dorians, and also because they thought that the proposed town would lie conveniently for the purposes of the war against the Athenians. A fleet might be got ready there against Euboea, with the advantage of a short passage to the island; and the town would also be useful as a station on the road to Thrace. In short, everything made the Lacedaemonians eager to found the place. After first consulting the

god at Delphi and receiving a favourable answer, they sent off the colonists, Spartans, and
Perioeci, inviting also any of the rest of the
Hellenes who might wish to accompany them,
except Ionians, Achaeans, and certain other nationalities; three Lacedaemonians leading as
founders of the colony, Leon, Alcidas, and
Damagon. The settlement effected, they fortified anew the city, now called Heraclea, distant
about four miles and a half from Thermopylae
and two miles and a quarter from the sea, and
commenced building docks, closing the side
towards Thermopylae just by the pass itself,
in order that they might be easily defended.

[93] The foundation of this town, evidently
meant to annoy Euboea (the passage across to
Cenaeum in that island being a short one), at
first caused some alarm at Athens, which the
event however did nothing to justify, the town
never giving them any trouble. The reason
of this was as follows. The Thessalians, who
were sovereign in those parts, and whose territory was menaced by its foundation, were
afraid that it might prove a very powerful
neighbour, and accordingly continually harassed and made war upon the new settlers,
until they at last wore them out in spite of
their originally considerable numbers, people
flocking from all quarters to a place founded
by the Lacedaemonians, and thus thought secure of prosperity. On the other hand the Lacedaemonians themselves, in the persons of their
governors, did their full share towards ruining
its prosperity and reducing its population, as
they frightened away the greater part of the
inhabitants by governing harshly and in some
cases not fairly, and thus made it easier for
their neighbours to prevail against them.

[94] The same summer, about the same time
that the Athenians were detained at Melos,
their fellow citizens in the thirty ships cruising
round Peloponnese, after cutting off some
guards in an ambush at Ellomenus in Leucadia, subsequently went against Leucas itself
with a large armament, having been reinforced by the whole levy of the Acarnanians
except Oeniadae, and by the Zacynthians and
Cephallenians and fifteen ships from Corcyra.
While the Leucadians witnessed the devastation of their land, without and within the
isthmus upon which the town of Leucas and
the temple of Apollo stand, without making
any movement on account of the overwhelming numbers of the enemy, the Acarnanians
urged Demosthenes, the Athenian general, to
build a wall so as to cut off the town from the

continent, a measure which they were convinced would secure its capture and rid them
once and for all of a most troublesome enemy.

Demosthenes however had in the meanwhile been persuaded by the Messenians that
it was a fine opportunity for him, having so
large an army assembled, to attack the Aetolians, who were not only the enemies of Naupactus, but whose reduction would further
make it easy to gain the rest of that part of the
continent for the Athenians. The Aetolian nation, although numerous and warlike, yet
dwelt in unwalled villages scattered far apart,
and had nothing but light armour, and might,
according to the Messenians, be subdued without much difficulty before succours could arrive. The plan which they recommended was
to attack first the Apodotians, next the Ophi-
nians, and after these the Eurytanians, who are
the largest tribe in Aetolia, and speak, as is
said, a language exceedingly difficult to understand, and eat their flesh raw. These once subdued, the rest would easily come in.

[95] To this plan Demosthenes consented,
not only to please the Messenians, but also in
the belief that by adding the Aetolians to his
other continental allies he would be able, without aid from home, to march against the Boeotians by way of Ozolian Locris to Kytinium in
Doris, keeping Parnassus on his right until he
descended to the Phocians, whom he could
force to join him if their ancient friendship for
Athens did not, as he anticipated, at once decide them to do so. Arrived in Phocis he was
already upon the frontier of Boeotia. He accordingly weighed from Leucas, against the
wish of the Acarnanians, and with his whole
armament sailed along the coast to Sollium,
where he communicated to them his intention;
and upon their refusing to agree to it on account of the non-investment of Leucas, himself with the rest of the forces, the Cephallenians, the Messenians, and Zacynthians, and
three hundred Athenian marines from his own
ships (the fifteen Corcyraean vessels having
departed), started on his expedition against
the Aetolians. His base he established at Oeneon in Locris, as the Ozolian Locrians were allies of Athens and were to meet him with all
their forces in the interior. Being neighbours
of the Aetolians and armed in the same way,
it was thought that they would be of great
service upon the expedition, from their acquaintance with the localities and the warfare
of the inhabitants.

[96] After bivouacking with the army in the

precinct of Nemean Zeus, in which the poet Hesiod is said to have been killed by the people of the country, according to an oracle which had foretold that he should die in Nemea, Demosthenes set out at daybreak to invade Aetolia. The first day he took Potidania, the next Krokyle, and the third Tichium, where he halted and sent back the booty to Eupalium in Locris, having determined to pursue his conquests as far as the Ophionians, and, in the event of their refusing to submit, to return to Naupactus and make them the objects of a second expedition. Meanwhile the Aetolians had been aware of his design from the moment of its formation, and as soon as the army invaded their country came up in great force with all their tribes; even the most remote Ophionians, the Bomiensians, and Calliensians, who extend towards the Malian Gulf, being among the number.

[97] The Messenians, however, adhered to their original advice. Assuring Demosthenes that the Aetolians were an easy conquest, they urged him to push on as rapidly as possible, and to try to take the villages as fast as he came up to them, without waiting until the whole nation should be in arms against him. Led on by his advisers and trusting in his fortune, as he had met with no opposition, without waiting for his Locrian reinforcements, who were to have supplied him with the light-armed darters in which he was most deficient, he advanced and stormed Aegitium, the inhabitants flying before him and posting themselves upon the hills above the town, which stood on high ground about nine miles from the sea. Meanwhile the Aetolians had gathered to the rescue, and now attacked the Athenians and their allies, running down from the hills on every side and darting their javelins, falling back when the Athenian army advanced, and coming on as it retired; and for a long while the battle was of this character, alternate advance and retreat, in both which operations the Athenians had the worst.

[98] Still as long as their archers had arrows left and were able to use them, they held out, the light-armed Aetolians retiring before the arrows; but after the captain of the archers had been killed and his men scattered, the soldiers, wearied out with the constant repetition of the same exertions and hard pressed by the Aetolians with their javelins, at last turned and fled, and falling into pathless gullies and places that they were unacquainted with, thus perished, the Messenian Chromon, their guide,

having also unfortunately been killed. A great many were overtaken in the pursuit by the swift-footed and light-armed Aetolians, and fell beneath their javelins; the greater number however missed their road and rushed into the wood, which had no ways out, and which was soon fired and burnt round them by the enemy. Indeed the Athenian army fell victims to death in every form, and suffered all the vicissitudes of flight; the survivors escaped with difficulty to the sea and Oeneon in Locris, whence they had set out. Many of the allies were killed, and about one hundred and twenty Athenian heavy infantry, not a man less, and all in the prime of life. These were by far the best men in the city of Athens that fell during this war. Among the slain was also Procles, the colleague of Demosthenes. Meanwhile the Athenians took up their dead under truce from the Aetolians, and retired to Naupactus, and from thence went in their ships to Athens; Demosthenes staying behind in Naupactus and in the neighbourhood, being afraid to face the Athenians after the disaster.

[99] About the same time the Athenians on the coast of Sicily sailed to Locris, and in a descent which they made from the ships defeated the Locrians who came against them, and took a fort upon the river Halex.

[100] The same summer the Aetolians, who before the Athenian expedition had sent an embassy to Corinth and Lacedaemon, composed of Tolophus, an Ophionian, Boriades, an Eurytanian, and Tisander, an Apodotian, obtained that an army should be sent them against Naupactus, which had invited the Athenian invasion. The Lacedaemonians accordingly sent off towards autumn three thousand heavy infantry of the allies, five hundred of whom were from Heraclea, the newly founded city in Trachis, under the command of Eurylochus, a Spartan, accompanied by Macarius and Menedaïus, also Spartans.

[101] The army having assembled at Delphi, Eurylochus sent a herald to the Ozolian Locrians; the road to Naupactus lying through their territory, and he having besides conceived the idea of detaching them from Athens. His chief abettors in Locris were the Amphissians, who were alarmed at the hostility of the Phocians. These first gave hostages themselves, and induced the rest to do the same for fear of the invading army; first, their neighbours the Myonians, who held the most difficult of the passes, and after them the Ipnians, Messapians, Tritaeans, Chalaeans, Tolophoni-

ans, Hessians, and Oeanthians, all of whom joined in the expedition; the Olpaeans contenting themselves with giving hostages, without accompanying the invasion; and the Hyaeans refusing to do either, until the capture of Polis, one of their villages.

[102] His preparations completed, Eurylochus lodged the hostages in Kytinium, in Doris, and advanced upon Naupactus through the country of the Locrians, taking upon his way Oeneon and Eupalium, two of their towns that refused to join him. Arrived in the Naupactian territory, and having been now joined by the Aetolians, the army laid waste the land and took the suburb of the town, which was unfortified; and after this Molycrium also, a Corinthian colony subject to Athens. Meanwhile the Athenian Demosthenes, who since the affair in Aetolia had remained near Naupactus, having had notice of the army and fearing for the town, went and persuaded the Acarnanians, although not without difficulty because of his departure from Leucas, to go to the relief of Naupactus. They accordingly sent with him on board his ships a thousand heavy infantry, who threw themselves into the place and saved it; the extent of its wall and the small number of its defenders otherwise placing it in the greatest danger. Meanwhile Eurylochus and his companions, finding that this force had entered and that it was impossible to storm the town, withdrew, not to Peloponnese, but to the country once called Aeolis, and now Calydon and Pleuron, and to the places in that neighbourhood, and Proschium in Aetolia; the Ambraciots having come and urged them to combine with them in attacking Amphilochian Argos and the rest of Amphilochia and Acarnania; affirming that the conquest of these countries would bring all the continent into alliance with Lacedaemon. To this Eurylochus consented, and dismissing the Aetolians, now remained quiet with his army in those parts, until the time should come for the Ambraciots to take the field, and for him to join them before Argos.

Summer was now over. *[103]* The winter ensuing, the Athenians in Sicily with their Hellenic allies, and such of the Sicel subjects or allies of Syracuse as had revolted from her and joined their army, marched against the Sicel town Inessa, the acropolis of which was held by the Syracusans, and after attacking it without being able to take it, retired. In the retreat, the allies retreating after the Athenians were attacked by the Syracusans from the fort, and a large part of their army routed with great slaughter. After this, Laches and the Athenians from the ships made some descents in Locris, and defeating the Locrians, who came against them with Proxenus, son of Capaton, upon the river Caïcinus, took some arms and departed.

[104] The same winter the Athenians purified Delos, in compliance, it appears, with a certain oracle. It had been purified before by Pisistratus the tyrant; not indeed the whole island, but as much of it as could be seen from the temple. All of it was, however, now purified in the following way. All the sepulchres of those that had died in Delos were taken up, and for the future it was commanded that no one should be allowed either to die or to give birth to a child in the island; but that they should be carried over to Rhenea, which is so near to Delos that Polycrates, tyrant of Samos, having added Rhenea to his other island conquests during his period of naval ascendancy, dedicated it to the Delian Apollo by binding it to Delos with a chain.

The Athenians, after the purification, celebrated, for the first time, the quinquennial festival of the Delian games. Once upon a time, indeed, there was a great assemblage of the Ionians and the neighbouring islanders at Delos, who used to come to the festival, as the Ionians now do to that of Ephesus, and athletic and poetical contests took place there, and the cities brought choirs of dancers. Nothing can be clearer on this point than the following verses of Homer, taken from a hymn to Apollo:

Phoebus, where'er thou strayest, far or near,
Delos was still of all thy haunts most dear.
Thither the robed Ionians take their way
With wife and child to keep thy holiday,
Invoke thy favour on each manly game,
And dance and sing in honour of thy name.

That there was also a poetical contest in which the Ionians went to contend, again is shown by the following, taken from the same hymn. After celebrating the Delian dance of the women, he ends his song of praise with these verses, in which he also alludes to himself:

Well, may Apollo keep you all! and so,
Sweethearts, good-bye—yet tell me not I go
Out from your hearts; and if in after hours
Some other wanderer in this world of ours
Touch at your shores, and ask your maidens here
Who sings the songs the sweetest to your ear,
Think of me then, and answer with a smile,
'A blind old man of Scio's rocky isle.'

Homer thus attests that there was anciently a great assembly and festival at Delos. In later times, although the islanders and the Athenians continued to send the choirs of dancers with sacrifices, the contests and most of the ceremonies were abolished, probably through adversity, until the Athenians celebrated the games upon this occasion with the novelty of horse-races.

[105] The same winter the Ambraciots, as they had promised Eurylochus when they retained his army, marched out against Amphilochian Argos with three thousand heavy infantry, and invading the Argive territory occupied Olpae, a stronghold on a hill near the sea, which had been formerly fortified by the Acarnanians and used as the place of assizes for their nation, and which is about two miles and three-quarters from the city of Argos upon the sea-coast. Meanwhile the Acarnanians went with a part of their forces to the relief of Argos, and with the rest encamped in Amphilochia at the place called Crenae, or the Wells, to watch for Eurylochus and his Peloponnesians, and to prevent their passing through and effecting their junction with the Ambraciots; while they also sent for Demosthenes, the commander of the Aetolian expedition, to be their leader, and for the twenty Athenian ships that were cruising off Peloponnese under the command of Aristotle, son of Timocrates, and Hierophon, son of Antimnestus. On their part, the Ambraciots at Olpae sent a messenger to their own city, to beg them to come with their whole levy to their assistance, fearing that the army of Eurylochus might not be able to pass through the Acarnanians, and that they might themselves be obliged to fight single-handed, or be unable to retreat, if they wished it, without danger.

[106] Meanwhile Eurylochus and his Peloponnesians, learning that the Ambraciots at Olpae had arrived, set out from Proschium with all haste to join them, and crossing the Achelous advanced through Acarnania, which they found deserted by its population, who had gone to the relief of Argos; keeping on their right the city of the Stratians and its garrison, and on their left the rest of Acarnania. Traversing the territory of the Stratians, they advanced through Phytia, next, skirting Medeon, through Limnaea; after which they left Acarnania behind them and entered a friendly country, that of the Agraeans. From thence they reached and crossed Mount Thymaus, which belongs to the Agraeans, and descended into the Argive territory after nightfall, and passing between the city of Argos and the Acarnanian posts at Crenae, joined the Ambraciots at Olpae.

[107] Uniting here at daybreak, they sat down at the place called Metropolis, and encamped. Not long afterwards the Athenians in the twenty ships came into the Ambracian Gulf to support the Argives, with Demosthenes and two hundred Messenian heavy infantry, and sixty Athenian archers. While the fleet off Olpae blockaded the hill from the sea, the Acarnanians and a few of the Amphilochians, most of whom were kept back by force by the Ambraciots, had already arrived at Argos, and were preparing to give battle to the enemy, having chosen Demosthenes to command the whole of the allied army in concert with their own generals. Demosthenes led them near to Olpae and encamped, a great ravine separating the two armies. During five days they remained inactive; on the sixth both sides formed in order of battle. The army of the Peloponnesians was the largest and outflanked their opponents; and Demosthenes fearing that his right might be surrounded, placed in ambush in a hollow way overgrown with bushes some four hundred heavy infantry and light troops, who were to rise up at the moment of the onset behind the projecting left wing of the enemy, and to take them in the rear. When both sides were ready they joined battle; Demosthenes being on the right wing with the Messenians and a few Athenians, while the rest of the line was made up of the different divisions of the Acarnanians, and of the Amphilochian carters. The Peloponnesians and Ambraciots were drawn up pell-mell together, with the exception of the Mantineans, who were massed on the left, without however reaching to the extremity of the wing, where Eurylochus and his men confronted the Messenians and Demosthenes.

[108] The Peloponnesians were now well engaged and with their outflanking wing were upon the point of turning their enemy's right; when the Acarnanians from the ambuscade set upon them from behind, and broke them at the first attack, without their staying to resist; while the panic into which they fell caused the flight of most of their army, terrified beyond measure at seeing the division of Eurylochus and their best troops cut to pieces. Most of the work was done by Demosthenes and his Messenians, who were posted in this part of the field. Meanwhile the Ambraciots (who are the

best soldiers in those countries) and the troops upon the right wing, defeated the division opposed to them and pursued it to Argos. Returning from the pursuit, they found their main body defeated; and hard pressed by the Acarnanians, with difficulty made good their passage to Olpae, suffering heavy loss on the way, as they dashed on without discipline or order, the Mantineans excepted, who kept their ranks best of any in the army during the retreat.

The battle did not end until the evening. [109] The next day Menedaïus, who on the death of Eurylochus and Macarius had succeeded to the sole command, being at a loss after so signal a defeat how to stay and sustain a siege, cut off as he was by land and by the Athenian fleet by sea, and equally so how to retreat in safety, opened a parley with Demosthenes and the Acarnanian generals for a truce and permission to retreat, and at the same time for the recovery of the dead. The dead they gave back to him, and setting up a trophy took up their own also to the number of about three hundred. The retreat demanded they refused publicly to the army; but permission to depart without delay was secretly granted to the Mantineans and to Menedaïus and the other commanders and principal men of the Peloponnesians by Demosthenes and his Acarnanian colleagues; who desired to strip the Ambraciots and the mercenary host of foreigners of their supporters; and, above all, to discredit the Lacedaemonians and Peloponnesians with the Hellenes in those parts, as traitors and self-seekers.

While the enemy was taking up his dead and hastily burying them as he could, and those who obtained permission were secretly planning their retreat, [110] word was brought to Demosthenes and the Acarnanians that the Ambraciots from the city, in compliance with the first message from Olpae, were on the march with their whole levy through Amphilochia to join their countrymen at Olpae, knowing nothing of what had occurred. Demosthenes prepared to march with his army against them, and meanwhile sent on at once a strong division to beset the roads and occupy the strong positions. [111] In the meantime the Mantineans and others included in the agreement went out under the pretence of gathering herbs and firewood, and stole off by twos and threes, picking on the way the things which they professed to have come out for, until they had gone some distance from Olpae, when they

quickened their pace. The Ambraciots and such of the rest as had accompanied them in larger parties, seeing them going on, pushed on in their turn, and began running in order to catch them up. The Acarnanians at first thought that all alike were departing without permission, and began to pursue the Peloponnesians; and believing that they were being betrayed, even threw a dart or two at some of their generals who tried to stop them and told them that leave had been given. Eventually, however, they let pass the Mantineans and Peloponnesians, and slew only the Ambraciots, there being much dispute and difficulty in distinguishing whether a man was an Ambraciot or a Peloponnesian. The number thus slain was about two hundred; the rest escaped into the bordering territory of Agraea, and found refuge with Salynthius, the friendly king of the Agraeans.

[112] Meanwhile the Ambraciots from the city arrived at Idomene. Idomene consists of two lofty hills, the higher of which the troops sent on by Demosthenes succeeded in occupying after nightfall, unobserved by the Ambraciots, who had meanwhile ascended the smaller and bivouacked under it. After supper Demosthenes set out with the rest of the army, as soon as it was evening; himself with half his force making for the pass, and the remainder going by the Amphilochian hills. At dawn he fell upon the Ambraciots while they were still abed, ignorant of what had passed, and fully thinking that it was their own countrymen— Demosthenes having purposely put the Messenians in front with orders to address them in the Doric dialect, and thus to inspire confidence in the sentinels, who would not be able to see them as it was still night. In this way he routed their army as soon as he attacked it, slaying most of them where they were, the rest breaking away in flight over the hills. The roads, however, were already occupied, and while the Amphilochians knew their own country, the Ambraciots were ignorant of it and could not tell which way to turn, and had also heavy armour as against a light-armed enemy, and so fell into ravines and into the ambushes which had been set for them, and perished there. In their manifold efforts to escape some even turned to the sea, which was not far off, and seeing the Athenian ships coasting alongshore just while the action was going on, swam off to them, thinking it better in the panic they were in, to perish, if perish they must, by the hands of the Athenians, than by

those of the barbarous and detested Amphilochians. Of the large Ambraciot force destroyed in this manner, a few only reached the city in safety; while the Acarnanians, after stripping the dead and setting up a trophy, returned to Argos.

[*113*] The next day arrived a herald from the Ambraciots who had fled from Olpae to the Agraeans, to ask leave to take up the dead that had fallen after the first engagement, when they left the camp with the Mantineans and their companions, without, like them, having had permission to do so. At the sight of the arms of the Ambraciots from the city, the herald was astonished at their number, knowing nothing of the disaster and fancying that they were those of their own party. Some one asked him what he was so astonished at, and how many of them had been killed, fancying in his turn that this was the herald from the troops at Idomene. He replied: "About two hundred"; upon which his interrogator took him up, saying: "Why, the arms you see here are of more than a thousand." The herald replied: "Then they are not the arms of those who fought with us?" The other answered: "Yes, they are, if at least you fought at Idomene yesterday." "But we fought with no one yesterday; but the day before in the retreat." "However that may be, we fought yesterday with those who came to reinforce you from the city of the Ambraciots." When the herald heard this and knew that the reinforcement from the city had been destroyed, he broke into wailing and, stunned at the magnitude of the present evils, went away at once without having performed his errand, or again asking for the dead bodies. Indeed, this was by far the greatest disaster that befell any one Hellenic city in an equal number of days during this war; and I have not set down the number of the dead, because the amount stated seems so out of proportion to the size of the city as to be incredible. In any case I know that if the Acarnanians and Amphilochians had wished to take Ambracia as the Athenians and Demosthenes advised, they would have done so without striking a blow; as it was, they feared that if the Athenians had it they would be worse neighbours to them than the present.

[*114*] After this the Acarnanians allotted a third of the spoils to the Athenians, and divided the rest among their own different towns. The share of the Athenians was captured on the voyage home; the arms now deposited in the Attic temples are three hundred panoplies, which the Acarnanians set apart for Demosthenes, and which he brought to Athens in person, his return to his country after the Aetolian disaster being rendered less hazardous by this exploit. The Athenians in the twenty ships also went off to Naupactus. The Acarnanians and Amphilochians, after the departure of Demosthenes and the Athenians, granted the Ambraciots and Peloponnesians who had taken refuge with Salynthius and the Agraeans a free retreat from Oeniadae, to which place they had removed from the country of Salynthius, and for the future concluded with the Ambraciots a treaty and alliance for one hundred years, upon the terms following. It was to be a defensive, not an offensive alliance; the Ambraciots could not be required to march with the Acarnanians against the Peloponnesians, nor the Acarnanians with the Ambraciots against the Athenians; for the rest the Ambraciots were to give up the places and hostages that they held of the Amphilochians, and not to give help to Anactorium, which was at enmity with the Acarnanians. With this arrangement they put an end to the war. After this the Corinthians sent a garrison of their own citizens to Ambracia, composed of three hundred heavy infantry, under the command of Xenocleides, son of Euthycles, who reached their destination after a difficult journey across the continent. Such was the history of the affair of Ambracia.

[*115*] The same winter the Athenians in Sicily made a descent from their ships upon the territory of Himera, in concert with the Sicels, who had invaded its borders from the interior, and also sailed to the islands of Aeolus. Upon their return to Rhegium they found the Athenian general, Pythodorus, son of Isolochus, come to supersede Laches in the command of the fleet. The allies in Sicily had sailed to Athens and induced the Athenians to send out more vessels to their assistance, pointing out that the Syracusans who already commanded their land were making efforts to get together a navy, to avoid being any longer excluded from the sea by a few vessels. The Athenians proceeded to man forty ships to send to them, thinking that the war in Sicily would thus be the sooner ended, and also wishing to exercise their navy. One of the generals, Pythodorus, was accordingly sent out with a few ships; Sophocles, son of Sostratides, and Eurymedon, son of Thucles, being destined to follow with the main body. Meanwhile Pythodorus had taken the command of Laches' ships, and towards the end of winter sailed

against the Locrian fort, which Laches had formerly taken, and returned after being defeated in battle by the Locrians.

[*116*] In the first days of this spring, the stream of fire issued from Etna, as on former occasions, and destroyed some land of the Catanians, who live upon Mount Etna, which is the largest mountain in Sicily. Fifty years, it is said, had elapsed since the last eruption, there having been three in all since the Hellenes have inhabited Sicily. Such were the events of this winter; and with it ended the sixth year of this war, of which Thucydides was the historian.

The Fourth Book

‏⋙⋙⋙⋙⋙⋙⋙⋙⋙⋙⋙⋙⋙⋘⋘⋘⋘⋘⋘⋘⋘⋘⋘⋘⋘⋘⋘⋘‏

CHAPTER XII

Seventh Year of the War—Occupation of Pylos—
Surrender of the Spartan Army in Sphacteria

[*1*] NEXT summer, about the time of the corn's coming into ear, ten Syracusan and as many Locrian vessels sailed to Messina, in Sicily, and occupied the town upon the invitation of the inhabitants; and Messina revolted from the Athenians. The Syracusans contrived this chiefly because they saw that the place afforded an approach to Sicily, and feared that the Athenians might hereafter use it as a base for attacking them with a larger force; the Locrians because they wished to carry on hostilities from both sides of the strait and to reduce their enemies, the people of Rhegium. Meanwhile, the Locrians had invaded the Rhegian territory with all their forces, to prevent their succouring Messina, and also at the instance of some exiles from Rhegium who were with them; the long factions by which that town had been torn rendering it for the moment incapable of resistance, and thus furnishing an additional temptation to the invaders. After devastating the country the Locrian land forces retired, their ships remaining to guard Messina, while others were being manned for the same destination to carry on the war from thence.

[*2*] About the same time in the spring, before the corn was ripe, the Peloponnesians and their allies invaded Attica under Agis, the son of Archidamus, king of the Lacedaemonians, and sat down and laid waste the country. Meanwhile the Athenians sent off the forty ships which they had been preparing to Sicily, with the remaining generals Eurymedon and Sophocles; their colleague Pythodorus having already preceded them thither. These had also instructions as they sailed by to look to the Corcyraeans in the town, who were being plundered by the exiles in the mountain. To support these exiles sixty Peloponnesian vessels had lately sailed, it being thought that the famine raging in the city would make it easy for them to reduce it. Demosthenes also, who had remained without employment since his return from Acarnania, applied and obtained permission to use the fleet, if he wished it, upon the coast of Peloponnese.

[*3*] Off Laconia they heard that the Peloponnesian ships were already at Corcyra, upon which Eurymedon and Sophocles wished to hasten to the island, but Demosthenes required them first to touch at Pylos and do what was wanted there, before continuing their voyage. While they were making objections, a squall chanced to come on and carried the fleet into Pylos. Demosthenes at once urged them to fortify the place, it being for this that he had come on the voyage, and made them observe there was plenty of stone and timber on the spot, and that the place was strong by nature, and together with much of the country round unoccupied; Pylos, or Coryphasium, as the Lacedaemonians call it, being about forty-five miles distant from Sparta, and situated in the old country of the Messenians. The commanders told him that there was no lack of desert headlands in Peloponnese if he wished to put the city to expense by occupying them. He, however, thought that this place was distinguished from others of the kind by having a harbour close by; while the Messenians, the old natives of the country, speaking the same dialect as the Lacedaemonians, could do them the greatest mischief by their incursions from it, and would at the same time be a trusty garrison.

[*4*] After speaking to the captains of companies on the subject, and failing to persuade either the generals or the soldiers, he remained inactive with the rest from stress of weather;

until the soldiers themselves wanting occupation were seized with a sudden impulse to go round and fortify the place. Accordingly they set to work in earnest, and having no iron tools, picked up stones, and put them together as they happened to fit, and where mortar was needed, carried it on their backs for want of hods, stooping down to make it stay on, and clasping their hands together behind to prevent it falling off; sparing no effort to be able to complete the most vulnerable points before the arrival of the Lacedaemonians, most of the place being sufficiently strong by nature without further fortifications.

[5] Meanwhile the Lacedaemonians were celebrating a festival, and also at first made light of the news, in the idea that whenever they chose to take the field the place would be immediately evacuated by the enemy or easily taken by force; the absence of their army before Athens having also something to do with their delay. The Athenians fortified the place on the land side, and where it most required it, in six days, and leaving Demosthenes with five ships to garrison it, with the main body of the fleet hastened on their voyage to Corcyra and Sicily.

[6] As soon as the Peloponnesians in Attica heard of the occupation of Pylos, they hurried back home; the Lacedaemonians and their king Agis thinking that the matter touched them nearly. Besides having made their invasion early in the season, and while the corn was still green, most of their troops were short of provisions: the weather also was unusually bad for the time of year, and greatly distressed their army. Many reasons thus combined to hasten their departure and to make this invasion a very short one; indeed they only stayed fifteen days in Attica.

[7] About the same time the Athenian general Simonides getting together a few Athenians from the garrisons, and a number of the allies in those parts, took Eion in Thrace, a Mendaean colony and hostile to Athens, by treachery, but had no sooner done so than the Chalcidians and Bottiaeans came up and beat him out of it, with the loss of many of his soldiers.

[8] On the return of the Peloponnesians from Attica, the Spartans themselves and the nearest of the Perioeci at once set out for Pylos, the other Lacedaemonians following more slowly, as they had just come in from another campaign. Word was also sent round Peloponnese to come up as quickly as possible to Pylos;

while the sixty Peloponnesian ships were sent for from Corcyra, and being dragged by their crews across the isthmus of Leucas, passed unperceived by the Athenian squadron at Zacynthus, and reached Pylos, where the land forces had arrived before them. Before the Peloponnesian fleet sailed in, Demosthenes found time to send out unobserved two ships to inform Eurymedon and the Athenians on board the fleet at Zacynthus of the danger of Pylos and to summon them to his assistance. While the ships hastened on their voyage in obedience to the orders of Demosthenes, the Lacedaemonians prepared to assault the fort by land and sea, hoping to capture with ease a work constructed in haste, and held by a feeble garrison. Meanwhile, as they expected the Athenian ships to arrive from Zacynthus, they intended, if they failed to take the place before, to block up the entrances of the harbour to prevent their being able to anchor inside it. For the island of Sphacteria, stretching along in a line close in front of the harbour, at once makes it safe and narrows its entrances, leaving a passage for two ships on the side nearest Pylos and the Athenian fortifications, and for eight or nine on that next the rest of the mainland: for the rest, the island was entirely covered with wood, and without paths through not being inhabited, and about one mile and five furlongs in length. The inlets the Lacedaemonians meant to close with a line of ships placed close together, with their prows turned towards the sea, and, meanwhile, fearing that the enemy might make use of the island to operate against them, carried over some heavy infantry thither, stationing others along the coast. By this means the island and the continent would be alike hostile to the Athenians, as they would be unable to land on either; and the shore of Pylos itself outside the inlet towards the open sea having no harbour, and, therefore, presenting no point which they could use as a base to relieve their countrymen, they, the Lacedaemonians, without sea-fight or risk would in all probability become masters of the place, occupied as it had been on the spur of the moment, and unfurnished with provisions. This being determined, they carried over to the island the heavy infantry, drafted by lot from all the companies. Some others had crossed over before in relief parties, but these last who were left there were four hundred and twenty in number, with their Helot attendants, commanded by Epitadas, son of Molobrus.

[9] Meanwhile Demosthenes, seeing the Lacedaemonians about to attack him by sea

and land at once, himself was not idle. He drew up under the fortification and enclosed in a stockade the galleys remaining to him of those which had been left him, arming the sailors taken out of them with poor shields made most of them of osier, it being impossible to procure arms in such a desert place, and even these having been obtained from a thirty-oared Messenian privateer and a boat belonging to some Messenians who happened to have come to them. Among these Messenians were forty heavy infantry, whom he made use of with the rest. Posting most of his men, unarmed and armed, upon the best fortified and strong points of the place towards the interior, with orders to repel any attack of the land forces, he picked sixty heavy infantry and a few archers from his whole force, and with these went outside the wall down to the sea, where he thought that the enemy would most likely attempt to land. Although the ground was difficult and rocky, looking towards the open sea, the fact that this was the weakest part of the wall would, he thought, encourage their ardour, as the Athenians, confident in their naval superiority, had here paid little attention to their defences, and the enemy if he could force a landing might feel secure of taking the place. At this point, accordingly, going down to the water's edge, he posted his heavy infantry to prevent, if possible, a landing, and encouraged them in the following terms:

[10] "Soldiers and comrades in this adventure, I hope that none of you in our present strait will think to show his wit by exactly calculating all the perils that encompass us, but that you will rather hasten to close with the enemy, without staying to count the odds, seeing in this your best chance of safety. In emergencies like ours calculation is out of place; the sooner the danger is faced the better. To my mind also most of the chances are for us, if we will only stand fast and not throw away our advantages, overawed by the numbers of the enemy. One of the points in our favour is the awkwardness of the landing. This, however, only helps us if we stand our ground. If we give way it will be practicable enough, in spite of its natural difficulty, without a defender; and the enemy will instantly become more formidable from the difficulty he will have in retreating, supposing that we succeed in repulsing him, which we shall find it easier to do, while he is on board his ships, than after he has landed and meets us on equal terms. As to his numbers, these need not too much alarm

you. Large as they may be he can only engage in small detachments, from the impossibility of bringing to. Besides, the numerical superiority that we have to meet is not that of an army on land with everything else equal, but of troops on board ship, upon an element where many favourable accidents are required to act with effect. I therefore consider that his difficulties may be fairly set against our numerical deficiencies, and at the same time I charge you, as Athenians who know by experience what landing from ships on a hostile territory means, and how impossible it is to drive back an enemy determined enough to stand his ground and not to be frightened away by the surf and the terrors of the ships sailing in, to stand fast in the present emergency, beat back the enemy at the water's edge, and save yourselves and the place."

[11] Thus encouraged by Demosthenes, the Athenians felt more confident, and went down to meet the enemy, posting themselves along the edge of the sea. The Lacedaemonians now put themselves in movement and simultaneously assaulted the fortification with their land forces and with their ships, forty-three in number, under their admiral, Thrasymelidas, son of Cratesicles, a Spartan, who made his attack just where Demosthenes expected. The Athenians had thus to defend themselves on both sides, from the land and from the sea; the enemy rowing up in small detachments, the one relieving the other—it being impossible for many to bring to at once—and showing great ardour and cheering each other on, in the endeavour to force a passage and to take the fortification. He who most distinguished himself was Brasidas. Captain of a galley, and seeing that the captains and steersmen, impressed by the difficulty of the position, hung back even where a landing might have seemed possible, for fear of wrecking their vessels, he shouted out to them, that they must never allow the enemy to fortify himself in their country for the sake of saving timber, but must shiver their vessels and force a landing; and bade the allies, instead of hesitating in such a moment to sacrifice their ships for Lacedaemon in return for her many benefits, to run them boldly aground, land in one way or another, and make themselves masters of the place and its garrison.

[12] Not content with this exhortation, he forced his own steersman to run his ship ashore, and stepping on to the gangway, was endeavouring to land, when he was cut down

by the Athenians, and after receiving many wounds fainted away. Falling into the bows, his shield slipped off his arm into the sea, and being thrown ashore was picked up by the Athenians, and afterwards used for the trophy which they set up for this attack. The rest also did their best, but were not able to land, owing to the difficulty of the ground and the unflinching tenacity of the Athenians. It was a strange reversal of the order of things for Athenians to be fighting from the land, and from Laconian land too, against Lacedaemonians coming from the sea; while Lacedaemonians were trying to land from shipboard in their own country, now become hostile, to attack Athenians, although the former were chiefly famous at the time as an inland people and superior by land, the latter as a maritime people with a navy that had no equal.

[13] After continuing their attacks during that day and most of the next, the Peloponnesians desisted, and the day after sent some of their ships to Asine for timber to make engines, hoping to take by their aid, in spite of its height, the wall opposite the harbour, where the landing was easiest. At this moment the Athenian fleet from Zacynthus arrived, now numbering fifty sail, having been reinforced by some of the ships on guard at Naupactus and by four Chian vessels. Seeing the coast and the island both crowded with heavy infantry, and the hostile ships in harbour showing no signs of sailing out, at a loss where to anchor, they sailed for the moment to the desert island of Prote, not far off, where they passed the night. The next day they got under way in readiness to engage in the open sea if the enemy chose to put out to meet them, being determined in the event of his not doing so to sail in and attack him. The Lacedaemonians did not put out to sea, and having omitted to close the inlets as they had intended, remained quiet on shore, engaged in manning their ships and getting ready, in the case of any one sailing in, to fight in the harbour, which is a fairly large one.

[14] Perceiving this, the Athenians advanced against them by each inlet, and falling on the enemy's fleet, most of which was by this time afloat and in line, at once put it to flight, and giving chase as far as the short distance allowed, disabled a good many vessels, and took five, one with its crew on board; dashing in at the rest that had taken refuge on shore, and battering some that were still being manned, before they could put out, and lashing on to their own ships and towing off empty others

whose crews had fled. At this sight the Lacedaemonians, maddened by a disaster which cut off their men on the island, rushed to the rescue, and going into the sea with their heavy armour, laid hold of the ships and tried to drag them back, each man thinking that success depended on his individual exertions. Great was the *mêlée,* and quite in contradiction to the naval tactics usual to the two combatants; the Lacedaemonians in their excitement and dismay being actually engaged in a sea-fight on land, while the victorious Athenians, in their eagerness to push their success as far as possible, were carrying on a land-fight from their ships. After great exertions and numerous wounds on both sides they separated, the Lacedaemonians saving their empty ships, except those first taken; and both parties returning to their camp, the Athenians set up a trophy, gave back the dead, secured the wrecks, and at once began to cruise round and jealously watch the island, with its intercepted garrison, while the Peloponnesians on the mainland, whose contingents had now all come up, stayed where they were before Pylos.

[15] When the news of what had happened at Pylos reached Sparta, the disaster was thought so serious that the Lacedaemonians resolved that the authorities should go down to the camp, and decide on the spot what was best to be done. There, seeing that it was impossible to help their men, and not wishing to risk their being reduced by hunger or overpowered by numbers, they determined, with the consent of the Athenian generals, to conclude an armistice at Pylos and send envoys to Athens to obtain a convention, and to endeavour to get back their men as quickly as possible.

[16] The generals accepting their offers, an armistice was concluded upon the terms following:

That the Lacedaemonians should bring to Pylos and deliver up to the Athenians the ships that had fought in the late engagement, and all in Laconia that were vessels of war, and should make no attack on the fortification either by land or by sea.

That the Athenians should allow the Lacedaemonians on the mainland to send to the men in the island a certain fixed quantity of corn ready kneaded, that is to say, two quarts of barley meal, one pint of wine, and a piece of meat for each man, and half the same quantity for a servant.

That this allowance should be sent in under the eyes of the Athenians, and that no boat should sail to the island except openly.

That the Athenians should continue to guard the island the same as before, without however landing upon it, and should refrain from attacking the Peloponnesian troops either by land or by sea.

That if either party should infringe any of these terms in the slightest particular, the armistice should be at once void.

That the armistice should hold good until the return of the Lacedaemonian envoys from Athens—the Athenians sending them thither in a galley and bringing them back again—and upon the arrival of the envoys should be at an end, and the ships be restored by the Athenians in the same state as they received them.

Such were the terms of the armistice, and the ships were delivered over to the number of sixty, and the envoys sent off accordingly. Arrived at Athens they spoke as follows:

[17] "Athenians, the Lacedaemonians sent us to try to find some way of settling the affair of our men on the island, that shall be at once satisfactory to our interests, and as consistent with our dignity in our misfortune as circumstances permit. We can venture to speak at some length without any departure from the habit of our country. Men of few words where many are not wanted, we can be less brief when there is a matter of importance to be illustrated and an end to be served by its illustration. Meanwhile we beg you to take what we may say, not in a hostile spirit, nor as if we thought you ignorant and wished to lecture you, but rather as a suggestion on the best course to be taken, addressed to intelligent judges. You can now, if you choose, employ your present success to advantage, so as to keep what you have got and gain honour and reputation besides, and you can avoid the mistake of those who meet with an extraordinary piece of good fortune, and are led on by hope to grasp continually at something further, through having already succeeded without expecting it. While those who have known most vicissitudes of good and bad, have also justly least faith in their prosperity; and to teach your city and ours this lesson experience has not been wanting.

[18] "To be convinced of this you have only to look at our present misfortune. What power in Hellas stood higher than we did? and yet we are come to you, although we formerly thought ourselves more able to grant what we are now here to ask. Nevertheless, we have not been brought to this by any decay in our power, or

through having our heads turned by aggrandizement; no, our resources are what they have always been, and our error has been an error of judgment, to which all are equally liable. Accordingly, the prosperity which your city now enjoys, and the accession that it has lately received, must not make you fancy that fortune will be always with you. Indeed sensible men are prudent enough to treat their gains as precarious, just as they would also keep a clear head in adversity, and think that war, so far from staying within the limit to which a combatant may wish to confine it, will run the course that its chances prescribe; and thus, not being puffed up by confidence in military success, they are less likely to come to grief, and most ready to make peace, if they can, while their fortune lasts. This, Athenians, you have a good opportunity to do now with us, and thus to escape the possible disasters which may follow upon your refusal, and the consequent imputation of having owed to accident even your present advantages, when you might have left behind you a reputation for power and wisdom which nothing could endanger.

[19] "The Lacedaemonians accordingly invite you to make a treaty and to end the war, and offer peace and alliance and the most friendly and intimate relations in every way and on every occasion between us; and in return ask for the men on the island, thinking it better for both parties not to stand out to the end, on the chance of some favourable accident enabling the men to force their way out, or of their being compelled to succumb under the pressure of blockade. Indeed if great enmities are ever to be really settled, we think it will be, not by the system of revenge and military success, and by forcing an opponent to swear to a treaty to his disadvantage, but when the more fortunate combatant waives these his privileges, to be guided by gentler feelings, conquers his rival in generosity, and accords peace on more moderate conditions than he expected. From that moment, instead of the debt of revenge which violence must entail, his adversary owes a debt of generosity to be paid in kind, and is inclined by honour to stand to his agreement. And men oftener act in this manner towards their greatest enemies than where the quarrel is of less importance; they are also by nature as glad to give way to those who first yield to them, as they are apt to be provoked by arrogance to risks condemned by their own judgment.

[20] "To apply this to ourselves: if peace

was ever desirable for both parties, it is surely so at the present moment, before anything irremediable befall us and force us to hate you eternally, personally as well as politically, and you to miss the advantages that we now offer you. While the issue is still in doubt, and you have reputation and our friendship in prospect, and we the compromise of our misfortune before anything fatal occur, let us be reconciled, and for ourselves choose peace instead of war, and grant to the rest of the Hellenes a remission from their sufferings, for which be sure they will think they have chiefly you to thank. The war that they labour under they know not which began, but the peace that concludes it, as it depends on your decision, will by their gratitude be laid to your door. By such a decision you can become firm friends with the Lacedaemonians at their own invitation, which you do not force from them, but oblige them by accepting. And from this friendship consider the advantages that are likely to follow: when Attica and Sparta are at one, the rest of Hellas, be sure, will remain in respectful inferiority before its heads."

[21] Such were the words of the Lacedaemonians, their idea being that the Athenians, already desirous of a truce and only kept back by their opposition, would joyfully accept a peace freely offered, and give back the men. The Athenians, however, having the men on the island, thought that the treaty would be ready for them whenever they chose to make it, and grasped at something further. Foremost to encourage them in this policy was Cleon, son of Cleaenetus, a popular leader of the time and very powerful with the multitude, who persuaded them to answer as follows: First, the men in the island must surrender themselves and their arms and be brought to Athens. Next, the Lacedaemonians must restore Nisaea, Pegae, Troezen, and Achaia, all places acquired not by arms, but by the previous convention, under which they had been ceded by Athens herself at a moment of disaster, when a truce was more necessary to her than at present. This done they might take back their men, and make a truce for as long as both parties might agree.

[22] To this answer the envoys made no reply, but asked that commissioners might be chosen with whom they might confer on each point, and quietly talk the matter over and try to come to some agreement. Hereupon Cleon violently assailed them, saying that he knew from the first that they had no right intentions, and that it was clear enough now by their refusing to speak before the people, and wanting to confer in secret with a committee of two or three. No, if they meant anything honest let them say it out before all. The Lacedaemonians, however, seeing that whatever concessions they might be prepared to make in their misfortune, it was impossible for them to speak before the multitude and lose credit with their allies for a negotiation which might after all miscarry, and on the other hand, that the Athenians would never grant what they asked upon moderate terms, returned from Athens without having effected anything.

[23] Their arrival at once put an end to the armistice at Pylos, and the Lacedaemonians asked back their ships according to the convention. The Athenians, however, alleged an attack on the fort in contravention of the truce, and other grievances seemingly not worth mentioning, and refused to give them back, insisting upon the clause by which the slightest infringement made the armistice void. The Lacedaemonians, after denying the contravention and protesting against their bad faith in the matter of the ships, went away and earnestly addressed themselves to the war. Hostilities were now carried on at Pylos upon both sides with vigour. The Athenians cruised round the island all day with two ships going different ways; and by night, except on the seaward side in windy weather, anchored round it with their whole fleet, which, having been reinforced by twenty ships from Athens come to aid in the blockade, now numbered seventy sail; while the Peloponnesians remained encamped on the continent, making attacks on the fort, and on the look-out for any opportunity which might offer itself for the deliverance of their men.

[24] Meanwhile the Syracusans and their allies in Sicily had brought up to the squadron guarding Messina the reinforcement which we left them preparing, and carried on the war from thence, incited chiefly by the Locrians from hatred of the Rhegians, whose territory they had invaded with all their forces. The Syracusans also wished to try their fortune at sea, seeing that the Athenians had only a few ships actually at Rhegium, and hearing that the main fleet destined to join them was engaged in blockading the island. A naval victory, they thought, would enable them to blockade Rhegium by sea and land, and easily to reduce it; a success which would at once place their affairs upon a solid basis, the prom-

ontory of Rhegium in Italy and Messina in Sicily being so near each other that it would be impossible for the Athenians to cruise against them and command the strait. The strait in question consists of the sea between Rhegium and Messina, at the point where Sicily approaches nearest to the continent, and is the Charybdis through which the story makes Ulysses sail; and the narrowness of the passage and the strength of the current that pours in from the vast Tyrrhenian and Sicilian mains, have rightly given it a bad reputation.

[25] In this strait the Syracusans and their allies were compelled to fight, late in the day, about the passage of a boat, putting out with rather more than thirty ships against sixteen Athenian and eight Rhegian vessels. Defeated by the Athenians they hastily set off, each for himself, to their own stations at Messina and Rhegium, with the loss of one ship; night coming on before the battle was finished. After this the Locrians retired from the Rhegian territory, and the ships of the Syracusans and their allies united and came to anchor at Cape Pelorus, in the territory of Messina, where their land forces joined them. Here the Athenians and Rhegians sailed up, and seeing the ships unmanned, made an attack, in which they in their turn lost one vessel, which was caught by a grappling iron, the crew saving themselves by swimming. After this the Syracusans got on board their ships, and while they were being towed alongshore to Messina, were again attacked by the Athenians, but suddenly got out to sea and became the assailants, and caused them to lose another vessel. After thus holding their own in the voyage alongshore and in the engagement as above described, the Syracusans sailed on into the harbour of Messina.

Meanwhile the Athenians, having received warning that Camarina was about to be betrayed to the Syracusans by Archias and his party, sailed thither; and the Messinese took this opportunity to attack by sea and land with all their forces their Chalcidian neighbour, Naxos. The first day they forced the Naxians to keep their walls, and laid waste their country; the next they sailed round with their ships, and laid waste their land on the river Akesines, while their land forces menaced the city. Meanwhile the Sicels came down from the high country in great numbers, to aid against the Messinese; and the Naxians, elated at the sight, and animated by a belief that the Leontines and their other Hellenic allies were com-

ing to their support, suddenly sallied out from the town, and attacked and routed the Messinese, killing more than a thousand of them; while the remainder suffered severely in their retreat home, being attacked by the barbarians on the road, and most of them cut off. The ships put in to Messina, and afterwards dispersed for their different homes. The Leontines and their allies, with the Athenians, upon this at once turned their arms against the now weakened Messina, and attacked, the Athenians with their ships, on the side of the harbour, and the land forces on that of the town. The Messinese, however, sallying out with Demoteles and some Locrians who had been left to garrison the city after the disaster, suddenly attacked and routed most of the Leontine army, killing a great number; upon seeing which the Athenians landed from their ships, and falling on the Messinese in disorder chased them back into the town, and setting up a trophy retired to Rhegium. After this the Hellenes in Sicily continued to make war on each other by land, without the Athenians.

[26] Meanwhile the Athenians at Pylos were still besieging the Lacedaemonians in the island, the Peloponnesian forces on the continent remaining where they were. The blockade was very laborious for the Athenians from want of food and water; there was no spring except one in the citadel of Pylos itself, and that not a large one, and most of them were obliged to grub up the shingle on the sea beach and drink such water as they could find. They also suffered from want of room, being encamped in a narrow space; and as there was no anchorage for the ships, some took their meals on shore in their turn, while the others were anchored out at sea. But their greatest discouragement arose from the unexpectedly long time which it took to reduce a body of men shut up in a desert island, with only brackish water to drink, a matter which they had imagined would take them only a few days. The fact was that the Lacedaemonians had made advertisement for volunteers to carry into the island ground corn, wine, cheese, and any other food useful in a siege; high prices being offered, and freedom promised to any of the Helots who should succeed in doing so. The Helots accordingly were most forward to engage in this risky traffic, putting off from this or that part of Peloponnese, and running in by night on the seaward side of the island. They were best pleased, however, when they could catch a wind to carry them in. It was more

easy to elude the look-out of the galleys, when it blew from the seaward, as it became impossible for them to anchor round the island; while the Helots had their boats rated at their value in money, and ran them ashore, without caring how they landed, being sure to find the soldiers waiting for them at the landing-places. But all who risked it in fair weather were taken. Divers also swam in under water from the harbour, dragging by a cord in skins poppy-seed mixed with honey, and bruised linseed; these at first escaped notice, but afterwards a look-out was kept for them. In short, both sides tried every possible contrivance, the one to throw in provisions, and the other to prevent their introduction.

[27] At Athens, meanwhile, the news that the army was in great distress, and that corn found its way in to the men in the island, caused no small perplexity; and the Athenians began to fear that winter might come on and find them still engaged in the blockade. They saw that the convoying of provisions round Peloponnese would be then impossible. The country offered no resources in itself, and even in summer they could not send round enough. The blockade of a place without harbours could no longer be kept up; and the men would either escape by the siege being abandoned, or would watch for bad weather and sail out in the boats that brought in their corn. What caused still more alarm was the attitude of the Lacedaemonians, who must, it was thought by the Athenians, feel themselves on strong ground not to send them any more envoys; and they began to repent having rejected the treaty. Cleon, perceiving the disfavour with which he was regarded for having stood in the way of the convention, now said that their informants did not speak the truth; and upon the messengers recommending them, if they did not believe them, to send some commissioners to see, Cleon himself and Theagenes were chosen by the Athenians as commissioners. Aware that he would now be obliged either to say what had been already said by the men whom he was slandering, or be proved a liar if he said the contrary, he told the Athenians, whom he saw to be not altogether disinclined for a fresh expedition, that instead of sending commissioners and wasting their time and opportunities, if they believed what was told them, they ought to sail against the men. And pointing at Nicias, son of Niceratus, then general, whom he hated, he tauntingly said that it would be easy, if they had men for gen-

erals, to sail with a force and take those in the island, and that if he had himself been in command, he would have done it.

[28] Nicias, seeing the Athenians murmuring against Cleon for not sailing now if it seemed to him so easy, and further seeing himself the object of attack, told him that for all that the generals cared, he might take what force he chose and make the attempt. At first Cleon fancied that this resignation was merely a figure of speech, and was ready to go, but finding that it was seriously meant, he drew back, and said that Nicias, not he, was general, being now frightened, and having never supposed that Nicias would go so far as to retire in his favour. Nicias, however, repeated his offer, and resigned the command against Pylos, and called the Athenians to witness that he did so. And as the multitude is wont to do, the more Cleon shrank from the expedition and tried to back out of what he had said, the more they encouraged Nicias to hand over his command, and clamoured at Cleon to go. At last, not knowing how to get out of his words, he undertook the expedition, and came forward and said that he was not afraid of the Lacedaemonians, but would sail without taking any one from the city with him, except the Lemnians and Imbrians that were at Athens, with some targeteers that had come up from Aenus, and four hundred archers from other quarters. With these and the soldiers at Pylos, he would within twenty days either bring the Lacedaemonians alive, or kill them on the spot. The Athenians could not help laughing at his fatuity, while sensible men comforted themselves with the reflection that they must gain in either circumstance; either they would be rid of Cleon, which they rather hoped, or if disappointed in this expectation, would reduce the Lacedaemonians.

[29] After he had settled everything in the assembly, and the Athenians had voted him the command of the expedition, he chose as his colleague Demosthenes, one of the generals at Pylos, and pushed forward the preparations for his voyage. His choice fell upon Demosthenes because he heard that he was contemplating a descent on the island; the soldiers distressed by the difficulties of the position, and rather besieged than besiegers, being eager to fight it out, while the firing of the island had increased the confidence of the general. He had been at first afraid, because the island having never been inhabited was almost entirely covered with wood and without paths, thinking this

to be in the enemy's favour, as he might land with a large force, and yet might suffer loss by an attack from an unseen position. The mistakes and forces of the enemy the wood would in a great measure conceal from him, while every blunder of his own troops would be at once detected, and they would be thus able to fall upon him unexpectedly just where they pleased, the attack being always in their power. If, on the other hand, he should force them to engage in the thicket, the smaller number who knew the country would, he thought, have the advantage over the larger who were ignorant of it, while his own army might be cut off imperceptibly, in spite of its numbers, as the men would not be able to see where to succour each other.

[30] The Aetolian disaster, which had been mainly caused by the wood, had not a little to do with these reflections. Meanwhile, one of the soldiers who were compelled by want of room to land on the extremities of the island and take their dinners, with outposts fixed to prevent a surprise, set fire to a little of the wood without meaning to do so; and as it came on to blow soon afterwards, almost the whole was consumed before they were aware of it. Demosthenes was now able for the first time to see how numerous the Lacedaemonians really were, having up to this moment been under the impression that they took in provisions for a smaller number; he also saw that the Athenians thought success important and were anxious about it, and that it was now easier to land on the island, and accordingly got ready for the attempt, sent for troops from the allies in the neighbourhood, and pushed forward his other preparations. At this moment Cleon arrived at Pylos with the troops which he had asked for, having sent on word to say that he was coming. The first step taken by the two generals after their meeting was to send a herald to the camp on the mainland, to ask if they were disposed to avoid all risk and to order the men on the island to surrender themselves and their arms, to be kept in gentle custody until some general convention should be concluded.

[31] On the rejection of this proposition the generals let one day pass, and the next, embarking all their heavy infantry on board a few ships, put out by night, and a little before dawn landed on both sides of the island from the open sea and from the harbour, being about eight hundred strong, and advanced with a run against the first post in the island.

The enemy had distributed his force as follows: In this first post there were about thirty heavy infantry; the centre and most level part, where the water was, was held by the main body, and by Epitadas their commander; while a small party guarded the very end of the island, towards Pylos, which was precipitous on the sea-side and very difficult to attack from the land, and where there was also a sort of old fort of stones rudely put together, which they thought might be useful to them, in case they should be forced to retreat. Such was their disposition.

[32] The advanced post thus attacked by the Athenians was at once put to the sword, the men being scarcely out of bed and still arming, the landing having taken them by surprise, as they fancied the ships were only sailing as usual to their stations for the night. As soon as day broke, the rest of the army landed, that is to say, all the crews of rather more than seventy ships, except the lowest rank of oars, with the arms they carried, eight hundred archers, and as many targeteers, the Messenian reinforcements, and all the other troops on duty round Pylos, except the garrison on the fort. The tactics of Demosthenes had divided them into companies of two hundred, more or less, and made them occupy the highest points in order to paralyse the enemy by surrounding him on every side and thus leaving him without any tangible adversary, exposed to the cross-fire of their host; plied by those in his rear if he attacked in front, and by those on one flank if he moved against those on the other. In short, wherever he went he would have the assailants behind him, and these light-armed assailants, the most awkward of all; arrows, darts, stones, and slings making them formidable at a distance, and there being no means of getting at them at close quarters, as they could conquer flying, and the moment their pursuer turned they were upon him. Such was the idea that inspired Demosthenes in his conception of the descent, and presided over its execution.

[33] Meanwhile the main body of the troops in the island (that under Epitadas), seeing their outpost cut off and an army advancing against them, serried their ranks and pressed forward to close with the Athenian heavy infantry in front of them, the light troops being upon their flanks and rear. However, they were not able to engage or to profit by their superior skill, the light troops keeping them in check on either side with their missiles, and

the heavy infantry remaining stationary instead of advancing to meet them; and although they routed the light troops wherever they ran up and approached too closely, yet they retreated fighting, being lightly equipped, and easily getting the start in their flight, from the difficult and rugged nature of the ground, in an island hitherto desert, over which the Lacedaemonians could not pursue them with their heavy armour.

[34] After this skirmishing had lasted some little while, the Lacedaemonians became unable to dash out with the same rapidity as before upon the points attacked, and the light troops, finding that they now fought with less vigour, became more confident. They could see with their own eyes that they were many times more numerous than the enemy; they were now more familiar with his aspect and found him less terrible, the result not having justified the apprehensions which they had suffered, when they first landed in slavish dismay at the idea of attacking Lacedaemonians; and accordingly their fear changing to disdain, they now rushed all together with loud shouts upon them, and pelted them with stones, darts, and arrows, whichever came first to hand. The shouting accompanying their onset confounded the Lacedaemonians, unaccustomed to this mode of fighting; dust rose from the newly burnt wood, and it was impossible to see in front of one with the arrows and stones flying through clouds of dust from the hands of numerous assailants. The Lacedaemonians had now to sustain a rude conflict; their caps would not keep out the arrows, darts had broken off in the armour of the wounded, while they themselves were helpless for offence, being prevented from using their eyes to see what was before them, and unable to hear the words of command for the hubbub raised by the enemy; danger encompassed them on every side, and there was no hope of any means of defence or safety.

[35] At last, after many had been already wounded in the confined space in which they were fighting, they formed in close order and retired on the fort at the end of the island, which was not far off, and to their friends who held it. The moment they gave way, the light troops became bolder and pressed upon them, shouting louder than ever, and killed as many as they came up with in their retreat, but most of the Lacedaemonians made good their escape to the fort, and with the garrison in it ranged themselves all along its whole extent to repulse the enemy wherever it was assailable. The Athenians pursuing, unable to surround and hem them in, owing to the strength of the ground, attacked them in front and tried to storm the position. For a long time, indeed for most of the day, both sides held out against all the torments of the battle, thirst, and sun, the one endeavouring to drive the enemy from the high ground, the other to maintain himself upon it, it being now more easy for the Lacedaemonians to defend themselves than before, as they could not be surrounded on the flanks.

[36] The struggle began to seem endless, when the commander of the Messenians came to Cleon and Demosthenes, and told them that they were losing their labour: but if they would give him some archers and light troops to go round on the enemy's rear by a way he would undertake to find, he thought he could force the approach. Upon receiving what he asked for, he started from a point out of sight in order not to be seen by the enemy, and creeping on wherever the precipices of the island permitted, and where the Lacedaemonians, trusting to the strength of the ground, kept no guard, succeeded after the greatest difficulty in getting round without their seeing him, and suddenly appeared on the high ground in their rear, to the dismay of the surprised enemy and the still greater joy of his expectant friends. The Lacedaemonians thus placed between two fires, and in the same dilemma, to compare small things with great, as at Thermopylae, where the defenders were cut off through the Persians getting round by the path, being now attacked in front and behind, began to give way, and overcome by the odds against them and exhausted from want of food, retreated.

The Athenians were already masters of the approaches [37] when Cleon and Demosthenes perceiving that, if the enemy gave way a single step further, they would be destroyed by their soldiery, put a stop to the battle and held their men back; wishing to take the Lacedaemonians alive to Athens, and hoping that their stubbornness might relax on hearing the offer of terms, and that they might surrender and yield to the present overwhelming danger. Proclamation was accordingly made, to know if they would surrender themselves and their arms to the Athenians to be dealt with at their discretion.

[38] The Lacedaemonians hearing this offer, most of them lowered their shields and waved their hands to show that they accepted it. Hostilities now ceased, and a parley was

held between Cleon and Demosthenes and Styphon, son of Pharax, on the other side; since Epitadas, the first of the previous commanders, had been killed, and Hippagretas, the next in command, left for dead among the slain, though still alive, and thus the command had devolved upon Styphon according to the law, in case of anything happening to his superiors. Styphon and his companions said they wished to send a herald to the Lacedaemonians on the mainland, to know what they were to do. The Athenians would not let any of them go, but themselves called for heralds from the mainland, and after questions had been carried backwards and forwards two or three times, the last man that passed over from the Lacedaemonians on the continent brought this message: "The Lacedaemonians bid you to decide for yourselves so long as you do nothing dishonourable"; upon which after consulting together they surrendered themselves and their arms. The Athenians, after guarding them that day and night, the next morning set up a trophy in the island, and got ready to sail, giving their prisoners in batches to be guarded by the captains of the galleys; and the Lacedaemonians sent a herald and took up their dead. The number of the killed and prisoners taken in the island was as follows: four hundred and twenty heavy infantry had passed over; three hundred all but eight were taken alive to Athens; the rest were killed. About a hundred and twenty of the prisoners were Spartans. The Athenian loss was small, the battle not having been fought at close quarters.

[39] The blockade in all, counting from the fight at sea to the battle in the island, had lasted seventy-two days. For twenty of these, during the absence of the envoys sent to treat for peace, the men had provisions given them, for the rest they were fed by the smugglers. Corn and other victual was found in the island; the commander Epitadas having kept the men upon half rations. The Athenians and Peloponnesians now each withdrew their forces from Pylos, and went home, and crazy as Cleon's promise was, he fulfilled it, by bringing the men to Athens within the twenty days as he had pledged himself to do.

[40] Nothing that happened in the war surprised the Hellenes so much as this. It was the opinion that no force or famine could make the Lacedaemonians give up their arms, but that they would fight on as they could, and die with them in their hands: indeed people could scarcely believe that those who had surren-dered were of the same stuff as the fallen; and an Athenian ally, who some time after insultingly asked one of the prisoners from the island if those that had fallen were men of honour, received for answer that the *atraktos*—that is, the arrow—would be worth a great deal if it could tell men of honour from the rest; in allusion to the fact that the killed were those whom the stones and the arrows happened to hit.

[41] Upon the arrival of the men the Athenians determined to keep them in prison until the peace, and if the Peloponnesians invaded their country in the interval, to bring them out and put them to death. Meanwhile the defence of Pylos was not forgotten; the Messenians from Naupactus sent to their old country, to which Pylos formerly belonged, some of the likeliest of their number, and began a series of incursions into Laconia, which their common dialect rendered most destructive. The Lacedaemonians, hitherto without experience of incursions or a warfare of the kind, finding the Helots deserting, and fearing the march of revolution in their country, began to be seriously uneasy, and in spite of their unwillingness to betray this to the Athenians began to send envoys to Athens, and tried to recover Pylos and the prisoners. The Athenians, however, kept grasping at more, and dismissed envoy after envoy without their having effected anything. Such was the history of the affair of Pylos.

CHAPTER XIII

Seventh and Eighth Years of the War—End of Corcyraean Revolution—Peace of Gela—Capture of Nisaea

[42] THE same summer, directly after these events, the Athenians made an expedition against the territory of Corinth with eighty ships and two thousand Athenian heavy infantry, and two hundred cavalry on board horse transports, accompanied by the Milesians, Andrians, and Carystians from the allies, under the command of Nicias, son of Niceratus, with two colleagues. Putting out to sea they made land at daybreak between Chersonese and Rheitus, at the beach of the country underneath the Solygian hill, upon which the Dorians in old times established themselves and carried on war against the Aeolian inhabitants of Corinth, and where a village now stands called Solygia. The beach where the fleet came to is about a mile and a half from the

village, seven miles from Corinth, and two and a quarter from the Isthmus. The Corinthians had heard from Argos of the coming of the Athenian armament, and had all come up to the Isthmus long before, with the exception of those who lived beyond it, and also of five hundred who were away in garrison in Ambracia and Leucadia; and they were there in full force watching for the Athenians to land. These last, however, gave them the slip by coming in the dark; and being informed by signals of the fact, the Corinthians left half their number at Cenchreae, in case the Athenians should go against Crommyon, and marched in all haste to the rescue.

[43] Battus, one of the two generals present at the action, went with a company to defend the village of Solygia, which was unfortified; Lycophron remaining to give battle with the rest. The Corinthians first attacked the right wing of the Athenians, which had just landed in front of Chersonese, and afterwards the rest of the army. The battle was an obstinate one, and fought throughout hand to hand. The right wing of the Athenians and Carystians, who had been placed at the end of the line, received and with some difficulty repulsed the Corinthians, who thereupon retreated to a wall upon the rising ground behind, and throwing down the stones upon them, came on again singing the paean, and being received by the Athenians, were again engaged at close quarters. At this moment a Corinthian company having come to the relief of the left wing, routed and pursued the Athenian right to the sea, whence they were in their turn driven back by the Athenians and Carystians from the ships. Meanwhile the rest of the army on either side fought on tenaciously, especially the right wing of the Corinthians, where Lycophron sustained the attack of the Athenian left, which it was feared might attempt the village of Solygia.

[44] After holding on for a long while without either giving way, the Athenians aided by their horse, of which the enemy had none, at length routed the Corinthians, who retired to the hill and, halting, remained quiet there, without coming down again. It was in this rout of the right wing that they had the most killed, Lycophron their general being among the number. The rest of the army, broken and put to flight in this way without being seriously pursued or hurried, retired to the high ground and there took up its position. The Athenians, finding that the enemy no longer

offered to engage them, stripped his dead and took up their own and immediately set up a trophy. Meanwhile, the half of the Corinthians left at Cenchreae to guard against the Athenians sailing on Crommyon, although unable to see the battle for Mount Oneion, found out what was going on by the dust, and hurried up to the rescue; as did also the older Corinthians from the town, upon discovering what had occurred. The Athenians seeing them all coming against them, and thinking that they were reinforcements arriving from the neighbouring Peloponnesians, withdrew in haste to their ships with their spoils and their own dead, except two that they left behind, not being able to find them, and going on board crossed over to the islands opposite, and from thence sent a herald, and took up under truce the bodies which they had left behind. Two hundred and twelve Corinthians fell in the battle, and rather less than fifty Athenians.

[45] Weighing from the islands, the Athenians sailed the same day to Crommyon in the Corinthian territory, about thirteen miles from the city, and coming to anchor laid waste the country, and passed the night there. The next day, after first coasting along to the territory of Epidaurus and making a descent there, they came to Methana between Epidaurus and Troezen, and drew a wall across and fortified the isthmus of the peninsula, and left a post there from which incursions were henceforth made upon the country of Troezen, Haliae, and Epidaurus. After walling off this spot, the fleet sailed off home.

[46] While these events were going on, Eurymedon and Sophocles had put to sea with the Athenian fleet from Pylos on their way to Sicily and, arriving at Corcyra, joined the townsmen in an expedition against the party established on Mount Istone, who had crossed over, as I have mentioned, after the revolution, and become masters of the country, to the great hurt of the inhabitants. Their stronghold having been taken by an attack, the garrison took refuge in a body upon some high ground and there capitulated, agreeing to give up their mercenary auxiliaries, lay down their arms, and commit themselves to the discretion of the Athenian people. The generals carried them across under truce to the island of Ptychia, to be kept in custody until they could be sent to Athens, upon the understanding that, if any were caught running away, all would lose the benefit of the treaty. Meanwhile the leaders of the Corcyraean commons, afraid that the Athe-

nians might spare the lives of the prisoners, had recourse to the following stratagem. They gained over some few men on the island by secretly sending friends with instructions to provide them with a boat, and to tell them, as if for their own sakes, that they had best escape as quickly as possible, as the Athenian generals were going to give them up to the Corcyraean people.

[47] These representations succeeding, it was so arranged that the men were caught sailing out in the boat that was provided, and the treaty became void accordingly, and the whole body were given up to the Corcyraeans. For this result the Athenian generals were in a great measure responsible; their evident disinclination to sail for Sicily, and thus to leave to others the honour of conducting the men to Athens, encouraged the intriguers in their design and seemed to affirm the truth of their representations. The prisoners thus handed over were shut up by the Corcyraeans in a large building, and afterwards taken out by twenties and led past two lines of heavy infantry, one on each side, being bound together, and beaten and stabbed by the men in the lines whenever any saw pass a personal enemy; while men carrying whips went by their side and hastened on the road those that walked too slowly.

[48] As many as sixty men were taken out and killed in this way without the knowledge of their friends in the building, who fancied they were merely being moved from one prison to another. At last, however, someone opened their eyes to the truth, upon which they called upon the Athenians to kill them themselves, if such was their pleasure, and refused any longer to go out of the building, and said they would do all they could to prevent any one coming in. The Corcyraeans, not liking themselves to force a passage by the doors, got up on the top of the building, and breaking through the roof, threw down the tiles and let fly arrows at them, from which the prisoners sheltered themselves as well as they could. Most of their number, meanwhile, were engaged in dispatching themselves by thrusting into their throats the arrows shot by the enemy, and hanging themselves with the cords taken from some beds that happened to be there, and with strips made from their clothing; adopting, in short, every possible means of self-destruction, and also falling victims to the missiles of their enemies on the roof. Night came on while these horrors were enacting, and

most of it had passed before they were concluded. When it was day the Corcyraeans threw them in layers upon wagons and carried them out of the city. All the women taken in the stronghold were sold as slaves. In this way the Corcyraeans of the mountain were destroyed by the commons; and so after terrible excesses the party strife came to an end, at least as far as the period of this war is concerned, for of one party there was practically nothing left. Meanwhile the Athenians sailed off to Sicily, their primary destination, and carried on the war with their allies there.

[49] At the close of the summer, the Athenians at Naupactus and the Acarnanians made an expedition against Anactorium, the Corinthian town lying at the mouth of the Ambracian Gulf, and took it by treachery; and the Acarnanians themselves, sending settlers from all parts of Acarnania, occupied the place.

Summer was now over. [50] During the winter ensuing, Aristides, son of Archippus, one of the commanders of the Athenian ships sent to collect money from the allies, arrested at Eion, on the Strymon, Artaphernes, a Persian, on his way from the King to Lacedaemon. He was conducted to Athens, where the Athenians got his dispatches translated from the Assyrian character and read them. With numerous references to other subjects, they in substance told the Lacedaemonians that the King did not know what they wanted, as of the many ambassadors they had sent him no two ever told the same story; if however they were prepared to speak plainly they might send him some envoys with this Persian. The Athenians afterwards sent back Artaphernes in a galley to Ephesus, and ambassadors with him, who heard there of the death of King Artaxerxes, son of Xerxes, which took place about that time, and so returned home.

[51] The same winter the Chians pulled down their new wall at the command of the Athenians, who suspected them of meditating an insurrection, after first however obtaining pledges from the Athenians, and security as far as this was possible for their continuing to treat them as before. Thus the winter ended, and with it ended the seventh year of this war of which Thucydides is the historian.

[52] In the first days of the next summer there was an eclipse of the sun at the time of new moon, and in the early part of the same month an earthquake. Meanwhile, the Mitylenian and other Lesbian exiles set out, for the most part from the continent, with mercen-

aries hired in Peloponnese, and others levied on the spot, and took Rhoeteum, but restored it without injury on the receipt of two thousand Phocaean staters. After this they marched against Antandrus and took the town by treachery, their plan being to free Antandrus and the rest of the Actaean towns, formerly owned by Mitylene but now held by the Athenians. Once fortified there, they would have every facility for ship-building from the vicinity of Ida and the consequent abundance of timber, and plenty of other supplies, and might from this base easily ravage Lesbos, which was not far off, and make themselves masters of the Aeolian towns on the continent.

While these were the schemes of the exiles, [53] the Athenians in the same summer made an expedition with sixty ships, two thousand heavy infantry, a few cavalry, and some allied troops from Miletus and other parts, against Cythera, under the command of Nicias, son of Niceratus, Nicostratus, son of Diotrephes, and Autocles, son of Tolmaeus. Cythera is an island lying off Laconia, opposite Malea; the inhabitants are Lacedaemonians of the class of the Perioeci; and an officer called the Judge of Cythera went over to the place annually from Sparta. A garrison of heavy infantry was also regularly sent there, and great attention paid to the island, as it was the landing-place for the merchantmen from Egypt and Libya, and at the same time secured Laconia from the attacks of privateers from the sea, at the only point where it is assailable, as the whole coast rises abruptly towards the Sicilian and Cretan seas.

[54] Coming to land here with their armament, the Athenians with ten ships and two thousand Milesian heavy infantry took the town of Scandea, on the sea; and with the rest of their forces landing on the side of the island looking towards Malea, went against the lower town of Cythera, where they found all the inhabitants encamped. A battle ensuing, the Cytherians held their ground for some little while, and then turned and fled into the upper town, where they soon afterwards capitulated to Nicias and his colleagues, agreeing to leave their fate to the decision of the Athenians, their lives only being safe. A correspondence had previously been going on between Nicias and certain of the inhabitants, which caused the surrender to be effected more speedily, and upon terms more advantageous, present and future, for the Cytherians; who would otherwise have been expelled by the Athenians on account of their being Lacedaemonians and their island being so near to Laconia. After the capitulation, the Athenians occupied the town of Scandea near the harbour, and appointing a garrison for Cythera, sailed to Asine, Helus, and most of the places on the sea, and making descents and passing the night on shore at such spots as were convenient, continued ravaging the country for about seven days.

[55] The Lacedaemonians seeing the Athenians masters of Cythera, and expecting descents of the kind upon their coasts, nowhere opposed them in force, but sent garrisons here and there through the country, consisting of as many heavy infantry as the points menaced seemed to require, and generally stood very much upon the defensive. After the severe and unexpected blow that had befallen them in the island, the occupation of Pylos and Cythera, and the apparition on every side of a war whose rapidity defied precaution, they lived in constant fear of internal revolution, and now took the unusual step of raising four hundred horse and a force of archers, and became more timid than ever in military matters, finding themselves involved in a maritime struggle, which their organization had never contemplated, and that against Athenians, with whom an enterprise unattempted was always looked upon as a success sacrificed. Besides this, their late numerous reverses of fortune, coming close one upon another without any reason, had thoroughly unnerved them, and they were always afraid of a second disaster like that on the island, and thus scarcely dared to take the field, but fancied that they could not stir without a blunder, for being new to the experience of adversity they had lost all confidence in themselves.

[56] Accordingly they now allowed the Athenians to ravage their seaboard, without making any movement, the garrisons in whose neighbourhood the descents were made always thinking their numbers insufficient, and sharing the general feeling. A single garrison which ventured to resist, near Cotyrta and Aphrodisia, struck terror by its charge into the scattered mob of light troops, but retreated, upon being received by the heavy infantry, with the loss of a few men and some arms, for which the Athenians set up a trophy, and then sailed off to Cythera. From thence they sailed round to Epidaurus Limera, ravaged part of the country, and so came to Thyrea in the Cynurian territory, upon the Argive and Laconian border. This district had been given by its

Lacedaemonian owners to the expelled Aeginetans to inhabit, in return for their good offices at the time of the earthquake and the rising of the Helots; and also because, although subjects of Athens, they had always sided with Lacedaemon.

[57] While the Athenians were still at sea, the Aeginetans evacuated a fort which they were building upon the coast, and retreated into the upper town where they lived, rather more than a mile from the sea. One of the Lacedaemonian district garrisons which was helping them in the work, refused to enter here with them at their entreaty, thinking it dangerous to shut themselves up within the wall, and retiring to the high ground remained quiet, not considering themselves a match for the enemy. Meanwhile the Athenians landed, and instantly advanced with all their forces and took Thyrea. The town they burnt, pillaging what was in it; the Aeginetans who were not slain in action they took with them to Athens, with Tantalus, son of Patrocles, their Lacedaemonian commander, who had been wounded and taken prisoner. They also took with them a few men from Cythera whom they thought it safest to remove. These the Athenians determined to lodge in the islands: the rest of the Cytherians were to retain their lands and pay four talents tribute; the Aeginetans captured were to be all put to death, on account of the old inveterate feud; and Tantalus to share the imprisonment of the Lacedaemonians taken on the island.

[58] The same summer, the inhabitants of Camarina and Gela in Sicily first made an armistice with each other, after which embassies from all the other Sicilian cities assembled at Gela to try to bring about a pacification. After many expressions of opinion on one side and the other, according to the griefs and pretensions of the different parties complaining, Hermocrates, son of Hermon, a Syracusan, the most influential man among them, addressed the following words to the assembly:

[59] "If I now address you, Sicilians, it is not because my city is the least in Sicily or the greatest sufferer by the war, but in order to state publicly what appears to me to be the best policy for the whole island. That war is an evil is a proposition so familiar to every one that it would be tedious to develop it. No one is forced to engage in it by ignorance, or kept out of it by fear, if he fancies there is anything to be gained by it. To the former the gain appears greater than the danger, while the latter would rather stand the risk than put up with any immediate sacrifice. But if both should happen to have chosen the wrong moment for acting in this way, advice to make peace would not be unserviceable; and this, if we did but see it, is just what we stand most in need of at the present juncture.

"I suppose that no one will dispute that we went to war at first in order to serve our own several interests, that we are now, in view of the same interests, debating how we can make peace; and that if we separate without having as we think our rights, we shall go to war again. [60] And yet, as men of sense, we ought to see that our separate interests are not alone at stake in the present congress: there is also the question whether we have still time to save Sicily, the whole of which in my opinion is menaced by Athenian ambition; and we ought to find in the name of that people more imperious arguments for peace than any which I can advance, when we see the first power in Hellas watching our mistakes with the few ships that she has at present in our waters, and under the fair name of alliance speciously seeking to turn to account the natural hostility that exists between us. If we go to war, and call in to help us a people that are ready enough to carry their arms even where they are not invited; and if we injure ourselves at our own expense, and at the same time serve as the pioneers of their dominion, we may expect, when they see us worn out, that they will one day come with a larger armament, and seek to bring all of us into subjection.

[61] "And yet as sensible men, if we call in allies and court danger, it should be in order to enrich our different countries with new acquisitions, and not to ruin what they possess already; and we should understand that the intestine discords which are so fatal to communities generally, will be equally so to Sicily, if we, its inhabitants, absorbed in our local quarrels, neglect the common enemy. These considerations should reconcile individual with individual, and city with city, and unite us in a common effort to save the whole of Sicily. Nor should any one imagine that the Dorians only are enemies of Athens, while the Chalcidian race is secured by its Ionian blood; the attack in question is not inspired by hatred of one of two nationalities, but by a desire for the good things in Sicily, the common property of us all. This is proved by the Athenian reception of the Chalcidian invitation: an ally who has never given them any assistance what-

ever, at once receives from them almost more than the treaty entitles him to. That the Athenians should cherish this ambition and practise this policy is very excusable; and I do not blame those who wish to rule, but those who are over-ready to serve. It is just as much in men's nature to rule those who submit to them, as it is to resist those who molest them; one is not less invariable than the other. Meanwhile all who see these dangers and refuse to provide for them properly, or who have come here without having made up their minds that our first duty is to unite to get rid of the common peril, are mistaken. The quickest way to be rid of it is to make peace with each other; since the Athenians menace us not from their own country, but from that of those who invited them here. In this way instead of war issuing in war, peace quietly ends our quarrels; and the guests who come hither under fair pretences for bad ends, will have good reason for going away without having attained them.

[62] "So far as regards the Athenians, such are the great advantages proved inherent in a wise policy. Independently of this, in the face of the universal consent that peace is the first of blessings, how can we refuse to make it amongst ourselves; or do you not think that the good which you have, and the ills that you complain of, would be better preserved and cured by quiet than by war; that peace has its honours and splendours of a less perilous kind, not to mention the numerous other blessings that one might dilate on, with the not less numerous miseries of war? These considerations should teach you not to disregard my words, but rather to look in them every one for his own safety. If there be any here who feels certain either by right or might to effect his object, let not this surprise be to him too severe a disappointment. Let him remember that many before now have tried to chastise a wrongdoer, and failing to punish their enemy have not even saved themselves; while many who have trusted in force to gain an advantage, instead of gaining anything more, have been doomed to lose what they had. Vengeance is not necessarily successful because wrong has been done, or strength sure because it is confident; but the incalculable element in the future exercises the widest influence, and is the most treacherous, and yet in fact the most useful of all things, as it frightens us all equally, and thus makes us consider before attacking each other.

[63] "Let us therefore now allow the undefined fear of this unknown future, and the

immediate terror of the Athenians' presence, to produce their natural impression, and let us consider any failure to carry out the programmes that we may each have sketched out for ourselves as sufficiently accounted for by these obstacles, and send away the intruder from the country; and if everlasting peace be impossible between us, let us at all events make a treaty for as long a term as possible, and put off our private differences to another day. In fine, let us recognize that the adoption of my advice will leave us each citizens of a free state, and as such arbiters of our own destiny, able to return good or bad offices with equal effect; while its rejection will make us dependent on others, and thus not only impotent to repel an insult, but on the most favourable supposition, friends to our direst enemies, and at feud with our natural friends.

[64] "For myself, though, as I said at first, the representative of a great city, and able to think less of defending myself than of attacking others, I am prepared to concede something in prevision of these dangers. I am not inclined to ruin myself for the sake of hurting my enemies, or so blinded by animosity as to think myself equally master of my own plans and of fortune which I cannot command; but I am ready to give up anything in reason. I call upon the rest of you to imitate my conduct of your own free will, without being forced to do so by the enemy. There is no disgrace in connections giving way to one another, a Dorian to a Dorian, or a Chalcidian to his brethren; above and beyond this we are neighbours, live in the same country, are girt by the same sea, and go by the same name of Sicilians. We shall go to war again, I suppose, when the time comes, and again make peace among ourselves by means of future congresses; but the foreign invader, if we are wise, will always find us united against him, since the hurt of one is the danger of all; and we shall never, in future, invite into the island either allies or mediators. By so acting we shall at the present moment do for Sicily a double service, ridding her at once of the Athenians, and of civil war, and in future shall live in freedom at home, and be less menaced from abroad."

[65] Such were the words of Hermocrates. The Sicilians took his advice, and came to an understanding among themselves to end the war, each keeping what they had—the Camarinaeans taking Morgantina at a price fixed to be paid to the Syracusans—and the allies of the Athenians called the officers in command, and

told them that they were going to make peace and that they would be included in the treaty. The generals assenting, the peace was concluded, and the Athenian fleet afterwards sailed away from Sicily. Upon their arrival at Athens, the Athenians banished Pythodorus and Sophocles, and fined Eurymedon for having taken bribes to depart when they might have subdued Sicily. So thoroughly had the present prosperity persuaded the citizens that nothing could withstand them, and that they could achieve what was possible and impracticable alike, with means ample or inadequate it mattered not. The secret of this was their general extraordinary success, which made them confuse their strength with their hopes.

[66] The same summer the Megarians in the city, pressed by the hostilities of the Athenians, who invaded their country twice every year with all their forces, and harassed by the incursions of their own exiles at Pegae, who had been expelled in a revolution by the popular party, began to ask each other whether it would not be better to receive back their exiles, and free the town from one of its two scourges. The friends of the emigrants, perceiving the agitation, now more openly than before demanded the adoption of this proposition; and the leaders of the commons, seeing that the sufferings of the times had tired out the constancy of their supporters, entered in their alarm into correspondence with the Athenian generals, Hippocrates, son of Ariphron, and Demosthenes, son of Alcisthenes, and resolved to betray the town, thinking this less dangerous to themselves than the return of the party which they had banished. It was accordingly arranged that the Athenians should first take the long walls extending for nearly a mile from the city to the port of Nisaea, to prevent the Peloponnesians coming to the rescue from that place, where they formed the sole garrison to secure the fidelity of Megara; and that after this the attempt should be made to put into their hands the upper town, which it was thought would then come over with less difficulty.

[67] The Athenians, after plans had been arranged between themselves and their correspondents both as to words and actions, sailed by night to Minoa, the island off Megara, with six hundred heavy infantry under the command of Hippocrates, and took post in a quarry not far off, out of which bricks used to be taken for the walls; while Demosthenes, the other commander, with a detachment of Plataean light troops and another of Peripoli, placed himself in ambush in the precinct of Enyalius, which was still nearer. No one knew of it, except those whose business it was to know that night. A little before daybreak, the traitors in Megara began to act. Every night for a long time back, under pretence of marauding, in order to have a means of opening the gates, they had been used, with the consent of the officer in command, to carry by night a sculling boat upon a cart along the ditch to the sea, and so to sail out, bringing it back again before day upon the cart, and taking it within the wall through the gates, in order, as they pretended, to baffle the Athenian blockade at Minoa, there being no boat to be seen in the harbour. On the present occasion the cart was already at the gates, which had been opened in the usual way for the boat, when the Athenians, with whom this had been concerted, saw it, and ran at the top of their speed from the ambush in order to reach the gates before they were shut again, and while the cart was still there to prevent their being closed; their Megarian accomplices at the same moment killing the guard at the gates. The first to run in was Demosthenes with his Plataeans and Peripoli, just where the trophy now stands; and he was no sooner within the gates than the Plataeans engaged and defeated the nearest party of Peloponnesians who had taken the alarm and come to the rescue, and secured the gates for the approaching Athenian heavy infantry.

[68] After this, each of the Athenians as fast as they entered went against the wall. A few of the Peloponnesian garrison stood their ground at first, and tried to repel the assault, and some of them were killed; but the main body took fright and fled; the night attack and the sight of the Megarian traitors in arms against them making them think that all Megara had gone over to the enemy. It so happened also that the Athenian herald of his own idea called out and invited any of the Megarians that wished, to join the Athenian ranks; and this was no sooner heard by the garrison than they gave way, and, convinced that they were the victims of a concerted attack, took refuge in Nisaea. By daybreak, the walls being now taken and the Megarians in the city in great agitation, the persons who had negotiated with the Athenians, supported by the rest of the popular party which was privy to the plot, said that they ought to open the gates and march out to battle. It had been concerted between them that the Athenians should rush

in, the moment that the gates were opened, while the conspirators were to be distinguished from the rest by being anointed with oil, and so to avoid being hurt. They could open the gates with more security, as four thousand Athenian heavy infantry from Eleusis, and six hundred horse, had marched all night, according to agreement, and were now close at hand. The conspirators were all ready anointed and at their posts by the gates, when one of their accomplices denounced the plot to the opposite party, who gathered together and came in a body, and roundly said that they must not march out—a thing they had never yet ventured on even when in greater force than at present—or wantonly compromise the safety of the town, and that if what they said was not attended to, the battle would have to be fought in Megara. For the rest, they gave no signs of their knowledge of the intrigue, but stoutly maintained that their advice was the best, and meanwhile kept close by and watched the gates, making it impossible for the conspirators to effect their purpose.

[69] The Athenian generals seeing that some obstacle had arisen, and that the capture of the town by force was no longer practicable, at once proceeded to invest Nisaea, thinking that, if they could take it before relief arrived, the surrender of Megara would soon follow. Iron, stone-masons, and everything else required quickly coming up from Athens, the Athenians started from the wall which they occupied, and from this point built a cross wall looking towards Megara down to the sea on either side of Nisaea; the ditch and the walls being divided among the army, stones and bricks taken from the suburb, and the fruit-trees and timber cut down to make a palisade wherever this seemed necessary; the houses also in the suburb with the addition of battlements sometimes entering into the fortification. The whole of this day the work continued, and by the afternoon of the next the wall was all but completed, when the garrison in Nisaea, alarmed by the absolute want of provisions, which they used to take in for the day from the upper town, not anticipating any speedy relief from the Peloponnesians, and supposing Megara to be hostile, capitulated to the Athenians on condition that they should give up their arms, and should each be ransomed for a stipulated sum; their Lacedaemonian commander, and any others of his countrymen in the place, being left to the discretion of the Athenians. On these conditions they surrendered and came out, and the Athenians broke down the long walls at their point of junction with Megara, took possession of Nisaea, and went on with their other preparations.

[70] Just at this time the Lacedaemonian Brasidas, son of Tellis, happened to be in the neighbourhood of Sicyon and Corinth, getting ready an army for Thrace. As soon as he heard of the capture of the walls, fearing for the Peloponnesians in Nisaea and the safety of Megara, he sent to the Boeotians to meet him as quickly as possible at Tripodiscus, a village so called of the Megarid, under Mount Geraneia, and went himself, with two thousand seven hundred Corinthian heavy infantry, four hundred Phliasians, six hundred Sicyonians, and such troops of his own as he had already levied, expecting to find Nisaea not yet taken. Hearing of its fall (he had marched out by night to Tripodiscus), he took three hundred picked men from the army, without waiting till his coming should be known, and came up to Megara unobserved by the Athenians, who were down by the sea, ostensibly, and really if possible, to attempt Nisaea, but above all to get into Megara and secure the town. He accordingly invited the townspeople to admit his party, saying that he had hopes of recovering Nisaea.

[71] However, one of the Megarian factions feared that he might expel them and restore the exiles; the other that the commons, apprehensive of this very danger, might set upon them, and the city be thus destroyed by a battle within its gates under the eyes of the ambushed Athenians. He was accordingly refused admittance, both parties electing to remain quiet and await the event; each expecting a battle between the Athenians and the relieving army, and thinking it safer to see their friends victorious before declaring in their favour.

Unable to carry his point, Brasidas went back to the rest of the army. [72] At daybreak the Boeotians joined him. Having determined to relieve Megara, whose danger they considered their own, even before hearing from Brasidas, they were already in full force at Plataea, when his messenger arrived to add spurs to their resolution; and they at once sent on to him two thousand two hundred heavy infantry, and six hundred horse, returning home with the main body. The whole army thus assembled numbered six thousand heavy infantry. The Athenian heavy infantry were drawn up by Nisaea and the sea; but the light troops being scattered over the plain were attacked by the Boeotian horse and driven to the sea, being taken entirely by surprise, as on previous occasions no relief had ever come to the Megarians from any quarter. Here the Boeotians were in their turn charged and engaged by the Athenian horse, and a cavalry action ensued which lasted a long time, and in which both parties claimed the victory. The Athenians killed and stripped the leader of the Boeotian horse and some few of his comrades who had charged right up to Nisaea, and remaining masters of the bodies gave them back under truce, and set up a trophy; but regarding the action as a whole the forces separated without either side having gained a decisive advantage, the Boeotians returning to their army and the Athenians to Nisaea.

[73] After this Brasidas and the army came nearer to the sea and to Megara, and taking up a convenient position, remained quiet in order of battle, expecting to be attacked by the Athenians and knowing that the Megarians were waiting to see which would be the victor. This attitude seemed to present two advantages. Without taking the offensive or willingly provoking the hazards of a battle, they openly showed their readiness to fight, and thus without bearing the burden of the day would fairly reap its honours; while at the same time they effectually served their interests at Megara. For if they had failed to show themselves they would not have had a chance, but would have certainly been considered vanquished, and have lost the town. As it was, the Athenians might possibly not be inclined to accept their challenge, and their object would be attained without fighting. And so it turned out. The Athenians formed outside the long walls and, the enemy not attacking, there remained motionless; their generals having decided that the risk was too unequal. In fact most of their objects had been already attained; and they would have to begin a battle against superior numbers, and if victorious could only gain Megara, while a defeat would destroy the flower of their heavy soldiery. For the enemy it was different; as even the states actually represented in his army risked each only a part of its entire force, he might well be more audacious. Accordingly, after waiting for some time without either side attacking, the Athenians withdrew to Nisaea, and the Peloponnesians after them to the point from which they had set out. The friends of the Megarian exiles now threw aside their hesitation, and opened the gates to Brasidas and the commanders from the different states—looking upon him as the victor and upon the Athenians as having declined the battle—and receiving them into the town proceeded to discuss matters with them; the party in correspondence with the Athenians being paralysed by the turn things had taken.

[74] Afterwards Brasidas let the allies go home, and himself went back to Corinth, to prepare for his expedition to Thrace, his original destination. The Athenians also returning home, the Megarians in the city most implicated in the Athenian negotiation, knowing that they had been detected, presently disappeared; while the rest conferred with the friends of the exiles, and restored the party at Pegae, after binding them under solemn oaths to take no vengeance for the past, and only to consult the real interests of the town. However, as soon as they were in office, they held a review of the heavy infantry, and separating the battalions, picked out about a hundred of their enemies, and of those who were thought to be most involved in the correspondence with the Athenians, brought them before the people, and compelling the vote to be given openly, had them condemned and executed, and established a close oligarchy in the town—a revolution which lasted a very long while, although effected by a very few partisans.

CHAPTER XIV

Eighth and Ninth Years of the War—Invasion of Boeotia—Fall of Amphipolis—Brilliant Successes of Brasidas

[75] THE same summer the Mitylenians were about to fortify Antandrus, as they had intended, when Demodocus and Aristides, the commanders of the Athenian squadron engaged in levying subsidies, heard on the Hellespont of what was being done to the place (Lamachus their colleague having sailed with ten ships into the Pontus) and conceived fears of its becoming a second Anaia—the place in which the Samian exiles had established themselves to annoy Samos, helping the Peloponnesians by sending pilots to their navy, and keeping the city in agitation and receiving all its outlaws. They accordingly got together a force from the allies and set sail, defeated in battle the troops that met them from Antandrus, and retook the place. Not long after, Lamachus, who had sailed into the Pontus, lost his ships at anchor in the river Calex, in the territory of Heraclea, rain having fallen in the interior and the flood coming suddenly down

upon them; and himself and his troops passed by land through the Bithynian Thracians on the Asiatic side, and arrived at Chalcedon, the Megarian colony at the mouth of the Pontus.

[76] The same summer the Athenian general, Demosthenes, arrived at Naupactus with forty ships immediately after the return from the Megarid. Hippocrates and himself had had overtures made to them by certain men in the cities in Boeotia, who wished to change the constitution and introduce a democracy as at Athens; Ptoeodorus, a Theban exile, being the chief mover in this intrigue. The seaport town of Siphae, in the bay of Crisae, in the Thespian territory, was to be betrayed to them by one party; Chaeronea (a dependency of what was formerly called the Minyan, now the Boeotian, Orchomenus) to be put into their hands by another from that town, whose exiles were very active in the business, hiring men in Peloponnese. Some Phocians also were in the plot, Chaeronea being the frontier town of Boeotia and close to Phanotis in Phocia. Meanwhile the Athenians were to seize Delium, the sanctuary of Apollo, in the territory of Tanagra looking towards Euboea; and all these events were to take place simultaneously upon a day appointed, in order that the Boeotians might be unable to unite to oppose them at Delium, being everywhere detained by disturbances at home. Should the enterprise succeed, and Delium be fortified, its authors confidently expected that even if no revolution should immediately follow in Boeotia, yet with these places in their hands, and the country being harassed by incursions, and a refuge in each instance near for the partisans engaged in them, things would not remain as they were, but that the rebels being supported by the Athenians and the forces of the oligarchs divided, it would be possible after a while to settle matters according to their wishes.

[77] Such was the plot in contemplation. Hippocrates with a force raised at home awaited the proper moment to take the field against the Boeotians; while he sent on Demosthenes with the forty ships above mentioned to Naupactus, to raise in those parts an army of Acarnanians and of the other allies, and sail and receive Siphae from the conspirators; a day having been agreed on for the simultaneous execution of both these operations. Demosthenes on his arrival found Oeniadae already compelled by the united Acarnanians to join the Athenian confederacy, and himself raising all the allies in those countries marched against

and subdued Salynthius and the Agraeans; after which he devoted himself to the preparations necessary to enable him to be at Siphae by the time appointed.

[78] About the same time in the summer, Brasidas set out on his march for the Thracian places with seventeen hundred heavy infantry, and arriving at Heraclea in Trachis, from thence sent on a messenger to his friends at Pharsalus, to ask them to conduct himself and his army through the country. Accordingly there came to Melitia in Achaia Panaerus, Dorus, Hippolochidas, Torylaus, and Strophacus, the Chalcidian *proxenus,* under whose escort he resumed his march, being accompanied also by other Thessalians, among whom was Niconidas from Larissa, a friend of Perdiccas. It was never very easy to traverse Thessaly without an escort; and throughout all Hellas for an armed force to pass without leave through a neighbour's country was a delicate step to take. Besides this the Thessalian people had always sympathized with the Athenians. Indeed if instead of the customary close oligarchy there had been a constitutional government in Thessaly, he would never have been able to proceed; since even as it was, he was met on his march at the river Enipeus by certain of the opposite party who forbade his further progress, and complained of his making the attempt without the consent of the nation. To this his escort answered that they had no intention of taking him through against their will; they were only friends in attendance on an unexpected visitor. Brasidas himself added that he came as a friend to Thessaly and its inhabitants, his arms not being directed against them but against the Athenians, with whom he was at war, and that although he knew of no quarrel between the Thessalians and Lacedaemonians to prevent the two nations having access to each other's territory, he neither would nor could proceed against their wishes; he could only beg them not to stop him. With this answer they went away, and he took the advice of his escort, and pushed on without halting, before a greater force might gather to prevent him. Thus in the day that he set out from Melitia he performed the whole distance to Pharsalus, and encamped on the river Apidanus; and so to Phacium, and from thence to Perrhaebia. Here his Thessalian escort went back, and the Perrhaebians, who are subjects of Thessaly, set him down at Dium in the dominions of Perdiccas, a Macedonian town under Mount Olympus, looking towards Thessaly.

[79] In this way Brasidas hurried through Thessaly before any one could be got ready to stop him, and reached Perdiccas and Chalcidice. The departure of the army from Peloponnese had been procured by the Thracian towns in revolt against Athens and by Perdiccas, alarmed at the successes of the Athenians. The Chalcidians thought that they would be the first objects of an Athenian expedition, not that the neighbouring towns which had not yet revolted did not also secretly join in the invitation; and Perdiccas also had his apprehensions on account of his old quarrels with the Athenians, although not openly at war with them, and above all wished to reduce Arrhabaeus, king of the Lyncestians. It had been less difficult for them to get an army to leave Peloponnese, because of the ill fortune of the Lacedaemonians at the present moment. *[80]* The attacks of the Athenians upon Peloponnese, and in particular upon Laconia, might, it was hoped, be diverted most effectually by annoying them in return, and by sending an army to their allies, especially as they were willing to maintain it and asked for it to aid them in revolting. The Lacedaemonians were also glad to have an excuse for sending some of the Helots out of the country, for fear that the present aspect of affairs and the occupation of Pylos might encourage them to move. Indeed fear of their numbers and obstinacy even persuaded the Lacedaemonians to the action which I shall now relate, their policy at all times having been governed by the necessity of taking precautions against them. The Helots were invited by a proclamation to pick out those of their number who claimed to have most distinguished themselves against the enemy, in order that they might receive their freedom; the object being to test them, as it was thought that the first to claim their freedom would be the most high-spirited and the most apt to rebel. As many as two thousand were selected accordingly, who crowned themselves and went round the temples, rejoicing in their new freedom. The Spartans, however, soon afterwards did away with them, and no one ever knew how each of them perished. The Spartans now therefore gladly sent seven hundred as heavy infantry with Brasidas, who recruited the rest of his force by means of money in Peloponnese.

[81] Brasidas himself was sent out by the Lacedaemonians mainly at his own desire, although the Chalcidians also were eager to have a man so thorough as he had shown himself whenever there was anything to be done

at Sparta, and whose after-service abroad proved of the utmost use to his country. At the present moment his just and moderate conduct towards the towns generally succeeded in procuring their revolt, besides the places which he managed to take by treachery; and thus when the Lacedaemonians desired to treat, as they ultimately did, they had places to offer in exchange, and the burden of war meanwhile shifted from Peloponnese. Later on in the war, after the events in Sicily, the present valour and conduct of Brasidas, known by experience to some, by hearsay to others, was what mainly created in the allies of Athens a feeling for the Lacedaemonians. He was the first who went out and showed himself so good a man at all points as to leave behind him the conviction that the rest were like him.

[82] Meanwhile his arrival in the Thracian country no sooner became known to the Athenians than they declared war against Perdiccas, whom they regarded as the author of the expedition, and kept a closer watch on their allies in that quarter.

[83] Upon the arrival of Brasidas and his army, Perdiccas immediately started with them and with his own forces against Arrhabaeus, son of Bromerus, king of the Lyncestian Macedonians, his neighbour, with whom he had a quarrel and whom he wished to subdue. However, when he arrived with his army and Brasidas at the pass leading into Lyncus, Brasidas told him that before commencing hostilities he wished to go and try to persuade Arrhabaeus to become the ally of Lacedaemon, this latter having already made overtures intimating his willingness to make Brasidas arbitrator between them, and the Chalcidian envoys accompanying him having warned him not to remove the apprehensions of Perdiccas, in order to ensure his greater zeal in their cause. Besides, the envoys of Perdiccas had talked at Lacedaemon about his bringing many of the places round him into alliance with them; and thus Brasidas thought he might take a larger view of the question of Arrhabaeus. Perdiccas however retorted that he had not brought him with him to arbitrate in their quarrel, but to put down the enemies whom he might point out to him; and that while he, Perdiccas, maintained half his army it was a breach of faith for Brasidas to parley with Arrhabaeus. Nevertheless Brasidas disregarded the wishes of Perdiccas and held the parley in spite of him, and suffered himself to be persuaded to lead off the army without invading the country of Arrha-

baeus; after which Perdiccas, holding that faith had not been kept with him, contributed only a third instead of half of the support of the army.

[84] The same summer, without loss of time, Brasidas marched with the Chalcidians against Acanthus, a colony of the Andrians, a little before vintage. The inhabitants were divided into two parties on the question of receiving him; those who had joined the Chalcidians in inviting him, and the popular party. However, fear for their fruit, which was still out, enabled Brasidas to persuade the multitude to admit him alone, and to hear what he had to say before making a decision; and he was admitted accordingly and appeared before the people, and not being a bad speaker for a Lacedaemonian, addressed them as follows:

[85] "Acanthians, the Lacedaemonians have sent out me and my army to make good the reason that we gave for the war when we began it, viz., that we were going to war with the Athenians in order to free Hellas. Our delay in coming has been caused by mistaken expectations as to the war at home, which led us to hope, by our own unassisted efforts and without your risking anything, to effect the speedy downfall of the Athenians; and you must not blame us for this, as we are now come the moment that we were able, prepared with your aid to do our best to subdue them. Meanwhile I am astonished at finding your gates shut against me, and at not meeting with a better welcome. We Lacedaemonians thought of you as allies eager to have us, to whom we should come in spirit even before we were with you in body; and in this expectation undertook all the risks of a march of many days through a strange country, so far did our zeal carry us. It will be a terrible thing if after this you have other intentions, and mean to stand in the way of your own and Hellenic freedom. It is not merely that you oppose me yourselves; but wherever I may go people will be less inclined to join me, on the score that you, to whom I first came—an important town like Acanthus, and prudent men like the Acanthians—refused to admit me. I shall have nothing to prove that the reason which I advance is the true one; it will be said either that there is something unfair in the freedom which I offer, or that I am here in insufficient force and unable to protect you against an attack from Athens. Yet when I went with the army which I now have to the relief of Nisaea, the Athenians did not venture to engage me al-

though in greater force than I; and it is not likely they will ever send across sea against you an army as numerous as they had at Nisaea. [86] And for myself, I have come here not to hurt but to free the Hellenes, witness the solemn oaths by which I have bound my government that the allies that I may bring over shall be independent; and besides my object in coming is not by force or fraud to obtain your alliance, but to offer you mine to help you against your Athenian masters. I protest, therefore, against any suspicions of my intentions after the guarantees which I offer, and equally so against doubts of my ability to protect you, and I invite you to join me without hesitation.

"Some of you may hang back because they have private enemies, and fear that I may put the city into the hands of a party: none need be more tranquil than they. I am not come here to help this party or that; and I do not consider that I should be bringing you freedom in any real sense, if I should disregard your constitution, and enslave the many to the few or the few to the many. This would be heavier than a foreign yoke; and we Lacedaemonians, instead of being thanked for our pains, should get neither honour nor glory, but, contrariwise, reproaches. The charges which strengthen our hands in the war against the Athenians would on our own showing be merited by ourselves, and more hateful in us than in those who make no pretensions to honesty; as it is more disgraceful for persons of character to take what they covet by fair-seeming fraud than by open force; the one aggression having for its justification the might which fortune gives, the other being simply a piece of clever roguery. [87] A matter which concerns us thus nearly we naturally look to most jealously; and over and above the oaths that I have mentioned, what stronger assurance can you have, when you see that our words, compared with the actual facts, produce the necessary conviction that it is our interest to act as we say?

"If to these considerations of mine you put in the plea of inability, and claim that your friendly feeling should save you from being hurt by your refusal; if you say that freedom, in your opinion, is not without its dangers, and that it is right to offer it to those who can accept it, but not to force it on any against their will, then I shall take the gods and heroes of your country to witness that I came for your good and was rejected, and shall do my best to compel you by laying waste your land. I shall do so without scruple, being justified by the necessity which constrains me, first, to prevent the Lacedaemonians from being damaged by you, their friends, in the event of your non-adhesion, through the moneys that you pay to the Athenians; and secondly, to prevent the Hellenes from being hindered by you in shaking off their servitude. Otherwise indeed we should have no right to act as we propose; except in the name of some public interest, what call should we Lacedaemonians have to free those who do not wish it? Empire we do not aspire to: it is what we are labouring to put down; and we should wrong the greater number if we allowed you to stand in the way of the independence that we offer to all. Endeavour, therefore, to decide wisely, and strive to begin the work of liberation for the Hellenes, and lay up for yourselves endless renown, while you escape private loss, and cover your commonwealth with glory."

[88] Such were the words of Brasidas. The Acanthians, after much had been said on both sides of the question, gave their votes in secret, and the majority, influenced by the seductive arguments of Brasidas and by fear for their fruit, decided to revolt from Athens; not however admitting the army until they had taken his personal security for the oaths sworn by his government before they sent him out, assuring the independence of the allies whom he might bring over. Not long after, Stagirus, a colony of the Andrians, followed their example and revolted.

Such were the events of this summer. [89] It was in the first days of the winter following that the places in Boeotia were to be put into the hands of the Athenian generals, Hippocrates and Demosthenes, the latter of whom was to go with his ships to Siphae, the former to Delium. A mistake, however, was made in the days on which they were each to start; and Demosthenes, sailing first to Siphae, with the Acarnanians and many of the allies from those parts on board, failed to effect anything, through the plot having been betrayed by Nicomachus, a Phocian from Phanotis, who told the Lacedaemonians, and they the Boeotians. Succours accordingly flocked in from all parts of Boeotia, Hippocrates not being yet there to make his diversion, and Siphae and Chaeronea were promptly secured, and the conspirators, informed of the mistake, did not venture on any movement in the towns.

[90] Meanwhile Hippocrates made a levy in mass of the citizens, resident aliens, and for-eigners in Athens, and arrived at his destination after the Boeotians had already come back from Siphae, and encamping his army began to fortify Delium, the sanctuary of Apollo, in the following manner. A trench was dug all round the temple and the consecrated ground, and the earth thrown up from the excavation was made to do duty as a wall, in which stakes were also planted, the vines round the sanctuary being cut down and thrown in, together with stones and bricks pulled down from the houses near; every means, in short, being used to run up the rampart. Wooden towers were also erected where they were wanted, and where there was no part of the temple buildings left standing, as on the side where the gallery once existing had fallen in. The work was begun on the third day after leaving home, and continued during the fourth, and till dinner-time on the fifth, when most of it being now finished the army removed from Delium about a mile and a quarter on its way home. From this point most of the light troops went straight on, while the heavy infantry halted and remained where they were; Hippocrates having stayed behind at Delium to arrange the posts, and to give directions for the completion of such part of the outworks as had been left unfinished.

[91] During the days thus employed the Boeotians were mustering at Tanagra, and by the time that they had come in from all the towns, found the Athenians already on their way home. The rest of the eleven Boeotarchs were against giving battle, as the enemy was no longer in Boeotia, the Athenians being just over the Oropian border, when they halted; but Pagondas, son of Aeolidas, one of the Boeotarchs of Thebes (Arianthides, son of Lysimachidas, being the other), and then commander-in-chief, thought it best to hazard a battle. He accordingly called the men to him, company after company, to prevent their all leaving their arms at once, and urged them to attack the Athenians, and stand the issue of a battle, speaking as follows:

[92] "Boeotians, the idea that we ought not to give battle to the Athenians, unless we came up with them in Boeotia, is one which should never have entered into the head of any of us, your generals. It was to annoy Boeotia that they crossed the frontier and built a fort in our country; and they are therefore, I imagine, our enemies wherever we may come up with them, and from wheresoever they may have come to act as enemies do. And if any one has taken up

with the idea in question for reasons of safety, it is high time for him to change his mind. The party attacked, whose own country is in danger, can scarcely discuss what is prudent with the calmness of men who are in full enjoyment of what they have got, and are thinking of attacking a neighbour in order to get more. It is your national habit, in your country or out of it, to oppose the same resistance to a foreign invader; and when that invader is Athenian, and lives upon your frontier besides, it is doubly imperative to do so. As between neighbours generally, freedom means simply a determination to hold one's own; and with neighbours like these, who are trying to enslave near and far alike, there is nothing for it but to fight it out to the last. Look at the condition of the Euboeans and of most of the rest of Hellas, and be convinced that others have to fight with their neighbours for this frontier or that, but that for us conquest means one frontier for the whole country, about which no dispute can be made, for they will simply come and take by force what we have. So much more have we to fear from this neighbour than from another. Besides, people who, like the Athenians in the present instance, are tempted by pride of strength to attack their neighbours, usually march most confidently against those who keep still, and only defend themselves in their own country, but think twice before they grapple with those who meet them outside their frontier and strike the first blow if opportunity offers. The Athenians have shown us this themselves; the defeat which we inflicted upon them at Coronea, at the time when our quarrels had allowed them to occupy the country, has given great security to Boeotia until the present day. Remembering this, the old must equal their ancient exploits, and the young, the sons of the heroes of that time, must endeavour not to disgrace their native valour; and trusting in the help of the god whose temple has been sacrilegiously fortified, and in the victims which in our sacrifices have proved propitious, we must march against the enemy, and teach him that he must go and get what he wants by attacking someone who will not resist him, but that men whose glory it is to be always ready to give battle for the liberty of their own country, and never unjustly to enslave that of others, will not let him go without a struggle."

[93] By these arguments Pagondas persuaded the Boeotians to attack the Athenians, and quickly breaking up his camp led his army forward, it being now late in the day. On nearing the enemy, he halted in a position where a hill intervening prevented the two armies from seeing each other, and then formed and prepared for action. Meanwhile Hippocrates at Delium, informed of the approach of the Boeotians, sent orders to his troops to throw themselves into line, and himself joined them not long afterwards, leaving about three hundred horse behind him at Delium, at once to guard the place in case of attack, and to watch their opportunity and fall upon the Boeotians during the battle. The Boeotians placed a detachment to deal with these, and when everything was arranged to their satisfaction appeared over the hill, and halted in the order which they had determined on, to the number of seven thousand heavy infantry, more than ten thousand light troops, one thousand horse, and five hundred targeteers. On their right were the Thebans and those of their province, in the centre the Haliartians, Coronaeans, Copaeans, and the other people around the lake, and on the left the Thespians, Tanagraeans, and Orchomenians, the cavalry and the light troops being at the extremity of each wing. The Thebans formed twenty-five shields deep, the rest as they pleased. Such was the strength and disposition of the Boeotian army.

[94] On the side of the Athenians, the heavy infantry throughout the whole army formed eight deep, being in numbers equal to the enemy, with the cavalry upon the two wings. Light troops regularly armed there were none in the army, nor had there ever been any at Athens. Those who had joined in the invasion, though many times more numerous than those of the enemy, had mostly followed unarmed, as part of the levy in mass of the citizens and foreigners at Athens, and having started first on their way home were not present in any number. The armies being now in line and upon the point of engaging, Hippocrates, the general, passed along the Athenian ranks, and encouraged them as follows:

[95] "Athenians, I shall only say a few words to you, but brave men require no more, and they are addressed more to your understanding than to your courage. None of you must fancy that we are going out of our way to run this risk in the country of another. Fought in their territory the battle will be for ours: if we conquer, the Peloponnesians will never invade your country without the Boeotian horse, and in one battle you will win Boeotia and in a manner free Attica. Advance to meet them then like citizens of a country in

which you all glory as the first in Hellas, and like sons of the fathers who beat them at Oenophyta with Myronides and thus gained possession of Boeotia."

[96] Hippocrates had got half through the army with his exhortation, when the Boeotians, after a few more hasty words from Pagondas, struck up the paean, and came against them from the hill; the Athenians advancing to meet them, and closing at a run. The extreme wing of neither army came into action, one like the other being stopped by the water-courses in the way; the rest engaged with the utmost obstinacy, shield against shield. The Boeotian left, as far as the centre, was worsted by the Athenians. The Thespians in that part of the field suffered most severely. The troops alongside them having given way, they were surrounded in a narrow space and cut down fighting hand to hand; some of the Athenians also fell into confusion in surrounding the enemy and mistook and so killed each other. In this part of the field the Boeotians were beaten, and retreated upon the troops still fighting; but the right, where the Thebans were, got the better of the Athenians and shoved them further and further back, though gradually at first. It so happened also that Pagondas, seeing the distress of his left, had sent two squadrons of horse, where they could not be seen, round the hill, and their sudden appearance struck a panic into the victorious wing of the Athenians, who thought that it was another army coming against them. At length in both parts of the field, disturbed by this panic, and with their line broken by the advancing Thebans, the whole Athenian army took to flight. Some made for Delium and the sea, some for Oropus, others for Mount Parnes, or wherever they had hopes of safety, pursued and cut down by the Boeotians, and in particular by the cavalry, composed partly of Boeotians and partly of Locrians, who had come up just as the rout began. Night however coming on to interrupt the pursuit, the mass of the fugitives escaped more easily than they would otherwise have done. The next day the troops at Oropus and Delium returned home by sea, after leaving a garrison in the latter place, which they continued to hold notwithstanding the defeat.

[97] The Boeotians set up a trophy, took up their own dead, and stripped those of the enemy, and leaving a guard over them retired to Tanagra, there to take measures for attacking Delium. Meanwhile a herald came from the Athenians to ask for the dead, but was met and turned back by a Boeotian herald, who told him that he would effect nothing until the return of himself the Boeotian herald, and who then went on to the Athenians, and told them on the part of the Boeotians that they had done wrong in transgressing the law of the Hellenes. Of what use was the universal custom protecting the temples in an invaded country, if the Athenians were to fortify Delium and live there, acting exactly as if they were on unconsecrated ground, and drawing and using for their purposes the water which they, the Boeotians, never touched except for sacred uses? Accordingly for the god as well as for themselves, in the name of the deities concerned, and of Apollo, the Boeotians invited them first to evacuate the temple, if they wished to take up the dead that belonged to them.

[98] After these words from the herald, the Athenians sent their own herald to the Boeotians to say that they had not done any wrong to the temple, and for the future would do it no more harm than they could help; not having occupied it originally in any such design, but to defend themselves from it against those who were really wronging them. The law of the Hellenes was that conquest of a country, whether more or less extensive, carried with it possession of the temples in that country, with the obligation to keep up the usual ceremonies, at least as far as possible. The Boeotians and most other people who had turned out the owners of a country, and put themselves in their places by force, now held as of right the temples which they originally entered as usurpers. If the Athenians could have conquered more of Boeotia this would have been the case with them: as things stood, the piece of it which they had got they should treat as their own, and not quit unless obliged. The water they had disturbed under the impulsion of a necessity which they had not wantonly incurred, having been forced to use it in defending themselves against the Boeotians who had first invaded Attica. Besides, anything done under the pressure of war and danger might reasonably claim indulgence even in the eye of the god; or why, pray, were the altars the asylum for involuntary offences? Transgression also was a term applied to presumptuous offenders, not to the victims of adverse circumstances. In short, which were most impious—the Boeotians who wished to barter dead bodies for holy places, or the Athenians who refused to give up holy places to obtain what was theirs by right? The condition of evacuating Boeotia

must therefore be withdrawn. They were no longer in Boeotia. They stood where they stood by the right of the sword. All that the Boeotians had to do was to tell them to take up their dead under a truce according to the national custom.

[99] The Boeotians replied that if they were in Boeotia, they must evacuate that country before taking up their dead; if they were in their own territory, they could do as they pleased: for they knew that, although the Oropid where the bodies as it chanced were lying (the battle having been fought on the borders) was subject to Athens, yet the Athenians could not get them without their leave. Besides, why should they grant a truce for Athenian ground? And what could be fairer than to tell them to evacuate Boeotia if they wished to get what they asked? The Athenian herald accordingly returned with this answer, without having accomplished his object.

[100] Meanwhile the Boeotians at once sent for darters and slingers from the Malian Gulf, and with two thousand Corinthian heavy infantry who had joined them after the battle, the Peloponnesian garrison which had evacuated Nisaea, and some Megarians with them, marched against Delium, and attacked the fort, and after divers efforts finally succeeded in taking it by an engine of the following description. They sawed in two and scooped out a great beam from end to end, and fitting it nicely together again like a pipe, hung by chains a cauldron at one extremity, with which communicated an iron tube projecting from the beam, which was itself in great part plated with iron. This they brought up from a distance upon carts to the part of the wall principally composed of vines and timber, and when it was near, inserted huge bellows into their end of the beam and blew with them. The blast passing closely confined into the cauldron, which was filled with lighted coals, sulphur and pitch, made a great blaze, and set fire to the wall, which soon became untenable for its defenders, who left it and fled; and in this way the fort was taken. Of the garrison some were killed and two hundred made prisoners; most of the rest got on board their ships and returned home.

[101] Soon after the fall of Delium, which took place seventeen days after the battle, the Athenian herald, without knowing what had happened, came again for the dead, which were now restored by the Boeotians, who no longer answered as at first. Not quite five hundred Boeotians fell in the battle, and nearly one thousand Athenians, including Hippocrates the general, besides a great number of light troops and camp followers.

Soon after this battle Demosthenes, after the failure of his voyage to Siphae and of the plot on the town, availed himself of the Acarnanian and Agraean troops and of the four hundred Athenian heavy infantry which he had on board, to make a descent on the Sicyonian coast. Before however all his ships had come to shore, the Sicyonians came up and routed and chased to their ships those that had landed, killing some and taking others prisoners; after which they set up a trophy, and gave back the dead under truce.

About the same time with the affair of Delium took place the death of Sitalces, king of the Odrysians, who was defeated in battle, in a campaign against the Triballi; Seuthes, son of Sparadocus, his nephew, succeeding to the kingdom of the Odrysians, and of the rest of Thrace ruled by Sitalces.

[102] The same winter Brasidas, with his allies in the Thracian places, marched against Amphipolis, the Athenian colony on the river Strymon. A settlement upon the spot on which the city now stands was before attempted by Aristagoras, the Milesian (when he fled from King Darius), who was however dislodged by the Edonians; and thirty-two years later by the Athenians, who sent thither ten thousand settlers of their own citizens, and whoever else chose to go. These were cut off at Drabescus by the Thracians. Twenty-nine years after, the Athenians returned (Hagnon, son of Nicias, being sent out as leader of the colony) and drove out the Edonians, and founded a town on the spot, formerly called Ennea Hodoi or Nine Ways. The base from which they started was Eion, their commercial seaport at the mouth of the river, not more than three miles from the present town, which Hagnon named Amphipolis, because the Strymon flows round it on two sides, and he built it so as to be conspicuous from the sea and land alike, running a long wall across from river to river, to complete the circumference.

[103] Brasidas now marched against this town, starting from Arne in Chalcidice. Arriving about dusk at Aulon and Bromiscus, where the lake of Bolbe runs into the sea, he supped there, and went on during the night. The weather was stormy and it was snowing a little, which encouraged him to hurry on, in order, if possible, to take every one at Amphipolis

by surprise, except the party who were to be-tray it. The plot was carried on by some natives of Argilus, an Andrian colony, residing in Am-phipolis, where they had also other accomplices gained over by Perdiccas or the Chalcidians. But the most active in the matter were the in-habitants of Argilus itself, which is close by, who had always been suspected by the Athe-nians, and had had designs on the place. These men now saw their opportunity arrive with Brasidas, and having for some time been in correspondence with their countrymen in Am-phipolis for the betrayal of the town, at once received him into Argilus, and revolted from the Athenians, and that same night took him on to the bridge over the river; where he found only a small guard to oppose him, the town be-ing at some distance from the passage, and the walls not reaching down to it as at present. This guard he easily drove in, partly through there being treason in their ranks, partly from the stormy state of the weather and the sud-denness of his attack, and so got across the bridge, and immediately became master of all the property outside; the Amphipolitans hav-ing houses all over the quarter.

[104] The passage of Brasidas was a com-plete surprise to the people in the town; and the capture of many of those outside, and the flight of the rest within the wall, combined to produce great confusion among the citizens; especially as they did not trust one another. It is even said that if Brasidas, instead of stop-ping to pillage, had advanced straight against the town, he would probably have taken it. In fact, however, he established himself where he was and overran the country outside, and for the present remained inactive, vainly awaiting a demonstration on the part of his friends within. Meanwhile the party opposed to the traitors proved numerous enough to prevent the gates being immediately thrown open, and in concert with Eucles, the general, who had come from Athens to defend the place, sent to the other commander in Thrace, Thucydides, son of Olorus, the author of this history, who was at the isle of Thasos, a Parian colony, half a day's sail from Amphipolis, to tell him to come to their relief. On receipt of this message he at once set sail with seven ships which he had with him, in order, if possible, to reach Amphipolis in time to prevent its capitulation, or in any case to save Eion.

[105] Meanwhile Brasidas, afraid of suc-cours arriving by sea from Thasos, and learn-ing that Thucydides possessed the right of working the gold mines in that part of Thrace, and had thus great influence with the inhabi-tants of the continent, hastened to gain the town, if possible, before the people of Amphi-polis should be encouraged by his arrival to hope that he could save them by getting to-gether a force of allies from the sea and from Thrace, and so refuse to surrender. He accord-ingly offered moderate terms, proclaiming that any of the Amphipolitans and Athenians who chose, might continue to enjoy their property with full rights of citizenship; while those who did not wish to stay had five days to depart, taking their property with them.

[106] The bulk of the inhabitants, upon hearing this, began to change their minds, especially as only a small number of the citi-zens were Athenians, the majority having come from different quarters, and many of the prisoners outside had relations within the walls. They found the proclamation a fair one in comparison of what their fear had sug-gested; the Athenians being glad to go out, as they thought they ran more risk than the rest, and further, did not expect any speedy relief, and the multitude generally being content at being left in possession of their civic rights, and at such an unexpected reprieve from dan-ger. The partisans of Brasidas now openly ad-vocated this course, seeing that the feeling of the people had changed, and that they no longer gave ear to the Athenian general pres-ent; and thus the surrender was made and Brasidas was admitted by them on the terms of his proclamation. In this way they gave up the city, and late in the same day Thucydides and his ships entered the harbour of Eion, Brasi-das having just got hold of Amphipolis, and having been within a night of taking Eion: had the ships been less prompt in relieving it, in the morning it would have been his.

[107] After this Thucydides put all in order at Eion to secure it against any present or fu-ture attack of Brasidas, and received such as had elected to come there from the interior ac-cording to the terms agreed on. Meanwhile Brasidas suddenly sailed with a number of boats down the river to Eion to see if he could not seize the point running out from the wall, and so command the entrance; at the same time he attempted it by land, but was beaten off on both sides and had to content himself with arranging matters at Amphipolis and in the neighbourhood. Myrcinus, an Edonian town, also came over to him; the Edonian king Pittacus having been killed by the sons of Go-

axis and his own wife Brauro; and Galepsus and Oesime, which are Thasian colonies, not long after followed its example. Perdiccas too came up immediately after the capture and joined in these arrangements.

[*108*] The news that Amphipolis was in the hands of the enemy caused great alarm at Athens. Not only was the town valuable for the timber it afforded for shipbuilding, and the money that it brought in; but also, although the escort of the Thessalians gave the Lacedaemonians a means of reaching the allies of Athens as far as the Strymon, yet as long as they were not masters of the bridge but were watched on the side of Eion by the Athenian galleys, and on the land side impeded by a large and extensive lake formed by the waters of the river, it was impossible for them to go any further. Now, on the contrary, the path seemed open. There was also the fear of the allies revolting, owing to the moderation displayed by Brasidas in all his conduct, and to the declarations which he was everywhere making that he was sent out to free Hellas. The towns subject to the Athenians, hearing of the capture of Amphipolis and of the terms accorded to it, and of the gentleness of Brasidas, felt most strongly encouraged to change their condition, and sent secret messages to him, begging him to come on to them; each wishing to be the first to revolt. Indeed there seemed to be no danger in so doing; their mistake in their estimate of the Athenian power was as great as that power afterwards turned out to be, and their judgment was based more upon blind wishing than upon any sound prevision; for it is a habit of mankind to entrust to careless hope what they long for, and to use sovereign reason to thrust aside what they do not fancy. Besides the late severe blow which the Athenians had met with in Boeotia, joined to the seductive, though untrue, statements of Brasidas, about the Athenians not having ventured to engage his single army at Nisaea, made the allies confident, and caused them to believe that no Athenian force would be sent against them. Above all the wish to do what was agreeable at the moment, and the likelihood that they should find the Lacedaemonians full of zeal at starting, made them eager to venture. Observing this, the Athenians sent garrisons to the different towns, as far as was possible at such short notice and in winter; while Brasidas sent dispatches to Lacedaemon asking for reinforcements, and himself made preparations for building galleys in the Strymon. The Lacedae-

monians however did not send him any, partly through envy on the part of their chief men, partly because they were more bent on recovering the prisoners of the island and ending the war.

[*109*] The same winter the Megarians took and razed to the foundations the long walls which had been occupied by the Athenians; and Brasidas after the capture of Amphipolis marched with his allies against Acte, a promontory running out from the King's dike with an inward curve, and ending in Athos, a lofty mountain looking towards the Aegean Sea. In it are various towns, Sane, an Andrian colony, close to the canal, and facing the sea in the direction of Euboea; the others being Thyssus, Cleone, Acrothoi, Olophyxus, and Dium, inhabited by mixed barbarian races speaking the two languages. There is also a small Chalcidian element; but the greater number are Tyrrheno-Pelasgians once settled in Lemnos and Athens, and Bisaltians, Crestonians, and Edonians; the towns being all small ones. Most of these came over to Brasidas; but Sane and Dium held out and saw their land ravaged by him and his army.

[*110*] Upon their not submitting, he at once marched against Torone in Chalcidice, which was held by an Athenian garrison, having been invited by a few persons who were prepared to hand over the town. Arriving in the dark a little before daybreak, he sat down with his army near the temple of the Dioscuri, rather more than a quarter of a mile from the city. The rest of the town of Torone and the Athenians in garrison did not perceive his approach; but his partisans knowing that he was coming (a few of them had secretly gone out to meet him) were on the watch for his arrival, and were no sooner aware of it than they took in to them seven light-armed men with daggers, who alone of twenty men ordered on this service dared to enter, commanded by Lysistratus an Olynthian. These passed through the sea wall, and without being seen went up and put to the sword the garrison of the highest post in the town, which stands on a hill, and broke open the postern on the side of Canastraeum.

[*111*] Brasidas meanwhile came a little nearer and then halted with his main body, sending on one hundred targeteers to be ready to rush in first, the moment that a gate should be thrown open and the beacon lighted as agreed. After some time passed in waiting and wondering at the delay, the targeteers by de-

grees got up close to the town. The Toronaeans inside at work with the party that had entered had by this time broken down the postern and opened the gates leading to the market-place by cutting through the bar, and first brought some men round and let them in by the postern, in order to strike a panic into the surprised townsmen by suddenly attacking them from behind and on both sides at once; after which they raised the fire-signal as had been agreed, and took in by the market gates the rest of the targeteers.

[112] Brasidas seeing the signal told the troops to rise, and dashed forward amid the loud hurrahs of his men, which carried dismay among the astonished townspeople. Some burst in straight by the gate, others over some square pieces of timber placed against the wall (which has fallen down and was being rebuilt) to draw up stones; Brasidas and the greater number making straight uphill for the higher part of the town, in order to take it from top to bottom, and once for all, while the rest of the multitude spread in all directions.

[113] The capture of the town was effected before the great body of the Toronaeans had recovered from their surprise and confusion; but the conspirators and the citizens of their party at once joined the invaders. About fifty of the Athenian heavy infantry happened to be sleeping in the market-place when the alarm reached them. A few of these were killed fighting; the rest escaped, some by land, others to the two ships on the station, and took refuge in Lecythus, a fort garrisoned by their own men in the corner of the town running out into the sea and cut off by a narrow isthmus; where they were joined by the Toronaeans of their party.

[114] Day now arrived, and the town being secured, Brasidas made a proclamation to the Toronaeans who had taken refuge with the Athenians, to come out, as many as chose, to their homes without fearing for their rights or persons, and sent a herald to invite the Athenians to accept a truce, and to evacuate Lecythus with their property, as being Chalcidian ground. The Athenians refused this offer, but asked for a truce for a day to take up their dead. Brasidas granted it for two days, which he employed in fortifying the houses near, and the Athenians in doing the same to their positions. Meanwhile he called a meeting of the Toronaeans, and said very much what he had said at Acanthus, namely, that they must not look upon those who had negotiated with him

for the capture of the town as bad men or as traitors, as they had not acted as they had done from corrupt motives or in order to enslave the city, but for the good and freedom of Torone; nor again must those who had not shared in the enterprise fancy that they would not equally reap its fruits, as he had not come to destroy either city or individual. This was the reason of his proclamation to those that had fled for refuge to the Athenians: he thought none the worse of them for their friendship for the Athenians; he believed that they had only to make trial of the Lacedaemonians to like them as well, or even much better, as acting much more justly: it was for want of such a trial that they were now afraid of them. Meanwhile he warned all of them to prepare to be staunch allies, and for being held responsible for all faults in future: for the past, they had not wronged the Lacedaemonians but had been wronged by others who were too strong for them, and any opposition that they might have offered him could be excused.

[115] Having encouraged them with this address, as soon as the truce expired he made his attack upon Lecythus; the Athenians defending themselves from a poor wall and from some houses with parapets. One day they beat him off; the next the enemy were preparing to bring up an engine against them from which they meant to throw fire upon the wooden defences, and the troops were already coming up to the point where they fancied they could best bring up the engine, and where place was most assailable; meanwhile the Athenians put a wooden tower upon a house opposite, and carried up a quantity of jars and casks of water and big stones, and a large number of men also climbed up. The house thus laden too heavily suddenly broke down with a loud crash; at which the men who were near and saw it were more vexed than frightened; but those not so near, and still more those furthest off, thought that the place was already taken at that point, and fled in haste to the sea and the ships.

[116] Brasidas, perceiving that they were deserting the parapet, and seeing what was going on, dashed forward with his troops, and immediately took the fort, and put to the sword all whom he found in it. In this way the place was evacuated by the Athenians, who went across in their boats and ships to Pallene. Now there is a temple of Athene in Lecythus, and Brasidas had proclaimed in the moment of making the assault that he would give thirty

silver minae to the man first on the wall. Being now of opinion that the capture was scarcely due to human means, he gave the thirty minae to the goddess for her temple, and razed and cleared Lecythus, and made the whole of it consecrated ground. The rest of the winter he spent in settling the places in his hands, and in making designs upon the rest; and with the expiration of the winter the eighth year of this war ended.

[*117*] In the spring of the summer following, the Lacedaemonians and Athenians made an armistice for a year; the Athenians thinking that they would thus have full leisure to take their precautions before Brasidas could procure the revolt of any more of their towns, and might also, if it suited them, conclude a general peace; the Lacedaemonians divining the actual fears of the Athenians, and thinking that after once tasting a respite from trouble and misery they would be more disposed to consent to a reconciliation, and to give back the prisoners, and make a treaty for the longer period. The great idea of the Lacedaemonians was to get back their men while Brasidas's good fortune lasted: further successes might make the struggle a less unequal one in Chalcidice, but would leave them still deprived of their men, and even in Chalcidice not more than a match for the Athenians and by no means certain of victory. An armistice was accordingly concluded by Lacedaemon and her allies upon the terms following:

[*118*] 1. *As to the temple and oracle of the Pythian Apollo, we are agreed that whosoever will shall have access to it, without fraud or fear, according to the usages of his forefathers. The Lacedaemonians and the allies present agree to this, and promise to send heralds to the Boeotians and Phocians, and to do their best to persuade them to agree likewise.*

2. *As to the treasure of the god, we agree to exert ourselves to detect all malversators, truly and honestly following the customs of our forefathers, we and you and all others willing to do so, all following the customs of our forefathers. As to these points the Lacedaemonians and the other allies are agreed as has been said.*

3. *As to what follows, the Lacedaemonians and the other allies agree, if the Athenians conclude a treaty, to remain, each of us in our own territory, retaining our respective acquisitions: the garrison in Coryphasium keeping within Buphras and Tomeus: that in Cythera attempting no communication with the Peloponnesian confederacy, neither we with them, nor they*

with us: that in Nisaea and Minoa not crossing the road leading from the gates of the temple of Nisus to that of Poseidon and from thence straight to the bridge at Minoa: the Megarians and the allies being equally bound not to cross this road, and the Athenians retaining the island they have taken, without any communication on either side: as to Troezen, each side retaining what it has, and as was arranged with the Athenians.

4. *As to the use of the sea, so far as refers to their own coast and to that of their confederacy, that the Lacedaemonians and their allies may voyage upon it in any vessel rowed by oars and of not more than five hundred talents tonnage, not a vessel of war.*

5. *That all heralds and embassies, with as many attendants as they please, for concluding the war and adjusting claims, shall have free passage, going and coming, to Peloponnese or Athens by land and by sea.*

6. *That during the truce, deserters whether bond or free shall be received neither by you, nor by us.*

7. *Further, that satisfaction shall be given by you to us and by us to you according to the public law of our several countries, all disputes being settled by law without recourse to hostilities.*

The Lacedaemonians and allies agree to these articles; but if you have anything fairer or juster to suggest, come to Lacedaemon and let us know: whatever shall be just will meet with no objection either from the Lacedaemonians or from the allies. Only let those who come come with full powers, as you desire us. The truce shall be for one year.

Approved by the people.

The tribe of Acamantis had the prytany, Phoenippus was secretary, Niciades chairman. Laches moved, in the name of the good luck of the Athenians, that they should conclude the armistice upon the terms agreed upon by the Lacedaemonians and the allies. It was agreed accordingly in the popular assembly that the armistice should be for one year, beginning that very day, the fourteenth of the month of Elaphebolion; during which time ambassadors and heralds should go and come between the two countries to discuss the bases of a pacification. That the generals and prytanes should call an assembly of the people, in which the Athenians should first consult on the peace, and on the mode in which the embassy for putting an end to the war should be admitted. That the embassy now present should at once take the engagement before the people to keep well and truly this truce for one year.

[*119*] On these terms the Lacedaemonians concluded with the Athenians and their allies on the twelfth day of the Spartan month Gerastius; the allies also taking the oaths. Those who concluded and poured the libation were Taurus, son of Echetimides, Athenaeus, son of Pericleidas, and Philocharidas, son of Eryxidaïdas, Lacedaemonians; Aeneas, son of Ocytus, and Euphamidas, son of Aristonymus, Corinthians; Damotimus, son of Naucrates, and Onasimus, son of Megacles, Sicyonians; Nicasus, son of Cecalus, and Menecrates, son of Amphidorus, Megarians; and Amphias, son of Eupaïdas, an Epidaurian; and the Athenian generals Nicostratus, son of Diitrephes, Nicias, son of Niceratus, and Autocles, son of Tolmaeus. Such was the armistice, and during the whole of it conferences went on on the subject of a pacification.

[*120*] In the days in which they were going backwards and forwards to these conferences, Scione, a town in Pallene, revolted from Athens, and went over to Brasidas. The Scionaeans say that they are Pallenians from Peloponnese, and that their first founders on their voyage from Troy were carried in to this spot by the storm which the Achaeans were caught in, and there settled. The Scionaeans had no sooner revolted than Brasidas crossed over by night to Scione, with a friendly galley ahead and himself in a small boat some way behind; his idea being that if he fell in with a vessel larger than the boat he would have the galley to defend him, while a ship that was a match for the galley would probably neglect the small vessel to attack the large one, and thus leave him time to escape. His passage effected, he called a meeting of the Scionaeans and spoke to the same effect as at Acanthus and Torone, adding that they merited the utmost commendation, in that, in spite of Pallene within the isthmus being cut off by the Athenian occupation of Potidaea and of their own practically insular position, they had of their own free will gone forward to meet their liberty instead of timorously waiting until they had been by force compelled to their own manifest good. This was a sign that they would valiantly undergo any trial, however great; and if he should order affairs as he intended, he should count them among the truest and sincerest friends of the Lacedaemonians, and would in every other way honour them.

[*121*] The Scionaeans were elated by his language, and even those who had at first disapproved of what was being done catching the general confidence, they determined on a vigorous conduct of the war, and welcomed Brasidas with all possible honours, publicly crowning him with a crown of gold as the liberator of Hellas; while private persons crowded round him and decked him with garlands as though he had been an athlete. Meanwhile Brasidas left them a small garrison for the present and crossed back again, and not long afterwards sent over a larger force, intending with the help of the Scionaeans to attempt Mende and Potidaea before the Athenians should arrive; Scione, he felt, being too like an island for them not to relieve it. He had besides intelligence in the above towns about their betrayal.

[*122*] In the midst of his designs upon the towns in question, a galley arrived with the commissioners carrying round the news of the armistice, Aristonymus for the Athenians and Athenaeus for the Lacedaemonians. The troops now crossed back to Torone, and the commissioners gave Brasidas notice of the convention. All the Lacedaemonian allies in Thrace accepted what had been done; and Aristonymus made no difficulty about the rest, but finding, on counting the days, that the Scionaeans had revolted after the date of the convention, refused to include them in it. To this Brasidas earnestly objected, asserting that the revolt took place before, and would not give up the town. Upon Aristonymus reporting the case to Athens, the people at once prepared to send an expedition to Scione. Upon this, envoys arrived from Lacedaemon, alleging that this would be a breach of the truce, and laying claim to the town upon the faith of the assertion of Brasidas, and meanwhile offering to submit the question to arbitration. Arbitration, however, was what the Athenians did not choose to risk; being determined to send troops at once to the place, and furious at the idea of even the islanders now daring to revolt, in a vain reliance upon the power of the Lacedaemonians by land. Besides the facts of the revolt were rather as the Athenians contended, the Scionaeans having revolted two days after the convention. Cleon accordingly succeeded in carrying a decree to reduce and put to death the Scionaeans; and the Athenians employed the leisure which they now enjoyed in preparing for the expedition.

[*123*] Meanwhile Mende revolted, a town

in Pallene and a colony of the Eretrians, and was received without scruple by Brasidas, in spite of its having evidently come over during the armistice, on account of certain infringements of the truce alleged by him against the Athenians. This audacity of Mende was partly caused by seeing Brasidas forward in the matter and by the conclusions drawn from his refusal to betray Scione; and besides, the conspirators in Mende were few, and, as I have already intimated, had carried on their practices too long not to fear detection for themselves, and not to wish to force the inclination of the multitude. This news made the Athenians more furious than ever, and they at once prepared against both towns. Brasidas, expecting their arrival, conveyed away to Olynthus in Chalcidice the women and children of the Scionaeans and Mendaeans, and sent over to them five hundred Peloponnesian heavy infantry and three hundred Chalcidian targeteers, all under the command of Polydamidas.

Leaving these two towns to prepare together against the speedy arrival of the Athenians, [124] Brasidas and Perdiccas started on a second joint expedition into Lyncus against Arrhabaeus; the latter with the forces of his Macedonian subjects, and a corps of heavy infantry composed of Hellenes domiciled in the country; the former with the Peloponnesians whom he still had with him and the Chalcidians, Acanthians, and the rest in such force as they were able. In all there were about three thousand Hellenic heavy infantry, accompanied by all the Macedonian cavalry with the Chalcidians, near one thousand strong, besides an immense crowd of barbarians. On entering the country of Arrhabaeus, they found the Lyncestians encamped awaiting them, and themselves took up a position opposite. The infantry on either side were upon a hill, with a plain between them, into which the horse of both armies first galloped down and engaged a cavalry action. After this the Lyncestian heavy infantry advanced from their hill to join their cavalry and offered battle; upon which Brasidas and Perdiccas also came down to meet them, and engaged and routed them with heavy loss; the survivors taking refuge upon the heights and there remaining inactive. The victors now set up a trophy and waited two or three days for the Illyrian mercenaries who were to join Perdiccas. Perdiccas then wished to go on and attack the villages of Arrhabaeus, and to sit still no longer; but Brasidas, afraid that the Athenians might sail up during his ab-

sence, and of something happening to Mende, and seeing besides that the Illyrians did not appear, far from seconding this wish was anxious to return.

[125] While they were thus disputing, the news arrived that the Illyrians had actually betrayed Perdiccas and had joined Arrhabaeus; and the fear inspired by their warlike character made both parties now think it best to retreat. However, owing to the dispute, nothing had been settled as to when they should start; and night coming on, the Macedonians and the barbarian crowd took fright in a moment in one of those mysterious panics to which great armies are liable; and persuaded that an army many times more numerous than that which had really arrived was advancing and all but upon them, suddenly broke and fled in the direction of home, and thus compelled Perdiccas, who at first did not perceive what had occurred, to depart without seeing Brasidas, the two armies being encamped at a considerable distance from each other. At daybreak Brasidas, perceiving that the Macedonians had gone on, and that the Illyrians and Arrhabaeus were on the point of attacking him, formed his heavy infantry into a square, with the light troops in the centre, and himself also prepared to retreat. Posting his youngest soldiers to dash out wherever the enemy should attack them, he himself with three hundred picked men in the rear intended to face about during the retreat and beat off the most forward of their assailants. Meanwhile, before the enemy approached, he sought to sustain the courage of his soldiers with the following hasty exhortation:

[126] "Peloponnesians, if I did not suspect you of being dismayed at being left alone to sustain the attack of a numerous and barbarian enemy, I should just have said a few words to you as usual without further explanation. As it is, in the face of the desertion of our friends and the numbers of the enemy, I have some advice and information to offer, which, brief as they must be, will, I hope, suffice for the more important points. The bravery that you habitually display in war does not depend on your having allies at your side in this or that encounter, but on your native courage; nor have numbers any terrors for citizens of states like yours, in which the many do not rule the few, but rather the few the many, owing their position to nothing else than to superiority in the field. Inexperience now makes you afraid of barbarians; and yet the trial of strength

which you had with the Macedonians among them, and my own judgment, confirmed by what I hear from others, should be enough to satisfy you that they will not prove formidable. Where an enemy seems strong but is really weak, a true knowledge of the facts makes his adversary the bolder, just as a serious antagonist is encountered most confidently by those who do not know him. Thus the present enemy might terrify an inexperienced imagination; they are formidable in outward bulk, their loud yelling is unbearable, and the brandishing of their weapons in the air has a threatening appearance. But when it comes to real fighting with an opponent who stands his ground, they are not what they seemed; they have no regular order that they should be ashamed of deserting their positions when hard pressed; flight and attack are with them equally honourable, and afford no test of courage; their independent mode of fighting never leaving any one who wants to run away without a fair excuse for so doing. In short, they think frightening you at a secure distance a surer game than meeting you hand to hand; otherwise they would have done the one and not the other. You can thus plainly see that the terrors with which they were at first invested are in fact trifling enough, though to the eye and ear very prominent. Stand your ground therefore when they advance, and again wait your opportunity to retire in good order, and you will reach a place of safety all the sooner, and will know for ever afterwards that rabble such as these, to those who sustain their first attack, do but show off their courage by threats of the terrible things that they are going to do, at a distance, but with those who give way to them are quick enough to display their heroism in pursuit when they can do so without danger."

[127] With this brief address Brasidas began to lead off his army. Seeing this, the barbarians came on with much shouting and hubbub, thinking that he was flying and that they would overtake him and cut him off. But wherever they charged they found the young men ready to dash out against them, while Brasidas with his picked company sustained their onset. Thus the Peloponnesians withstood the first attack, to the surprise of the enemy, and afterwards received and repulsed them as fast as they came on, retiring as soon as their opponents became quiet. The main body of the barbarians ceased therefore to molest the Hellenes with Brasidas in the open

country, and leaving behind a certain number to harass their march, the rest went on after the flying Macedonians, slaying those with whom they came up, and so arrived in time to occupy the narrow pass between two hills that leads into the country of Arrhabaeus. They knew that this was the only way by which Brasidas could retreat, and now proceeded to surround him just as he entered the most impracticable part of the road, in order to cut him off.

[128] Brasidas, perceiving their intention, told his three hundred to run on without order, each as quickly as he could, to the hill which seemed easiest to take, and to try to dislodge the barbarians already there, before they should be joined by the main body closing round him. These attacked and overpowered the party upon the hill, and the main army of the Hellenes now advanced with less difficulty towards it—the barbarians being terrified at seeing their men on that side driven from the height and no longer following the main body, who, they considered, had gained the frontier and made good their escape. The heights once gained, Brasidas now proceeded more securely, and the same day arrived at Arnisa, the first town in the dominions of Perdiccas. The soldiers, enraged at the desertion of the Macedonians, vented their rage on all their yokes of oxen which they found on the road, and on any baggage which had tumbled off (as might easily happen in the panic of a night retreat), by unyoking and cutting down the cattle and taking the baggage for themselves. From this moment Perdiccas began to regard Brasidas as an enemy and to feel against the Peloponnesians a hatred which could not be congenial to the adversary of the Athenians. However, he departed from his natural interests and made it his endeavour to come to terms with the latter and to get rid of the former.

[129] On his return from Macedonia to Torone, Brasidas found the Athenians already masters of Mende, and remained quiet where he was, thinking it now out of his power to cross over into Pallene and assist the Mendaeans, but he kept good watch over Torone. For about the same time as the campaign in Lyncus, the Athenians sailed upon the expedition which we left them preparing against Mende and Scione, with fifty ships, ten of which were Chians, one thousand Athenian heavy infantry and six hundred archers, one hundred Thracian mercenaries and some targeteers drawn from their allies in the neighbourhood, under

the command of Nicias, son of Niceratus, and Nicostratus, son of Diitrephes. Weighing from Potidaea, the fleet came to land opposite the temple of Poseidon, and proceeded against Mende; the men of which town, reinforced by three hundred Scionaeans, with their Peloponnesian auxiliaries, seven hundred heavy infantry in all, under Polydamidas, they found encamped upon a strong hill outside the city. These Nicias, with one hundred and twenty light-armed Methonaeans, sixty picked men from the Athenian heavy infantry, and all the archers, tried to reach by a path running up the hill, but received a wound and found himself unable to force the position; while Nicostratus, with all the rest of the army, advancing upon the hill, which was naturally difficult, by a different approach further off, was thrown into utter disorder; and the whole Athenian army narrowly escaped being defeated. For that day, as the Mendaeans and their allies showed no signs of yielding, the Athenians retreated and encamped, and the Mendaeans at nightfall returned into the town.

[130] The next day the Athenians sailed round to the Scione side, and took the suburb, and all day plundered the country, without any one coming out against them, partly because of intestine disturbances in the town; and the following night the three hundred Scionaeans returned home. On the morrow Nicias advanced with half the army to the frontier of Scione and laid waste the country; while Nicostratus with the remainder sat down before the town near the upper gate on the road to Potidaea. The arms of the Mendaeans and of their Peloponnesian auxiliaries within the wall happened to be piled in that quarter, where Polydamidas accordingly began to draw them up for battle, encouraging the Mendaeans to make a sortie. At this moment one of the popular party answered him factiously that they would not go out and did not want a war, and for thus answering was dragged by the arm and knocked about by Polydamidas. Hereupon the infuriated commons at once seized their arms and rushed at the Peloponnesians and at their allies of the opposite faction. The troops thus assaulted were at once routed, partly from the suddenness of the conflict and partly through fear of the gates being opened to the Athenians, with whom they imagined that the attack had been concerted. As many as were not killed on the spot took refuge in the citadel, which they had held from the first; and the whole Athenian army, Nicias having by

this time returned and being close to the city, now burst into Mende, which had opened its gates without any convention, and sacked it just as if they had taken it by storm, the generals even finding some difficulty in restraining them from also massacring the inhabitants. After this the Athenians told the Mendaeans that they might retain their civil rights, and themselves judge the supposed authors of the revolt; and cut off the party in the citadel by a wall built down to the sea on either side, appointing troops to maintain the blockade. Having thus secured Mende, they proceeded against Scione.

[131] The Scionaeans and Peloponnesians marched out against them, occupying a strong hill in front of the town, which had to be captured by the enemy before they could invest the place. The Athenians stormed the hill, defeated and dislodged its occupants, and, having encamped and set up a trophy, prepared for the work of circumvallation. Not long after they had begun their operations, the auxiliaries besieged in the citadel of Mende forced the guard by the sea-side and arrived by night at Scione, into which most of them succeeded in entering, passing through the besieging army.

[132] While the investment of Scione was in progress, Perdiccas sent a herald to the Athenian generals and made peace with the Athenians, through spite against Brasidas for the retreat from Lyncus, from which moment indeed he had begun to negotiate. The Lacedaemonian Ischagoras was just then upon the point of starting with an army overland to join Brasidas; and Perdiccas, being now required by Nicias to give some proof of the sincerity of his reconciliation to the Athenians, and being himself no longer disposed to let the Peloponnesians into his country, put in motion his friends in Thessaly, with whose chief men he always took care to have relations, and so effectually stopped the army and its preparation that they did not even try the Thessalians. Ischagoras himself, however, with Ameinias and Aristeus, succeeded in reaching Brasidas; they had been commissioned by the Lacedaemonians to inspect the state of affairs, and brought out from Sparta (in violation of all precedent) some of their young men to put in command of the towns, to guard against their being entrusted to the persons upon the spot. Brasidas accordingly placed Clearidas, son of Cleonymus, in Amphipolis, and Pasitelidas, son of Hegesander, in Torone.

[133] The same summer the Thebans dis-

mantled the wall of the Thespians on the charge of Atticism, having always wished to do so, and now finding it an easy matter, as the flower of the Thespian youth had perished in the battle with the Athenians. The same summer also the temple of Hera at Argos was burnt down, through Chrysis, the priestess, placing a lighted torch near the garlands and then falling asleep, so that they all caught fire and were in a blaze before she observed it. Chrysis that very night fled to Phlius for fear of the Argives, who, agreeably to the law in such a case, appointed another priestess named Phaeinis. Chrysis at the time of her flight had been priestess for eight years of the present war and half the ninth. At the close of the summer the investment of Scione was completed, and the Athenians, leaving a detachment to maintain the blockade, returned with the rest of their army.

[*134*] During the winter following, the Athenians and Lacedaemonians were kept quiet by the armistice; but the Mantineans and Tegeans, and their respective allies, fought a battle at Laodicium, in the Oresthid. The victory remained doubtful, as each side routed one of the wings opposed to them, and both set up trophies and sent spoils to Delphi. After heavy loss on both sides the battle was undecided, and night interrupted the action; yet the Tegeans passed the night on the field and set up a trophy at once, while the Mantineans withdrew to Bucolion and set up theirs afterwards.

[*135*] At the close of the same winter, in fact almost in spring, Brasidas made an attempt upon Potidaea. He arrived by night, and succeeded in planting a ladder against the wall without being discovered, the ladder being planted just in the interval between the passing round of the bell and the return of the man who brought it back. Upon the garrison, however, taking the alarm immediately afterwards, before his men came up, he quickly led off his troops, without waiting until it was day. So ended the winter and the ninth year of this war of which Thucydides is the historian.

The Fifth Book

CHAPTER XV

Tenth Year of the War—Death of Cleon and Brasidas—Peace of Nicias

[1] THE next summer the truce for a year ended, after lasting until the Pythian games. During the armistice the Athenians expelled the Delians from Delos, concluding that they must have been polluted by some old offence at the time of their consecration, and that this had been the omission in the previous purification of the island, which, as I have related, had been thought to have been duly accomplished by the removal of the graves of the dead. The Delians had Atramyttium in Asia given them by Pharnaces, and settled there as they removed from Delos.

[2] Meanwhile Cleon prevailed on the Athenians to let him set sail at the expiration of the armistice for the towns in the direction of Thrace with twelve hundred heavy infantry and three hundred horse from Athens, a large force of the allies, and thirty ships. First touching at the still besieged Scione, and taking some heavy infantry from the army there, he next sailed into Cophos, a harbour in the territory of Torone, which is not far from the town. From thence, having learnt from deserters that Brasidas was not in Torone, and that its garrison was not strong enough to give him battle, he advanced with his army against the town, sending ten ships to sail round into the harbour. He first came to the fortification lately thrown up in front of the town by Brasidas in order to take in the suburb, to do which he had pulled down part of the original wall and made it all one city. [3] To this point Pasitelidas, the Lacedaemonian commander, with such garrison as there was in the place, hurried to repel the Athenian assault; but finding himself hard pressed, and seeing the ships that had been sent round sailing into the harbour,

Pasitelidas began to be afraid that they might get up to the city before its defenders were there and, the fortification being also carried, he might be taken prisoner, and so abandoned the outwork and ran into the town. But the Athenians from the ships had already taken Torone, and their land forces following at his heels burst in with him with a rush over the part of the old wall that had been pulled down, killing some of the Peloponnesians and Toronaeans in the *mêlée,* and making prisoners of the rest, and Pasitelidas their commander amongst them. Brasidas meanwhile had advanced to relieve Torone, and had only about four miles more to go when he heard of its fall on the road, and turned back again. Cleon and the Athenians set up two trophies, one by the harbour, the other by the fortification and, making slaves of the wives and children of the Toronaeans, sent the men with the Peloponnesians and any Chalcidians that were there, to the number of seven hundred, to Athens; whence, however, they all came home afterwards, the Peloponnesians on the conclusion of peace, and the rest by being exchanged against other prisoners with the Olynthians. About the same time Panactum, a fortress on the Athenian border, was taken by treachery by the Boeotians. Meanwhile Cleon, after placing a garrison in Torone, weighed anchor and sailed around Athos on his way to Amphipolis.

[4] About the same time Phaeax, son of Erasistratus, set sail with two colleagues as ambassador from Athens to Italy and Sicily. The Leontines, upon the departure of the Athenians from Sicily after the pacification, had placed a number of new citizens upon the roll, and the commons had a design for redividing the land; but the upper classes, aware of their intention, called in the Syracusans and expelled the commons. These last were scattered in various directions; but the upper classes came to an

482

agreement with the Syracusans, abandoned and laid waste their city, and went and lived at Syracuse, where they were made citizens. Afterwards some of them were dissatisfied, and leaving Syracuse occupied Phocaeae, a quarter of the town of Leontini, and Bricinniae, a strong place in the Leontine country, and being there joined by most of the exiled commons carried on war from the fortifications. The Athenians hearing this, sent Phaeax to see if they could not by some means so convince their allies there and the rest of the Sicilians of the ambitious designs of Syracuse as to induce them to form a general coalition against her, and thus save the commons of Leontini. Arrived in Sicily, Phaeax succeeded at Camarina and Agrigentum, but meeting with a repulse at Gela did not go on to the rest, as he saw that he should not succeed with them, but returned through the country of the Sicels to Catana, and after visiting Bricinniae as he passed, and encouraging its inhabitants, sailed back to Athens.

[5] During his voyage along the coast to and from Sicily, he treated with some cities in Italy on the subject of friendship with Athens, and also fell in with some Locrian settlers exiled from Messina, who had been sent thither when the Locrians were called in by one of the factions that divided Messina after the pacification of Sicily, and Messina came for a time into the hands of the Locrians. These being met by Phaeax on their return home received no injury at his hands, as the Locrians had agreed with him for a treaty with Athens. They were the only people of the allies who, when the reconciliation between the Sicilians took place, had not made peace with her; nor indeed would they have done so now, if they had not been pressed by a war with the Hipponians and Medmaeans who lived on their border, and were colonists of theirs. Phaeax meanwhile proceeded on his voyage, and at length arrived at Athens.

[6] Cleon, whom we left on his voyage from Torone to Amphipolis, made Eion his base, and after an unsuccessful assault upon the Andrian colony of Stagirus, took Galepsus, a colony of Thasos, by storm. He now sent envoys to Perdiccas to command his attendance with an army, as provided by the alliance; and others to Thrace, to Polles, king of the Odomantians, who was to bring as many Thracian mercenaries as possible; and himself remained inactive in Eion, awaiting their arrival. Informed of this, Brasidas on his part took up a position of observation upon Cerdylium, a place situated in the Argilian country on high ground across the river, not far from Amphipolis, and commanding a view on all sides, and thus made it impossible for Cleon's army to move without his seeing it; for he fully expected that Cleon, despising the scanty numbers of his opponent, would march against Amphipolis with the force that he had got with him. At the same time Brasidas made his preparations, calling to his standard fifteen hundred Thracian mercenaries and all the Edonians, horse and targeteers; he also had a thousand Myrcinian and Chalcidian targeteers, besides those in Amphipolis, and a force of heavy infantry numbering altogether about two thousand, and three hundred Hellenic horse. Fifteen hundred of these he had with him upon Cerdylium; the rest were stationed with Clearidas in Amphipolis.

[7] After remaining quiet for some time, Cleon was at length obliged to do as Brasidas expected. His soldiers, tired of their inactivity, began also seriously to reflect on the weakness and incompetence of their commander, and the skill and valour that would be opposed to him, and on their own original unwillingness to accompany him. These murmurs coming to the ears of Cleon, he resolved not to disgust the army by keeping it in the same place, and broke up his camp and advanced. The temper of the general was what it had been at Pylos, his success on that occasion having given him confidence in his capacity. He never dreamed of any one coming out to fight him, but said that he was rather going up to view the place; and if he waited for his reinforcements, it was not in order to make victory secure in case he should be compelled to engage, but to be enabled to surround and storm the city. He accordingly came and posted his army upon a strong hill in front of Amphipolis, and proceeded to examine the lake formed by the Strymon, and how the town lay on the side of Thrace. He thought to retire at pleasure without fighting, as there was no one to be seen upon the wall or coming out of the gates, all of which were shut. Indeed, it seemed a mistake not to have brought down engines with him; he could then have taken the town, there being no one to defend it.

[8] As soon as Brasidas saw the Athenians in motion he descended himself from Cerdylium and entered Amphipolis. He did not venture to go out in regular order against the Athenians: he mistrusted his strength, and

thought it inadequate to the attempt; not in numbers—these were not so unequal—but in quality, the flower of the Athenian army being in the field, with the best of the Lemnians and Imbrians. He therefore prepared to assail them by stratagem. By showing the enemy the number of his troops, and the shifts which he had been put to to arm them, he thought that he should have less chance of beating him than by not letting him have a sight of them, and thus learn how good a right he had to despise them. He accordingly picked out a hundred and fifty heavy infantry and, putting the rest under Clearidas, determined to attack suddenly before the Athenians retired; thinking that he should not have again such a chance of catching them alone, if their reinforcements were once allowed to come up; and so calling all his soldiers together in order to encourage them and explain his intention, spoke as follows:

[9] "Peloponnesians, the character of the country from which we have come, one which has always owed its freedom to valour, and the fact that you are Dorians and the enemy you are about to fight Ionians, whom you are accustomed to beat, are things that do not need further comment. But the plan of attack that I propose to pursue, this it is as well to explain, in order that the fact of our adventuring with a part instead of with the whole of our forces may not damp your courage by the apparent disadvantage at which it places you. I imagine it is the poor opinion that he has of us, and the fact that he has no idea of any one coming out to engage him, that has made the enemy march up to the place and carelessly look about him as he is doing, without noticing us. But the most successful soldier will always be the man who most happily detects a blunder like this, and who carefully consulting his own means makes his attack not so much by open and regular approaches, as by seizing the opportunity of the moment; and these stratagems, which do the greatest service to our friends by most completely deceiving our enemies, have the most brilliant name in war. Therefore, while their careless confidence continues, and they are still thinking, as in my judgment they are now doing, more of retreat than of maintaining their position, while their spirit is slack and not high-strung with expectation, I with the men under my command will, if possible, take them by surprise and fall with a run upon their centre; and do you, Clearidas, afterwards, when you see me already upon them, and, as is likely, dealing terror among them, take with you the Amphipolitans, and the rest of the allies, and suddenly open the gates and dash at them, and hasten to engage as quickly as you can. That is our best chance of establishing a panic among them, as a fresh assailant has always more terrors for an enemy than the one he is immediately engaged with. Show yourself a brave man, as a Spartan should; and do you, allies, follow him like men, and remember that zeal, honour, and obedience mark the good soldier, and that this day will make you either free men and allies of Lacedaemon, or slaves of Athens; even if you escape without personal loss of liberty or life, your bondage will be on harsher terms than before, and you will also hinder the liberation of the rest of the Hellenes. No cowardice then on your part, seeing the greatness of the issues at stake, and I will show that what I preach to others I can practise myself."

[10] After this brief speech Brasidas himself prepared for the sally, and placed the rest with Clearidas at the Thracian gates to support him as had been agreed. Meanwhile he had been seen coming down from Cerdylium and then in the city, which is overlooked from the outside, sacrificing near the temple of Athene; in short, all his movements had been observed, and word was brought to Cleon, who had at the moment gone on to look about him, that the whole of the enemy's force could be seen in the town, and that the feet of horses and men in great numbers were visible under the gates, as if a sally were intended. Upon hearing this he went up to look, and having done so, being unwilling to venture upon the decisive step of a battle before his reinforcements came up, and fancying that he would have time to retire, bid the retreat be sounded and sent orders to the men to effect it by moving on the left wing in the direction of Eion, which was indeed the only way practicable. This however not being quick enough for him, he joined the retreat in person and made the right wing wheel round, thus turning its unarmed side to the enemy. It was then that Brasidas, seeing the Athenian force in motion and his opportunity come, said to the men with him and the rest: "Those fellows will never stand before us, one can see that by the way their spears and heads are going. Troops which do as they do seldom stand a charge. Quick, someone, and open the gates I spoke of, and let us be out and at them with no fears

for the result." Accordingly issuing out by the palisade gate and by the first in the long wall then existing, he ran at the top of his speed along the straight road, where the trophy now stands as you go by the steepest part of the hill, and fell upon and routed the centre of the Athenians, panic-stricken by their own disorder and astounded at his audacity. At the same moment Clearidas in execution of his orders issued out from the Thracian gates to support him, and also attacked the enemy. The result was that the Athenians, suddenly and unexpectedly attacked on both sides, fell into confusion; and their left towards Eion, which had already got on some distance, at once broke and fled. Just as it was in full retreat and Brasidas was passing on to attack the right, he received a wound; but his fall was not perceived by the Athenians, as he was taken up by those near him and carried off the field. The Athenian right made a better stand, and though Cleon, who from the first had no thought of fighting, at once fled and was overtaken and slain by a Myrcinian targeteer, his infantry forming in close order upon the hill twice or thrice repulsed the attacks of Clearidas, and did not finally give way until they were surrounded and routed by the missiles of the Myrcinian and Chalcidian horse and the targeteers. Thus the Athenian army was all now in flight; and such as escaped being killed in the battle, or by the Chalcidian horse and the targeteers, dispersed among the hills, and with difficulty made their way to Eion. The men who had taken up and rescued Brasidas, brought him into the town with the breath still in him: he lived to hear of the victory of his troops, and not long after expired. The rest of the army returning with Clearidas from the pursuit stripped the dead and set up a trophy.

[11] After this all the allies attended in arms and buried Brasidas at the public expense in the city, in front of what is now the market-place, and the Amphipolitans, having enclosed his tomb, ever afterwards sacrifice to him as a hero and have given to him the honour of games and annual offerings. They constituted him the founder of their colony, and pulled down the Hagnonic erections, and obliterated everything that could be interpreted as a memorial of his having founded the place; for they considered that Brasidas had been their preserver, and courting as they did the alliance of Lacedaemon for fear of Athens, in their present hostile relations with the latter they could no longer with the same advantage or

satisfaction pay Hagnon his honours. They also gave the Athenians back their dead. About six hundred of the latter had fallen and only seven of the enemy, owing to there having been no regular engagement, but the affair of accident and panic that I have described. After taking up their dead the Athenians sailed off home, while Clearidas and his troops remained to arrange matters at Amphipolis.

[12] About the same time three Lacedaemonians—Ramphias, Autocharidas, and Epicydidas—led a reinforcement of nine hundred heavy infantry to the towns in the direction of Thrace, and arriving at Heraclea in Trachis reformed matters there as seemed good to them. While they delayed there, this battle took place and so the summer ended.

[13] With the beginning of the winter following, Ramphias and his companions penetrated as far as Pierium in Thessaly; but as the Thessalians opposed their further advance, and Brasidas whom they came to reinforce was dead, they turned back home, thinking that the moment had gone by, the Athenians being defeated and gone, and themselves not equal to the execution of Brasidas's designs. The main cause however of their return was because they knew that when they set out Lacedaemonian opinion was really in favour of peace.

[14] Indeed it so happened that directly after the battle of Amphipolis and the retreat of Ramphias from Thessaly, both sides ceased to prosecute the war and turned their attention to peace. Athens had suffered severely at Delium, and again shortly afterwards at Amphipolis, and had no longer that confidence in her strength which had made her before refuse to treat, in the belief of ultimate victory which her success at the moment had inspired; besides, she was afraid of her allies being tempted by her reverses to rebel more generally, and repented having let go the splendid opportunity for peace which the affair of Pylos had offered. Lacedaemon, on the other hand, found the event of the war to falsify her notion that a few years would suffice for the overthrow of the power of the Athenians by the devastation of their land. She had suffered on the island a disaster hitherto unknown at Sparta; she saw her country plundered from Pylos and Cythera; the Helots were deserting, and she was in constant apprehension that those who remained in Peloponnese would rely upon those outside and take advantage of the situation to renew their old attempts at revolution. Besides this, as chance would have it, her thirty years'

truce with the Argives was upon the point of expiring; and they refused to renew it unless Cynuria were restored to them; so that it seemed impossible to fight Argos and Athens at once. She also suspected some of the cities in Peloponnese of intending to go over to the enemy, as was indeed the case.

[15] These considerations made both sides disposed for an accommodation; the Lacedaemonians being probably the most eager, as they ardently desired to recover the men taken upon the island, the Spartans among whom belonged to the first families and were accordingly related to the governing body in Lacedaemon. Negotiations had been begun directly after their capture, but the Athenians in their hour of triumph would not consent to any reasonable terms; though after their defeat at Delium, Lacedaemon, knowing that they would be now more inclined to listen, at once concluded the armistice for a year, during which they were to confer together and see if a longer period could not be agreed upon.

[16] Now, however, after the Athenian defeat at Amphipolis, and the death of Cleon and Brasidas, who had been the two principal opponents of peace on either side—the latter from the success and honour which war gave him, the former because he thought that, if tranquillity were restored, his crimes would be more open to detection and his slanders less credited—the foremost candidates for power in either city, Pleistoanax, son of Pausanias, king of Lacedaemon, and Nicias, son of Niceratus, the most fortunate general of his time, each desired peace more ardently than ever. Nicias, while still happy and honoured, wished to secure his good fortune, to obtain a present release from trouble for himself and his countrymen, and hand down to posterity a name as an ever-successful statesman, and thought the way to do this was to keep out of danger and commit himself as little as possible to fortune, and that peace alone made this keeping out of danger possible. Pleistoanax, again, was assailed by his enemies for his restoration, and regularly held up by them to the prejudice of his countrymen, upon every reverse that befell them, as though his unjust restoration were the cause; the accusation being that he and his brother Aristocles had bribed the prophetess of Delphi to tell the Lacedaemonian deputations which successively arrived at the temple to bring home the seed of the demigod son of Zeus from abroad, else they would have to plough with a silver share. In this way, it was

insisted, in time he had induced the Lacedaemonians in the nineteenth year of his exile to Lycaeum (whither he had gone when banished on suspicion of having been bribed to retreat from Attica, and had built half his house within the consecrated precinct of Zeus for fear of the Lacedaemonians), to restore him with the same dances and sacrifices with which they had instituted their kings upon the first settlement of Lacedaemon. [17] The smart of this accusation, and the reflection that in peace no disaster could occur, and that when Lacedaemon had recovered her men there would be nothing for his enemies to take hold of (whereas, while war lasted, the highest station must always bear the scandal of everything that went wrong), made him ardently desire a settlement. Accordingly this winter was employed in conferences; and as spring rapidly approached, the Lacedaemonians sent round orders to the cities to prepare for a fortified occupation of Attica, and held this as a sword over the heads of the Athenians to induce them to listen to their overtures; and at last, after many claims had been urged on either side at the conferences, a peace was agreed on upon the following basis. Each party was to restore its conquests, but Athens was to keep Nisaea; her demand for Plataea being met by the Thebans asserting that they had acquired the place not by force or treachery, but by the voluntary adhesion upon agreement of its citizens; and the same, according to the Athenian account, being the history of her acquisition of Nisaea. This arranged, the Lacedaemonians summoned their allies, and all voting for peace except the Boeotians, Corinthians, Eleans, and Megarians, who did not approve of these proceedings, they concluded the treaty and made peace, each of the contracting parties swearing to the following articles:

[18] *The Athenians and Lacedaemonians and their allies made a treaty, and swore to it, city by city, as follows;*

1. *Touching the national temples, there shall be a free passage by land and by sea to all who wish it, to sacrifice, travel, consult, and attend the oracle or games, according to the customs of their countries.*

2. *The temple and shrine of Apollo at Delphi and the Delphians shall be governed by their own laws, taxed by their own state, and judged by their own judges, the land and the people, according to the custom of their country.*

3. *The treaty shall be binding for fifty years upon the Athenians and the allies of the Athenians, and upon the Lacedaemonians and the allies of the Lacedaemonians, without fraud or hurt by land or by sea.*

4. *It shall not be lawful to take up arms, with intent to do hurt, either for the Lacedaemonians and their allies against the Athenians and their allies, or for the Athenians and their allies against the Lacedaemonians and their allies, in any way or means whatsoever. But should any difference arise between them they are to have recourse to law and oaths, according as may be agreed between the parties.*

5. *The Lacedaemonians and their allies shall give back Amphipolis to the Athenians. Nevertheless, in the case of cities given up by the Lacedaemonians to the Athenians, the inhabitants shall be allowed to go where they please and to take their property with them: and the cities shall be independent, paying only the tribute of Aristides. And it shall not be lawful for the Athenians or their allies to carry on war against them after the treaty has been concluded, so long as the tribute is paid. The cities referred to are Argilus, Stagirus, Acanthus, Scolus, Olynthus, and Spartolus. These cities shall be neutral, allies neither of the Lacedaemonians nor of the Athenians: but if the cities consent, it shall be lawful for the Athenians to make them their allies, provided always that the cities wish it. The Mecybernaeans, Sanaeans, and Singaeans shall inhabit their own cities, as also the Olynthians and Acanthians: but the Lacedaemonians and their allies shall give back Panactum to the Athenians.*

6. *The Athenians shall give back Coryphasium, Cythera, Methana, Pteleum, and Atalanta to the Lacedaemonians, and also all Lacedaemonians that are in the prison at Athens or elsewhere in the Athenian dominions, and shall let go the Peloponnesians besieged in Scione, and all others in Scione that are allies of the Lacedaemonians, and all whom Brasidas sent in there, and any others of the allies of the Lacedaemonians that may be in the prison at Athens or elsewhere in the Athenian dominions.*

7. *The Lacedaemonians and their allies shall in like manner give back any of the Athenians or their allies that they may have in their hands.*

8. *In the case of Scione, Torone, and Sermylium, and any other cities that the Athenians may have, the Athenians may adopt such measures as they please.*

9. *The Athenians shall take an oath to the Lacedaemonians and their allies, city by city. Every man shall swear by the most binding oath of his country, seventeen from each city. The oath shall be as follows; "I will abide by this agreement and treaty honestly and without deceit." In the same way an oath shall be taken by the Lacedaemonians and their allies to the Athenians: and the oath shall be renewed annually by both parties. Pillars shall be erected at Olympia, Pythia, the Isthmus, at Athens in the Acropolis, and at Lacedaemon in the temple at Amyclae.*

10. *If anything be forgotten, whatever it be, and on whatever point, it shall be consistent with their oath for both parties, the Athenians and Lacedaemonians, to alter it, according to their discretion.*

[19] *The treaty begins from the ephoralty of Pleistolas in Lacedaemon, on the 27th day of the month of Artemisium, and from the archonship of Alcaeus at Athens, on the 25th day of the month of Elaphebolion. Those who took the oath and poured the libations for the Lacedaemonians were Pleistoanax, Agis, Pleistolas, Damagetis, Chionis, Metagenes, Acanthus, Daithus, Ischagoras, Philocharidas, Zeuxidas, Antippus, Tellis, Alcinadas, Empedias, Menas, and Laphilus: for the Athenians, Lampon, Isthmonicus, Nicias, Laches, Euthydemus, Procles, Pythodorus, Hagnon, Myrtilus, Thrasycles, Theagenes, Aristocrates, Iolcius, Timocrates, Leon, Lamachus, and Demosthenes.*

[20] This treaty was made in the spring, just at the end of winter, directly after the city festival of Dionysus, just ten years, with the difference of a few days, from the first invasion of Attica and the commencement of this war. This must be calculated by the seasons rather than by trusting to the enumeration of the names of the several magistrates or offices of honour that are used to mark past events. Accuracy is impossible where an event may have occurred in the beginning, or middle, or at any period in their tenure of office. But by computing by summers and winters, the method adopted in this history, it will be found that, each of these amounting to half a year, there were ten summers and as many winters contained in this first war.

[21] Meanwhile the Lacedaemonians, to whose lot it fell to begin the work of restitution, immediately set free all the prisoners of war in their possession, and sent Ischagoras, Menas, and Philocharidas as envoys to the towns in the direction of Thrace, to order Cle-

aridas to hand over Amphipolis to the Athenians, and the rest of their allies each to accept the treaty as it affected them. They, however, did not like its terms, and refused to accept it; Clearidas also, willing to oblige the Chalcidians, would not hand over the town, averring his inability to do so against their will. Meanwhile he hastened in person to Lacedaemon with envoys from the place, to defend his disobedience against the possible accusations of Ischagoras and his companions, and also to see whether it was too late for the agreement to be altered; and on finding the Lacedaemonians were bound, quickly set out back again with instructions from them to hand over the place, if possible, or at all events to bring out the Peloponnesians that were in it.

[22] The allies happened to be present in person at Lacedaemon, and those who had not accepted the treaty were now asked by the Lacedaemonians to adopt it. This, however, they refused to do, for the same reasons as before, unless a fairer one than the present were agreed upon; and remaining firm in their determination were dismissed by the Lacedaemonians, who now decided on forming an alliance with the Athenians, thinking that Argos, who had refused the application of Ampelidas and Lichas for a renewal of the treaty, would without Athens be no longer formidable, and that the rest of the Peloponnese would be most likely to keep quiet, if the coveted alliance of Athens were shut against them. Accordingly, after conference with the Athenian ambassadors, an alliance was agreed upon and oaths were exchanged, upon the terms following:

[23] 1. *The Lacedaemonians shall be allies of the Athenians for fifty years.*

2. *Should any enemy invade the territory of Lacedaemon and injure the Lacedaemonians, the Athenians shall help them in such way as they most effectively can, according to their power. But if the invader be gone after plundering the country, that city shall be the enemy of Lacedaemon and Athens, and shall be chastised by both, and one shall not make peace without the other. This to be honestly, loyally, and without fraud.*

3. *Should any enemy invade the territory of Athens and injure the Athenians, the Lacedaemonians shall help them in such way as they most effectively can, according to their power. But if the invader be gone after plundering the country, that city shall be the enemy of Lacedaemon and Athens, and shall be chastised by both, and one shall not make peace without* the other. This to be honestly, loyally, and without fraud.

4. *Should the slave population rise, the Athenians shall help the Lacedaemonians with all their might, according to their power.*

5. *This treaty shall be sworn to by the same persons on either side that swore to the other. It shall be renewed annually by the Lacedaemonians going to Athens for the Dionysia, and the Athenians to Lacedaemon for the Hyacinthia, and a pillar shall be set up by either party: at Lacedaemon near the statue of Apollo at Amyclae, and at Athens on the Acropolis near the statue of Athene. Should the Lacedaemonians and Athenians see fit to add to or take away from the alliance in any particular, it shall be consistent with their oaths for both parties to do so, according to their discretion.*

[24] *Those who took the oath for the Lacedaemonians were Pleistoanax, Agis, Pleistolas, Damagetus, Chionis, Metagenes, Acanthus, Daithus, Ischagoras, Philocharidas, Zeuxidas, Antippus, Alcinadas, Tellis, Empedias, Menas, and Laphilus; for the Athenians, Lampon, Isthmionicus, Laches, Nicias, Euthydemus, Procles, Pythodorus, Hagnon, Myrtilus, Thrasycles, Theagenes, Aristocrates, Iolcius, Timocrates, Leon, Lamachus, and Demosthenes.*

This alliance was made not long after the treaty; and the Athenians gave back the men from the island to the Lacedaemonians, and the summer of the eleventh year began. This completes the history of the first war, which occupied the whole of the ten years previously.

CHAPTER XVI

Feeling against Sparta in Peloponnese—League of the Mantineans, Eleans, Argives, and Athenians—Battle of Mantinea and breaking up of the League

[25] AFTER the treaty and the alliance between the Lacedaemonians and Athenians, concluded after the ten years' war, in the ephorate of Pleistolas at Lacedaemon, and the archonship of Alcaeus at Athens, the states which had accepted them were at peace; but the Corinthians and some of the cities in Peloponnese trying to disturb the settlement, a fresh agitation was instantly commenced by the allies against Lacedaemon. Further, the Lacedaemonians, as time went on, became suspected by the Athenians through their not performing some of the provisions in the treaty; and though for six years and ten months they abstained from in-

vasion of each other's territory, yet abroad an unstable armistice did not prevent either party doing the other the most effectual injury, until they were finally obliged to break the treaty made after the ten years' war and to have recourse to open hostilities.

[26] The history of this period has been also written by the same Thucydides, an Athenian, in the chronological order of events by summers and winters, to the time when the Lacedaemonians and their allies put an end to the Athenian empire, and took the Long Walls and Piraeus. The war had then lasted for twenty-seven years in all. Only a mistaken judgment can object to including the interval of treaty in the war. Looked at by the light of facts it cannot, it will be found, be rationally considered a state of peace, where neither party either gave or got back all that they had agreed, apart from the violations of it which occurred on both sides in the Mantinean and Epidaurian wars and other instances, and the fact that the allies in the direction of Thrace were in as open hostility as ever, while the Boeotians had only a truce renewed every ten days. So that the first ten years' war, the treacherous armistice that followed it, and the subsequent war will, calculating by the seasons, be found to make up the number of years which I have mentioned, with the difference of a few days, and to afford an instance of faith in oracles being for once justified by the event. I certainly all along remember from the beginning to the end of the war its being commonly declared that it would last thrice nine years. I lived through the whole of it, being of an age to comprehend events, and giving my attention to them in order to know the exact truth about them. It was also my fate to be an exile from my country for twenty years after my command at Amphipolis; and being present with both parties, and more especially with the Peloponnesians by reason of my exile, I had leisure to observe affairs somewhat particularly. I will accordingly now relate the differences that arose after the ten years' war, the breach of the treaty, and the hostilities that followed.

[27] After the conclusion of the fifty years' truce and of the subsequent alliance, the embassies from Peloponnese which had been summoned for this business returned from Lacedaemon. The rest went straight home, but the Corinthians first turned aside to Argos and opened negotiations with some of the men in office there, pointing out that Lacedaemon could have no good end in view, but only the subjugation of Peloponnese, or she would never have entered into treaty and alliance with the once detested Athenians, and that the duty of consulting for the safety of Peloponnese had now fallen upon Argos, who should immediately pass a decree inviting any Hellenic state that chose, such state being independent and accustomed to meet fellow powers upon the 'fair and equal ground of law and justice, to make a defensive alliance with the Argives; appointing a few individuals with plenipotentiary powers, instead of making the people the medium of negotiation, in order that, in the case of an applicant being rejected, the fact of his overtures might not be made public. They said that many would come over from hatred of the Lacedaemonians. After this explanation of their views, the Corinthians returned home.

[28] The persons with whom they had communicated reported the proposal to their government and people, and the Argives passed the decree and chose twelve men to negotiate an alliance for any Hellenic state that wished it, except Athens and Lacedaemon, neither of which should be able to join without reference to the Argive people. Argos came into the plan the more readily because she saw that war with Lacedaemon was inevitable, the truce being on the point of expiring; and also because she hoped to gain the supremacy of Peloponnese. For at this time Lacedaemon had sunk very low in public estimation because of her disasters, while the Argives were in a most flourishing condition, having taken no part in the Attic war, but having on the contrary profited largely by their neutrality. The Argives accordingly prepared to receive into alliance any of the Hellenes that desired it.

[29] The Mantineans and their allies were the first to come over through fear of the Lacedaemonians. Having taken advantage of the war against Athens to reduce a large part of Arcadia into subjection, they thought that Lacedaemon would not leave them undisturbed in their conquests, now that she had leisure to interfere, and consequently gladly turned to a powerful city like Argos, the historical enemy of the Lacedaemonians, and a sister democracy. Upon the defection of Mantinea, the rest of Peloponnese at once began to agitate the propriety of following her example, conceiving that the Mantineans would not have changed sides without good reason; besides which they were angry with Lacedaemon among other reasons for having inserted in the treaty with Athens that it should be con-

sistent with their oaths for both parties, Lacedaemonians and Athenians, to add to or take
away from it according to their discretion. It
was this clause that was the real origin of the
panic in Peloponnese, by exciting suspicions of
a Lacedaemonian and Athenian combination
against their liberties: any alteration should
properly have been made conditional upon the
consent of the whole body of the allies. With
these apprehensions there was a very general
desire in each state to place itself in alliance
with Argos.

[30] In the meantime the Lacedaemonians
perceiving the agitation going on in Peloponnese, and that Corinth was the author of it
and was herself about to enter into alliance
with the Argives, sent ambassadors thither in
the hope of preventing what was in contemplation. They accused her of having brought it all
about, and told her that she could not desert
Lacedaemon and become the ally of Argos,
without adding violation of her oaths to the
crime which she had already committed in not
accepting the treaty with Athens, when it had
been expressly agreed that the decision of the
majority of the allies should be binding, unless
the gods or heroes stood in the way. Corinth
in her answer, delivered before those of her
allies who had like her refused to accept the
treaty, and whom she had previously invited
to attend, refrained from openly stating the injuries she complained of, such as the non-re-
covery of Sollium or Anactorium from the
Athenians, or any other point in which she
thought she had been prejudiced, but took
shelter under the pretext that she could not
give up her Thracian allies, to whom her separate individual security had been given, when
they first rebelled with Potidaea, as well as
upon subsequent occasions. She denied, therefore, that she committed any violation of her
oaths to the allies in not entering into the
treaty with Athens; having sworn upon the
faith of the gods to her Thracian friends, she
could not honestly give them up. Besides, the
expression was, "unless the gods or heroes
stand in the way." Now here, as it appeared to
her, the gods stood in the way. This was what
she said on the subject of her former oaths. As
to the Argive alliance, she would confer with
her friends and do whatever was right. The
Lacedaemonian envoys returning home, some
Argive ambassadors who happened to be in
Corinth pressed her to conclude the alliance
without further delay, but were told to attend
at the next congress to be held at Corinth.

[31] Immediately afterwards an Elean embassy arrived, and first making an alliance with
Corinth went on from thence to Argos, according to their instructions, and became allies of
the Argives, their country being just then at
enmity with Lacedaemon and Lepreum. Some
time back there had been a war between the
Lepreans and some of the Arcadians; and the
Eleans being called in by the former with the
offer of half their lands, had put an end to the
war, and leaving the land in the hands of its
Leprean occupiers had imposed upon them the
tribute of a talent to the Olympian Zeus. Till
the Attic war this tribute was paid by the Lepreans, who then took the war as an excuse for
no longer doing so, and upon the Eleans using
force appealed to Lacedaemon. The case was
thus submitted to her arbitrament; but the
Eleans, suspecting the fairness of the tribunal,
renounced the reference and laid waste the
Leprean territory. The Lacedaemonians nevertheless decided that the Lepreans were independent and the Eleans aggressors, and as the
latter did not abide by the arbitration, sent a
garrison of heavy infantry into Lepreum. Upon
this the Eleans, holding that Lacedaemon had
received one of their rebel subjects, put forward the convention providing that each confederate should come out of the Attic war in
possession of what he had when he went into
it, and considering that justice had not been
done them went over to the Argives, and now
made the alliance through their ambassadors,
who had been instructed for that purpose. Immediately after them the Corinthians and the
Thracian Chalcidians became allies of Argos.
Meanwhile the Boeotians and Megarians, who
acted together, remained quiet, being left to
do as they pleased by Lacedaemon, and thinking that the Argive democracy would not suit
so well with their aristocratic government as
the Lacedaemonian constitution.

[32] About the same time in this summer
Athens succeeded in reducing Scione, put the
adult males to death, and, making slaves of the
women and children, gave the land for the
Plataeans to live in. She also brought back the
Delians to Delos, moved by her misfortunes in
the field and by the commands of the god at
Delphi. Meanwhile the Phocians and Locrians
commenced hostilities. The Corinthians and
Argives, being now in alliance, went to Tegea
to bring about its defection from Lacedaemon,
seeing that, if so considerable a state could be
persuaded to join, all Peloponnese would be
with them. But when the Tegeans said that

they would do nothing against Lacedaemon, the hitherto zealous Corinthians relaxed their activity, and began to fear that none of the rest would now come over. Still they went to the Boeotians and tried to persuade them to alliance and a common action generally with Argos and themselves, and also begged them to go with them to Athens and obtain for them a ten days' truce similar to that made between the Athenians and Boeotians not long after the fifty years' treaty, and, in the event of the Athenians refusing, to throw up the armistice, and not make any truce in future without Corinth. These were the requests of the Corinthians. The Boeotians stopped them on the subject of the Argive alliance, but went with them to Athens, where however they failed to obtain the ten days' truce; the Athenian answer being that the Corinthians had truce already, as being allies of Lacedaemon. Nevertheless the Boeotians did not throw up their ten days' truce, in spite of the prayers and reproaches of the Corinthians for their breach of faith; and these last had to content themselves with a *de facto* armistice with Athens.

[*33*] The same summer the Lacedaemonians marched into Arcadia with their whole levy under Pleistoanax, son of Pausanias, king of Lacedaemon, against the Parrhasians, who were subjects of Mantinea, and a faction of whom had invited their aid. They also meant to demolish, if possible, the fort of Cypsela which the Mantineans had built and garrisoned in the Parrhasian territory, to annoy the district of Sciritis in Laconia. The Lacedaemonians accordingly laid waste the Parrhasian country, and the Mantineans, placing their town in the hands of an Argive garrison, addressed themselves to the defence of their confederacy, but being unable to save Cypsela or the Parrhasian towns went back to Mantinea. Meanwhile the Lacedaemonians made the Parrhasians independent, razed the fortress, and returned home.

[*34*] The same summer the soldiers from Thrace who had gone out with Brasidas came back, having been brought from thence after the treaty by Clearidas; and the Lacedaemonians decreed that the Helots who had fought with Brasidas should be free and allowed to live where they liked, and not long afterwards settled them with the Neodamodes at Lepreum, which is situated on the Laconian and Elean border; Lacedaemon being at this time at enmity with Elis. Those however of the Spartans who had been taken prisoners on the

island and had surrendered their arms might, it was feared, suppose that they were to be subjected to some degradation in consequence of their misfortune, and so make some attempt at revolution, if left in possession of their franchise. These were therefore at once disfranchised, although some of them were in office at the time, and thus placed under a disability to take office, or buy and sell anything. After some time, however, the franchise was restored to them.

[*35*] The same summer the Dians took Thyssus, a town on Acte by Athos in alliance with Athens. During the whole of this summer intercourse between the Athenians and Peloponnesians continued, although each party began to suspect the other directly after the treaty, because of the places specified in it not being restored. Lacedaemon, to whose lot it had fallen to begin by restoring Amphipolis and the other towns, had not done so. She had equally failed to get the treaty accepted by her Thracian allies, or by the Boeotians or the Corinthians; although she was continually promising to unite with Athens in compelling their compliance, if it were longer refused. She also kept fixing a time at which those who still refused to come in were to be declared enemies to both parties, but took care not to bind herself by any written agreement. Meanwhile the Athenians, seeing none of these professions performed in fact, began to suspect the honesty of her intentions, and consequently not only refused to comply with her demands for Pylos, but also repented having given up the prisoners from the island, and kept tight hold of the other places, until Lacedaemon's part of the treaty should be fulfilled. Lacedaemon, on the other hand, said she had done what she could, having given up the Athenian prisoners of war in her possession, evacuated Thrace, and performed everything else in her power. Amphipolis it was out of her ability to restore; but she would endeavour to bring the Boeotians and Corinthians into the treaty, to recover Panactum, and send home all the Athenian prisoners of war in Boeotia. Meanwhile she required that Pylos should be restored, or at all events that the Messenians and Helots should be withdrawn, as her troops had been from Thrace, and the place garrisoned, if necessary, by the Athenians themselves. After a number of different conferences held during the summer, she succeeded in persuading Athens to withdraw from Pylos the Messenians and the rest of the Helots and deserters from Laconia,

who were accordingly settled by her at Cranii in Cephallenia. Thus during this summer there was peace and intercourse between the two peoples.

[*36*] Next winter, however, the ephors under whom the treaty had been made were no longer in office, and some of their successors were directly opposed to it. Embassies now arrived from the Lacedaemonian confederacy, and the Athenians, Boeotians, and Corinthians also presented themselves at Lacedaemon, and after much discussion and no agreement between them, separated for their several homes; when Cleobulus and Xenares, the two ephors who were the most anxious to break off the treaty, took advantage of this opportunity to communicate privately with the Boeotians and Corinthians, and, advising them to act as much as possible together, instructed the former first to enter into alliance with Argos, and then try and bring themselves and the Argives into alliance with Lacedaemon. The Boeotians would so be least likely to be compelled to come into the Attic treaty; and the Lacedaemonians would prefer gaining the friendship and alliance of Argos even at the price of the hostility of Athens and the rupture of the treaty. The Boeotians knew that an honourable friendship with Argos had been long the desire of Lacedaemon; for the Lacedaemonians believed that this would considerably facilitate the conduct of the war outside Peloponnese. Meanwhile they begged the Boeotians to place Panactum in her hands in order that she might, if possible, obtain Pylos in exchange for it, and so be more in a position to resume hostilities with Athens.

[*37*] After receiving these instructions for their governments from Xenares and Cleobulus and their friends at Lacedaemon, the Boeotians and Corinthians departed. On their way home they were joined by two persons high in office at Argos, who had waited for them on the road, and who now sounded them upon the possibility of the Boeotians joining the Corinthians, Eleans, and Mantineans in becoming the allies of Argos, in the idea that if this could be effected they would be able, thus united, to make peace or war as they pleased either against Lacedaemon or any other power. The Boeotian envoys were pleased at thus hearing themselves accidentally asked to do what their friends at Lacedaemon had told them; and the two Argives perceiving that their proposal was agreeable, departed with a promise to send ambassadors to the Boeotians. On their

arrival the Boeotians reported to the Boeotarchs what had been said to them at Lacedaemon and also by the Argives who had met them, and the Boeotarchs, pleased with the idea, embraced it with the more eagerness from the lucky coincidence of Argos soliciting the very thing wanted by their friends at Lacedaemon. Shortly afterwards ambassadors appeared from Argos with the proposals indicated; and the Boeotarchs approved of the terms and dismissed the ambassadors with a promise to send envoys to Argos to negotiate the alliance.

[*38*] In the meantime it was decided by the Boeotarchs, the Corinthians, the Megarians, and the envoys from Thrace first to interchange oaths together to give help to each other whenever it was required and not to make war or peace except in common; after which the Boeotians and Megarians, who acted together, should make the alliance with Argos. But before the oaths were taken the Boeotarchs communicated these proposals to the four councils of the Boeotians, in whom the supreme power resides, and advised them to interchange oaths with all such cities as should be willing to enter into a defensive league with the Boeotians. But the members of the Boeotian councils refused their assent to the proposal, being afraid of offending Lacedaemon by entering into a league with the deserter Corinth; the Boeotarchs not having acquainted them with what had passed at Lacedaemon and with the advice given by Cleobulus and Xenares and the Boeotian partisans there, namely, that they should become allies of Corinth and Argos as a preliminary to a junction with Lacedaemon; fancying that, even if they should say nothing about this, the councils would not vote against what had been decided and advised by the Boeotarchs. This difficulty arising, the Corinthians and the envoys from Thrace departed without anything having been concluded; and the Boeotarchs, who had previously intended after carrying this to try and effect the alliance with Argos, now omitted to bring the Argive question before the councils, or to send to Argos the envoys whom they had promised; and a general coldness and delay ensued in the matter.

[*39*] In this same winter Mecyberna was assaulted and taken by the Olynthians, having an Athenian garrison inside it.

All this while negotiations had been going on between the Athenians and Lacedaemonians about the conquests still retained by each, and Lacedaemon, hoping that if Athens were to get back Panactum from the Boeotians she might herself recover Pylos, now sent an embassy to the Boeotians, and begged them to place Panactum and their Athenian prisoners in her hands, in order that she might exchange them for Pylos. This the Boeotians refused to do, unless Lacedaemon made a separate alliance with them as she had done with Athens. Lacedaemon knew that this would be a breach of faith to Athens, as it had been agreed that neither of them should make peace or war without the other; yet wishing to obtain Panactum which she hoped to exchange for Pylos, and the party who pressed for the dissolution of the treaty strongly affecting the Boeotian connection, she at length concluded the alliance just as winter gave way to spring; and Panactum was instantly razed. And so the eleventh year of the war ended.

[40] In the first days of the summer following, the Argives, seeing that the promised ambassadors from Boeotia did not arrive, and that Panactum was being demolished, and that a separate alliance had been concluded between the Boeotians and Lacedaemonians, began to be afraid that Argos might be left alone, and all the confederacy go over to Lacedaemon. They fancied that the Boeotians had been persuaded by the Lacedaemonians to raze Panactum and to enter into the treaty with the Athenians, and that Athens was privy to this arrangement, and even her alliance, therefore, no longer open to them—a resource which they had always counted upon, by reason of the dissensions existing, in the event of the non-continuance of their treaty with Lacedaemon. In this strait the Argives, afraid that, as the result of refusing to renew the treaty with Lacedaemon and of aspiring to the supremacy in Peloponnese, they would have the Lacedaemonians, Tegeans, Boeotians, and Athenians on their hands all at once, now hastily sent off Eustrophus and Aeson, who seemed the persons most likely to be acceptable, as envoys to Lacedaemon, with the view of making as good a treaty as they could with the Lacedaemonians, upon such terms as could be got, and being left in peace.

[41] Having reached Lacedaemon, their ambassadors proceeded to negotiate the terms of the proposed treaty. What the Argives first demanded was that they might be allowed to refer to the arbitration of some state or private person the question of the Cynurian land, a piece of frontier territory about which they have always been disputing, and which con-

tains the towns of Thyrea and Anthene, and is occupied by the Lacedaemonians. The Lacedaemonians at first said that they could not allow this point to be discussed, but were ready to conclude upon the old terms. Eventually, however, the Argive ambassadors succeeded in obtaining from them this concession: For the present there was to be a truce for fifty years, but it should be competent for either party, there being neither plague nor war in Lacedaemon or Argos, to give a formal challenge and decide the question of this territory by battle, as on a former occasion, when both sides claimed the victory; pursuit not being allowed beyond the frontier of Argos or Lacedaemon. The Lacedaemonians at first thought this mere folly; but at last, anxious at any cost to have the friendship of Argos, they agreed to the terms demanded, and reduced them to writing. However, before any of this should become binding, the ambassadors were to return to Argos and communicate with their people and, in the event of their approval, to come at the feast of the Hyacinthia and take the oaths.

The envoys returned accordingly. [42] In the meantime, while the Argives were engaged in these negotiations, the Lacedaemonian ambassadors—Andromedes, Phaedimus, and Antimenidas—who were to receive the prisoners from the Boeotians and restore them and Panactum to the Athenians, found that the Boeotians had themselves razed Panactum, upon the plea that oaths had been anciently exchanged between their people and the Athenians, after a dispute on the subject to the effect that neither should inhabit the place, but that they should graze it in common. As for the Athenian prisoners of war in the hands of the Boeotians, these were delivered over to Andromedes and his colleagues, and by them conveyed to Athens and given back. The envoys at the same time announced the razing of Panactum, which to them seemed as good as its restitution, as it would no longer lodge an enemy of Athens. This announcement was received with great indignation by the Athenians, who thought that the Lacedaemonians had played them false, both in the matter of the demolition of Panactum, which ought to have been restored to them standing, and in having, as they now heard, made a separate alliance with the Boeotians, in spite of their previous promise to join Athens in compelling the adhesion of those who refused to accede to the treaty. The Athenians also considered the other points in which Lacedaemon had failed in her compact, and thinking that they had been over-reached, gave an angry answer to the ambassadors and sent them away.

[43] The breach between the Lacedaemonians and Athenians having gone thus far, the party at Athens, also, who wished to cancel the treaty, immediately put themselves in motion. Foremost amongst these was Alcibiades, son of Clinias, a man yet young in years for any other Hellenic city, but distinguished by the splendour of his ancestry. Alcibiades thought the Argive alliance really preferable, not that personal pique had not also a great deal to do with his opposition; he being offended with the Lacedaemonians for having negotiated the treaty through Nicias and Laches, and having overlooked him on account of his youth, and also for not having shown him the respect due to the ancient connection of his family with them as their *proxeni*, which, renounced by his grandfather, he had lately himself thought to renew by his attentions to their prisoners taken in the island. Being thus, as he thought, slighted on all hands, he had in the first instance spoken against the treaty, saying that the Lacedaemonians were not to be trusted, but that they only treated, in order to be enabled by this means to crush Argos, and afterwards to attack Athens alone; and now, immediately upon the above occurring, he sent privately to the Argives, telling them to come as quickly as possible to Athens, accompanied by the Mantineans and Eleans, with proposals of alliance; as the moment was propitious and he himself would do all he could to help them.

[44] Upon receiving this message and discovering that the Athenians, far from being privy to the Boeotian alliance, were involved in a serious quarrel with the Lacedaemonians, the Argives paid no further attention to the embassy which they had just sent to Lacedaemon on the subject of the treaty, and began to incline rather towards the Athenians, reflecting that, in the event of war, they would thus have on their side a city that was not only an ancient ally of Argos, but a sister democracy and very powerful at sea. They accordingly at once sent ambassadors to Athens to treat for an alliance, accompanied by others from Elis and Mantinea.

At the same time arrived in haste from Lacedaemon an embassy consisting of persons reputed well disposed towards the Athenians—Philocharidas, Leon, and Endius—for fear that the Athenians in their irritation might conclude alliance with the Argives, and also to ask back Pylos in exchange for Panactum, and in defence of the alliance with the Boeotians to plead that it had not been made to hurt the Athenians. [45] Upon the envoys speaking in the senate upon these points, and stating that they had come with full powers to settle all others at issue between them, Alcibiades became afraid that, if they were to repeat these statements to the popular assembly, they might gain the multitude, and the Argive alliance might be rejected, and accordingly had recourse to the following stratagem. He persuaded the Lacedaemonians by a solemn assurance that if they would say nothing of their full powers in the assembly, he would give back Pylos to them (himself, the present opponent of its restitution, engaging to obtain this from the Athenians), and would settle the other points at issue. His plan was to detach them from Nicias and to disgrace them before the people, as being without sincerity in their intentions, or even common consistency in their language, and so to get the Argives, Eleans, and Mantineans taken into alliance. This plan proved successful. When the envoys appeared before the people, and upon the question being put to them, did not say as they had said in the senate, that they had come with full powers, the Athenians lost all patience, and carried away by Alcibiades, who thundered more loudly than ever against the Lacedaemonians, were ready instantly to introduce the Argives and their companions and to take them into alliance. An earthquake, however, occurring, before anything definite had been done, this assembly was adjourned.

[46] In the assembly held the next day, Nicias, in spite of the Lacedaemonians having been deceived themselves, and having allowed him to be deceived also in not admitting that they had come with full powers, still maintained that it was best to be friends with the Lacedaemonians, and, letting the Argive proposals stand over, to send once more to Lacedaemon and learn her intentions. The adjournment of the war could only increase their own prestige and injure that of their rivals; the excellent state of their affairs making it their interest to preserve this prosperity as long as possible, while those of Lacedaemon were so desperate that the sooner she could try her fortune again the better. He succeeded accordingly in persuading them to send ambassadors, himself being among the number, to invite the Lacedaemonians, if they were really sincere, to re-

store Panactum intact with Amphipolis, and to abandon their alliance with the Boeotians (unless they consented to accede to the treaty), agreeably to the stipulation which forbade either party to treat without the other. The ambassadors were also directed to say that the Athenians, had they wished to play false, might already have made alliance with the Argives, who were indeed come to Athens for that very purpose, and went off furnished with instructions as to any other complaints that the Athenians had to make. Having reached Lacedaemon, they communicated their instructions, and concluded by telling the Lacedaemonians that unless they gave up their alliance with the Boeotians, in the event of their not acceding to the treaty, the Athenians for their part would ally themselves with the Argives and their friends. The Lacedaemonians, however, refused to give up the Boeotian alliance—the party of Xenares the ephor, and such as shared their view, carrying the day upon this point—but renewed the oaths at the request of Nicias, who feared to return without having accomplished anything and to be disgraced; as was indeed his fate, he being held the author of the treaty with Lacedaemon. When he returned, and the Athenians heard that nothing had been done at Lacedaemon, they flew into a passion, and deciding that faith had not been kept with them, took advantage of the presence of the Argives and their allies, who had been introduced by Alcibiades, and made a treaty and alliance with them upon the terms following:

[47] *The Athenians, Argives, Mantineans, and Eleans, acting for themselves and the allies in their respective empires, made a treaty for a hundred years, to be without fraud or hurt by land and by sea.*

1. *It shall not be lawful to carry on war, either for the Argives, Eleans, Mantineans, and their allies, against the Athenians, or the allies in the Athenian empire: or for the Athenians and their allies against the Argives, Eleans, Mantineans, or their allies, in any way or means whatsoever.*
The Athenians, Argives, Eleans, and Mantineans shall be allies for a hundred years upon the terms following:

2. *If an enemy invade the country of the Athenians, the Argives, Eleans, and Mantineans shall go to the relief of Athens, according as the Athenians may require by message, in such way as they most effectually can, to the best of their power. But if the invader be gone after plundering the territory, the offending*
state shall be the enemy of the Argives, Mantineans, Eleans, and Athenians, and war shall be made against it by all these cities: and no one of the cities shall be able to make peace with that state, except all the above cities agree to do so.*

3. *Likewise the Athenians shall go to the relief of Argos, Mantinea, and Elis, if an enemy invade the country of Elis, Mantinea, or Argos, according as the above cities may require by message, in such way as they most effectually can, to the best of their power. But if the invader be gone after plundering the territory, the state offending shall be the enemy of the Athenians, Argives, Mantineans, and Eleans, and war shall be made against it by all these cities, and peace may not be made with that state except all the above cities agree to it.*

4. *No armed force shall be allowed to pass for hostile purposes through the country of the powers contracting, or of the allies in their respective empires, or to go by sea, except all the cities—that is to say, Athens, Argos, Mantinea, and Elis—vote for such passage.*

5. *The relieving troops shall be maintained by the city sending them for thirty days from their arrival in the city that has required them, and upon their return in the same way: if their services be desired for a longer period, the city that sent for them shall maintain them, at the rate of three Aeginetan obols per day for a heavy-armed soldier, archer, or light soldier, and an Aeginetan drachma for a trooper.*

6. *The city sending for the troops shall have the command when the war is in its own country: but in case of the cities resolving upon a joint expedition the command shall be equally divided among all the cities.*

7. *The treaty shall be sworn to by the Athenians for themselves and their allies, by the Argives, Mantineans, Eleans, and their allies, by each state individually. Each shall swear the oath most binding in his country over fullgrown victims: the oath being as follows:*

"I WILL STAND BY THE ALLIANCE AND ITS ARTICLES, JUSTLY, INNOCENTLY, AND SINCERELY, AND I WILL NOT TRANSGRESS THE SAME IN ANY WAY OR MEANS WHATSOEVER."

The oath shall be taken at Athens by the Senate and the magistrates, the Prytanes administering it: at Argos by the Senate, the Eighty, and the Artynae, the Eighty administering it: at Mantinea by the Demiurgi, the Senate, and the other magistrates, the Theori and Polemarchs administering it: at Elis by the

Demiurgi, the magistrates, and the Six Hundred, the Demiurgi and the Thesmophylaces administering it. The oaths shall be renewed by the Athenians going to Elis, Mantinea, and Argos thirty days before the Olympic games: by the Argives, Mantineans, and Eleans going to Athens ten days before the great feast of the Panathenaea. The articles of the treaty, the oaths, and the alliance shall be inscribed on a stone pillar by the Athenians in the citadel, by the Argives in the market-place, in the temple of Apollo: by the Mantineans in the temple of Zeus, in the market-place: and a brazen pillar shall be erected jointly by them at the Olympic games now at hand. Should the above cities see good to make any addition in these articles, whatever all the above cities shall agree upon, after consulting together, shall be binding.

[48] Although the treaty and alliances were thus concluded, still the treaty between the Lacedaemonians and Athenians was not renounced by either party. Meanwhile Corinth, although the ally of the Argives, did not accede to the new treaty, any more than she had done to the alliance, defensive and offensive, formed before this between the Eleans, Argives, and Mantineans, when she declared herself content with the first alliance, which was defensive only, and which bound them to help each other, but not to join in attacking any. The Corinthians thus stood aloof from their allies, and again turned their thoughts towards Lacedaemon.

[49] At the Olympic games which were held this summer, and in which the Arcadian Androsthenes was victor the first time in the wrestling and boxing, the Lacedaemonians were excluded from the temple by the Eleans, and thus prevented from sacrificing or contending, for having refused to pay the fine specified in the Olympic law imposed upon them by the Eleans, who alleged that they had attacked Fort Phyrcus, and sent heavy infantry of theirs into Lepreum during the Olympic truce. The amount of the fine was two thousand minae, two for each heavy-armed soldier, as the law prescribes. The Lacedaemonians sent envoys, and pleaded that the imposition was unjust; saying that the truce had not yet been proclaimed at Lacedaemon when the heavy infantry were sent off. But the Eleans affirmed that the armistice with them had already begun (they proclaim it first among themselves), and that the aggression of the Lacedaemonians had taken them by surprise while they were living quietly as in time of peace, and not expecting anything. Upon this the Lacedaemonians submitted, that if the Eleans really believed that they had committed an aggression, it was useless after that to proclaim the truce at Lacedaemon; but they had proclaimed it notwithstanding, as believing nothing of the kind, and from that moment the Lacedaemonians had made no attack upon their country. Nevertheless the Eleans adhered to what they had said, that nothing would persuade them that an aggression had not been committed; if, however, the Lacedaemonians would restore Lepreum, they would give up their own share of the money and pay that of the god for them.

[50] As this proposal was not accepted, the Eleans tried a second. Instead of restoring Lepreum, if this was objected to, the Lacedaemonians should ascend the altar of the Olympian Zeus, as they were so anxious to have access to the temple, and swear before the Hellenes that they would surely pay the fine at a later day. This being also refused, the Lacedaemonians were excluded from the temple, the sacrifice, and the games, and sacrificed at home; the Lepreans being the only other Hellenes who did not attend. Still the Eleans were afraid of the Lacedaemonians sacrificing by force, and kept guard with a heavy-armed company of their young men; being also joined by a thousand Argives, the same number of Mantineans, and by some Athenian cavalry who stayed at Harpina during the feast. Great fears were felt in the assembly of the Lacedaemonians coming in arms, especially after Lichas, son of Arcesilaus, a Lacedaemonian, had been scourged on the course by the umpires; because, upon his horses being the winners, and the Boeotian people being proclaimed the victor on account of his having no right to enter, he came forward on the course and crowned the charioteer, in order to show that the chariot was his. After this incident all were more afraid than ever, and firmly looked for a disturbance: the Lacedaemonians, however, kept quiet, and let the feast pass by, as we have seen. After the Olympic games, the Argives and the allies repaired to Corinth to invite her to come over to them. There they found some Lacedaemonian envoys; and a long discussion ensued, which after all ended in nothing, as an earthquake occurred, and they dispersed to their different homes.

Summer was now over. [51] The winter following a battle took place between the Heracleots in Trachinia and the Aenianians, Dolopians, Malians, and certain of the Thessalians, all tribes bordering on and hostile to the town, which directly menaced their country. Accordingly, after having opposed and harassed it from its very foundation by every means in their power, they now in this battle defeated the Heracleots, Xenares, son of Cnidis, their Lacedaemonian commander, being among the slain. Thus the winter ended and the twelfth year of this war ended also. *[52]* After the battle, Heraclea was so terribly reduced that in the first days of the summer following the Boeotians occupied the place and sent away the Lacedaemonian Agesippidas for misgovernment, fearing that the town might be taken by the Athenians while the Lacedaemonians were distracted with the affairs of Peloponnese. The Lacedaemonians, nevertheless, were offended with them for what they had done.

The same summer Alcibiades, son of Clinias, now one of the generals at Athens, in concert with the Argives and the allies, went into Peloponnese with a few Athenian heavy infantry and archers and some of the allies in those parts whom he took up as he passed, and with this army marched here and there through Peloponnese, and settled various matters connected with the alliance, and among other things induced the Patrians to carry their walls down to the sea, intending himself also to build a fort near the Achaean Rhium. However, the Corinthians and Sicyonians, and all others who would have suffered by its being built, came up and hindered him.

[53] The same summer war broke out between the Epidaurians and Argives. The pretext was that the Epidaurians did not send an offering for their pasture-land to Apollo Pythaeus, as they were bound to do, the Argives having the chief management of the temple; but, apart from this pretext, Alcibiades and the Argives were determined, if possible, to gain possession of Epidaurus, and thus to ensure the neutrality of Corinth and give the Athenians a shorter passage for their reinforcements from Aegina than if they had to sail round Scyllaeum. The Argives accordingly prepared to invade Epidaurus by themselves, to exact the offering.

[54] About the same time the Lacedaemonians marched out with all their people to Leuctra upon their frontier, opposite to Mount Lycaeum, under the command of Agis, son of Archidamus, without any one knowing their destination, not even the cities that sent the contingents. The sacrifices, however, for crossing the frontier not proving propitious, the Lacedaemonians returned home themselves, and sent word to the allies to be ready to march after the month ensuing, which happened to be the month of Carneus, a holy time for the Dorians. Upon the retreat of the Lacedaemonians the Argives marched out on the last day but three of the month before Carneus, and keeping this as the day during the whole time that they were out, invaded and plundered Epidaurus. The Epidaurians summoned their allies to their aid, some of whom pleaded the month as an excuse; others came as far as the frontier of Epidaurus and there remained inactive.

[55] While the Argives were in Epidaurus embassies from the cities assembled at Mantinea, upon the invitation of the Athenians. The conference having begun, the Corinthian Euphamidas said that their actions did not agree with their words; while they were sitting deliberating about peace, the Epidaurians and their allies and the Argives were arrayed against each other in arms; deputies from each party should first go and separate the armies, and then the talk about peace might be resumed. In compliance with this suggestion, they went and brought back the Argives from Epidaurus, and afterwards reassembled, but without succeeding any better in coming to a conclusion; and the Argives a second time invaded Epidaurus and plundered the country. The Lacedaemonians also marched out to Caryae; but the frontier sacrifices again proving unfavourable, they went back again, and the Argives, after ravaging about a third of the Epidaurian territory, returned home. Meanwhile a thousand Athenian heavy infantry had come to their aid under the command of Alcibiades, but finding that the Lacedaemonian expedition was at an end, and that they were no longer wanted, went back again.

So passed the summer. *[56]* The next winter the Lacedaemonians managed to elude the vigilance of the Athenians, and sent in a garrison of three hundred men to Epidaurus, under the command of Agesippidas. Upon this the Argives went to the Athenians and complained of their having allowed an enemy to pass by sea, in spite of the clause in the treaty by which the allies were not to allow an enemy to pass through their country. Unless, therefore, they now put the Messenians and Helots in Pylos to annoy the Lacedaemonians, they, the Argives, should consider that faith had not been kept with them. The Athenians were persuaded by Alcibiades to inscribe at the bottom of the Laconian pillar that the Lacedaemonians had not kept their oaths, and to convey the Helots at Cranii to Pylos to plunder the country; but for the rest they remained quiet as before. During this winter hostilities went on between the Argives and Epidaurians, without any pitched battle taking place, but only forays and ambuscades, in which the losses were small and fell now on one side and now on the other. At the close of the winter, towards the beginning of spring, the Argives went with scaling ladders to Epidaurus, expecting to find it left unguarded on account of the war and to be able to take it by assault, but returned unsuccessful. And the winter ended, and with it the thirteenth year of the war ended also.

[57] In the middle of the next summer the Lacedaemonians, seeing the Epidaurians, their allies, in distress, and the rest of Peloponnese either in revolt or disaffected, concluded that it was high time for them to interfere if they wished to stop the progress of the evil, and accordingly with their full force, the Helots included, took the field against Argos, under the command of Agis, son of Archidamus, king of the Lacedaemonians. The Tegeans and the other Arcadian allies of Lacedaemon joined in the expedition. The allies from the rest of Peloponnese and from outside mustered at Phlius; the Boeotians with five thousand heavy infantry and as many light troops, and five hundred horse and the same number of dismounted troopers; the Corinthians with two thousand heavy infantry; the rest more or less as might happen; and the Phliasians with all their forces, the army being in their country.

[58] The preparations of the Lacedaemonians from the first had been known to the Argives, who did not, however, take the field until the enemy was on his road to join the rest at Phlius. Reinforced by the Mantineans with their allies, and by three thousand Elean heavy infantry, they advanced and fell in with the Lacedaemonians at Methydrium in Arcadia. Each party took up its position upon a hill, and the Argives prepared to engage the Lacedaemonians while they were alone; but Agis eluded them by breaking up his camp in the night, and proceeded to join the rest of the allies at Phlius. The Argives discovering this at daybreak, marched first to Argos and then to the Nemean road, by which they expected the Lacedaemonians and their allies would come down. However, Agis, instead of taking this road as they expected, gave the Lacedaemonians, Arcadians, and Epidaurians their orders, and went along another difficult road, and descended into the plain of Argos. The Corinthians, Pellenians, and Phliasians marched by another steep road; while the Boeotians, Megarians, and Sicyonians had instructions to come down by the Nemean road where the Argives were posted, in order that, if the enemy advanced into the plain against the troops of Agis, they might fall upon his rear with their cavalry. These dispositions concluded, Agis invaded the plain and began to ravage Saminthus and other places.

[59] Discovering this, the Argives came up from Nemea, day having now dawned. On their way they fell in with the troops of the Phliasians and Corinthians, and killed a few of the Phliasians and had perhaps a few more of their own men killed by the Corinthians. Meanwhile the Boeotians, Megarians, and Sicyonians, advancing upon Nemea according to their instructions, found the Argives no longer there, as they had gone down on seeing their property ravaged, and were now forming for battle, the Lacedaemonians imitating their example. The Argives were now completely surrounded; from the plain the Lacedaemonians and their allies shut them off from their city; above them were the Corinthians, Phliasians, and Pellenians; and on the side of Nemea the Boeotians, Sicyonians, and Megarians. Meanwhile their army was without cavalry, the Athenians alone among the allies not having yet arrived. Now the bulk of the Argives and their allies did not see the danger of their position, but thought that they could not have a fairer field, having intercepted the Lacedaemonians in their own country and close to the city. Two men, however, in the Argive army, Thrasylus, one of the five generals, and Alciphron, the Lacedaemonian *proxenus,* just as the armies were upon the point of engaging, went and held a parley with Agis and urged him not to bring on a battle, as the Argives were ready to refer to fair and equal arbitration whatever complaints the Lacedaemonians might have against them, and to make a treaty and live in peace in future.

[60] The Argives who made these statements did so upon their own authority, not by order of the people, and Agis on his accepted their proposals, and without himself either consulting the majority, simply communicated the matter to a single individual, one of the high officers accompanying the expedition, and granted the Argives a truce for four months,

in which to fulfil their promises; after which he immediately led off the army without giving any explanation to any of the other allies. The Lacedaemonians and allies followed their general out of respect for the law, but amongst themselves loudly blamed Agis for going away from so fair a field (the enemy being hemmed in on every side by infantry and cavalry) without having done anything worthy of their strength. Indeed this was by far the finest Hellenic army ever yet brought together; and it should have been seen while it was still united at Nemea, with the Lacedaemonians in full force, the Arcadians, Boeotians, Corinthians, Sicyonians, Pellenians, Phliasians and Megarians, and all these the flower of their respective populations, thinking themselves a match not merely for the Argive confederacy, but for another such added to it. The army thus retired blaming Agis, and returned every man to his home. The Argives however blamed still more loudly the persons who had concluded the truce without consulting the people, themselves thinking that they had let escape with the Lacedaemonians an opportunity such as they should never see again; as the struggle would have been under the walls of their city, and by the side of many and brave allies. On their return accordingly they began to stone Thrasylus in the bed of the Charadrus, where they try all military causes before entering the city. Thrasylus fled to the altar, and so saved his life; his property however they confiscated.

[61] After this arrived a thousand Athenian heavy infantry and three hundred horse, under the command of Laches and Nicostratus; whom the Argives, being nevertheless loath to break the truce with the Lacedaemonians, begged to depart, and refused to bring before the people, to whom they had a communication to make, until compelled to do so by the entreaties of the Mantineans and Eleans, who were still at Argos. The Athenians, by the mouth of Alcibiades their ambassador there present, told the Argives and the allies that they had no right to make a truce at all without the consent of their fellow confederates, and now that the Athenians had arrived so opportunely the war ought to be resumed. These arguments proving successful with the allies, they immediately marched upon Orchomenos, all except the Argives, who, although they had consented like the rest, stayed behind at first, but eventually joined the others. They now all sat down and besieged Orchomenos, and made assaults upon it; one of their

reasons for desiring to gain this place being that hostages from Arcadia had been lodged there by the Lacedaemonians. The Orchomenians, alarmed at the weakness of their wall and the numbers of the enemy, and at the risk they ran of perishing before relief arrived, capitulated upon condition of joining the league, of giving hostages of their own to the Mantineans, and giving up those lodged with them by the Lacedaemonians. [62] Orchomenos thus secured, the allies now consulted as to which of the remaining places they should attack next. The Eleans were urgent for Lepreum; the Mantineans for Tegea; and the Argives and Athenians giving their support to the Mantineans, the Eleans went home in a rage at their not having voted for Lepreum; while the rest of the allies made ready at Mantinea for going against Tegea, which a party inside had arranged to put into their hands.

[63] Meanwhile the Lacedaemonians, upon their return from Argos after concluding the four months' truce, vehemently blamed Agis for not having subdued Argos, after an opportunity such as they thought they had never had before; for it was no easy matter to bring so many and so good allies together. But when the news arrived of the capture of Orchomenos, they became more angry than ever, and, departing from all precedent, in the heat of the moment had almost decided to raze his house, and to fine him ten thousand drachmae. Agis however entreated them to do none of these things, promising to atone for his fault by good service in the field, failing which they might then do to him whatever they pleased; and they accordingly abstained from razing his house or fining him as they had threatened to do, and now made a law, hitherto unknown at Lacedaemon, attaching to him ten Spartans as counsellors, without whose consent he should have no power to lead an army out of the city.

[64] At this juncture arrived word from their friends in Tegea that, unless they speedily appeared, Tegea would go over from them to the Argives and their allies, if it had not gone over already. Upon this news a force marched out from Lacedaemon, of the Spartans and Helots and all their people, and that instantly and upon a scale never before witnessed. Advancing to Orestheum in Maenalia, they directed the Arcadians in their league to follow close after them to Tegea, and, going on themselves as far as Orestheum, from thence sent back the sixth part of the Spartans, consisting

of the oldest and youngest men, to guard their homes, and with the rest of their army arrived at Tegea; where their Arcadian allies soon after joined them. Meanwhile they sent to Corinth, to the Boeotians, the Phocians, and Locrians, with orders to come up as quickly as possible to Mantinea. These had but short notice; and it was not easy except all together, and after waiting for each other, to pass through the enemy's country, which lay right across and blocked up the line of communication. Nevertheless they made what haste they could. Meanwhile the Lacedaemonians with the Arcadian allies that had joined them, entered the territory of Mantinea, and encamping near the temple of Heracles began to plunder the country.

[65] Here they were seen by the Argives and their allies, who immediately took up a strong and difficult position, and formed in order of battle. The Lacedaemonians at once advanced against them, and came on within a stone's throw or javelin's cast, when one of the older men, seeing the enemy's position to be a strong one, hallooed to Agis that he was minded to cure one evil with another; meaning that he wished to make amends for his retreat, which had been so much blamed, from Argos, by his present untimely precipitation. Meanwhile Agis, whether in consequence of this halloo or of some sudden new idea of his own, quickly led back his army without engaging, and entering the Tegean territory, began to turn off into that of Mantinea the water about which the Mantineans and Tegeans are always fighting, on account of the extensive damage it does to whichever of the two countries it falls into. His object in this was to make the Argives and their allies come down from the hill, to resist the diversion of the water, as they would be sure to do when they knew of it, and thus to fight the battle in the plain. He accordingly stayed that day where he was, engaged in turning off the water. The Argives and their allies were at first amazed at the sudden retreat of the enemy after advancing so near, and did not know what to make of it; but when he had gone away and disappeared, without their having stirred to pursue him, they began anew to find fault with their generals, who had not only let the Lacedaemonians get off before, when they were so happily intercepted before Argos, but who now again allowed them to run away, without any one pursuing them, and to escape at their leisure while the Argive army was leisurely betrayed.

The generals, half-stunned for the moment, afterwards led them down from the hill, and went forward and encamped in the plain, with the intention of attacking the enemy.

[66] The next day the Argives and their allies formed in the order in which they meant to fight, if they chanced to encounter the enemy; and the Lacedaemonians returning from the water to their old encampment by the temple of Heracles, suddenly saw their adversaries close in front of them, all in complete order, and advanced from the hill. A shock like that of the present moment the Lacedaemonians do not ever remember to have experienced: there was scant time for preparation, as they instantly and hastily fell into their ranks, Agis, their king, directing everything, agreeably to the law. For when a king is in the field all commands proceed from him: he gives the word to the Polemarchs; they to the Lochages; these to the Pentecostyes; these again to the Enomotarchs, and these last to the Enomoties. In short all orders required pass in the same way and quickly reach the troops; as almost the whole Lacedaemonian army, save for a small part, consists of officers under officers, and the care of what is to be done falls upon many.

[67] In this battle the left wing was composed of the Sciritae, who in a Lacedaemonian army have always that post to themselves alone; next to these were the soldiers of Brasidas from Thrace, and the Neodamodes with them; then came the Lacedaemonians themselves, company after company, with the Arcadians of Heraea at their side. After these were the Maenalians, and on the right wing the Tegeans with a few of the Lacedaemonians at the extremity; their cavalry being posted upon the two wings. Such was the Lacedaemonian formation. That of their opponents was as follows: On the right were the Mantineans, the action taking place in their country; next to them the allies from Arcadia; after whom came the thousand picked men of the Argives, to whom the state had given a long course of military training at the public expense; next to them the rest of the Argives, and after them their allies, the Cleonaeans and Orneans, and lastly the Athenians on the extreme left, and their own cavalry with them.

[68] Such were the order and the forces of the two combatants. The Lacedaemonian army looked the largest; though as to putting down the numbers of either host, or of the contingents composing it, I could not do so with any accuracy. Owing to the secrecy of their gov-

ernment the number of the Lacedaemonians was not known, and men are so apt to brag about the forces of their country that the estimate of their opponents was not trusted. The following calculation, however, makes it possible to estimate the numbers of the Lacedaemonians present upon this occasion. There were seven companies in the field without counting the Sciritae, who numbered six hundred men: in each company there were four Pentecostyes, and in the Pentecosty four Enomoties. The first rank of the Enomoty was composed of four soldiers: as to the depth, although they had not been all drawn up alike, but as each captain chose, they were generally ranged eight deep; the first rank along the whole line, exclusive of the Sciritae, consisted of four hundred and forty-eight men.

[69] The armies being now on the eve of engaging, each contingent received some words of encouragement from its own commander. The Mantineans were reminded that they were going to fight for their country and to avoid returning to the experience of servitude after having tasted that of empire; the Argives, that they would contend for their ancient supremacy, to regain their once equal share of Peloponnese of which they had been so long deprived, and to punish an enemy and a neighbour for a thousand wrongs; the Athenians, of the glory of gaining the honours of the day with so many and brave allies in arms, and that a victory over the Lacedaemonians in Peloponnese would cement and extend their empire, and would besides preserve Attica from all invasions in future. These were the incitements addressed to the Argives and their allies. The Lacedaemonians meanwhile, man to man, and with their war-songs in the ranks, exhorted each brave comrade to remember what he had learnt before; well aware that the long training of action was of more saving virtue than any brief verbal exhortation, though never so well delivered.

[70] After this they joined battle, the Argives and their allies advancing with haste and fury, the Lacedaemonians slowly and to the music of many flute-players—a standing institution in their army, that has nothing to do with religion, but is meant to make them advance evenly, stepping in time, without breaking their order, as large armies are apt to do in the moment of engaging.

[71] Just before the battle joined, King Agis resolved upon the following manœuvre. All armies are alike in this: on going into action they get forced out rather on their right wing, and one and the other overlap with this adversary's left; because fear makes each man do his best to shelter his unarmed side with the shield of the man next him on the right, thinking that the closer the shields are locked together the better will he be protected. The man primarily responsible for this is the first upon the right wing, who is always striving to withdraw from the enemy his unarmed side; and the same apprehension makes the rest follow him. On the present occasion the Mantineans reached with their wing far beyond the Sciritae, and the Lacedaemonians and Tegeans still farther beyond the Athenians, as their army was the largest. Agis, afraid of his left being surrounded, and thinking that the Mantineans outflanked it too far, ordered the Sciritae and Brasideans to move out from their place in the ranks and make the line even with the Mantineans, and told the Polemarchs Hipponoidas and Aristocles to fill up the gap thus formed, by throwing themselves into it with two companies taken from the right wing; thinking that his right would still be strong enough and to spare, and that the line fronting the Mantineans would gain in solidity.

[72] However, as he gave these orders in the moment of the onset, and at short notice, it so happened that Aristocles and Hipponoidas would not move over, for which offence they were afterwards banished from Sparta, as having been guilty of cowardice; and the enemy meanwhile closed before the Sciritae (whom Agis on seeing that the two companies did not move over ordered to return to their place) had time to fill up the breach in question. Now it was, however, that the Lacedaemonians, utterly worsted in respect of skill, showed themselves as superior in point of courage. As soon as they came to close quarters with the enemy, the Mantinean right broke their Sciritae and Brasideans, and, bursting in with their allies and the thousand picked Argives into the unclosed breach in their line, cut up and surrounded the Lacedaemonians, and drove them in full rout to the wagons, slaying some of the older men on guard there. But the Lacedaemonians, worsted in this part of the field, with the rest of their army, and especially the centre, where the three hundred knights, as they are called, fought round King Agis, fell on the older men of the Argives and the five companies so named, and on the Cleonaeans, the Orneans, and the Athenians next them, and instantly routed them; the greater number not even

waiting to strike a blow, but giving way the moment that they came on, some even being trodden under foot, in their fear of being overtaken by their assailants.

[73] The army of the Argives and their allies, having given way in this quarter, was now completely cut in two, and the Lacedaemonian and Tegean right simultaneously closing round the Athenians with the troops that outflanked them, these last found themselves placed between two fires, being surrounded on one side and already defeated on the other. Indeed they would have suffered more severely than any other part of the army, but for the services of the cavalry which they had with them. Agis also on perceiving the distress of his left opposed to the Mantineans and the thousand Argives, ordered all the army to advance to the support of the defeated wing; and while this took place, as the enemy moved past and slanted away from them, the Athenians escaped at their leisure, and with them the beaten Argive division. Meanwhile the Mantineans and their allies and the picked body of the Argives ceased to press the enemy, and seeing their friends defeated and the Lacedaemonians in full advance upon them, took to flight. Many of the Mantineans perished; but the bulk of the picked body of the Argives made good their escape. The flight and retreat, however, were neither hurried nor long; the Lacedaemonians fighting long and stubbornly until the rout of their enemy, but that once effected, pursuing for a short time and not far.

[74] Such was the battle, as nearly as possible as I have described it; the greatest that had occurred for a very long while among the Hellenes, and joined by the most considerable states. The Lacedaemonians took up a position in front of the enemy's dead, and immediately set up a trophy and stripped the slain; they took up their own dead and carried them back to Tegea, where they buried them, and restored those of the enemy under truce. The Argives, Orneans, and Cleonaeans had seven hundred killed; the Mantineans two hundred, and the Athenians and Aeginetans also two hundred, with both their generals. On the side of the Lacedaemonians, the allies did not suffer any loss worth speaking of: as to the Lacedaemonians themselves it was difficult to learn the truth; it is said, however, that there were slain about three hundred of them.

[75] While the battle was impending, Pleistoanax, the other king, set out with a reinforcement composed of the oldest and young-

est men, and got as far as Tegea, where he heard of the victory and went back again. The Lacedaemonians also sent and turned back the allies from Corinth and from beyond the Isthmus, and returning themselves dismissed their allies, and kept the Carnean holidays, which happened to be at that time. The imputations cast upon them by the Hellenes at the time, whether of cowardice on account of the disaster in the island, or of mismanagement and slowness generally, were all wiped out by this single action: fortune, it was thought, might have humbled them, but the men themselves were the same as ever.

The day before this battle, the Epidaurians with all their forces invaded the deserted Argive territory, and cut off many of the guards left there in the absence of the Argive army. After the battle three thousand Elean heavy infantry arriving to aid the Mantineans, and a reinforcement of one thousand Athenians, all these allies marched at once against Epidaurus, while the Lacedaemonians were keeping the Carnea, and dividing the work among them began to build a wall round the city. The rest left off; but the Athenians finished at once the part assigned to them round Cape Heraeum; and having all joined in leaving a garrison in the fortification in question, they returned to their respective cities.

Summer now came to an end. [76] In the first days of the next winter, when the Carnean holidays were over, the Lacedaemonians took the field, and arriving at Tegea sent on to Argos proposals of accommodation. They had before had a party in the town desirous of overthrowing the democracy; and after the battle that had been fought, these were now far more in a position to persuade the people to listen to terms. Their plan was first to make a treaty with the Lacedaemonians, to be followed by an alliance, and after this to fall upon the commons. Lichas, son of Arcesilaus, the Argive *proxenus,* accordingly arrived at Argos with two proposals from Lacedaemon, to regulate the conditions of war or peace, according as they preferred the one or the other. After much discussion, Alcibiades happening to be in the town, the Lacedaemonian party, who now ventured to act openly, persuaded the Argives to accept the proposal for an accommodation; which ran as follows:

[77] *The assembly of the Lacedaemonians agrees to treat with the Argives upon the terms following:*

1. *The Argives shall restore to the Orcho-*

menians their children, and to the Maenalians their men, and shall restore the men they have in Mantinea to the Lacedaemonians.

2. They shall evacuate Epidaurus, and raze the fortification there. If the Athenians refuse to withdraw from Epidaurus, they shall be declared enemies of the Argives and of the Lacedaemonians, and of the allies of the Lacedaemonians and the allies of the Argives.

3. If the Lacedaemonians have any children in their custody, they shall restore them every one to his city.

4. As to the offering to the god, the Argives, if they wish, shall impose an oath upon the Epidaurians, but, if not, they shall swear it themselves.

5. All the cities in Peloponnese, both small and great, shall be independent according to the customs of their country.

6. If any of the powers outside Peloponnese invade Peloponnesian territory, the parties contracting shall unite to repel them, on such terms as they may agree upon, as being most fair for the Peloponnesians.

7. All allies of the Lacedaemonians outside Peloponnese shall be on the same footing as the Lacedaemonians, and the allies of the Argives shall be on the same footing as the Argives, being left in enjoyment of their own possessions.

8. This treaty shall be shown to the allies, and shall be concluded, if they approve; if the allies think fit, they may send the treaty to be considered at home.

[78] The Argives began by accepting this proposal, and the Lacedaemonian army returned home from Tegea. After this intercourse was renewed between them, and not long afterwards the same party contrived that the Argives should give up the league with the Mantineans, Eleans, and Athenians, and should make a treaty and alliance with the Lacedaemonians; which was consequently done upon the terms following:

[79] The Lacedaemonians and Argives agree to a treaty and alliance for fifty years upon the terms following:

1. All disputes shall be decided by fair and impartial arbitration, agreeably to the customs of the two countries.

2. The rest of the cities in Peloponnese may be included in this treaty and alliance, as independent and sovereign, in full enjoyment of what they possess; all disputes being decided by fair and impartial arbitration, agreeably to the customs of the said cities.

3. All allies of the Lacedaemonians outside Peloponnese shall be upon the same footing as the Lacedaemonians themselves, and the allies of the Argives shall be upon the same footing as the Argives themselves, continuing to enjoy what they possess.

4. If it shall be anywhere necessary to make an expedition in common, the Lacedaemonians and Argives shall consult upon it and decide, as may be most fair for the allies.

5. If any of the cities, whether inside or outside Peloponnese, have a question whether of frontiers or otherwise, it must be settled; but if one allied city should have a quarrel with another allied city, it must be referred to some third city thought impartial by both parties. Private citizens shall have their disputes decided according to the laws of their several countries.

[80] The treaty and above alliance concluded, each party at once released everything whether acquired by war or otherwise, and thenceforth acting in common voted to receive neither herald nor embassy from the Athenians unless they evacuated their forts and withdrew from Peloponnese, and also to make neither peace nor war with any, except jointly. Zeal was not wanting: both parties sent envoys to the Thracian places and to Perdiccas, and persuaded the latter to join their league. Still he did not at once break off from Athens, although minded to do so upon seeing the way shown him by Argos, the original home of his family. They also renewed their old oaths with the Chalcidians and took new ones: the Argives, besides, sent ambassadors to the Athenians, bidding them evacuate the fort at Epidaurus. The Athenians, seeing their own men outnumbered by the rest of the garrison, sent Demosthenes to bring them out. This general, under colour of a gymnastic contest which he arranged on his arrival, got the rest of the garrison out of the place, and shut the gates behind them. Afterwards the Athenians renewed their treaty with the Epidaurians, and by themselves gave up the fortress.

[81] After the defection of Argos from the league, the Mantineans, though they held out at first, in the end finding themselves powerless without the Argives, themselves too came to terms with Lacedaemon, and gave up their sovereignty over the towns. The Lacedaemonians and Argives, each a thousand strong, now took the field together, and the former first went by themselves to Sicyon and made the government there more oligarchical than before, and then both, uniting, put down the de-

mocracy at Argos and set up an oligarchy favourable to Lacedaemon. These events occurred at the close of the winter, just before spring; and the fourteenth year of the war ended. *[82]* The next summer the people of Dium, in Athos, revolted from the Athenians to the Chalcidians, and the Lacedaemonians settled affairs in Achaea in a way more agreeable to the interests of their country. Meanwhile the popular party at Argos little by little gathered new consistency and courage, and waited for the moment of the Gymnopaedic festival at Lacedaemon, and then fell upon the oligarchs. After a fight in the city, victory declared for the commons, who slew some of their opponents and banished others. The Lacedaemonians for a long while let the messages of their friends at Argos remain without effect. At last they put off the Gymnopaediae and marched to their succour, but learning at Tegea the defeat of the oligarchs, refused to go any further in spite of the entreaties of those who had escaped, and returned home and kept the festival. Later on, envoys arrived with messages from the Argives in the town and from the exiles, when the allies were also at Sparta; and after much had been said on both sides, the Lacedaemonians decided that the party in the town had done wrong, and resolved to march against Argos, but kept delaying and putting off the matter. Meanwhile the commons at Argos, in fear of the Lacedaemonians, began again to court the Athenian alliance, which they were convinced would be of the greatest service to them; and accordingly proceeded to build long walls to the sea, in order that in case of a blockade by land; with the help of the Athenians they might have the advantage of importing what they wanted by sea. Some of the cities in Peloponnese were also privy to the building of these walls; and the Argives with all their people, women and slaves not excepted, addressed themselves to the work, while carpenters and masons came to them from Athens.

Summer was now over. *[83]* The winter following the Lacedaemonians, hearing of the walls that were building, marched against Argos with their allies, the Corinthians excepted, being also not without intelligence in the city itself; Agis, son of Archidamus, their king, was in command. The intelligence which they counted upon within the town came to nothing; they however took and razed the walls which were being built, and after capturing the Argive town Hysiae and killing all the freemen that fell into their hands, went back and dispersed every man to his city. After this the Argives marched into Phlius and plundered it for harbouring their exiles, most of whom had settled there, and so returned home. The same winter the Athenians blockaded Macedonia, on the score of the league entered into by Perdiccas with the Argives and Lacedaemonians, and also of his breach of his engagements on the occasion of the expedition prepared by Athens against the Chalcidians in the direction of Thrace and against Amphipolis, under the command of Nicias, son of Niceratus, which had to be broken up mainly because of his desertion. He was therefore proclaimed an enemy. And thus the winter ended, and the fifteenth year of the war ended with it.

CHAPTER XVII

Sixteenth Year of the War—The Melian Conference—Fate of Melos

[84] THE next summer Alcibiades sailed with twenty ships to Argos and seized the suspected persons still left of the Lacedaemonian faction to the number of three hundred, whom the Athenians forthwith lodged in the neighbouring islands of their empire. The Athenians also made an expedition against the isle of Melos with thirty ships of their own, six Chian, and two Lesbian vessels, sixteen hundred heavy infantry, three hundred archers, and twenty mounted archers from Athens, and about fifteen hundred heavy infantry from the allies and the islanders. The Melians are a colony of Lacedaemon that would not submit to the Athenians like the other islanders, and at first remained neutral and took no part in the struggle, but afterwards upon the Athenians using violence and plundering their territory, assumed an attitude of open hostility. Cleomedes, son of Lycomedes, and Tisias, son of Tisimachus, the generals, encamping in their territory with the above armament, before doing any harm to their land, sent envoys to negotiate. These the Melians did not bring before the people, but bade them state the object of their mission to the magistrates and the few; upon which the Athenian envoys spoke as follows:

[85] Athenians. Since the negotiations are not to go on before the people, in order that we may not be able to speak straight on without interruption, and deceive the ears of the multitude by seductive arguments which would pass without refutation (for we know that this

is the meaning of our being brought before the few), what if you who sit there were to pursue a method more cautious still? Make no set speech yourselves, but take us up at whatever you do not like, and settle that before going any farther. And first tell us if this proposition of ours suits you.

[86] The Melian commissioners answered:

Melians. To the fairness of quietly instructing each other as you propose there is nothing to object; but your military preparations are too far advanced to agree with what you say, as we see you are come to be judges in your own cause, and that all we can reasonably expect from this negotiation is war, if we prove to have right on our side and refuse to submit, and in the contrary case, slavery.

[87] *Athenians.* If you have met to reason about presentiments of the future, or for anything else than to consult for the safety of your state upon the facts that you see before you, we will give over; otherwise we will go on.

[88] *Melians.* It is natural and excusable for men in our position to turn more ways than one both in thought and utterance. However, the question in this conference is, as you say, the safety of our country; and the discussion, if you please, can proceed in the way which you propose.

[89] *Athenians.* For ourselves, we shall not trouble you with specious pretences—either of how we have a right to our empire because we overthrew the Mede, or are now attacking you because of wrong that you have done us—and make a long speech which would not be believed; and in return we hope that you, instead of thinking to influence us by saying that you did not join the Lacedaemonians, although their colonists, or that you have done us no wrong, will aim at what is feasible, holding in view the real sentiments of us both; since you know as well as we do that right, as the world goes, is only in question between equals in power, while the strong do what they can and the weak suffer what they must.

[90] *Melians.* As we think, at any rate, it is expedient—we speak as we are obliged, since you enjoin us to let right alone and talk only of interest—that you should not destroy what is our common protection, the privilege of being allowed in danger to invoke what is fair and right, and even to profit by arguments not strictly valid if they can be got to pass current. And you are as much interested in this as any, as your fall would be a signal for the heaviest vengeance and an example

for the world to meditate upon.

[91] *Athenians.* The end of our empire, if end it should, does not frighten us: a rival empire like Lacedaemon, even if Lacedaemon was our real antagonist, is not so terrible to the vanquished as subjects who by themselves attack and overpower their rulers. This, however, is a risk that we are content to take. We will now proceed to show you that we are come here in the interest of our empire, and that we shall say what we are now going to say, for the preservation of your country; as we would fain exercise that empire over you without trouble, and see you preserved for the good of us both.

[92] *Melians.* And how, pray, could it turn out as good for us to serve as for you to rule?

[93] *Athenians.* Because you would have the advantage of submitting before suffering the worst, and we should gain by not destroying you.

[94] *Melians.* So that you would not consent to our being neutral, friends instead of enemies, but allies of neither side.

[95] *Athenians.* No; for your hostility cannot so much hurt us as your friendship will be an argument to our subjects of our weakness, and your enmity of our power.

[96] *Melians.* Is that your subjects' idea of equity, to put those who have nothing to do with you in the same category with peoples that are most of them your own colonists, and some conquered rebels?

[97] *Athenians.* As far as right goes they think one has as much of it as the other, and that if any maintain their independence it is because they are strong, and that if we do not molest them it is because we are afraid; so that besides extending our empire we should gain in security by your subjection; the fact that you are islanders and weaker than others rendering it all the more important that you should not succeed in baffling the masters of the sea.

[98] *Melians.* But do you consider that there is no security in the policy which we indicate? For here again if you debar us from talking about justice and invite us to obey your interest, we also must explain ours, and try to persuade you, if the two happen to coincide. How can you avoid making enemies of all existing neutrals who shall look at our case and conclude from it that one day or another you will attack them? And what is this but to make greater the enemies that you have already, and to force others to become so who would otherwise have never thought of it?

[*99*] *Athenians.* Why, the fact is that continentals generally give us but little alarm; the liberty which they enjoy will long prevent their taking precautions against us; it is rather islanders like yourselves, outside our empire, and subjects smarting under the yoke, who would be the most likely to take a rash step and lead themselves and us into obvious danger.

[*100*] *Melians.* Well then, if you risk so much to retain your empire, and your subjects to get rid of it, it were surely great baseness and cowardice in us who are still free not to try everything that can be tried, before submitting to your yoke.

[*101*] *Athenians.* Not if you are well advised, the contest not being an equal one, with honour as the prize and shame as the penalty, but a question of self-preservation and of not resisting those who are far stronger than you are.

[*102*] *Melians.* But we know that the fortune of war is sometimes more impartial than the disproportion of numbers might lead one to suppose; to submit is to give ourselves over to despair, while action still preserves for us a hope that we may stand erect.

[*103*] *Athenians.* Hope, danger's comforter, may be indulged in by those who have abundant resources, if not without loss at all events without ruin; but its nature is to be extravagant, and those who go so far as to put their all upon the venture see it in its true colours only when they are ruined; but so long as the discovery would enable them to guard against it, it is never found wanting. Let not this be the case with you, who are weak and hang on a single turn of the scale; nor be like the vulgar, who, abandoning such security as human means may still afford, when visible hopes fail them in extremity, turn to invisible, to prophecies and oracles, and other such inventions that delude men with hopes to their destruction.

[*104*] *Melians.* You may be sure that we are as well aware as you of the difficulty of contending against your power and fortune, unless the terms be equal. But we trust that the gods may grant us fortune as good as yours, since we are just men fighting against unjust, and that what we want in power will be made up by the alliance of the Lacedaemonians, who are bound, if only for very shame, to come to the aid of their kindred. Our confidence, therefore, after all is not so utterly irrational.

[*105*] *Athenians.* When you speak of the favour of the gods, we may as fairly hope for that as yourselves; neither our pretensions nor our conduct being in any way contrary to what men believe of the gods, or practise among themselves. Of the gods we believe, and of men we know, that by a necessary law of their nature they rule wherever they can. And it is not as if we were the first to make this law, or to act upon it when made: we found it existing before us, and shall leave it to exist for ever after us; all we do is to make use of it, knowing that you and everybody else, having the same power as we have, would do the same as we do. Thus, as far as the gods are concerned, we have no fear and no reason to fear that we shall be at a disadvantage. But when we come to your notion about the Lacedaemonians, which leads you to believe that shame will make them help you, here we bless your simplicity but do not envy your folly. The Lacedaemonians, when their own interests or their country's laws are in question, are the worthiest men alive; of their conduct towards others much might be said, but no clearer idea of it could be given than by shortly saying that of all the men we know they are most conspicuous in considering what is agreeable honourable, and what is expedient just. Such a way of thinking does not promise much for the safety which you now unreasonably count upon.

[*106*] *Melians.* But it is for this very reason that we now trust to their respect for expediency to prevent them from betraying the Melians, their colonists, and thereby losing the confidence of their friends in Hellas and helping their enemies.

[*107*] *Athenians.* Then you do not adopt the view that expediency goes with security, while justice and honour cannot be followed without danger; and danger the Lacedaemonians generally court as little as possible.

[*108*] *Melians.* But we believe that they would be more likely to face even danger for our sake, and with more confidence than for others, as our nearness to Peloponnese makes it easier for them to act, and our common blood ensures our fidelity.

[*109*] *Athenians.* Yes, but what an intending ally trusts to is not the goodwill of those who ask his aid, but a decided superiority of power for action; and the Lacedaemonians look to this even more than others. At least, such is their distrust of their home resources that it is only with numerous allies that they attack a neighbour; now is it likely that while we are masters of the sea they will cross over to an island?

[*110*] *Melians.* But they would have others to send. The Cretan Sea is a wide one, and it is more difficult for those who command it to intercept others, than for those who wish to elude them to do so safely. And should the Lacedaemonians miscarry in this, they would fall upon your land, and upon those left of your allies whom Brasidas did not reach; and instead of places which are not yours, you will have to fight for your own country and your own confederacy.

[*111*] *Athenians.* Some diversion of the kind you speak of you may one day experience, only to learn, as others have done, that the Athenians never once yet withdrew from a siege for fear of any. But we are struck by the fact that, after saying you would consult for the safety of your country, in all this discussion you have mentioned nothing which men might trust in and think to be saved by. Your strongest arguments depend upon hope and the future, and your actual resources are too scanty, as compared with those arrayed against you, for you to come out victorious. You will therefore show great blindness of judgment, unless, after allowing us to retire, you can find some counsel more prudent than this. You will surely not be caught by that idea of disgrace, which in dangers that are disgraceful, and at the same time too plain to be mistaken, proves so fatal to mankind; since in too many cases the very men that have their eyes perfectly open to what they are rushing into, let the thing called disgrace, by the mere influence of a seductive name, lead them on to a point at which they become so enslaved by the phrase as in fact to fall wilfully into hopeless disaster, and incur disgrace more disgraceful as the companion of error, than when it comes as the result of misfortune. This, if you are well advised, you will guard against; and you will not think it dishonourable to submit to the greatest city in Hellas, when it makes you the moderate offer of becoming its tributary ally, without ceasing to enjoy the country that belongs to you; nor when you have the choice given you between war and security, will you be so blinded as to choose the worse. And it is certain that those who do not yield to their equals, who keep terms with their superiors, and are moderate towards their inferiors, on the whole succeed best. Think over the matter, therefore, after our withdrawal, and reflect once and again that it is for your country that you are consulting, that you have not more than one, and that upon this one deliberation depends its prosperity or ruin.

[*112*] The Athenians now withdrew from the conference; and the Melians, left to themselves, came to a decision corresponding with what they had maintained in the discussion, and answered: "Our resolution, Athenians, is the same as it was at first. We will not in a moment deprive of freedom a city that has been inhabited these seven hundred years; but we put our trust in the fortune by which the gods have preserved it until now, and in the help of men, that is, of the Lacedaemonians; and so we will try and save ourselves. Meanwhile we invite you to allow us to be friends to you and foes to neither party, and to retire from our country after making such a treaty as shall seem fit to us both."

[*113*] Such was the answer of the Melians. The Athenians now departing from the conference said: "Well, you alone, as it seems to us, judging from these resolutions, regard what is future as more certain than what is before your eyes, and what is out of sight, in your eagerness, as already coming to pass; and as you have staked most on, and trusted most in, the Lacedaemonians, your fortune, and your hopes, so will you be most completely deceived."

[*114*] The Athenian envoys now returned to the army; and the Melians showing no signs of yielding, the generals at once betook themselves to hostilities, and drew a line of circumvallation round the Melians, dividing the work among the different states. Subsequently the Athenians returned with most of their army, leaving behind them a certain number of their own citizens and of the allies to keep guard by land and sea. The force thus left stayed on and besieged the place.

[*115*] About the same time the Argives invaded the territory of Phlius and lost eighty men cut off in an ambush by the Phliasians and Argive exiles. Meanwhile the Athenians at Pylos took so much plunder from the Lacedaemonians that the latter, although they still refrained from breaking off the treaty and going to war with Athens, yet proclaimed that any of their people that chose might plunder the Athenians. The Corinthians also commenced hostilities with the Athenians for private quarrels of their own; but the rest of the Peloponnesians stayed quiet. Meanwhile the Melians attacked by night and took the part of the Athenian lines over against the market, and killed some of the men, and brought in corn and all else that they could find useful to

them, and so returned and kept quiet, while the Athenians took measures to keep better guard in future.

Summer was now over. [*116*] The next winter the Lacedaemonians intended to invade the Argive territory, but arriving at the frontier found the sacrifices for crossing unfavourable, and went back again. This intention of theirs gave the Argives suspicions of certain of their fellow citizens, some of whom they arrested; others, however, escaped them. About the same time the Melians again took another part of the Athenian lines which were but feebly garrisoned. Reinforcements afterwards arriving from Athens in consequence, under the command of Philocrates, son of Demeas, the siege was now pressed vigorously; and some treachery taking place inside, the Melians surrendered at discretion to the Athenians, who put to death all the grown men whom they took, and sold the women and children for slaves, and subsequently sent out five hundred colonists and inhabited the place themselves.

The Sixth Book

➤➤➤ ➤➤➤ ➤➤➤ ➤➤➤ ➤➤➤ ➤➤➤ ➤➤➤ ➤➤➤ ➤➤➤ ➤➤➤ ➤➤➤ ➤➤➤ ➤➤➤ ⤶⤶⤶ ⤶⤶⤶ ⤶⤶⤶ ⤶⤶⤶ ⤶⤶⤶ ⤶⤶⤶ ⤶⤶⤶ ⤶⤶⤶ ⤶⤶⤶ ⤶⤶⤶ ⤶⤶⤶ ⤶⤶⤶

CHAPTER XVIII

Seventeenth Year of the War—The Sicilian Campaign—Affair of the Hermae—Departure of the Expedition

[1] THE same winter the Athenians resolved to sail again to Sicily, with a greater armament than that under Laches and Eurymedon, and, if possible, to conquer the island; most of them being ignorant of its size and of the number of its inhabitants, Hellenic and barbarian, and of the fact that they were undertaking a war not much inferior to that against the Peloponnesians. For the voyage round Sicily in a merchantman is not far short of eight days; and yet, large as the island is, there are only two miles of sea to prevent its being mainland.

[2] It was settled originally as follows, and the peoples that occupied it are these. The earliest inhabitants spoken of in any part of the country are the Cyclopes and Laestrygones; but I cannot tell of what race they were, or whence they came or whither they went, and must leave my readers to what the poets have said of them and to what may be generally known concerning them. The Sicanians appear to have been the next settlers, although they pretend to have been the first of all and aborigines; but the facts show that they were Iberians, driven by the Ligurians from the river Sicanus in Iberia. It was from them that the island, before called Trinacria, took its name of Sicania, and to the present day they inhabit the west of Sicily. On the fall of Ilium, some of the Trojans escaped from the Achaeans, came in ships to Sicily, and settled next to the Sicanians under the general name of Elymi; their towns being called Eryx and Egesta. With them settled some of the Phocians carried on their way from Troy by a storm, first to Libya, and afterwards from thence to Sicily.

The Sicels crossed over to Sicily from their first home Italy, flying from the Opicans, as tradition says and as seems not unlikely, upon rafts, having watched till the wind set down the strait to effect the passage; although perhaps they may have sailed over in some other way. Even at the present day there are still Sicels in Italy; and the country got its name of Italy from Italus, a king of the Sicels, so called. These went with a great host to Sicily, defeated the Sicanians in battle and forced them to remove to the south and west of the island, which thus came to be called Sicily instead of Sicania, and after they crossed over continued to enjoy the richest parts of the country for near three hundred years before any Hellenes came to Sicily; indeed they still hold the centre and north of the island. There were also Phoenicians living all round Sicily, who had occupied promontories upon the sea coasts and the islets adjacent for the purpose of trading with the Sicels. But when the Hellenes began to arrive in considerable numbers by sea, the Phoenicians abandoned most of their stations, and drawing together took up their abode in Motye, Soloeis, and Panormus, near the Elymi, partly because they confided in their alliance, and also because these are the nearest points for the voyage between Carthage and Sicily.

These were the barbarians in Sicily, settled as I have said. [3] Of the Hellenes, the first to arrive were Chalcidians from Euboea with Thucles, their founder. They founded Naxos and built the altar to Apollo Archegetes, which now stands outside the town, and upon which the deputies for the games sacrifice before sailing from Sicily. Syracuse was founded the year afterwards by Archias, one of the Heraclids from Corinth, who began by driving out the Sicels from the island upon which the inner city now stands, though it is no longer surrounded by water: in process of time the outer town also was taken within the walls and became populous. Meanwhile Thucles and the Chalcidians set out from Naxos in the fifth year after the foundation of Syracuse, and drove out the Sicels by arms and founded Leontini and afterwards Catana; the Catanians themselves choosing Evarchus as their founder.

[4] About the same time Lamis arrived in Sicily with a colony from Megara, and after founding a place called Trotilus beyond the river Pantacyas, and afterwards leaving it and for a short while joining the Chalcidians at Leontini, was driven out by them and founded Thapsus. After his death his companions were driven out of Thapsus, and founded a place called the Hyblaean Megara; Hyblon, a Sicel king, having given up the place and inviting them thither. Here they lived two hundred and forty-five years; after which they were expelled from the city and the country by the Syracusan tyrant Gelo. Before their expulsion, however, a hundred years after they had settled there, they sent out Pamillus and founded Selinus; he having come from their mother country Megara to join them in its foundation. Gela was founded by Antiphemus from Rhodes and Entimus from Crete, who joined in leading a colony thither, in the forty-fifth year after the foundation of Syracuse. The town took its name from the river Gelas, the place where the citadel now stands, and which was first fortified, being called Lindii. The institutions which they adopted were Dorian. Near one hundred and eight years after the foundation of Gela, the Geloans founded Acragas (Agrigentum), so called from the river of that name, and made Aristonous and Pystilus their founders; giving their own institutions to the colony. Zancle was originally founded by pirates from Cuma, the Chalcidian town in the country of the Opicans: afterwards, however, large numbers came from Chalcis and the rest of Euboea, and helped to people the place; the founders being Perieres and Crataemenes from Cuma and Chalcis respectively. It first had the name of Zancle given it by the Sicels, because the place is shaped like a sickle, which the Sicels call *zanclon;* but upon the original settlers being afterwards expelled by some Samians and other Ionians who landed in Sicily flying from the Medes, and the Samians in their turn not long afterwards by Anaxilas, tyrant of Rhegium, the town was by him colonized with a mixed population, and its name changed to Messina, after his old country.

[5] Himera was founded from Zancle by Euclides, Simus, and Sacon, most of those who went to the colony being Chalcidians; though they were joined by some exiles from Syracuse, defeated in a civil war, called the Myletidae. The language was a mixture of Chalcidian and Doric, but the institutions which prevailed were the Chalcidian. Acrae and Casmenae were founded by the Syracusans; Acrae seventy years after Syracuse, Casmenae nearly twenty after Acrae. Camarina was first founded by the Syracusans, close upon a hundred and thirty-five years after the building of Syracuse; its founders being Daxon and Menecolus. But the Camarinaeans being expelled by arms by the Syracusans for having revolted, Hippocrates, tyrant of Gela, some time later receiving their land in ransom for some Syracusan prisoners, resettled Camarina, himself acting as its founder. Lastly, it was again depopulated by Gelo, and settled once more for the third time by the Geloans.

[6] Such is the list of the peoples, Hellenic and barbarian, inhabiting Sicily, and such the magnitude of the island which the Athenians were now bent upon invading; being ambitious in real truth of conquering the whole, although they had also the specious design of succouring their kindred and other allies in the island. But they were especially incited by envoys from Egesta, who had come to Athens and invoked their aid more urgently than ever. The Egestaeans had gone to war with their neighbours the Selinuntines upon questions of marriage and disputed territory, and the Selinuntines had procured the alliance of the Syracusans, and pressed Egesta hard by land and sea. The Egestaeans now reminded the Athenians of the alliance made in the time of Laches, during the former Leontine war, and begged them to send a fleet to their aid, and among a number of other considerations urged as a capital argument that if the Syracusans were allowed to go unpunished for their depopulation of Leontini, to ruin the allies still left to Athens in Sicily, and to get the whole power of the island into their hands, there would be a danger of their one day coming with a large force, as Dorians, to the aid of their Dorian brethren, and as colonists, to the aid of the Peloponnesians who had sent them out, and joining these in pulling down the Athenian empire. The Athenians would, therefore, do well to unite with the allies still left to them, and to make a stand against the Syracusans; especially as they, the Egestaeans, were

prepared to furnish money sufficient for the war. The Athenians, hearing these arguments constantly repeated in their assemblies by the Egestaeans and their supporters, voted first to send envoys to Egesta, to see if there was really the money that they talked of in the treasury and temples, and at the same time to ascertain in what posture was the war with the Selinuntines.

[7] The envoys of the Athenians were accordingly dispatched to Sicily. The same winter the Lacedaemonians and their allies, the Corinthians excepted, marched into the Argive territory, and ravaged a small part of the land, and took some yokes of oxen and carried off some corn. They also settled the Argive exiles at Orneae, and left them a few soldiers taken from the rest of the army; and after making a truce for a certain while, according to which neither Orneatae nor Argives were to injure each other's territory, returned home with the army. Not long afterwards the Athenians came with thirty ships and six hundred heavy infantry, and the Argives joining them with all their forces, marched out and besieged the men in Orneae for one day; but the garrison escaped by night, the besiegers having bivouacked some way off. The next day the Argives, discovering it, razed Orneae to the ground, and went back again; after which the Athenians went home in their ships. Meanwhile the Athenians took by sea to Methone on the Macedonian border some cavalry of their own and the Macedonian exiles that were at Athens, and plundered the country of Perdiccas. Upon this the Lacedaemonians sent to the Thracian Chalcidians, who had a truce with Athens from one ten days to another, urging them to join Perdiccas in the war, which they refused to do. And the winter ended, and with it ended the sixteenth year of this war of which Thucydides is the historian.

[8] Early in the spring of the following summer the Athenian envoys arrived from Sicily, and the Egestaeans with them, bringing sixty talents of uncoined silver, as a month's pay for sixty ships, which they were to ask to have sent them. The Athenians held an assembly and, after hearing from the Egestaeans and their own envoys a report, as attractive as it was untrue, upon the state of affairs generally, and in particular as to the money, of which, it was said, there was abundance in the temples and the treasury, voted to send sixty ships to Sicily, under the command of Alcibiades, son of Clinias, Nicias, son of Niceratus, and Lama-

chus, son of Xenophanes, who were appointed with full powers; they were to help the Egestaeans against the Selinuntines, to restore Leontini upon gaining any advantage in the war, and to order all other matters in Sicily as they should deem best for the interests of Athens. Five days after this a second assembly was held, to consider the speediest means of equipping the ships, and to vote whatever else might be required by the generals for the expedition; and Nicias, who had been chosen to the command against his will, and who thought that the state was not well advised, but upon a slight and specious pretext was aspiring to the conquest of the whole of Sicily, a great matter to achieve, came forward in the hope of diverting the Athenians from the enterprise, and gave them the following counsel:

[9] "Although this assembly was convened to consider the preparations to be made for sailing to Sicily, I think, notwithstanding, that we have still this question to examine, whether it be better to send out the ships at all, and that we ought not to give so little consideration to a matter of such moment, or let ourselves be persuaded by foreigners into undertaking a war with which we have nothing to do. And yet, individually, I gain in honour by such a course, and fear as little as other men for my person—not that I think a man need be any the worse citizen for taking some thought for his person and estate; on the contrary, such a man would for his own sake desire the prosperity of his country more than others—nevertheless, as I have never spoken against my convictions to gain honour, I shall not begin to do so now, but shall say what I think best. Against your character any words of mine would be weak enough, if I were to advise your keeping what you have got and not risking what is actually yours for advantages which are dubious in themselves, and which you may or may not attain. I will, therefore, content myself with showing that your ardour is out of season, and your ambition not easy of accomplishment.

[10] "I affirm, then, that you leave many enemies behind you here to go yonder and bring more back with you. You imagine, perhaps, that the treaty which you have made can be trusted; a treaty that will continue to exist nominally, as long as you keep quiet—for nominal it has become, owing to the practices of certain men here and at Sparta—but which in the event of a serious reverse in any quarter would not delay our enemies a moment in at-

tacking us; first, because the convention was forced upon them by disaster and was less honourable to them than to us; and secondly, because in this very convention there are many points that are still disputed. Again, some of the most powerful states have never yet accepted the arrangement at all. Some of these are at open war with us; others (as the Lacedaemonians do not yet move) are restrained by truces renewed every ten days, and it is only too probable that if they found our power divided, as we are hurrying to divide it, they would attack us vigorously with the Siceliots, whose alliance they would have in the past valued as they would that of few others. A man ought, therefore, to consider these points, and not to think of running risks with a country placed so critically, or of grasping at another empire before we have secured the one we have already; for in fact the Thracian Chalcidians have been all these years in revolt from us without being yet subdued, and others on the continents yield us but a doubtful obedience. Meanwhile the Egestaeans, our allies, have been wronged, and we run to help them, while the rebels who have so long wronged us still wait for punishment.

[11] "And yet the latter, if brought under, might be kept under; while the Sicilians, even if conquered, are too far off and too numerous to be ruled without difficulty. Now it is folly to go against men who could not be kept under even if conquered, while failure would leave us in a very different position from that which we occupied before the enterprise. The Siceliots, again, to take them as they are at present, in the event of a Syracusan conquest (the favourite bugbear of the Egestaeans, would to my thinking be even less dangerous to us than before. At present they might possibly come here as separate states for love of Lacedaemon; in the other case one empire would scarcely attack another; for after joining the Peloponnesians to overthrow ours, they could only expect to see the same hands overthrow their own in the same way. The Hellenes in Sicily would fear us most if we never went there at all, and next to this, if after displaying our power we went away again as soon as possible. We all know that that which is farthest off, and the reputation of which can least be tested, is the object of admiration; at the least reverse they would at once begin to look down upon us, and would join our enemies here against us. You have yourselves experienced this with regard to the Lacedaemonians and their allies, whom your unexpected success, as compared with what you feared at first, has made you suddenly despise, tempting you further to aspire to the conquest of Sicily. Instead, however, of being puffed up by the misfortunes of your adversaries, you ought to think of breaking their spirit before giving yourselves up to confidence, and to understand that the one thought awakened in the Lacedaemonians by their disgrace is how they may even now, if possible, overthrow us and repair their dishonour; inasmuch as military reputation is their oldest and chiefest study. Our struggle, therefore, if we are wise, will not be for the barbarian Egestaeans in Sicily, but how to defend ourselves most effectually against the oligarchical machinations of Lacedaemon.

[12] "We should also remember that we are but now enjoying some respite from a great pestilence and from war, to the no small benefit of our estates and persons, and that it is right to employ these at home on our own behalf, instead of using them on behalf of these exiles whose interest it is to lie as fairly as they can, who do nothing but talk themselves and leave the danger to others, and who if they succeed will show no proper gratitude, and if they fail will drag down their friends with them. And if there be any man here, overjoyed at being chosen to command, who urges you to make the expedition, merely for ends of his own—especially if he be still too young to command—who seeks to be admired for his stud of horses, but on account of its heavy expenses hopes for some profit from his appointment, do not allow such a one to maintain his private splendour at his country's risk, but remember that such persons injure the public fortune while they squander their own, and that this is a matter of importance, and not for a young man to decide or hastily to take in hand.

[13] "When I see such persons now sitting here at the side of that same individual and summoned by him, alarm seizes me; and I, in my turn, summon any of the older men that may have such a person sitting next him not to let himself be shamed down, for fear of being thought a coward if he do not vote for war, but, remembering how rarely success is got by wishing and how often by forecast, to leave to them the mad dream of conquest, and as a true lover of his country, now threatened by the greatest danger in its history, to hold up his hand on the other side; to vote that the Siceliots be left in the limits now existing between us, limits of which no one can complain (the

Ionian sea for the coasting voyage, and the Sicilian across the open main), to enjoy their own possessions and to settle their own quarrels; that the Egestaeans, for their part, be told to end by themselves with the Selinuntines the war which they began without consulting the Athenians; and that for the future we do not enter into alliance, as we have been used to do, with people whom we must help in their need, and who can never help us in ours.

[14] "And you, Prytanis, if you think it your duty to care for the commonwealth, and if you wish to show yourself a good citizen, put the question to the vote, and take a second time the opinions of the Athenians. If you are afraid to move the question again, consider that a violation of the law cannot carry any prejudice with so many abettors, that you will be the physician of your misguided city, and that the virtue of men in office is briefly this, to do their country as much good as they can, or in any case no harm that they can avoid."

[15] Such were the words of Nicias. Most of the Athenians that came forward spoke in favour of the expedition, and of not annulling what had been voted, although some spoke on the other side. By far the warmest advocate of the expedition was, however, Alcibiades, son of Clinias, who wished to thwart Nicias both as his political opponent and also because of the attack he had made upon him in his speech, and who was, besides, exceedingly ambitious of a command by which he hoped to reduce Sicily and Carthage, and personally to gain in wealth and reputation by means of his successes. For the position he held among the citizens led him to indulge his tastes beyond what his real means would bear, both in keeping horses and in the rest of his expenditure; and this later on had not a little to do with the ruin of the Athenian state. Alarmed at the greatness of his licence in his own life and habits, and of the ambition which he showed in all things soever that he undertook, the mass of the people set him down as a pretender to the tyranny, and became his enemies; and although publicly his conduct of the war was as good as could be desired, individually, his habits gave offence to every one, and caused them to commit affairs to other hands, and thus before long to ruin the city. Meanwhile he now came forward and gave the following advice to the Athenians:

[16] "Athenians, I have a better right to command than others—I must begin with this as Nicias has attacked me—and at the same time I believe myself to be worthy of it. The things for which I am abused, bring fame to my ancestors and to myself, and to the country profit besides. The Hellenes, after expecting to see our city ruined by the war, concluded it to be even greater than it really is, by reason of the magnificence with which I represented it at the Olympic games, when I sent into the lists seven chariots, a number never before entered by any private person, and won the first prize, and was second and fourth, and took care to have everything else in a style worthy of my victory. Custom regards such displays as honourable, and they cannot be made without leaving behind them an impression of power. Again, any splendour that I may have exhibited at home in providing choruses or otherwise, is naturally envied by my fellow citizens, but in the eyes of foreigners has an air of strength as in the other instance. And this is no useless folly, when a man at his own private cost benefits not himself only, but his city: nor is it unfair that he who prides himself on his position should refuse to be upon an equality with the rest. He who is badly off has his misfortunes all to himself, and as we do not see men courted in adversity, on the like principle a man ought to accept the insolence of prosperity; or else, let him first mete out equal measure to all, and then demand to have it meted out to him. What I know is that persons of this kind and all others that have attained to any distinction, although they may be unpopular in their lifetime in their relations with their fellow-men and especially with their equals, leave to posterity the desire of claiming connection with them even without any ground, and are vaunted by the country to which they belonged, not as strangers or ill-doers, but as fellow-countrymen and heroes. Such are my aspirations, and however I am abused for them in private, the question is whether any one manages public affairs better than I do. Having united the most powerful states of Peloponnese, without great danger or expense to you, I compelled the Lacedaemonians to stake their all upon the issue of a single day at Mantinea; and although victorious in the battle, they have never since fully recovered confidence.

[17] "Thus did my youth and so-called monstrous folly find fitting arguments to deal with the power of the Peloponnesians, and by its ardour win their confidence and prevail. And do not be afraid of my youth now, but while I am still in its flower, and Nicias appears fortunate, avail yourselves to the utmost of the serv-

ices of us both. Neither rescind your resolution to sail to Sicily, on the ground that you would be going to attack a great power. The cities in Sicily are peopled by motley rabbles, and easily change their institutions and adopt new ones in their stead; and consequently the inhabitants, being without any feeling of patriotism, are not provided with arms for their persons, and have not regularly established themselves on the land; every man thinks that either by fair words or by party strife he can obtain something at the public expense, and then in the event of a catastrophe settle in some other country, and makes his preparations accordingly. From a mob like this you need not look for either unanimity in counsel or concert in action; but they will probably one by one come in as they get a fair offer, especially if they are torn by civil strife as we are told. Moreover, the Siceliots have not so many heavy infantry as they boast; just as the Hellenes generally did not prove so numerous as each state reckoned itself, but Hellas greatly over-estimated their numbers, and has hardly had an adequate force of heavy infantry throughout this war. The states in Sicily, therefore, from all that I can hear, will be found as I say, and I have not pointed out all our advantages, for we shall have the help of many barbarians, who from their hatred of the Syracusans will join us in attacking them; nor will the powers at home prove any hindrance, if you judge rightly. Our fathers with these very adversaries, which it is said we shall now leave behind us when we sail, and the Mede as their enemy as well, were able to win the empire, depending solely on their superiority at sea. The Peloponnesians had never so little hope against us as at present; and let them be ever so sanguine, although strong enough to invade our country even if we stay at home, they can never hurt us with their navy, as we leave one of our own behind us that is a match for them.

[18] "In this state of things what reason can we give to ourselves for holding back, or what excuse can we offer to our allies in Sicily for not helping them? They are our confederates, and we are bound to assist them, without objecting that they have not assisted us. We did not take them into alliance to have them to help us in Hellas, but that they might so annoy our enemies in Sicily as to prevent them from coming over here and attacking us. It is thus that empire has been won, both by us and by all others that have held it, by a constant readiness to support all, whether barbarians or Hel-

lenes, that invite assistance; since if all were to keep quiet or to pick and choose whom they ought to assist, we should make but few new conquests, and should imperil those we have already won. Men do not rest content with parrying the attacks of a superior, but often strike the first blow to prevent the attack being made. And we cannot fix the exact point at which our empire shall stop; we have reached a position in which we must not be content with retaining but must scheme to extend it, for, if we cease to rule others, we are in danger of being ruled ourselves. Nor can you look at inaction from the same point of view as others, unless you are prepared to change your habits and make them like theirs.

"Be convinced, then, that we shall augment our power at home by this adventure abroad, and let us make the expedition, and so humble the pride of the Peloponnesians by sailing off to Sicily, and letting them see how little we care for the peace that we are now enjoying; and at the same time we shall either become masters, as we very easily may, of the whole of Hellas through the accession of the Sicilian Hellenes, or in any case ruin the Syracusans, to the no small advantage of ourselves and our allies. The faculty of staying if successful, or of returning, will be secured to us by our navy, as we shall be superior at sea to all the Siceliots put together. And do not let the do-nothing policy which Nicias advocates, or his setting of the young against the old, turn you from your purpose, but in the good old fashion by which our fathers, old and young together, by their united counsels brought our affairs to their present height, do you endeavour still to advance them; understanding that neither youth nor old age can do anything the one without the other, but that levity, sobriety, and deliberate judgment are strongest when united, and that, by sinking into inaction, the city, like everything else, will wear itself out, and its skill in everything decay; while each fresh struggle will give it fresh experience, and make it more used to defend itself not in word but in deed. In short, my conviction is that a city not inactive by nature could not choose a quicker way to ruin itself than by suddenly adopting such a policy, and that the safest rule of life is to take one's character and institutions for better and for worse, and to live up to them as closely as one can."

[19] Such were the words of Alcibiades. After hearing him and the Egestaeans and some Leontine exiles, who came forward re-

minding them of their oaths and imploring their assistance, the Athenians became more eager for the expedition than before. Nicias, perceiving that it would be now useless to try to deter them by the old line of argument, but thinking that he might perhaps alter their resolution by the extravagance of his estimates, came forward a second time and spoke as follows:

[20] "I see, Athenians, that you are thoroughly bent upon the expedition, and therefore hope that all will turn out as we wish, and proceed to give you my opinion at the present juncture. From all that I hear we are going against cities that are great and not subject to one another, or in need of change, so as to be glad to pass from enforced servitude to an easier condition, or in the least likely to accept our rule in exchange for freedom; and, to take only the Hellenic towns, they are very numerous for one island. Besides Naxos and Catana, which I expect to join us from their connection with Leontini, there are seven others armed at all points just like our own power, particularly Selinus and Syracuse, the chief objects of our expedition. These are full of heavy infantry, archers, and darters, have galleys in abundance and crowds to man them; they have also money, partly in the hands of private persons, partly in the temples at Selinus, and at Syracuse first-fruits from some of the barbarians as well. But their chief advantage over us lies in the number of their horses, and in the fact that they grow their corn at home instead of importing it.

[21] "Against a power of this kind it will not do to have merely a weak naval armament, but we shall want also a large land army to sail with us, if we are to do anything worthy of our ambition, and are not to be shut out from the country by a numerous cavalry; especially if the cities should take alarm and combine, and we should be left without friends (except the Egestaeans) to furnish us with horse to defend ourselves with. It would be disgraceful to have to retire under compulsion, or to send back for reinforcements, owing to want of reflection at first: we must therefore start from home with a competent force, seeing that we are going to sail far from our country, and upon an expedition not like any which you may have undertaken in the quality of allies, among your subject states here in Hellas, where any additional supplies needed were easily drawn from the friendly territory; but we are cutting ourselves off, and going to a land entirely strange, from which during four months in winter it is not even easy for a messenger to get to Athens.

[22] "I think, therefore, that we ought to take great numbers of heavy infantry, both from Athens and from our allies, and not merely from our subjects, but also any we may be able to get for love or for money in Peloponnese, and great numbers also of archers and slingers, to make head against the Sicilian horse. Meanwhile we must have an overwhelming superiority at sea, to enable us the more easily to carry in what we want; and we must take our own corn in merchant vessels, that is to say, wheat and parched barley, and bakers from the mills compelled to serve for pay in the proper proportion; in order that in case of our being weather-bound the armament may not want provisions, as it is not every city that will be able to entertain numbers like ours. We must also provide ourselves with everything else as far as we can, so as not to be dependent upon others; and above all we must take with us from home as much money as possible, as the sums talked of as ready at Egesta are readier, you may be sure, in talk than in any other way.

[23] "Indeed, even if we leave Athens with a force not only equal to that of the enemy except in the number of heavy infantry in the field, but even at all points superior to him, we shall still find it difficult to conquer Sicily or save ourselves. We must not disguise from ourselves that we go to found a city among strangers and enemies, and that he who undertakes such an enterprise should be prepared to become master of the country the first day he lands, or failing in this to find everything hostile to him. Fearing this, and knowing that we shall have need of much good counsel and more good fortune—a hard matter for mortal man to aspire to—I wish as far as may be to make myself independent of fortune before sailing, and when I do sail, to be as safe as a strong force can make me. This I believe to be surest for the country at large, and safest for us who are to go on the expedition. If any one thinks differently I resign to him my command."

[24] With this Nicias concluded, thinking that he should either disgust the Athenians by the magnitude of the undertaking, or, if obliged to sail on the expedition, would thus do so in the safest way possible. The Athenians, however, far from having their taste for the voyage taken away by the burdensomeness of

the preparations, became more eager for it than ever; and just the contrary took place of what Nicias had thought, as it was held that he had given good advice, and that the expedition would be the safest in the world. All alike fell in love with the enterprise. The older men thought that they would either subdue the places against which they were to sail, or at all events, with so large a force, meet with no disaster; those in the prime of life felt a longing for foreign sights and spectacles, and had no doubt that they should come safe home again; while the idea of the common people and the soldiery was to earn wages at the moment, and make conquests that would supply a never-ending fund of pay for the future. With this enthusiasm of the majority, the few that liked it not, feared to appear unpatriotic by holding up their hands against it, and so kept quiet.

[25] At last one of the Athenians came forward and called upon Nicias and told him that he ought not to make excuses or put them off, but say at once before them all what forces the Athenians should vote him. Upon this he said, not without reluctance, that he would advise upon that matter more at leisure with his colleagues; as far however as he could see at present, they must sail with at least one hundred galleys—the Athenians providing as many transports as they might determine, and sending for others from the allies—not less than five thousand heavy infantry in all, Athenian and allied, and if possible more; and the rest of the armament in proportion; archers from home and from Crete, and slingers, and whatever else might seem desirable, being got ready by the generals and taken with them.

[26] Upon hearing this the Athenians at once voted that the generals should have full powers in the matter of the numbers of the army and of the expedition generally, to do as they judged best for the interests of Athens. After this the preparations began; messages being sent to the allies and the rolls drawn up at home. And as the city had just recovered from the plague and the long war, and a number of young men had grown up and capital had accumulated by reason of the truce, everything was the more easily provided.

In the midst of these preparations [27] all the stone Hermae in the city of Athens, that is to say the customary square figures, so common in the doorways of private houses and temples, had in one night most of them their faces mutilated. No one knew who had done it, but large public rewards were offered to

find the authors; and it was further voted that any one who knew of any other act of impiety having been committed should come and give information without fear of consequences, whether he were citizen, alien, or slave. The matter was taken up the more seriously, as it was thought to be ominous for the expedition, and part of a conspiracy to bring about a revolution and to upset the democracy.

[28] Information was given accordingly by some resident aliens and body servants, not about the Hermae but about some previous mutilations of other images perpetrated by young men in a drunken frolic, and of mock celebrations of the mysteries, averred to take place in private houses. Alcibiades being implicated in this charge, it was taken hold of by those who could least endure him, because he stood in the way of their obtaining the undisturbed direction of the people, and who thought that if he were once removed the first place would be theirs. These accordingly magnified the matter and loudly proclaimed that the affair of the mysteries and the mutilation of the Hermae were part and parcel of a scheme to overthrow the democracy, and that nothing of all this had been done without Alcibiades; the proofs alleged being the general and undemocratic licence of his life and habits.

[29] Alcibiades repelled on the spot the charges in question, and also before going on the expedition, the preparations for which were now complete, offered to stand his trial, that it might be seen whether he was guilty of the acts imputed to him; desiring to be punished if found guilty, but, if acquitted, to take the command. Meanwhile he protested against their receiving slanders against him in his absence, and begged them rather to put him to death at once if he were guilty, and pointed out the imprudence of sending him out at the head of so large an army, with so serious a charge still undecided. But his enemies feared that he would have the army for him if he were tried immediately, and that the people might relent in favour of the man whom they already caressed as the cause of the Argives and some of the Mantineans joining in the expedition, and did their utmost to get this proposition rejected, putting forward other orators who said that he ought at present to sail and not delay the departure of the army, and be tried on his return within a fixed number of days; their plan being to have him sent for and brought home for trial upon some graver charge, which they would the more easily get

up in his absence. Accordingly it was decreed that he should sail.

[*30*] After this the departure for Sicily took place, it being now about midsummer. Most of the allies, with the corn transports and the smaller craft and the rest of the expedition, had already received orders to muster at Corcyra, to cross the Ionian Sea from thence in a body to the Iapygian promontory. But the Athenians themselves, and such of their allies as happened to be with them, went down to Piraeus upon a day appointed at daybreak, and began to man the ships for putting out to sea. With them also went down the whole population, one may say, of the city, both citizens and foreigners; the inhabitants of the country each escorting those that belonged to them, their friends, their relatives, or their sons, with hope and lamentation upon their way, as they thought of the conquests which they hoped to make, or of the friends whom they might never see again, considering the long voyage which they were going to make from their country. Indeed, at this moment, when they were now upon the point of parting from one another, the danger came more home to them than when they voted for the expedition; although the strength of the armament, and the profuse provision which they remarked in every department, was a sight that could not but comfort them. As for the foreigners and the rest of the crowd, they simply went to see a sight worth looking at and passing all belief.

[*31*] Indeed this armament that first sailed out was by far the most costly and splendid Hellenic force that had ever been sent out by a single city up to that time. In mere number of ships and heavy infantry that against Epidaurus under Pericles, and the same when going against Potidaea under Hagnon, was not inferior; containing as it did four thousand Athenian heavy infantry, three hundred horse, and one hundred galleys accompanied by fifty Lesbian and Chian vessels and many allies besides. But these were sent upon a short voyage and with a scanty equipment. The present expedition was formed in contemplation of a long term of service by land and sea alike, and was furnished with ships and troops so as to be ready for either as required. The fleet had been elaborately equipped at great cost to the captains and the state; the treasury giving a drachma a day to each seaman, and providing empty ships, sixty men-of-war and forty transports, and manning these with the best crews obtainable; while the captains gave a bounty in

addition to the pay from the treasury to the *thranitae* and crews generally, besides spending lavishly upon figure-heads and equipments, and one and all making the utmost exertions to enable their own ships to excel in beauty and fast sailing. Meanwhile the land forces had been picked from the best musterrolls, and vied with each other in paying great attention to their arms and personal accoutrements. From this resulted not only a rivalry among themselves in their different departments, but an idea among the rest of the Hellenes that it was more a display of power and resources than an armament against an enemy. For if any one had counted up the public expenditure of the state, and the private outlay of individuals—that is to say, the sums which the state had already spent upon the expedition and was sending out in the hands of the generals, and those which individuals had expended upon their personal outfit, or as captains of galleys had laid out and were still to lay out upon their vessels; and if he had added to this the journey money which each was likely to have provided himself with, independently of the pay from the treasury, for a voyage of such length, and what the soldiers or traders took with them for the purpose of exchange—it would have been found that many talents in all were being taken out of the city. Indeed the expedition became not less famous for its wonderful boldness and for the splendour of its appearance, than for its overwhelming strength as compared with the peoples against whom it was directed, and for the fact that this was the longest passage from home hitherto attempted, and the most ambitious in its objects considering the resources of those who undertook it.

[*32*] The ships being now manned, and everything put on board with which they meant to sail, the trumpet commanded silence, and the prayers customary before putting out to sea were offered, not in each ship by itself, but by all together to the voice of a herald; and bowls of wine were mixed through all the armament, and libations made by the soldiers and their officers in gold and silver goblets. In their prayers joined also the crowds on shore, the citizens and all others that wished them well. The hymn sung and the libations finished, they put out to sea, and first sailing out in column then raced each other as far as Aegina, and so hastened to reach Corcyra, where the rest of the allied forces were also assembling.

CHAPTER XIX

Seventeenth Year of the War—Parties at Syracuse
—Story of Harmodius and Aristogiton—Disgrace
of Alcibiades

MEANWHILE at Syracuse news came in from many quarters of the expedition, but for a long while met with no credence whatever. Indeed, an assembly was held in which speeches, as will be seen, were delivered by different orators, believing or contradicting the report of the Athenian expedition; among whom Hermocrates, son of Hermon, came forward, being persuaded that he knew the truth of the matter, and gave the following counsel:

[33] "Although I shall perhaps be no better believed than others have been when I speak upon the reality of the expedition, and although I know that those who either make or repeat statements thought not worthy of belief not only gain no converts but are thought fools for their pains, I shall certainly not be frightened into holding my tongue when the state is in danger, and when I am persuaded that I can speak with more authority on the matter than other persons. Much as you wonder at it, the Athenians nevertheless have set out against us with a large force, naval and military, professedly to help the Egestaeans and to restore Leontini, but really to conquer Sicily, and above all our city, which once gained, the rest, they think, will easily follow. Make up your minds, therefore, to see them speedily here, and see how you can best repel them with the means under your hand, and do not be taken off your guard through despising the news, or neglect the common weal through disbelieving it. Meanwhile those who believe me need not be dismayed at the force or daring of the enemy. They will not be able to do us more hurt than we shall do them; nor is the greatness of their armament altogether without advantage to us. Indeed, the greater it is the better, with regard to the rest of the Siceliots, whom dismay will make more ready to join us; and if we defeat or drive them away, disappointed of the objects of their ambition (for I do not fear for a moment that they will get what they want), it will be a most glorious exploit for us, and in my judgment by no means an unlikely one. Few indeed have been the large armaments, either Hellenic or barbarian, that have gone far from home and been successful. They cannot be more numerous than the people of the country and their neighbours, all of whom fear leagues together; and if they miscarry for want of supplies in a foreign land, to those against whom their plans were laid none the less they leave renown, although they may themselves have been the main cause of their own discomfort. Thus these very Athenians rose by the defeat of the Mede, in a great measure due to accidental causes, from the mere fact that Athens had been the object of his attack; and this may very well be the case with us also.

[34] "Let us, therefore, confidently begin preparations here; let us send and confirm some of the Sicels, and obtain the friendship and alliance of others, and dispatch envoys to the rest of Sicily to show that the danger is common to all, and to Italy to get them to become our allies, or at all events to refuse to receive the Athenians. I also think that it would be best to send to Carthage as well; they are by no means there without apprehension, but it is their constant fear that the Athenians may one day attack their city, and they may perhaps think that they might themselves suffer by letting Sicily be sacrificed, and be willing to help us secretly if not openly, in one way if not in another. They are the best able to do so, if they will, of any of the present day, as they possess most gold and silver, by which war, like everything else, flourishes. Let us also send to Lacedaemon and Corinth, and ask them to come here and help us as soon as possible, and to keep alive the war in Hellas. But the true thing of all others, in my opinion, to do at the present moment, is what you, with your constitutional love of quiet, will be slow to see, and what I must nevertheless mention. If we Siceliots, all together, or at least as many as possible besides ourselves, would only launch the whole of our actual navy with two months' provisions, and meet the Athenians at Tarentum and the Iapygian promontory, and show them that before fighting for Sicily they must first fight for their passage across the Ionian Sea, we should strike dismay into their army, and set them on thinking that we have a base for our defensive—for Tarentum is ready to receive us—while they have a wide sea to cross with all their armament, which could with difficulty keep its order through so long a voyage, and would be easy for us to attack as it came on slowly and in small detachments. On the other hand, if they were to lighten their vessels, and draw together their fast sailers and with these attack us, we could either fall upon them when they were wearied with rowing, or

if we did not choose to do so, we could retire to Tarentum; while they, having crossed with few provisions just to give battle, would be hard put to it in desolate places, and would either have to remain and be blockaded, or to try to sail along the coast, abandoning the rest of their armament, and being further discouraged by not knowing for certain whether the cities would receive them. In my opinion this consideration alone would be sufficient to deter them from putting out from Corcyra; and what with deliberating and reconnoitring our numbers and whereabouts, they would let the season go on until winter was upon them, or, confounded by so unexpected a circumstance, would break up the expedition, especially as their most experienced general has, as I hear, taken the command against his will, and would grasp at the first excuse offered by any serious demonstration of ours. We should also be reported, I am certain, as more numerous than we really are, and men's minds are affected by what they hear, and besides the first to attack, or to show that they mean to defend themselves against an attack, inspire greater fear because men see that they are ready for the emergency. This would just be the case with the Athenians at present. They are now attacking us in the belief that we shall not resist, having a right to judge us severely because we did not help the Lacedaemonians in crushing them; but if they were to see us showing a courage for which they are not prepared, they would be more dismayed by the surprise than they could ever be by our actual power. I could wish to persuade you to show this courage; but if this cannot be, at all events lose not a moment in preparing generally for the war; and remember all of you that contempt for an assailant is best shown by bravery in action, but that for the present the best course is to accept the preparations which fear inspires as giving the surest promise of safety, and to act as if the danger was real. That the Athenians are coming to attack us, and are already upon the voyage, and all but here—this is what I am sure of."

[35] Thus far spoke Hermocrates. Meanwhile the people of Syracuse were at great strife among themselves; some contending that the Athenians had no idea of coming and that there was no truth in what he said; some asking if they did come what harm they could do that would not be repaid them tenfold in return; while others made light of the whole affair and turned it into ridicule. In short, there

were few that believed Hermocrates and feared for the future. Meanwhile Athenagoras, the leader of the people and very powerful at that time with the masses, came forward and spoke as follows:

[36] "For the Athenians, he who does not wish that they may be as misguided as they are supposed to be, and that they may come here to become our subjects, is either a coward or a traitor to his country; while as for those who carry such tidings and fill you with so much alarm, I wonder less at their audacity than at their folly if they flatter themselves that we do not see through them. The fact is that they have their private reasons to be afraid, and wish to throw the city into consternation to have their own terrors cast into the shade by the public alarm. In short, this is what these reports are worth; they do not arise of themselves, but are concocted by men who are always causing agitation here in Sicily. However, if you are well advised, you will not be guided in your calculation of probabilities by what these persons tell you, but by what shrewd men and of large experience, as I esteem the Athenians to be, would be likely to do. Now it is not likely that they would leave the Peloponnesians behind them, and before they have well ended the war in Hellas wantonly come in quest of a new war quite as arduous in Sicily; indeed, in my judgment, they are only too glad that we do not go and attack them, being so many and so great cities as we are.

[37] "However, if they should come as is reported, I consider Sicily better able to go through with the war than Peloponnese, as being at all points better prepared, and our city by itself far more than a match for this pretended army of invasion, even were it twice as large again. I know that they will not have horses with them, or get any here, except a few perhaps from the Egestaeans; or be able to bring a force of heavy infantry equal in number to our own, in ships which will already have enough to do to come all this distance, however lightly laden, not to speak of the transport of the other stores required against a city of this magnitude, which will be no slight quantity. In fact, so strong is my opinion upon the subject, that I do not well see how they could avoid annihilation if they brought with them another city as large as Syracuse, and settled down and carried on war from our frontier; much less can they hope to succeed with all Sicily hostile to them, as all Sicily will be,

and with only a camp pitched from the ships, and composed of tents and bare necessaries, from which they would not be able to stir far for fear of our cavalry.

[38] "But the Athenians see this as I tell you, and as I have reason to know are looking after their possessions at home, while persons here invent stories that neither are true nor ever will be. Nor is this the first time that I see these persons, when they cannot resort to deeds, trying by such stories and by others even more abominable to frighten your people and get into their hands the government: it is what I see always. And I cannot help fearing that trying so often they may one day succeed, and that we, as long as we do not feel the smart, may prove too weak for the task of prevention, or, when the offenders are known, of pursuit. The result is that our city is rarely at rest, but is subject to constant troubles and to contests as frequent against herself as against the enemy, not to speak of occasional tyrannies and infamous cabals. However, I will try, if you will support me, to let nothing of this happen in our time, by gaining you, the many, and by chastising the authors of such machinations, not merely when they are caught in the act— a difficult feat to accomplish—but also for what they have the wish though not the power to do; as it is necessary to punish an enemy not only for what he does, but also beforehand for what he intends to do, if the first to relax precaution would not be also the first to suffer. I shall also reprove, watch, and on occasion warn the few—the most effectual way, in my opinion, of turning them from their evil courses. And after all, as I have often asked, what would you have, young men? Would you hold office at once? The law forbids it, a law enacted rather because you are not competent than to disgrace you when competent. Meanwhile you would not be on a legal equality with the many! But how can it be right that citizens of the same state should be held unworthy of the same privileges?

[39] "It will be said, perhaps, that democracy is neither wise nor equitable, but that the holders of property are also the best fitted to rule. I say, on the contrary, first, that the word demos, or people, includes the whole state, oligarchy only a part; next, that if the best guardians of property are the rich, and the best counsellors the wise, none can hear and decide so well as the many; and that all these talents, severally and collectively, have their just place in a democracy. But an oligarchy gives the many their share of the danger, and not content with the largest part takes and keeps the whole of the profit; and this is what the powerful and young among you aspire to, but in a great city cannot possibly obtain.

[40] "But even now, foolish men, most senseless of all the Hellenes that I know, if you have no sense of the wickedness of your designs, or most criminal if you have that sense and still dare to pursue them—even now, if it is not a case for repentance, you may still learn wisdom, and thus advance the interest of the country, the common interest of us all. Reflect that in the country's prosperity the men of merit in your ranks will have a share and a larger share than the great mass of your fellow countrymen, but that if you have other designs you run a risk of being deprived of all; and desist from reports like these, as the people know your object and will not put up with it. If the Athenians arrive, this city will repulse them in a manner worthy of itself; we have moreover, generals who will see to this matter. And if nothing of this be true, as I incline to believe, the city will not be thrown into a panic by your intelligence, or impose upon itself a self-chosen servitude by choosing you for its rulers; the city itself will look into the matter, and will judge your words as if they were acts, and, instead of allowing itself to be deprived of its liberty by listening to you, will strive to preserve that liberty, by taking care to have always at hand the means of making itself respected."

[41] Such were the words of Athenagoras. One of the generals now stood up and stopped any other speakers coming forward, adding these words of his own with reference to the matter in hand: "It is not well for speakers to utter calumnies against one another, or for their hearers to entertain them; we ought rather to look to the intelligence that we have received, and see how each man by himself and the city as a whole may best prepare to repel the invaders. Even if there be no need, there is no harm in the state being furnished with horses and arms and all other insignia of war; and we will undertake to see to and order this, and to send round to the cities to reconnoitre and do all else that may appear desirable. Part of this we have seen to already, and whatever we discover shall be laid before you." After these words from the general, the Syracusans departed from the assembly.

[42] In the meantime the Athenians with all their allies had now arrived at Corcyra.

Here the generals began by again reviewing the armament, and made arrangements as to the order in which they were to anchor and encamp, and dividing the whole fleet into three divisions, allotted one to each of their number, to avoid sailing all together and being thus embarrassed for water, harbourage, or provisions at the stations which they might touch at, and at the same time to be generally better ordered and easier to handle, by each squadron having its own commander. Next they sent on three ships to Italy and Sicily to find out which of the cities would receive them, with instructions to meet them on the way and let them know before they put in to land.

[43] After this the Athenians weighed from Corcyra, and proceeded to cross to Sicily with an armament now consisting of one hundred and thirty-four galleys in all (besides two Rhodian fifty-oars), of which one hundred were Athenian vessels—sixty men-of-war, and forty troopships—and the remainder from Chios and the other allies; five thousand and one hundred heavy infantry in all, that is to say, fifteen hundred Athenian citizens from the rolls at Athens and seven hundred Thetes shipped as marines, and the rest allied troops, some of them Athenian subjects, and besides these five hundred Argives, and two hundred and fifty Mantineans serving for hire; four hundred and eighty archers in all, eighty of whom were Cretans, seven hundred slingers from Rhodes, one hundred and twenty light-armed exiles from Megara, and one horse-transport carrying thirty horses.

[44] Such was the strength of the first armament that sailed over for the war. The supplies for this force were carried by thirty ships of burden laden with corn, which conveyed the bakers, stone-masons, and carpenters, and the tools for raising fortifications, accompanied by one hundred boats, like the former pressed into the service, besides many other boats and ships of burden which followed the armament voluntarily for purposes of trade; all of which now left Corcyra and struck across the Ionian Sea together. The whole force making land at the Iapygian promontory and Tarentum, with more or less good fortune, coasted along the shores of Italy, the cities shutting their markets and gates against them, and according them nothing but water and liberty to anchor, and Tarentum and Locri not even that, until they arrived at Rhegium, the extreme point of Italy. Here at length they reunited, and not gaining admission within the walls pitched a camp outside the city in the precinct of Artemis, where a market was also provided for them, and drew their ships on shore and kept quiet. Meanwhile they opened negotiations with the Rhegians, and called upon them as Chalcidians to assist their Leontine kinsmen; to which the Rhegians replied that they would not side with either party, but should await the decision of the rest of the Italiots, and do as they did. Upon this the Athenians now began to consider what would be the best action to take in the affairs of Sicily, and meanwhile waited for the ships sent on to come back from Egesta, in order to know whether there was really there the money mentioned by the messengers at Athens.

[45] In the meantime came in from all quarters to the Syracusans, as well as from their own officers sent to reconnoitre, the positive tidings that the fleet was at Rhegium; upon which they laid aside their incredulity and threw themselves heart and soul into the work of preparation. Guards or envoys, as the case might be, were sent round to the Sicels, garrisons put into the posts of the Peripoli in the country, horses and arms reviewed in the city to see that nothing was wanting, and all other steps taken to prepare for a war which might be upon them at any moment.

[46] Meanwhile the three ships that had been sent on came from Egesta to the Athenians at Rhegium, with the news that so far from there being the sums promised, all that could be produced was thirty talents. The generals were not a little disheartened at being thus disappointed at the outset, and by the refusal to join in the expedition of the Rhegians, the people they had first tried to gain and had had most reason to count upon, from their relationship to the Leontines and constant friendship for Athens. If Nicias was prepared for the news from Egesta, his two colleagues were taken completely by surprise. The Egestaeans had had recourse to the following stratagem, when the first envoys from Athens came to inspect their resources. They took the envoys in question to the temple of Aphrodite at Eryx and showed them the treasures deposited there: bowls, wine-ladles, censers, and a large number of other pieces of plate, which from being in silver gave an impression of wealth quite out of proportion to their really small value. They also privately entertained the ships' crews, and collected all the cups of gold and silver that they could find in Egesta itself or could borrow in the neighbouring Phoeni-

cian and Hellenic towns, and each brought them to the banquets as their own; and as all used pretty nearly the same, and everywhere a great quantity of plate was shown, the effect was most dazzling upon the Athenian sailors, and made them talk loudly of the riches they had seen when they got back to Athens. The dupes in question—who had in their turn persuaded the rest—when the news got abroad that there was not the money supposed at Egesta, were much blamed by the soldiers.

Meanwhile the generals consulted upon what was to be done. [47] The opinion of Nicias was to sail with all the armament to Selinus, the main object of the expedition, and if the Egestaeans could provide money for the whole force, to advise accordingly; but if they could not, to require them to supply provisions for the sixty ships that they had asked for, to stay and settle matters between them and the Selinuntines either by force or by agreement, and then to coast past the other cities, and after displaying the power of Athens and proving their zeal for their friends and allies, to sail home again (unless they should have some sudden and unexpected opportunity of serving the Leontines, or of bringing over some of the other cities), and not to endanger the state by wasting its home-resources.

[48] Alcibiades said that a great expedition like the present must not disgrace itself by going away without having done anything; heralds must be sent to all the cities except Selinus and Syracuse, and efforts be made to make some of the Sicels revolt from the Syracusans, and to obtain the friendship of others, in order to have corn and troops; and first of all to gain the Messinese, who lay right in the passage and entrance to Sicily, and would afford an excellent harbour and base for the army. Thus, after bringing over the towns and knowing who would be their allies in the war, they might at length attack Syracuse and Selinus; unless the latter came to terms with Egesta and the former ceased to oppose the restoration of Leontini.

[49] Lamachus, on the other hand, said that they ought to sail straight to Syracuse, and fight their battle at once under the walls of the town while the people were still unprepared, and the panic at its height. Every armament was most terrible at first; if it allowed time to run on without showing itself, men's courage revived, and they saw it appear at last almost with indifference. By attacking suddenly, while Syracuse still trembled at their coming, they would have the best chance of gaining a victory for themselves and of striking a complete panic into the enemy by the aspect of their numbers—which would never appear so considerable as at present—by the anticipation of coming disaster, and above all by the immediate danger of the engagement. They might also count upon surprising many in the fields outside, incredulous of their coming; and at the moment that the enemy was carrying in his property the army would not want for booty if it sat down in force before the city. The rest of the Siceliots would thus be immediately less disposed to enter into alliance with the Syracusans, and would join the Athenians, without waiting to see which were the strongest. They must make Megara their naval station as a place to retreat to and a base from which to attack: it was an uninhabited place at no great distance from Syracuse either by land or by sea.

[50] After speaking to this effect, Lamachus nevertheless gave his support to the opinion of Alcibiades. After this Alcibiades sailed in his own vessel across to Messina with proposals of alliance, but met with no success, the inhabitants answering that they could not receive him within their walls, though they would provide him with a market outside. Upon this he sailed back to Rhegium. Immediately upon his return the generals manned and victualled sixty ships out of the whole fleet and coasted along to Naxos, leaving the rest of the armament behind them at Rhegium with one of their number. Received by the Naxians, they then coasted on to Catana, and being refused admittance by the inhabitants, there being a Syracusan party in the town, went on to the river Terias. Here they bivouacked, and the next day sailed in single file to Syracuse with all their ships except ten which they sent on in front to sail into the great harbour and see if there was any fleet launched, and to proclaim by herald from shipboard that the Athenians were come to restore the Leontines to their country, as being their allies and kinsmen, and that such of them, therefore, as were in Syracuse should leave it without fear and join their friends and benefactors the Athenians. After making this proclamation and reconnoitring the city and the harbours, and the features of the country which they would have to make their base of operations in the war, they sailed back to Catana.

[51] An assembly being held here, the inhabitants refused to receive the armament, but

invited the generals to come in and say what they desired; and while Alcibiades was speaking and the citizens were intent on the assembly, the soldiers broke down an ill-walled-up postern gate without being observed, and getting inside the town, flocked into the market-place. The Syracusan party in the town no sooner saw the army inside than they became frightened and withdrew, not being at all numerous; while the rest voted for an alliance with the Athenians and invited them to fetch the rest of their forces from Rhegium. After this the Athenians sailed to Rhegium, and put off, this time with all the armament, for Catana, and fell to work at their camp immediately upon their arrival.

[52] Meanwhile word was brought them from Camarina that if they went there the town would go over to them, and also that the Syracusans were manning a fleet. The Athenians accordingly sailed alongshore with all their armament, first to Syracuse, where they found no fleet manning, and so always along the coast to Camarina, where they brought to at the beach, and sent a herald to the people, who, however, refused to receive them, saying that their oaths bound them to receive the Athenians only with a single vessel, unless they themselves sent for more. Disappointed here, the Athenians now sailed back again, and after landing and plundering on Syracusan territory and losing some stragglers from their light infantry through the coming up of the Syracusan horse, so got back to Catana.

[53] There they found the *Salaminia* come from Athens for Alcibiades, with orders for him to sail home to answer the charges which the state brought against him, and for certain others of the soldiers who with him were accused of sacrilege in the matter of the mysteries and of the Hermae. For the Athenians, after the departure of the expedition, had continued as active as ever in investigating the facts of the mysteries and of the Hermae, and, instead of testing the informers, in their suspicious temper welcomed all indifferently, arresting and imprisoning the best citizens upon the evidence of rascals, and preferring to sift the matter to the bottom sooner than to let an accused person of good character pass unquestioned, owing to the rascality of the informer. The commons had heard how oppressive the tyranny of Pisistratus and his sons had become before it ended, and further that that tyranny had been put down at last, not by themselves and Harmodius, but by the Lacedaemonians, and so were always in fear and took everything suspiciously.

[54] Indeed, the daring action of Aristogiton and Harmodius was undertaken in consequence of a love affair, which I shall relate at some length, to show that the Athenians are not more accurate than the rest of the world in their accounts of their own tyrants and of the facts of their own history. Pisistratus dying at an advanced age in possession of the tyranny, was succeeded by his eldest son, Hippias, and not Hipparchus, as is vulgarly believed. Harmodius was then in the flower of youthful beauty, and Aristogiton, a citizen in the middle rank of life, was his lover and possessed him. Solicited without success by Hipparchus, son of Pisistratus, Harmodius told Aristogiton, and the enraged lover, afraid that the powerful Hipparchus might take Harmodius by force, immediately formed a design, such as his condition in life permitted, for overthrowing the tyranny. In the meantime Hipparchus, after a second solicitation of Harmodius, attended with no better success, unwilling to use violence, arranged to insult him in some covert way. Indeed, generally their government was not grievous to the multitude, or in any way odious in practice; and these tyrants cultivated wisdom and virtue as much as any, and without exacting from the Athenians more than a twentieth of their income, splendidly adorned their city, and carried on their wars, and provided sacrifices for the temples. For the rest, the city was left in full enjoyment of its existing laws, except that care was always taken to have the offices in the hands of some one of the family. Among those of them that held the yearly archonship at Athens was Pisistratus, son of the tyrant Hippias, and named after his grandfather, who dedicated during his term of office the altar to the twelve gods in the market-place, and that of Apollo in the Pythian precinct. The Athenian people afterwards built on to and lengthened the altar in the market-place, and obliterated the inscription; but that in the Pythian precinct can still be seen, though in faded letters, and is to the following effect:

> *Pisistratus, the son of Hippias,*
> *Set up this record of his archonship*
> *In precinct of Apollo Pythias.*

[55] That Hippias was the eldest son and succeeded to the government, is what I positively assert as a fact upon which I have had more exact accounts than others, and may be also ascertained by the following circumstance.

He is the only one of the legitimate brothers that appears to have had children; as the altar shows, and the pillar placed in the Athenian Acropolis, commemorating the crime of the tyrants, which mentions no child of Thessalus or of Hipparchus, but five of Hippias, which he had by Myrrhine, daughter of Callias, son of Hyperechides; and naturally the eldest would have married first. Again, his name comes first on the pillar after that of his father; and this too is quite natural, as he was the eldest after him, and the reigning tyrant. Nor can I ever believe that Hippias would have obtained the tyranny so easily, if Hipparchus had been in power when he was killed, and he, Hippias, had had to establish himself upon the same day; but he had no doubt been long accustomed to overawe the citizens, and to be obeyed by his mercenaries, and thus not only conquered, but conquered with ease, without experiencing any of the embarrassment of a younger brother unused to the exercise of authority. It was the sad fate which made Hipparchus famous that got him also the credit with posterity of having been tyrant.

[56] To return to Harmodius; Hipparchus having been repulsed in his solicitations insulted him as he had resolved, by first inviting a sister of his, a young girl, to come and bear a basket in a certain procession, and then rejecting her, on the plea that she had never been invited at all owing to her unworthiness. If Harmodius was indignant at this, Aristogiton for his sake now became more exasperated than ever; and having arranged everything with those who were to join them in the enterprise, they only waited for the great feast of the Panathenaea, the sole day upon which the citizens forming part of the procession could meet together in arms without suspicion. Aristogiton and Harmodius were to begin, but were to be supported immediately by their accomplices against the bodyguard. The conspirators were not many, for better security, besides which they hoped that those not in the plot would be carried away by the example of a few daring spirits, and use the arms in their hands to recover their liberty.

[57] At last the festival arrived; and Hippias with his bodyguard was outside the city in the Ceramicus, arranging how the different parts of the procession were to proceed. Harmodius and Aristogiton had already their daggers and were getting ready to act, when seeing one of their accomplices talking familiarly with Hippias, who was easy of access to every one, they

took fright, and concluded that they were discovered and on the point of being taken; and eager if possible to be revenged first upon the man who had wronged them and for whom they had undertaken all this risk, they rushed, as they were, within the gates, and meeting with Hipparchus by the Leocorium recklessly fell upon him at once, infuriated, Aristogiton by love, and Harmodius by insult, and smote him and slew him. Aristogiton escaped the guards at the moment, through the crowd running up, but was afterwards taken and dispatched in no merciful way: Harmodius was killed on the spot.

[58] When the news was brought to Hippias in the Ceramicus, he at once proceeded not to the scene of action, but to the armed men in the procession, before they, being some distance away, knew anything of the matter, and composing his features for the occasion, so as not to betray himself, pointed to a certain spot, and bade them repair thither without their arms. They withdrew accordingly, fancying he had something to say; upon which he told the mercenaries to remove the arms, and there and then picked out the men he thought guilty and all found with daggers, the shield and spear being the usual weapons for a procession.

[59] In this way offended love first led Harmodius and Aristogiton to conspire, and the alarm of the moment to commit the rash action recounted. After this the tyranny pressed harder on the Athenians, and Hippias, now grown more fearful, put to death many of the citizens, and at the same time began to turn his eyes abroad for a refuge in case of revolution. Thus, although an Athenian, he gave his daughter, Archedice, to a Lampsacene, Aeantides, son of the tyrant of Lampsacus, seeing that they had great influence with Darius. And there is her tomb in Lampsacus with this inscription:

Archedice lies buried in this earth,
Hippias her sire, and Athens gave her birth;
Unto her bosom pride was never known,
Though daughter, wife, and sister to the throne.

Hippias, after reigning three years longer over the Athenians, was deposed in the fourth by the Lacedaemonians and the banished Alcmaeonidae, and went with a safe conduct to Sigeum, and to Aeantides at Lampsacus, and from thence to King Darius; from whose court he set out twenty years after, in his old age, and came with the Medes to Marathon.

[60] With these events in their minds, and

recalling everything they knew by hearsay on the subject, the Athenian people grow difficult of humour and suspicious of the persons charged in the affair of the mysteries, and persuaded that all that had taken place was part of an oligarchical and monarchical conspiracy. In the state of irritation thus produced, many persons of consideration had been already thrown into prison, and far from showing any signs of abating, public feeling grew daily more savage, and more arrests were made; until at last one of those in custody, thought to be the most guilty of all, was induced by a fellow prisoner to make a revelation, whether true or not is a matter on which there are two opinions, no one having been able, either then or since, to say for certain who did the deed. However this may be, the other found arguments to persuade him, that even if he had not done it, he ought to save himself by gaining a promise of impunity, and free the state of its present suspicions; as he would be surer of safety if he confessed after promise of impunity than if he denied and were brought to trial. He accordingly made a revelation, affecting himself and others in the affair of the Hermae; and the Athenian people, glad at last, as they supposed, to get at the truth, and furious until then at not being able to discover those who had conspired against the commons, at once let go the informer and all the rest whom he had not denounced, and bringing the accused to trial executed as many as were apprehended, and condemned to death such as had fled and set a price upon their heads. In this it was, after all, not clear whether the sufferers had been punished unjustly, while in any case the rest of the city received immediate and manifest relief.

[61] To return to Alcibiades: public feeling was very hostile to him, being worked on by the same enemies who had attacked him before he went out; and now that the Athenians fancied that they had got at the truth of the matter of the Hermae, they believed more firmly than ever that the affair of the mysteries also, in which he was implicated, had been contrived by him in the same intention and was connected with the plot against the democracy. Meanwhile it so happened that, just at the time of this agitation, a small force of Lacedaemonians had advanced as far as the Isthmus, in pursuance of some scheme with the Boeotians. It was now thought that this had come by appointment, at his instigation, and not on account of the Boeotians, and that, if the citi-

zens had not acted on the information received, and forestalled them by arresting the prisoners, the city would have been betrayed. The citizens went so far as to sleep one night armed in the temple of Theseus within the walls. The friends also of Alcibiades at Argos were just at this time suspected of a design to attack the commons; and the Argive hostages deposited in the islands were given up by the Athenians to the Argive people to be put to death upon that account: in short, everywhere something was found to create suspicion against Alcibiades. It was therefore decided to bring him to trial and execute him, and the *Salaminia* was sent to Sicily for him and the others named in the information, with instructions to order him to come and answer the charges against him, but not to arrest him, because they wished to avoid causing any agitation in the army or among the enemy in Sicily, and above all to retain the services of the Mantineans and Argives, who, it was thought, had been induced to join by his influence. Alcibiades, with his own ship and his fellow accused, accordingly sailed off with the *Salaminia* from Sicily, as though to return to Athens, and went with her as far as Thurii, and there they left the ship and disappeared, being afraid to go home for trial with such a prejudice existing against them. The crew of the *Salaminia* stayed some time looking for Alcibiades and his companions, and at length, as they were nowhere to be found, set sail and departed. Alcibiades, now an outlaw, crossed in a boat not long after from Thurii to Peloponnese; and the Athenians passed sentence of death by default upon him and those in his company.

CHAPTER XX

Seventeenth and Eighteenth Years of the War— Inaction of the Athenian Army—Alcibiades at Sparta—Investment of Syracuse

[62] THE Athenian generals left in Sicily now divided the armament into two parts, and, each taking one by lot, sailed with the whole for Selinus and Egesta, wishing to know whether the Egestaeans would give the money, and to look into the question of Selinus and ascertain the state of the quarrel between her and Egesta. Coasting along Sicily, with the shore on their left, on the side towards the Tyrrhene Gulf, they touched at Himera, the only Hellenic city in that part of the island, and being refused admission resumed their voyage. On their way they took Hyccara, a petty Sicanian

seaport, nevertheless at war with Egesta, and making slaves of the inhabitants gave up the town to the Egestaeans, some of whose horse had joined them; after which the army proceeded through the territory of the Sicels until it reached Catana, while the fleet sailed along the coast with the slaves on board. Meanwhile Nicias sailed straight from Hyccara along the coast and went to Egesta and, after transacting his other business and receiving thirty talents, rejoined the forces. They now sold their slaves for the sum of one hundred and twenty talents, and sailed round to their Sicel allies to urge them to send troops; and meanwhile went with half their own force to the hostile town of Hybla in the territory of Gela, but did not succeed in taking it.

Summer was now over. *[63]* The winter following, the Athenians at once began to prepare for moving on Syracuse, and the Syracusans on their side for marching against them. From the moment when the Athenians failed to attack them instantly as they at first feared and expected, every day that passed did something to revive their courage; and when they saw them sailing far away from them on the other side of Sicily, and going to Hybla only to fail in their attempts to storm it, they thought less of them than ever, and called upon their generals, as the multitude is apt to do in its moments of confidence, to lead them to Catana, since the enemy would not come to them. Parties also of the Syracusan horse employed in reconnoitring constantly rode up to the Athenian armament, and among other insults asked them whether they had not really come to settle with the Syracusans in a foreign country rather than to resettle the Leontines in their own.

[64] Aware of this, the Athenian generals determined to draw them out in mass as far as possible from the city, and themselves in the meantime to sail by night alongshore, and take up at their leisure a convenient position. This they knew they could not so well do, if they had to disembark from their ships in front of a force prepared for them, or to go by land openly. The numerous cavalry of the Syracusans (a force which they were themselves without) would then be able to do the greatest mischief to their light troops and the crowd that followed them; but this plan would enable them to take up a position in which the horse could do them no hurt worth speaking of, some Syracusan exiles with the army having told them of the spot near the Olympieum, which they

afterwards occupied. In pursuance of their idea, the generals imagined the following stratagem. They sent to Syracuse a man devoted to them, and by the Syracusan generals thought to be no less in their interest; he was a native of Catana, and said he came from persons in that place, whose names the Syracusan generals were acquainted with, and whom they knew to be among the members of their party still left in the city. He told them that the Athenians passed the night in the town, at some distance from their arms, and that if the Syracusans would name a day and come with all their people at daybreak to attack the armament, they, their friends, would close the gates upon the troops in the city, and set fire to the vessels, while the Syracusans would easily take the camp by an attack upon the stockade. In this they would be aided by many of the Catanians, who were already prepared to act, and from whom he himself came.

[65] The generals of the Syracusans, who did not want confidence, and who had intended even without this to march on Catana, believed the man without any sufficient inquiry, fixed at once a day upon which they would be there, and dismissed him, and the Selinuntines and others of their allies having now arrived, gave orders for all the Syracusans to march out in mass. Their preparations completed, and the time fixed for their arrival being at hand, they set out for Catana, and passed the night upon the river Symaethus, in the Leontine territory. Meanwhile the Athenians no sooner knew of their approach than they took all their forces and such of the Sicels or others as had joined them, put them on board their ships and boats, and sailed by night to Syracuse. Thus, when morning broke the Athenians were landing opposite the Olympieum ready to seize their camping ground, and the Syracusan horse having ridden up first to Catana and found that all the armament had put to sea, turned back and told the infantry, and then all turned back together, and went to the relief of the city.

[66] In the meantime, as the march before the Syracusans was a long one, the Athenians quietly sat down their army in a convenient position, where they could begin an engagement when they pleased, and where the Syracusan cavalry would have least opportunity of annoying them, either before or during the action, being fenced off on one side by walls, houses, trees, and by a marsh, and on the other by cliffs. They also felled the neighbouring

trees and carried them down to the sea, and formed a palisade alongside of their ships, and with stones which they picked up and wood hastily raised a fort at Daskon, the most vulnerable point of their position, and broke down the bridge over the Anapus. These preparations were allowed to go on without any interruption from the city, the first hostile force to appear being the Syracusan cavalry, followed afterwards by all the foot together. At first they came close up to the Athenian army, and then, finding that they did not offer to engage, crossed the Helorine road and encamped for the night.

[67] The next day the Athenians and their allies prepared for battle, their dispositions being as follows: Their right wing was occupied by the Argives and Mantineans, the centre by the Athenians, and the rest of the field by the other allies. Half their army was drawn up eight deep in advance, half close to their tents in a hollow square, formed also eight deep, which had orders to look out and be ready to go to the support of the troops hardest pressed. The camp followers were placed inside this reserve. The Syracusans, meanwhile, formed their heavy infantry sixteen deep, consisting of the mass levy of their own people, and such allies as had joined them, the strongest contingent being that of the Selinuntines; next to them the cavalry of the Geloans, numbering two hundred in all, with about twenty horse and fifty archers from Camarina. The cavalry was posted on their right, full twelve hundred strong, and next to it the darters. As the Athenians were about to begin the attack, Nicias went along the lines, and addressed these words of encouragement to the army and the nations composing it:

[68] "Soldiers, a long exhortation is little needed by men like ourselves, who are here to fight in the same battle, the force itself being, to my thinking, more fit to inspire confidence than a fine speech with a weak army. Where we have Argives, Mantineans, Athenians, and the first of the islanders in the ranks together, it were strange indeed, with so many and so brave companions in arms, if we did not feel confident of victory; especially when we have mass levies opposed to our picked troops, and what is more, Siceliots, who may disdain us but will not stand against us, their skill not being at all commensurate to their rashness. You may also remember that we are far from home and have no friendly land near, except what your own swords shall win you; and here

I put before you a motive just the reverse of that which the enemy are appealing to; their cry being that they shall fight for their country, mine that we shall fight for a country that is not ours, where we must conquer or hardly get away, as we shall have their horse upon us in great numbers. Remember, therefore, your renown, and go boldly against the enemy, thinking the present strait and necessity more terrible than they."

[69] After this address Nicias at once led on the army. The Syracusans were not at that moment expecting an immediate engagement, and some had even gone away to the town, which was close by; these now ran up as hard as they could and, though behind time, took their places here or there in the main body as fast as they joined it. Want of zeal or daring was certainly not the fault of the Syracusans, either in this or the other battles, but although not inferior in courage, so far as their military science might carry them, when this failed them they were compelled to give up their resolution also. On the present occasion, although they had not supposed that the Athenians would begin the attack, and although constrained to stand upon their defence at short notice, they at once took up their arms and advanced to meet them. First, the stone-throwers, slingers, and archers of either army began skirmishing, and routed or were routed by one another, as might be expected between light troops; next, soothsayers brought forward the usual victims, and trumpeters urged on the heavy infantry to the charge; and thus they advanced, the Syracusans to fight for their country, and each individual for his safety that day and liberty hereafter; in the enemy's army, the Athenians to make another's country theirs and to save their own from suffering by their defeat; the Argives and independent allies to help them in getting what they came for, and to earn by victory another sight of the country they had left behind; while the subject allies owed most of their ardour to the desire of self-preservation, which they could only hope for if victorious; next to which, as a secondary motive, came the chance of serving on easier terms, after helping the Athenians to a fresh conquest.

[70] The armies now came to close quarters, and for a long while fought without either giving ground. Meanwhile there occurred some claps of thunder with lightning and heavy rain, which did not fail to add to the fears of the party fighting for the first time, and very

little acquainted with war; while to their more experienced adversaries these phenomena appeared to be produced by the time of year, and much more alarm was felt at the continued resistance of the enemy. At last the Argives drove in the Syracusan left, and after them the Athenians routed the troops opposed to them, and the Syracusan army was thus cut in two and betook itself to flight. The Athenians did not pursue far, being held in check by the numerous and undefeated Syracusan horse, who attacked and drove back any of their heavy infantry whom they saw pursuing in advance of the rest; in spite of which the victors followed so far as was safe in a body, and then went back and set up a trophy. Meanwhile the Syracusans rallied at the Helorine road, where they re-formed as well as they could under the circumstances, and even sent a garrison of their own citizens to the Olympieum, fearing that the Athenians might lay hands on some of the treasures there. The rest returned to the town.

[71] The Athenians, however, did not go to the temple, but collected their dead and laid them upon a pyre, and passed the night upon the field. The next day they gave the enemy back their dead under truce, to the number of about two hundred and sixty, Syracusans and allies, and gathered together the bones of their own, some fifty, Athenians and allies, and taking the spoils of the enemy, sailed back to Catana. It was now winter; and it did not seem possible for the moment to carry on the war before Syracuse, until horse should have been sent for from Athens and levied among the allies in Sicily—to do away with their utter inferiority in cavalry—and money should have been collected in the country and received from Athens, and until some of the cities, which they hoped would be now more disposed to listen to them after the battle, should have been brought over, and corn and all other necessaries provided, for a campaign in the spring against Syracuse.

[72] With this intention they sailed off to Naxos and Catana for the winter. Meanwhile the Syracusans burned their dead, and then held an assembly, in which Hermocrates, son of Hermon, a man who with a general ability of the first order had given proofs of military capacity and brilliant courage in the war, came forward and encouraged them, and told them not to let what had occurred make them give way, since their spirit had not been conquered, but their want of discipline had done the mischief. Still they had not been beaten by so much as might have been expected, especially as they were, one might say, novices in the art of war, an army of artisans opposed to the most practised soldiers in Hellas. What had also done great mischief was the number of the generals (there were fifteen of them) and the quantity of orders given, combined with the disorder and insubordination of the troops. But if they were to have a few skilful generals, and used this winter in preparing their heavy infantry, finding arms for such as had not got any, so as to make them as numerous as possible, and forcing them to attend to their training generally, they would have every chance of beating their adversaries, courage being already theirs and discipline in the field having thus been added to it. Indeed, both these qualities would improve, since danger would exercise them in discipline, while their courage would be led to surpass itself by the confidence which skill inspires. The generals should be few and elected with full powers, and an oath should be taken to leave them entire discretion in their command: if they adopted this plan, their secrets would be better kept, all preparations would be properly made, and there would be no room for excuses.

[73] The Syracusans heard him, and voted everything as he advised, and elected three generals, Hermocrates himself, Heraclides, son of Lysimachus, and Sicanus, son of Execestes. They also sent envoys to Corinth and Lacedaemon to procure a force of allies to join them, and to induce the Lacedaemonians for their sakes openly to address themselves in real earnest to the war against the Athenians, that they might either have to leave Sicily or be less able to send reinforcements to their army there.

[74] The Athenian forces at Catana now at once sailed against Messina, in the expectation of its being betrayed to them. The intrigue, however, after all came to nothing: Alcibiades, who was in the secret, when he left his command upon the summons from home, foreseeing that he would be outlawed, gave information of the plot to the friends of the Syracusans in Messina, who had at once put to death its authors, and now rose in arms against the opposite faction with those of their way of thinking, and succeeded in preventing the admission of the Athenians. The latter waited for thirteen days, and then, as they were exposed to the weather and without provisions, and met with no success, went back to Naxos, where they made places for their ships to lie in, erected a palisade round their camp, and re-

tired into winter quarters; meanwhile they sent a galley to Athens for money and cavalry to join them in the spring. *[75]* During the winter the Syracusans built a wall on to the city, so as to take in the statue of Apollo Temenites, all along the side looking towards Epipolae, to make the task of circumvallation longer and more difficult, in case of their being defeated, and also erected a fort at Megara and another in the Olympieum, and stuck palisades along the sea wherever there was a landing place. Meanwhile, as they knew that the Athenians were wintering at Naxos, they marched with all their people to Catana, and ravaged the land and set fire to the tents and encampment of the Athenians, and so returned home. Learning also that the Athenians were sending an embassy to Camarina, on the strength of the alliance concluded in the time of Laches, to gain, if possible, that city, they sent another from Syracuse to oppose them. They had a shrewd suspicion that the Camarinaeans had not sent what they did send for the first battle very willingly; and they now feared that they would refuse to assist them at all in future, after seeing the success of the Athenians in the action, and would join the latter on the strength of their old friendship. Hermocrates, with some others, accordingly arrived at Camarina from Syracuse, and Euphemus and others from the Athenians; and an assembly of the Camarinaeans having been convened, Hermocrates spoke as follows, in the hope of prejudicing them against the Athenians:

[76] "Camarinaeans, we did not come on this embassy because we were afraid of your being frightened by the actual forces of the Athenians, but rather of your being gained by what they would say to you before you heard anything from us. They are come to Sicily with the pretext that you know, and the intention which we all suspect, in my opinion less to restore the Leontines to their homes than to oust us from ours; as it is out of all reason that they should restore in Sicily the cities that they lay waste in Hellas, or should cherish the Leontine Chalcidians because of their Ionian blood, and keep in servitude the Euboean Chalcidians, of whom the Leontines are a colony. No; but the same policy which has proved so successful in Hellas is now being tried in Sicily. After being chosen as the leaders of the Ionians and of the other allies of Athenian origin, to punish the Mede, the Athenians accused some of failure in military service, some of fighting against each other, and

others, as the case might be, upon any colourable pretext that could be found, until they thus subdued them all. In fine, in the struggle against the Medes, the Athenians did not fight for the liberty of the Hellenes, or the Hellenes for their own liberty, but the former to make their countrymen serve them instead of him, the latter to change one master for another, wiser indeed than the first, but wiser for evil.

[77] "But we are not now come to declare to an audience familiar with them the misdeeds of a state so open to accusation as is the Athenian, but much rather to blame ourselves, who, with the warnings we possess in the Hellenes in those parts that have been enslaved through not supporting each other, and seeing the same sophisms being now tried upon ourselves—such as restorations of Leontine kinsfolk and support of Egestaean allies—do not stand together and resolutely show them that here are no Ionians, or Hellespontines, or islanders, who change continually, but always serve a master, sometimes the Mede and sometimes some other, but free Dorians from independent Peloponnese, dwelling in Sicily. Or, are we waiting until we be taken in detail, one city after another; knowing as we do that in no other way can we be conquered, and seeing that they turn to this plan, so as to divide some of us by words, to draw some by the bait of an alliance into open war with each other, and to ruin others by such flattery as different circumstances may render acceptable? And do we fancy when destruction first overtakes a distant fellow countryman that the danger will not come to each of us also, or that he who suffers before us will suffer in himself alone?

[78] "As for the Camarinaean who says that it is the Syracusan, not he, that is the enemy of the Athenian, and who thinks it hard to have to encounter risk in behalf of my country, I would have him bear in mind that he will fight in my country, not more for mine than for his own, and by so much the more safely in that he will enter on the struggle not alone, after the way has been cleared by my ruin, but with me as his ally, and that the object of the Athenian is not so much to punish the enmity of the Syracusan as to use me as a blind to secure the friendship of the Camarinaean. As for him who envies or even fears us (and envied and feared great powers must always be), and who on this account wishes Syracuse to be humbled to teach us a lesson, but would still have her survive, in the interest of his own security the wish that he in-

dulges is not humanly possible. A man can control his own desires, but he cannot likewise control circumstances; and in the event of his calculations proving mistaken, he may live to bewail his own misfortune, and wish to be again envying my prosperity. An idle wish, if he now sacrifice us and refuse to take his share of perils which are the same, in reality though not in name, for him as for us; what is nominally the preservation of our power being really his own salvation. It was to be expected that you, of all people in the world, Camarinaeans, being our immediate neighbours and the next in danger, would have foreseen this, and instead of supporting us in the lukewarm way that you are now doing, would rather come to us of your own accord, and be now offering at Syracuse the aid which you would have asked for at Camarina, if to Camarina the Athenians had first come, to encourage us to resist the invader. Neither you, however, nor the rest have as yet bestirred yourselves in this direction.

[79] "Fear perhaps will make you study to do right both by us and by the invaders, and plead that you have an alliance with the Athenians. But you made that alliance, not against your friends, but against the enemies that might attack you, and to help the Athenians when they were wronged by others, not when as now they are wronging their neighbours. Even the Rhegians, Chalcidians though they be, refuse to help to restore the Chalcidian Leontines; and it would be strange if, while they suspect the gist of this fine pretence and are wise without reason, you, with every reason on your side, should yet choose to assist your natural enemies, and should join with their direst foes in undoing those whom nature has made your own kinsfolk. This is not to do right; but you should help us without fear of their armament, which has no terrors if we hold together, but only if we let them succeed in their endeavours to separate us; since even after attacking us by ourselves and being victorious in battle, they had to go off without effecting their purpose.

[80] "United, therefore, we have no cause to despair, but rather new encouragement to league together; especially as succour will come to us from the Peloponnesians, in military matters the undoubted superiors of the Athenians. And you need not think that your prudent policy of taking sides with neither, because allies of both, is either safe for you or fair to us. Practically it is not as fair as it pretends to be. If the vanquished be defeated, and the victor

conquer, through your refusing to join, what is the effect of your abstention but to leave the former to perish unaided, and to allow the latter to offend unhindered? And yet it were more honourable to join those who are not only the injured party, but your own kindred, and by so doing to defend the common interests of Sicily and save your friends the Athenians from doing wrong.

"In conclusion, we Syracusans say that it is useless for us to demonstrate either to you or to the rest what you know already as well as we do; but we entreat, and if our entreaty fail, we protest that we are menaced by our eternal enemies the Ionians, and are betrayed by you our fellow Dorians. If the Athenians reduce us, they will owe their victory to your decision, but in their own name will reap the honour, and will receive as the prize of their triumph the very men who enabled them to gain it. On the other hand, if we are the conquerors, you will have to pay for having been the cause of our danger. Consider, therefore; and now make your choice between the security which present servitude offers and the prospect of conquering with us and so escaping disgraceful submission to an Athenian master and avoiding the lasting enmity of Syracuse."

[81] Such were the words of Hermocrates; after whom Euphemus, the Athenian ambassador, spoke as follows:

[82] "Although we came here only to renew the former alliance, the attack of the Syracusans compels us to speak of our empire and of the good right we have to it. The best proof of this the speaker himself furnished, when he called the Ionians eternal enemies of the Dorians. It is the fact; and the Peloponnesian Dorians being our superiors in numbers and next neighbours, we Ionians looked out for the best means of escaping their domination. After the Median War we had a fleet, and so got rid of the empire and supremacy of the Lacedaemonians, who had no right to give orders to us more than we to them, except that of being the strongest at that moment; and being appointed leaders of the King's former subjects, we continue to be so, thinking that we are least likely to fall under the dominion of the Peloponnesians, if we have a force to defend ourselves with, and in strict truth having done nothing unfair in reducing to subjection the Ionians and islanders, the kinsfolk whom the Syracusans say we have enslaved. They, our kinsfolk, came against their mother country, that is to say against us, together with the

Mede, and, instead of having the courage to revolt and sacrifice their property as we did when we abandoned our city, chose to be slaves themselves, and to try to make us so.

[83] "We, therefore, deserve to rule because we placed the largest fleet and an unflinching patriotism at the service of the Hellenes, and because these, our subjects, did us mischief by their ready subservience to the Medes; and, desert apart, we seek to strengthen ourselves against the Peloponnesians. We make no fine profession of having a right to rule because we overthrew the barbarian single-handed, or because we risked what we did risk for the freedom of the subjects in question any more than for that of all, and for our own: no one can be quarrelled with for providing for his proper safety. If we are now here in Sicily, it is equally in the interest of our security, with which we perceive that your interest also coincides. We prove this from the conduct which the Syracusans cast against us and which you somewhat too timorously suspect; knowing that those whom fear has made suspicious may be carried away by the charm of eloquence for the moment, but when they come to act follow their interests.

"Now, as we have said, fear makes us hold our empire in Hellas, and fear makes us now come, with the help of our friends, to order safely matters in Sicily, and not to enslave any but rather to prevent any from being enslaved. [84] Meanwhile, let no one imagine that we are interesting ourselves in you without your having anything to do with us, seeing that, if you are preserved and able to make head against the Syracusans, they will be less likely to harm us by sending troops to the Peloponnesians. In this way you have everything to do with us, and on this account it is perfectly reasonable for us to restore the Leontines, and to make them, not subjects like their kinsmen in Euboea, but as powerful as possible, to help us by annoying the Syracusans from their frontier. In Hellas we are alone a match for our enemies; and as for the assertion that it is out of all reason that we should free the Sicilian, while we enslave the Chalcidian, the fact is that the latter is useful to us by being without arms and contributing money only; while the former, the Leontines and our other friends, cannot be too independent.

[85] "Besides, for tyrants and imperial cities nothing is unreasonable if expedient, no one a kinsman unless sure; but friendship or enmity is everywhere an affair of time and circumstance. Here, in Sicily, our interest is not to weaken our friends, but by means of their strength to cripple our enemies. Why doubt this? In Hellas we treat our allies as we find them useful. The Chians and Methymnians govern themselves and furnish ships; most of the rest have harder terms and pay tribute in money; while others, although islanders and easy for us to take, are free altogether, because they occupy convenient positions round Peloponnese. In our settlement of the states here in Sicily, we should, therefore, naturally be guided by our interest, and by fear, as we say, of the Syracusans. Their ambition is to rule you, their object to use the suspicions that we excite to unite you, and then, when we have gone away without effecting anything, by force or through your isolation, to become the masters of Sicily. And masters they must become, if you unite with them; as a force of that magnitude would be no longer easy for us to deal with united, and they would be more than a match for you as soon as we were away.

[86] "Any other view of the case is condemned by the facts. When you first asked us over, the fear which you held out was that of danger to Athens if we let you come under the dominion of Syracuse; and it is not right now to mistrust the very same argument by which you claimed to convince us, or to give way to suspicion because we are come with a larger force against the power of that city. Those whom you should really distrust are the Syracusans. We are not able to stay here without you, and if we proved perfidious enough to bring you into subjection, we should be unable to keep you in bondage, owing to the length of the voyage and the difficulty of guarding large, and in a military sense continental, towns: they, the Syracusans, live close to you, not in a camp, but in a city greater than the force we have with us, plot always against you, never let slip an opportunity once offered, as they have shown in the case of the Leontines and others, and now have the face, just as if you were fools, to invite you to aid them against the power that hinders this, and that has thus far maintained Sicily independent. We, as against them, invite you to a much more real safety, when we beg you not to betray that common safety which we each have in the other, and to reflect that they, even without allies, will, by their numbers, have always the way open to you, while you will not often have the opportunity of defending yourselves with such numerous auxiliaries; if, through your sus-

picions, you once let these go away unsuccessful or defeated, you will wish to see if only a handful of them back again, when the day is past in which their presence could do anything for you.

[87] "But we hope, Camarinaeans, that the calumnies of the Syracusans will not be allowed to succeed either with you or with the rest: we have told you the whole truth upon the things we are suspected of, and will now briefly recapitulate, in the hope of convincing you. We assert that we are rulers in Hellas in order not to be subjects; liberators in Sicily that we may not be harmed by the Sicilians; that we are compelled to interfere in many things, because we have many things to guard against; and that now, as before, we are come as allies to those of you who suffer wrong in this island, not without invitation but upon invitation. Accordingly, instead of making yourselves judges or censors of our conduct, and trying to turn us, which it were now difficult to do, so far as there is anything in our interfering policy or in our character that chimes in with your interest, this take and make use of; and be sure that, far from being injurious to all alike, to most of the Hellenes that policy is even beneficial. Thanks to it, all men in all places, even where we are not, who either apprehend or meditate aggression, from the near prospect before them, in the one case, of obtaining our intervention in their favour, in the other, of our arrival making the venture dangerous, find themselves constrained, respectively, to be moderate against their will, and to be preserved without trouble of their own. Do not you reject this security that is open to all who desire it, and is now offered to you; but do like others, and instead of being always on the defensive against the Syracusans, unite with us, and in your turn at last threaten them."

[88] Such were the words of Euphemus. What the Camarinaeans felt was this. Sympathizing with the Athenians, except in so far as they might be afraid of their subjugating Sicily, they had always been at enmity with their neighbour Syracuse. From the very fact, however, that they were their neighbours, they feared the Syracusans most of the two, and being apprehensive of their conquering even without them, both sent them in the first instance the few horsemen mentioned, and for the future determined to support them most in fact, although as sparingly as possible; but for the moment in order not to seem to slight the Athenians, especially as they had been successful in the engagement, to answer both alike. Agreeably to this resolution they answered that as both the contending parties happened to be both allies of theirs, they thought it most consistent with their oaths at present to side with neither; with which answer the ambassadors of either party departed.

In the meantime, while Syracuse pursued her preparations for war, the Athenians were encamped at Naxos, and tried by negotiation to gain as many of the Sicels as possible. Those more in the low lands, and subjects of Syracuse, mostly held aloof; but the peoples of the interior who had never been otherwise than independent, with few exceptions, at once joined the Athenians, and brought down corn to the army, and in some cases even money. The Athenians marched against those who refused to join, and forced some of them to do so; in the case of others they were stopped by the Syracusans sending garrisons and reinforcements. Meanwhile the Athenians moved their winter quarters from Naxos to Catana, and reconstructed the camp burnt by the Syracusans, and stayed there the rest of the winter. They also sent a galley to Carthage, with proffers of friendship, on the chance of obtaining assistance, and another to Tyrrhenia; some of the cities there having spontaneously offered to join them in the war. They also sent round to the Sicels and to Egesta, desiring them to send them as many horses as possible, and meanwhile prepared bricks, iron, and all other things necessary for the work of circumvallation, intending by the spring to begin hostilities.

In the meantime the Syracusan envoys dispatched to Corinth and Lacedaemon tried as they passed along the coast to persuade the Italiots to interfere with the proceedings of the Athenians, which threatened Italy quite as much as Syracuse, and having arrived at Corinth made a speech calling on the Corinthians to assist them on the ground of their common origin. The Corinthians voted at once to aid them heart and soul themselves, and then sent on envoys with them to Lacedaemon, to help them to persuade her also to prosecute the war with the Athenians more openly at home and to send succours to Sicily. The envoys from Corinth having reached Lacedaemon found there Alcibiades with his fellow refugees, who had at once crossed over in a trading vessel from Thurii, first to Cyllene in Elis, and afterwards from thence to Lacedaemon; upon the Lacedaemonians' own invitation, after first obtaining a safe conduct, as he feared them for the part he had taken in the affair of Mantinea. The result was that the Corinthians, Syracusans, and Alcibiades, pressing all the same request in the assembly of the Lacedaemonians, succeeded in persuading them; but as the ephors and the authorities, although resolved to send envoys to Syracuse to prevent their surrendering to the Athenians, showed no disposition to send them any assistance, Alcibiades now came forward and inflamed and stirred the Lacedaemonians by speaking as follows:

[89] "I am forced first to speak to you of the prejudice with which I am regarded, in order that suspicion may not make you disinclined to listen to me upon public matters. The connection with you as your *proxeni,* which the ancestors of our family by reason of some discontent renounced, I personally tried to renew by my good offices towards you, in particular upon the occasion of the disaster at Pylos. But although I maintained this friendly attitude, you yet chose to negotiate the peace with the Athenians through my enemies, and thus to strengthen them and to discredit me. You had therefore no right to complain if I turned to the Mantineans and Argives, and seized other occasions of thwarting and injuring you; and the time has now come when those among you, who in the bitterness of the moment may have been then unfairly angry with me, should look at the matter in its true light, and take a different view. Those again who judged me unfavourably, because I leaned rather to the side of the commons, must not think that their dislike is any better founded. We have always been hostile to tyrants, and all who oppose arbitrary power are called commons; hence we continued to act as leaders of the multitude; besides which, as democracy was the government of the city, it was necessary in most things to conform to established conditions. However, we endeavoured to be more moderate than the licentious temper of the times; and while there were others, formerly as now, who tried to lead the multitude astray—the same who banished me—our party was that of the whole people, our creed being to do our part in preserving the form of government under which the city enjoyed the utmost greatness and freedom, and which we had found existing. As for democracy, the men of sense among us knew what it was, and I perhaps as well as any, as I have the more cause to complain of it; but there is nothing new to be said of a

patent absurdity; meanwhile we did not think it safe to alter it under the pressure of your hostility.

[90] "So much then for the prejudices with which I am regarded: I now can call your attention to the questions you must consider, and upon which superior knowledge perhaps permits me to speak. We sailed to Sicily first to conquer, if possible, the Siceliots, and after them the Italiots also, and finally to assail the empire and city of Carthage. In the event of all or most of these schemes succeeding, we were then to attack Peloponnese, bringing with us the entire force of the Hellenes lately acquired in those parts, and taking a number of barbarians into our pay, such as the Iberians and others in those countries, confessedly the most warlike known, and building numerous galleys in addition to those which we had already, timber being plentiful in Italy; and with this fleet blockading Peloponnese from the sea and assailing it with our armies by land, taking some of the cities by storm, drawing works of circumvallation round others, we hoped without difficulty to effect its reduction, and after this to rule the whole of the Hellenic name. Money and corn meanwhile for the better execution of these plans were to be supplied in sufficient quantities by the newly acquired places in those countries, independently of our revenues here at home.

[91] "You have thus heard the history of the present expedition from the man who most exactly knows what our objects were; and the remaining generals will, if they can, carry these out just the same. But that the states in Sicily must succumb if you do not help them, I will now show. Although the Siceliots, with all their inexperience, might even now be saved if their forces were united, the Syracusans alone, beaten already in one battle with all their people and blockaded from the sea, will be unable to withstand the Athenian armament that is now there. But if Syracuse falls, all Sicily falls also, and Italy immediately afterwards; and the danger which I just now spoke of from that quarter will before long be upon you. None need therefore fancy that Sicily only is in question; Peloponnese will be so also, unless you speedily do as I tell you, and send on board ship to Syracuse troops that shall be able to row their ships themselves, and serve as heavy infantry the moment that they land; and what I consider even more important than the troops, a Spartan as commanding officer to discipline the forces already on foot and to

compel recusants to serve. The friends that you have already will thus become more confident, and the waverers will be encouraged to join you. Meanwhile you must carry on the war here more openly, that the Syracusans, seeing that you do not forget them, may put heart into their resistance, and that the Athenians may be less able to reinforce their armament. You must fortify Decelea in Attica, the blow of which the Athenians are always most afraid and the only one that they think they have not experienced in the present war; the surest method of harming an enemy being to find out what he most fears, and to choose this means of attacking him, since every one naturally knows best his own weak points and fears accordingly. The fortification in question, while it benefits you, will create difficulties for your adversaries, of which I shall pass over many, and shall only mention the chief. Whatever property there is in the country will most of it become yours, either by capture or surrender; and the Athenians will at once be deprived of their revenues from the silver mines at Laurium, of their present gains from their land and from the law courts, and above all of the revenue from their allies, which will be paid less regularly, as they lose their awe of Athens and see you addressing yourselves with vigour to the war. [92] The zeal and speed with which all this shall be done depends, Lacedaemonians, upon yourselves; as to its possibility, I am quite confident, and I have little fear of being mistaken.

"Meanwhile I hope that none of you will think any the worse of me if, after having hitherto passed as a lover of my country, I now actively join its worst enemies in attacking it, or will suspect what I say as the fruit of an outlaw's enthusiasm. I am an outlaw from the iniquity of those who drove me forth, not, if you will be guided by me, from your service; my worst enemies are not you who only harmed your foes, but they who forced their friends to become enemies; and love of country is what I do not feel when I am wronged, but what I felt when secure in my rights as a citizen. Indeed I do not consider that I am now attacking a country that is still mine; I am rather trying to recover one that is mine no longer; and the true lover of his country is not he who consents to lose it unjustly rather than attack it, but he who longs for it so much that he will go all lengths to recover it. For myself, therefore, Lacedaemonians, I beg you to use me without scruple for danger and trouble of every kind,

and to remember the argument in every one's mouth, that if I did you great harm as an enemy, I could likewise do you good service as a friend, inasmuch as I know the plans of the Athenians, while I only guessed yours. For yourselves I entreat you to believe that your most capital interests are now under deliberation; and I urge you to send without hesitation the expeditions to Sicily and Attica; by the presence of a small part of your forces you will save important cities in that island, and you will destroy the power of Athens both present and prospective; after this you will dwell in security and enjoy the supremacy over all Hellas, resting not on force but upon consent and affection."

[93] Such were the words of Alcibiades. The Lacedaemonians, who had themselves before intended to march against Athens, but were still waiting and looking about them, at once became much more in earnest when they received this particular information from Alcibiades, and considered that they had heard it from the man who best knew the truth of the matter. Accordingly they now turned their attention to the fortifying of Decelea and sending immediate aid to the Sicilians; and naming Gylippus, son of Cleandridas, to the command of the Syracusans, bade him consult with that people and with the Corinthians and arrange for succours reaching the island, in the best and speediest way possible under the circumstances. Gylippus desired the Corinthians to send him at once two ships to Asine, and to prepare the rest that they intended to send, and to have them ready to sail at the proper time. Having settled this, the envoys departed from Lacedaemon.

In the meantime arrived the Athenian galley from Sicily sent by the generals for money and cavalry; and the Athenians, after hearing what they wanted, voted to send the supplies for the armament and the cavalry. And the winter ended, and with it ended the seventeenth year of the present war of which Thucydides is the historian.

[94] The next summer, at the very beginning of the season, the Athenians in Sicily put out from Catana, and sailed along shore to Megara in Sicily, from which, as I have mentioned above, the Syracusans expelled the inhabitants in the time of their tyrant Gelo, themselves occupying the territory. Here the Athenians landed and laid waste the country, and after an unsuccessful attack upon a fort of the Syracusans, went on with the fleet and

army to the river Terias, and advancing inland laid waste the plain and set fire to the corn; and after killing some of a small Syracusan party which they encountered, and setting up a trophy, went back again to their ships. They now sailed to Catana and took in provisions there, and going with their whole force against Centoripa, a town of the Sicels, acquired it by capitulation, and departed, after also burning the corn of the Inessaeans and Hybleans. Upon their return to Catana they found the horsemen arrived from Athens, to the number of two hundred and fifty (with their equipments, but without their horses which were to be procured upon the spot), and thirty mounted archers and three hundred talents of silver.

[95] The same spring the Lacedaemonians marched against Argos, and went as far as Cleonae, when an earthquake occurred and caused them to return. After this the Argives invaded the Thyreatid, which is on their border, and took much booty from the Lacedaemonians, which was sold for no less than twenty-five talents. The same summer, not long after, the Thespian commons made an attack upon the party in office, which was not successful, but succours arrived from Thebes, and some were caught, while others took refuge at Athens.

[96] The same summer the Syracusans learned that the Athenians had been joined by their cavalry, and were on the point of marching against them; and seeing that without becoming masters of Epipolae, a precipitous spot situated exactly over the town, the Athenians could not, even if victorious in battle, easily invest them, they determined to guard its approaches, in order that the enemy might not ascend unobserved by this, the sole way by which ascent was possible, as the remainder is lofty ground, and falls right down to the city, and can all be seen from inside; and as it lies above the rest the place is called by the Syracusans Epipolae or Overtown. They accordingly went out in mass at daybreak into the meadow along the river Anapus, their new generals, Hermocrates and his colleagues, having just come into office, and held a review of their heavy infantry, from whom they first selected a picked body of six hundred, under the command of Diomilus, an exile from Andros, to guard Epipolae, and to be ready to muster at a moment's notice to help wherever help should be required.

[97] Meanwhile the Athenians, the very same morning, were holding a review, having already made land unobserved with all the armament from Catana, opposite a place called Leon, not much more than half a mile from Epipolae, where they disembarked their army, bringing the fleet to anchor at Thapsus, a peninsula running out into the sea, with a narrow isthmus, and not far from the city of Syracuse either by land or water. While the naval force of the Athenians threw a stockade across the isthmus and remained quiet at Thapsus, the land army immediately went on at a run to Epipolae, and succeeded in getting up by Euryelus before the Syracusans perceived them, or could come up from the meadow and the review. Diomilus with his six hundred and the rest advanced as quickly as they could, but they had nearly three miles to go from the meadow before reaching them. Attacking in this way in considerable disorder, the Syracusans were defeated in battle at Epipolae and retired to the town, with a loss of about three hundred killed, and Diomilus among the number. After this the Athenians set up a trophy and restored to the Syracusans their dead under truce, and next day descended to Syracuse itself; and no one coming out to meet them, reascended and built a fort at Labdalum, upon the edge of the cliffs of Epipolae, looking towards Megara, to serve as a magazine for their baggage and money, whenever they advanced to give battle or to work at the lines.

[98] Not long afterwards three hundred cavalry came to them from Egesta, and about a hundred from the Sicels, Naxians, and others; and thus, with the two hundred and fifty from Athens, for whom they had got horses from the Egestaeans and Catanians, besides others that they bought, they now mustered six hundred and fifty cavalry in all. After posting a garrison in Labdalum, they advanced to Syca, where they sat down and quickly built the Circle or centre of their wall of circumvallation. The Syracusans, appalled at the rapidity with which the work advanced, determined to go out against them and give battle and interrupt it; and the two armies were already in battle array, when the Syracusan generals observed that their troops found such difficulty in getting into line, and were in such disorder, that they led them back into the town, except part of the cavalry. These remained and hindered the Athenians from carrying stones or dispersing to any great distance, until a tribe of the Athenian heavy infantry, with all the cavalry, charged and routed the Syracusan horse with some loss; after which they set

up a trophy for the cavalry action.

[99] The next day the Athenians began building the wall to the north of the Circle, at the same time collecting stone and timber, which they kept laying down towards Trogilus along the shortest line for their works from the great harbour to the sea; while the Syracusans, guided by their generals, and above all by Hermocrates, instead of risking any more general engagements, determined to build a counterwork in the direction in which the Athenians were going to carry their wall. If this could be completed in time, the enemy's lines would be cut; and meanwhile, if he were to attempt to interrupt them by an attack, they would send a part of their forces against him, and would secure the approaches beforehand with their stockade, while the Athenians would have to leave off working with their whole force in order to attend to them. They accordingly sallied forth and began to build, starting from their city, running a cross wall below the Athenian Circle, cutting down the olives and erecting wooden towers. As the Athenian fleet had not yet sailed round into the great harbour, the Syracusans still commanded the seacoast, and the Athenians brought their provisions by land from Thapsus.

[100] The Syracusans now thought the stockades and stonework of their counterwall sufficiently far advanced; and as the Athenians, afraid of being divided and so fighting at a disadvantage, and intent upon their own wall, did not come out to interrupt them, they left one tribe to guard the new work and went back into the city. Meanwhile the Athenians destroyed their pipes of drinking-water carried underground into the city; and watching until the rest of the Syracusans were in their tents at midday, and some even gone away into the city, and those in the stockade keeping but indifferent guard, appointed three hundred picked men of their own, and some men picked from the light troops and armed for the purpose, to run suddenly as fast as they could to the counterwork, while the rest of the army advanced in two divisions, the one with one of the generals to the city in case of a sortie, the other with the other general to the stockade by the postern gate. The three hundred attacked and took the stockade, abandoned by its garrison, who took refuge in the outworks round the statue of Apollo Temenites. Here the pursuers burst in with them, and after getting in were beaten out by the Syracusans, and some few of the Argives and Athenians slain; after

which the whole army retired, and having demolished the counterwork and pulled up the stockade, carried away the stakes to their own lines, and set up a trophy.

[101] The next day the Athenians from the Circle proceeded to fortify the cliff above the marsh which on this side of Epipolae looks towards the great harbour; this being also the shortest line for their work to go down across the plain and the marsh to the harbour. Meanwhile the Syracusans marched out and began a second stockade, starting from the city, across the middle of the marsh, digging a trench alongside to make it impossible for the Athenians to carry their wall down to the sea. As soon as the Athenians had finished their work at the cliff they again attacked the stockade and ditch of the Syracusans. Ordering the fleet to sail round from Thapsus into the great harbour of Syracuse, they descended at about dawn from Epipolae into the plain, and laying doors and planks over the marsh, where it was muddy and firmest, crossed over on these, and by daybreak took the ditch and the stockade, except a small portion which they captured afterwards. A battle now ensued, in which the Athenians were victorious, the right wing of the Syracusans flying to the town and the left to the river. The three hundred picked Athenians, wishing to cut off their passage, pressed on at a run to the bridge, when the alarmed Syracusans, who had with them most of their cavalry, closed and routed them, hurling them back upon the Athenian right wing, the first tribe of which was thrown into a panic by the shock. Seeing this, Lamachus came to their aid from the Athenian left with a few archers and with the Argives, and crossing a ditch, was left alone with a few that had crossed with him, and was killed with five or six of his men. These the Syracusans managed immediately to snatch up in haste and get across the river into a place of security, themselves retreating as the rest of the Athenian army now came up.

[102] Meanwhile those who had at first fled for refuge to the city, seeing the turn affairs were taking, now rallied from the town and formed against the Athenians in front of them, sending also a part of their number to the Circle on Epipolae, which they hoped to take while denuded of its defenders. These took and destroyed the Athenian outwork of a thousand feet, the Circle itself being saved by Nicias, who happened to have been left in it through illness, and who now ordered the servants to set fire to the engines and timber

thrown down before the wall; want of men, as he was aware, rendering all other means of escape impossible. This step was justified by the result, the Syracusans not coming any further on account of the fire, but retreating. Meanwhile succours were coming up from the Athenians below, who had put to flight the troops opposed to them; and the fleet also, according to orders, was sailing from Thapsus into the great harbour. Seeing this, the troops on the heights retired in haste, and the whole army of the Syracusans re-entered the city, thinking that with their present force they would no longer be able to hinder the wall reaching the sea.

[103] After this the Athenians set up a trophy and restored to the Syracusans their dead under truce, receiving in return Lamachus and those who had fallen with him. The whole of their forces, naval and military, being now with them, they began from Epipolae and the cliffs and enclosed the Syracusans with a double wall down to the sea. Provisions were now brought in for the armament from all parts of Italy; and many of the Sicels, who had hitherto been looking to see how things went, came as allies to the Athenians: there also arrived three ships of fifty oars from Tyrrhenia. Meanwhile everything else progressed favourably for their hopes. The Syracusans began to despair of finding safety in arms, no relief having reached them from Peloponnese, and were now proposing terms of capitulation among themselves and to Nicias, who after the death of Lamachus was left sole commander. No decision was come to, but, as was natural with men in difficulties and besieged more straitly than before, there was much discussion with Nicias and still more in the town. Their present misfortunes had also made them suspicious of one another; and the blame of their disasters was thrown upon the ill-fortune or treachery of the generals under whose command they had happened; and these were deposed and others, Heraclides, Eucles, and Tellias, elected in their stead.

[104] Meanwhile the Lacedaemonian, Gylippus, and the ships from Corinth were now off Leucas, intent upon going with all haste to the relief of Sicily. The reports that reached them being of an alarming kind, and all agreeing in the falsehood that Syracuse was already completely invested, Gylippus abandoned all hope of Sicily, and wishing to save Italy, rapidly crossed the Ionian Sea to Tarentum with the Corinthian, Pythen, two Laconian, and two Corinthian vessels, leaving the Corinthians to follow him after manning, in addition to their own ten, two Leucadian and two Ambraciot ships. From Tarentum Gylippus first went on an embassy to Thurii, and claimed anew the rights of citizenship which his father had enjoyed; failing to bring over the townspeople, he weighed anchor and coasted along Italy. Opposite the Terinaean Gulf he was caught by the wind which blows violently and steadily from the north in that quarter, and was carried out to sea; and after experiencing very rough weather, remade Tarentum, where he hauled ashore and refitted such of his ships as had suffered most from the tempest. Nicias heard of his approach, but, like the Thurians, despised the scanty number of his ships, and set down piracy as the only probable object of the voyage, and so took no precautions for the present.

[105] About the same time in this summer, the Lacedaemonians invaded Argos with their allies, and laid waste most of the country. The Athenians went with thirty ships to the relief of the Argives, thus breaking their treaty with the Lacedaemonians in the most overt manner. Up to this time incursions from Pylos, descents on the coast of the rest of Peloponnese, instead of on the Laconian, had been the extent of their co-operation with the Argives and Mantineans; and although the Argives had often begged them to land, if only for a moment, with their heavy infantry in Laconia, lay waste ever so little of it with them, and depart, they had always refused to do so. Now, however, under the command of Phytodorus, Laespodius, and Demaratus, they landed at Epidaurus Limera, Prasiae, and other places, and plundered the country; and thus furnished the Lacedaemonians with a better pretext for hostilities against Athens. After the Athenians had retired from Argos with their fleet, and the Lacedaemonians also, the Argives made an incursion into the Phliasid, and returned home after ravaging their land and killing some of the inhabitants.

The Seventh Book

CHAPTER XXI

Eighteenth and Nineteenth Years of the War—
Arrival of Gylippus at Syracuse—Fortification of
Decelea—Successes of the Syracusans

[1] AFTER refitting their ships, Gylippus and Pythen coasted along from Tarentum to Epizephyrian Locris. They now received the more correct information that Syracuse was not yet completely invested, but that it was still possible for an army arriving at Epipolae to effect an entrance; and they consulted, accordingly, whether they should keep Sicily on their right and risk sailing in by sea, or, leaving it on their left, should first sail to Himera and, taking with them the Himeraeans and any others that might agree to join them, go to Syracuse by land. Finally they determined to sail for Himera, especially as the four Athenian ships which Nicias had at length sent off, on hearing that they were at Locris, had not yet arrived at Rhegium. Accordingly, before these reached their post, the Peloponnesians crossed the strait and, after touching at Rhegium and Messina, came to Himera. Arrived there, they persuaded the Himeraeans to join in the war, and not only to go with them themselves but to provide arms for the seamen from their vessels which they had drawn ashore at Himera; and they sent and appointed a place for the Selinuntines to meet them with all their forces. A few troops were also promised by the Geloans and some of the Sicels, who were now ready to join them with much greater alacrity, owing to the recent death of Archonidas, a powerful Sicel king in that neighbourhood and friendly to Athens, and owing also to the vigour shown by Gylippus in coming from Lacedaemon. Gylippus now took with him about seven hundred of his sailors and marines, that number only having arms, a thousand heavy infantry and light troops from Himera with a body of a hundred horse, some light troops and cavalry from Selinus, a few Geloans, and Sicels numbering a thousand in all, and set out on his march for Syracuse.

[2] Meanwhile the Corinthian fleet from Leucas made all haste to arrive; and one of their commanders, Gongylus, starting last with a single ship, was the first to reach Syracuse, a little before Gylippus. Gongylus found the Syracusans on the point of holding an assembly to consider whether they should put an end to the war. This he prevented, and reassured them by telling them that more vessels were still to arrive, and that Gylippus, son of Cleandridas, had been dispatched by the Lacedaemonians to take the command. Upon this the Syracusans took courage, and immediately marched out with all their forces to meet Gylippus, who they found was now close at hand. Meanwhile Gylippus, after taking Ietae, a fort of the Sicels, on his way, formed his army in order of battle, and so arrived at Epipolae, and ascending by Euryelus, as the Athenians had done at first, now advanced with the Syracusans against the Athenian lines. His arrival chanced at a critical moment. The Athenians had already finished a double wall of six or seven furlongs to the great harbour, with the exception of a small portion next the sea, which they were still engaged upon; and in the remainder of the circle towards Trogilus on the other sea, stones had been laid ready for building for the greater part of the distance, and some points had been left half finished, while others were entirely completed. The danger of Syracuse had indeed been great.

[3] Meanwhile the Athenians, recovering from the confusion into which they had been at first thrown by the sudden approach of Gylippus and the Syracusans, formed in order of battle. Gylippus halted at a short distance off and sent on a herald to tell them that, if they

would evacuate Sicily with bag and baggage within five days' time, he was willing to make a truce accordingly. The Athenians treated this proposition with contempt, and dismissed the herald without an answer. After this both sides began to prepare for action. Gylippus, observing that the Syracusans were in disorder and did not easily fall into line, drew off his troops more into the open ground, while Nicias did not lead on the Athenians but lay still by his own wall. When Gylippus saw that they did not come on, he led off his army to the citadel of the quarter of Apollo Temenites, and passed the night there. On the following day he led out the main body of his army, and, drawing them up in order of battle before the walls of the Athenians to prevent their going to the relief of any other quarter, dispatched a strong force against Fort Labdalum, and took it, and put all whom he found in it to the sword, the place not being within sight of the Athenians. On the same day an Athenian galley that lay moored off the harbour was captured by the Syracusans.

[4] After this the Syracusans and their allies began to carry a single wall, starting from the city, in a slanting direction up Epipolae, in order that the Athenians, unless they could hinder the work, might be no longer able to invest them. Meanwhile the Athenians, having now finished their wall down to the sea, had come up to the heights; and part of their wall being weak, Gylippus drew out his army by night and attacked it. However, the Athenians who happened to be bivouacking outside took the alarm and came out to meet him, upon seeing which he quickly led his men back again. The Athenians now built their wall higher, and in future kept guard at this point themselves, disposing their confederates along the remainder of the works, at the stations assigned to them. Nicias also determined to fortify Plemmyrium, a promontory over against the city, which juts out and narrows the mouth of the Great Harbour. He thought that the fortification of this place would make it easier to bring in supplies, as they would be able to carry on their blockade from a less distance, near to the port occupied by the Syracusans; instead of being obliged, upon every movement of the enemy's navy, to put out against them from the bottom of the great harbour. Besides this, he now began to pay more attention to the war by sea, seeing that the coming of Gylippus had diminished their hopes by land. Accordingly, he conveyed over his ships

and some troops, and built three forts in which he placed most of his baggage, and moored there for the future the larger craft and men-of-war. This was the first and chief occasion of the losses which the crews experienced. The water which they used was scarce and had to be fetched from far, and the sailors could not go out for firewood without being cut off by the Syracusan horse, who were masters of the country; a third of the enemy's cavalry being stationed at the little town of Olympieum, to prevent plundering incursions on the part of the Athenians at Plemmyrium. Meanwhile Nicias learned that the rest of the Corinthian fleet was approaching, and sent twenty ships to watch for them, with orders to be on the look-out for them about Locris and Rhegium and the approach to Sicily.

[5] Gylippus, meanwhile, went on with the wall across Epipolae, using the stones which the Athenians had laid down for their own wall, and at the same time constantly led out the Syracusans and their allies, and formed them in order of battle in front of the lines, the Athenians forming against him. At last he thought that the moment was come, and began the attack; and a hand-to-hand fight ensued between the lines, where the Syracusan cavalry could be of no use; and the Syracusans and their allies were defeated and took up their dead under truce, while the Athenians erected a trophy. After this Gylippus called the soldiers together, and said that the fault was not theirs but his; he had kept their lines too much within the works, and had thus deprived them of the services of their cavalry and darters. He would now, therefore, lead them on a second time. He begged them to remember that in material force they would be fully a match for their opponents, while, with respect to moral advantages, it were intolerable if Peloponnesians and Dorians should not feel confident of overcoming Ionians and islanders with the motley rabble that accompanied them, and of driving them out of the country.

[6] After this he embraced the first opportunity that offered of again leading them against the enemy. Now Nicias and the Athenians held the opinion that even if the Syracusans should not wish to offer battle, it was necessary for them to prevent the building of the cross wall, as it already almost overlapped the extreme point of their own, and if it went any further it would from that moment make no difference whether they fought ever so many successful actions, or never fought at all. They

accordingly came out to meet the Syracusans. Gylippus led out his heavy infantry further from the fortifications than on the former occasion, and so joined battle; posting his horse and darters upon the flank of the Athenians in the open space, where the works of the two walls terminated. During the engagement the cavalry attacked and routed the left wing of the Athenians, which was opposed to them; and the rest of the Athenian army was in consequence defeated by the Syracusans and driven headlong within their lines. The night following the Syracusans carried their wall up to the Athenian works and passed them, thus putting it out of their power any longer to stop them, and depriving them, even if victorious in the field, of all chance of investing the city for the future.

[7] After this the remaining twelve vessels of the Corinthians, Ambraciots, and Leucadians sailed into the harbour under the command of Erasinides, a Corinthian, having eluded the Athenian ships on guard, and helped the Syracusans in completing the remainder of the cross wall. Meanwhile Gylippus went into the rest of Sicily to raise land and naval forces, and also to bring over any of the cities that either were lukewarm in the cause or had hitherto kept out of the war altogether. Syracusan and Corinthian envoys were also dispatched to Lacedaemon and Corinth to get a fresh force sent over, in any way that might offer, either in merchant vessels or transports, or in any other manner likely to prove successful, as the Athenians too were sending for reinforcements; while the Syracusans proceeded to man a fleet and to exercise, meaning to try their fortune in this way also, and generally became exceedingly confident.

[8] Nicias perceiving this, and seeing the strength of the enemy and his own difficulties daily increasing, himself also sent to Athens. He had before sent frequent reports of events as they occurred, and felt it especially incumbent upon him to do so now, as he thought that they were in a critical position, and that, unless speedily recalled or strongly reinforced from home, they had no hope of safety. He feared, however, that the messengers, either through inability to speak, or through failure of memory, or from a wish to please the multitude, might not report the truth, and so thought it best to write a letter, to ensure that the Athenians should know his own opinion without its being lost in transmission, and be able to decide upon the real facts of the case.

His emissaries, accordingly, departed with the letter and the requisite verbal instructions; and he attended to the affairs of the army, making it his aim now to keep on the defensive and to avoid any unnecessary danger.

[9] At the close of the same summer the Athenian general Euetion marched in concert with Perdiccas with a large body of Thracians against Amphipolis, and failing to take it brought some galleys round into the Strymon, and blockaded the town from the river, having his base at Himeraeum.

Summer was now over. [10] The winter ensuing, the persons sent by Nicias, reaching Athens, gave the verbal messages which had been entrusted to them, and answered any questions that were asked them, and delivered the letter. The clerk of the city now came forward and read out to the Athenians the letter, which was as follows:

[11] "Our past operations, Athenians, have been made known to you by many other letters; it is now time for you to become equally familiar with our present condition, and to take your measures accordingly. We had defeated in most of our engagements with them the Syracusans, against whom we were sent, and we had built the works which we now occupy, when Gylippus arrived from Lacedaemon with an army obtained from Peloponnese and from some of the cities in Sicily. In our first battle with him we were victorious; in the battle on the following day we were overpowered by a multitude of cavalry and darters, and compelled to retire within our lines. We have now, therefore, been forced by the numbers of those opposed to us to discontinue the work of circumvallation, and to remain inactive; being unable to make use even of all the force we have, since a large portion of our heavy infantry is absorbed in the defence of our lines. Meanwhile the enemy have carried a single wall past our lines, thus making it impossible for us to invest them in future, until this cross wall be attacked by a strong force and captured. So that the besieger in name has become, at least from the land side, the besieged in reality; as we are prevented by their cavalry from even going for any distance into the country.

[12] "Besides this, an embassy has been dispatched to Peloponnese to procure reinforcements, and Gylippus has gone to the cities in Sicily, partly in the hope of inducing those that are at present neutral to join him in the war, partly of bringing from his allies addi-

tional contingents for the land forces and material for the navy. For I understand that they contemplate a combined attack, upon our lines with their land forces and with their fleet by sea. You must none of you be surprised that I say by sea also. They have discovered that the length of the time we have now been in commission has rotted our ships and wasted our crews, and that with the entireness of our crews and the soundness of our ships the pristine efficiency of our navy has departed. For it is impossible for us to haul our ships ashore and careen them, because, the enemy's vessels being as many or more than our own, we are constantly anticipating an attack. Indeed, they may be seen exercising, and it lies with them to take the initiative; and not having to maintain a blockade, they have greater facilities for drying their ships.

[13] "This we should scarcely be able to do, even if we had plenty of ships to spare, and were freed from our present necessity of exhausting all our strength upon the blockade. For it is already difficult to carry in supplies past Syracuse; and were we to relax our vigilance in the slightest degree it would become impossible. The losses which our crews have suffered and still continue to suffer arise from the following causes. Expeditions for fuel and for forage, and the distance from which water has to be fetched, cause our sailors to be cut off by the Syracusan cavalry; the loss of our previous superiority emboldens our slaves to desert; our foreign seamen are impressed by the unexpected appearance of a navy against us, and the strength of the enemy's resistance; such of them as were pressed into the service take the first opportunity of departing to their respective cities; such as were originally seduced by the temptation of high pay, and expected little fighting and large gains, leave us either by desertion to the enemy or by availing themselves of one or other of the various facilities of escape which the magnitude of Sicily affords them. Some even engage in trade themselves and prevail upon the captains to take Hyccaric slaves on board in their place; thus they have ruined the efficiency of our navy.

[14] "Now I need not remind you that the time during which a crew is in its prime is short, and that the number of sailors who can start a ship on her way and keep the rowing in time is small. But by far my greatest trouble is, that holding the post which I do, I am prevented by the natural indocility of the Athenian seaman from putting a stop to these evils;

and that meanwhile we have no source from which to recruit our crews, which the enemy can do from many quarters, but are compelled to depend both for supplying the crews in service and for making good our losses upon the men whom we brought with us. For our present confederates, Naxos and Catana, are incapable of supplying us. There is only one thing more wanting to our opponents, I mean the defection of our Italian markets. If they were to see you neglect to relieve us from our present condition, and were to go over to the enemy, famine would compel us to evacuate, and Syracuse would finish the war without a blow.

"I might, it is true, have written to you something different and more agreeable than this, but nothing certainly more useful, if it is desirable for you to know the real state of things here before taking your measures. Besides I know that it is your nature to love to be told the best side of things, and then to blame the teller if the expectations which he has raised in your minds are not answered by the result; and I therefore thought it safest to declare to you the truth.

[15] "Now you are not to think that either your generals or your soldiers have ceased to be a match for the forces originally opposed to them. But you are to reflect that a general Sicilian coalition is being formed against us; that a fresh army is expected from Peloponnese, while the force we have here is unable to cope even with our present antagonists; and you must promptly decide either to recall us or to send out to us another fleet and army as numerous again, with a large sum of money, and someone to succeed me, as a disease in the kidneys unfits me for retaining my post. I have, I think, some claim on your indulgence, as while I was in my prime I did you much good service in my commands. But whatever you mean to do, do it at the commencement of spring and without delay, as the enemy will obtain his Sicilian reinforcements shortly, those from Peloponnese after a longer interval; and unless you attend to the matter the former will be here before you, while the latter will elude you as they have done before."

[16] Such were the contents of Nicias's letter. When the Athenians had heard it they refused to accept his resignation, but chose him two colleagues, naming Menander and Euthydemus, two of the officers at the seat of war, to fill their places until their arrival, that Nicias might not be left alone in his sickness to

bear the whole weight of affairs. They also voted to send out another army and navy, drawn partly from the Athenians on the muster-roll, partly from the allies. The colleagues chosen for Nicias were Demosthenes, son of Alcisthenes, and Eurymedon, son of Thucles. Eurymedon was sent off at once, about the time of the winter solstice, with ten ships, a hundred and twenty talents of silver, and instructions to tell the army that reinforcements would arrive, and that care would be taken of them; [17] but Demosthenes stayed behind to organize the expedition, meaning to start as soon as it was spring, and sent for troops to the allies, and meanwhile got together money, ships, and heavy infantry at home.

The Athenians also sent twenty vessels round Peloponnese to prevent any one crossing over to Sicily from Corinth or Peloponnese. For the Corinthians, filled with confidence by the favourable alteration in Sicilian affairs which had been reported by the envoys upon their arrival, and convinced that the fleet which they had before sent out had not been without its use, were now preparing to dispatch a force of heavy infantry in merchant vessels to Sicily, while the Lacedaemonians did the like for the rest of Peloponnese. The Corinthians also manned a fleet of twenty-five vessels, intending to try the result of a battle with the squadron on guard at Naupactus, and meanwhile to make it less easy for the Athenians there to hinder the departure of their merchantmen, by obliging them to keep an eye upon the galleys thus arrayed against them.

[18] In the meantime the Lacedaemonians prepared for their invasion of Attica, in accordance with their own previous resolve, and at the instigation of the Syracusans and Corinthians, who wished for an invasion to arrest the reinforcements which they heard that Athens was about to send to Sicily. Alcibiades also urgently advised the fortification of Decelea, and a vigorous prosecution of the war. But the Lacedaemonians derived most encouragement from the belief that Athens, with two wars on her hands, against themselves and against the Siceliots, would be more easy to subdue, and from the conviction that she had been the first to infringe the truce. In the former war, they considered, the offence had been more on their own side, both on account of the entrance of the Thebans into Plataea in time of peace, and also of their own refusal to listen to the Athenian offer of arbitration, in spite of the clause in the former treaty that where arbitration should be offered there should be no appeal to arms. For this reason they thought that they deserved their misfortunes, and took to heart seriously the disaster at Pylos and whatever else had befallen them. But when, besides the ravages from Pylos, which went on without any intermission, the thirty Athenian ships came out from Argos and wasted part of Epidaurus, Prasiae, and other places; when upon every dispute that arose as to the interpretation of any doubtful point in the treaty, their own offers of arbitration were always rejected by the Athenians, the Lacedaemonians at length decided that Athens had now committed the very same offence as they had before done, and had become the guilty party; and they began to be full of ardour for the war. They spent this winter in sending round to their allies for iron, and in getting ready the other implements for building their fort; and meanwhile began raising at home, and also by forced requisitions in the rest of Peloponnese, a force to be sent out in the merchantmen to their allies in Sicily. Winter thus ended, and with it the eighteenth year of this war of which Thucydides is the historian.

[19] In the first days of the spring following, at an earlier period than usual, the Lacedaemonians and their allies invaded Attica, under the command of Agis, son of Archidamus, king of the Lacedaemonians. They began by devastating the parts bordering upon the plain, and next proceeded to fortify Decelea, dividing the work among the different cities. Decelea is about thirteen or fourteen miles from the city of Athens, and the same distance or not much further from Boeotia; and the fort was meant to annoy the plain and the richest parts of the country, being in sight of Athens. While the Peloponnesians and their allies in Attica were engaged in the work of fortification, their countrymen at home sent off, at about the same time, the heavy infantry in the merchant vessels to Sicily; the Lacedaemonians furnishing a picked force of Helots and Neodamodes (or freedmen), six hundred heavy infantry in all, under the command of Eccritus, a Spartan; and the Boeotians three hundred heavy infantry, commanded by two Thebans, Xenon and Nicon, and by Hegesander, a Thespian. These were among the first to put out into the open sea, starting from Taenarus in Laconia. Not long after their departure the Corinthians sent off a force of five hundred heavy infantry, consisting partly of

men from Corinth itself, and partly of Arcadian mercenaries, placed under the command of Alexarchus, a Corinthian. The Sicyonians also sent off two hundred heavy infantry at the same time as the Corinthians, under the command of Sargeus, a Sicyonian. Meantime the five-and-twenty vessels manned by Corinth during the winter lay confronting the twenty Athenian ships at Naupactus until the heavy infantry in the merchantmen were fairly on their way from Peloponnese; thus fulfilling the object for which they had been manned originally, which was to divert the attention of the Athenians from the merchantmen to the galleys.

[20] During this time the Athenians were not idle. Simultaneously with the fortification of Decelea, at the very beginning of spring, they sent thirty ships round Peloponnese, under Charicles, son of Apollodorus, with instructions to call at Argos and demand a force of their heavy infantry for the fleet, agreeably to the alliance. At the same time they dispatched Demosthenes to Sicily, as they had intended, with sixty Athenian and five Chian vessels, twelve hundred Athenian heavy infantry from the muster-roll, and as many of the islanders as could be raised in the different quarters, drawing upon the other subject allies for whatever they could supply that would be of use for the war. Demosthenes was instructed first to sail round with Charicles and to operate with him upon the coasts of Laconia, and accordingly sailed to Aegina and there waited for the remainder of his armament, and for Charicles to fetch the Argive troops.

[21] In Sicily, about the same time in this spring, Gylippus came to Syracuse with as many troops as he could bring from the cities which he had persuaded to join. Calling the Syracusans together, he told them that they must man as many ships as possible, and try their hand at a sea-fight, by which he hoped to achieve an advantage in the war not unworthy of the risk. With him Hermocrates actively joined in trying to encourage his countrymen to attack the Athenians at sea, saying that the latter had not inherited their naval prowess nor would they retain it for ever; they had been landsmen even to a greater degree than the Syracusans, and had only become a maritime power when obliged by the Mede. Besides, to daring spirits like the Athenians, a daring adversary would seem the most formidable; and the Athenian plan of paralysing by the boldness of their attack a neighbour

often not their inferior in strength could now be used against them with as good effect by the Syracusans. He was convinced also that the unlooked-for spectacle of Syracusans daring to face the Athenian navy would cause a terror to the enemy, the advantages of which would far outweigh any loss that Athenian science might inflict upon their inexperience. He accordingly urged them to throw aside their fears and to try their fortune at sea; and the Syracusans, under the influence of Gylippus and Hermocrates, and perhaps some others, made up their minds for the sea-fight and began to man their vessels.

[22] When the fleet was ready, Gylippus led out the whole army by night; his plan being to assault in person the forts on Plemmyrium by land, while thirty-five Syracusan galleys sailed according to appointment against the enemy from the great harbour, and the forty-five remaining came round from the lesser harbour, where they had their arsenal, in order to effect a junction with those inside and simultaneously to attack Plemmyrium, and thus to distract the Athenians by assaulting them on two sides at once. The Athenians quickly manned sixty ships, and with twenty-five of these engaged the thirty-five of the Syracusans in the great harbour, sending the rest to meet those sailing round from the arsenal; and an action now ensued directly in front of the mouth of the great harbour, maintained with equal tenacity on both sides; the one wishing to force the passage, the other to prevent them.

[23] In the meantime, while the Athenians in Plemmyrium were down at the sea, attending to the engagement, Gylippus made a sudden attack on the forts in the early morning and took the largest first, and afterwards the two smaller, whose garrisons did not wait for him, seeing the largest so easily taken. At the fall of the first fort, the men from it who succeeded in taking refuge in their boats and merchantmen, found great difficulty in reaching the camp, as the Syracusans were having the best of it in the engagement in the great harbour, and sent a fast-sailing galley to pursue them. But when the two others fell, the Syracusans were now being defeated; and the fugitives from these sailed alongshore with more ease. The Syracusan ships fighting off the mouth of the harbour forced their way through the Athenian vessels and sailing in without any order fell foul of one another, and transferred the victory to the Athenians; who not only routed the squadron in question, but

also that by which they were at first being defeated in the harbour, sinking eleven of the
Syracusan vessels and killing most of the men,
except the crews of three ships whom they
made prisoners. Their own loss was confined
to three vessels; and after hauling ashore the
Syracusan wrecks and setting up a trophy
upon the islet in front of Plemmyrium, they
retired to their own camp.

[24] Unsuccessful at sea, the Syracusans had
nevertheless the forts in Plemmyrium, for
which they set up three trophies. One of the
two last taken they razed, but put in order and
garrisoned the two others. In the capture of
the forts a great many men were killed and
made prisoners, and a great quantity of property was taken in all. As the Athenians had
used them as a magazine, there was a large
stock of goods and corn of the merchants inside, and also a large stock belonging to the
captains; the masts and other furniture of forty
galleys being taken, besides three galleys which
had been drawn up on shore. Indeed the first
and chiefest cause of the ruin of the Athenian
army was the capture of Plemmyrium; even
the entrance of the harbour being now no
longer safe for carrying in provisions, as the
Syracusan vessels were stationed there to prevent it, and nothing could be brought in without fighting; besides the general impression of
dismay and discouragement produced upon
the army.

[25] After this the Syracusans sent out
twelve ships under the command of Agatharchus, a Syracusan. One of these went to Peloponnese with ambassadors to describe the
hopeful state of their affairs, and to incite the
Peloponnesians to prosecute the war there even
more actively than they were now doing, while
the eleven others sailed to Italy, hearing that
vessels laden with stores were on their way to
the Athenians. After falling in with and destroying most of the vessels in question, and
burning in the Caulonian territory a quantity
of timber for shipbuilding, which had been got
ready for the Athenians, the Syracusan squadron went to Locri, and one of the merchantmen from Peloponnese coming in, while they
were at anchor there, carrying Thespian heavy
infantry, took these on board and sailed alongshore towards home. The Athenians were on
the look-out for them with twenty ships at
Megara, but were only able to take one vessel
with its crew; the rest getting clear off to Syracuse. There was also some skirmishing in the
harbour about the piles which the Syracusans

had driven in the sea in front of the old docks,
to allow their ships to lie at anchor inside,
without being hurt by the Athenians sailing up
and running them down. The Athenians
brought up to them a ship of ten thousand talents burden furnished with wooden turrets
and screens, and fastened ropes round the piles
from their boats, wrenched them up and broke
them, or dived down and sawed them in two.
Meanwhile the Syracusans plied them with
missiles from the docks, to which they replied
from their large vessel; until at last most of the
piles were removed by the Athenians. But the
most awkward part of the stockade was the
part out of sight: some of the piles which had
been driven in did not appear above water, so
that it was dangerous to sail up, for fear of running the ships upon them, just as upon a reef,
through not seeing them. However divers
went down and sawed off even these for reward; although the Syracusans drove in others. Indeed there was no end to the contrivances to which they resorted against each other, as might be expected between two hostile
armies confronting each other at such a short
distance: and skirmishes and all kinds of other
attempts were of constant occurrence. Meanwhile the Syracusans sent embassies to the cities, composed of Corinthians, Ambraciots, and
Lacedaemonians, to tell them of the capture of
Plemmyrium, and that their defeat in the sea-
fight was due less to the strength of the enemy
than to their own disorder; and generally, to
let them know that they were full of hope, and
to desire them to come to their help with ships
and troops, as the Athenians were expected
with a fresh army, and if the one already there
could be destroyed before the other arrived, the
war would be at an end.

While the contending parties in Sicily were
thus engaged, [26] Demosthenes, having now
got together the armament with which he was
to go to the island, put out from Aegina, and
making sail for Peloponnese, joined Charicles
and the thirty ships of the Athenians. Taking
on board the heavy infantry from Argos they
sailed to Laconia, and, after first plundering
part of Epidaurus Limera, landed on the coast
of Laconia, opposite Cythera, where the temple of Apollo stands, and, laying waste part of
the country, fortified a sort of isthmus, to
which the Helots of the Lacedaemonians
might desert, and from whence plundering incursions might be made as from Pylos. Demosthenes helped to occupy this place, and then
immediately sailed on to Corcyra to take up

some of the allies in that island, and so to proceed without delay to Sicily; while Charicles waited until he had completed the fortification of the place and, leaving a garrison there, returned home subsequently with his thirty ships and the Argives also.

[27] This same summer arrived at Athens thirteen hundred targeteers, Thracian swordsmen of the tribe of the Dii, who were to have sailed to Sicily with Demosthenes. Since they had come too late, the Athenians determined to send them back to Thrace, whence they had come; to keep them for the Decelean war appearing too expensive, as the pay of each man was a drachma a day. Indeed since Decelea had been first fortified by the whole Peloponnesian army during this summer, and then occupied for the annoyance of the country by the garrisons from the cities relieving each other at stated intervals, it had been doing great mischief to the Athenians; in fact this occupation, by the destruction of property and loss of men which resulted from it, was one of the principal causes of their ruin. Previously the invasions were short, and did not prevent their enjoying their land during the rest of the time: the enemy was now permanently fixed in Attica; at one time it was an attack in force, at another it was the regular garrison overrunning the country and making forays for its subsistence, and the Lacedaemonian king, Agis, was in the field and diligently prosecuting the war; great mischief was therefore done to the Athenians. They were deprived of their whole country: more than twenty thousand slaves had deserted, a great part of them artisans, and all their sheep and beasts of burden were lost; and as the cavalry rode out daily upon excursions to Decelea and to guard the country, their horses were either lamed by being constantly worked upon rocky ground, or wounded by the enemy.

[28] Besides, the transport of provisions from Euboea, which had before been carried on so much more quickly overland by Decelea from Oropus, was now effected at great cost by sea round Sunium; everything the city required had to be imported from abroad, and instead of a city it became a fortress. Summer and winter the Athenians were worn out by having to keep guard on the fortifications, during the day by turns, by night all together, the cavalry excepted, at the different military posts or upon the wall. But what most oppressed them was that they had two wars at once, and had thus reached a pitch of frenzy which no one

would have believed possible if he had heard of it before it had come to pass. For could any one have imagined that even when besieged by the Peloponnesians entrenched in Attica, they would still, instead of withdrawing from Sicily, stay on there besieging in like manner Syracuse, a town (taken as a town) in no way inferior to Athens, or would so thoroughly upset the Hellenic estimate of their strength and audacity, as to give the spectacle of a people which, at the beginning of the war, some thought might hold out one year, some two, none more than three, if the Peloponnesians invaded their country, now seventeen years after the first invasion, after having already suffered from all the evils of war, going to Sicily and undertaking a new war nothing inferior to that which they already had with the Peloponnesians? These causes, the great losses from Decelea, and the other heavy charges that fell upon them, produced their financial embarrassment; and it was at this time that they imposed upon their subjects, instead of the tribute, the tax of a twentieth upon all imports and exports by sea, which they thought would bring them in more money; their expenditure being now not the same as at first, but having grown with the war while their revenues decayed.

[29] Accordingly, not wishing to incur expense in their present want of money, they sent back at once the Thracians who came too late for Demosthenes, under the conduct of Diitrephes, who was instructed, as they were to pass through the Euripus, to make use of them if possible in the voyage alongshore to injure the enemy. Diitrephes first landed them at Tanagra and hastily snatched some booty; he then sailed across the Euripus in the evening from Chalcis in Euboea and disembarking in Boeotia led them against Mycalessus. The night he passed unobserved near the temple of Hermes, not quite two miles from Mycalessus, and at daybreak assaulted and took the town, which is not a large one; the inhabitants being off their guard and not expecting that any one would ever come up so far from the sea to molest them, the wall too being weak, and in some places having tumbled down, while in others it had not been built to any height, and the gates also being left open through their feeling of security. The Thracians bursting into Mycalessus sacked the houses and temples, and butchered the inhabitants, sparing neither youth nor age, but killing all they fell in with, one after the other, children

and women, and even beasts of burden, and whatever other living creatures they saw; the Thracian race, like the bloodiest of the barbarians, being even more so when it has nothing to fear. Everywhere confusion reigned and death in all its shapes; and in particular they attacked a boys' school, the largest that there was in the place, into which the children had just gone, and massacred them all. In short, the disaster falling upon the whole town was unsurpassed in magnitude, and unapproached by any in suddenness and in horror.

[30] Meanwhile the Thebans heard of it and marched to the rescue, and overtaking the Thracians before they had gone far, recovered the plunder and drove them in panic to the Euripus and the sea, where the vessels which brought them were lying. The greatest slaughter took place while they were embarking, as they did not know how to swim, and those in the vessels on seeing what was going on on shore moored them out of bowshot: in the rest of the retreat the Thracians made a very respectable defence against the Theban horse, by which they were first attacked, dashing out and closing their ranks according to the tactics of their country, and lost only a few men in that part of the affair. A good number who were after plunder were actually caught in the town and put to death. Altogether the Thracians had two hundred and fifty killed out of thirteen hundred, the Thebans and the rest who came to the rescue about twenty, troopers and heavy infantry, with Scirphondas, one of the Boeotarchs. The Mycalessians lost a large proportion of their population.

While Mycalessus thus experienced a calamity for its extent as lamentable as any that happened in the war, [31] Demosthenes, whom we left sailing to Corcyra, after the building of the fort in Laconia, found a merchantman lying at Phea in Elis, in which the Corinthian heavy infantry were to cross to Sicily. The ship he destroyed, but the men escaped, and subsequently got another in which they pursued their voyage. After this, arriving at Zacynthus and Cephallenia, he took a body of heavy infantry on board, and sending for some of the Messenians from Naupactus, crossed over to the opposite coast of Acarnania, to Alyzia, and to Anactorium which was held by the Athenians. While he was in these parts he was met by Eurymedon returning from Sicily, where he had been sent, as has been mentioned, during the winter, with the money for the army, who told him the news, and also

that he had heard, while at sea, that the Syracusans had taken Plemmyrium. Here, also, Conon came to them, the commander at Naupactus, with news that the twenty-five Corinthian ships stationed opposite to him, far from giving over the war, were meditating an engagement; and he therefore begged them to send him some ships, as his own eighteen were not a match for the enemy's twenty-five. Demosthenes and Eurymedon, accordingly, sent ten of their best sailers with Conon to reinforce the squadron at Naupactus, and meanwhile prepared for the muster of their forces; Eurymedon, who was now the colleague of Demosthenes, and had turned back in consequence of his appointment, sailing to Corcyra to tell them to man fifteen ships and to enlist heavy infantry; while Demosthenes raised slingers and darters from the parts about Acarnania.

[32] Meanwhile the envoys, already mentioned, who had gone from Syracuse to the cities after the capture of Plemmyrium, had succeeded in their mission, and were about to bring the army that they had collected, when Nicias got scent of it, and sent to the Centoripae and Alicyaeans and other of the friendly Sicels, who held the passes, not to let the enemy through, but to combine to prevent their passing, there being no other way by which they could even attempt it, as the Agrigentines would not give them a passage through their country. Agreeably to this request the Sicels laid a triple ambuscade for the Siceliots upon their march, and attacking them suddenly, while off their guard, killed about eight hundred of them and all the envoys, the Corinthian only excepted, by whom fifteen hundred who escaped were conducted to Syracuse.

[33] About the same time the Camarinaeans also came to the assistance of Syracuse with five hundred heavy infantry, three hundred darters, and as many archers, while the Geloans sent crews for five ships, four hundred darters, and two hundred horse. Indeed almost the whole of Sicily, except the Agrigentines, who were neutral, now ceased merely to watch events as it had hitherto done, and actively joined Syracuse against the Athenians.

While the Syracusans after the Sicel disaster put off any immediate attack upon the Athenians, Demosthenes and Eurymedon, whose forces from Corcyra and the continent were now ready, crossed the Ionian Gulf with all their armament to the Iapygian promontory, and starting from thence touched at the Choerades Isles lying off Iapygia, where they took on board a hundred and fifty Iapygian darters of the Messapian tribe, and after renewing an old friendship with Artas the chief, who had furnished them with the darters, arrived at Metapontium in Italy. Here they persuaded their allies the Metapontines to send with them three hundred darters and two galleys, and with this reinforcement coasted on to Thurii, where they found the party hostile to Athens recently expelled by a revolution, and accordingly remained there to muster and review the whole army, to see if any had been left behind, and to prevail upon the Thurians resolutely to join them in their expedition, and in the circumstances in which they found themselves to conclude a defensive and offensive alliance with the Athenians.

[34] About the same time the Peloponnesians in the twenty-five ships stationed opposite to the squadron at Naupactus to protect the passage of the transports to Sicily had got ready for engaging, and manning some additional vessels, so as to be numerically little inferior to the Athenians, anchored off Erineus in Achaia in the Rhypic country. The place off which they lay being in the form of a crescent, the land forces furnished by the Corinthians and their allies on the spot came up and ranged themselves upon the projecting headlands on either side, while the fleet, under the command of Polyanthes, a Corinthian, held the intervening space and blocked up the entrance. The Athenians under Diphilus now sailed out against them with thirty-three ships from Naupactus, and the Corinthians, at first not moving, at length thought they saw their opportunity, raised the signal, and advanced and engaged the Athenians. After an obstinate struggle, the Corinthians lost three ships, and without sinking any altogether, disabled seven of the enemy, which were struck prow to prow and had their foreships stove in by the Corinthian vessels, whose cheeks had been strengthened for this very purpose. After an action of this even character, in which either party could claim the victory (although the Athenians became masters of the wrecks through the wind driving them out to sea, the Corinthians not putting out again to meet them), the two combatants parted. No pursuit took place, and no prisoners were made on either side; the Corinthians and Peloponnesians who were fighting near the shore escaping with ease, and none of the Athenian vessels having been sunk. The Athenians now sailed back to Naupactus, and the Corinthians im-

mediately set up a trophy as victors, because they had disabled a greater number of the enemy's ships. Moreover they held that they had not been worsted, for the very same reason that their opponent held that he had not been victorious; the Corinthians considering that they were conquerors, if not decidedly conquered, and the Athenians thinking themselves vanquished, because not decidedly victorious. However, when the Peloponnesians sailed off and their land forces had dispersed, the Athenians also set up a trophy as victors in Achaia, about two miles and a quarter from Erineus, the Corinthian station.

This was the termination of the action at Naupactus. [35] To return to Demosthenes and Eurymedon: the Thurians having now got ready to join in the expedition with seven hundred heavy infantry and three hundred darters, the two generals ordered the ships to sail along the coast to the Crotonian territory, and meanwhile held a review of all the land forces upon the river Sybaris, and then led them through the Thurian country. Arrived at the river Hylias, they here received a message from the Crotonians, saying that they would not allow the army to pass through their country; upon which the Athenians descended towards the shore, and bivouacked near the sea and the mouth of the Hylias, where the fleet also met them, and the next day embarked and sailed along the coast touching at all the cities except Locri, until they came to Petra in the Rhegian territory.

[36] Meanwhile the Syracusans hearing of their approach resolved to make a second attempt with their fleet and their other forces on shore, which they had been collecting for this very purpose in order to do something before their arrival. In addition to other improvements suggested by the former sea-fight which they now adopted in the equipment of their navy, they cut down their prows to a smaller compass to make them more solid and made their cheeks stouter, and from these let stays into the vessels' sides for a length of six cubits within and without, in the same way as the Corinthians had altered their prows before engaging the squadron at Naupactus. The Syracusans thought that they would thus have an advantage over the Athenian vessels, which were not constructed with equal strength, but were slight in the bows, from their being more used to sail round and charge the enemy's side than to meet him prow to prow, and that the battle being in the great harbour, with a great

many ships in not much room, was also a fact in their favour. Charging prow to prow, they would stave in the enemy's bows, by striking with solid and stout beaks against hollow and weak ones; and secondly, the Athenians for want of room would be unable to use their favourite manœuvre of breaking the line or of sailing round, as the Syracusans would do their best not to let them do the one, and want of room would prevent their doing the other. This charging prow to prow, which had hitherto been thought want of skill in a helmsman, would be the Syracusans' chief manœuvre, as being that which they should find most useful, since the Athenians, if repulsed, would not be able to back water in any direction except towards the shore, and that only for a little way, and in the little space in front of their own camp. The rest of the harbour would be commanded by the Syracusans; and the Athenians, if hard pressed, by crowding together in a small space and all to the same point, would run foul of one another and fall into disorder, which was, in fact, the thing that did the Athenians most harm in all the sea-fights, they not having, like the Syracusans, the whole harbour to retreat over. As to their sailing round into the open sea, this would be impossible, with the Syracusans in possession of the way out and in, especially as Plemmyrium would be hostile to them, and the mouth of the harbour was not large.

[37] With these contrivances to suit their skill and ability, and now more confident after the previous sea-fight, the Syracusans attacked by land and sea at once. The town force Gylippus led out a little the first and brought them up to the wall of the Athenians, where it looked towards the city, while the force from the Olympieum, that is to say, the heavy infantry that were there with the horse and the light troops of the Syracusans, advanced against the wall from the opposite side; the ships of the Syracusans and allies sailing out immediately afterwards. The Athenians at first fancied that they were to be attacked by land only, and it was not without alarm that they saw the fleet suddenly approaching as well; and while some were forming upon the walls and in front of them against the advancing enemy, and some marching out in haste against the numbers of horse and darters coming from the Olympieum and from outside, others manned the ships or rushed down to the beach to oppose the enemy, and when the ships were manned put out with seventy-five sail

against about eighty of the Syracusans.

[38] After spending a great part of the day in advancing and retreating and skirmishing with each other, without either being able to gain any advantage worth speaking of, except that the Syracusans sank one or two of the Athenian vessels, they parted, the land force at the same time retiring from the lines. The next day the Syracusans remained quiet, and gave no signs of what they were going to do; but Nicias, seeing that the battle had been a drawn one, and expecting that they would attack again, compelled the captains to refit any of the ships that had suffered, and moored merchant vessels before the stockade which they had driven into the sea in front of their ships, to serve instead of an enclosed harbour, at about two hundred feet from each other, in order that any ship that was hard pressed might be able to retreat in safety and sail out again at leisure. These preparations occupied the Athenians all day until nightfall.

[39] The next day the Syracusans began operations at an earlier hour, but with the same plan of attack by land and sea. A great part of the day the rivals spent as before, confronting and skirmishing with each other; until at last Ariston, son of Pyrrhicus, a Corinthian, the ablest helmsman in the Syracusan service, persuaded their naval commanders to send to the officials in the city, and tell them to move the sale market as quickly as they could down to the sea, and oblige every one to bring whatever eatables he had and sell them there, thus enabling the commanders to land the crews and dine at once close to the ships, and shortly afterwards, the selfsame day, to attack the Athenians again when they were not expecting it.

[40] In compliance with this advice a messenger was sent and the market got ready, upon which the Syracusans suddenly backed water and withdrew to the town, and at once landed and took their dinner upon the spot; while the Athenians, supposing that they had returned to the town because they felt they were beaten, disembarked at their leisure and set about getting their dinners and about their other occupations, under the idea that they done with fighting for that day. Suddenly the Syracusans had manned their ships and again sailed against them; and the Athenians, in great confusion and most of them fasting, got on board, and with great difficulty put out to meet them. For some time both parties remained on the defensive without engaging, until the Athenians at last resolved not to let

themselves be worn out by waiting where they were, but to attack without delay, and giving a cheer, went into action. The Syracusans received them, and charging prow to prow as they had intended, stove in a great part of the Athenian foreships by the strength of their beaks; the darters on the decks also did great damage to the Athenians, but still greater damage was done by the Syracusans who went about in small boats, ran in upon the oars of the Athenian galleys, and sailed against their sides, and discharged from thence their darts upon the sailors.

[41] At last, fighting hard in this fashion, the Syracusans gained the victory, and the Athenians turned and fled between the merchantmen to their own station. The Syracusan ships pursued them as far as the merchantmen, where they were stopped by the beams armed with dolphins suspended from those vessels over the passage. Two of the Syracusan vessels went too near in the excitement of victory and were destroyed, one of them being taken with its crew. After sinking seven of the Athenian vessels and disabling many, and taking most of the men prisoners and killing others, the Syracusans retired and set up trophies for both the engagements, being now confident of having a decided superiority by sea, and by no means despairing of equal success by land.

CHAPTER XXII

Nineteenth Year of the War—Arrival of Demosthenes—Defeat of the Athenians at Epipolae—Folly and Obstinacy of Nicias

In the meantime, while the Syracusans were preparing for a second attack upon both elements, [42] Demosthenes and Eurymedon arrived with the succours from Athens, consisting of about seventy-three ships, including the foreigners; nearly five thousand heavy infantry, Athenian and allied; a large number of darters, Hellenic and barbarian, and slingers and archers and everything else upon a corresponding scale. The Syracusans and their allies were for the moment not a little dismayed at the idea that there was to be no term or ending to their dangers, seeing, in spite of the fortification of Decelea, a new army arrive nearly equal to the former, and the power of Athens proving so great in every quarter. On the other hand, the first Athenian armament regained a certain confidence in the midst of its misfortunes. Demosthenes, seeing how matters stood, felt that he could not drag on and fare as Ni-

cias had done, who by wintering in Catana instead of at once attacking Syracuse had allowed the terror of his first arrival to evaporate in contempt, and had given time to Gylippus to arrive with a force from Peloponnese, which the Syracusans would never have sent for if he had attacked immediately; for they fancied that they were a match for him by themselves, and would not have discovered their inferiority until they were already invested, and even if they then sent for succours, they would no longer have been equally able to profit by their arrival. Recollecting this, and well aware that it was now on the first day after his arrival that he like Nicias was most formidable to the enemy, Demosthenes determined to lose no time in drawing the utmost profit from the consternation at the moment inspired by his army; and seeing that the counterwall of the Syracusans, which hindered the Athenians from investing them, was a single one, and that he who should become master of the way up to Epipolae, and afterwards of the camp there, would find no difficulty in taking it, as no one would even wait for his attack, made all haste to attempt the enterprise. This he took to be the shortest way of ending the war, as he would either succeed and take Syracuse, or would lead back the armament instead of frittering away the lives of the Athenians engaged in the expedition and the resources of the country at large.

First therefore the Athenians went out and laid waste the lands of the Syracusans about the Anapus and carried all before them as at first by land and by sea, the Syracusans not offering to oppose them upon either element, unless it were with their cavalry and darters from the Olympieum. [43] Next Demosthenes resolved to attempt the counterwall first by means of engines. As however the engines that he brought up were burnt by the enemy fighting from the wall, and the rest of the forces repulsed after attacking at many different points, he determined to delay no longer, and having obtained the consent of Nicias and his fellow commanders, proceeded to put in execution his plan of attacking Epipolae. As by day it seemed impossible to approach and get up without being observed, he ordered provisions for five days, took all the masons and carpenters, and other things, such as arrows, and everything else that they could want for the work of fortification if successful, and, after the first watch, set out with Eurymedon and Menander and the whole army for

Epipolae, Nicias being left behind in the lines. Having come up by the hill of Euryelus (where the former army had ascended at first) unobserved by the enemy's guards, they went up to the fort which the Syracusans had there, and took it, and put to the sword part of the garrison. The greater number, however, escaped at once and gave the alarm to the camps, of which there were three upon Epipolae, defended by outworks, one of the Syracusans, one of the other Siceliots, and one of the allies; and also to the six hundred Syracusans forming the original garrison for this part of Epipolae. These at once advanced against the assailants and, falling in with Demosthenes and the Athenians, were routed by them after a sharp resistance, the victors immediately pushing on, eager to achieve the objects of the attack without giving time for their ardour to cool; meanwhile others from the very beginning were taking the counterwall of the Syracusans, which was abandoned by its garrison, and pulling down the battlements. The Syracusans and the allies, and Gylippus with the troops under his command, advanced to the rescue from the outworks, but engaged in some consternation (a night attack being a piece of audacity which they had never expected), and were at first compelled to retreat. But while the Athenians, flushed with their victory, now advanced with less order, wishing to make their way as quickly as possible through the whole force of the enemy not yet engaged, without relaxing their attack or giving them time to rally, the Boeotians made the first stand against them, attacked them, routed them, and put them to flight.

[44] The Athenians now fell into great disorder and perplexity, so that it was not easy to get from one side or the other any detailed account of the affair. By day certainly the combatants have a clearer notion, though even then by no means of all that takes place, no one knowing much of anything that does not go on in his own immediate neighbourhood; but in a night engagement (and this was the only one that occurred between great armies during the war) how could any one know anything for certain? Although there was a bright moon they saw each other only as men do by moonlight, that is to say, they could distinguish the form of the body, but could not tell for certain whether it was a friend or an enemy. Both had great numbers of heavy infantry moving about in a small space. Some of the Athenians were already defeated, while others were com-

ing up yet unconquered for their first attack. A large part also of the rest of their forces either had only just got up, or were still ascending, so that they did not know which way to march. Owing to the rout that had taken place all in front was now in confusion, and the noise made it difficult to distinguish anything. The victorious Syracusans and allies were cheering each other on with loud cries, by night the only possible means of communication, and meanwhile receiving all who came against them; while the Athenians were seeking for one another, taking all in front of them for enemies, even although they might be some of their now flying friends; and by constantly asking for the watchword, which was their only means of recognition, not only caused great confusion among themselves by asking all at once, but also made it known to the enemy, whose own they did not so readily discover, as the Syracusans were victorious and not scattered, and thus less easily mistaken. The result was that if the Athenians fell in with a party of the enemy that was weaker than they, it escaped them through knowing their watchword; while if they themselves failed to answer they were put to the sword. But what hurt them as much, or indeed more than anything else, was the singing of the paean, from the perplexity which it caused by being nearly the same on either side; the Argives and Corcyraeans and any other Dorian peoples in the army, struck terror into the Athenians whenever they raised their paean, no less than did the enemy. Thus, after being once thrown into disorder, they ended by coming into collision with each other in many parts of the field, friends with friends, and citizens with citizens, and not only terrified one another, but even came to blows and could only be parted with difficulty. In the pursuit many perished by throwing themselves down the cliffs, the way down from Epipolae being narrow; and of those who got down safely into the plain, although many, especially those who belonged to the first armament, escaped through their better acquaintance with the locality, some of the newcomers lost their way and wandered over the country, and were cut off in the morning by the Syracusan cavalry and killed.

[45] The next day the Syracusans set up two trophies, one upon Epipolae where the ascent had been made, and the other on the spot where the first check was given by the Boeotians; and the Athenians took back their dead under truce. A great many of the Athenians

and allies were killed, although still more arms were taken than could be accounted for by the number of the dead, as some of those who were obliged to leap down from the cliffs without their shields escaped with their lives and did not perish like the rest.

[46] After this the Syracusans, recovering their old confidence at such an unexpected stroke of good fortune, dispatched Sicanus with fifteen ships to Agrigentum where there was a revolution, to induce if possible the city to join them; while Gylippus again went by land into the rest of Sicily to bring up reinforcements, being now in hope of taking the Athenian lines by storm, after the result of the affair on Epipolae.

[47] In the meantime the Athenian generals consulted upon the disaster which had happened, and upon the general weakness of the army. They saw themselves unsuccessful in their enterprises, and the soldiers disgusted with their stay; disease being rife among them owing to its being the sickly season of the year, and to the marshy and unhealthy nature of the spot in which they were encamped; and the state of their affairs generally being thought desperate. Accordingly, Demosthenes was of opinion that they ought not to stay any longer; but agreeably to his original idea in risking the attempt upon Epipolae, now that this had failed, he gave his vote for going away without further loss of time, while the sea might yet be crossed, and their late reinforcement might give them the superiority at all events on that element. He also said that it would be more profitable for the state to carry on the war against those who were building fortifications in Attica, than against the Syracusans whom it was no longer easy to subdue; besides which it was not right to squander large sums of money to no purpose by going on with the siege.

[48] This was the opinion of Demosthenes. Nicias, without denying the bad state of their affairs, was unwilling to avow their weakness, or to have it reported to the enemy that the Athenians in full council were openly voting for retreat; for in that case they would be much less likely to effect it when they wanted without discovery. Moreover, his own particular information still gave him reason to hope that the affairs of the enemy would soon be in a worse state than their own, if the Athenians persevered in the siege; as they would wear out the Syracusans by want of money, especially with the more extensive command of the sea now given them by their present navy. Be-

sides this, there was a party in Syracuse who wished to betray the city to the Athenians, and kept sending him messages and telling him not to raise the siege. Accordingly, knowing this and really waiting because he hesitated between the two courses and wished to see his way more clearly, in his public speech on this occasion he refused to lead off the army, saying he was sure the Athenians would never approve of their returning without a vote of theirs. Those who would vote upon their conduct, instead of judging the facts as eye-witnesses like themselves and not from what they might hear from hostile critics, would simply be guided by the calumnies of the first clever speaker; while many, indeed most, of the soldiers on the spot, who now so loudly proclaimed the danger of their position, when they reached Athens would proclaim just as loudly the opposite, and would say that their generals had been bribed to betray them and return. For himself, therefore, who knew the Athenian temper, sooner than perish under a dishonourable charge and by an unjust sentence at the hands of the Athenians, he would rather take his chance and die, if die he must, a soldier's death at the hand of the enemy. Besides, after all, the Syracusans were in a worse case than themselves. What with paying mercenaries, spending upon fortified posts, and now for a full year maintaining a large navy, they were already at a loss and would soon be at a standstill: they had already spent two thousand talents and incurred heavy debts besides, and could not lose even ever so small a fraction of their present force through not paying it, without ruin to their cause; depending as they did more upon mercenaries than upon soldiers obliged to serve, like their own. He therefore said that they ought to stay and carry on the siege, and not depart defeated in point of money, in which they were much superior.

[49] Nicias spoke positively because he had exact information of the financial distress at Syracuse, and also because of the strength of the Athenian party there which kept sending him messages not to raise the siege; besides which he had more confidence than before in his fleet, and felt sure at least of its success. Demosthenes, however, would not hear for a moment of continuing the siege, but said that if they could not lead off the army without a decree from Athens, and if they were obliged to stay on, they ought to remove to Thapsus or Catana; where their land forces would have a

wide extent of country to overrun, and could live by plundering the enemy, and would thus do them damage; while the fleet would have the open sea to fight in, that is to say, instead of a narrow space which was all in the enemy's favour, a wide sea-room where their science would be of use, and where they could retreat or advance without being confined or circumscribed either when they put out or put in. In any case he was altogether opposed to their staying on where they were, and insisted on removing at once, as quickly and with as little delay as possible; and in this judgment Eurymedon agreed. Nicias however still objecting, a certain diffidence and hesitation came over them, with a suspicion that Nicias might have some further information to make him so positive.

CHAPTER XXIII

Nineteenth Year of the War—Battles in the Great Harbour—Retreat and Annihilation of the Athenian Army

WHILE the Athenians lingered on in this way without moving from where they were, [*50*] Gylippus and Sicanus now arrived at Syracuse. Sicanus had failed to gain Agrigentum, the party friendly to the Syracusans having been driven out while he was still at Gela; but Gylippus was accompanied not only by a large number of troops raised in Sicily, but by the heavy infantry sent off in the spring from Peloponnese in the merchantmen, who had arrived at Selinus from Libya. They had been carried to Libya by a storm, and having obtained two galleys and pilots from the Cyrenians, on their voyage alongshore had taken sides with the Euesperitae and had defeated the Libyans who were besieging them, and from thence coasting on to Neapolis, a Carthaginian mart, and the nearest point to Sicily, from which it is only two days' and a night's voyage, there crossed over and came to Selinus. Immediately upon their arrival the Syracusans prepared to attack the Athenians again by land and sea at once. The Athenian generals seeing a fresh army come to the aid of the enemy, and that their own circumstances, far from improving, were becoming daily worse, and above all distressed by the sickness of the soldiers, now began to repent of not having removed before; and Nicias no longer offering the same opposition, except by urging that there should be no open voting, they gave orders as secretly as possible for all to be prepared to sail out from

the camp at a given signal. All was at last ready, and they were on the point of sailing away, when an eclipse of the moon, which was then at the full, took place. Most of the Athenians, deeply impressed by this occurrence, now urged the generals to wait; and Nicias, who was somewhat over-addicted to divination and practices of that kind, refused from that moment even to take the question of departure into consideration, until they had waited the thrice nine days prescribed by the soothsayers.

The besiegers were thus condemned to stay in the country; [*51*] and the Syracusans, getting wind of what had happened, became more eager than ever to press the Athenians, who had now themselves acknowledged that they were no longer their superiors either by sea or by land, as otherwise they would never have planned to sail away. Besides which the Syracusans did not wish them to settle in any other part of Sicily, where they would be more difficult to deal with, but desired to force them to fight at sea as quickly as possible, in a position favourable to themselves. Accordingly they manned their ships and practised for as many days as they thought sufficient. When the moment arrived they assaulted on the first day the Athenian lines, and upon a small force of heavy infantry and horse sallying out against them by certain gates, cut off some of the former and routed and pursued them to the lines, where, as the entrance was narrow, the Athenians lost seventy horses and some few of the heavy infantry.

[*52*] Drawing off their troops for this day, on the next the Syracusans went out with a fleet of seventy-six sail, and at the same time advanced with their land forces against the lines. The Athenians put out to meet them with eighty-six ships, came to close quarters, and engaged. The Syracusans and their allies first defeated the Athenian centre, and then caught Eurymedon, the commander of the right wing, who was sailing out from the line more towards the land in order to surround the enemy, in the hollow and recess of the harbour, and killed him and destroyed the ships accompanying him; after which they now chased the whole Athenian fleet before them and drove them ashore.

[*53*] Gylippus seeing the enemy's fleet defeated and carried ashore beyond their stockades and camp, ran down to the breakwater with some of his troops, in order to cut off the men as they landed and make it easier for the

Syracusans to tow off the vessels by the shore being friendly ground. The Tyrrhenians who guarded this point for the Athenians, seeing them come on in disorder, advanced out against them and attacked and routed their van, hurling it into the marsh of Lysimeleia. Afterwards the Syracusan and allied troops arrived in greater numbers, and the Athenians fearing for their ships came up also to the rescue and engaged them, and defeated and pursued them to some distance and killed a few of their heavy infantry. They succeeded in rescuing most of their ships and brought them down by their camp; eighteen however were taken by the Syracusans and their allies, and all the men killed. The rest the enemy tried to burn by means of an old merchantman which they filled with faggots and pine-wood, set on fire, and let drift down the wind which blew full on the Athenians. The Athenians, however, alarmed for their ships, contrived means for stopping it and putting it out, and checking the flames and the nearer approach of the merchantman, thus escaped the danger.

[54] After this the Syracusans set up a trophy for the sea-fight and for the heavy infantry whom they had cut off up at the lines, where they took the horses; and the Athenians for the rout of the foot driven by the Tyrrhenians into the marsh, and for their own victory with the rest of the army.

[55] The Syracusans had now gained a decisive victory at sea, where until now they had feared the reinforcement brought by Demosthenes, and deep, in consequence, was the despondency of the Athenians, and great their disappointment, and greater still their regret for having come on the expedition. These were the only cities that they had yet encountered, similar to their own in character, under democracies like themselves, which had ships and horses, and were of considerable magnitude. They had been unable to divide and bring them over by holding out the prospect of changes in their governments, or to crush them by their great superiority in force, but had failed in most of their attempts, and being already in perplexity, had now been defeated at sea, where defeat could never have been expected, and were thus plunged deeper in embarrassment than ever.

[56] Meanwhile the Syracusans immediately began to sail freely along the harbour, and determined to close up its mouth, so that the Athenians might not be able to steal out in future, even if they wished. Indeed, the Syra-

cusans no longer thought only of saving themselves, but also how to hinder the escape of the enemy; thinking, and thinking rightly, that they were now much the stronger, and that to conquer the Athenians and their allies by land and sea would win them great glory in Hellas. The rest of the Hellenes would thus immediately be either freed or released from apprehension, as the remaining forces of Athens would be henceforth unable to sustain the war that would be waged against her; while they, the Syracusans, would be regarded as the authors of this deliverance, and would be held in high admiration, not only with all men now living but also with posterity. Nor were these the only considerations that gave dignity to the struggle. They would thus conquer not only the Athenians but also their numerous allies, and conquer not alone, but with their companions in arms, commanding side by side with the Corinthians and Lacedaemonians, having offered their city to stand in the van of danger, and having been in a great measure the pioneers of naval success.

Indeed, there were never so many peoples assembled before a single city, if we except the grand total gathered together in this war under Athens and Lacedaemon. [57] The following were the states on either side who came to Syracuse to fight for or against Sicily, to help to conquer or defend the island. Right or community of blood was not the bond of union between them, so much as interest or compulsion as the case might be. The Athenians themselves being Ionians went against the Dorians of Syracuse of their own free will; and the peoples still speaking Attic and using the Athenian laws, the Lemnians, Imbrians, and Aeginetans, that is to say the then occupants of Aegina, being their colonists, went with them. To these must be also added the Hestiaeans dwelling at Hestiaea in Euboea. Of the rest some joined in the expedition as subjects of the Athenians, others as independent allies, others as mercenaries. To the number of the subjects paying tribute belonged the Eretrians, Chalcidians, Styrians, and Carystians from Euboea; the Ceans, Andrians, and Tenians from the islands; and the Milesians, Samians, and Chians from Ionia. The Chians, however, joined as independent allies, paying no tribute, but furnishing ships. Most of these were Ionians and descended from the Athenians, except the Carystians, who are Dryopes, and although subjects and obliged to serve, were still Ionians fighting against Dorians. Besides these there were men of Aeolic race, the Methymnians, subjects who provided ships, not tribute, and the Tenedians and Aenians who paid tribute. These Aeolians fought against their Aeolian founders, the Boeotians in the Syracusan army, because they were obliged, while the Plataeans, the only native Boeotians opposed to Boeotians, did so upon a just quarrel. Of the Rhodians and Cytherians, both Dorians, the latter, Lacedaemonian colonists, fought in the Athenian ranks against their Lacedaemonian countrymen with Gylippus; while the Rhodians, Argives by race, were compelled to bear arms against the Dorian Syracusans and their own colonists, the Geloans, serving with the Syracusans. Of the islanders round Peloponnese, the Cephallenians and Zacynthians accompanied the Athenians as independent allies, although their insular position really left them little choice in the matter, owing to the maritime supremacy of Athens, while the Corcyraeans, who were not only Dorians but Corinthians, were openly serving against Corinthians and Syracusans, although colonists of the former and of the same race as the latter, under colour of compulsion, but really out of free will through hatred of Corinth. The Messenians, as they are now called in Naupactus and from Pylos, then held by the Athenians, were taken with them to the war. There were also a few Megarian exiles, whose fate it was to be now fighting against the Megarian Selinuntines.

The engagement of the rest was more of a voluntary nature. It was less the league than hatred of the Lacedaemonians and the immediate private advantage of each individual that persuaded the Dorian Argives to join the Ionian Athenians in a war against Dorians; while the Mantineans and other Arcadian mercenaries, accustomed to go against the enemy pointed out to them at the moment, were led by interest to regard the Arcadians serving with the Corinthians as just as much their enemies as any others. The Cretans and Aetolians also served for hire, and the Cretans who had joined the Rhodians in founding Gela, thus came to consent to fight for pay against, instead of for, their colonists. There were also some Acarnanians paid to serve, although they came chiefly for love of Demosthenes and out of goodwill to the Athenians whose allies they were. These all lived on the Hellenic side of the Ionian Gulf. Of the Italiots, there were the Thurians and Metapontines, dragged into the quarrel by the stern necessities of a time of revolution; of the Siceliots, the Naxians and the Catanians; and of the barbarians, the Egestaeans, who called in the Athenians, most of the Sicels, and outside Sicily some Tyrrhenian enemies of Syracuse and Iapygian mercenaries.

Such were the peoples serving with the Athenians. [58] Against these the Syracusans had the Camarinaeans their neighbours, the Geloans who live next to them; then passing over the neutral Agrigentines, the Selinuntines settled on the farther side of the island. These inhabit the part of Sicily looking towards Libya; the Himeraeans came from the side towards the Tyrrhenian Sea, being the only Hellenic inhabitants in that quarter, and the only people that came from thence to the aid of the Syracusans. Of the Hellenes in Sicily the above peoples joined in the war, all Dorians and independent, and of the barbarians the Sicels only, that is to say, such as did not go over to the Athenians. Of the Hellenes outside Sicily there were the Lacedaemonians, who provided a Spartan to take the command, and a force of Neodamodes or Freedmen, and of Helots; the Corinthians, who alone joined with naval and land forces, with their Leucadian and Ambraciot kinsmen; some mercenaries sent by Corinth from Arcadia; some Sicyonians forced to serve, and from outside Peloponnese the Boeotians. In comparison, however, with these foreign auxiliaries, the great Siceliot cities furnished more in every department—numbers of heavy infantry, ships, and horses, and an immense multitude besides having been brought together; while in comparison, again, one may say, with all the rest put together, more was provided by the Syracusans themselves, both from the greatness of the city and from the fact that they were in the greatest danger.

[59] Such were the auxiliaries brought together on either side, all of which had by this time joined, neither party experiencing any subsequent accession. It was no wonder, therefore, if the Syracusans and their allies thought that it would win them great glory if they could follow up their recent victory in the seafight by the capture of the whole Athenian armada, without letting it escape either by sea or by land. They began at once to close up the Great Harbour by means of boats, merchant vessels, and galleys moored broadside across its mouth, which is nearly a mile wide, and made all their other arrangements for the event of the Athenians again venturing to fight at sea. There was, in fact, nothing little either in their plans or their ideas.

[60] The Athenians, seeing them closing up the harbour and informed of their further designs, called a council of war. The generals and colonels assembled and discussed the difficulties of the situation; the point which pressed most being that they no longer had provisions for immediate use (having sent on to Catana to tell them not to send any, in the belief that they were going away), and that they would not have any in future unless they could command the sea. They therefore determined to evacuate their upper lines, to enclose with a cross wall and garrison a small space close to the ships, only just sufficient to hold their stores and sick, and manning all the ships, seaworthy or not, with every man that could be spared from the rest of their land forces, to fight it out at sea, and, if victorious, to go to Catana, if not, to burn their vessels, form in close order, and retreat by land for the nearest friendly place they could reach, Hellenic or barbarian. This was no sooner settled than carried into effect; they descended gradually from the upper lines and manned all their vessels, compelling all to go on board who were of age to be in any way of use. They thus succeeded in manning about one hundred and ten ships in all, on board of which they embarked a number of archers and darters taken from the Acarnanians and from the other foreigners, making all other provisions allowed by the nature of their plan and by the necessities which imposed it. All was now nearly ready, and Nicias, seeing the soldiery disheartened by their unprecedented and decided defeat at sea, and by reason of the scarcity of provisions eager to fight it out as soon as possible, called them all together, and first addressed them, speaking as follows:

[61] "Soldiers of the Athenians and of the allies, we have all an equal interest in the coming struggle, in which life and country are at stake for us quite as much as they can be for the enemy; since if our fleet wins the day, each can see his native city again, wherever that city may be. You must not lose heart, or be like men without any experience, who fail in a first essay and ever afterwards fearfully forebode a future as disastrous. But let the Athenians among you who have already had experience of many wars, and the allies who have joined us in so many expeditions, remember the surprises of war, and with the hope that fortune will not be always against us, prepare to fight again in a manner worthy of the number which you see yourselves to be.

[62] "Now, whatever we thought would be of service against the crush of vessels in such a narrow harbour, and against the force upon the decks of the enemy, from which we suffered before, has all been considered with the helmsmen, and, as far as our means allowed, provided. A number of archers and darters will go on board, and a multitude that we should not have employed in an action in the open sea, where our science would be crippled by the weight of the vessels; but in the present landfight that we are forced to make from shipboard all this will be useful. We have also discovered the changes in construction that we must make to meet theirs; and against the thickness of their cheeks, which did us the greatest mischief, we have provided grapplingirons, which will prevent an assailant backing water after charging, if the soldiers on deck here do their duty; since we are absolutely compelled to fight a land battle from the fleet, and it seems to be our interest neither to back water ourselves, nor to let the enemy do so, especially as the shore, except so much of it as may be held by our troops, is hostile ground.

[63] "You must remember this and fight on as long as you can, and must not let yourselves be driven ashore, but once alongside must make up your minds not to part company until you have swept the heavy infantry from the enemy's deck. I say this more for the heavy infantry than for the seamen, as it is more the business of the men on deck; and our land forces are even now on the whole the strongest. The sailors I advise, and at the same time implore, not to be too much daunted by their misfortunes, now that we have our decks better armed and a greater number of vessels. Bear in mind how well worth preserving is the pleasure felt by those of you who through your knowledge of our language and imitation of our manners were always considered Athenians, even though not so in reality, and as such were honoured throughout Hellas, and had your full share of the advantages of our empire, and more than your share in the respect of our subjects and in protection from ill treatment. You, therefore, with whom alone we freely share our empire, we now justly require not to betray that empire in its extremity, and in scorn of Corinthians, whom you have often conquered, and of Siceliots, none of whom so much as presumed to stand against us when our navy was in its prime, we ask you to repel them, and to show that even in sickness and disaster your skill is more than a

match for the fortune and vigour of any other.

[64] "For the Athenians among you I add once more this reflection: You left behind you no more such ships in your docks as these, no more heavy infantry in their flower; if you do aught but conquer, our enemies here will immediately sail thither, and those that are left of us at Athens will become unable to repel their home assailants, reinforced by these new allies. Here you will fall at once into the hands of the Syracusans—I need not remind you of the intentions with which you attacked them— and your countrymen at home will fall into those of the Lacedaemonians. Since the fate of both thus hangs upon this single battle, now, if ever, stand firm, and remember, each and all, that you who are now going on board are the army and navy of the Athenians, and all that is left of the state and the great name of Athens, in whose defence if any man has any advantage in skill or courage, now is the time for him to show it, and thus serve himself and save all."

[65] After this address Nicias at once gave orders to man the ships. Meanwhile Gylippus and the Syracusans could perceive by the preparations which they saw going on that the Athenians meant to fight at sea. They had also notice of the grappling-irons, against which they specially provided by stretching hides over the prows and much of the upper part of their vessels, in order that the irons when thrown might slip off without taking hold. All being now ready, the generals and Gylippus addressed them in the following terms:

[66] "Syracusans and allies, the glorious character of our past achievements and the no less glorious results at issue in the coming battle are, we think, understood by most of you, or you would never have thrown yourselves with such ardour into the struggle; and if there be any one not as fully aware of the facts as he ought to be, we will declare them to him. The Athenians came to this country first to effect the conquest of Sicily, and after that, if successful, of Peloponnese and the rest of Hellas, possessing already the greatest empire yet known, of present or former times, among the Hellenes. Here for the first time they found in you men who faced their navy which made them masters everywhere; you have already defeated them in the previous sea-fights, and will in all likelihood defeat them again now. When men are once checked in what they consider their special excellence, their whole opinion of themselves suffers more than if they had not at first believed in their superiority, the unexpected shock to their pride causing them to give way more than their real strength warrants; and this is probably now the case with the Athenians.

[67] "With us it is different. The original estimate of ourselves which gave us courage in the days of our unskilfulness has been strengthened, while the conviction superadded to it that we must be the best seamen of the time, if we have conquered the best, has given a double measure of hope to every man among us; and, for the most part, where there is the greatest hope, there is also the greatest ardour for action. The means to combat us which they have tried to find in copying our armament are familiar to our warfare, and will be met by proper provisions; while they will never be able to have a number of heavy infantry on their decks, contrary to their custom, and a number of darters (born landsmen, one may say, Acarnanians and others, embarked afloat, who will not know how to discharge their weapons when they have to keep still), without hampering their vessels and falling all into confusion among themselves through fighting not according to their own tactics. For they will gain nothing by the number of their ships—I say this to those of you who may be alarmed by having to fight against odds—as a quantity of ships in a confined space will only be slower in executing the movements required, and most exposed to injury from our means of offence. Indeed, if you would know the plain truth, as we are credibly informed, the excess of their sufferings and the necessities of their present distress have made them desperate; they have no confidence in their force, but wish to try their fortune in the only way they can, and either to force their passage and sail out, or after this to retreat by land, it being impossible for them to be worse off than they are.

[68] "The fortune of our greatest enemies having thus betrayed itself, and their disorder being what I have described, let us engage in anger, convinced that, as between adversaries, nothing is more legitimate than to claim to sate the whole wrath of one's soul in punishing the aggressor, and nothing more sweet, as the proverb has it, than the vengeance upon an enemy, which it will now be ours to take. That enemies they are and mortal enemies you all know, since they came here to enslave our country, and if successful had in reserve for our men all that is most dreadful, and for our children and wives all that is most dishonourable,

and for the whole city the name which conveys the greatest reproach. None should therefore relent or think it gain if they go away without further danger to us. This they will do just the same, even if they get the victory; while if we succeed, as we may expect, in chastising them, and in handing down to all Sicily her ancient freedom strengthened and confirmed, we shall have achieved no mean triumph. And the rarest dangers are those in which failure brings little loss and success the greatest advantage."

[69] After the above address to the soldiers on their side, the Syracusan generals and Gylippus now perceived that the Athenians were manning their ships, and immediately proceeded to man their own also. Meanwhile Nicias, appalled by the position of affairs, realizing the greatness and the nearness of the danger now that they were on the point of putting out from shore, and thinking, as men are apt to think in great crises, that when all has been done they have still something left to do, and when all has been said that they have not yet said enough, again called on the captains one by one, addressing each by his father's name and by his own, and by that of his tribe, and adjured them not to belie their own personal renown, or to obscure the hereditary virtues for which their ancestors were illustrious: he reminded them of their country, the freest of the free, and of the unfettered discretion allowed in it to all to live as they pleased; and added other arguments such as men would use at such a crisis, and which, with little alteration, are made to serve on all occasions alike— appeals to wives, children, and national gods— without caring whether they are thought commonplace, but loudly invoking them in the belief that they will be of use in the consternation of the moment. Having thus admonished them, not, he felt, as he would, but as he could, Nicias withdrew and led the troops to the sea, and ranged them in as long a line as he was able, in order to aid as far as possible in sustaining the courage of the men afloat; while Demosthenes, Menander, and Euthydemus, who took the command on board, put out from their own camp and sailed straight to the barrier across the mouth of the harbour and to the passage left open, to try to force their way out.

[70] The Syracusans and their allies had already put out with about the same number of ships as before, a part of which kept guard at the outlet, and the remainder all round the rest of the harbour, in order to attack the Athenians on all sides at once; while the land forces held themselves in readiness at the points at which the vessels might put into the shore. The Syracusan fleet was commanded by Sicanus and Agatharchus, who had each a wing of the whole force, with Pythen and the Corinthians in the centre. When the rest of the Athenians came up to the barrier, with the first shock of their charge they overpowered the ships stationed there, and tried to undo the fastenings; after this, as the Syracusans and allies bore down upon them from all quarters, the action spread from the barrier over the whole harbour, and was more obstinately disputed than any of the preceding ones. On either side the rowers showed great zeal in bringing up their vessels at the boatswains' orders, and the helmsmen great skill in manœuvring, and great emulation one with another; while the ships once alongside, the soldiers on board did their best not to let the service on deck be outdone by the others; in short, every man strove to prove himself the first in his particular department. And as many ships were engaged in a small compass (for these were the largest fleets fighting in the narrowest space ever known, being together little short of two hundred), the regular attacks with the beak were few, there being no opportunity of backing water or of breaking the line; while the collisions caused by one ship chancing to run foul of another, either in flying from or attacking a third, were more frequent. So long as a vessel was coming up to the charge the men on the decks rained darts and arrows and stones upon her; but once alongside, the heavy infantry tried to board each other's vessel, fighting hand to hand. In many quarters it happened, by reason of the narrow room, that a vessel was charging an enemy on one side and being charged herself on another, and that two or sometimes more ships had perforce got entangled round one, obliging the helmsmen to attend to defence here, offence there, not to one thing at once, but to many on all sides; while the huge din caused by the number of ships crashing together not only spread terror, but made the orders of the boatswains inaudible. The boatswains on either side in the discharge of their duty and in the heat of the conflict shouted incessantly orders and appeals to their men; the Athenians they urged to force the passage out, and now if ever to show their mettle and lay hold of a safe return to their country; to the Syracusans and their allies they cried that it would be glorious to prevent the

escape of the enemy, and, conquering, to exalt the countries that were theirs. The generals, moreover, on either side, if they saw any in any part of the battle backing ashore without being forced to do so, called out to the captain by name and asked him—the Athenians, whether they were retreating because they thought the thrice hostile shore more their own than that sea which had cost them so much labour to win; the Syracusans, whether they were flying from the flying Athenians, whom they well knew to be eager to escape in whatever way they could.

[71] Meanwhile the two armies on shore, while victory hung in the balance, were a prey to the most agonizing and conflicting emotions; the natives thirsting for more glory than they had already won, while the invaders feared to find themselves in even worse plight than before. The all of the Athenians being set upon their fleet, their fear for the event was like nothing they had ever felt; while their view of the struggle was necessarily as chequered as the battle itself. Close to the scene of action and not all looking at the same point at once, some saw their friends victorious and took courage and fell to calling upon heaven not to deprive them of salvation, while others who had their eyes turned upon the losers, wailed and cried aloud, and, although spectators, were more overcome than the actual combatants. Others, again, were gazing at some spot where the battle was evenly disputed; as the strife was protracted without decision, their swaying bodies reflected the agitation of their minds, and they suffered the worst agony of all, ever just within reach of safety or just on the point of destruction. In short, in that one Athenian army as long as the sea-fight remained doubtful there was every sound to be heard at once, shrieks, cheers, "We win," "We lose," and all the other manifold exclamations that a great host would necessarily utter in great peril; and with the men in the fleet it was nearly the same; until at last the Syracusans and their allies, after the battle had lasted a long while, put the Athenians to flight, and with much shouting and cheering chased them in open rout to the shore. The naval force, one one way, one another, as many as were not taken afloat now ran ashore and rushed from on board their ships to their camp; while the army, no more divided, but carried away by one impulse, all with shrieks and groans deplored the event, and ran down, some to help the ships, others to guard what was left of their wall, while the

remaining and most numerous part already began to consider how they should save themselves. Indeed, the panic of the present moment had never been surpassed. They now suffered very nearly what they had inflicted at Pylos; as then the Lacedaemonians with the loss of their fleet lost also the men who had crossed over to the island, so now the Athenians had no hope of escaping by land, without the help of some extraordinary accident.

[72] The sea-fight having been a severe one, and many ships and lives having been lost on both sides, the victorious Syracusans and their allies now picked up their wrecks and dead, and sailed off to the city and set up a trophy. The Athenians, overwhelmed by their misfortune, never even thought of asking leave to take up their dead or wrecks, but wished to retreat that very night. Demosthenes, however, went to Nicias and gave it as his opinion that they should man the ships they had left and make another effort to force their passage out next morning; saying that they had still left more ships fit for service than the enemy, the Athenians having about sixty remaining as against less than fifty of their opponents. Nicias was quite of his mind; but when they wished to man the vessels, the sailors refused to go on board, being so utterly overcome by their defeat as no longer to believe in the possibility of success.

Accordingly they all now made up their minds to retreat by land. [73] Meanwhile the Syracusan Hermocrates—suspecting their intention, and impressed by the danger of allowing a force of that magnitude to retire by land, establish itself in some other part of Sicily, and from thence renew the war—went and stated his views to the authorities, and pointed out to them that they ought not to let the enemy get away by night, but that all the Syracusans and their allies should at once march out and block up the roads and seize and guard the passes. The authorities were entirely of his opinion, and thought that it ought to be done, but on the other hand felt sure that the people, who had given themselves over to rejoicing, and were taking their ease after a great battle at sea, would not be easily brought to obey; besides, they were celebrating a festival, having on that day a sacrifice to Heracles, and most of them in their rapture at the victory had fallen to drinking at the festival, and would probably consent to anything sooner than to take up their arms and march out at that moment. For these reasons the thing appeared impracticable to the magistrates; and Hermocrates, finding himself unable to do anything further with them, had now recourse to the following stratagem of his own. What he feared was that the Athenians might quietly get the start of them by passing the most difficult places during the night; and he therefore sent, as soon as it was dusk, some friends of his own to the camp with some horsemen who rode up within earshot and called out to some of the men, as though they were well-wishers of the Athenians, and told them to tell Nicias (who had in fact some correspondents who informed him of what went on inside the town) not to lead off the army by night as the Syracusans were guarding the roads, but to make his preparations at his leisure and to retreat by day. After saying this they departed; and their hearers informed the Athenian generals, [74] who put off going for that night on the strength of this message, not doubting its sincerity.

Since after all they had not set out at once, they now determined to stay also the following day to give time to the soldiers to pack up as well as they could the most useful articles, and, leaving everything else behind, to start only with what was strictly necessary for their personal subsistence. Meanwhile the Syracusans and Gylippus marched out and blocked up the roads through the country by which the Athenians were likely to pass, and kept guard at the fords of the streams and rivers, posting themselves so as to receive them and stop the army where they thought best; while their fleet sailed up to the beach and towed off the ships of the Athenians. Some few were burned by the Athenians themselves as they had intended; the rest the Syracusans lashed on to their own at their leisure as they had been thrown up on shore, without any one trying to stop them, and conveyed to the town.

[75] After this, Nicias and Demosthenes now thinking that enough had been done in the way of preparation, the removal of the army took place upon the second day after the sea-fight. It was a lamentable scene, not merely from the single circumstance that they were retreating after having lost all their ships, their great hopes gone, and themselves and the state in peril; but also in leaving the camp there were things most grievous for every eye and heart to contemplate. The dead lay unburied, and each man as he recognized a friend among them shuddered with grief and horror; while the living whom they were leaving behind, wounded or sick, were to the living far more shocking than the dead, and more to be pitied than those who had perished. These fell to entreating and bewailing until their friends knew not what to do, begging them to take them and loudly calling to each individual comrade or relative whom they could see, hanging upon the necks of their tent-fellows in the act of departure, and following as far as they could, and, when their bodily strength failed them, calling again and again upon heaven and shrieking aloud as they were left behind. So that the whole army being filled with tears and distracted after this fashion found it not easy to go, even from an enemy's land, where they had already suffered evils too great for tears and in the unknown future before them feared to suffer more. Dejection and self-condemnation were also rife among them. Indeed they could only be compared to a starved-out town, and that no small one, escaping; the whole multitude upon the march being not less than forty thousand men. All carried anything they could which might be of use, and the heavy infantry and troopers, contrary to their wont, while under arms carried their own victuals, in some cases for want of servants, in others through not trusting them; as they had long been deserting and now did so in greater numbers than ever. Yet even thus they did not carry enough, as there was no longer food in the camp. Moreover their disgrace generally, and the universality of their sufferings, however to a certain extent alleviated by being borne in company, were still felt at the moment a heavy burden, especially when they contrasted the splendour and glory of their setting out with the humiliation in which it had ended. For this was by far the greatest reverse that ever befell an Hellenic army. They had come to enslave others, and were departing in fear of being enslaved themselves: they had sailed out with prayer and paeans, and now started to go back with omens directly contrary; travelling by land instead of by sea, and trusting not in their fleet but in their heavy infantry. Nevertheless the greatness of the danger still impending made all this appear tolerable.

[76] Nicias seeing the army dejected and greatly altered, passed along the ranks and encouraged and comforted them as far as was possible under the circumstances, raising his voice still higher and higher as he went from one company to another in his earnestness, and in his anxiety that the benefit of his words might reach as many as possible:

[77] "Athenians and allies, even in our present position we must still hope on, since men have ere now been saved from worse straits than this; and you must not condemn yourselves too severely either because of your disasters or because of your present unmerited sufferings. I myself who am not superior to any of you in strength—indeed you see how I am in my sickness—and who in the gifts of fortune am, I think, whether in private life or otherwise, the equal of any, am now exposed to the same danger as the meanest among you; and yet my life has been one of much devotion toward the gods, and of much justice and without offence toward men. I have, therefore, still a strong hope for the future, and our misfortunes do not terrify me as much as they might. Indeed we may hope that they will be lightened: our enemies have had good fortune enough; and if any of the gods was offended at our expedition, we have been already amply punished. Others before us have attacked their neighbours and have done what men will do without suffering more than they could bear; and we may now justly expect to find the gods more kind, for we have become fitter objects for their pity than their jealousy. And then look at yourselves, mark the numbers and efficiency of the heavy infantry marching in your ranks, and do not give way too much to despondency, but reflect that you are yourselves at once a city wherever you sit down, and that there is no other in Sicily that could easily resist your attack, or expel you when once established. The safety and order of the march is for yourselves to look to; the one thought of each man being that the spot on which he may be forced to fight must be conquered and held as his country and stronghold. Meanwhile we shall hasten on our way night and day alike, as our provisions are scanty; and if we can reach some friendly place of the Sicels, whom fear of the Syracusans still keeps true to us, you may forthwith consider yourselves safe. A message has been sent on to them with directions to meet us with supplies of food. To sum up, be convinced, soldiers, that you must be brave, as there is no place near for your cowardice to take refuge in, and that if you now escape from the enemy, you may all see again what your hearts desire, while those of you who are Athenians will raise up again the great power of the state, fallen though it be. Men make the city and not walls or ships without men in them."

[78] As he made this address, Nicias went along the ranks, and brought back to their place any of the troops that he saw straggling out of the line; while Demosthenes did as much for his part of the army, addressing them in words very similar. The army marched in a hollow square, the division under Nicias leading, and that of Demosthenes following, the heavy infantry being outside and the baggage-carriers and the bulk of the army in the middle. When they arrived at the ford of the river Anapus there they found drawn up a body of the Syracusans and allies, and routing these, made good their passage and pushed on, harassed by the charges of the Syracusan horse and by the missiles of their light troops. On that day they advanced about four miles and a half, halting for the night upon a certain hill. On the next they started early and got on about two miles further, and descended into a place in the plain and there encamped, in order to procure some eatables from the houses, as the place was inhabited, and to carry on with them water from thence, as for many furlongs in front, in the direction in which they were going, it was not plentiful. The Syracusans meanwhile went on and fortified the pass in front, where there was a steep hill with a rocky ravine on each side of it, called the Acraean cliff. The next day the Athenians advancing found themselves impeded by the missiles and charges of the horse and darters, both very numerous, of the Syracusans and allies; and after fighting for a long while, at length retired to the same camp, where they had no longer provisions as before, it being impossible to leave their position by reason of the cavalry.

[79] Early next morning they started afresh and forced their way to the hill, which had been fortified, where they found before them the enemy's infantry drawn up many shields deep to defend the fortification, the pass being narrow. The Athenians assaulted the work, but were greeted by a storm of missiles from the hill, which told with the greater effect through its being a steep one, and unable to force the passage, retreated again and rested. Meanwhile occurred some claps of thunder and rain, as often happens towards autumn, which still further disheartened the Athenians, who thought all these things to be omens of their approaching ruin. While they were resting, Gylippus and the Syracusans sent a part of their army to throw up works in their rear on the way by which they had advanced; however, the Athenians immediately sent some of

their men and prevented them; after which they retreated more towards the plain and halted for the night. When they advanced the next day the Syracusans surrounded and attacked them on every side, and disabled many of them, falling back if the Athenians advanced and coming on if they retired, and in particular assaulting their rear, in the hope of routing them in detail, and thus striking a panic into the whole army. For a long while the Athenians persevered in this fashion, but after advancing for four or five furlongs halted to rest in the plain, the Syracusans also withdrawing to their own camp.

[80] During the night Nicias and Demosthenes, seeing the wretched condition of their troops, now in want of every kind of necessary, and numbers of them disabled in the numerous attacks of the enemy, determined to light as many fires as possible, and to lead off the army, no longer by the same route as they had intended, but towards the sea in the opposite direction to that guarded by the Syracusans. The whole of this route was leading the army not to Catana but to the other side of Sicily, towards Camarina, Gela, and the other Hellenic and barbarian towns in that quarter. They accordingly lit a number of fires and set out by night. Now all armies, and the greatest most of all, are liable to fears and alarms, especially when they are marching by night through an enemy's country and with the enemy near; and the Athenians falling into one of these panics, the leading division, that of Nicias, kept together and got on a good way in front, while that of Demosthenes, comprising rather more than half the army, got separated and marched on in some disorder. By morning, however, they reached the sea, and getting into the Helorine road, pushed on in order to reach the river Cacyparis, and to follow the stream up through the interior, where they hoped to be met by the Sicels whom they had sent for. Arrived at the river, they found there also a Syracusan party engaged in barring the passage of the ford with a wall and a palisade, and forcing this guard, crossed the river and went on to another called the Erineus, according to the advice of their guides.

[81] Meanwhile, when day came and the Syracusans and allies found that the Athenians were gone, most of them accused Gylippus of having let them escape on purpose, and hastily pursuing by the road which they had no difficulty in finding that they had taken, overtook them about dinner-time. They first came up with the troops under Demosthenes, who were behind and marching somewhat slowly and in disorder, owing to the night panic above referred to, and at once attacked and engaged them, the Syracusan horse surrounding them with more ease now that they were separated from the rest, and hemming them in on one spot. The division of Nicias was five or six miles on in front, as he led them more rapidly, thinking that under the circumstances their safety lay not in staying and fighting, unless obliged, but in retreating as fast as possible, and only fighting when forced to do so. On the other hand, Demosthenes was, generally speaking, harassed more incessantly, as his post in the rear left him the first exposed to the attacks of the enemy; and now, finding that the Syracusans were in pursuit, he omitted to push on, in order to form his men for battle, and so lingered until he was surrounded by his pursuers and himself and the Athenians with him placed in the most distressing position, being huddled into an enclosure with a wall all round it, a road on this side and on that, and olive-trees in great number, where missiles were showered in upon them from every quarter. This mode of attack the Syracusans had with good reason adopted in preference to fighting at close quarters, as to risk a struggle with desperate men was now more for the advantage of the Athenians than for their own; besides, their success had now become so certain that they began to spare themselves a little in order not to be cut off in the moment of victory, thinking too that, as it was, they would be able in this way to subdue and capture the enemy.

[82] In fact, after plying the Athenians and allies all day long from every side with missiles, they at length saw that they were worn out with their wounds and other sufferings; and Gylippus and the Syracusans and their allies made a proclamation, offering their liberty to any of the islanders who chose to come over to them; and some few cities went over. Afterwards a capitulation was agreed upon for all the rest with Demosthenes, to lay down their arms on condition that no one was to be put to death either by violence or imprisonment or want of the necessaries of life. Upon this they surrendered to the number of six thousand in all, laying down all the money in their possession, which filled the hollows of four shields, and were immediately conveyed by the Syracusans to the town.

Meanwhile Nicias with his division arrived that day at the river Erineus, crossed over, and posted his army upon some high ground upon the other side. *[83]* The next day the Syracusans overtook him and told him that the troops under Demosthenes had surrendered, and invited him to follow their example. Incredulous of the fact, Nicias asked for a truce to send a horseman to see, and upon the return of the messenger with the tidings that they had surrendered, sent a herald to Gylippus and the Syracusans, saying that he was ready to agree with them on behalf of the Athenians to repay whatever money the Syracusans had spent upon the war if they would let his army go; and offered until the money was paid to give Athenians as hostages, one for every talent. The Syracusans and Gylippus rejected this proposition, and attacked this division as they had the other, standing all round and plying them with missiles until the evening. Food and necessaries were as miserably wanting to the troops of Nicias as they had been to their comrades; nevertheless they watched for the quiet of the night to resume their march. But as they were taking up their arms the Syracusans perceived it and raised their paean, upon which the Athenians, finding that they were discovered, laid them down again, except about three hundred men who forced their way through the guards and went on during the night as they were able.

[84] As soon as it was day Nicias put his army in motion, pressed, as before, by the Syracusans and their allies, pelted from every side by their missiles, and struck down by their javelins. The Athenians pushed on for the Assinarus, impelled by the attacks made upon them from every side by a numerous cavalry and the swarm of other arms, fancying that they should breathe more freely if once across the river, and driven on also by their exhaustion and craving for water. Once there they rushed in, and all order was at an end, each man wanting to cross first, and the attacks of the enemy making it difficult to cross at all; forced to huddle together, they fell against and trod down one another, some dying immediately upon the javelins, others getting entangled together and stumbling over the articles of baggage, without being able to rise again. Meanwhile the opposite bank, which was steep, was lined by the Syracusans, who showered missiles down upon the Athenians, most of them drinking greedily and heaped together in disorder in the hollow bed of the river. The Peloponnesians also came down and butchered them, especially those in the water, which was thus immediately spoiled, but which they went on drinking just the same, mud and all, bloody as it was, most even fighting to have it.

[85] At last, when many dead now lay piled one upon another in the stream, and part of the army had been destroyed at the river, and the few that escaped from thence cut off by the cavalry, Nicias surrendered himself to Gylippus, whom he trusted more than he did the Syracusans, and told him and the Lacedaemonians to do what they liked with him, but to stop the slaughter of the soldiers. Gylippus, after this, immediately gave orders to make prisoners; upon which the rest were brought together alive, except a large number secreted by the soldiery, and a party was sent in pursuit of the three hundred who had got through the guard during the night, and who were now taken with the rest. The number of the enemy collected as public property was not considerable; but that secreted was very large, and all Sicily was filled with them, no convention having been made in their case as for those taken with Demosthenes. Besides this, a large portion were killed outright, the carnage being very great, and not exceeded by any in this Sicilian war. In the numerous other encounters upon the march, not a few also had fallen. Nevertheless many escaped, some at the moment, others served as slaves, and then ran away subsequently. These found refuge at Catana.

[86] The Syracusans and their allies now mustered and took up the spoils and as many prisoners as they could, and went back to the city. The rest of their Athenian and allied captives were deposited in the quarries, this seeming the safest way of keeping them; but Nicias and Demosthenes were butchered, against the will of Gylippus, who thought that it would be the crown of his triumph if he could take the enemy's generals to Lacedaemon. One of them, as it happened, Demosthenes, was one of her greatest enemies, on account of the affair of the island and of Pylos; while the other, Nicias, was for the same reasons one of her greatest friends, owing to his exertions to procure the release of the prisoners by persuading the Athenians to make peace. For these reasons the Lacedaemonians felt kindly towards him; and it was in this that Nicias himself mainly confided when he surrendered to Gylippus. But some of the Syra-

cusans who had been in correspondence with him were afraid, it was said, of his being put to the torture and troubling their success by his revelations; others, especially the Corinthians, of his escaping, as he was wealthy, by means of bribes, and living to do them further mischief; and these persuaded the allies and put him to death. This or the like was the cause of the death of a man who, of all the Hellenes in my time, least deserved such a fate, seeing that the whole course of his life had been regulated with strict attention to virtue.

[87] The prisoners in the quarries were at first hardly treated by the Syracusans. Crowded in a narrow hole, without any roof to cover them, the heat of the sun and the stifling closeness of the air tormented them during the day, and then the nights, which came on autumnal and chilly, made them ill by the violence of the change; besides, as they had to do everything in the same place for want of room, and the bodies of those who died of their wounds or from the variation in the temperature, or from similar causes, were left heaped together one upon another, intolerable stenches arose; while hunger and thirst never ceased to afflict them, each man during eight months having only half a pint of water and a pint of corn given him daily. In short, no single suffering to be apprehended by men thrust into such a place was spared them. For some seventy days they thus lived all together, after which all, except the Athenians and any Siceliots or Italiots who had joined in the expedition, were sold. The total number of prisoners taken it would be difficult to state exactly, but it could not have been less than seven thousand.

This was the greatest Hellenic achievement of any in this war, or, in my opinion, in Hellenic history; at once most glorious to the victors, and most calamitous to the conquered. They were beaten at all points and altogether; all that they suffered was great; they were destroyed, as the saying is, with a total destruction, their fleet, their army, everything was destroyed, and few out of many returned home. Such were the events in Sicily.

The Eighth Book

⫸ ⫸ ⫸ ⫸ ⫸ ⫸ ⫸ ⫸ ⫸ ⫸ ⫸ ⫸ ⫸ ⫸ ⫸ ⫷ ⫷ ⫷ ⫷ ⫷ ⫷ ⫷ ⫷ ⫷ ⫷ ⫷ ⫷ ⫷ ⫷ ⫷

CHAPTER XXIV

Nineteenth and Twentieth Years of the War—Revolt of Ionia—Intervention of Persia—The War in Ionia

[*1*] WHEN the news was brought to Athens, for a long while they disbelieved even the most respectable of the soldiers who had themselves escaped from the scene of action and clearly reported the matter, a destruction so complete not being thought credible. When the conviction was forced upon them, they were angry with the orators who had joined in promoting the expedition, just as if they had not themselves voted it, and were enraged also with the reciters of oracles and soothsayers, and all other omen-mongers of the time who had encouraged them to hope that they should conquer Sicily. Already distressed at all points and in all quarters, after what had now happened, they were seized by a fear and consternation quite without example. It was grievous enough for the state and for every man in his proper person to lose so many heavy infantry, cavalry, and able-bodied troops, and to see none left to replace them; but when they saw, also, that they had not sufficient ships in their docks, or money in the treasury, or crews for the ships, they began to despair of salvation. They thought that their enemies in Sicily would immediately sail with their fleet against Piraeus, inflamed by so signal a victory; while their adversaries at home, redoubling all their preparations, would vigorously attack them by sea and land at once, aided by their own revolted confederates. Nevertheless, with such means as they had, it was determined to resist to the last, and to provide timber and money, and to equip a fleet as they best could, to take steps to secure their confederates and above all Euboea, to reform things in the city upon a more economical footing, and to elect a board of elders to advise upon the state of affairs as occasion should arise. In short, as is the way of a democracy, in the panic of the moment they were ready to be as prudent as possible.

These resolves were at once carried into effect. Summer was now over. [*2*] The winter ensuing saw all Hellas stirring under the impression of the great Athenian disaster in Sicily. Neutrals now felt that even if uninvited they ought no longer to stand aloof from the war, but should volunteer to march against the Athenians, who, as they severally reflected, would probably have come against them if the Sicilian campaign had succeeded. Besides, they considered that the war would now be short, and that it would be creditable for them to take part in it. Meanwhile the allies of the Lacedaemonians felt all more anxious than ever to see a speedy end to their heavy labours. But above all, the subjects of the Athenians showed a readiness to revolt even beyond their ability, judging the circumstances with passion, and refusing even to hear of the Athenians being able to last out the coming summer. Beyond all this, Lacedaemon was encouraged by the near prospect of being joined in great force in the spring by her allies in Sicily, lately forced by events to acquire their navy. With these reasons for confidence in every quarter, the Lacedaemonians now resolved to throw themselves without reserve into the war, considering that, once it was happily terminated, they would be finally delivered from such dangers as that which would have threatened them from Athens, if she had become mistress of Sicily, and that the overthrow of the Athenians would leave them in quiet enjoyment of the supremacy over all Hellas.

[*3*] Their king, Agis, accordingly set out at once during this winter with some troops from Decelea, and levied from the allies contribu-

tions for the fleet, and turning towards the Malian Gulf exacted a sum of money from the Oetaeans by carrying off most of their cattle in reprisal for their old hostility, and, in spite of the protests and opposition of the Thessalians, forced the Achaeans of Phthiotis and the other subjects of the Thessalians in those parts to give him money and hostages, and deposited the hostages at Corinth, and tried to bring their countrymen into the confederacy. The Lacedaemonians now issued a requisition to the cities for building a hundred ships, fixing their own quota and that of the Boeotians at twenty-five each; that of the Phocians and Locrians together at fifteen; that of the Corinthians at fifteen; that of the Arcadians, Pellenians, and Sicyonians together at ten; and that of the Megarians, Troezenians, Epidaurians, and Hermionians together at ten also; and meanwhile made every other preparation for commencing hostilities by the spring.

[4] In the meantime the Athenians were not idle. During this same winter, as they had determined, they contributed timber and pushed on their ship-building, and fortified Sunium to enable their corn-ships to round it in safety, and evacuated the fort in Laconia which they had built on their way to Sicily; while they also, for economy, cut down any other expenses that seemed unnecessary, and above all kept a careful look-out against the revolt of their confederates.

[5] While both parties were thus engaged, and were as intent upon preparing for the war as they had been at the outset, the Euboeans first of all sent envoys during this winter to Agis to treat of their revolting from Athens. Agis accepted their proposals, and sent for Alcamenes, son of Sthenelaïdas, and Melanthus from Lacedaemon, to take the command in Euboea. These accordingly arrived with some three hundred Neodamodes, and Agis began to arrange for their crossing over. But in the meanwhile arrived some Lesbians, who also wished to revolt; and these being supported by the Boeotians, Agis was persuaded to defer acting in the matter of Euboea, and made arrangements for the revolt of the Lesbians, giving them Alcamenes, who was to have sailed to Euboea, as governor, and himself promising them ten ships, and the Boeotians the same number. All this was done without instructions from home, as Agis while at Decelea with the army that he commanded had power to send troops to whatever quarter he pleased, and to levy men and money. During this period,

one might say, the allies obeyed him much more than they did the Lacedaemonians in the city, as the force he had with him made him feared at once wherever he went. While Agis was engaged with the Lesbians, the Chians and Erythraeans, who were also ready to revolt, applied, not to him but at Lacedaemon; where they arrived accompanied by an ambassador from Tissaphernes, the commander of King Darius, son of Artaxerxes, in the maritime districts, who invited the Peloponnesians to come over, and promised to maintain their army. The King had lately called upon him for the tribute from his government, for which he was in arrears, being unable to raise it from the Hellenic towns by reason of the Athenians; and he therefore calculated that by weakening the Athenians he should get the tribute better paid, and should also draw the Lacedaemonians into alliance with the King; and by this means, as the King had commanded him, take alive or dead Amorges, the bastard son of Pissuthnes, who was in rebellion on the coast of Caria.

While the Chians and Tissaphernes thus joined to effect the same object, [6] about the same time Calligeitus, son of Laophon, a Megarian, and Timagoras, son of Athenagoras, a Cyzicene, both of them exiles from their country and living at the court of Pharnabazus, son of Pharnaces, arrived at Lacedaemon upon a mission from Pharnabazus, to procure a fleet for the Hellespont; by means of which, if possible, he might himself effect the object of Tissaphernes' ambition and cause the cities in his government to revolt from the Athenians, and so get the tribute, and by his own agency obtain for the King the alliance of the Lacedaemonians.

The emissaries of Pharnabazus and Tissaphernes treating apart, a keen competition now ensued at Lacedaemon as to whether a fleet and army should be sent first to Ionia and Chios, or to the Hellespont. The Lacedaemonians, however, decidedly favoured the Chians and Tissaphernes, who were seconded by Alcibiades, the family friend of Endius, one of the ephors for that year. Indeed, this is how their house got its Laconic name, Alcibiades being the family name of Endius. Nevertheless the Lacedaemonians first sent to Chios Phrynis, one of the Perioeci, to see whether they had as many ships as they said, and whether their city generally was as great as was reported; and upon his bringing word that they had been told the truth, immediately entered into alli-

ance with the Chians and Erythraeans, and
voted to send them forty ships, there being already, according to the statement of the Chians, not less than sixty in the island. At first
the Lacedaemonians meant to send ten of
these forty themselves, with Melanchridas
their admiral; but afterwards, an earthquake
having occurred, they sent Chalcideus instead
of Melanchridas, and instead of the ten ships
equipped only five in Laconia. And the winter
ended, and with it ended also the nineteenth
year of this war of which Thucydides is the
historian.

[7] At the beginning of the next summer
the Chians were urging that the fleet should be
sent off, being afraid that the Athenians, from
whom all these embassies were kept a secret,
might find out what was going on, and the
Lacedaemonians at once sent three Spartans to
Corinth to haul the ships as quickly as possible
across the Isthmus from the other sea to that
on the side of Athens, and to order them all to
sail to Chios, those which Agis was equipping
for Lesbos not excepted. The number of ships
from the allied states was thirty-nine in all.

[8] Meanwhile Calligeitus and Timagoras
did not join on behalf of Pharnabazus in the
expedition to Chios or give the money—twenty-five talents—which they had brought with
them to help in dispatching a force, but determined to sail afterwards with another force
by themselves. Agis, on the other hand, seeing
the Lacedaemonians bent upon going to Chios
first, himself came in to their views; and the
allies assembled at Corinth and held a council,
in which they decided to sail first to Chios under the command of Chalcideus, who was
equipping the five vessels in Laconia, then to
Lesbos, under the command of Alcamenes, the
same whom Agis had fixed upon, and lastly to
go to the Hellespont, where the command was
given to Clearchus, son of Ramphias. Meanwhile they would take only half the ships
across the Isthmus first, and let those sail off at
once, in order that the Athenians might attend
less to the departing squadron than to those
to be taken across afterwards, as no care had
been taken to keep this voyage secret through
contempt of the impotence of the Athenians,
who had as yet no fleet of any account upon the
sea. Agreeably to this determination, twenty-
one vessels were at once conveyed across the
Isthmus.

[9] They were now impatient to set sail, but
the Corinthians were not willing to accompany
them until they had celebrated the Isthmian

festival, which fell at that time. Upon this Agis
proposed to them to save their scruples about
breaking the Isthmian truce by taking the expedition upon himself. The Corinthians not
consenting to this, a delay ensued, during
which the Athenians conceived suspicions of
what was preparing at Chios, and sent Aristocrates, one of their generals, and charged
them with the fact, and, upon the denial of the
Chians, ordered them to send with them a contingent of ships, as faithful confederates. Sev-
en were sent accordingly. The reason of the
dispatch of the ships lay in the fact that the
mass of the Chians were not privy to the negotiations, while the few who were in the secret
did not wish to break with the multitude until
they had something positive to lean upon, and
no longer expected the Peloponnesians to arrive by reason of their delay.

[10] In the meantime the Isthmian games
took place, and the Athenians, who had been
also invited, went to attend them, and now
seeing more clearly into the designs of the
Chians, as soon as they returned to Athens
took measures to prevent the fleet putting out
from Cenchreae without their knowledge. After the festival the Peloponnesians set sail with
twenty-one ships for Chios, under the command of Alcamenes. The Athenians first sailed
against them with an equal number, drawing
off towards the open sea. The enemy, however,
turning back before he had followed them far,
the Athenians returned also, not trusting the
seven Chian ships which formed part of their
number, and afterwards manned thirty-seven
vessels in all and chased him on his passage
alongshore into Spiraeum, a desert Corinthian
port on the edge of the Epidaurian frontier.
After losing one ship out at sea, the Peloponnesians got the rest together and brought them
to anchor. The Athenians now attacked not
only from the sea with their fleet, but also disembarked upon the coast; and a *mêlée* ensued
of the most confused and violent kind, in
which the Athenians disabled most of the enemy's vessels and killed Alcamenes their commander, losing also a few of their own men.

[11] After this they separated, and the Athenians, detaching a sufficient number of ships
to blockade those of the enemy, anchored with
the rest at the islet adjacent, upon which they
proceeded to encamp, and sent to Athens for
reinforcements; the Peloponnesians having
been joined on the day after the battle by the
Corinthians, who came to help the ships, and
by the other inhabitants in the vicinity not

long afterwards. These saw the difficulty of keeping guard in a desert place, and in their perplexity at first thought of burning the ships, but finally resolved to haul them up on shore and sit down and guard them with their land forces until a convenient opportunity for escaping should present itself. Agis also, on being informed of the disaster, sent them a Spartan of the name of Thermon. The Lacedaemonians first received the news of the fleet having put out from the Isthmus, Alcamenes having been ordered by the ephors to send off a horseman when this took place, and immediately resolved to dispatch their own five vessels under Chalcideus, and Alcibiades with him. But while they were full of this resolution came the second news of the fleet having taken refuge in Spiraeum; and disheartened at their first step in the Ionian war proving a failure, they laid aside the idea of sending the ships from their own country, and even wished to recall some that had already sailed.

[12] Perceiving this, Alcibiades again persuaded Endius and the other ephors to persevere in the expedition, saying that the voyage would be made before the Chians heard of the fleet's misfortune, and that as soon as he set foot in Ionia, he should, by assuring them of the weakness of the Athenians and the zeal of Lacedaemon, have no difficulty in persuading the cities to revolt, as they would readily believe his testimony. He also represented to Endius himself in private that it would be glorious for him to be the means of making Ionia revolt and the King become the ally of Lacedaemon, instead of that honour being left to Agis (Agis, it must be remembered, was the enemy of Alcibiades); and Endius and his colleagues thus persuaded, he put to sea with the five ships and the Lacedaemonian Chalcideus, and made all haste upon the voyage.

[13] About this time the sixteen Peloponnesian ships from Sicily, which had served through the war with Gylippus, were caught on their return off Leucadia and roughly handled by the twenty-seven Athenian vessels under Hippocles, son of Menippus, on the lookout for the ships from Sicily. After losing one of their number, the rest escaped from the Athenians and sailed into Corinth.

[14] Meanwhile Chalcideus and Alcibiades seized all they met with on their voyage, to prevent news of their coming, and let them go at Corycus, the first point which they touched at in the continent. Here they were visited by some of their Chian correspondents and, being urged by them to sail up to the town without announcing their coming, arrived suddenly before Chios. The many were amazed and confounded, while the few had so arranged that the council should be sitting at the time; and after speeches from Chalcideus and Alcibiades stating that many more ships were sailing up, but saying nothing of the fleet being blockaded in Spiraeum, the Chians revolted from the Athenians, and the Erythraeans immediately afterwards. After this three vessels sailed over to Clazomenae, and made that city revolt also; and the Clazomenians immediately crossed over to the mainland and began to fortify Polichna, in order to retreat there, in case of necessity, from the island where they dwelt.

While the revolted places were all engaged in fortifying and preparing for the war, [15] news of Chios speedily reached Athens. The Athenians thought the danger by which they were now menaced great and unmistakable, and that the rest of their allies would not consent to keep quiet after the secession of the greatest of their number. In the consternation of the moment they at once took off the penalty attaching to whoever proposed or put to the vote a proposal for using the thousand talents which they had jealously avoided touching throughout the whole war, and voted to employ them to man a large number of ships, and to send off at once under Strombichides, son of Diotimus, the eight vessels, forming part of the blockading fleet at Spiraeum, which had left the blockade and had returned after pursuing and failing to overtake the vessels with Chalcideus. These were to be followed shortly afterwards by twelve more under Thrasycles, also taken from the blockade. They also recalled the seven Chian vessels, forming part of their squadron blockading the fleet in Spiraeum, and giving the slaves on board their liberty, put the freemen in confinement, and speedily manned and sent out ten fresh ships to blockade the Peloponnesians in the place of all those that had departed, and decided to man thirty more. Zeal was not wanting, and no effort was spared to send relief to Chios.

[16] In the meantime Strombichides with his eight ships arrived at Samos, and, taking one Samian vessel, sailed to Teos and required them to remain quiet. Chalcideus also set sail with twenty-three ships for Teos from Chios, the land forces of the Clazomenians and Erythraeans moving alongshore to support him. Informed of this in time, Strombichides put out from Teos before their arrival, and while

out at sea, seeing the number of the ships from Chios, fled towards Samos, chased by the enemy. The Teians at first would not receive the land forces, but upon the flight of the Athenians took them into the town. There they waited for some time for Chalcideus to return from the pursuit, and as time went on without his appearing, began themselves to demolish the wall which the Athenians had built on the land side of the city of the Teians, being assisted by a few of the barbarians who had come up under the command of Stages, the lieutenant of Tissaphernes.

[*17*] Meanwhile Chalcideus and Alcibiades, after chasing Strombichides into Samos, armed the crews of the ships from Peloponnese and left them at Chios, and filling their places with substitutes from Chios and manning twenty others, sailed off to effect the revolt of Miletus. The wish of Alcibiades, who had friends among the leading men of the Milesians, was to bring over the town before the arrival of the ships from Peloponnese, and thus, by causing the revolt of as many cities as possible with the help of the Chian power and of Chalcideus, to secure the honour for the Chians and himself and Chalcideus, and, as he had promised, for Endius who had sent them out. Not discovered until their voyage was nearly completed, they arrived a little before Strombichides and Thrasycles (who had just come with twelve ships from Athens, and had joined Strombichides in pursuing them), and occasioned the revolt of Miletus. The Athenians sailing up close on their heels with nineteen ships found Miletus closed against them, and took up their station at the adjacent island of Lade. The first alliance between the King and the Lacedaemonians was now concluded immediately upon the revolt of the Milesians, by Tissaphernes and Chalcideus, and was as follows:

[*18*] *The Lacedaemonians and their allies made a treaty with the King and Tissaphernes upon the terms following:*

1. *Whatever country or cities the King has, or the King's ancestors had, shall be the King's: and whatever came in to the Athenians from these cities, either money or any other thing, the King and the Lacedaemonians and their allies shall jointly hinder the Athenians from receiving either money or any other thing.*

2. *The war with the Athenians shall be carried on jointly by the King and by the Lacedaemonians and their allies: and it shall not be lawful to make peace with the Athenians except both agree, the King on his side and the*

Lacedaemonians and their allies on theirs.

3. *If any revolt from the King, they shall be the enemies of the Lacedaemonians and their allies. And if any revolt from the Lacedaemonians and their allies, they shall be the enemies of the King in like manner.*

[*19*] This was the alliance. After this the Chians immediately manned ten more vessels and sailed for Anaia, in order to gain intelligence of those in Miletus, and also to make the cities revolt. A message, however, reaching them from Chalcideus to tell them to go back again, and that Amorges was at hand with an army by land, they sailed to the temple of Zeus, and there sighting ten more ships sailing up with which Diomedon had started from Athens after Thrasycles, fled, one ship to Ephesus, the rest to Teos. The Athenians took four of their ships empty, the men finding time to escape ashore; the rest took refuge in the city of the Teians; after which the Athenians sailed off to Samos, while the Chians put to sea with their remaining vessels, accompanied by the land forces, and caused Lebedos to revolt, and after it Erae. After this they both returned home, the fleet and the army.

[*20*] About the same time the twenty ships of the Peloponnesians in Spiraeum, which we left chased to land and blockaded by an equal number of Athenians, suddenly sallied out and defeated the blockading squadron, took four of their ships, and, sailing back to Cenchreae, prepared again for the voyage to Chios and Ionia. Here they were joined by Astyochus as high admiral from Lacedaemon, henceforth invested with the supreme command at sea. The land forces now withdrawing from Teos, Tissaphernes repaired thither in person with an army and completed the demolition of anything that was left of the wall, and so departed. Not long after his departure Diomedon arrived with ten Athenian ships, and, having made a convention by which the Teians admitted him as they had the enemy, coasted along to Erae, and, failing in an attempt upon the town, sailed back again.

[*21*] About this time took place the rising of the commons at Samos against the upper classes, in concert with some Athenians, who were there in three vessels. The Samian commons put to death some two hundred in all of the upper classes, and banished four hundred more, and themselves took their land and houses; after which the Athenians decreed their independence, being now sure of their fidelity, and the commons henceforth gov-

erned the city, excluding the landholders from all share in affairs, and forbidding any of the commons to give his daughter in marriage to them or to take a wife from them in future.

[22] After this, during the same summer, the Chians, whose zeal continued as active as ever, and who even without the Peloponnesians found themselves in sufficient force to effect the revolt of the cities and also wished to have as many companions in peril as possible, made an expedition with thirteen ships of their own to Lesbos; the instructions from Lacedaemon being to go to that island next, and from thence to the Hellespont. Meanwhile the land forces of the Peloponnesians who were with the Chians and of the allies on the spot, moved alongshore for Clazomenae and Cuma, under the command of Eualas, a Spartan; while the fleet under Diniadas, one of the Perioeci, first sailed up to Methymna and caused it to revolt, and, leaving four ships there, with the rest procured the revolt of Mitylene.

[23] In the meantime Astyochus, the Lacedaemonian admiral, set sail from Cenchreae with four ships, as he had intended, and arrived at Chios. On the third day after his arrival, the Athenian ships, twenty-five in number, sailed to Lesbos under Diomedon and Leon, who had lately arrived with a reinforcement of ten ships from Athens. Late in the same day Astyochus put to sea, and taking one Chian vessel with him sailed to Lesbos to render what assistance he could. Arrived at Pyrrha, and from thence the next day at Eresus, he there learned that Mitylene had been taken, almost without a blow, by the Athenians, who had sailed up and unexpectedly put into the harbour, had beaten the Chian ships, and landing and defeating the troops opposed to them had become masters of the city. Informed of this by the Eresians and the Chian ships, which had been left with Eubulus at Methymna, and had fled upon the capture of Mitylene, and three of which he now fell in with, one having been taken by the Athenians, Astyochus did not go on to Mitylene, but raised and armed Eresus, and, sending the heavy infantry from his own ships by land under Eteonicus to Antissa and Methymna, himself proceeded alongshore thither with the ships which he had with him and with the three Chians, in the hope that the Methymnians upon seeing them would be encouraged to persevere in their revolt. As, however, everything went against him in Lesbos, he took up his own force and sailed back to Chios; the

land forces on board, which were to have gone to the Hellespont, being also conveyed back to their different cities. After this six of the allied Peloponnesian ships at Cenchreae joined the forces at Chios. The Athenians, after restoring matters to their old state in Lesbos, set sail from thence and took Polichna, the place that the Clazomenians were fortifying on the continent, and carried the inhabitants back to their town upon the island, except the authors of the revolt, who withdrew to Daphnus; and thus Clazomenae became once more Athenian.

[24] The same summer the Athenians in the twenty ships at Lade, blockading Miletus, made a descent at Panormus in the Milesian territory, and killed Chalcideus the Lacedaemonian commander, who had come with a few men against them, and the third day after sailed over and set up a trophy, which, as they were not masters of the country, was however pulled down by the Milesians. Meanwhile Leon and Diomedon with the Athenian fleet from Lesbos issuing from the Oenussae, the isles off Chios, and from their forts of Sidussa and Pteleum in the Erythraeid, and from Lesbos, carried on the war against the Chians from the ships, having on board heavy infantry from the rolls pressed to serve as marines. Landing in Cardamyle and in Bolissus they defeated with heavy loss the Chians that took the field against them and, laying desolate the places in that neighbourhood, defeated the Chians again in another battle at Phanae, and in a third at Leuconium. After this the Chians ceased to meet them in the field, while the Athenians devastated the country, which was beautifully stocked and had remained uninjured ever since the Median wars. Indeed, after the Lacedaemonians, the Chians are the only people that I have known who knew how to be wise in prosperity, and who ordered their city the more securely the greater it grew. Nor was this revolt, in which they might seem to have erred on the side of rashness, ventured upon until they had numerous and gallant allies to share the danger with them, and until they perceived the Athenians after the Sicilian disaster themselves no longer denying the thoroughly desperate state of their affairs. And if they were thrown out by one of the surprises which upset human calculations, they found out their mistake in company with many others who believed, like them, in the speedy collapse of the Athenian power. While they were thus blockaded from the sea and plundered by land, some of the citizens under-

took to bring the city over to the Athenians. Apprised of this the authorities took no action themselves, but brought Astyochus, the admiral, from Erythrae, with four ships that he had with him, and considered how they could most quietly, either by taking hostages or by some other means, put an end to the conspiracy.

While the Chians were thus engaged, [25] a thousand Athenian heavy infantry and fifteen hundred Argives (five hundred of whom were light troops furnished with armour by the Athenians), and one thousand of the allies, towards the close of the same summer sailed from Athens in forty-eight ships, some of which were transports, under the command of Phrynichus, Onomacles, and Scironides, and putting into Samos crossed over and encamped at Miletus. Upon this the Milesians came out to the number of eight hundred heavy infantry, with the Peloponnesians who had come with Chalcideus, and some foreign mercenaries of Tissaphernes, Tissaphernes himself and his cavalry, and engaged the Athenians and their allies. While the Argives rushed forward on their own wing with the careless disdain of men advancing against Ionians who would never stand their charge, and were defeated by the Milesians with a loss little short of three hundred men, the Athenians first defeated the Peloponnesians, and driving before them the barbarians and the ruck of the army, without engaging the Milesians, who after the rout of the Argives retreated into the town upon seeing their comrades worsted, crowned their victory by grounding their arms under the very walls of Miletus. Thus, in this battle, the Ionians on both sides overcame the Dorians, the Athenians defeating the Peloponnesians opposed to them, and the Milesians the Argives. After setting up a trophy, the Athenians prepared to draw a wall round the place, which stood upon an isthmus; thinking that, if they could gain Miletus, the other towns also would easily come over to them.

[26] Meanwhile about dusk tidings reached them that the fifty-five ships from Peloponnese and Sicily might be instantly expected. Of these the Siceliots, urged principally by the Syracusan Hermocrates to join in giving the finishing blow to the power of Athens, furnished twenty-two—twenty from Syracuse, and two from Silenus; and the ships that we left preparing in Peloponnese being now ready, both squadrons had been entrusted to Therimenes, a Lacedaemonian, to take to Astyochus, the admiral. They now put in first at Leros the island off Miletus, and from thence, discovering that the Athenians were before the town, sailed into the Iasic Gulf, in order to learn how matters stood at Miletus. Meanwhile Alcibiades came on horseback to Teichiussa in the Milesian territory, the point of the gulf at which they had put in for the night, and told them of the battle in which he had fought in person by the side of the Milesians and Tissaphernes, and advised them, if they did not wish to sacrifice Ionia and their cause, to fly to the relief of Miletus and hinder its investment.

[27] Accordingly they resolved to relieve it the next morning. Meanwhile Phrynichus, the Athenian commander, had received precise intelligence of the fleet from Leros, and when his colleagues expressed a wish to keep the sea and fight it out, flatly refused either to stay himself or to let them or any one else do so if he could help it. Where they could hereafter contend, after full and undisturbed preparation, with an exact knowledge of the number of the enemy's fleet and of the force which they could oppose to him, he would never allow the reproach of disgrace to drive him into a risk that was unreasonable. It was no disgrace for an Athenian fleet to retreat when it suited them: put it as they would, it would be more disgraceful to be beaten, and to expose the city not only to disgrace, but to the most serious danger. After its late misfortunes it could hardly be justified in voluntarily taking the offensive even with the strongest force, except in a case of absolute necessity: much less then without compulsion could it rush upon peril of its own seeking. He told them to take up their wounded as quickly as they could and the troops and stores which they had brought with them, and leaving behind what they had taken from the enemy's country, in order to lighten the ships, to sail off to Samos, and there concentrating all their ships to attack as opportunity served. As he spoke so he acted; and thus not now more than afterwards, nor in this alone but in all that he had to do with, did Phrynichus show himself a man of sense. In this way that very evening the Athenians broke up from before Miletus, leaving their victory unfinished, and the Argives, mortified at their disaster, promptly sailed off home from Samos.

[28] As soon as it was morning the Peloponnesians weighed from Teichiussa and put into Miletus after the departure of the Athenians; they stayed one day, and on the next took with them the Chian vessels originally chased into

port with Chalcideus, and resolved to sail back for the tackle which they had put on shore at Teichiussa. Upon their arrival Tissaphernes came to them with his land forces and induced them to sail to Iasus, which was held by his enemy Amorges. Accordingly they suddenly attacked and took Iasus, whose inhabitants never imagined that the ships could be other than Athenian. The Syracusans distinguished themselves most in the action. Amorges, a bastard of Pissuthnes and a rebel from the King, was taken alive and handed over to Tissaphernes, to carry to the King, if he chose, according to his orders: Iasus was sacked by the army, who found a very great booty there, the place being wealthy from ancient date. The mercenaries serving with Amorges the Peloponnesians received and enrolled in their army without doing them any harm, since most of them came from Peloponnese, and handed over the town to Tissaphernes with all the captives, bond or free, at the stipulated price of one Doric stater a head; after which they returned to Miletus. Pedaritus, son of Leon, who had been sent by the Lacedaemonians to take the command at Chios, they dispatched by land as far as Erythrae with the mercenaries taken from Amorges; appointing Philip to remain as governor of Miletus.

Summer was now over. [29] The winter following, Tissaphernes put Iasus in a state of defence, and passing on to Miletus distributed a month's pay to all the ships as he had promised at Lacedaemon, at the rate of an Attic drachma a day for each man. In future, however, he was resolved not to give more than three obols, until he had consulted the King; when if the King should so order he would give, he said, the full drachma. However, upon the protest of the Syracusan general Hermocrates (for as Therimenes was not admiral, but only accompanied them in order to hand over the ships to Astyochus, he made little difficulty about the pay), it was agreed that the amount of five ships' pay should be given over and above the three obols a day for each man; Tissaphernes paying thirty talents a month for fifty-five ships, and to the rest, for as many ships as they had beyond that number, at the same rate.

[30] The same winter the Athenians in Samos, having been joined by thirty-five more vessels from home under Charminus, Strombichides, and Euctemon, called in their squadron at Chios and all the rest, intending to blockade Miletus with their navy, and to send a fleet and an army against Chios; drawing lots for the respective services. This intention they carried into effect; Strombichides, Onamacles, and Euctemon sailing against Chios, which fell to their lot, with thirty ships and a part of the thousand heavy infantry, who had been to Miletus, in transports; while the rest remained masters of the sea with seventy-four ships at Samos, and advanced upon Miletus.

[31] Meanwhile Astyochus, whom we left at Chios collecting the hostages required in consequence of the conspiracy, stopped upon learning that the fleet with Therimenes had arrived, and that the affairs of the league were in a more flourishing condition, and putting out to sea with ten Peloponnesian and as many Chian vessels, after a futile attack upon Pteleum, coasted on to Clazomenae, and ordered the Athenian party to remove inland to Daphnus, and to join the Peloponnesians, an order in which also joined Tamos the king's lieutenant in Ionia. This order being disregarded, Astyochus made an attack upon the town, which was unwalled, and having failed to take it was himself carried off by a strong gale to Phocaea and Cuma, while the rest of the ships put in at the islands adjacent to Clazomenae—Marathussa, Pele, and Drymussa. Here they were detained eight days by the winds, and, plundering and consuming all the property of the Clazomenians there deposited, put the rest on shipboard and sailed off to Phocaea and Cuma to join Astyochus.

[32] While he was there, envoys arrived from the Lesbians who wished to revolt again. With Astyochus they were successful; but the Corinthians and the other allies being averse to it by reason of their former failure, he weighed anchor and set sail for Chios, where they eventually arrived from different quarters, the fleet having been scattered by a storm. After this Pedaritus, whom we left marching along the coast from Miletus, arrived at Erythrae, and thence crossed over with his army to Chios, where he found also about five hundred soldiers who had been left there by Chalcideus from the five ships with their arms. Meanwhile some Lesbians making offers to revolt, Astyochus urged upon Pedaritus and the Chians that they ought to go with their ships and effect the revolt of Lesbos, and so increase the number of their allies, or, if not successful, at all events harm the Athenians. The Chians, however, turned a deaf ear to this, and Pedaritus flatly refused to give up to him the Chian vessels.

[33] Upon this Astyochus took five Corinthian and one Megarian vessel, with another from Hermione, and the ships which had come with him from Laconia, and set sail for Miletus to assume his command as admiral; after telling the Chians with many threats that he would certainly not come and help them if they should be in need. At Corycus in the Erythraeid he brought to for the night; the Athenian armament sailing from Samos against Chios being only separated from him by a hill, upon the other side of which it brought to; so that neither perceived the other. But a letter arriving in the night from Pedaritus to say that some liberated Erythraean prisoners had come from Samos to betray Erythrae, Astyochus at once put back to Erythrae, and so just escaped falling in with the Athenians. Here Pedaritus sailed over to join him; and after inquiry into the pretended treachery, finding that the whole story had been made up to procure the escape of the men from Samos, they acquitted them of the charge, and sailed away, Pedaritus to Chios and Astyochus to Miletus as he had intended.

[34] Meanwhile the Athenian armament sailing round Corycus fell in with three Chian men-of-war off Arginus, and gave immediate chase. A great storm coming on, the Chians with difficulty took refuge in the harbour; the three Athenian vessels most forward in the pursuit being wrecked and thrown up near the city of Chios, and the crews slain or taken prisoners. The rest of the Athenian fleet took refuge in the harbour called Phoenicus, under Mount Mimas, and from thence afterwards put into Lesbos and prepared for the work of fortification.

[35] The same winter the Lacedaemonian Hippocrates sailed out from Peloponnese with ten Thurian ships under the command of Dorieus, son of Diagoras, and two colleagues, one Laconian and one Syracusan vessel, and arrived at Cnidus, which had already revolted at the instigation of Tissaphernes. When their arrival was known at Miletus, orders came to them to leave half their squadron to guard Cnidus, and with the rest to cruise round Triopium and seize all the merchantmen arriving from Egypt. Triopium is a promontory of Cnidus and sacred to Apollo. This coming to the knowledge of the Athenians, they sailed from Samos and captured the six ships on the watch at Triopium, the crews escaping out of them. After this the Athenians sailed into Cnidus and made an assault upon the town,

which was unfortified, and all but took it; and the next day assaulted it again, but with less effect, as the inhabitants had improved their defences during the night, and had been reinforced by the crews escaped from the ships at Triopium. The Athenians now withdrew, and after plundering the Cnidian territory sailed back to Samos.

[36] About the same time Astyochus came to the fleet at Miletus. The Peloponnesian camp was still plentifully supplied, being in receipt of sufficient pay, and the soldiers having still in hand the large booty taken at Iasus. The Milesians also showed great ardour for the war. Nevertheless the Peloponnesians thought the first convention with Tissaphernes, made with Chalcideus, defective, and more advantageous to him than to them, and consequently while Therimenes was still there concluded another, which was as follows:

[37] The convention of the Lacedaemonians and the allies with King Darius and the sons of the King, and with Tissaphernes for a treaty and friendship, as follows:

1. Neither the Lacedaemonians nor the allies of the Lacedaemonians shall make war against or otherwise injure any country or cities that belong to King Darius or did belong to his father or to his ancestors; neither shall the Lacedaemonians nor the allies of the Lacedaemonians exact tribute from such cities. Neither shall King Darius nor any of the subjects of the King make war against or otherwise injure the Lacedaemonians or their allies.

2. If the Lacedaemonians or their allies should require any assistance from the King, or the King from the Lacedaemonians or their allies, whatever they both agree upon they shall be right in doing.

3. Both shall carry on jointly the war against the Athenians and their allies: and if they make peace, both shall do so jointly.

4. The expense of all troops in the King's country, sent for by the King, shall be borne by the King.

5. If any of the states comprised in this convention with the King attack the King's country, the rest shall stop them and aid the King to the best of their power. And if any in the King's country or in the countries under the King's rule attack the country of the Lacedaemonians or their allies, the King shall stop it and help them to the best of his power.

[38] After this convention Therimenes handed over the fleet to Astyochus, sailed off in a small boat, and was lost. The Athenian ar-

mament had now crossed over from Lesbos to Chios, and being master by sea and land began to fortify Delphinium, a place naturally strong on the land side, provided with more than one harbour, and also not far from the city of Chios. Meanwhile the Chians remained inactive. Already defeated in so many battles, they were now also at discord among themselves; the execution of the party of Tydeus, son of Ion, by Pedaritus upon the charge of Atticism, followed by the forcible imposition of an oligarchy upon the rest of the city, having made them suspicious of one another; and they therefore thought neither themselves not the mercenaries under Pedaritus a match for the enemy. They sent, however, to Miletus to beg Astyochus to assist them, which he refused to do, and was accordingly denounced at Lacedaemon by Pedaritus as a traitor. Such was the state of the Athenian affairs at Chios; while their fleet at Samos kept sailing out against the enemy in Miletus, until they found that he would not accept their challenge, and then retired again to Samos and remained quiet.

[39] In the same winter the twenty-seven ships equipped by the Lacedaemonians for Pharnabazus through the agency of the Megarian Calligeitus, and the Cyzicene Timagoras, put out from Peloponnese and sailed for Ionia about the time of the solstice, under the command of Antisthenes, a Spartan. With them the Lacedaemonians also sent eleven Spartans as advisers to Astyochus; Lichas, son of Arcesilaus, being among the number. Arrived at Miletus, their orders were to aid in generally superintending the good conduct of the war; to send off the above ships or a greater or less number to the Hellespont to Pharnabazus, if they thought proper, appointing Clearchus, son of Ramphias, who sailed with them, to the command; and further, if they thought proper, to make Antisthenes admiral, dismissing Astyochus, whom the letters of Pedaritus had caused to be regarded with suspicion. Sailing accordingly from Malea across the open sea, the squadron touched at Melos and there fell in with ten Athenian ships, three of which they took empty and burned. After this, being afraid that the Athenian vessels escaped from Melos might, as they in fact did, give information of their approach to the Athenians at Samos, they sailed to Crete, and having lengthened their voyage by way of precaution made land at Caunus in Asia, from whence considering themselves in safety they

sent a message to the fleet at Miletus for a convoy along the coast.

[40] Meanwhile the Chians and Pedaritus, undeterred by the backwardness of Astyochus, went on sending messengers pressing him to come with all the fleet to assist them against their besiegers, and not to leave the greatest of the allied states in Ionia to be shut up by sea and overrun and pillaged by land. There were more slaves at Chios than in any one other city except Lacedaemon, and being also by reason of their numbers punished more rigorously when they offended, most of them, when they saw the Athenian armament firmly established in the island with a fortified position, immediately deserted to the enemy, and through their knowledge of the country did the greatest mischief. The Chians therefore urged upon Astyochus that it was his duty to assist them, while there was still a hope and a possibility of stopping the enemy's progress, while Delphinium was still in process of fortification and unfinished, and before the completion of a higher rampart which was being added to protect the camp and fleet of their besiegers. Astyochus now saw that the allies also wished it and prepared to go, in spite of his intention to the contrary owing to the threat already referred to.

[41] In the meantime news came from Caunus of the arrival of the twenty-seven ships with the Lacedaemonian commissioners; and Astyochus, postponing everything to the duty of convoying a fleet of that importance, in order to be more able to command the sea, and to the safe conduct of the Lacedaemonians sent as spies over his behaviour, at once gave up going to Chios and set sail for Caunus. As he coasted along he landed at the Meropid Cos and sacked the city, which was unfortified and had been lately laid in ruins by an earthquake, by far the greatest in living memory, and, as the inhabitants had fled to the mountains, overran the country and made booty of all it contained, letting go, however, the free men. From Cos arriving in the night at Cnidus he was constrained by the representations of the Cnidians not to disembark the sailors, but to sail as he was straight against the twenty Athenian vessels, which with Charminus, one of the commanders at Samos, were on the watch for the very twenty-seven ships from Peloponnese which Astyochus was himself sailing to join; the Athenians in Samos having heard from Melos of their approach, and Charminus being on the look-out off Syme, Chalce, Rhodes, and

Lycia, as he now heard that they were at Caunus.

[42] Astyochus accordingly sailed as he was to Syme, before he was heard of, in the hope of catching the enemy somewhere out at sea. Rain, however, and foggy weather encountered him, and caused his ships to straggle and get into disorder in the dark. In the morning his fleet had parted company and was most of it still straggling round the island, and the left wing only in sight of Charminus and the Athenians, who took it for the squadron which they were watching for from Caunus, and hastily put out against it with part only of their twenty vessels, and attacking immediately sank three ships and disabled others, and had the advantage in the action until the main body of the fleet unexpectedly hove in sight, when they were surrounded on every side. Upon this they took to flight, and after losing six ships with the rest escaped to Teutlussa or Beet Island, and from thence to Halicarnassus. After this the Peloponnesians put into Cnidus and, being joined by the twenty-seven ships from Caunus, sailed all together and set up a trophy in Syme, and then returned to anchor at Cnidus.

[43] As soon as the Athenians knew of the sea-fight, they sailed with all the ships at Samos to Syme, and, without attacking or being attacked by the fleet at Cnidus, took the ships' tackle left at Syme, and touching at Lorymi on the mainland sailed back to Samos. Meanwhile the Peloponnesian ships, being now all at Cnidus, underwent such repairs as were needed; while the eleven Lacedaemonian commissioners conferred with Tissaphernes, who had come to meet them, upon the points which did not satisfy them in the past transactions, and upon the best and mutually most advantageous manner of conducting the war in future. The severest critic of the present proceedings was Lichas, who said that neither of the treaties could stand, neither that of Chalcideus, nor that of Therimenes; it being monstrous that the King should at this date pretend to the possession of all the country formerly ruled by himself or by his ancestors—a pretension which implicitly put back under the yoke all the islands—Thessaly, Locris, and everything as far as Boeotia—and made the Lacedaemonians give to the Hellenes instead of liberty a Median master. He therefore invited Tissaphernes to conclude another and a better treaty, as they certainly would not recognize those existing and did not want any of his pay upon such conditions. This offended Tissaphernes so much

that he went away in a rage without settling anything.

CHAPTER XXV

*Twentieth and Twenty-first Years of the War—
Intrigues of Alcibiades—Withdrawal of the Persian Subsidies—Oligarchical Coup d'Etat at Athens—Patriotism of the Army at Samos*

[44] THE Peloponnesians now determined to sail to Rhodes, upon the invitation of some of the principal men there, hoping to gain an island powerful by the number of its seamen and by its land forces, and also thinking that they would be able to maintain their fleet from their own confederacy, without having to ask for money from Tissaphernes. They accordingly at once set sail that same winter from Cnidus, and first put in with ninety-four ships at Camirus in the Rhodian country, to the great alarm of the mass of the inhabitants, who were not privy to the intrigue, and who consequently fled, especially as the town was unfortified. They were afterwards, however, assembled by the Lacedaemonians together with the inhabitants of the two other towns of Lindus and Ialysus; and the Rhodians were persuaded to revolt from the Athenians and the island went over to the Peloponnesians. Meanwhile the Athenians had received the alarm and set sail with the fleet from Samos to forestall them, and came within sight of the island, but being a little too late sailed off for the moment to Chalce, and from thence to Samos, and subsequently waged war against Rhodes, issuing from Chalce, Cos, and Samos.

The Peloponnesians now levied a contribution of thirty-two talents from the Rhodians, after which they hauled their ships ashore and for eighty days remained inactive. [45] During this time, and even earlier, before they removed to Rhodes, the following intrigues took place. After the death of Chalcideus and the battle at Miletus, Alcibiades began to be suspected by the Peloponnesians; and Astyochus received from Lacedaemon an order from them to put him to death, he being the personal enemy of Agis, and in other respects thought unworthy of confidence. Alcibiades in his alarm first withdrew to Tissaphernes, and immediately began to do all he could with him to injure the Peloponnesian cause. Henceforth becoming his adviser in everything, he cut down the pay from an Attic drachma to three obols a day, and even this not paid too regularly; and told Tissaphernes to say to the Peloponnesians that the Athenians, whose maritime experience was of an older date than their own, only gave their men three obols, not so much from poverty as to prevent their seamen being corrupted by being too well off, and injuring their condition by spending money upon enervating indulgences, and also paid their crews irregularly in order to have a security against their deserting in the arrears which they would leave behind them. He also told Tissaphernes to bribe the captains and generals of the cities, and so to obtain their connivance —an expedient which succeeded with all except the Syracusans, Hermocrates alone opposing him on behalf of the whole confederacy. Meanwhile the cities asking for money Alcibiades sent off, by roundly telling them in the name of Tissaphernes that it was great impudence in the Chians, the richest people in Hellas, not content with being defended by a foreign force, to expect others to risk not only their lives but their money as well in behalf of their freedom; while the other cities, he said, had had to pay largely to Athens before their rebellion, and could not justly refuse to contribute as much or even more now for their own selves. He also pointed out that Tissaphernes was at present carrying on the war at his own charges, and had good cause for economy, but that as soon as he received remittances from the king he would give them their pay in full and do what was reasonable for the cities.

[46] Alcibiades further advised Tissaphernes not to be in too great a hurry to end the war, or to let himself be persuaded to bring up the Phoenician fleet which he was equipping, or to provide pay for more Hellenes, and thus put the power by land and sea into the same hands; but to leave each of the contending parties in possession of one element, thus enabling the king when he found one troublesome to call in the other. For if the command of the sea and land were united in one hand, he would not know where to turn for help to overthrow the dominant power; unless he at last chose to stand up himself, and go through with the struggle at great expense and hazard. The cheapest plan was to let the Hellenes wear each other out, at a small share of the expense and without risk to himself. Besides, he would find the Athenians the most convenient partners in empire as they did not aim at conquests on shore, and carried on the war upon principles and with a practice most advantageous to the King; being prepared to combine to conquer the sea for Athens, and for the King all the Hellenes inhabiting his country, whom the Peloponnesians, on the contrary, had come to liberate. Now it was not likely that the Lacedaemonians would free the Hellenes from the Hellenic Athenians, without freeing them also from the barbarian Mede, unless overthrown by him in the meanwhile. Alcibiades therefore urged him to wear them both out at first, and, after docking the Athenian power as much as he could, forthwith to rid the country of the Peloponnesians. In the main Tissaphernes approved of this policy, so far at least as could be conjectured from his behaviour; since he now gave his confidence to Alcibiades in recognition of his good advice, and kept the Peloponnesians short of money, and would not let them fight at sea, but ruined their cause by pretending that the Phoenician fleet would arrive, and that they would thus be enabled to contend with the odds in their favour, and so made their navy lose its efficiency, which had been very remarkable, and generally betrayed a coolness in the war that was too plain to be mistaken.

[47] Alcibiades gave this advice to Tissaphernes and the King, with whom he then was, not merely because he thought it really the best, but because he was studying means to effect his restoration to his country, well knowing that if he did not destroy it he might one day hope to persuade the Athenians to recall him, and thinking that his best chance of persuading them lay in letting them see that he possessed the favour of Tissaphernes. The event proved him to be right. When the Athenians at Samos found that he had influence with Tissaphernes, principally of their own motion (though partly also through Alcibiades himself sending word to their chief men to tell the best men in the army that, if there were only an oligarchy in the place of the rascally democracy that had banished him, he would be glad to return to his country and to make Tissaphernes their friend), the captains and chief men in the armament at once embraced the idea of subverting the democracy.

[48] The design was first mooted in the camp, and afterwards from thence reached the city. Some persons crossed over from Samos and had an interview with Alcibiades, who immediately offered to make first Tissaphernes, and afterwards the King, their friend, if they would give up the democracy and make it possible for the King to trust them. The higher class, who also suffered most severely from the war, now conceived great hopes of getting the government into their own hands, and

of triumphing over the enemy. Upon their return to Samos the emissaries formed their partisans into a club, and openly told the mass of the armament that the King would be their friend, and would provide them with money, if Alcibiades were restored and the democracy abolished. The multitude, if at first irritated by these intrigues, were nevertheless kept quiet by the advantageous prospect of the pay from the King; and the oligarchical conspirators, after making this communication to the people, now re-examined the proposals of Alcibiades among themselves, with most of their associates. Unlike the rest, who thought them advantageous and trustworthy, Phrynichus, who was still general, by no means approved of the proposals. Alcibiades, he rightly thought, cared no more for an oligarchy than for a democracy, and only sought to change the institutions of his country in order to get himself recalled by his associates; while for themselves their one object should be to avoid civil discord. It was not the King's interest, when the Peloponnesians were now their equals at sea, and in possession of some of the chief cities in his empire, to go out of his way to side with the Athenians whom he did not trust, when he might make friends of the Peloponnesians who had never injured him. And as for the allied states to whom oligarchy was now offered, because the democracy was to be put down at Athens, he well knew that this would not make the rebels come in any the sooner, or confirm the loyal in their allegiance; as the allies would never prefer servitude with an oligarchy or democracy to freedom with the constitution which they actually enjoyed, to whichever type it belonged. Besides, the cities thought that the so-called better classes would prove just as oppressive as the commons, as being those who originated, proposed, and for the most part benefited from the acts of the commons injurious to the confederates. Indeed, if it depended on the better classes, the confederates would be put to death without trial and with violence; while the commons were their refuge and the chastiser of these men. This he positively knew that the cities had learned by experience, and that such was their opinion. The propositions of Alcibiades, and the intrigues now in progress, could therefore never meet with his approval.

[49] However, the members of the club assembled, agreeably to their original determination, accepted what was proposed, and prepared to send Pisander and others on an embassy to Athens to treat for the restoration of Alcibiades and the abolition of the democracy in the city, and thus to make Tissaphernes the friend of the Athenians.

[50] Phrynichus now saw that there would be a proposal to restore Alcibiades, and that the Athenians would consent to it; and fearing after what he had said against it that Alcibiades, if restored, would revenge himself upon him for his opposition, had recourse to the following expedient. He sent a secret letter to the Lacedaemonian admiral Astyochus, who was still in the neighbourhood of Miletus, to tell him that Alcibiades was ruining their cause by making Tissaphernes the friend of the Athenians, and containing an express revelation of the rest of the intrigue, desiring to be excused if he sought to harm his enemy even at the expense of the interests of his country. However, Astyochus, instead of thinking of punishing Alcibiades, who, besides, no longer ventured within his reach as formerly, went up to him and Tissaphernes at Magnesia, communicated to them the letter from Samos, and turned informer, and, if report may be trusted, became the paid creature of Tissaphernes, undertaking to inform him as to this and all other matters; which was also the reason why he did not remonstrate more strongly against the pay not being given in full. Upon this Alcibiades instantly sent to the authorities at Samos a letter against Phrynichus, stating what he had done, and requiring that he should be put to death. Phrynichus distracted, and placed in the utmost peril by the denunciation, sent again to Astyochus, reproaching him with having so ill kept the secret of his previous letter, and saying that he was now prepared to give them an opportunity of destroying the whole Athenian armament at Samos; giving a detailed account of the means which he should employ, Samos being unfortified, and pleading that, being in danger of his life on their account, he could not now be blamed for doing this or anything else to escape being destroyed by his mortal enemies. This also Astyochus revealed to Alcibiades.

[51] Meanwhile Phrynichus having had timely notice that he was playing him false, and that a letter on the subject was on the point of arriving from Alcibiades, himself anticipated the news, and told the army that the enemy, seeing that Samos was unfortified and the fleet not all stationed within the harbour, meant to attack the camp, that he could be certain of this intelligence, and that they must

fortify Samos as quickly as posible, and generally look to their defences. It will be remembered that he was general, and had himself
authority to carry out these measures. Accordingly they addressed themselves to the work of
fortification, and Samos was thus fortified
sooner than it would otherwise have been. Not
long afterwards came the letter from Alcibiades, saying that the army was betrayed by
Phrynichus, and the enemy about to attack it.
Alcibiades, however, gained no credit, it being
thought that he was in the secret of the enemy's designs, and had tried to fasten them
upon Phrynichus, and to make out that he was
their accomplice, out of hatred; and consequently far from hurting him he rather bore
witness to what he had said by this intelligence.

[52] After this Alcibiades set to work to persuade Tissaphernes to become the friend of
the Athenians. Tissaphernes, although afraid
of the Peloponnesians because they had more
ships in Asia than the Athenians, was yet disposed to be persuaded if he could, especially
after his quarrel with the Peloponnesians at
Cnidus about the treaty of Therimenes. The
quarrel had already taken place, as the Peloponnesians were by this time actually at
Rhodes; and in it the original argument of Alcibiades touching the liberation of all the
towns by the Lacedaemonians had been veri-
fied by the declaration of Lichas that it was
impossible to submit to a convention which
made the King master of all the states at any
former time ruled by himself or by his fathers.

While Alcibiades was besieging the favour
of Tissaphernes with an earnestness proportioned to the greatness of the issue, [53] the
Athenian envoys who had been dispatched
from Samos with Pisander arrived at Athens,
and made a speech before the people, giving a
brief summary of their views, and particularly
insisting that, if Alcibiades were recalled and
the democratic constitution changed, they
could have the King as their ally, and would be
able to overcome the Peloponnesians. A number of speakers opposed them on the question
of the democracy, the enemies of Alcibiades
cried out against the scandal of a restoration
to be effected by a violation of the constitution,
and the Eumolpidae and Ceryces protested in
behalf of the mysteries, the cause of his banishment, and called upon the gods to avert his
recall; when Pisander, in the midst of much
opposition and abuse, came forward, and taking each of his opponents aside asked him the
following question: In the face of the fact that

the Peloponnesians had as many ships as their
own confronting them at sea, more cities in alliance with them, and the King and Tissaphernes to supply them with money, of which the
Athenians had none left, had he any hope of
saving the state, unless someone could induce
the King to come over to their side? Upon their
replying that they had not, he then plainly
said to them: "This we cannot have unless we
have a more moderate form of government,
and put the offices into fewer hands, and so
gain the King's confidence, and forthwith restore Alcibiades, who is the only man living
that can bring this about. The safety of the
state, not the form of its government, is for the
moment the most pressing question, as we can
always change afterwards whatever we do not
like."

[54] The people were at first highly irritated at the mention of an oligarchy, but upon
understanding clearly from Pisander that this
was the only resource left, they took counsel of
their fears, and promised themselves some day
to change the government again, and gave
way. They accordingly voted that Pisander
should sail with ten others and make the best
arrangement that they could with Tissaphernes and Alcibiades. At the same time the people, upon a false accusation of Pisander, dismissed Phrynichus from his post together with
his colleague Scironides, sending Diomedon
and Leon to replace them in the command of
the fleet. The accusation was that Phrynichus
had betrayed Iasus and Amorges; and Pisander brought it because he thought him a man
unfit for the business now in hand with Alcibiades. Pisander also went the round of all
the clubs already existing in the city for help in
lawsuits and elections, and urged them to
draw together and to unite their efforts for the
overthrow of the democracy; and after taking
all other measures required by the circumstances, so that no time might be lost, set off
with his ten companions on his voyage to Tissaphernes.

[55] In the same winter Leon and Diomedon, who had by this time joined the fleet,
made an attack upon Rhodes. The ships of the
Peloponnesians they found hauled up on shore,
and, after making a descent upon the coast and
defeating the Rhodians who appeared in the
field against them, withdrew to Chalce and
made that place their base of operations instead of Cos, as they could better observe from
thence if the Peloponnesian fleet put out to sea.
Meanwhile Xenophantes, a Laconian, came to

Rhodes from Pedaritus at Chios, with the news that the fortification of the Athenians was now finished, and that, unless the whole Peloponnesian fleet came to the rescue, the cause in Chios must be lost. Upon this they resolved to go to his relief. In the meantime Pedaritus, with the mercenaries that he had with him and the whole force of the Chians, made an assault upon the work round the Athenian ships and took a portion of it, and got possession of some vessels that were hauled up on shore, when the Athenians sallied out to the rescue, and first routing the Chians, next defeated the remainder of the force round Pedaritus, who was himself killed, with many of the Chians, a great number of arms being also taken.

[56] After this the Chians were besieged even more straitly than before by land and sea, and the famine in the place was great. Meanwhile the Athenian envoys with Pisander arrived at the court of Tissaphernes, and conferred with him about the proposed agreement. However, Alcibiades, not being altogether sure of Tissaphernes (who feared the Peloponnesians more than the Athenians, and besides wished to wear out both parties, as Alcibiades himself had recommended), had recourse to the following stratagem to make the treaty between the Athenians and Tissaphernes miscarry by reason of the magnitude of his demands. In my opinion Tissaphernes desired this result, fear being his motive; while Alcibiades, who now saw that Tissaphernes was determined not to treat on any terms, wished the Athenians to think, not that he was unable to persuade Tissaphernes, but that after the latter had been persuaded and was willing to join them, they had not conceded enough to him. For the demands of Alcibiades, speaking for Tissaphernes, who was present, were so extravagant that the Athenians, although for a long while they agreed to whatever he asked, yet had to bear the blame of failure: he required the cession of the whole of Ionia, next of the islands adjacent, besides other concessions, and these passed without opposition; at last, in the third interview, Alcibiades, who now feared a complete discovery of his inability, required them to allow the King to build ships and sail along his own coast wherever and with as many as he pleased. Upon this the Athenians would yield no further, and concluding that there was nothing to be done, but that they had been deceived by Alcibiades, went away in a passion and proceeded to Samos.

[57] Tissaphernes immediately after this, in the same winter, proceeded along shore to Caunus, desiring to bring the Peloponnesian fleet back to Miletus, and to supply them with pay, making a fresh convention upon such terms as he could get, in order not to bring matters to an absolute breach between them. He was afraid that if many of their ships were left without pay they would be compelled to engage and be defeated, or that their vessels being left without hands the Athenians would attain their objects without his assistance. Still more he feared that the Peloponnesians might ravage the continent in search of supplies. Having calculated and considered all this, agreeably to his plan of keeping the two sides equal, he now sent for the Peloponnesians and gave them pay, and concluded with them a third treaty in words following:

[58] *In the thirteenth year of the reign of Darius, while Alexippidas was ephor at Lacedaemon, a convention was concluded in the plain of the Maeander by the Lacedaemonians and their allies with Tissaphernes, Hieramenes, and the sons of Pharnaces, concerning the affairs of the King and of the Lacedaemonians and their allies.*

1. *The country of the King in Asia shall be the King's, and the King shall treat his own country as he pleases.*

2. *The Lacedaemonians and their allies shall not invade or injure the King's country: neither shall the King invade or injure that of the Lacedaemonians or of their allies. If any of the Lacedaemonians or of their allies invade or injure the King's country, the Lacedaemonians and their allies shall prevent it: and if any from the King's country invade or injure the country of the Lacedaemonians or of their allies, the King shall prevent it.*

3. *Tissaphernes shall provide pay for the ships now present, according to the agreement, until the arrival of the King's vessels: but after the arrival of the King's vessels the Lacedaemonians and their allies may pay their own ships if they wish it. If, however, they choose to receive the pay from Tissaphernes, Tissaphernes shall furnish it: and the Lacedaemonians and their allies shall repay him at the end of the war such moneys as they shall have received.*

4. *After the King's vessels have arrived, the ships of the Lacedaemonians and of their allies and those of the King shall carry on the war jointly, according as Tissaphernes and the Lacedaemonians and their allies shall think best. If they wish to make peace with the Athe-*

nians, they shall make peace also jointly.

[59] This was the treaty. After this Tissaphernes prepared to bring up the Phoenician fleet according to agreement, and to make good his other promises, or at all events wished to make it appear that he was so preparing.

[60] Winter was now drawing towards its close, when the Boeotians took Oropus by treachery, though held by an Athenian garrison. Their accomplices in this were some of the Eretrians and of the Oropians themselves, who were plotting the revolt of Euboea, as the place was exactly opposite Eretria, and while in Athenian hands was necessarily a source of great annoyance to Eretria and the rest of Euboea. Oropus being in their hands, the Eretrians now came to Rhodes to invite the Peloponnesians into Euboea. The latter, however, were rather bent on the relief of the distressed Chians, and accordingly put out to sea and sailed with all their ships from Rhodes. Off Triopium they sighted the Athenian fleet out at sea sailing from Chalce, and, neither attacking the other, arrived, the latter at Samos, the Peloponnesians at Miletus, seeing that it was no longer possible to relieve Chios without a battle. And this winter ended, and with it ended the twentieth year of this war of which Thucydides is the historian.

[61] Early in the spring of the summer following, Dercyllidas, a Spartan, was sent with a small force by land to the Hellespont to effect the revolt of Abydos, which is a Milesian colony; and the Chians, while Astyochus was at a loss how to help them, were compelled to fight at sea by the pressure of the siege. While Astyochus was still at Rhodes they had received from Miletus, as their commander after the death of Pedaritus, a Spartan named Leon, who had come out with Antisthenes, and twelve vessels which had been on guard at Miletus, five of which were Thurian, four Syracusans, one from Anaia, one Milesian, and one Leon's own. Accordingly the Chians marched out in mass and took up a strong position, while thirty-six of their ships put out and engaged thirty-two of the Athenians; and after a tough fight, in which the Chians and their allies had rather the best of it, as it was now late, retired to their city.

[62] Immediately after this Dercyllidas arrived by land from Miletus; and Abydos in the Hellespont revolted to him and Pharnabazus, and Lampsacus two days later. Upon receipt of this news Strombichides hastily sailed from Chios with twenty-four Athenian ships, some transports carrying heavy infantry being of the number, and defeating the Lampsacenes who came out against him, took Lampsacus, which was unfortified, at the first assault, and making prize of the slaves and goods restored the freemen to their homes, and went on to Abydos. The inhabitants, however, refusing to capitulate, and his assaults failing to take the place, he sailed over to the coast opposite, and appointed Sestos, the town in the Chersonese held by the Medes at a former period in this history, as the centre for the defence of the whole Hellespont.

[63] In the meantime the Chians commanded the sea more than before; and the Peloponnesians at Miletus and Astyochus, hearing of the sea-fight and of the departure of the squadron with Strombichides, took fresh courage. Coasting along with two vessels to Chios, Astyochus took the ships from that place, and now moved with the whole fleet upon Samos, from whence, however, he sailed back to Miletus, as the Athenians did not put out against him, owing to their suspicions of one another. For it was about this time, or even before, that the democracy was put down at Athens. When Pisander and the envoys returned from Tissaphernes to Samos they at once strengthened still further their interest in the army itself, and instigated the upper class in Samos to join them in establishing an oligarchy, the very form of government which a party of them had lately risen to avoid. At the same time the Athenians at Samos, after a consultation among themselves, determined to let Alcibiades alone, since he refused to join them, and besides was not the man for an oligarchy; and now that they were once embarked, to see for themselves how they could best prevent the ruin of their cause, and meanwhile to sustain the war, and to contribute without stint money and all else that might be required from their own private estates, as they would henceforth labour for themselves alone.

[64] After encouraging each other in these resolutions, they now at once sent off half the envoys and Pisander to do what was necessary at Athens (with instructions to establish oligarchies on their way in all the subject cities which they might touch at), and dispatched the other half in different directions to the other dependencies. Diitrephes also, who was in the neighbourhood of Chios, and had been elected to the command of the Thracian towns, was sent off to his government, and arriving at Thasos abolished the democracy there. Two

months, however, had not elapsed after his departure before the Thasians began to fortify their town, being already tired of an aristocracy with Athens, and in daily expectation of freedom from Lacedaemon. Indeed there was a party of them (whom the Athenians had banished), with the Peloponnesians, who with their friends in the town were already making every exertion to bring a squadron, and to effect the revolt of Thasos; and this party thus saw exactly what they most wanted done, that is to say, the reformation of the government without risk, and the abolition of the democracy which would have opposed them. Things at Thasos thus turned out just the contrary to what the oligarchical conspirators at Athens expected; and the same in my opinion was the case in many of the other dependencies; as the cities no sooner got a moderate government and liberty of action, than they went on to absolute freedom without being at all seduced by the show of reform offered by the Athenians.

[65] Pisander and his colleagues on their voyage alongshore abolished, as had been determined, the democracies in the cities, and also took some heavy infantry from certain places as their allies, and so came to Athens. Here they found most of the work already done by their associates. Some of the younger men had banded together, and secretly assassinated one Androcles, the chief leader of the commons, and mainly responsible for the banishment of Alcibiades; Androcles being singled out both because he was a popular leader and because they sought by his death to recommend themselves to Alcibiades, who was, as they supposed, to be recalled, and to make Tissaphernes their friend. There were also some other obnoxious persons whom they secretly did away with in the same manner. Meanwhile their cry in public was that no pay should be given except to persons serving in the war, and that not more than five thousand should share in the government, and those such as were most able to serve the state in person and in purse.

[66] But this was a mere catchword for the multitude, as the authors of the revolution were really to govern. However, the Assembly and the Council of the Bean still met notwithstanding, although they discussed nothing that was not approved of by the conspirators, who both supplied the speakers and reviewed in advance what they were to say. Fear, and the sight of the numbers of the conspirators, closed the mouths of the rest; or if any ventured to rise in opposition, he was presently put to death in some convenient way, and there was neither search for the murderers nor justice to be had against them if suspected; but the people remained motionless, being so thoroughly cowed that men thought themselves lucky to escape violence, even when they held their tongues. An exaggerated belief in the numbers of the conspirators also demoralized the people, rendered helpless by the magnitude of the city, and by their want of intelligence with each other, and being without means of finding out what those numbers really were. For the same reason it was impossible for any one to open his grief to a neighbour and to concert measures to defend himself, as he would have had to speak either to one whom he did not know, or whom he knew but did not trust. Indeed all the popular party approached each other with suspicion, each thinking his neighbour concerned in what was going on, the conspirators having in their ranks persons whom no one could ever have believed capable of joining an oligarchy; and these it was who made the many so suspicious, and so helped to procure impunity for the few, by confirming the commons in their mistrust of one another.

[67] At this juncture arrived Pisander and his colleagues, who lost no time in doing the rest. First they assembled the people, and moved to elect ten commissioners with full powers to frame a constitution, and that when this was done they should on an appointed day lay before the people their opinion as to the best mode of governing the city. Afterwards, when the day arrived, the conspirators enclosed the assembly in Colonus, a temple of Poseidon, a little more than a mile outside the city; when the commissioners simply brought forward this single motion, that any Athenian might propose with impunity whatever measure he pleased, heavy penalties being imposed upon any who should indict for illegality, or otherwise molest him for so doing. The way thus cleared, it was now plainly declared that all tenure of office and receipt of pay under the existing institutions were at an end, and that five men must be elected as presidents, who should in their turn elect one hundred, and each of the hundred three apiece; and that this body thus made up to four hundred should enter the council chamber with full powers and govern as they judged best, and should convene the five thousand whenever they pleased.

[68] The man who moved this resolution was Pisander, who was throughout the chief

ostensible agent in putting down the democracy. But he who concerted the whole affair, and prepared the way for the catastrophe, and who had given the greatest thought to the matter, was Antiphon, one of the best men of his day in Athens; who, with a head to contrive measures and a tongue to recommend them, did not willingly come forward in the assembly or upon any public scene, being ill looked upon by the multitude owing to his reputation for talent; and who yet was the one man best able to aid in the courts, or before the assembly, the suitors who required his opinion. Indeed, when he was afterwards himself tried for his life on the charge of having been concerned in setting up this very government, when the Four Hundred were overthrown and hardly dealt with by the commons, he made what would seem to be the best defence of any known up to my time. Phrynichus also went beyond all others in his zeal for the oligarchy. Afraid of Alcibiades, and assured that he was no stranger to his intrigues with Astyochus at Samos, he held that no oligarchy was ever likely to restore him, and once embarked in the enterprise, proved, where danger was to be faced, by far the staunchest of them all. Theramenes, son of Hagnon, was also one of the foremost of the subverters of the democracy—a man as able in council as in debate. Conducted by so many and by such sagacious heads, the enterprise, great as it was, not unnaturally went forward; although it was no light matter to deprive the Athenian people of its freedom, almost a hundred years after the deposition of the tyrants, when it had been not only not subject to any during the whole of that period, but accustomed during more than half of it to rule over subjects of its own.

[69] The assembly ratified the proposed constitution, without a single opposing voice, and was then dissolved; after which the Four Hundred were brought into the council chamber in the following way. On account of the enemy at Decelea, all the Athenians were constantly on the wall or in the ranks at the various military posts. On that day the persons not in the secret were allowed to go home as usual, while orders were given to the accomplices of the conspirators to hang about, without making any demonstration, at some little distance from the posts, and in case of any opposition to what was being done, to seize the arms and put it down. There were also some Andrians and Tenians, three hundred Carystians, and some of the settlers in Aegina come with their own

arms for this very purpose, who had received similar instructions. These dispositions completed, the Four Hundred went, each with a dagger concealed about his person, accompanied by one hundred and twenty Hellenic youths, whom they employed wherever violence was needed, and appeared before the Councillors of the Bean in the council chamber, and told them to take their pay and be gone; themselves bringing it for the whole of the residue of their term of office, and giving it to them as they went out.

[70] Upon the Council withdrawing in this way without venturing any objection, and the rest of the citizens making no movement, the Four Hundred entered the council chamber, and for the present contented themselves with drawing lots for their Prytanes, and making their prayers and sacrifices to the gods upon entering office, but afterwards departed widely from the democratic system of government, and except that on account of Alcibiades they did not recall the exiles, ruled the city by force; putting to death some men, though not many, whom they thought it convenient to remove, and imprisoning and banishing others. They also sent to Agis, the Lacedaemonian king, at Decelea, to say that they desired to make peace, and that he might reasonably be more disposed to treat now that he had them to deal with instead of the inconstant commons.

[71] Agis, however, did not believe in the tranquillity of the city, or that the commons would thus in a moment give up their ancient liberty, but thought that the sight of a large Lacedaemonian force would be sufficient to excite them if they were not already in commotion, of which he was by no means certain. He accordingly gave to the envoys of the Four Hundred an answer which held out no hopes of an accommodation, and sending for large reinforcements from Peloponnese, not long afterwards, with these and his garrison from Decelea, descended to the very walls of Athens; hoping either that civil disturbances might help to subdue them to his terms, or that, in the confusion to be expected within and without the city, they might even surrender without a blow being struck; at all events he thought he would succeed in seizing the Long Walls, bared of their defenders. However, the Athenians saw him come close up, without making the least disturbance within the city; and sending out their cavalry, and a number of their heavy infantry, light troops, and archers, shot down some of his soldiers who approached

too near, and got possession of some arms and dead. Upon this Agis, at last convinced, led his army back again and, remaining with his own troops in the old position at Decelea, sent the reinforcement back home, after a few days' stay in Attica. After this the Four Hundred persevering sent another embassy to Agis, and now meeting with a better reception, at his suggestion dispatched envoys to Lacedaemon to negotiate a treaty, being desirous of making peace.

[72] They also sent ten men to Samos to reassure the army, and to explain that the oligarchy was not established for the hurt of the city or the citizens, but for the salvation of the country at large; and that there were five thousand, not four hundred only, concerned; although, what with their expeditions and employments abroad, the Athenians had never yet assembled to discuss a question important enough to bring five thousand of them together. The emissaries were also told what to say upon all other points, and were so sent off immediately after the establishment of the new government, which feared, as it turned out justly, that the mass of seamen would not be willing to remain under the oligarchical constitution, and, the evil beginning there, might be the means of their overthrow.

[73] Indeed at Samos the question of the oligarchy had already entered upon a new phase, the following events having taken place just at the time that the Four Hundred were conspiring. That part of the Samian population which has been mentioned as rising against the upper class, and as being the democratic party, had now turned round, and yielding to the solicitations of Pisander during his visit, and of the Athenians in the conspiracy at Samos, had bound themselves by oaths to the number of three hundred, and were about to fall upon the rest of their fellow citizens, whom they now in their turn regarded as the democratic party. Meanwhile they put to death one Hyperbolus, an Athenian, a pestilent fellow that had been ostracized, not from fear of his influence or position, but because he was a rascal and a disgrace to the city; being aided in this by Charminus, one of the generals, and by some of the Athenians with them, to whom they had sworn friendship, and with whom they perpetrated other acts of the kind, and now determined to attack the people. The latter got wind of what was coming, and told two of the generals, Leon and Diomedon, who, on account of the credit which they enjoyed

with the commons, were unwilling supporters of the oligarchy; and also Thrasybulus and Thrasyllus, the former a captain of a galley, the latter serving with the heavy infantry, besides certain others who had ever been thought most opposed to the conspirators, entreating them not to look on and see them destroyed, and Samos, the sole remaining stay of their empire, lost to the Athenians. Upon hearing this, the persons whom they addressed now went round the soldiers one by one, and urged them to resist, especially the crew of the *Paralus,* which was made up entirely of Athenians and freemen, and had from time out of mind been enemies of oligarchy, even when there was no such thing existing; and Leon and Diomedon left behind some ships for their protection in case of their sailing away anywhere themselves. Accordingly, when the Three Hundred attacked the people, all these came to the rescue, and foremost of all the crew of the *Paralus;* and the Samian commons gained the victory, and putting to death some thirty of the Three Hundred, and banishing three others of the ringleaders, accorded an amnesty to the rest, and lived together under a democratic government for the future.

[74] The ship *Paralus,* with Chaereas, son of Archestratus, on board, an Athenian who had taken an active part in the revolution, was now without loss of time sent off by the Samians and the army to Athens to report what had occurred; the fact that the Four Hundred were in power not being yet known. When they sailed into harbour the Four Hundred immediately arrested two or three of the Parali and, taking the vessel from the rest, shifted them into a troopship and set them to keep guard round Euboea. Chaereas, however, managed to secrete himself as soon as he saw how things stood, and returning to Samos, drew a picture to the soldiers of the horrors enacting at Athens, in which everything was exaggerated; saying that all were punished with stripes, that no one could say a word against the holders of power, that the soldiers' wives and children were outraged, and that it was intended to seize and shut up the relatives of all in the army at Samos who were not of the government's way of thinking, to be put to death in case of their disobedience; besides a host of other injurious inventions.

[75] On hearing this the first thought of the army was to fall upon the chief authors of the oligarchy and upon all the rest concerned. Eventually, however, they desisted from this

idea upon the men of moderate views opposing it and warning them against ruining their cause, with the enemy close at hand and ready for battle. After this, Thrasybulus, son of Lycus, and Thrasyllus, the chief leaders in the revolution, now wishing in the most public manner to change the government at Samos to a democracy, bound all the soldiers by the most tremendous oaths, and those of the oligarchical party more than any, to accept a democratic government, to be united, to prosecute actively the war with the Peloponnesians, and to be enemies of the Four Hundred, and to hold no communication with them. The same oath was also taken by all the Samians of full age; and the soldiers associated the Samians in all their affairs and in the fruits of their dangers, having the conviction that there was no way of escape for themselves or for them, but that the success of the Four Hundred or of the enemy at Miletus must be their ruin.

[76] The struggle now was between the army trying to force a democracy upon the city, and the Four Hundred an oligarchy upon the camp. Meanwhile the soldiers forthwith held an assembly, in which they deposed the former generals and any of the captains whom they suspected, and chose new captains and generals to replace them, besides Thrasybulus and Thrasyllus, whom they had already. They also stood up and encouraged one another, and among other things urged that they ought not to lose heart because the city had revolted from them, as the party seceding was smaller and in every way poorer in resources than themselves. They had the whole fleet with which to compel the other cities in their empire to give them money just as if they had their base in the capital, having a city in Samos which, so far from wanting strength, had when at war been within an ace of depriving the Athenians of the command of the sea, while as far as the enemy was concerned they had the same base of operations as before. Indeed, with the fleet in their hands, they were better able to provide themselves with supplies than the government at home. It was their advanced position at Samos which had throughout enabled the home authorities to command the entrance into Piraeus; and if they refused to give them back the constitution, they would now find that the army was more in a position to exclude them from the sea than they were to exclude the army. Besides, the city was of little or no use towards enabling them to overcome the enemy; and they had lost nothing in losing those

who had no longer either money to send them (the soldiers having to find this for themselves), or good counsel, which entitles cities to direct armies. On the contrary, even in this the home government had done wrong in abolishing the institutions of their ancestors, while the army maintained the said institutions, and would try to force the home government to do so likewise. So that even in point of good counsel the camp had as good counsellors as the city. Moreover, they had but to grant him security for his person and his recall, and Alcibiades would be only too glad to procure them the alliance of the King. And above all, if they failed altogether, with the navy which they possessed, they had numbers of places to retire to in which they would find cities and lands.

[77] Debating together and comforting themselves after this manner, they pushed on their war measures as actively as ever; and the ten envoys sent to Samos by the Four Hundred, learning how matters stood while they were still at Delos, stayed quiet there.

[78] About this time a cry arose among the soldiers in the Peloponnesian fleet at Miletus that Astyochus and Tissaphernes were ruining their cause. Astyochus had not been willing to fight at sea—either before, while they were still in full vigour and the fleet of the Athenians small, or now, when the enemy was, as they were informed, in a state of sedition and his ships not yet united—but kept them waiting for the Phoenician fleet from Tissaphernes, which had only a nominal existence, at the risk of wasting away in inactivity. While Tissaphernes not only did not bring up the fleet in question, but was ruining their navy by payments made irregularly, and even then not made in full. They must therefore, they insisted, delay no longer, but fight a decisive naval engagement. The Syracusans were the most urgent of any.

[79] The confederates and Astyochus, aware of these murmurs, had already decided in council to fight a decisive battle; and when the news reached them of the disturbance at Samos, they put to sea with all their ships, one hundred and ten in number, and, ordering the Milesians to move by land upon Mycale, set sail thither. The Athenians with the eighty-two ships from Samos were at the moment lying at Glauce in Mycale, a point where Samos approaches near to the continent; and, seeing the Peloponnesian fleet sailing against them, retired into Samos, not thinking themselves numerically strong enough to stake their

all upon a battle. Besides, they had notice from Miletus of the wish of the enemy to engage, and were expecting to be joined from the Hellespont by Strombichides, to whom a messenger had been already dispatched, with the ships that had gone from Chios to Abydos. The Athenians accordingly withdrew to Samos, and the Peloponnesians put in at Mycale, and encamped with the land forces of the Milesians and the people of the neighbourhood. The next day they were about to sail against Samos, when tidings reached them of the arrival of Strombichides with the squadron from the Hellespont, upon which they immediately sailed back to Miletus. The Athenians, thus reinforced, now in their turn sailed against Miletus with a hundred and eight ships, wishing to fight a decisive battle, but, as no one put out to meet them, sailed back to Samos.

CHAPTER XXVI

Twenty-first Year of the War—Recall of Alcibiades to Samos—Revolt of Euboea and Downfall of the Four Hundred—Battle of Cynossema

[80] IN the same summer, immediately after this, the Peloponnesians having refused to fight with their fleet united, through not thinking themselves a match for the enemy, and being at a loss where to look for money for such a number of ships, especially as Tissaphernes proved so bad a paymaster, sent off Clearchus, son of Ramphias, with forty ships to Pharnabazus, agreeably to the original instructions from Peloponnese; Pharnabazus inviting them and being prepared to furnish pay, and Byzantium besides sending offers to revolt to them. These Peloponnesian ships accordingly put out into the open sea, in order to escape the observation of the Athenians, and being overtaken by a storm, the majority with Clearchus got into Delos, and afterwards returned to Miletus, whence Clearchus proceeded by land to the Hellespont to take the command: ten, however, of their number, under the Megarian Helixus, made good their passage to the Hellespont, and effected the revolt of Byzantium. After this, the commanders at Samos were informed of it, and sent a squadron against them to guard the Hellespont; and an encounter took place before Byzantium between eight vessels on either side.

[81] Meanwhile the chiefs at Samos, and especially Thrasybulus, who from the moment that he had changed the government had remained firmly resolved to recall Alcibiades, at last in an assembly brought over the mass of the soldiery, and upon their voting for his recall and amnesty, sailed over to Tissaphernes and brought Alcibiades to Samos, being convinced that their only chance of salvation lay in his bringing over Tissaphernes from the Peloponnesians to themselves. An assembly was then held in which Alcibiades complained of and deplored his private misfortune in having been banished, and speaking at great length upon public affairs, highly incited their hopes for the future, and extravagantly magnified his own influence with Tissaphernes. His object in this was to make the oligarchical government at Athens afraid of him, to hasten the dissolution of the clubs, to increase his credit with the army at Samos and heighten their own confidence, and lastly to prejudice the enemy as strongly as possible against Tissaphernes, and blast the hopes which they entertained. Alcibiades accordingly held out to the army such extravagant promises as the following: that Tissaphernes had solemnly assured him that if he could only trust the Athenians they should never want for supplies while he had anything left, no, not even if he should have to coin his own silver couch, and that he would bring the Phoenician fleet now at Aspendus to the Athenians instead of to the Peloponnesians; but that he could only trust the Athenians if Alcibiades were recalled to be his security for them.

[82] Upon hearing this and much more besides, the Athenians at once elected him general together with the former ones, and put all their affairs into his hands. There was now not a man in the army who would have exchanged his present hopes of safety and vengeance upon the Four Hundred for any consideration whatever; and after what they had been told they were now inclined to disdain the enemy before them, and to sail at once for Piraeus. To the plan of sailing for Piraeus, leaving their more immediate enemies behind them, Alcibiades opposed the most positive refusal, in spite of the numbers that insisted upon it, saying that now that he had been elected general he would first sail to Tissaphernes and concert with him measures for carrying on the war. Accordingly, upon leaving this assembly, he immediately took his departure in order to have it thought that there was an entire confidence between them, and also wishing to increase his consideration with Tissaphernes, and to show that he had now been elected general and was in a position to

do him good or evil as he chose; thus managing to frighten the Athenians with Tissaphernes and Tissaphernes with the Athenians.

[83] Meanwhile the Peloponnesians at Miletus heard of the recall of Alcibiades and, already distrustful of Tissaphernes, now became far more disgusted with him than ever. Indeed after their refusal to go out and give battle to the Athenians when they appeared before Miletus, Tissaphernes had grown slacker than ever in his payments; and even before this, on account of Alcibiades, his unpopularity had been on the increase. Gathering together, just as before, the soldiers and some persons of consideration besides the soldiery began to reckon up how they had never yet received their pay in full; that what they did receive was small in quantity, and even that paid irregularly, and that unless they fought a decisive battle or removed to some station where they could get supplies, the ships' crews would desert; and that it was all the fault of Astyochus, who humoured Tissaphernes for his own private advantage.

[84] The army was engaged in these reflections, when the following disturbance took place about the person of Astyochus. Most of the Syracusan and Thurian sailors were freemen, and these the freest crews in the armament were likewise the boldest in setting upon Astyochus and demanding their pay. The latter answered somewhat stiffly and threatened them, and when Dorieus spoke up for his own sailors even went so far as to lift his baton against him; upon seeing which the mass of men, in sailor fashion, rushed in a fury to strike Astyochus. He, however, saw them in time and fled for refuge to an altar; and they were thus parted without his being struck. Meanwhile the fort built by Tissaphernes in Miletus was surprised and taken by the Milesians, and the garrison in it turned out—an act which met with the approval of the rest of the allies, and in particular of the Syracusans, but which found no favour with Lichas, who said moreover that the Milesians and the rest in the King's country ought to show a reasonable submission to Tissaphernes and to pay him court, until the war should be happily settled. The Milesians were angry with him for this and for other things of the kind, and upon his afterwards dying of sickness, would not allow him to be buried where the Lacedaemonians with the army desired.

[85] The discontent of the army with Astyochus and Tissaphernes had reached this pitch, when Mindarus arrived from Lacedaemon to succeed Astyochus as admiral, and assumed the command. Astyochus now set sail for home; and Tissaphernes sent with him one of his confidants, Gaulites, a Carian, who spoke the two languages, to complain of the Milesians for the affair of the fort, and at the same time to defend himself against the Milesians, who were, as he was aware, on their way to Sparta chiefly to denounce his conduct, and had with them Hermocrates, who was to accuse Tissaphernes of joining with Alcibiades to ruin the Peloponnesian cause and of playing a double game. Indeed Hermocrates had always been at enmity with him about the pay not being restored in full; and eventually when he was banished from Syracuse, and new commanders—Potamis, Myscon, and Demarchus —had come out to Miletus to the ships of the Syracusans, Tissaphernes, pressed harder than ever upon him in his exile, and among other charges against him accused him of having once asked him for money, and then given himself out as his enemy because he failed to obtain it.

While Astyochus and the Milesians and Hermocrates made sail for Lacedaemon, Alcibiades had now crossed back from Tissaphernes to Samos. [86] After his return the envoys of the Four Hundred sent, as has been mentioned above, to pacify and explain matters to the forces at Samos, arrived from Delos; and an assembly was held in which they attempted to speak. The soldiers at first would not hear them, and cried out to put to death the subverters of the democracy, but at last, after some difficulty, calmed down and gave them a hearing. Upon this the envoys proceeded to inform them that the recent change had been made to save the city, and not to ruin it or to deliver it over to the enemy, for they had already had an opportunity of doing this when he invaded the country during their government; that all the Five Thousand would have their proper share in the government; and that their hearers' relatives had neither outrage, as Chaereas had slanderously reported, nor other ill treatment to complain of, but were all in undisturbed enjoyment of their property just as they had left them. Besides these they made a number of other statements which had no better success with their angry auditors; and amid a host of different opinions the one which found most favour was that of sailing to Piraeus. Now it was that Alcibiades for the first time did the state a service, and one of the most signal kind. For when the Athenians at Samos were bent upon sailing against their countrymen, in which case Ionia and the Hellespont would most certainly at once have passed into possession of the enemy, Alcibiades it was who prevented them. At that moment, when no other man would have been able to hold back the multitude, he put a stop to the intended expedition, and rebuked and turned aside the resentment felt, on personal grounds, against the envoys; he dismissed them with an answer from himself, to the effect that he did not object to the government of the Five Thousand, but insisted that the Four Hundred should be deposed and the Council of Five Hundred reinstated in power: meanwhile any retrenchments for economy, by which pay might be better found for the armament, met with his entire approval. Generally, he bade them hold out and show a bold face to the enemy, since if the city were saved there was good hope that the two parties might some day be reconciled, whereas if either were once destroyed, that at Samos, or that at Athens, there would no longer be any one to be reconciled to. Meanwhile arrived envoys from the Argives, with offers of support to the Athenian commons at Samos: these were thanked by Alcibiades, and dismissed with a request to come when called upon. The Argives were accompanied by the crew of the *Paralus,* whom we left placed in a troopship by the Four Hundred with orders to cruise round Euboea, and who being employed to carry to Lacedaemon some Athenian envoys sent by the Four Hundred— Laespodias, Aristophon, and Melesias—as they sailed by Argos laid hands upon the envoys, and delivering them over to the Argives as the chief subverters of the democracy, themselves, instead of returning to Athens, took the Argive envoys on board, and came to Samos in the galley which had been confided to them.

[*87*] The same summer at the time that the return of Alcibiades coupled with the general conduct of Tissaphernes had carried to its height the discontent of the Peloponnesians, who no longer entertained any doubt of his having joined the Athenians, Tissaphernes wishing, it would seem, to clear himself to them of these charges, prepared to go after the Phoenician fleet to Aspendus, and invited Lichas to go with him; saying that he would appoint Tamos as his lieutenant to provide pay for the armament during his own absence. Accounts differ, and it is not easy to ascertain with what intention he went to Aspen-

dus, and did not bring the fleet after all. That one hundred and forty-seven Phoenician ships came as far as Aspendus is certain; but why they did not come on has been variously accounted for. Some think that he went away in pursuance of his plan of wasting the Peloponnesian resources, since at any rate Tamos, his lieutenant, far from being any better, proved a worse paymaster than himself: others that he brought the Phoenicians to Aspendus to exact money from them for their discharge, having never intended to employ them: others again that it was in view of the outcry against him at Lacedaemon, in order that it might be said that he was not in fault, but that the ships were really manned and that he had certainly gone to fetch them. To myself it seems only too evident that he did not bring up the fleet because he wished to wear out and paralyse the Hellenic forces, that is, to waste their strength by the time lost during his journey to Aspendus, and to keep them evenly balanced by not throwing his weight into either scale. Had he wished to finish the war, he could have done so, assuming of course that he made his appearance in a way which left no room for doubt; as by bringing up the fleet he would in all probability have given the victory to the Lacedaemonians, whose navy, even as it was, faced the Athenian more as an equal than as an inferior. But what convicts him most clearly, is the excuse which he put forward for not bringing the ships. He said that the number assembled was less than the King had ordered; but surely it would only have enhanced his credit if he spent little of the King's money and effected the same end at less cost. In any case, whatever was his intention, Tissaphernes went to Aspendus and saw the Phoenicians; and the Peloponnesians at his desire sent a Lacedaemonian called Philip with two galleys to fetch the fleet.

[*88*] Alcibiades finding that Tissaphernes had gone to Aspendus, himself sailed thither with thirteen ships, promising to do a great and certain service to the Athenians at Samos, as he would either bring the Phoenician fleet to the Athenians, or at all events prevent its joining the Peloponnesians. In all probability he had long known that Tissaphernes never meant to bring the fleet at all, and wished to compromise him as much as possible in the eyes of the Peloponnesians through his apparent friendship for himself and the Athenians, and thus in a manner to oblige him to join their side.

While Alcibiades weighed anchor and sailed eastward straight for Phaselis and Caunus, [89] the envoys sent by the Four Hundred to Samos arrived at Athens. Upon their delivering the message from Alcibiades, telling them to hold out and to show a firm front to the enemy, and saying that he had great hopes of reconciling them with the army and of overcoming the Peloponnesians, the majority of the members of the oligarchy, who were already discontented and only too much inclined to be quit of the business in any safe way that they could, were at once greatly strengthened in their resolve. These now banded together and strongly criticized the administration, their leaders being some of the principal generals and men in office under the oligarchy, such as Theramenes, son of Hagnon, Aristocrates, son of Scellias, and others; who, although among the most prominent members of the government (being afraid, as they said, of the army at Samos, and most especially of Alcibiades, and also lest the envoys whom they had sent to Lacedaemon might do the state some harm without the authority of the people), without insisting on objections to the excessive concentration of power in a few hands, yet urged that the Five Thousand must be shown to exist not merely in name but in reality, and the constitution placed upon a fairer basis. But this was merely their political cry; most of them being driven by private ambition into the line of conduct so surely fatal to oligarchies that arise out of democracies. For all at once pretend to be not only equals but each the chief and master of his fellows; while under a democracy a disappointed candidate accepts his defeat more easily, because he has not the humiliation of being beaten by his equals. But what most clearly encouraged the malcontents was the power of Alcibiades at Samos, and their own disbelief in the stability of the oligarchy; and it was now a race between them as to which should first become the leader of the commons.

[90] Meanwhile the leaders and members of the Four Hundred most opposed to a democratic form of government—Phrynichus who had had the quarrel with Alcibiades during his command at Samos, Aristarchus the bitter and inveterate enemy of the commons, and Pisander and Antiphon and others of the chiefs who already as soon as they entered upon power, and again when the army at Samos seceded from them and declared for a democracy, had sent envoys from their own body to Lacedaemon and made every effort for peace, and

had built the wall in Eetionia—now redoubled their exertions when their envoys returned from Samos, and they saw not only the people but their own most trusted associates turning against them. Alarmed at the state of things at Athens as at Samos, they now sent off in haste Antiphon and Phrynichus and ten others with injunctions to make peace with Lacedaemon upon any terms, no matter what, that should be at all tolerable. Meanwhile they pushed on more actively than ever with the wall in Eetionia. Now the meaning of this wall, according to Theramenes and his supporters, was not so much to keep out the army of Samos, in case of its trying to force its way into Piraeus, as to be able to let in, at pleasure, the fleet and army of the enemy. For Eetionia is a mole of Piraeus, close alongside of the entrance of the harbour, and was now fortified in connection with the wall already existing on the land side, so that a few men placed in it might be able to command the entrance; the old wall on the land side and the new one now being built within on the side of the sea, both ending in one of the two towers standing at the narrow mouth of the harbour. They also walled off the largest porch in Piraeus which was in immediate connection with this wall, and kept it in their own hands, compelling all to unload there the corn that came into the harbour, and what they had in stock, and to take it out from thence when they sold it.

[91] These measures had long provoked the murmurs of Theramenes, and when the envoys returned from Lacedaemon without having effected any general pacification, he affirmed that this wall was like to prove the ruin of the state. At this moment forty-two ships from Peloponnese, including some Siceliot and Italiot vessels from Locri and Tarentum, had been invited over by the Euboeans and were already riding off Las in Laconia preparing for the voyage to Euboea, under the command of Agesandridas, son of Agesander, a Spartan. Theramenes now affirmed that this squadron was destined not so much to aid Euboea as the party fortifying Eetionia, and that unless precautions were speedily taken the city would be surprised and lost. This was no mere calumny, there being really some such plan entertained by the accused. Their first wish was to have the oligarchy without giving up the empire; failing this to keep their ships and walls and be independent; while, if this also were denied them, sooner than be the first victims of the restored democracy, they were resolved to call

in the enemy and make peace, give up their walls and ships, and at all costs retain possession of the government, if their lives were only assured to them.

[92] For this reason they pushed forward the construction of their work with posterns and entrances and means of introducing the enemy, being eager to have it finished in time. Meanwhile the murmurs against them were at first confined to a few persons and went on in secret, until Phrynichus, after his return from the embassy to Lacedaemon, was laid wait for and stabbed in full market by one of the Peripoli, falling down dead before he had gone far from the council chamber. The assassin escaped; but his accomplice, an Argive, was taken and put to the torture by the Four Hundred, without their being able to extract from him the name of his employer, or anything further than that he knew of many men who used to assemble at the house of the commander of the Peripoli and at other houses. Here the matter was allowed to drop. This so emboldened Theramenes and Aristocrates and the rest of their partisans in the Four Hundred and out of doors, that they now resolved to act. For by this time the ships had sailed round from Las, and anchoring at Epidaurus had overrun Aegina; and Theramenes asserted that, being bound for Euboea, they would never have sailed in to Aegina and come back to anchor at Epidaurus, unless they had been invited to come to aid in the designs of which he had always accused the government. Further inaction had therefore now become impossible. In the end, after a great many seditious harangues and suspicions, they set to work in real earnest. The heavy infantry in Piraeus building the wall in Eetionia, among whom was Aristocrates, a colonel, with his own tribe, laid hands upon Alexicles, a general under the oligarchy and the devoted adherent of the cabal, and took him into a house and confined him there. In this they were assisted by one Hermon, commander of the Peripoli in Munychia, and others, and above all had with them the great bulk of the heavy infantry. As soon as the news reached the Four Hundred, who happened to be sitting in the council chamber, all except the disaffected wished at once to go to the posts where the arms were, and menaced Theramenes and his party. Theramenes defended himself, and said that he was ready immediately to go and help to rescue Alexicles; and taking with him one of the generals belonging to his party, went down to Piraeus, followed by Aristarchus and some young men of the cavalry. All was now panic and confusion. Those in the city imagined that Piraeus was already taken and the prisoner put to death, while those in Piraeus expected every moment to be attacked by the party in the city. The older men, however, stopped the persons running up and down the town and making for the stands of arms; and Thucydides the Pharsalian, *proxenus* of the city, came forward and threw himself in the way of the rival factions, and appealed to them not to ruin the state, while the enemy was still at hand waiting for his opportunity, and so at length succeeded in quieting them and in keeping their hands off each other. Meanwhile Theramenes came down to Piraeus, being himself one of the generals, and raged and stormed against the heavy infantry, while Aristarchus and the adversaries of the people were angry in right earnest. Most of the heavy infantry, however, went on with the business without faltering, and asked Theramenes if he thought the wall had been constructed for any good purpose, and whether it would not be better that it should be pulled down. To this he answered that if they thought it best to pull it down, he for his part agreed with them. Upon this the heavy infantry and a number of the people in Piraeus immediately got up on the fortification and began to demolish it. Now their cry to the multitude was that all should join in the work who wished the Five Thousand to govern instead of the Four Hundred. For instead of saying in so many words "all who wished the commons to govern," they still disguised themselves under the name of the Five Thousand; being afraid that these might really exist, and that they might be speaking to one of their number and get into trouble through ignorance. Indeed this was why the Four Hundred neither wished the Five Thousand to exist, nor to have it known that they did not exist; being of opinion that to give themselves so many partners in empire would be downright democracy, while the mystery in question would make the people afraid of one another.

[93] The next day the Four Hundred, although alarmed, nevertheless assembled in the council chamber, while the heavy infantry in Piraeus, after having released their prisoner Alexicles and pulled down the fortification, went with their arms to the theatre of Dionysus, close to Munychia, and there held an assembly in which they decided to march into

the city, and setting forth accordingly halted in the Anaceum. Here they were joined by some delegates from the Four Hundred, who reasoned with them one by one, and persuaded those whom they saw to be the most moderate to remain quiet themselves, and to keep in the rest; saying that they would make known the Five Thousand, and have the Four Hundred chosen from them in rotation, as should be decided by the Five Thousand, and meanwhile entreated them not to ruin the state or drive it into the arms of the enemy. After a great many had spoken and had been spoken to, the whole body of heavy infantry became calmer than before, absorbed by their fears for the country at large, and now agreed to hold upon an appointed day an assembly in the theatre of Dionysus for the restoration of concord.

[94] When the day came for the assembly in the theatre, and they were upon the point of assembling, news arrived that the forty-two ships under Agesandridas were sailing from Megara along the coast of Salamis. The people to a man now thought that it was just what Theramenes and his party had so often said, that the ships were sailing to the fortification, and concluded that they had done well to demolish it. But though it may possibly have been by appointment that Agesandridas hovered about Epidaurus and the neighbourhood, he would also naturally be kept there by the hope of an opportunity arising out of the troubles in the town. In any case the Athenians, on receipt of the news, immediately ran down in mass to Piraeus, seeing themselves threatened by the enemy with a worse war than their war among themselves, not at a distance, but close to the harbour of Athens. Some went on board the ships already afloat, while others launched fresh vessels, or ran to defend the walls and the mouth of the harbour.

[95] Meanwhile the Peloponnesian vessels sailed by, and rounding Sunium anchored between Thoricus and Prasiae, and afterwards arrived at Oropus. The Athenians, with revolution in the city, and unwilling to lose a moment in going to the relief of their most important possession (for Euboea was everything to them now that they were shut out from Attica), were compelled to put to sea in haste and with untrained crews, and sent Thymochares with some vessels to Eretria. These upon their arrival, with the ships already in Euboea, made up a total of thirty-six vessels, and were immediately forced to engage. For Agesandridas, after his crews had dined, put out from Oro-

pus, which is about seven miles from Eretria by sea; and the Athenians, seeing him sailing up, immediately began to man their vessels. The sailors, however, instead of being by their ships, as they supposed, were gone away to purchase provisions for their dinner in the houses in the outskirts of the town; the Eretrians having so arranged that there should be nothing on sale in the marketplace, in order that the Athenians might be a long time in manning their ships, and, the enemy's attack taking them by surprise, might be compelled to put to sea just as they were. A signal also was raised in Eretria to give them notice in Oropus when to put to sea. The Athenians, forced to put out so poorly prepared, engaged off the harbour of Eretria, and after holding their own for some little while notwithstanding, were at length put to flight and chased to the shore. Such of their number as took refuge in Eretria, which they presumed to be friendly to them, found their fate in that city, being butchered by the inhabitants; while those who fled to the Athenian fort in the Eretrian territory, and the vessels which got to Chalcis, were saved. The Peloponnesians, after taking twenty-two Athenian ships, and killing or making prisoners of the crews, set up a trophy, and not long afterwards effected the revolt of the whole of Euboea (except Oreus, which was held by the Athenians themselves), and made a general settlement of the affairs of the island.

[96] When the news of what had happened in Euboea reached Athens, a panic ensued such as they had never before known. Neither the disaster in Sicily, great as it seemed at the time, nor any other had ever so much alarmed them. The camp at Samos was in revolt; they had no more ships or men to man them; they were at discord among themselves and might at any moment come to blows; and a disaster of this magnitude coming on the top of all, by which they lost their fleet, and worst of all Euboea, which was of more value to them than Attica, could not occur without throwing them into the deepest despondency. Meanwhile their greatest and most immediate trouble was the possibility that the enemy, emboldened by his victory, might make straight for them and sail against Piraeus, which they had no longer ships to defend; and every moment they expected him to arrive. This, with a little more courage, he might easily have done, in which case he would either have increased the dissensions of the city by his presence, or, if he had stayed to besiege it, have compelled the fleet

from Ionia, although the enemy of the oligarchy, to come to the rescue of their country and of their relatives, and in the meantime would have become master of the Hellespont, Ionia, the islands, and of everything as far as Euboea, or, to speak roundly, of the whole Athenian empire. But here, as on so many other occasions, the Lacedaemonians proved the most convenient people in the world for the Athenians to be at war with. The wide difference between the two characters, the slowness and want of energy of the Lacedaemonians as contrasted with the dash and enterprise of their opponents, proved of the greatest service, especially to a maritime empire like Athens. Indeed this was shown by the Syracusans, who were most like the Athenians in character, and also most successful in combating them.

[97] Nevertheless, upon receipt of the news, the Athenians manned twenty ships and called immediately a first assembly in the Pnyx, where they had been used to meet formerly, and deposed the Four Hundred and voted to hand over the government to the Five Thousand, of which body all who furnished a suit of armour were to be members, decreeing also that no one should receive pay for the discharge of any office, or if he did should be held accursed. Many other assemblies were held afterwards, in which law-makers were elected and all other measures taken to form a constitution. It was during the first period of this constitution that the Athenians appear to have enjoyed the best government that they ever did, at least in my time. For the fusion of the high and the low was effected with judgment, and this was what first enabled the state to raise up her head after her manifold disasters. They also voted for the recall of Alcibiades and of other exiles, and sent to him and to the camp at Samos, and urged them to devote themselves vigorously to the war.

[98] Upon this revolution taking place, the party of Pisander and Alexicles and the chiefs of the oligarchs immediately withdrew to Decelea, with the single exception of Aristarchus, one of the generals, who hastily took some of the most barbarian of the archers and marched to Oenoe. This was a fort of the Athenians upon the Boeotian border, at that moment besieged by the Corinthians, irritated by the loss of a party returning from Decelea, who had been cut off by the garrison. The Corinthians had volunteered for this service, and had called upon the Boeotians to assist them. After communicating with them, Aristarchus deceived the garrison in Oenoe by telling them that their countrymen in the city had compounded with the Lacedaemonians, and that one of the terms of the capitulation was that they must surrender the place to the Boeotians. The garrison believed him as he was general, and besides knew nothing of what had occurred owing to the siege, and so evacuated the fort under truce. In this way the Boeotians gained possession of Oenoe, and the oligarchy and the troubles at Athens ended.

[99] To return to the Peloponnesians in Miletus. No pay was forthcoming from any of the agents deputed by Tissaphernes for that purpose upon his departure for Aspendus; neither the Phoenician fleet nor Tissaphernes showed any signs of appearing, and Philip, who had been sent with him, and another Spartan, Hippocrates, who was at Phaselis, wrote word to Mindarus, the admiral, that the ships were not coming at all, and that they were being grossly abused by Tissaphernes. Meanwhile Pharnabazus was inviting them to come, and making every effort to get the fleet and, like Tissaphernes, to cause the revolt of the cities in his government still subject to Athens, founding great hopes on his success; until at length, at about the period of the summer which we have now reached, Mindarus yielded to his importunities, and, with great order and at a moment's notice, in order to elude the enemy at Samos, weighed anchor with seventy-three ships from Miletus and set sail for the Hellespont. Thither sixteen vessels had already preceded him in the same summer, and had overrun part of the Chersonese. Being caught in a storm, Mindarus was compelled to run in to Icarus and, after being detained five or six days there by stress of weather, arrived at Chios.

[100] Meanwhile Thrasyllus had heard of his having put out from Miletus, and immediately set sail with fifty-five ships from Samos, in haste to arrive before him in the Hellespont. But learning that he was at Chios, and expecting that he would stay there, he posted scouts in Lesbos and on the continent opposite to prevent the fleet moving without his knowing it, and himself coasted along to Methymna, and gave orders to prepare meal and other necessaries, in order to attack them from Lesbos in the event of their remaining for any length of time at Chios. Meanwhile he resolved to sail against Eresus, a town in Lesbos which had revolted, and, if he could, to take it. For some of the principal Methymnian exiles had carried

over about fifty heavy infantry, their sworn associates, from Cuma, and hiring others from the continent, so as to make up three hundred in all, chose Anaxander, a Theban, to command them, on account of the community of blood existing between the Thebans and the Lesbians, and first attacked Methymna. Balked in this attempt by the advance of the Athenian guards from Mitylene, and repulsed a second time in a battle outside the city, they then crossed the mountain and effected the revolt of Eresus. Thrasyllus accordingly determined to go there with all his ships and to attack the place. Meanwhile Thrasybulus had preceded him thither with five ships from Samos, as soon as he heard that the exiles had crossed over, and coming too late to save Eresus, went on and anchored before the town. Here they were joined also by two vessels on their way home from the Hellespont, and by the ships of the Methymnians, making a grand total of sixty-seven vessels; and the forces on board now made ready with engines and every other means available to do their utmost to storm Eresus.

[101] In the meantime Mindarus and the Peloponnesian fleet at Chios, after taking provisions for two days and receiving three Chian pieces of money for each man from the Chians, on the third day put out in haste from the island; in order to avoid falling in with the ships at Eresus, they did not make for the open sea, but keeping Lesbos on their left, sailed for the continent. After touching at the port of Carteria, in the Phocaeid, and dining, they went on along the Cumaean coast and supped at Arginusae, on the continent over against Mitylene. From thence they continued their voyage along the coast, although it was late in the night, and arriving at Harmatus on the continent opposite Methymna, dined there; and swiftly passing Lectum, Larisa, Hamaxitus, and the neighbouring towns, arrived a little before midnight at Rhoeteum. Here they were now in the Hellespont. Some of the ships also put in at Sigeum and at other places in the neighbourhood.

[102] Meanwhile the warnings of the fire signals and the sudden increase in the number of fires on the enemy's shore informed the eighteen Athenian ships at Sestos of the approach of the Peloponnesian fleet. That very night they set sail in haste just as they were, and, hugging the shore of the Chersonese, coasted along to Elaeus, in order to sail out into the open sea away from the fleet of the enemy.

After passing unobserved the sixteen ships at Abydos, which had nevertheless been warned by their approaching friends to be on the alert to prevent their sailing out, at dawn they sighted the fleet of Mindarus, which immediately gave chase. All had not time to get away; the greater number however escaped to Imbros and Lemnos, while four of the hindmost were overtaken off Elaeus. One of these was stranded opposite to the temple of Protesilaus and taken with its crew, two others without their crews; the fourth was abandoned on the shore of Imbros and burned by the enemy.

[103] After this the Peloponnesians were joined by the squadron from Abydos, which made up their fleet to a grand total of eighty-six vessels; they spent the day in unsuccessfully besieging Elaeus, and then sailed back to Abydos. Meanwhile the Athenians, deceived by their scouts, and never dreaming of the enemy's fleet getting by undetected, were tranquilly besieging Eresus. As soon as they heard the news they instantly abandoned Eresus, and made with all speed for the Hellespont, and after taking two of the Peloponnesian ships which had been carried out too far into the open sea in the ardour of the pursuit and now fell in their way, the next day dropped anchor at Elaeus, and, bringing back the ships that had taken refuge at Imbros, during five days prepared for the coming engagement.

[104] After this they engaged in the following way. The Athenians formed in column and sailed close alongshore to Sestos; upon perceiving which the Peloponnesians put out from Abydos to meet them. Realizing that a battle was now imminent, both combatants extended their flank; the Athenians along the Chersonese from Idacus to Arrhiani with seventy-six ships; the Peloponnesians from Abydos to Dardanus with eighty-six. The Peloponnesian right wing was occupied by the Syracusans, their left by Mindarus in person with the best sailers in the navy; the Athenian left by Thrasyllus, their right by Thrasybulus, the other commanders being in different parts of the fleet. The Peloponnesians hastened to engage first, and outflanking with their left the Athenian right sought to cut them off, if possible, from sailing out of the straits, and to drive their centre upon the shore, which was not far off. The Athenians perceiving their intention extended their own wing and outsailed them, while their left had by this time passed the point of Cynossema. This, however, obliged them to thin and weaken their centre, espe-

cially as they had fewer ships than the enemy, and as the coast round Point Cynossema formed a sharp angle which prevented their seeing what was going on on the other side of it.

[*105*] The Peloponnesians now attacked their centre and drove ashore the ships of the Athenians, and disembarked to follow up their victory. No help could be given to the centre either by the squadron of Thrasybulus on the right, on account of the number of ships attacking him, or by that of Thrasyllus on the left, from whom the point of Cynossema hid what was going on, and who was also hindered by his Syracusan and other opponents, whose numbers were fully equal to his own. At length, however, the Peloponnesians in the confidence of victory began to scatter in pursuit of the ships of the enemy, and allowed a considerable part of their fleet to get into disorder. On seeing this the squadron of Thrasybulus discontinued their lateral movement and, facing about, attacked and routed the ships opposed to them, and next fell roughly upon the scattered vessels of the victorious Peloponnesian division, and put most of them to flight without a blow. The Syracusans also had by this time given way before the squadron of Thrasyllus, and now openly took to flight upon seeing the flight of their comrades.

[*106*] The rout was now complete. Most of the Peloponnesians fled for refuge first to the river Midius, and afterwards to Abydos. Only a few ships were taken by the Athenians; as owing to the narrowness of the Hellespont the enemy had not far to go to be in safety. Nevertheless nothing could have been more opportune for them than this victory. Up to this time they had feared the Peloponnesian fleet, owing to a number of petty losses and to the disaster in Sicily; but they now ceased to mistrust themselves or any longer to think their enemies good for anything at sea. Meanwhile they took from the enemy eight Chian vessels, five Corinthian, two Ambraciot, two Boeotian, one Leucadian, Lacedaemonian, Syracusan, and Pellenian, losing fifteen of their own. After setting up a trophy upon Point Cynossema, securing the wrecks, and restoring to the enemy his dead under truce, they sent off a galley to Athens with the news of their victory. The arrival of this vessel with its unhoped-for good news, after the recent disasters of Euboea, and in the revolution at Athens, gave fresh courage to the Athenians, and caused them to believe that if they put their shoulders

to the wheel their cause might yet prevail.

[*107*] On the fourth day after the sea-fight the Athenians in Sestos having hastily refitted their ships sailed against Cyzicus, which had revolted. Off Harpagium and Priapus they sighted at anchor the eight vessels from Byzantium, and, sailing up and routing the troops on shore, took the ships, and then went on and recovered the town of Cyzicus, which was unfortified, and levied money from the citizens. In the meantime the Peloponnesians sailed from Abydos to Elaeus, and recovered such of their captured galleys as were still uninjured, the rest having been burned by the Elaeusians, and sent Hippocrates and Epicles to Euboea to fetch the squadron from that island.

[*108*] About the same time Alcibiades returned with his thirteen ships from Caunus and Phaselis to Samos, bringing word that he had prevented the Phoenician fleet from joining the Peloponnesians, and had made Tissaphernes more friendly to the Athenians than before. Alcibiades now manned nine more ships, and levied large sums of money from the Halicarnassians, and fortified Cos. After doing this and placing a governor in Cos, he sailed back to Samos, autumn being now at hand. Meanwhile Tissaphernes, upon hearing that the Peloponnesian fleet had sailed from Miletus to the Hellespont, set off again back from Aspendus, and made all sail for Ionia. While the Peloponnesians were in the Hellespont, the Antandrians, a people of Aeolic extraction, conveyed by land across Mount Ida some heavy infantry from Abydos, and introduced them into the town; having been illtreated by Arsaces, the Persian lieutenant of Tissaphernes. This same Arsaces had, upon pretence of a secret quarrel, invited the chief men of the Delians to undertake military service (these were Delians who had settled at Atramyttium after having been driven from their homes by the Athenians for the sake of purifying Delos); and after drawing them out from their town as his friends and allies, had laid wait for them at dinner, and surrounded them and caused them to be shot down by his soldiers. This deed made the Antandrians fear that he might some day do them some mischief; and as he also laid upon them burdens too heavy for them to bear, they expelled his garrison from their citadel.

[*109*] Tissaphernes, upon hearing of this act of the Peloponnesians in addition to what had occurred at Miletus and Cnidus, where his garrisons had been also expelled, now saw that the

breach between them was serious; and fearing further injury from them, and being also vexed to think that Pharnabazus should receive them, and in less time and at less cost perhaps succeed better against Athens than he had done, determined to rejoin them in the Hellespont, in order to complain of the events at Antandros and excuse himself as best he could in the matter of the Phoenician fleet and of the other charges against him. Accordingly he went first to Ephesus and offered sacrifice to Artemis. . . .

[When the winter after this summer is over the twenty-first year of this war will be completed.]

MAPS: THUCYDIDES

ADRIATIC SEA

Ortona

Rome

CAMPANIA

Pontiae Is.

Cumae
Neapolis

IAPYGIA

Posidonia

LUCANIA

Metapontum
Choerades Is.
Tarentum

Heraclea
Siris
Callipolis

TYRRHENIAN

SEA

Sybaris

Thurii

MAGNA

Crotona

Terina

GRAECIA

IONIAN

Lipara Is.

Caulonia
Epizephyrian Locris

SEA

Messana
Rhegium

Panormus

Segesta
Himera

Lilybaeum

Petra

Naxos

Selinus

Catana

SICILY

Minoa

Agrigentum

Leontini

Gela

Syracuse

Camarina

|||||||| IONIANS

━━━ DORIANS

▦▦▦ AEOLIANS

0   100   200 MILES

I. THE GREEK

HAEMUS MT.

EUXINE
(BLACK)
SEA

Beroea•

T H R A C E

PAEONIA

ILLYRIS

Epidamnus•

MACEDONIA

•Apollonia

•Aulon

EPIRUS

Corcyra•

PROPONTIS

Byzantium•
Selymbria
•Cypsela   Perinthus
                  Dascylium
Amphipolis   PHRYGIA
Pella•   •Thasos   Chersonese
Therma   Hellespont
Methone•   Olynthus   Sestos Cyzicus
Pydna•   Potidaea   Imbros Abydos Lampsacus
         Mende Torone Sigeum Troy TROAD
              Scione   Antandrus
                  Lemnos   Lectum Pr. Adramyttium
                                Methymna   MYSIA
Larissa•   Antissa•   Pergamum   Macestus R.
THESSALY   Eresus• Mytilene
Pharsalus•   Lesbos
                      Scyros•   Myrina
Ambracia•   Phocaea•   Cyme   LYDIA Hermus R.
Anactorium•   Clazomenae Sardis•
Leucas•   AETOLIA   Chios   Erythrae Teos Colophon
                Phocis Chalcis•   Chios   Myonnesus Ephesus Maeander R.
Cephallenia   Delphi BOEOTIA   Lebedus Samos Priene Myus
                Thespiae• Thebes•   Icaria   Samos   Miletus CARIA
                Plataea• Decelea   Myconos• Iassus
Zacynthus• ACHAIA Megara• ATHENS•   Tenos•   Halicarnassus
           Patrae• Sicyon• ATTICA•   Andros•   Cos• Caunus
ELIS PELOPON- Corinth•   Naxos• Cnidus• Syme• Cynossema Pr.
Elis• ARCADIA Argos• Epidaurus•   Paros•   Ialyssus•
Olympia• Mantinea• Troezen•   Thera   Lindus•
NESUS   Tegea• ARGOLIS   RHODES
MESSENIA Messene• SPARTA•
Pylos• LACONIA   •Cythera
Sphacteria•
                        Cythera•
                  Aegilia•
                                       •Carpathus

||||||| ATHENS & ALLIES

≡≡≡≡ SPARTA & ALLIES

                  Cydonia•
                    Cnossus•
            CRETE   •Gortyn

·V·R·

WORLD, 431 B.C.

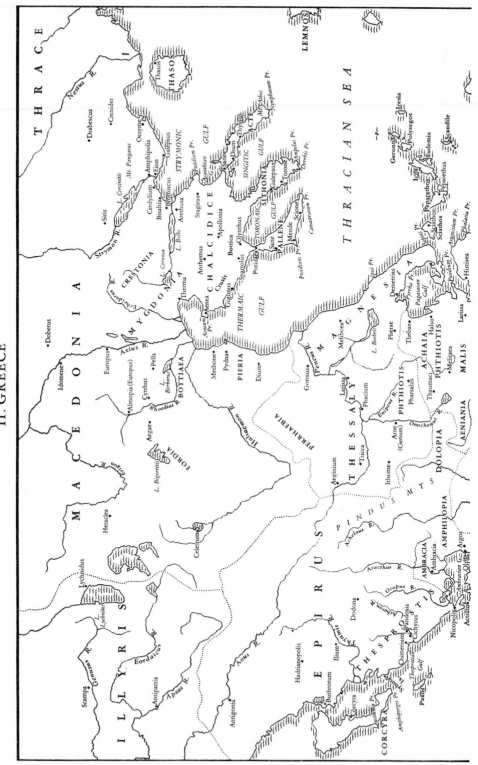

II. GREECE

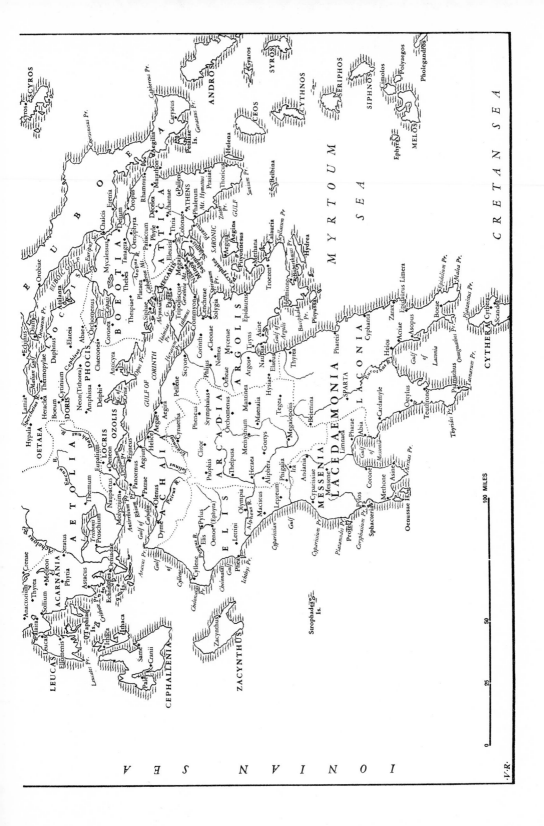

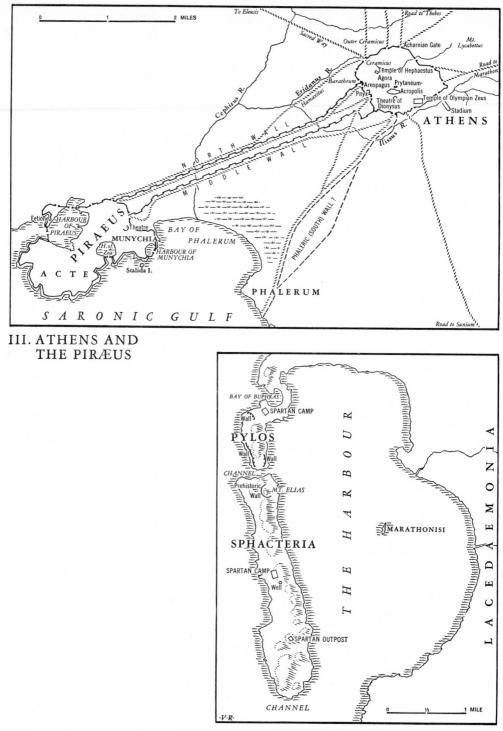

III. ATHENS AND THE PIRÆUS

2 MILES

To Eleusis
Road to Thebes
Sacred Way
Outer Ceramicus
Acharnian Gate
Mt. Lycabettus
Ceramicus
Temple of Hephaestus
Eridanus R.
Agora
Barathrum
Prytaneum
Road to Marathon
Areopagus
Ilamaxitus
Acropolis
Pnyx
Temple of Olympian Zeus
Theatre of Dionysus
Stadium
ATHENS
Cephissus R.
Ilissus R.
NORTH WALL
MIDDLE WALL
Eetionea
HARBOUR OF PIRÆUS
Theatre
BAY OF PHALERUM
PHALERIC (SOUTH) WALL ?
PIRÆUS
MUNYCHIA
H. of Zea
HARBOUR OF MUNYCHIA
Stalida I.
ACTE
PHALERUM
SARONIC GULF
Road to Sunium

IV. PYLOS AND SPHACTERIA

BAY OF BUPHRAS
SPARTAN CAMP
Wall
PYLOS
Wall
Wall
CHANNEL
Prehistoric Wall
MT. ELIAS
THE HARBOUR
MARATHONISI
SPHACTERIA
SPARTAN CAMP
Well
SPARTAN OUTPOST
CHANNEL
LACEDÆMONIA
·V·R·
1 MILE

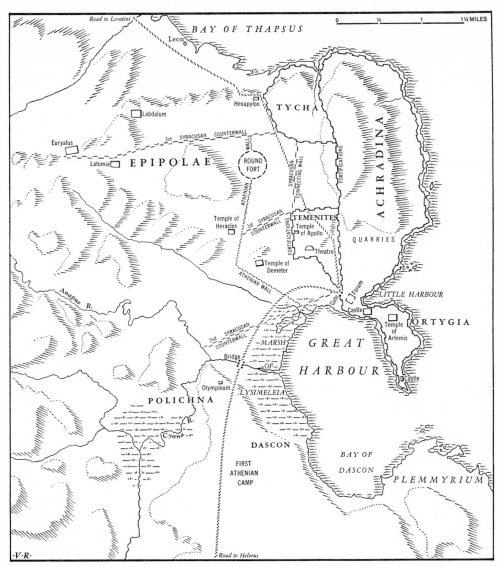

Road to Leontini

BAY OF THAPSUS

0   ½   1   1½ MILES

Leon.

Hexapylon

TYCHA

Labdalum

ACHRADINA

Euryalus

3rd SYRACUSAN COUNTERWALL

ROUND
FORT

Latomia

EPIPOLAE

SYRACUSAN
CONNECTING WALL

WALL

FORTIFICATIONS

ATHENIAN

1st
SYRACUSAN
COUNTERWALL

TEMENITES

Temple of
Heracles

Temple
of Apollo

QUARRIES

FORTIFICATION

Theatre

Temple of
Demeter

ATHENIAN WALL

Anapus R.

Forum

LITTLE HARBOUR

Gate

Castle

2nd SYRACUSAN
COUNTERWALL

Temple
of
Artemis

ORTYGIA

MARSH

GREAT

Bridge

OF

HARBOUR

Olympieum

LYSIMELEIA

Castle

R.

POLICHNA

Cyane

DASCON

FIRST
ATHENIAN
CAMP

BAY OF
DASCON

PLEMMYRIUM

·V·R·

Road to Helorus

V. SYRACUSE, 415–413 B.C.

Index

Terias, river, 522, 535
Terinaean, Gulf, 537
Teutiaplus, 423
Teutlussa, or Beet Island, 574
Thapsus, 510, 535, 536, 537, 551
Thasos, revolt of, 374, 579, 580; Thucydides at, 473
Theaenetus, son of Tolmides, 421
Theagenes, tyrant of Megara, 380, 454, 487, 488
Thebans, surprise Plataea, 387, 542; why they joined Xerxes, 432; procure from the Lacedaemonians the slaughter of the Plataeans, 434; at Delium, 470; their treatment of the Thespians, 480, 481; in Boeotia, 546. *See* Boeotians
Thebes, 371, 422, 535
Themistocles, author of the naval greatness of Athens, and founder of the Athenian empire, 353, 367, 372; implicated in the treason of Pausanias, 383; ostracized and residing at Argos, 383; his interview with Admetus, 383; flight to Persia and death, 383, 384
Theori, 495
Thera, 389
Theramenes, son of Hagnon, Athenian politician, 581, 587, 588, 589
Therimenes, Spartan commander, 570, 571, 572, 574, 577
Therme, 395
Thermopylae, 415, 440, 456
Theseus, 391, 392, 525
Thesmophylaces, 496
Thespians, suffer heavy loss at Delium, 470, 471; how rewarded by the Thebans, 480, 481; factions of, 535
Thesprotis, 356, 361, 409
Thessalians, 374, 393, 415, 440, 466, 474, 480, 485, 497, 565
Thessalus, 524
Thetes, poorest class of Athenian citizens, 521
Thirty Years' Truce, 377
Thoricus, 589
Thracians, 374, 472, 483, 490; invade Macedonia, 414, 415; raid Boeotia, 545, 546
Thrasybulus and Thrasyllus, leaders of the patriotic movement in the army of Samos, 582, 583, 584; win the battle of Cynossema, 592
Thrasycles, Athenian commander, 487, 488, 567, 568
Thrasylus, Argive general, 498, 499
Thrasymelidas, son of Cratesicles, Spartan admiral, 449
Thria, 393
Thrius, 377
Thronium, 394
Thucles, 509, 510
Thucydides, son of Olorus, when he began his history, 349; his mode of dealing with mythical traditions, 351, 352, 394; his conception of history, 354; his account of the plague, 399; his reflections on the Corcyraean revolution, 436, 437; commands at Amphipolis, 473;

possessed property in Thrace, 473; exiled, 489; his admiration for Sparta, 569; his aristocratic feeling, 581
Thuriats, 374
Thurii, in Lucania, 525, 532, 537, 547, 554, 579, 585
Thyamis, river, 361
Thymaus, Mount, 443
Thymochares, Athenian commander, 589
Thyrea, 394, 460, 461, 493, 535
Thyssus, 474, 491
Tichium, 441
Tilataeans, 414
Timagoras, a Cyzicene, 565, 566, 573,
Timagoras, a Tegean, 404
Timanthes, 356
Timocrates, Athenian leader, 487, 488
Timocrates, Spartan officer, 410, 413
Timoxenus, son of Timocrates, Corinthian commander, 395
Tisamenus, 439
Tisander, an Apodotian, 441
Tisias, son of Tisimachus, Athenian general, 504
Tissaphernes, Persian satrap, 565, 570, 571, 575, 583-586, 590, 592, 593; his treaties with the Peloponnesians, 568, 572, 574, 578, 579
Tlepolemus, 377
Tolmides, son of Tolmaeus, Athenian admiral, 376, 377
Tolophonians, 441, 442
Tolophus, an Ophionian, 441
Torone, 474, 475, 477, 479, 482, 487
Torylaus, 466
Trachinians, 439, 496
Tragia, 377
Treres, 414
Triballi, 414, 472
Trinacria, 509
Triopium, promontory of Cnidus, 572, 579
Tripodiscus, 464
Tritaeans, 441
Troezen, 356, 377, 401, 452, 458, 476, 565
Trogilus, 536, 538
Trojan War, 350-352, 353, 509
Trotilus, 510
Tydeus, son of Ion, 573
Tyndareus, 351
Tyrrhene Gulf, 525
Tyrrhenians, 474, 532, 537, 553, 554

Ulysses, 453

White Castle, 375

Xenares, son of Cnidis, Lacedaemonian commander, 492, 495, 497
Xenoclides, son of Euthycles, Corinthian admiral, 360, 445
Xenon, Theban commander, 542
Xenophantes, a Laconian, 577
Xenophon, son of Euripides, 405, 408
Xerxes, 353, 378, 381, 383, 430

THE GREAT IDEAS, Volumes 2 and 3